THE OFFICIAL

1987 PRICE GUIDE TO

Antiques and Collectibles

FROM THE EDITORS
OF THE HOUSE OF COLLECTIBLES

SEVENTH EDITION
THE HOUSE OF COLLECTIBLES
NEW YORK, NEW YORK 10022

Important Notice. The format of *The Official Price Guide Series*, published by *The House of Collectibles,* is based on the following proprietary features: *All facts and prices are compiled through a nationwide sampling of information* obtained from noteworthy experts, auction houses, and specialized dealers. *Detailed "indexed" format* enables quick retrieval of information for positive identification. *Encapsulated histories* precede each category to acquaint the collector with the specific traits that are peculiar to that area of collecting. *Valuable collecting information* is provided for both the novice as well as the seasoned collector: How to begin a collection; how to buy, sell and trade; care and storage techniques; tips on restoration; grading guidelines; lists of periodicals, clubs, museums, auction houses, dealers, etc. *An average price range* takes geographic location and condition into consideration when reporting collector value. *An inventory checklist system* is provided for cataloging a collection.

All of the information, including valuations, in this book has been compiled from the most reliable sources, and every effort has been made to eliminate errors and questionable data. Nevertheless the possibility of error, in a work of such immense scope, always exists. The publisher will not be held responsible for losses which may occur in the purchase, sale, or other transaction of items because of information contained herein. Readers who feel they have discovered errors are invited to *write* and inform us, so they may be corrected in subsequent editions. Those seeking further information on the topics covered in this book are advised to refer to the complete line of Official Price Guides published by The House of Collectibles.

Published by: The House of Collectibles
201 East 50th Street
New York, New York 10022

Distributed by Ballantine Books, a division of Random House, Inc., New York and simultaneously in Canada by Random House of Canada Limited, Toronto.

Manufactured in the United States of America

Library of Congress Catalog Card Number: 84-642991

ISBN: 0-87637-517-4

10 9 8 7 6 5 4 3 2 1

TABLE OF CONTENTS

ACKNOWLEDGMENTS

The House of Collectibles would like to express its appreciation to the following individuals and organizations for their assistance in the preparation of this publication: Phillips-Fine Art Auctioneers and Appraisers, 867 Madison Avenue, NY; The Topps Chewing Gum Co., Brooklyn, NY; The Fleer Corp., Philadelphia, PA; Juke Box Saturday Nite, Steve Schussler, Chicago, IL; Carousel Midwest, Dale Sorenson, North Lake, WI; Clocks and Things, Cindy and Joseph Fanelli, NY; Abe Kessler Appraisal Service, Queens Village, NY; Central Florida Depression Glass Club, Elizabeth Faust, Five Points Antique, Longwood, FL; Millie Downey, Millie's Glass and China Shop, Orlando FL; Alfred J. Young, Police Academy Museum, NY; Kruse Auction International Auburn, IN; Donald Z. Sokal, Airplanes, Pottstown, PA; Rita Nolth, Tacoma, WA; Michael Auclair Lace, NY; Selma Sternheim, Majolica, Monsey, NY; Eugene H. Brown, Lightbulbs, Dodge City, KS; George S. James Pen Fancier's Club, Washington, DC; Fridolt Johnson, Bookplates, Woodstock, NY; H.D. Lazuras, Toy Trains, Panorama City, CA; C.B. Goodman, Telegraphical, Chicago, IL; Antique Galleria, Ken Cooynan, Pasadena, CA; Dale Rogalsky, Beer Cans, Gainesville, FL; Mrs. M. Marshall, Pottery, Richmond, VA; Richard Rounsaville, Brookside Country Club, Golf Collectibles, Macungie, PA; Fred Ruckewich, Bottles, Cheyenne, WY; David Nago, Pottery; Sven Stau, Ginger Beer Bottles, Buffalo, NY; and South Street Antiques, Charlottesville, VA.

A special mention of Shirley Smith of Shirley's Antiques for her considerable knowledge of the antiques market, 750 Highway 50, Winter Garden, FL 32787; and Ted Salveson of the *Salveson's Coin Machine Trader,* a monthly newsletter. For information, write Mr. Salveson at PO Box 602, Huron, SD 57350.

Also, a special thanks extended to Ted Hake of Hake's Americana & Collectibles for providing many photos for this book. Since 1967, Mr. Hake has published catalogs specializing in radio premiums, movie and television items, comic and cowboy collectibles and Disneyana. For a sample of his next catalog, send $2.00 to: Hake's Americana, Box 1444Y, York, PA 17405.

In addition, The House of Collectibles would like to thank Charles J. Jordan for providing the special feature section on collectibles for the future. Mr. Jordan is a well-known expert on collectibles.

NOTE TO READERS

MARKET REVIEW

As we pass into the second half of the 1980s, we see many interesting trends emerging in the antiques and collectibles markets. Collector interest continues to grow in every field as more and more people join the ranks of collectors each day. There is every reason to suspect that these trends are reflecting the interests and leisure time activities of the country as a whole.

For instance, the public looks to the future as an exciting time—a time full of potential and expansion, and perhaps a return to the pioneering spirit that helped build this country. As enthusiasm for space travel grows, so does the market for such collectibles as toy robots, Star Trek and Star Wars items, and Flash Gordon memorabilia, among others.

The country is also in an economic upswing that is affecting every aspect of our lives. Now, more than ever, people are enjoying their interests and looking for new ways to expand their knowledge, their collections, and their circles of friends in various collecting fields.

We found furniture, as usual, to be a reliable indicator of the antique trade as a whole. Top of the line items such as Louis XVI furniture are, as always, doing well. Examples include a set of Louis XVI mahogany cabinets which sold for $264,000 at Sotheby's; also sold at Sotheby's was a Louis XVI chandelier for $148,000. A very unusual 21″ Shaker table brought an unexpected $38,000 at a private auction. These are solid investments and will continue to command high prices. Victorian furniture is also doing extremely well. Watch for oak to really come alive again this year, especially in the East.

Lower priced items are also doing well as people are searching for what will be collectible in the future. We have included a section on *Future Collectibles* in this edition for the first time this year, as we feel this was an integral part of the market in the past year. In future collectibles, watch out for an issue of Statue of Liberty commemorative coins, including a $5 piece depicting the famous statue, a $1 piece showing Ellis Island, and a half-dollar piece dedicated to the contribution of immigrants toward the building of America.

Relatively low-priced items, such as glassware and games, are doing exceptionally well. A good example, is an 1896 Egerton R. Williams baseball game that brought a record $1250 at a private sale. This kind of item is accessible to the mid-range collector and is also easy to enjoy.

One trend that has really taken our notice is that moderately expensive items—those between $500 and $3000—are not showing much strength, with the exception of furniture. These items are seen as risky by many collectors and dealers alike. They are not guaranteed investments like the "top of the line" items mentioned previously, and they might be too expensive to take a risk with. In this category we include tall case clocks and the more expensive pottery. There still is a market out there, and many items will continue to fetch a good price, but numerous people have reported a weakening in this price range.

Another major trend noticed this past year was that many new items came to be of interest to collectors. We first noticed this trend during the early 70s, with the tremendous boost in interest in comics and comic art. At the present time, it has grown even more to include a wide variety of memorabilia.

As always, the value of an item depends not only on what it is but where it was sold. Different parts of the country reported differing lists of gainers and losers. Bottles, an affordable and ever-popular item, showed strength and stability in the Southeast, but seemed soft in the North and West. Dealers from

New England and Canada reported high prices and slow sales, whereas the Western dealers felt a general slackening of interest.

Another area that displayed regional differences was that of pottery. It was noted that Californians felt a great interest in the pottery made in their area. Easterners, on the other hand, varied their collections among different manufacturers around the country. Again, the low end of the price range did very well while the middle range suffered. Some dealers reported trouble moving some of the more expensive items, such as George Ohr and the high end of Bennington, but the collectors we spoke to said interest was still there.

There has been a slight pause in the growth of the Orientalia market as a whole, although specific areas are doing quite well. A pair of cloisonne peacocks recently sold for $35,200 despite a pre-sale estimate of $14,000–$18,000. Prices for Chinese paintings are greatly on the rise, as is Oriental furniture. The auction houses were humming along, although without the sensational sales of a few years ago. A selection of twelve fine Oriental rugs at *Sotheby's* brought good response and high prices. The East and West coasts both reported continued growth and interest, but the Southeast seemed to show a softening. The place to watch is the Southwest, as the market there is growing rapidly.

Americana continued to show great strength throughout the nation. There are so many fields of interest within this one category that picking out certain highlights is always a difficult task, but certainly decoys have to be on everyone's mind as a big gainer. It all started back in 1983 when prices for the best specimens started to edge up around $30,000. That year a Crowell goose went for $45,000.

In 1984, interest remained high as auctions offered thousands of lots, and buyers responded with high prices. At three major houses—*Julia, Oliver* and *Bourne*—decoy sales combined to total as much as $1.3 million. Many felt the market had peaked. But the following year turned out to be even better as record prices were realized.

Beer cans had a good year, with growth in prices as well as in the actual range of what is considered collectible. The more unusual cans were growing tremendously while the cans sporting more decorative artwork also increased, but at a slower pace.

What a year for toys! Prices were up, and once again the realm of what is considered collectible grew nicely. The big fields were space toys and Teddy bears, but the market, as a whole, was very strong.

Toy soldiers were active this year, and good sales were reported. At a show at *Phillips* auction house in New York City, a rare double figure of John Maurewarde attacking Le Bourg di Pre was expected to fetch $600–$800, but ended up bringing $1,350. Another highly priced item was a mounted figure of Sir William Beauchamp, carrying a pre-sale estimate of $550–$650 that reined in $1,500. Another mounted figure, of Sir John Slinton, went for $1,000.

Celluloids were also available at the *Phillips* show, and a celluloid of Walt Disney's *Ugly Duckling* was taken home for $700. The big price, though, was a celluloid of *Snow White Kissing Bashful* that brought in $1,300. Another celluloid of the *Seven Dwarfs* came in slightly lower at $1,200.

An interesting selection of majolica from the collection of the late chef James Beard was put on sale in October at *Doyle Galleries,* and collector response was excellent. Some outstanding prices from that sale included a set of eight 19th century Minton majolica sardine plates, estimated to go for $800–$1,200, which ended up selling for $3,500. A 19th century majolica oval fish platter that was predicted to go for $600–$900 eventually sold for $2,100. But the big surprise came when a continental faience soup tureen—estimated at $400–$600—was taken home for $4,000. A pair of 19th century stoneware rustic garden seats that were modeled after trunk and bark examples topped the whole sale at $5,500.

Glassware had a big year, and Depression-era glass led the way. Prices are low, and the mid-range collector can afford just about anything he or she wants. Fine art glass is holding its own but is apparently not gaining substantially. Again, it's the smaller items that are really taking off. Carnival glass is strong and will continue to do well in the coming year.

Limited editions moved ahead steadily in the past year, and we like this hobby's stability and accessibility to the public. There are some folks who say that collector plates are the third most popular hobby in the world. Many fine artists presented excellent work in 1985 and will probably continue to do so in 1986. We expect continued growth and a healthy market.

Music collectibles are always a lot of fun, as they are things which everyone can appreciate. Adults love to collect memorabilia of their favorite musicians. Last year was a turning point, as prices were rising and the field came into the public eye more than in any preceding year.

Beatles memorabilia did very well, as did items associated with the great classical composers. Presleyana did not fare quite as well, although no major losses are reported.

We see two trends: first, look for more limited editions in records and memorabilia; and second, don't be surprised by rising prices for antique musical instruments.

Keep your eyes open for the future. We see a great many objects that are becoming delightful collector pieces that were once regarded as mundane. Keeping that in mind may help to give us a new outlook on the objects which pass through our hands each day. Enjoy the beauty of these things; most of all —keep your eyes open and think!

We have noticed one final trend, and we find it to be perhaps the most pleasing of all. People are going about their collecting with more and more intentions of actually using and enjoying their pieces. While this book is a price guide, the editors realize that monetary value is not the sole motivation for the collecting hobbyist. Also important is the pleasure one experiences when surrounded by special things with special memories. Your specialty may be music, art, plates, dolls, games, carpets, furniture, or decoys, but no matter where your collector interest lies, the enjoyment of your hobby and, most of all, the enjoyment of the people who share it with you can be the greatest payoff for the time and energy you have invested in it. We believe that one of life's greatest joys lies in the camaraderie that can be found in fun-loving people sharing an interest.

AN IN-DEPTH OVERVIEW OF THE MARKETPLACE

AMERICANA

Optimism was the key word in Americana this past year, as both prices and the number of collectors enjoyed steady gains.

What is Americana? It is antiques and collectibles that represent periods or figures from America's history. It is fun to note how many things we use every day that will one day be collectible.

Americana antiques and collectibles span a broad range. On the one hand, there are the affordable and durable kitchen and household collectibles and primitives found in abundance at local flea markets and garage sales. Then there is the more fragile, more valuable items, such as the molded copper and zinc Indian weather vane that sold for over $41,000, or the small, Shaker-style oval box that sold for over $3,000.

Noteworthy Americana on today's secondary market includes decoys, tramp art, advertising collectibles, and kitchen and household collectibles. Decoy collectors might want to call this past year "Decoy Year" and justifiably so. Prices went sky-high with no end in sight. Several days of auctions at the big decoy houses—*Julia, Oliver* and *Bourne*—took in just under $2 million. Some special sales included a Blair pintail that went for $22,000 and a Ward Brothers black duck for $38,000. The big hit of the season, though, came early in the year when a Bowman golden plover was purchased for $50,000. This was the highest price ever paid for a decoy.

Even with all of these big prices, the dealers we spoke to are still enthusiastic about small sales, as they know that interest is on the rise and the market is strong.

Tramp art is the name given to a form of 19th century American folk art, but it has just recently been receiving attention because of the folk art craze currently sweeping the country. Tramp art can usually be found in flea markets, out-of-the-way junk shops, and garage sales. It received its name from its unusual, transient artists (hobos or tramps). Tramp art items include elaborately carved picture frames, odd shaped boxes, lighting devices, and furniture.

Collectors of advertising memorabilia have plenty to be pleased about this year. A museum consisting of a plethora of *Nabisco* brand products and other related items recently opened in New Jersey. Items such as posters, biscuit tins, and signs are displayed, depicting the history of the company as well as the age of advertising in America.

In addition, an advertising art collector recently sold his collection, spanning 25 years. One of the most significant items was a 1922 five-panel *Coca-Cola* screen priced at $22,500. Also, a 1928 *General Electric* calendar with artwork by Norman Rockwell sold for $400.

Americana items appeal to the casual collector as well. The casual collector is one who is searching for a few items to decorate his home or office. Especially appealing to this type of collector are baskets, fruit crate art, decoys, carousel animals, Disneyana, and railroadiana. Fortunately, enough of these items exist to satisfy the interests of both the casual and the serious collector.

Kitchenware, as a whole, showed fewer sales, but the veteran collector knows that things will change. We look to this area for growth in 1986.

Most of all, Americana is fun. What will be collectible years from now? It might be something that is used every day by all of us. Keep looking, keep thinking, and most of all have fun with it.

CARS

Last year we predicted a good year for investments in cars, and we think we can safely say the same for the coming year. Prices appreciated well, and collector interest grew just as fast.

Old favorites like the 1953 Corvette convertibles were selling for about $32,000 in 1985. A classic 1937 Cadillac Series 90-coupe Fleetwood body could be expected to bring in as much as $100,000. The early touring cars still seemed to be undervalued, as a 1908 Model T Ford might fetch $20,000, but we expect prices for these items to be on the rise very soon.

Auctions were also important this year, as many high prices were realized. During one sale at the Henry Ford Museum in Dearborn, Michigan, transportation items that dated back two hundred years were offered. Some highlights included a 1928 Bugatti Sports car for $92,500, a Benz Phaeton for $51,500 and, to top them all, a V-12 Lincoln Royal Limo that sold for an outstanding $210,000. Also sold that day were 40 stationary steam engines at up to $6,900 each, and a variety of other transportation items including motorcycles, locomotives, motor-dynamos, and machine tools. A James Spencer lathe brought $1,000.

The really spectacular sales this year were from William Harrah's collection. A 1934 LeBaron V-12 Runabout Speedster sold for $710,000. However, the big winner was a 1929 Duesenberg Murphy, which brought down the house at a cool million. This can only mean great things for the classic car collectors.

The other area to watch this year is car-related merchandise. Items such as license plates, advertisements, toys, pedal cars, and club insignia will all develop greater followings in the coming year.

Because of the sophistication needed to be even a minimally competent collector in this field, no beginner should venture out without belonging to a specialized car club (see our section on clubs in *The Official Price Guide to Collector Cars,* published by The House of Collectibles) and without first doing extensive research. A mistake in this hobby can be a costly one; therefore it pays to keep up with the current trends and to consult a professional before making a purchase.

EPHEMERA

These items have enjoyed a genuine rekindling of interest in the 1980s. While the term *ephemera* refers to anything made of paper which is considered to be collectible, in practice, only items with genuine celebrity or historical appeal are truly valuable as collectors' items.

Autographs, for instance, are a part of ephemera with which everyone has had contact. An autograph is especially valuable when written on something that could further add to its value. For example, an autographed promotion photo of Grace Kelly sold recently for $130. A one-page letter penned by Thomas Jefferson brought $3,000. Items such as personal checks and passports are also valuable if associated with a well-known figure.

Postcards are also very popular. The cards that cost a penny years ago have long since multiplied in value. Prices vary greatly in accordance with age, size of issue, and subject matter. Rare old Coca-Cola cards can bring as much as $180. Religious theme cards are also very popular, and many old sets remain. An antique issue of ten different cards each illustrating one of the Ten Commandments can bring in up to $115. Another favorite is an eight-card set with the Lord's Prayer which, in excellent condition, will bring its owner up to $100. Cards devoted to a holiday can also be quite valuable. Lounsburt's set of four April Fools' day cards can often fetch as much as $100.

Books have always been an integral part of ephemera, with the current year being no exception. As we reported last year, if you're fortunate enough to own one of the 250 copies of James Joyce's *Ulysses* signed by Joyce and illustrator Henri Matisse, you are at least $2,500 richer. But this past year will become known as the year when even the lesser known authors started to rein in the big money. An auction held in 1985 of Gene Stratton Porter's books did exceptionally well. Examples include a copy of *Metropolitan Magazine* containing her first published work, which sold for $300. A handwritten poem of hers, critiquing

Walt Whitman, sold for $225. Two first editions also did well. An autographed copy of *Firebird* sold for $1850 while a *Freckles* first edition went for $1050. The item which really made everyone take notice, though, was a copy of *Jesus of the Emerald* which brought $2,500, a price previously unheard of outside of the big names.

The bargain of the year that we heard of was a 1931 Boy Scout calendar with artwork by Norman Rockwell. Someone took it home for $90. We think that is a good investment.

What's in the future for ephemera? Be sure to check our section on *Future Collectibles* but, just as a hint, watch out for Statue of Liberty paper items and printed World's Fair memorabilia. Both are exciting areas and should be watched carefully.

GLASSWARE

A very good year was reported from all parts of the country and from all levels of the market. Depression glass was phenomenally strong this year. Elegant patterns and Carnival also did very well, but the big news was Depression glass. Good prices, good supply, and heavy collector interest fueled strong activity, especially in Heisey.

The Heisey Collectors of America (HCA) made headlines this year by buying the original molds used to make the glass. The cost was $229,150, and the money was donated entirely by members and friends of the HCA. Included in the sale were 4,000 Heisey molds, hundreds of etching plates (at least 75 of which are new), and thousands of mold drawings. How will this affect prices for Heisey? Well, the HCA has said that the molds will mainly be used to make a few pieces for the Heisey museum, but that they will market the Williamsburg pattern. Since there will be no drastic increase of Heisey on the marketplace, prices should remain strong. If someone else had bought the molds and had mass-produced them, it would have become extremely difficult to distinguish the original pieces from the new editions. As a result, Heisey prices most likely would have dropped.

Elsewhere in glass. Carnival is ever popular. Unique pieces have always been avidly sought after, and 1985 was no exception. Farmyard must always be mentioned; these pieces are so rarely on the market that their appearance always causes a stir. Regal Iris, Peter Rabbit, Christmas Compôte, and Perfection are also valuable to own. We think that Wide Panel might be a pattern to watch in the coming year. Elegance is back in vogue, and people are impressed with Wide Panel's style.

Cut glass is still a buyer's market and has been for a couple of years; but we don't think that is going to last too long. We expect that now is a good time to acquire cut glass, especially the finer pieces. While they may cost a little more, their value should increase—and you can enjoy a beautiful possession!

Many people expected a move away from Tiffany to the cheaper art glass, but so far the move has been mainly to smaller Tiffany. The larger pieces will, of course, still hold excellent value, but the prices are currently more than most collectors can afford. For instance, a favrille glass and and bronze Crocus lamp recently sold at *Doyle's* for $12,000. As the years go by, less and less high-end Tiffany will be available on the market.

JEWELRY

Interest in jewelry marches to a steady drumbeat, and sales remained strong throughout the past year—in shops, shows, flea markets, and auctions. Although trends shift with geographical areas and age groups, there are collectible items in every price range, for every taste [from $18 for a small, sterling silver flower pin (1940) to a matched pair of 1″ gold bangle bracelets in mint condition for $3,000]. Collectors of jewelry are becoming more educated every year with the proliferation of flea markets, household sales, and auctions across the country. As tastes become upgraded, we find that interest in antique jewelry becomes heightened. For the past several years, large antique brooches and bar pins have been a prime target. The serious collector was most interested in the true Art Deco pieces from the Edwardian era. At the other end of the spectrum, costume jewelry continued as the height of fashion, with collectible items such as gaudy plastic beads from the 1950's, in every color, for as little as $10.

In the mid-Atlantic market, consumers were looking for quality and value at affordable prices. Smaller items with some unusual characteristic, in the price range of $35–$100, were considered to be a quality purchase with little strain on the pocketbook. The East Coast and the deep South preferred antique jewelry of good value, in the mid-price range of $1,000–$4,000. A trend toward the finer pieces from the less expensive pieces (under $500) developed in 1985. There was little fluctuation in price, which held steady throughout the year.

The consumer maintained an interest in earrings of all kinds. As a trend toward silver developed, particularly in the mid-Atlantic states, clip-on earrings from the 1930s and 1940s were hot items. Silver belt buckles were popular. We found, in general, an upward trend in silver items. People are also beginning to mix silver and gold.

A great demand for cultured pearls was evident. Affordable necklaces of seed pearls were popular at shows, selling from $400–$600. Also in demand were crystal beads from the late 1920s, which ranged from plain glass beads at the low end of the spectrum to antique Czechoslavakian and Austrian crystal, faceted beads, which commanded a slightly higher price.

Watches have lost popularity, as has Art Nouveau, because there are so many reproductions being made today.

Following the dictates of current designers, the fashion-conscious young professional has become addicted to large, chunky pieces of jewelry from the 1940s and 1950s. Once again, costume jewelry is at the height of fashion, and prices remain comparatively low. This trend remains strong.

LIMITED EDITIONS

The market this year was similar to that of 1984: lots of shows, dealers, collectors and, most of all, plates. The difference in 1985, especially during the last half, was that sales were generally much livelier. Dealers across the country reported excellent movement of their merchandise, along with good prices and an influx of new customers. Plates have always been very popular, but the ranks of collectors are growing ever larger. The vast choice now available may cause the veteran collector to be wary, but it seems to be attracting many new people to the hobby.

The most perplexing question in this field is: What are the qualities that make a plate popular and valuable? Sometimes it's the artist, sometimes the subject, or sometimes the beauty of the piece. Whatever it is, we have found that no one can really predict the future of a specific plate. Perhaps its a combination of variety and the unknown that stimulates this hobby.

Many series were popular this past year, but the one most often mentioned to us was the *Gone With the Wind* collection. First put out in 1978, these plates are still being issued and their value remains high. Norman Rockwell plates have always been solid investments and should continue to be, and holiday editions remain a favorite. Series based on films are generally active, although the *Oklahoma* series did not do as well as expected. Editions based on television productions are emerging and selling well, and we can expect more entertainment-based editions in 1986.

Limited edition collectors are unique in that they are often collectors of other types of items as well. They are often knowledgeable about many different fields within antiques and collectibles. Plate collecting very possibly grew out of antique collecting, and the two are very closely related. The trend in 1986 is that people will collect items that relate to their limited editions. For instance, a collector of antique dolls will also collect plates depicting antique dolls; likewise, a hummel plate collector may also collect hummel figurines.

This year may have marked the opposite end of the market swing that we saw starting in the early 1970s. The market was not strong then, and some collectors lost faith. The market has slowly turned around over the past decade, and we will see more and more strength in the coming year.

What were the best plates? In a field where everyone has his own favorites, there is no clear answer. As for market value, there was gradual growth but no major changes. Boehm's Butterfly, Hard Fruit, Soft Fruit, and Seashell were all valued at around $400, and Borsato's plaques still remain high at about $1,700. DeGrazia's work is still highly valued; for instance, his Los Niños will bring its owner $1,400, even though the issue price was only $35. If you're fortunate enough to have one of the 500 plates that he signed, you add $1,200 to that for a $2,600 value. Gunnar Nylun's "Bringing Home the Tree" has stayed steady for the past few years at about $550 while the grandfather of them all —Bing and Grondahl's 1895 "Behind the Frozen Window" by Grans August Hallin—also stayed steady at about $4,000.

A sale held in Elgin, Illinois turned in some good prices. An Albino Ware plate entitled "Fishing Boats" sold for $302.50. Hummels were also popular as Hummel #71, "Stormy Weather," sold for $341 and #203, "Signs of Spring," sold for $262. There was an 1897 Bing and Grondahl Christmas plate at the same show that topped them all at $495.

MUSIC

This was one of the most interesting years for music collectibles in quite a while. Great auctions were happening all over, and high prices were realized. Supplies are growing every day with collectibility keeping pace with interest.

Recently, a big find was a crate full of music scores by George Gershwin, Cole Porter, and Richard Rogers, among others. Much of the material found was unpublished, making it a real find. Sheet music, on the whole, has been a field of steady collector interest and should continue to do well.

An 1892 Steinway & Sons satinwood grand piano was purchased for $11,000 at Sloan's. Supplies of this sort are finite, and we look for large price increases.

An absolutely fantastic collection of music items was auctioned last year in Geneva, New York. Items from many facets of this field were offered and quickly taken up.

"Nipper," the dog on the RCA advertisements listening to "his master's voice," had a very good year: a 40-inch Nipper brought in $800 at the Geneva sale, while a smaller version sold for $725. Organs did well, as an 1886 paper roller rolled out of the showroom for $950, and a concert roller organ sold for $550. Phonographs were abundant, with some real beauties on sale. A 1903 Victor VI, with an oak base and horn, sold for $1,000, whereas a 1902 Victor MS with horn played a softer tune for $900. A 1901 Victor Royal came in nicely at $525, and a beautiful Edison Cygnet was a good deal at $400. Several portable antique phonographs were also available, ranging in price from $60 to $100.

Some miscellaneous items were also available, and they included a set of three mini 1930s Chevrolet advertisement records which sold for $130, and a set of talking book records for $60.

Limited editions have also hit the music field. We saw two really interesting offers this year. *Fantasy Records* is now offering 3,000 copy editions of *Original Jazz Classics* for only $8.95. These are re-releases, so you are not getting the original copies, but they are of high quality: the jacket, cover, and liner notes are all recreated, as well as the tunes.

The second limited release was *50 Years Adrift,* by Derek Taylor. It is a beautiful book, bound in calf leather with gilt-edge pages. Taylor was the press agent for the Beatles and many other big-name Rock and Roll bands throughout the 1960s and 1970s. The price of this highly collectible volume is $350, so it is not for everyone, but there are no plans for a less expensive edition; the print run is limited to 2,000 copies.

Jukeboxes were a favorite this year; some prices from a *Doyle's* auction include a Wurlitzer 1015 for $5,750; a Wurlitzer 850 for $6,500; and a Wurlitzer 1100 for $2,000.

PRINTS

Boosted by a series of important art shows and exhibitions across the country, print collecting remained strong. In particular, interest in Americana and country prints continued to swell. Artists P. Buckley Moss and Charles Wysocki enjoyed continued popularity. Leading the sales were old prints by Norman Rockwell and Currier & Ives.

Judging by the large attendance at events such as the exhibition of Cowboy Artists of America at the Phoenix, Arizona Museum, the annual Wildlife and Western Art Exhibition in Minneapolis (sponsored by the National Wildlife and Western Art Collectors Society), and an important charity in New York City for cancer research, hosted by such luminaries as Perry Como, Silver Porter and Armand Hammer, the area of Western art is drawing new and enthusiastic collectors, taking a seat beside wildlife art at the top of the market.

Prominent artists associated with Western art and wildlife art are Bev Doolittle, nominated as "Western Artist of the Year," and Guy Coheleach, "Wildlife Artist of the Year," as well as David Maass, Olaf Weighorst, Owen Gromme, and Robert Abbett. Bob Timberlake opened his fifth one-man show in New York; Charles Harper was selected in Kentucky for a state promotion project as "Water Awareness" for a painting for poster distribution; Jim Harrison was chosen by the Women Involved in Rural Electrification (WIRE) to execute a commemorative painting for the celebration of their 50th anniversary; and Ray Harm was the Appalachian Gold Medallion winner, from the University of Charleston, South Carolina, as an artist whose work represents the area in "a profound and compelling way."

On the international scene, selected works of wildlife artist John Ruthven were chosen by the United States government for inclusion in the cultural exchange program with the Soviet Union.

TOYS

Last year we warned you to hang on to your hats, as toy prices were so unpredictable that any guess was hazardous. Although values are still far from uniform among the various categories of toys, we can now venture to say that the trend is definitely upward and will continue for some time—at least through the year.

Among the leaders during this past year were mechanical banks, toy trains, Mickey Mouse items, pull toys, and dolls. Perhaps the biggest movers this year, though, were stuffed animals, Teddy bears in particular. A Steiff Teddy auctioned for $2,530 at *Christie's East*. Also of great interest at that show was a bisque-headed Bebe which brought in $18,700, and a Mignot "War of the World" diorama which sold for $3,300. A set of Buck Rogers action figures by Britains brought a deserved $1,540, owing to its rarity.

At *Sotheby's,* pull toys and boats were a great hit, as a tin riverboat pull toy marked "Puritan" (c. 1880) by James Fallows & Sons brought in $22,000. At the same sale, two Marklin ships also sold well: the first was a tin reproduction of the battleship *Oregon* that cruised out at $17,000; the other was a tin clockwork oceanliner marked *Carmania* that sold for $12,000. Finally, a delightful, manually operated tin Ferris wheel brought in $13,200.

Another big area was toy robots and space toys. The collectibility of toy robots has grown so much in the last few years that even specimens of unknown manufacturers, such as the "Robot 2500," can commonly bring three-figure sums in excellent condition. A "Robby Space Patrol" robot will bring its seller about $1,750 (if you can find one; owners are not letting go of these). Dealers and collectors couldn't get enough robots this year, as the trade papers were full of ads offering thousands of dollars for rare specimens and collections. Flash Gordon items have also greatly appreciated in value and are currently holding steady. The most interesting aspect of these items lies in their vast diversity of quality and affordability.

Howdy Doody continued his remarkable career on the collectibles stage with an increase in popularity and in prices. These items are notable for two reasons: first, Howdy Doody achieved popularity initially through television, without the help of movies or comics; second, so many Howdy Doody items were produced that it seemed that the market would be saturated. This did not turn out to be true as Howdy Doody toys—the largest collection devoted to a single television character—have remained steady and profitable.

The field of toy soldiers remained healthy and displayed great strength. Collectors in this field are also tremendously original as they recreate the famous battles of history. This hobby is a true art devoted to the faithful reproduction of events that shaped the world. Prices are up and interest never flags in this enjoyable hobby. A Britains pre-war set known as "The Full Band of the Coldstream Guards" sold for $605. Upward trends will continue through 1986.

The common denominator of toy collectors is that fun and profit can indeed combine to boost the popularity of this growing hobby. We expect toys to keep their strength throughout the coming year. We see space toys as leading the way, but toys of all types will continue to perform well.

INVESTING

Investment in collectors' items on a *grand scale* began overseas slightly before it began in the U.S. In Japan and Western Europe, where inflation was more drastic than in America, investors were turning to art and antiques in the early seventies. When prices for collectibles boomed abroad, as of course they did from the super-strong competition, the effect was dramatic on the U.S. market. Foreign investors by the score started buying from American dealers to take advantage of the savings. But the savings did not last long. Very shortly, U.S. prices for art, antiques and other collectibles were on a par with those of Japan and Western Europe. And the level of investor buying in all these far-flung regions of the globe was about the same as it is today.

Today, as we approach the late 1980s, antiques, art, coins and other "collectible investing" has been with us long enough to give us a fairly good perspective on its long-term potential, and to draw some conclusions which would have been impossible to arrive at (without a crystal ball) as recently as five years ago.

Collectible investment has proven itself more resilient than its critics believed. They were convinced that the first wave of heavy selling by investors—returning their purchases to the marketplace and taking their profit on them—would seriously reduce values and discourage any further investment. These collectibles would, they felt, be treated in the same manner as declining stocks.

Well, the first wave of heavy investment selling has come and gone, followed by more selling, in a rather balanced flow since the late seventies. A very sizable amount of the merchandise bought by investors during the 1970s has gone back on the market, and some of it has passed through the hands of dealers and/or auctioneers half a dozen times since then. The disaster predicted by critics did not occur. Some slumps were evident in certain areas of collectibles, but these have occurred historically through the years without any influence from investors. In most cases, the slumps were not of long duration because new investors came in to snatch up bargains that resulted from falling prices.

The first requirement for successful investing is that the buyer knows what he's purchasing—what sort of investment prospects it has, and whether the particular specimen merits investment.

In other words, you cannot simply "invest in collectibles." You choose your subject, analyze the field, and buy methodically.

Even then, you are not GUARANTEED success. But your chances of turning a profit, on a well-selected collector's item bought for investment, are unquestionably in your favor.

So many subtle considerations are involved that we cannot detail them all here. For a much more thorough exploration of investing in collectors' items—with all the pros, cons, and professional strategy—the interested reader is advised to consult the series of books on that subject published by The House of Collectibles. These include *The Official Investors' Guide to Gold, Silver and Diamonds; The Official Investors' Guide to Gold Coins; The Official Investors Guide to Silver Coins;* and *The Official Investors Guide to Silver Dollars.* The basic methods outlined in these works can be applied to any types of collectors' items.

The person who contemplates investing is, often, misled by the changing values of collectors' items. This is one basic "hurdle" for a new investor to clear. For example, someone has purchased a certain antique five years ago for $100. He opens a magazine today and discovers an advertisement offering the item for $200. The instinctive reaction is that he could double his money, in five years, by purchasing additional specimens for investment. There ARE some collectors' items, in fact quite a few of them, on which the investor can profit in five years or even less. But in this example, he would be ill-advised to go out and put a great deal of money into the item that rose from $100 to $200. The simple fact is that you DON'T double your money on something which rises in value that gradually. You may actually end up taking a loss on it, depending on circumstances.

Let's explore things a bit further.

When that item is selling for $200, this represents the retail market value—such as is given in the listings section of this book for thousands and thousands of collectors' items. If YOU, as a private owner, sell the item to a dealer, you will not receive $200. You may get only 50% of the retail market value, which means getting back the $100 you paid for it five years ago. But you still aren't even "breaking even." In the meantime, inflation has reduced the buying power of money. One hundred dollars isn't worth as much today as it was five years ago. You would need to receive close to $200 just to break even, in terms of the actual value of the money. So what appears on paper or in your imagination to be an excellent investment is really not one at all.

To be a worthwhile investment, an item would need to recover the cost price (when sold); PLUS compensate for the declining value of the dollar; PLUS leave you a profit when BOTH OF THESE FACTORS have been taken into consideration. To accomplish this, the investment item needs to rise in value at a fast pace. In addition, YOU the investor must watch the market and be aware of developments occurring on collectibles at that time—so you can seize the proper moment to sell.

BUILDING A COLLECTION

Virtually every type of collector's item offers the possibility of building a collection, and adopting a hobby that can last a lifetime. All of those listed in this book, as obscure or remote as some may appear, fall into that category. And there are numerous others, hundreds in fact, which space limitations prevent us from covering. A visit to any antique shop will introduce you to many of them. So will a casual glance through the hobbyist periodicals, which are available at your public library.

Collecting need not be expensive. And it needn't be time-consuming, if you don't want it to be. This depends on you, and on what you want from your hobby. The goals and motives of collectors are diverse. Some collectors receive most of their pleasure and satisfaction from seeing their collection grow. Others enjoy the hunt and chase—tracking down hard-to-find items, following their trail wherever it leads. To them, browsing for three hours in a crowded antique shop and leaving with dust-laden hands and clothing is a prime exhilaration. And still others enjoy collecting because it leads to meeting other collectors and widening their circle of friends and social activities.

Your selection of a collecting interest depends on finances, space, and other considerations, but mainly on your own personal tastes and inclinations. It's largely a matter of what you'll be most comfortable with. Looking through this book will provide a kaleidoscope of suggestions. While you're thinking, here are some points to ponder. Most areas of collecting can be pursued inexpensively and adapted to fit just about any budget. But this is not, unfortunately, true of EVERY type of collectible. You cannot collect Tiffany lamps or Currier & Ives lithographs without spending rather substantial amounts for each acquisition. This has nothing to do with the size or scope of the particular hobby. Competition is a factor in price, but so is availability. There are millions of coin and stamp collectors—far more than for Tiffany lamps—yet the vast majority of stamps and coins are inexpensive. These are hobbies in which great rarities exist alongside pieces that can be bought for a few pennies. Book collecting is another pursuit in which prices run the scale from zero to lofty heights. Original art, antique furniture, and porcelain are others in that category (plenty to choose from, pricewise). And there are some collecting areas in which the MOST valuable existing items are not expensive at all.

One thing you may want to consider in thinking about your choice of a collecting hobby is whether you'd like to collect objects that bear a DIRECT relationship to each other, such as sets. Set collecting can be done with material which was originally issued as a set (as in silverware), or carries dates or numbers that permit set assembly (such as comic books or coins). A typical example of a "set collection" is a run of Lincoln cents, beginning with the earliest one for 1909 and continuing up to the present. With this sort of collection, you always have a clear direction and you don't lose sight of your purpose. But for many people, set collecting is not creative enough. Each component in the set is, in many instances, very similar to every other component. A group of 70 Lincoln cents on which all the "heads" (obverse sides) are identical except for the dates is simply boring in the view of some hobbyists. They want more variety. If you fall into that category, set collecting is definitely not for you!

Another point to consider is whether you'd like to participate in a well-established hobby that's amply supplied with reference literature, clubs and periodicals, or get in on the "ground floor" of one that's just in the process of developing. There are pros and cons on both sides of the fence, so it becomes, as usual, a matter of personal preference. With a well-established hobby, you receive the benefit of all the work already done by experts in terms of research, classification, and inquiry into fakes and counterfeits. On the other hand, items in such a group all carry an equally well-established market value, so there is less chance of finding bargains or making any discoveries on your own. In a hobby which has not yet been well developed, you could get some really excellent buys (things that might be soaring skyward in values, next year or five years from now), but they'll be somewhat harder to find and possibly trickier to authenticate. In some instances, if the hobby is really new, the dealers may not have had the chance to accumulate much knowledge and will hesitate to proclaim an item "genuine" or "fake."

But what it really boils down to is: What do you like? What do you enjoy owning, looking at, handling, thinking about? Do you like detective shows on TV? You might be at home collecting first editions of detective novels; or police memorabilia; or old "wanted" posters.

Like pets? Many collections have been made of animal-motif items, such as porcelain dogs and cats, or mechanical banks in the shape of animals.

Are you a travel enthusiast? Stamps and coins take you to faraway places. So do foreign banknotes and many other collectibles.

Into cooking? There are old and scarce and very curious cookbooks to be collected, as well as the implements used by our forebears in cooking and eating.

In other words, just about anything that interests you can be turned into a hobby, even if you never thought about it from the standpoint of "collecting." For the sports fans, there are baseball and football cards, autographs, team equipment, yearbooks and plenty of other collectibles. For the car buff, there are antique components rescued from vintage autos, as well as all kinds of automotive ephemera.

And how about your job? Love it or hate it, it occupies a good deal of your attention. Are you ever curious about the way your predecessors in that type of job worked 50 to 100 years ago? The implements they used? Quite a few collectors get curious enough to become historians of their profession.

More doctors and dentists build collections around their profession than anyone else. In the hobbyist publications, you will encounter many ads placed by doctors and dentists, seeking to buy medical or dental memorabilia of yester-year. These are, of course, ideal fields for collecting, because the professions are very old, have a well-documented history, and have produced a vast quantity of collectible items of every description.

Think about your job, and whether it might contain the spark for a collection.

CONDITION

The condition, or physical preservation, of collectors' items is receiving increasing attention. Collectors are becoming more demanding with regard to condition. For investors, condition is of extreme importance, since it has been shown beyond a doubt that collectors' items in the best grades of condition rise sharpest in value.

Nearly ALL collectors' items in well-preserved condition have a higher rarity factor than the VERY SAME ITEMS in lesser condition. This is because the majority of existing specimens are, almost invariably, in less than outstanding condition. With some items, there may be one "mint" specimen in circulation for every ten showing signs of wear, use or abuse. With others, the ratio could be 1-to-100 or even 1-to-1000. It varies, of course, with the type of collectible, the age, and other factors.

Condition, therefore, is a prime influence in buying or selling collectors' items. Whether the beginning collector is really concerned about condition or not, he needs to learn something about it and its effect on prices. Otherwise he is likely to see bargains where they do not exist, or accuse a seller of overpricing when a premium is being charged because of noteworthy condition. If you're bidding at auction sales, you must be even MORE alert to condition and the difference it makes in values.

No grading system fits all varieties of collectors' items. Each item has to be judged in terms of its material, age, the use for which it was intended, and other considerations. Something made as a household decoration to be hung on a wall and admired is in a far different category than a tool or cooking utensil. You would not expect a 19th century sledgehammer to be free of any nicks and scratches.

Don't expect the impossible, but don't settle for slipshod specimens of items that could have been much better preserved.

FAKES

Develop a critical sense, a vital quality which the bargain-hunter and casual shopper usually lack.

In nearly all cases, fakes fall into one of the following categories:

1. The outright fake. This is what most people think of as a fake, being unaware that other kinds exist. An outright fake is made wholly by the faker,

"from scratch." He obtains materials and uses his own processes to create the object, and his goal is to defraud the eventual buyer.

2. The honest reproduction. These are multiplying in number. An honest reproduction is a facsimile of a collector's item made as a decoration, souvenir, curio, or for some other legitimate purpose without the intent to defraud. They are, however, sometimes mistaken for originals.

3. The doctored item. This is a genuine collector's item which the faker changes in some way or other to make it appear more valuable, such as a coin on which a mintmark is removed or a silver porringer to which an inscription and date are added.

4. The hybrid. These are objects made from components of two or more collectors' items. Hybrids occur most frequently in furniture. A faker will take two tables, one with good legs and the other with a good top, and meld the well-preserved components.

Of these four categories of fakes, objects falling into the first (outright fakes) are automatically worthless, except for intrinsic value if they happen to contain a precious metal.

Honest reproductions can, and usually do, have some value, but the value is considerably less than that of the model. There are occasional exceptions to this rule. When a reproduction is made as a limited edition, in a deluxe manner using the best materials and workmanship, it can be a desirable collector's item in itself and POSSIBLY of even greater value than the original. Some reproductions of antique firearms (for example) attain very high collector value.

Doctored items tend to be considered "spoiled" by collectors, even if they had a substantial value originally. As for the last category, hybrids, these are very commonplace on the antique market and are sold regularly. While the collector value or historical value of any hybrid is open to debate, there is definitely a good demand for them. They have the look of an antique and have a utilitarian value, if the object is a piece of furniture; and many noncollecting buyers will ask no further questions. So it is open to argument, really, whether the maker of hybrids can be called a faker.

One of your chief weapons against buying fakes (of any variety) is to buy only from the more respected sources of supply. This advice makes obvious sense. Specialist dealers who handle just one type of collector's item are likely to be expert on that type of collector's item. The specialist dealers, because of their reputation for knowing their subject, are very seldom offered fakes for sale. Anyone who knowingly wants to sell a fake will, nine times in ten, take it to a general antique dealer. This may mean a little lower price, but the danger of detection is lower too, and this is what counts in such situations. The less careful and less expert the dealer is, the more careful and more expert his customers must be!

BUYING TIPS

BUYING FROM DEALERS

There may be occasional problems or drawbacks in buying from dealers, but on the whole they serve a vital purpose. Most of the collecting hobbies covered in this book could not exist without the professional dealers. They do the legwork for you in finding the material and bringing a large selection of it together for your perusal. They serve as a kind of buffer between you and the counterfeiters and forgers who manufacture bogus collectibles. Sometimes fakes do get on dealers' shelves; but without the dealers as a line of defense, things would be far worse. Dealers can be helpful to you in many ways. They have contacts within the trade which would be hard for a private hobbyist to duplicate. If they know exactly what type of item you're looking for, even if it's something very offbeat or scarce, they can usually find it for you.

There are basically two types of dealers in collectors' items. The first is the general dealer. Most antique dealers fall into that category. They offer a broad variety of collectors' items, and possibly some objects which could not be called collectors' items, but are decorative or interesting. The second type is the specialist dealer. He sells primarily—or exclusively—collectors' items of a certain kind, such as stamps, comic books, or prints. Today there are specialist dealers for nearly every type of collectible. Naturally the bigger hobbies have the most specialist dealers; thousands of dealers specialize in coins, for example, while only a handful restrict themselves to something like firefighting memorabilia. This is governed strictly by the degree of hobbyist activity and the amount of money being spent in each field. What are the basic differences in buying from a general dealer as opposed to buying from a specialist?

In the shops of general antique dealers, you will find many of the identical items offered by specialist dealers. There IS a difference, though. The prices are usually a bit lower. When you buy from a general dealer, you will usually pay a lower price for the same item than if you had acquired it from a specialist. The savings might be only five or ten percent, but it could be as much as fifty percent or even more.

The general dealer does not have as large a selection of specialist items. If you collect Depression Glass, for example, the general dealer might have a dozen pieces—or perhaps he might have none at all. A specialist dealer in glassware will be displaying HUNDREDS of examples of Depression Glass. The general antique dealer does not, in most instances, profess to be an expert on everything in his stock. His wares represent a conglomeration of his purchases from many different sources, and he offers them "as they come." Not all general antique dealers fall into that category, as some deal in a higher grade of merchandise and have experts on their staff to appraise and identify incoming stock. In return for the opportunity to get a bargain, the onus falls upon you, the customer, to decide whether an item is exactly what it appears to be.

The specialist dealer goes to more trouble than the general dealer. He inspects his merchandise more carefully. He has expert knowledge of his pet subject and, usually, a reputation within the field. There is very little likelihood that fakes, counterfeits, or restorations can slip by him.

Price Variations. The question most often asked by beginners about buying in antique shops is: How firm are the prices? What will happen if I make a counter-offer? Will the dealer be offended? Do I stand much chance of getting an item for less than the named price?

The situation is generally this: the dealer has a price in mind (it may be tagged on the item, or truly "in mind") that he would LIKE to get—a price that would cover his cost and leave a favorable margin of profit. It may be double the sum he paid, or even triple: this varies depending on the item and its nature, and also his style and volume of business. A dealer will be more apt to show flexibility on a price if the item has been in stock for months or (in some cases) a year or more. When stock is relatively new, the dealer holds out, hoping that it will sell for the full price he wishes to get. As time passes and it fails to sell, it becomes evident that the price may need to be adjusted. With some dealers, the waiting period before price adjustment is very short, as they like to turn over their stock rapidly.

The term "reducing the price" is apt to be misleading. To determine whether the reduction results in a favorable buy, you would need to know if the ORIGINAL price was in line with the true market value. If a dealer prices something at $300 when the average market price is $200, he can reduce it by 20% and still be charging more than most of his competitors.

As far as the reaction you'll receive from dickering, this varies with the dealers. Some are insulted. Some pretend to be insulted, but aren't. Some welcome a no-holds-barred discussion about price, because it gets the customer talking and a talking customer is likely to end up buying. You're apt to get a more favorable reception by not drawing attention to flaws or taking a an overly casual approach. The skilled bargainer always takes a positive attitude about the item under discussion. He never asks for a discount because the item isn't EXACTLY what he really wants. Rather, he acknowledges his interest in it, and says something like, "if I could get this for $50, I wouldn't hesitate a minute," or words to that effect. If you have experience at all with antique shops and their proprietors, you can usually tell when dickering will be successful and when it won't. If you and the owner are TOO far apart in price, it's just a waste of your time to get into a bargaining session. Don't delude yourself into believing that you can work the price down to half the original sum. In most cases, a discount of ten or fifteen percent is the most you're going to get—because ten percent off the PRICE means at least twenty percent off the PROFIT in most cases. There are many possible variations on approaches to bargaining—far too numerous to enter into here. One novel method is worth mentioning. There was a collector who would browse around an antique shop until he found something he wanted, say a tin pelican priced at $30. He would pretend he hadn't seen the item, then casually ask the dealer, "Do you happen to have any tin pelicans for around $20?" This is a very effective approach, because it establishes YOUR price range before the dealer has the chance to establish HIS price range. It's a way of bargaining without appearing to be bargaining.

BUYING AT AUCTIONS

Auction buying is exciting, and offers more opportunities for bargains than in buying from dealers, but carries somewhat greater risks. As a rule, auction buying is more suitable for the experienced collector. But there is no reason why a beginner, using caution and common sense, cannot attend auctions and try his luck in the competition.

If you buy at an auction, you are apt to be involved in bidding under a broad variety of circumstances. You will sometimes be bidding on a lot for which YOUR maximum bid represents one-tenth the sum another bidder is ready, willing, and able to pay. And you will, just as frequently or perhaps more so, come prepared to give a small fortune for an item that not a single other bidder wants. The price that something brings at an auction is not, therefore, an indication of its value, but only of its value to the bidders in that particular sale. If sold again the next day, with different bidders on the floor, it could go considerably higher or lower.

If it sounds as though auction buying entails a substantial measure of uncertainty, it does indeed. But if you know the mechanics of auctions, have a relatively cool head and sound judgment about collectors' items, you can do very well in the auction arena. The important thing is to keep a reign on your emotions and not overpay unless the item is something extra-special. Also important is to know what you're bidding on: if it's authentic, if it's in good condition, and whether it truly merits the size of the bid you intend to place.

If you're going to attend the sale, don't fail to also attend the *presale exhibition.*

You could (as many bidders do) wander around the presale exhibit and see what catches your fancy. This is time-consuming, though, and a better approach is to check off—in the catalogue—lots which SEEM as though they appeal to you. Then, at the presale exhibit, you can go directly to them and spend your time giving each a thorough examination.

As you make your inspections, mark your bid limit for each item in the catalogue. This is the time to think about price, not during the heat of competition. At the presale exhibit, you're not being influenced by the prices OTHER bidders are willing to pay. You can make a much sounder judgment of how much you want it and how much it's worth to you in dollars and cents.

SELLING TIPS

Many factors enter into the price you receive (or the price you're offered) when selling collectibles. Let's take a look at some of them:

1. Dealer's stock on hand. This, of course, varies from dealer to dealer, and even among the same dealers at different times of the year. You aren't in a position to know what kind of stock the dealer has on hand, or what he has coming in, yet this does play a role in determining (a) whether he'll be interested in purchasing your antiques, and (b) the extent of investment he cares to make in them. When a dealer says he's overstocked, this is not necessarily a ploy to induce you to accept a low price. All dealers in collectors' items DO become overstocked periodically—and they become *understocked,* too. It all hinges on the pace at which material moves in and out, and that's governed largely by circumstances over which the dealer has only partial control. Sometimes he'll go for weeks without anyone offering to sell him anything. Then armies of sellers all arrive at the same time. This works fine if the volume and flow of buying is comparable to that of selling. But if the dealer has been buying more than he's been selling, he has no choice but to slow down for a while. No dealer likes to bypass the opportunity to buy worthwhile merchandise, but he can't have more cash going out than coming in.

2. The dealer's clientele. Every dealer—whether he sells antiques, militaria, dolls, or whatever—has his own special group of customers, who are the life and blood of his business. Some of them are sure to be general collectors, but others are specialists, and the specialties of these clients can be very exclusive in some cases. An antique dealer may have a customer who wants nothing but augers (old tools uses to bore holes in wood). You could survey ninety-nine other antique dealers and find NONE who have customers for augers, but this particular dealer has one—and an avid one to boot. The customer possibly has one of the largest collections of augers in the country. He wants to buy any specimens and ALL specimens that he can find, regardless of size, shape or color. He never says "no" to an auger. Consequently, the dealer knows he can sell any augers that come into his stock. When an auger is offered to him, he automatically buys it, and he may pay a higher proportion of the retail value than he pays for other antiques. He has a sure sale at a sure price, so his degree of risk is just about zero.

The type of items that a dealer displays in his shop may be a clue to those in which he's most interested in buying. Certainly if you find an antique shop whose stock consists mainly of glass, this would be a more likely place to sell a collection of glassware than to a "general" antique shop. But it does not always work that way. In the example given above, of augers, you would not find a single auger in the shop, even though its proprietor would rather buy them than anything else. Why? Because every one he purchases is sold immediately to his special customer, without ever going out on display in the shop. This is the situation with many kinds of merchandise in many collectors' shops. What you see "out front" displayed to the public is the general stock. Articles that have been bought for special clients aren't around any longer.

3. Geographical location. With some types of collectors' items the PLACE of sale can be a factor in their price. Values given in this book are averages for the country as a whole. If an item has definite *regional interest,* it can be counted on to sell somewhat higher in that locality and usually a bit lower than the average elsewhere. More collectors' items have regional interest than you might imagine, though it is not usually strong enough to influence the value by more than 10% or at the most 15%.

It also happens, sometimes, that certain collecting hobbies thrive a bit stronger in some parts of the country than others, for no really explainable reason. This has been the case with knife collecting, to name one; it has been more popular in the southern states than elsewhere. In the earlier days of *rock 'n roll record collecting,* nearly all collecting activity was confined to New York and California (this has since changed). Comic book collecting was a big hobby in New York before it surfaced anywhere else.

4. Condition. It is an inescapable fact that when an item is worn, damaged, or otherwise not in the best of condition, it is not worth the full retail value. It may still be collectible and salable to a dealer, but it represents a kind of question mark for him. Maybe if the item was in "mint" condition he would not hesitate to purchase it. In inferior condition, he will automatically wonder how long it will take to sell, and whether it will sell at all. Some dealers do not care to stock damaged or defective items. Others will do so, in certain cases, but their buying offer will be CONSIDERABLY less than their offer for a mint or near-mint specimen. It may be just ten percent of the retail value of a mint specimen or even less. If that seems unfair, you should stop to consider that the dealer is in a bind when he handles merchandise of that nature. He has to offer his customers a very healthy discount on it, possibly selling it for a third as much as a mint specimen. Therefore he can put very little money into it.

If you have a collection which is mostly in good condition but contains some defective items, it may be best to REMOVE the defective items before offering it for sale. These sub-par components in a collection will always catch the dealer's eye and may give him a negative feeling toward the collection as a whole. Then, when you discuss price, the dealer is sure to point out the inferior condition of these items. Just like your garden, your collection may need weeding out before selling it. Put it in the best shape you can, and you'll stand an excellent chance of getting a satisfactory price for it.

SELLING BY AUCTION

Maybe you enjoy buying at auction. Have you considered the possibility of selling your collection in that fashion, when the time comes to sell?

Auction sales have become a much more popular method for selling all types of collectors' items. The chief attraction of selling by auction is that you have the chance, with a little luck, of realizing more than a dealer would pay for your collection. A dealer has to resell the material, so of course he takes a deduction from its retail market value in figuring up his purchase price. At auction, the sky is the limit. If two or three determined bidders lock horns on something YOU own, they could drive the price up far beyond the retail market value. Even after the auctioneer's "house commission" is deducted from the selling price, you would end up doing better than selling outright to a dealer.

Of course, it doesn't always work that way. Auctions are unpredictable. Just as you have the opportunity, at auction, of realizing more than a dealer would pay, the possibility also exists that your collection will bring LESS than a dealer would have given. Those are the breaks of the auction game.

Consider the type of collection you have for sale, its contents and value, and you may be able to judge fairly accurately which method of sale holds out the brighter prospects.

The best types of collections to sell by auction are those which are highly specialized and those containing a large proportion of investment items. But as you will see by attending auctions or just reading the reports of them, many collections are sold—thousands of them annually—which do not fall into either of these categories. Their owners chose the auction route, when they could have sold to a dealer and received quicker payment.

There are all types of auctions. They range from posh sales of art and jewels, accompanied by lavish catalogues which serve as reference books in themselves. At a sale of this type, bids totaling more than a million dollars might be recorded in less than a hour. At the other end of the scale are country auctions and estate sales, at which anything under the sun is apt to turn up and where lots can go for as low as $1 each. (But do not underestimate the country or estate sale, either—when desirable collectors' items are included, as they sometimes are, dealers and collectors flock to them and the prices can get very, very strong.)

Some auctioneers are specialists while others handle whatever comes along, so long as it falls in the nature of secondhand property. The biggest groups of specialist auctioneers are those handling coins and stamps. Material of this nature requires specialist knowledge to appraise and classify, so it is very seldom sold by the general art or antique auctioneers. If you have a specialized collection, it is advisable (when selling by auction) to seek out an auctioneer whose sales are geared to that type of merchandise. Such an auctioneer has an established mailing list of active buyers for THAT PARTICULAR KIND OF COLLECTIBLE, and you're sure to do much better pricewise than if you select a local auctioneer just because of convenience.

The procedures vary among auction houses in terms of the arrangements made with sellers and also the actual rules and regulations of their sales. The amount of their commission varies, too, but this usually proves to be a rather minor detail. You should not automatically choose the auctioneer who offers the lowest commission rate (i.e., the percentage he deducts from the sale price of each lot before settling with the owner). When one house is operating on a ten percent commission and another on fifteen percent, it might seem as though the ten percent house is the obvious choice. This just isn't so. Usually when an auctioneer is charging slightly higher commission rates than the competition, it's because he spends a great deal more in advertising and promoting his sales, and on the preparation of his catalogues. Therefore, the prices realized at his sales are likely to be MUCH higher—so you would do better selling through him, even though his commission rate might seem discouraging. A low commission rate is, often, an indication that the house has a hard time attracting property for sale. When an auction house has an established record of successful sales and satisfied clients, it has no problem getting material to sell. So do not allow yourself to be influenced by differences in commission rates.

When you put material up for sale by auction, it is never sold immediately. It has to be lotted and catalogued and the catalogues have to be distributed. All of this takes time. It may be two to three months, between placing the merchandise in the auctioneer's hands and the actual date of sale. And, thereafter, it might be another 30 days before you receive settlement. Settlement is seldom made quickly. Each auction house works by contract. You and the auctioneer sign a sales contract at the time of placing the material in the auctioneer's care. The contract spells out all these details — the rate of commission, the sale date, and the length of waiting time between the sale date and receiving your payment.

FLEA MARKET DIRECTORY

The following flea markets are listed in alphabetical order according to state. Within each state the listings are in alphabetical order according to city or town. If you would like to have your flea market listed free of charge in the next edition of this book, please send us your information using the format found below. We provide this directory as a service to our readers and would like to expand it to include as many flea markets as possible.

One word of caution—be sure to verify flea market dates and hours of operation before driving long distances to attend.

CALIFORNIA

GARDEN GROVE
Westminister Abbey
Antique Mall 11751
Westminister Ave.
Daily 10:00–5:00, Friday 10:00–9:00
PM Closed Tuesday

CONNECTICUT

JEWETT CITY
College Mart Flea Market
Indoor/outdoor, all year round since 1982
1 mile off I-395, exit 84 or 85;
follow Flea Market signs to
Wedgewood Drive. (203) 642-6248
Sundays 9 AM–4 PM
100 dealers presently
Free parking and admission

FLORIDA

BRANDON
Joe & Jackie's Flea Market
3 miles north of Brandon between
Parsons and Kingsway on Hwy. 574
Daily (305) 689-6318

FT. LAUDERDALE
Oakland Park Boulevard
Flea Market
3161 W. Oakland Park Blvd.

HIALEAH *(Miami area)*
DAV Swap Meet
1000 E. 56th St. (305) 685-1296

HIALEAH GARDENS *(Miami area)*
Palmetto Flea Market
7705 NW 103rd St.
(305) 821-8901 822-4478 825-9605

LAKELAND—AUBURNDALE
International Market World
Highway 92 East of Lakeland
Friday, Saturday and Sunday
(813) 665-0062

MIAMI
Flea Bazaar
14501 W. Dixie Hwy.
(305) 945-3553

MIAMI
Metro Flea Markets
701 SW 27th Ave.
(305) 541-3400

MIAMI
Turnpike Drive In Theatre Flea
Market
12850 WN 27th Ave.
Wednesday, Friday, Saturday,
Sunday (305) 681-7150

MIAMI
119th St. Flea Market
1701 NW 119th Street
(305) 687-0521

MIAMI BEACH
World's Largest Indoor Flea Market
1901 Convention Center Dr.
(305) 673-8071

NORTH MIAMI
Seventh Avenue Flea Market Inc.
13995 NW 7th Ave.
(305) 688-3852

NORTH MIAMI
North Miami Flea Market
14135 NW 7th Ave.
(305) 685-7721

MT DORA
Florida Twin Markets, Jim Renninger
—proprietor Highway 441 in Mt.
Dora, ½ mile north of Highway 46
Every Saturday and Sunday 8 AM–5
PM
(305) 886-8946

ORLANDO
Bobbie's Flea Market
5620 W. Colonial Dr.
Daily (305) 298-0386

ORLANDO
House of Bargains
6021 E. Colonial Dr.
Thursday through Sunday (305)
273-5555

ORLANDO
Northgate Flea Market
1725 Lee Rd
Weekends (305) 293-3600

ORLANDO
Orlando Flea Market
5022 S. Orange Blossom Trail
(305) 857-0048

PALMETTO *(Tampa area)*
Country Fair
U.S. Highway 301 and 41
(813) 722-5633

PLANT CITY *(Tampa area)*
Country Village Flea Market
One mile north of 1-4 Exit 13 on St.
Rd. 39
Wednesday, Saturday and Sunday
(813) 752-4670

SANFORD *(Orlando area)*
Flea World
Hwy. 17-92 between Orlando and
Sanford
Friday, Saturday, Sunday 8 AM–5
PM
(305) 645-1792

SARASOTA
Trail Outdoor Flea Market
6801 Tamiami Tr N, across 41 from
Sarasota airport
(813) 355-6329

TAMPA
Bargain Barn Flea Market
2400 Gehman PL.
(813) 248-1208

TAMPA
Buccaneer Flea Market Inc.
4260 Dale Mabry Highway S
(813) 831-4499

TAMPA
Oldsmar Flea Market
180 Race Track Rd.
(813) 855-5306

TAMPA
Seminole Flea Market
7407 Hillsborough Ave.
(813) 623-5662

TAMPA
Top Value Flea Market
8120 Anderson Rd. corner of
Anderson and Waters
Saturday and Sunday (813)
884-7810

THONOTOSSASA *(Tampa area)*
North 301 Flea World Inc.
11802 US Hwy. 301 N, one mile
north of Fowler Ave.
Thursday, Friday, Saturday,
Sunday 8 AM–5 PM (813) 896-1344

VENICE
Dome Flea Market
5115 St. Rd. 775, one mile off 41
(813) 493-2446

WEST PALM BEACH
Farmer's Flea Market
1200 S. Congress Ave.
(305) 965-1500

WEST PALM BEACH
West 45th Street Flea Market
3500 45th St.
(305) 684-8444

GEORGIA

ATLANTA
A Flea Market at Moreland Ave.
1400 Moreland Ave. SE
Every Friday and Saturday from 10
AM to 7 PM
Sunday from 12 AM to 6 PM
(404) 627-0831

ATLANTA
Arnold's Flea Market
2298 Cascade Rd. SW
Every day (404) 752-9507

ATLANTA
Flea Market at Forest Square
4855 Jonesboro Rd. FPK. just
outside 1-285
1½ miles south
Friday and Saturday 10 AM–9 PM
Sunday 12 AM–6 PM
(404) 361-1221

ATLANTA
Flossie's Flea Market
636 Lindbergh Way NE, behind
Victoria Station at Piedmont
Monday through Saturday 11 AM–6
PM
(404) 237-6273

ATLANTA
Funtown Flea Market
500 Northside Dr. SW
(404) 659-9806

ATLANTA
Golden Key Flea Market
833 Cascade Rd. SW
(404) 758-8780

ATLANTA
Scavenger Hunt on Peachtree
4090 Peachtree NE
Seven days a week 10 AM–6 PM
(404) 237-9789

ATLANTA
The Second Act Inc.
82 Peachtree St. SW, one block
from Five Points
(404) 523-9490

CHAMBLEE *(Atlanta area)*
North Perimeter Flea Market
5000 Buford Highway
(404) 451-2893

CHAMBLEE *(Atlanta area)*
Atlanta Flea Market and Antique
Center
5360 Peachtree Industrial Blvd.
Cham.
(404) 458-0456

DECATUR *(Atlanta area)*
Bailey's Flea Markets
3372 Memorial Drive
(404) 298-9726

DECATUR *(Atlanta area)*
Decatur Flea Market
724 W. College Ave.
(404) 378-4784

DECATUR *(Atlanta area)*
Kudzu Flea Market
2874 Ponce de Leon Blvd.
(404) 373-6498

DECATUR *(Atlanta area)*
Let's Make a Deal Flea Market
205 E. Ponce De Leon at Church
(404) 377-8676

DECATUR *(Atlanta area)*
Sims Flea Market
902 W. College Ave. between East
Lake Marta Station and Agnes Scott
College
Monday through Saturday 9 AM–6
PM (404) 371-8032

ILLINOIS

AMBOY
Antique Show and Flea Market
Route 30, 4-H Fairgrounds
Third Sunday in each month
8 AM–4 PM

BELLEVILLE
Belleville Flea Market
Route 13 and 159, just off 460,
Belleclair Exposition Center
Third weekend of every month

BELVIDERE
Boone County Flea Market
Boone County Fairgrounds
Check ahead of time; the dates vary

BLOOMINGTON
McLean County Flea Market
McLean County Fairgrounds
Check ahead

CHICAGO
A Mart Flea Market
1839 S. Pulaski Rd.
(312) 542-6619

CHICAGO
Archer & Damen Flea Mart
3450 S. Archer
(312) 927-3556

CHICAGO
Buyers Flea Market
1126 N. Kolmar
(312) 227-1889

CHICAGO
The Christian Hope Enterprise
8357 S. Halstead
(312) 488-5025

CHICAGO
First Chicago Flea Market
4840 N. Pulaski Rd.
(312) 545-3149

CHICAGO
North Side Flea Market
5906 N. Clark
(312) 334-8982

CHICAGO
Paris Flea Market
Sheridan Drive in Theatre,
7701 South Harlem Ave.
Every weekend (312) 233-2551

CHICAGO
Roseland Great American Flea
Market
10131 S. Michigan Ave.
(312) 995-5503

CICERO *(Chicago area)*
Flap Jaws Flea Market
1823 Cicero
Every day (312) 656-3616

ROCKFORD
Greater Rockford Indoor-Outdoor
Antique Market
Highway 251 South, corner of 11th
St. and Sandy Hollow Road
Every weekend 9 AM–5 PM
(815) 397-6683

SPRINGFIELD
The Springfield Antique Show and
Flea Market Clark County
Fairgrounds
(Next to exit 59 on I-70)
Third weekend of every month
except July
(513) 325-0053

St. CHARLES
Kane County Fairgrounds
Route No. 64
First Sunday of every month 7
AM–4 PM

WHEATON
Dupage Antique and Collectible
Market
Dupage County Fairgrounds
22 miles West of Chicago's Loop &
7 miles west of Charles, Illinois
Third Sunday of each month except
July 8 AM–4 PM

INDIANA

CEDAR LAKE
The Barn & Field Flea Market
151 St. and Parrish, one mile east
on Route 41
Every weekend (219) 696-7368

CENTERVILLE
Webb's Antique Mall
200 W. Union and 106 E.
Main
Daily 9 AM to 6 PM

EATON
Robyn's Nest Flea Market and
Antiques
103 W. Harris St.
Monday through Saturday
9:30 AM–5 PM

FRANKLIN
Antique Show and Flea
Market
4-H Fairgrounds
Third weekend of every month
(317) 535-5084

FT WAYNE
The Speedway Mall
across from 84 Lumber
Friday, Saturday and Sunday
(219) 484-1239

INDIANAPOLIS
The Antique Mall
3444 N. Shadeland Ave.
Every day

INDIANAPOLIS
Traylor's Flea Market
7159 E. 46th Street
Every weekend

INDIANAPOLIS
West Washington Flea
Market
6445 W. Washington St.
Every Friday, Saturday and
Sunday (317) 244-0941

MUNCIE
Highway 28 Flea Market
State Road 28, east of Highway 3
North
Every weekend, 9 AM–6 PM
(317) 282-5414

NEW WHITELAND
The New Whiteland Flea Market
1-465 on U.S. 31, 10 miles south of
Indianapolis
Friday, Saturday, Sunday
(317) 535-5907

RICHMOND
Yester Years Flea Market
The Old Melody Skating Rink
1505 S. 9th Street
Thursday 11 AM–5 PM, Friday 11
AM–7 PM, Saturday and Sunday 9
AM–5 PM

SOUTH BEND
Thieve's Market
2309 E. Edison at Ironwood
Every weekend

KENTUCKY

LOUISVILLE
Louisville Antique Mall
900 Gross Avenue
Daily 10 AM–6 PM
Monday-Saturday; 1–5 PM Sunday
(502) 635-2852

LOUISIANA

BATON ROUGE
Deep South
5350 Florida Blvd.
Friday, Saturday, Sunday
(504) 923-0142

LAFAYETTE
Deep South
3124 NE Evangeline Thorway
Friday, Saturday, Sunday
(318) 237-5529

MASSACHUSETTS

NORTON
Norton Flea Market
Route140,takeexit11offRoute495
Every Sunday

MICHIGAN

YPSILANTI
Giant Flea Market
214 East Michigan at Park
Every weekend (313) 971-7676,
487-5890 (weekends)

MISSOURI

SPRINGFIELD
Olde Towne Antique Mall and Flea
Market
Every day except Thursday
(417) 831-6665

SPRINGFIELD
Park Central Flea Market
429 Boonville
Every day (417) 831-7516

SPRINGFIELD
Viking Flea Market
North Grant and Chase
Every day except Wednesday
(417) 869-4237

NEVADA

LAS VEGAS
Tanner's Flea Market
Nevada Convention Center
Call (702) 382-8355 for dates

NEW YORK

BROOKLYN
Duffield Flea Market
223 Duffield Street between
Fulton and Willoughby
Monday through Saturday 11 AM–6
PM
(212) 625-7579

DELKALB JUNCTION
Antiques Flea Market
Route 11
Every Friday 10 AM–4 PM,
Saturday and Sunday 9 AM–5 PM
(315) 347-3393

DUANESBURG
Gordon Reid's Pine Grove Farm
Antique Flea Market
Junction of U. S. Rte. 20, NY Route
7 and I-88
1985 Dates: May 3–4; July 5–6;
Sept. 6–7
(518) 895-2300

MANHATTAN
The Canal Street Flea Market
CornerofCanal&Greene(parkinglot)
Saturday and Sunday, 9 AM–6 PM
(213) 226-7541

OHIO

AMHERST
Jamie's Flea Market
West of Route 58 on Route 113
Wednesday evenings, Saturday and
Sunday
(216) 986-4402

AURORA
Aurora Farms Flea Market
Route 43, one mile south of Route
82
Every Wednesday and Sunday
(216) 562-2000

CINCINNATI
Ferguson Antiques Mall and Flea
Market
3742 Kellog Ave.
Every Saturday and Sunday
(513) 321-7341

CINCINNATI
Paris Flea Market
Ferguson Hills Drive In Theatre,
2310 Ferguson Road
Every Saturday and Sunday
(513) 223-0222 weekdays;
451-1271 weekend

CINCINNATI
Strickers Grove
Route 128, one mile south of
Ross
Every Thursday, June through
September
(513) 733-5885

DAYTON
Paris Flea Market
Dixie Drive in Theatre
6201 N. Dixie
Every Saturday and Sunday 7 AM–4
PM
(513) 223-0222 weekdays;
890-5513 weekend

FERNALD *(Cincinnati area)*
Web Flea Market
1-74, Exit 7, north 5 miles to New
Haven Road
Every Saturday and Sunday
(513) 738-2678

MONTPELIER
Fairgrounds Flea Market
Williams County Fairgrounds
Every Thursday—(419) 636-6085
L & K Promotions
Rt 1, Montpelier, OH 43543

SPRINGFIELD
Antique Show and Flea
Market
Clark County Fairgrounds
Call for information:
(513) 399-7351 or 399-2261

TIFFIN
Tiffin Flea Market
Seneca County Fairgrounds
April through October
Call for information:
(419) 983-5084

WILMINGTON-WAYNESVILLE
Caesar Creek Flea Market
Intersection of 1-71 and State
Route 73
Every Saturday and Sunday
(513) 382-1669

PENNSYLVANIA

BEAVER FALLS
The Antique Emporium
818 7th Ave.
Everyday except Monday
(412) 847-1919

MANSFIELD
Antique Show and Flea
Market
Richland County Fairgrounds
Last weekend of the month,
February through November

RHODE ISLAND

ASHAWAY
Ashaway Flea Market
Route 3 (Exit 1 off I-95S near
Mystic Seaport)
Saturday and Sunday, 9 AM–5 PM
(401) 377-4947

PAWTUCKET
American Flea Market
Narragansett Race Track
Call for directions
Saturday, Sunday and Holidays, 8
AM–4 PM
(401) 726-0081

VERMONT

MANCHESTER CENTER
Manchester Flea Market
Route 11 & 30
East 3 miles on Rte. 11 and 30
from the junction of Rte. 7
Saturdays, May through October
(802) 362-1631

VIRGINIA

NORFOLK
Big Top Flea Market
Indoors/Outdoors
7600 Sewells Pt. Rd.
Tuesday-Sunday, 9:30 AM–4:30 PM

GREAT BRIDGE
Oak Grove Flea Market
910 Oak Grove Rd.
I-64 Exit 168, South 2 miles
Saturday and Sunday 10 AM–6 PM.
All year round.
(804) 482-1030, 547-1500

PUBLICATIONS

Periodicals for collectors include those of a general or specialized nature. Since magazines are prone to ownership or address changes, the information below is not guaranteed for long-term accuracy.

AMERICAN ART AND ANTIQUES
1515 Broadway, New York City, NY 10036

AMERICAN INDIAN ART
7045 Third Avenue, Scottsdale, AZ 85251

AMERICAN RIFLEMAN
National Rifle Association
1600 Rhode Island Avenue, N.W., Washington, D.C. 20036

ANTIQUE COLLECTING
P.O. Box 327, Ephrata, PA 17522

ANTIQUE COLLECTOR
Chestergate House, Vauxhall Bridge Road, London SW1V 1HF, England

ANTIQUE MARKET REPORT
P.O. Box 12830, Wichita, KS 67235

ANTIQUE MONTHLY
P.O. Drawer 2, Tuscaloosa, AL 35401

ANTIQUE REVIEW
P.O. Box 538, Worthington, OH 43085

ANTIQUE TOY WORLD
3941 Belle Plaine, Chicago, IL 60618

ANTIQUE TRADER
P.O. Box 1050
Dubuque, IA 52001

ANTIQUES (The Magazine Antiques)
551 Fifth Avenue, New York City, NY 10017

ANTIQUES AND THE ARTS WEEKLY
Newtown Bee, Newtown, CT 06470

ANTIQUES DEALER
1115 Clifton Avenue, P.O. Box 2147, Clifton, NJ 07015

ANTIQUES JOURNAL
P.O. Box 1046, Dubuque, IA 52001

ANTIQUES WORLD
P.O. Box 990, Farmingdale, L.I., NY 11737

ARMS GAZETTE
13222 Saticoy Street, North Hollywood, CA 91605 *(firearms)*

BANKNOTE REPORTER
Iola, WI 54945 *(paper money)*

BIE NEWSLETTER
4601 NE Third Avenue, Ft. Lauderdale, FL 33308 *(odd and error coins)*

BLUE RIDGE COIN NEWS
Banner Publishing Co., Camden, SC 29020

CLARION, THE (America's Folk Art Magazine)
49 West 53rd Street, New York City, NY 10019

CLASSICS READER
Box 1191, Station Q, Toronto, Canada M4T 2P4 *(comics)*

COINage
16001 Ventura Boulevard, Encino, CA 91316

COIN HOBBY NEWS
300 Booth Street, Anamosa, IA 52205

COIN PRICES
Iola, WI 54945

COINS MAGAZINE
Iola, WI 54945

COIN SLOT
P.O. Box 612, Wheatridge, CO 80033 *(coin-operated machines)*

COIN WHOLESALER
P.O. Box 893, Chattanooga, TN 37401

COIN WORLD
P.O. Box 150, Sydney, OH 45367

COLLECTIBLES MONTHLY
P.O. Box 2023, York, PA 17405

COLLECTOR EDITIONS QUARTERLY
170 Fifth Avenue, New York City, NY 10010

COLLECTOR'S DREAM
P.O. Box 127, Station T Toronto, Canada M6B3Z9

COLLECTOR'S MART
15100 Kellogg, Wichita, KS 67235

COLLECTOR'S NEWS
P.O. Box 156, Grundy Center, IA 50638

COLLECTOR'S PARADISE
P.O. Box 3658, Cranston, RI 02910

COLLECTOR'S SHOWCASE
P.O. Box 6929, San Diego, CA 92106

COLLECTORS UNITED
P.O. Box 1160, Chatsworth, GA 30705 *(dolls)*

COLONIAL NEWSLETTER
P.O. Box 4411, Huntsville, AL 35802 *(colonial coins)*

COMIC INFORMER
3131 West Alabama, Houston, TX 77098

COMIC TIMES
305 Broad, New York City, NY 10007

COMIXINE
10 Geneva Drive, Redcar, Cleveland T510 1JP, United Kingdom

DEPRESSION GLASS DAZE
P.O. Box 57, Otisville, MI 48463

DOLL TIMES
1675, Orchid, Aurora, IL 60505

DYNAZINE
8 Palmer Drive, Canton, MA 02021 *(comics)*

ERB-DOM
Route 2, Box 119, Clinton, LA 70722 *(Edgar Rice Burroughs)*

ERRORSCOPE
P.O. Box 695, Sidney, OH 45365 *(coin errors)*

ERROR TRENDS
P.O. Box 158, Oceanside, NY 11572 *(coin errors)*

ESSAY-PROOF JOURNAL
225 South Fischer Avenue, Jefferson, WI 53549 *(coins)*

FANTASY TRADER
34 Heworth Hall Drive, York, England *(comics)*

FANTASY UNLIMITED
47 Hesperus Crescent, Millwall, London, E.14, England *(comics)*

FUTURE GOLD
4146 Marlene Drive, Toledo, OH 43606 *(investment)*

GOBRECHT JOURNAL
5718 King Arthur Drive, Kettering, OH 45429 *(relating to life and work of Christian Gobrecht, 19th century coin designer)*

GOLDMINE
770 East State Street, Iola, WI 54990

GRAPHIC TIMES
25 Cowles Street, Bridgeport, CT 06607

GUN REPORT
P.O. Box 111, Aledo, IL 61231

HEISEY NEWS
Heisey Collectors of America, Inc., P.O. Box 27, Newark, OH 43055

HOBBIES
1006 South Michigan Avenue, Chicago, IL 60605

INDIAN TRADER
P.O. Box 31235, Billings, MT 59107 *(Indian relics)*

INSIGHT ON COLLECTABLES
P.O. Box 130, Durham, Ontario N0G 1R0

JOEL SATER'S ANTIQUE NEWS
P.O. Box B, Marietta, PA 17547

JOURNAL OF NUMISMATICS AND FINE ARTS
P.O. Box 777, Encino, CA 91316 *(ancient coins and classical antiquities)*

JUKEBOX TRADER
P.O. Box 1081, Des Moines, IA 50311

LINN'S STAMP NEWS
P.O. Box 29, Sidney, OH 45365

LOOSE CHANGE
21176 South Alameda Street, Long Beach, CA 90810 *(coin-operated machines)*

MAINE ANTIQUES DIGEST
P.O. Box 358, Waldboro, ME 05472

MEMORY LANE
P.O. Box 1627, Lubbock, TX 79408

MOVIE COLLECTOR'S WORLD
P.O. Box 309, Fraser, MI 48026

NATIONAL ANTIQUES COURIER
P.O. Box 500, Warwick, MD 21912

NATIONAL VALENTINE COLLECTORS ASSOC.
Box 1404, Santa Ana, CA 92702

NEW ENGLAND COUNTRY ANTIQUES
4 Church Street, Ware, MA 01082

NEW YORK ANTIQUE ALMANAC
P.O. Box 335, Lawrence, NY 11559

NEW YORK/PENNSYLVANIA COLLECTOR
Wolfe Publications, 4 South Main Street, Pittsford, NY 14534

NINETEENTH CENTURY (Forbes)
60 Fifth Avenue, New York City, NY 10011

NUMISMATIC NEWS
Iola, WI 54945

NUMISMATIST, THE
P.O. Box 2366, Colorado Springs, CO 80901

OHIO ANTIQUE REVIEW
72 North Street, Worthington, OH 43085

OLD CARS WEEKLY
Iola, WI 54990

OLD TOY SOLDIER NEWSLETTER
209 North Lombard, Oak Park, IL 60302

THE ORIENTALIA JOURNAL
P.O. Box 94, Dept. T, Little Neck, NY 11363

OWL'S NEST
P.O. Box 5491, Fresno, CA 93755 *(owl-motif items)*

PAPER & ADVERTISING COLLECTOR
P.O. Box 500, Mount Joy, PA 17552

PEN FANCIER
169 Overcash, Dunedin, FL 33528 *(writing instruments)*

POLITICAL COLLECTOR
503 Madison Avenue, York, PA 17404

POSTCARD COLLECTOR
700 E. State Street, Iola, WI 54990

PRINTS
P.O. Box 1468, Alton, IL 62002

RECORD PROFILE MAGAZINE, INC.
4361 Greenfield, Suite 201, Southfield, MI 48075

TAMS JOURNAL
P.O. Box 127, Scandinavia, WI 54977 *(tokens and medals)*

THE DOLL AND TOY COLLECTOR
International Collectors Publications, Inc.
468 Seventh Street, Brooklyn, NY 11215

THE MILK ROUTE
4 Oxbow Road, Westport, CT 16880

THE PLATE COLLECTOR
Collector's Media, Inc.
P.O. Box 1729, San Marcos, TX 78667

THE SHAKER MESSENGER
P.O. Box 45, Holland, MI 49423

WHEELS OF TIME
American Truck Historical Society
Saunders Building, 201 Office Park Drive, Birmingham, AL 35223

THE WILDLIFE COLLECTABLES JOURNAL
P.O. Box 130, Durham, Ontario N0G 1R0

WORLD COIN NEWS
Iola, WI 54945

WORLD WIDE AVON NEWS
44021 7th Street East, Lancaster, CA 93534

HOW TO USE THIS BOOK

The editors of this book have tried to include as many of the major collecting categories as possible. We have also included unusual, yet interesting collecting areas. We have not intended to cover each subject thoroughly, instead an overview of each collecting market is given. For more information on most of the categories listed, consult the complete series of *The Official Price Guides,* published by The House of Collectibles.

The sections in this book have been alphabetized for easy reference. Within each section is information describing the topic and alphabetized listings. Each listing provides relevant information about the item.

A price range is shown for each item. It represents a range of dealers average retail sums and auction results. A third price column shows last year's average value for each item. This feature measures market performance and should be helpful to investors, dealers, and collectors.

ADVERTISING COLLECTIBLES

TOPIC: Advertising collectibles are considered to be any items with a company's name or logo on them.

TYPES: Advertising collectibles can be found in any form. Common items used for advertising range from ashtrays to posters to yo-yos.

PERIOD: Advertising has been around almost since humanity became literate, but advertising collectibles of interest to the modern enthusiast began around 1800. Pre-1900 items are scarce and valuable.

MATERIALS: These items are usually made of ceramics, glass, paper or tin, although the material depends on the item.

COMMENTS: Many large companies (such as Coca-Cola) put much effort into producing promotional items that are now very collectible. Because of this, a collector may focus on procuring items that pertain to a particular company. Other enthusiasts, however, collect a certain item (mirrors, for example) regardless of the company or product that is advertised.

ADDITIONAL TIPS: The listings in this section are arranged in the following order: item, company or product advertised, title, description, what it was used for, material, shape, size and date manufactured. Other information was included where relevant.

	Current Price Range		P/Y Average
☐ **Ashtray,** Armstrong tire, clear, red decal, round, 5⅞" diameter	9.00	12.00	10.50
☐ **Ashtray,** Bacardi rum, white china, round, 4½" diameter	3.50	7.00	5.00
☐ **Ashtray,** Budweiser, glass, round, 5" diameter	3.00	5.00	4.00
☐ **Ashtray,** Camel cigarettes, Camel logo in center, tin, round, 3½" diameter	1.50	2.50	2.00
☐ **Ashtray,** Chivas Regal, Wade china, triangular with rounded sides, 11½"	5.00	9.00	7.00

	Current Price Range		P/Y Average

☐ **Ashtray,** Firestone Tire, 1936 Texas Central Expo **13.00 18.00 15.00**

☐ **Ashtray,** Goodrich, for Silvertown Heavy Duty Cord, round, 6⅜″ diameter **6.00 12.00 9.00**

☐ **Ashtray,** Goodrich, for Silvertown Cord tires, 1776 decal, round, 6¼″ diameter **10.00 16.00 13.00**

☐ **Ashtray,** Labatt's Stout-Lager-Ales, cream-colored porcelain, round, 6½″ diameter **3.00 7.00 5.00**

☐ **Ashtray,** Michelob Beer, round, 5½″ diameter **3.00 7.00 5.00**

☐ **Ashtray,** Pennsylvania, for Balloon Cord tires, round, 6⅛″ diameter **8.00 12.00 10.00**

☐ **Ashtray,** Salem Cigarettes, metal, round, 3½″ diameter .... **.50 1.50 1.00**

☐ **Ashtray,** White Horse Whiskey, white, figural horse head, 5″ x 3¾″ **8.00 10.00 9.00**

☐ **Ashtray,** Winston Cigarettes, tin .... **.03 .07 .05**

☐ **Ashtray,** Winston Cigarettes, Winston logo in center, tin, round, 3½″ diameter **1.50 2.50 2.00**

☐ **Bag,** Knox Knit Hosiery, picture of woman, 5″ x 7″ **1.00 2.00 1.50**

☐ **Bank,** Pepsi Cola, 75 Year Commemorative, red, tin can style, 1973 .... **2.00 5.00 3.50**

☐ **Bank,** R.C.A. Dog, "Nipper," ceramic, 6½″ tall **8.00 12.00 10.00**

☐ **Bank,** Texaco Oil Can, one quart, 1970s **1.00 3.50 2.25**

☐ **Banner,** De Soto Auto, red, gold and black fringed silk, 38″ x 66″, 1951 .... **55.00 65.00 60.00**

☐ **Bell,** Cherry Smash, porcelain, 6″ high **1.25 2.25 1.75**

☐ **Bell,** Full O' Juice, porcelain, 4″ high **1.50 2.65 2.07**

☐ **Bell,** Honeymoon Tobacco, porcelain, 4″ high **1.50 2.50 2.00**

☐ **Bell,** Minister Beer, porcelain, 4″ high **1.25 2.50 1.87**

☐ **Blotter,** Jersey Cream, picture of children, 4″ x 9″, 1920s **1.00 3.00 2.00**

☐ **Blotter,** Smith Brother's Chewing Gum and Cough Drops, c. 1930 .... **10.00 15.00 12.50**

☐ **Book,** Kellogg's, "Kellogg's Funny Jungleland Moving Pictures," 6″ x 8″, 1909 .... **35.00 42.00 39.00**

☐ **Booklet,** Budweiser Beer, 20 pages, 5″ x 7″ 1965 .... **.50 2.00 1.25**

☐ **Booklet,** Camel Cigarettes, "Know Your Nerves," 3″ x 4″, 1934 .... **12.00 16.00 14.00**

☐ **Booklet,** Hire's Root Beer, "Hire's Magic Story," 1934 .... **13.00 17.00 15.00**

☐ **Booklet,** Old Dutch Cleanser, 3″ x 6″ **2.00 6.00 4.00**

☐ **Booklet,** Royal Baking Powder, "The Comical Cruises of Captain Cooky," 1926 .... **14.00 18.00 16.00**

☐ **Booklet,** Royal Baking Powder, making biscuits, 1927 .... **2.50 3.50 3.00**

☐ **Booklet,** Rumford Baking Powder **2.50 3.50 3.00**

☐ **Bottle Carrier,** Coca-Cola, holds six miniature bottles, 2″ tall, 1953 .... **.75 2.00 1.25**

☐ **Bottle Opener,** Coca-Cola, cast iron **1.00 2.00 1.50**

☐ **Bottle Opener,** Dr. Pepper, cast iron **1.00 2.00 1.50**

☐ **Bottle Opener,** Falstaff, cast iron **1.00 2.00 1.50**

☐ **Bottle Opener,** Pepsi Cola, cast iron **1.00 2.00 1.50**

	Current Price Range		P/Y Average
☐ **Bottle Opener,** Seven-Up, cast iron	1.00	2.00	1.50
☐ **Bottle Opener,** Squirt, cast iron	1.00	2.00	1.50
☐ **Box,** Barricini Candies, resembles wood, 9″ x 7″ x 2″ with 12″ x 9″ base	8.00	12.00	10.00
☐ **Box,** Chandler's One-Day Tablets, 1″ x 5″ x 6″	.25	.50	.37
☐ **Box,** Coca-Cola, red and gold snap lid, for pencils, 1″ x 3″ x 8″, 1937	18.00	30.00	24.00
☐ **Box,** Portola Tuna, picture of Portola and tuna, cardboard, 8½″ x 14″ 1929	3.50	7.00	5.00
☐ **Box,** Solace Tobacco, blue with gold print, cardboard, 8½″ x 11″ x 5″, 1862	35.00	45.00	40.00
☐ **Calendar,** Alka Seltzer, 1942	3.50	5.75	4.25
☐ **Calendar,** Blatz Beer, girl in red, 1904	135.00	175.00	155.00
☐ **Calendar,** Camel Cigarettes, 1963	32.00	38.00	35.00
☐ **Calendar,** Coca Cola, pictures of beautiful women, six pages, 13″ x 17″, 1957	20.00	25.00	22.50
☐ **Calendar,** Dr. Mile's Remedies, picture of girl and boy, 1908	12.50	16.50	14.00
☐ **Calendar,** Dr. Pepper, 1950	22.00	27.00	24.00
☐ **Calendar,** Equitable Life Insurance, 1904	20.00	28.00	24.00
☐ **Calendar,** Fairy Soap, picture of Naval officer, 1899	13.00	19.00	16.00
☐ **Cannister,** Sir Walter Raleigh Smoking Tobacco, round	18.00	22.00	20.00
☐ **Catalog,** Lionel Trains, 8″ x 11″, 1958	3.00	6.00	4.50
☐ **Catalog,** Williams Manufacturing Company, picture of the factory, for baskets, 1891	20.00	25.00	22.50
☐ **Catalog,** Wurlitzer Juke Box, 8″ x 11″, 1950s	2.00	5.00	3.50
☐ **Chalkboard,** Hires Root Beer, for restaurants, tin, 10″ x 20″, 1940s	16.00	20.00	18.00
☐ **Clicker,** Butternut Break, tincricket, 1¾″ diameter, c. 1930	.75	1.75	1.25
☐ **Clock,** Anheuser Busch, wood	25.00	30.00	27.50
☐ **Clock,** Bardahl Petroleum, square, electric	40.00	48.00	44.00
☐ **Clock,** Canada Dry Sport Cola, 13″ x 18″	25.00	30.00	27.50
☐ **Clock,** Coca-Cola, metal, round	35.00	45.00	40.00
☐ **Clock,** Falstaff Beer, illuminated	50.00	58.00	54.00
☐ **Clock,** Florsheim Shoes, wood, illuminated	35.00	45.00	40.00
☐ **Clock,** General Electric, metal, refrigerator style	50.00	60.00	55.00
☐ **Clock,** Mr. Peanut, with alarm	25.00	30.00	27.50
☐ **Clock,** Pearl Beer, illuminated	30.00	40.00	35.00
☐ **Clock,** Seven-Up, metal, round	30.00	40.00	35.00
☐ **Clock,** St. Joseph's Aspirin for Children, 14″ diameter......................................	55.00	65.00	60.00
☐ **Coaster,** Olympia Beer, metal, round, 3½″ diameter	.50	1.10	.85
☐ **Comb,** Coca-Cola, red, plastic, embossed, pocket-size, 1960s	1.00	4.00	2.50
☐ **Decal,** Bull Dog Malt Liquor, picture of a bulldog, square, 7″, 1940s	3.00	7.00	6.00
☐ **Decal,** Planters and Clark Bar, for candy machine, 4″ x 8″, 1950s	1.25	2.00	1.62

	Current Price Range		P/Y Average
☐ **Decal,** Red Goose Shoes, 1930s	1.00	3.00	2.00
☐ **Decal,** Seven-Up, 4″ x 4″, 1931–57	1.50	3.00	2.25
☐ **Decal,** Triple AAA, 5¢ Root Beer, picture of a girl, 6″ x 9″, 1940s	1.00	4.00	2.50
☐ **Doll,** Campbell Kid, early 1900s style clothing, rag	23.00	28.00	25.00
☐ **Door Handle,** Dandy Bread, picture of loaf and slices, metal, 3″ x 13″, 1940s	12.00	17.00	15.00
☐ **Fan,** 666 Liquid Medicine, picture of two children on a horse, wicker handle, c. 1935	1.50	2.50	2.00
☐ **Figurine,** R.C.A. Dog, "Nipper," ceramic, 3″ . .	3.00	4.50	3.75
☐ **Folder,** Philadelphia Buckeye Wood Pumps, 6″ x 14″	9.00	14.00	11.50
☐ **Key Chain,** Mr. Peanut, 5″	.50	1.50	1.00
☐ **Key Holder,** Dr. Pepper, 1″ x 2″, 1930s	1.50	3.00	2.25
☐ **License Plate,** Coca-Cola, red and white, embossed, 6″ x 12″, 1970s	2.50	5.00	3.75
☐ **License Plate Top,** Ford, reflective, metal, 3″ x 10″, 1952	12.00	15.00	14.00
☐ **Lighter,** Camel Cigarettes, metal	2.50	4.50	3.50
☐ **Magazine Ad,** any automobile, 1911–1920	2.50	3.50	3.50
☐ **Magazine Ad,** any automobile, 1921–1930	1.50	2.00	1.75
☐ **Magazine Ad,** Coca-Cola, pre-1900	14.00	18.00	16.00
☐ **Magazine Ad,** Coca-Cola, 1901–1910	9.00	12.00	10.50
☐ **Magazine Ad,** Coca-Cola, 1911–1920	6.00	8.00	7.00
☐ **Magazine Ad,** Coca-Cola, 1921–1930	3.00	4.00	3.50
☐ **Magazine Ad,** any photograph, pre-1900	4.00	5.50	4.75
☐ **Magazine Ad,** radio, 1920–1925	3.00	4.00	3.50
☐ **Magazine Ad,** TV set, pre-1945	2.00	3.00	2.50
☐ **Matchbook,** Hires Root Beer, miniature, 1940s	.50	1.25	.87
☐ **Mirror,** Aunt Jemima, from Breakfast Club, round	.75	1.25	1.00
☐ **Mirror,** Coca-Cola, pocket-size, 2″ x 3″	.25	1.25	.75
☐ **Mirror,** Palmolive Soap, picture of the Dionne Quintuplets and doctor	.50	1.50	1.00
☐ **Mug,** Anheuser-Busch, crockery, embossed with eagle, 7″ tall, 1940	10.00	15.00	12.50
☐ **Pen Holders,** Falstaff Beer, for a pocket, 1960s	1.00	3.00	2.00
☐ **Pin,** Coca-Cola, bottle cap style, for a lapel, enameled, 1968	3.00	5.00	4.00
☐ **Pitcher,** Ambassador Scotch, white	8.00	10.00	9.00
☐ **Pitcher,** Glenfiddich, black	8.00	10.00	9.00
☐ **Poster,** Granger Pipe Tobacco, picture of Joe Heistand Champion trap shooter, 14″ x 20″ . . .	25.00	30.00	27.50
☐ **Poster,** Planters Presents Sheindele the Chazente, cardboard, 11″ x 17″	22.00	27.00	24.00
☐ **Poster,** Shoat Sale, announcing auction of 175 pigs, 12″ x 19″, c. 1920	7.00	10.00	8.50
☐ **Poster,** Yeast Foam, picture of a little girl, tin rimmed, 10″ x 14″, 1920s	18.00	22.00	20.00
☐ **Pot Holders,** Campbell Kid 8¼″ x 8½″, set of two	8.00	12.00	10.00

Mr. Peanut Peanut Butter Maker, *plastic,* $25.00

	Current Price Range		P/Y Average
☐ **Sign,** American Argiculturist, tin, embossed, 6½" x 13½", 1920s	7.00	10.00	8.50
☐ **Sign,** Arrow Trailer Rentals, picture of U.S. map, embossed, 14" x 18", 1940s	12.00	16.00	14.00
☐ **Sign,** Barnum's Animal Crackers, commemorative, tin 4" diameter, 6" tall, 1979	3.00	5.00	4.00
☐ **Sign,** Bayer Aspirin, tin, 15" x 18"	25.00	35.00	30.00
☐ **Sign,** Beechnut Tobacco, rectangular	12.00	17.00	14.50
☐ **Sign,** Borden, glass, 12" x 20	62.00	72.00	68.00
☐ **Sign,** Budweiser, plastic, with bottle, lighted, 5" x 12"	12.00	18.00	15.00
☐ **Sign,** Bunny Bread, red and white, tin, embossed, 3½" x 28", 1930s	8.00	12.00	10.00
☐ **Sign,** Burma shave, wooden, 10" x 3½"	1.50	2.50	2.00
☐ **Sign,** Busch Ginger Ale, picture of eagle, porcelain, 10" x 20", 1920s	75.00	85.00	80.00
☐ **Sign,** Camel Cigarettes, picture of blond woman, cardboard, 20" x 11", c. 1941	13.00	18.00	15.00

	Current Price Range		P/Y Average

Sign, Canadian Club, for a ceiling fan, round, 7" diameter, 1930	2.50	5.00	3.75
Sign, Coca-Cola, "Join the Friendly Circle," c. 1954	25.00	35.00	30.00
Sign, Coors Beer, picture of lake and mountain, lighted	25.00	35.00	30.00
Sign, Dr. Meyer's Foot Soap, picture of hands holding soap, cardboard, 7" x 10"	4.00	6.00	5.00
Sign, Dr. Nutt Soda, tin, embossed, 10" x 13", 1920s	25.00	32.00	30.00
Sign, Dr. Pepper, red and white, tin, 6" x 18", 1950s	7.00	11.00	9.00
Sign, DuBois Budweiser, tin, 21" x 13"	18.00	22.00	20.00
Sign, Dull Durham, cardboard, 14" x 22"	35.00	45.00	40.00
Sign, Dutch Boy, "wet paint," picture of boy, cardboard, 6" x 9", 1930s	2.00	5.00	3.50
Sign, Fairy Soap, 5¢, for a trolley car, rectangular	85.00	115.00	100.00
Sign, Ford Tractor, masonite, 11" x 21", 1942	20.00	25.00	22.50
Sign, Free Lance Cigar, cardboard, embossed, 8" x 10", c. 1910	8.00	12.00	10.00
Sign, Goodyear Tires, oval	22.00	26.00	24.00
Sign, Hires Root Beer, paper, 28" x 12"	40.00	50.00	45.00
Sign, Ivory Soap, picture of child holding soap, for a trolley car, 20" x 10"	68.00	85.00	77.00
Sign, Kelloggs Corn Flakes, picture of infant in wicker basket, tin, rectangular	70.00	88.00	79.00
Sign, Marvels Cigarettes, picture of two cigarette packages, tin, embossed, 3½" x 16", 1930s ..	16.00	21.00	19.00
Sign, Narragansett Lager, red with silver and gold letters, 20" x 10"	69.00	89.00	79.00
Sign, Old Milwaukee Beer, picture of woman in Victorian clothing, plastic, 15" x 22"	17.00	25.00	21.00
Sign, Olympia Gold, cardboard, 12" x 10"	5.00	10.00	7.50
Sign, Orange Crush, picture of pinup girl, cardboard, 12" x 15", 1950s	4.00	6.00	5.00
Sign, Orange Crush, 12" x 32", 1940s	25.00	30.00	27.50
Sign, Ritz Crackers, cardboard, rectangular ...	30.00	40.00	35.00
Sign, Rochelle Lime-Dry, cardboard, embossed, 10" x 15", 1920s	2.50	3.50	3.00
Sign, Salvation Army, red and white, porcelain, square, 16", 1940s	22.00	27.00	25.00
Sign, Schaefer Beer, wood, barrel-shaped, 14" x 16"	24.00	30.00	27.00
Sign, Smith Brothers Cough Drops, 5¢, for a trolley car	85.00	115.00	100.00
Sign, Sun Maid Raisins, for a trolley car	40.00	50.00	45.00
Sign, 2-Room Apartments, brass, 1½" x 7", c. 1940	2.00	6.00	4.00
Sign, Uneeda Biscuits, cardboard, 10" x 13" ..	25.00	35.00	30.00
Sign, Viceroy Cigarettes, tin	22.00	33.00	27.00
Sign, Virginia Cigarettes, picture of bathing beauty, tin, 14" x 21", 1930s	50.00	62.00	56.00

	Current Price Range		P/Y Average

☐ **Sign,** White Rock Mineral Water, tin, 4″ x 12″,
1910 .... 8.00 12.00 10.00
☐ **Sign,** Whitman's Chocolate Candy, 13″ x 18″ 50.00 68.00 59.00
☐ **Sign,** Wrigley's Gum, picture of Wrigley arrow
boy, for a streetcar, 10″ x 20″, 1920s 35.00 42.00 39.00
☐ **Sign,** Wrigley's Gum, picture of Wrigley arrow
man, for a streetcar, 10″ x 20″, 1920 .... 30.00 39.00 34.00
☐ **Sign,** Woo Chong Import Co., picture of oriental
women and art objects, paper, 21″ x 31″, c. 1920
.... 30.00 40.00 35.00
☐ **Sign,** Wunder Bread, cardboard, 6″ x 9″, 1910 8.00 12.00 10.00
☐ **Silverware,** Campbell Kid, three piece place set-
ting 14.00 18.00 16.00
☐ **Spoon,** A & P, for measuring coffee, yellow, plas-
tic .... .50 1.00 .75
☐ **Thermometer,** B-1 Soda, tin, 5″ x 16″, 1940s 16.00 21.00 19.00
☐ **Thermometer,** Carstairs, "Join the Carstairs
Crowd," round 25.00 35.00 30.00
☐ **Thermometer,** Coca-Cola, tin, embossed, 16″,
1960s 5.00 8.00 6.50
☐ **Thermometer,** Coca-Cola, gold, bottle shape, 7″
.... 20.00 30.00 25.00
☐ **Thermometer,** Coca-Cola, bottle shape, 27″ .. 50.00 60.00 55.00
☐ **Thermometer,** Coca-Cola, "Things Go Better
With Coke," 17½″ 22.00 30.00 26.00
☐ **Thermometer,** Copenhagen Chewing Tobacco,
12″ 12.00 18.00 15.00
☐ **Thermometer,** Dr. Pepper, 17″ 25.00 35.00 30.00
☐ **Thermometer,** Gilbey's Gin, 9″ 46.00 56.00 50.00
☐ **Thermometer,** Hires Root Beer, bottle shape,
27″ 45.00 55.00 50.00
☐ **Thermometer,** Morton Salt, picture of girl under
umbrella, metal 6.00 8.50 7.25
☐ **Thermometer,** Old Dutch Root Beer, windmills,
26″ 25.00 35.00 30.00
☐ **Thermometer,** Royal Crown Cola, 27″ 24.00 30.00 27.00
☐ **Thermometer,** Vernor's Ginger Ale, 12″ diame-
ter 43.00 53.00 48.00
☐ **Thimble,** Cherry Smash, porcelain .... .75 1.25 1.00
☐ **Thimble,** Coca-Cola, yellow, red and white .... .75 2.00 1.37
☐ **Thimble,** Deppen Beer, porcelain .... .50 1.25 .87
☐ **Thimble,** Minster Wooden Shoe, porcelain .... .75 1.25 1.00
☐ **Thimble,** Peerless Ice Cream, porcelain ...... .50 1.25 .87
☐ **Thimble,** Red Heart Beer, porcelain .... .75 1.25 1.00
☐ **Thimble,** Schuster's Root Beer, porcelain ..... .50 1.25 .87
☐ **Thimble,** Simms Roasted Coffee, porcelain ... .75 1.25 1.00
☐ **Thimble,** Watkins Cinnamon, porcelain .... .75 1.25 1.00
☐ **Tray,** Beck's Brewing, picture of a buffalo, round,
13″ diameter, c. 1950s 18.00 22.00 20.00
☐ **Tray,** Bromo Seltzer, for tips 60.00 70.00 65.00
☐ **Tray,** Carnation Milk, for tips 42.00 52.00 47.00
☐ **Tray,** Climax Furnaces and Stoves, picture of a
Roman soldier holding a torch, c. 1910 .... 75.00 85.00 80.00

	Current Price Range		P/Y Average
☐ **Tray,** Coca-Cola, girl with menu, c. 1950	20.00	30.00	25.00
☐ **Tray,** Coca-Cola, hostess, c. 1936	50.00	70.00	60.00
☐ **Tray,** Coca-Cola, Santa Claus, c. 1973	21.00	31.00	26.00
☐ **Tray,** Coors, metal, round, 13″ diameter	4.00	5.00	4.50
☐ **Tray,** Coors Beer, picture of a glass and bottle of beer	25.00	32.00	23.50
☐ **Tray,** Cracker Jack, tin	10.00	15.00	12.50
☐ **Tray,** Dr. Pepper, picture of a lion, steel, 12″ x 15″	2.00	4.00	3.00
☐ **Tray,** Falstaff Beer, picture of Sir Falstaf holding a bottle and tray, round, 12″ diameter, 1940s	22.00	28.00	25.00
☐ **Tray,** Franklin Life Insurance, for tips	22.00	28.00	25.00
☐ **Tray,** Genessee 12 Horse Ale, picture of horse team, round, 13″ diameter	35.00	45.00	40.00
☐ **Tray,** Hemmer's Ice Cream	50.00	58.00	54.00
☐ **Tray,** Hires Root Beer, c. 1910	82.00	98.00	90.00
☐ **Tray,** J. Leinenkugel Brewing Co., picture of Brewmaster testing beer	2.00	4.00	3.00
☐ **Tray,** Jenny Gasoline, for tips	38.00	48.00	40.00
☐ **Tray,** Lowenbrau, metal, round, 12″ diameter	3.00	4.50	3.75
☐ **Tray,** Miller High Life, for tips	7.00	12.00	10.00
☐ **Tray,** Miller High Life, picture of girl on moon, metal, round, 12″ diameter	2.50	4.50	3.50
☐ **Tray,** Miller High Life, picture of girl on moon, round, 13″ diameter, c. 1940s	35.00	60.00	47.00
☐ **Tray,** Miller Lite, metal, round, 13″ diameter ...	3.00	4.50	3.75
☐ **Tray,** Old Reliable Coffee, for tips	27.00	37.00	30.00
☐ **Tray,** Pacific Beer, picture of Mount Tacoma, 12″ diameter, 1912	45.00	65.00	55.00
☐ **Tray,** Pepsi Cola, picture of Pepsi Blue Lady, for change, 4½″ x 6″	1.00	2.50	1.75
☐ **Tray,** Pepsi Cola, picture of Pepsi Blue Lady, steel, 12″ x 15″	2.00	4.00	3.00
☐ **Tray,** Pepsi Cola, "Hits the Spot," picture of children under tree	25.00	35.00	30.00
☐ **Tray,** Prudential Insurance, for tips	7.00	17.00	12.00
☐ **Tray,** R.C.A. Dog, "Nipper," steel, oval, 12″ x 15″	2.00	3.00	2.50
☐ **Tray,** Roi-Tan Cigars, for tips	40.00	50.00	45.00
☐ **Tray,** Schlitz Beer, "Schliterland," 12″, 1957 ..	6.00	8.00	7.00
☐ **Tray,** Sears, Roebuck and Company, for tips ..	47.00	57.00	50.00
☐ **Tray,** Stroh's Beer, c. 1901	35.00	45.00	40.00
☐ **Tray,** White Rock, for change, oval, 12″ x 15″	2.00	3.00	2.50
☐ **Tray,** White Rock, for tips	38.00	48.00	40.00
☐ **Tray,** Wrigley's Gum, for tips	20.00	30.00	25.00
☐ **Watch,** Campbell Kid, adult style	60.00	70.00	65.00
☐ **Watch,** Campbell Kid, children's style	17.00	23.00	20.00
☐ **Yo-Yo,** Coca-Cola, bottle cap style, 2″ diameter	2.50	6.00	4.00

AKRO AGATE

DESCRIPTION: This glass is found in a wide range of colors and types, including clear, opaque and marbleized. The patterns listed here are children's dishes.

HISTORY: The Akro Agate Company of Akron, Ohio began producing marbles and toys in 1911. For economic reasons the company moved to Clarksburg, West Virginia several years later. By the late 1920s Akro Agate was the largest marble producer in the country. However, competition soon forced the company into diversification, and in 1935 new lines were introduced which included ashtrays and children's dishes. When the Brilliant Glass Company burned in 1936, Akro Agate bought the surviving molds and materials and began producing bathroom fixtures, flower pots, planters, vases and novelty items. They also produced a full line of children's dishes in transparent, opaque and marbleized glass which were very popular in the early 1940s. However, as plastic was developed Akro Agate wares suffered a decline in popularity and finally closed down in 1951.

COLORS: Crystal; transparent amber, various shades of green, blue, brown, yellow, etc.; translucent amber; satin lemonade and oxblood; opaque white, various shades of blue, green, yellow, black amethyst, beige; marbled blue-white, brown-white, green-white, red-white, orange-white, pumpkin-white, lemonade-oxblood and shiny black opaque.

MARKS: A Flying Crow: Made in USA; Westite: Ramses (embossed); Ashtrays: 245, 246, 249, 252; Flower Pots: 297, 296, 305, 307; Bowls/Candlesticks: 320, 321, 323, 340; Six sided small urn: 764; Cornucopia Vase: 765.

CHIQUITA

Green opaque is the most common color found in this pattern made for J. Pressman.

	Current Price Range		P/Y Average
Complete Set 16 pieces, in box			
□ green opaque	48.00	60.00	51.00
□ cobalt	110.00	125.00	114.00
□ crystal	150.00	180.00	160.00
□ baked-on color	57.00	60.00	58.00
Complete Set, 22 pieces, in box			
□ green opaque	63.00	75.00	65.00
Creamer, 1½"			
□ green opaque	4.00	5.00	4.25
□ cobalt	9.00	10.00	9.25
□ crystal	13.00	15.00	13.50
□ baked-on color	5.50	6.50	5.75
Cup, 1½"			
□ green opaque	3.50	4.50	3.75
□ cobalt	5.00	6.00	5.25
□ crystal	10.00	12.00	10.50
□ baked-on color	4.25	5.00	4.50
Plate, 3¾"			
□ green opaque	2.00	2.50	2.15
□ cobalt	5.25	6.00	5.50
□ crystal	10.00	12.00	10.50
□ baked-on color	1.75	2.25	1.85
Saucer, 3⅛"			
□ green opaque	1.75	2.25	1.85
□ cobalt	2.75	3.25	2.85
□ crystal	4.75	5.75	5.00
□ baked-on color	1.25	1.50	1.30
Sugar, 1½"			
□ green opaque	3.75	4.25	3.85
□ cobalt	7.00	8.00	7.25
□ crystal	11.00	13.00	11.50
□ baked-on color	4.25	4.75	4.35

CONCENTRIC RIB

	Current Price Range		P/Y Average
Complete Set, 7 pieces, in box			
□ green and white	23.00	27.00	24.50
□ other opaque colors	27.00	32.00	28.00
Creamer, 1¼"			
□ green and white	3.75	4.75	4.00
□ other opaque colors	4.50	6.00	5.00
Cup, 1¼"			
□ green and white	2.25	2.75	2.35
□ other opaque colors	2.75	3.75	3.00
Saucer, 2¾"			
□ green and white	1.75	2.25	1.85
□ other opaque colors	1.75	2.50	2.00
Sugar, 1¼"			
□ green and white	4.00	5.00	4.25
□ other opaque colors	4.50	6.00	5.00

	Current Price Range		P/Y Average

CONCENTRIC RING

Made in a large and small children's size, this pattern is similar to Concentric Rib. However, Concentric Ring is of better quality than Concentric Rib.

Complete Set, 21 pieces, large size, in box
☐ cobalt	335.00	385.00	345.00
☐ blue marble	430.00	470.00	440.00

Complete Set, 16 pieces, small size, in box
☐ cobalt	240.00	270.00	250.00
☐ blue marble	300.00	335.00	310.00

Cereal Bowl, 3⅜″
☐ cobalt	24.00	26.00	24.50
☐ blue marble	29.00	33.00	30.00
☐ other opaque colors	16.00	19.00	17.00

Creamer, 1⅜″
☐ cobalt	23.00	26.00	24.00
☐ blue marble	32.00	37.00	33.00
☐ other opaque colors	11.00	14.00	12.00

Creamer, 1¼″
☐ cobalt	19.00	22.00	20.00
☐ blue marble	25.00	28.00	26.00
☐ other opaque colors	9.00	11.00	9.50

Cup, 1⅜″
☐ cobalt	23.00	26.00	24.00
☐ blue marble	27.00	31.00	28.00
☐ other opaque colors	13.00	15.00	13.50

Cup, 1¼″
☐ cobalt	25.00	28.00	26.00
☐ blue marble	28.00	31.00	29.00
☐ other opaque colors	9.00	11.00	9.50

Plate, 4¼″
☐ cobalt	11.00	14.00	12.00
☐ blue marble	16.00	19.00	17.00
☐ other opaque colors	6.50	8.00	7.00

Plate, 3¼″
☐ cobalt	11.00	13.00	11.50
☐ blue marble	12.00	14.00	12.50
☐ other opaque colors	4.50	6.00	5.00

Saucer, 3⅛″
☐ cobalt	6.00	8.00	6.50
☐ blue marble	8.50	10.00	9.00
☐ other opaque colors	4.50	5.50	4.75

Saucer, 2¾″
☐ cobalt	8.00	10.00	8.50
☐ blue marble	9.00	11.00	9.50
☐ other opaque colors	3.00	4.00	3.25

Sugar, 1⅞″
☐ cobalt	31.00	34.00	32.00
☐ blue marble	37.00	42.00	39.00
☐ other opaque colors	17.00	20.00	18.00

	Current Price Range		P/Y Average
Sugar, 1¼″			
☐ cobalt	19.00	22.00	20.00
☐ blue marble	25.00	27.00	25.50
☐ other opaque colors	9.00	11.00	9.50

INTERIOR PANEL

This pattern was made in a large and a small children's size.

Complete Set, 21 pieces, in box, large size			
☐ green	130.00	145.00	135.00
☐ yellow	110.00	130.00	115.00
☐ blue and white	305.00	330.00	310.00
☐ red and white	330.00	360.00	335.00
☐ green and white	245.00	275.00	250.00
☐ lemonade and oxblood	320.00	350.00	330.00
Complete Set, 8 pieces, in box, small size			
☐ pink	38.00	50.00	40.00
☐ green	38.00	50.00	40.00
☐ blue	110.00	115.00	105.00
☐ yellow	110.00	115.00	105.00
☐ green	33.00	45.00	35.00
☐ topaz	33.00	45.00	35.00
☐ blue and white	105.00	120.00	110.00
☐ red and white	90.00	100.00	93.00
☐ green and white	60.00	70.00	63.00
Complete Set, 16 pieces, in box, small size			
☐ pink	110.00	125.00	115.00
☐ green	110.00	125.00	115.00
☐ blue	215.00	240.00	220.00
☐ yellow	215.00	240.00	220.00
☐ green	80.00	95.00	85.00
☐ topaz	80.00	95.00	85.00
☐ blue and white	215.00	230.00	220.00
☐ red and white	200.00	225.00	210.00
☐ green and white	120.00	140.00	125.00
Creamer, 1⅜″			
☐ blue and white	21.00	24.00	22.00
☐ red and white	23.00	26.00	24.00
☐ green and white	17.00	19.00	17.50
☐ lemonade and oxblood	23.00	27.00	24.00
☐ green	10.00	12.00	10.50
☐ topaz	9.00	11.00	9.50
Creamer, 1¼″			
☐ pink	21.00	23.00	21.50
☐ green	21.00	23.00	21.50
☐ blue	25.00	28.00	26.00
☐ yellow	25.00	28.00	26.00
☐ green	9.00	11.00	9.50
☐ topaz	9.00	11.00	9.50
☐ blue and white	21.00	24.00	22.00
☐ red and white	23.00	27.00	24.00
☐ green and white	14.00	17.00	15.00

	Current Price Range		P/Y Average
Cup, 1⅜″			
☐ green	5.50	7.00	6.00
☐ topaz	4.50	6.00	5.00
☐ blue and white	19.00	21.00	19.50
☐ red and white	20.00	23.00	21.00
☐ green and white	14.00	17.00	15.00
☐ lemonade and oxblood	19.00	22.00	20.00
Cup, 1¼″			
☐ pink	7.00	9.00	7.50
☐ green	7.00	9.00	7.50
☐ blue	24.00	27.00	25.00
☐ yellow	24.00	27.00	25.00
☐ green	6.00	7.50	6.50
☐ topaz	6.00	7.50	6.50
☐ blue and white	19.00	22.00	20.00
☐ red and white	21.00	24.00	22.00
☐ green and white	14.00	17.00	15.00
Plate, 4¼″			
☐ green	4.50	6.00	5.00
☐ topaz	3.50	6.00	4.00
☐ blue and white	9.00	11.00	9.50
☐ red and white	9.00	11.00	9.50
☐ green and white	7.50	10.00	8.00
☐ lemonade and oxblood	10.00	12.00	10.50
Plate, 3¾″			
☐ pink	4.00	5.00	4.25
☐ green	4.00	5.00	4.25
☐ blue	4.50	6.50	5.00
☐ yellow	4.50	6.50	5.00
☐ green	3.00	4.00	3.25
☐ topaz	3.00	4.00	3.25
☐ blue and white	9.00	10.00	9.25
☐ red and white	6.50	8.00	7.00
☐ green and white	5.50	7.00	6.00
Saucer, 3⅛″			
☐ green	3.00	4.00	3.25
☐ topaz	2.50	3.50	3.00
☐ blue and white	6.50	8.00	7.00
☐ red and white	7.50	9.00	8.00
☐ green and white	6.50	8.00	7.00
☐ lemonade and oxblood	6.50	8.00	7.00
Saucer, 2⅜″			
☐ pink	3.00	4.00	3.25
☐ green	3.00	4.00	3.25
☐ blue	6.00	8.00	6.50
☐ yellow	6.00	8.00	6.50
☐ green	3.25	4.00	3.50
☐ topaz	3.25	4.00	3.50
☐ blue and white	6.50	8.00	7.00
☐ red and white	6.50	8.00	7.00
☐ green and white	3.25	4.00	3.50

	Current Price Range		P/Y Average
Sugar, 1⅞"			
☐ green	14.00	17.00	15.00
☐ topaz	14.00	17.00	15.00
☐ blue and white	29.00	32.00	30.00
☐ red and white	30.00	33.00	31.00
☐ green and white	22.00	25.00	23.00
☐ lemonade and oxblood	30.00	33.00	31.00
Sugar, 1¼"			
☐ pink	21.00	24.00	22.00
☐ green	21.00	24.00	22.00
☐ blue	25.00	28.00	26.00
☐ yellow	25.00	28.00	26.00
☐ green	9.00	11.00	9.50
☐ topaz	9.00	11.00	9.50
☐ blue and white	21.00	24.00	22.00
☐ red and white	23.00	26.00	24.00
☐ green and white	15.00	18.00	16.00

ALMANACS

DESCRIPTION: Almanacs are annual publications that include astrological and meterological data as well as general information of the year. Farmers use the information in almanacs to determine how weather and other variables may affect their crops.

VARIATIONS: A variety of almanacs have been published. Among the best known are the *Farmer's Almanac* and *Poor Richard's Almanack.*

PERIOD: Almanacs date to the 17th century.

COMMENTS: Collectors are primarily concerned with almanacs published before 1800. Publisher and literary content are also factors in determining price and importance.

ADDITIONAL TIPS: Almanac listings are in chronological order, and the name of the publisher is given. Prices from year to year vary greatly. For additional information refer to *The Official Price Guide to Paper Collectibles,* published by The House of Collectibles.

Almanacs, *advertising Seven Barks, 1900s,*
$8.00-$10.00

	Current Price Range		P/Y Average
☐ **The New-England Almanack,** Lodowick, 1695	3000.00	3750.00	3400.00
☐ **The Farmer's Almanack,** Whittemore, 1714 ..	900.00	1200.00	1050.00
☐ **An Almanack of the Coelestial Motions and Aspects,** Travis, 1717	300.00	375.00	337.00
☐ **The New-England Diary,** Bowen, 1724	350.00	435.00	392.00
☐ **The New-England Diary,** Bowen, 1725	330.00	390.00	360.00
☐ **The Rhode-Island Almanack,** Stafford, 1738	1100.00	1375.00	1237.00
☐ **Poor Job's Almanack,** Shepherd (James Franklin), 1753	1400.00	1900.00	1650.00
☐ **An Astronomical Diary; Or, An Almanack,** Ames, 1753	240.00	315.00	277.00
☐ **An Astronomical Diary,** Ames, 1764	75.00	95.00	85.00
☐ **The New-England Almanack,** West, 1775	240.00	315.00	277.00
☐ **The North-American's Almanack,** Stearns, 1775	90.00	120.00	110.00
☐ **Bickerstaff's Boston Almanack,** 1775	170.00	210.00	190.00
☐ **Bickerstaff's Boston Almanack,** 1778	150.00	180.00	165.00
☐ **American Almanack,** Russell, 1782	90.00	115.00	105.00
☐ **Webster's Connecticut Pocket Almanack,** Nickerstaff, 1787	145.00	180.00	165.00
☐ **An Astronomical Diary,** Strong, 1788	115.00	150.00	132.00
☐ **An Astronomical Diary,** Sewall, 1794	115.00	150.00	132.00
☐ **Strong's Almanack,** 1796	115.00	150.00	132.00
☐ **Farmer's Almanack,** Thomas, 1799	27.00	36.00	32.00

	Current Price Range		P/Y Average
☐ Greenleaf's New-York, Connecticut and New Jersey Almanack, 1801	90.00	115.00	105.00
☐ New England Almanack, Daboll, 1805	35.00	47.00	41.00
☐ New England Almanack, Daboll, 1808	22.00	30.00	26.00
☐ New England Almanack, Daboll, 1810	33.00	41.00	37.00
☐ Law's Boston, 1812	16.00	21.00	19.00
☐ New England Almanack, Daboll, 1813	27.00	36.00	32.00
☐ New England Almanack, Daboll, 1816	28.00	35.00	31.00
☐ National Comic Almanack, 1851	10.00	14.00	12.00
☐ True Americans Almanack, 1855	50.00	65.00	57.00
☐ Western Almanack, 1867	16.00	21.00	19.00
☐ Hagerstown Town and Country Almanack, 1869	8.00	12.00	10.00
☐ Farmer and Mechanics Almanac, Scovill, 1871	10.00	14.00	12.00
☐ Tarrytown Almanack, 1872	9.00	13.00	11.00
☐ United States Almanack, Hostetter, 1874	9.00	13.00	11.00
☐ Hagerstown Almanack, Gruber, 1880	9.00	13.00	11.00
☐ Humans and Horses, 1881	11.00	16.00	13.00
☐ Presto-Fertilizer Co., 1885	7.00	10.00	8.50
☐ Mandrahe Bitters Almanack, 1886	8.00	11.00	9.50
☐ Kendall Doctor At Home	8.00	11.00	9.50
☐ Williams And Clark Fertilizers, colored cover, 1888	9.00	13.00	11.00
☐ Wright's Pictorial Family Almanack, 1888	9.00	13.00	11.00
☐ Home Almanack, 1897	5.00	7.00	6.00
☐ Barker's Guide/Cookbook, 1900	11.00	15.00	13.50
☐ Swamp Root, 1902	4.00	6.00	5.00
☐ Diamond Dye #6, 1908	11.00	15.00	13.00
☐ Ranson's, 1912	7.00	10.00	8.50
☐ Royster's, 1912	6.00	8.00	7.00
☐ Dr. Ayer's (American Health), 1915	6.00	8.00	7.00
☐ Lady's Birthday Almanack, 1917	7.00	10.00	8.50
☐ Poor Richard's Almanack, 1919	6.00	8.00	7.00
☐ Hood Farm, 1923	6.00	8.00	7.00

AMERICAN INDIAN ARTIFACTS

TOPIC: American Indian artifacts are appreciating quickly as more and more people are attracted to these unique and historical items.

TYPES: Types of artifacts range from jewelry to woven products to weapons.

PERIOD: Though some items may be prehistoric, as a rule these collectibles will date from around 1600 to 1925. More recent artifacts are usually valued according to rarity and quality of workmanship.

ORIGIN: These artifacts may originate anywhere in the United States, but the Plains and the Southwest have provided a disproportionate amount of items.

MATERIALS: The material depends on the artifact, and so leather, stone, wood and ceramics are used extensively.

COMMENTS: Many collectors focus on specific tribes and items, such as Navajo rugs or Hopi Kachina dolls. Others do not limit themselves so strictly, and may collect all Indian artifacts from a certain period or area.

ADDITIONAL TIPS: The following listings are organized by item. The tribe name follows, and the description after that will include types, colors and decorations. The material is next, followed by the dimensions of the item and the date, if known. Other information was included where relevant.

	Current Price Range		P/Y Average
☐ **Armband,** Sioux, beaded, green and white, set of two	45.00	75.00	60.00
☐ **Arrow,** Yuma, cane and hardwood, 37".c. 1890	30.00	49.00	40.00
☐ **Axe,** Creek, wraparound eye, steel head, handle 20", head 6", c. 1837	125.00	175.00	150.00
☐ **Bag,** Araphaho, beaded, white, black and pink, buffalo hide, 5" x 8", c. 1885	65.00	95.00	80.00

Hopi Kachina Dolls, *pair, 75 years old,* $1000.00

	Current Price Range		P/Y Average
☐ **Bag,** Cheyenne, beaded, red, yellow and blue, 2" diameter	15.00	25.00	20.00
☐ **Bag,** Chippewa, beaded, peco edging, 4" wide, 6" long	25.00	45.25	35.00
☐ **Basket,** Cherokee, red and black, tub-shaped, split oak, 5" wide, 6" high	45.00	57.25	51.00
☐ **Basket,** Chocataw, for berries, cane, 6" high . .	15.00	25.25	20.00
☐ **Basket,** Jicarilla, multicolored, 13" x 18" x 3"	125.00	145.25	135.00
☐ **Basket,** Maidu, tray type, redbud motif, 15" diameter, 7" high	115.00	140.25	127.00
☐ **Basket,** Objibwa, painted, splint and sweet grass, c. 1895	20.00	35.25	27.00
☐ **Basket,** Paiute, wedding type, 13" wide, 4" high	85.00	145.25	115.00
☐ **Basket,** Washo, three rod style, 14" wide, 8" high	165.00	275.00	220.00
☐ **Belt,** Apache, children's, beaded, white, blue and red, 2" x 27"	125.00	225.00	175.00
☐ **Belt,** Cheyenne, square conchos style	65.00	95.00	80.00
☐ **Blanket,** Navajo, red, black, brown, orange and white, nine spot pattern	1200.00	1650.00	1400.00
☐ **Blanket,** Navajo, red, blue, black, green, yellow, fourth phase nine spot pattern	1500.00	1800.00	1650.00
☐ **Blanket,** Navajo, red, white, blue and black, nine spot pattern with diamond shapes	1800.00	2100.00	1950.00
☐ **Bolo,** Navajo, turquoise stone	25.00	45.00	35.00
☐ **Boot Liners,** Eskimo, woven	35.00	45.00	40.00

	Current Price Range		P/Y Average
☐ **Bracelet,** Navajo, silver and petrified wood, c. 1945	70.00	95.00	85.00
☐ **Bracelet,** Zuni, turquoise and coral	90.00	110.00	100.00
☐ **Broach,** Navajo, silver, turquoise, c. 1910	45.00	75.00	60.00
☐ **Brow Band,** Sioux, quilled, purple, white and red, 15" x 4", c. 1905	80.00	110.00	95.00
☐ **Canoe,** Chippewa, miniature, quilled, diamond and cross pattern, birch, 12" long, 3" high	25.00	42.00	34.00
☐ **Canteen,** Acoma, fineline, with heart-line deer, 7" tall, c. 1975	48.00	72.00	60.00
☐ **Club,** Apache, "flop-knob" type, stone, wood and rawhide	100.00	125.00	112.00
☐ **Club,** Shoshone, stone, wood and rawhide, 22"	35.00	55.00	45.00
☐ **Club,** Sioux, stone, wood and rawhide	27.00	37.00	30.00
☐ **Coat,** Cheyenne, beaded, leather, c. 1900	250.00	395.00	322.00
☐ **Cradleboard,** Apache, beaded, rawhide and wood, c. 1900	110.00	135.00	122.00
☐ **Doll,** Hopi, Kachina type, corn cob style body, 6" tall	23.00	42.00	31.00
☐ **Doll,** Hopi, Kachina type, 8" tall, c. 1963	40.00	55.00	47.00
☐ **Doll,** Hopi, Kachina type, 7" tall, c. 1915	45.00	65.00	55.00
☐ **Doll,** Hopi, Kachina type, leather clothing, 15" tall	80.00	98.00	89.00
☐ **Doll,** Plains, beaded, rawhide, 11" tall, c. 1915	50.00	65.00	57.00
☐ **Doll,** Plains, "scalp" type, rawhide, 1800s	185.00	225.00	205.00
☐ **Drum,** Apache, ceremonial, leather and brass, 7" wide, 3" wide	75.00	125.00	105.00
☐ **Drum,** Pawnee, 10" wide, 4" high	15.00	23.00	19.00
☐ **Drum,** Yaqui, leather and wood, 7" wide, 24" tall	48.00	78.00	63.00
☐ **Effigy,** Papago, 4" wide, 6" high	35.00	55.00	45.00
☐ **Fan,** Navajo, peyote type, goose feathers	35.00	48.00	42.00
☐ **Fob,** Kickapoo, beaded, black and white, diamond design, 2" x 6"	28.00	48.00	38.00
☐ **Hat,** Hupa, bands, step design	135.00	175.00	155.00
☐ **Head Band,** Comanche, beaded, red, blue and white, diamond design, 1" x 23"	23.00	33.00	30.00
☐ **Hobbles,** Navajo, rawhide, c. 1890	18.00	30.00	24.00
☐ **Jar,** Hohokam, shoulder type, painted, 6" wide, 4" high	175.00	280.00	225.00
☐ **Jar,** Papago, redware, 10" tall	80.00	115.00	95.00
☐ **Jar,** Zuni, head pot, red, green and white, 10" wide, 8" high, c. 1922	335.00	435.00	385.00
☐ **Knife Case,** Sioux, beaded, quilled, 7½", c. 1885	210.00	250.00	230.00
☐ **Knife Sheath,** Osage, beaded, white, green, blue and red, 8"	85.00	130.00	107.00
☐ **Leggings,** Nez Perce, men's style, beaded, fringed, c. 1915	220.00	260.00	245.00
☐ **Leggings,** Osage, men's style, blue, c. 1880 ..	150.00	175.00	162.00
☐ **Leggings,** Plains, beaded, blue and white, rawhide, c. 1925	180.00	225.00	102.00

Zuni Grain Jar, *archaic, museum quality,* **$5,000.00 +**

	Current Price Range		P/Y Average
☐ **Moccasins,** Apache, beaded, black and white, set of two	80.00	115.00	97.00
☐ **Moccasins,** Arapaho, blue, yellow and green, set of two	60.00	110.00	75.00
☐ **Moccasins,** Sioux, children's, beaded, green, red and white, set of two	45.00	75.00	60.00
☐ **Moccasins,** Sioux, beaded, white, red and blue, set of two	138.00	178.00	158.00
☐ **Necklace,** Blackfoot, beaded, rawhide, 37" ...	40.00	60.00	50.00
☐ **Paddle,** Creek, mush style, 24", 1800s	28.00	48.00	38.00
☐ **Paddles,** Haida, painted, 56", set of two	70.00	90.00	80.00
☐ **Pillow Cover,** Plains Cree, beaded, leather, fringed, 17" x 20"	310.00	350.00	330.00
☐ **Pin,** Zuni, Rainbird Kachina Dancer motif	75.00	90.00	82.00
☐ **Pipe,** Calumet, catlinite bowl and stem, toma-hawk shape, c. 1850	400.00	450.00	425.00
☐ **Plaque,** Hopi, red, green and black, coil ware, 15" wide	80.00	129.00	105.00
☐ **Pot,** Papago, black and red, chain design, 7" wide, 7" tall, c. 1910	25.00	42.00	33.00
☐ **Pot,** Zia, bird type, 7½" wide, 6" high, c. 1980	80.00	95.00	87.50
☐ **Pouch,** Cheyenne, medicine type, beaded, blue, leather	28.00	38.00	32.00
☐ **Purse,** Comanche, red, white, and green, fret de-sign, 3½" wide, 5" long	45.00	58.00	52.00

	Current Price Range		P/Y Average
☐ **Rattle,** Hopi, white and black, gourd style, feather streamers	18.00	28.00	20.00
☐ **Ring,** Navajo, horseshoe design, silver, turquoise stone	12.00	18.00	15.00
☐ **Rug,** Navajo, blue and white, Yei figure design, 24″ x 15″, c. 1978	75.00	95.00	85.00
☐ **Rug,** Navajo, red, black and white, diamond motif, c. 1935	700.00	900.00	800.00
☐ **Saddle,** Kiowa, tacked, 18″ long, 12″ high, c. 1858	225.00	295.00	260.00
☐ **Saddlebag,** Parfleche, multicolored, fringed, 11″ x 10″	185.00	215.00	200.00
☐ **Saddle Blanket,** Plateau, elkhide, c. 1885	330.00	370.00	350.00
☐ **Serape,** Navajo, orange, blue, green, yellow and gray, 45″ x 65″, c. 1890	3000.00	3700.00	3400.00
☐ **Serape,** Navajo, blue, white and red, late teraced stsyle, 52″ x 68″, c. 1890	4200.00	4600.00	4400.00
☐ **Serape,** Navajo, blue, white and red, 54″ x 72″	8700.00	10500.00	9600.00
☐ **Snowshoes,** Chippewa, wood and rawhide, 29″, c. 1875	150.00	175.00	162.00
☐ **Totem Pole,** Tsimshian, carved faces, painted, 12″ long	65.00	89.00	77.00
☐ **Vase,** Hopi, wedding type, 10″	165.00	195.00	180.00
☐ **Vase,** Jemez, wedding type, red and green, 12″ tall	75.00	125.00	100.00
☐ **Wrist Band,** Hopi, net woven, c. 1895	30.00	45.00	37.00
☐ **Yoke,** Mohave, beaded, 17″ wide, 9″ long	20.00	35.00	27.00

ANIMAL COLLECTIBLES

DESCRIPTION: Animal collectibles are highly popular among all types of collectors. The older Steiff bears, for instance, are experiencing stiff competition from the new, limited edition issues. Collectible bears and cats are extremely popular in the current market.

COMMENTS: The following list is merely a sample guide to the animal collectibles currently available on today's retail and secondary markets. All categories, bears, cats, cows, dogs, pigs, rabbits and unicorns, are listed alphabetically.

ADDITIONAL TIPS: For further information, refer to the directory located in the front of this book.

	Current Price Range		P/Y Average

BEARS

☐ **Aloysius,** North American Bear Co., plaid ribbon, brown, 20″	35.00	45.00	37.00
☐ **Amelia Bearhart,** North American Bear Co., flight suit, hat and goggles, discontinued	45.00	55.00	47.00
☐ **Anniversary Bear,** Merry Thought, commemorative, has growling mechanism, offwhite	100.00	150.00	105.00
☐ **Baby Bear,** Bear Haus USA, tan, jointed, #1301, 14″	12.00	15.00	13.00
☐ **Baby Bear,** Bear Haus USA, tan, jointed, #3019, 10″	10.00	15.00	11.00
☐ **Bare Bear,** North American Bear Co.	35.00	45.00	37.00
☐ **Bentley Bear,** Dakin, jointed, has growling mechanism, 21″	35.00	45.00	37.00
☐ **Bialosky Bear,** North American Bear Co., sailor middy, 13″	25.00	35.00	26.00
☐ **Bialosky Bear,** North American Bear Co., sailor middy, 18″	45.00	55.00	47.00
☐ **Bialosky Bear,** North American Bear Co., satin tuxedo, 18″	45.00	55.00	47.00
☐ **Edwardian Bear,** Merry Thought, mohair, jointed, has growling mechanism, #HE18	80.00	110.00	84.00
☐ **Humphrey Beargurt,** North American Bear Co., trench coat and hat, 19″	40.00	50.00	42.00
☐ **Kareem Abdul Jabear,** North American Bear Co., black bear in basketball uniform	40.00	50.00	42.00
☐ **Lauren Bearcall,** North American Bear Co., in fur coat and veiled hat	40.00	50.00	42.00
☐ **Little Bear,** Bear Haus USA, tan, jointed, #1502, 12″	11.00	16.00	12.00
☐ **Mama Bear,** Bear Haus USA, tan, jointed, #3100, 14″	15.00	20.00	16.00
☐ **Margaret Strong Teddy Bear,** Steiff, mohair, voice box	185.00	200.00	195.00
☐ **Merry Bear,** Merry Thought, mohair, green embroidered scarf, #M914	50.00	60.00	55.00
☐ **Mikhail Bearishnikov,** North American Bear Co., in ballet tights, 19″	40.00	50.00	42.00
☐ **Papa Bear,** Bear Haus USA, tan, jointed, #3008, 16″	15.00	20.00	16.00
☐ **Richard Steiff Bear,** copy of original Steiff Teddy, limited edition, 1983, 12″	85.00	95.00	89.00
☐ **Running Bear,** jogging suit with hood	40.00	50.00	42.00
☐ **Scarlett O'Beara,** North American Bear Co., in traditional southern belle style	40.00	50.00	42.00
☐ **Teddy Bear,** plush brown, glass eyes, red ribbon, 7¾″	50.00	60.00	55.50

	Current Price Range		P/Y Average

☐ **Teddy Bear,** baby rattle, sterling silver, with teething ring	80.00	100.00	91.00
☐ **Teddy Bear,** cookbook, 1907	35.00	55.00	46.00
☐ **Teddy Bear,** on wheels, riding toy, brown mohair body stuffed with straw, glass eyes, embroidered nose, growler	1000.00	1500.00	1260.00
☐ **Teddy Bear,** tray, rectangular, c. 1906	40.00	50.00	46.00
☐ **Theodore Bear,** Dakin, jointed, 12″	8.00	12.00	9.00
☐ **Theodore Bear,** Dakin, jointed, 15″	11.00	18.00	12.00
☐ **William Shakesbear,** North American Bear Co., Shakespearean costume, 19″	40.00	50.00	42.00
☐ **Zsa Zsa Gabear,** North American Bear Co., fancy gown, 19″	40.00	50.00	42.00

CATS

☐ **Black Cat Kitchen Set,** oil and vinegar bottles	15.00	25.00	20.00
☐ **Black Cat Pretzel Holder,** tail serves as dowel to collect pretzels, cat in arched position, plaster of paris, USA	4.00	10.00	6.00
☐ **Cat Ashtray,** black cat, red bow around neck, green eyes	12.00	17.00	15.50
☐ **Cat Baby Fork,** silver plate, "Puss 'N' Boots"	12.00	17.00	14.50
☐ **Cat Bank,** plaster, painted a rust hue, black whiskers, 10″ high	80.00	100.00	90.00
☐ **Cat Bookends,** "Halloween Cat", cast iron, signed	40.00	60.00	51.00
☐ **Cat Candy Dish,** Fenton Carnival glass, features Chessie, 1970	100.00	130.00	118.00
☐ **Cat Candy Dish,** Fenton rosalene glass, features Chessie, 1977	90.00	120.00	100.00
☐ **Cat Candy Mold,** tin, 3½″	20.00	30.00	24.00
☐ **Cat Doorstop,** cast iron, full figure	85.00	105.00	96.00
☐ **Cat Figurine,** Mama cat, in pink bonnet, washing the face of a kitten, both in standing position	45.00	60.00	56.50
☐ **Cat Napkin Ring,** silver plate, from the Victorian era	90.00	110.00	100.00
☐ **Cat Postcards,** cats dressed up as various people, set of 18	20.00	30.00	27.50
☐ **Cat Prints,** Currier and Ives, unframed	115.00	175.00	130.00
☐ **Cat String Holder,** white cat bust, ceramic ...	20.00	30.00	27.00
☐ **Garfield,** Dakin, 7″	6.00	12.00	8.00
☐ **Garfield,** Dakin, 9″	10.00	15.00	11.00
☐ **Lizzy Cat,** Steiff, 1982	35.00	45.00	37.00

COWS

☐ **Cow,** fabric covered and painted, black hooves, brown spots, glass eyes, carved wooden base, 4¼″ high	20.00	30.00	24.50
☐ **Flora The Cow,** Steiff, white, beige, #3792/25, 10″	60.00	80.00	63.00

	Current Price Range		P/Y Average

DOGS

☐ **Dog Ashtray,** Scotty dog, plastic, black and white	12.00	20.00	17.00
☐ **Bookends,** German Shepherds, bronze, manufactured by Armor Bronze, New York	120.00	140.00	132.00
☐ **Dog Bootscraper,** Scotty in standing position, c. 1920s	8.00	15.00	12.00
☐ **Dog Matchstrike,** figural bulldog	40.00	50.00	45.00
☐ **Dog Planter,** Scotty, with ashtray, china	5.00	10.00	8.00
☐ **Dog Rattle,** with teething ring, sterling	50.00	90.00	72.00

PIGS

☐ **Pig,** brown and white stuffed	35.00	45.00	40.00
☐ **Pig Ashtray,** two pigs peering at camera, pale pink bisque	70.00	90.00	80.00
☐ **Pig Figurine,** pig driving jalopy, 3¾"	40.00	60.00	49.75
☐ **Pig Figurine,** pig peeking out of baby bassinet, 3½"	40.00	60.00	49.75
☐ **Pig Figurine,** pig sits beside "Boston Baked Beans" pot, 2½"	30.00	50.00	39.50
☐ **Pig Milk Pitcher,** dressed in evening finery, 4"	10.00	20.00	14.50
☐ **Pig Pillow,** quilted pattern	7.00	17.00	13.50

RABBITS

☐ **Benjamin Bunny,** Beatrix Potter	20.00	30.00	25.00
☐ **Bunnykins,** Autumn Days	10.00	20.00	16.50
☐ **Bunnykins,** Springtime	12.00	20.00	16.50
☐ **Mrs. Rabbit and Bunnies,** Beatrix Potter	22.00	32.00	27.00
☐ **Punning The Rabbit,** Steiff, mohair, sitting in a crouched position, #2960/25, c. 1960s, 10" ..	65.00	79.00	69.00
☐ **Rabbit Cake Mold,** in two pieces, cast iron, 11"	30.00	50.00	42.00
☐ **Rabbit Figurine,** Peter Rabbit, Anri	60.00	80.00	70.00
☐ **Running Rabbit,** Steiff, mohair, #131400, c. 1950s, 6"	100.00	130.00	105.00

UNICORNS

☐ **Unicorn,** Steuben crystal, etched signature, 7" high	710.00	910.00	810.00

ANIMATED CELS

DESCRIPTION: Animated cels are sheets of celluloid with painted designs used to produce color cartoons and full length animated features. Some films use part animation and part live actors as in Disney's *Song of the South* and the Beatles' *Yellow Submarine.* Cels which combine live actors and animation are equally collectible as fully animated cels.

ORIGIN: After Walt Disney Productions' release of *Snow White* in 1937, art dealers and collectors began forseeing a market for animated cels. The public acceptance of the fanciful characters in *Snow White* encouraged Disney to preserve the cels. During the 1930s and 1940s, animated cels continued to sell well fetching prices from $5 to $50. Today animated cels of that era sell for hundreds of dollars.

MAKER: Although the animated works of Walt Disney Productions and Fleischer Studios are highly collectible, animated cels preceding the 1920s are extremely desirable.

COMMENTS: Animated cels are produced by many notable cartoonists including Walter Lantz, the creator of Woody Woodpecker and Charles Jones, the originator of the Roadrunner. Disney's works are perhaps the most desirable of all since the studio often ignored production cost in order to produce detailed cels for the cartoon features.

CARE AND CONDITION: Special care should be taken with all animated cels especially those produced prior to 1951. Cels made before 1951 were made of cellulose nitrate, a flammable material which could be a serious fire hazard if stored incorrectly. After 1951, a less flammable celluloid was used. All cels, especially nitrate cels, should be stored individually in closed metal containers. Keep the containers in a cool, well-ventilated area. Do not wrap the cels in paper before storing.

ADDITIONAL TIPS: A glass mount is better than a cardboard mount. If one used cardboard, it should be made of 100 percent rag stock. Always display any cel away from heat or humidity.

Original Hand Painted Cel By Chuck Jones,
©*Warner Brothers, Inc., 1980,* **$30.00-$40.00**

	Current Price Range		P/Y Average
☐ **Adventures of Ichabod Crane and Mr. Toad,** Walt Disney Productions, full figure of Mr. Toad with whip, clicking heels together, full color, 5¼" x 6½", 1949	275.00	280.00	277.50
☐ **Alice in Wonderland,** Walt Disney Productions, full figure of caterpillar smoking pipe, color, 5" x 5½", 1951	175.00	200.00	187.00
☐ **Alice in Wonderland,** Walt Disney Productions, two cels which combine to produce a scene of the Dodo and a pair of birds, figures are one cel and the ocean another, full color, 7½" x 11", 1951	130.00	160.00	145.00
☐ **Alice in Wonderland,** Walt Disney Productions, full figure of the White Rabbit in three piece suit carrying umbrella, full color, 4" x 4½", 1951 . .	175.00	200.00	187.00
☐ **Art of Skiing, The,** Walt Disney Productions, air brushed background showing Goofy colliding with a tree, bears WDP stamp and Courvoisier label on reverse, 8¼" x 7½", 1941	310.00	335.00	322.00
☐ **Bambi,** Walt Disney Productions, air brushed and watercolor background showing Bambi, Thumper and friends watching a butterfly, bears Courvoisier label on reverse, 7½" x 9¼", 1942	1100.00	1300.00	1200.00
☐ **Bugs Bunny,** Chuck Jones Studio, full figure of Bugs Bunny with right leg raised, full color, 2½" x 6½", 1970	60.00	65.00	62.50

	Current Price Range		P/Y Average

☐ **Casper the Friendly Ghost,** Famous Studios, full figure of Casper, hands at side, full color, 2" x 3½", 1950s **30.00   40.00   35.00**

☐ **Cinderella,** Walt Disney Productions, showing the fairy waving her wand, bears WDP copyright on reverse, 6" x 9", 1950 .... **95.00   110.00   100.00**

☐ **Cinderella,** Walt Disney Productions, showing the Grand Duke in gray and blue uniform, 12½" x 15½", 1950 .... **70.00   80.00   75.00**

☐ **Dumbo,** Walt Disney Productions, showing Dumbo cradled in his mother's trunk, 7" x 5½", 1941 .... **1250.00   2450.00   1850.00**

☐ **Fantasia,** Walt Disney Productions, showing a centaurette holding a flower from the Pastoral Symphony, 10" x 12", 1940 .... **110.00   135.00   125.00**

☐ **Fantasia,** Walt Disney Productions, showing nineteen Milkwood fairies against pine tree branches and a gray background, bears Courvoisier label on reverse, 10" x 19", 1940 .... **610.00   660.00   635.00**

☐ **Lady and the Tramp,** Walt Disney Productions, showing Lady, 8" x 10", 1955 .... **100.00   135.00   115.00**

☐ **Mary Poppins,** Walt Disney Productions, showing pair of penguins and two small birds flying overhead, full color, 5½" x 6½", 1964 .... **160.00   200.00   180.00**

☐ **Mickey Mouse Club,** Walt Disney Productions, showing full figure of Jiminy Cricket with a yo-yo, 5½" x 6", 1950s **140.00   150.00   145.00**

☐ **Peter Pan,** Walt Disney Productions, showing Wendy with hands out and palms upraised, mouth open, full color, 3½" x 4¼", 1953 ..... **100.00   130.00   115.00**

☐ **Peter Pan,** Walt Disney Productions, showing John holding an umbrella and wearing a silk hat, full color, 5½" x 7", 1953 .... **90.00   110.00   100.00**

☐ **Pink Panther,** Depattee-Frelang Studio, showing Pink Panther on a steel structure high above street, 10" x 12½", 1965 .... **195.00   210.00   202.00**

☐ **Pinocchio,** Walt Disney Productions, showing Jiminy Cricket on the sea floor startled by a fish, bears Courvoisier label on reverse, 5½" x 6½", 1940 .... **430.00   460.00   445.00**

☐ **Sinking of the Lusitania, The,** Winsor McCay, showing the sinking of the Lusitania, 7½" x 9", 1918 .... **500.00   800.00   650.00**

☐ **Sleeping Beauty,** Walt Disney Productions, showing Prince Philip on horseback bearing a sword and shield, full color, 5¼" x 7", 1959 .. **220.00   250.00   235.00**

☐ **Snoopy,** CBS Television, showing Snoopy in tennis clothes and racket, 10¼" x 12½", 1970s **55.00   65.00   60.00**

☐ **Snow White,** Walt Disney Productions, showing Dopey standing with squirrels running past him, 8½" x 8½", 1937 .... **335.00   360.00   347.00**

☐ **Snow White,** Walt Disney Productions, showing Bashful, 7" x 5", 1937 .... **260.00   280.00   270.00**

	Current Price Range		P/Y Average
☐ **You're An Education,** Warner Brothers Studio, Hep Cat blowing a yellow trombone, 8″ x 11″, 1938	70.00	90.00	80.00

ART DECO

TOPIC: ART DECO See Icart; Lalique.

DESCRIPTION: Art Deco is essentially a design movement which was named for an important exhibition in Paris in 1925 called "l'Exposition Internationale des Arts Decoratifs." The show came, however, at least five years after the movement was underway.

PERIOD: Today, we call the 1920s and 1930s the period of Art Deco. Designers were inspired by Cubist art and artifacts from ancient Egypt and North and Central America. These are all characterized by strong color and abstract geometric design. There is some time overlap with the Art Nouveau period, but the major differences are characterized by the "modernist" look of Art Deco.

TYPES: The range of Art Deco collectibles is great—from plastic bracelets to custom-designed glass vases.

Furniture in sleek modernistic lines was produced and often lacquered in black or white.

COMMENTS: The sleek designs of Art Deco are currently very popular once again. California is the leading edge of this movement with the "Hollywood" style of the 1920s and 30s being particularly popular.

ADDITIONAL TIPS: Many Art Deco items can be purchased very inexpensively at second hand shops and thrift stores across the country. Look for geometric motifs, sleek styling, pastel colors, black or white enameling, chrome, and smoked glass in a wide variety of items. These include lamp bases, smoking accoutrements, vases, mirrors, vanity accessories, dishes, glassware, figurines, objets d'art and furniture. Old bedroom suites from the 1920s abound. It is quite possible to acquire a complete bedroom suite including bed, night stands, chest of drawers, dresser and vanity for under $200. Don't be put off by the old wood veneer finish. These sets can be enameled in black, white, or even pastel colors with dazzling results!

RECOMMENDED READING: For more information on Art Deco, you may refer to the following books published by The House of Collectibles:

The Official Price Guide to Glassware
The Official Price Guide to Antique Jewelry
The Official Price Guide to Collector Prints
The Official Price Guide to Pottery and Porcelain
The Official Price Guide to Wicker
The Official Identification Guide to Glassware
The Official Identification Guide to Pottery and Porcelain

Vogue magazine promotional, *Art Deco style, brass, 1926,* **$70.00-$90.00**

	Current Price Range		P/Y Average
☐ **Andirons,** brass, pair	255.00	300.00	270.00
☐ **Ashtray,** bronze and onyx figural, onyx bowl with flower head supporting a ballerina, inscribed Lorenzl, 12¾", c. 1925	900.00	1150.00	990.00
☐ **Bar pin,** platinum, diamond, jade and onyx with white gold clasp, c. 1925	900.00	1150.00	990.00
☐ **Bedroom Suite,** Heywood Wakefield, four piece set includes dressing table with large round mirror, tabouret, four drawer dresser, and night stand, black enamel, c. 1935	2800.00	3200.00	2850.00
☐ **Chair,** occasional, black vinyl upholstery, rounded back, lower arms cut out, circular seat, white apron, 33" high by 25" wide, c. 1925 ...	175.00	225.00	187.00
☐ **Cigar box,** Tiffany & Company, rectangular, cedar lining, c. 1925	400.00	450.00	410.00
☐ **Cigarette case,** silver and blue enamel	195.00	215.00	200.00
☐ **Clock,** desk, black onyx and sterling silver, Zenith, fifteen jewel movement, three adjustments, 2⅜"	285.00	340.00	305.00

	Current Price Range		P/Y Average

☐ **Clock,** desk, jade and enamel, square form, blue enamelled hands and black Roman numerals, Cartier, 1¼" .... | 2500.00 | 3500.00 | 2800.00

☐ **Clock,** desk, rock crystal gold, enamel and diamonds, Cartier, c. 1935 .... | 3400.00 | 4000.00 | 3600.00

☐ **Clock,** glass and chrome-plated bronze, chrome face, black glass and chrome base, 8¾", c. 1930 .... | 305.00 | 475.00 | 315.00

☐ **Comb case,** six cabochon sapphires in gold motif, sterling silver, c. 1935 .... | 500.00 | 600.00 | 515.00

☐ **Compact,** black with diamond corners, black enamel link chain attached to finger ring ...... | 1050.00 | 1320.00 | 1150.00

☐ **Compact,** rectangular, gold enamel and diamonds, Cartier, c. 1930 .... | 3400.00 | 4000.00 | 3600.00

☐ **Desk,** curved with twin pedestal, cabinet and four drawers on either side of a large central drawer, unsigned, French, 56" long .... | 325.00 | 400.00 | 360.00

☐ **Desk,** drop front, English, c. 1935 .... | 1200.00 | 1800.00 | 1375.00

☐ **Figure,** dancer, exotic silvered figure, marble base, inscribed Fayral, c. 1925 .... | 610.00 | 835.00 | 700.00

☐ **Figure,** dancer, gilt-bronze nude figure with outstretched arms supporting a drapery, inscribed A. Kelety, 14½", c. 1930 .... | 790.00 | 1200.00 | 900.00

☐ **Figure,** dancer, swaying, inscribed CJR Colinet, 18½", c. 1925 .... | 680.00 | 790.00 | 700.00

☐ **Figure,** Pierette and Pierrot, bronze, green marble base, inscribed Lorenzl, 16¾", c. 1925 .... | 1375.00 | 1870.00 | 1500.00

☐ **Figure,** young sailor, bronze and ivory, marked "BRONZE," plinth inscribed A. Jorel, 9", early 20th century .... | 390.00 | 500.00 | 425.00

☐ **Figure,** young woman, bronze and tortoise shell .... | 830.00 | 1025.00 | 900.00

☐ **Figure,** young woman, bronze and ivory, onyx base, Bessie Callender, 17", c. 1930 .... | 1015.00 | 1410.00 | 1150.00

☐ **Figure,** young woman, silvered and gilt-bronze figure riding on elephant, onyx and marble base, French, 24", c. 1925 .... | 1650.00 | 2100.00 | 1750.00

☐ **Floor Lamp,** skyscraper style with checkerboard design, marked Warren Allen with date of January, 1929, 55½" .... | 275.00 | 335.00 | 290.00

☐ **Footstool,** upholstered and aluminum, designed by Deskey, c. 1931 .... | 460.00 | 680.00 | 550.00

☐ **Hall Rack,** wrought iron, made in Belgium, has pivoting mirror with hooks at either side, base serves as umbrella stand, six feet by three feet | 325.00 | 380.00 | 340.00

☐ **Lamp,** alabaster and metal, figural, female holding torch, diamond shaped base, 22½" ...... | 350.00 | 450.00 | 380.00

☐ **Lamps,** pair, chromed metal, small circular base, cylindrical standard, one-piece bowl shaped shade, French, 19", c. 1925 .... | 1400.00 | 1600.00 | 1425.00

☐ **Lapel watch,** black onyx panel, pin has rosecut diamonds, platinum and gold watch, Dreicer & Co. .... | 1485.00 | 1870.00 | 1575.00

	Current Price Range		P/Y Average
☐ **Necklace,** faceted black glass rectangles, oval faceted pastes, black metal mountings, 15″ long, Czechoslovakian, c. 1920–30	45.00	55.00	47.50
☐ **Necklace,** fancy aluminum and round black glass beads, 16½″ long, c. 1920–30	120.00	140.00	122.00
☐ **Necklace,** fancy green and white plastic beads, 20″ long, c. 1920–30	45.00	55.00	44.00
☐ **Necklace,** fancy pumpkin, orange and amber colored plastic beads, 16½″ long, c. 1920–30	35.00	45.00	35.50
☐ **Necklace,** geometric motif, beige, apple green and white plastic beads, 17″ long, c. 1920–30	35.00	45.00	35.00
☐ **Necklace,** oval and round bittersweet amber colored plastic beads, 15½″ long, c. 1920–30 ...	25.00	35.00	27.50
☐ **Necklace,** round jade green ceramic beads spaced with white metal fancy links, 15½″ long, c. 1920–30	35.00	45.00	35.50
☐ **Necklace,** three pendants of round pastes sandwiched between two round amber glass beads, chain of small cherry red plastic tubes, 22½″ long, c. 1920–30	35.00	5.00	35.50
☐ **Necklace,** triple pendant, 14K gold, American, c. 1930	750.00	950.00	765.00
☐ **Picture,** reverse painting on glass by W. Fager, floral motif, enclosed in gilt wire frame, 22″ ...	80.00	100.00	87.00
☐ **Picture Frame,** standing, bronze with black marble base, 14¼″ wide, 13½″ tall	90.00	110.00	96.00
☐ **Picture Frames,** set of four wall hanging frames, with reverse silkscreen decoration on glass, 12″ x 10″	110.00	140.00	120.00
☐ **Rack,** hall, lacquer and brass, mirror plate, brass holders, black support, French, 5′1″, c. 1930 ..	425.00	530.00	475.00
☐ **Ring,** one round diamond approx. .50 ct., one round diamond approx. .25 ct., 16 round diamonds approx. .32 ct., 14K white gold, c. 1935	1800.00	2200.00	1875.00
☐ **Ring,** one round diamond approx. .50 ct., six baguette diamonds, 20 round diamonds, platinum, c. 1930	2000.00	2400.00	2075.00
☐ **Ring,** one round diamond approx. 1.90 cts., six baguette diamonds, round diamonds, platinum, c. 1930	7000.00	8500.00	7200.00
☐ **Ring,** oval black onyx center, two round diamonds, 14K gold, c. 1925	475.00	575.00	490.00
☐ **Ring,** platinum, cabochon sapphire and six baguette diamonds	1800.00	2300.00	2000.00
☐ **Ring,** platinum, diamond and ruby, wide band	500.00	720.00	600.00
☐ **Watch,** wrist, square geometric motif, 64 round diamonds approx. 1.26 cts., 20 baguette diamonds approx. 1.06 cts., 14K white gold, maker: Hamilton, 22 jewels, c. 1930	3200.00	3400.00	3225.00
☐ **Watch,** ring, oval motif, polychrome enamels, white enamel dial, steel hands, 18K gold case, c. 1930	1700.00	1900.00	1750.00

ART GLASS
(See also Daum Nancy; Gallé; Lalique; Tiffany Glass)

DESCRIPTION: Collectible art glass refers to various types of decorative glass which was developed all over the world and hand worked in one or all stages of development from the last half of the nineteenth century until the 1930s and 1940s. It includes glass from the Victorian, Art Nouveau and Art Deco periods. Victorian Art Glass consists of the Amberina, Burmese, Peach-Blow, Opal, Silverina, Agate, Crown Milano, Napoli, Satin and Royal Flemish, to name a few. With the decline of the Victorian period and the emergence of Art Nouveau, iridized glass appeared, made in America by Louis Comfort Tiffany and Steuben, in Austria by Lotz, in France by Galle, and in England by Thomas Webb and Sons.

Art Deco replaced Art Nouveau in the 1920s and the Lalique glass of France epitomized the sleek styles of the day.

CARE: The utmost care must be exercised in cleaning art glass. Enameled or flashed pieces can be damaged by washing. It is always wise to first wipe the object with a dry, flannel cloth, buffing gently to remove accumulated dirt and dust. Then, if need be, use a damp cloth and wipe carefully. Dry the piece thoroughly. If a piece needs washing use only mild soap in lukewarm water. Do not soak. Wash and dry quickly.

REPAIRS: Repairs must be made by an expert. To find one in your area, call local galleries or museums. But remember, generally speaking, any serious damage renders art glass virtually worthless. Most damaged glass is impossible to repair.

RECOMMENDED READING: For further information refer to *The Official Price Guide to Glassware* and *The Official Identification Guide to Glassware,* published by The House of Collectibles.

	Current Price Range		P/Y Average

AGATA

☐ **Spooner,** green opaque, very good mottling and gold band, 4½" high	625.00	725.00	635.00

	Current Price Range		P/Y Average

☐ **Tumbler,** green opaque, excellent mottling and gold band, bottom has optic rib, 3¾" high **575.00 675.00 585.00**

☐ **Tumbler,** green opaque, good mottling and gold band, glass is somewhat thick, 3¾" high **475.00 575.00 485.00**

☐ **Tumbler,** green opaque, good mottling and gold band, bottom has optic rib, 3¾" high **525.00 625.00 535.00**

AMBER

☐ **Beer Stein,** amber applied handle, green applied berry prunts, pewter base and hinged lid with thumbpiece, hold ¼ liter, 6⅞" high, 3" diameter **180.00 230.00 190.00**

☐ **Beer Stein,** amber applied handle, applied green berry prunts, pewter base and lid, 6¾" high, 3" diameter **180.00 230.00 190.00**

☐ **Cologne Bottle,** cut glass with matching stopper, 7" high, 3¾" diameter **150.00 200.00 155.00**

☐ **Liqueur Cruet,** pewter stopper, pewter mounted, 8" high, 3" diameter **100.00 130.00 105.00**

☐ **Liqueur Cruet,** swirl, amber rigaree, applied foot, pewter stopper, 8½" high, 3⅛" diameter **120.00 150.00 125.00**

☐ **Vinegar Cruet,** applied handle and ball stopper with enameled decorations, enameled, white dabs and blue fans on cruet, bulbous shaped mouth, 6¾" high, 3½" diameter **130.00 180.00 135.00**

☐ **Vinegar Cruet,** inverted thumbprint style, applied handle and bubble stopper, bulbous shape, 5¼" high, 3" diameter **100.00 150.00 110.00**

AMBERINA

☐ **Bowl,** swirl, deep fluted, rich cranberry shades evenly to amber, amber wafer foot, decorated with gold branches, berries and leaves, 7½" x 10¾" **350.00 450.00 365.00**

☐ **Bowl,** swirl, fluted, rich red shades to amber, irridized finish, 4" high, 7⅝" diameter **140.00 190.00 150.00**

☐ **Champagne Glass,** hollow stem, 6" high **175.00 250.00 185.00**

☐ **Cruet,** Mt. Washington, Venetian Diamond, deep fuschia shading to honey amber, original stopper **250.00 350.00 275.00**

☐ **Fingerbowl and Underplate,** Libbey, bowl is more red than underplate which is fuschia, 2½" high, signed LIBBEY, 1917 .... **525.00 625.00 535.00**

☐ **Mug,** bulbous, amber handle, 4" high **105.00 125.00 110.00**

☐ **Pitcher,** diamond quilted, applied amber handle, red shaded to amber, round mouth, shape of tankard, belltone, 7" high, 4⅛" diameter **350.00 400.00 375.00**

☐ **Salt and Pepper Shakers,** set, inverted thumbprint, deepest fuschia color, original tops, 1880s **250.00 350.00 265.00**

☐ **Spooner,** Mt. Washington, diamond quilted, deep fuschia, square top **275.00 350.00 290.00**

	Current Price Range		P/Y Average

☐ **Tumber,** cranberry shaded to amberina quilted design, 3″ high **40.00 65.00 35.00**

☐ **Tumbler,** deep cranberry, evenly to amber, 5½″ high **75.00 90.00 80.00**

☐ **Vase,** flower petal shaped top, fancy amber applied spiral trim, cranberry shades evenly to amber, 10″ high, 5⅝″ diameter **140.00 190.00 150.00**

☐ **Vase,** Libbey, deep cranberry vase tapers to amber stem, 11¼″ high **435.00 500.00 470.00**

☐ **Vase,** swirl, fan shaped top, rich cranberry shaded to golden amber, amber edging around top, amber applied wishbone feet, 8⅛″ high, 6⅜″ diameter **135.00 195.00 130.00**

☐ **Vases,** Jack-In-Pulpit, decorated in gold with amber edging around top, cranberry shaded to amber, decoration of flowers and leaves in heavy gold, pair, 14¾″ high, 5⅜″ diameter **475.00 520.00 480.00**

☐ **Whiskey Tumber,** diamond quilted, deep red shaded to amber, belltone, 2⅝″ high, 2⅛″ diameter **170.00 200.00 185.00**

AMBERINA, REVERSE

☐ **Pitcher,** bulbous, olive amber shades evenly to cranberry, round mouth, clear reeded applied handle, colored enameled leaves and flowers, red and green jewel decorations, 7⅞″ high, 5¼″ diameter **225.00 325.00 240.00**

☐ **Salt Shaker,** inverted baby thumbprint, pewter top **150.00 220.00 160.00**

☐ **Tumbler,** amber shaded to cranberry at base, pink, yellow and blue enameled flowers with applied red jewels to centers, 5⅛″ high, 2⅝″ diameter **90.00 130.00 95.00**

ARGY-ROUSSEAU

☐ **Bowl,** pate-de-verre, cylinder shape tapering towards the base, red background, molded with pineapples and leaves inside medallion-like designs which encircle the shoulder in a band, in black and red, signed, 4½″ diameter, c. 1925 **1100.00 1400.00 1150.00**

☐ **Bowl,** pate-de-verre, expanding cylinder, mottled lavender and green background, molds with roses, signed, 2¾″ high, c. 1925 .... **800.00 1200.00 850.00**

☐ **Box,** covered, circular, light amber, orange, and gray, molded with leaves, strapwork, and stars with a red mask on the lid, signed, 6″ diameter, c. 1925 .... **2200.00 2800.00 2250.00**

BOHEMIAN

☐ **Bowl,** overlay of cobalt, cut hobstars and fans, starcut design on base, tapered sides, round shape, 3½″ high, 12″ diameter **60.00 80.00 70.00**

	Current Price Range		P/Y Average
☐ **Bowl,** overlay of cobalt, cut hobstars and fans, tapered sides, starcut design on base, tapered sides, round shape, 3½" high, 12" diameter ..	65.00	85.00	70.00
☐ **Cake Plate,** overlay of amethyst, cut wave design surrounding hobstars and diamonds, notched and scalloped rim, 11¼" diameter ...	42.00	62.00	50.00
☐ **Cologne Bottle,** ruby red with frosting around center, ruby circles and medallion have etched scene of deer, ruby cut stopper, 7⅜" high, 2½" diameter	155.00	205.00	160.00
☐ **Compote,** overlay of green, triangles with caning, thumbprints and sunburst design, notched and paneled shafts, starcut design on base, 6" high, 7½" diameter	37.50	75.00	45.00
☐ **Decanter,** cobalt with bullseye and fan cuts, paneled neck, clear stopper, 12½" high	55.00	75.00	65.00
☐ **Dish,** overlay of green with three large cut fans, thumbprint and marquise on border, footed, round shape, 3¼" high, 8" diameter	45.00	65.00	50.00
☐ **Vase,** overlay of amethyst, graduated sizes of cut panels, 10" high	25.00	50.00	35.00
☐ **Vase,** overlay of cobalt, trumpet shape, cut pinwheels, diamonds and fans, 12" high	62.50	105.00	80.00

Bohemian Decanter, *cranberry forest design, etched, 15" high,* **$185.00-$200.00**

	Current Price Range		P/Y Average

☐ **Vase,** overlay of cobalt, trumpet shape, graduated sizes of cut panels, 7″ high 30.00 50.00 40.00

☐ **Vase,** overlay of cranberry, cut spiked diamond and notched leaves, tapered base, cylindrical shape 62.50 82.50 70.00

☐ **Vase,** overlay with diamond cuts 80.00 110.00 90.00

BRISTOL

☐ **Cologne Bottle,** finish of apple green satin, green reeded handles trimmed in gold, matching scalloped stopper, 9⅜″ high, 3⅜″ diameter ... 130.00 190.00 140.00

☐ **Lustres,** gold decorated blue combination of glossy and satin finish, each lustre has eight crystal cut, spear point prisms, 10¾″ high, 5″ diameter 320.00 370.00 325.00

☐ **Sweetmeat Jar,** of pink overlay, silver plated lid, handle and rim around base, white interior, floral decoration of blue and white and enameled duck in flight, 5″ high 3″ diameter 120.00 160.00 135.00

☐ **Vase,** decorated turquoise blue, gray, purple and yellow bird of enamel on front, flowers of pink and white with green leaves, bug decoration on back, dots of white and bands of gold adorn pedestal base, flattened oval shape, 2½″ high, 4¼″ diameter 200.00 240.00 210.00

☐ **Vase,** of pink overlay, scalloped cut top with gold trim, decorated in blue, white and orange enameled flowers, white heron outlined in blue dot pattern, 15″ high, 5″ diameter 210.00 270.00 230.00

☐ **Vases,** narrow necks, globular shape, 6½″ high 25.00 40.00 30.00

BURGUN & SCHVERER

☐ **Bowl,** half-spherical, wide mouth with sawtooth, light green streaked with red, enameled with cherry blossoms and leaves in light pink, white, green, and brown, overlaid and carved in clear, gilding, 7″ diameter, c. 1895. 4000.00 6000.00 4100.00

☐ **Bowl,** waisted dome body, flaring rolled lip, lobed circular foot, brownish-yellow streaked with green background, cut with wild animals and flowers within black enamel bands, background cut with spiraling garlands, enameled orange leaves around mouth, 5⅛″ diameter, c. 1895 3000.00 4000.00 3250.00

☐ **Bowl,** wide circular body, waisted standard, slightly flaring foot, sawtooth rim, light green with red-streaked background, enameled with poppies, grass, and leaves in light pink, white, green, and brown, overlaid clear with carving, gilding, 6″, diameter, c. 1895 .... 4000.00 5000.00 4100.00

☐ **Vase,** bulbous body, cylinder neck slightly expanding towards sawtooth lip, pale yellow with brown streaks, enameled with flowers and leaves

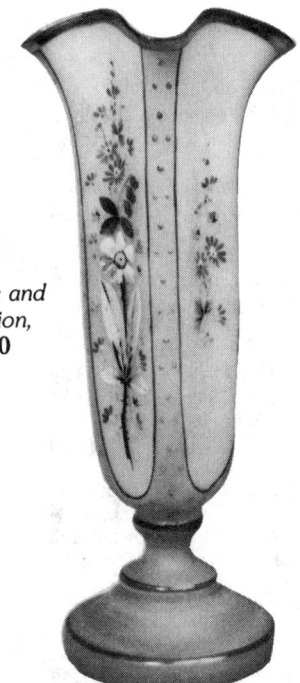

Bristol Vase, *frosted mauve and white, enamel floral decoration,* 10½" *high,* **$85.00-$100.00**

	Current Price Range		P/Y Average
in blue and green, overlaid in clear, an applied scroll of foliage twining around neck, gilding, 5½" high, c. 1895	2000.00	3000.00	2100.00
☐ **Vase,** bulbous body with long cylinder neck, gray shading towards base to lavender, overlaid in clear, carved with flowers and leaves of white, light yellow, and green, sawtooth neck, gilding, 5¾" high, c. 1895	2000.00	3000.00	2100.00
☐ **Vase,** cabinet, baluster shape, sawtooth neck, yellow and beige background, overlaid in clear, carved with flowers and leaves of lavender, white, green, and brown, gilding, 5¼" high, c. 1895	3000.00	4000.00	3100.00
☐ **Vase,** cabinet, spherical body, short cylinder neck with flaring lip, three clear feet, frosted gray with lavender streaked background, overlaid in lavender, cut with bleeding hearts and leaves, gilding highlights, 3⅛" high, c. 1895	600.00	800.00	615.00

	Current Price Range		P/Y Average

BURMESE

☐ **Cruet,** Mt. Washington, acid finish, melon ribbed, undecorated, second fired yellow edge on spout, very fine color, 6½" high .... | 900.00 | 1400.00 | 950.00

☐ **Cruet,** Mt. Washington, acid finish, ribbed, matching ribbed stopper, yellow handle, 7" high, 3¾" diameter .... | 775.00 | 900.00 | 785.00

☐ **Fairy Lamp,** acid finish, superb color, deep salmon pink shades evenly to creamy yellow, rare pressed burmese base, clear inside cup, base marked Clarke, 5" high, 3⅞" diameter ... | 375.00 | 475.00 | 385.00

☐ **Fairy Lamp,** acid finish, superb color, rich salmon pink shades evenly to yellow, on matching ruffed reversible base, clear marked Clarke cup, 5¾" high, 7" diameter .... | 525.00 | 725.00 | 525.00

☐ **Fairy Lamp,** Webb, acid finish, dome on signed Clarkes candle cup .... | 225.00 | 250.00 | 230.00

☐ **Fairy Lamp,** Webb, acid finish, gold decorated Aladdin shape muted green Tunnecliffe pottery-base, shade is decorated with red flowers and green leaves, base marked Clarke inside, 6½" high .... | 675.00 | 750.00 | 685.00

☐ **Fairy Lamp,** Webb, acid finish, superb color, matching unsigned fluted burmese bowl base with three yellow feet, pressed burmese insert signed Clarke, clear candle cup, large burmese dome shade, 6½" high, 4¼" diameter .... | 700.00 | 810.00 | 700.00

☐ **Muffineer,** Mt. Washington, acid finish, white and colored dots form delicate blossoms, attributed to Timothy Canty, 4½" high .... | 575.00 | 650.00 | 580.00

☐ **Rosebowl,** miniature, Webb, acid finish, crimped top, decorated with red berries, green and brown leaves, unsigned, 2½" high, 2¾" diameter .... | 275.00 | 350.00 | 285.00

☐ **Sugar and Creamer Set,** Mt. Washington, acid finish, no decoration, 3¾" creamer has applied handle, open sugar is 2⅛" high .... | 550.00 | 650.00 | 575.00

☐ **Table Lamp,** probably Mt. Washington, shade has satin exterior, shiny interior, fine color, base is originally Kerosene, converted to electricity, made of Brittania metal in England, has embossed florals, shade is 10" diameter, total height is 15" .... | 1000.00 | 2000.00 | 1200.00

☐ **Toothpick Holder,** acid finish, bulbous with square top, decorated with dainty brown leaves, white and blue enameled flowers, 3" high, 2½" diameter .... | 230.00 | 330.00 | 245.00

☐ **Toothpick Holder,** acid finish, square top, 2⅝" high, 2½" diameter .... | 145.00 | 180.00 | 135.00

☐ **Vase,** acid finish, ribbed, scalloped top, 3¾" high, 2½" diameter .... | 150.00 | 230.00 | 165.00

☐ **Vase,** shiny finish, ruffled top, 3¾" high, 3" diameter .... | 150.00 | 200.00 | 160.00

	Current Price Range		P/Y Average

☐ **Vase,** acid finish, salmon pink shades evenly to yellow, enameled decoration features red buds and green leaves unsigned but attributed to Webb, 8″ high, 4″ diameter **700.00   900.00   725.00**

☐ **Vase,** acid finish, undecorated, 3¾″ high, 5¼″ diameter at widest point **175.00   275.00   180.00**

☐ **Vase,** Mt. Washington, beautiful coloration, enameled multicolor stylized blossoms and foliage, two applied handles, 10½″ high **1150.00   1350.00   1200.00**

☐ **Vase,** Mt. Washington, bottle, acid finish, salmon pink evenly shaded to yellow, white enameled mums and dainty green foliage, 6⅜″ high, 3¼″ diameter **225.00   325.00   250.00**

☐ **Vase,** Mt. Washington, bulbous base, long slender neck, decorated with sacred ibis, oasis scene in raised gold, 12″ high, 7″ diameter at widest point **2500.00   3500.00   750.00**

☐ **Vase,** Mt. Washington, egg shaped, acid finish, decorated with daisies and foliage in three shades of gold enamel, designs outlined in raised gold, 9″ high, 4¾″ diameter at widest point . . .   **650.00   750.00   75.00**

☐ **Vase,** Mt. Washington, jack-in-pulpit, acid finish, very good color, flared crimped top, 12½″ high, 5″ diameter at top **600.00   700.00   625.00**

☐ **Vase,** Mt. Washington, teardrop shape, elaborate blossom and foliage multicolored and gold decoration, raised gold dots, fancy scrolls, 10½″ high, 5½″ diameter at widest point **1500.00   2500.00   1750.00**

☐ **Vase,** Webb, acid finish, flower petal top, salmon pink shades evenly to yellow, decorated with green leaves and red berries, 3⅜″ high, 3⅛″ diameter **300.00   385.00   315.00**

☐ **Vase,** Webb, acid finish, fluted top, slightly embossed striped effect, 3½″ high, 3″ diameter   **175.00   270.00   185.00**

☐ **Vase,** Webb, acid finish, ruffled top and base, 4½″ high, 2¾″ diameter **175.00   270.00   185.00**

☐ **Vase,** Webb, acid finish, ruffled top, salmon pink shades evenly to yellow, decorated with lavender five petal flower, green and brown leaves, unsigned, 4⅛″ high, 2¾″ diameter **295.00   395.00   300.00**

☐ **Vase,** Webb, acid finish, ruffled top, widely flared, ball shape body, unsigned, 3⅛″ high. **175.00   275.00   180.00**

☐ **Vase,** Webb, acid finish, salmon pink shades evenly to yellow, decorated with green foliage and red buds, unusual shape, 4⅜″ high, 2½″ diameter **300.00   400.00   325.00**

☐ **Vase,** Webb, Queen's, acid finish, bottle, salmon pink shades evenly to yellow green ivy leaf enameled decoration, signed Thos. Webb Queens Burmese Ware, 7¾″ high, 4½″ diameter **800.00   1000.00   825.00**

	Current Price Range		P/Y Average

☐ **Vase,** Webb, Queen's, acid finish, flower petal top, salmon pink shades evenly to yellow, decorated with green and brown leaves, red berries, signed Thos. Webb Queens Burmese Ware, 2¾" high, 3¼" diameter 375.00 475.00 400.00

☐ **Vase,** Webb, Queen's, acid finish, flower shaped top, unusual frosted edging, salmon pink shades evenly to yellow, tan pine cone enameled decoration, signed Thos. Webb Queens Burmese Ware, 5⅝" high, 3⅛" diameter 500.00 700.00 550.00

☐ **Whiskey Tumbler,** Mt. Washington, acid finish, diamond quilted, reheated yellow top edge, 2¾" high, 2¼" diameter 150.00 220.00 165.00

CAMEO

☐ **Bowl,** English, ribbed, thin outer layer of various pink shades, white inner layer, acid cut back in fish scale motif, decorated with morning glory vine and butterfly in gold enamel, 3" base, 7½" at widest point, 6¼" top diameter, signed in enamel G.L.F., paper label Whitlow collection 950.00 1125.00 950.00

☐ **Perfume Bottle,** English, round, dark blue ground, profusely decorated with deeply carved and finely detailed white blossoms, foliage and butterfly, sterling, screw-type stopper, 7¼" high, 5" diameter 1800.00 2500.00 1900.00

☐ **Vase,** English, four layers, white to red to clear to green, depicts raspberries and foliage, very elaborate top border, 7" high, 4½" diameter at widest point, unsigned 2000.00 3000.00 2250.00

☐ **Vase,** signed by Michel Paris, translucent, frosted background with brown cut to yellow, sailboat scene, three detailed acid cuttings, 8½" high, 3½" diameter 800.00 850.00 820.00

CASED

☐ **Lustres,** white with cranberry banding, circular medallions, hand painted flowers, ruffled rims, pedestal bases, spearpoint prisms, 12⅝" high 70.00 160.00 110.00

☐ **Perfume Bottle,** decorated yellow, clear ball stopper has covering of gold, sanded gold leaves and ribbon studded with applied jewels of green and red, 5½" high, 2⅛" diameter 100.00 140.00 110.00

☐ **Rose Bowl,** amethyst, applied flower in white with transparent, applied branch and leaf, 3¾" high, 4" diameter, rare 150.00 200.00 175.00

☐ **Rose Bowl,** pink hobnail design, eight crimp top, 3⅛" high, 3⅝" diameter 90.00 130.00 115.00

	Current Price Range		P/Y Average

CORALENE

☐ **Pitcher,** orange glass, amber applied handle and rigaree of amber surrounds neck, water lilies of white and green leaves in Coralene beading decoration, 6¼" high, 4" diameter. 210.00 250.00 215.00

☐ **Lamp Base,** satin glass of decorated yellow, fern leaf sprays of pale yellow in beaded Coralene of yellow, original brass burner, 7⅝" high, 3" diameter 150.00 200.00 160.00

☐ **Vase,** seaweed decoration on pale blue diamond quilted mother of pearl, coralene blossoms have applied jewel center, 7" high 450.00 550.00 475.00

☐ **Vase,** seaweed, pink decoration on gold diamond quilted mother of pearl, 6¾" high 450.00 550.00 475.00

CRANBERRY

☐ **Bowl,** applied crystal berries on top edge, berry pontil plus three crystal fans applied around top, three reeded scroll feet, 5½" high, 5½" diameter 280.00 330.00 290.00

☐ **Bowl,** clear reeded scroll feet, six clear berry prunts around top, three crystal fan shaped applied designs on bowl, berry on base, 5⅜" high, 6⅛" diameter 230.00 310.00 250.00

☐ **Bowl,** two rows of crystal applied shell trim, applied rigaree around center, three crystal reeded scroll feet, base has berry prunt, 4¾" high, 8" diameter. 420.00 480.00 430.00

☐ **Cologne Bottle,** frosted with gold decorations, clear ball stopper adorned in gold, 5¾" high, 3⅛" diameter 180.00 220.00 185.00

☐ **Fairy Lamp,** frosted, shade has crimped top, signed Clarke base, 3¾" high, 2⅞" diameter 110.00 150.00 115.00

☐ **Liqueur Set on Tray,** decorated in heavy gold, tray has square, scalloped edge, 8" diameter, bottle has applique on sides with flower basket and butterfly decoration, 9¼" high, set of six glasses, matching, 2" high 255.00 315.00 255.00

☐ **Lustres,** clear crystal prisms, pair, 11" high . . . 110.00 160.00 130.00

☐ **Pitcher,** inverted thumbprint, bulbous with square top, clear applied handles, 5⅞" high, 3½" diameter 85.00 120.00 90.00

☐ **Pitcher,** inverted thumbprint with applied handle 8½" high, 4½" diameter 280.00 305.00 290.00

☐ **Vase,** decorated with gold enamel and blue and white forget-me-nots, 11" high, 4" diameter . . . 120.00 160.00 130.00

☐ **Vase,** ewer, Moser-type, enameled, clear twig handle, 11½" high 40.00 77.00 45.00

☐ **Vase,** fan shaped, deep cranberry color, clear applied ruffle around top edge, clear applied wishbone feet, decorated with small enameled multicolored leaves, blue and white flowers on gold panel, 10¾" high 190.00 235.00 190.00

Cranberry Pickle Castor, *sterling holder with fork, 11¾″ high,* **$225.00-$250.00**

Cranberry Thumbprint Basket, *applied crystal handle, 10″ high,* **65.00-$80.00**

	Current Price Range		P/Y Average
☐ **Vase,** hand painted circular plaque of young child in porcelain, some fired gold foliage and bird design, pedestal base, inverted heart shape, 5″ high	35.00	65.00	45.00
☐ **Vases,** pair, decorated with gold sanded flowers and leaves outlined in white with blue centers, small white enameled flowers and branches, gold sanded top and bottom bands, 10″ high, 3¾″ diameter	275.00	330.00	285.00
☐ **Vases,** pair, deep cranberry color, lavishly decorated with gold, blue and white flowers and leaves, 11″ high, 4″ diameter	300.00	400.00	325.00

	Current Price Range		P/Y Average

☐ **Water Pitcher,** optic effect, clear applied handle, very large, 12¾" high, 6¼" diameter **250.00 320.00   275.00**

☐ **Wine Glasses,** cranberry bowls with clear stems and feet, belltone, set of six, 5⅛, 2¼" diameter
. . . . **160.00 200.00   165.00**

CROWN MILANO

☐ **Ewer,** Mt. Washington, applied handle, profuse eight-color geometric decoration, 13" high, unsigned **1600.00 2000.00 1700.00**

☐ **Ewer,** Mt. Washington, unusual pastel lilac decoration depicts reclining shepherdess with her sheep, back decorated with birds and roses, raised gold wreaths surround both panels, small pastel lilac wreaths elsewhere, 10½" high, 8½" diameter across front **2500.00 3500.00 2650.00**

☐ **Cracker Jar,** Mt. Washington, melon ribbed, cream ground, colorful nasturtuim enameled decoration, silver plated bail and lid, lid is signed J.P.C.E.P.N.S., 8" high to top of fully extended bail, 7" diameter **500.00 600.00   530.00**

Crown Milano Biscuit Jar, *enamel decoration, silver plated lid,* **$900.00-$1000.00**

	Current Price Range		P/Y Average

☐ **Decanter,** with hollow stopper, shiny finish, decorated with exquisite enamel roses and profuse gold scrolls on neck and stopper, 10″ high and 6″ wide at bulbous base, rare early Albertine/Crown Milano signature **1000.00 1400.00 1150.00**

☐ **Jam Jar,** white body, slightest hint of pink at shoulders and base, decorated with very delicate blue and white forget-me-nots, silver plated lid and bail is signed Sant & Co., signed jar, body is 4″ high, overall height to top of extended bail is 7″ **350.00 450.00 375.00**

☐ **Pickle Castor,** Mt. Washington-Pairpoint, pansy decoration, silver plated lid signed M.W., holder has Pairpoint mark, both resilvered, bowl is 4″ high, 4½″ diameter, holder is 10″ tall **1000.00 1200.00 1025.00**

☐ **Plate,** rose and fired gold scrolling, enameled dots on three reserves, 11″ diameter **120.00 180.00 150.00**

☐ **Rose Bowl,** Mt. Washington, all over decoration of roses, buds, leaves, gold trim, purple numbered pontil **360.00 450.00 365.00**

☐ **Salt Shaker,** cockle shell, Mt. Washington, white satin body, dainty enamel blossoms, silver plated top shaped like seashell **385.00 485.00 390.00**

☐ **Tray,** Mt. Washington, shiny finish, rolled and serrated edges, enamel thistle and foliage decoration, outlined with raised gold, 9½″ long, 7″ wide, signed **825.00 1000.00 40.00**

☐ **Urn,** with rare crown shaped lid, raised gold blossom and foliage decoration, 16½″ high, 8″ wide, 5½″ deep, signed **2800.00 3300.00 2900.00**

☐ **Vase,** early Guba, tall and slender, shiny finish, decorated with four flying ducks over raised gold wheat field, 17″ high, 4½″ diameter, signed with Crown Milano/Albertine mark which features a crown within a crown **3500.00 4200.00 3650.00**

☐ **Vase,** Guba, decorated with five ducks on front, three in back, two applied handles, excellent professional repair to base **2000.00 2250.00 2100.00**

☐ **Vase,** Mt. Washington, bulbous, cream colored body with slender neck, gold blossoms and jewels covered with gold enamel, 12½″ high, signed **825.00 1000.00 840.00**

☐ **Vase,** Mt. Washington, cone shaped, enamel floral bouquet decoration, 8¾″ high, signed **850.00 975.00 865.00**

☐ **Vase,** square shaped, rounded corners, two delicate applied handles, decorated with pastel enamels in tiny free form geometric patterns, 8″ high, unsigned **720.00 820.00 730.00**

☐ **Vase,** Mt. Washington, square with rounded corners, two applied scroll handles, cream ground, decoration of gold and colorful enamel oak leaves and gold acorns, original paper label, 8¼″ high **950.00 1100.00 975.00**

	Current Price Range		P/Y Average

D'ARGENTHAL

☐ **Bowl,** double-conical shape, wide with waisted neck and foot, slightly flaring rim, yellow background, overlaid in red, carved with roses, leaves, and branches, signed, 12" diameter, c. 1900 .. — 1000.00 — 1400.00 — 1100.00

☐ **Bowl,** swollen spherical, indulated rim scalloped, yellow background, overlaid in maroon, cut with roses, signed, 6" diameter, c. 1900 .... — 600.00 — 700.00 — 650.00

☐ **Box,** covered, shallow circular shape, dark yellow background, overlaid in brown and umber, cut with wildflowers and leaves, signed, 3¾" diameter, c. 1915 .... — 400.00 — 600.00 — 425.00

☐ **Vase,** baluster shape, light yellow background splashed with red, overlaid in red, cut with landscape of lake, arched bridge, and trees, signed, 13¾" high, c. 1910 .... — 2000.00 — 3000.00 — 2100.00

☐ **Vase,** baluster shape, turquoise background, overlaid in dark blue, cut with flowers and leaves, signed 7" high, c. 1900 .... — 400.00 — 500.00 — 425.00

☐ **Vase,** cameo, pastoral scene with house, trees and mountain-top chateau in background, signed, 6¾" high, 4⅛" diameter .... — 480.00 — 575.00 — 530.00

☐ **Vase,** cameo, light brown background with dark brown floral pattern, signed, 14" high, 6" diameter .... — 655.00 — 725.00 — 665.00

☐ **Vase,** cylinder shape tapering towards lip, short circular foot, orange-yellow background, overlaid in red, cut with leafy branches, trumpet blossoms, signed, 11¾" high, c. 1900 .... — 700.00 — 1000.00 — 750.00

DESIRE CHRISTIAN

☐ **Bowl,** bulbous shape, wide mouth, short circular foot, pale green shading to lime green and turquoise, overlaid in lime green, carved lily pads, blossoms, and flying dragonfly, signed, 6" diameter, c. 1895 .... — 1200.00 — 1400.00 — 1250.00

☐ **Vase,** bud, compressed spherical body with long cylinder neck tapering towards flared rim, dark burnt brown with lavender tinge shading to olive green and beige, overlaid in lavender, carved with milkweeds, leaves, and grass, signed, 12⅝" high, c. 1895 .... — 3000.00 — 4000.00 — 3100.00

☐ **Vase,** elongated cylinder expanding to swollen neck, knopped base, spreading foot, gray splashed with red background, carved with two orchids on two long stems and leaves and grass around base, signed, 14⅜" high, c. 1895 ..... — 2000.00 — 3000.00 — 2100.00

DE VEZ

☐ **Vase,** acid finish background, dark green shaded to rose landscape scene in three acid cuttings, signed, 9⅜" high, 2⅝" diameter .... — 620.00 — 680.00 — 630.00

	Current Price Range		P/Y Average

☐ **Vase,** acid finish background of blue with mountain landscape scenes on three, detailed acid cuttings, signed, 11½" high, 3¾" diameter **720.00 770.00 730.00**

☐ **Vase,** acid finish background of shell pink with navy blue shaded to yellow shaded to pink in three acid cuttings, mountain scene, signed, 6½" high, 2⅞" diameter **630.00 690.00 640.00**

☐ **Vase,** bulbous body sloping towards long cylinder neck, light pink background, overlaid in yellow and blue, cut with scene with squirrels in trees in the foreground and mountains in the distance, signed, 13" high, c. 1900 .... **1100.00 1400.00 1150.00**

☐ **Vase,** cylinder shape expanding toward a flaring rim, flaring circular foot, yellow background splashed with orange and green, cut with river scene, signed, 5¼" high, c. 1910 .... **700.00 800.00 725.00**

☐ **Vase,** cylinder shape tapering toward the neck, milky, overlaid in lavender shading to pink, cut with cartouches enclosing river landscape, signed, 9¾" high, c. 1900 .... **800.00 1000.00 810.00**

☐ **Vase,** elongated pear shape, short cylinder neck, yellow background streaked with orange, overlaid in dark blue, cut with river scene, signed, 5½" high, c. 1910 .... **700.00 800.00 725.00**

☐ **Vase,** pear shape body, long cylinder neck, flared rim, yellow background, overlaid in orange and blue, cut with a river scene, signed, 6" high, c. 1910 .... **700.00 800.00 725.00**

☐ **Vase,** trumpet, acid finish background, navy blue shaded to rose in three acid cuttings, bird on branch, foliage frames scene, gold plated brass base with leaves, 18¾" high, 6⅜" diameter .. **2000.00 2200.00 2100.00**

DURAND

☐ **Plate,** flashed ruby with white pulled feathers, hatched pontil, underside features Bridgeton Rose engraving by Charles Link, 8" diameter **275.00 375.00 285.00**

☐ **Vase,** baluster shape, waisted and flaring neck, flattened circular foot, amber iridescence with opalescent trails, 8⅛" high, c. 1900–1930 .... **300.00 400.00 350.00**

☐ **Vase,** bulbous shape, iridescent blue, wide flared neck, 8½" high **175.00 230.00 210.00**

☐ **Vase,** compressed bulbous, flattened shoulders, waisted and lobed neck, flaring rim, blue iridescence, signed, 8½" diameter, c. 1905–1930 ... **350.00 450.00 375.00**

☐ **Vase,** compressed spherical base, cylinder neck expanding into trumpet-shape, green background, undulating bands in amber iridescence, signed, 12" high, c. 1905–1930 .... **1200.00 1600.00 1250.00**

☐ **Vase,** compressed spherical body, lobed neck, blue, 8½" high **350.00 450.00 375.00**

	Current Price Range		P/Y Average

☐ **Vase,** compressed spherical, trumpet-like neck, short circular foot, blue iridescence, signed, 9¼" high, c. 1905–1930 .... 300.00 400.00 350.00

☐ **Vase,** conical, iridescent gold leaf and vine design, flared rim, 7" high 250.00 400.00 310.00

☐ **Vase,** cylindrical, flaring rim, circular base, amber decorated with opalescent interlacing designs, 8⅛" high 700.00 800.00 725.00

☐ **Vase,** cylindrical, iridescent platinum "King Tut" pattern, wide, narrow mouth, 8" high 250.00 400.00 310.00

☐ **Vase,** cylindrical, scalloped rim, short circular base, opalescent glass decorated with green hearts and vines, 11" high 700.00 800.00 725.00

☐ **Vase,** cylindrical, expanding towards the shoulders, waisted neck, flaring rim, flattened circular foot, blue iridescent, amber iridescent foot, signed, 14¼" high 300.00 400.00 375.00

☐ **Vase,** cylindrical, swollen shoulders, everted lip, silvery-blue, signed, 6⅛" high, c. 1905–1920 .. 300.00 500.00 375.00

☐ **Vase,** elongated ovoid, waisted neck, flattened flaring rim, short circular foot, blue iridescent background, opalescent clinging heart vine, 10½" high, c. 1905–1930 .... 300.00 500.00 375.00

☐ **Vase,** ovoid shape, flaring neck, iridescent blue, signed, 10¼" high, c. 1905–1925 .... 400.00 500.00 425.00

☐ **Vase,** urn shape, blue iridescent background, with white heart and trailing vine overlay, 7⅛" high, 1905–1925 .... 400.00 600.00 425.00

LE VERRE FRANÇAIS

☐ **Vase,** cameo, ovoid-shaped, waisted neck, flaring rim, mottled pink background, cut in daisies around the shoulder, overlaid in lavender deepening to amethyst around the base, 4½" high, c. 1925 .... 200.00 300.00 250.00

☐ **Vase,** cameo, trumpet-shaped, mottled orange and yellow background, cut with bouquets of flowers and leaves in bright orange darkening to a deep purple, signed, 18⅛" high, c. 1925 .... 200.00 300.00 250.00

☐ **Vase,** compressed spherical tapering to trumpet-shaped neck, green background, overlaid in mottled orange, brown, and green, carved with flowers with honeycomb pattern around the base, 16¾" high, c. 1920 .... 400.00 600.00 425.00

☐ **Vase,** cylinder body tapering towards neck, waisted neck and foot slightly flaring rim, mottled pink background, overlaid in orange shading to green and turquoise, cut with blossoms and leaves, honeycomb design on neck, 26" high, c. 1930 .... 600.00 800.00 650.00

Le Verre Français Vase,
*French Cameo glass, orange
and blue, signed, 5" high,*
$600.00–$700.00

	Current Price Range		P/Y Average
☐ **Vase,** spherical-shaped with thin cylinder neck, flaring rim, yellow background, cut in flowers and tendrils in blue and orange, signed, 12" high, c. 1925	250.00	400.00	275.00

LOETZ

☐ **Biscuit Jar,** iridescent purple shaded to black, swing handle, silverplate lid, 9" high	65.00	125.00	90.00
☐ **Bowl,** bulbous body with waisted base and neck, flaring rim, magenta background, silvery-blue designs of ripples, 10" diameter, c. 1900	925.00	1125.00	950.00
☐ **Bowl,** bulbous shape, green iridescent, swirl decoration, pinched form, 5½" high	82.50	135.00	100.00
☐ **Bowl,** circular, green iridescent, fluted, 7½" diameter	70.00	100.00	85.00
☐ **Bowl,** deeply curved, pinched rim which curves in, clear, silvery-blue oil spots, 7" high, c. 1900	100.00	150.00	115.00
☐ **Bowl,** ovoid shape, crimped lip and sides, slightly flaring rim, short circular foot, oil-spotted yellow background with blue striations, 10¼" long, c. 1900	900.00	1000.00	920.00
☐ **Bowl,** ovoid-shaped, silvery amber iridescent background, amber iridescent wave pattern, ruffled neck, unsigned, c. 1900	310.00	415.00	310.00

	Current Price Range		P/Y Average

☐ **Lamp,** iridescent cylinder body with spherical shade, sits in bronze stand which encircles the cylinder body and ends in a triangular base, body in salmon with amber and silvery-blue oil spots, 19½″ high, c. 1900 .... **600.00   1000.00   700.00**

☐ **Lamp,** melon-shaped base, silvery-blue oil spots, helmet-shaped shade in avocado green, both with four vertical hobnail band, 11″ high, c. 1900 .... **1000.00   1500.00   1100.00**

☐ **Vase,** baluster body, expanding to swollen ovoid at upper portion, waisted neck, flaring lip, flaring circular foot, amber iridescent background, loops and trails in orange, silvery-blue, and amber iridescent, 6¼″ high, c. 1900 .... **600.00   800.00   650.00**

☐ **Vase,** baluster shape, flaring lip, spreading circular base, pale iridescent orange, orange straited lappets around lip, rose spotting around the foot, 8¼″ high, c. 1900 .... **200.00   300.00   220.00**

☐ **Vase,** baluster shape, triangular mouth, orange oil spots, loops and swirls in silvery-blue and iridescent amber, 8¼″ high, c. 1900 .... **200.00   300.00   215.00**

☐ **Vase,** bulbous base tapering to long cylinder neck, everted rim, light orange background, lavender feathering, silvery-blue iridescent oil spots, overlaid in silver, 10½″ high, c. 1900 .... **600.00   1000.00   650.00**

☐ **Vase,** blue and green, iridescent pinched shoulder and ruffled collar, Loetz Austria etched on bottom, 7″ high **335.00   430.00   375.00**

☐ **Vase,** purple, wide lip on top, unsigned, 6½″ **190.00   210.00   190.00**

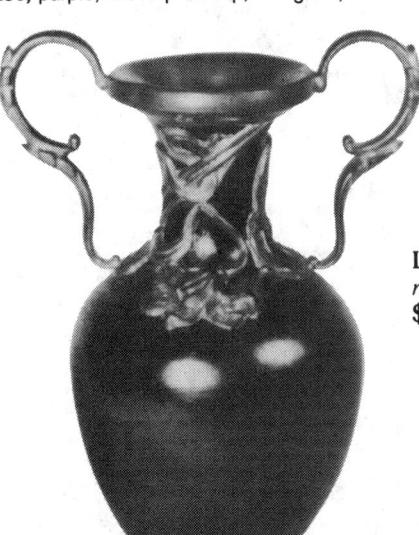

Loetz Vase, *Art Nouveau design, metallic overlay, 6″ high,* **$345.00-$370.00**

MARY GREGORY

	Current Price Range		P/Y Average
☐ **Box,** cobalt blue, round, hinged lid, ormolu feet, white enameled decoration depicts young girl holding bird, white floral sprays, 5″ high, 5⅜″ diameter	350.00	450.00	365.00
☐ **Box,** emerald green, puffy shape, lift off lid, white enameled decoration depicts young girl, 3″ high, 3⅝″ diameter	90.00	130.00	95.00
☐ **Box,** lime green, hinged lid, white enameled decoration depicts young boy, hinged, 1¾″ high, 2⅜″ diameter	120.00	150.00	125.00
☐ **Box,** patch, cobalt, round, hinged lid, white enameled decoration depicts little boy, white enamel dots around sides, 1⅛″ high, 2″ diameter	150.00	180.00	155.00
☐ **Box,** patch, round, lime green, white enameled decoration depicts young girl, hinged, 1⅜″ high, 2⅛″ diameter	120.00	150.00	125.00
☐ **Box,** sapphire blue, round, hinged lid, white enameled decoration depicts young girl, white dot trim around sides, 2⅝″ high, 3¼″ diameter	130.00	175.00	135.00
☐ **Plate,** cobalt, white enameled decoration depicts girl with butterfly net, original ormolu compote stand, three round rings hang from holder, 6¼″ diameter	140.00	170.00	145.00
☐ **Spa Glass,** amber, flattened oval shape, white enameled decoration depicts little girl carrying basket, 4⅛″ high, 2⅜″ diameter	90.00	120.00	95.00
☐ **Tumbler,** cranberry, white enameled decoration depicts young girl, 4¼″ high, 2½″ diameter	50.00	85.00	60.00
☐ **Vase,** covered, cobalt blue, white enameled decoration depicts young girl carrying flower basket, enameled dot bands around top and lid, 14″ high, 5½″ diameter	275.00	375.00	285.00
☐ **Vase,** cranberry, white enameled decoration depicts young boy wearing hat, 7¾″ high	100.00	150.00	110.00
☐ **Vase,** sapphire blue, cut scalloped top, white enameled decoration depicts young boy holding goblet, fancy metal base mount of plated brass with woman's head handles on each side, 14¼″ high, 3¾″ diameter	200.00	275.00	220.00
☐ **Wine Bottle,** cranberry, white enameled decoration depicts girl holding bouquet, original clear bubble stopper, 9″ high, 3⅛″ diameter	140.00	170.00	145.00

MOSER

☐ **Box,** decorated amethyst, three applied salamanders in amber for feet that are trimmed in gold, amber salamander trimmed in gold on lid, enameled flowers of pink and green foliage, hinged, 4⅜″ high	600.00	650.00	610.00
☐ **Decanter,** with glass stopper, clear evenly to green, signed, 8″ high	175.00	200.00	185.00

Moser Cup and Saucer, *lavender with gold gild decor,*
$150.00–$170.00

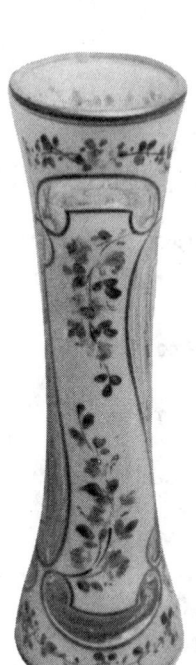

Moser Karsbad Bud Vase, *cut
scroll design frames enamel floral
decor, 6" high,*
$125.00–$150.00

	Current Price Range		P/Y Average
☐ **Juice Glass,** cranberry, gold enamel branches, yellow, pink, turquoise and blue enamel leaves, leaves and veins outlined in raised gold, acorns, gold band at rim and base, 4" high	150.00	225.00	175.00
☐ **Libation Jug,** enameled decorations, strap, twig handle, signed, 9½" high	35.00	80.00	45.00
☐ **Tumbler,** crystal top shades to blue at base, engraved with ruffed grouse and landscape scene, acid cut decorative band atrim with gold enamel, cutting at base, 5" high, 3" diameter, signed ..	350.00	400.00	360.00
☐ **Vase,** decorated opaque pink shaded to clear, four amber reeded applied scroll feet covered in gold, gold rigaree on sides of vase, enameled eagle in relief on front, multicolored oak leaves, enameled insect decoration, applied glass acorns, 7⅞" high, 7" diameter	1500.00	2000.00	1600.00

	Current Price Range		P/Y Average

☐ **Vase Ewer,** gold over crystal, enameled, multi-colored flowers and green leaves, pedestal base, 5¾" high, 2¾" diameter 150.00   200.00   160.00

☐ **Vase,** opalescent deep pink at top shading to almost clear at base, applied crimped glass handles burnished with gold on each end of the flattened oval shape body, parrot, acorns, leaves and branches in relief and gold and multicolor enamel decoration, elaborate decoration around neck, 7½" high, 7¾" at widest point, 2½" deep, Moser signature 850.00   950.00   875.00

☐ **Vase,** multicolored enameled grape leaves and bee with applied yellow and red grape bunches, four applied feet of amber rosette, 5½" high, 2¼" diameter 350.00   400.00   360.00

MOTHER-OF-PEARL

☐ **Bowl,** blue diamond quilted, oblong, four applied feet, 8" long, 7" wide, 3" high 275.00   375.00   275.00

☐ **Creamer,** satin, blue raindrop, bulbous, round top, white lining, blue frosted reeded applied handle, 4½" high, 3⅛" diameter 200.00   250.00   215.00

☐ **Fairy Lamp,** satin glass, swirl shaded pink, white interior, clear insert cup for bulb, ruffled lampshade and base, 5" high, 5½" diameter 420.00   480.00   435.00

☐ **Fruit Bowl,** thin pink interior layer, air trap of interlocking diamond mother of pearl, thick exterior layer of white glass, thorn handle at one end, 10½" long, 5¾" high 530.00   630.00   540.00

☐ **Peg Lamp,** swirl satin glass ruffled shade and font, clear chimney, classical lady candlestick of heavy brass, 19½" high, 3½" diameter 620.00   700.00   640.00

☐ **Perfume Bottle,** satin glass, diamond quilted blue, white interior, silver top, 4½" high, 2⅝" diameter 275.00   325.00   270.00

MULLER FRERES

☐ **Bowl,** inverted cone shape, waisted neck and foot, flaring rim, short circular foot, overlaid, carved, and enameled in flurogravure, harvest scene of workers in rust, orange and ochre, signed, 6¼" high, c. 1900 . . . . 2000.00   3000.00   2250.00

☐ **Ewer,** inverted cone shape, cylinder neck, upright spout, applied c-scroll handle, waisted short circular foot, frosted and green background, overlaid, carved, and enameled in flurogravure with blossoms and leaves, signed, 19" high, c. 1900 . . . . 2000.00   3000.00   2200.00

☐ **Vase,** baluster shape, waisted neck, spreading circular foot, frosted blue background, overlaid, carved, and enameled in flurogravure in yellow and off-white, winter scene with two dogs and hanging pheasant, signed, 9" high, c. 1900 . . . 1800.00   2200.00   1900.00

	Current Price Range		P/Y Average

☐ **Vase,** bulbous double gourd shape, background of purple acid with cameo carved decoration, narrow neck, signed, 6¼″ high 350.00 500.00 400.00

☐ **Vase,** bulbous shape, waisted neck, lobed lip, orange background, overlaid in black, cut with country landscape, signed, 4¼″ high, c. 1910 700.00 900.00 725.00

☐ **Vase,** cameo, depicts storks with frosted yellow and gold background of water, 7½″ high, 4″ diameter 1450.00 1650.00 1535.00

☐ **Vase,** cylinder body expanding towards shoulder, cylinder neck, applied serpentine handle, green background, enameled in flurogravure of branches of berries and leaves, in orange, brown, mustard, and gray, signed, 10¼″ high, c. 1910 1000.00 1400.00 1100.00

☐ **Vase,** frosted pink background, with red roses, signed, 7¾″ high, 3¾″ diameter 1145.00 1235.00 1180.00

OPALESCENT

☐ **Bowl,** diamond quilted light green shaded to pink, ruffled, polished pewter frame, 17¾″ high, 11¾″ diameter 210.00 250.00 215.00

☐ **Bowl,** flashed rainbow, fluted edge, decorated with enamel florals, 5″ high 2780.00 330.00 275.00

☐ **Ewer,** striped white shaded to green, vaseline applied leaf and handle, appliqued flowers in pink, 8½″ high, 3″ diameter 130.00 180.00 140.00

☐ **Fairy Lamp,** amber swirl, signed Clarke base, shaped like a pyramid, 3¾″ high, 3⅛″ diameter
.... 100.00 120.00 110.00

☐ **Fairy Lamp,** blue swirl satin finish, light blue glass cup and candle cup, matching square ruffled base, rare, 6½″ high, 5¾″ diameter 530.00 590.00 540.00

☐ **Fairy Lamp,** pink and white frosted swirl decoration, dome shape, signed Clarke candle cup, matching square ruffled vase, 5½″ high, 6″ diameter 520.00 600.00 535.00

☐ **Fairy Lamp,** pressed glass, blue embossed rib design, signed Clarke base, 3¾″ high, 2⅞″ diameter...................................... 100.00 150.00 110.00

☐ **Vase,** Jack-In-Pulpit, fluted with purple edge, 7″ high, 3⅞″ diameter 70.00 100.00 80.00

☐ **Vase,** white opalescent Monot Stumpf, pink shaded to off-white, pantin fan shape, belltone, interior is of lustered glass, 7″ high, 6⅛″ diameter 220.00 270.00 230.00

☐ **Vase,** white opalescent Monot Stumpf, pink shaded to striped white, pantin ruffled fan shape, belltone, 7¾″ high, 7½″ diameter 280.00 330.00 290.00

☐ **Water Tumbler,** cranberry, ten row hobnail, 3¾″ high, 2¾″ diameter 125.00 160.00 140.00

☐ **Water Tumbler,** decorated peach, white flowers have gold leaves and centers, 4″ high, 2¾″ diameter...................................... 50.00 100.00 80.00

	Current Price Range		P/Y Average

☐ **Water Tumbler,** lavender, light row hobnail, 3¾″ high, 2¾″ diameter .... | 125.00 | 160.00 | 140.00

ORREFORS

☐ **Beaker,** cylinder body, flaring neck, four ball feet set on flattened dome base, clear, etched jungle scene with men, women, children, palm trees, exotic birds, squirrels, and monkeys, signed, 10½″ high, c. 1930 .... | 1000.00 | 1400.00 | 1100.00

☐ **Bottle,** cylinder body, short cylinder neck, elongated dome stopper, light green, clear, decorated internally with sea grass and starfish in maroon, signed, 6¼″ high, c. 1938 .... | 1200.00 | 1400.00 | 1275.00

☐ **Bottle,** cylinder, thick-walled, clear, cartouche with dove and strapework, signed 6¼″ diameter, c. 1940 .... | 2500.00 | 3000.00 | 2600.00

☐ **Bottle,** circular, thick-walled, stepped interior, green garlands and air bubbles embedded in walls, signed, 6½″ diameter, c. 1940 .... | 600.00 | 700.00 | 620.00

☐ **Bottle,** cylinder with expanding neck, clear, cut with hunting scenes, signed, 8¾″ long, c. 1927 .... | 700.00 | 800.00 | 780.00

☐ **Bottle,** flaring, blue-tinted background, engraved scene of two maidens catching a dolphin in a net on one side, engraved dolphin on the other, stylized sunset and clouds above, scalloped border engraved around the rim, withstand, 8½″ long, c. 1925 .... | 500.00 | 700.00 | 550.00

☐ **Bottle,** octagon shape, light gray, cut with nude females and foliage, signed, 11½″ long, c. 1928 .... | 550.00 | 650.00 | 575.00

OVERLAY

☐ **Bowl,** shaded pink, fan shape with amber applied edging, hobnail effect around top, ormolu holder with tassels, 7¼″ high, 9¾″ diameter .... | 260.00 | 300.00 | 265.00

☐ **Fairy Lamp,** candy striped in pink, matching candle cup, embossed, pink rib dome shade, clear applied feet, ruffled base, white interior, three parts, 5¼″ high, 4⅜″ diameter .... | 375.00 | 420.00 | 380.00

☐ **Fairy Lamp,** dark green, shade has white interior, signed Clarke base, 4⅜″ high, 3⅞″ diameter | 130.00 | 180.00 | 140.00

☐ **Fairy Lamp Shade,** dark green with white interior, signed Clarke base, 4½″ high, 4″ diameter .... | 120.00 | 170.00 | 125.00

☐ **Finger Lamp and Chimney,** blue, shaded, clear reeded applied handle, pink and white enameled flowers and gold color foilage, 5½″ high, 4¼″ diameter .... | 125.00 | 165.00 | 130.00

☐ **Finger Lamp and Chimney,** pink shaded, clear handle, red roses trimmed in green and dots of white, 6″ high, 5″ diameter .... | 175.00 | 225.00 | 200.00

	Current Price Range		P/Y Average

☐ **Finger Lamp and Chimney,** satin, lemon yellow, embossed shell and leaf, frosted reeded applied handle, 5" high, 3⅞" diameter 150.00 180.00 160.00

☐ **Finger Lamp,** blue, shaded, clear reeded, applied handle, embossed designs, 6" high, 4¼" diameter 135.00 175.00 140.00

☐ **Goblet,** white on crystal, dainty multicolor floral decoration, white cut to clear and outlined in gold in places, continental 140.00 160.00 145.00

☐ **Hand Lamp and Chimney,** shaded chartreuse green, clear reeded applied handle, scroll decoration in beige, base has panelled pattern, 5" high, 3⅝" diameter 130.00 180.00 140.00

☐ **Rose Bowl,** diamond quilted rose satin cut velvet, eight crimp top, white interior, 3½" high, 3¼" diameter 220.00 270.00 230.00

☐ **Rose Bowl,** shaded blue with embossed swirl rib design, eight crimp top, white interior, 5" high, 6" diameter 180.00 210.00 185.00

☐ **Table Lamp,** mushroom shape shade has pink embossed flowers and a ruffled top and clear chimney, white interior, silverplated base, 17¼" high, 6" diameter 330.00 380.00 340.00

☐ **Vase,** Jack-In-Pulpit, amber edged ruffled top, pink and white applied flowers with amber leaves on cream, white interior, 6⅞" high, 6⅛" diameter 150.00 200.00 160.00

☐ **Vase,** Jack-In-Pulpit, cranberry edged, white background, 7½" high, 6" diameter 130.00 180.00 140.00

☐ **Vase,** Jack-In-Pulpit, decorated blue with multicolored, enameled flowers, branches and butterfly, decorated blue interior, 5⅝" high, 4⅝" diameter 130.00 170.00 135.00

☐ **Vase,** Jack-In-Pulpit, green, white background, clear applied feet, 7" high, 5" diameter 120.00 150.00 130.00

☐ **Vase,** Jack-In-Pulpit, purple, ruffled top, white background, 7½" high, 6" diameter 130.00 180.00 140.00

☐ **Vase,** Jack-In-Pulpit, purple shaded to lavender, ruffled, 7¼" high, 6" diameter 120.00 170.00 125.00

☐ **Vase,** Jack-In-Pulpit, shaded green, clear applied feet, scalloped edges, 6⅝" high, 5½" diameter 120.00 170.00 125.00

☐ **Vase,** Jack-In-Pulpit, shaded maroon, white background, ruffled edging, 7" high, 6½" diameter 140.00 175.00 150.00

☐ **Vase,** pink, large applied crystal flower and branch, crystal around base, white interior, 8¾" high, 4⅜" diameter 130.00 180.00 140.00

☐ **Vase,** silver floral leaves and swag etched over green, narrow, flaring neck, pear shape, 5" high 40.00 80.00 50.00

☐ **Vases,** white with enameled blue flowers, clear applied edge around ruffled top, ormolu handled holder, pink interior, 12¾" high, 7" diameter .. 260.00 310.00 265.00

	Current Price Range		P/Y Average

☐ **Water Tumbler,** overlay of decorated shaded pink, with satin blue and white flower with green leaves, gold trim, white interior, 4⅛" high, 3" diameter **150.00 200.00 160.00**

OVERSHOT

☐ **Fairy Lamp,** amber embossed swirl, signed Clarke base, 3½" high, 2⅞" diameter **120.00 170.00 125.00**

☐ **Fairy Lamp,** cranberry, embossed hob design, signed Clarke base, 4" high, 3" diameter **140.00 200.00 160.00**

☐ **Fairy Lamp,** cranberry, embossed ribs, signed Clarke base, 3¾" high, 2⅞" diameter **135.00 195.00 155.00**

☐ **Fairy Lamp,** opaque yellow, with embossed swirl pattern, signed Clarke base, 3½" high, 2⅞" diameter **150.00 200.00 170.00**

☐ **Pitcher,** ruffled, pink and white spatter glass, bulbous three way top, clear reeded applied handle, 7⅞" high, 5¼" diameter **150.00 200.00 160.00**

PEACHBLOW

☐ **Bowl,** New England, flared scalloped rim, 2¾" high, 5½" at widest point **700.00 800.00 725.00**

☐ **Bowl,** porridge, New England, shiny finish, deep rich color dominates, 2¾" high, 4½" diameter **400.00 475.00 425.00**

☐ **Cruet,** Wheeling, deepest mahogany color at top gradually shading to cream at base, clear amber faceted handle, reeded handle, 6¾" high **1100.00 1400.00 1200.00**

☐ **Pitcher,** Wheeling, shiny finish, exquisite color, applied amber handle, 9½" high **1000.00 1500.00 1100.00**

☐ **Shade,** gas light, New England, shiny finish, very good color, 4½" high, 6¼" diameter at top, 2¼" fitting, rare **350.00 450.00 375.00**

☐ **Sugar and Creamer Set,** Mt. Washington, pink to gray shading, egg-shell thin glass, squatty creamer is 1¾" high and 5½" across including extension of two applied handles, corset shaped pitcher is 3¾" high and 2" wide at base **4000.00 5000.00 4300.00**

☐ **Toothpick Holder,** ruffled rim, cylindrical shape, 2¼" high **110.00 130.00 120.00**

☐ **Tumbler,** New England, shiny finish, wild rose upper half, 3¾" high **350.00 425.00 375.00**

☐ **Vase,** bulbous, gold and silver butterfly on gold and silver background, with blue trim, 4¼" high, 4⅜" diameter **260.00 295.00 270.00**

☐ **Vase,** Hummingbird on gold and silver background, narrow neck, 10½" high, 6" diameter **435.00 510.00 460.00**

☐ **Vase,** lily, New England, shiny finish, deep wild rose color covers 3" of this 9¾" high piece . . . **750.00 850.00 775.00**

☐ **Vase,** Mt. Washington, acid finish, cast in Webb Burmese shape, pink shaded to blue, flower top, very rare, 3¼" high, 3" diameter **800.00 1200.00 850.00**

	Current Price Range		P/Y Average

☐ **Vase,** Mt. Washington, trumpet (lily), acid finish, pink shaded to blue, rare, 6¼" high, 2½" diameter **900.00** **1400.00** **1000.00**

☐ **Vase,** New England, Wild Rose, satin finish, double gourd, deepest raspberry shading to white, 7" high, 1880s **500.00** **700.00** **550.00**

☐ **Vase,** satin finish, ribbed pear design, narrow neck, 9" high **75.00** **110.00** **75.00**

☐ **Vase,** Webb, glossy, dark red and pink with raised gold prunus, cream lining, 3¼" high, 2⅜" diameter **250.00** **450.00** **275.00**

☐ **Vase,** Webb, glossy, rose red and pink with raised gold prunus and bird decoration, cream lining, 9" high, 4" diameter **400.00** **700.00** **450.00**

☐ **Vase,** Webb, satin, rose and pink with floral and butterfly decoration in heavy gold, cream lining, 8" high, 3" diameter **375.00** **600.00** **425.00**

☐ **Vase,** Webb, two applied handles, raised gold, green and silver decoration features squirrels, grapes and grape vines, 10" high **455.00** **575.00** **475.00**

☐ **Vases,** rose shaded to cream, Japanese style blossoming branches, slender necks, pair, 7" high **210.00** **310.00** **250.00**

☐ **Water Pitcher,** Wheeling, finest color, square top, applied amber handle, 10" high **1000.00** **1500.00** **1200.00**

POMONA

☐ **Juice Glass,** first grind, delicate hobnail interior, tapered, 3¾" high, base 1½" in diameter, 2¼" in diameter at top **70.00** **87.50** **65.00**

☐ **Lemonade Pitcher,** first grind, cylindrical shape, two rows of blue tinted cornflowers, 12" high, 4" diameter at base, 3" diameter at top **950.00** **1075.00** **975.00**

☐ **Pitcher,** New England, first grind, miniature, square top **93.00** **135.00** **100.00**

☐ **Tumbler,** New England, second grind, cornflower staining **67.50** **105.00** **70.00**

☐ **Water Carafe,** New England, second grind, cornflower staining **175.00** **225.00** **185.00**

☐ **Water Set,** pitcher and six tumblers, first grind, pitcher is 6¾" high **700.00** **900.00** **725.00**

☐ **Water Tumbler,** New England, blue cornflower pattern, second grind, 3¾" high, 2½" diameter **160.00** **200.00** **165.00**

QUEZAL

☐ **Bowl,** circular, shallow, flaring lip, mounted on circular base, iridescent, signed, 11¾" diameter, c. 1901–1925 . . . . **300.00** **400.00** **320.00**

☐ **Dish,** circular shape, two ribbed handles, amber iridescence, 5½" diameter, c. 1901–1925 . . . . . **125.00** **175.00** **135.00**

☐ **Light Shade,** flower form, with scalloping, flared rim, iridescent yellow, signed, 5¼" high, c. 1900 . . . . **150.00** **200.00** **150.00**

	Current Price Range		P/Y Average

☐ **Vase,** elongated baluster, domed foot, light yellow background, green feather designs, highlighted with amber iridescence, 19½" high, c. 1901–1925 . . . . 1000.00 1400.00 1100.00

☐ **Vase,** Jack-In-The-Pulpit, flower face slightly ruffled, thin cylinder stem, flattened circular foot, opalescent, amber iridescent, striated green feathering, amber iridescence on foot, signed, 10¼" high, c. 1901–1925 . . . . 1500.00 2000.00 1600.00

☐ **Vase,** ovoid body with vertical lobing, wide cylinder neck, slightly flaring lip, opalescent background, green and amber iridescent draping bands, applied stringing in free form design, 6¼" high, c. 1901–1925 . . . . 1400.00 1600.00 1480.00

☐ **Vase,** pear shape, amber iridescent, overlaid in silver, chased with flowers and leaves, strapwork, signed, 8¾" high, c. 1905–1920 . . . . 600.00 1000.00 700.00

SATIN

☐ **Bowl Vase,** decorated yellow webb with prunus blossoms and butterfly in heavy gold, trimmed in gold, 3½" high, 4¼" diameter 350.00 400.00 375.00

☐ **Bride's Bowl,** overlay of decorated pink, white on bottom, maroon flowers, green, yellow and lavender leaves, frosted, ruffled edging, gold trim, 4½" high, 10½" x 9¼" 270.00 350.00 310.00

☐ **Ewer,** overlay of decorated, shaded pink, applied frosted handle, small flowers of white and branches of gold, three petal top, white interior, 7¾" high, 3¼" diameter 110.00 160.00 130.00

☐ **Ewer,** overlay of decorated, shaded pink, applied frosted handle, enameled flowers of white and pink, foliage of gold, white interior, 8½" high, 4¼" diameter 140.00 190.00 165.00

☐ **Ewer,** overlay of decorated, shaded pink, frosted, applied handle, with enameled flowers of white and pink with yellow centers, three petal top, white interior, 9¼" high, 3¾" diameter . . . 120.00 170.00 145.00

☐ **Fairy Lamp,** Webb-like decoration, brown and tan leaves with cones on cream background, signed Clarke base, rare, 5⅝" high, 3⅞" diameter 240.00 300.00 245.00

☐ **Lacemaker's Lamp,** shade has embossed leaves, scrolls and overlapping petals with chimney, brass handled base, 18" high, 10" diameter 520.00 570.00 530.00

☐ **Peg Lamps,** shaded yellow, embossed completely, set in candleholders made of brass, 17" high, 6" diameter, pair 1300.00 1500.00 1350.00

☐ **Perfume Bottle,** decorated Webb, ivory, prunus blossoms and butterfly in heavy gold, silver, hallmarked top, 3¼" high, 2⅜" diameter 260.00 300.00 275.00

	Current Price Range		P/Y Average

☐ **Rose Bowl,** embossed flowers of rose shaded to pink, white interior, eight crimp top, 3½″ high, 4″ diameter **130.00 180.00 155.00**

☐ **Rose Bowl,** overlay of blue diamond quilted cut velvet, four crimp, white interior, 3¼″ high, 3½″ diameter **175.00 220.00 185.00**

☐ **Rose Bowl,** overlay of decorated blue, egg shape, florals in cream with typical coralene foliage, frosted petal applied feet, eight crimp top, white interior, 6¼″ high, 3½″ diameter **150.00 200.00 155.00**

☐ **Rose Bowl,** overlay of decorated blue, flowers in white and pink with Monarch butterfly decoration, petal applied feet, four crimp top, white interior, 5½″ high, 4½″ diameter **150.00 200.00 155.00**

☐ **Rose Bowl,** overlay of decorated light blue, applied, frosted feet of leaf motif, enameled daisies of white and foliage of cream, center of flower has red jewel, light crimp top, white interior, 4½″ high, 4½″ diameter **150.00 200.00 175.00**

☐ **Rose Bowl,** overlay of decorated rose, applied, frosted petal feet, decoration of green foliage and morning glory of tan and cream, four crimp top, 5¼″ high, 4½″ diameter **155.00 200.00 170.00**

☐ **Rose Bowl,** overlay of decorated rose shaded to pink, egg shape, mauve and yellow pansies, frosted petal applied feet, four crimp top, white lining, 5½″ high, 3⅜″ diameter **150.00 200.00 155.00**

☐ **Vase,** circular pinched form, flared rim of petal design, 8″ high **35.00 60.00 45.00**

☐ **Vase,** overlay of diamond quilted, rose cut velvet, white interior, ruffled, 7¼″ high, 3¼″ diameter **200.00 240.00 205.00**

☐ **Vases,** overlay of decorated rose shaded to pink, with enameled flowers of white, foliage of gold, white interior, 6⅞″ high, 4½″ diameter, pair ... **220.00 300.00 250.00**

☐ **Water Tumbler,** decorated shaded pink overlay, enameled flowers of blue and white with green and yellow leaves, white interior, 4¼″ high, 3″ diameter **150.00 200.00 160.00**

SPATTER

☐ **Box,** cased glass, egg shaped, decorated yellow, three applied feet in clear gold, branches and leaves of gold and white, floral decoration is blue bell shaped, 7½″ high, 4½″ diameter **260.00 300.00 270.00**

☐ **Jar,** yellow, small forget-me-nots in blue, applied finial is clear, lid, 6¼″ high, 3½″ diameter **75.00 100.00 80.00**

☐ **Finger Lamp and Chimney,** peach with white and brown spatter, clear applied handle, 6¼″ high, 4¼″ diameter **130.00 180.00 150.00**

☐ **Vase,** Jack-In-Pulpit, ruffled, diamond quilted, green, white and peach, 9¼″ high, 5½″ diameter **80.00 120.00 90.00**

	Current Price Range		P/Y Average

☐ **Water Tumbler,** green and white embossed swirl, 3¾" high, 2¾" diameter 60.00   100.00   70.00

STEUBEN

☐ **Bowl,** circular shape, incurved neck and flaring rim, amber aurene and calcite, 5½" diameter, c. 1902–1932 . . . .   160.00   210.00   175.00

☐ **Bowl,** lobed circular, short circular foot, clear, scrolling flowers in dark blue, dark blue band at rim, 5¼" diameter, c. 1930 . . . .   3500.00   4500.00   3700.00

☐ **Compote,** blue aurene and calcite, inside iridescent blue, 6" high, c. 1902–1932 . . . .   200.00   400.00   210.00

☐ **Figure,** fish rising from a breaking wave, scalloped base, 5¾" high, c. 1940 . . . .   3000.00   4000.00   3200.00

☐ **Finger Bowls,** bell shape, on pedestal base of selenium red, fluted body, 5" diameter, c. 1930   40.00   50.00   42.00

☐ **Flask,** flattened circular body, cylindrical neck, handles, sides have irregular air trapped bubbles, blue neck to white shoulders, signed, 10" high, c. 1925 . . . .   600.00   700.00   620.00

☐ **Glasses,** wine, crystal, bell shape with fluting, long pedestal stems of selenium red, 5" high, c. 1930 . . . .   40.00   50.00   43.00

☐ **Goblets,** crystal, inverted bell shape, fluted, long pedestal stem with circular base, stems selenium red, 8⅜" high, c. 1930 . . . .   50.00   65.00   42.00

☐ **Vase,** baluster body, short waisted neck, spreading circular foot, amber body decorated with gold peacock feathering, signed, 8½" high 1400.00   1600.00   1480.00

☐ **Vase,** baluster shape, cylinder neck slightly flaring, knopped at bottom of base, domed and flattened circular foot, off-white background with green feathering, amber iridescent clinging hearts and vines, 10" high, c. 1905–1925 . . . . .   1600.00   1800.00   1680.00

Steuben Dish, *calcite finish, gold over white, 10" diameter,*
$300.00–$350.00

	Current Price Range		P/Y Average

☐ **Vase,** trumpet shape on slightly domed circular foot, amber iridescent, signed, 8⅛" high, c. 1904–1930 .... 400.00 500.00 410.00

STEVENS AND WILLIAMS

☐ **Fairy Lamp,** satin finish, striped green and white, base is signed Clarke, 5¼" high, 4" diameter 200.00 250.00 225.00

☐ **Plate,** Pastil, blue with fleur-de-lis, signed, 7¾" diameter 40.00 80.00 55.00

☐ **Vase,** Arboresque, frosted cranberry with opaque white, frosted, reeded applied handles and pedestal foot, ruffled top, 6⅛" high, 3⅛" diameter...................................... 140.00 180.00 145.00

☐ **Vase,** cream colored ribbed tubular body on random molded amber base, caramel Northwood pull up decoration, applied glass branches and blue flower, 5½" high 650.00 675.00 665.00

☐ **Vase,** green rib design, pinched floral form, 6" diameter.................................... 35.00 67.50 40.00

☐ **Vase,** overlay amber applied edging around ruffle, off-white opaque with amber branches with multicolored flowers and leaves, pink interior, 6⅝" high, 3¼" diameter 150.00 200.00 160.00

☐ **Vase,** overlay, amber handle and branch on white background with amber plum, pink and amber leaf, square top in pink, amber edging, 8" high, 3½" diameter 125.00 175.00 130.00

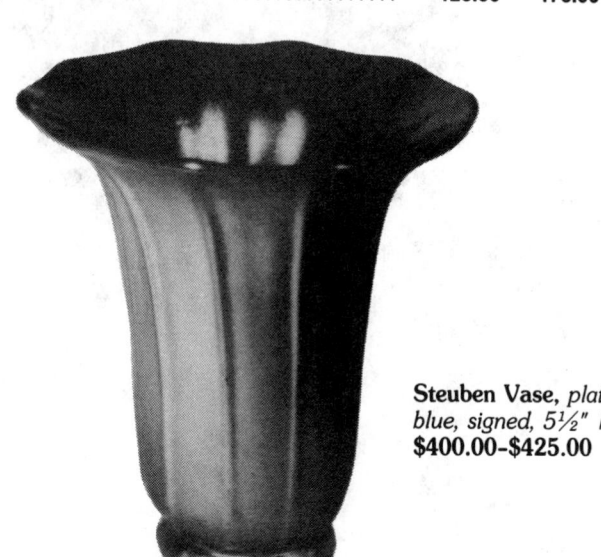

Steuben Vase, *platinum finish, blue, signed, 5½" high,* **$400.00–$425.00**

	Current Price Range		P/Y Average

THOMAS WEBB AND SONS

☐ **Berry Bowl and Underplate,** alexandrite, crimped edge bowl is 5″ in diameter, matching underplate is 6½″ diameter, set is 2¼″ high .. 1000.00 1100.00 1050.00

☐ **Bowl,** fruit, white opal exterior lined with thin pink glass, two tone gold decoration of bird and flowering branch, three heavy textured applied feet, 6″ high, 8″ diameter, signed with spider Webb mark over E 450.00 550.00 475.00

☐ **Decanter,** bell shape, paneled and tapered sides, signed, 11¾″ high 55.00 80.00 70.00

Stevens & Williams Vase, *cranberry, applied feet and filigree, 6¼″ high,* $245.00-$260.00

	Current Price Range		P/Y Average

☐ **Bottle,** perfume, inverted teardrop shape, cylinder neck with silver, domed lid, red background, overlaid in white, cut on one side with wildflowers and leaves, the other side with ferns, 4¼″ high 800.00   1000.00   900.00

☐ **Bottle,** perfume, squared, cylinder neck with silver, flaring rim, flattened knop, dark green background, overlaid in white, cut with blossoms and leaves, signed, 5¼″ high, c. 1901 . . . .   3000.00   4000.00   3300.00

☐ **Bottle,** spherical body, cylinder neck of applied silver, flattened lid, turquoise background, overlaid in white, cut with shells and underwater plants, 3⅞″ high, c. 1900 . . . .   1600.00   2000.00   1800.00

☐ **Bowl,** squared, lobed at lip tapering to spherical shape, short circular foot, red background, overlaid in white, cut with roses, poppies, and bowknots, floral band around lip, 6½″ diameter, c. 1895 . . . .   4000.00   5000.00   4100.00

☐ **Decanter,** bulbous body, long cylinder neck tapering, silver domed cover with hinge, silver neck band chased with foliage and anchored with a chain hooked to lug handle on shoulder, greenish-yellow background, overlaid in pink and white, cut with apple blossoms, 9½″ high, c. 1886 . . . .   6000.00   8000.00   6500.00

☐ **Plaque,** circular shape, dark brown background, overlaid in white, carved with birds perched in blossoming branches in green, pink, blue, and rust, stylized border around rim, signed, 18¼″ diameter, c. 1890 . . . .   3500.00   4500.00   3600.00

☐ **Potpourri Jar,** ivory satin, decorated with panels of enameled pink, blue and yellow flowers, green leaves, all outlined in gold, green bands with gold trim and decoration gold washed ormulu feet, pierced top rim and lid with hinged inside cover, very ornate, 6½″ high, 4¾″ diameter 500.00   700.00   550.00

☐ **Rose Bowl,** blue ground with white morning glory blossoms and foliage, reverse side has butterfly, three applied blue feet, one of which has been ground, 4″ high, 6″ diameter 730.00   975.00   740.00

☐ **Rose Bowl,** miniature, chartreuse green satin overlay ground with white cut to pink carved flowers and foliage, white lining, unsigned, 2½″ high, 2¾″ diameter 900.00   1200.00   950.00

☐ **Rose Bowl,** satin glass, peachblow, signed, 6″ high 120.00   175.00   125.00

☐ **Toothpick Holder,** Alexandrite, rare, 2½″ high   900.00   1000.00   925.00

☐ **Vase,** acid cut back, cream colored background, decorated with pink flowers outlined heavily in gold, gold spider in web decoration 450.00   500.00   470.00

☐ **Vase,** baluster shape, yellow background, overlaid in pink and white, cut with apple blossoms, leaves, and butterfly, 6½″ high, c. 1895 . . . . . .   400.00   500.00   420.00

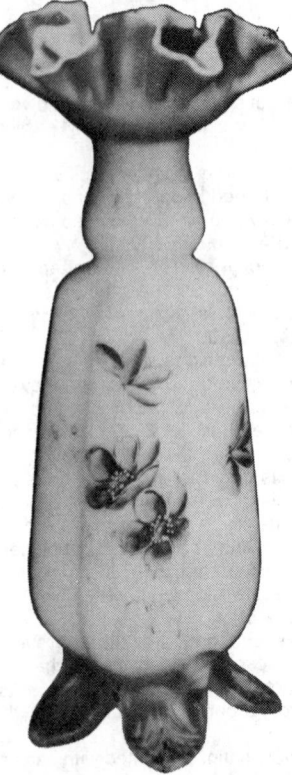

Thomas Webb and Sons Vase,
Peachblow, enamel floral decor,
9½" high, **$300.00-$400.00**

	Current Price Range		P/Y Average
☐ **Vase,** bulbous body, acid red background with white floral decoration, narrow neck, bulbous shape, 5½" high	575.00	700.00	620.00
☐ **Vase,** bulbous body, cylinder neck, peach shading to light, overlaid in white, cut with poppies and leaves, 7½" high, c. 1895	4000.00	6000.00	4150.00
☐ **Vase,** bulbous body, long cylinder neck, greenish-gray background, overlaid in white and pink, cut with morning glories and leaves, stylized coils around neck, 8½" high, c. 1890	4000.00	6000.00	4300.00

ART NOUVEAU

TOPIC: ART NOUVEAU See Daum Nancy; Galle; Lalique; Maxfield Parrish; Tiffany.

DESCRIPTION: Art Nouveau is the term applied to an international style of decorative art which flourished around the world from the 1880s to 1920s. The Art Nouveau style was a rebellion against the imitativeness of the Victorian period and the mass production of the Industrial Revolution. It came out of the Arts and Crafts movement in England and the belief of its founder, William Morris, that all decorative arts should be handmade. The Art Nouveau style is characterized by a return to nature in motifs executed by sensual, flowing lines with a heavy oriental influence.

PERIOD: The period of Art Nouveau decorative and fine arts ranges from the last fifteen years or so of the 19th century to the second decade of the 20th century. The name derives from the 1895 opening of a design shop in Paris, L'Art Nouveau.

TYPES: The Art Nouveau style was interpreted in jewelry, ceramics, glass, textiles, furniture, metalwork and architecture. Two of the most important aspects of Art Nouveau are asymmetry and femininity. There is a wide use of maidens with flowing hair, flowers, scrolls, tendrils, snakes and anything else with sinuous curves. Art Nouveau objects, particularly fine jewelry, are in great demand today.

COMMENTS: The works of Louis Comfort Tiffany are considered to be the finest examples of Art Nouveau artistry in America.

RECOMMENDED READING: For more in-depth information on Art Nouveau, you may refer to *The Official Price Guide to Glassware* and *The Official Price Guide to Jewelry,* published by The House of Collectibles.

	Current Price Range		P/Y Average
☐ **Andirons,** pair, bronze finials, patinated metal bases, finials are molded with the face of a woman, 28″, c. 1900	1575.00	1950.00	1600.00

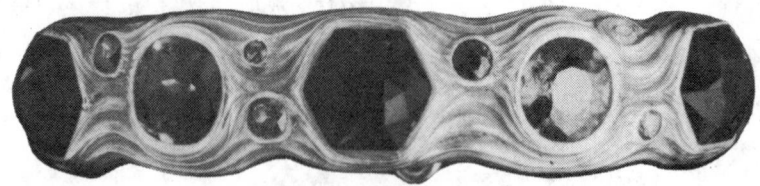

Bracelet,
Art Nouveau motif in a swirl design, faceted amethyst and colored stones, gold, Tiffany & Co., early 1900s,
$5500.00-$6000.00

	Current Price Range		P/Y Average
☐ **Basket,** silver, four flower molded feet, calla lily handles, Austrian, Maker's Mark R. O., 14″, c. 1900	550.00	650.00	580.00
☐ **Bell,** bronze, curtsying woman in gown, inscribed P. Tereszczuk, 2½″, c. 1900	255.00	340.00	290.00
☐ **Bookends,** metal, painted gold, figure of young knight and his lady, square plinth, 7¾″	55.00	65.00	50.00
☐ **Bookends,** reclining nude female figure on rocky base, inscribed S. Morani, 7½″, c. 1914	120.00	180.00	135.00
☐ **Bookends,** bronze busts, brown and green patinas, inscribed Gruber, pair, 5″, late 19th c.	560.00	670.00	595.00
☐ **Bracelet,** bangle, Art Nouveau motif in a swirl design with faceted amethyst and colored stones, gold, maker: Tiffany & Co., American, c. 1915	5500.00	6000.00	5650.00
☐ **Bracelet,** bangle, water lily motif, chased, blank initial medallions, gold, probable maker: Riker Bros., Newark, NJ, American, c. 1900	2000.00	2200.00	2050.00
☐ **Bracelet,** lady head bracelet, two Georgian chains with eight miniatures of ladies heads, heads in Art Nouveau style, c. 1890–1920	2300.00	2700.00	2340.00
☐ **Brooch,** Art Nouveau motif, 11 round diamonds approx. .90 ct., one pearl, lapel watch holder, gold, c. 1890	1800.00	1900.00	1825.00
☐ **Brooch,** dragon, diamond mouth, ruby eye, gold, c. 1880	650.00	800.00	675.00
☐ **Brooch,** fire opal, old mine diamonds, gold, c. 1890	1400.00	1500.00	1425.00
☐ **Brooch,** flower motif, translucent pink and yellow enamel flowers with seed pearls, rose diamond in silver leaves, gold, c. 1905	2500.00	2900.00	2550.00
☐ **Brooch,** flowers, ivory with opals, 3½″ Dia.	495.00	535.00	495.00
☐ **Brooch,** flowing scroll motif, 11 round diamonds approx. 3.75 cts., gold and platinum, c. 1900	3400.00	3800.00	3450.00
☐ **Brooch,** gold Egyptian goddess, outspread wings and serpent tail, Austrian, maker's mark M.L., 2⅛″ Dia., c. 1920	420.00	510.00	445.00
☐ **Brooch,** gold eagle with outstretched wings, open beak and curled talons, French, 2¼″ Dia., c. 1910	450.00	535.00	475.00

	Current Price Range		P/Y Average

Brooch, ladies heads motif, carved, gold, c. 1900 .... 140.00 160.00 145.00

Brooch, leaf motif, translucent enamel, seed pearls, gold, c. 1900, pair 450.00 500.00 460.00

Brooch, lily-of-the-valley flower motif, seed pearls, translucent green enamel, gold, c. 1915, pair 425.00 475.00 435.00

Brooch, medallion portrait of a winged warrior with helmet, gold, 1″ diameter, inscribed: V. Prouve, French, c. 1900–10 .... 1500.00 1700.00 1550.00

Brooch, miniature of a lady, translucent pink and red enamel, emeralds in tiara, six cabochon opals in bar, engraved, gold, c. 1900 .... 1500.00 1700.00 1550.00

Brooch, pelican, translucent pink and yellow enamel body, baroque pearl, green translucent plique-a-jour wings with rose diamonds in edges, c. 1890–1910 .... 4500.00 5000.00 4575.00

Brooch, peridot, seed pearls, 14K gold, c. 1890 .... 250.00 275.00 260.00

Brooch, scroll freeform motif, 14 old mine diamonds, round and rose diamonds, 18K gold, c. 1890–1900 .... 2500.00 2900.00 2575.00

Brooch, translucent enamel portrait of a lady, diamonds in headband, two pearls, gold, c. 1890–1910 .... 1500.00 1700.00 1575.00

Brooch, tulip motif, rubies, sapphires, diamonds, pink tourmadend, pink sapphires, old mine diamonds, natural pearls, blue green and orange translucent enamel, platinum, gold, c. 1900 ... 16000.00 18000.00 16500.00

Centerpiece bowl, sterling silver, undulating rim, embossed floral chasing, the torso of a young girl on one end with torso of young boy on the other, footed, Gorham, 23″, c. 1900 .... 8500.00 11500.00 8750.00

Chatelaine, morning glory plaque with memo pad, pencil and glass scent bottle, white metal, c. 1895 .... 180.00 200.00 190.00

Desk set, sterling silver, etched with flowers, leaves and children's faces, includes ruler, quill holder/sharpener, glass inkwell with hinged silver lid on stand and four corner blotter mounts, Tiffany & Company, c. 1900 .... 775.00 1150.00 900.00

Clock, desk type, nude nymph, metal case ... 58.00 90.00 70.00

Dining room suite, buffet, table sideboard and five chairs, Belgian, c. 1900 .... 3200.00 3900.00 3400.00

Locket, medallion portrait of a lady and birds, 14K gold, c. 1900 .... 400.00 500.00 410.00

Locket, medallion portrait of a lady, rose diamonds, slides to open, gold, maker: Diolot, c. 1890 .... 2000.00 2200.00 2050.00

Locket, swirl motif, one round diamond, 14K gold, American, c. 1900 .... 375.00 475.00 385.00

Match safe, cigar cutter base, engraved initials, sterling silver, c. 1910 .... 175.00 225.00 185.00

	Current Price Range		P/Y Average

☐ **Miniature,** portrait of a lady, round diamonds in border, 18K gold, signed: Gollay Fils & Stah, Geneve, c. 1890 .... **2200.00 2400.00 2225.00**

☐ **Mirror,** hand, with woman's head and flowing hair, flowers and swans, sterling silver, Unger Bros., c. 1900 .... **105.00 160.00 125.00**

☐ **Mirror,** vanity, brass, c. 1900 .... **60.00 88.00 68.00**

☐ **Necklace,** choker, Art Nouveau scroll links, lozenge-shape peridots, 54 old mine diamonds approx. 4.50 cts., forms two bracelets, maker: Harvey & Gore, English, c. late 19th **6250.00 6750.00 6300.00**

☐ **Necklace,** flower and festoon motif, seed pearls, one fresh water pearl, red glass, enamel, gold, c. 1890–1910 .... **575.00 675.00 585.00**

☐ **Necklace,** flower motif, blue and green plique a jour enamel, fresh water pearls, silver, c. 1900 **650.00 850.00 675.00**

☐ **Necklace,** flower motif, oval cabochon opals, demantoid garnets, c. 1900 .... **4400.00 4600.00 4475.00**

☐ **Necklace,** flower motif, pearls, one fresh water pearl, lime green to pale rose plique a jour enamel, "900" silver, French **1000.00 1200.00 1050.00**

☐ **Necklace,** flowers and fleur-de-lys motif, enameled, seven pearls, gold, c. 1890–1910 .... **675.00 875.00 695.00**

☐ **Necklace,** lady with dragonfly wing motif, green and blue plique-a-jour wings with one calibre sapphire surrounded by rose diamonds, one Holland-rose diamond set in hair of lady, 11 calibre sapphires in tail, two baroque pearls, opaque enamelled cattails, detachable pin and chain, gold, c. late 19th **22000.00 26000.00 23000.00**

☐ **Necklace,** leaf and swirl motif, translucent green and yellow enamel, one oval and two round faceted peridots, one large baroque pearl suspended from center, smaller baroque pearls spaced in chain, 14K gold, American, c. 1890–1910 .... **675.00 875.00 695.00**

☐ **Necklace,** leaf motif, peridots, seed pearls, citrines, green enamel, 18K gold **2000.00 2200.00 2075.00**

☐ **Necklace,** openwork pendant with one small round diamond and a fresh water pearl drop attached to a double link chain spaced with seed pearls, gold, c. 1900 .... **475.00 575.00 485.00**

☐ **Pendant,** flower motif, pearls, fresh water pearls, green enamel leaves, pink enamel flower, "900" silver, c. 1900 .... **275.00 375.00 285.00**

☐ **Vase,** bronze, tapered cylindrical with four dragonflies forming handles, inscribed H.E.-T., 10″ H., c. 1900 .... **200.00 310.00 245.00**

☐ **Vase,** cameo glass, cranberry and mauve, inscribed Galle, 5¼″ H., c. 1900 .... **425.00 535.00 465.00**

☐ **Vase,** enamel cameo glass, russet, mustard and dark green on brown and mustard ground, Daum Nancy, 5″ H., c. 1900 .... **305.00 425.00 355.00**

	Current Price Range		P/Y Average
☐ **Vase,** girl with doves, German, 12″ H., c. 1900	240.00	300.00	255.00
☐ **Vase,** pottery, cherry blossoms in shades of white, iron-red, tan and brown, sea blue at base, Rookwood, 9″ H., c. 1883	680.00	1200.00	880.00
☐ **Vase,** pottery, forest scene, dolphin handles enameled in gilt, Amphora, 7¼″ H., c. 1920 . . .	425.00	635.00	515.00
☐ **Vase,** pottery, iridescent with tendrils and leafage, amber, green and red glaze, French, 6½″ H., c. 1900	175.00	230.00	190.00
☐ **Wall shelf,** fruitwood frame and shelf, cameo glass half moon panel depicting idyllic landscape, signed Jacques/Gruber, 20″, c. 1900	1350.00	1950.00	1450.00
☐ **Watch fob,** Art Nouveau motif, two cabochon sardonyx stones in fob, gold, c. 1890	675.00	725.00	685.00

AUDUBON PRINTS

DESCRIPTION: John James Audubon is a name synonymous with bird pictures. His "Birds of America" series is recognized worldwide.

PERIOD: Between 1826 and 1842, Audubon traveled throughout the United States and Canada gathering material to paint this famous work.

COMMENTS: Today, experts believe there are less than 200 sets of "Birds of America" actually bound in volumes. The work was engraved by R. Havell and son in London. There are 435 plates in a complete set.

ADDITIONAL TIPS: This section lists many of the original prints in the set with the current market price. For a complete list of all the prints refer to *The Official Price Guide to Collector Prints* published by The House of Collectibles.

PLATE NUMBER	SUBJECT	CURRENT RETAIL PRICE
☐ 1	Turkey Cock	30,000.00
☐ 2	Yellow-billed Cuckoo	2,090.00
☐ 3	Prothonotary Warbler	990.00
☐ 4	Purple Finch	825.00
☐ 5	Bonaparte's Flycatcher	715.00
☐ 6	Hen Turkey	14,300.00

PLATE NUMBER	SUBJECT	CURRENT RETAIL PRICE
☐ 7	Purple Grackle	3,960.00
☐ 8	White-throated Sparrow	1,760.00
☐ 9	Selby's Flycatcher	605.00
☐ 10	Brown Lark	715.00
☐ 11	Bird of Washington	5,225.00
☐ 12	Baltimore Oriole	6,325.00
☐ 13	Snow Bird	715.00
☐ 14	Prairie Warbler	1,320.00
☐ 15	Blue Yellow-backed Warbler	1,760.00
☐ 16	Great Footed Hawk	3,080.00
☐ 17	Carolina Pigeon	12,100.00
☐ 18	Bewick's Wren	1,045.00
☐ 19	Louisiana Water Thrush	825.00
☐ 20	Blue-winged Yellow Warbler	2,200.00
☐ 21	Mockingbird	7,150.00
☐ 22	Purple Martin	2,640.00
☐ 23	Maryland Yellow Throat	1,430.00
☐ 24	Roscoe's Yellow Throat	825.00
☐ 25	Song Sparrow	715.00
☐ 26	Carolina Parrot	17,600.00
☐ 27	Red-headed Woodpecker	3,410.00
☐ 28	Solitary Flycatcher	1,045.00
☐ 29	Towhe Bunting	1,980.00
☐ 30	Vigor's Vireo	1,430.00
☐ 31	White-headed Eagle	7,425.00
☐ 32	Black-billed Cuckoo	5,775.00
☐ 33	American Goldfinch	2,640.00
☐ 34	Worm-eating Warbler	1,430.00
☐ 35	Children's Warbler	1,045.00
☐ 36	Stanley Hawk	3,520.00
☐ 37	Golden-winged Woodpecker	3,520.00
☐ 38	Kentucky Warbler	1,320.00
☐ 39	Crested Titmouse	2,145.00
☐ 40	American Redstart	1,870.00
☐ 41	Ruffed Grouse	10,175.00
☐ 42	Orchard's Oriole	3,630.00
☐ 43	Cedar Waxwing	3,520.00
☐ 44	Summer Tanager	3,850.00
☐ 45	Traill's Flycatcher	1,100.00
☐ 169	Mangrove Cuckoo	1,850.00
☐ 170	Gray Tyrant	935.00
☐ 171	Barn Owl	9,000.00
☐ 172	Blue-headed Pigeon	2,000.00
☐ 173	Barn Swallow	2,500.00
☐ 174	Olive Sided Flycatcher	660.00
☐ 175	Marsh Wren	1,650.00
☐ 176	Spotted Grouse	6,000.00
☐ 177	White-crowned Pigeon	7,150.00
☐ 178	Orange-crowned Warbler	825.00
☐ 179	Wood Wren	2,650.00
☐ 180	Pine Finch	1,350.00
☐ 181	Golden Eagle	4,000.00
☐ 182	Ground Dove	3,250.00
☐ 183	Golden-crested Wren	900.00

PLATE 203 HAVELL EDITION "Fresh Water Marsh Wren (King Rall)"

PLATE NUMBER	SUBJECT	CURRENT RETAIL PRICE
☐ 184	Mangrove Hummingbird	2,650.00
☐ 185	Bachman's Warbler	2,750.00
☐ 186	Pinnated Grouse	7,250.00
☐ 187	Boat-tailed Grackle	3,500.00
☐ 188	Tree Sparrow	1,300.00
☐ 189	Snow Bunting	1,000.00
☐ 190	Yellow-bellied Woodpecker	1,600.00
☐ 191	Willow Grouse	5,500.00
☐ 192	Great American Shrike	1,500.00
☐ 193	Lincoln Finch	2,300.00
☐ 194	Canadian Titmouse	1,200.00
☐ 195	Ruby-crowned Wren	2,000.00
☐ 196	Labrador Falcon	3,500.00
☐ 197	American Crossbill	2,500.00
☐ 198	Worm-eating Warbler	1,650.00
☐ 199	Little Owl	1,500.00
☐ 200	Shore Lark	700.00
☐ 201	Canada Goose	21,000.00
☐ 202	Red-throated Diver	4,500.00
☐ 203	Fresh Water Marsh Wren	2,750.00
☐ 204	Salt Water Marsh Wren	1,850.00
☐ 205	Virginia Rail	2,000.00
☐ 206	Summer or Wood Duck	13,750.00
☐ 207	Booby Gannet	3,250.00
☐ 208	Esquimaux Curlew	715.00
☐ 209	Wilson's Plover	385.00
☐ 210	Least Bittern	2,500.00
☐ 211	Great Blue Heron	42,000.00

PLATE NUMBER	SUBJECT	CURRENT RETAIL PRICE
☐ 212	Common Gull	1,900.00
☐ 213	Puffin	2,475.00
☐ 214	Razor Bill	935.00
☐ 215	Phalarope	660.00
☐ 216	Wood Ibis	10,450.00
☐ 217	Louisiana Heron	15,400.00
☐ 218	Foolish Guillemar	715.00
☐ 219	Black Guillemar	577.00
☐ 220	Piping Plover	550.00
☐ 221	Mallard Duck	25,500.00
☐ 222	White Ibis	9,250.00
☐ 223	Pied Oyster Catcher	825.00
☐ 224	Kittiwake Gull	825.00
☐ 225	Kildeer Plover	715.00
☐ 226	Whooping Crane	14,000.00
☐ 227	Pin-tailed Duck	7,250.00
☐ 228	Green-wing Teal	5,500.00
☐ 229	Scaup Duck	3,850.00
☐ 230	Ruddy Plover	850.00
☐ 231	Long-billed Curlew	20,000.00
☐ 232	Hooded Merganser	4,500.00
☐ 233	Sora or Rail	1,700.00
☐ 234	Tufted Duck	3,250.00
☐ 235	Sooty Tern	900.00
☐ 236	Night Heron	10,500.00
☐ 237	Great Esquimaux Curlew	2,400.00
☐ 238	Great Marbled Codwit	2,500.00
☐ 239	American Coot	2,400.00
☐ 240	Roseate Tern	3,000.00
☐ 311	White Pelican	30,000.00
☐ 312	Old Squaw	3,200.00
☐ 313	Blue-winged Teal	5,000.00
☐ 314	Laughing Gull	880.00
☐ 315	Sandpiper	1,100.00
☐ 317	Surf Scoter	1,540.00
☐ 318	Avocet	3,000.00
☐ 319	Lesser Tern	2,000.00
☐ 320	Little Sandpiper	1,600.00
☐ 321	Roseate Spoonbill	28,750.00
☐ 322	Red-head Duck	6,500.00
☐ 323	Black Skimmer	3,500.00
☐ 324	Bonaparte's Gull	2,500.00
☐ 325	Bufflehead	5,000.00
☐ 326	Gannet	6,000.00
☐ 327	Shoveller Duck	8,500.00
☐ 328	Blackneck Stilt	3,000.00
☐ 329	Yellow Rail	850.00
☐ 330	Plover	385.00
☐ 331	American Merganser	6,500.00
☐ 332	Labrador Duck	4,300.00
☐ 333	Green Heron	5,700.00
☐ 334	Black-bellied Plover	550.00
☐ 335	Red-bellied Sandpiper	1,100.00
☐ 336	Yellow Crowned Night Heron	7,370.00

PLATE NUMBER	SUBJECT	CURRENT RETAIL PRICE
☐ 337	American Bittern	3,500.00
☐ 338	Bemaculated Duck	5,000.00
☐ 339	Little Auk	900.00
☐ 340	Stormy Petrel	700.00
☐ 341	Great Auk	5,000.00
☐ 342	Golden-eyed Duck	4,500.00
☐ 343	Ruddy Duck	4,150.00
☐ 344	Long-legged Sandpiper	1,000.00
☐ 345	American Widgeon	4,300.00
☐ 346	Black Throated Diver	9,750.00
☐ 347	American Bittern	3,500.00
☐ 348	Gadwall Duck	5,000.00
☐ 349	Least Water Hen	1,500.00
☐ 350	Rocky Mountain Plover	385.00
☐ 351	Great Cinereous Owl	6,200.00
☐ 352	Black-winged Hawk	1,650.00
☐ 353	Titmouse, Etc.	1,700.00
☐ 354	Louisiana Tanager	3,000.00
☐ 355	MacGillivray's Finch	1,400.00
☐ 356	Marsh Hawk	3,750.00
☐ 357	American Magpie	3,000.00
☐ 358	Pine Grosbeak	880.00
☐ 359	Arkansas Flycatcher	1,210.00
☐ 360	Winter and Rock Wren	1,900.00

Red Breasted Merganser, *plate 401,*
$6500.00

PLATE NUMBER	SUBJECT	CURRENT RETAIL PRICE
☐ 361	Long-tailed Grouse	3,500.00
☐ 362	Yellow-billed Magpie	2,640.00
☐ 363	Bohemian Chatterer	1,500.00
☐ 364	White-winged Grossbill	2,000.00
☐ 365	Lapland Longspur	990.00
☐ 366	Iceland Falcon	25,500.00
☐ 367	Band-tailed Pigeon	4,750.00
☐ 368	Rock Grouse	3,300.00
☐ 369	Mountain Mockingbird	1,400.00
☐ 370	American Water Ouzel	700.00
☐ 371	Cock of the Plains	6,000.00
☐ 372	Common Buzzard	3,000.00
☐ 373	Evening Grosbeak	1,100.00
☐ 374	Sharp Shinned Hawk	990.00
☐ 375	Lesser Red Poll	850.00
☐ 376	Trumpeter Swan	9,500.00
☐ 377	Scolopaceys Courlan	3,000.00
☐ 378	Hawk Owl	1,900.00
☐ 379	Ruff-necked Hummingbird	2,860.00

AUTOGRAPHS

DESCRIPTION: Original autographs of celebrities, including Presidents, entertainers, writers and artists, are fairly available and always sought after.

PERIOD: Autographs exist dating to the middle ages.

COMMENTS: Autographs have established cash values though they vary greatly in price because each specimen is unique. Single signatures are generally less expensive than signatures that are part of a letter. Often values depend on buyer demand.

ADDITIONAL TIPS: A holograph letter, AL, is a letter written entirely in the person's handwriting. A letter with the body written or typed by a secretary is referred to as an L. D is for a signed document, and N is for a signed note.

Listed alphabetically by celebrity name, prices are given for ALs, Ls, signed photo, manuscript page, document and plain signatures. For further information on autographs see *The Official Price Guide to Old Books and Autographs,* published by The House of Collectibles.

Give tea to my Third: 'tis a name I assign
To plate, pictures, or wine,
Which is yours and not mine.

Give no tea to my Whole: it will keep her awake,
And her small head will ache,
And a riot she'll make,
Till, for quietness' sake,
You supply her with cake.

Lewis Carroll.
Mar. 16. 1880.

Portion Of A Page of Verse, *written and signed by Lewis Carroll,*
$750.00–$1000.00

AMERICAN PRESIDENTS

	ALs	Ls	Document	Signed Photo	Plain Signature
☐ Washington, George	$8000.00–35,000.00	$1800.00–9500.00	$1500.00–4000.00		$450.00–600.00
☐ Adams, John	4000.00–7000.00	1250.00–4000.00	1000.00–2500.00		300.00–400.00
☐ Jefferson, Thomas	6000.00–30,000.00	2000.00–8000.00	1200.00–3000.00		400.00–500.00
☐ Madison, James	1000.00–3000.00	500.00–1400.00	200.00–800.00		100.00–150.00
☐ Monroe, James	500.00–1500.00	450.00–1200.00	150.00–300.00		75.00–100.00
☐ Adams, John Q.............	750.00–1500.00	450.00–1200.00	150.00–300.00		80.00–125.00
☐ Jackson, Andrew	1750.00–3000.00	700.00–2000.00	400.00–650.00		150.00–200.00
☐ Van Buren, Martin	500.00–1000.00	300.00–600.00	150.00–200.00		65.00–85.00
☐ Harrison, William H.	1000.00–1500.00	300.00–1000.00	350.00–475.00		80.00–100.00
☐ Tyler, John	600.00–1000.00	350.00–600.00	150.00–200.00		60.00–75.00
☐ Polk, James K.............	500.00–1000.00	350.00–600.00	150.00–200.00		60.00–70.00
☐ Taylor, Zachary	750.00–2000.00	350.00–1100.00	275.00–600.00		60.00–100.00
☐ Fillmore, Millard	275.00–400.00	175.00–300.00	100.00–200.00		50.00–60.00
☐ Pierce, Franklin	250.00–400.00	150.00–175.00	100.00–200.00		50.00–60.00
☐ Buchanan, James	250.00–	175.00–	100.00–		50.00–

	ALs	Ls	Document	Signed Photo	Plain Signature
	400.00	275.00	200.00		60.00
☐ Lincoln, Abraham	5000.00–	2000.00–	750.00–	4000.00–	350.00–
	25,000.00	12,000.00	2500.00	7000.00	350.00
☐ Johnson, Andrew	1000.00–	400.00–	150.00–	1800.00–	50.00–
	2000.00	1000.00	200.00	2500.00	60.00
☐ Grant, U. S.	750.00–	400.00–	85.00–	100.00–	40.00–
	1200.00	750.00	150.00	175.00	45.00
☐ Hayes, R. B.	250.00–	150.00	65.00–	250.00–	30.00–
	500.00	150.00	65.00	300.00	38.00
☐ Garfield, James	350.00–	200.00–	100.00–	350.00–	38.00–
	600.00	350.00	90.00	700.00	50.00
☐ Arthur, Chester A.	200.00–	120.00–	60.00–	850.00–	30.00–
	300.00	250.00	85.00	1200.00	38.00
☐ Cleveland, Grover	175.00–	80.00–	50.00–	100.00–	26.00–
	250.00	120.00	70.00	200.00	32.00
☐ Harrison, Benjamin	300.00–	145.00–	65.00–	325.00–	28.00–
	400.00	175.00	85.00	450.00	32.00
☐ McKinley, William	500.00–	190.00–	95.00–	175.00–	38.00–
	750.00	300.00	140.00	225.00	42.00
☐ Roosevelt, Theodore	300.00–	100.00–	60.00–	100.00–	32.00–
	350.00	190.00	60.00	400.00	38.00
☐ Taft, William H.	150.00–	90.00–	45.00–	150.00–	28.00–
	200.00	100.00	50.00	180.00	35.00
☐ Wilson, Woodrow	500.00–	140.00–	60.00–	160.00–	38.00–
	700.00	190.00	70.00	220.00	45.00
☐ Harding, Warren G.........	700.00–	250.00–	60.00–	110.00–	28.00–
	900.00	350.00	75.00	140.00	35.00
☐ Coolidge, Calvin	475.00–	140.00–	75.00–	75.00–	28.00–
	700.00	180.00	70.00	100.00	35.00
☐ Hoover, Herbert	4000.00–	150.00–	45.00–	150.00–	28.00–
	6000.00	190.00	60.00	200.00	35.00
☐ Roosevelt, Franklin	600.00–	100.00–	95.00–	120.00–	33.00–
	1000.00	265.00	150.00	180.00	39.00
☐ Truman, Harry	1200.00–	140.00–	80.00–	150.00–	39.00–
	2000.00	350.00	120.00	180.00	45.00
☐ Eisenhower, Dwight	1000.00–	200.00–	80.00–	200.00–	28.00–
	1500.00	275.00	100.00	300.00	35.00
☐ Kennedy, John F.	1500.00–	450.00–	175.00–	500.00–	100.00–
	4000.00	900.00	350.00	1000.00	150.00
☐ Johnson, Lyndon B.	1300.00–	300.00–	80.00–	140.00–	35.00–
	1800.00	500.00	100.00	190.00	48.00
☐ Nixon, Richard M	4500.00–	450.00–	150.00–	250.00–	75.00–
	6500.00	800.00	190.00	375.00	100.00
☐ Ford, Gerald	700.00–	250.00–	80.00–	140.00–	28.00–
	1000.00	400.00	110.00	190.00	35.00
☐ Carter, James	700.00–	200.00–	70.00–	120.00–	25.00–
	1000.00	350.00	90.00	150.00	35.00
☐ Reagan, Ronald	1000.00–	175.00–	85.00–	70.00–	25.00–
	1500.00	250.00	125.00	100.00	30.00

ARTISTS

	ALS		S	
☐ Barbieri, Giovanni Francesco	600.00–	800.00	150.00–	170.00
☐ Benson, Frank W.	18.00–	23.00	4.00–	6.00
☐ Cass, George N.	12.00–	15.00	2.50–	3.50
☐ Cellini, Benvenuto	3750.00–	6000.00	350.00–	450.00
☐ Cezanne, Paul	400.00–	700.00	30.00–	40.00
☐ Chagall, Marc	170.00–	200.00	22.00–	28.00
☐ Church, Frederick S.	110.00–	140.00	12.00–	15.00
☐ Corot, Camille	85.00–	100.00	17.00–	22.00
☐ Cruikshank, George	100.00–	150.00	12.00–	17.00
☐ DaVinci, Leonardo	35000.00–	60000.00	1750.00–	2250.00
☐ Degas, Edgar	375.00–	550.00	60.00–	75.00
☐ Duran, Carolus	18.00–	23.00	2.50–	3.50
☐ Eastlake, Sir Charles L.	85.00–	100.00	8.00–	10.00
☐ Fildes, Sir Luke	18.00–	23.00	3.00–	4.00
☐ Forain, Jean	12.00–	15.00	3.00–	4.00
☐ Forrester, Alfred Henry	28.00–	34.00	3.00–	4.00
☐ Gauguin, Paul	650.00–	850.00	22.00–	28.00
☐ Gibson, Charles D.	50.00–	70.00	7.00–	10.00
☐ Gifford, R. Swain	8.00–	10.00	2.50–	3.50
☐ Landseer, Sir Edwin	22.00–	27.00	3.50–	4.75
☐ Lawrence, Sir Thomas	120.00–	150.00	6.00–	8.00
☐ Lear, Edward	175.00–	225.00	12.00–	15.00
☐ Leslie, C. R.	40.00–	50.00	4.00–	6.00
☐ Low, Will H.	9.00–	12.00	2.50–	3.75
☐ Matisse, Henri	140.00–	190.00	20.00–	30.00
☐ Menzel, Morlan	18.00–	25.00	2.50–	3.75
☐ Michelangelo Buonarroti	15000.00–	22000.00	1250.00–	1600.00
☐ Millais, J. E.	28.00–	34.00	4.00–	6.00
☐ Modigliani, Amedeo	700.00–	1000.00	70.00–	100.00
☐ Monet, Claude	70.00–	100.00	12.00–	15.00
☐ Morghen, Raphael	60.00–	80.00	6.00–	8.00
☐ Pissarro, Camille	140.00–	190.00	25.00–	33.00
☐ Raphael, Sanzio	35000.00–	60000.00	1750.00–	2500.00
☐ Redoute, Pierre J.	80.00–	100.00	6.00–	8.00
☐ Rembrant van Rijn	75000.00–	150000.00	4000.00–	6000.00
☐ Remington, Frederick	500.00–	900.00	30.00–	50.00
☐ Renoir, Pierre A.	350.00–	500.00	60.00–	85.00
☐ Rossetti, Dante G.	250.00–	350.00	30.00–	40.00
☐ Rouault, George S.	150.00–	200.00	25.00–	35.00
☐ Rubens, Peter Paul	9000.00–	12000.00	700.00–	1000.00
☐ Sargent, J. S.	110.00–	150.00	12.00–	15.00
☐ Sully, Thomas	110.00–	150.00	12.00–	15.00
☐ West, Benjamin	170.00–	200.00	12.00–	15.00
☐ Whistler, James A. M.	120.00–	160.00	17.00–	22.00
☐ Wyeth, N. C.	70.00–	100.00	7.00–	10.00

AUTHORS

AMERICAN

	ALS		MS Page	
☐ Alcott, Louisa M.	$250.00–	$350.00	$500.00–	$700.00
☐ Aldrich, Thomas B.	100.00–	130.00	200.00–	275.00
☐ Alger, Horatio	30.00–	40.00	200.00–	275.00
☐ Bates, Arlo	12.00–	16.00	17.00–	22.00
☐ Botta, Ann Lynch	8.00–	10.00	12.00–	15.00

	ALS		MS Page	
☐ Brooks, Fred Emerson	8.00–	10.00	12.00–	15.00
☐ Browne, Chas. F. (Artemus Ward)	22.00–	26.00	28.00–	35.00
☐ Bryant, William C.	75.00–	95.00	150.00–	190.00
☐ Burnett, Frances H.	17.00–	22.00	30.00–	35.00
☐ Burroughs, John	35.00–	50.00	75.00–	100.00
☐ Butler, Ellis P.	8.00–	10.00	14.00–	18.00
☐ Curtis, George W.	14.00–	18.00	16.00–	20.00
☐ Dana, R. H., Jr.	42.00–	53.00	100.00–	150.00
☐ Davis, Richard H.	8.00–	10.00	14.00–	18.00
☐ Dixon, Thomas	6.00–	8.00	12.00–	15.00
☐ Dodge, Mary Mapes	18.00–	24.00	22.00–	28.00
☐ Field, Eugene	72.00–	93.00	150.00–	200.00
☐ Field, Kate	6.00–	8.00	12.00–	15.00
☐ Fiske, John	10.00–	14.00	12.00–	15.00
☐ Flagg, Wilson	8.00–	10.00	12.00–	15.00
☐ Guiterman, Arthur	6.00–	8.00	12.00–	15.00
☐ Hale, Edward E.	14.00–	18.00	22.00–	28.00
☐ Harris, Joel C.	100.00–	150.00	300.00–	400.00
☐ Hawthorne, Nathaniel	1500.00–	2000.00	2000.00–	3000.00
☐ Headley, Joel T.	6.00–	8.00	12.00–	15.00
☐ Hearn, Lafcadio	250.00–	400.00	400.00–	700.00
☐ Hemingway, Ernest	1500.00–	3500.00	3000.00–	5000.00
☐ Hubbard, Elbert	18.00–	23.00	35.00–	40.00
☐ Huneker, James	8.00–	10.00	18.00–	23.00
☐ Irving, Washington	1000.00–	1500.00	3000.00–	4000.00
☐ Jackson, Helen Hunt	8.00–	10.00	18.00–	23.00
☐ Jewett, Sarah	14.00–	18.00	22.00–	27.00
☐ Kilmer, Joyce	175.00–	225.00	400.00–	500.00
☐ Longfellow, H. W.	150.00–	180.00	250.00–	300.00
☐ Lowell, Amy	100.00–	150.00	275.00–	325.00
☐ Lowell, James R.	45.00–	60.00	120.00–	160.00
☐ McCutcheon, George B.	8.00–	10.00	17.00–	22.00
☐ Markham, Edwin	17.00–	23.00	35.00–	40.00
☐ Melville, Herman	3750.00–	6000.00	4500.00–	7000.00
☐ Mencken, H. L.	75.00–	100.00	100.00–	200.00
☐ Morley, Christopher	40.00–	55.00	60.00–	80.00
☐ Nye, E. W.	55.00–	70.00	110.00–	140.00
☐ O'Neill, Eugene	800.00–	2000.00	1500.00–	2250.00
☐ O'Reilly, John B.	22.00–	27.00	60.00–	75.00
☐ Parsons, T. W.	8.00–	10.00	18.00–	23.00
☐ Payne, John H.	175.00–	225.00	325.00–	400.00
☐ Percival, J. G.	60.00–	80.00	120.00–	150.00
☐ Pierpont, John	30.00–	40.00	60.00–	80.00
☐ Porter, W. S. (O. Henry)	800.00–	1000.00	800.00–	1000.00
☐ Prescott, Mary N.	30.00–	40.00	60.00–	80.00
☐ Randall, James R.	120.00–	150.00	300.00–	375.00
☐ Sikes, William W.	12.00–	22.00	30.00–	35.00
☐ Stockton, Frank	40.00–	50.00	85.00–	110.00
☐ Stoddard, R. H.	30.00–	40.00	60.00–	80.00
☐ Stowe, H. B.	140.00–	170.00	400.00–	550.00
☐ Tarkington, Booth	175.00–	225.00	250.00–	350.00
☐ Taylor, Bayard	40.00–	50.00	80.00–	100.00
☐ Terhune, Albert P.	17.00–	22.00	28.00–	33.00
☐ Thoreau, Henry D.	1200.00–	1500.00	1750.00–	2250.00

	ALS		MS Page	
☐ Thorpe, Thomas B.	40.00–	50.00	80.00–	100.00
☐ Tomlinson, Everett	14.00–	18.00	30.00–	40.00
☐ Wolfe, Thomas	400.00–	700.00	1200.00–	1600.00

AVIATION MEMORABILIA

DESCRIPTION: Aviation memorabilia includes any item dealing with airplanes. From commercial airlines to the air force, hobbyists are collecting any type of aviation memorabilia available.

TYPES: Stewardess wings, pilot goggles, pins, buttons, helmets, entire airplanes or just parts of airplanes are all types of memorabilia collected by hobbyists.

COMMENTS: Finding aviation collectibles could be difficult. A good source to contact is the World Airline Hobby Club, 3381 Apple Tree Lane, Erlanger, KY 41018.

	Current Price Range		P/Y Average
☐ **Activity Book For Children,** cut-out book with seven different planes of the classic era including Lockheed Vega, Stinson, Curtiss Robin, Spirit of St. Louis, full color, 10″ x 15″, 1930, price is for an intact specimen	40.00	55.00	44.00
☐ **Bombadeer's Panel,** with wing lights, bomb bay lights, bomb salvo switch, door on/off switch, World War II	100.00	150.00	117.50
☐ **Book,** The Romance Of Air Fighting by R.W. Anderson, soft cover, 31 pages, published in Great Britain, 1917	35.00	45.00	38.00
☐ **Book,** Signal Corps Pilot's Book, used by a cadet in 1917, hardcover, 5½″ x 6″	50.00	65.00	55.00
☐ **Booklet,** Souvenir of the Harvard/Boston Aviation Meet, 1911, with photographs of Glen Curtis, Willard, Graham White and many other notables of the Wright Brothers era	100.00	130.00	110.00
☐ **Button,** brass, pictures world globe and reads "U.S. Air Mail," c. 1930	10.00	15.00	11.00

	Current Price Range		P/Y Average

	Current Price Range	P/Y Average
□ **Cap,** canvas with built-in earphones, bakelite phones, c. 1930–1934	50.00 65.00	54.75
□ **Cockpit Instrument Panel (fragment),** portion of instrument panel from World War II craft, un-identified, with starter, landing lights, light prop, feathering switch, some wiring, 10″ x 12″	100.00 150.00	117.50
□ **Coffee Mug,** porcelain, reads Tactical Air Command/General White, white with gold, 3″	15.00 20.00	16.75
□ **Drinking Cup,** leather, Pan American Airways System, 4″, c. 1930	15.00 20.00	17.00
□ **Game,** Flying For Fun, aviation card game based on stunt pilot maneuvers, boxed with instructions, 1928	40.00 50.00	43.00
□ **Game, Squadron Scramble,** card game, World War II era picturing many different allied and axis aircraft, no indication of publisher	25.00 33.00	28.00
□ **Magazine, The Alexander Aircrafter,** September, 1927, full color cover, 22 pages, 5½″ x 8″	30.00 35.00	31.00
□ **Military Pass to MacDill Air Field, Florida,** dated August 14, 1942	13.00 17.00	14.25
□ **Notebook,** personal notes of 2nd Lieut. L.H. Thayer taken in Officer's Training Course at Kelly Field, Texas, from January to April, 1918, including nomenclature and diagrams	75.00 100.00	82.00
□ **Pamphlet,** National Air Races, International Aeronautical Exposition, details of prizes with entry blank, features nonstop flight New York to Los Angeles, Orville Wright listed as Chairman, 8″ x 11″, 1928	50.00 65.00	56.00
□ **Pilot Goggles,** bakelite with elastic band, screw off lenses, made by Wilson, c. 1930	35.00 45.00	38.50
□ **Pilot Goggles,** fur lined, yellow tinted lenses, elastic band, c. 1920–1930	30.00 40.00	32.50
□ **Pinback Button,** Autogiro, full color celluloid premium from Bond's Bread	7.00 10.00	7.75
□ **Pinback Button,** Byrd's Floyd Bennet, full color celluloid premium from Bond's Bread	7.00 10.00	7.75
□ **Pinback Button,** Earhart's Friendship, full color celluloid premium from Bond's Bread	7.00 10.00	7.75
□ **Pinback Button,** The Hero Of Niagara: Lincoln Beachey, black and white portrait of the famous pioneer aviator and stunt pilot, 1¾″, 1915	55.00 70.00	59.00
□ **Pocket Watch,** Graf Zeppelin, silvered case has embossed view of New York City skyline, black and gold dial, reads "Trail Blazers Around The World: Magellan 1522, c. 1929–1930	275.00 325.00	290.00
□ **Postcard,** biplane over Paris, black and white, unused, c. 1910–1912	14.00 18.00	15.20
□ **Postcard,** Hanriot Monoplane in flight with Hanriot at controls, black and white, unused	19.00 24.00	21.00
□ **Postcard,** Hudson-Fulton Celebration, $10,000 prize contest to any aviator who could fly from New York City to Albany, reproduction of Biedermann painting, 1909	25.00 32.00	27.00

	Current Price Range		P/Y Average
☐ **Slides,** set of one hundred study slides of planes in silhouette enclosed in original box, World War II	60.00	80.00	67.00
☐ **Trade Catalogue,** Bird Aircraft Corporation, seventeen page catalogue of airplanes available for sale, 1931	35.00	43.00	37.00
☐ **Watch Fob,** aluminum shell, pictures dirigible, reads "U.S. Navy, Duralumin," c. 1930s	25.00	30.00	26.00
☐ **Wreck Fragment,** piece of a Douglas SBD-3 dive bomber salvaged from wreckage, yellow metal with portions of attached canvas, 5", World War II	20.00	25.00	20.25

AVON BOTTLES

DESCRIPTION: The oldest toiletry company that issues decorative bottles, Avon is the modern leader in the non-liquor bottle field.

TYPES: There are a variety of Avon bottle types, including figurals shaped as animals, people, cars, etc., cologne bottles, hand lotion bottles, among others.

PERIOD: Based on door-to-door sales, Avon began as the California Perfume Company more than 50 years ago. Since 1939 the name Avon has been used exclusively.

COMMENTS: Everything relating to Avon, including bottles, brochures and magazine ads, is highly collectible. Older Avon memorabilia is usually of more value than recent products.

ADDITIONAL TIPS: The listings in this section are alphabetized by item name, followed by date of issue, description and, when possible, issue date. For more information, consult *The Official Price Guide to Bottles, Old and New,* published by The House of Collectibles.

WOMEN'S FIGURALS

	Current Price Range		P/Y Average
☐ **Baby Owl,** clear glass, gold cap, 1 oz. 1975–76. Original price $2.00	2.00	4.00	2.50

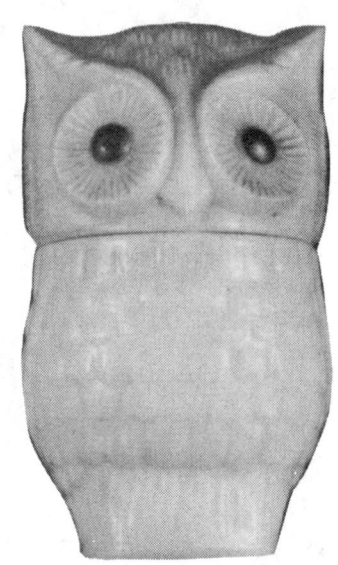

Avon Bottle,
owl cream sachet,
1½ oz., 1972,
$5.00-$6.50

	Current Price Range		P/Y Average
☐ **Bath Urn,** white glass and cap with gold top band under the cap, 5 oz., 1971–73	4.00	6.00	4.25
☐ **Bath Treasure Snail decanter,** clear glass, gold head, 6 oz., 1973–76. Original price $6.00	6.00	8.00	6.50
☐ **Beautiful Awakening,** clear glass, painted gold in shape of an alarm clock, with clock face on front, 3 oz., 1973–74	5.00	7.00	5.50
☐ **Betsy Ross decanter,** clear glass painted white, 4 oz., 1976. Original price $10.00	8.00	12.00	8.50
☐ **Bird of Paradise cologne,** blue glass, gold cap, 1.5 oz., 1975–76. Original price $3.00	3.00	5.00	3.50
☐ **La Belle Telephone,** telephone figurine, clear glass, gold top, 1 oz., 1974–76. Original price $7.00	7.00	9.00	7.50
☐ **Lady Bug perfume decanter,** frosted glass, gold cap, ¼ oz., 1975–76. Original price $4.00	3.00	5.00	3.50
☐ **Lady Spaniel,** opal glass, plastic head, 1.5 oz., 1974–76. Original price $3.00	3.00	5.00	3.50
☐ **Leisure Hours,** white milk glass in shape of clock with face of clock design on the front, gold cap, 5 oz., 1970–72. Original price $4.00	4.00	6.00	4.50
☐ **Love Song decanter,** frosted glass, gold cap, 6 oz., 1973–75. Original price $6.00	5.50	7.50	5.75
☐ **Magic Pumpkin Coach,** clear glass, gold cap, 1 oz., 1976. Original price $5.00	2.50	4.50	2.75
☐ **Ming Blue Lamp,** blue glass in shape of lamp, white plastic shade, 5 oz., 1974–76. Original price $6.00	6.00	8.00	6.50

	Current Price Range		P/Y Average
☐ **Ming Cat cologne,** tall seated cat, white glass, blue trim, neck ribbon, 6 oz., 1971	8.00	11.00	8.50
☐ **One dram perfume,** clear glass with ribbing, gold cap, 1974–76. Original price $4.25	3.00	5.00	3.50
☐ **Parisian Garden perfume,** white milk glass, in shape of pitcher with floral design on front, gold cap, 3.3 oz., 1974–75. Original price $5.00	5.00	7.00	5.50
☐ **Parlor Lamp,** lower portion in white milk glass, top portion in light amber glass, gold cap, 3 oz., 1971–72. Original price $7.00	8.00	11.00	8.50
☐ **Partridge cologne decanger,** white milk glass, white plastic lid, 5 oz., 1973–75. Original price $5.00	5.00	7.00	5.50
☐ **Roaring Twenties fashion figurine,** clear glass painted purple, plastic purple top, 3 oz., 1972–74	6.00	8.00	6.50
☐ **Robin Red-Breast cologne decanter,** red frosted glass, silver plastic, 2 oz., 1974–75. Original price $4.00	4.00	6.00	4.50
☐ **Royal Coach,** white milk glass, in shape of coach with gold cap on top, 5 oz., 1972–73. Original price $5.00	5.00	7.00	5.50

BANKS

TOPIC: Banks make saving coins more enjoyable. Besides providing a receptacle for a hoard of coins, they are interesting and amusing in themselves.

TYPES: Banks are either still or mechanical. Still banks are simply receptacles and do not move or react when a coin is deposited. Mechanical banks, however, respond to the coin (via a series of levers and springs) and put on a small show for the depositor.

PERIOD: Still banks were first made in the United States in the early 1790s; mechanical banks were introduced about seventy years later.

MATERIALS: Cast iron is the favorite material for banks.

COMMENTS: Banks make good collectibles because they are entertaining, attractive and often ingenious.

Bank, *tin, lithographed, Towle's Log Cabin Syrup, made in Hong Kong, 1950s,* $13.00–$20.00

		Current Price Range		P/Y Average
☐ **Airplane,** tin, single propeller, length 8″		50.00	60.00	55.00
☐ **Alamo,** replica of Alamo, height 1⅞″		80.00	90.00	85.00
☐ **Alice In Wonderland,** English, cube with embossed designs on each side, brass, height 4¼″		60.00	110.00	85.00
☐ **Alphabet,** drum shaped, children's scenes around the outside, band with alphabet around the top, tin, height 3″		30.00	40.00	35.00
☐ **Alphabet,** multisided spherical object, each side has embossed letter, height 3¼″		85.00	135.00	110.00
☐ **Amish Lady,** carries food on a plate in her left hand, height 5½″		55.00	65.00	60.00
☐ **Animal Bank,** drum shaped, embossed designs of animals around the outside, height 3″		30.00	40.00	35.00
☐ **Apple,** apple sits on apple leaves, height 3½″		110.00	210.00	150.00
☐ **Apple,** apple sits on embossed stand, medallion on front of apple, height 2½″		110.00	210.00	150.00
☐ **Armored Bank,** tin, length 6¼″		30.00	40.00	35.00
☐ **Atlas,** statuette of Atlas carrying the world on his shoulders, height 4¾″		110.00	310.00	160.00
☐ **Baseball On Three Bats,** three bats criscrossed to form a stand with a disproportionately large baseball between them, height 5″		85.00	135.00	110.00

	Current Price Range		P/Y Average

	Current Price Range		P/Y Average
☐ **Baseball,** painted white with red tiger head on one side and red pegasus (Mobil gas) on the other, glass	30.00	40.00	35.00
☐ **Battleship,** not authentic appearing, height 8½"	160.00	260.00	210.00
☐ **Battleship Maine,** does not appear authentic, "Maine" embossed on front, height 4½"	185.00	220.00	195.00
☐ **Battleship Oregon,** not authentic appearing, "Oregon" embossed on the side, height 6¼"	270.00	300.00	285.00
☐ **Blanket Chest,** rectangular shaped, two medieval window shapes on front, height 2"	385.00	485.00	435.00
☐ **Boot,** old fashioned shoe, height 3"	60.00	110.00	85.00
☐ **Boy Scout,** holds flag pole to his right side, height 6"	135.00	150.00	142.50
☐ **Boy With Top Hat,** German, white metal, height 4½"	20.00	30.00	25.00
☐ **Brinks Armored Truck,** Die Cast, height 4¾" . . .	40.00	50.00	45.00
☐ **Buffalo,** authentic looking, height 3"	50.00	60.00	65.00
☐ **Buffalo,** "Amherst Stoves," printed on the side, height 5"	85.00	135.00	110.00
☐ **Century Of Progress,** long building with one tall tower in the center, height 6⅞"	360.00	460.00	410.00
☐ **Charlie Chaplin,** glass, candy container, height 3¾"	70.00	80.00	75.00
☐ **Chest,** embossed designs, height 2"	50.00	60.00	55.00
☐ **Chest,** lid opens up, height 6"	40.00	50.00	45.00
☐ **Christmas Bank,** tin, cylinder shape, design on the outside, height 3"	30.00	40.00	35.00
☐ **Church,** pot metal, bell tower, height 4"	30.00	40.00	35.00
☐ **Church,** cathedral style, tall bell tower on one side, height 6"	55.00	65.00	50.00
☐ **Churchill,** bust, composition, height 4¾"	40.00	50.00	45.00
☐ **Coronation Crown,** four shell feet, beaded border over the top, height 4½"	80.00	90.00	85.00
☐ **Cottage,** two storied with small chimneys on each side, height 3⅝"	45.00	55.00	45.00
☐ **Cottage,** pot metal, single storied, height 2" . .	50.00	60.00	55.00
☐ **Cow,** authentic looking, height 2½"	50.00	60.00	55.00
☐ **Cow,** authentic looking, height 3½"	50.00	60.00	55.00
☐ **Coronation Crown Prince Phillip,** pot metal, height 3¾"	15.00	25.00	20.00
☐ **County Bank,** English, height 4¼"	60.00	110.00	85.00
☐ **Crystal Bank,** cylinder shade glass with domed top, three feet	20.00	30.00	25.00
☐ **Cup,** tin, with lid and handle, height 2½"	12.00	16.00	12.00
☐ **Fez,** Shriner's hat with tassel, height 1½"	110.00	210.00	160.00
☐ **Fireman,** height 5½"	85.00	135.00	110.00
☐ **Football Player,** old fashioned uniform, height 5¾"	110.00	210.00	150.00
☐ **Football Player With Ball Overhead,** disproportionately, height 5"	110.00	160.00	130.00
☐ **Fort Dearborn,** three-storied, log building, height 6"	60.00	110.00	85.00

	Current Price Range		P/Y Average

☐ **Fortune Ship,** small pole, one mast, "Marie" and "U.S.A." printed on the side 85.00 135.00 110.00

☐ **French Artillery Hat,** height 1¾" 45.00 75.00 60.00

☐ **General Butler,** comical looking character, with large mustache, height 6½" 160.00 260.00 210.00

☐ **General Sherman,** rides rearing horse, height 5½" 135.00 235.00 185.00

☐ **German Ship,** length 7¼" 85.00 135.00 110.00

☐ **Globe On Arc,** on pedestal stand 110.00 210.00 150.00

☐ **Globe With Eagle,** pedestal foot, small eagle on top 160.00 260.00 210.00

☐ **Globe Savings Fund,** height 7" 85.00 135.00 110.00

☐ **Goose,** authentic looking, height 4" 60.00 110.00 85.00

☐ **Goose,** "Red Goose Shoes" printed on side, height 4½" 50.00 60.00 55.00

☐ **Goose,** height 5" 70.00 80.00 75.00

☐ **Grapette Cat,** with label, glass 5.00 7.00 5.00

☐ **Grapette Cat,** without label, glass 5.00 7.00 6.00

☐ **Grapette Clown,** glass 5.00 7.00 6.00

☐ **Grapette Elephant,** glass 5.00 7.00 6.00

☐ **Grandpa Dukes,** comical head with flat hat, height 2¼" 30.00 40.00 35.00

☐ **Grandpa's Hat,** upside down, top hat, height 2¼" 60.00 110.00 85.00

☐ **Guardhouse,** tin, soldier stands in archway, large striping on building, height 3½" 40.00 50.00 45.00

☐ **Hand Grenade,** height 3¾" 70.00 80.00 75.00

☐ **Happy Fats,** chubby figure stands on drum, candy container, height 4½" 165.00 200.00 180.00

☐ **Hen On Nest,** height 3" 110.00 210.00 155.00

☐ **Hippo,** authentic looking, height 2½" 110.00 210.00 155.00

☐ **Indian Family,** combination busts of Indian, squaw, and papoose, height 3¾" 80.00 90.00 85.00

☐ **Indian Maiden,** pot metal, wears headband and one feather at the side, height 3½" 25.00 35.00 30.00

☐ **Iron Maiden,** canister shape with head on the top, height 4¾" 110.00 210.00 160.00

☐ **Jarmulowsky Building,** brick design, height 8" 85.00 135.00 110.00

☐ **Keene Savings Bank,** tin, replica of a bank, double doors 75.00 105.00 90.00

☐ **Key,** stands on end, height 5½" 60.00 110.00 85.00

☐ **Koop's Mustard Barrel Bank,** glass 10.00 12.00 10.00

☐ **Kroger's Country Club Mustard Barrel Bank,** glass 10.00 12.00 10.00

☐ **Ladies Slipper,** old-fashioned style, height 2½" 55.00 65.00 60.00

☐ **Liberty Bell,** amber, iridescent, glass 10.00 14.00 10.00

☐ **Liberty Bell,** embossed lettering, height 4" ... 60.00 110.00 85.00

☐ **Lighthouse,** keeper's house with tall tower, domed top, on rocky base 110.00 210.00 185.00

☐ **Lucky Joe Mustard,** with paper lips, glass 15.00 23.00 18.00

☐ **Lucky Joe Mustard,** without paper lips, glass 10.00 14.00 12.00

☐ **Mail Box,** pot metal, type that attaches or inserts into a wall, height 5¼" 12.00 22.00 15.00

	Current Price Range		P/Y Average
☐ **Mail Box,** free standing type, four legs, "Letters" embossed on front, height 5½"	45.00	75.00	50.00
☐ **Mail Box,** small box type on pedestal stand, "Airmail U.S." embossed on front, height 6½"	60.00	110.00	85.00
☐ **Globe Savings Fund,** height 7"	85.00	135.00	110.00
☐ **Mickey Mouse With Banjo,** pot metal, sits on drum with one leg dangling over the side, height 5"	60.00	110.00	85.00
☐ **Miniature Taxi,** height 2½"	160.00	260.00	210.00
☐ **Rearing Horse On Oval Base,** "Beauty" printed on side of horse, height 4¾"			
☐ **Rearing Horse On Pebbled Base,** height 7½"	85.00	135.00	110.00
☐ **Reclining Man,** pottery, fat, hands behind head, feet crossed	35.00	85.00	50.00
☐ **½ red Goose Shoes,** name printed on goose's wing, height 3¾"	85.00	135.00	110.00
☐ **Refrigerator,** height 3¾"	40.00	50.00	45.00
☐ **Reid Library,** replica, height 5½"	60.00	110.00	85.00
☐ **Rocking Chair,** unusual design, openwork, height 6½"	160.00	260.00	210.00
☐ **Roly Poly Monkey,** tin, globe shaped body with ovoid head, cone hat, height 6"	30.00	40.00	35.00
☐ **Round Clown,** spherical with nub feet, height 2¼"	30.00	40.00	35.00

Mechanical Bank, *cast iron, Trick Dog, no underplate, repainted,* $125.00-$150.00

	Current Price Range		P/Y Average
☐ **Safe,** rectangular, free standing with four feet, height 3″	15.00	25.00	17.00
☐ **Safe,** free standing, double doors, height 6″ ..	45.00	75.00	55.00
☐ **Sailor,** saluting with one hand, holds paddle at his side with other hand, height 5¾″	85.00	135.00	110.00
☐ **Santa,** holds a toy in each hand, height 5½″	160.00	260.00	210.00
☐ **Santa With Pack,** peaked hat, simplistic face	135.00	185.00	160.00

BARBED WIRE

DESCRIPTION: Barbed wire was first used by Western farmers who installed it on their land to deter cattlemen. Railroads used it in some areas to keep cattle and buffalo off the tracks.

VARIATIONS: There are various types of barbed wire including ribbon wire, double round wire with two points and single round wire with two points.

ORIGIN: The first wire fencing was patented in 1853. Between 1868 and 1900 more than 750 patents were issued for various barbed wire styles.

COMMENTS: Barbed wire is collectible because of its historical importance during the settlement of western territories.

ADDITIONAL TIPS: Prices vary from $1 to more than $400 for a stick, which is an 18 inch piece of barbed wire.

The listings in this section are alphabetical according to barbed wire type. When available, the date of manufacture is given. Along with the price range, a previous year average price is included.

SINGLE ROUND WITH TWO POINTS

☐ **Bakers Single Strand,** c. 1883	3.15	5.15	3.50
☐ **Charles D. Rogers,** c. 1888	3.15	5.15	3.50
☐ **Dobbs and Booth Single Line,** c. 1875	5.15	7.15	5.50
☐ **Gunderson,** c. 1881	5.15	7.15	5.50
☐ **Half-Hitch,** c. 1877	3.50	7.00	3.75
☐ **H. M. Rose Wrap Barb,** c. 1877	3.25	5.25	4.00
☐ **L. E. Sunderland No Kink,** c. 1884	3.15	5.15	4.15
☐ **Mack's Alternate,** c. 1875	12.50	18.50	15.50

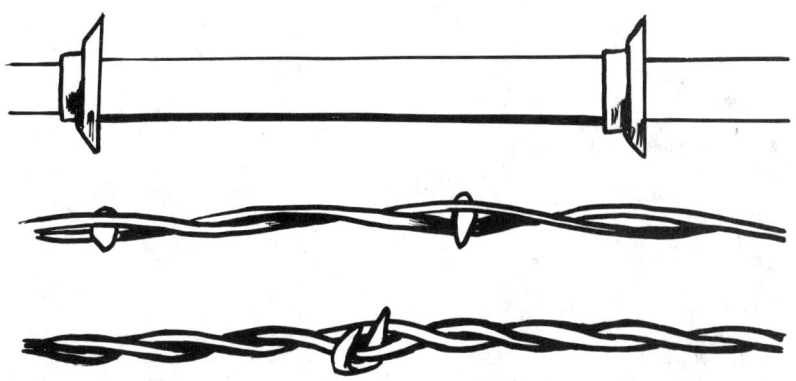

From Top to Bottom: *Brinkerhoff Ribbon wire, Daniel C. Stover two line wire and Scutt's Single Clip wire, late 1800s,* $20.00-$30.00

	Current Price Range		P/Y Average
☐ **Nelson Clip,** c. 1876	85.00	105.00	95.00
☐ **Putnams Flat Under Barb,** c. 1877	16.00	21.00	16.50
☐ **R. Emerson,** c. 1876	165.00	195.00	180.00
☐ **Rose Kink Line,** c. 1877	4.00	6.00	4.75
☐ **Single Line Wide Wrap Barb,** c. 1878	85.00	105.00	95.00
☐ **Sunderland Hammered Barb,** c. 1884	3.75	4.75	4.50
☐ **"Two Point Ripple Wire"**	7.50	9.50	8.50

DOUBLE ROUND WITH TWO POINTS

	Current Price Range		P/Y Average
☐ **Australian Loose Wrap**	4.00	6.00	3.75
☐ **Baker's Half-Round Barb**	2.50	3.50	2.00
☐ **C. H. Salisbury,** c. 1876	15.00	20.00	16.00
☐ **Decker Parallel,** c. 1884	7.00	9.00	6.00
☐ **Figure 8 Barb, Wright,** c. 1881	22.00	28.00	23.00
☐ **"Forked Tongue,"** c. 1887	4.00	6.00	4.50
☐ **Haish's Original "S,"** c. 1875	3.00	5.00	3.50
☐ **Glidden Barb on Both Lines**	4.50	7.50	5.00
☐ **J. D. Curtis "Twisted Point"**	2.50	3.50	2.50
☐ **J. D. Nadlehoffer,** c. 1878	45.00	60.00	50.00
☐ **Kangaroo Wire,** c. 1876	4.00	6.50	4.50
☐ **L. E. Sunderland Barb on Two Line Wire,** c. 1884	110.00	140.00	115.00
☐ **Missouri Hump Wire Staple Barb,** c. 1876 . . .	9.00	12.00	9.50
☐ **Peter P. Hill Parallel,** c. 1876	160.00	185.00	150.00
☐ **Rose Barb on Copper Lines,** c. 1877	5.50	7.50	5.50
☐ **W. Edenborn**	4.00	6.00	4.50
☐ **W. Edenborn's Locked in Barb,** c. 1885	3.00	5.00	3.50

RIBBON WIRE

	Current Price Range		P/Y Average
☐ **Allis Barbless Ribbon and Single Wire,** c. 1881	16.00	24.00	16.00

	Current Price Range		P/Y Average
☐ Allis Flat Ribbon Barb, c. 1892	16.00	24.00	16.00
☐ Brinkerhoff's Ribbon Barb, c. 1881	4.50	6.50	5.00
☐ Cast Iron Buckthorn	6.50	10.00	8.00
☐ Factory Splice on Thin Barbed Ribbon, c. 1892	40.00	55.00	40.00
☐ F. D. Ford Flat Ribbon, c. 1885	4.50	6.50	5.00
☐ John Hallner's "Greenbriar," c. 1878	1.75	4.00	2.00
☐ Harbaugh's Torn Ribbon, c. 1881	6.50	10.50	7.50
☐ Kelly's Split Ribbon, c. 1868	22.00	35.00	25.00
☐ Kelmer Ornamental Fence, c. 1885	16.00	20.00	16.00
☐ "Open Face" by Brinkerhoff, c. 1881	8.00	12.00	9.00
☐ Scutt's Smooth Ribbon	14.00	24.00	14.00
☐ Scutt's Ridged Ribbon, c. 1883	55.00	70.00	55.00
☐ Three-Quarter Inch Ribbon	10.00	16.00	10.00
☐ Very Light and Narrow Ribbon, c. 1868	60.00	70.00	60.00

BASEBALL CARDS

DESCRIPTION: Baseball cards usually have the picture of a baseball player on one side and the player's baseball record on the other. Baseball cards were made in different sizes depending on the era and the company.

ORIGIN: Baseball cards were introduced in the mid-1880s. At first they were made exclusively by tobacco companies for distribution with cigarettes or other tobacco products. From 1900 to 1930, other firms also printed baseball cards, but not on a regular basis. The modern era of baseball cards began during the Depression when gum companies began packaging cards along with bubblegum. At first, the motive was to simply boost gum sales, but as the public became more interested in the cards, card issuing developed into a thriving industry.

TYPES: There are basically two types of cards—cards from before the 1930s and the modern cards after the 1930s.

COMPANIES: Major companies that produced baseball cards in the late 1800s and early 1900s include Goodwin and Company, Allen and Ginter, P.H. Mayo and Brothers Tobacco Company and D. Buchner.

Since the early 1930s, modern card companies like Goudey Gum Company, Delong Gum Company and Frank H. Fleer have been major card producers. The Topps Chewing Gum Company, which began distributing cards in the 1970s, is one which most people associate with baseball cards.

ADDITIONAL INFORMATION: For more information, consult *The Official Price Guide to Baseball Cards,* published by The House of Collectibles.

Barney McCosky, *outfielder, Philadelphia Athletics, No. 84 in 1951 Bowman Gum card series,* **$2.00–$2.25**

MEAT PACKERS CARDS

Hunter's Wieners, set of 29 cards, 2″ x 4¾″, issued in 1955, depicts players, coaches, etc. of the St. Louis Cardinals, the cards are not numbered, this set was locally distributed in the St. Louis area, had a small printing and became very scarce within a few years of its appearance, the most valuable single card is that of Stan Musial, now selling for $85–110, the rest are bringing $70–90.

	G-VG		FINE	
☐ Complete set	650.00	825.00	1150.00	1475.00

Hygrade Meats, set of nine cards, 3¾″ x 4½″, issued in 1957, depicts members of the Seattle Pacific Coast League team, the cards are not numbered, values:

	G-VG		FINE	
☐ **Dick Aylward**	23.00	31.00	45.00	60.00
☐ **Bob Balcena**	23.00	31.00	45.00	60.00
☐ **Jim Dyck**	23.00	31.00	45.00	60.00
☐ **Mario Fricane**	23.00	31.00	45.00	60.00
☐ **Bill Glynn**	23.00	31.00	45.00	60.00
☐ **Bill Kennedy**	23.00	31.00	45.00	60.00
☐ **Ray Orteig**	23.00	31.00	45.00	60.00
☐ **Joe Taylor**	23.00	31.00	45.00	60.00

	G-VG		FINE	
☐ Maury Wills	55.00	70.00	100.00	135.00
☐ Complete set	280.00	340.00	500.00	750.00

Koester's Bread, set of 52 cards, 3½″ x 2″, issued in 1921, depicts members of the New York Giants and New York Yankees, and is entitled "World Series Issue" (these teams met in the World Series of 1921, the first so-called "subway series" to be played in New York), the cards are unnumbered, more valuable specimens:

☐ New York Giants—Frankie Frisch	18.00	24.00	39.00	49.00
☐ New York Giants—George Kelly	16.00	22.00	33.00	42.00
☐ New York Giants—John McGraw	19.00	25.00	40.00	50.00
☐ New York Giants—Charles D. Stengel	23.00	32.00	45.00	60.00
☐ New York Yankees—Waite Hoyt	15.00	20.00	30.00	39.00
☐ New York Yankees—Carl Mays	16.00	22.00	33.00	42.00
☐ New York Yankees—Babe Ruth	28.00	37.00	55.00	75.00
☐ Complete set	850.00	1075.00	1675.00	2000.00

Red Heart Dog Food, set of 33 cards, 2½″ x 3¾″, issued in 1954, depicts players from the American and National Leagues, the cards are not numbered, this set would appear to be somewhat scarcer than the current market value indicates.

☐ Complete set	65.00	85.00	120.00	155.00

Stahl-Meyer Frankfurters, set of 12 cards, 3¼″ x 4½″, issued in 1953, depicts players from the New York Yankees, New York Giants, and Brooklyn Dodgers, this set was distributed exclusively in the New York metropolitan area, the cards are not numbered, more valuable specimens:

☐ Roy Campanella	33.00	42.00	60.00	80.00
☐ Gil Hodges	45.00	60.00	85.00	110.00
☐ Monte Irvin	37.00	50.00	75.00	95.00
☐ Mickey Mantle	37.00	50.00	75.00	95.00
☐ Duke Snider	33.00	42.00	60.00	80.00
☐ Complete set	415.00	490.00	725.00	900.00

Sugardale Meats, set of four cards, 3¾″ x 5¼″, issued in 1962, depicts members of the Pittsburgh Pirates, cards are lettered, values:

☐ A. Dick Groat	10.00	14.00	20.00	28.00
☐ B. Roberto Clemente	17.00	22.00	33.00	42.00
☐ C. Don Hoak	10.00	14.00	20.00	28.00
☐ D. Dick Stuart	10.00	14.00	20.00	28.00
☐ Complete set	78.00	105.00	120.00	145.00

TOBACCO CARDS

Fatima Cigarettes, set of 16 cards, 5¾″ x 2½″, issued in 1913, depicts group portraits of all the major league teams then in existence (8 National League, 8 American League), the cards are not numbered, values:

American League

☐ Boston	24.00	33.00	45.00	60.00
☐ Chicago	16.00	22.00	31.00	40.00
☐ Cleveland	16.00	22.00	31.00	40.00
☐ Detroit	36.00	46.00	70.00	95.00

	G-VG		FINE	
☐ New York	32.00	42.00	60.00	80.00
☐ Philadelphia	17.00	22.00	33.00	42.00
☐ St. Louis	60.00	80.00	110.00	140.00
☐ Washington...........................	17.00	22.00	33.00	42.00
National League				
☐ Boston	16.00	22.00	31.00	40.00
☐ Brooklyn	16.00	22.00	31.00	40.00
☐ Chicago	16.00	22.00	31.00	40.00
☐ Cincinnati	16.00	22.00	31.00	40.00
☐ New York	16.00	22.00	31.00	40.00
☐ Philadelphia	16.00	22.00	31.00	40.00
☐ Pittsburgh	16.00	22.00	31.00	40.00
☐ St. Louis	33.00	43.00	65.00	85.00
☐ Complete set	475.00	600.00	875.00	1195.00

Fez Cigarettes, set of 126 cards (of which 100 are baseball players, the balance boxers), entitled "Prominent Baseball Players and Athletes," 5¾" x 8", issued in 1911, depicts players of the National and American Leagues, the identical set was also distributed with Old Mill cigarettes; values are the same regardless of the imprint, more valuable specimens:

	G-VG		FINE	
☐ # 5 Sam Crawford	20.00	27.00	40.00	55.00
☐ # 6 Hal Chase	17.00	22.00	33.00	43.00
☐ # 8 Fred Clarke	18.00	23.00	35.00	45.00
☐ # 9 Ty Cobb	23.00	32.00	45.00	57.00
☐ # 23 Nap Lajoie	20.00	27.00	40.00	55.00
☐ # 26 John McGraw	20.00	27.00	40.00	55.00
☐ # 27 Christy Mathewson	25.00	35.00	45.00	60.00
☐ # 35 Joe Tinker	16.00	21.00	32.00	41.00
☐ # 36 Tris Speaker	21.00	29.00	43.00	59.00
☐ # 39 Rube Waddell	24.00	38.00	47.00	62.00
☐ # 42 Cy Young........................	21.00	29.00	43.00	59.00
☐ # 47 Frank Chance	19.00	24.00	36.00	47.00
☐ # 80 Chief Bender	20.00	25.00	38.00	52.00
☐ # 87 Eddie Collins	21.00	27.00	40.00	55.00
☐ # 125 Ed Walsh	17.25	22.25	33.00	40.00
☐ Complete set (including boxers)	no recent recorded sales, price would be over $3000.00 (FINE)			

Note: Cards of boxers are omitted from the above listing.

BASKETS

TOPIC: The art of basketry is indeed a reflection of America's cultural past. Long before this nation's first colonization, the American Indian had achieved artistic excellence as a basket weaver. Indian baskets are said to be the world's finest. Each basket was woven for a specific purpose and with the utmost care. These baskets were not only used to hold food and water and for ceremonial purposes, but some were also used for cooking. The work is unique because only materials from nature—pine needles, straw, leaves, willow, porcupine quills, vines, reeds and grass were used. Dyes were made from bark, roots or berries. Their distinctive designs have made them sought-after by most basket enthusiasts.

TYPES: There are several types of basket construction. Wickerwork, the most common and widely used technique, is nothing more than an over and under pattern. Twining is similar except that two strands are twisted as they are woven over and under, producing a finer weave. Plaiting gives a checkerboard effect and can be either a tight weave or left with some open spaces. Twillwork is much the same except that a diagonal effect is achieved by changing the number of strands over which the weaver passes. Coiling is the most desirable weave for the collector. This technique has been carefully refined since its conception around 7000 BC. Fibers are wrapped around and stitched together to form the basket's shape. Most of these pieces were either used for ceremonial purposes or for holding liquids, since the containers made in this fashion were tightly woven and leakproof.

COMMENTS: Baskets are available in a wide range of prices and types. Because of their decorative appeal they are now avidly sought by collectors. They may be collected by general category such as Indian, Appalachian, Nantucket, etc., or simply acquired in a wide variety of types and styles.

ADDITIONAL TIPS: Baskets are easy to care for but a few basic rules must be followed.

1. Never wash an Indian basket. Dust it gently using a very soft sable artist's brush.

2. Do not subject Indian baskets to the sun as it will fade the patterns.

3. Do not wash any basket made of pine needles, straw, grass or leaves.

4. Willow, oak, hickory and rattan baskets may be washed in a mild solution of Murphy's Oil Soap and dried in a sunny location.

Basket, *Indian, coiled, 1880s,* $200.00–$220.00

	Current Price Range		P/Y Average
☐ **American Indian,** 10″ Dia.	180.00	220.00	155.00
☐ **Apache burden basket,** 2½″ x 2½″	25.00	35.00	22.50
☐ **Apache burden basket,** rawhide bottom, plain, 11½″ H.	300.00	375.00	300.00
☐ **Apache burden basket,** geometric pattern, tin cones hanging from leather straps, 6½″ x 5″	60.00	75.00	62.00
☐ **Apache burden basket,** negative pattern, tin cones hanging from leather straps, 12″ x 10½″	225.00	300.00	238.00
☐ **Apache coiled storage basket,** round body, dark brown with geometric motifs, 12½″ H.	725.00	925.00	800.00
☐ **Apache coiled storage basket,** round body, flaring rim, dark brown with animals and human figures, 16¾″ H.	725.00	925.00	800.00
☐ **Apache coiled basket,** flat base, dark brown with snowflake motif, 8⅜″ Dia.	325.00	425.00	350.00
☐ **Apache grain barrel basket,** geometric design with human figures, 10″ x 11″	375.00	475.00	400.00
☐ **Apache plaque basket,** geometric design, 16″ x 5″	550.00	650.00	575.00
☐ **Apache miniature basket,** star design, 5½″ x 1″	145.00	210.00	160.00
☐ **Apache tray,** 10½″ Dia., c. 1890s	110.00	160.00	125.00
☐ **Apache wedding basket,** 13″ Dia., c. 1880	30.00	45.00	32.00
☐ **Bannock berry basket,** 8″ x 8½″	55.00	80.00	58.00
☐ **Buttocks basket,** tightly woven splint, 7″	150.00	190.00	155.00

	Current Price Range		P/Y Average

- [ ] **California,** tightly woven, light brown, diamond motif, 5¾″ Dia. 150.00 175.00 138.00
- [ ] **Caushatta effigy baskets,** pine cones and needles: Crawfish, 9″ x 6½″ 25.00 35.00 22.50
- [ ] Crab, 6″ x 5″ 25.00 35.00 22.50
- [ ] Alligator, 9″ x 2¾″ 25.00 35.00 22.50
- [ ] Turtle, 6½″ x 3″ 25.00 35.00 22.50
- [ ] **Cheese basket,** splint 125.00 175.00 100.00
- [ ] **Cheese shaker,** round, 12 ″ Dia. 250.00 275.00 225.00
- [ ] **Chehalis basket,** geometric and cross design, 4¼″ x 6¼″ 200.00 250.00 160.00
- [ ] **Chemehuevi basket,** two concentric geometric bands, 11½″ x 2″ 350.00 450.00 375.00
- [ ] **Clothes basket,** round with two handles 75.00 95.00 62.00
- [ ] **Cowlitz lidded basket,** 3″ x 4¼″ 80.00 130.00 100.00
- [ ] **Drying basket,** New England, 30″ x 48″, shallow rim, 1850s 325.00 500.00 330.00
- [ ] **Field basket,** oak splint, 1880s 100.00 175.00 110.00
- [ ] **Havasupi coiled basket,** triangle design, 11¾″ Dia. 175.00 200.00 150.00
- [ ] **Hopi coiled basket,** rectangular body in brown, orange and yellow raincloud and thunder motif, 5⅝″ 110.00 160.00 125.00
- [ ] **Hopi corn sifter basket,** wicker with hoop around top, spiral design 80.00 110.00 82.00
- [ ] **Hopi coiled bowl basket,** floral design, 9¼″ Dia. 90.00 140.00 110.00
- [ ] **Hopi coiled plaque,** 14½″ Dia., c. 1930 ...... 110.00 160.00 125.00
- [ ] **Hopi tray,** mythological motif, 11″ Dia. 80.00 130.00 100.00
- [ ] **Japanese,** tightly woven in brown and tan, circular, 7½″ Dia. 55.00 80.00 62.00
- [ ] **Karok basket,** oval, bottom inverted, 10″ x 7″ 110.00 160.00 125.00
- [ ] **Klamath tray,** 14″ Dia., c. 1900 .... 210.00 260.00 225.00
- [ ] **Laundry basket,** oak splint, 1910 .... 50.00 70.00 55.00
- [ ] **Lilooet basket,** 12½″ x 16″ 160.00 210.00 175.00
- [ ] **Maidu basket tray,** 8½″ Dia. 60.00 80.00 65.00
- [ ] **Makah basket,** zigzag designs, 7″ Dia. 55.00 80.00 62.00
- [ ] **Mandan basket,** wood splint, circular 180.00 230.00 200.00
- [ ] **Mission basket tray,** 12″ Dia. 330.00 410.00 360.00
- [ ] **Miwok basket,** 7″ Dia., c. 1900 .... 230.00 280.00 250.00
- [ ] **Modoc basketcap,** diamond design, 6″ Dia. .. 120.00 140.00 125.00
- [ ] **Nantucket lightship basket,** 5″ x 10″ 400.00 465.00 415.00
- [ ] **Navajo wedding basket,** 10″ Dia. 130.00 180.00 150.00
- [ ] **Nootka whaler's hat,** 10½″ x 10½″ 230.00 280.00 250.00
- [ ] **Paiute coiled basket,** exterior is beaded, 5″ Dia. 180.00 210.00 182.00
- [ ] **Paiute lidded basket,** 10″ H., c. 1900 .... 90.00 125.00 100.00
- [ ] **Paiute water jar,** horse-hair handles, 5½″ x 7½″ 80.00 110.00 82.00
- [ ] **Panamint basket,** reverse diamond design, 10½″ x 4″ 310.00 410.00 350.00
- [ ] **Papago basket,** geometric design, 13″ Dia. 80.00 110.00 82.00
- [ ] **Papago coiled basket,** body woven in dark brown with bands of swastikas, 11⅝″ Dia. 230.00 280.00 250.00

	Current Price Range		P/Y Average

☐ **Papago plaque,** concentric square design, 15″ Dia. 130.00 180.00 150.00

☐ **Papago waste paper basket,** men and dogs motif, 10″ Dia. 100.00 130.00 110.00

☐ **Pima basket bowl,** 16″ Dia. 260.00 335.00 295.00

☐ **Pima coiled basket,** flat base, flaring body, dark brown with pattern of human figures, 11¼″ Dia. 260.00 360.00 300.00

☐ **Pima coiled basket,** shallow, dark brown with crosses in the field, 9¼″ Dia. 110.00 160.00 125.00

☐ **Pima grain barrel,** geometric design, 11″ Dia. 430.00 530.00 475.00

☐ **Pima plaque,** 11″ Dia. 180.00 230.00 200.00

☐ **Pomo basket,** decorated with feathers, 12″ Dia. 180.00 230.00 200.00

☐ **Sewing basket,** wicker 55.00 80.00 58.00

☐ **Skokomish berry basket,** 7″ x 8″ 110.00 135.00 112.50

☐ **Southwest coiled storage basket,** flat base, dark brown with arrow motifs, 27″ H. 730.00 830.00 775.00

☐ **Splint collecting basket,** tightly woven, 8″ x 9″ 55.00 85.00 62.00

☐ **Splint cradle,** hooded, c. early 19th century, 19″ x 8″ 100.00 130.00 110.00

☐ **Splint hickory basket,** open handles 55.00 80.00 58.00

☐ **Splint,** oval, with wooded handles 145.00 195.00 150.00

☐ **Splint,** back pack 65.00 165.00 90.00

☐ **Split,** oak buttocks 55.00 80.00 58.00

☐ **Split,** oak buttocks, large 80.00 160.00 120.00

☐ **Tlingit basket,** geometric design, 6″ Dia. 330.00 380.00 350.00

☐ **Tlingit basket,** 5″ Dia., c. 1880 .... 330.00 380.00 350.00

☐ **Tlingit lidded basket,** 4½″ x 6½″ 430.00 510.00 460.00

☐ **Tlingit twined spruce root basket,** cylindrical body, pale yellow bands with orange zigzag decoration, 5″ Dia. 360.00 460.00 400.00

☐ **Tulare basket,** step pattern, squaw stitch, 7½″ Dia. 130.00 210.00 162.00

☐ **Tulare basket,** rattlesnake design 110.00 135.00 112.50

☐ **Tulare coiled basket,** flat base, rounded sides, rattlesnake bands in black and reddish brown, 14½″ Dia. 1250.00 1350.00 1150.00

☐ **Washo basket,** tightly woven, band design, 7″ Dia. 85.00 115.00 80.00

☐ **Washo basket,** geometric design, 7″ 65.00 95.00 75.00

☐ **Washo coiled trinket basket,** red, blue, black and green on white ground, 4¼″ Dia. 110.00 160.00 125.00

BATMAN

DESCRIPTION: Batman is one of the early comic strip superheroes.

VARIATIONS: Included among Batman memorabilia are comics, toy cars and toy figures.

ORIGIN: The first Batman comic was published more than 40 years ago, and "Batman" was a popular TV show in the 1960s.

ADDITIONAL TIPS: Only Batman memorabilia has been listed here. For Batman comics, look in the comics chapter of this book. For further information, see *The Official Price Guide to Comic Books and Collectibles,* published by The House of Collectibles.

Batman Coloring Book,
Western Publishing Company, Inc.
$4.00–$6.00

	Current Price Range		P/Y Average
☐ **Bank,** ceramic figure of Batman, 7″	30.00	45.00	37.50
☐ **Bank,** ceramic figures of Batman and Robin, c. 1966	70.00	90.00	75.00
☐ **Batbike,** toy, c. 1978	5.00	7.00	6.00
☐ **Batmobile,** toy, c. 1966	5.00	7.00	6.00
☐ **Batmobile And Batbike,** Corgi, c. 1968	10.00	15.00	12.50
☐ **Book,** *Batman and Robin,* hardcover, *From The 30s to the 70s,* 7½″ x 10½″, Bonanza, c. 1971	12.50	17.50	15.00
☐ **Book,** *Batman and Robin: From Alfred to Zowie!* by Ruthanna Thomas, Golden Press, 1966, book is die cut in shape of Batman's head	1.75	2.50	1.75
☐ **Book And Record Set,** *Gorilla City and Mystery of the Scarecrow Corpse,* Peter Pan Industries/National Periodical Publications, 1976	4.50	5.75	4.50
☐ **Bookends,** Batman and Robin, 4″ x 7″, c. 1966	25.00	50.00	35.00
☐ **Bubble Bath,** Avon, plastic Batmobile bottle which originally contained bubble bath	7.00	10.00	8.00
☐ **Button,** Batman and Robin Official Member, full color, 3½″, mid 1960s	6.50	8.50	7.00
☐ **Button,** lithographed tin, Batman in flight, TV inspired, 1966	7.50	11.00	8.50
☐ **Charm Bracelet,** with five figures (Batman, Robin, Penguin, The Riddler, The Joker), on original store card, 1966	12.00	16.00	12.00
☐ **Clock,** Bradley/National Periodical Publications, lucite desk model, c. 1966	15.00	18.00	16.00
☐ **Coloring Book,** Western Publishing Co., with the Western series number 1002, undated	4.50	6.25	5.00
☐ **Coloring Book,** *Batman Meets Blockbuster,* Whitman, 8″ x 10¾″, 1956	4.00	4.75	4.20
☐ **Costume,** with mask, gray outfit, large yellow monogram with black bat on chest, blue cape, black half-mask, c. 1960	30.00	40.00	33.00
☐ **Figurine,** plastic, Wilton/National Periodical Publications, 4″	2.50	3.50	2.65
☐ **Game,** Hasbro, 1965	11.00	15.00	11.00
☐ **Game,** board game, Milton Bradley/National Periodical Publications, assorted playing pieces, box measures 9½″ x 19″	12.00	16.00	12.00
☐ **Jigsaw Puzzle,** three scenes of Batman and The Joker taken from Neal Adams' artwork in Batman Comics #251	20.00	25.00	20.50
☐ **License Plate,** 4″ x 7¼″, 1966	6.75	9.50	7.50
☐ **License Plate,** metal, 6″ x 12″, National Periodical Publications, c. 1966	6.00	9.00	7.50
☐ **Lunch Box And Thermos Set**	35.00	45.00	26.00
☐ **Model Kit,** Aurora, unopened, 1964	30.00	38.00	34.00
☐ **Mug,** white plastic with illustrations of Batman and Robin by Carmine Infantino	31.00	40.00	30.00
☐ **Music Box,** Price/National Periodical Publications, figural ceramic, 7″, late 1970s	24.50	31.00	25.50

	Current Price Range		P/Y Average
☐ **Music Box,** The Joker, Price/National Periodical Publications, figural ceramic, 7″, late 1970s ...	22.00	29.00	24.00
☐ **Music Box,** Penguin, Price/National Periodical Publications, figural ceramic, 7″, late 1970s ...	22.00	29.00	24.00
☐ **Music Box,** The Riddler, Price/National Periodical Publications, figural ceramic, 7″, late 1970s	22.00	29.00	24.00
☐ **Paint By Numbers Set,** Hasbro, reproduction of the cover of Batman Comics #1 to be colored	6.75	11.00	7.50
☐ **Phonograph Record,** 12″ LP on 20th Century Fox label, sleeve has photos of Burt Ward and Adam West with wording, "Exclusive Original Television Soundtrack Album . . . Hear the Actual Television Voices of Batman and Robin, Plus Great Villains: The Penguin, Zelda, Mr. Freeze, The Riddler," etc.	23.00	30.00	21.50
☐ **Presto Paints,** undated	19.00	24.00	21.00
☐ **Token,** Batcoin #16, picturing Robin and The Riddler, TV inspired, 1966	4.25	5.50	4.00
☐ **Wallet,** 1966	12.00	16.50	13.00
☐ **Wristwatch,** Dabs, in box, c. 1977	32.00	39.00	32.50

BATTLESTAR GALACTICA

TOPIC: Battlestar Galactica was originally a science fiction movie and later a television show. It starred Lorne Greene, Richard Hatch and Dirk Benedict. The story involves a group of humans whose ancestors settled a distant part of the universe. These people are attacked and nearly annihilated by hostile "Cylons" (alien creatures who control an army of robots). The survivors flee in a small fleet of spaceships led by a battlestar (fighting spaceship) called "The Galactica." The fleet's destination is earth. The Cylons are in constant pursuit.

TYPES: Memorabilia from Battlestar Galactica may come in the form of trading cards, toys, posters or other promotional items.

PERIOD: The television show ran in 1978.

COMMENTS: Although Battlestar Galactica experienced a limited run on television, it was popular and collectors still treasure memorabilia from the show.

Battlestar Galactica Rub N' Play Magic Transfer Set, *made by Colorforms, under license from Universal City Studios, set of transfer sheets with likenesses of characters, 1978,* **$3.00-$5.00**

ADDITIONAL TIPS: For more complete listings, please refer to *The Official Price Guide to Science Fiction and Fantasy Books and Collectibles,* published by the House of Collectibles.

	Current Price Range		P/Y Average
☐ **Posters,** set of four, small	12.00	15.00	13.50
☐ **Poster,** standard size	10.00	13.00	11.50
☐ **Scripts,** group of four, "The Super Scout" and "The Night the Cyclone Landed," total of 219 pages	40.00	50.00	42.00
☐ **Trading cards,** full set of 132, Topps, 2½" x 3½", 1978	12.00	15.00	13.00
☐ **Trading Card,** Topps, A Direct Hit, #116, 2½" x 3½", 1978	.10	.13	.11
☐ **Trading card,** Topps, A Planet in Peril, #101, 2½" x 3½", 1978........................	.09	.12	.10
☐ **Trading card,** Topps, A World in Flames, 11, 2½" x 3½", 1978........................	.09	.12	.10
☐ **Trading card,** Topps, Adar's Final Moments, #13, 2½" x 3½", 1978	.09	.12	.10
☐ **Trading card,** Topps, Annihilation of the Human Colonies, #19, 2½" x 3½", 1978	.10	.12	.11
☐ **Trading card,** Topps, An Ovion Warrior, #59, 2½" x 3½", 1978.........................	.10	.12	.11
☐ **Trading card,** Topps, Conferring with Seetol, #55, 2½" x 3½", 1978	.09	.13	.11

	Current Price Range		P/Y Average
☐ **Trading card,** Topps, Escape from Fiery Death, #57, 2½" x 3½", 1978	.09	.12	.10
☐ **Trading card,** Topps, For the Love of Gold Cubits, #7, 2½" x 3½", 1978	.10	.13	.11
☐ **Trading card,** Topps, Hitting Outrageously High Notes, #70, 2½" x 3½", 1978	.09	.12	.10
☐ **Trading card,** Topps, Landram to the Rescue, #123, 2½" x 3½", 1978	.09	.12	.10
☐ **Trading card,** Topps, Night of the Metal Monsters, #90, 2½" x 3½", 1978	.09	.12	.11
☐ **Trading card,** Topps, Panic in Caprica Mall, #15, 2½" x 3½", 1978	.10	.13	.11
☐ **Trading card,** Topps, Richard Hatch is Captain Apollo, #3, 2½" x 3½", 1978	.09	.12	.10
☐ **Trading card,** Topps, The President's Council, #14, 2½" x 3½", 1978	.09	.13	.11
☐ **Trading card,** Topps, War of the Wiles, #69, 2½" x 3½", 1978	.09	.12	.11
☐ **Trading card,** Topps, Where the Elite Meet, #64, 2½" x 3½", 1978	.10	.12	.11

THE BEATLES

VARIATIONS: There is an unlimited variety of Beatles memorabilia. Records are quite collectible as well as buttons, posters and other souvenir items.

ORIGIN: The Beatles formed in Liverpool, England in the late 50s and early 60s. Band members included Paul McCartney, John Lennon, Ringo Starr and George Harrison. They took America by storm in 1964 when they appeared on the Ed Sullivan Show. Credited with starting the musical British invasion, The Beatles contributed much to rock and roll.

COMMENTS: The Beatles, along with Elvis Presley, are more collected than other recording artists. From the start of Beatlemania, anything Beatle related has become collectible.

ADDITIONAL TIPS: The listings in this section include memorabilia and records. The memorabilia section is listed alphabetically by item. Records are also listed alphabetically by title, followed by whether the record is an LP or a 45, the record company, issue number and other pertinent information.

For further information, refer to *The Official Price Guide to Records,* or *The Official Price Guide to Music Collectibles,* published by The House of Collectibles.

Beatles, *still, if signed would be worth considerably more,*
$1.50-$2.00

	Current Price Range		P/Y Average
☐ **Bandaid Dispenser,** promotional item from "Help"	3.00	6.00	3.50
☐ **Bank,** date register bank, with pictures and signatures, 1964	15.00	30.00	22.50
☐ **Belt buckle,** with "Beatles" and illustrations ..	60.00	80.00	70.00
☐ **Book,** *A Cellarful of Noise* by Brian Epstein, clothbound reprint of the now-scarce 1964 first edition	15.00	22.00	15.00
☐ **Book,** *A Day in the Life* by Tom Schultheiss, paperback, 334 pages	10.00	15.00	9.50
☐ **Book,** *A Hard Day's Night* by John Burke, published by Dell, paperback	15.00	25.00	17.50
☐ **Book,** *A Spaniard in the Works* by John Lennon, clothbound first edition	25.00	35.00	22.50

This price represents the average range but published offers differ considerably. When autographed by Lennon it is, of course, worth substantially more.

	Current Price Range		P/Y Average

☐ **Book,** *The Beatles Down Under* by Glenn Baker, paperback, 128 pages **15.00 20.00 15.00**
Story of the group's Australian tour.

☐ **Book,** *The Beatles' England* by David Bacon and Norman Maslov, paperback, 138 pages **11.00 16.00 12.50**

☐ **Book,** *The Beatles for the Record,* authorship uncredited, 96 pages, measures 12" square ... **10.00 17.00 9.50**

☐ **Book,** *The Beatles Forever* by Nicholas Schaffner, clothbound, 218 pages **15.00 20.00 15.00**
An identical edition in paperback is selling at $6–8.

☐ **Book,** *The Beatles in Their Own Words* by Miles (author who uses no last name), paperback ... **7.00 10.00 6.00**

☐ **Book,** *The Beatles on Record* by J. P. Russell, paperback, 682 pages **7.00 10.00 6.00**

☐ **Book,** *The Beatles' Record in Australia* by Bruce Hamlin, paperback, published in Australia **10.00 17.00 9.50**

☐ **Book,** *The Beatles Reader* by Charles P. Neises, clothbound **15.00 20.00 15.00**

☐ **Book,** *The Beatles Who's Who* by Bill Harry, paperback, 190 pages **8.00 15.00 9.00**
Biographies of everyone who played a role in the Beatles' lives.

☐ **Book,** *The Book of Lennon* by Bill Harry, paperback, 223 pages **10.00 15.00 10.50**

☐ **Book,** *Come Together* by Jon Wiener, paperback, 379 pages. **13.00 15.00 11.50**

☐ **Book,** *The Complete Beatles Quiz Book* by Edwin Goodgold and Dan Carlinsky, clothbound, 128 pages **3.50 5.00 3.25**

☐ **Book,** *Dakota Days* by John Green, clothbound, 260 pages **14.00 20.00 12.50**

☐ **Book,** *George Harrison Yesterday and Today* by Ross Michaels, paperback, 96 pages, published in Great Britain **6.00 8.00 7.00**

☐ **Book,** *Growing Up With the Beatles* by Rom Schaumburg, paperback, 160 pages **8.00 10.00 8.50**

☐ **Book,** *In His Own Write* by John Lennon, clothbound first edition **50.00 75.00 27.50**
Multiply that by about ten if it's personally autographed.

☐ **Book,** *Lennon and Me* by Pete Shotton, paperback, 399 pages **3.50 5.00 4.00**

☐ **Book,** *Lennon and McCartney* by Malcolm Doney, clothbound, 126 pages **10.00 12.50 9.50**

☐ **Book,** *John Lennon: A Family Album* by Nishi F. Saimaru, paperback, 128 pages **35.00 43.00 36.00**

☐ **Book,** *John Lennon in His Own Words,* by Miles (author who uses no last name), paperback ... **7.50 10.00 6.00**

☐ **Button,** movie promo, "I've Got My Beatles Movie Tickets, Have You?", 2¼" **1.50 2.00 1.15**

☐ **Car mascots,** bobbing headed Beatles, set of four **700.00 900.00 800.00**

	Current Price Range		P/Y Average
☐ **Cards,** autographed wallet photo card, 2½″ x 3″, 1964	1.00	1.50	.88
☐ **Cards,** gum cards, set of 65, question and answer series, color, Topps, 1964	50.00	65.00	52.50
☐ **Cards,** gum cards, set of 50, Yellow Submarine, Primrose Confectionary (Britain), 1968	100.00	125.00	105.00
☐ **Card,** individual gum card, question and answer series, color, 1964	.80	1.50	1.00
☐ **Card,** individual gum card, Yellow Submarine, Primrose Confectionary (Britain), 1968	1.30	2.25	1.65
☐ **Cards,** playing cards with picture of group, 1964	4.00	7.50	4.75
☐ **Change purse,** picture of the Beatles, 1964	2.50	5.00	3.25
☐ **Coasters,** set of six plastic coasters with illustrations and words, c. 1960s	30.00	50.00	30.00
☐ **Coloring book,** "Beatles Coloring Book," Saalfield Publishing Co., 1964	51.00	67.50	57.50
☐ **Comb,** John Lennon promotional	1.00	3.00	1.00
☐ **Coin,** brass commemorative U.S. visit coin, 1964	7.00	15.00	10.00
☐ **Dolls,** blow up dolls, 16″, 1966, set of four	50.00	75.00	50.00
☐ **Doll,** John Lennon, fully dressed, base of doll is a radio, 8½″	15.00	25.00	19.50
☐ **Game,** The Beatles Flip Your Wig Game, Milton Bradley, 1964	40.00	55.00	47.50
☐ **Hair brush,** 1964	10.00	15.00	12.50
☐ **Ink stamp,** self inking stamps, set of four, 1964	9.50	20.00	15.00
☐ **Jigsaw puzzle,** for fan club members, not sold in stores, 8½″ x 11″, 1964	7.50	15.00	10.00
☐ **Key fob,** figural, promotional item for 1965 Shea Stadium Concert	1.00	2.00	1.15
☐ **Key ring,** John Lennon, "Walls and Bridges" album, 1972	1.00	2.00	1.15
☐ **Lunchbox,** laminated tin with color drawings of the Beatles	200.00	215.00	192.50
☐ **Magazine,** Rolling Stone, featuring John Lennon as "Man of the Year," 1970	35.00	50.00	37.50
☐ **Mirror,** black and white picture pocket mirror, features picture of group playing, 1964	1.00	2.00	1.15
☐ **Mirror,** color picture of the Beatles, 1964	2.00	5.00	2.25
☐ **Pencil,** picture of Beatles, set of four, 1964	3.50	4.00	3.50
☐ **Pencil case,** picture of Beatles, 1964	7.50	17.50	10.00
☐ **Pen,** magic picture pen, color photo	2.00	6.00	4.00
☐ **Pennant,** felt pennant with "Beatles" in block letters and illustrations of the group	50.00	65.00	50.00
☐ **Pin,** flasher pin flashes from group shot to four heads	1.75	3.50	2.25
☐ **Pin,** "I Like Beatles" flasher pin	1.75	2.50	1.50
☐ **Pin,** "I'm a Beatles Booster," 1965	1.50	2.00	1.15
☐ **Pin,** John Lennon "Give Peace a Chance"	1.50	2.00	1.15
☐ **Pin,** John Lennon "Remember Love," 1¼″	1.00	2.75	1.15
☐ **Pin,** official fan pin, 2¼″, 1965	1.00	1.75	1.15
☐ **Pin,** tin litho picture of Beatles, 1964	1.00	1.75	1.15

	Current Price Range		P/Y Average
☐ **Pin,** Yellow Submarine, 1966	1.00	1.75	1.15
☐ **Pocketbook,** canvas, illustrated with "Beatles" and pictures	42.00	54.00	45.00
☐ **Pocket knife,** John Lennon, "In Memory of a Great Beatle," 1980	1.50	3.50	2.00
☐ **Poster,** Beatles at London Paladium, full color, 20" x 27", 1963, reissued in 1975	1.50	3.50	2.00
☐ **Poster,** fan club souvenir poster, full color, 20" x 30", 1968	175.00	250.00	200.00
☐ **Poster,** features 12 full color Beatles photos, 24" x 28", 1979	2.00	4.00	2.50
☐ **Poster,** John Lennon commemorative, 1980 ..	5.00	10.00	2.00
☐ **Poster,** John Lennon, "Imagine There's No Lennon," 17" x 25", 1980	5.00	10.00	2.25
☐ **Poster,** record shop poster advertising "A Hard Day's Night"	175.00	230.00	172.50
☐ **Press kit,** Paul McCartney, Apple, 1970	75.00	90.00	70.00
☐ **Press kit,** Paul McCartney and Wings, 1973 ..	85.00	125.00	95.00
☐ **Program,** George Harrison, 1974 concert tour program	5.00	7.50	5.25
☐ **Record fob,** metal with faces of the Beatles, 1964	1.00	2.00	1.15
☐ **Ring,** individual color flasher ring, set of four ..	1.00	2.00	1.15
☐ **Ruler,** 12", with signatures, photos and information, 1965	3.50	6.00	4.00
☐ **Scarf,** colored with pictures and signatures, 1964	6.00	15.00	8.50
☐ **Strap,** for carrying schoolbooks, features "Beatles" with musical notes	15.00	22.00	17.50
☐ **Tablecloth,** printed with illustrations of the Beatles	75.00	100.00	72.50
☐ **Tickets,** concert tickets	45.00	100.00	47.50
☐ **Tie tack,** official fan club item, black and gold, 1964	2.00	5.00	2.25
☐ **Tie tack,** raised figural face, set of four, 1964	30.00	35.00	12.00
☐ **Whistle,** police style from the movie "Help," 1966	3.50	5.00	2.75
☐ **Wig,** long hair Beatles wig	40.00	60.00	37.50
☐ **Wrist watch,** full color picture on dial	10.00	50.00	20.00
☐ **Writing table,** cover photo of the Beatles			35.00

RECORDS

☐ **Abbey Road,** LP, Apple, 383, stereo	8.00	20.00	14.00
☐ **All You Need Is Love/Baby You're A Rich Man,** 45, Capitol, 5964, promotional copy	40.00	80.00	57.50
☐ Orange label	2.50	5.00	3.25
☐ **And I Love Her/If I Fell,** 45, Capitol, 5235, orange label	2.50	5.00	3.25
☐ Picture sleeve	15.00	30.00	18.00
☐ **The Beatles,** LP, Apple, 101, stereo	15.00	30.00	21.50
☐ **The Beatles, 1962–1966,** 2 LP, Apple, 3403, stereo	12.00	16.00	9.50

	Current Price Range		P/Y Average
☐ **The Beatles, 1967–1970,** 2LP, Apple, 3404, stereo	12.00	16.00	9.50
☐ **The Beatles Second Album,** LP, Capitol, 2080, stereo, green label	11.00	25.00	17.00
☐ Black label	9.00	19.00	13.00
☐ **Christmas Fan Club Album,** LP, Apple, 100, stereo	35.00	80.00	54.00
☐ **Come Together/Something,** 45, Apple, 2654, Apple and Capitol markings	4.00	10.00	6.25
☐ **Do You Want To Know A Secret?/Thank You Girl,** 45, Capitol Starline, 6064	8.00	25.00	14.00
☐ **Do You Want To Know A Secret?/Thank You Girl,** 45, Vee Jay, 587, label name in brackets	6.00	15.00	9.50
☐ **Do You Want To Know A Secret?/Thank You Girl,** 45, Vee Jay, 587, label name in oval with a picture sleeve	35.00	65.00	41.00
☐ **The Early Beatles,** LP, Capitol, 2309, stereo, green label	8.50	15.00	10.00
☐ Black label	8.00	16.00	11.25
☐ **Eight Days A Week/I Don't Want To Spoil The Party,** 45, Capitol, 5371, orange label	3.00	5.00	3.25
☐ **From Me To You/Please Please Me,** 45, Vee Jay, 581, picture sleeve with label name in brackets	55.00	130.00	80.00
☐ **A Hard Day's Night/I Should Have Known Better,** 45, Capitol, 5222, orange label	3.00	6.00	3.25
☐ Picture sleeve	10.00	22.50	14.50
☐ **Hey Jude/Revolution,** 45, Apple, 2276	5.00	10.00	4.75
☐ **Hey Jude,** LP, Apple, 385, stereo	8.00	15.00	6.50
☐ **I Want To Hold Your Hand/I Saw Her Standing There,** 45, Apple, 5112	5.00	10.00	4.00
☐ **I Want To Hold Your Hand/I Saw Her Standing There,** 45, Capitol, 5112, orange label	4.00	6.00	3.00
☐ Orange, yellow label	5.00	10.00	5.75
☐ **In The Beginning,** LP, Polydor, 24-4504, stereo	7.00	13.00	13.00
☐ **Lady Madonna/The Inner Light,** 45, Capitol, 2138, orange label	4.50	7.50	3.25
☐ Orange and yellow label	15.00	20.00	5.75
☐ **Let It Be/You Know My Name,** 45, Apple, 2764			
☐ **Let It Be,** LP, Apple, 3401, stereo	4.00	9.00	4.00
☐ **The Long and Winding Road/For Your Blue,** 45, Apple, 2832	4.00	9.00	4.00
☐ Picture sleeve	11.00	35.00	14.75
☐ **Magical Mystery Tour,** LP, Apple, 2835, stereo	10.00	18.00	9.50
☐ **Meet The Beatles,** LP, Apple, 2047, stereo . . .	6.00	12.00	6.50
☐ **Meet The Beatles,** LP, Capitol, 2047, stereo, green label	13.00	18.00	10.00
☐ Black label	22.50	35.50	15.50
☐ **My Bonnie/The Saints,** 45, Polydor, 66-833, Tony Sheridan and the Beatles, most valuable Beatles 45	1500.00	3100.00	2200.00

	Current Price Range		P/Y Average
☐ **Please Please Me/Ask Me Why,** 45, Vee Jay, 498, Beatles is misspelled, "Beattles," and it is in thick letters	145.00	315.00	202.50
☐ **Revolver,** LP, Apple, 2576, stereo	8.00	18.00	8.00
☐ **Revolver,** LP, EMI, 2576, mono	9.00	15.00	10.00
☐ **Rubber Soul,** LP, Apple, 2442, stereo	8.00	18.00	8.00
☐ **Rubber Soul,** LP, EMI, 1267, mono	15.00	25.00	15.00
☐ **Sergeant Pepper's Lonely Hearts Club Band,** LP, Apple, 2652, stereo	8.00	16.00	8.00
☐ **Twist And Shout,** LP, Capitol, 6054, stereo ...	9.50	20.00	12.00
☐ **With the Beatles,** LP, EMI, 1206, mono	7.00	10.00	6.00
☐ **Twist And Shout/There's A Place,** 45, Capitol Starline, 6061	10.00	25.00	6.50
☐ **Yellow Submarine,** LP, Apple, 153, stereo	8.00	14.00	4.00
☐ **Yesterday/Act Naturally,** 45, Apple, 5498	4.00	8.00	4.00
☐ **Yesterday/Act Naturally,** 45, Capitol, 5498, orange label	5.00	9.00	3.25
☐ Orange and yellow label, picture sleeve	11.50	32.00	16.75
☐ **Yesterday And Today,** LP, Apple, 2553, stereo			
☐ **Yesterday And Today,** LP, Capitol, 2553, stereo, butcher cover	295.00	585.00	420.00
☐ Revised cover	150.00	300.00	210.00
☐ New Cover	8.00	22.00	14.50

BEER CANS

DESCRIPTION: Beer cans are highly collectible items. Beer cans were produced in different shapes, the most common include flat tops, cone tops and pull tabs.

PERIOD: Cans were first produced by breweries in 1935. The first cans were called flat tops because of the shape of the can top. Cone tops were produced shortly afterward, but they were not as popular with consumers, therefore by the 1960s they were virtually extinct. Today, cans with pull tabs are being produced.

ADDITIONAL TIPS: There are different ways to have a beer can collection. Some hobbyists collect full cans or empties while others collect unfinished cans called flats. See *The Official Price Guide to Beer Cans,* published by the House of Collectibles, for more detailed information about this subject.

	Current Price Range		P/Y Average

CONE TOPS

☐ **Altes Lager,** Tivoli, 12 oz., silver and black—CROWNTAINER	45.00	55.00	45.00
☐ **American,** American, 12 oz., red, white, blue and gold, brand name in blue script lettering	105.00	127.50	112.00
☐ **Bavarian's Old Style,** Bavarian, 12 oz., white, gold and red, brand name in gold lettering (very ornate) with red initials	72.00	90.00	77.00
☐ **Becker's Uinta Club Mellow,** Becker, 12 oz., silver, blue and red, bucking bronco symbol	140.00	175.00	150.00
Note: This is the correct spelling: Uinta. But it frequently appears as "unita" on trade lists.			
☐ **Ben Brew,** Franklin, 12 oz., yellow and gold, brand name in blue, red ribbon with "100% Grain Beer"	95.00	115.00	105.00
☐ **Sunshine,** Barbey, 12 oz., white and brown, brand name in white lettering against brown band, slogan "Since 1861" near top with sunburst—CROWNTAINER	620.00	700.00	550.00
☐ **Sunshine Vitamin D,** Schlitz, 12 oz., brown and white	52.00	65.00	58.50
☐ **Topaz,** Koller, 12 oz., silver, red stripes near bottom—CROWNTAINER	135.00	160.00	90.00
☐ **Topper Draught,** Standard, gallon	32.00	43.00	37.50
☐ **Tropical Premium,** Florida, 12 oz., brown and white, slogan "Taste Tells"	480.00	575.00	527.00
☐ **Wagner's Gambrinus,** Wagner, 12 oz., gold and multi-colored	120.00	150.00	135.00
☐ **Wiedemann,** Wiedemann, 12 oz.,- CROWNTAINER	80.00	100.00	45.00

FLAT TOPS

☐ **A-1 Pilsner,** Arizona, 12 oz., white with "A-1" in block characters within gold frame	37.00	45.00	41.00
☐ **A-1 Pilsner,** Arizona, 12 oz., white and red, oval medallion with white lettering on red background	52.00	65.00	58.50
☐ **Banner Extra Dry,** Cumberland, 12 oz., white and red, "Premium Beer" in blue	15.00	20.00	17.50
☐ **Bantam,** Goebel, 8 oz., squat, white and dark green	26.00	33.00	29.50
☐ **Bantam Ale,** Goebel, 8 oz., squat, white and light green	31.00	40.00	35.50
☐ **Bartels Pure,** Lion, 12 oz., white and red, illustration of man with long beard	65.00	80.00	72.50
☐ **Bavarian Jay Vee,** Grace, 12 oz., blue and white	90.00	115.00	105.00

Cone Top, Eastside Beer,
Los Angeles Brewing Co.,
12 oz., **$35.00–$45.00**

(photo courtesy of
©Rogalski Brothers,
Gainesville, FL, 1984)

	Current Price Range		P/Y Average
☐ **Becker's,** Becker, 12 oz., red, white and blue, brand name in white against red background ..	32.00	41.00	36.50
☐ **Becker's Best,** Becker, 12 oz., silver with black lettering	76.00	95.00	85.00
☐ **Burger,** Burger, 12 oz., white and red, letters in brand name have no black outlines and the red is a strong burgundy-red	10.00	14.00	12.00
☐ **Burgemeister Premium,** Warsaw, 12 oz., cream white, red and gold, light gold banding at top and bottom	3.00	4.00	3.50
☐ **Country Club,** Goetz, 12 oz., white, red and gold	18.00	23.00	20.50
☐ **Country Club Malt Liquor,** Goetz, 8 oz., squat, white with "Country Club" in red, gold band at bottom	21.00	29.00	26.00
☐ **Drewry's Extra Dry,** Drewry, 16 oz., blue shield, no crown, brand name in white	16.00	21.00	19.00
☐ **Drewry's Lager,** Drewry, 12 oz., silver red and black	21.00	28.00	24.50
☐ **Drewry's Malt Liquor,** Drewry, 12 oz., red, green and white, brand name in white lettering on green background, slogan "A Man's Drink" at bottom	235.00	290.00	262.00

	Current Price Range		P/Y Average
☐ **Highlander Premium,** Missoula, 12 oz., red and white, white portion of can has slight greyish tinge (revised version)	13.00	16.50	14.75
☐ **Hillman's Export,** Best, 12 oz., brown and black, grained effect	50.00	65.00	57.50
☐ **Hillman's Superb,** Empire, 12 oz., blue and gold	62.00	78.00	69.00
☐ **Hillman's Superb,** United States Brewing, 12 oz., blue and gold	60.00	75.00	67.50
☐ **Hofbrau,** Hofbrau, 12 oz., cream white and red, illustration of German village inn	16.00	21.00	19.00
☐ **Hoffman House,** Walter, 12 oz., white, brown and red	5.00	6.50	5.75
☐ **Holiday Special,** Potosi, 12 oz., white and brown with blue bands at top and bottom	12.00	16.00	14.00
☐ **Holihan's Light Ale,** Diamond Springs, red and cream white	55.00	70.00	62.00
☐ **Krueger,** Krueger, 12 oz., pink, dark red and silver, without traditional company symbol (pictorial letter "K")	24.00	32.00	28.00
☐ **Krueger,** Krueger, 12 oz., yellow, red and white, "Light Lager" in black	42.00	53.00	48.50
☐ **Meister Brau,** Peter Hand, 12 oz., white, gold and red, red band at top	5.00	7.00	6.00
☐ **Mile Hi,** Tivoli, 12 oz., red, white and blue, illustration of Colorado mountain	43.00	54.00	48.00
☐ **Mile Hi,** Tivoli, 12 oz., red, white and blue, illustration of Colorado mountain, reads "Light Premium Quality" in bands at bottom, mountain illustration has dark blue background	35.00	44.00	42.00
☐ **Miller Select,** Miller, 12 oz., red, white and blue, quarter-moon emblem in blue medallion	48.00	62.00	57.50
☐ **Milwaukee's Best,** Gettelman, 12 oz., blue and white, illustration of stein	16.00	21.00	19.00
☐ **Milwaukee Premium,** Waukee, 12 oz., white, red and gold	13.00	18.00	15.00
☐ **Mitchell's Premium,** Mitchell, 12 oz., red, white and blue	82.00	100.00	91.00
☐ **Old Milwaukee,** Schlitz, 12 oz., gold and red, scene within rectangular frame	25.00	33.00	29.00
☐ **Old Milwaukee,** Schlitz, 12 oz., red and white, dark printing on shield symbol	5.00	7.00	6.00
☐ **Pabst Blue Ribbon,** Pabst, 12 oz., red, white and blue	5.75	7.25	6.50
☐ **Pabst Blue Ribbon,** Pabst, 12 oz., gold, white and blue, slogan above gold band at bottom ..	7.00	9.50	8.50
☐ **Pabst Blue Ribbon,** Pabst, 12 oz., gold, white and blue, slogan on gold band at bottom	7.00	9.50	8.50
☐ **Pfeiffer's,** Pfeiffer, 12 oz., gold, white and red, horizontal striping	8.00	11.00	9.50
☐ **Pickwick Ale,** Haffenreffer, 12 oz., gold, black and white	100.00	130.00	115.00
☐ **Piel's,** Piel's, 12 oz., gold, silver and black, brand name in white	10.00	13.75	11.57

	Current Price Range		P/Y Average

PULL TABS

	Current Price Range		P/Y Average
☐ **A-1 Light Pilsner,** National, 12 oz., cream white and brown	.60	.90	.50
☐ **ABC Premium,** Garden State, 16 oz., dark red and white	3.00	3.75	2.87
☐ **ABC Premium,** Wagner, 12 oz., red and white, "AGED" in rectangular frame	2.50	2.95	2.12
☐ **ABC Premium Ale,** Eastern, 12 oz., dark green with "AGED" in rectangular frame	1.10	1.45	1.02
☐ **Ballantine Ale,** Falstaff, 16 oz.	1.50	2.00	1.45
☐ **Ballantine Bock,** Ballantine, 12 oz., gold with ram's head in red circle	2.25	3.00	2.25
☐ **Ballantine Bock,** Falstaff, 12 oz., gold with ram's head in red circle	1.05	1.35	1.00
☐ **Ballantine Draft,** Falstaff, 12 oz., white with "Draft" in large red letters, "Genuine" in red letters at top, three-ring sign in gold	1.10	1.40	1.00
☐ **Black Dallas Malt Liquor,** Walter, 12 oz., blue and black, evening skyline	27.50	35.00	27.50
☐ **Black Horse Ale,** Black Horse, 12 oz., white, red and black, profile portrait of black horse	1.25	1.50	1.05
☐ **Buckhorn,** Olympia, 12 oz., yellow with illustration of antelope head in gold medallion, brand name in silver lettering.....................	.65	.85	.55
☐ **Buckhorn,** Olympia, 12 oz., dark yellow with illustration of antelope head in dark brassy gold medallion, brand name in bluish silver	.65	.85	.55
☐ **Budweiser,** Anheuser-Busch, 12 oz., white and red, current	.60	.80	.50
☐ **Budweiser,** Anheuser-Busch, 12 oz., red and white, "Tab Top" lettered around base	2.70	3.70	2.75
☐ **Budweiser,** Anheuser-Busch, 16 oz., "Tab Top"	5.00	6.75	4.87
☐ **Budweiser Malt Liquor,** Anheuser-Busch, 12 oz., black, brand name in red	2.35	3.00	2.05
☐ **Budweiser Malt Liquor,** Anheuser-Busch, 16 oz.	12.00	15.00	11.62
☐ **Buffalo,** Blitz Weinhard, 12 oz., light brown with illustration of buffalo	1.40	1.90	1.25
☐ **Busch Bavarian,** Anheuser-Busch, 12 oz., white and blue, snow-covered mountains, no clouds in background	2.00	3.00	2.12
☐ **Busch Bavarian,** Anheuser-Busch, 12 oz., white and blue, snow-covered mountains, no clouds in background, does not read "Tab Top," brand name encircled by thin red frame	.60	.80	.50
☐ **Carling's Black Label,** Carling, 12 oz., red and black, brand name within tilted medallion, "Carling" in red within medallion, coat-of-arms in gold, gold band at top	.50	.85	.60
☐ **Carling's Tuborg,** Carling, 12 oz., dark gold and dark red	.50	.85	.50

	Current Price Range		P/Y Average

☐ **Cascade,** Blitz Weinhard, 12 oz., blue and white, brand name in white on blue background	2.00	2.95	2.17
☐ **Cascade,** Blitz Weinhard, 16 oz., does not state "King Size"	2.50	3.25	2.25
☐ **Cascade,** Blitz Weinhard, 16 oz., states "King Size" near top	12.25	16.25	13.00
☐ **Cee Bee,** Colonial, 12 oz., red and white	11.00	14.00	11.62
☐ **Hof-Brau,** General, 12 oz., red and white, brand name in bright blue lettering, bright blue frame around medallion	.85	1.45	1.00
☐ **Hof-Brau,** Maier, 12 oz., red and white, brand name in grey-blue lettering	8.00	10.00	5.50
☐ **Kingsbury Real Draft,** Kingsbury, 12 oz., white, brown and red, lower portion of can has wood-grain finish	7.00	9.00	6.50
☐ **Kingsbury Wisconsin Pale,** Kingsbury, 12 oz., red, white and blue	5.75	7.50	5.50
☐ **Knickerbocker Natural,** Jacob Ruppert, 7 oz., white with red and blue ribbons, blue lettering	6.00	7.25	5.50
☐ **Koch's Golden Anniversary,** Koch, 12 oz., red, white and gold, "The Best in Flavor" at top of can	.50	.70	.50
☐ **Kodiak Ale,** Schmidt, 12 oz., blue and gold, illustration of mountain peaks	1.00	1.30	1.05
☐ **Koehler,** Erie, 12 oz., dark blue and white, no bright orange trim around brand name	14.50	18.00	15.00
☐ **Koehler,** Erie, 12 oz., dark blue and white, bright orange trim around brand name	3.25	4.00	3.12
☐ **Koehler,** Erie, 12 oz., blue and white	1.25	1.75	1.45
☐ **Koehler,** Erie, 12 oz., blue and white, Bicentennial	.90	1.20	1.05
☐ **Koehler,** Erie, 12 oz., red and white, Bicentennial	.90	1.20	1.05
☐ **Koehler Lager,** Erie, 12 oz., red and white ...	1.75	2.25	2.00
☐ **Koenig Brau,** Koenig Brau, 12 oz., gold and white	6.25	8.00	7.12
☐ **Lucky Lager,** Lucky Lager, 12 oz., pale blue and gold, brand name slightly curved	4.00	6.00	5.00
☐ **Lucky Lager,** Lucky, 16 oz.	14.00	17.00	14.00
☐ **Lucky Light Draft,** General, 12 oz., white and tan, pictorial illustration and lengthy text	.90	1.20	1.05
☐ **Lucky Malt Liquor,** Lucky, 16 oz.	25.00	33.00	29.00
☐ **Lucky Red Carpet,** General, 12 oz., red and white	.90	1.20	1.05
☐ **Maier Select,** Maier, 12 oz., red, white and blue, blue leaf near top	4.00	6.00	5.00
☐ **Malt Duck Grape,** National, 12 oz., purple and white	39.00	50.00	40.00
☐ **Manheim,** Reading, 12 oz., red and white	8.00	11.00	9.50
☐ **Mark Meister Premium Lager,** Eastern, 12 oz., blue and white	5.00	7.00	6.00
☐ **Mark V,** Pittsburgh, 12 oz., red, white and blue, brand name in black	1.75	2.35	2.05

	Current Price Range		P/Y Average
☐ **Mark V,** Pittsburgh, 12 oz., red, white and blue, brand name in blue	.65	.85	.75
☐ **Miller High Life,** Miller, 12 oz., gold, white and red...	.40	.60	.50
☐ **Old Crown,** Old Crown, 12 oz., white and red, without symbol (figure of man)	.90	1.20	1.05
☐ **Old Crown,** Old Crown, 12 oz., white and red, with symbol (figure of man)	2.20	2.75	2.25
☐ **Old Crown Bock,** Old Crown, 12 oz., brown and white, illustration of ram's head	1.75	2.50	2.12
☐ **Schlitz,** Schlitz, 12 oz., white and brown, slogan "The Beer That Made Milwaukee Famous" is printed in dark brown scrip letters	.90	1.20	1.05
☐ **Schlitz,** Schlitz, 12 oz., white and brown, slogan "The Beer That Made Milwaukee Famous" is printed in dark brown script letters, dated 1971	.80	1.05	.92
☐ **Schlitz Malt Liquor,** Schlitz, 12 oz., white and gold, brand name blue	3.10	4.25	3.12
☐ **Schlitz Malt Liquor,** Schlitz, 12 oz., blue, black and white, illustration	.90	1.20	1.05
☐ **Schlitz Malt Liquor,** Schlitz, 16 oz., dark blue bull	1.00	1.35	1.17
☐ **Schlitz Stout Malt Liquor,** Schlitz, 12 oz., white and gold, blue lettering, "Stout" positioned above "Malt Liquor" instead of all on one line	3.25	4.25	3.37
☐ **Stag,** Stag, 12 oz., gold, white and red, small brand name	.40	.60	.50
☐ **Stag,** Carling, 16 oz., "Half Quart" in large white letters near top	4.50	6.00	5.25
☐ **Stag,** Carling, 16 oz., does not state "Half Quart"	1.75	2.25	2.00
☐ **Stallion XII,** Gold Medal, 12 oz., gold, white and red, illustration of horse	75.00	95.00	85.00
☐ **Standard Cream Ale,** Standard Rochester, 12 oz., green, white and gold	14.00	18.00	16.00
☐ **Standard Dry Ale,** Eastern, 12 oz., blue, white and gold	.85	1.15	1.00
☐ **Standard Dry Ale,** Standard Rochester, 12 oz., blue, white and gold	3.75	4.75	4.25
☐ **Stegmaier Bock,** Stegmaier, 12 oz., brown and white, slogan "Truly Brewed"	2.00	2.75	1.25
☐ **Stegmaier Gold Medal,** Stegmaier, 12 oz., gold and white	.90	1.20	1.05
☐ **Winchester Malt Liquor,** Walter, 12 oz., pale blue	4.50	5.75	5.12
☐ **Winchester Malt Liquor,** Walter, 16 oz.	12.00	16.00	14.00
☐ **Wisconsin Club Premium Pilsner,** Huber, 12 oz., white and gold, brand name in white	1.00	1.35	1.17
☐ **Wisconsin Gold Label,** Huber, 12 oz., white and gold, brand name in gold, very ornate gold designing......................................	.90	1.20	1.05
☐ **Wisconsin Gold Label Premium,** Huber, 12 oz., gold and white............................	5.75	7.25	6.50

	Current Price Range		P/Y Average
☐ **Wisconsin Holiday,** Holiday, 12 oz., white and red	1.80	2.25	2.02
☐ **Wisconsin Holiday,** Huber, 12 oz., white and red	1.00	1.30	1.15
☐ **Wisconsin Premium,** Heileman, 12 oz., white, red and blue, small map of Wisconsin	1.00	1.30	1.15
☐ **Wunderbar,** Minneapolis Brewing, 12 oz., light gold and dark gold with blue and white	14.00	17.50	11.00
☐ **Wunderbrau Malt Beverage, Near Beer,** Erie, 12 oz., blue and white, coat of arms	14.50	19.00	13.62
☐ **Yorktown Extra Fine Premium,** Reading, 12 oz., red, white and black	9.00	12.00	10.50
☐ **Yuengling Premium,** Yuengling, 12 oz., silver and red, eagle symbol near top, in red	.90	1.20	1.05

BELLS

TOPIC: Bells have been used for thousands of years to signal important events such as births, weddings, enemy attacks and holidays.

TYPES: Bells can be divided into many categories, including closed and open mouth bells, figurine bells, jingle bells, chimes and gongs.

PERIODS: Bells have existed for thousands of years, although they were introduced to Europe about 1500 years ago.

MATERIALS: Brass, iron, silver, gold, bronze, wood, glass and porcelain are frequently used to make bells.

COMMENTS: Bells are very popular among collectors because of their interesting shapes and musical qualities.

☐ **Alaska bell,** colored totem handle, original	42.00	58.00	48.00
☐ **Alexander's helmet bell,** no clapper, 5½″ Dia.	13.00	18.00	14.00
☐ **Bayreuther bell,** hand painted porcelain, lilies of the valley	72.00	92.00	80.00
☐ **Brass bell,** stork	34.00	50.00	38.00
☐ **Brass clapper bell**	110.00	130.00	112.50

Call Bell, *dome shaped, round base, spring operated clapper,* **$20.00-$45.00**

	Current Price Range		P/Y Average
☐ **Brass dinner bell**	8.00	12.00	7.50
☐ **Brass hotel call bell,** 4″ Dia.	50.00	65.00	52.00
☐ **Brass musical chime bell**	32.00	68.00	42.00
☐ **Brass school bell,** 4⅜″ Dia., c. 1910	20.00	28.00	21.00
☐ **Brass bell,** wooden handle, 4″	12.00	18.00	12.50
☐ **Brass bell,** wooden handle, 6″	18.00	22.00	20.00
☐ **Brass bell,** wooden handle, 7″	28.00	38.00	30.00
☐ **Brass bell,** wooden handle, 8″	28.00	38.00	30.00
☐ **Bronze art figurine bells,** very detailed, rare	210.00	360.00	275.00
☐ **Bronze bell,** angel holder	95.00	115.00	100.00
☐ **Cast iron bell,** mechanical	130.00	160.00	138.00
☐ **Charlie Chaplin bell,** solid brass, cane and typical pose	18.00	22.00	17.50
☐ **China bell,** cobalt, 5″	50.00	63.00	52.00
☐ **China bell,** German, painted clown	68.00	82.00	72.00
☐ **Chinese brass gong bell,** 9″	45.00	60.00	48.00
☐ **Church bell,** solid brass, single tier	110.00	135.00	112.50
☐ **Church bell,** solid brass, triple tier	180.00	220.00	195.00
☐ **Church bell,** old, 1100 pounds	575.00	675.00	600.00
☐ **Church bell,** without wheel	130.00	160.00	138.00
☐ **Coast Guard,** brass, Herculoy, mounted on walnut base, 16″, 1945	625.00	825.00	690.00
☐ **Conestoga,** graduated on strap (4), brass	210.00	260.00	225.00
☐ **Cow bell,** iron ring with strap attachment	32.00	48.00	38.00
☐ **Cow bell,** leather collar	12.00	16.00	12.50
☐ **Cow bell,** clapper	28.00	38.00	30.00

	Current Price Range		P/Y Average
☐ **Cow bells,** hand riveted	28.00	38.00	30.00
☐ **Crystal bell,** faceted drummer boy handle, Blair-Reubel	35.00	50.00	38.00
☐ **Cutter bells,** 4 bells, 2½"–2¾" Dia.	45.00	60.00	48.00
☐ **Cutter-type bell,** iron strap	80.00	110.00	82.00
☐ **Damascus bell,** bronze, inlaid gold and green leaves with red berries	55.00	75.00	60.00
☐ **Dinner bell,** crystal	55.00	75.00	60.00
☐ **Dinner bell,** enamel on metal	55.00	75.00	60.00
☐ **Dinner bell,** nickel	13.00	17.00	12.50
☐ **Dinner bell,** ornate sterling silver	65.00	90.00	72.00
☐ **Dog bells,** sculptured handles, pair, 4"	80.00	110.00	87.50
☐ **Doorbell,** Abbe's patent double strike	35.00	50.00	38.00
☐ **Door bell,** brass	55.00	75.00	60.00
☐ **Early American thumbprint bell,** design around skirt	50.00	65.00	48.00
☐ **Elephant bell,** brass	45.00	60.00	48.00
☐ **Elephant bell,** cloisonne	110.00	130.00	112.00
☐ **Fire Alarm bell**	48.00	58.00	48.00
☐ **Fire Truck bell,** eagle mounted on top of original mounting bracket, nickel plated, c. 1925	700.00	900.00	760.00
☐ **Fire Truck bell,** solid brass, brass acorn finial, polished, 10", c. 1920	450.00	550.00	480.00
☐ **Fire Truck bell,** solid brass, brass finial, 10", c. 1900	175.00	225.00	195.00
☐ **French flint glass bell,** cordinated handle and clapper	420.00	495.00	430.00
☐ **Glass bell,** amber, glass	120.00	185.00	112.00
☐ **Glass bell,** Bristol, 11½"	120.00	185.00	112.00
☐ **Glass bell,** Bristol wedding bell, 14"	130.00	160.00	138.00
☐ **Glass bell,** carnival	18.00	22.00	17.50
☐ **Glass bell,** cranberry glass, clear handle	160.00	200.00	170.00
☐ **Glass bell,** clear dark green	90.00	115.00	90.00
☐ **Glass bell,** cut glass including handle	145.00	175.00	150.00
☐ **Glass bell,** nailsea bell, solid glass handle, loops and swirls in color	210.00	260.00	225.00
☐ **Glass Bell,** Venetian, ruby red, enamel decoration	90.00	110.00	90.00
☐ **Glass Bell,** Venetian glass bell, latticino, pink, 14"	160.00	195.00	165.00
☐ **Glass Bell,** Venetian, goose bell	22.00	32.00	25.00
☐ **Hand bell,** brass	110.00	135.00	112.50
☐ **Hand bell,** brass with decorations	80.00	110.00	82.00
☐ **Hand bell,** brass with wooden handle	110.00	135.00	112.50
☐ **Iron bell,** bronze, lion and sun motif, bas relief	90.00	110.00	90.00
☐ **Iron bell,** cow	18.00	22.00	17.50
☐ **Iron bell,** dinner	110.00	135.00	112.50
☐ **Iron bell,** farm	230.00	280.00	250.00
☐ **Iron bell,** sleigh	60.00	78.00	60.00
☐ **Johannes Afine bell,** (Joseph Von Ende) bronze, wreath and cherub, bas relief	95.00	120.00	105.00
☐ **Lady sculptured bell,** 4"	160.00	190.00	170.00
☐ **Lennox-Imperial bell,** off-white porcelain, 18K gold, 6"	60.00	80.00	65.00

	Current Price Range		P/Y Average
☐ **Locomotive bell,** brass, New York City, brass finial, polished, 17″, c. 1920–1930	550.00	650.00	580.00
☐ **Locomotive bell,** steam bell by Howard, brass, from narrow guage era, 13″	800.00	1000.00	860.00
☐ **Locomotive bell,** with yoke and cradle, from steam locomotive, 17″	1200.00	1600.00	1375.00
☐ **Majolica bell,** dog	40.00	55.00	42.00
☐ **Mass bell,** solid brass	80.00	110.00	82.00
☐ **Meissen bells,** decorated, antique	110.00	135.00	112.50
☐ **Meissen bells,** raised decorations	210.00	260.00	225.00
☐ **Meneely bell,** bronze, original clapper, polished, 19″, 1858	775.00	975.00	850.00
☐ **Meneely Tower bell,** raised letters, large brass hexball finial, 28″, weights about 950 pounds with cradle, age undetermined	3600.00	4400.00	3775.00
☐ **Mission bell,** min. clapper	80.00	110.00	82.00
☐ **Mission bell,** Spanish	110.00	135.00	112.50
☐ **Navy bell,** main deck bell from battleship, brass, large raised letters, large brass finial, 25″, c. 1920–1930	3000.00	3400.00	325.00
☐ **Pewter sterling bell**	22.00	32.00	25.00
☐ **Pressed glass bell,** smokey	6.00	12.00	7.50
☐ **Quimper lady bell,** colored, 8″	75.00	95.00	80.00
☐ **Roeland Ghend,** bronze, sand cast, crusade handle	65.00	85.00	70.00
☐ **Saddle chimes,** set of 3 with pinwheel on each	145.00	175.00	150.00
☐ **School bell,** bronze, 20″ iron yoke, Jones and Hitchcock, c. 1856	860.00	960.00	900.00
☐ **School bell,** metal, wooden handles, small . . .	80.00	110.00	82.00
☐ **School bell,** metal, wooden handle, large	90.00	110.00	90.00
☐ **School bell,** 5″	50.00	65.00	52.00
☐ **School bell,** 6½″	72.00	92.00	80.00
☐ **School bell,** 8¼″	95.00	115.00	100.00
☐ **School bell,** 9½″	95.00	115.00	100.00
☐ **Sculptured bell,** lady 4″	55.00	75.00	60.00
☐ **Sculptured bell,** little boy on a coal pile, original clapper, detailed	155.00	190.00	170.00
☐ **Sculptured bell,** old woman on the green from "Canterbury Tales", detailed	110.00	160.00	125.00
☐ **Sheep bell**	55.00	75.00	60.00
☐ **Ship bell,** brass, c. 1845	210.00	260.00	235.00
☐ **Ship bell,** brass dolphin	225.00	250.00	235.00
☐ **Ship bell,** H.M.S. Wilstar, c. 1880, 14″ diameter	475.00	575.00	510.00
☐ **Ship bell,** nickel plated bronze, acorn finial, matching bronze mounting bracket, 10″, c. 1910	275.00	325.00	290.00
☐ **Silver-plated bell,** wooden handle, 7″ H.	40.00	50.00	45.00
☐ **Silver-plated call bell,** foot operated, embossed trim, 36″ H.	80.00	92.00	85.00
☐ **Sleigh bells,** leather strap of 17 bells	210.00	260.00	225.00
☐ **Sleigh bells,** leather strap of 20 bells	260.00	285.00	262.00

	Current Price Range		P/Y Average
☐ **Sleigh bells,** iron string of 25 bells	280.00	330.00	300.00
☐ **Sleigh bells,** brass string of 25 bells	230.00	280.00	250.00
☐ **Sleigh bells,** all brass, 29 bells mounted on a jointed brass strap, old	170.00	205.00	178.00
☐ **Soldier,** roman	55.00	75.00	60.00
☐ **Sterling silver bell,** Reed & Barton, "Pointed Antique"	25.00	32.00	29.00
☐ **Sterling silver bell,** twisted handle, engraved scroll design	30.00	36.00	33.00
☐ **Sterling silver bell,** woman	120.00	150.00	132.00
☐ **Swedish bell,** heavy brass, double throated, 2¾″ Dia.	20.00	26.00	20.50
☐ **Swedish bell,** heavy brass, triple throated, 3″ Dia.	22.00	32.00	25.00
☐ **Town Crier,** long with wooden handle	110.00	135.00	112.50
☐ **Trolley car,** 8″ Dia.	80.00	110.00	82.00
☐ **Turtle,** German mechanical	80.00	110.00	82.00
☐ **Waterford crystal bell**	60.00	80.00	65.00
☐ **Wedgwood,** porcelain, c. 1979	30.00	40.00	30.00

BELT BUCKLES

DESCRIPTION: Belt buckles have become a very popular collectible as the interest in vintage clothing has grown. They can be found in thrift shops and second hand clothing stores as well as in pawn shops, antique shops and flea markets. They have been made in a wide variety of styles, utilizing many different materials.

RECOMMENDED READING: For further information you may refer to *The Official Price Guide to Antique Jewelry* by Arthur Guy Kaplan, published by The House of Collectibles.

☐ **Buckle and button set,** translucent apple green enamel, silver, English, c. 1920–30	220.00	240.00	225.00
☐ **Cameo motif,** carved lava, gold plated, c. late 19th	220.00	240.00	225.00

Scroll Motif Buckles, *gold, c. 1900,* $700.00–$800.00

	Current Price Range		P/Y Average
□ **Circular motif buckle,** with beaded edge and slide with beaded edge, sterling silver, American, c. 1896	135.00	145.00	137.00
□ **Cluster motif pair of buckles,** rhinestone, white metal, c. 1930–40	10.00	15.00	11.00
□ **Fan and scroll motif buckle,** champleve opaque black and white enamel, gold, c. 1870	1200.00	1300.00	1210.00
□ **Fancy shape motif pair of buckles,** rhinestone, white metal, c. 1930–40	12.00	18.00	13.00
□ **Oval Etruscan granulation motif, buckle pin,** gold, c. 1870	240.00	260.00	247.00
□ **Oval motif,** paste, silver	400.00	500.00	410.00
□ **Oval motif pair of buckles,** cut steel, c. late 19th	35.00	45.00	37.00
□ **Oval wreath motif pair of buckles,** cut steel, c. late 19th	25.00	30.00	26.00
□ **Rectangular buckle,** and floral motif slide, floral motif belt, sterling silver, American, c. 1896 ...	75.00	85.00	78.00
□ **Rectangular buckle,** and floral motif slide, floral motif belt, sterling silver, American, c. 1896 ...	75.00	85.00	78.00
□ **Rectangular buckle,** with beaded rim and slide, sterling silver, American, c. 1896	85.00	110.00	88.00
□ **Rectangular flower motif pair of buckles,** cut steel, marked: France, c. late 19th	40.00	50.00	42.00
□ **Rectangular motif buckle,** 64 emerald-cut sapphires, 114 round diamonds, platinum, gold, French, c. 1890	3200.00	3400.00	3250.00
□ **Rectangular motif pair of buckles,** silver plated, c. mid 20th	12.00	18.00	13.00
□ **Rectangular motif pair of buckles,** silver plated, c. mid 20th	10.00	15.00	11.00
□ **Rectangular pair of buckles,** engraved, sterling silver, c. 1920	50.00	60.00	55.00
□ **Ribbon and leaf motif,** gold, French, c. 1870	950.00	1100.00	955.00
□ **Scroll motif buckles,** gold, c. 1900	700.00	800.00	710.00
□ **Scroll motif buckle,** gold, c. 1890	500.00	600.00	520.00
□ **Scroll motif buckle and slide,** sterling silver, American, c. 1896	160.00	180.00	165.00

	Current Price Range		P/Y Average
☐ **Scroll motif buckle and slide,** with beaded rim, sterling silver, American, c. 1896	130.00	140.00	135.00
☐ **Scroll and flower motif,** cloisonne and guilloche enamel, Arts and Crafts, c. late 19th	250.00	300.00	255.00
☐ **Shell motif buckle,** two round diamonds, six round demantoid garnets, gold, c. 1880	1300.00	1400.00	1350.00
☐ **Snake motif buckle,** enamelled, three round diamonds, gold, c. 19th	1600.00	1800.00	1650.00
☐ **Square crescent motif pair of buckles,** cut steel, c. 19th	35.00	40.00	
☐ **36.00**			
☐ **Square motif buckle,** seed pearl border, cobalt blue enamel, 14K gold, c. 1920	300.00	350.00	310.00
☐ **Square motif buckle,** with beaded edge and slide with beaded edge, sterling silver, American, c. 1896	155.00	165.00	160.00
☐ **Wide rectangular motif buckle and slide,** sterling silver, American, c. 1896	85.00	110.00	90.00

BENNINGTON POTTERY

TOPIC: Bennington ranks in a special class among American pottery. It was the first U.S. factory to gain an international reputation, and the first to produce truly creative artistic works. The popularity of Bennington among collectors stretches back before the beginning of the America's antique trade. By as early as 1890, the wares had become solidly established as collectors' items. Since the factory's operations closed in 1858, all of its products have been ranked as antiques for many years.

HISTORY: The period of true Bennington was brief, extending from 1842 to 1858, but this may be deceiving since the output during those 16 years was heavy. For the actual beginnings of Bennington, we must delve into the 18th century. In 1793, John Norton established a pottery works of rather humble proportions in the town of Bennington, Vermont. Its products were red earthenware and mason's bricks. During the War of 1812, Norton installed a stoneware kiln and began making English-style wares. Brown glazed wares were also produced. The earlier Bennington wares were all sold locally, apparently without any effort to invade the more lucrative market of the mid-Atlantic states. From all available information, it seems that production during these years was modest. Things took a dramatic change in the winter of 1842 to 1843, when Julius Norton (a grandson of the founder) went into partnership with Christopher Fenton. The aim of this new alliance was to diversify the Bennington line and bring it fully up to par with the imported English stonewares. With the kind of ambition that characterized few American potters of that era, Norton and Fenton set out to duplicate the much admired bold finished surface of Rockingham wares. This they accomplished and many collectors would agree that they surpassed Rockingham.

STYLE: The Bennington products were marvels of free-spirited design. Among the best known are its stoneware figures with mottled, deep-brown color. The same type of unique coloration also appears on water pitchers, conventional tableware and other items. In 1849, the company filed for a patent on colored glazes, the first of its kind in the United States. The secret of the Bennington process was to take the fired wares and coat them with metallic oxides. Next they were dipped in flint enamel—the glaze was not brush-painted. The myth of brush-painted glaze on Bennington stoneware was probably inspired by what appear to be brush markings. These, however, were the result of natural texturing as the liquid glaze gradually solidified. If the glaze was thick on some areas of a piece, which was almost inevitable from the dipping process, it gathered into the crevices before drying. Much to the credit of Bennington, it never strove to achieve a smooth ware, free of mottling. The company was quite proud of the individuality of its product, and public response confirmed this confidence. In its time, however, the popularity of Bennington was small compared to heights reached later on the antique market.

The company underwent several name changes. From the original name of "Norton and Fenton," it became "Fenton's Works," then "Lyman, Fenton and Co." Finally, the name was changed to "United States Pottery" in 1850 which was in use at the time of the company's collapse in 1858.

In addition to the instantly recognizable wares mentioned above, Bennington also produced parianware. This was a minor phase of its operations.

MARKS: The earliest mark upon the association of Norton and Fenton in 1842, was a circle composed of the wording NORTON & FENTON, BENNINGTON, Vt. Block lettering was used without any symbol. When the company name was changed, after Norton left in 1847, the mark became FENTON'S WORKS; BENNINGTON, VERMONT enclosed in a rectangular decorative border. This distinctive mark was set in two styles of lettering with FENTON'S WORKS in slanting characters resembling italics. The address was set in standard vertical lettering. The next mark, that of Lyman, Fenton and Co., was contained within a plain oval frame and read LYMAN FENTON & CO., FENTON'S ENAMEL, PATENTED 1849, BENNINGTON, Vt. This ushered in the era of colored glazes. Within this mark, the year (1849) is very prominently displayed. When the name became United States Pottery Co., two different marks were introduced, both reading UNITED STATES POTTERY Co., BENNINGTON, Vt. One carries the wording within an oval frame and contains two small ornamental flourishes; the other is a modified diamond-shape composed of decorative printer's type, but without further ornamentation.

	Current Price Range		P/Y Average
☐ **Baker,** 10″, oval, mottled brown glaze	65.00	85.00	68.00
☐ **Basin,** 12″, mottled brown Rockingham glaze	70.00	80.00	72.00
☐ **Bed Pan,** mottled brown Rockingham glaze . . .	70.00	80.00	72.00
☐ **Bottle,** 10½″, figure of coachman wearing hat and cape without tassels, c. 1847–58	200.00	225.00	210.00
☐ **Bowl,** 6″, Rockingham glaze, bell-shaped	90.00	100.00	95.00
☐ **Bowl,** 7½″, mottled brown glaze	90.00	100.00	95.00
☐ **Bowl,** 9″, mottled brown Rockingham glaze . . .	70.00	80.00	72.00
☐ **Bowl,** 10″ oval, mottled brown Rockingham glaze	70.00	80.00	72.00
☐ **Box, covered,** 5¾″ oval, all white, parian, shell-molded base and lid with shell finial	80.00	95.00	82.00
☐ **Box,** 5¾″, square, all white parian, shell finial	95.00	105.00	97.00
☐ **Box,** 4⅜″, square, parian, top with figure, Lion of Lucerne	120.00	130.00	122.00
☐ **Candlesticks,** 11″, mottled brown glaze, pair	225.00	270.00	215.00
☐ **Churn,** mottled brown glaze, wooden lid and dasher	230.00	270.00	235.00
☐ **Compote,** on low footed base, molded design on body	120.00	130.00	122.00
☐ **Creamer,** cow, mottled brown glaze	180.00	200.00	185.00
☐ **Cream pot,** 1 qt., cobalt floral, covered, J. & E. Norton	145.00	160.00	147.00
☐ **Crock,** 2 gal., gray, cobalt blue foliage, impressed "E. Norton & Co., Bennington, Vt.", c. 1883–94	140.00	50.00	142.00
☐ **Crock,** 4 gal., yellow-brown with "4" impressed with cobalt blue	310.00	350.00	315.00
☐ **Crock,** 6-gal., handled, gray, cobalt blue floral & ribbon motif, impressed "E. & L.P. Norton, Bennington, Vt." c. 1861–81	160.00	175.00	165.00
☐ **Cuspidor,** 8½″, mottled brown glaze, shell pattern	130.00	150.00	135.00
☐ **Dish,** 2½″, brown Rockingham glaze	60.00	70.00	62.00
☐ **Dove,** 7½″, modeled in flight, molded feathers, made to hang, c. 1847–48	550.00	570.00	555.00
☐ **Egg cup,** molded lily pad feet, all white, set of 6	130.00	150.00	135.00
☐ **Flask,** 5½″, yellow and brown glaze	480.00	520.00	485.00
☐ **Flower pot,** 6″, Rockingham glaze, eagles in relief on sides	30.00	40.00	32.00
☐ **Inkwell,** 5″ x 2½″, mottled brown Rockingham glaze	120.00	140.00	122.00
☐ **Inkwell,** 4 quill holes, usual color, design in relief	210.00	250.00	215.00
☐ **Inkwell,** cylindrical, Rockingham glaze	105.00	125.00	110.00
☐ **Jar,** covered, two handled, mottled brown Rockingham glaze, impressed 1849	555.00	565.00	560.00
☐ **Jar,** 1 gal., gray stoneware, cobalt blue, butterfly and floral decor, impressed "E. & L. Norton, Bennington, Vt."	125.00	135.00	117.00
☐ **Jar,** 2 gal, 11″, ovoid, handled, gray, cobalt blue floral motif, impressed "E. & L.P. Norton, Bennington, Vt.," c. 1861–81	200.00	220.00	210.00

	Current Price Range		P/Y Average
☐ **Jug,** 11¼", gray, cobalt blue bird motif, impressed "J. & E. Norton, Bennington, Vt." c. 1850–59	230.00	240.00	235.00
☐ **Jug,** 16", gray, cobalt blue floral spray, impressed "Julius Norton, Bennington, Vt.," c. 1838–45	240.00	250.00	242.00
☐ **Jug,** 1 gal., gray stoneware, cobalt blue tree, design, marked "E. Norton, Bennington, Vt.," c. 1881–83	140.00	150.00	142.00
☐ **Jug,** 1 gal., 10½", gray, cobalt blue bird and branch motif, impressed "J. Norton & Co., Bennington, Vt."	230.00	250.00	227.00
☐ **Jug,** 1½ gal., 9½", mottled brown glaze	150.00	170.00	155.00
☐ **Jug,** 2 gal., gray, brushed cobalt blue rabbit motif, impressed "Julius Norton, Bennington, Vt."	230.00	240.00	235.00
☐ **Jug,** gal., gray, cobalt blue floral spray, impressed "J. & E. Norton, Bennington, Vt.," c. 1850–59	230.00	240.00	235.00
☐ **Jug,** 2 gal., gray stoneware with cobalt blue scrolling feather design, impressed "E. & L.P. Norton, Bennington, Vt."	130.00	175.00	135.00
☐ **Jug,** 2 gal., blue and green, flint enamel	100.00	115.00	105.00
☐ **Jug,** 2 gal, 13½", gray, cobalt blue bird motif, impressed "J. & E. Norton, Bennington, Vt.," c. 1850–59	335.00	350.00	340.00
☐ **Jug,** 3 gal., 16", gray stoneware with cobalt blue floral decor, impressed "E. & L.P., Bennington, Vt.," 1861–81	130.00	175.00	135.00
☐ **Jug,** 3 gal., ovoid, gray stoneware with cobalt blue floral decor, impressed "Norton & Fenton, Bennington, Vt."	150.00	170.00	155.00
☐ **Mug,** 6", Rockingham glaze	110.00	125.00	115.00
☐ **Ornament,** form of a cow with tree trunk at rear, dark brown and yellow-brown glaze with some green	975.00	1000.00	950.00
☐ **Pie plate,** 10½", mottled brown Rockingham glaze	120.00	140.00	125.00
☐ **Pitcher,** 5½", tulip and sun flower pamotif	55.00	65.00	60.00
☐ **Pitcher,** 7", hunting scene with dogs and hunters on horseback in relief, mottle brown Rockingham glaze	100.00	110.00	102.00
☐ **Pitcher,** 7½", parian, relief-molded white palm trees and exotic flowers designed for syrup cover, marked "U.S.P." on base	100.00	110.00	102.00
☐ **Pitcher,** 8¼", tulip and heart, flint enamel	160.00	180.00	165.00
☐ **Pitcher,** 8½", parian, blue and white, molded grape cluster leaves	120.00	130.00	122.00
☐ **Pitcher,** 8¾", Rockingham glaze, castle scene	360.00	400.00	365.00
☐ **Pitcher,** 10", hunting scene, mottled brown Rockingham glaze	330.00	340.00	332.00
☐ **Pitcher,** 11", hexagonal, brown birds and flowers	280.00	330.00	285.00
☐ **Snuff jar,** 3⅞", flint enamel, flat bottom	760.00	850.00	765.00
☐ **Teapot,** 7¾", "Rebecca at the Well"	70.00	80.00	72.00

	Current Price Range		P/Y Average
☐ **Teapot,** 2 qt., mottled brown glaze	125.00	140.00	127.00
☐ **Tile,** 7″, mottled olive brown glaze, impressed 1849	530.00	540.00	532.00
☐ **Tobacco jar,** 11″, mottled brown glaze, covered	210.00	250.00	215.00
☐ **Toby creamer,** 6⅛″, mottled brown Rocking- ham glaze, seated Toby	340.00	375.00	345.00
☐ **Vase,** basket of roses in medallion	30.00	38.00	32.00
☐ **Vase,** 7¼″, mottled brown glaze, ear of corn shape	100.00	120.00	105.00
☐ **Vase,** 7½″, all white, parian	50.00	60.00	52.00
☐ **Vase,** 7½″, flint enamel, tulip in relief	260.00	300.00	265.00

BIBLES

DESCRIPTION: The Bible, comprised of the Old and New Testaments, is the religious book used by Christians.

PERIOD: The Bible holds the distinction of being the first book ever printed. Johann Gutenberg printed it during the middle 1400s. Since then, the Bible has been reprinted more than any other book.

COMMENTS: There are several ways to collect Bibles. Some collectors buy only the rare Bibles of the 15th and 16th centuries. Others specialize in minia-ture Bibles or Bibles that have been translated into several languages. Another popular way to collect Bibles is specializing in first editions.

ADDITIONAL TIPS: This section is organized according to date beginning with the 1500s through the 1800s. For more information, consult *The Official Price Guide to Old Books and Autographs,* published by The House of Collectibles.

☐ **English,** includes Tyndals Prologues, London, N. Hyll, 1551	650.00	900.00	775.00
☐ **English,** Breeches Bible, with the Book of Com- mon Prayer, London, Barker, 1578	350.00	500.00	425.00
☐ **English,** London, Barker, 1583	350.00	500.00	425.00
☐ **English,** London, Barker, 1594	250.00	325.00	287.00

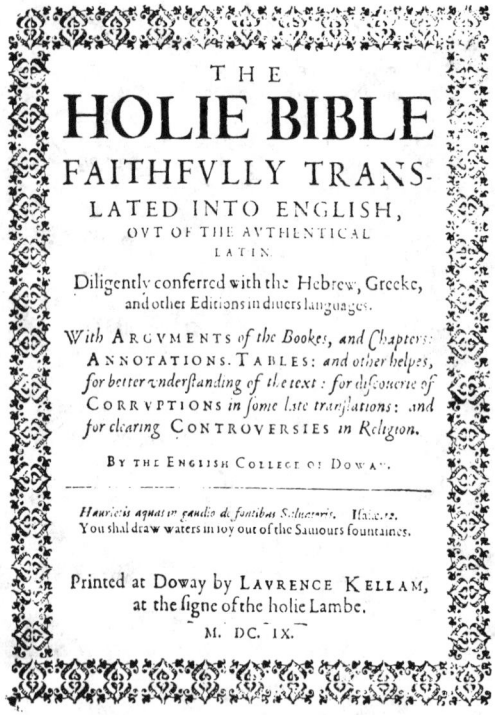

Title Page Of The First Edition Of The Roman Catholic Old Testament In English, *printed in Douai, France which was spelled "Doway."*
$200.00-$235.00

	Current Price Range		P/Y Average
☐ **English,** London, Barker, 1606	85.00	120.00	102.00
☐ **English,** Breeches Bible, London, R. Barker, 1608	275.00	350.00	312.00
☐ **English,** The New Testament, London, Barker, 1612	50.00	75.00	62.00
☐ **English,** The Holy Bible, London, Barker, 1615	125.00	185.00	155.00
☐ **English,** New Testament, Cambridge, England, 1628	130.00	175.00	152.00
☐ **English,** The Holy Bible, Cambridge, England, 1630	125.00	160.00	137.00
☐ **English,** London, Barker and Bill, 1630	450.00	650.00	530.00
☐ **English,** London, H. Hill and J. Field, 1660	325.00	400.00	362.00
☐ **English,** London, 1711	100.00	135.00	117.00
☐ **English,** Baskett Bible, Oxford, 1759, two volumes	120.00	150.00	135.00

	Current Price Range		P/Y Average
□ **English,** Blayney's Bible, Oxford, 1769	140.00	190.00	165.00
□ **English,** Old and New Testament, illustrated with engravings by Fittler, London, Bensley, 1795, two volumes	120.00	150.00	135.00
□ **American,** Philadelphia, 1794, pocket size	45.00	65.00	55.00
□ **American,** Philadelphia, 1813	300.00	400.00	350.00
□ **American,** N.Y., 1822, pocket size	75.00	100.00	87.00
□ **American,** Brattleboro, Vt., 1823	300.00	400.00	350.00

BICENTENNIAL

DESCRIPTION: The bicentennial, celebrated on July 4, 1976, was the 200th birthday of the United States as an independent nation. It was on July 4, 1776 that the Declaration of Independence was signed in Philadelphia, PA and the U.S. declared its freedom from England.

PERIOD: Bicentennial memorabilia was produced from the early 1970s until 1976.

COMMENTS: A variety of bicentennial commemoratives were made, from inexpensive trinkets to fine plates and silver.

ADDITIONAL TIPS: The listings are alphabetical by item. Other information includes, when possible, a description of the item, manufacturer, country of manufacture, production quantity and date. The first price listed is the issue price of the item; the second price is the current value of the item.

For more information on bicentennial memorabilia refer to *The Official Guide to Collector Plates* and *The Official Guide to American Silver and Silver Plate,* published by The House of Collectibles.

□ **Knife,** The American Eagle Bicentennial Series, commemorative set of five knives, handcrafted, solid nickel silver bolsters, brass linings, stainless steel blades	165.00	195.00	180.00
□ **Medal,** July 4, 1976, set of 12, sterling silver, 39 mm., Franklin Mint, U.S., production quantity 4,675, 1976 .... each	25.00	45.00	35.00

	Current Price Range		P/Y Average
☐ ....set	245.00	325.00	275.00
☐ **Medal,** sterling silver, 64 mm., Franklin Mint, U.S., production quantity 18,849, 1975–1976 ..	80.00	105.00	90.00
☐ **Medal,** sterling silver, 32 mm., Franklin Mint, U.S., production quantity 238,192, 1976	15.00	27.00	20.00
☐ **Medal,** thirteen original states, set of 13 medals, sterling silver, 39 mm., Franklin Mint, U.S., production quantity, 10,264 .... each	20.00	31.00	22.00
☐ ....set	250.00	305.00	275.00
☐ **Plate,** Across the Delaware, Wedgwood, Great Britain, 1975...............................	45.00	90.00	67.00
☐ **Plate,** Boston Tea Party, silver, Gorham Collection, U.S., production quantity 750, 1973	560.00	630.00	590.00
☐ **Plate,** Burning of the Gaspee, pewter, Gorham Collection, U.S., production quantity 5,000, 1971	40.00	50.00	45.00
☐ **Plate,** Calm Before the Storm, Armstrong's, U.S., production quantity 250, 1971	255.00	280.00	265.00
☐ **Plate,** Constellation, Kirk, U.S., production quantity 825, 1972...............................	80.00	90.00	82.00
☐ **Plate,** Crossing the Delaware, Stieff, U.S., production quantity 10,000, 1975	55.00	60.00	57.00
☐ **Plate,** The Declaration, Castleton China, U.S., production quantity 7,600, 1973.............	65.00	70.00	67.00
☐ **Plate,** The Declaration, porcelain, scalloped border, 9¾", Haviland, France, production quantity 10,000, 1976	40.00	50.00	42.00
☐ **Plate,** Declaration Signed, Wedgwood, Great Britain, 1976...............................	47.00	62.00	53.00
☐ **Plate,** E. Pluribus Unum, Bing and Grondahl, Denmark, 1976	55.00	60.00	56.00
☐ **Plate,** Eagle, blue satin glass, Fenton Art Glass, U.S., 1974	20.00	30.00	22.00
☐ **Plate,** Eagle, chocolate glass, Fenton Art Glass, U.S. 1975	16.00	29.00	22.00
☐ **Plate,** Eagle, white satin glass, Fenton Art Glass, U.S. 1976	16.00	29.00	22.00
☐ **Plate,** First in War, Ridgewood, U.S. production quantity 12,500, 1974	42.00	45.00	43.00
☐ **Plate,** Gaspee Incident, Armstrong's, U.S., production quantity 175, 1972	260.00	270.00	262.00
☐ **Plate,** Independence Hall, Bayel of France, France, production quantity 500, 1975	62.00	65.00	62.50
☐ **Plate,** John Hancock Signs the Declaration of Independence, sterling silver, bas-relief, 24kt gold inlaid and electro plated, 8", Franklin Mint, U.S. production quantity 10,166, 1976.............	180.00	215.00	195.00
☐ **Plate,** Liberty Bell, Bayel of France, France, production quantity 500, 1974	55.00	60.00	57.00
☐ **Plate,** Monticello, damascene silver, Reed and Barton, U.S., production quantity 1,000, 1972	80.00	90.00	82.00
☐ **Plate,** Mt. Vernon, damascene silver, Reed and Barton, U.S., 1973	80.00	90.00	82.00

	Current Price Range		P/Y Average
☐ **Plate,** A New Dawn, Castleton China, U.S., production quantity 7,600, 1972	65.00	67.00	66.00
☐ **Plate,** One Nation, Castleton China, U.S., production quantity 7,600, 1974	65.00	67.00	66.00
☐ **Plate,** Paul Revere, porcelain, scalloped border, 9¾″, Haviland, France, production quantity 10,000, 1975	35.00	55.00	42.00

BICYCLES

ORIGIN: A steerable wooden horse on wheels, the Draisienne, is considered to be the first modern bicycle. It was built in 1818. The first pedal driven bike appeared in Scotland in 1839. Later versions include the Velocipede, the High-Wheeler and the safety bike.

MAKER: Top manufacturers of the early bicycle were the Wright Brothers of Dayton, Ohio, and Columbia.

COMMENTS: Bicycles built before 1900 are the most collectible. Of particular note are the 1861 Velocipede with front wheel pedals and the 1885 Rover. Tricycles and quadricycles are especially rare and collectible.

ADDITIONAL TIPS: The listings are in alphabetical order; they are followed by the year of manufacture. Prices include a current price range as well as an average price for the previous year.

☐ **Adult tricycle,** 1885	5000.00	5800.00	5200.00
☐ **Boneshaker,** 1850	1750.00	2500.00	2100.00
☐ **Boneshaker,** 1870	1250.00	1800.00	1400.00
☐ **Buggy spoked triangle pedal high wheeler,** 1886	600.00	700.00	630.00
☐ **Chainless,** 1853	160.00	225.00	190.00
☐ **Chainless safety,** 1900	225.00	280.00	240.00
☐ **Columbia chainless,** 1856	225.00	280.00	240.00
☐ **Columbia high wheeler,** 1901	1350.00	2000.00	1500.00
☐ **Columbia,** three wheeler tandem tricycle, 1888	3350.00	4000.00	3500.00
☐ **Eagle,** 50 inch high wheeler, 1872	2250.00	2800.00	2500.00
☐ **Eagle,** high wheeler with brake, 1865	3250.00	4000.00	3500.00
☐ **Fifty inch high wheeler,** 1878	1350.00	1800.00	1450.00

Child's Bike, *Otto, iron, weighs 60 pounds, 1887,*
$250.00-$500.00

	Current Price Range		P/Y Average
☐ **Fifty-six inch high wheeler,** 1898	720.00	950.00	800.00
☐ **High wheeler bicycle,** 1885	1250.00	1850.00	1450.00
☐ **Scooter,** 1927	225.00	290.00	240.00
☐ **Solid tire safety,** 1890	820.00	1500.00	1000.00
☐ **Spring fork,** 1862	650.00	800.00	725.00
☐ **Tandem,** 1914	275.00	350.00	300.00
☐ **Tandem,** adult tricycle, 1885	6500.00	7500.00	7000.00
☐ **Tandem,** bicycle, 1895	380.00	500.00	425.00
☐ **Two wheeler,** 1896	380.00	500.00	425.00
☐ **Two wheeler,** 1914	150.00	200.00	175.00

BLACK MEMORABILIA

DESCRIPTION: A wide variety of items depicting blacks was produced from 1900 to 1960. Many were advertising promotions featuring Uncle Remus and Aunt Jemima type characters. Figural mammy kitchenware, slavery postcards, cast iron banks and doorstops, chalkware statues, dolls, figurines, etc., were very popular.

COMMENTS: Many of these items were extremely derogatory in nature and depicted blacks as slovenly and ignorant. The civil rights movement of the 1960s put an end to the production of racist depictions of blacks.

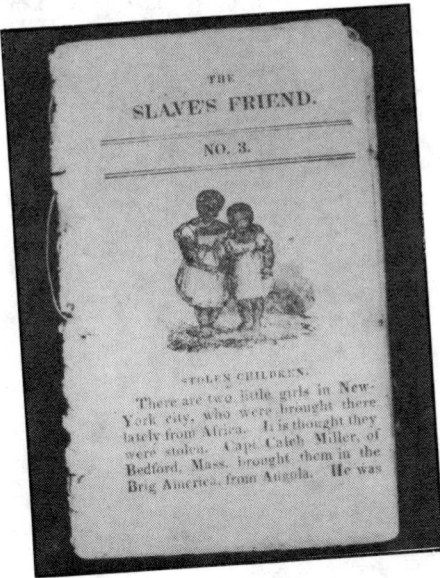

The Slave's Friend,
miniature children's magazine,
1842, **$40.00–$50.00**

	Current Price Range		P/Y Average
☐ **Advertising Poster,** Cascarets laxative, pullman passenger and black porter, wording "Is the road clear?" lithographed on heavy cardboard, 13″ x 17″	60.00	80.00	64.00
☐ **Advertising Sign,** Coon's Ice Cream, cardboard trimmed in tin, lithographed, red, cream with black stripes, 21″ x 60″, c. 1920	110.00	135.00	117.00
☐ **Bank,** Aunt Jemima, new, cast iron, 8″	8.00	10.00	9.00
☐ **Bell,** Mammy, new, bisque, red and yellow dress with white apron, holding mixing bowl	4.00	5.00	4.50
☐ **Book,** *Old Voices* by Howard Weeden, published by Doubleday, collection of black poetry, pictorial cover, 1904	25.00	30.00	26.25
☐ **Book,** *Ten Little Nigger Girls,* children's book with full color cover and colored illustrations along with rhymes, published in New York by E.P. Dutton, 9″ x 11″, c. 1900–1910	175.00	225.00	190.00
☐ **Booklet,** advertising, Excelsier Improved Varnish, 1940s, cover depicts black boy, read "Won't Turn White," eight pages long	1.00	2.00	1.50
☐ **Broom Holder,** Mammy, cast iron	140.00	145.00	142.00
☐ **Button,** advertising, new, black boy holding raccoon, Two Coons Axle Grease, color, 2¼″	1.00	2.00	1.50
☐ **Button,** advertising, new, Black Man, Georgia Cane Syrup, color, 2¼″	1.00	1.50	1.25
☐ **Button,** advertising, new, Pickaninny Girl with Watermelon, color, 2¼″	1.00	1.50	1.25
☐ **Candy Box,** Amos n' Andy	75.00	80.00	77.00
☐ **Cookie Jar,** Mammy, new, bisque, very colorful, 9½″	15.50	18.50	16.50
☐ **Cookie Jar,** Mammy, new, Rockingham Pottery, lid is on belly, brown and red with white trim, 9″	16.50	18.50	17.00
☐ **Doll,** Aunt Jemima Pancake Flour, cloth, uncut	65.00	70.00	67.00

Black Musicians, *Made in Japan,* $90.00–$125.00

	Current Price Range		P/Y Average

☐ **Doll,** baby, new, bisque, jointed arms and legs, three braided pigtails, red polka dot dress, 3½"
.... 5.00   6.00   5.00

☐ **Doll,** black baby, bisque, three patches of hair with ribbon, handpainted features, made in Japan, 3", c. 1930–1940 .... 80.00   100.00   84.00

☐ **Doll,** black girl, bisque, jointed, made in Japan, 4½", c. 1940 .... 30.00   40.00   32.00

☐ **Doll,** Bye-Lo Baby, new, black bisque head, arms and legs, lace trimmed gown and bonnet, 11"   9.00   11.00   10.00

☐ **Doll,** girl, new, bisque, jointed arms and legs, three braided pigtails, red polka dot dress, 6"   7.00   8.00   7.50

☐ **Doll,** Mammy, new, bisque head, arms, legs, stuffed body, fully dressed in colorful outfit with apron and bandana 16" 11.00   15.00   12.00

☐ **Doll,** Mammy, rag, new, Mammy flips over to Southern Belle doll, 14" 6.50   8.50   7.50

☐ **Doll,** Uncle Mose, cloth, uncut 65.00   70.00   67.00

☐ **Figurine,** Black Boy Eating Watermelon, new, bisque, colorful, 2" 2.50   3.50   2.75

☐ **Figurine,** Black Boy on Potty, bisque, dressed in yellow nightgown and red night cap, holding a slice of watermelon 4.00   6.00   4.75

☐ **Figurines,** set of five, new, New Orleans Jazz Band, bisque, five musicians dressed in tuxedos playing banjo, clarinet, horn, saxophone and drums, 3" 17.00   20.00   18.50

☐ **Figurine,** same as set above except old, made in Japan 90.00   125.00   95.00

☐ **Game,** Comic Conversation Cards, question and answer cards with black themes, lithograph of black man and woman on box lid playing the game, published by Ottmann, box measures 5¼" x 7¼", c. 1910 .... 175.00   225.00   190.00

☐ **Jigsaw Puzzle,** Amos and Andy, Pepsodent premium (they were sponsors of the show), full color, 8" x 10", c. 1930–1935 .... 100.00   130.00   110.00
Note: Price is for specimen in the original mailing envelope.

☐ **Kewpie,** vinyl, Rose O'Neill wings, 4½" 1.50   2.50   1.75

☐ **Label,** cane syrup, Uncle Remus, 1924, stone lithograph, says "Dis' Sho' Am Good," 6¾" x 20"
.... 8.00   8.50   8.25

☐ **Medal,** anti-slavery, white metal (imitation silver), British and Foreign Antislavery Society, pictures kneeling slave with legend, "Am I Not a Man and a Brother," also reads "A Voice from Great Britain to America," 1834 .... 90.00   115.00   97.00

☐ **Mirror,** advertising, Merrick Thread, depicts black boy hanging by thread over open mouthed alligator, saying "Fooled Dis Time Cully Dis Cotton Ain't Gwine To Break," 2" x 3" 1.50   2.50   1.75

Figurine, *German Bisque,* $75.00

	Current Price Range		P/Y Average
☐ **Mirror,** Aunt Jemima, round, color	1.00	1.50	1.25
☐ **Oven Paddle,** Mammy, new, wooden, full color picture of Mammy, 15½″	2.50	4.50	2.75
☐ **Pail,** peanut butter, pickaninny	20.00	25.00	22.00
☐ **Phonograph Record,** "Coon Band Contest," Columbia Wax Cylinder #531412, banjo solo, artist unbilled, c. 1890	40.00	60.00	45.00
☐ **Phonograph Record,** "If the Man in the Moon Were a Coon," Oxford Wax Cylinder #33083, soprano solo, artist unbilled, c. 1905	28.00	42.00	31.00
☐ **Photograph,** carte-de-visite of Sojourner Truth, early female activist for black equality, holds photo in her lap of Abraham Lincoln	200.00	250.00	215.00
☐ **Pin Back,** Aunt Jemima, color, 2¼″	1.00	1.50	1.25
☐ **Postcards,** set of twelve, shows different scenes of slavery, color...........................	6.00	8.00	6.50
☐ **Postcards,** 1940s, set of 25 assorted, Ashville Postcard Company, full color, variety of subjects including comical, Mammy, plantation, pickaninnies, etc	12.00	15.00	13.00
☐ **Poster,** broadside, anti-slavery, "Remarks on the Slave Trade" by Samuel Wood, 362 Pearl Street, New York City, woodcut of deck plan of slave ship showing overcrowding and atrocities to which slaves were subjected, 7¼″ x 12½″, undated, c. 1830–1840	600.00	800.00	640.00

	Current Price Range		P/Y Average

☐ **Print,** "Pore Lil Mose," lithographed page from book of the same name by cartoonist R.F. Outcault, full color, typical stereotyped likenesses and dialogue, 10" x 14", c. 1900–1905 .... **40.00 50.00 43.00**
Note: This value is for a single illustrated page. Complete copies of the book are rare.

☐ **Puzzle Postcard,** "Pick the Pickaninnies" by Ulman Manufacturing Company, lithographed card with five folding flaps, 3½" x 5½", 1907 **65.00 85.00 72.00**
Note: The flaps picture white and black children. Object of the puzzle is to fold the flaps so that only black children can be seen.

☐ **Salt and Pepper Shakers,** Aunt Jemima and Uncle Mose, new, ceramic, colorful, pair, 3¾" **4.00 5.00 4.50**

☐ **Salt and Pepper Shakers,** Mammy and Chef, new, porcelain, colorful, pair, 4½" **4.00 5.00 4.50**

☐ **Salt and Pepper Shakers,** Mammy, new, bisque, colorful, pair, 3" **4.00 5.00 4.50**

☐ **Salt and Pepper Shakers,** Mammy, new, celluloid, colorful, pair, 5" **3.50 5.50 4.50**

☐ **Sampler,** embroidered, pictures black boy and black girl dancing with wording "We're Free," red and black on white background, 8" x 6", 1863 **250.00 300.00 260.00**

☐ **Sheet Music,** "Three Little Words" from the motion picture "Check and Double Check," pictures Amos and Andy on cover, 9" x 12", 1930 ..... **20.00 30.00 23.00**

☐ **Sign,** railroad station sign for rest rooms with arrow pointing in one direction for "white," another for "colored," reverse painting on glass, B. & J. Signs, 12" x 4", 1929 .... **75.00 100.00 82.00**

☐ **Sign,** Picaninny Freeze, Hendler's Ice Cream, full color cartoon of black baby eating slice of watermelon with price 5¢, 11" x 14", 1922 .... **50.00 65.00 54.00**

☐ **String Holder,** Mammy, new, chalkware, wall mounted **8.00 9.00 8.50**

☐ **Thermometer,** composition, standing figural showing stereotyped wide-eyed black boy looking out from behind thermometer, wearing diaper, almost certainly a carnival giveaway, 5½", c. 1940–1950 .... **40.00 50.00 43.00**

☐ **Thermometer,** Mammy, new, metal picture of Mammy cooking, 7½" **2.00 3.00 2.50**

☐ **Thimble,** Mammy, bisque, new, figural, very colorful **2.00 3.00 2.50**

☐ **Token,** anti-slavery, front shows black beside tree waiting to board African slave ship, reverse reads "American Colonization Society, One Cent, Founded AD 1816," apparently dates from 1830s **175.00 225.00 190.00**

☐ **Toothpick Holder,** Mammy, new, bisque, colorful, 3" **2.00 3.00 2.50**

	Current Price Range		P/Y Average
☐ **Toy,** Alabama Coon Jigger, clockwork, lithographed tin figure of black man attached to tin base by rod, "dances" when wound up, made in Germany for Strauss of New York, M.I.B., 10", 1912	325.00	400.00	340.00
☐ **Toy,** Amos and Andy Fresh Air Taxi by Marx, lithographed tin, clockwork motor, 8", 1930 . . .	400.00	500.00	430.00
☐ **Toy,** dancing black man, carved and painted wood, fixed to bamboo rod and paddle, jointed at arms, hips and knees, unmarked, possibly folk art, figure is 4" tall with 26" paddle, c. early 1900s	200.00	250.00	215.00
☐ **Toy,** dancing black man, sheet metal figure mounted on a wood frame, curved arms, painted, believed to be the work of a blacksmith, figure is 11" tall and the frame measures 20", mid 1800s	700.00	875.00	740.00
☐ **Toy,** Jazzbo Jim, "The Dancer on the Roof," clockwork, lithographed tin figure of black man who dances on roof of house, made by Ferdinand Strauss, 10", c. 1920	325.00	400.00	355.00
☐ **Toy,** Mammy by Lindstrom, clockwork, lithographed tin, figure of black woman wearing apron, shakes when wound, 8", c. 1930–1940	200.00	250.00	215.00
☐ **Tape Measure,** Aunt Jemima, new, retractable, colorful	1.50	2.50	1.75
☐ **Wall Plaques,** Mammy and Chef chalkware, new, with hooks for hanging pot holders, 6"	7.00	8.00	7.50
☐ **Wall Plaques,** set of two, black boy and girl with umbrellas, new, chalkware, 8"	9.00	10.00	9.50

BOEHM

ORIGIN: Edward Marshall Boehm founded a pottery studio in Trenton, New Jersey in 1949. Following Mr. Boehm's death, his wife Helen took over the company. In addition to the Trenton studio there are Boehm studios in England.

The information here, including the prices listed below, is secondhand material gleaned from trade journals and Boehm advertising material. Boehm figurines are beautifully made and show a great deal of time and attention to detail. They are owned by American presidents as well as the crowned heads of Europe and the entire world.

PRICES: Following are selected auction results for items which are no longer being made. Because they are all pre-1971 items, it is assumed they were made in Trenton.

RECOMMENDED READING: For further information refer to *The Official Price Guide to Pottery and Porcelain* published by The House of Collectibles.

	Current Price Range		P/Y Average
☐ Blue Grosbeak	900.00	1100.00	925.00
☐ Bobolink	1000.00	1200.00	1050.00
☐ Boxer, large size	1050.00	1200.00	1075.00
☐ Carolina Wrens	5000.00	5750.00	5100.00
☐ Catbird	1675.00	1975.00	1700.00
☐ Crested Flycatcher	2150.00	2550.00	2200.00
☐ Downy Woodpecker	1350.00	1550.00	1400.00
☐ Fledgling Blue Jay	150.00	160.00	152.00
☐ Fledgling Canada Warbler	1450.00	1650.00	1500.00
☐ Fledgling Goldfinch	190.00	220.00	192.00
☐ Fledgling Magpie	680.00	800.00	690.00
☐ Fledgling Red Poll	170.00	190.00	175.00
☐ Green Jays	4425.00	4925.00	4450.00
☐ Lazuli Bunting Paperweight	130.00	140.00	132.00
☐ Mourning Doves	4625.00	5125.00	4650.00
☐ Nuthatch	235.00	285.00	240.00
☐ Oven-Bird	1350.00	1550.00	1355.00
☐ Parula Warbler	2350.00	2850.00	2355.00
☐ Polo Player	3750.00	4300.00	3775.00
☐ Prothonotary Warblers	420.00	470.00	425.00
☐ Road Runner	4400.00	4800.00	4450.00
☐ Rufous Hummingbirds	1800.00	2100.00	1850.00
☐ Scottish Terrier	460.00	550.00	470.00
☐ Standing Poodle, apricot-colored	1450.00	1650.00	1475.00
☐ Thoroughbred and Exercise Boy, decorated	6800.00	8000.00	6900.00
☐ Towhee	1850.00	2150.00	1900.00
☐ Tufted Titmice	1075.00	1275.00	1100.00
☐ Varied Buntings	4625.00	5125.00	4650.00
☐ Whippets	3250.00	4000.00	3275.00

Note: Current items range all the way from an $18 cup and saucer to a $35,000 Prince Rudolph's Blue Bird of Paradise.

BOOKPLATES

TOPIC: Bookplates are printed paper labels which identify the owner of a book.

PERIOD: These items were produced primarily during the 1600s and 1700s.

ORIGIN: The first bookplates were printed in Germany in the 15th century.

MATERIALS: Paper was used to make bookplates.

COMMENTS: Many enthusiasts collect bookplates that have similar designs, while others do not limit themselves. In Europe, where bookplate collecting is presently very popular, it is common to buy mixed packets of bookplates, much as mixed packets of stamps are offered to stamp collectors in the United States.

ADDITIONAL TIPS: The following listings are organized by artist.

	Current Price Range		P/Y Average
☐ **Bell, Robert,** design for Fanny Nicholson, c. 1900	7.00	9.00	8.10
☐ **Gill, Eric,** design for Scott Cunningham	7.00	10.00	8.50
☐ **Kent, Rockwell,** most designs	6.00	9.00	7.00
☐ **Parrish, Maxfield**	9.00	16.00	12.50
☐ **American Bookplates,** 18th century, except Revere or Hurd	6.00	8.00	6.50
☐ **Armorials,** 18th century, not done for famous people	4.75	8.00	5.00
☐ **Mixed Packet,** 50 different, 18th century	12.00	18.00	12.50
☐ **Mixed Packet,** 100 different, 18th century	25.00	40.00	28.00
☐ **Mixed Packet,** 50 different, 19th century	8.00	11.00	9.50
☐ **Mixed Packet,** 100 different, 19th century	14.00	17.00	14.50

BOOKS

TOPIC: Books have been extremely important in man's history, for they allow him to record information and distribute it to others in unaltered form.

TYPES: Books fall into two categories, fiction and non-fiction. The non-fiction books can be further subdivided by the subjects they deal with, such as medicine or natural history.

PERIOD: Books were first printed around 1450, although handwritten books were in existence earlier than that.

MATERIALS: Paper was used almost exclusively in producing books.

COMMENTS: Many book collectors limit themselves to one or two favorite writers or a favorite subject, since the field of book collecting is vast. A collection is judged on quality rather than quantity, since the number of books that would be appropriate in a collection is so large.

CONDITION: It is important that the book be in good condition. Books with water damage, fire damage, broken bindings or missing pages are worth significantly less than similar books in good condition.

TIPS: For further information please refer to *The Official Price Guide to Old Books and Autographs,* published by The House of Collectibles.

	Current Price Range		P/Y Average
☐ **Bronte, Charlotte,** *Jane Eyre,* London, 1847, three vols.	1100.00	1450.00	1150.00
☐ **Bronte, Charlotte,** *Shirley,* London, 1849, three vols.	1650.00	2175.00	1700.00
☐ **Bronte, Charlotte,** *The Professor,* London, 1857, two vols.	160.00	200.00	165.00
☐ **Bronte, Emily,** *Wuthering Heights,* London, 1847, three vols. The third volume is titled *Agnes Grey.* Only 1,000 copies were printed, though this was not a "limited edition" in the true sense of the term	10500.00	14500.00	10500.00
☐ **Brooke, Rupert,** *1914 and Other Poems,* London, 1915, softbound	40.00	55.00	46.00

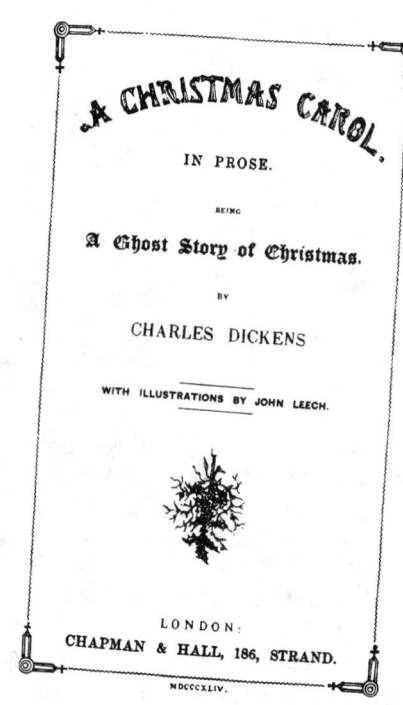

.A CHRISTMAS CAROL.

IN PROSE.

BEING

A Ghost Story of Christmas.

BY

CHARLES DICKENS

WITH ILLUSTRATIONS BY JOHN LEECH.

LONDON:
CHAPMAN & HALL, 186, STRAND.

MDCCCXLIV.

A Christmas Carol,
*title page, first edition,
by Charles Dickens,*
$400.00–$500.00

	Current Price Range		P/Y Average
☐ Brooke, Rupert, *Lithuania*, Chicago, 1915	165.00	190.00	170.00
☐ Brooke, Rupert, *Letters from America*, London, 1916	40.00	55.00	47.00
☐ Brooke, Rubert, *The Old Vicarage*, London, 1916, softbound	90.00	115.00	100.00
☐ Brooks, Van Wyck, *The Confident Years*, n.p., N.Y., 1922	32.00	38.00	32.00
☐ Brooks, Van Wyck, *The American Caravan*, N.Y., 1927	22.00	28.00	20.00
☐ Brooks, Van Wyck, *Sketches in Criticism*, N.Y., 1932	30.00	35.00	31.00
☐ Browning, Elizabeth B., *Two Poems*, London, 1854, softbound	42.00	57.00	46.00
☐ Browning, Elizabeth B., *Aurora Leigh*, N.Y., 1857, first American edition	42.00	57.00	46.00
☐ Browning, Elizabeth B., *Poems Before Congress*, London, 1860, blindstamped cloth	125.00	155.00	133.00
☐ Browning, Elizabeth B., *Last Poems*, London, 1862, purple cloth........................	63.00	82.00	69.00
☐ Browning, Elizabeth B., *Psyche Apocalypse*, London, 1876, softbound	52.00	73.00	59.00
☐ Browning, Elizabeth B., *Sonnets from the Portuguese*, London, 1887, one of eight copies on vellum	465.00	580.00	500.00

	Current Price Range		P/Y Average

☐ **Browning, Robert,** *Paracelsus,* London, 1835, boards with paper label 465.00 540.00 480.00

☐ **Clemens, Samuel Langhorne,** *Mark Twain, The Celebrated Jumping Frog of Calaveras County and Other Sketches,* edited by John Paul. The first issue has traditionally been identified by a page of yellow ads before the titlepage, and a normal letter "i" in "this" on page 198, last line. An effort is now under way to fix priority on basis of binding. The bindings are in assorted colors, but in some the gold-stamped frog adorning the front cover is at the center, in others at the lower left. It is believed (cautiously) the former represents an earlier or at least scarcer state, N.Y., 1867 . . . . 2200.00 2750.00 2400.00

☐ **Dickens, Charles,** *The Adventures of Oliver Twist,* London, 1846, third edition, ten parts, green wrappers 950.00 1275.00 1050.00

☐ **Dickens, Charles,** *The Adventures of Oliver Twist,* London, 1846, hard covers 275.00 325.00 265.00

☐ **Dickens, Charles,** *Nicholas Nickleby,* first issue has misspelling "vister" for "sister," page 123, line 17 of part four, London, 1838–1839, 19 parts, green wrappers 475.00 575.00 460.00

☐ **Dickinson, Emily,** *Poems,* edited by M.L. Todd and T.W. Higginson, Boston, 1890 . . . . 350.00 425.00 355.00

☐ **Eliot, T.S.,** *Charles Whibley,* London, 1931, softbound 40.00 55.00 47.00

☐ **Eliot, T.S.,** *After Strange Gods,* London, 1934 60.00 80.00 70.00

☐ **Eliot, T.S.,** *The Rock,* London, 1934 . . . . 35.00 45.00 40.00

☐ **Eliot, T.S.,** *Murder in the Cathedral,* London, 1935 . . . . 28.00 35.00 31.00

☐ **Eliot, T.S.,** *Four Quartets,* N.Y., 1943 . . . . 1250.00 1600.00 1400.00

☐ **Faulkner, William,** *Mosquitoes,* N.Y., 1927, blue cloth 1525.00 1950.00 1600.00

☐ **Faulkner, William,** *Sartoris,* N.Y., n.d., 1929 . . . 615.00 825.00 700.00

☐ **Faulkner, William,** *These Thirteen,* N.Y., n.d., 1931 . . . . 52.00 67.00 56.00

☐ **Faulkner, William,** *Idyll in the Desert,* N.Y., 1931, limited sign edition 670.00 835.00 700.00

☐ **Faulkner, William,** *Sanctuary,* N.Y., n.d., 1931 1050.00 1500.00 1200.00

☐ **Faulkner, William,** *Light in August,* N.Y., n.d., 1932 . . . . 120.00 145.00 125.00

☐ **Faulkner, William,** *Miss Zilphia Gant,* N.Y., 1932 . . . . 620.00 825.00 700.00

☐ **Faulkner, William,** *Salmagundi,* Milwaukee, 1932, softbound, limited edition 515.00 720.00 600.00

☐ **Garside, Alston H.,** *Cotton Goes to Market,* N.Y., 1934, 411 pp. 25.00 30.00 27.00

☐ **Gates, Charles M.,** *Messages of the Governors of the Territory of Washington to the Legislative Assembly,* 1854–1889, Seattle, 1940, 297 pp., softbound 35.00 42.00 38.00

	Current Price Range		P/Y Average

☐ **Hemingway, Ernest,** *The Sun Also Rises,* first state copies have misspelling "stopped" on page 181, line 26, N.Y., 1926, black cloth 675.00 825.00 700.00

☐ **Hemingway, Ernest,** *Men Without Women,* N.Y., 1927, weighs 15 to 15½ ounces in the first state 260.00 320.00 260.00

☐ **Hemingway, Ernest,** *Death in the Afternoon,* N.Y., 1932, black cloth, for fine copy in dustjacket 450.00 575.00 450.00

☐ **Hemingway, Ernest,** *Winner Take Nothing,* N.Y., 1933, black cloth 160.00 210.00 170.00

☐ **Hemingway, Ernest,** *God Rest You Merry Gentlemen,* N.Y., 1933, red cloth 365.00 435.00 380.00

☐ **Hemingway, Ernest,** *Green Hills of Africa,* N.Y., 1935, green cloth 115.00 145.00 127.00

☐ **Highbee, Elias and Thompson, R.B.,** *The Petition of the Latter-Day Saints, commonly known as Mormons,* Washington, D.C., 1840, 13 pp., softbound 220.00 270.00 240.00

☐ **Hill, Jasper S.,** *The Letters of A Young Miner, Covering the Adventures of Jasper S. Hill during the California Goldrush,* 1848–1852, San Francisco, 1964, 111 pp., limited to 475 copies, with a folding map 65.00 80.00 72.00

☐ **Smith, Samuel,** *Memoirs of the Life of Samuel Smith,* Middleborough, Mass., 1853 . . . . 140.00 170.00 155.00

☐ **Smith, Samuel,** *History of the Province of Pennsylvania,* Philadelphia, 1913, 231 pp. 15.00 20.00 17.00

☐ **Smith, Sara S.,** *The Founders of the Massachusetts Bay Colony,* Pittsfield, Mass., 1897, 372 pp., bound in cloth 40.00 50.00 44.00

☐ **Steinbeck, John,** *Saint Katy the Virgin,* N.p., n.d. (N.Y., 1936), limited to 199 signed copies, rare 1200.00 1500.00 1350.00

☐ **Steinbeck, John,** *Nothing So Monstrous,* N.Y., 1936, limited to 370 copies 300.00 375.00 330.00

☐ **Steinbeck, John,** *In Dubious Battle,* N.Y., n.d., 1936, orange cloth 125.00 160.00 136.00

☐ **Steinbeck, John,** *The Red Pony,* N.Y., 1937, limited to 699 signed copies, boxed 150.00 180.00 166.00

☐ **Steinbeck, John,** *Of Mice and Men,* N.Y., n.d., 1937, beige cloth 90.00 115.00 100.00

☐ **Wilder, Thornton,** *The Angel That Troubled the Waters,* N.Y., 1928, limited, signed 38.00 48.00 40.00

☐ **Wilder, Thornton,** *The Long Christmas Dinner,* N.Y., 1931 . . . . 38.00 48.00 40.00

☐ **Wilder, Thornton,** *The Ides of March,* N.Y., 1948, limited to 750, signed 85.00 110.00 95.00

☐ **Williams, Tennessee,** *The Glass Menagerie,* N.Y., 1945 . . . . 125.00 150.00 133.00

☐ **Williams, Tennessee,** *A Streetcar Named Desire,* n.p., n.d., (Norfolk, 1947) 125.00 150.00 133.00

☐ **Williams, Tennessee,** *The Roman Spring of Mrs. Stone,* n.p., n.d., (N.Y., 1950), limited to 500, signed 185.00 235.00 205.00

	Current Price Range		P/Y Average

	Current Price Range		P/Y Average
☐ **Williams, Tennessee,** *Cat on a Hot Tin Roof,* n.p., n.d., (N.Y., 1955)	50.00	70.00	45.00

BOTTLES

DESCRIPTION: With the availability of cheaper containers made of plastic, aluminum and paper, glass bottles are declining rapidly as a form of storage. With the decline of bottle production, more collectors are realizing how important old bottles are, especially as they relate to history.

TYPES: There are many types of bottles found on the collectible market including ale and gin, beer, cosmetic, bitters, crocks, cure, food, ink, medicine, mineral water, poison, pontil, soda and spirits. Because of their collector appeal, flasks, fruit jars and Hutchinson bottles are listed separately.

ADDITIONAL TIPS: This section is organized alphabetically by bottle type. For additional information on bottles, consult *The Official Price Guide to Bottles Old & New,* published by The House of Collectibles.

☐ **Bitters,** Baker's High Life, the Great Nerve Tonic embossed on back, tapered top, machine made, pint	15.00	25.00	20.00
☐ **Bitters,** Baxter's Mandrake, Lord Bros. Prop. Burlington, Vt. on vertical panels, amethyst, 6½"	10.00	20.00	15.00
☐ **Bitters,** Begg's Dandelion Bitters in three lines, tapered top, base to neck a plain band, amber, 7¾"	21.00	26.00	22.50
☐ **Bitters,** Dr. Boyce's Tonic label, sample size, twelve panels, aqua, 4½"	10.00	15.00	14.75
☐ **Bitters,** The Bitters Pharmacy on label, clear, 4½"	4.00	6.00	5.00
☐ **Bitters,** Caroni, pint, amber	10.00	20.00	15.00
☐ **Bitters,** Celery & Chamomile on label, square, amber, 10"	10.00	20.00	15.00
☐ **Bitters,** Dr. E. Chyder Stomach Bitters, N.O., amber, 10"	18.00	23.00	20.00

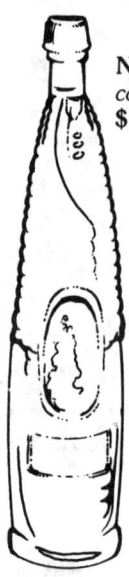

National Bitters Bottle, *ear of corn design, burgundy, 12½",* **$160.00–$400.00**

S. T. Drake's Plantation Bitters Jar, *square body, expanded lip, golden amber, 9½",* **$160.00–$400.00**

	Current Price Range		P/Y Average
□ **Bitters,** Compound Calisaya Bitters in two lines, tapered top, square, amber, 9½"	14.00	18.00	15.75
□ **Bitters,** Fer-Kina Galeno on shoulder, beer type bottle, brown, machine made, 10⅛"	10.00	15.00	12.50
□ **Cure,** Dr. Taylor's Sure Chill Cure, on side Richardson Taylor Med. Co., ring top, aqua, 5½" ..	5.00	10.00	7.00
□ **Cure,** Twenty-Four Hour Cure Guaranteed, ring top, clear, 5"	8.00	12.00	9.50
□ **Cure,** Veno's Lightning Cough Cure, double ring top, aqua, 7¼"	7.00	10.00	8.25
□ **Cure,** White's Quick Healing Cure, amber, 6¼"	9.00	12.00	10.25
□ **Cure,** Wood's Great Peppermint Cure for Coughs and Colds, clear, 6½"	7.00	10.00	8.50
□ **Food,** Hires Improved Root Beer, Panel, Mfg. by The Charles Hires Co., panel, Philadelphia Pa., U.S.A., panel, Make five Gallons of a Delicious Drink, aqua, 4¾"	5.00	7.00	4.60
□ **Food,** Joslyn's Maple Syrup, eight sides, round lip, aqua, 8"	5.00	8.00	6.50
□ **Food,** Kelloggs, oval, clear	2.00	3.05	1.40
□ **Food,** Mason, Belvidere, III in center, Dairy in a circle, ½ pt. base M, dots on shoulder, clear ..	12.00	18.00	14.50
□ **Food,** My Wife's Salad Dressing, machine made, blue green, 8"	5.00	8.00	6.20
□ **Food,** Nut House, figure of house, store jar, ball shape, clear	14.00	18.00	14.50
□ **Food,** Peppermint, marble in center of neck, aqua, 7¼	10.00	13.00	9.90

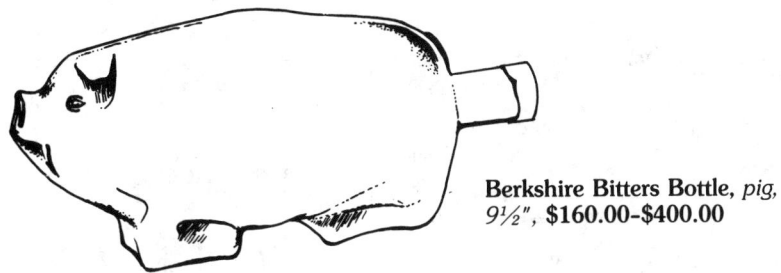

Berkshire Bitters Bottle, *pig,*
9½", **$160.00-$400.00**

American Life Bitters Bottle,
cabin design, amber, 9", **$160.00-$400.00**

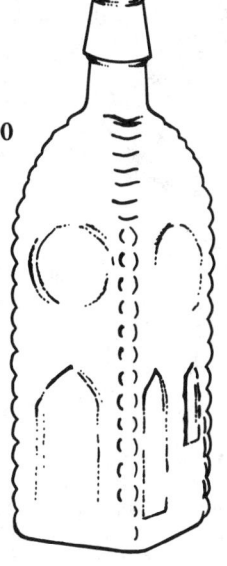

	Current Price Range		P/Y Average
☐ **Food,** Planters, same in back, square, glass top with peanut nobs, clear	30.00	40.00	31.00
☐ **Food,** Red Snapper Sauce Co., Memphis, Tenn., six sides, clear, 9½"	9.00	13.00	9.75
☐ **Food,** Warsaw Pickle Co., aqua, 8¾"	7.00	10.00	8.20
☐ **Ink,** Angus & Co., cone, aqua, 3½"	5.00	7.00	4.75
☐ **Ink,** Arnold's round, clear or amethyst, 2½" . . .	6.00	8.00	5.75
☐ **Ink,** B&B, pottery bottle, tan, 7½"	7.00	9.00	6.50
☐ **Ink,** Billing & Co., Banker's Writing Ink, aqua, 2"	14.00	20.00	12.00

	Current Price Range		P/Y Average

□ **Medicine,** Balsam of Honey, pontil, aqua, 3¼″ 25.00 35.00 29.00
□ **Medicine,** Dr. Barkman's Never Failing Liniment printed on front, light green, 6¼″ 5.00 7.00 5.75
□ **Medicine,** T.B. Barton, clear or amethyst, 4½″ 3.00 5.00 3.75
□ **Medicine,** Batemans Drops, vertical, cylindrical, amethyst, 5¼″ 3.00 5.00 4.00
□ **Medicine,** Dr. Bell's, The E.E. Sutherland Medicine Co., Paducah, Ky., Pine Tar Honey, aqua, 5½″ 7.00 12.00 3.75
□ **Medicine,** Borax, clear, 5¼″ 12.00 18.00 14.50
□ **Medicine,** B & P, amber, Lyons Powder on shoulder of opposite side, 4¼″ 3.00 5.00 3.75
□ **Medicine,** F. Brown's, aqua, 5½″ 5.00 8.00 4.75
□ **Medicine,** Brown Sarsaparilla, aqua, 9½″ 6.00 9.00 7.50
□ **Medicine,** Brown's Instant Relief for Pain, aqua, embossed, 5¼″ 3.00 5.00 3.75
□ **Medicine,** Burnett, clear, 6¾″ 8.00 11.00 9.25
□ **Medicine,** California Fig Syrup Co., Califig, Sterling Products Successor on front, rectangular, clear, 6¾″ 3.00 5.00 3.60
□ **Mineral,** San Francisco Glass works, tapered neck, blob top, green, 6⅞″ 14.00 19.00 16.00

 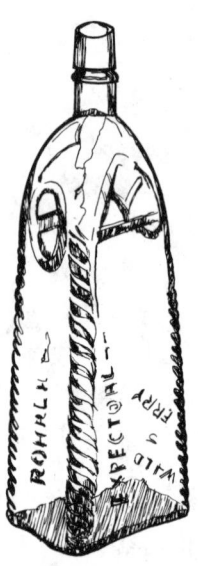 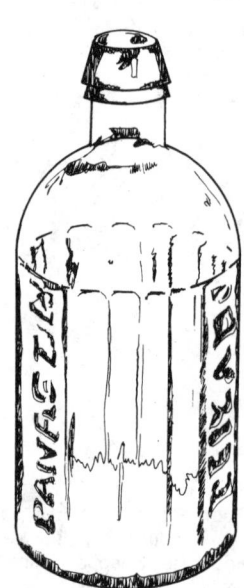

Left to Right: *Vaughn's Vegetable Lithontriptic Mixture Medicine Bottle, blue, 8½″; Rohrer's Wild Cherry Tonic Medicine Bottle, pyramid shape, amber, 10½″; Swaim's Panacea Medicine Bottle, yellow green, 8¼″,*
$45.00-$75.00

	Current Price Range		P/Y Average
☐ **Mineral,** Saratoga Spring, honey amber, 9¾"	30.00	40.00	34.00
☐ **Mineral,** Shasta Water Co., Mineral Water Co., amber, 10½"	7.00	9.00	7.70
☐ **Mineral,** UTE Chief of Mineral Water, Maniton, Colo., U.T. on base, crown top, clear or purple, 8"	5.00	8.00	6.50
☐ **Mineral,** Veronica Mineral Water printed around shoulder, square, amber, clear 10¼"	8.00	11.00	9.50
☐ **Mineral,** Weller Bottling Works, Saratoga, N.Y., blob top, aqua	8.00	12.00	9.75
☐ **Mineral,** Adam W. Young, Canton, Ohio, graduated collar, aqua, 9¼"	7.00	9.00	7.70
☐ **Poison,** Baltimore, MD. printed on bottom, amber, 3"	3.00	4.00	3.25
☐ **Poison,** Browns Rat Killer, under it C. Wakefield Co., applied lip, aqua, 3"	7.00	11.00	8.50
☐ **Poison,** DPS, skull and cross on front, cross on four sides, ring top, cobalt	8.00	12.00	10.00
☐ **Poison,** Eli Lilly & Co., Poison on each panel, amber, 2"	7.00	10.00	8.50
☐ **Poison,** Evans Medical Ltd., Liverpool, label, Chloroform B.A. Poison, number and U.Y.B. under bottom, ABM, amber, 6½"	5.00	8.00	6.50
☐ **Poison,** F.S. & Co. on base, Poison vertically, surrounded by dots, two sides plain, ringtop, amber, 2¾"	11.00	16.00	13.00
☐ **Poison,** R.C. Millings Bed Bug Poison, Charleston, S.C. shoulder strap on side, clear, 6¼"	12.00	17.00	14.00
☐ **Poison,** Rat Poison printed horizontal on round bottle, clear or amethyst, 2½"	18.00	26.00	21.00
☐ **Poison,** Tincture Iodine printed in three lines under skull and crossbones, square, amber	6.00	9.00	7.50
☐ **Poison,** Triloids printed on one panel of bottle, Poison on another, cobalt, 3¼"	6.00	9.00	7.50
☐ **Poison,** Wyeth Poison printed vertical on back, round ring base and top, cobalt, 2¼"	10.00	15.00	12.00
☐ **Pontil,** Allen Mrs. S.A. printed on one side, on front World's Hair Balsam, 355 Broone St printed in three lines, aqua, 6½"	19.00	27.00	22.00
☐ **Pontil,** Bake's Dr. printed on front, tapered top, pale aqua, 5"	24.00	37.00	29.00
☐ **Pontil,** Balsam of Honey printed on three lines, round bottle, ring top, aqua, 3"	19.00	27.00	23.00
☐ **Pontil,** Brown's, F., Ess of Jamaica Ginger, Philad. printed on four lines, tapered top, oval, aqua, 5½"	10.00	15.00	12.00
☐ **Pontil,** Cannington Shaw & Co., St. Helens on top of L.D. beaded decoration around shoulder	14.00	21.00	17.00
☐ **Pontil,** Cooke's Carmine Ink printed on two lines, bell shaped, ring top, aqua, 1½"	15.00	21.00	17.50
☐ **Pontil,** Dalby's Carminate printed on two lines, round, light ring top, 3¾"	20.00	27.00	24.00
☐ **Pontil,** Harrison's Columbia Ink printed on three lines, round, ring top, cobalt, 4½"	30.00	42.00	33.00

	Current Price Range		P/Y Average

☐ **Pontil,** Hauel, J., Phila. on two lines in sunken panel, oval, light ring top, aqua, 3¾" **12.00 18.00 14.00**

☐ **Pontil,** Hoover, Phila. 12 panels, ring top, light green **18.00 27.00 22.00**

☐ **Pontil,** Snuff, label, flare top, short neck, beveled corners, olive amber, 4½" **12.00 18.00 14.50**

☐ **Pontil,** Taylor & Co., Varparaiso Chile printed on three lines, blob top, dark green, 7¼" **45.00 63.00 52.00**

☐ **Spirits,** Acker Merrall, label, A9 on bottom, amber, 11" **8.00 11.00 9.50**

☐ **Spirits,** Bailey's Whiskey, clear or amethyst, 9¾" **8.00 11.00 9.75**

☐ **Spirits,** B&B, clear or amber **4.00 6.00 4.75**

☐ **Spirits,** Belle of Nelson, label, whiskey, M.M. on bottom, clear, 12" **7.00 10.00 7.25**

☐ **Spirits,** E.R. Betterton & Co., distillers Chattanooga, Tenn. printed on three lines in sunken panel on back, raised panel plain, flask, three ribs on each side, twenty ribs around neck, on bottom a diamond with letter Y, brown **7.00 10.00 8.75**

BOXES

DESCRIPTION: Versatile and charming, boxes not only have a variety of uses but they are also quite collectible.

MATERIALS: Boxes are made using a variety of materials including straw, wood, china and glass.

COMMENTS: In the 18th and 19th centuries boxes were mostly for utilitarian use such as perishable food storage. Special boxes were made to hold such items as wedding dresses. Small boxes, for trinkets, matches or cigarettes, seem to be especially intricate and collectible.

ADDITIONAL TIPS: The listings in this section are alphabetical according to type of box, followed by descriptions and date.

☐ **Apple Box,** footed, smoked finish **260.00 310.00 275.00**

☐ **Apple Box,** pine, painted, 11" x 8½" **55.00 80.00 62.00**

	Current Price Range		P/Y Average
☐ **Ballot Box,** maple, oblong, sliding top	105.00	135.00	120.00
☐ **Band Box,** oval, painted, schoolhouse, flowers and trees on lid, 9″ x 6″	1400.00	1900.00	1600.00
☐ **Band Box,** man and woman with flowers on lid, flowers on sides	1300.00	1800.00	1500.00
☐ **Band Box,** hunter shooting deer	600.00	700.00	585.00
☐ **Bible Box,** carved oak, English, mid 1600's . . .	430.00	480.00	450.00
☐ **Book-shaped Box,** inlaid, large	85.00	110.00	90.00
☐ **Book-shaped Box,** with name and dated 1861	325.00	375.00	350.00
☐ **Book-shaped Box,** Pennsylvania German, painted wood	55.00	110.00	75.00
☐ **Book-shaped Box,** inlaid colored wax hearts, stars	30.00	45.00	38.00
☐ **Box,** Wilcox, quadruple plate, scrolls, pointer dogs, lock lion's paw feet, 9″ x 5″	185.00	210.00	182.00
☐ **Brass Box,** covered with leather, shape of coffin	50.00	70.00	55.00
☐ **Bride's Box,** painted flowers, dark green, c. 1817	275.00	325.00	275.00
☐ **Bride's Box,** oval, painted bride and groom with floral motif, 18″	385.00	435.00	400.00
☐ **Bride's Box,** German or Pennsylvania German, oval, 19th c.	210.00	260.00	225.00
☐ **Butter Box,** six individual containers	110.00	145.00	118.00
☐ **Candle Box,** cherry, carved, scalloped arch . . .	410.00	460.00	425.00
☐ **Candle Box,** geometric design, carved and inlaid, 8″	110.00	145.00	118.00
☐ **Candle Box,** pine, sliding lid, red border, knob on lid, 14″	385.00	430.00	400.00
☐ **Candle Box,** tin, hanging, round	180.00	230.00	200.00
☐ **Cheese Box,** tree and leaf design, inlaid mahogany, 7″ Dia.	380.00	430.00	400.00
☐ **Cigar Box,** coromandel with brass fittings, mid 19th c.	180.00	230.00	200.00
☐ **Cigarette Box,** "Wavecrest," cream, blue, white, pink forget-me-nots, word "Cigarettes," 4″ H.	260.00	310.00	275.00
☐ **Cigarette Box,** cloisonne, cylindrical, unmarked	65.00	110.00	80.00
☐ **Cigarette or Chocolate Box,** brass, Princess Mary, WW1, with Mary, and names of Allies around lid	38.00	48.00	40.00
☐ **Cigarette Box,** green, Lenox wreath mark, Lenox	29.00	33.00	31.00
☐ **Cigarette Box,** pink daisy design, square with lid, 4½″, Southern Potteries	6.00	8.00	7.00
☐ **Cigarette Box,** rounded corners, ribbing, relief apple blossom design, green with white flowers, Lenox wreath mark, Lenox	49.00	55.00	52.00
☐ **Cigarette Box,** rounded corners, ribbing, relief apple blossom design, Lenox wreath mark, Lenox	34.00	38.00	36.00
☐ **Cigarette Box,** white with Lenox Rose trim, Lenox wreath mark, Lenox	43.00	48.00	45.00

Cigarette Box, *Lenox, shape #3033, rose design,* $50.00–$55.00

	Current Price Range		P/Y Average
☐ **Cigarette Box,** white with Ming trim, Lenox wreath mark, Lenox	49.00	55.00	52.00
☐ **Coin Box,** oak, changer, c. 1823	260.00	310.00	275.00
☐ **Collar Box,** man's, with drawer, black with red lining	9.00	13.00	10.00
☐ **Cookie Box,** round with lid and handle, Pennsylvania Dutch design	280.00	330.00	300.00
☐ **Cutlery Box,** triple compartments, walnut, 10″ x 16″	60.00	70.00	60.00
☐ **Deed Box,** wood, carved	80.00	105.00	82.00
☐ **Desk Box,** mahoghany, compartments for writing tools and ink, original hardware, 5″ x 4½″ x 14″	280.00	330.00	300.00
☐ **Desk Box,** painted red, slant lid, 17½″ W.	110.00	135.00	112.00
☐ **Dome Top Box,** bird motif, 10″ W.	460.00	510.00	475.00
☐ **Dresser Box,** orange plush with molded celluloid trim, all tools intact	30.00	40.00	30.00
☐ **Glove Box,** coromandel, gilt brass with green stones inlaid	65.00	95.00	75.00
☐ **Glove Box,** covered with wallpaper	80.00	110.00	82.00
☐ **Hat Box,** covered with bird motif wallpaper ...	135.00	160.00	138.00
☐ **Hat Box,** wooden, original finish and hardware, c. 1874–90	110.00	135.00	112.00
☐ **Herb Box,** oval, original paint and lid	280.00	330.00	300.00
☐ **Jewel Box,** miniature, antique Japanese bronze d'or and black laquer, gold design, two drawers, footed, 2½″ x 2″, 19th century	300.00	360.00	325.00
☐ **Jewelry Box,** plated silver (replated), cherubs playing, 8″ x 6″ x 3″	110.00	160.00	125.00

	Current Price Range		P/Y Average

☐ **Jewel Casket,** Simpson, Hall and Miller silver-plate, round on pedestal with three cupids with wings, finial, another cherub **110.00 160.00   125.00**

☐ **Jewel Box,** Jenning Bros. ormolu, scenes of lovers, children in relief, pink plush lining, 2½″ H. **22.00   32.00   25.00**

☐ **Jewel Box,** Pairpont "Wavecrest," 9″ Dia. **725.00 825.00   750.00**

☐ **Jewel Box,** "Wavecrest," ormolu mounts, square shape, 7″ x 7″ x 5″ **425.00 475.00   425.00**

☐ **Knife Box,** curly maple, dovetailed **55.00   70.00   58.00**

☐ **Knife Box,** pine, scalloped, dovetailed **160.00 185.00   162.00**

☐ **Knife Box,** walnut, carved handle **110.00 135.00   112.00**

☐ **Lacquered Box,** octagonal, yellow with Oriental designs, early 19th c. **280.00 330.00   300.00**

☐ **Lap desk,** brass inlaid, walnut, 15″ W. **140.00 190.00   150.00**

☐ **Leather Box,** pressed design **14.00   20.00   15.00**

☐ **Lectern Box,** carved, painted, with carved book on top **17000.00 18000.00   17000.00**

☐ **Lunch Box,** oval, 19th c. **45.00   55.00   45.00**

☐ **Lunch Box,** tin, Art Deco design, nursery characters **45.00   55.00   45.00**

☐ **Match Box,** shaped like treasure chest with acorn finial, unmarked, 3″, Willets Manufacturing Company **40.00   50.00   43.00**

☐ **Match Box,** wooden, carved, 5″ H. **32.00   42.00   35.00**

☐ **Miniature Box,** antique Satsuma, rectangular, children and swans on cover and interior, 3½″, 18th century **300.00 360.00   330.00**

☐ **Pantry Box,** Scandinavian Bentwood **110.00 150.00   125.00**

☐ **Pantry Box,** varnished, 10″ **28.00   42.00   32.00**

☐ **Pantry Box,** two-fingered round, small size ... **110.00 150.00   120.00**

☐ **Pantry Box,** three-fingered oval, painted red (possibly Shaker) **135.00 180.00   150.00**

☐ **Pantry Box,** oval, two-fingered, c. 1820 ...... **135.00 180.00   150.00**

☐ **Pantry Boxes,** five graduated, round, painted **160.00 210.00   180.00**

☐ **Patch Box,** Royal Bayreuth tapestry, five sheep on lid, gray mark, 2½″ x 1½″ **140.00 180.00   150.00**

☐ **Pencil Box,** sliding lid, dovetailed **22.00   32.00   25.00**

☐ **Pipe Box,** pine, drawer, dovetailed **330.00 360.00   338.00**

☐ **Pottery Box,** covered, oval, all white with shell molded base, shell finial on lid, 5¾″, Bennington **80.00   95.00   84.00**

☐ **Pottery Box,** square with Lion of Lucerne figure, Bennington **120.00 130.00   124.00**

☐ **Rouge Box,** round, embossed rims and ornate finial, undecorated, C.A.C. green palette mark, Lenox **40.00   50.00   44.00**

☐ **Salt Box,** curved front, flat black, painted red **55.00   70.00   62.00**

☐ **Salt Box,** maple and cherry, striped wood, hinged cover, hanging **110.00 135.00   112.00**

☐ **Salt Box,** pine, dovetailed, open, hanging **90.00   110.00   92.00**

☐ **Salt Box,** walnut, dovetailed, slant lid, hanging **140.00 170.00   150.00**

☐ **Salt Box,** Pennsylvania Dutch design, two compartments, open **180.00 210.00   182.00**

	Current Price Range		P/Y Average
☐ **Seed Box,** compartments, sliding lid	135.00	160.00	138.00
☐ **Shaving Box,** brush	45.00	55.00	45.00
☐ **Snuff Box,** Austrian silver gilt, musical with sectional comb, 9 cm., hallmarked Vienna, c. 1828	2300.00	2700.00	2460.00
☐ **Snuff Box,** French tortoiseshell, musical with sectional comb, 9 cm., c. 1810	1200.00	1800.00	1450.00
☐ **Snuff Box,** Mauchline ware, boxwood, 3½″ W.	55.00	80.00	62.00
☐ **Snuff Box,** horn, acorn-shaped, screw-on top, 1¾″	28.00	38.00	30.00
☐ **Snuff Box,** pewter	38.00	48.00	40.00
☐ **Snuff Box,** treenware, 2¾″ Dia.	18.00	24.00	18.00
☐ **Spice Box,** cherry, nine drawers, original, 13″ H.	150.00	175.00	152.00
☐ **Spice Box,** curly maple, twelve drawers, brass pulls	315.00	365.00	325.00
☐ **Spice Box,** oak, eight drawers, wooden pulls, hanging	80.00	110.00	82.00
☐ **Spice Box,** pine, eight drawers, porcelain pulls, hanging	100.00	130.00	102.00
☐ **Spice Box,** tin, eight drawers, painted black ...	100.00	130.00	102.00
☐ **Spice Box,** walnut, two drawers, carved back, dovetailed	280.00	330.00	300.00
☐ **Stamp Box,** brass, footed, covered	45.00	55.00	45.00
☐ **Stamp Box,** pewter, hinged top	65.00	85.00	70.00
☐ **Stamp Box,** sterling with enameled lid, chair and finger ring	28.00	38.00	30.00
☐ **Stationery Box,** walnut with brass and ivory decoration, 7″ H., late 19th c.	120.00	170.00	135.00
☐ **Tea caddy,** Marguetry, English, c. 1780	550.00	650.00	662.00
☐ **Tea caddy,** imitation tortoise shell, green, English, early 19th c.	230.00	280.00	250.00
☐ **Tin Box,** with brass rings, hand embossed arch and bullseye, c. 1880	30.00	40.00	33.00
☐ **Tin Box,** "Breethem" breath sweetener box, picture of a woman and product slogan	1.50	3.00	2.10
☐ **Tobacco Box,** Pennsylvania Dutch design, 19″ H.	55.00	70.00	62.00
☐ **Tool Box,** oak	28.00	32.00	30.00
☐ **Tool Box,** child's, with tools, c. 1930	45.00	55.00	45.00
☐ **Tramp Art Box,** footed, geometic design, hinged top, 14″ x 15″	185.00	210.00	182.00
☐ **Tramp Art Wall Boxes,** small	32.00	48.00	38.00
☐ **Trinket Box,** Art Deco, woman on cover, 6½″, Fulper Pottery	195.00	205.00	199.00
☐ **Trinket Box,** painted, one drawer	325.00	375.00	325.00
☐ **Trinket Box,** papier mache and antique sulphide, design features four women, 2¾″, 18th century	350.00	400.00	360.00
☐ **Trinket Box,** rectangle, hand painted red roses with gold trim, 2″ x 4″, Lenox palette mark, Lenox	75.00	85.00	77.00
☐ **Trinket Box,** round, Ming pattern, 3¾″, Lenox wreath mark, Lenox	115.00	125.00	119.00

	Current Price Range		P/Y Average
☐ **Trinket Box,** round, undecorated, 3¾″, Lenox pallette mark, Lenox	42.00	48.00	44.00
☐ **Trinket Box,** wooden, carved, painted flowers, 6″ H.	325.00	375.00	325.00
☐ **Wall Box,** open top, painted brown, 19th c. . . .	160.00	210.00	175.00
☐ **Writing Box,** oak, English, 13½″ W., 18th c. . .	135.00	185.00	150.00
☐ **Writing Box,** Shaker, two drawers	135.00	185.00	150.00

BOXING

DESCRIPTION: Boxing draws many fans into its realm each year. This fascinating sport keeps collectors on their toes searching for memorabilia relating to their favorite athlete.

PERIOD: Boxing began in the late 1800s and has continued to thrive through the twentieth century.

TYPE: There are many different items boxing enthusiasts can collect including autographed photos, magazines, posters, cards and programs.

ADDITIONAL TIPS: This section is alphabetized according to item. For more information about boxing memorabilia, consult *The Official Price Guide to Sports Collectibles,* published by The House of Collectibles.

	Current Price Range		P/Y Average
☐ **Autograph, Muhammad Ali,** plain card ink . . .	4.00	6.00	4.75
☐ **Autograph, Muhammad Ali,** plain card, pencil	3.00	4.00	3.25
☐ **Autograph, Mahammad Ali,** 8″ x 10″, black and white photo, ink	12.00	17.00	14.00
☐ **Autograph, Muhammad Ali,** 8″ x 10″, color photo, ink	15.00	20.00	17.00
☐ **Autograph, Cassius Clay,** plain card, ink	50.00	70.00	59.00
☐ **Autograph, Cassius Clay,** plain card, pencil . .	40.00	50.00	45.00
☐ **Autograph, James Corbett,** small photo, ink	50.00	65.00	57.00
☐ **Autograph, Jack Dempsey,** plain card, ink . . .	5.00	8.00	6.00
☐ **Autograph, George Foreman,** plain card, ink	1.00	2.00	1.30
☐ **Autograph, George Foreman,** 8″ x 10″, black and white photo, ink	2.00	4.00	3.00

Poster,
*Sugar Ray Leonard vs.
Thomas Hearnes for the
Welterweight Championship,
September 16, 1981,
Caesar's Palace, Las Vegas,
full color, signed "Moss,"
24" × 18½",*
$15.00-$25.00

	Current Price Range		P/Y Average
☐ Autograph, **Joe Frazier,** plain card, ink	1.00	2.00	1.30
☐ Autograph, **Joe Frazier,** 8" x 10", black and white photo, ink	2.00	4.00	3.00
☐ Autograph, **Rocky Graziano,** plain card, ink ..	1.00	2.00	1.30
☐ Autograph, **Rocky Graziano,** 8" x 10", black and white photo, ink	2.00	4.00	3.00
☐ Autograph, **James Jeffries,** plain card, ink ...	20.00	25.00	22.00
☐ Autograph, **James Jeffries,** check, ink	50.00	65.00	57.00
☐ Autograph, **James Jeffries,** letter, ink	60.00	80.00	70.00
☐ Autograph, **Stanley Ketchel,** plain card, ink ..	23.00	29.00	26.00
☐ Autograph, **Stanley Ketchel,** letter, ink	42.00	57.00	48.00
☐ Autograph, **Sugar Ray Leonard,** plain card, ink	1.00	2.00	1.30
☐ Autograph, **Sugar Ray Leonard,** 8" x 10", black and white photo, ink	2.00	4.00	3.00
☐ Autograph, **Joe Louis,** plain card, ink	15.00	20.00	17.00
☐ Autograph, **Rocky Marciano,** plain card, ink	20.00	30.00	25.00
☐ Autograph, **Rocky Marciano,** 8" x 10", black and white photo, ink	30.00	40.00	35.00
☐ Autograph, **Harry Wills,** plain card, ink	18.00	24.00	21.00
☐ Autograph, **Harry Wills,** contract, ink	300.00	400.00	345.00
☐ Boxing Card, **Tommy Loughran,** Knock-Out Bubble Gum Cards, Leaf Gum Cards, 1948 ...	1.00	2.00	1.30
☐ **Same as Above, Harry Greb**	1.00	2.00	1.30
☐ Boxing Card, **George Carpenter,** Magnoms Cigarettes, British Boxing Card, 1914, 25 cards in set	2.00	3.00	2.40

	Current Price Range		P/Y Average
☐ **Same as Above,** complete set	25.00	35.00	29.00
☐ **Boxing Card, Willy Beecher,** Mecca Cigarettes, early 1900s	1.00	2.00	1.30
☐ **Same as Above, Joe Coburn**	1.00	2.00	1.30
☐ **Same as Above, Pal Moore**	1.00	2.00	1.30
☐ **Boxing Card, Gene Tunney,** Pugilists in Action, British Cigarette Card, 1928, 50 cards in set ...	2.00	3.00	2.40
☐ **Same as Above, Mickey Walker**	1.00	2.00	1.30
☐ **Same as Above,** complete set	50.00	60.00	54.00
☐ **Boxing Cards, Jimmy Flood,** Topps Ringside, 1950s	1.00	2.00	1.30
☐ **Same as Above, Randy Turpin**	2.00	4.00	2.80
☐ **Same as Above, Tony Zale**	2.00	4.00	2.80
☐ **Boxing Card, William Papke,** Turkey Red Cigarette Cards, early 1900s	30.00	35.00	32.00
☐ **Same as Above, Tommy Murphy**	20.00	25.00	22.00
☐ **Same as Above, Johnny Coulon**	15.00	20.00	17.00
☐ **Magazine,** Boxing Illustrated, 1975, Ali vs. Frazier "Super Fight III"	3.00	4.00	3.20
☐ **Magazine,** Ring Magazine, most single issues, 1922	28.00	35.00	31.00
☐ **Magazine,** World Boxing Magazine, May, 1974	1.00	2.00	1.30
☐ **Poster, Muhammad Ali,** exhibition against unnamed opponent, May 29, 1979, Royal Albert Hall, London, paper, 16" x 23"	9.00	19.00	13.00
☐ **Poster, Joe Brown vs. Dave Charnley,** February 25, 1963, Manchester, England, paper 6½" x 8"	4.00	8.00	6.00
☐ **Poster, George Foreman vs. Joe Roman,** Heavyweight Championship, August 31, 1973, Tokyo, Japan, cardboard, 14" x 22"	17.00	29.00	22.00
☐ **Poster, Marvin Hagler vs. Fully Obel,** Middleweight Championship, January 17, 1981, Boston, 18" x 23"	16.00	27.00	21.00
☐ **Poster, Andy Kendall vs. Mike Quarry,** October 3, 1973, Orlando, Florida, cardboard, 14" x 22"	9.00	17.00	13.00
☐ **Poster, Sugar Ray Leonard vs. Pete Ranzany,** Welterweight Championship, August 12, 1979, Las Vegas, paper, 19" x 25"	15.00	27.00	19.00
☐ **Poster, Joe Louis vs. Tony Galento,** Heavyweight Championship, June 28, 1939, New York, theater film poster, 14" x 22"	40.00	60.00	50.00
☐ **Poster, Leon Spinks,** exhibition with unnamed opponents, Freeport, Bahamas, cardboard, 14" x 22"	15.00	27.00	21.00
☐ **Poster, Leon Spinks vs. Muhammad Ali,** Heavyweight Championship, September 15, 1978, 21" x 28"	4.00	10.00	6.00
☐ **Program, Max Baer vs. Tony Galento,** Heavyweight Championship, July 2, 1940, Vienna, Austria, 18 pp.	7.00	9.00	8.00

	Current Price Range		P/Y Average
☐ **Program, Rocky Graziano vs. Charley Fusari,** Middleweight bout, September 14, 1949, Polo Grounds, New York, 24 pp.	25.00	30.00	27.00
☐ **Program, Sugar Ray Leonard vs. Bruce Finch,** Welterweight Championship, February 15, 1982, Centennial Coliseum, Reno, Nevada, 32 pp.	9.00	12.00	10.00
☐ **Program, Ernie Terrell vs. George Chuvalo,** November 1, 1965, Toronto, Canada, autographed by Chuvalo	15.00	20.00	17.00

BRASS

DESCRIPTION: Brass is an alloy of copper and zinc and has been used since antiquity. Because of its malleable nature it can be fashioned into a wide variety of utensils, tools and decorative objects.

COMMENTS: Decorative brassware has been imported from the Orient since the turn of the century. These wares feature very intricate engraving and tooling. Brass is very durable and, although it tarnishes quickly, it can be polished and restored to its lovely golden color very easily. Brassware can often be found in garage sales very cheaply as many people are unwilling to polish it regularly.

☐ **Andirons,** pair, solid brass fluted column and ball finial with solid brass feet, 20½"	110.00	120.00	112.50
☐ **Ashtray,** brass dog standing on edge, marked China, 4½"	18.00	20.00	18.50
☐ **Ashtray,** fashioned from World War II artillery shell, very heavy, marked FSC 8/19/43, 7-V 50 cal., 4½"	10.00	15.00	10.50
☐ **Ashtray,** ivy leaf shape, marked English Ivy by Cambron, 5¾" x 4½"	12.00	15.00	12.50
☐ **Ashtray,** shaped like coal scuttle, enameled with scene of men studying books around table, marked China	10.00	12.00	10.50

	Current Price Range		P/Y Average
☐ **Mint Dish,** hand tooled floral and leaf band and center, pedestal base, marked India, 5"x2" ...	8.00	10.00	8.50
☐ **Mug,** no handle, 3"x3"	3.00	4.00	3.25
☐ **Pig,** solid, 2½"	10.00	12.00	11.00
☐ **Pig,** solid, 3"	15.00	17.00	16.00
☐ **Pig,** solid, 4¼"	24.00	28.00	25.00
☐ **Plate,** covered with tooled leaf engraving, 4¾"	4.00	5.00	4.25
☐ **Plate,** heavy cast brass with scalloped rim, features people in elaborate relief at center and around rim	6.00	8.00	6.50
☐ **Platter,** pedestal, marked China, 8"	19.00	21.00	18.50
☐ **Soap Dish,** Victorian bath tub with four curved feet, 5½"x2⅜"	9.00	11.00	10.00
☐ **Spittoon,** 6⅝"x4¾"	32.00	35.00	33.00
☐ **Table Lighter,** engraved leaves, marked India, 4½"	8.00	10.00	8.50
☐ **Table Top,** round, brass clad, covered with intricate Mid-Eastern engraving and caligraphy, 24" diameterx1⅝" thick	130.00	150.00	140.00
☐ **Tongs,** claw end, hanging ring, 11"	15.00	18.00	16.50
☐ **Tray,** hammered, 5½"	4.00	5.00	4.25
☐ **Tray,** octagonal, hammered, 15"x10"	15.00	16.00	15.50
☐ **Tray,** two handles, engraved peacocks and flowers, marked India, 29"x8"	24.00	28.00	25.00
☐ **Vase,** bronze birds and flowers, marked China, 6"	28.00	32.00	28.50
☐ **Vase,** heavy, square top, two Foo dog handles, marked China, 9½"	65.00	75.00	67.50
☐ **Wall Brush Set,** includes mirror, and two bristle brushes with leaf scroll tooling, brushes hang from two hooks below mirror	45.00	48.00	46.00
☐ **Wax Seal,** bee shape	3.00	4.00	3.25
☐ **Wax Seal,** leaf shape	3.00	4.00	3.25

BREWERIANA

TOPIC: Breweriana is beer-related memorabilia.

TYPES: Popular types of breweriana include serving trays, coasters, bottle and can openers and advertising signs.

PERIOD: Breweriana that dates back to 17th century England can be found, but most collectible breweriana was made after 1800. Contemporary products such as advertising mirrors are presently quite popular.

COMMENTS: Although some breweriana enthusiasts collect beer cans and beer bottles also, many limit themselves to breweriana and a specific company. Others collect certain items such as ashtrays.

ADDITIONAL TIPS: The following listings are arranged by company. For more extensive listings, refer to *The Official Price Guide to Beer Cans,* published by The House of Collectibles.

Iroquois Tray, *made by Charles Snowk, 1905, scarce, 12"*
$350.00–$400.00
(photo courtesy of ©Paul Michel, Buffalo, NY, 1984)

	Current Price Range		P/Y Average
☐ **Albion,** mirror, "Gold Medal Award from the 1924 Breweries Exhibition, To Albion Brewery, Championship Cup and Gold Medal Ales," 7"x9"	130.00	170.00	150.00
☐ **American,** non-illuminated sign, glass and wood, "Brewer's Best Premium," 13"x13"	22.00	28.00	25.00
☐ **American,** poster, "Salute to National Tavern Month," 11¼"x14"	.40	.60	.50

	Current Price Range		P/Y Average

☐ **Ballantine,** coaster, circular, red and black, "We Serve Ballantine Ale and Beer," probably late 1940's, 4¼" 4.00   6.00   5.00

☐ **Ballantine,** foam scraper, white and red, smile mug with logo and "Ballantine Draught Beer," dated 1964, 9" 8.50   11.50   10.00

☐ **Ballantine,** opener, copper plated, front: "Ballantine Ale and Beer" with three-ring sign, reverse: "Ballantine Ale and Beer," stamped Vaughn, 1,996,550 . . . .   4.25   5.00   4.62

☐ **Ballantine,** opener, front: "Drink Ballantine Ale and Beer," three-ring sign at top; reverse: blank 7.00   9.00   8.00

☐ **Ballantine,** tray, three-ring sign with beer mug in red, yellow and black on white background 6.50   9.50   8.00

☐ **Ballantine's Ale and Beer,** tray, three ring sign, 11¾" 10.00   14.00   12.00

☐ **Barbey's Sunshine,** tray, "Since 1861," gold with blue background, rounded sizes 31.00   39.00   36.00

☐ **Bavarian,** coaster, circular, red and black, "Bavarian Type Beer, Mount Carbon Brewery, Pottsville, Pa., Union Made," 1940's, 4¼" 3.50   4.50   4.00

☐ **Blatz,** illuminated sign, octagonal, brand name at center, mounted on pillar-type decorative bar with brass finial, gold and brown, 14"x7" 8.00   10.00   9.00

☐ **Blatz,** miniature bottle, 4" 13.00   17.00   15.00

☐ **Braumeister,** coaster, oval, red, blue and yellow, "Braumeister Special Pilsner Beer, Milwaukee's Choicest, Independent Milwaukee Brewery," World War II era, 4¼" 4.00   6.00   5.00

☐ **Black Horse Ale,** tap marker 6.50   8.50   7.50

☐ **Brunswick Bock,** poster, "Brunswick Bock Beer," ram's head in white against green background, 1930's–40's, 23"x34" 60.00   80.00   70.00

☐ **Budweiser,** opener, wooden bottle with Bud label 10.00   14.00   12.00

☐ **Budweiser,** paper hat, white with red lettering, "We Feature Budweiser Beer," c. 1950–60 . . . .   8.50   11.50   10.00

☐ **Budweiser,** tip tray, Budweiser logo and "King of Beers," red with white lettering, rectangular, 3"x7" 10.00   14.00   12.00

☐ **Budweiser,** tray, "Duquoine State Fair, 50th Anniversary," gold and red, cream white background, 11¾" 13.00   17.00   15.00

☐ **Budweiser,** tray, "King of Beers," eagle and trademark in red, green and yellow on white, 13¼" 9.00   12.00   10.50

☐ **Budweiser,** tray, "Where There's Life, There's Budweiser," red, white and blue, 13¼" 11.00   15.00   13.00

☐ **Columbia,** tray, hops and stars, multicolored with gold, 11¾" 19.00   25.00   22.00

☐ **Columbia Five Star,** tray, Shenandoah, Pennsylvania, grain, hops and shield in multicolors and gold 22.00   28.00   26.00

	Current Price Range		P/Y Average

☐ **Coors,** tray, "America's Fine Light Beer," white lion, red striped background, 13¼" .... — 8.00 — 10.00 — 9.00

☐ **Coors,** poster, reprint, "Coors Golden Brewery, Golden, Colo.," Gibson girl, 14"x19" .... — 8.50 — 11.50 — 10.00

☐ **Dinkel Acker,** plastic, white with black and yellow border, logo and brand name .... — .90 — 1.20 — 1.05

☐ **Edelweiss,** non-illuminated sign, "Stop Here for Edelwiss Light Beer," thick cardboard in black, red, yellow and white, has circle marked "Special" with space for price to be written, c. 1950–60 .... — 22.00 — 28.00 — 25.00

☐ **Esslinger,** salt and pepper set, 4" .... — 21.00 — 27.00 — 24.00

☐ **Esslinger's,** opener, "Esslinger's Premium Beer, Over the Top" .... — 8.00 — 10.00 — 9.00

☐ **Falls City,** tray, "70th Anniversary," illustration of brewery, multicolors, 11¾" .... — 19.00 — 25.00 — 22.00

☐ **F and S Beer and Ale,** tray, multicolored drum major .... — 22.00 — 29.00 — 25.00

☐ **Genesee,** tray, "Ask for Jenny," illustration of Jenny, white, black and yellow against reddish background, 11¾" .... — 14.00 — 18.00 — 16.00

☐ **Genesee,** tray, still life with pheasant on table, multicolored, 11¾" .... — 15.00 — 19.00 — 17.00

☐ **Gibbons Mellow-Pure Beer and Ale,** tray, white, black and red, 11¾" .... — 13.00 — 17.00 — 15.00

☐ **Gibbons Premium,** tray, "Gibbons is Good," white with black and red lettering, 13¼" ...... — 8.00 — 10.00 — 9.00

☐ **Grain Belt,** tray, logo with grain, hops, mug and lake in background, multicolored, 13¼" .... — 12.00 — 16.00 — 14.00

☐ **Hamm's,** tray, bear with lake in woodland scene, multicolored, 11¾" .... — 14.00 — 18.00 — 16.00

☐ **Hamm's,** tray, canoer on lake, multicolored, 13¼" .... — 15.00 — 19.00 — 17.00

☐ **Hamm's,** tray, lion crest in gold with white lettering on red background, 13¼" .... — 8.00 — 10.00 — 9.00

☐ **Hamm's,** tray, woodland scene with hiker and bear, multicolored, 13¼" .... — 15.00 — 19.00 — 17.00

☐ **Hamm's Preferred Stock,** tray, view of brewery on front and reverse of tray, red and black against white background, 13¼" .... — 24.00 — 32.00 — 28.00

☐ **Heineken,** pocket knife-opener combination, brand name on handle, "Solingen, Germany" on base of blade .... — 44.00 — 52.00 — 49.00

☐ **Heineken,** shoe, wood, "Heineken Beer," yellow with illustration of Dutch boy and windmill, 10" — 22.00 — 28.00 — 25.00

☐ **Hofbrau Bavaria,** mug, ceramic .... — 4.00 — 6.00 — 5.00

☐ **Holsten,** ashtray, ceramic, circular, "Holsten Beer" in black lettering on white, made in Germany, 4" .... — 17.00 — 23.00 — 20.00

☐ **Iroquois,** coaster, red and white, head of Indian chief, "Iroquois Indian Head Beer and Ale, Iroquois Beverage Corp., Buffalo, N.Y.," c. 1940–50, 4" .... — 5.00 — 7.00 — 6.00

	Current Price Range		P/Y Average

☐ **Iroquois,** tip tray, Indian chief trademark with "Iroquois Brewery, Buffalo," circular, c. 1930–40, 4½" ... **100.00 140.00 120.00**

☐ **Jacob Ruppert,** non-illuminated sign, oval, wire stand-up device on back, "Ruppert Beer and Ale, New York," reverse-painted on glass, black with silver lettering, imitation wood frame, 18"x12" **50.00 70.00 60.00**

☐ **Knickerbocker,** opener, "Jacob Ruppert Brewery, New York, The Brew that Satisfies, Save this Opener, Order by the Case" ... **17.00 23.00 20.00**

☐ **Kuebler,** tip tray, "Kuebler Beer, Easton, Pa., 1852," black and orange, illustration of top-hatted man with mug, circular, believed to date from late 1940's, 4½" ... **35.00 45.00 40.00**

☐ **Lone Star,** tray, star logo in gold and red against white background, 13¼" ... **11.00 15.00 13.00**

☐ **Lowenbrau,** tray, gold heraldic lion, blue background, 13¼" ... **5.00 7.00 6.00**

☐ **McSorley's Cream Stock Ale,** tray, tavern interior scene, dated 1936, 11¾" ... **40.00 50.00 45.00**

☐ **Michelob,** coaster, circular, red and black, emblem on front, on back: "Have a Michelob, It's an Unexpected Pleasure," c. 1970–80, 3½" ... **.90 1.20 1.05**

☐ **Miller Lite,** non-illuminated sign, plastic, white with blue lettering, 18"x14" ... **4.00 5.00 4.50**

☐ **Old German,** thermometer, circular, 10" diameter ... **22.00 28.00 25.00**

☐ **Old German,** tie clip, "Herman" ... **13.00 17.00 15.00**

☐ **Old Shay Ale,** ashtray, metallic, silver color, "Old Shay Ale, Product of Fort Pitt Brewing Co., Jeannette, Pa. Plant" in black lettering ... **13.00 17.00 15.00**

☐ **Old Style,** illuminated sign, octagonal, brand name at center, mounted on pillar-type decorative bar with brass finial, gold and brown, 14"x7" ... **8.00 10.00 9.00**

☐ **Pabst Blue Ribbon,** illuminated sign, standard logo, raised seal and lettering in a plaque-like frame, blue and white, 15"x20" ... **16.00 20.00 18.00**

☐ **Pabst Blue Ribbon,** illuminated sign, circular, silver and gold mug with large brand name at top of frame, logo at bottom, 15"x15" ... **10.00 14.00 12.00**

☐ **Pabst Blue Ribbon,** tray, girl in flapper outfit, multicolored, 13¼" ... **7.00 9.00 8.00**

☐ **Pabst Blue Ribbon,** tray, 1976 Bicentennial tray with view of old brewery, 13¼" ... **7.00 9.00 8.00**

☐ **Piel's** tray, "Enjoy Piel's Beer," multicolored caricatures of Bert and Harry Piel, white background, 13¼" ... **15.00 19.00 17.00**

☐ **Piel's Light,** tray, elf carrying tray, multicolored against gold background, 11¾" ... **15.00 19.00 17.00**

☐ **Rheingold Extra Dry,** tray, Liebman, black and white on red background, 11¾" ... **7.00 9.00 8.00**

	Current Price Range		P/Y Average
☐ **Rheingold Extra Dry Lager,** tray, logo in black and red against white background, red sides, 13¼″	8.00	10.00	9.00
☐ **Ruppert Knickerbocker,** tray, Father Knickerbocker, multicolored, 13¼″	10.00	14.00	12.00
☐ **Ruppert Old Knickerbocker,** tray, eagle in gold and white, gold and red on red background, 13¼″	18.00	24.00	21.00
☐ **Schaefer,** tray, logo and grain symbol in red, white and gold, repeated on reverse, 13¼″ ...	7.00	9.00	8.00
☐ **Schaefer,** tray, red and white with mottos, 11¾″	9.00	13.00	11.00
☐ **Schlitz,** illuminated sign, shield-shaped, "Light Beer" with word "Light" in very large lettering, decorative molding, gold and yellow, 20″x18″	21.00	27.00	24.00
☐ **Schmidt's,** non-illuminated sign, "Schmidt's of Philadelphia, Beer and Ale," small sign on black wooden stand, black with silver lettering, c. 1940–50, 8″x6″	43.00	57.00	50.00
☐ **Whitebread,** astray, plastic, circular, blue, "Whitebread Tankard Helps me Excel," made in Great Britain, 9″	4.00	6.00	5.00
☐ **Yuengling,** coaster, circular, green and red, front: "Yuengling Premium Beer, Since 1829," reverse: "America's Oldest Breweries," 3¼″	1.85	2.30	2.10
☐ **Yuengling,** opener, "Drink Yuengling's Beer and Ale, D.G. Yuengling & Son, Inc., Pottsville, Pa."	8.00	10.00	9.00

BRITISH ROYALTY MEMORABILIA

VARIATIONS: A wide variety of British Royalty commemoratives have been made, from inexpensive tourist trinkets to fine pieces of porcelain.

COMMENTS: The pageantry and elegance that surrounds British royalty intrigues and attracts collectors of royalty memorabilia.

Royal Baby Doll, *commemorating the birth of Prince William of Wales, born June 21, 1982, Heirloom series, limited edition of 2,500,* **$275.00-$325.00**

ADDITIONAL TIPS: This section is listed alphabetically according to item. Included after the item are the royal figures being honored, and when available, special events, decoration on the item, color, special features, maker, height and price.

	Current Price Range		P/Y Average
☐ **Ashtray,** King Edward VIII, Edward's head and flags, Paladin china, 4½"	5.00	10.00	7.00
☐ **Box,** King George VI and Queen Elizabeth, king, queen, two princesses, tin, 5"x4"x3"	12.00	18.00	14.00
☐ **Box,** Prince Albert, impressed head of prince, round, brass, 2½"	20.00	30.00	24.00
☐ **Covered Jar,** Queen Elizabeth II, Coronation 1953, cream pottery with gold scrolls, portrait, coat of arms, 5"	40.00	50.00	45.00
☐ **Cover Jar,** Queen Victoria, cover shaped like Victoria's head with necklace, veil, crown, round jar has coat of arms, milkglass, 8"	55.00	65.00	60.00

	Current Price Range		P/Y Average
☐ **Cup,** King George V and Queen Mary, Coronation 1911, king, queen, prince of Wales, enamel	50.00	60.00	53.00
☐ **Cup,** King George V and Queen Mary, Coronation 1911, portraits of royal couple, monograms, crowns, Royal Doulton	45.00	55.00	50.00
☐ **Cup,** King George V and Queen Mary, Silver Jubilee, king, queen, flags, green glass, handle	25.00	35.00	28.00
☐ **Cup,** King Edward VII and Queen Alexandra, Coronation 1902, photos of royal couple, flags, enamel, 3½″	45.00	55.00	48.00
☐ **Cup,** King George VI and Queen Elizabeth, family portrait of king, queen and two princesses, roses, thistles, castles, Spode, 3½″	30.00	40.00	33.00
☐ **Cup,** Queen Elizabeth II, Coronation 1953, green garland, raised heads of Elizabeth and Philip, red glaze interior, tan and white outside, double handle	25.00	35.00	31.00
☐ **Cup,** Queen Victoria, scroll design with portrait of queen, palace, enamel	45.00	55.00	50.00
☐ **Finger Bowl,** King Gerorge V and Queen Mary, Coronation 1911, portraits of royal couple, flags, flowers	45.00	55.00	50.00
☐ **Mug,** King Edward VIII, color portrait, lion, unicorn, flags, ribbon, china, 3″	15.00	25.00	20.00
☐ **Mug,** King Edward VIII, Coronation 1937, Edward's head on red background in blue frame, oak leaves, 3½″	25.00	35.00	30.00
☐ **Mug,** King Edward VIII, family motto, crown, oak branches, tapered, 3½″	25.00	35.00	30.00
☐ **Mug,** King Edward VIII, picture of king on front, medallion on back blue and white, Wedgwood, 3½″	25.00	35.00	30.00
☐ **Mug,** King Edward VIII, official design, "May 1937 Coronation of King Edward VIII," around rim, bulbous handle, 4½″	30.00	40.00	37.00
☐ **Mug,** King Edward VII and Queen Alexandra, Coronation 1902, picture of royal couple, crown, coat of arms, Royal Doulton, 4″	40.00	50.00	44.00
☐ **Mug,** King George VI and Queen Elizabeth, king and queen in gold frames, flags, crown, china, ″	10.00	20.00	14.00
☐ **Mug,** Queen Elizabeth II, Coronation 1953, date of coronation around rim, portrait of queen surrounded by leaves and flowers, Copeland Spode, handle, 3½″	15.00	25.00	20.00
☐ **Mug,** Queen Elizabeth II, Coronation 1953, portrait of queen, lion, unicorn, flags, ribbons, handleless, flared, 3½″	25.00	35.00	28.00
☐ **Mug,** Queen Elizabeth II, gold framed picture of Elizabeth, blue ribbons, pink roses, Royal Albert bone china, handle, 4½″	30.00	40.00	33.00

	Current Price Range		P/Y Average

□ **Mug,** Queen Elizabeth II, official design with photo, flags, crown and flowers, Johnson Brothers, glazed pottery, 3½″ **15.00 25.00 20.00**

□ **Mug,** Queen Elizabeth II, photo in frame, lion, unicorn, flags, handle, 3½″ **15.00 25.00 18.00**

□ **Mug,** Queen Elizabeth II, photo of queen surrounded by roses, shamrocks, daffodils, thistles, Tuscan bone china, handle, 3½″ **25.00 35.00 28.00**

□ **Mug,** Queen Elizabeth II, picture of queen on front, coat of arms on back, green, handle, 3″ **8.00 15.00 12.00**

□ **Mug,** Queen Elizabeth II, picture of queen on front, coat of arms on back, pink, handle, 3″ .. **8.00 15.00 12.00**

□ **Mug,** Queen Elizabeth II, raised head of queen, thistles, daffodils, roses, shamrocks, white glazed pottery, handle, 3½″ **15.00 25.00 18.00**

□ **Mug,** Queen Elizabeth II, Silver Jubilee, photo of queen, handle, 3½″ **20.00 30.00 25.00**

□ **Mug,** Queen Elizabeth II, Silver Jubilee, portrait, Royal Worcester fine porcelain, 3½″ **25.00 35.00 30.00**

□ **Pierced Dish,** King George VI and Queen Elizabeth, figures of king and queen impressed in bowl of dish, round, 5″ **25.00 35.00 30.00**

□ **Pitcher,** King Edward VII and Queen Alexandra, 25th wedding anniversary, flat sided **60.00 70.00 65.00**

□ **Pitcher,** King Edward VII and Queen Alexandra, young royal couple as Prince and Princess of Wales, flow blue, 7″ **90.00 100.00 93.00**

□ **Pitcher,** King George V and Queen Mary, portraits of king and queen, flags, flowers, china, rose and white, 5″ **35.00 45.00 40.00**

□ **Pitcher,** King George V and Queen Mary, royal couple in garlands of roses, saying on back, clear and frosted glass, 4″ **30.00 40.00 37.00**

□ **Pitcher,** Queen Victoria, 50th Anniversary, picture of queen, sayings, white, flat sided, 5″ ... **80.00 90.00 85.00**

□ **Picture,** Queen Victoria, figure and flowers in enamel, black glazed redware, 6″ **90.00 100.00 95.00**

□ **Plate,** King Edward VIII, Edward's head with crown, flags, square, 8½″ **15.00 25.00 20.00**

□ **Plate,** King Edward VII, photograph of Edward, fleur-de-lis border, glass, 7″ **20.00 30.00 24.00**

□ **Plate,** King Edward VII and Queen Alexandra, portrait of Edward, scalloped border, white around rim, flow blue, 9″ **35.00 45.00 40.00**

□ **Plate,** King George V and Queen Mary, picture of royal couple, coat of arms, color with blue border, 6″ **25.00 35.00 30.00**

□ **Plate,** Queen Alexandra, photograph of Alexandra, fleur-de-lis border, glass, 7″ **20.00 30.00 25.00**

□ **Plate,** Queen Elizabeth II, large painted crown, bright colors on white china, 5½″ **8.00 14.00 11.00**

□ **Plate,** Queen Elizabeth II, oak leaves, acorns, portrait, square **20.00 30.00 25.00**

	Current Price Range		P/Y Average
☐ **Plate,** Queen Elizabeth II, official pottery makers design, square, 8″	15.00	25.00	20.00
☐ **Plate,** Queen Elizabeth II, official pottery makers design, 9″	20.00	30.00	25.00
☐ **Plate,** Queen Victoria, portrait of queen surrounded by emblems of Canadian provinces ..	25.00	35.00	30.00
☐ **Plaque,** Queen Elizabeth II, Coronation 1953, round, brass, 8″	20.00	30.00	25.00
☐ **Sugar and Creamer,** King Edward VIII, Edward's head, gold leaves, decorations	30.00	40.00	35.00
☐ **Sugar and Creamer,** Queen Elizabeth II, photograph, flags, flowers, bone china	35.00	45.00	40.00
☐ **Tea Set,** King Edward VII and Queen Alexandra, 6½″, teapot, sugar and creamer, 9″ cake plate, decorated with coat of arms, figures, white glazed Foley china with gold trim, melon shaped	300.00	350.00	325.00
☐ **Tumbler,** Queen Victoria, silhouette of queen, garland, black milk glass, 5″	20.00	30.00	24.00
☐ **Tumbler,** Queen Victoria, triple rows of beading, "To Commemorate Queen Victoria's Reign of 60 Years," clear, heavy	25.00	35.00	30.00
☐ **Vase,** King George VI and Queen Elizabeth, Coronation 1937, shamrocks, thistles, roses, crystal, cut, etched, flared, 8″	40.00	50.00	45.00

BRONZE

DESCRIPTION: Sculptures and other decorative objects were cast in bronze, and usually made in limited numbers.

TYPES: Bronze statues were often made in classical styles, such as gods and goddesses, animals and warriors; also vases, urns, bookends and similar items.

PERIOD: Though bronze sculpture is of ancient origin, most of the collectible specimens on the market are Victorian to early 20th century.

CARE AND CONDITION: Clean and polish bronze with a good bronze polish. This will guard against corrosion.

	Current Price Range		P/Y Average

☐ **Ashtray,** bronze resting on onyx base, the tray measures 6″, the base 4½″x7″ . . . . 27.00 · 34.00 · 30.00

☐ **Bonheur, Rosa,** set of bookends modeled after a work by her, picturing horses in relief . . . . 50.00 · 60.00 · 55.00

☐ **Bookends,** set with anchor motif . . . . 30.00 · 35.00 · 32.00

☐ **Book Rack,** Bradley and Hubbard, expandable, leafwork motif with screen sides . . . . 40.00 · 50.00 · 44.00

☐ **DeAngelis, Sabatino,** figure of an armored horseman, signed Sabatino DeAngelis, and Fils (son), Naples, 1908, mounted on a green marble base . . . . 300.00 · 400.00 · 340.00

☐ **Diana The Huntress,** anonymous bronze sculpture of the mythological goddess with quiver, mounted on a bronze stand, French, undated, probably late 19th century, 33½″ . . . . 900.00 · 1150.00 · 950.00

☐ **D'Ore, Jean B.,** bronze sculpture of an angel, signed, 17″ . . . . 1000.00 · 1500.00 · 1200.00

☐ **Horse And Dog,** modeled after a work by P.J. Mene, horse is shown bending over the dog, signed, 18″ . . . . 2200.00 · 2800.00 · 2500.00

☐ **Jockey And Horse,** modeled after a work by Yves Benoist Gironiere, horse in racing motion, signed, 31″ in length by 13″ high . . . . 1600.00 · 2000.00 · 1750.00

☐ **Mercury,** modeled after a work by Jean de Bologne, large room-size mythological bronze, intended as a corner piece for large room, mounted on marble platform, 49½″ . . . . 800.00 · 1100.00 · 950.00

☐ **Milles, Carl,** figure of man in frock coat, kneeling, signed and dated 1948 and bearing the number four along with a foundry mark, 17″ . . . . 1200.00 · 1600.00 · 1300.00

☐ **Mongniez, J.,** figural grouping, sculptured bronze, signed . . . . 1200.00 · 1450.00 · 1300.00

☐ **Picault, E.,** bronze sculpture of an unidentified nobleman, signed . . . . 2200.00 · 2800.00 · 2450.00

☐ **Portrait Bust,** man in ribboned hat, modeled after a work by C. Kauba, signed, marked Gershutz with the mold number 4529, 5″ . . . . 110.00 · 140.00 · 125.00

☐ **Temple Musicians,** set of eight figurines of various musicians, all seated, wearing head-dresses and elaborate costumes, playing different musical instruments, ranging in height from 3″ to 3½″, set . . . . 135.00 · 170.00 · 150.00

☐ **Turtle,** French bronze sculpture in the likeness of a turtle, unsigned, 6½″ . . . . 180.00 · 220.00 · 200.00

BUCK ROGERS

DESCRIPTION: Buck Rogers began as a futuristic comic strip hero conceived by Philip Nowlan in 1929. Since then, comic books, radio programs, television series and movies have been produced about this early spaceman.

TYPES: Because of its popularity among children, all types of items including premiums, toys, school supplies and dishes have featured Buck Rogers characters.

COMMENTS: Collectors of Buck Rogers memorabilia will find that items produced in its early years are usually more valuable then recent objects.

	Current Price Range		P/Y Average
☐ **Badge,** Buck Rogers Solar Scout badge, Cream of Wheat premium, dated 1935	37.00	48.00	40.00
☐ **Button,** Buck Rogers in the 25th Century, celluloid, multicolored	38.00	50.00	40.00
☐ **Button,** Buck Rogers Satellite Pioneer, lithographed tin in red, white and black, illustration of space vehicle with balcony encircling it, astronauts walking on balcony, words, "Rocket Rangers" in small letters	100.00	125.00	105.00
☐ **Button,** Buck Rogers Solar Scout membership button, Cream of Wheat premium, celluloid, 1935	21.00	27.00	22.50
☐ **Figure,** Buck Rogers in the 25th Century, Ardella, Mego, plastic, 1979	10.00	15.00	10.50
☐ **Figure,** Buck Rogers in the 25th Century, Draco, Mego, plastic, 1979	9.50	12.50	10.50
☐ **Figure,** Buck Rogers in the 25th Century, Killer Kane, Mego, plastic, 1979	9.50	12.50	10.50
☐ **Gun,** Buck Rogers Atomic Pistol, Daisy Manufacturing Co., Plymouth, Michigan, cast pot metal with chrome plating, beaded grip.	50.00	70.00	60.00
☐ **Gun,** Buck Rogers Copper Disintegrator Cap gun, cast iron, picture of Buck Rogers with wording "Buck Rogers in the 25th Century"	125.00	155.00	135.00

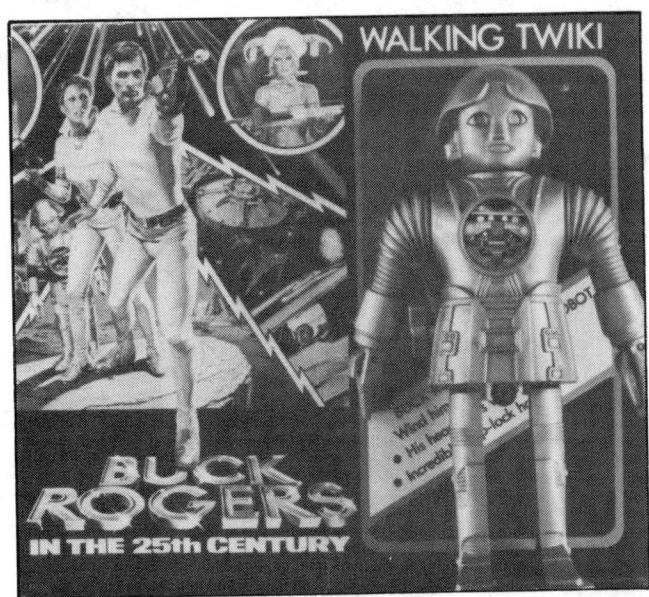

Buck Rogers Walking Twiki, *made by Mego under license from Robert C. Dille, hard molded plastic, head turns when he walks, has grip lock hands, 6½", 1979,* $5.00–$8.00

	Current Price Range		P/Y Average
☐ **Gun,** Buck Rogers Pocket Pistol, Daisy Manufacturing Co., lithographed tin	100.00	130.00	120.00
☐ **Gun,** Buck Rogers Rubber Band Gun, Onward School Supply Co., large lithographed cardboard card from which the gun and targets punch out	43.00	52.00	45.00
☐ **Gun,** Buck Rogers Sonic Ray Gun, Norton Engineering and Manufacturing Co., Chicago, plastic, battery powered	33.00	42.00	35.00
☐ **Holster,** Buck Rogers combat set holster, 1934	100.00	120.00	110.00
☐ **Kite,** Buck Rogers Strato-Kite, Aero Kite Co., 1946	45.00	55.00	40.00
☐ **Matchbook Cover,** Buck Rogers, carries ad for ice cream with ad for Buck Rogers radio network program	8.00	11.00	8.50
☐ **Pencil Case,** Buck Rogers Pencil Case, cardboard, multicolored, top has picture of Buck Rogers, 1938	25.00	35.00	30.00
☐ **Printing Set,** Buck Rogers, set of 22 stamps used to create comic book stories	130.00	170.00	125.00
☐ **Rocket Ships,** Buck Rogers Battlecruiser, Tootsie Toy Co., lithographed tin, blue and yellow, moves on string or wire, 1937	70.00	90.00	70.00

	Current Price Range		P/Y Average
☐ **Rocket Ship,** Buck Rogers Laserscope Fighter, Mego, plastic, complex design, 1979	20.00	25.00	21.50
☐ **Rocket Ship,** Buck Rogers Tootsietoy Rocket Ship # 1033, Attack Ship, cast metal, white and red	150.00	200.00	145.00

BUTTONS

DESCRIPTION: Dating to the 13th century, buttons were first used for decoration. Early buttons had very elaborate and exquisite designs. Later buttons were more commonly used as fasteners. Both types are collectible.

VARIATIONS: A variety of button types have been made including, heads of famous people, animals, picture buttons, story buttons, sporting buttons, among others. "Realistics" were plastic buttons made in the 1930s and 1940s that looked like everyday items in miniature. Examples include fruit, animals and food.

MAKER: Most antique and collectible buttons on the market today are American, French or English made.

MATERIALS: Buttons have been made from materials including painted tin, metal, mother-of-pearl, pewter, brass, glass, gilt, plastic, ivory, ceramic, cloisonne and celluloid.

MARKS: Some early buttons, from the 18th and 19th centuries, had backmarks which identify the maker. Some collectors collect by backmark rather than by button design.

COMMENTS: Currently buttons from the 18th century to the present are the most available and collectible. They are a lovely and usually inexpensive collectible.

ADDITIONAL TIPS: The listings are arranged alphabetically by button material. A description follows.

For further button information, contact: The National Button Society, Box 39, Eastwood, Kentucky 40018.

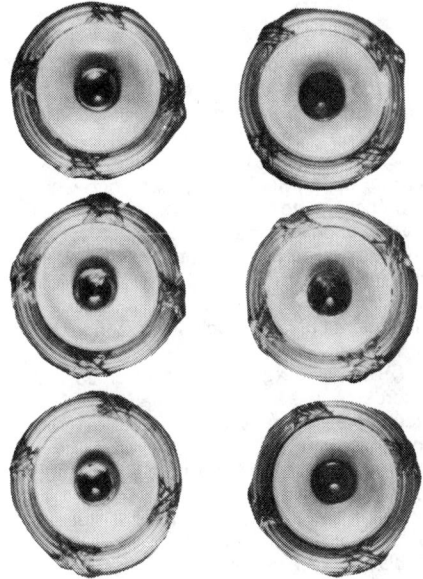

Buttons,
mother of pearl,
sapphire inset,
Tiffany & Co., 1915,
$675.00-$800.00

	Current Price Range		P/Y Average
☐ **Black Glass,** cameo head	12.50	20.00	14.00
☐ **Black Glass,** elephant under palm tree	7.50	13.00	8.50
☐ **Black Glass,** faceted ball, gold foil top	35.00	45.00	37.00
☐ **Black Glass,** mountain with house scene, beaded gilt edge	35.00	45.00	37.00
☐ **Black Glass,** shape of a slipper	10.00	15.00	12.00
☐ **Black Onyx,** with 14K gold, ball shaped, 19th century	60.00	70.00	63.00
☐ **Black Onyx,** gold filled, ball shaped, 19th century	20.00	25.00	21.00
☐ **Brass,** Aesop's Fable, frog and rabbit	21.50	30.00	24.00
☐ **Brass,** Aesop's Fable, two mice	35.00	45.00	37.00
☐ **Brass,** angry rooster	10.00	15.00	12.00
☐ **Brass,** cherubs with cornucopia and goat	4.50	8.00	6.50
☐ **Brass,** children playing game, Victorian era ...	21.00	30.00	24.00
☐ **Brass,** dancing gypsy girl with goat	48.00	60.00	53.00
☐ **Brass Disc,** bridge and river scene, black and white	75.00	105.00	84.00
☐ **Brass,** Indian hunter	35.00	45.00	37.00
☐ **Brass,** mother feeding child, high relief	21.50	30.00	25.00
☐ **Brass,** rooster standing on wheat shaft	16.00	25.00	18.00
☐ **Celluloid,** angel head, gold background, gilt rims	35.00	45.00	37.00
☐ **Celluloid,** Count Fersen, floral brass frame ...	21.00	30.00	22.00
☐ **Celluloid,** Duchess of Devonshire, pastel colors	42.00	55.00	47.00

	Current Price Range		P/Y Average
☐ **Celluloid,** Marie Antoinette	10.00	15.00	12.00
☐ **Ceramic,** bird, black and white	25.00	35.00	28.00
☐ **Ceramic,** bird with branch in beak, scalloped border	35.00	45.00	37.00
☐ **Ceramic,** cupid, scroll design on edge	45.00	55.00	47.00
☐ **Cloisonne,** birds flying, brass, black and white with red background	82.00	115.00	95.00
☐ **Enamel,** lighthouse with boat scene	47.00	58.00	50.00
☐ **Enamel,** lady riding bicycle, cut steel border . . .	62.00	77.00	65.00
☐ **Enamel,** maiden, blue and white, diamond paste border	52.00	67.00	55.00
☐ **Enamel,** portrait of lady, black background, 18th c.	62.00	78.00	65.00
☐ **Enamel,** rose colored scene on white, embossed scroll border	200.00	245.00	220.00
☐ **Enamel,** with seed pearls and 14K gold, ladybug design, 19th century	575.00	600.00	580.00
☐ **Enamel,** shepherdess, light purple, diamond paste border	47.00	58.00	50.00
☐ **Enamel,** star shape decorated with cut steels	16.00	25.00	20.00
☐ **Enamel,** woman at fountain	55.00	75.00	60.00
☐ **Glass,** black liberty cap and flag, silver frame, 18th c.	55.00	75.00	60.00
☐ **Glass,** French Revolution motif, copper rim . . .	70.00	88.00	74.00
☐ **Glass,** molded opaque, brown bird design	25.00	35.00	28.00
☐ **Gold,** 14K, ball shape with ribbing, 19th century	60.00	70.00	63.00
☐ **Gold,** 14K, button set with chain, 19th century	50.00	60.00	52.00
☐ **Gold,** 14K, engraved collar button, 19th century	30.00	35.00	31.00
☐ **Gold,** 14K, pearl shape, 19th century	60.00	70.00	63.00
☐ **Gold,** 14K, scrolled edge design, 19th century	60.00	70.00	63.00
☐ **Gold,** woven hair under swirls, cartwheel design, 19th century	110.00	130.00	118.00
☐ **Gold,** woven hair under swirls, cartwheel design with scalloped edge, 19th century	130.00	150.00	138.00
☐ **Gold-filled,** ball shape with ribbing, 19th century	20.00	25.00	21.00
☐ **Gold Plated,** dragon	7.50	13.00	8.00
☐ **Ivory,** carved Royal Salamander	30.00	40.00	34.00
☐ **Ivory,** cut-out girl and bird, blue background . .	150.00	180.00	155.00
☐ **Ivory,** painted cherub in chariot drawn by two horses	90.00	110.00	95.00
☐ **Ivory,** painted girl and dog chasing butterflies	90.00	110.00	95.00
☐ **Ivory,** painted lady and dog, silver rim	48.00	60.00	53.00
☐ **Ivory,** painted Oriental head	35.00	45.00	40.00
☐ **Mother-of-pearl,** 14K gold, simple button, 19th century	75.00	85.00	80.00
☐ **Oriental,** fan design, multicolored, scalloped border	30.00	40.00	33.00
☐ **Oriental,** floral motif, enameled	35.00	45.00	37.00
☐ **Pewter,** owl's head	4.50	8.00	5.50

	Current Price Range		P/Y Average
☐ **Pierced Brass,** Little Red Riding Hood	13.00	20.00	15.00
☐ **Porcelain,** cherub catching butterflies, pink, black and white	20.00	30.00	23.00
☐ **Porcelain,** cupid, scroll design on edge	48.00	65.00	52.00
☐ **Porcelain,** flowers and butterfly, 18th c.	17.50	30.00	20.00
☐ **Porcelain,** pasture scene with children	30.00	40.00	34.00
☐ **Porcelain,** with gold, painted angels, 19th century	520.00	540.00	528.00
☐ **Silver,** Bacchus, God of Wine, etched design	25.00	35.00	27.00
☐ **Stamped Brass,** two children fighting and pulling hair	21.00	30.00	24.00
☐ **Steel,** floral design	4.50	8.00	5.50
☐ **Turquoise,** with 14K gold, button set with chain, 19th century	95.00	105.00	98.00
☐ **Victorian,** figure, black glass disc	8.50	14.00	9.00
☐ **Wedgwood,** classic figures, white relief on blue, cut steel border, 18th c.	250.00	295.00	270.00
☐ **Wedgwood,** classic figure, white on royal blue, gilt rim, 18th c.	235.00	275.00	245.00
☐ **Wedgwood,** classical figures, white relief on light blue	52.00	70.00	60.00
☐ **Wedgwood,** floral design, diamond paste border, silver frame	200.00	250.00	215.00
☐ **Wedgwood,** warrior, white relief on royal blue, copper border	225.00	275.00	230.00

CAMBRIDGE GLASS

HISTORY: The Cambridge Glass Co., located in the Ohio town of the same name, was chiefly a producer of cut glass, though it sold other types as well. Its operations were very extensive and for many years, especially during the 1920s and 1930s, it maintained a near monopoly on the manufacture of cut glass tableware. Some of its designs were most creative.

COMMENTS: The glassware listed here has come to be known as "elegant" depression glass.

MARKS: Most Cambridge elegant depression glass was unmarked. A triangle with a C inside or "Near-cut" appears on some pieces of Cambridge glass.

RECOMMENDED READING: For further information refer to *The Official Price Guide to Depression Glass,* published by The House of Collectibles.

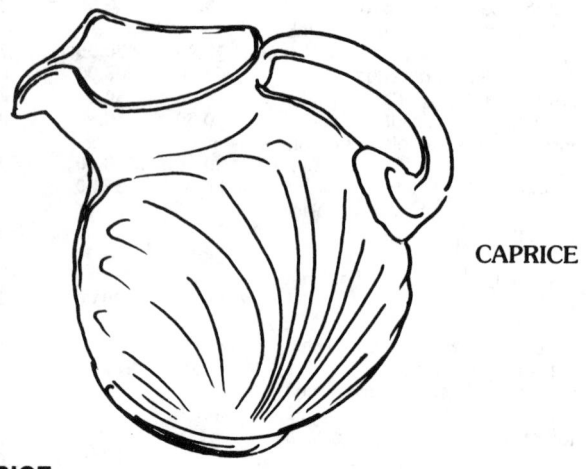

CAPRICE

CAPRICE

Caprice was first made in the 1940s. Colors are crystal, blue, amber and amethyst. Pieces in blue are the most collectible and sought after.

	Current Price Range		P/Y Average
Ashtray, triangle shape, 4½"			
☐ blue	14.00	19.50	14.00
☐ crystal	10.00	13.00	10.00
Bon Bon Dish, square with handle, 6"			
☐ blue	26.00	34.00	28.00
☐ crystal	16.00	20.00	17.00
Bread And Butter Plate, 6½"			
☐ blue	17.00	21.00	18.00
☐ crystal	11.00	14.00	12.00
Cake Plate, footed, 13"			
☐ blue	240.00	280.00	240.00
☐ crystal	97.00	110.00	98.00
Candy Box, footed, with lid, 6"			
☐ blue	84.00	95.00	86.00
☐ crystal	47.00	55.00	50.00
Claret Goblet, 4½ oz.			
☐ blue	42.00	52.00	42.00
☐ crystal	25.00	32.00	25.00
Coaster, 3½"			
☐ blue	25.00	30.00	25.00
☐ crystal	13.00	18.00	15.00

	Current Price Range		P/Y Average
Cocktail Goblet, 3½ oz.			
☐ blue	39.50	47.50	39.00
☐ crystal	24.50	30.00	24.00
Creamer, medium			
☐ blue	13.00	18.00	14.50
☐ crystal	7.00	10.00	7.00
Decanter, with stopper, 36 oz.			
☐ blue	130.00	170.00	140.00
☐ crystal	72.00	90.00	77.00
Dinner Plate, 9½"			
☐ blue	87.00	110.00	90.00
☐ crystal	35.00	45.00	37.00
Luncheon Plate, 8½"			
☐ blue	25.50	32.50	24.00
☐ crystal	13.00	19.00	14.00
Pitcher, ball shaped, 32 oz.			
☐ blue	172.00	190.00	175.00
☐ crystal	90.00	110.00	90.00
Rose Bowl, footed, 8"			
☐ blue	95.00	108.00	95.00
☐ crystal	60.00	70.00	60.00
Salad Bowl, footed, 8"			
☐ blue	42.00	52.00	42.00
☐ crystal	24.00	34.00	25.00
Salad Plate, 7½"			
☐ blue	21.00	25.50	20.00
☐ crystal	14.50	18.00	14.00
Sherbet, tall, 7 oz.			
☐ blue	27.00	35.00	25.00
☐ crystal	20.00	26.00	20.00
Sugar, medium size			
☐ blue	15.00	20.00	15.00
☐ crystal	9.00	11.00	7.50
Tumbler, footed, 3 oz.			
☐ blue	23.00	27.00	22.00
☐ crystal	17.00	22.00	16.00
Tumbler, footed, 5 oz.			
☐ blue	23.00	28.00	22.00
☐ crystal	17.00	22.00	16.00
Tumbler, footed, 10 oz.			
☐ blue	32.00	38.50	32.00
☐ crystal	20.00	25.00	20.00
Tumbler, footed, 12 oz.			
☐ blue	35.00	42.50	35.00
☐ crystal	23.00	30.00	22.00
Vase, 5½"			
☐ blue	60.00	70.00	59.00
☐ crystal	45.00	54.00	45.00

	Current Price Range		P/Y Average
Vase, 8½″			
☐ blue	70.00	100.00	89.00
☐ crystal	55.00	75.00	54.00
Wine Goblet, 3 oz.			
☐ blue	50.00	55.00	45.00
☐ crystal	27.00	35.00	27.00

DECAGON

Made in the shape of a decagon, this pattern was produced in the 1930s. Colors range from pastels to red and cobalt blue.

Almond Bowl, 2½″			
☐ green	9.00	12.00	9.50
☐ pink	9.00	12.00	9.50
☐ light blue	9.00	12.00	9.50
☐ red	16.00	21.00	16.50
☐ cobalt	16.00	21.00	16.50
Berry Bowl, 10″			
☐ green	9.00	12.00	9.50
☐ pink	9.00	12.00	9.50
☐ light blue	9.00	12.00	9.50
☐ red	16.00	21.00	16.00
☐ cobalt	16.00	21.00	16.00
Bon Bon Bowl, handles, 5½″			
☐ green	9.50	12.50	9.50
☐ pink	9.50	12.50	9.50
☐ light blue	9.50	12.50	9.50
☐ red	16.00	21.00	16.00
☐ cobalt	16.00	21.00	16.00

DECAGON

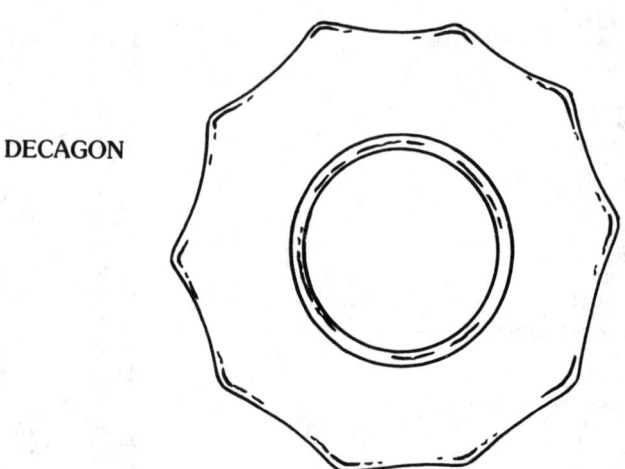

	Current Price Range		P/Y Average
Bread And Butter Plate, 6¼″			
☐ pink	2.50	5.50	2.50
☐ green	2.50	4.50	2.50
☐ light blue	2.50	4.50	2.50
☐ red	4.75	6.75	4.50
☐ cobalt	4.75	6.75	4.50
Celery Tray, 11″			
☐ green	9.00	12.00	9.50
☐ pink	9.00	12.00	9.50
☐ light blue	9.00	12.00	9.50
☐ red	19.00	23.00	19.00
☐ cobalt	19.00	23.00	19.00
Cereal Bowl, bell shaped, 6″			
☐ green	7.00	9.00	6.50
☐ pink	7.00	9.00	6.50
☐ light blue	7.00	9.00	6.50
☐ red	12.00	15.50	12.00
☐ cobalt	12.00	15.50	12.50
Cereal Bowl, flat rim, 6″			
☐ green	6.50	7.50	5.50
☐ pink	6.50	7.50	5.50
☐ light blue	6.50	7.50	5.50
☐ red	10.50	13.00	10.50
☐ cobalt	10.50	13.00	10.50
Comport, 7″			
☐ green	16.00	21.00	16.00
☐ pink	16.00	21.00	16.00
☐ light blue	16.00	21.00	16.00
☐ red	26.00	32.00	26.00
☐ cobalt	26.00	32.00	26.00
Cream Soup, with liner			
☐ green	9.00	12.00	9.00
☐ pink	9.00	12.00	9.00
☐ light blue	9.00	12.00	9.00
☐ red	14.00	18.00	14.00
☐ cobalt	14.00	18.00	14.00
Creamer, footed			
☐ green	8.00	11.50	8.50
☐ pink	8.00	11.50	8.50
☐ light blue	8.00	11.50	8.50
☐ red	19.00	24.00	19.00
☐ cobalt	19.00	24.00	19.00
Creamer, scalloped edge			
☐ green	7.00	10.50	7.50
☐ pink	7.00	10.50	7.50
☐ light blue	7.00	10.50	7.50
☐ red	17.50	21.50	17.00
☐ cobalt	17.50	21.50	17.00
Cruet, handle, stopper, 6 oz.			
☐ pink	21.50	26.00	21.00
☐ green	21.50	26.00	21.00

	Current Price Range		P/Y Average
☐ light blue	21.50	26.00	21.00
☐ red	36.00	42.50	37.00
☐ cobalt	36.00	42.50	37.00
Cup			
☐ green	5.50	7.50	5.50
☐ pink	5.50	7.50	5.50
☐ light blue	5.50	7.50	6.50
☐ red	9.00	12.00	9.50
☐ cobalt	9.00	12.00	9.50
Dinner Plate, 9½"			
☐ green	9.00	12.00	9.50
☐ pink	9.00	12.00	9.50
☐ light blue	9.00	12.00	9.50
☐ red	16.00	21.00	16.00
☐ cobalt	16.00	21.00	16.00
Grill Plate, 10"			
☐ green	7.00	10.00	7.50
☐ pink	7.00	10.00	7.50
☐ light blue	7.00	10.00	7.50
☐ red	13.00	17.50	13.00
☐ cobalt	13.00	17.50	13.00
Mayonnaise Dish, with liner and ladle			
☐ green	17.50	22.00	17.00
☐ pink	17.50	22.00	17.00
☐ light blue	17.50	22.00	17.00
☐ red	27.50	35.00	28.00
☐ cobalt	27.50	35.00	28.00
Pickle Tray, 9"			
☐ green	9.00	12.50	9.50
☐ pink	9.00	12.50	9.50
☐ light blue	9.00	12.50	9.50
☐ red	16.50	22.00	16.00
☐ cobalt	16.50	22.00	16.00
Plate, handles, 7"			
☐ pink	9.00	12.00	8.50
☐ green	9.00	12.00	8.50
☐ light blue	9.00	12.00	8.50
☐ red	14.00	18.00	14.00
☐ cobalt	14.00	18.00	14.00
Salad Plate, 8½"			
☐ green	6.00	8.00	5.50
☐ pink	6.00	8.00	5.50
☐ light blue	6.00	8.00	5.50
☐ red	9.50	12.50	9.50
☐ cobalt	9.50	12.50	9.50
Sauce Boat, with saucer			
☐ green	21.50	25.00	21.00
☐ pink	21.50	25.00	21.00
☐ light blue	21.50	25.00	21.00
☐ red	37.50	45.00	38.00
☐ cobalt	37.50	45.00	38.00

	Current Price Range		P/Y Average
Saucer			
☐ green	1.00	2.00	1.00
☐ pink	1.00	2.00	1.00
☐ light blue	1.00	2.00	1.00
☐ red	1.75	3.75	2.00
☐ cobalt	1.75	3.75	2.00
Service Tray, handles, 13″			
☐ green	19.50	23.00	19.00
☐ pink	19.50	23.00	19.00
☐ light blue	19.50	23.00	19.00
☐ red	27.50	35.50	28.00
☐ cobalt	27.50	35.50	28.00
Sugar, footed			
☐ green	7.50	10.50	7.50
☐ pink	7.50	10.50	7.50
☐ light blue	7.50	10.50	7.50
☐ red	17.50	21.50	17.00
☐ cobalt	17.50	21.50	17.00
Sugar, scalloped edge			
☐ green	7.00	10.00	6.50
☐ pink	7.00	10.00	6.50
☐ light blue	7.00	10.00	6.50
☐ red	16.00	21.50	16.00
☐ cobalt	16.00	21.50	16.00
Vegetable Bowl, oval, 9½″			
☐ green	11.50	14.50	11.50
☐ pink	11.50	14.50	11.50
☐ light blue	11.50	14.50	11.50
☐ red	21.50	25.50	21.00
☐ cobalt	21.50	25.50	21.00

CAMERAS

DESCRIPTION: Camera collecting is a favorite hobby for thousands of people. Not only do hobbyists collect cameras, but everything associated with photography including film, postcards that picture cameras, ads selling cameras and signs from photo stores.

TYPES: Box, folding, panoramic, miniature and 35 mm cameras are all favorite types to collect.

ORIGIN: Although the photographic process was invented by Louis Jacques Mande Daguerre of Paris in 1839, it wasn't until the late 1800s that photography was accessible to the masses. An American, George Eastman, was a major influence in manufacturing cameras to sell to the public.

COMMENTS: Since Kodak was the first company to successfully produce cameras for the public, its cameras are very popular collector's items.

ADDITIONAL INFORMATION: For more information about camera collectibles, consult *The Official Price Guide to Collectible Cameras,* published by The House of Collectibles.

An original Jiffy Kodak camera

	Current Price Range		P/Y Average
☐ **Kodak,** Autographic Junior No. 1, F77/100 mm lens, 1915	15.00	25.00	20.00
☐ **Kodak,** Brownie, No.2, 50th Anniversary box camera giveaway, 1930	15.00	20.00	17.50
☐ **Kodak,** Bulls-Eye No.3, uses 124 film, 1910 ...	40.00	50.00	45.00
☐ **Kodak,** Duo-620 Series II folding camera, f3.5/75 mm lens, 1940	50.00	60.00	55.00
☐ **Kodak,** Eureka No.4, uses 109 film, 1899	85.00	95.00	80.00
☐ **Kodak,** Folding Pocket No.3, uses 122 film, 1905	30.00	50.00	40.00
☐ **Kodak,** Ordinary, box, wooden, 4"x5", 1890s	800.00	1200.00	1000.00
☐ **Kodak,** Premo, box camera, achromatic lens, automatic shutter, 4"x5", 1910	20.00	30.00	25.00

	Current Price Range		P/Y Average
☐ **Kodak,** Quick Focus, achromatic lens, rotary shutter, 3¼"x5½", 1908	125.00	150.00	137.00
☐ **Kodak,** Vest Pocket Kodak Model B, rotary shutter, 1930s	80.00	120.00	100.00
☐ **Leica,** model IIc, highest shutter speed 500, 1940s	150.00	200.00	175.00
☐ **Minolta,** Semi-Automatic, folding, Promar lens, 1937	40.00	60.00	50.00
☐ **Nikon,** Model S, later replaced by Model S2, 1951	100.00	125.00	112.00
☐ **Pentacon,** model FBM, exposure meter, 1957	55.00	80.00	67.00
☐ **Peerless,** box camera, uses glass plates	60.00	80.00	70.00
☐ **Rex Magazine Camera, Co.,** 4"x5", 1899	175.00	220.00	200.00
☐ **Teddy Camera Co.,** Model A, takes direct positive prints, developing tank below camera, 1924	325.00	425.00	375.00

CANES AND WALKING STICKS

TOPIC: Canes and walking sticks were popular accessories in the 17th and 18th centuries. They were both fashionable and utilitarian, because they could be used for protection if needed.

TYPES: Canes are either simple walking sticks or "gadget" canes which conceal a sword, pistol, musical instrument or other device.

PERIOD: Canes are descendents of the sticks early man used to defend himself, and as such date back into early human history. The stylish canes of Europe came into vogue in the 17th and 18th centuries, while the 19th century saw gadget canes reaching a peak of popularity.

MATERIAL: Wood is used for the shafts of almost all canes. Handles may be made out of wood, ivory, bone or metal.

COMMENTS: Canes are fascinating collectibles whether they contain concealed devices or not. The ones that do are particularly interesting because ingenious guns or other weapons may be hidden in them. It is advisable to use caution when handling old canes because a concealed weapon might be inadvertently triggered.

ADDITIONAL TIPS: When buying a cane or walking stick, examine it closely for indications of hidden compartments. Many devices are so well concealed in canes that they go undiscovered for years.

	Current Price Range		P/Y Average
☐ **Amethyst,** cut glass handle	180.00	220.00	190.00
☐ **Bamboo,** curved handle	17.00	20.00	18.00
☐ **Blown Glass,** green	85.00	95.00	87.00
☐ **Bottle Cane,** glass liner holds liquor, 36″	150.00	180.00	160.00
☐ **Clenched Hand,** ivory	180.00	280.00	195.00
☐ **Dog's Head,** Fox Terrier, plainted and carved wood	210.00	230.00	215.00
☐ **Dog's Head,** wood with brown eyes, c. 1900 ..	40.00	60.00	45.00
☐ **Dog's Head,** glass eyes, c. 1900	45.00	60.00	47.00
☐ **Hound's Head,** ivory	70.00	115.00	85.00
☐ **Monkey,** hand carved	95.00	120.00	105.00
☐ **Mother-Of-Pearl,** gold	65.00	85.00	70.00
☐ **Parade Cane,** china clown head	40.00	50.00	42.00
☐ **Umbrella Cane,** wood case, 34″	90.00	120.00	95.00
☐ **Walking Stick,** gold head	110.00	130.00	115.00
☐ **Walking Stick,** sterling head	50.00	60.00	52.00

CARNIVAL GLASS

DESCRIPTION: In 1905, Taffeta, or Carnival glass as it has come to be known, was born out of the turn of the century craze for iridescent art glass. Using mass production and new chemical techniques, Carnival glass was widely produced toward the end of the Art Nouveau period. Tastes changed, however, ushering in the streamlined Art Deco period. Even though it continued to be produced until 1930, by 1925 Carnival glass was on the way out. With a dwindling market, this glass was sold by the trainload to fairs and carnivals to be given away as prizes. Hence, it has come to be called Carnival glass.

ADDITIONAL TIPS: Intense collector interest has already driven the prices of Carnival glass into the astronomical range. An amethyst Carnival farmyard plate sold for $8,000 just this year. The tables have really been turned in this field over the years as this originally cheap imitation of Art glass now far exceeds in value the high quality glass it sought to imitate. Long regarded with disdain by serious dealers, collectors and auction houses, Carnival glass is now turning up on the most prestigious auction blocks in the country. Carnival glass auctions demonstrated one thing clearly: Carnival glass continues to command higher and higher prices with no ceiling in sight. Examples of auction results are: rare, one-of-a-kind Acan Burrs aqua-opalescent punch bowl, base and five cups, $12,500; purple Christmas compote, $1550; large green Hobstar and Feather rosebowl, $1150; amethyst Inverted Thistle pitcher, $2100; teal blue Grape and Cable plate, $1150; and amethyst Farmyard bowl, $1400.

RECOMMENDED READING: For more in-depth information on Carnival glass, you may refer to *The Official Price Guide to Carnival Glass, The Official Price Guide to Glassware* and *The Official Identification Guide to Glassware,* published by The House of Collectibles.

Bowl, *Marigold Carnival Glass, Luster Rose pattern, three footed, marked,* **$85.00-$100.00**
(photo courtesy of ©BJ Warner, Surfside Beach, SC, 1984)

	Current Price Range		P/Y Average
ACORN—Fenton			
Bowl, diameter 7″–8½″			
☐ marigold	22.00	32.50	25.00
☐ purple	30.00	52.00	30.00
☐ green	30.00	52.00	30.00

	Current Price Range		P/Y Average
☐ blue	30.00	52.00	30.00
☐ amethyst	30.00	52.00	30.00
☐ peach opalescent	120.00	135.00	125.00
☐ vaseline	110.00	125.00	115.00
☐ red	225.00	325.00	260.00

Plate, diameter 9″
☐ marigold	120.00	135.00	125.00
☐ purple	285.00	340.00	300.00
☐ green	285.00	340.00	300.00
☐ blue	285.00	340.00	300.00
☐ amethyst	285.00	340.00	300.00

APPLE BLOSSOMS—Dugan

Bowl, 7″–9″
☐ marigold	35.00	45.00	37.50
☐ purple	40.00	50.00	42.00
☐ green	40.00	50.00	42.00
☐ blue	40.00	50.00	42.00
☐ amethyst	40.00	50.00	42.00
☐ white	60.00	80.00	65.00
☐ ices	60.00	80.00	65.00

Plate, diameter 8½″
☐ marigold	45.00	57.50	48.50
☐ purple	65.00	85.00	70.00
☐ green	65.00	85.00	70.00
☐ blue	65.00	85.00	70.00
☐ amethyst	65.00	85.00	70.00
☐ white	85.00	110.00	90.00
☐ ice blue	85.00	110.00	90.00
☐ ice green	85.00	110.00	90.00

BANDED DRAPE—Fenton

Tumbler
☐ marigold	17.50	22.50	18.50
☐ blue	30.00	33.50	30.00
☐ amethyst	30.00	33.50	30.00
☐ ice green	36.00	42.50	39.50
☐ white	37.50	44.00	39.50

Water Pitcher
☐ marigold	70.00	85.00	72.00
☐ blue	185.00	200.00	190.00
☐ amethyst	185.00	200.00	190.00
☐ ice green	240.00	275.00	245.00
☐ white	240.00	275.00	245.00

BEADED CABLE—Northwood

Candy Dish
☐ marigold	22.50	30.00	25.00
☐ purple	32.50	40.00	35.00
☐ green	32.50	40.00	35.00
☐ blue	32.50	40.00	35.00

	Current Price Range		P/Y Average
☐ amethyst	32.50	40.00	35.00
Rose Bowl			
☐ marigold	32.50	40.00	35.00
☐ purple	50.00	62.50	52.00
☐ green	50.00	62.50	52.00
☐ blue	50.00	62.50	52.00
☐ amethyst	50.00	62.50	52.00
☐ aqua opalescent	175.00	225.00	180.00
☐ ices	175.00	190.00	180.00

CHRYSANTHEMUM—Fenton

Bowl, flat, diameter 10″

☐ marigold	35.50	41.00	35.00
☐ blue	47.00	55.00	50.00
☐ green	47.00	55.00	50.00
☐ ice green	95.00	110.00	100.00
☐ white	95.00	110.00	100.00
☐ red	500.00	600.00	550.00

Bowl, footed, diameter 10″

☐ marigold	33.00	37.00	35.00
☐ blue	47.00	55.00	50.00
☐ green	47.00	55.00	50.00
☐ ice green	95.00	110.00	100.00
☐ white	95.00	110.00	100.00
☐ red	500.00	600.00	525.00

ELKS—Fenton

Bowl, Detroit

☐ purple	325.00	375.00	330.00
☐ green	325.00	375.00	330.00
☐ blue	325.00	375.00	330.00
☐ amethyst	325.00	375.00	330.00

Bowl, Parkersburg

☐ purple	350.00	425.00	360.00
☐ green	350.00	425.00	360.00
☐ blue	350.00	425.00	360.00
☐ amethyst	350.00	425.00	360.00

CAROUSEL ANIMALS

DESCRIPTION: The collecting of carousel animals is one of the most unusual areas of collectibles. These beautiful, hand-carved and sculptured creations are true examples of a lost art.

PERIOD: The "golden age" of carousel animals in America began shortly after the Civil War. Circuses at that time were beginning to incorporate rides into their side-shows, and larger more elaborate rides were being set up at permanent amusement parks. By 1890 the carousel or "merry-go-round" had become a standard attraction at all amusement parks and many other places of entertainment. They became so popular that a number of public parks installed them, including New York's Central Park, whose 19th century carousel is still in operation. Outstanding quality in carousel animals called for expert wood carvers. Most of those who worked in America were Italians who had learned the art of wood carving in Italy.

	Current Price Range		P/Y Average
☐ **Armitage Hershell Jumpers,** track type, no holes through horse, c. 1890	825.00	925.00	875.00
☐ **Carmel Borrelli,** 60"x50"	3000.00	3500.00	3250.00
☐ **Carmel Borrelli,** 54"x56"	3500.00	4000.00	3750.00
☐ **Carmel Borrelli,** 49"x49"	2500.00	3000.00	2750.00
☐ **Carmel Borrelli,** stander	3500.00	4000.00	3750.00
☐ **Dentzel Jumping Mare,** Pittsburg, PA Carousel	2500.00	3000.00	2750.00
☐ **Metal Illions Jumper,** off kiddie machine, 36"	200.00	220.00	210.00
☐ **Muller,** medium stander, 71"	2000.00	2500.00	2250.00
☐ **Muller Dentzel,** parrots on back of saddle, 79	3800.00	4000.00	3900.00
☐ **Parker,** large flowers with jewel centers	1000.00	1200.00	1100.00
☐ **Parker Jumper,** super sweet horse	900.00	1000.00	950.00
☐ **Parker Style Aluminum Horse,** 52"x29"	400.00	500.00	450.00
☐ **Spillman,** nice flowing mane, shield, 66"	1000.00	1200.00	1100.00
☐ **Trojan Jumper,** 66"	750.00	950.00	850.00

Jumping Horse, *Philadelphia Toboggan Co., carved by Frank Caretta,* **$900.00-$1500.00**

CARS

PERIOD: While groundwork for the automobile was laid in the 18th century, it wasn't until 1896 that Henry Ford operated his first car—a twin cylinder, four-horse power quadricycle. Since then the car business and car collecting business has blossomed, and car collectors specialize in cars from that early date up to the more current cars of the 1970s. Car collecting is only about thirty years old, but it is a solid hobby.

COMMENTS: At first the collector car hobby centered around the Brass Era of the 1930s and 1940s. The pace of car collecting quickened in the 50s, and the nostalgia boom of the 1960s produced an increased interest in the Brass Era and Classic Car era. Today collectors buy a variety of cars, from the early ones to the muscle cars of the 1960s.

ADDITIONAL TIPS: The listings in this section are alphabetical according to the car maker. Following the maker is the date of manufacture, model, type of engine, type of body and price range. Prices do vary according to the condition of the car.

For further information see *The Official Price Guide to Collector Cars,* published by the House of Collectibles.

YEAR	MODEL	ENGINE	BODY	F	G	E
B.M.W. (Deutschland, Germany, 1928-to-date)						
1932	320	1971cc	Touring	6800	14000	22000
1935	315	1.5 Litre	Cabriolet	3250	6800	12500
1953	Type 328		Drop Head Coupe	2100	4400	9800
1965	2000 CS		Coupe	3800	6800	13000
1972	Sport	6 cyl.	Sedan	3600	4900	9900
BUICK (United States, 1903-to-date)						
1903	Model B	2 cyl.	Touring Runabout	28500	66000	175000
1904	Model B	2 cyl.	Touring	12000	34000	83000
1905	Model C	2 cyl.	Touring	7000	10200	24200
1906	Model G	2 cyl.	Runabout	4940	11100	30700
1907	Model G	4 cyl.	Runabout	5600	11400	32000
1908	Model D	4 cyl.	Roadster	6040	12000	34000
1909	Model 10	4 cyl.	Roadster	3525	6770	15200
1910	Model 14	2 cyl.	Roadster	4500	11700	29000
1911	Model 33	4 cyl.	Roadster	4650	7250	12375
1912	Model 35	4 cyl.	Touring	3400	11300	26000
1913	McLaughlin	4 cyl.	Touring	2800	9450	24000
1914	Model 24	4 cyl.	Roadster	2700	9230	24000
1915	C-25	4 cyl.	Touring	6000	9550	14550
1916	D-35	6 cyl.	Touring	4500	10900	26600
1917	D-44	6 cyl.	Roadster	4300	7500	13500
1918	G-47	6 cyl.	Sedan	4000	7000	13000
1919	H-44	6 cyl.	Roadster	4000	6575	13000
1920	K-50	6 cyl.	Touring	4000	6575	13000
1921	21–46	6 cyl.	Coupe	3400	9200	14500
1922	22–44	6 cyl.	Sport Roadster	5000	11400	28500
1923	23–44	4 cyl.	Roadster	3900	10000	28000
1924	24–55	6 cyl.	Sport Touring	4700	10000	29500
1925	Standard	6 cyl.	Coach	3900	7100	22000
1926	40	6 cyl.	Touring	4800	11400	28500
1927	Master 6	6 cyl.	Roadster	5300	100000	29000
1928	28–54	6 cyl.	Sport Roadster	4500	13500	30600
1929	Big Six	6 cyl.	Cabriolet	4700	13200	30700
1930	30–46 S	6 cyl.	Sport Coupe	3200	6400	13000
1931	94	8 cyl.	Roadster	8900	23000	42000
1932	90	8 cyl.	Phaeton	6700	14000	34000
1933	90	8 cyl.	7 Passenger Sedan	3000	6000	17100
1934	40	8 cyl.	2 Door Sedan	2500	5000	13000
1935	66	8 cyl.	Sport Coupe Rumble Seat	3900	8200	15000

YEAR	MODEL	ENGINE	BODY	F	G	E
1936	Special	8 cyl.	Sport Coupe	4200	7200	14000
1937	Special	8 cyl.	2 Door Sedan	1500	3300	10000
1938	Roadmaster	8 cyl.	Sedan	1575	3250	10500
1939	Special	8 cyl.	Convertible Phaeton	5000	8000	16000
1940	Super	8 cyl.	Coupe	2200	4200	10200
1941	Special (44-S)	8 cyl.	Coupe	2300	6200	12900
1942	Roadmaster	8 cyl.	Sedan	2300	6200	12900
1946	Super	8 cyl.	2 Door Sedan	2300	4700	10200
1947	Super	8 cyl.	Convertible	5100	7800	14400
1948	Super	8 cyl.	Convertible	3550	6550	14200
1949	Super	8 cyl.	Sedanet	2000	4000	7550

CADILLAC (United States 1903-to-date)

YEAR	MODEL	ENGINE	BODY	F	G	E
1903	A	1 cyl.	Touring	4700	11000	25500
1904	A	1 cyl.	Roadster	4800	8050	23500
1905	B	1 cyl.	Roadster	3900	9700	26500
1906	K	1 cyl.	Runabout	3700	8800	24500
1907	K	1 cyl.	Roadster	4000	9500	26100
1908	T	1 cyl.	Runabout	4000	6000	20000
1909	30	4 cyl.	Touring	4000	6000	21000
1910	30	4 cyl.	Town	4300	11200	28600
1912	30	4 cyl.	Opera Coupe	3450	9200	15700
1913	30	4 cyl.	6 Passenger Touring	4400	6600	24000
1914	30	4 cyl.	Touring	4200	7000	29300
1915	51	(V) 8 cyl.	Touring	4500	11300	29300
1916	53	(V) 8 cyl.	Touring	4500	11300	29300
1917	55	(V) 8 cyl.	Touring	4200	8900	23000
1918	57	(V) 8 cyl.	7 Passenger Touring	4200	8900	23000
1919	57	(V) 8 cyl.	Touring	3700	5000	18000
1920	59	(V) 8 cyl.	7 Passenger Touring	3700	7900	22000
1921	59	(V) 8 cyl.	7 Passenger Touring	3800	8000	21500
1922	61	(V) 8 cyl.	7 Passenger Phaeton	4600	8500	25000
1923	61	(V) 8 cyl.	Sport Phaeton	4400	8200	29300
1924	V-63	(V) 8 cyl.	Phaeton	6600	11500	34500
1925	V-63	(V) 8 cyl.	Dual Cowl Phaeton	8450	20950	46000
1926	314	(V) 8 cyl.	Sedan	3650	8400	16750
1927	314	(V) 8 cyl.	Town Sedan	4700	9900	22000
1928	Fleetwood	(V) 8 cyl.	Cabriolet	8600	16800	33500
1929	341-B SM		Town Sedan	8575	13500	42500
1930	353	(V) 8 cyl.	Coupe Roadster	7000	12500	29800
1931	452	(V) 16 cyl.	Sedan	12600	22000	46000
1932	355B	(V) 8 cyl.	Club Sedan	6400	16700	26200
1933	355C	(V) 8 cyl.	Convertible Sedan	13600	37500	69000

CHEVROLET (United States, 1911-to-date)

YEAR	MODEL	ENGINE	BODY	F	G	E
1912	Classic Six	6 cyl.	Touring	5700	9300	32000
1913	Baby Grand	4 cyl.	Touring	3900	11400	24000
1914	Baby Grand	4 cyl.	Touring	4100	10900	26000
1915	Baby Grand	4 cyl.	Touring	3400	11400	26000

YEAR	MODEL	ENGINE	BODY	F	G	E
1916	Special	6 cyl.	Roadster	4700	11500	22700
1917	D	(V) 8 cyl.	Roadster	6800	13100	27000
1918	490	4 cyl.	Coupe	1900	2900	7100
1919	490	4 cyl.	Touring	3300	4500	15100
1920	490	4 cyl.	Coupe	2100	3100	8200
1921	490	4 cyl.	Touring	3300	4500	15100
1922	FB	4 cyl.	Sport Touring	4100	10600	18800
1923	FB	4 cyl.	Sedan	1800	5200	10900
1924	Superior	4 cyl.	Sedan	2700	4900	12900
1925	Superior	4 cyl.	Roadster	3100	4300	14500
1926	Superior V	4 cyl.	Coupe	2500	4900	13000
1927	AA	4 cyl.	Roadster	3400	4400	14600
1928	AB	4 cyl.	Sedan	2000	3000	7600
1929	AC	6 cyl.	Touring	4300	6600	24000

FORD (United States, 1903-to-date)

YEAR	MODEL	ENGINE	BODY	F	G	E
1903	A	2 cyl.	Runabout	9600	13000	25500
1904	A-AC	2 cyl.	Runabout	6900	17650	29250
1905	C	2 cyl.	Runabout	4600	9825	18850
1906	F	2 cyl.	Touring	5000	9600	20000
1907	N	4 cyl.	Runabout	5000	8600	14500
1907	K	6 cyl.	Runabout	19375	57700	115000
1908	S	4 cyl.	Runabout	2800	6500	17800
1909	T	4 cyl.	Town	4600	9725	20950
1910	T	4 cyl.	Runabout	3100	6900	14000
1911	T	4 cyl.	Tourabout	5000	8500	18850
1912	T	4 cyl.	Roadster	3100	6900	15500
1913	T	4 cyl.	Touring	4000	7200	15500

Ford, Model T Touring Car, *1915,* **$3000.00-$14000.00**
(photo courtesy of ©James Lemen, Summit Point, WV)

YEAR	MODEL	ENGINE	BODY	F	G	E
1913	T	4 cyl.	Town	3600	7225	18850
1914	T	4 cyl.	Roadster	3500	7200	14500
1915	T	4 cyl.	Coupelet	3700	7840	21950
1916	T	4 cyl.	Roadster	2500	4800	14860
1917	T	4 cyl.	Center Door Sedan	3600	5400	9000
1918	T	4 cyl.	Roadster	2300	3600	11200
1918	T	4 cyl.	Touring	2000	4000	13495
1918	T	4 cyl.	Center Door Sedan	3600	4600	9000
1919	T	4 cyl.	Roadster	2600	3600	10500
1920	T	4 cyl.	Coupe	1600	2500	6500
1921	T	4 cyl.	Roadster	1600	3500	10000
1922	T	4 cyl.	Roadster	1600	3000	11500
1922	T	4 cyl.	Touring	1600	3000	11500
1923	T	4 cyl.	Roadster	1600	3000	11500
1924	T	4 cyl.	Roadster	2095	4000	10500
1925	T	4 cyl.	Fordor	2000	3800	12235
1926	T	4 cyl.	Roadster	2000	3800	11500
1927	T	4 cyl.	Fordor	1900	3200	5800
1928	AR	4 cyl.	Touring	4600	10400	24050
1928	A	4 cyl.	Fordor	1900	4800	7500
1929	A	4 cyl.	Roadster	4000	9400	26000
1930	A	4 cyl.	Victoria	2800	5650	14450
1931	A	4 cyl.	Roadster	4300	7400	26500
1931	A	4 cyl.	Town Sedan	2700	6200	13600
1932	B	4 cyl.	Roadster	6500	10000	28500
1933	40	(V) 8 cyl.	Cabriolet	5600	8200	23500
1934	40	(V) 8 cyl.	Roadster	6000	9000	30500
1935	48	(V) 8 cyl.	Station Wagon	3700	6000	13100
1935	48	(V) 8 cyl.	Sedan Delivery	2800	7200	14600
1936	68	(V) 8 cyl.	Roadster	7400	11200	27100
1937	78	(V) 8 cyl.	Station Wagon	4000	6000	14500
1938	Standard	(V) 8 cyl.	Coupe	2000	3800	7500
1939	Deluxe	(V) 8 cyl.	Fordor	1750	3600	6700
1939	Deluxe	(V) 8 cyl.	Station Wagon	3100	6000	13500
1940	Standard	(V) 8 cyl.	Coupe	2600	4100	10600
1941		(V) 8 cyl.	Pickup	1300	4400	8400
1942	Special	6 cyl.	Coupe	1900	4000	7200

MERCEDES-BENZ (1926-to-date)

YEAR	MODEL	ENGINE	BODY	F	G	E
1901		4 cyl.	Phaeton	13000	26000	52000
1901		4 cyl.	Racing	19000	39000	82000
1902		4 cyl.	Tonneau	13000	26000	52000
1902		4 cyl.	Touring	15000	33000	70000
1903	'60'	4 cyl.	Racing	19000	39000	115000
1904	Simplex	4 cyl.	Tonneau	19000	39000	115000
1905		4 cyl.	Tonneau	22000	42000	88000
1906	45	4 cyl.	Limousine	13000	26000	52000
1907		6 cyl.	Landaulet	13000	26000	49000
1908		6 cyl.	Landaulet	9800	19000	39000
1909		6 cyl.	Sport	9600	19000	39000
1910	14/30	4 cyl.	Sport	6700	13000	26000
1911	16/40	4 cyl.	Phaeton	15000	32000	67000
1912	14/30	4 cyl.	Limousine	7900	14000	33000
1913	38/70	4 cyl.	Sport Phaeton	11000	26000	61000
1914	GP	4 cyl.	Racing	9100	15000	35000

YEAR	MODEL	ENGINE	BODY	F	G	E
1915		4 cyl.	Sport	6700	16000	41000
1916		6 cyl.	Racing	7900	23000	60000
1917		6 cyl.	Limousine	7900	14000	30000
1918		6 cyl.	Limousine	7900	14000	31000
1919		4 cyl.	Racing	9400	27000	61000
1920		6 cyl.	Coupe	5900	11000	23000
1921	6/18	4 cyl.	Sport	7900	19000	44000
1922	10/40/65	4 cyl.	Touring	11000	23000	62000
1923	24/100/140	6 cyl.	Touring	13000	26000	71000
1924	25-40	6 cyl.	Touring	10400	23000	64000
1925	SS	6 cyl.	Touring	19000	52000	120000
1926	K	6 cyl.	Touring	13000	26000	78000
1927	SS	6 cyl.	Touring	26000	94000	240000
1928		8 cyl.	Convertible	19000	39000	97000
1929	K	8 cyl.	Limousine	16000	33000	52000

CHALKWARE

DESCRIPTION: Items made from plaster of paris and painted in bright colors are called chalkware.

TYPES: Animal and bird figurines were the main items produced as chalkware.

PERIOD: Chalkware, which was produced as a cheap imitation of Staffordshire and Bennington ware, was found in middle class homes during the 1800s.

COMMENTS: Chalkware is now associated with Folk Art and can be found in antiques stores specializing in that area.

ADDITIONAL TIPS: Animals with nodding heads are especially rare. Few were produced and even fewer have survived through the years.

	Current Price Range		P/Y Average
☐ **Bank,** apple with red cheeks	28.00	32.00	27.50
☐ **Basket,** fruit filled	310.00	360.00	325.00
☐ **Bird,** nesting	260.00	310.00	280.00
☐ **Black Boy with Watermelon,** 4″	18.00	22.00	17.50
☐ **Bookends,** pirates, painted, pair	42.00	48.00	42.00
☐ **Boy,** reading books, 10½″	90.00	110.00	92.00

	Current Price Range		P/Y Average
☐ **Cat,** 4½″	160.00	185.00	162.00
☐ **Cat,** 10½″	185.00	235.00	200.00
☐ **Charley McCarthy,** 15″	22.00	28.00	22.50
☐ **Dancing Lady,** 14″	18.00	32.00	22.00
☐ **Deer,** 9½″	435.00	485.00	450.00
☐ **Dog,** 8½″	135.00	155.00	138.00
☐ **Dove,** green with blue wings, 12″	210.00	235.00	212.00
☐ **Dove,** green and yellow wings, 6″	260.00	310.00	275.00
☐ **Duck,**	140.00	165.00	142.00
☐ **Eagle,** spread, 9½″	285.00	335.00	300.00
☐ **Gnome,** German, 11″, 1930s	22.00	28.00	22.50
☐ **Horn of Plenty,** 14″	18.00	32.00	22.00
☐ **Indian,** Cigar Store, reclining, 23″	210.00	235.00	212.00
☐ **Lamb,** gray body, 8½″	260.00	310.00	275.00
☐ **Lamb,** rectangular base, 6½″	135.00	160.00	138.00
☐ **Owl,** 12″	185.00	210.00	182.00
☐ **Parrot,** 10½″	1300.00	1600.00	1400.00
☐ **Pigeon,** 10″	135.00	160.00	138.00
☐ **Poodles,** 7¾″	185.00	235.00	200.00
☐ **Rabbit,** sitting, 8″	160.00	185.00	162.00
☐ **Rooster,** 6″	335.00	385.00	350.00
☐ **Santa Claus,** 24″	155.00	180.00	160.00
☐ **Sheep,** mother with babies, 7″	185.00	210.00	182.00
☐ **Shepherd,** German, 17½″	85.00	105.00	85.00
☐ **Squirrel,** 10″	185.00	210.00	182.00
☐ **Stag,** rectangular base, 15″	260.00	310.00	275.00

CHILDREN'S BOOKS

DESCRIPTION: A children's book is any title written specifically for children, usually between the ages of three and thirteen.

VALUE: Condition and author play important roles in determining value. The more notable authors usually command higher prices. Lewis Carroll is a good example of an author whose children's books are extremely valuable.

COMMENTS: Children's books of the 1800s are especially collectible.

	Current Price Range		P/Y Average

☐ **Abbott, Jacob,** *Rollo's Correspondence,* Boston, 1841 . . . . **100.00 150.00   125.00**

☐ **Abbott, Jacob,** *Marco Baul's Travels and Adventures: Erie Canal,* Boston, 1848, colored frontispiece and four colored plates **55.00   75.00   65.00**

☐ **Abbott, Jacob,** *Rollo at School,* Boston, 1849 **175.00 225.00   200.00**

☐ **Adams, Hannah,** *An Abridgement of the History of New England for the Use of Young Persons,* Boston, 1807, second edition **20.00   30.00   25.00**

☐ **Aikin, Lucy,** *Juvenile Correspondence, or Letters . . . for Children of Both Sexes,* Boston, 1822, calf **30.00   40.00   35.00**

☐ **Alcott, Louisa M.,** *Little Women,* Boston, 1869, second issue **70.00   90.00   80.00**

☐ **Alcott, Louisa M.,** *Little Men,* Boston, 1871 . . . **240.00 315.00   277.00**

☐ **Alcott, Louisa M.,** *Silver Pitchers,* Boston, 1876
. . . . **35.00   42.00   38.00**

☐ **Alcott, Louisa M.,** *Jo's Boys,* Boston, 1886 . . . **35.00   42.00   38.00**

☐ **Berquin, M.,** *The Blossoms of Morality; Intended for the Amusement and Instruction of Young Ladies and Gentlemen,* London, 1821, quarter roan, gilt **12.00   15.00   13.50**

☐ **Berquin, M.,** *The Beauties of the Children's Friend,* Boston, 1827 . . . . **35.00   45.00   40.00**

☐ **Bible in Miniature,** *Thumb Bible,* Troy, N.Y., 1823, measures 2"x1⅝" **150.00 200.00   175.00**

☐ **Bible Natural History,** containing a description of Quadrupeds, Birds, Trees, Plants, Insects, etc., mentioned in the Holy Scriptures, London, 1852 . . . . **6.00   8.00   7.00**

☐ **Bisset, J.,** *The Orphan Boy,* A Pathetic Tale, founded on fact, Birmingham, n.d., 1799, third edition **18.00   23.00   20.00**

☐ **Blewitt, Mrs. Octavian,** *The Rose and the Lily,* A Fairy Tale, London, 1877 . . . . **8.00   10.00   9.00**

☐ **Book of Riddles,** N.Y., 1816, 28 pp., softbound, on some copies the wrapper incorrectly reads *History of Insects,* rare **150.00 200.00   175.00**

☐ **Bouton, Eliz. Gladwin,** *Grandmother's Doll,* N.Y., n.d., 1931 . . . . **45.00   60.00   53.00**

☐ **Brereton, Captain F.S.,** *In the Grip of the Mullah,* A Tale of Adventure in Somililand, London, 1904
. . . . **8.00   10.00   9.00**

☐ **Brereton, Captain F.S.,** *The Hero of Panama,* A Tale of the Great Canal, London, 1912 . . . . **8.00   10.00   9.00**

☐ **Browning, Robert,** *The Pied Piper of Hamelin,* London, n.d. **25.00   30.00   27.50**

☐ **Burnett, Francis H.,** *Little Lord Fauntleroy,* N.Y., 1886 . . . . **150.00 200.00   175.00**

☐ **Burnett, Francis H.,** *Editha's Burglar,* Boston, 1888, second issue **15.00   20.00   17.50**

☐ **Butterworth, Hezekiah,** *Zig-Zag Journeys in Europe,* Boston, 1880, first edition **40.00   50.00   45.00**

Roy Rogers Plate And Bowl, *set,* **$10.00-$15.00**
(photo courtesy of ©Hake's Americana, York, PA, 1984)

	Current Price Range		P/Y Average
☐ **Bowl,** glass, Shirley Temple, blue, 6½″	50.00	65.00	55.00
☐ **Butter Dish,** pattern glass, Bead and Scroll, clear, with dome lid, 4″	135.00	155.00	140.00
☐ **Casserole,** Blue Willow, Made in Japan, 4¾″	15.00	20.00	17.50
☐ **Casserole,** Blue Willow, Made in Japan, 5″ . . .	15.00	20.00	17.50
☐ **Casserole,** Blue Willow, Occupied Japan	15.00	20.00	17.50
☐ **Casserole,** graniteware, blue and white, with lid, 2⅞″	42.00	50.00	43.00
☐ **Casserole,** Noritake, Bluebird, 6″	30.00	40.00	35.00
☐ **Casserole,** Pagodas, England, with lid, 5½″ . .	40.00	50.00	42.00
☐ **Coffee Pot,** aluminum, tapered with full length wooded handle, hinged lid is embossed with advertising slogan "Drink Thomson Malted Milk," lid has wooden knob, 5″, 1930s	15.00	20.00	17.50
☐ **Coffee Pot,** tin, hinged top with wooden knob, tapered sides, long spout, curved full length handle, engraved decoration, 5½″, 1890	25.00	35.00	30.00
☐ **Creamer,** Blue Willow, Made in Japan, 1½″ . .	6.00	8.00	7.00
☐ **Creamer,** Blue Willow, Made in Japan, 2″	6.00	8.00	7.00
☐ **Creamer,** Blue Willow, Occupied Japan	5.00	10.00	7.50
☐ **Creamer,** depression glass, Cherry Blossom, pink, 2¾″	25.00	30.00	27.50
☐ **Creamer,** depression glass, Doric and Pansy, pink, 2¾″	25.00	30.00	27.00
☐ **Creamer,** glass, Akro Agate, Chiquita, green opaque, 1½″	3.50	4.50	4.00
☐ **Creamer,** Noritake, Bluebird, 1⅞″	10.00	15.00	12.00
☐ **Creamer,** pattern glass, Acorn, clear, 3½″	70.00	80.00	72.00
☐ **Creamer,** Sunset, Made in Japan, 1⅞″	3.00	5.00	3.25
☐ **Creamer,** Water Hen, England, 3⅛″	20.00	25.00	21.00

	Current Price Range		P/Y Average

Crock, lid, brown and gray, 4″, 1920s	9.00	15.00	12.50
Cup And Saucer, Blue Willow, Made in Japan, 1⅛″ cup, 3⅜″ diameter saucer	6.00	8.00	6.50
Cup And Saucer, Blue Willow, Made in Japan, 3½″ cup, 3¾″ diameter saucer	6.50	10.00	7.50
Cup And Saucer, Blue Willow, Occupied Japan	10.00	12.00	11.00
Cup And Saucer, depression glass, Cherry Blossom, pink, 1½″ cup, diameter of saucer is 4½″	25.00	28.00	26.00
Cup And Saucer, depression glass, Doric and Pansy, ultramarine, 1½″ cup, diameter of saucer is 4½″	25.00	30.00	22.00
Cup And Saucer, Noritake, Bluebird	7.00	12.00	10.00
Cup And Saucer, Noritake, Silhouette, pale lavender with black silhouette of little girl pushing a doll buggy, 1¼″ cup, 3¾″ saucer	9.00	12.00	10.00
Cup And Saucer, Silhouette, Made in Japan, 1½″ cup, diameter of saucer is 3¾″	6.00	8.00	6.50
Cup And Saucer, Sunset, Made in Japan, 1¼″ cup, diameter of saucer is 3⅜″	6.00	8.00	6.50
Cup And Saucer, Water Hen, England, 2″ cup, 4½″ diameter saucer	15.00	18.00	16.50
Dishpan, aluminum, flat sides, rolled edge, loop handles, 4″	4.00	8.00	5.00
Frying Pan, graniteware, blue and white, 4½″	28.00	35.00	30.00
Grater, graniteware, blue and white, 4″	50.00	55.00	52.00
Gravy Boat, Blue Marble, England, 1½″	28.00	33.00	30.00
Gravy Boat, Blue Willow, Made in Japan	15.00	20.00	17.50
Grill Plate, Blue Willow, Made in Japan, 5″ ...	15.00	20.00	17.50
Mold, graniteware, blue and white, fluted, 2¾″	30.00	35.00	32.00
Mug, glass, Hopalong Cassidy, white milk glass with black enameled picture of Hopalong Cassidy, 3″	5.00	7.00	5.50
Penny Candy Tray, with spoon, pressed tin, shaped like cream skimmer, originally sold in 1920s filled with candy, 3″x1″x⅛″	5.00	10.00	7.50
Pitcher And Wash Bowl, ironstone, white background with pastel green shading, 24 Kt gold bands, roses, scalloped edges, scroll handle, 4″, 1890	25.00	30.00	27.50
Pitcher And Wash Bowl, porcelain, very fancy, pitcher is 4″ tall, bowl has 5″ diameter, white with pale green and gold trim, decorated with roses, marked with gold crown, the letter L and the number 5725	60.00	70.00	65.00
Pitcher, graniteware, blue and white, 2½″	40.00	48.00	42.00
Plate, Blue Marble, England, 4″	9.00	12.00	10.00
Plate, Blue Willow, Made in Japan, 3¾″	2.00	4.00	2.50
Plate, Blue Willow, Made in Japan, 5″	13.00	15.00	14.00
Plate, Blue Willow, Occupied Japan	3.50	5.00	4.00
Plate, depression glass, Cherry Blossom, pink, 5⅞″	7.00	9.00	8.00

	Current Price Range		P/Y Average

☐ **Plate,** depression glass, Doric and Pansy, pink, 5⅞" 6.00 8.00 7.00

☐ **Plate,** glass, Akro Agate, Concentric Rib, green opaque, 3¼" 1.50 2.50 1.75

☐ **Plate,** glass, Hopalong Cassidy, white milk glass with black enameled picture of Hopalong Cassidy and his horse, 7" 14.00 18.00 15.00

☐ **Plate,** Noritake, Bluebird, 4¼" 3.50 5.00 4.00

☐ **Plate,** Pagodas, England, 4½" 10.00 12.00 10.00

☐ **Plate,** Sunset, Made in Japan, 4¼" 1.00 2.00 1.25

☐ **Platter,** Blue Marble, England, 4½" 25.00 30.00 27.00

☐ **Platter,** Blue Willow, Made in Japan, 4⅝" 7.00 10.00 7.50

☐ **Platter,** Blue Willow, Made in Japan, 6" 7.00 10.00 7.50

☐ **Platter,** Blue Willow, Occupied Japan 10.00 15.00 12.00

☐ **Platter,** Noritake, Bluebird, 7⅛" 10.00 15.00 12.00

☐ **Platter,** Pagodas, England, 7⅛" 25.00 32.00 27.00

☐ **Presentation Cup,** porcelain, "To My Sister," pink roses, 24 Kt scrolling, closed loop handle, 2⅜", 1890 . . . . 15.00 20.00 17.50

☐ **Sugar Bowl,** Blue Willow, Made in Japan, with lid, 2" 7.00 10.00 8.50

☐ **Sugar Bowl,** Blue Willow, Made in Japan, with lid, 2¾" 5.00 10.00 6.00

☐ **Sugar Bowl,** Blue Willow, Occupied Japan, with lid 10.00 15.00 12.00

☐ **Sugar Bowl,** depression glass, Cherry Blossom, pink, 2⅝" 20.00 25.00 22.00

☐ **Sugar Bowl,** depression glass, Doric and Pansy, pink, 2½" 20.00 24.00 21.00

☐ **Sugar Bowl,** Noritake, Bluebird, with lid, 2¾" 14.00 20.00 15.00

☐ **Sugar Bowl,** pattern glass, Block, blue, with lid, 4½" 90.00 105.00 95.00

☐ **Sugar Bowl,** Sunset, Made in Japan, with lid, 3⅛" 3.00 5.00 3.50

☐ **Sugar Bowl,** Water Hen, England, with lid, 4½" 25.00 30.00 26.50

☐ **Table Utensils,** tin, ten pieces, five knives with two piece riveted bone handles, five forks, 3½", 1910 . . . . 25.00 35.00 30.00

☐ **Teapot,** Blue Willow, Made in Japan, with lid, 2⅝" 35.00 45.00 32.00

☐ **Teapot,** Blue Willow, Made in Japan, with lid, 3¾" 30.00 40.00 32.00

☐ **Teapot,** Blue Willow, Occupied Japan, with lid 20.00 25.00 17.50

☐ **Teapot,** glass, Akro Agate, J.P., Transparent green, with lid, 1½" 25.00 30.00 26.50

☐ **Teapot,** Noritake, Bluebird, with lid, 3½" 30.00 40.00 35.00

☐ **Teapot,** Noritake, Silhouette, pale lavender with black silhouette of little girl pushing a doll buggy, 3½" 30.00 40.00 32.00

☐ **Teapot,** Silhouette, Made in Japan, with lid, 4" 6.00 8.00 6.50

☐ **Teapot,** Sunset, Made in Japan, with lid, 3¾" 5.00 7.00 5.50

	Current Price Range		P/Y Average
☐ **Teapot,** Water Hen, England, with lid, 5¼″ ...	35.00	40.00	36.50
☐ **Tea Set,** china, nine pieces, covered teapot, creamer, covered sugar, two cups, two saucers, white with blue shading, 24 Kt gold decoration, scalloped edges, tallest piece is 5½″, German, 1910	75.00	100.00	85.00
☐ **Tea Set,** depression glass, Homespun, fourteen pieces, pink, original box	190.00	220.00	195.00
☐ **Tea Set,** glass, Akro Agate, Chiquita, twenty-two pieces, green opaque, original box	55.00	75.00	60.00
☐ **Tea Set,** glass, Akro Agate, Concentric Ring, twenty-one pieces, marbleized blue, original box	400.00	475.00	420.00
☐ **Tea Set,** glass, Akro Agate, Interior Panel, eight pieces, transparent topaz, original box	25.00	42.00	30.00
☐ **Tea Set,** Palissy china, twenty-three pieces, covered teapot, creamer, covered sugar, six cups, six saucers, six plates, white with brown flower berry and leaf decoration, gold trim, very elaborate shape, teapot is 4½″ high, perfect condition, Palissy blue mark, early 1800s	150.00	250.00	175.00
☐ **Tea Set,** porcelain, eight pieces, covered teapot, creamer, covered sugar, two cups, two saucers, teddy bear decoration	8.00	10.00	8.50
☐ **Tea Set,** porcelain, seven pieces, covered teapot, sugar, creamer, two cups, two saucers, Dolly Dingle decoration	6.00	10.00	7.50
☐ **Tea Set,** porcelain, seven pieces, covered teapot, sugar, creamer, two cups, two saucers, Peter Rabbit decoration	6.00	10.00	7.50
☐ **Toleware,** tin, set of three pieces, pitcher, cup, saucer, pitcher is 2″, cup is 1⅝″, painted blue and cream with still life scenes, 1920	9.00	15.00	12.00
☐ **Tureen,** Blue Willow, Made in Japan, with lid, 4″	15.00	20.00	17.00
☐ **Tureen,** Blue Willow, Occupied Japan, with lid	20.00	25.00	22.00
☐ **Tureen,** ironstone, lid, moss rose decoration, rococo styling, 24 Kt trim on handles, 1890	25.00	35.00	30.00
☐ **Tureen,** semi-porcelain, Johnson Brothers, lid, white with gold trim and sprays of tiny roses, 7″x4½″, 1800s	50.00	60.00	55.00
☐ **Turkey Roasting Pan,** aluminum, oval, lid, riveted iron handles on ends of pan and top of lid, 5½″x3½″x1½″, 1920s	5.00	10.00	7.50

CHRISTMAS DECORATIONS

DESCRIPTION: Christmas tree ornaments were first manufactured and sold to consumers in the 1870s. Replacing homemade decorations, most of these early ones were simple shapes made in small German villages. Dresden ornaments are the rarest and most valuable. Being made of embossed cardboard and covered with metallic paper, these intricate handcrafted specimens were soon superceded by easily produced blown glass items. It is estimated that by the 1920s, over 5,000 different designs were used for ornaments.

COMMENTS: Age, rarity and, therefore, value are determined by the ornament's construction, design, patina and the material of which it is made. The best place to find old ornaments at a reasonable price is most likely in great-grandma's attic. Since they are in great demand at the moment, dealer prices are high, even for specimens in average condition.

ADDITIONAL TIPS: Also quite collectible are Christmas tree lights dating from the 1920s and 1930s, even if they no longer work. The most collectible of these are the blown glass ones made in molds in Occupied Japan. A variety of shapes and sizes are available.

	Current Price Range		P/Y Average
☐ **Light,** Andy Gump, milk glass	15.00	17.00	16.00
☐ **Light,** bear with guitar, milk glass	15.00	17.00	16.00
☐ **Light,** blue bird, milk glass	15.00	17.00	16.00
☐ **Light,** clock	15.00	17.00	16.00
☐ **Light,** clown, milk glass	20.00	24.00	22.00
☐ **Light,** elephant, milk glass	7.00	9.00	8.00
☐ **Light,** fish, milk glass	13.00	15.00	14.00
☐ **Light,** gingerbread man	13.00	15.00	14.00
☐ **Light,** grapes, milk glass	8.00	10.00	9.00
☐ **Light,** house, milk glass	13.00	15.00	14.00
☐ **Light,** Humpty Dumpty, milk glass	15.00	17.00	16.00
☐ **Light,** lantern	13.00	15.00	14.00
☐ **Light,** parrot, milk glass	7.00	9.00	8.00
☐ **Light,** Pinocchio	20.00	22.00	21.00

Ornament, Gorham,
silver plated,
$13.00-$17.00

	Current Price Range		P/Y Average
☐ **Light,** Puss N' Boots, milk glass	20.00	22.00	21.00
☐ **Light,** Santa, painted	20.00	22.00	21.00
☐ **Light,** snowman, milk glass	13.00	15.00	14.00
☐ **Light,** zeppelin with flag	20.00	22.00	21.00
☐ **Ornament,** angel's face, blown glass, 2½" ...	22.00	28.00	24.00
☐ **Ornament,** baby in bunting, blown glass, embossed script lettering, 4"	65.00	85.00	73.00
☐ **Ornament,** ball, amber	23.00	25.00	24.00
☐ **Ornament,** ball, canary, blown glass	20.00	22.00	21.00
☐ **Ornament,** basket, fruit filled, blown glass	23.00	25.00	24.00
☐ **Ornament,** bear with muff, blown glass	48.00	50.00	49.00
☐ **Ornament,** camel, Dresden	30.00	32.00	31.00
☐ **Ornament,** carrot, blown glass, embossed detail, pre-1920, 4"	40.00	50.00	43.00
☐ **Ornament,** child, milk glass	10.00	12.00	11.00
☐ **Ornament,** church, blown glass.............	30.00	32.00	31.00
☐ **Ornament,** clown head, blown glass	53.00	55.00	54.00
☐ **Ornament,** cuckoo clock, blown glass, white/orange/green, embossed and painted ..	22.00	28.00	23.50
☐ **Ornament,** doll's head, blown glass, silver and flesh color with blown glass eyes, 3"	50.00	70.00	55.00
☐ **Ornament,** elephant, mercury glass with blown milk glass tusks, label reads "Made in Germany," 4"	30.00	40.00	33.00
☐ **Ornament,** fence, wood	23.00	25.00	24.00
☐ **Ornament,** fish, blown glass	53.00	55.00	54.00

	Current Price Range		P/Y Average
☐ Ornament, football player, milk glass	20.00	22.00	21.00
☐ Ornament, Foxy Grandpa, blown glass with applied legs, 4½"	150.00	175.00	160.00
Note: High value because this was an early comic strip character.			
☐ Ornament, girl, blown glass	34.00	36.00	35.00
☐ Ornament, girl's head, blown glass with blown glass eyes, 2½"	25.00	30.00	26.75
☐ Ornament, Happy Hooligan, blown glass with applied legs, 4½"	200.00	250.00	215.00
Note: Happy Hooligan, a comic strip character of the early 1900s, was created by Frederick Burr Opper.			
☐ Ornament, heart, blown glass, large	35.00	37.00	36.00
☐ Ornament, icicle, glass	20.00	24.00	22.00
☐ Ornament, lamp	55.00	57.00	56.00
☐ Ornament, lion, Dresden	20.00	22.00	21.00
☐ Ornament, man in the moon, blown glass, green, 3"	36.00	44.00	39.00
☐ Ornament, monkey holding stick, blown glass, 2½"	50.00	65.00	56.00
☐ Ornament, musical instrument	20.00	22.00	21.00
☐ Ornament, peacock, blown glass, brush tail . . .	20.00	22.00	21.00
☐ Ornament, penguin, blown glass, blue, silver, red, embossed feet, 1¾"	37.00	45.00	40.00
☐ Ornament, pinecone, blown glass	7.00	9.00	8.00
☐ Ornament, pipe, blown glass	23.00	25.00	24.00
☐ Ornament, pocket watch, blown glass with paper watch face, pre-1920, 2"	40.00	50.00	43.00
☐ Ornament, purse, blown glass	33.00	35.00	34.00
☐ Ornament, Santa, celluloid	33.00	35.00	34.00
☐ Ornament, Santa carrying bag of toys, blown glass, 2½"	18.00	23.00	20.00
☐ Ornament, Santa, with plaster face	23.00	25.00	24.00
☐ Ornament, Scottie dog, blown glass, yellow and blue, size unavailable	50.00	65.00	55.00
☐ Ornament, smiling snowman with broom, blown glass, pre-1920, 3½"	35.00	45.00	36.75
☐ Ornament, stag, blown glass, blue with gold antlers, label reads "Made in Germany," 3", ...	30.00	40.00	33.00
☐ Ornament, star, Dresden	20.00	22.00	21.00
☐ Ornament, swan, blown glass	23.00	25.00	24.00
☐ Ornament, teapot	23.00	25.00	24.00
☐ Ornament, turkey, blown glass with tinsel wings and tail, 5"	10.00	15.00	12.00
☐ Ornament, umbrella, tinsel	23.00	25.00	24.00

CHROME

DESCRIPTION: Glossy metal used in various types of manufacturing, such as decorative trimmings on autos and trucks, sailboats, etc.

TYPES: Chrome collectibles include not only auto items, which are perhaps the most familiar to the general public, but a wide variety of decorative household objects and novelties.

PERIOD: Chrome came into extensive use in the 1920s and has remained popular thereafter. It was one of the more important substances of the Art Deco era.

CARE AND CONDITION: Clean with any metal cleaning polish recommended for use on chrome. Do not use an abrasive tool, nor even steel wool, as this will result in fine scratches that mar the surface. As chrome is very durable, it presents no problem in storage or display.

	Current Price Range		P/Y Average
□ **Bud Vase,** chased, 4½″ cylinder resting on a 3½″ base	16.00	20.00	18.00
□ **Cocktail Set,** shaker with six matching flared goblets, height of goblets 7″, set	30.00	35.00	32.00
□ **Cocktail Shaker,** footed, etched banding with grape leaf cluster motif, red plastic handle, 11¾″	10.00	14.00	12.00
□ **Cocktail Shaker,** grape etching, with cap and lid	9.00	12.00	10.25
□ **Cordial Dispenser,** clear glass and chrome, plunger type with six jiggers, the glass decorated with horizontal ribbing, jiggers have plastic belts, set	22.00	28.00	24.00
□ **Cordial Dispenser,** keg resting on pedestal with six small mugs, price for full set	14.00	18.00	16.00
□ **Farber Cocktail Shaker And Six Glasses,** hammered texture, shaker with plastic handle (black), height of glasses 6¼″, set	27.00	34.00	30.00

	Current Price Range		P/Y Average
☐ **Lazy Susan,** 2-tier bar, green plastic central handle, top has six small jiggers with green and yellow striping, bottle has twelve jiggers, set	32.00	40.00	35.00
☐ **Liquer Dispenser,** decorative sphere with six shot glasses, set	20.00	25.00	22.00
☐ **Tray,** large, ceramic with chrome trim and chrome handles, the ceramic painted with purple grapes, 13¾" diameter	21.00	28.00	23.00

CIGAR BOX LABELS

TOPIC: Cigar box labels are brightly colored, artistically decorated labels that adorn cigar boxes.

TYPES: The major types of cigar box labels are inside lids (which are placed on the inside lid of the box), box end labels (which are placed on the ends of the box) and box sealers (which seal the lid to the sides).

PERIOD: These labels came into use in the middle of the 19th century.

MAKERS: Witsch & Schmitt of New York created many artistic labels.

COMMENTS: Labels which were damaged while being removed from their boxes are automatically worth less. In the early 1900s printers often sold unused bands directly to collectors.

ADDITIONAL TIPS: Most labels in the ten to fifteen dollar price range are multi-colored stone lithographs dating from around 1900. Prices decrease as age decreases.

☐ **Acropolis,** inside lid, 6"x9", c. 1920	3.00	5.50	4.25
☐ **A Dream,** small boy riding bicycle, full colors, 4"x5½"	20.00	25.00	21.25
☐ **Africora,** box end label, 4"x4"	.50	1.50	1.00
☐ **Alcazar,** inside lid, 6"x9", c. 1920	1.00	3.00	2.00
☐ **American Twins,** pictures twin girls, full colors, 6"x9", c. 1880–1890	40.00	50.00	43.00
Note: This brand of cigar was sold by the pair.			
☐ **Barrister,** inside lid, 6"x9", c. 1895	8.00	11.00	9.50

Labels, *cigar box, 1900s, each,* $10.00–$20.00

	Current Price Range		P/Y Average
☐ **Barrister,** inside lid, 6″x9″, c. 1895	8.00	11.00	9.50
☐ **Big Five,** inside lid, 6″x9″, c. 1935	.20	.30	.25
☐ **Big Wolf,** box sealer, 2″x3″	.50	1.50	1.00
☐ **Blue Bird,** inside lid, 6″x9″, c. 1930	1.00	3.00	2.00
☐ **Blue Goose,** box end label, 4″x4″	.20	.30	.25
☐ **Blue Goose,** inside lid, 6″x9″, c. 1935	.50	1.50	1.00
☐ **Brick House,** box end label, 2″x5″	.25	.75	.50
☐ **Calendar,** inside lid, 6″x9″, c. 1905	13.00	18.00	15.50
☐ **Castellanos,** inside lid, 6″x9″, c. 1930	1.00	3.00	2.00
☐ **Castle Hall,** inside lid, 6″x9″, c. 1940	.25	.75	.50

	Current Price Range		P/Y Average
☐ **Christy Girl,** box end label, 4"x4"	.50	1.50	1.00
☐ **Christy Girl,** inside lid, 6"x9", c. 1932	2.00	3.00	2.50
☐ **Clipper,** box end label, 4"x4"	1.00	3.00	2.00
☐ **Clubhouse,** box end label, 2"x5"	.20	.30	.25
☐ **College Inn,** box sealer, 2"x3"	.25	.75	.50
☐ **College Inn,** inside lid, 6"x9", c. 1910	8.00	12.00	10.00
☐ **Custom House,** inside lid, 6"x9", c. 1930	3.00	5.00	4.00
☐ **Damasco,** inside lid, 6"x9", c. 1900	13.00	17.00	15.00
☐ **Diamond Crown,** box end label, 2"x5"	.20	.30	.25
☐ **Diamond Crown,** inside lid, 6"x9", c. 1940 ...	.50	1.50	1.00
☐ **Don Alfonso,** inside lid, 6"x9", c. 1905	14.00	16.00	15.00
☐ **Don Nieto,** box end label, 2"x5"	.20	.30	.25
☐ **Don Nieto,** inside lid, 6"x9", c. 1940	.20	.30	.25
☐ **Duo Art,** box end label, 4"x4"	.25	.75	.50
☐ **Duo Art,** inside lid, 6"x9", c. 1930	.25	.75	.50
☐ **Edmund Halley,** inside lid, 6"x9", c. 1900	8.00	12.00	10.00
☐ **El Escudero,** box end label, 4"x4"	.20	.30	.25
☐ **El Escudero,** inside lid, 6"x9", c. 1940	.20	.30	.25
☐ **El Guardo,** inside lid, 6"x9", c. 1910	4.00	7.00	5.50
☐ **Elsie,** box end label, 4"x4"	.50	1.50	1.00
☐ **Farragut,** inside lid, 6"x9", c. 1905	8.00	13.00	10.50
☐ **Fidelity,** box end label, 4"x4"	.25	.75	.50
☐ **Fidelity,** inside lid, 6"x9", c. 1945	.25	.75	.50
☐ **First Blush,** box end label, 4"x4"	4.00	6.50	5.25
☐ **Flor de Franklin,** Benjamin Franklin flying a kite, full color, 3"x5"	30.00	35.00	31.50
☐ **For Cash Only,** illustration of man buying cigar at counter with female clerk behind counter, full color, 6"x6", believed to date from 1880s	40.00	50.00	43.00
Note: In the late 1800s many restaurants kept open boxes of cigars at the cashier's desk and patrons were welcome to take one for free. Better grade cigars were available for purchase, and this brand—For Cash Only—wanted to make certain it wasn't mistaken for a freebie.			
☐ **Fragancia,** box end label, 4"x4"	.50	1.50	1.00
☐ **Gallatin,** box end label, 2"x5"	.25	.75	.50
☐ **Garcia Y Garcia,** inside lid, 6"x9", c. 1937	.50	1.25	.80
☐ **Garcia Y Hermanos,** box end label, 4"x4"	4.00	6.00	5.00
☐ **Garcia Y Hermanos,** inside lid, 6"x9", c. 1920	3.50	5.50	4.50
☐ **Golden Horn,** pictures Arabian female, full colors, size unavailable, c. 1880–1890	25.00	30.00	26.00
☐ **Golden Sun,** box end label, 4"x4"	.25	.75	.50
☐ **Grand Council,** box end label, 4"x4"	1.00	3.00	2.00
☐ **Group of 40,** colored and gilded, includes Prudential, Airdale, Montebello, Lyra, Red Tips, others	17.00	25.00	20.50
☐ **Longfellow,** box end label, 2"x5"	.50	1.50	1.00
☐ **Lopez-Alvaraz,** box end label, 4"x4"	.20	.30	.25
☐ **Lord Puffer,** portrait of elegantly dressed man seated by fire with cigar and whisky nearby, 5½"x 8½"	25.00	30.00	26.75
☐ **Lord Vernon,** inside lid, 6"x9", c. 1930	2.00	4.50	3.25
☐ **Lucky Bill,** box end label, 2"x5"	.20	.30	.25

	Current Price Range		P/Y Average
☐ **Madrigal,** inside lid, 6″x9″, c. 1930	.25	.75	.50
☐ **Malta,** box end label, 4″x4″	.20	.30	.25
☐ **Manila Blunts,** inside lid, 6″x9″, c. 1942	.20	.30	.25
☐ **Memorata,** box end label, 4″x4″	4.00	6.00	5.00
☐ **Miss Pluck,** pictures woman and corset, full colors, 6″x9″, c. 1880–1890	35.00	45.00	37.00
☐ **Mission,** box end label, 4″x4″	.50	1.50	1.00
☐ **Moosariana,** box end label, 4″x4″	1.00	3.00	2.00
☐ **Moro Light,** inside lid, 6″x9″, c. 1938	.50	1.50	1.00
☐ **Navy Ribbon,** box end label, 2″x5″	.25	.75	.50
☐ **Newport Club,** men in top hats ride stage coach past hotel, full color, 4¼″x5¼″	20.00	25.00	21.75
☐ **Nutura,** box end label, 4″x4″	.20	.30	.25
☐ **Old Abe,** portrait of Abraham Lincoln in gray and white with embossed gold, 7″x9″	20.00	25.00	21.50
☐ **Old Hickory,** box end label, 4″x4″	.25	.75	.50
☐ **Old Hickory,** inside lid, 6″x9″, c. 1930	.50	1.50	1.00
☐ **Old Hickory,** portrait of Andrew Jackson, full color, 7″x8″	20.00	25.00	26.00
☐ **Our Bird,** pictures the Lindbergh aircraft Spirit of St. Louis, red/white/blue, 7″x9″	25.00	30.00	26.25
Note: As the historic Lindbergh flight was made in 1927 this label probably dates to the years immediately thereafter.			
☐ **Our Fire Laddies,** pictures uniformed firemen and engine, full colors, c. 1880	30.00	40.00	33.00
☐ **Our Kitties,** box sealer, 2″x3″	.25	.75	.50
☐ **Peace Time,** box end label, 4″x4″	.25	.75	.50
☐ **Peace Time,** inside lid, 6″x9″, c. 1927	.25	.75	.50
☐ **Pearl,** inside lid, 6″x9″, c. 1925	3.00	6.00	4.50
☐ **Pony Post,** box end label, 4″x4″	4.00	6.00	5.00
☐ **Prima Rosa,** inside lid, 6″x9″, c. 1930	2.00	3.50	2.75
☐ **Prize Beauty,** picture of a young girl, 1880s ..	4.00	6.50	5.75
☐ **Pug,** inside lid, 6″x9″, c. 1903	7.00	12.00	9.50
☐ **Quaker Quality,** box end label, 4″x4″	.50	1.50	1.00
☐ **Quaker Quality,** inside lid, 6″x9″, c. 1934	.50	1.50	1.00
☐ **Red Ball,** couple on ice skates pushing huge red ball, full color, 4¼″x5¼″	30.00	35.00	31.50
☐ **Red Cloud,** pictures Indian chief on horse, full colors, 6″x10″, undetermined age	25.00	30.00	26.25
☐ **Red Dandies,** inside lid, 6″x9″, c. 1900	14.00	16.50	15.25
☐ **Red Tips,** box end label, 2″x5″	.20	.30	.25
☐ **Regal X Ten,** inside lid, 6″x9″, c. 1920″	3.00	6.00	4.50
☐ **Reina Bella,** box end label, 4″x4″	.25	.75	.50
☐ **Rigoletto,** inside lid, 6″x9″, c. 1929″	1.00	3.00	2.00
☐ **Rolamo,** inside lid, 6″x9″, c. 1945	.20	.30	.25
☐ **Rosa Moro,** inside lid, 6″x9″, c. 1940	.25	.75	.50
☐ **Rosa Y O,** box sealer, 2″x3″	.25	.75	.50
☐ **Round-Up,** box end label, 2″x5″	.25	.75	.50

CIRCUS MEMORABILIA

DESCRIPTION: All circus-related items are considered collectible, including posters, photographs, ticket stubs, programs as well as large items such as cages and tents.

ORIGIN: The first American circus opened in 1793 in Philadelphia. The show was modeled after already established English circuses. The show traveled from town to town in order to entertain rural communities. About 30 years after the first American circus, tents and big tops were introduced. In 1919 the top three competing circuses, P.T. Barnum, James A. Bailey and Ringling Brothers combined their shows.

COMMENTS: The year 1984 marks the centennial for Ringling Brothers. This special celebration may add to the already high interest in circus memorabilia.

ADDITIONAL TIPS: The following listings are alphabetical according to title. A description and price range follow.

	Current Price Range		P/Y Average
☐ **Band Wagon,** horse drawn	400.00	450.00	405.00
☐ **Book,** *Barnum's Wonders,* An Illustrated History of the Hindoo Hairy Family and other Prodigious and Exclusive Features of "The Greatest Show on Earth," 16 pp., c. 1890	60.00	75.00	65.00
☐ **Book,** *Buffalo Bill's Wild West,* programmed and descriptive booklet, c. 1885	125.00	175.00	136.00
☐ **Book,** *Burdett Twins,* Fanny and Major, age, 22 years, height 38″, New York, c. 1890	55.00	75.00	60.00
☐ **Book,** *The Curious and Amusing Exhibition of The Educated Fleas,* by L. Bertolotto, 5th edition, 245 pp., New York, c. 1876	85.00	115.00	100.00
☐ **Book,** *Dr. Doolittle's Circus,* by Hugh Loftring, New York, c. 1924	90.00	120.00	95.00
☐ **Book,** *The Genial Showman,* depicts the life of Artemus Ward, New York, c. 1870	50.00	65.00	53.00

Booklet,
Ringling Bros. Barnum & Bailey, 1929,
$25.00–$35.00
(photo courtesy of ©Lou McCulloch, Highland, Heights, OH)

	Current Price Range		P/Y Average
☐ **Book,** *The Man of the Mountain,* by Frederic Farnsworth, Boston, c. 1818	150.00	180.00	160.00
☐ **Book,** *Tom Thumb,* life of Charles S. Stratton, 28″ high and 15 pounds, 24 pp. booklet, published by Barnum, New York, c. 1847	200.00	280.00	224.00
☐ **Booklet,** *Barnum and Bailey Circus,* color cover, features biographies, pictures and descriptions of the circus, c. 1910	65.00	85.00	70.00
☐ **Booklet,** *Forepaugh and Sells Circus,* color cover, features biographies, pictures and descriptions of the circus, c. 1910	55.00	75.00	60.00
☐ **Booklet,** *Walter L. Main Circus,* 8 pp., color, wraps	16.00	25.00	18.00
☐ **Broadside,** Bailey Bros. Circus, red, white, blue, 14″x41″	20.00	30.00	24.50
☐ **Broadside Handbills,** illustrated, 10″x28″, c. 1920s	20.00	30.00	23.00
☐ **Button,** "Souvenir Ringling Bros.—World's Greatest Shows," black and white, 1½″, c. 1900s	75.00	100.00	87.50
☐ **Courier,** Illustrated News, by P.T. Barnum, 16 pp., c. 1897	42.00	58.00	44.00
☐ **Cabinet Photo,** "Che—Mah, The Chinese Dwarf" from Barnum and Bailey, c. 1900	25.00	35.00	29.50
☐ **Elephant,** tin lithograph, Unique Art Mfg. Co., "Flying Circus" marked on base, c. 1930s	100.00	125.00	115.00

	Current Price Range		P/Y Average

☐ **Folder,** Barnum and Bailey, full color, 14 pp., c. 1910 .... 30.00 / 50.00 — 40.00

	Current Price Range		P/Y Average
☐ **Folder,** Barnum and Bailey, full color, 14 pp., c. 1910	30.00	50.00	40.00
☐ **Lithograph,** The Tigers Are Ferocious and They Bite, by Adam Forepaugh, c. 1880	135.00	175.00	160.00
☐ **Lithograph,** The Circus Kings of All Time, window card, 14"x22", mid 1830s	32.50	40.00	35.00
☐ **Herald Or Handbill,** Sparks Circus, c. 1921	16.00	25.00	18.00
☐ **Magazine,** Barnum and Bailey Circus, bright color cover, c. 1918	55.00	75.00	60.00
☐ **Magazine,** Magazine of Wonders and Daily Review, by Ringling Brothers, color, c. 1914	60.00	80.00	70.00
☐ **Photograph,** Downie Brothers Circus, groups of photos features various artists, 5"x7", c. 1930	35.00	50.00	40.00
☐ **Photograph,** Russell Brothers Circus, groups of photos features various artists, 5"x7", c. 1930	15.00	25.00	18.00
☐ **Poster,** Adam Forepaugh Circus and Roman Hippodrome, 7 part composite, 30½"x40", c. 1885	185.00	215.00	195.00
☐ **Poster,** Adam Forepaugh's "Queen of The Ring," 30"x40½" c. 1885	135.00	175.00	145.00
☐ **Poster,** Adam Forepaugh and Sells circus, pictures Aurora Zoaves	52.00	70.00	58.00
☐ **Poster,** Barnum and Bailey Circus, color, depicts naval battle against Spanish fleet, 25"x36", c. 1898	180.00	220.00	195.00
☐ **Poster,** Clyde Beatty Circus, action scene, 21"x28", c. 1930	75.00	100.00	80.00
☐ **Poster,** Clyde Beatty, training lions and tigers, c. 1930	80.00	100.00	89.00
☐ **Poster,** Dale's animal three-ring circus	15.50	25.00	18.00
☐ **Poster,** "Lady Viola, The Most Beautiful Tattoed Woman in The World," painted in oils over large photo, 40"x40", New York, c. 1925	450.00	495.00	460.00
☐ **Poster,** "Lilla," high-wire act, 34"x45", c. 1895	230.00	250.00	237.00
☐ **Poster,** "Princess Topaze, Star of The Casino de Paris," female midget, 35"x48"	300.00	340.00	310.00
☐ **Poster,** P.T. Barnum and Co., Lake Front, Chicago, Monday, July 19th	20.00	28.00	23.00
☐ **Poster,** "Terrell Jacobs The Liong King," 28"x40", c. 1935	60.00	70.00	63.00
☐ **Poster,** Terrell Jacobs in Big Top, surrounded by lions, 28"x40", c. 1934	75.00	85.00	77.00
☐ **Program,** Ringling Brothers, Barnum and Bailey, c. 1948	15.00	23.00	17.00
☐ **Program,** Hagenbeck-Wallas	20.00	28.00	23.00
☐ **Sheet Music,** Children At The Circus, c. 1909	25.00	35.00	28.00
☐ **Sheet Music,** Whe It's Circus Day Back Home, c. 1917	25.00	35.00	27.00
☐ **Song Book,** Barnum and London Musical Album, large size	25.00	35.00	27.00
☐ **Stationery,** Sparton Brothers, ornate, unused	4.50	8.00	6.00
☐ **Tickets,** Barnum's Circus, c. 1890	15.00	24.00	17.00
☐ **Tickets,** Hunts Brothers, illustrated with clown, 100 large, c. 1940s	10.00	15.00	12.00

	Current Price Range		P/Y Average
☐ **Ticket,** P.T. Barnum Circus, c. 1890	15.00	25.00	17.00
☐ **Toy,** Barnum and Bailey circus cage, elephant drawn, painted, stained and lithographed wood, c. 1930	180.00	280.00	220.00
☐ **Toy,** circus cage, decorative wagon, c. 1928 . .	150.00	200.00	175.00
☐ **Toy,** circus train, tin, eight pieces, c. 1950s . . .	112.00	140.00	117.00
☐ **Toy,,** clown, Rolly-Poly, Shoenhut, 9″	25.00	35.00	27.00
☐ **Toy,** clown, wooden, hinged	75.00	100.00	80.00
☐ **Toy,** elephant pulling animals in cage, mechanical, c. 1935	170.00	210.00	180.00
☐ **Toy,** lion cage, driver and lions	130.00	190.00	143.00
☐ **Toy,** tin clown holding balloon, long gown with feet protruding, 6⅞″, c. 1930	100.00	140.00	110.00
☐ **Toy Wagon,** wood and tin with scene of circus on wagon, 17½″ L.	115.00	160.00	130.00

CIVIL WAR MEMORABILIA

DESCRIPTION: The Civil War produced some of the most collectible antiques in today's marketplace. Items are available all over the world. Collecting Civil War memorabilia can be a most gratifying hobby for the collector as he delves into the history of each item and discovers the principles upon which this country has grown.

COMMENTS: The most sought-after collectible in this category is that of firearms. This period in time marked a technological transition from a single shot gun to one that would shoot several times, including the first machine gun. Other collectible areas include uniforms, buttons, belt buckles, canteens, knapsacks, insignias and personal effects, such as diaries, letters, and photographs.

ADDITIONAL TIPS: Auctions are a great place to pick up such items as well as dealer shops. Prices are as varied as the items so even the novice can afford to begin this type of collection.

RECOMMENDED READING: For more in-depth information and listings, you may refer to *The Official Price Guide to Military Collectibles* by Colonel Robert H. Rankin, published by The House of Collectibles.

AUTOGRAPHS (ALs stands for autographed letters)

	ALs		Document		Plain Signature	
☐ Ammen, Rear Admiral Daniel	$35.00–	$42.00	$18.00–	$23.00	$4.00–	$6.00
☐ Andrew, John A.	18.00–	23.00	8.00–	10.00	3.00–	4.00
☐ Anderson, James P.	36.00–	43.00	18.00–	23.00	5.00–	6.00
☐ Anderson, Brig. Gen. Robert	60.00–	75.00	25.00–	33.00	7.00–	11.00
☐ Augur, Christopher C.	14.00–	16.00	4.00–	7.00	1.00–	1.50
☐ Badeau, Adam	14.00–	16.00	4.00–	7.00	1.00–	1.50
☐ Banks, Nathaniel P.	50.00–	65.00	18.00–	23.00	8.00–	11.00
☐ Barnard, John G.	18.00–	22.00	8.00–	10.00	3.00–	5.00
☐ Beauregard, G. T.	275.00–	350.00	90.00–	110.00	14.00–	19.00
☐ Benton, James G.	10.00–	12.00	8.00–	9.00	2.00–	3.00
☐ Berdan, Hiram	43.00–	50.00	14.00–	18.00	4.00–	6.00
☐ Bocock, Thomas S.	20.00–	26.00	8.00–	10.00	2.00–	3.00
☐ Bonham, M. L.	14.00–	18.00	8.00–	10.00	2.00–	3.00
☐ Bragg, Braxton	42.00–	50.00	18.00–	23.00	8.00–	11.00
☐ Buchanan, Thomas McKean	125.00–	175.00	38.00–	50.00	20.00–	27.00
☐ Burnside, A. E.	90.00–	120.00	33.00–	45.00	12.00–	18.00
☐ Butterfield, Daniel	20.00–	28.00	10.00–	15.00	4.00–	7.00
☐ Cleburne, Patrick R.	240.00–	300.00	100.00–	140.00	35.00–	55.00
☐ Corse, Brig. Gen. John M. ...	14.00–	20.00	8.00–	11.00	3.00–	5.00
☐ Cosby, George B.	20.00–	28.00	10.00–	15.00	4.50–	7.00
☐ Crittenden, Thomas	20.00–	28.00	10.00–	15.00	4.50–	7.00
☐ Custer, George A.	850.00–	875.00	250.00–	330.00	60.00–	90.00
☐ Dahlgren, Rear Admiral John	33.00–	40.00	20.00–	28.00	4.50–	7.00
☐ Davis, Jefferson	1100.00–	2000.00	325.00–	475.00	50.00–	80.00
☐ Dix, Gen. John A.	45.00–	60.00	20.00–	28.00	4.50–	7.00
☐ Early, Jubal A.	90.00–	130.00	50.00–	70.00	8.00–	13.00
☐ Farragut, Admiral David G. ...	275.00–	350.00	125.00–	200.00	15.00–	22.00
☐ Floyd, John B.	20.00–	29.00	8.00–	13.00	3.00–	5.00
☐ Forney, Maj. Gen. John H. ..	20.00–	29.00	8.00–	13.00	3.00–	5.00
☐ Foster, John G.	17.00–	23.00	8.00–	12.00	3.00–	5.00
☐ Fremont, Gen. J. C.	35.00–	43.00	10.00–	15.00	6.00–	9.00
☐ French, Samuel G.	40.00–	56.00	10.00–	15.00	6.00–	9.00
☐ Gardner, Franklin	25.00–	35.00	8.00–	13.00	3.00–	5.00
☐ Garnett, Robert S.	32.00–	43.00	11.00–	18.00	3.00–	5.00
☐ Gilmore, Gen. Quincy A.	25.00–	34.00	8.00–	11.00	3.00–	5.00
☐ Gladden, Adley H.	70.00–	95.00	21.00–	30.00	10.00–	15.00
☐ Gordon, John B.	32.00–	42.00	10.00–	14.00	3.00–	5.00
☐ Gorgas, Josiah	32.00–	42.00	10.00–	14.00	3.00–	5.00
☐ Halleck, H. W.	45.00–	60.00	22.00–	29.00	5.00–	8.00
☐ Hancock, W. S.	35.00–	43.00	15.00–	20.00	3.00–	5.00
☐ Heintzelman, S. P.	22.00–	28.00	10.00–	14.00	3.00–	5.00
☐ Hooker, Gen. Joseph	34.00–	42.00	12.00–	19.00	5.00–	8.00
☐ Humphries, A. A.	34.00–	42.00	12.00–	19.00	5.00–	8.00
☐ Ingraham, Duncan N.	40.00–	58.00	15.00–	20.00	5.00–	8.00
☐ Iverson, Alfred	35.00–	45.00	15.00–	20.00	3.00–	5.00
☐ Jackson, "Stonewall"	2800.00–	4500.00	700.00–	1200.00	150.00–	200.00
☐ Jackson, W. H.	36.00–	47.00	15.00–	20.00	6.00–	9.00
☐ Johnston, Joseph E.	45.00–	60.00	20.00–	32.00	6.00–	9.00
☐ Jones, David R.	95.00–	130.00	45.00–	70.00	15.00–	22.00

	ALs	Document	Plain Signature
☐ Kearny, Philip	200.00– 275.00	70.00– 95.00	20.00– 28.00
☐ Lee, FitzHugh	32.00– 45.00	15.00– 20.00	3.00– 5.00
☐ Lee, Robert E.	500.00– 900.00	200.00– 325.00	80.00– 110.00
☐ Logan, Maj. Gen. John A. ...	26.00– 35.00	15.00– 10.00	4.00– 7.00
☐ Longstreet, James	26.00– 35.00	10.00– 15.00	4.00– 7.00
☐ Luce, Admiral Stephen	33.00– 40.00	10.00– 15.00	4.00– 7.00
☐ Lyon, Gen. Nathaniel	110.00– 150.00	45.00– 70.00	20.00– 28.00
☐ Mahone, William	33.00– 40.00	10.00– 15.00	4.00– 7.00
☐ McArthur, John	40.00– 50.00	15.00– 22.00	4.00– 7.00
☐ McClellan, Geo. B.	58.00– 75.00	22.00– 32.00	6.00– 9.00
☐ Mason, James M.	275.00– 350.00	80.00– 120.00	20.00– 29.00
☐ Meade, George G.	45.00– 58.00	18.00– 26.00	6.00– 10.00
☐ Meagher, Thomas F.	26.00– 36.00	10.00– 15.00	4.00– 7.00
☐ Mosby, John S.	26.00– 36.00	10.00– 15.00	4.00– 7.00
☐ Pickett, George E.	300.00– 415.00	115.00– 170.00	18.00– 25.00
☐ Porter, Admiral David D.	110.00– 170.00	50.00– 75.00	8.00– 12.00
☐ Porter, FitzJohn	45.00– 65.00	15.00– 23.00	5.00– 8.00
☐ Porter, Horace	33.00– 42.00	15.00– 23.00	3.00– 5.00
☐ Price, Sterling	40.00– 60.00	20.00– 29.00	5.00– 8.00
☐ Pryor, Roger A.	47.00– 75.00	20.00– 29.00	5.00– 8.00
☐ Ransom, Robert, Jr.	60.00– 100.00	22.00– 30.00	5.00– 8.00
☐ Reagan, John H.	33.00– 47.00	15.00– 22.00	4.00– 7.00
☐ Richardson, J. B.	33.00– 47.00	15.00– 22.00	4.00– 7.00
☐ Ripley, R. S.	38.00– 50.00	15.00– 22.00	4.00– 7.00
☐ Rosecrans, W. S.	80.00– 110.00	22.00– 28.00	8.00– 12.00
☐ Scott, Winfield	200.00– 300.00	80.00– 130.00	15.00– 20.00
☐ Seddon, James A.	110.00– 150.00	35.00– 50.00	7.00– 12.00
☐ Seward, William H.	150.00– 210.00	47.00– 65.00	10.00– 15.00
☐ Sherman, William T.	220.00– 300.00	70.00– 100.00	15.00– 22.00
☐ Sigel, Franz	37.00– 50.00	15.00– 22.00	4.00– 7.00
☐ Sneed, John L. T.	40.00– 62.00	22.00– 28.00	5.00– 8.00
☐ Stanton, Edwin M.	130.00– 220.00	45.00– 85.00	10.00– 15.00
☐ Stephens, Alexander H.	80.00– 110.00	23.00– 32.00	5.00– 8.00
☐ Sumner, Charles	80.00– 110.00	23.00– 32.00	5.00– 8.00
☐ Taylor, Richard	100.00– 140.00	35.00– 50.00	8.00– 11.00
☐ Thomas, Maj. Gen. George H.	150.00– 200.00	47.00– 62.00	11.00– 15.00
☐ Thompson, M. J.	110.00– 140.00	35.00– 50.00	8.00– 11.00
☐ Toombs, Robert	90.00– 110.00	22.00– 28.00	5.00– 9.00
☐ Twiggs, David E.	40.00– 65.00	15.00– 22.00	4.00– 7.00
☐ Waterhouse, Richard	50.00– 75.00	15.00– 22.00	5.00– 8.00
☐ Welles, Gideon	75.00– 110.00	22.00– 28.00	5.00– 8.00
☐ Wheeler, Gen. Joseph	50.00– 75.00	22.00– 28.00	5.00– 8.00
☐ Winslow, Admiral John A. ...	75.00– 110.00	30.00– 39.00	5.00– 8.00
☐ Wool, John E.	50.00– 75.00	22.00– 28.00	3.00– 5.00

MISCELLANEOUS

	Current Price Range		P/Y Average
☐ Bayonet Scrabbard Tip, excavated	2.00	3.00	2.40
☐ Belt, Union, infantry, oval belt plate marked SNY, issued by the state of New York early in the war, black bridle leather belt	325.00	350.00	337.50

	Current Price Range		P/Y Average
Belt, Union, infantry, standard issue leather belt with U.S. oval buckle	75.00	80.00	77.50
Belt Plate, rectangular with eagle motif, M1851, used from the 1850s into the early days of the Civil War	100.00	125.00	110.00
Blanket, Union, Regular Army issue, medium brown, very fine condition	300.00	325.00	312.50
Bond, Confederate States of America, $500 coupon bond, issued under Act of February 17, 1864, vignette of sailing vessel, printed by Evans and Cogswell of Columbia, South Carolina	1100.00	1500.00	1275.00
Bond, Confederate States of America, $1,000 coupon bond, issued under Act of August 19, 1861, pictures C.G. Memminger, printed by B. Duncan of Columbia, South Carolina	60.00	80.00	67.00
Bond, State of Louisiana $500 coupon bond, issued under Act of January 13, 1862, typeset, signed by governor and other state officials, state seal vignette at upper center	185.00	230.00	205.00
Book, *The Story of the Fourth Regiment, Ohio Volunteer Cavalry,* 216 pages, published 1912	5.00	7.00	5.60
Books, *Miller's Photographic History,* set of ten volumes, contains original photographs on nearly every page, 8"x11", each is around 350 pages, published in 1911, the classic Civil War reference work	330.00	350.00	340.00
Buckle, Confederate, forked tongue, found buried near Fredericksburg, Virginia, 3⅝"x2¼" ...	190.00	200.00	195.00
Bugle, cavalry, solid brass, 8½"	365.00	385.00	375.00
Bugle, infantry, 17¾"	320.00	330.00	325.00
Bullet, .44 cal. Colt Dragoon	.60	1.00	.80
As Above, .44 cal. Colt Army	.80	1.35	1.05
Bullet, .52 cal. Sharps carbine	.60	1.00	.80
Bullet, .58 cal. Gardner, Confederate States of America	.75	1.25	1.00
Bullet, .58 cal. U.S. standard "minie ball"	.50	1.00	.75
Candleholder, camp, spike on bottom and side, cast iron, 4½"	45.00	50.00	47.50
Canteen, smooth body pattern, tin spout, thought to be Confederate. It is very difficult to distinguish Union from Confederate canteens	50.00	65.00	54.00
Cap Pouch, black leather, stamped "Ohio" ...	70.00	100.00	82.00
Card Game, "The Commander of Our Forces," in multi colored box picturing Zouaves and ironclad ships, price is for specimen in box and with original instruction sheet	45.00	60.00	51.00
Cartridge And Bullet, .56 cal. Spencer carbine	2.00	3.00	2.40
Cartridge Box, black leather, brass U.S. box plate, tin inserts, average condition	35.00	45.00	38.00
Cavalry Boots, leather, very tall above-knee type, soft tops to conform with leg contour, square toes, high heels, spurs missing, 31" high, pair	400.00	500.00	430.00

	Current Price Range		P/Y Average

☐ **Cavalry Bugle,** solid brass, dark patina, cord rings on inside of loops, 8½" in length, diameter across bell 3⅝" 300.00 400.00 335.00

☐ **Drummer's Plate,** solid brass, worn on drum sling, iron wire hooks, stamped in back is C.L. Carrington/AP/4th, excellent condition, 3¼" wide by 3½" high 225.00 250.00 237.50

☐ **Drumsticks,** rosewood, pair 90.00 100.00 95.00

☐ **Envelope,** at left a portrait of Liberty seated with sixth corp's badge, gold link, by Magnuss 20.00 25.00 21.75
Note: Value is for specimen bearing a common or damaged postage stamp. A stamp of premium value would of course add value to the item as a whole.

☐ **Flag,** Confederate, regimental battle flag of the Confederate Army of Northern Virginia, infantry size, 4'x4', superb condition, very rare .... 9500.00 — —

☐ **Flag,** Confederate, small version used to show patriotism during parades and rallies, polished cotton on wooden stick, 6"x8", excellent condition, 1863 .... 65.00 75.00 70.00

☐ **Flag,** Confederate, small type used in local parades and celebrations, 8"x11", with original carrying stick 50.00 65.00 54.00

☐ **Flask,** whiskey, Confederate, glass body with pewter top and cup which slides over lower half of flask, engraved, 7", marked on bottom by hand Richmond/1863/B.A./1st VA. REG. 175.00 195.00 185.00

☐ **Grape Shot,** solid iron, approximately 4½" diameter 40.00 55.00 44.00
Note: These come in various sizes, all the way up to huge ones that can hardly be lifted. One word of caution: not all are solid. Some are powder loaded and set with a percussion fuse. Even after 120 years they can still explode.

☐ **Gun Wrench,** Springfield type, excavated 2.00 3.00 2.40

☐ **Holster,** Confederate, full flap holster for dragoon sized revolver, brass stud closure, single wide belt loop on back, typical reddish brown Richmond leather, excellent condition 475.00 500.00 487.50

☐ **Hook,** brass, for knapsack, excavated .... .50 .75 .62

☐ **Infantry Bugle,** brass, engraved, chain guard for mouthpiece, 17¾" in length, 6" diameter across bell 225.00 300.00 260.00

☐ **Jacket,** Union, artillery shell, regulation issue, dark blue with red piping, twenty eagle buttons, fully lined, small to medium, excellent condition 475.00 500.00 487.50

☐ **Kit,** boot care, black japanned tin hinged case lid, contains three compartments which hold cake of saddle soap, chamois, and four brushes, marked Tiffany & Co. in gold letters on lid 185.00 205.00 195.00

	Current Price Range		P/Y Average

☐ **Knapsack,** Confederate, box style, black oil cloth over wood frame with leather reinforced corners, white buff straps, imported from England, marked "S.Isaacs Campbell/London." **150.00 170.00 160.00**

☐ **Knapsack,** Union, so-called "softpack" without wooden frame, made of tar-covered fabric, leather straps and shoulder sling, sling has inspection stamp **35.00 45.00 38.00**

☐ **Lantern,** camp and signal, tin, japanned finish, scalloped peaked roof, cylindrical body with large glass lens on door, oil burner, wire loop handles, wire belt hook, 6½", excellent condition **65.00 85.00 75.00**

☐ **Letter,** Confederate, written by General John Bell Hood, commander of the Texas Cavalry, 8"x10", dated March 2, 1864, framed **175.00 185.00 180.00**

☐ **Letter,** soldier's letter by Union Lieutenant writing to wife of a Colonel in his unit who was taken ill, reporting on his condition, has had fever averaging 103 for twenty days, 7¾"x12¼", August 16, 1863 .... **16.00 20.00 17.00**
Note: We list this specimen as an example only. Civil War soldiers' letters vary considerably in price depending on content.

☐ **Lincoln Portrait Bust,** stamped on copper sheet with very detailed relief, coated with frosted silver plate, applied to velvetized tin background and mounted in a circular frame of gilded plaster over wood, bust is 7" high, frame is 16" in diameter, done at the end of the Civil War, signed and dated, J. Powell, Patented 1865 .... **250.00 270.00 260.00**

☐ **Map,** Confederate, pocket map of Virginia published by West & Johnston in Richmond, 1862 **325.00 350.00 337.50**

☐ **Mirror,** cased, recovered from battlefield of Chicamauga **35.00 45.00 38.00**

☐ **Musket,** Confederate, 3 band rifled, marked Potts & Hunt, London, good condition **775.00 825.00 800.00**

☐ **Musket Hammer,** escavated **3.00 4.00 3.50**
Note: Whenever a Civil War relic is identified by a dealer as "excavated," this means it was in the ground for a century or more and is rusty, twisted, etc.

☐ **Naval Cutlass,** model 1860, brass hilt, half-basket guard, leather grip, blade dated 1862 and hallmarked U.S.N. **210.00 265.00 230.00**

☐ **Officers Frock Coat,** Union, field grade officers model, regulation army, finest quality materials and workmanship, double breasted with eighteen buttons bearing the Rhode Island state seal, excellent condition **600.00 650.00 625.00**

☐ **Stereopticon Photo,** view of contraband camp at Harper's Ferry, Virginia, #369 from the John Soule series of Civil War views, 1865 .... **26.00 34.00 28.75**

	Current Price Range		P/Y Average
☐ **Stereopticon Photo,** view of the headquarters of General Meade at the battle of Gettysburg, #557 from the W.H. Tipton series of Gettysburg views, undated	25.00	30.00	26.75
☐ **Stereopticon Photo,** view of the interior of Fort Sumpter looking toward Morris Island, #343 from the John Soule series of Civil War views, 1865	25.00	30.00	26.00
☐ **Sword,** Foot Officer's, double sided engraved blade, American eagle and floral patterns on one side of blade, Union inscription, leather grip, leather scabbard	280.00	335.00	300.00
☐ **Sword Belt,** Confederate, consists of two piece sword belt plate on original belt, plate marked CS	975.00	1000.00	987.50
☐ **Sword,** officers, staff and field, rayskin grips, Horstmann blade, etched eagle, scabbard is brass mounted steel	650.00	660.00	655.00
☐ **Trousers,** red wool for Zouaves or other units wearing red trousers, part machine and part hand sewn, pewter buttons, believed to be made in France	600.00	800.00	675.00

CLOCKS

TOPIC: Clocks, of course, are devices that measure time in hours, minutes and sometimes seconds. Usually they have circular faces with arabic or roman numerals. Two or three hands on the face are standard.

TYPES: There are numerous types of clocks, including alarm clocks, atmospheric clocks, dresser clocks, gingerbread clocks, tall case (Grandfather) clocks, mantel clocks, regulator clocks, travel clocks and wall clocks.

PERIOD: Most collectors focus on 18th and 19th century clocks. Domestic clocks originated around the 1500s.

ORIGIN: Clocks developed in Europe.

MATERIALS: Clock cases may be of wood, glass, plastic, metal or porcelain. The works are metal.

MAKERS: Seth Thomas is one of the most famous clockmakers from New England. Well-known clock companies include: Ansonia, W.L. Gilbert, E. Ingraham, Jerome, New Haven and Waterbury.

COMMENTS: Clocks cover a great range of sizes, varieties and designs. The collector can focus on a specific type of clock, such as a wall clock, and further specialize in banjo style specimens.

ADDITIONAL TIPS: The listings are arranged in the following order: type of clock, manufacturer, style, material, description, dimensions and date. For further information, please refer to *The Official Price Guide to Antique Clocks,* published by The House of Collectibles.

Ingraham 8 Day Clock, *strikes half hour and hour,*
$90.00–$125.00

	Current Price Range		P/Y Average
☐ **Alarm Clock,** Victorian, cherrywood	35.00	56.00	45.50
☐ **Atmospheric Clock,** Lecoultre, brass and glass, 9½″ H.	225.00	300.00	262.00
☐ **Carriage Clock,** French, hourly bell, one piece case, 6½″ H., c. 1845	950.00	1050.00	1000.00
☐ **Carriage Clock,** French, porcelain, 6¼″ H., c. 1880	2100.00	2500.00	2300.00
☐ **Carriage Clock,** French, by Margaine, gilded brass, 7″ H.	1000.00	1250.00	1125.00
☐ **Carriage Clock,** Japan, tin, music box alarm, 6″ H., 5¼″ W.	55.00	75.00	65.00
☐ **Carriage Clock,** tin, music box alarm, 6″x5½″	40.00	60.00	50.00
☐ **Carriage Clock,** Waterbury, gilded metal, 6″ H.	180.00	235.00	207.00
☐ **Dresser Clock,** New Haven, Art Noveau, 7¼″ H.	40.00	55.00	48.00

	Current Price Range		P/Y Average
☐ **Dresser Clock,** Gilbert, wood, key wind, 8″x5″	15.00	25.00	20.00
☐ **Dresser Clock,** Western Clock Company, brass, 5″ H.	25.00	40.00	32.00
☐ **Gingerbread Clock,** elaborate decoration	110.00	135.00	122.00
☐ **Gingerbread Clock,** Gilbert, grape design	110.00	130.00	120.00
☐ **Gingerbread Clock,** Victorian, oak, eglomise painting, 21″x14″	70.00	100.00	85.00
☐ **Mantel Clock,** American, onyx, c. 1880	175.00	250.00	212.00
☐ **Mantel Clock,** American Bisque, wedgwood style, c. 1865	175.00	245.00	210.00
☐ **Mantel Clock,** Ansonia, ceramic	175.00	225.00	200.00
☐ **Mantel Clock,** Ansonia, slate, gilded, 15″x10″x6″	245.00	295.00	270.00
☐ **Mantel Clock,** French, Art Deco, brass and marble, c. 1900	350.00	450.00	400.00
☐ **Mantel Clock,** Empire, 14″ H., 9½″ W.	40.00	60.00	50.00
☐ **Mantel Clock,** French, bronze and beveled glass, key wind, 10½″ H.	265.00	345.00	305.00
☐ **Mantel Clock,** French, by Chardon, bronze, on rhinoceros base, 18″ H., 13½″ L.	1750.00	2300.00	1900.00
☐ **Mantel Clock,** French, d'ore bronze, porcelain plaques, 14″ H., 14″ W.	1200.00	1550.00	1325.00
☐ **Mantel Clock,** French, Empire, bronze, 18¼″ H., c. 1815	850.00	950.00	900.00
☐ **Mantel Clock,** French, Empire, gilt metal, 18½″ H.	70.00	100.00	85.00
☐ **Mantel Clock,** French, marble and d'ore bronze, pillars, 24″ H.	550.00	650.00	600.00
☐ **Mantel Clock,** German, mahogany, scrolled, 21½″ L.	80.00	120.00	100.00
☐ **Mantel Clock,** Ingraham, banjo shape, 40″ ...	320.00	400.00	360.00
☐ **Mantel Clock,** Ingraham, wood, black, gilt	125.00	200.00	162.00
☐ **Mantel Clock,** Italian, baroque, brass, 15″ H.	200.00	280.00	240.00
☐ **Mantel Clock,** marble and onyx, columns, 10¾″ H., 1800s	55.00	85.00	70.00
☐ **Mantel Clock,** Parisien, bronze, pendulum, 24″ H.	3600.00	4100.00	3850.00
☐ **Mantel Clock,** rococo, porcelain, painted, 11½″ H., c. 1900	225.00	265.00	245.00
☐ **Mantel Clock,** Sessions	40.00	55.00	48.00
☐ **Mantel Clock,** Seth Thomas, key wind, domed case	30.00	50.00	40.00
☐ **Mantel Clock,** Seth Thomas, marbleized, lions	60.00	85.00	72.00
☐ **Mantel Clock,** Seth Thomas, pillars and scrolls, 32″ H., 16½″ W., 1800s	175.00	250.00	200.00
☐ **Mantel Clock,** Victorian, rococo, gilt metal, 11½″ H.	120.00	150.00	135.00
☐ **Mantel Clock,** Victorian, walnut, pendulum, 19½″x12″	225.00	325.00	275.00
☐ **Mantel Clock,** Waterbury, pillars and ornaments	40.00	60.00	50.00
☐ **Regulator Clock,** Waterbury, mahogany, pendulum, 22″	180.00	230.00	205.00

	Current Price Range		P/Y Average
☐ **Tall Case Clock,** Chippendale, Boston, mahogany, calendar, seconds dial, 94½″ H., 17½″ W., 8½″ Dp., c. 1800	7500.00	8000.00	7750.00
☐ **Tall Case Clock,** Colonial Manufacturing Company, German works, 73¼″ H.	800.00	1100.00	950.00
☐ **Tall Case Clock,** Federal, Massachusetts, maple, 85″ H., 17½″ W., 10½″ Dp., c. 1800 . .	2700.00	3200.00	2950.00
☐ **Tall Case Clock,** Jacobean, Colonial Manufacturing Company, oak, German works, strikes on the quarter hour, half hour and hour, 86″ H., 20¼″ W.	1300.00	1750.00	1525.00
☐ **Travel Clock,** Swiss, silver, 3½″x3″	50.00	85.00	67.00
☐ **Wall Clock,** Gilbert, calendar, for a school, octagonal, 24½″ H.	80.00	130.00	105.00
☐ **Wall Clock,** Dutch, friese, painted, 41¾″ H., c. 1865	190.00	400.00	295.00
☐ **Wall Clock,** Dutch, Stoeltjes, wood and lead, gilded, pendulum, c. 1860	200.00	300.00	250.00
☐ **Wall Clock,** French, brass, round, strikes on hour, pendulum	325.00	475.00	400.00
☐ **Wall Clock,** German, walnut, 38″ H.	190.00	290.00	240.00
☐ **Wall Clock,** New Haven, banjo shape, 30″ H.	100.00	140.00	120.00
☐ **Wall Clock,** New Haven, banjo shape, 33″ H.	110.00	160.00	135.00
☐ **Wall Clock,** Sessions, banjo shape, 28″ H. . . .	130.00	150.00	140.00
☐ **Wall Clock,** Tiffany, New York, bronze, banjo shape, 38″ H., 1800s	5000.00	5700.00	5350.00
☐ **Wall Clock,** Victorian, painted, gilded, 11″ diameter	40.00	60.00	50.00

CLOTHING

DESCRIPTION: Vintage clothing is collected by those who wish to add it to their wardrobes as well as by collectors who wish only to display it.

VARIATIONS: Clothes of all ages are collectible. Currently, the most sought after are Victorian era clothes as well as clothes from the 1920s, 1930s and 1940s.

MATERIALS: Among the popular material types collected are silk, taffeta, silk velvet, chiffon, crepe de chine and beadwork. Current fashions are rarely made of such fine fabrics so such clothes are especially collectible.

COMMENTS: As with any collectible, clothing becomes less valuable when damaged. Alterations and construction details are factors in determining price, while skilled workmanship or handmade trims often increase value. Clothing with beadwork is also a good investment.

CARE AND CONDITION: Vintage clothing requires careful handling. Textiles are perishable: light, humidity, dust and body oil are potentially harmful. The acids in wood, cardboard and tissue paper can also hurt clothing. When storing pieces, it is best to wrap items in white sheets and use mothballs. Hang light-weight clothing on padded hangers, and store heavy clothing laid flat.

ADDITIONAL TIPS: The listings are alphabetical according to clothing item. Also included is a description and, when available, date. For further information on vintage clothing, contact The Costume Society of America, c/o The Costume Institute, The Metropolitan Museum of Art, NY, NY 10028.

Vintage Jacket, *black bouclé with ecru cotton lace insert,* **$40.00-$50.00**

	Current Price Range		P/Y Average
☐ **Apron,** embroidered, Hungarian, c. 1930	32.00	45.00	38.00
☐ **Baby Shoes,** hand stitched satin shoes with mocassin style lowers and double-ribbon drawstring through uppers	10.00	20.00	13.00
☐ **Baby Shoes,** kidskin leather button shoes, three buttons on uppers, c. 1880	35.00	65.00	45.00
☐ **Baby Shoes,** velvet top button shoes, leather lowers, five buttons on uppers, c. 1880	50.00	75.00	60.00

	Current Price Range		P/Y Average
□ **Baby Slippers,** white kid Mary Janes, strap, fastened with mother-of-pearl button, soft leather sole	30.00	50.00	40.00
□ **Bonnet,** for Christening, lace with white silk tie ribbons	25.00	45.00	35.00
□ **Coin Purse,** nickel plated metal with mother-of-pearl panels, compartments in red leatherette	12.00	20.00	14.00
□ **Dress,** black faille damask, cap sleeves, tie belt, c. 1940	50.00	90.00	60.00
□ **Dress,** floor length, horizontal stripes and metallic thread, tiered	60.00	100.00	80.00
□ **Dress,** for child, tucked bib, lace trim, embroidered	30.00	60.00	40.00
□ **Dress,** handmade traveling dress, c. 1890s . . .	200.00	240.00	210.00
□ **Dress,** for infant, lace, long sleeves	20.00	50.00	35.00
□ **Dress,** for infant, scalloped collar, embroidered	25.00	50.00	37.00
□ **Dress and Jacket,** blue lace over rose, velvet ribbon straps, short jacket	40.00	75.00	55.00
□ **Evening Bag,** Victorian, crochet flowers, metal beads	115.00	130.00	120.00
□ **Evening Bag,** Victorian, petit point flowers on silk	115.00	130.00	122.00
□ **Gloves,** cotton crochet, c. 1890	14.50	22.00	16.00
□ **Gloves,** long, brown suede	8.00	16.00	11.00
□ **Gloves,** short, white kid	8.00	16.00	13.00
□ **Gloves,** white cotton	8.00	16.00	13.00
□ **Hat,** fox fur	15.00	30.00	18.00
□ **Hat,** man's beaver top hat	45.00	65.00	55.00
□ **Mantilla,** Blonde de Caen lace, cream colored, c. 1820	120.00	160.00	130.00
□ **Mantilla,** black lace	45.00	60.00	53.00
□ **Purse,** clear crystal beads, white cloth liner, drawstring, beaded decoration, c. 1920s	20.00	40.00	30.00
□ **Robe,** embroidered silk, Japanese, c. 1890 . . .	282.00	350.00	300.00
□ **Shawl,** peach silk, bright silk embroidered flowers, c. 1920s	165.00	225.00	180.00
□ **Skirt,** crocheted, floor length, fringed bottom . .	30.00	50.00	40.00
□ **Wedding Gown,** lace, satin, pearls and white beaded flowers, high neck, cap sleeves, train, c. 1960s	75.00	150.00	100.00

COCA-COLA COLLECTIBLES

DESCRIPTION: Coca-Cola collectibles are any items made by or for the largest soft drink company in the world, the Coca-Cola Company. Although this company produces several types of cola, its most popular soft drink is Coke.

ORIGIN: The Coca-Cola Company produced its first bottle in Atlanta, GA in 1886. It was created by John Pemberton, an Atlanta pharmacist. The familiar Coca-Cola logo was created by Pemberton's bookkeeper, Frank Robinson.

COMMENTS: Although the company produced thousands of different items promoting its soft drinks, because of the large number of Coca-Cola collectors, many items are valued higher than similar objects for other soft drink companies advertising memorabilia.

	Current Price Range		P/Y Average
☐ **Ashtray,** aluminum, c. 1955	3.00	6.00	3.00
☐ **Ashtray And Match Holder,** c. 1940	180.00	200.00	177.00
☐ **Ashtray,** metal, c. 1963	18.00	22.00	17.50
☐ **Ashtray,** Mexican, painted aluminum	3.00	4.00	2.50
☐ **Ashtray,** picture of Atlanta plant	18.00	22.00	20.00
☐ **Ashtray,** set of card suites, c. 1940	55.00	60.00	52.00
☐ **Badge,** Coca-Cola Vendor's License, brass 1¾"	1.00	4.00	3.00
☐ **Bank,** Coca-Cola, metal cap	1.00	2.00	1.50
☐ **Bank,** pop bottle machine, tin	28.00	38.00	30.00
☐ **Bingo Game**	55.00	65.00	55.00
☐ **Blackboard,** c. 1939	38.00	48.00	40.00
☐ **Blotter,** "Delicious and Refreshing," c. 1904 . .	11.00	14.00	10.50
☐ **Blotter,** "Duster Girl" in auto, c. 1904	11.00	14.00	10.50
☐ **Blotter,** "Icy Style COLD Refreshment," c. 1939	7.00	9.00	7.00
☐ **Blotter,** "Restores Energy and Strengthens Nerves," c. 1906	9.00	11.00	9.00
☐ **Blotter,** Santa Claus with children, c. 1938	7.00	9.00	8.00
☐ **Blotter,** Sprite with bottle-top hat, c. 1953	3.25	4.25	3.50

Radio, *speaker behind
Coca-Cola logo, 1930's.*
$325.00-$350.00

	Current Price Range		P/Y Average
☐ **Blotter,** Sprite with bottle-top hat, c. 1956	2.25	3.25	2.50
☐ **Book Cover,** c. 1939	6.50	8.50	7.00
☐ **Book Cover,** c. 1951	6.00	8.00	6.00
☐ **Bookmark,** Coke can, c. 1960	9.00	12.00	9.00
☐ **Bookmark,** Hilda Clark, c. 1899	140.00	160.00	142.00
☐ **Bookmark,** Hilda Clark, c. 1900	135.00	155.00	138.00
☐ **Bookmark,** little girl with bird house, c. 1904 ..	160.00	180.00	160.00
☐ **Bookmark,** Lillian Russel, c. 1904	80.00	90.00	80.00
☐ **Bookmark,** owl on perch, c. 1906	105.00	115.00	100.00
☐ **Bookmark,** Valentine, c. 1899	110.00	130.00	110.00
☐ **Bookmark,** Victorian Lady	175.00	190.00	172.00
☐ **Bottle Holder Protector,** paper envelope, c. 1932	6.00	8.00	6.00
☐ **Bottle Holder Protector,** six bottle type, c. 1933	38.00	45.00	37.50
☐ **Bottle,** "Best by a Dam Site," c. 1936........	38.00	45.00	37.50
☐ **Bottle,** light green, c. 1905	12.00	16.00	11.00
☐ **Bottle,** applied paper label, c. 1915	38.00	42.00	37.50
☐ **Bottle,** display 20" H., red or clear, c. 1923 ...	125.00	235.00	120.00

	Current Price Range		P/Y Average
☐ **Bottle,** Donald Duck, 7 oz., painted	5.00	10.00	6.00
☐ **Cigarette Lighter,** aluminum, c. 1963	8.00	12.00	8.50
☐ **Cigarette Lighter,** Coke bottle shape, c. 1940	9.00	14.00	10.00
☐ **Cigarette Lighter,** Coke can, c. 1950	28.00	32.00	27.50
☐ **Cigarette Lighter,** music box plays "Dixie" ...	20.00	28.00	22.00
☐ **Cigarette Lighter,** musical, c. 1960	30.00	38.00	32.00
☐ **Clock,** brass mantle type, c. 1954	95.00	125.00	190.00
☐ **Clock,** dome style, c. 1950	185.00	200.00	192.00
☐ **Clock,** electric brass wall model, c. 1915	260.00	310.00	270.00
☐ **Clock,** leather boudoir, c. 1919	220.00	260.00	230.00
☐ **Clock,** re-issue of Betty, c. 1974	55.00	75.00	65.00
☐ **Clock,** small boudoir style, c. 1915	250.00	270.00	250.00
☐ **Clock,** spring operated wall style, brass pendulum	310.00	360.00	325.00
☐ **Clock,** walnut wall model, c. 1960	225.00	250.00	225.00
☐ **Cooler,** c. 1930	310.00	385.00	340.00
☐ **Cuff Links,** bottle cap, c. 1954	8.00	12.00	9.00
☐ **Cuff Links,** blue pearl	75.00	90.00	78.00
☐ **Cuff Links,** gold burnish links and tie clip, c. 1952	14.00	18.00	14.00
☐ **Cuff Links,** salesman's sterling silver links and tie tack, c. 1930	55.00	65.00	55.00
☐ **Cuff Links,** sterling silver, c. 1923	50.00	60.00	48.00
☐ **Cutouts,** uncut, c. 1930	85.00	115.00	92.00
☐ **Cutouts,** uncut, c. 1932	55.00	80.00	62.00
☐ **Dice,** white and red imprint, pair	1.00	2.00	1.50
☐ **Door Pull,** bottle shape	48.00	58.00	50.00
☐ **Flashlight,** bottle shaped plastic	6.00	8.00	6.00
☐ **Fountain Dispenser**	85.00	120.00	85.00
☐ **Glass,** 5¢ with arrow, c. 1905	130.00	155.00	132.00
☐ **Glass,** flair type, c. 1900	185.00	195.00	180.00
☐ **Glass,** flair lip, c. 1923	35.00	45.00	35.00
☐ **Glass,** fountain type with syrup line, c. 1900 ...	52.00	62.00	55.00
☐ **Glass,** fountain type, no syrup line	8.00	12.00	8.50
☐ **Glass,** home promotion type, red and white ...	4.00	6.00	4.00
☐ **Glass,** pewter, c. 1930	72.00	82.00	75.00
☐ **Ice Pick and Opener,** c. 1940	8.00	12.00	8.50
☐ **Key Chain,** amber replica bottle with brass chain, c. 1964	6.00	8.00	6.00
☐ **Key Chain,** car key style, c. 1950	28.00	32.00	27.50
☐ **Key Chain,** red with gold bottle, c. 1955	18.00	28.00	20.00
☐ **Key Chain,** 50th Anniversary Celebration, c. 1936	12.00	18.00	12.50
☐ **Knife,** pocket, "Enjoy Coca-Cola"	80.00	110.00	82.00
☐ **Knife,** pocket, two blades	12.00	18.00	12.50
☐ **Menu Board,** tin, c. 1940	42.00	62.00	50.00
☐ **Milk Glass,** light shade, c. 1920	385.00	410.00	382.00
☐ **Mirror,** pocket-size, "Bathing Beauty," c. 1918	285.00	300.00	282.00
☐ **Mirror,** pocket-size, "Betty," c. 1914	110.00	130.00	110.00
☐ **Mirror,** pocket-size, "Coca-Cola Girl," c. 1909	130.00	150.00	135.00
☐ **Mirror,** pocket-size, "Coca-Cola Girl," c. 1911	130.00	150.00	130.00
☐ **Mirror,** pocket-size, "Drink Coca-Cola 5¢," c. 1914	260.00	285.00	262.00

	Current Price Range		P/Y Average
☐ **Mirror**, pocket-size, "Elaine," c. 1917	155.00	165.00	155.00
☐ **Mirror**, pocket-size, "Enjoy Thirst," c. 1930 ...	80.00	95.00	82.00
☐ **Mirror**, pocket-size, "Garden Girl," c. 1920 ...	260.00	285.00	262.00
☐ **Mirror**, pocket-size, "Juanita," oval, c. 1905 ...	195.00	210.00	292.00
☐ **Mirror**, pocket-size, "Lillian Russel," round, c. 1904	72.00	82.00	75.00
☐ **Mirror**, pocket-size, oval, c. 1903	140.00	160.00	140.00
☐ **Mirror**, pocket-size, "Relieves Fatigue," c. 1906	160.00	190.00	170.00
☐ **Mirror**, pocket-size, "St. Louis Exposition," c. 1904	110.00	120.00	105.00
☐ **Mirror**, pocket-size, "St. Louis Fair," c. 1904 ..	135.00	150.00	138.00
☐ **Music Box**, cooler, c. 1951	55.00	80.00	62.00
☐ **Note Book**, brown leather, embossed, c. 1903	280.00	360.00	372.00
☐ **Note Pad**, celluloid covered, c. 1902	80.00	100.00	85.00
☐ **Opener**, bone handle knife, c. 1908	140.00	160.00	140.00
☐ **Opener**, Nashville Anniversary, c. 1952	55.00	70.00	58.00
☐ **Opener**, skate key style, c. 1935	38.00	48.00	40.00
☐ **Opener**, "Starr X," c. 1925	3.00	5.00	3.00
☐ **Opener**, stationary wall model, c. 1900	22.00	28.00	22.00
☐ **Paperweight**, Coca-Cola gum, c. 1916	80.00	90.00	80.00
☐ **Paperweight**, "Coke is Coca-Cola," c. 1948 ..	75.00	95.00	80.00
☐ **Paperweight**, hollow glass, tin bottom, c. 1909	260.00	285.00	262.00
☐ **Pen**, ball point with telephone dialer	6.00	8.00	6.00
☐ **Pen**, baseball bat, c. 1940	22.00	33.00	25.00
☐ **Pencil Box**, c. 1930	40.00	55.00	42.00
☐ **Pencil Holder**, celluloid, c. 1910	130.00	140.00	130.00
☐ **Pencil Holder**, miniature ceramic, c. 1960	70.00	80.00	70.00
☐ **Pencil Holder**, tin, c. 1925	4.50	7.00	5.00
☐ **Pencil Sharpener**, plastic, c. 1960	6.00	12.00	7.50
☐ **Pencil Sharpener**, red metal, c. 1933	14.00	18.00	13.50
☐ **Playing Cards**, Airplane Spatter, (deck), c. 1942	12.00	18.00	11.00
☐ **Playing Cards**, Coca Cola Girls, (deck), c. 1909	52.00	62.00	55.00
☐ **Plate**, glass and Coke bottle, c. 1920	70.00	85.00	72.00
☐ **Pocket Knife**, Chicago World's Fair, 3½"	1.00	3.00	2.00
☐ **Pocket Knife**, Coca Cola in bottles, 3½"	1.00	3.00	2.00
☐ **Pocket Knife**, picture of Coke bottle, 3½"	1.00	3.00	2.00
☐ **Pocket Secretary**, leather bound, c. 1920	32.00	42.00	35.00
☐ **Postcard**, "All Over the World," c. 1913	115.00	125.00	112.00
☐ **Postcard**, "Duster Girl" driving car, c. 1906 ...	95.00	105.00	95.00
☐ **Postcard**, girl with picture hat, c. 1909	28.00	38.00	30.00
☐ **Postcard**, horse and delivery wagon, c. 1900	130.00	150.00	130.00
☐ **Postcard**, men in speedboat, c. 1913	105.00	120.00	105.00
☐ **Postcard**, picture of bottling plant, c. 1905	120.00	140.00	120.00
☐ **Postcard**, school teacher at blackboard, c. 1913	88.00	98.00	90.00
☐ **Postcard**, truck carrying cases of Coke, c. 1913	135.00	155.00	135.00
☐ **Postcard Set**, Dick Tracy series, c. 1942	140.00	160.00	145.00
☐ **Poster**, "Bathing Beauty," c. 1918	410.00	435.00	412.00

	Current Price Range		P/Y Average
☐ **Poster,** "Betty," c. 1914	260.00	280.00	260.00
☐ **Poster,** "Early Display with Young Lovers," c. 1891	460.00	490.00	465.00
☐ **Poster,** "Flapper Girl," c. 1929	160.00	180.00	160.00
☐ **Poster,** "Florine McKinney," c. 1936	40.00	50.00	40.00
☐ **Poster,** "Girl in Hammock," c. 1900	435.00	460.00	438.00
☐ **Poster,** "Hilda Clark Cuban," c. 1901	310.00	335.00	312.00
☐ **Tray,** "Hilda Clark," c. 1904	260.00	285.00	262.00
☐ **Tray,** "Johnny Weismuller and Maureen O'Sullivan," c. 1934	185.00	210.00	188.00
☐ **Tray,** "Juanita," round, c. 1905	150.00	175.00	158.00
☐ **Tray,** "Olympic Games," 15″ x 11″, c. 1976 ..	12.00	18.00	12.50
☐ **Tray** (serving), plastic, c. 1971	50.00	60.00	52.00
☐ **Tray,** replica of "Duster Girl," c. 1972	28.00	42.00	32.00
☐ **Tray,** "Sailor Girl," c. 1940	28.00	42.00	32.00
☐ **Tray,** "Saint Louis Fair," oval, c. 1904	160.00	190.00	170.00
☐ **Tray,** "Santa Claus," 15″ x 11 ″, c. 1973	22.00	32.00	25.00
☐ **Tray,** "Soda Fountain Clerk," c. 1927	80.00	110.00	82.00
☐ **Tray,** "Springboard Girl," c. 1939	45.00	60.00	46.00
☐ **Tray,** "Summer Girl," c. 1921	185.00	235.00	200.00
☐ **Tray,** T.V., candle design, c. 1972	20.00	28.00	21.00
☐ **Tray,** T.V., picnic basket	28.00	38.00	30.00
☐ **Tray,** T.V., Thanksgiving motif, c. 1961	20.00	28.00	21.00
☐ **Tray,** "Topless," c. 1908	510.00	710.00	600.00
☐ **Tray,** "Two Girls at Car," c. 1942	32.00	42.00	35.00
☐ **Tray,** "Vienna Art Nude," c. 1905	210.00	285.00	238.00
☐ **Tray,** "Western Bottling Co.," c. 1905	110.00	160.00	125.00
☐ **Vendor's Umbrella,** "Pause that Refreshes"	135.00	160.00	138.00
☐ **Wallet,** Coke bottle emblem, c. 1915	75.00	85.00	75.00
☐ **Wallet,** Coca-Cola script, c. 1922	88.00	98.00	90.00
☐ **Wallet,** embossed coin purse, c. 1906	150.00	165.00	148.00
☐ **Watch Fob,** bulldog, c. 1925	55.00	85.00	65.00
☐ **Watch Fob,** "Drink Coca-Cola in Bottles"	60.00	80.00	65.00

COINS

DESCRIPTION: Coins are metallic objects, usually circular, designed as a medium of exchange. The earlier series of U.S. coins comprised base metal for the lowest denominations; silver for the medium to high denominations; and gold for very high denominations up to $20. Today, all U.S. coins, regardless of denomination, are made of base metal; neither silver nor gold is used. For present-day U.S. coins of 10¢ and higher denominations, a nickel exterior coating is bonded to a copper interior. The front of a coin, which on U.S. issues carries a portrait, is called the "obverse." The back is the "reverse."

PERIOD: U.S. coins were first struck in 1793, though earlier coins issued by the colonial governments had preceded them. They have been struck continually since then, though with various changes in denominations and of course in designs. The U.S. has had coins with face values of 2¢, 3¢, 20¢ and other odd amounts.

MATERIALS: When precious metal was used in U.S. coins, it was usually a .900 grade. That is, silver coins were 90% silver vs. 10% copper; gold coins were 90% gold vs. 10% copper. The very earliest U.S. coins did not precisely conform to these standards, but all later ones did. Thus the term "coin silver" means .900 silver.

MARKS: While there are numerous types of marks that could potentially be found on coins (double strikes, small letters, etc.), the most frequent are the "Mint marks," which are placed intentionally. These are small letters indicating the Mint from which that particular coin has originated, such as S for San Francisco and D for Denver. Traditionally the Mint did not place any mark on its Philadelphia coins, but this practice has been changed in recent years.

ADDITIONAL TIPS: Do not attempt to clean or polish coins; the surfaces are much more delicate than you may imagine and can be easily injured. Though coin collecting is a hobby and pastime, coin buying is more akin to a science. Coin fakes are very numerous, often of high quality and undetectable except by a trained expert. It is therefore important to buy, as much as possible, from the recognized coin dealers rather than from flea markets or other questionable sources.

The following values were compiled with silver selling in the range of $8 to $10 per ounce. In the following listings, ABP means Average Buying Price.

For a complete explanation of coins, see *The Official Blackbook Price Guide to U.S. Coins,* published by The House of Collectibles.

SMALL CENTS—INDIAN HEAD, 1859–1887

DATE	MINTAGE	ABP	G-4 Good	F-12 Fine	EF-40 Ex. Fine	MS-60 Unc.	PRF-65 Proof
☐ 1859 Copper-Nickel	36,400,000	3.50	6.00	10.00	65.00	340.00	5500.00
☐ 1860 Copper-Nickel	20,566,000	2.00	5.00	7.00	25.00	130.00	2800.00
☐ 1861 Copper-Nickel	10,100,000	4.50	9.00	18.00	42.00	220.00	2800.00
☐ 1862 Copper-Nickel	28,075,000	2.00	4.00	6.00	22.00	110.00	2800.00
☐ 1863 Copper-Nickel	49,840,000	2.00	3.00	5.00	17.50	110.00	2800.00
☐ 1864 Copper-Nickel	13,740,000	4.00	8.00	13.00	33.00	145.00	2800.00
☐ 1864 Bronze	39,233,714	2.00	4.00	7.00	26.00	100.00	2400.00
☐ 1864 L on Ribbon		15.00	30.00	65.00	150.00	375.00	16,500.00
☐ 1865	35,429,286	1.25	3.00	7.00	25.00	75.00	1400.00
☐ 1866	9,826,500	8.00	18.00	40.00	110.00	300.00	1400.00
☐ 1867	9,821,000	8.00	18.00	40.00	110.00	300.00	1400.00
☐ 1868	10,266,500	8.00	18.00	40.00	110.00	300.00	1400.00
☐ 1869	6,420,000	12.00	32.00	70.00	170.00	400.00	1450.00
☐ 1869 over 8		45.00	85.00	220.00	500.00	1400.00	
☐ 1870	5,275,000	12.00	24.00	60.00	120.00	285.00	1625.00
☐ 1871	3,929,500	16.00	32.00	65.00	125.00	320.00	1625.00
☐ 1872	4,042,000	23.00	40.00	80.00	190.00	395.00	1625.00
☐ 1873	11,676,500	3.00	8.00	17.00	50.00	150.00	1500.00
☐ 1873 Doubled Liberty						EXTREMELY RARE	
☐ 1874	14,187,500	4.00	8.00	18.00	60.00	150.00	1315.00
☐ 1875	13,528,000	4.00	8.00	18.00	60.00	150.00	1315.00
☐ 1876	7,944,000	5.00	12.00	25.00	55.00	175.00	1600.00
☐ 1877	852,500	150.00	285.00	475.00	900.00	1750.00	4900.00
☐ 1878	5,799,850	4.50	11.00	26.00	55.00	200.00	2000.00
☐ 1879	16,231,000	2.00	3.00	8.00	22.00	80.00	1315.00
☐ 1880	38,964,955	.40	1.35	6.00	16.00	70.00	1315.00
☐ 1881	39,211,575	.40	1.35	3.75	16.00	70.00	1315.00
☐ 1882	38,581,100	.40	1.35	3.75	16.00	70.00	1315.00
☐ 1883	45,598,109	.40	1.35	3.75	18.00	70.00	1315.00
☐ 1884	23,261,742	.40	1.35	6.50	30.00	75.00	1315.00
☐ 1885	11,765,384	2.00	5.00	12.00	40.00	100.00	1600.00
☐ 1886	17,654,290	1.50	4.00	10.00	38.00	100.00	1600.00
☐ 1887	45,226,483	.40	1.25	2.50	10.00	70.00	1315.00

SMALL CENTS—LINCOLN HEAD, 1909–1920

(1909–1942 COMPOSITION-95/TIN AND ZINC)

DATE	MINTAGE	ABP	G-4 Good	F-12 Fine	VF-20 V. Fine	EF-40 Ex. Fine	MS-60 Unc.	PRF-65 Proof
☐ 1909	72,702,618	.25	.50	1.00	1.50	2.75	25.00	1000.00
☐ 1909 V.D.B.	27,995,000	1.15	1.85	2.75	3.10	4.00	20.00	2800.00
☐ 1909S	1,825,000	20.00	45.00	65.00	90.00	100.00	240.00	
☐ 1909S V.D.B.	484,000	100.00	200.00	300.00	380.00	425.00	600.00	
☐ 1910	146,801,218	.15	.30	.50	1.00	2.50	18.00	1200.00

Nickel, *Liberty Head, issued 1883–1912,* $20.00–$1500.00

DATE	MINTAGE	ABP	G-4 Good	F-12 Fine	VF-20 V. Fine	EF-40 Ex. Fine	MS-60 Unc.	PRF-65 Proof
☐ 1910S	6,045,000	2.50	5.00	10.00	12.00	20.00	100.00	
☐ 1911	101,177,787	.10	.20	.65	1.40	4.00	25.00	625.00
☐ 1911D	12,672,000	1.25	2.50	5.00	9.00	20.00	100.00	
☐ 1911S	4,026,000	6.00	9.00	13.00	17.00	27.00	115.00	
☐ 1912	68,153,060	.20	.30	1.70	4.00	7.50	30.00	500.00
☐ 1912D	10,411,000	2.00	3.00	7.50	12.00	30.00	145.00	
☐ 1912S	4,431,000	4.50	8.00	12.00	16.00	23.00	110.00	
☐ 1913	76,532,352	.20	.30	1.50	2.25	7.00	38.00	550.00
☐ 1913D	15,804,000	.80	1.25	3.50	6.00	17.00	75.00	
☐ 1913S	6,101,000	3.00	5.75	8.00	10.00	18.00	100.00	
☐ 1914	75,238,432	.20	.40	1.60	3.50	7.00	70.00	600.00
☐ 1914D	1,193,000	35.00	50.00	125.00	210.00	475.00	1800.00	
☐ 1914S	4,137,000	4.00	7.00	10.00	15.00	25.00	185.00	
☐ 1915	29,092,120	.20	.50	3.50	8.00	23.00	135.00	1000.00
☐ 1915D	22,050,000	.20	.45	1.25	5.00	11.00	60.00	
☐ 1915S	4,833,677	4.00	7.00	10.00	12.00	20.00	120.00	
☐ 1916	131,838,677	.08	.35	1.00	2.00	6.00	20.00	1000.00
☐ 1916D	35,956,000	.12	.35	.85	1.50	7.00	42.00	
☐ 1916S	22,510,000	.28	.60	1.25	2.00	7.50	80.00	
☐ 1917	196,429,785	.08	.25	.30	.70	2.75	22.00	
☐ 1917D	55,120,000	.10	.35	.75	2.50	6.00	75.00	
☐ 1917S	32,620,000	.10	.25	.75	2.25	6.00	80.00	
☐ 1918	288,104,634	.08	.22	.30	.60	2.00	25.00	
☐ 1918D	47,830,000	.10	.30	.75	2.50	7.00	75.00	
☐ 1918S	34,680,000	.12	.30	.60	2.25	5.50	80.00	
☐ 1919	392,021,000	.08	.15	.40	.60	2.00	20.00	

DATE	MINTAGE	ABP	G-4 Good	F-12 Fine	VF-20 V. Fine	EF-40 Ex. Fine	MS-60 Unc.	PRF-65 Proof
☐ 1919D	57,154,000	.10	.20	.65	2.50	5.25	50.00	
☐ 1919S	139,760,000	.10	.20	.40	.75	3.25	60.00	
☐ 1920	310,165,000	.08	.20	.40	1.00	3.00	20.00	
☐ 1920D	49,280,000	.08	.20	.60	2.00	4.00	60.00	
☐ 1920S	46,220,000	.08	.20	.60	2.00	4.00	95.00	

NICKELS—LIBERTY HEAD, 1883–1909

DATE	MINTAGE	ABP	G-4 Good	F-12 Fine	EF-40 Ex. Fine	MS-60 Unc.	PRF-65 Proof
☐ 1883 no cents	5,479,519	.75	2.00	4.50	11.00	55.00	3200.00
☐ 1883 w/cents	16,032,983	4.00	7.00	20.00	45.00	300.00	2000.00
☐ 1884	11,273,942	4.25	8.00	22.00	47.00	315.00	2000.00
☐ 1885	1,476,490	175.00	400.00	620.00	1000.00	1500.00	2650.00
☐ 1886	3,330,290	21.00	42.00	100.00	250.00	600.00	2500.00
☐ 1887	15,263,652	2.25	4.50	22.00	47.00	200.00	2000.00
☐ 1888	10,720,483	2.00	6.00	21.00	50.00	200.00	2000.00
☐ 1889	15,881,361	3.50	5.00	25.00	50.00	200.00	2000.00
☐ 1890	16,259,272	3.50	5.00	18.00	50.00	200.00	2000.00
☐ 1891	16,834,350	3.00	3.50	17.00	50.00	200.00	2000.00
☐ 1892	11,699,642	3.00	4.75	20.00	50.00	200.00	2000.00
☐ 1893	13,370,195	3.00	4.50	19.00	50.00	200.00	2000.00
☐ 1894	5,413,132	2.00	4.00	25.00	75.00	200.00	2000.00
☐ 1895	9,979,884	2.50	5.00	23.00	50.00	200.00	2000.00
☐ 1896	8,842,920	2.75	5.25	24.00	50.00	200.00	2000.00
☐ 1897	20,428,735	.40	1.10	5.00	35.00	100.00	2000.00
☐ 1898	12,532,087	.40	1.25	5.00	20.00	150.00	2000.00
☐ 1899	26,029,031	.22	1.00	2.50	20.00	100.00	2000.00
☐ 1900	27,255,995	.22	1.00	2.50	20.00	100.00	2000.00
☐ 1901	26,480,213	.22	1.00	2.50	20.00	100.00	2000.00
☐ 1902	31,480,579	.22	1.00	2.50	20.00	100.00	2000.00
☐ 1903	28,006,725	.22	1.00	2.50	20.00	100.00	2000.00
☐ 1904	21,404,984	.22	1.00	2.50	20.00	100.00	2000.00
☐ 1905	29,827,276	.22	1.00	2.50	20.00	100.00	2000.00
☐ 1906	38,613,725	.22	1.00	2.50	20.00	100.00	2000.00
☐ 1907	39,214,800	.22	1.00	2.50	20.00	100.00	2000.00
☐ 1908	22,686,177	.22	1.00	2.50	20.00	100.00	2000.00
☐ 1909	11,590,526	.40	1.00	2.50	20.00	100.00	2000.00

DIMES—MERCURY DIMES, 1916–1927

DATE	MINTAGE	ABP	G-4 Good	F-12 Fine	VF-20 V. Fine	EF-40 Ex. Fine	MS-60 Unc.
☐ 1916	22,180,000	.50	3.50	4.50	6.00	9.00	35.00
☐ 1916D	264,000	225.00	400.00	1000.00	1500.00	2000.00	2800.00
☐ 1916S	10,450,000	.50	2.50	6.00	8.00	14.00	47.00
☐ 1917	55,230,000	.50	1.75	2.50	5.00	7.00	28.00
☐ 1917D	9,402,000	.50	3.00	8.00	15.00	40.00	120.00
☐ 1917S	27,330,000	.50	2.00	3.00	6.00	8.00	55.00
☐ 1918	26,680,000	.50	2.25	4.00	10.00	22.00	65.00
☐ 1918D	22,674,800	.50	2.25	3.75	8.00	19.00	85.00
☐ 1918S	19,300,000	.50	3.00	4.00	7.00	14.00	50.00
☐ 1919	35,740,000	.50	1.50	3.00	5.00	8.00	39.00
☐ 1919D	9,939,000	.50	3.50	5.50	14.00	30.00	100.00

DATE	MINTAGE	ABP	G-4 Good	F-12 Fine	VF-20 V. Fine	EF-40 Ex. Fine	MS-60 Unc.
☐ 1919S	8,850,000	.50	3.25	5.00	12.00	26.00	100.00
☐ 1920	59,030,000	.50	1.35	2.00	4.50	7.00	30.00
☐ 1920D	19,171,000	.50	2.20	4.00	6.50	14.00	70.00
☐ 1920S	13,820,000	.50	2.20	4.00	6.50	13.00	70.00
☐ 1921	1,230,000	15.00	28.00	70.00	150.00	400.00	600.00
☐ 1921D	1,080,000	16.00	34.00	60.00	175.00	420.00	650.00
☐ 1923*	50,130,000	.50	2.50	3.50	4.00	7.00	20.00
☐ 1923S	6,440,000	.50	2.20	4.00	7.00	18.00	85.00
☐ 1924	24,010,000	.50	2.20	3.50	4.50	7.00	50.00
☐ 1924D	6,810,000	.50	2.20	6.00	8.00	24.00	100.00
☐ 1924S	7,120,000	.50	2.15	6.00	8.00	24.00	100.00
☐ 1925	25,610,000	.50	2.15	4.00	5.00	8.00	42.00
☐ 1925D	5,117,000	2.00	5.00	10.00	24.00	60.00	220.00
☐ 1925S	5,850,000	.50	2.00	3.50	6.50	18.00	120.00
☐ 1926	32,160,000	.50	2.00	3.00	3.75	6.00	20.00
☐ 1926D	6,828,000	.50	2.00	3.00	6.00	14.00	70.00
☐ 1926S	1,520,000	3.50	8.00	16.00	32.00	80.00	350.00
☐ 1927	28,080,000	.50	2.00	3.00	5.00	6.00	20.00
☐ 1927D	4,812,000	.50	3.00	8.00	15.00	32.00	120.00

*All dimes with 23D date are counterfeit.

QUARTERS—WASHINGTON, 1932–1943

DATE	MINTAGE	ABP	G-4 Good	F-12 Fine	EF-40 Ex. Fine	MS-60 Unc.	PRF-65 Proof
☐ 1932	5,404,000	1.20	2.75	4.00	10.00	30.00	
☐ 1932D	436,800	22.00	42.00	60.00	160.00	475.00	
☐ 1932S	408,000	15.00	30.00	35.00	60.00	250.00	
☐ 1934	31,912,052	1.20	2.50	6.00	10.00	40.00	
☐ 1934 Double Die			35.00	40.00	100.00	250.00	
☐ 1934D	3,527,200	1.20	2.50	8.00	20.00	135.00	
☐ 1935	32,484,000	1.20		5.00	10.00	32.00	
☐ 1935D	5,780,000	1.20		6.00	18.00	130.00	
☐ 1935S	5,550,000	1.20		7.00	14.00	100.00	
☐ 1936	41,303,837	1.20		6.00	11.00	40.00	1500.00
☐ 1936D	5,374,000	1.20		6.00	28.00	200.00	
☐ 1936S	3,828,000	1.20		7.00	11.50	150.00	
☐ 1937	19,701,542	1.20		5.00	8.00	30.00	450.00
☐ 1937D	7,189,600	1.20		5.00	10.00	45.00	
☐ 1937S	1,652,000	1.20		6.00	18.00	150.00	
☐ 1938	9,480,045	1.20		4.00	15.00	65.00	425.00
☐ 1938S	2,832,000	1.20		6.00	12.00	50.00	
☐ 1939	33,548,795	1.20		4.00	8.00	18.00	275.00
☐ 1939D	7,092,000	1.20		6.00	11.00	50.00	
☐ 1939S	2,628,000	1.20		6.00	12.00	50.00	
☐ 1940	35,715,246	1.20		5.00	8.00	15.00	210.00
☐ 1940D	2,797,600	1.20		6.00	12.00	95.00	
☐ 1940S	8,244,000	1.20		4.00	8.00	15.00	
☐ 1941	79,047,287	1.20		2.00	2.50	10.00	170.00
☐ 1941D	16,714,800	1.20		2.00	2.50	25.00	
☐ 1941S	16,080,000	1.20		2.00	2.50	28.00	
☐ 1942	102,117,123	1.20		2.00	2.50	9.00	170.00
☐ 1942D	17,487,200	1.20		2.00	2.50	15.00	
☐ 1942S	19,384,000	1.20		2.00	2.50	60.00	

DATE	MINTAGE	ABP	G-4 Good	F-12 Fine	EF-40 Ex. Fine	MS-60 Unc.	PRF-65 Proof
☐ 1943 99,700,000		1.20		2.00	2.50	10.00	
☐ 1943D 16,095,600		1.20		2.00	2.50	15.00	

HALF DOLLARS—LIBERTY WALKING, 1916–1936

DATE	MINTAGE	ABP	G-4 Good	F-12 Fine	EF-40 Ex. Fine	MS-60 Unc.	PRF-65 Proof
☐ 1916 608,000		8.00	15.00	40.00	150.00	385.00	
☐ 1916D on obverse 1,014,400		8.00	20.00	30.00	130.00	400.00	
☐ 1916S on obverse 508,000		16.00	30.00	75.00	200.00	600.00	1800.00
☐ 1917 12,292,000		2.40	4.00	9.00	25.00	140.00	
☐ 1917D on obverse 765,400		7.00	14.00	22.00	160.00	500.00	
☐ 1917D on reverse 1,940,000		2.40	6.00	20.00	125.00	550.00	
☐ 1917S on obverse 952,000		7.00	14.00	35.00	200.00	700.00	1800.00
☐ 1917S on reverse 6,554,000		2.40	5.00	12.00	40.00	260.00	
☐ 1918 6,634,000		2.40	6.00	15.00	115.00	325.00	
☐ 1918D 3,853,040		2.40	6.00	15.00	130.00	700.00	
☐ 1918S 10,282,000		2.40	6.00	12.00	40.00	275.00	
☐ 1919 962,000		2.40	9.00	25.00	300.00	1000.00	
☐ 1919D 1,165,000		2.40	15.00	25.00	375.00	2100.00	
☐ 1919S 1,552,000		2.40	12.00	18.00	325.00	1800.00	
☐ 1920 6,372,000		2.40	4.00	10.00	50.00	250.00	
☐ 1920D 1,551,000		2.40	4.00	18.00	250.00	900.00	
☐ 1920S 4,624,000		2.40	4.00	12.00	125.00	800.00	
☐ 1921 246,000		35.00	65.00	150.00	850.00	2000.00	
☐ 1921D 208,000		55.00	115.00	200.00	950.00	2200.00	
☐ 1921S 548,000		10.00	18.00	40.00	950.00	6000.00	
☐ 1923S 2,178,000		2.40	4.25	9.00	140.00	800.00	
☐ 1927S 2,393,000		2.40	4.25	9.00	75.00	700.00	
☐ 1928S 1,940,000		2.40	4.25	9.00	95.00	800.00	
☐ 1929D 1,001,200		2.40	4.25	9.00	70.00	375.00	
☐ 1929S 1,902,000		2.40	4.25	9.00	70.00	350.00	
☐ 1933S 1,786,000		2.40	4.25	9.00	55.00	325.00	
☐ 1934 6,964,000		2.40	4.00	6.00	12.00	90.00	
☐ 1934D 2,361,400		2.40	4.00	6.00	30.00	175.00	
☐ 1934S 3,652,000		2.40	4.00	6.00	22.00	350.00	
☐ 1935 9,162,000		2.40	4.00	6.00	15.00	75.00	
☐ 1935D 3,003,800		2.40	4.00	6.00	30.00	190.00	
☐ 1935S 2,854,000		2.40	4.00	6.00	22.00	210.00	
☐ 1936 12,617,901		2.40	4.00	6.00	12.00	70.00	3500.00

SILVER DOLLARS—LIBERTY HEAD OR "MORGAN," 1878–1892

DATE	MINTAGE	ABP	F-12 Fine	EX-40 Ex. Fine	MS-60 Unc.	PRF-65 Proof
☐ 1878 7 Tail Feathers 416,000		8.00	20.00	35.00	60.00	8000.00
☐ 1878 8 Tail Feathers 750,000		8.00	21.00	32.00	70.00	7000.00
☐ 1878 7 over 8 Tail Feathers		8.00	23.00	40.00	80.00	
☐ 1878CC 2,212,000		8.00	25.00	40.00	135.00	
☐ 1878S 9,774,000		8.00	18.00	20.00	65.00	
☐ 1879 14,807,100		8.00	16.00	20.00	50.00	6500.00
☐ 1879CC 756,000		15.00	35.00	175.00	1300.00	
☐ 1879O 2,887,000		8.00	14.00	17.50	60.00	
☐ 1879S 9,110,000		8.00	14.00	17.50	56.00	

DATE	MINTAGE	ABP	F-12 Fine	EX-40 Ex. Fine	MS-60 Unc.	PRF-65 Proof
☐ 1880	12,601,355	8.00	14.00	17.50	50.00	6000.00
☐ 1880CC	591,000	15.00	35.00	75.00	200.00	
☐ 1880 over 79CC		25.00	54.00	90.00	215.00	
☐ 1880O	5,305,000	8.00	14.00	20.00	75.00	
☐ 1880S	8,900,000	8.00	14.00	17.50	70.00	
☐ 1881	9,163,975	8.00	14.00	17.50	50.00	6000.00
☐ 1881CC	206,000	30.00	60.00	90.00	235.00	
☐ 1881O	5,708,000	8.00	14.00	19.00	50.00	
☐ 1881S	12,760,000	8.00	14.00	19.00	55.00	
☐ 1882	11,101,000	8.00	14.00	19.00	55.00	6000.00
☐ 1882CC	1,133,000	12.00	25.00	50.00	120.00	
☐ 1882O	6,090,000	8.00	14.00	18.00	50.00	
☐ 1882O, O over S		14.00	14.00	18.00	52.00	6000.00
☐ 1882S	9,250,000	8.00	14.00	18.00	55.00	
☐ 1883	12,191,039	8.00	14.00	18.00	50.00	6000.00
☐ 1883CC	1,204,000	12.00	25.00	50.00	115.00	
☐ 1883O	8,725,000	8.00	16.00	19.00	50.00	
☐ 1883S	6,250,000	8.00	16.00	25.00	475.00	
☐ 1884	14,070,875	8.00	16.50	21.00	65.00	6000.00
☐ 1884CC	1,136,000	20.00	40.00	70.00	110.00	
☐ 1884O	9,730,000	8.00	14.00	19.00	50.00	
☐ 1884S	3,200,000	8.00	18.00	30.00	1600.00	
☐ 1885	17,787,767	8.00	16.50	19.00	60.00	6000.00
☐ 1885CC	228,000	80.00	160.00	180.00	280.00	
☐ 1885O	9,185,000	8.00	14.00	19.00	60.00	
☐ 1885S	1,497,000	8.00	14.00	30.00	120.00	
☐ 1886	19,963,886	8.00	14.00	20.00	300.00	6000.00
☐ 1886O	10,710,000	8.00	14.00	20.00	300.00	
☐ 1886S	750,000	8.00	18.00	35.00	180.00	
☐ 1887	20,290,710	8.00	14.00	18.00	50.00	6000.00
☐ 1887O	11,550,000	8.00	14.00	18.00	70.00	
☐ 1887S	1,771,000	8.00	18.00	24.00	100.00	
☐ 1888	19,183,833	8.00	14.00	18.00	50.00	6000.00
☐ 1888O	12,150,000	8.00	14.00	18.00	60.00	
☐ 1888S	657,000	16.00	30.00	60.00	180.00	
☐ 1889	21,726,811	8.00	16.50	18.00	40.00	6000.00
☐ 1889CC	350,000	80.00	150.00	500.00	4000.00	
☐ 1889O	11,875,000	8.00	14.00	20.00	110.00	
☐ 1889S	700,000	8.00	34.00	55.00	80.00	
☐ 1890	16,802,590	8.00	14.00	20.00	60.00	6000.00
☐ 1890CC	2,309,041	16.00	29.00	48.00	240.00	
☐ 1890O	10,701,000	8.00	14.00	18.00	70.00	
☐ 1890S	8,230,373	8.00	14.00	18.00	70.00	
☐ 1891	8,694,206	8.00	14.00	24.00	100.00	6000.00
☐ 1891CC	1,618,000	12.00	25.00	50.00	250.00	
☐ 1891O	7,954,529	8.00	14.00	24.00	100.00	
☐ 1891S	5,296,000	8.00	14.00	23.00	65.00	
☐ 1892	1,037,245	8.00	15.00	28.00	175.00	6000.00
☐ 1892CC	1,352,000	15.00	30.00	85.00	375.00	
☐ 1892O	2,744,000	8.00	14.00	25.00	150.00	
☐ 1892S	1,200,000	10.00	20.00	100.00	4000.00	

COMIC ART

TOPIC: Original comic art consists of the drawings and paintings from which final printed reproductions are made.

TYPES: Comic art can be from comic strips that ran in a newspaper or from comic books. Original artwork for magazine cartoons also falls into this category but is considered a specialized field by collectors. The art may be a "penciled rough" (which is sketched very lightly in pencil), or a finished drawing (which has been enhanced by drawing ink).

PERIOD: With rare exceptions, comic art in America has been produced during the 1900s.

MAKERS: Famous comic artists include Walt Kelly, Alex Raymond, Jack Kirby and Arthur Suydam.

COMMENTS: Original art is unique and has more visual impact than the printed reproduction. Most of it is priced within the range of the average collector, although some art by famous artists is quite valuable.

ADDITIONAL TIPS: With original comic art, prices do not reflect scarcity. They are determined by the number of admirers a certain artist has, and how much these admirers are willing to pay for the work. For more information and more extensive listings, please refer to *The Official Price Guide to Comic Books and Collectibles,* published by The House of Collectibles. The following listings are organized by artist.

	Current Price Range		P/Y Average
ADAMS, NEAL			
☐ **Amazing Adventures # 18,** War of the Worlds, page 8, pencil layout on translucent paper, signed	30.00	40.00	34.00
☐ **Batman # 236,** cover, scene from story Wail of the Ghost Bride	275.00	325.00	290.00
☐ **Ben Casey,** daily strip for March 19, 1966	26.00	34.00	29.00

	Current Price Range		P/Y Average
☐ **Ben Casey,** daily strip for March 19, 1966	26.00	34.00	29.00
☐ **Ben Casey,** Sunday page for February 13, 1966	110.00	140.00	120.00
☐ **Black and white illustrations for 1976 D.C. calendar,** depicting Superman; inking by Giordano, 15″ x 14″	250.00	300.00	265.00
☐ **Brave And The Bold #83,** page 16 (featuring Batman and the Ten Titans)	30.00	40.00	33.00
☐ **Brave And The Bold #83,** page 24	40.00	50.00	44.00
☐ **Creepy #15,** large splash of Ty Rex	140.00	180.00	152.00
☐ **The Flash #226,** page one (Green Lantern story)	135.00	165.00	145.00
☐ **The Flash #226,** page one of second story (splash page) featuring The Green Lantern	130.00	170.00	145.00
☐ **The Flash #226,** page 5	110.00	140.00	122.00
☐ **The Flash #226,** page 7	110.00	140.00	122.00
☐ **The Green Lantern #78,** page 20, featuring The Black Canary	70.00	90.00	77.00
☐ **Justice League of America #79,** cover	110.00	140.00	123.00
☐ **Justice League of America #139,** cover without logo	110.00	140.00	122.00
☐ **Superboy #158,** cover	90.00	110.00	97.00
☐ **Teen Titans #22,** page 5, featuring Wonder Girl and Kid Flash, inking by Cardy	60.00	80.00	66.00
☐ **Tomahawk #128,** cover	130.00	170.00	143.00

BUSCEMA, JOHN

☐ **Avengers #82,** page 14	35.00	45.00	37.75
☐ **Captain America #115,** page 10, featuring The Red Skull	45.00	55.00	47.00
☐ **KaZar #7,** cover	45.00	55.00	47.00
☐ **Marvel Preview #27,** page 19, featuring The Phoenix	28.00	36.00	30.25
☐ **Marvel Two In One #8,** page 17	4.00	6.00	4.20
☐ **Peter Parker #38,** page 27	22.00	28.00	23.50
☐ **Savage Sword Of Conan #10,** page 57	26.00	34.00	27.80
☐ **Savage Sword Of Conan #10,** page 63	26.00	34.00	27.80
☐ **Savage Sword Of Conan #10,** page 64	26.00	34.00	27.80
☐ **Thor #226,** page 26, featuring Glactus and Hercules	17.00	23.00	18.35
☐ **Thor #241,** page 26	16.00	20.00	17.00

CHAN, ERNIE

☐ **Batman Family Giant #9,** cover	13.00	17.00	14.20
☐ **Conan The Barbarian,** daily strip for December 21, 1978, featuring Red Sonja	30.00	40.00	32.20
☐ **Conan The Barbarian,** daily strip for January 20, 1979, featuring The Great White Worm	30.00	40.00	32.20
☐ **Conan The Barbarian,** daily strip for January 22, 1979, featuring The Great White Worm	30.00	40.00	32.20
☐ **Conan The Barbarian,** daily strip for January 24, 1979, featuring The Great White Worm	30.00	40.00	32.20

	Current Price Range		P/Y Average
□ **Conan The Barbarian,** daily strip for February 23, 1979, featuring The Shadow Bats	30.00	40.00	32.20

FRAZETTA, FRANK

□ **Danger Is Our Business** #1, page 5, signed	1000.00	1200.00	1050.00
□ **Sketch of nude figure, described only as "small"**	350.00	450.00	365.00
□ **Yours, Mine And Ours,** watercolor for movie poster (Lucille Ball/Henry Fonda movie, 11″ x 15″	1600.00	2000.00	1715.00

FREAS, KELLY

□ Ace paperback cover of a spaceship and a city, from unidentified novel, 1967	26.00	34.00	29.00
□ Double page spread for a Marvel black and white horror magazine (specific title and issue not known)	110.00	140.00	122.50
□ Preliminary sketch (in ink) for title page of The Art of Science Fiction, 3″ x 18″	22.00	28.00	24.15

FREEMAN, GEORGE

□ Framed painting of Red Sonja battling cavemen; she has two swords and they have spears. No information on whether published or not, 13″ x 18″	300.00	350.00	310.00

FRENZ, RON

□ **KaZar** #16, page 9	8.50	11.50	9.35
□ **KaZar** #16, page 22	8.50	11.50	9.35
□ **KaZar** #17, page 4	17.00	23.00	18.15
□ **KaZar** #17, page 14	22.00	28.00	23.60
□ **Peter Parker** #80, page 10	6.50	8.50	6.80
□ **Peter Parker** #80, page 15	6.50	8.50	6.80

FULLER, VING

□ **Doc Syke,** Sunday page from 1946	42.00	58.00	47.00

GAMMILL, KERRY

□ **Marvel Team-Up** #127, page 2	14.00	18.00	14.20
□ **Marvel Team-Up** #127, page 3	11.00	15.00	11.75
□ **Marvel Team-Up** #127, page 5	14.00	18.00	14.20
□ **Marvel Team-Up** #127, page 8	11.00	15.00	11.75
□ **Marvel Team-Up** #127, page 9	14.00	18.00	14.20
□ **Marvel Team-Up** #127, page 10	11.00	15.00	11.75
□ **Marvel Team-Up** #127, page 12	14.00	18.00	14.20
□ **Marvel Team-Up** #127, page 13	14.00	18.00	14.20

	Current Price Range		P/Y Average

KIRBY, JACK AND NEAL ADAMS

☐ **Jimmy Olson #148,** cover 90.00 110.00 91.15

KIRBY, JACK AND MICKY DEMEO

☐ **Tales To Astonish #74,** page 3 (Hulk) 65.00 85.00 67.00
☐ **Tales To Astonish #74,** page 4 (Hulk) 65.00 85.00 67.00
☐ **Tales To Astonish #74,** page 5 (Hulk) 60.00 70.00 61.15
☐ **Tales To Astonish #74,** page 6 (Hulk) 40.00 50.00 42.20

MAYERICK, VAL

☐ **Micronauts #35,** page 1 (splash page) 40.00 50.00 42.25
☐ **Micronauts #35,** page 8 .... 22.00 28.00 23.15
☐ **Micronauts #35,** page 9 .... 22.00 28.00 23.15
☐ **Micronauts #35,** page 11 .... 17.00 23.00 17.70
☐ **Micronauts #35,** page 15 .... 13.00 17.00 13.45
☐ **Micronauts #35,** page 16 .... 22.00 28.00 23.15
☐ **Micronauts #35,** page 35 .... 22.00 28.00 23.15

MAXON, REX

☐ **Tarzan,** set of six daily strips from 1940, matted into an area 25″ x 36″ 175.00 215.00 187.50

MCCAY, WINSOR

☐ **Drawing Of Christ,** surrounded by followers, signed twice, believed to date from about 1900, 27″ x 11″ 700.00 900.00 785.00
☐ **Little Nemo,** Sunday pages, 1906 .... 5500.00 6200.00 5700.00
☐ **Dream Of The Rarebit Friend,** 1905 .... 1000.00 1200.00 1050.00

MCDONELL, LUKE

☐ **Iron Man #166,** page 18 .... 26.00 34.00 26.75
☐ **Iron Man #166,** page 22 .... 35.00 45.00 36.00
☐ **Iron Man #166,** page 31 .... 30.00 40.00 31.15
☐ **Iron Man #167,** page 19 .... 40.00 50.00 41.20
☐ **Micronauts #46,** page 5 .... 22.00 28.00 22.90
☐ **Micronauts #46,** page 7 .... 26.00 34.00 26.75
☐ **Micronauts #46,** page 10 .... 26.00 34.00 26.75
☐ **Micronauts #46,** page 12 .... 22.00 28.00 22.90

MYERS, RUSS

☐ **Broomhilda,** daily strip from 1970 .... 60.00 85.00 70.00
☐ **Broomhilda,** Sunday page from 1972 .... 140.00 165.00 150.00

NINO, ALEX

☐ **The Burial Of Death,** oil painting, 42″ x 60″ .. 900.00 1200.00 1025.00

	Current Price Range		P/Y Average

ROMITA, JOHN

☐ **Amazing Spiderman** #107, page 20	26.00	34.00	27.10
☐ **Amazing Spiderman** #39, page 7	60.00	70.00	61.75
☐ **Amazing Spiderman** #39, page 9	60.00	70.00	61.75
☐ **Amazing Spiderman** #39, page 11	60.00	70.00	61.75
☐ **Amazing Spiderman** #39, page 19	60.00	70.00	61.75
☐ **Amazing Spiderman** #41, page 1	65.00	85.00	67.90
☐ **Amazing Spiderman** #41, page 12	50.00	60.00	52.00
☐ **Amazing Spiderman** #41, page 14	50.00	60.00	52.00
☐ **Amazing Spiderman** #41, page 16	50.00	60.00	52.00
☐ **Amazing Spiderman** #41, page 17	50.00	60.00	52.00
☐ **Amazing Spiderman** #43, page 1 (splash page)	65.00	85.00	67.90
☐ **Amazing Spiderman** #43, page 8	52.00	68.00	53.85
☐ **Amazing Spiderman** #43, page 9	52.00	68.00	53.85
☐ **Amazing Spiderman** #43, page 12	52.00	68.00	53.85
☐ **Amazing Spiderman** #43, page 13	52.00	68.00	53.85
☐ **Amazing Spiderman** #43, page 16	52.00	68.00	53.85
☐ **Amazing Spiderman** #43, page 17	52.00	68.00	53.85
☐ **Amazing Spiderman** #43, page 19	52.00	68.00	53.85
☐ **Amazing Spiderman** #210, page 6	8.50	11.50	9.10
☐ **Amazing Spiderman** #210, page 13	8.50	11.50	9.10
☐ **Daredevil** #14, page 11, featuring Foggy and Karen	22.00	28.00	22.50
☐ **Dr. Strange** #7, page 32, featuring Clea and de-mons	20.00	25.00	21.10
☐ **Incredible Hulk** #196, cover	65.00	85.00	67.25

ROMITA, JOHN JR.

☐ **Amazing Spiderman** #244, cover	50.00	70.00	51.75
☐ **Amazing Spiderman** #245, cover	50.00	70.00	51.75

ROMITA, JOHN JR. AND LAYTON

☐ **Iron Man** #123, page 26	22.00	28.00	22.50

ROSENBERGER, JOHN

☐ **The Fly** #11, page 1	26.00	34.00	26.90
☐ **The Fly** #11, page 3	26.00	34.00	26.90
☐ **The Fly** #11, page 6	26.00	34.00	26.90
☐ **The Fly** #11, page 7	26.00	34.00	26.90
☐ **The Fly** #11, page 9	26.00	34.00	26.90
☐ **The Fly** #11, page 11	26.00	34.00	26.90

ROTH, WERNER

☐ **X-Men** #20, page 1 (splash page)	80.00	100.00	84.15
☐ **X-Men** #21, page 1 (splash page), without logo	55.00	75.00	57.75
☐ **X-Men** #33, page 1 (splash page)	80.00	100.00	84.15

	Current Price Range		P/Y Average

SUYDAM, ARTHUR

☐ **Epic** #1, page 3 of the story *Heads*	350.00	450.00	345.00
☐ **Epic** #1, page 4 of the story *Heads*	350.00	450.00	345.00
☐ **Epic** #1, page 5 of the story *Heads*	350.00	450.00	345.00
☐ **Heavy Metal** for January, 1980, page 1 of the story *Food For My Children* (splash page)	350.00	450.00	345.00
☐ **Heavy Metal** for January, 1980, page 2 of the story *Food For My Children*	325.00	375.00	305.00
☐ **Heavy Metal** for January, 1980, page 3 of the story *Food For My Children*	325.00	375.00	305.00
☐ **Heavy Metal** for January, 1980, page 4 of the story *Food For My Children*	325.00	375.00	305.00

SWAN, CURT

☐ **Action** #383, page 1 (splash page from *The Killer Costume*)	22.00	28.00	23.70
☐ **Action** #489, page 1	22.00	28.00	23.70
☐ **Action** #495, page 1	22.00	28.00	23.70
☐ **Action** #515, page 13	11.00	14.00	11.45
☐ **Action** #515, page 14	11.00	14.00	11.45
☐ **Action** #515, page 16	11.00	14.00	11.45
☐ **Action** #515, page 18 (featuring Superman) ..	16.00	20.00	16.90
☐ **Action** #515, page 20 (featuring Superman) ..	16.00	20.00	16.90
☐ **Action** #527, page 12	16.00	20.00	16.90
☐ **Action** #527, page 13	16.00	20.00	16.90
☐ **Action** #527, page 14	16.00	20.00	16.90
☐ **Action** #527, page 15	16.00	20.00	16.90
☐ **Adventure** #377, pencil for cover (unpublished)	110.00	140.00	117.00
☐ **D.C. Presents** #6, page 15	11.00	14.00	11.45
☐ **Jimmy Olson** #75, page 5	45.00	55.00	46.40
☐ **Jimmy Olson** #122, cover	22.00	28.00	23.10
☐ **Superboy** #62, page 1	60.00	80.00	62.75
☐ **Superman** #233, page 2, inking by Murphy Anderson	25.00	32.00	26.20
☐ **Superman** #233, page 10, inking by Murphy Anderson	28.00	38.00	29.40
☐ **Superman** #242, page 6, inking by Anderson	22.00	28.00	23.30
☐ **Superman** #261, a page featuring Star Sapphire	22.00	28.00	23.30

YOUNG, CHIC

☐ **Blondie**, Sunday page from May 31, 1931, 17" x 16"	350.00	425.00	375.00

COMIC BOOKS

TOPIC: Comic books are collections of sequential cartoons that tell a story. Each illustrated frame progresses the story line.

TYPES: Comic books are categorized by publisher; for instance, D-C/National Periodical, Fawcett and Marvel.

PERIOD: Most collectible comic books were published from 1940 to the early 1970s.

COMMENTS: Comic books make wonderful collectibles because they are both historic and artistic.

ADDITIONAL TIPS: The following listings are organized by publisher. The order of the remaining information is: name and date of the series, name of the issue, issue number, main characters and descriptive information. For more information and extensive listings, please refer to *The Official Price Guide to Comic Books and Collectibles,* published by The House of Collectibles.

D-C/NATIONAL PERIODICAL PUBLICATIONS

	Current Price Range		P/Y Average

ACTION COMICS, 1938

	Current Price Range		P/Y Average
☐ **7, Superman,** (Pep Morgan, Scoop Scanlon), *Adventures of Marco Polo,* Superman on cover	1500.00	1775.00	1615.00
☐ **14, Superman vs. Ultra,** (Pep Morgan, Chuck Dawson, Clip Carson), *Adventures of Marco Polo,* (Zatara) on cover	425.00	485.00	440.00
☐ **17, Superman vs. Ultra,** last installment of *Adventures of Marco Polo,* Superman on cover . .	360.00	410.00	375.00
☐ **18, Three Aces,** begins	375.00	425.00	390.00
☐ **19, Superman vs. Ultra,** (Chuck Dawson, Clip Carson, Three Aces), Superman on cover	335.00	375.00	345.00
☐ **20, Superman vs. Ultra**	335.00	375.00	345.00
☐ **22, Last Chuck Dawson,** (had appeared continuously from #1)	265.00	315.00	275.00

Left to Right: *#9, Four Favorites,* © *Ace Magazines,*
$33.00–$41.00; *#1, Lightning,* © *Ace Magazines,*
$125.00–$150.00

	Current Price Range		P/Y Average
☐ **23, Superman vs. Luthor,** Luthor shown with red hair initially, first appearance of (The Black Pirate), created by Sheldon Moldoff, this short-lived series ran for only nineteen issues and was never regarded as a major feature but it was superbly illustrated	385.00	450.00	405.00
☐ **33, Mr. America,** origin of Mr. America, created by artist Bernard Bailey	275.00	330.00	290.00
☐ **37, Superman Charged With Violation Of Law,** first appearance of Congo Bill, created by Whitney Ellsworth, first appeared as a minor feature in D-C's More Fun Comics for eleven issues, then was dropped. But one month later, Action Comics introduced a new series of Congo Bill in which he suddenly became a movie star. The movie serial turned out to be one of the better ones of the 1940's	230.00	285.00	245.00
☐ **42, Origin Of The Vigilante,** last (Black Pirate, Mr. America) uses his cape as a flying carpet for the first time, Vigilante soon became one of D-C's star attractions and he headlined their new entry, Leading Comics, which began as a quarterly publication in January 1942	275.00	330.00	290.00

	Current Price Range		P/Y Average

☐ **43, The Vigilante vs. The Shade,** (Billy Gunn) **220.00 270.00 235.00**

☐ **45, The Vigilante,** first appearance of (Stuff, the Chinatown Kid) **215.00 260.00 225.00**

☐ **46, The Vigilante vs. Rainbow Man** **215.00 260.00 225.00**

☐ **51, Superman vs. The Prankster,** first appearance of (The Prankster) **220.00 270.00 235.00**

☐ **52, Origin Of Americommando,** cover features montage with Superman, Zatara, Congo Bill and The Vigilante **175.00 230.00 180.00**

☐ **56, Americommando vs. Dr. Ito** **130.00 160.00 140.00**

☐ **60, Lois Lane, Superwoman** **175.00 230.00 185.00**

☐ **64, Superman vs. The Toyman,** first appearance of (The Toyman) **160.00 200.00 170.00**

☐ **68, Lois Lane's,** (niece Susie is introduced) . . . **130.00 160.00 145.00**

BATMAN (1940)

☐ **2, The Crime Master,** (Adam Lamb), *The Case of the Missing Link* (Hackett and Snead, Professor Drake) **1150.00 1375.00 1230.00**

☐ **3, The Ugliest Man In The World,** (Carlson, Ugly Horde, Detective McGonicle), *The Crime School for Boys* (Big Boy Daniels), *Batman vs. the Cat Woman,* first appearance of Cat Woman in costume, cover: Batman and Robin running toward reader with capes flying **700.00 875.00 760.00**

☐ **4, More Whirlwing Adventures Of Batman And Robin,** *Blackbeard's Crew and the Yacht Society* (Thatch), cover: Batman climbing rope ladder **575.00 700.00 615.00**

☐ **5, The Case Of The Honest Crook,** (Smiley Sikes), *The Riddle of the Missing Card* (Queenie, Diamond Jack Deegan, Clumbsy), cover: Batman weighing fugitives on balance scale, "scales of justice." Last issue to be published quarterly. Switches to semi-monthly (six issues per year) with #6 . . . . **500.00 625.00 545.00**

☐ **6, Suicide Beat,** (Jimmy Kelly, Fancy Dan, Alderman Skigg) **350.00 450.00 385.00**

☐ **7, The Trouble Trap,** (Linda Page, Commissioner Gordon), *The People vs. the Batman* (Horatio Delmar, Weasel Venner, Freddie Hill) **350.00 450.00 385.00**

☐ **8, The Strange Case Of Professor Radium,** (Professor Rose), *Stone Walls Do Not Prison A Make, The Superstition Murders* (Johnny Glim), *The Cross-Country Crimes* (Namtab I/Batman; Nabtab is Batman spelled backwards) **375.00 450.00 400.00**

☐ **9, The Case Of The Lucky Law Breakers,** *The White Whale* (Capt. Burly), (Bob Crachit, Timmy Cratchit) **325.00 400.00 350.00**

☐ **10, Sheriff Of Ghost Town,** (Five Aces Frogel), *Report Card Blues* (Tommy Trent) **300.00 375.00 330.00**

☐ **11, Four Birds Of A Feather,** (Buzzard Benny, Joe Crow, Canary, The Penguin), *Payment in Full* (Joe Dolan) **275.00 330.00 290.00**

	Current Price Range		P/Y Average

☐ **12, The Wizard Of Words,** (The Jocker), *They Thrill to Conquer* (Joe Kirk) 300.00 375.00 330.00

☐ **13, The Story Of The 17 Stones,** (Rocky Grimes), *Comedy of Tears* (The Joker) 275.00 335.00 295.00

☐ **14, Prescription For Happiness,** (Pills Mattson), Swastika over the White House (Count Felix, Fritz Hoffner), *The Case Batman Failed to Solve* ... 275.00 335.00 295.00

☐ **15, Your Face Is Your Fortune,** (Elva Barr), *The Loneliest Man in the World* (Dirk Dagner, Tom Wick), *The Boy who Wanted to be Robin* (Knuckles Conger, Bobby Deen) 260.00 320.00 287.50

☐ **16, Grade-A Crimes,** (Winthrop, character without first name), *Here Comes Alfred* (Alfred the Butler), *Adventures of the Branded Tree* (Squidge, character without first name), *The Joker Reforms* (Joe Kerswag) 295.00 340.00 310.00

☐ **17, Adventure Of The Vitamin Vandals,** (Archie Gibbons), *The Penguin Goes a-Hunting, Rogues' Pageant* (Alfred the Butler) 140.00 170.00 152.75

☐ **18, The Secret Of The Hunter's Inn,** (Alfred the Butler, Tweed Cousins), first appearance of Police Stories 140.00 170.00 152.75

☐ **19, Collector Of Millionaires,** (Ali, Ali's Health Resort), *The Case of the Timid Lion* (The Joker), *Atlantis Goes to War* (Emperor Taro, Empress Lanya) 140.00 170.00 152.75

☐ **20, The Centuries Of Crime,** (Ecla Tate, Swami Meera Kell, The Joker), *Bruce Wayne Loses the Guardianship of Dick Grayson* (Alfred the Butler, Fatso Foley), *The Trial of Titus Keyes* (Slick Fingers/George Collins) 145.00 175.00 155.00

☐ **21, Batman And Robin Whoop It Up In Four Whirlwind Action Stories,** *The Streamlined Rustlers* (Brule, character without first name), *His Lordship's Double* (Lord Hurley Burleigh C.L.J. Carruthers), *The Three Eccentrics* (The Penguin), Blitzkreig Bandats (Chopper Gant, Hannibal B. Brown) 140.00 170.00 148.00

☐ **47, Special! The Peril-Packed Inside Story Of The Origin Of Batman!,** (retold), *The Chain Gang Crimes* (Warden Beltt, Whiskers Mob), cover: Batman (as a boy) reading Gotham Gazette with headline *Socialite Thomas Wayne Slain By Mystery Killer!* Thomas Wayne was Batman's father. The Gotham Gazette neglected to mention that Batman's mother was killed at the same time, although it is not clear whether she was also slain by the gunman or suffered a fatal heart attack as an onlooker 235.00 285.00 247.00

☐ **48, The Thousand Secrets Of The Batcave,** (Wolf Brando), *Fowls of Fate* (The Penguin), *Crime from Tomorrow* (Morton, character without first name) 60.00 80.00 65.00

	Current Price Range		P/Y Average

☐ **49, Scoop Of The Century,** (Jervis Tetch, Vicki Vale), *Batman's Arabian Nights* (The Crier, Professor Carter Nichols, The Joker) **65.00 85.00 72.75**

☐ **50, The Second Boy Wonder,** (Waxey Wilson), *Lights—Camera—Crime* (Vicki Vale, Stilts Tyler, Tom Macon) **60.00 80.00 64.85**

☐ **51, The Stars Of Yesterday,** (Rufus Lane), Pee -Wee the Talking Penguin, The Wonderful Mr. Wimble (Warts) **55.00 75.00 60.00**

☐ **52, Batman And The Vikings,** (Olaf Erickson, Professor Carter Nichols), *The Man with the Automatic Brain* (Alfred the Butler), *The Happy Victims* (The Joker, Mrs. Carlin) **60.00 80.00 64.50**
Note: Batman and the Vikings is another Prof. Nichols time travel story. This one is about the Viking exploration of North America in the 10th century A.D.

☐ **57, The Walking Mummy,** (Andrews, character without a first name—he was a museum curator), *The Funny Man Crimes* (The Joker) **45.00 60.00 49.00**

☐ **58, The Brand Of A Hero,** (Joaquin Murieta), *The State Bird Crimes* (The Penguin), *The Black Diamond* (Bulls-Eye Kendall, Barracuda Brothers, Nitro Nelson) Joaquin Murieta was a real-life desperado of the Old West, here worked into a time-travel piece **45.00 60.00 49.00**

☐ **59, Batman In The Future,** (Erkham, character without first name), *The Man who Replaced Batman* (Deadshot/Floyd Lawton, Commissioner Gordon), *The Forbidden Celler* (Professor Vincent) **40.00 55.00 44.75**

☐ **60, The Auto Circus Mystery,** (Lucky Hooton) **35.00 45.00 38.00**

☐ **61, The Birth Of Batplane II,** (Boley Brothers), *Wheelchair Crimefighter* (Vicki Vale), *Mystery of the Winged People* (The Penguin) **37.00 48.00 40.00**

SUPERMAN (1939)

☐ **2, Superman vs. Luthor,** first appearance of Luthor **2300.00 3000.00 2350.00**

☐ **4, Superman vs. Luthor** **1275.00 1500.00 1270.00**

☐ **10, Superman vs. Luthor** **400.00 500.00 395.00**

☐ **12, Superman vs. Luthor** **400.00 500.00 395.00**

☐ **19, Superman Movie Cartoons,** redone into book format **320.00 375.00 310.00**

☐ **20, Cover Taken From Hardcovered Superman Book,** (by this time Superman products of all kinds were one the market) **320.00 375.00 310.00**

☐ **30, Superman vs. Mr. Mxyztplk,** first appearance of Mr. Mxyztplk; in later issues the name was spelled Mxyzptlk **235.00 285.00 215.00**

☐ **45, Lois Lane,** Superwoman (Hocus, Pocus) .. **210.00 260.00 190.00**

☐ **53, Anniversary Issue,** origin retold **245.00 310.00 215.00**

	Current Price Range		P/Y Average
☐ 54, **Superman vs. The Wrecker,** first appearance of the Wrecker	100.00	130.00	95.00
☐ 61, **Superman Returns To Krypton,** first Kryptonite story	150.00	200.00	145.00
☐ 76, **Guest Appearances By Batman And Robin**	275.00	340.00	245.00
☐ 78, **Lois Lane's Meeting With Lana Lang**	90.00	115.00	80.00
☐ 81, **Superman's Secret Workshop,** discovered by arch-foe Luthor	65.00	90.00	60.00
☐ 100, **Origin Retold,** for the second time	75.00	100.00	72.75
☐ 113, **The Superman Of The Past,** part I	28.00	37.00	26.75
☐ 114, **The Superman Of The Past,** part II	28.00	37.00	26.75
☐ 115, **The Superman Of The Past,** part III	28.00	37.00	26.75
☐ 123, **Girl Of Steel**	22.00	30.00	19.50
☐ 125, **Clark Kent In College**	26.00	33.00	21.75
☐ 127, **Return Of Titano**	25.00	32.00	22.00
☐ 128, **Kryptonite Story**	27.00	37.00	23.50
☐ 130, **Krypto Grows Up**	26.00	33.00	23.00
☐ 133, **How Parry White Hired Clark Kent**	20.00	25.00	17.25
☐ 135, **Lori Lemaris**	19.00	24.00	16.75
☐ 138, **Lori Lemaris**	19.00	24.00	16.75
☐ 139, **Story Of Red Kryptonite**	23.00	31.00	19.00
☐ 140, **Superman And The Son Of Bizarro**	19.00	24.00	18.00
☐ 141, **Superman Returns To Krypton And Meets Lyla Lerrol**	20.00	25.00	18.50
☐ 142, **Guest Appearances By Batman And Robin**	50.00	70.00	42.75
☐ 143, **Return Of Bizarro**	22.00	30.00	17.75
☐ 144, **Superboy's First Public Appearance**	28.00	37.00	23.50
☐ 145, **Great Boo-Boo**	16.00	21.00	14.75
☐ 146, **Superman's Life Story**	65.00	85.00	60.00
☐ 147, **Superman vs. The Legion Of Super Villains,** first appearance of *The Legion of Super Villains*	45.00	60.00	41.50
☐ 148, **Guest Appearance By Aquaman**	45.00	60.00	39.75
☐ 149, **Death Of Superman,** (fantasy)	50.00	70.00	43.50
☐ 156, **Last Days Of Superman,** with appearances by Batman and Robin	65.00	85.00	57.75
☐ 158, **Nightwing And Flamebird**	16.00	21.00	13.25

FAWCETT

CAPTAIN MARVEL (1941)

☐ 19, **Cover:** Santa Claus riding on Captain Marvel's back, with Mary Marvel alongside, wording (at upper right), "On sale every third Friday"	150.00	180.00	160.00
☐ 26, **Cover:** Captain Marvel soaring skyward against huge American flag, wording "War Stamps for Victory"	65.00	80.00	69.75
☐ 27, **Captain Marvel Joins The Navy,** cover: Captain Marvel rearing back to hurl bomb as if it were a football. Wording: "This is the insignia			

	Current Price Range		P/Y Average

recently adopted by a naval air squadron." (Referring to the lightning bolt on Captain Marvel's shirt-front) **60.00** **75.00** **63.25**

☐ **28, Cover:** Captain Marvel standing at attention with hands at sides, receiving medal being pinned on him by Unclm Sam while column of soldiers watch **55.00** **70.00** **58.15**

☐ **31, Captain Marvel In Buffalo, City Saved From Doom; Captain Marvel Fights His Own Conscience,** cover: Captain Marvel in close-up with an angel on one shoulder and a devil on the other (relating to the story, Captain Marvel fights his own conscience) **55.00** **70.00** **58.00**

☐ **42, Cover:** close-up portrait of Captain Marvel in Christmas wreath, wording "Season's Greetings" **40.00** **55.00** **44.50**

☐ **47, Cover:** Captain Marvel stands facing old man with long beard who holds scroll. On wall are names Solomon, Hercules, Atlas, Zeus, Achilles, Mercury. Also on cover, "Seventh War Loan, buy stamps and bonds" **40.00** **55.00** **44.50**

☐ **60, Captain Marvel Battles The Dread Atomic War,** cover: Captain Marvel in nuclear-devastated city, poised to catch falling atomic bomb in his arms **75.00** **100.00** **82.75**

☐ **70, Captain Marvel And The Horror In The Box,** cover: Captain Marvel, with astonished expression on face, peering into box that has a question mark on the lid **37.00** **45.00** **40.00**

☐ **73, Cover:** Captain Marvel speeds past sky-scraper (Woolworth Building in New York) **32.00** **38.00** **34.50**

☐ **97, Captain Marvel Is Wiped Out!,** cover: Captain Marvel standing full-length, while a hand with an eraser is "wiping out" the drawing. He exclaims, "Holy moley! What goes on?" **21.00** **27.00** **23.00**

☐ **104, Mr. Tawny's Masquerade,** cover: Mr. Tawny (with cape) delivering knockout punch, while Captain Marvel exclaims, "Attaboy, Mr. Tawny" **18.00** **24.00** **20.00**

☐ **112, Captain Marvel And The Strange Worrybird,** cover: Worrybird pacing ground with dark cloud of gloom over its head, as Captain Marvel stands by mystified **18.00** **24.00** **20.00**

MARVEL COMICS GROUP

AMAZING SPIDERMAN (1963)

☐ **1, Origin Retold,** *Spiderman vs. Chameleon,* (John Jameson, Fabulous Four), Ditko artwork, Lee stories, Dee lettering, inking unknown **1100.00** **1350.00** **1175.00**

	Current Price Range		P/Y Average
□ **2, Duel To The Death With The Vulture,** *Uncanny Threat of the Terrible Tinkerer,* Ditko artwork, Lee stories, Duffy lettering, inking unknown	420.00	500.00	460.00
□ **3, Spiderman vs. Dr. Octopus,** (Human Torch), Ditko artwork, Lee stories, Duffy lettering, inking unknown	220.00	260.00	237.00
□ **4, Nothing Can Stop The Sandman,** (Betty Brant), Ditko artwork, Lee stories	170.00	200.00	182.00
□ **5, Marked For Destruction By Dr. Doom,** (Fabulous Four), Ditko artwork, Lee stories, Rosen lettering	105.00	125.00	112.00
□ **6, Face To Face With The Lizard,** Ditko artwork, Lee stories, Simek lettering	105.00	125.00	112.00
□ **7, Return Of The Vulture,** Ditko artwork, Lee stories, Simek lettering	80.00	100.00	87.00
□ **8, Living Brain,** *Spiderman Tackles the Human Torch,* (Fabulous Four), Kirby and Ditko artwork, Lee stories, Simek lettering, Ditko inking	80.00	100.00	87.00
□ **9, Man Called Electro,** Ditko artwork, Lee stories, Simek lettering	80.00	100.00	87.00
□ **10, Enforcers,** (Fredrick Foswell, The Ox, Montana, Fancy Dan), Ditko artwork, Lee stories, Rosen lettering	80.00	100.00	87.00
□ **11, Turning Point,** (Spiderman Tracer, Dr. Octopus), Ditko artwork, Lee stories, Rosen lettering	45.00	60.00	52.00
□ **12, Unmasked By Dr. Octopus,** Ditko artwork, Lee stories, Simek lettering	45.00	60.00	52.00
□ **13, Menace Of Mysterio,** Ditko artwork, Lee stories, Simek lettering	45.00	60.00	52.00
□ **14, Green Goblin,** (Hulk, Enforcers, Ox, Montana, Fancy Dan), Ditko artwork, Lee stories, Simek lettering, (premium value because of Hulk appearance)	80.00	100.00	87.00
□ **15, Kraven The Hunter,** (Chameleon), Ditko artwork, Lee stories, Simek lettering	45.00	60.00	52.00

COOKBOOKS

PERIOD: Cookbooks have been published for close to 500 years.

ORIGIN: European in origin, the earliest cookbooks usually featured recipes for medicine.

COMMENTS: Rare first edition cookbooks, and those published before 1850, can be very expensive. However, most collectible cookbooks are reasonably priced. Many cookbooks from the early 20th century were given away as advertising premiums.

CONDITION: Cookbooks were usually heavily used so they are not in mint condition. Notations in margins are common.

ADDITIONAL TIPS: The following listings are alphabetical according to the author's name. For further information, refer to *The Official Guide to Kitchen Collectibles,* or *The Official Guide to Old Books and Autographs,* published by The House of Collectibles.

	Current Price Range		P/Y Average
☐ **Acton, Eliza,** *The English Bread-Book for Domestic Use,* practical receipes for many varieties of bread, etc. London, 1857, clothbound	40.00	53.00	45.00
☐ *Adventures In Good Cooking And The Art of Carving In The Home,* Duncan Hines, Inc., 1947	3.00	7.00	4.50
☐ **Allen, Elaine,** *Watkins Salad Book,* J.R. Watkins Co., 1946	6.00	10.00	8.50
☐ **Allen, H. Warner,** *Sherry,* London, 1934, clothbound	12.00	17.00	14.00
☐ **Allen, Mrs. Ida Cogswell Bailey,** *Golden Rule Cook Book,* Golden Rule House, 1918	10.00	30.00	17.50
☐ **Ames, Richard,** *The Bacchanalian Sessions; or, The Contenion of Liquors: With a Farewell to Wine,* by the author of *The Search After Claret,* London, for E. Hawkins, 1693	250.00	325.00	265.00
☐ **Ames, Richard,** *Fatal Friendship, or, The Drunkard's Misery,* being a satry against hard drinking, London, for Randal Taylor, 1693, bound in calf. "Satry" meant, of course, "satire"	230.00	275.00	245.00
☐ *Archdeacon's Kitchen Cabinet,* Chicago, 1876	30.00	45.00	40.00
☐ **Armstrong, John,** *The Young Women's Guide to Virtue, Economy and Happiness With a Complete and Elegant System of Domestic Cookery,*			

Advertising Cookbooks,
1920s, each, $5.00-$8.00

	Current Price Range		P/Y Average
Newcastle (England), n.d. (c. 1819), with engraved frontis and ten engraved plates, calfbound, mainly a handbook for young ladies who intended going into domestic service	**100.00**	**130.00**	**120.00**
□ **Cornerstones**—*A Cookbook by Assistance League,* Marshalltown, Iowa, spiral bound, 441 pp., 1976	**4.00**	**8.00**	**5.50**
□ *Could I Have Your Recipe?* An international Cookbook published by The United Nations Nursery School, Geneva, Switzerland, spiral bound, 287 pp., 1957	**4.00**	**8.00**	**5.50**
□ **Croly, Mrs. J.C.,** *Jennie June's American Cookery Book,* N.Y., 1870	**40.00**	**53.00**	**48.00**
□ *Dainty Dishes for Slender Incomes,* New York, 1900	**20.00**	**28.00**	**23.00**
□ **Darby, Charles,** *Bacchanalia,* or, *A Desscription of a Drunken Club,* London, for Robert Boulter, 1680, folio, 16 pp., calfbound	**300.00**	**400.00**	**320.00**

	Current Price Range		P/Y Average

☐ **Decker, John W.,** *Cheese Making,* Wisconsin, 1909 .... 25.00 33.00 26.00

☐ **Degraf, Mrs. Belle,** *Asparagus For Delicacy And Variety,* Canners League of California, c. 1920s 4.00 14.00 7.00

☐ **De Loup, Maximillan,** *The American Salad Book,* McClure, Phillips & Co., New York, 1901 29.00 45.00 37.00

☐ *Dining And Its Amenities,* by *A Lover of Good Cheer,* New York, 1907 .... 25.00 33.00 28.00

☐ **Escoffier, A.,** *A Guide to Modern Cookery,* McClure, Phillips & Co., New York, 1907 .... 50.00 70.00 59.00

☐ *Experienced American Housekeeper,* Hartford, 1836, with four engraved plates, one of which is a folding plate, price given is for a sound copy 130.00 170.00 140.00

☐ **Farley, John,** *The London Art of Cookery and Housekeeper's Complete Assistant,* eighth edition, London, John Fielding, J. Scatcherd and J. Whitacker, 1796, with portrait and 12 engraved plates, showing menus for every month of the year 190.00 235.00 190.00

☐ **Farmer, Fannie M.,** *Food And Cooking For The Sick And Convalescent,* Little, Brown & Co., Boston, 1911 .... 25.00 35.00 30.00

☐ *Fifty Good Ways of Serving Woodcock Macaroni,* New York, 1919 .... 6.00 10.00 8.00

☐ **Frederick, Mrs. Christine,** *Meals That Cook Themselves,* Sentinel Mfg. Co., New Haven, 1915 .... 10.00 15.00 13.00

☐ **Gillette, Mrs. F.L.,** *White House Cook Book,* Chicago, 1889 .... 75.00 95.00 80.00

☐ **Lemery, Louis,** *A Treatise of all Sorts of Foods, both Animal and Vegetable: also of Drinkables,* giving an account how to choose the best sort of all kinds, London, 1745, calf-bound 250.00 325.00 275.00

☐ **Leslie, Miss,** *75 Receipes for Pastry, Cakes and Sweetmeats,* by a Lady of Philadelphia, Boston, n.d. (1828) 150.00 200.00 175.00

☐ **Leslie, Miss,** *Directions for Cookery,* Philadelphia, 1863, 59th edition 20.00 27.00 23.00

☐ *Lessons of Thrift Published for General Benefit,* by a member of the Save-All Club, London, 1820, with 12 colored aquatints by Cruikshank, bound in gilt morocco. Though largely a satirical work, the illustrations give a fairly accurate view of (for example) proceedings in a no-frills chophouse of the era. Theft of tableware was such a problem that knives, forks, etc., were chained to the table 200.00 260.00 230.00

☐ **Lincoln, Mary,** *The Peerless Cook Book,* Boston, 1901, softbound 14.00 19.00 16.00

☐ **Lincoln, Mrs.,** *Boston Cook Book, What To Do and What Not To Do in Cooking,* Boston, 1884 475.00 575.00 550.00

☐ **Lincoln, Mrs.,** *Carving and Serving,* Boston, 1915 .... 17.00 23.00 20.00

	Current Price Range		P/Y Average
☐ **Lincoln, Mrs. D.A.,** *Boston School Kitchen Textbook,* Boston, 1887	25.00	33.00	28.00
☐ **Lippman, B.F.,** *Aunt Betty's Cook Book,* Cincinnati, 1918	15.00	21.00	17.00
☐ **Llanover, Lady Augusta,** *The First Principles of Good Cookery,* London, 1867, illustrated, clothbound	70.00	90.00	80.00
☐ **Lockhart, Marion,** *Standard Cook Book for All Occasions,* New York, 1925	12.00	17.00	15.00
☐ **McCann, Alfred W.,** *Thirty Cent Bread,* New York, 1917, bound in boards. Alfred W. McCann hosted the first food-and cooking radio show	14.00	19.00	17.00
☐ **MacDougall, A.F.,** *Coffee and Waffles,* New York, 1927	11.00	16.00	12.00
☐ **MacKenzie, Colin,** *MacKenzie's Five Thousand Receipes,* Philadelphia, 1825	150.00	190.00	175.00
☐ **Maddocks, Mildred,** *The Pure Food Cook Book,* New York, 1914	17.00	24.00	20.00
☐ **Manchester, Herbert,** *The Evolution of Cooking and Heating,* published by Fuller and Warren, 1917	55.00	70.00	60.00
☐ **Nelson, Harriet S.,** *Fruits and Their Cookery,* New York, 1921	14.00	19.00	17.00
☐ *New Family Receipe-Book,* containing 800 truly valuable receipts in various branches of domestic economy, selected from the works of British and foreign writers, London, 1811, half calf	80.00	100.00	90.00
☐ *New Family Receipe-Book,* containing 800 truly valuable receipts in various branches of domestic economy, selected from the works of British and foreign writers, London, 1837 edition, half calf	70.00	90.00	75.00
☐ **Nichol, Mary E.,** *366 Dinners,* by "M.E.N." New York, 1892	20.00	27.00	23.00
☐ **Nicholson, Elizabeth,** *What I Know;* or, *Hints on The Daily Duties of a Housekeeper,* Philadelphia, 1856	130.00	165.00	150.00
☐ **Norton, Caroline T.,** *The Rocky Mountain Cook Book,* Denver, 1903	30.00	39.00	32.00
☐ **Nutt, Frederick,** *The Complete Confectioner,* or, *The Whole Art of Confectionary Made* Easy, with receipes for liqueurs, home-made wines, etc., new edition, with additions, London, 1809, with ten plates, half calf	150.00	190.00	170.00
☐ **Owen, Catherine,** *Culture and Cooking,* New York, 1881	30.00	39.00	32.00
☐ **Owen, Catherine,** *Choice Cookery,* New York, 1889	30.00	39.00	32.00
☐ **Owens, Mrs. F.,** *Cook Book and Useful Household Hints,* Chicago, 1883	20.00	27.00	23.00
☐ **Panchard, E.,** *Meats, Poultry and Game,* New York, 1919	14.00	19.00	16.00
☐ **Parloa, Maria,** *The Appledore* Cook Book, Boston, 1878	25.00	33.00	28.00

	Current Price Range		P/Y Average
☐ **Parloa, Maria,** *Choice Receipts,* Dorchester (Mass)., 1895, softbound	12.00	17.00	14.00
☐ **Paul, Mrs. Sara T.,** *Cookery from Experience,* Philadelphia, 1875	25.00	33.00	28.00
☐ **Parker, T.N.,** *Remarks on The Malt Tax,* with reference to the debate in the House of Commons on the 10th March, 1835, Shrewsbury (England), 1835, 34 pp.	25.00	33.00	28.00
☐ **Pereira, J.,** *A Treatise on Food and Diet,* New York, 1843	45.00	60.00	52.00
☐ **Poindexter, Charlotte M.,** *Jane Hamilton's Recipes,* Chicago, 1909	17.00	23.00	20.00
☐ **Poole, H.M.,** *Fruits and How to Use Them,* New York, 1890	20.00	27.00	23.00

COOKIE CUTTERS

TOPIC: Cookie cutters are outlines or molds that shape cookie dough into a specific design.

TYPES: Cookie cutters are generally divided into the hand-crafted variety versus the manufactured variety. They can also be categorized according to shape or design.

PERIOD: Cookie cutters have been widely used since at least the 16th century. There is evidence that they have existed in some form for thousands of years.

ORIGIN: Cookie cutters are thought to have originated in Europe.

MATERIAL: The oldest cookie cutters are made of wood. These are seldom seen on the market today. Aluminum became popular around 1920, and plastic usurped aluminum around 1940. Other metals, especially tin, occur frequently also.

COMMENTS: Backplates can sometimes be used to approximate the date of manufacture of a cookie cutter. In the late 1800s, these backings were trimmed to echo the shape of the cutter design. After the turn of the century, backplates were usually rectangular.

ADDITIONAL TIPS: Scarcity and age are not good indicators of cutter prices. In general, the price depends on the quality of the piece and the interest the individual collector has in it. Cutters with names on them are often more valuable than similar nameless ones. The following listings are organized by design.

	Current Price Range		P/Y Average
☐ **Acorn,** metal, European	4.00	7.00	6.00
☐ **Animals,** tin	8.00	15.00	8.50
☐ **Bear,** metal, oval backplate, holes form a star	12.00	18.00	15.00
☐ **Bear,** metal, trimmed backplate, two holes, 6¼"	75.00	100.00	83.00
☐ **Bear,** tin, 4" high	15.00	25.00	16.00
☐ **Bird,** aluminum, 4¾"	1.00	2.50	1.75
☐ **Bird,** metal, flying, handle, 2¾" x 5¼"	20.00	29.00	24.50
☐ **Bird,** metal, flying, two holes, 4¾"	100.00	125.00	112.50
☐ **Bird,** metal, standing, one hole, 3¾"	20.00	30.00	25.00
☐ **Bird,** tin, 3" long	20.00	35.00	19.00
☐ **Butterfly,** tin	15.00	26.00	19.00
☐ **Cat,** metal, sitting, curling tail, one hole, handle, 5"	110.00	125.00	117.00
☐ **Cat,** metal, sitting, French	20.00	30.00	25.00
☐ **Chick,** metal, holes form a star, 4"	17.00	25.00	21.00
☐ **Chick,** tin	10.00	20.00	10.50
☐ **Christmas Tree,** metal, thick trunk, handle, 4⅝"	80.00	95.00	87.50
☐ **Christmas Tree,** tin, 4¾"	4.00	6.50	5.25
☐ **Circle,** aluminum, open handle, late 1800s	7.00	10.00	8.50
☐ **Circle,** metal, crimped, handle, 4"	5.00	8.00	6.50
☐ **Circle,** tin, handle, 3" diameter	2.00	4.00	3.00
☐ **Club (of cards),** tin, 3½" long, 1¾" high	1.00	3.00	2.00
☐ **Deer,** tin, jumping	30.00	42.00	31.00
☐ **Diamond,** metal, painted wood handle	.50	1.50	1.00
☐ **Dog,** metal, Husky, one hole, 3⅜" x 4⅜"	35.00	50.00	42.50
☐ **Donkey,** tin, lying down	16.00	26.00	19.00
☐ **Duck,** metal, 4"	5.00	8.00	7.00
☐ **Duck,** metal, embossed, "Davis Baking Powder"	4.00	8.00	6.00
☐ **Elephant,** metal, one hole, 4½"	100.00	115.00	107.50
☐ **Fish,** metal, handle, 6"	20.00	35.00	27.50

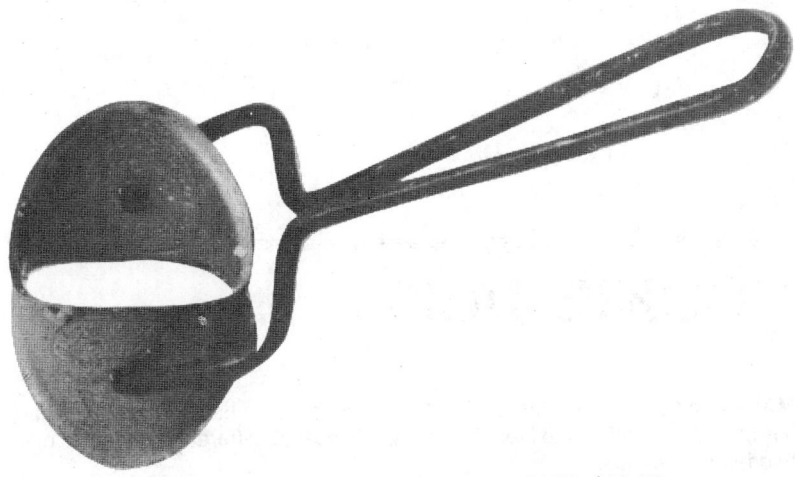

Cookie Cutter, *aluminum, late 19th c.,* **$6.50-$10.00**

	Current Price Range		P/Y Average
☐ **Gingerbread Man,** aluminum, 6″	3.50	6.50	5.00
☐ **Gingerbread Man,** plastic, with crown, yellow	1.00	3.50	2.25
☐ **Goose,** tin, flying	32.00	47.00	37.00
☐ **Guitar,** tin	20.00	30.00	21.00
☐ **Heart,** metal, painted wood handle	.50	1.50	1.00
☐ **Heart,** metal, two holes, handle, 4½″	40.00	65.00	47.50
☐ **Heart,** tin	4.00	10.00	5.50
☐ **Horse,** metal, prancing, three holes, 5¼″	135.00	160.00	148.00
☐ **Horse,** tin	12.00	24.00	13.00
☐ **Lamb,** aluminum, 4″	1.00	3.50	2.25
☐ **Leaf,** metal, crimped border, interior design ...	12.00	20.00	16.00
☐ **Lion,** metal, standing, two holes, 4½″	10.00	15.00	12.50
☐ **Man on Horseback,** tin	15.00	21.00	17.00
☐ **Man,** tin, stylized	20.00	30.00	21.00
☐ **Multiple Forms (animals),** metal, Mexican	3.00	7.00	5.00
☐ **Peacock,** tin	18.00	30.00	21.00
☐ **Pig,** tin	33.00	46.00	37.00
☐ **Pitcher,** metal, two holes, handle, 5¼″	90.00	110.00	100.00
☐ **Rabbit,** metal, handle, 3″	5.00	15.00	10.00
☐ **Rabbit,** tin	10.00	25.00	13.00
☐ **Santa Claus,** tin	11.00	18.00	13.00
☐ **Set,** tin, "Junior Card Party Cake Cutters," a heart, spade, diamond and club, 2″	10.00	15.00	12.50
☐ **Spade,** tin, handle, 3½″	2.00	4.00	3.00
☐ **Star in Crescent Moon,** metal, 2¾″	15.00	28.00	21.50
☐ **Star,** tin, six points	22.00	37.00	27.00
☐ **Swan,** metal, standing, two holes, 3¼″	25.00	40.00	32.50
☐ **Tulip,** metal, crimped border, contemporary ...	10.00	20.00	15.00
☐ **Whale,** metal, multiple holes, 3¾″	20.00	35.00	27.50
☐ **Woman,** aluminum, 5¼″	2.50	4.00	3.25
☐ **Woman,** metal, stylized, 3″	10.00	20.00	15.00

COOKIE JARS

MAKER: A variety of pottery and glassware companies have made cookie jars. It is sometimes difficult to identify the maker because different companies often used similar molds.

COMMENTS: Cookie jars are collected by those interested in pottery as well as those interested in kitchen items. Prices on cookie jars, unless very rare or very old, are usually moderate.

ADDITIONAL TIPS: The listings are alphabetical according to cookie jar shape. When available, a description, color, height and company are listed.

RECOMMENDED READING: For more information, see *The Official Price Guide to Pottery and Porcelain,* published by The House of Collectibles.

McCoy Cookie Jar, $10.00-$13.00

	Current Price Range		P/Y Average
☐ **Alice in Wonderland**	26.00	38.00	30.00
☐ **Animals,** "Cookies," in relief	19.00	36.00	24.00
☐ **Antique Wall Phone,** Cardinal pottery	15.00	25.00	28.00
☐ **Apple,** yellow, red, green, with lid	10.00	15.00	12.00
☐ **Autumn Leaf,** Hall China Company, c. 1936, 1939	75.00	80.00	77.00
☐ **Bananas,** McCoy pottery	16.00	24.00	18.00
☐ **Bear,** cookies in pocket, McCoy pottery	22.00	26.00	23.00
☐ **Bear,** manufactured by Royhimare	25.00	35.00	30.00
☐ **Bear,** McCoy pottery	20.00	26.00	22.00
☐ **Bear,** with open eyes, manufactured by A.B. Co.	20.00	30.00	24.50
☐ **Bears,** manufactured by Turnabout	12.00	17.00	14.50
☐ **Bell,** "Ring Fo Cookies," with lid	15.00	24.00	28.00
☐ **Bird Feed Sack,** manufactured by McCoy Pottery	10.00	20.00	16.00

	Current Price Range		P/Y Average
☐ **Bird,** flying, 9″ diameter	341.00	380.00	350.00
☐ **Brown,** with red flowers	14.00	20.00	16.00
☐ **Butter Churn,** flowers	19.00	25.00	22.00
☐ **Cat,** fluffy	23.00	33.00	26.00
☐ **Cat,** in basket	17.00	30.00	21.00
☐ **Cat,** leaves and flowers, with lid	15.00	23.00	18.00
☐ **Cat,** on beehive	17.00	26.00	20.00
☐ **Cat,** seated, yellow, black, pink, white	18.00	37.00	22.00
☐ **Chef,** manufactured by McCoy Pottery........	35.00	45.00	40.00
☐ **Chick,** on chicken........................	19.00	39.00	25.00
☐ **Chick,** wearing a beret, manufactured by A.B. Co..	25.00	35.00	27.00
☐ **Chick,** wearing a blue jacket	13.50	18.00	16.00
☐ **Clown,** head only, with black boater hat, lid is formed by hat, McCoy pottery	18.00	23.00	20.00
☐ **Clown,** in barrel, tan and white, McCoy pottery	16.00	24.00	18.00
☐ **Clown,** on stage, manufactured by A.B. Co. ...	25.00	37.00	29.00
☐ **Coffee Grinder,** with lid, McCoy pottery	18.00	25.00	20.00
☐ **Coffee Pot,** imprinted cookies and cup, white	14.00	20.00	16.00
☐ **Collegiate Owl,** manufactured by A.B. Co.	20.00	30.00	25.00
☐ **Cookie Boy,** manufactured by McCoy Pottery	25.00	35.00	29.00
☐ **Cookie Garage**	16.00	22.00	18.00
☐ **Cookie Truck,** manufactured by A.B. Co.	45.00	60.00	53.50
☐ **Coors USA**	25.00	35.00	30.00
☐ **Covered Wagon,** with lid, McCoy pottery	25.00	35.00	30.00
☐ **Cow,** manufactured by A.B. Co.	20.00	25.00	22.50
☐ **Cow,** manufactured by Brush	60.00	80.00	74.00
☐ **Daffodil,** gold trim, Hall China Company	27.00	33.00	30.00
☐ **Dog,** in basket............................	11.00	22.00	14.00
☐ **Donald Duck,** with nephews, Disney	32.00	40.00	35.00
☐ **Dutch Boy,** American Bisque	14.00	28.00	17.00
☐ **Dutch Boy,** manufactured by Shawnee	40.00	50.00	46.00
☐ **Dutch Girl,** brown, manufactured by Red Wing	35.00	45.00	39.50
☐ **Dutch Girl,** stoneware, manufactured by McCoy Pottery	20.00	30.00	24.50
☐ **Dutch Girl,** tulips on skirt	19.00	40.00	24.00
☐ **Dutch Windmill**	16.00	34.00	20.00
☐ **Ear of Corn,** manufactured by McCoy Pottery	55.00	65.00	59.50
☐ **Elephant,** grinning, blond, in blue bonnet and jacket, ice cream cone in trunk, with lid	16.00	24.00	18.00
☐ **Elephant,** honking, crossed legs	21.00	28.00	23.00
☐ **Elf's Head**	23.00	30.00	25.00
☐ **Farmer Pig,** manufactured by Shawnee	40.00	50.00	46.00
☐ **Fat Man**	16.00	28.00	20.00
☐ **Fat Policeman,** manufactured by R.R.P. Co. ..	25.00	35.00	29.50
☐ **Flowers,** stoneware, manufactured by McCoy Pottery	10.00	20.00	16.00
☐ **Flower Forms,** gold, pink, lilac, blue, raised gold stems, 2 handles	100.00	120.00	105.00
☐ **French Chef,** manufactured by Red Wing	40.00	45.00	42.50
☐ **Frog,** manufactured by Holiday	20.00	30.00	25.00
☐ **Frontier Scene,** manufactured by McCoy Pottery	25.00	35.00	29.50

	Current Price Range		P/Y Average
Gingerbread Man and Baker, "Cookies," hexagonal	16.00	24.00	18.00
Gingerbread Man, candy cane handle	32.00	60.00	36.00
Grandma, manufactured by A.B. Co.	35.00	45.00	39.50
Grandma, red skirt, glasses, hair bun forms lid	27.00	32.00	29.00
Hobby Horse, manufactured by McCoy Pottery	35.00	45.00	40.00
Honey Bear, manufactured by McCoy Pottery	20.00	30.00	27.50
Honeycomb, manufactured by McCoy Pottery	15.00	25.00	19.50
Humpty Dunpty, in cowboy attire, manufactured by Brugh	30.00	40.00	34.50
Humpty Dumpty, yellow, with lid	12.00	16.00	14.00
Jack-In-The-Box, manufactured by A.B. Co.	30.00	40.00	37.00
Kitchen Jar, pink, manufactured by Hull	7.00	15.00	9.50
Kitten, in basket, McCoy Pottery	22.00	26.00	24.00
Kitten, on barrel, manufactured by Hull	20.00	30.00	25.00
Kitten, on basketweave, manufactured by McCoy Pottery	30.00	40.00	34.50
Kitten, on beehive, manufactured by A.B. Co.	25.00	35.00	29.50
Lady Pig, manufactured by A.B. Co.	25.00	35.00	29.50
Lamb, manufactured by A.B. Co.	20.00	25.00	22.00
Lion, wears cowboy hat, manufactured by Balmont	30.00	40.00	34.50
Log Cabin, manufactured by McCoy Pottery	30.00	40.00	34.50
Ma and Pa Owls, manufactured by McCoy Pottery	25.00	35.00	29.50
Mammy, manufactured by McCoy Pottery	50.00	100.00	75.00
Mammy, red kerchief, "Mammy," Pearl china	18.00	25.00	20.00
Mickey And Minnie, manufactured by Turnabout	25.00	35.00	30.00
Milk Can, blue, white and gray, 9"	20.00	30.00	25.00
Monk, "Thou Shalt Not Steal"	26.00	50.00	35.00
Mother Goose, manufactured by McCoy Pottery	50.00	60.00	54.50
Owl, glossy brown, McCoy Pottery	15.00	25.00	18.00
Owl, white and brown, one eye closed, Shawnee Pottery Company	11.00	15.00	13.00
Pair of Boots, manufactured by A.B. Co.	40.00	50.00	44.50
Penguins, kissing, McCoy pottery	24.00	28.00	26.00
Picnic Basket, McCoy pottery	30.00	35.00	32.00
Pig, dressed as farmer, white, Shawnee Pottery Company	32.00	36.00	34.00
Pig, manufactured by Brush	60.00	80.00	74.00
Pig, Smiley, red bandana, flowers, Shawnee Pottery Company, with lid	30.00	40.00	35.00
Pineapple, McCoy Pottery	22.00	25.00	23.00
Polar Bear, manufactured by McCoy Pottery	22.00	32.00	27.00
Pot Belly Stove, black, McCoy Pottery	10.00	16.00	12.00
Puppy, holding sign, manufactured by McCoy Pottery	20.00	30.00	26.00
Puppy, in blue pot, manufactured by A.B. Co.	20.00	30.00	24.50
Rabbit In Hat, manufactured by A.B. Co.	30.00	45.00	39.00
Raggedy Ann, manufactured by McCoy Pottery	35.00	45.00	39.50

	Current Price Range		P/Y Average
☐ **Red And White,** with lid, 10″ diameter	26.00	50.00	35.00
☐ **Red Riding Hood,** with lid, Hull Pottery	30.00	40.00	33.00
☐ **Rooster,** tail is handle, with lid, pale green, Red Wing pottery	26.00	32.00	28.00
☐ **Rooster,** yellow, manufactured by McCoy Pottery	20.00	30.00	24.50
☐ **Sailor Boy,** manufactured by Shawnee	45.00	55.00	49.50
☐ **School Girl's Face,** glasses and pigtails, "Cooky," Abingdon Pottery	15.00	25.00	20.00
☐ **Schoolhouse Bell,** manufactured by A.B. Co.	20.00	30.00	24.50
☐ **Sheriff Pig,** manufactured by R.R.P. Co.	30.00	40.00	37.00
☐ **Strawberry,** manufactured by Sears	12.00	17.00	14.50
☐ **Strawberry,** McCoy Pottery	22.00	28.00	24.00
☐ **Sunset Scene,** house and church in background, jeweling on three legs and finial, 7½″	160.00	180.00	168.00
☐ **Teapot,** copper and bronze, McCoy Pottery ...	22.00	28.00	24.00
☐ **Toy Soldier,** manufactured by A.B. Co.	7.00	15.00	11.00
☐ **Train,** manufactured by A.B. Co.	25.00	35.00	29.50
☐ **Truck,** with perched bird, yellow	14.00	20.00	16.00
☐ **Tug Boat,** manufactured by A.B. Co.	55.00	65.00	59.50
☐ **Windmill,** blue, manufactured by McCoy Pottery	25.00	35.00	29.50
☐ **Wishing Well,** McCoy Pottery	16.00	24.00	18.00
☐ **Wise Bird,** manufactured by R.R.P. Co.	30.00	40.00	37.00
☐ **Woodsey Owl,** manufactured by McCoy Pottery	30.00	40.00	34.50

COPPER

DESCRIPTION: This versatile metal has been used extensively by mankind in every conceivable way. Copper is an excellent conductor of heat and electricity and is also very malleable. It has been made into wire, cooking utensils, coins, decorative objects and countless other useful items.

RECOMMENDED READING: For more in-depth information on copper you may refer to *From Hearth to Cookstove* by Linda Campbell Franklin and The *Official Price Guide to Kitchen Collectibles,* published by The House of Collectibles.

Copper Boiler, $75.00-$100.00

	Current Price Range		P/Y Average
☐ **Cream Skimmer**	35.00	45.00	36.00
☐ **Cup**	35.00	45.00	38.00
☐ **Dipper,** 19th century	55.00	72.00	63.00
☐ **Egg Poacher,** long iron handle, holds nine eggs	35.00	65.00	40.00
☐ **Egg Poacher,** two brass handles, holds 16 eggs, large	35.00	65.00	40.00
☐ **Dipper,** many types	25.00	50.00	35.00
☐ **Evaporating Pan,** iron bail handle, swinging, with ring handles	85.00	95.00	84.00
☐ **Funnel,** 23″ high	155.00	210.00	156.00
☐ **Funnel,** 8″ diameter	35.00	45.00	32.00
☐ **Funnel,** tube shaped, with screen attachment, 8″ diameter	35.00	45.00	32.00
☐ **Hot Water Bottle,** 12″	40.00	45.00	36.00
☐ **Hot Water Bottle,** egg shaped, with brass cap, unmarked	35.00	40.00	32.00
☐ **Hot Water Bottle,** circular, with brass cap, unmarked	35.00	40.00	33.00
☐ **Hot Water Bottle,** bail handle, brass lid, late 19th century	50.00	55.00	49.00
☐ **Hot Water Urn**	250.00	300.00	255.00
☐ **Hot Water Urn,** early 19th century	300.00	500.00	425.00
☐ **Kettle,** for apple butter, mid-1800's, dove-tail bottom, 25″ diameter	450.00	500.00	459.00

	Current Price Range		P/Y Average
☐ **Kettle,** apple butter, c. 1880–1900	75.00	125.00	82.00
☐ **Kettle,** copper with brass, wood handle, one gallon, Portugal	14.00	18.00	15.00
☐ **Kettle,** bail handle, iron, swinging, molded lip, iron stand	460.00	475.00	462.00
☐ **Kettle,** early 20th century	50.00	60.00	51.00
☐ **Kettle,** early 19th century	115.00	125.00	112.00
☐ **Kettle,** iron bail handle, jelly kettle	60.00	75.00	62.00
☐ **Kettle,** apple butter, used outdoors, 25″ diameter	110.00	130.00	115.00
☐ **Kettle,** apple butter, used outdoors, 28″ diameter	130.00	150.00	128.00
☐ **Kettle,** 19th century, kitchen, brass knop, 15″ high	90.00	110.00	92.00
☐ **Kettle,** mid 19th century, 9″	260.00	300.00	257.00
☐ **Kettle,** early American, 10″ in diameter, 15″ high	130.00	175.00	132.00
☐ **Lid,** set, 19th century, 6″ diameter	215.00	250.00	213.00
☐ **Measure,** pint	46.00	52.00	47.00
☐ **Measure,** quart	46.00	52.00	47.00
☐ **Measure,** set, one pint to 2½ quarts	170.00	190.00	172.00
☐ **Measure,** flared spout, soldered handle, narrowing sides, early 19th century, 11″	80.00	110.00	83.00
☐ **Measure,** set, 19th century, harvest measures	600.00	750.00	625.00
☐ **Measure,** 1 quart, handle, brass knob	50.00	60.00	55.00
☐ **Measure,** pours, sloping edges, holds one pint	25.00	30.00	26.00
☐ **Measure,** pours, sloping edges, holds one quart	30.00	35.00	32.00
☐ **Measures,** a trio of measures for rum, large to small, 19th century	600.00	750.00	615.00
☐ **Measuring Cups,** set, wide based, marked, seven in all, pure copper	1400.00	2000.00	1600.00
☐ **Milk Bucket,** iron bail, handle, late 19th century	100.00	125.00	105.00
☐ **Milk Churn,** 19th century, European, molded brass ring handles, 32″ high	850.00	1200.00	848.00
☐ **Milk Jug**	80.00	95.00	82.00
☐ **Milk Pail**	110.00	108.00	105.00
☐ **Mixing Bowl,** circular base, one handle, 15″ diameter, 8″ deep	45.00	65.00	48.00
☐ **Mixing Bowl,** 15″ diameter, 8″ deep	50.00	80.00	55.00
☐ **Miniatures,** pan, 5″ diameter, 8″ deep	10.00	16.00	14.00
☐ **Miniatures,** pan for frying, 5″ diameter, handle of heavy brass	12.00	22.00	16.00
☐ **Miniatures,** wash tub, brass trim, and handles, 3″ diameter	10.00	14.00	12.00
☐ **Miniatures,** kettle, pours, iron bail handle, swinging, 3″ diameter	9.00	14.00	12.00
☐ **Miniatures,** tea kettle, 2″ high, pure brass, European	7.00	12.00	8.00
☐ **Mold,** bird	30.00	45.00	32.00
☐ **Mold,** bundt	95.00	110.00	95.00
☐ **Mold,** Easter egg, rabbit	55.00	65.00	55.00
☐ **Mold,** jelly or pudding	50.00	70.00	53.00

	Current Price Range		P/Y Average
☐ **Mold,** quart size	30.00	45.00	32.00
☐ **Mold,** pint size	25.00	40.00	29.00
☐ **Mold,** circular base with fruit or floral motif, quart size	30.00	40.00	31.00
☐ **Mold,** circular base, with fruit or floral motif, pint size	15.00	26.00	15.00
☐ **Mold,** fluted with scroll design along edge, 8″	3.00	6.00	4.50
☐ **Mold,** twelve tube, c. 1860	130.00	150.00	129.00
☐ **Mold,** pan	140.00	155.00	138.00
☐ **Mold,** pan, iron, handle, hanging eye	150.00	165.00	149.00
☐ **Mold,** dull finish, copper handles, 6″ x 20″ diameter	150.00	165.00	149.00
☐ **Mold,** iron handle, 13″ diameter	70.00	75.00	68.00
☐ **Pitcher**	40.00	55.00	41.00
☐ **Plate,** 9″	10.00	20.00	12.00
☐ **Pot,** crafted by hand, handled, early 19th century, 15″ diameter	95.00	110.00	98.00
☐ **Pots,** hollow iron handles, tin interiors, with lids, set of three, 6″, 7″ and 8″ diameter	30.00	40.00	36.00
☐ **Reservoir,** from kitchen stove, 19″ x 8¾″ x 11½″	15.00	25.00	19.00
☐ **Salt Box**	50.00	65.00	52.00
☐ **Saucepan,** covered, one long brass handle, lined with tin, one quart	50.00	65.00	52.00
☐ **Saucepan,** covered, one long handle, lined with tin, two quart	50.00	67.00	52.00
☐ **Saucepan,** covered, one long brass handle, lined with tin, three quart	55.00	84.00	53.25
☐ **Saucepan,** covered, one long brass handle, lined with tin, four quart	60.00	93.00	65.00
☐ **Saucepan,** double boiler, one quart	35.00	43.00	39.00

COVERLETS

DESCRIPTION: Coverlets are bedspreads that have been woven on a loom.

VARIATIONS: The many types of designs produced by weavers fall into two categories: geometrics and Jacquards. The geometrics are the earliest coverlets made and they have small simple designs such as the star, diamond or snowball. The Jacquards, produced using a loom device made by Frenchman Joseph Jacquard, have curving, ornate designs such as flowers, birds and trees.

PERIOD: Coverlets were made from the 18th to the 20th century in the East, South and Midwest. Some are made today in isolated areas.

MAKER: The early geometric coverlets were woven at home usually by women. The Jacquards were more often made by professional male weavers. The Jacquard device enabled the weaver to put his name on his work, the simple loom didn't.

MATERIALS: Two threads are used in weaving. The warp threads, which are vertical, are usually cotton, and the weft threads are horizontal and usually wool. All-cotton or all-wool coverlets are fairly rare. Red and blue dye was primarily used until the middle of the 19th century when synthetic dyes brought a greater color variety.

COMMENTS: The Jacquards are more popular with collectors than the geometrics. Most coverlets, especially the geometrics, are reasonably priced. The Jacquards go for the highest prices. Prices are also higher for the more rare allcotton or all-wool coverlets. The development of the power loom brought an end to most manual loom weaving.

ADDITIONAL TIPS: The listings are identified as geometric or Jacquard. Following the identification are color, description and dates, when available.

RECOMMENDED READING: For further information contact the Colonial Coverlet Guild of America, 7931 Birchdale Ave., Elmwood Park, IL 60635.

	Current Price Range		P/Y Average
☐ **Geometric,** blue and white, double woven	175.00	210.00	185.00
☐ **Geometric,** blue and white, c. 1840	270.00	375.00	300.00
☐ **Geometric,** blue and white, design, c. 1830 ...	350.00	400.00	375.00
☐ **Geometric,** indigo and cream, double woven	300.00	400.00	320.00
☐ **Geometric,** log cabin design	300.00	375.00	315.00
☐ **Geometric,** red, white, blue, center seam	275.00	325.00	290.00
☐ **Jacquard,** black and white, birds and flowers	375.00	440.00	390.00
☐ **Jacquard,** blue and white, crossed rose sprays and stars center, potted rose plant border with eagle corners, double woven, c. 1850	750.00	800.00	760.00
☐ **Jacquard,** blue and white, floral and geometric motifs, house, horse and tree border, double woven, center seam, c. 1835	460.00	520.00	475.00
☐ **Jacquard,** blue and white, floral medallions and florals with American eagles and star border, double woven, c. 1830	575.00	650.00	600.00
☐ **Jacquard,** blue and white garlands and flowers, spread winged American Eagle, double woven, center seam, c. 1855	575.00	625.00	585.00
☐ **Jacquard,** blue and white, patriotic motif, signed, c. 1860	1050.00	1500.00	1200.00
☐ **Jacquard,** blue and white, rosettes, leaves, snowflakes, double woven	500.00	580.00	520.00

	Current Price Range		P/Y Average
☐ **Jacquard,** red and white, floral motif	350.00	450.00	365.00
☐ **Jacquard,** red and white, lilies and floral sprays, signed	375.00	425.00	385.00
☐ **Jacquard,** red, blue, green, white, double house border, single weave, center seam	750.00	800.00	765.00
☐ **Jacquard,** red, eagle motif, signed	400.00	450.00	410.00
☐ **Jacquard,** red, eagle motif, unsigned	400.00	480.00	415.00
☐ **Jacquard,** red, green, white, oak leaf and flower design	400.00	450.00	415.00
☐ **Jacquard,** red, gold, blue, stars and leaves with grapes on border, center seam, c. 1850	700.00	800.00	730.00
☐ **Jacquard,** red, tan, ivory, eagle motif, "Independence, Virtue, Liberty"	850.00	950.00	875.00
☐ **Jacquard,** red, white, blue, exotic birds	750.00	900.00	800.00
☐ **Jacquard,** red, white, blue, star and flower motif	350.00	450.00	365.00
☐ **Jacquard,** red, white, gold, bird medallions, double weave	340.00	420.00	360.00
☐ **Jacquard,** red, white, gold, green, central medallions and floral borders, double woven	350.00	450.00	365.00
☐ **Jacquard,** red, white, green, flowers, stars, spread winged American eagle	400.00	500.00	420.00
☐ **Jacquard,** tree of life, signed, c. 1948	525.00	550.00	600.00

CRACKER JACK MEMORABILIA

ORIGIN: This famous mixture of popcorn, peanuts, and molasses was developed in 1893 and sold at the Columbian Exposition in Chicago where it was an overnight sensation. In 1896 it was named Cracker Jack and in 1910 the prizes were introduced. At first coupons were used which the customer could trade for various prizes. The company began putting the actual prize in each box in 1912.

MATERIAL: Cracker Jack prizes have been made of lead, paper, porcelain, plastic, tin and wood.

	Current Price Range		P/Y Average

☐ **Clicker, Whistle,** metal, embossed CJ, 2″ 15.00 25.00 20.00
☐ **Corkscrew,** Angelus, metal, 3¾″ wide 25.00 50.00 37.50
☐ **Flip Book,** Charlie Chaplin, pre-1922 .... 50.00 75.00 62.50
☐ **Fortune Teller,** 2″ H. 25.00 50.00 37.50
☐ **Game # 1,** red, white and blue, 2½″ 20.00 50.00 35.00
☐ **Horse And Wagon,** metal, 2″ long 50.00 100.00 75.00
☐ **Hummer Band,** metal, embossed, 1″ diameter 15.00 25.00 20.00
☐ **Air Corps Wings,** metal, embossed 25.00 50.00 37.50
☐ **Badge,** junior detective, metal, embossed, 1¼″ 5.00 25.00 15.00
☐ **Baseball Card,** #124, Earl Moore, Buffalo Federals, red, white and black 25.00 75.00 50.00
☐ **Baseball Card,** #150, W.R. Johnston, Cleveland Americans, red, white, blue and black 25.00 75.00 50.00
☐ **Card,** #95, Victoria Cross Heroes series, 3″ x 2½″, made by Lowney 5.00 25.00 15.00
☐ **Charm For Bracelet,** blue celluloid, comical head of man fully shaped with chain attached to top of head 20.00 25.00 21.00
☐ **Clicker,** metal, black and silver, instructions on front, 2⅛″ H 5.00 25.00 15.00
☐ **Iron-Ons,** paper, set of four attached on a folded sheet, c. 1940–1950 .... 5.00 10.00 7.00
☐ **Jumper,** tin, frog, green and silver, 1⅞″, c. 1935 .... 25.00 35.00 28.00

Note: Jumpers were among the most numerous of Cracker Jacks premiums. These little novelties, always made of lightweight lithographed sheet tin, had a spring device on the underside. The end of the spring was pressed into a small wad of tar and the jumper placed on the ground. After a few seconds (or longer, depending on how hard you pressed) the spring worked itself free and the jumper sprang up into the air. Larger versions were commercially sold.

☐ **Magazine Advertisement,** Saturday Evening Post, June, 1919, red, white and blue 5.00 15.00 10.00
☐ **Magic Puzzle,** donkey, paper and plastic, 1½″ 5.00 15.00 10.00
☐ **Magic Puzzle,** fish 5.00 15.00 10.00
☐ **Magic Puzzle,** man with cigar, marked CJ Co. on reverse 5.00 15.00 10.00
☐ **Paper Booklet,** #12, Bess and Bill, 2½″ 15.00 50.00 32.50
☐ **Paper Frog,** outside is green black and white, opens to red and tan inside 15.00 25.00 20.00
☐ **Paper Golf Top,** red, white and blue, rules back, intact 15.00 50.00 32.50
☐ **Paper Prize,** Jack at the blackboard, turn dial and Jack writes and erases his name from blackboard, black, white, red, blue, and brown, 2″ square 25.00 75.00 50.00
☐ **Pin,** Lady 15.00 25.00 20.00
☐ **Pin,** Lady, celluloid, paper insert in back for "CJ 5 Cents" 15.00 25.00 20.00

	Current Price Range		P/Y Average
☐ **Pocket Watch**, tin, gold, black, and white, 1½" diameter	15.00	25.00	20.00
☐ **Postcard**, bears, #13	5.00	25.00	15.00
☐ **Postcard**, bears, #15	5.00	25.00	15.00
☐ **Puzzle Book**, #1, 4", copyright 1917	15.00	50.00	32.50
☐ **Puzzles**, #1–15, complete set	100.00	200.00	150.00
☐ **Rainbow Spinner**, blue and white on one side, other side is red, blue and yellow, 2½" long, 1940s	15.00	25.00	20.00
☐ **Sign**, cardboard, string at top for hanging, red, white and blue box on blue background, 11" x 15"	200.00	500.00	350.00
☐ **Spinner**, tin, red/white/blue with illustration of Cracker Jacks package, 1½"	10.00	15.00	12.00
Note: This was something like a top (very popular in the 1930s) but you spun it by hand without a string.			
☐ **Tin**, Coconut Corn Crisp, full color round tin, 8½" tall	45.00	60.00	49.00
☐ **Tin Stand-Up**, Harold Teen	25.00	50.00	37.50
☐ **Tin Stand-Up**, Orphan Annie	5.00	50.00	37.50
☐ **Tin Stand-Up**, Perry	25.00	50.00	37.50
☐ **Tin Top**	5.00	25.00	15.00
☐ **Tin Top**, fortune teller	25.00	50.00	37.50
☐ **Truck**, plastic, embossed on all four sides, gold, 1⅝" long, late 1940s	5.00	15.00	10.00
☐ **Truck**, tin, red, white and black, one side says Cracker Jack, the other says Angelus, 1⅝" long	15.00	25.00	20.00
☐ **Whistle**, metal, embossed CJ	15.00	50.00	32.50
☐ **Whistle**, paper, red and white, reverse marked CJ Whistle, 2" H	15.00	25.00	20.00
☐ **Whistle**, paper, 2⅜", rare	15.00	50.00	30.00
☐ **Whistle**, plastic, red and white, embossed, 1½", 1950s	5.00	15.00	10.00
☐ **Whistle**, tin, silver and blue, 2½", no later than 1940s	15.00	25.00	18.00

CROCKS

DESCRIPTION: A crock is a container made of thick earthenware. Early crocks were intended as storage containers for food.

PERIOD: Crocks were made in the U.S. as early as 1641. Most household crocks were made in the 19th century however, and those with an interior glaze were made after 1900.

COMMENTS: The automatic glassblowing machine, introduced in 1903, made glass bottle making easier and the use of pottery crocks declined. Today they are popular collectibles.

RECOMMENDED READING: For further information on crocks please refer to *The Official Price Guide to Bottles Old and New,* published by The House of Collectibles.

	Current Price Range		P/Y Average
☐ **Jug Style,** floral pattern, 2¾″ diameter	35.00	45.00	37.00
☐ **P.H. Alders, Compliments of The Eagle Saloon,** St. Joseph, MO, cream and brown, 3″ ..	35.00	45.00	37.00
☐ **Ale,** label, tan, 8½″	15.00	25.00	17.00
☐ **American Stone Ware,** in two lines, blue letters also near top a large six, gray, 13½″	32.00	42.00	35.00
☐ **F.A. Ames & Co.,** Owensboro KY in back, flat, tan and brown, 3½″	38.00	48.00	43.00
☐ **Anderson's Weiss Beers,** 7¼″	10.00	16.00	12.00
☐ **Armour & Company,** Chicago, jug, pouring spout, white, 7¼″	24.00	30.00	26.00
☐ **B. & J. Arnold,** London, England, Master Ink, dark brown, 9″	15.00	25.00	18.00
☐ **B & H,** cream, 3″	30.00	40.00	33.00
☐ **Bass & Co.,** NY, cream, 9½″	18.00	27.00	21.00
☐ **Bean Pot,** label, light blue, 4¼″	5.00	8.00	6.00
☐ **L. Beard,** on shoulder, cream and blue, blob top, 8½″	20.00	26.00	22.00
☐ **Bellarmine Jug,** superb mask, two horseshoe decorations below mask, 13″	26.00	36.00	30.00
☐ **Biscuit Slip Glaze Stone Porter,** blob top with small impressed ring for string, firmly impressed towards base, J, Heginbotham, Kings Arms,			

Western Stoneware Jar, *impressed Monmouth, Ill, 2,*
$45.00-$65.00

	Current Price Range		P/Y Average
Stayley Bridge, reserve has other letters impressed below shoulder which cannot be clearly deciphered: UBL?T ??? ?EA TODY, towards base are a further possible 14 characters which cannot be deciphered, MINT STATE and EARLY 1800's, 9½"	50.00	70.00	56.00
□ **Compliments of Beniss & Thompson,** Shelbyville, KY, tan and brown, 3¾"	30.00	42.00	35.00
□ **Jas. Benjamin, Stoneware Depot,** Cincinnati, OH, blue stencil lettering, mottled tan, 9"	38.00	48.00	42.00
□ **Jas. Benjamin, Stoneware Depot,** Cincinnati, OH, blue stencil lettering, tan, 13½"	38.00	48.00	42.00
□ **Black's Family Liquor Stone,** H.P. Black, 2042–43 Fresno in blue glaze letters, 1 gal. jug, ivory and dark brown	30.00	40.00	33.00
□ **Bitter,** label, olive, brown trim, 10¼"	35.00	50.00	40.00
□ **B.B. Bitter Mineral Water,** Bowling Green, MO, white, five gallon, 15"	35.00	50.00	38.00
□ **Black Family Liquor Store,** stamped in blue glaze, brown and tan, gallon	20.00	28.00	23.00
□ **Blanchflower & Sons,** homemade, four price medals, GT, Yarmouth, Norfolk, cream with black, six sided lid	20.00	28.00	22.00
□ **Blue Picture Print Ginger Jar,** picture extends entire circumference of jar, building and junk in sail, 3½"	25.00	35.00	27.00

	Current Price Range		P/Y Average

☐ **Blue Print Ointment Pot Beach & Barnicott,** successors to Dr. Roberts Bridgeport, poor man's friend, crisp print . . . . | 12.00 | 18.00 | 14.00

☐ **Blue Top And Print Cream Pot,** Golden Pastures, thick rich cream, chard, picture of maid milking cow . . . . | 14.00 | 21.00 | 16.00

☐ **Brownings Pale Ale,** Lewes, sparkled biscut glazed finish, string rim at neck, cork closure, impressed, 8¾″ . . . . | 18.00 | 24.00 | 20.00

☐ **Brownings Pale Ale,** Lewes, potters mark: Stephen Green's Lambeth . . . . | 18.00 | 24.00 | 20.00

☐ **Boston Baked Beans,** HHH on back, brick color. 1½″ . . . . | 6.00 | 10.00 | 7.00

☐ **Boston Baked Beans,** OK on back, brick color, 1½″ . . . . | 6.00 | 10.00 | 7.00

☐ **Bowers Three Thistles Snuff,** cream color with blue lettering, two to three gallon . . . . | 40.00 | 55.00 | 45.00

☐ **Burgess, John & Son,** anchovy paste, warehouse 107 stand, black print on white, 3½″, curved shoulder type, print 2″ x 2¾″ . . . . | 30.00 | 40.00 | 33.00

☐ **Bryant & Woodruff,** Pittsfield, ME, handled jug, blue gray, 7″ . . . . | 26.00 | 37.00 | 29.00

☐ **Bynol Malt & Oil,** Allen & Hanbury's, black on white, print 2¾″ x 3¾″, height, lots of writing on this pot, 4 1/5″ . . . . | 20.00 | 27.00 | 22.00

☐ **Butter,** no label, handle, blue-gray decoration, 4″ . . . . | 26.00 | 37.00 | 28.00

☐ **Butter,** no label, blue-gray decoration, 5¼″ . . . | 20.00 | 30.00 | 24.00

☐ **California Pop,** pat. Dec. 29, 1872, blob top, tan, 10½″ . . . . | 60.00 | 80.00 | 65.00

☐ **California Cough Balm,** dose teaspoon full, children ½, 10-brown, crock jug with handle, 3¼″ | 95.00 | 125.00 | 103.00

☐ **Cambridge Springs Mineral Water,** in two lines, 2½″, brown and tan . . . . | 20.00 | 30.00 | 23.00

☐ **Canning,** inscribed Hold Fast That Which is Good, dark brown, 6½″ . . . . | 25.00 | 36.00 | 28.00

☐ **Canning,** wax sealer, 6″ . . . . | 22.00 | 30.00 | 24.00

☐ **Canning,** wax sealer, reddish brown, 8″ . . . . . . | 22.00 | 30.00 | 24.00

☐ **Canning,** blue with a gray decorative design, 8½″ . . . . | 22.00 | 30.00 | 24.00

☐ **Canning,** mustard color, 7″ . . . . | 18.00 | 24.00 | 20.00

☐ **Canning,** maple leaf design in lid, caramel color, 6″ . . . . | 12.00 | 18.00 | 14.00

☐ **Canning,** brown, 5″ . . . . | 16.00 | 22.00 | 17.50

☐ **Canning,** wax channel, brown, 8½″ . . . . | 17.00 | 24.00 | 18.00

☐ **Canning,** reddish brown, green on the inside, 6¾″ . . . . | 18.00 | 24.00 | 19.00

☐ **Canning,** crude, brown, 4″ . . . . | 12.00 | 18.00 | 13.00

☐ **Canning,** wax sealer, dark brown, 5½″ . . . . | 16.00 | 24.00 | 18.00

☐ **Canning,** wax sealer, tan, 5½″ . . . . | 16.00 | 24.00 | 18.00

☐ **Canning,** wax sealer, dark brown, 5½″ . . . . | 12.00 | 17.00 | 14.00

☐ **Canning,** wax sealer, dark brown, 6½″ . . . . | 11.00 | 16.00 | 13.00

☐ **Canning,** wax sealer, mottled gray, 5″ . . . . | 10.00 | 15.00 | 12.00

	Current Price Range		P/Y Average
☐ **Canning,** wax sealer, brown, 5½"	13.00	18.00	14.50
☐ **Canning,** barrel, dark brown, 5½"	13.00	18.00	14.50
☐ **Canning,** lid, star design, dark brown, 8¾" ...	18.00	25.00	20.00
☐ **Canning,** dark brown, 7½"	16.00	22.00	17.00
☐ **Canning,** tan, 9"	18.00	25.00	20.00
☐ **Canning,** wax channel, brown, 7½"	18.00	25.00	20.00

CURRENCY

DESCRIPTION: Currency notes issued by the federal government, as a medium of exchange ("legal tender").

MAKER: Today all U.S. paper money is produced by the U.S. Department of Printing and Engraving at Washington, D.C. Early specimens were contracted for with private firms. From its origin to the present day, all U.S. paper money has been engraved. This is considered the most difficult process to counterfeit.

MATERIALS: A special paper is used for U.S. paper money, of high quality and with tiny blue and red threads running through it. This paper is not available to the public.

MARKS: Various standard markings appear on U.S. paper money, including the Treasury Seal, district number, district name, control number, and the serial number. The serial number is green and appears twice on each note, at the lower left and upper right. When the numbers on a note are not alike, or missing, or wrongly positioned, it is regarded as a freak note and commands a premium price.

COMMENTS: Traditionally, collectors were interested only in the early types or "large size" currency. (In 1929 the government reduced the physical size of notes to their present proportions.) Today, all paper money is collectible, though common specimens must be in strictly uncirculated condition to be regarded as such.

ADDITIONAL TIPS: Paper money deteriorates in circulation very rapidly. When a note is said to be uncirculated it has no creases, wrinkles, fading, or signs of fatigue; the paper is crisp and the printing fresh and bright. Notes in very deteriorated condition, with holes or corners missing, etc., are not deemed collectible unless the type is very rare.

Early U.S. paper money is often found with tiny pinholes, even when the condition is otherwise excellent. This is due to the common practice among old-time storekeepers of impaling notes on nails, before the use of cash registers. Since this defect is so commonplace, it does not cause a great reduction in value, unless the hole occurs on the portrait.

Twenty Dollar Note, *Federal reserve bank note, 1929, portrait of President Jackson, small size,* **$20.00–$100.00**

ONE DOLLAR NOTES (1969) FEDERAL RESERVE NOTES
(Small Size)   NOTE NO. 18A

SERIES OF 1969—ELSTON-KENNEDY, GREEN SEAL

Boston 2.70	Cleveland ...2.70	Chicago 2.70	Kansas City 2.70
New York 2.70	Richmond ...2.70	St. Louis 2.70	Dallas 2.70
Philadelphia ..2.70	Atlanta 2.70	Minneapolis 2.70	San Francisco ..2.70

SERIES OF 1969A—KABIS-KENNEDY, GREEN SEAL

Boston 2.70	Cleveland ...2.70	Chicago 2.70	Kansas City 2.70
New York 2.70	Richmond ...2.70	St. Louis 2.70	Dallas 2.70
Philadelphia ..2.70	Atlanta 2.70	Minneapolis 2.70	San Francisco ..2.70

SERIES OF 1969B—KABIS-CONNALLY, GREEN SEAL

Boston 2.70	Cleveland ...2.70	Chicago 2.70	Kansas City 2.70
New York 2.70	Richmond ...2.70	St. Louis 2.70	Dallas 2.70
Philadelphia ..2.70	Atlanta 2.70	Minneapolis 2.70	San Francisco ..2.70

SERIES OF 1969C—BANUELOS-CONNALLY, GREEN SEAL

Boston 2.15	Cleveland ...2.15	Chicago 2.15	Kansas City 2.15
New York 2.15	Richmond ...2.15	St. Louis 2.15	Dallas 2.15
Philadelphia ..2.15	Atlanta 2.15	Minneapolis 2.15	San Francisco ..2.15

SERIES OF 1969D—BANUELOS-CONNALLY, GREEN SEAL

Boston 2.15	Cleveland ...2.15	Chicago 2.15	Kansas City 2.15
New York 2.15	Richmond ...2.15	St. Louis 2.15	Dallas 2.15
Philadelphia ..2.15	Atlanta 2.15	Minneapolis 2.15	San Francisco ..2.15

SERIES OF 1974—NEFF-SIMON, GREEN SEAL

Boston 2.15	Cleveland ...2.15	Chicago 2.15	Kansas City 2.15
New York 2.15	Richmond ...2.15	St. Louis 2.15	Dallas 2.15
Philadelphia ..2.15	Atlanta 2.15	Minneapolis 2.15	San Francisco ..2.15

SERIES OF 1977—MORTON-BLUMENTHAL, GREEN SEAL

Boston 2.10	Cleveland ...2.10	Chicago 2.10	Kansas City 2.10
New York 2.10	Richmond ...2.10	St. Louis 2.10	Dallas 2.10
Philadelphia ..2.10	Atlanta 2.10	Minneapolis 2.10	San Francisco ..2.10

SERIES OF 1977A—MORTON-MILLER, GREEN SEAL

Boston 2.10	Cleveland ...2.10	Chicago 2.10	Kansas City 2.10
New York 2.10	Richmond ...2.10	St. Louis 2.10	Dallas 2.10
Philadelphia ..2.10	Atlanta 2.10	Minneapolis 2.10	San Francisco ..2.10

SERIES OF 1981—TORTEGA-REGAN, GREEN SEAL

Issued for all Federal Reserve Banks ....CURRENT

FIVE DOLLAR NOTES (1950–1963) FEDERAL RESERVE NOTES
(Small Size)   **NOTE NO. 57**

SERIES OF 1950—SIGNATURES OF CLARK-SNYDER, GREEN SEAL

BANK & CITY	A.B.P.	V.FINE	UNC.	BANK & CITY	A.B.P.	V.FINE	UNC.
☐ Boston	5.15	7.00	15.75	☐ Chicago	5.15	7.00	16.00
☐ New York	5.15	7.00	13.75	☐ St. Louis	5.15	7.00	17.00
☐ Philadelphia	5.15	7.00	15.00	☐ Minneapolis	5.15	7.00	17.50
☐ Cleveland	5.15	7.00	15.00	☐ Kansas City	5.15	7.00	17.00
☐ Richmond	5.15	7.00	14.75	☐ Dallas	5.15	7.00	17.00
☐ Atlanta	5.15	7.00	15.00	☐ San Francisco ...	5.15	7.00	16.00

SERIES OF 1950A—PRIEST-HUMPHREY, GREEN SEAL

Boston 14.25	Cleveland ..14.25	Chicago 14.25	Kansas City ...14.25
New York ...14.25	Richmond ..14.25	St. Louis 14.75	Dallas 14.25
Philadelphia .14.25	Atlanta 14.25	Minneapolis ...14.75	San Francisco .14.25

SERIES OF 1950B—PRIEST-ANDERSON, GREEN SEAL

Boston 13.60	Cleveland ..13.00	Chicago 12.00	Kansas City ...14.25
New York ...13.00	Richmond ..13.00	St. Louis 14.50	Dallas 13.80
Philadelphia .13.00	Atlanta 13.00	Minneapolis ...15.00	San Francisco .14.35

SERIES OF 1950C—SMITH-DILLON, GREEN SEAL

Boston 12.50	Cleveland ..12.85	Chicago 13.75	Kansas City ...13.65
New York ...12.25	Richmond ..12.85	St. Louis 12.85	Dallas 15.75
Philadelphia .12.85	Atlanta 12.85	Minneapolis ...13.75	San Francisco .14.25

SERIES OF 1950D—GRANAHAN-DILLON, GREEN SEAL

Boston 12.30	Cleveland ..12.30	Chicago 12.30	Kansas City ...12.75
New York ...12.30	Richmond ..12.30	St. Louis 12.30	Dallas 12.75
Philadelphia .12.30	Atlanta 12.30	Minneapolis ...12.75	San Francisco .12.30

SERIES OF 1950E—GRANAHAN-FOWLER, GREEN SEAL

New York ...16.25 Chicago ....17.00 San Francisco .16.50
This Note was issued by only three banks.

TEN DOLLAR NOTES (1934) FEDERAL RESERVE NOTES
(Small Size)   NOTE NO. 83B

SERIES OF 1934A—SIGNATURES OF JULIAN-MORGENTHAU, GREEN SEAL

BANK & CITY	A.B.P.	V.FINE	UNC.	BANK & CITY	A.B.P.	V.FINE	UNC.
☐ Boston	10.50	3.75	26.00	☐ Chicago	10.50	13.75	25.00
☐ New York	10.50	13.75	26.00	☐ St. Louis	10.50	13.75	31.00
☐ Philadelphia	10.50	13.75	26.00	☐ Minneapolis	10.50	13.75	31.00
☐ Cleveland	10.50	13.75	28.00	☐ Kansas City	10.50	13.75	25.00
☐ Richmond	10.50	13.75	29.00	☐ Dallas	10.50	13.75	25.00
☐ Atlanta	10.50	13.75	29.00	☐ San Francisco* ..	14.00	25.00	250.00

*San Francisco—1934A with brown seal and overprinted HAWAII on face and back, Special issue for use in combat areas during World War II. Value in V. Fine $45.00, Value in Unc. $220.00.

SERIES OF 1934B—SIGNATURES OF JULIAN-VINSON, GREEN SEAL

☐ Boston	10.75	15.00	29.00	☐ Chicago	10.75	15.00	29.00
☐ New York	10.75	15.00	29.00	☐ St. Louis	10.75	15.00	29.00
☐ Philadelphia	10.75	15.00	29.00	☐ Minneapolis	10.75	15.00	29.00
☐ Cleveland	10.75	15.00	31.00	☐ Kansas City	10.75	16.00	31.00
☐ Richmond	10.75	15.00	29.00	☐ Dallas	10.75	15.00	31.00
☐ Atlanta	10.75	15.00	29.00	☐ San Francisco ...	10.75	15.00	29.00

SERIES OF 1934C—SIGNATURES OF JULIAN-SNYDER, GREEN SEAL

☐ Boston	10.25	12.75	21.75	☐ Chicago	10.25	12.75	21.00
☐ New York	10.25	12.75	21.00	☐ St. Louis	10.25	12.75	21.00
☐ Philadelphia	10.25	12.75	21.00	☐ Minneapolis	10.25	12.75	22.00
☐ Cleveland	10.25	13.00	23.00	☐ Kansas City	10.25	12.75	22.00
☐ Richmond	10.25	12.75	21.00	☐ Dallas	10.25	12.75	22.00
☐ Atlanta	10.25	12.75	21.00	☐ San Francisco ...	10.25	12.75	21.00

SERIES OF 1934D—SIGNATURES OF CLARK-SNYDER, GREEN SEAL

☐ Boston	10.25	12.75	21.50	☐ Chicago	10.25	12.75	21.50
☐ New York	10.25	12.75	21.50	☐ St. Louis	10.25	12.75	21.50
☐ Philadelphia	10.25	12.75	21.50	☐ Minneapolis	10.25	12.75	23.00
☐ Cleveland	10.25	12.75	22.00	☐ Kansas City	10.25	12.75	23.50
☐ Richmond	10.25	12.75	21.50	☐ Dallas	10.25	12.75	22.00
☐ Atlanta	10.25	12.75	21.50	☐ San Francisco ...	10.25	12.75	21.50

TWENTY DOLLAR NOTES (1928) FEDERAL RESERVE NOTES
(Small Size)   NOTE NO. 99

SERIES OF 1928—SIGNATURES OF TATE-MELLON, GREEN SEAL

BANK & CITY	A.B.P.	V.FINE	UNC.	BANK & CITY	A.B.P.	V.FINE	UNC.
☐ Boston	22.00	28.00	65.00	☐ Chicago	22.00	28.00	53.00
☐ New York	22.00	28.00	57.00	☐ St. Louis	22.00	32.00	70.00
☐ Philadelphia	22.00	28.00	60.00	☐ Minneapolis	22.00	35.00	80.00
☐ Cleveland	22.00	28.00	60.00	☐ Kansas City	22.00	32.00	80.00
☐ Richmond	22.00	35.00	70.00	☐ Dallas	22.00	32.00	80.00
☐ Atlanta	22.00	32.00	65.00	☐ San Francisco	22.00	30.00	70.00

SERIES OF 1928A—SIGNATURES OF WOODS-MELLON, GREEN SEAL

BANK & CITY	A.B.P.	V.FINE	UNC.	BANK & CITY	A.B.P.	V.FINE	UNC.
☐ Boston	22.75	40.00	60.00	☐ Chicago	22.75	37.00	70.00
☐ New York	22.75	37.00	70.00	☐ St. Louis	22.75	40.00	65.00
☐ Philadelphia	22.75	37.00	60.00	☐ Minneapolis		NOT ISSUED	
☐ Cleveland	22.75	37.00	65.00	☐ Kansas City	22.75	45.00	85.00
☐ Richmond	22.75	40.00	70.00	☐ Dallas	22.75	35.00	75.00
☐ Atlanta	22.75	40.00	65.00	☐ San Francisco		NOT ISSUED	

TWENTY DOLLAR NOTES (1928) FEDERAL RESERVE NOTES
(Small Size)   NOTE NO. 100

SERIES OF 1928B—SIGNATURES OF WOODS-MELLON, GREEN SEAL
FACE AND BACK DESIGN SIMILAR TO PREVIOUS NOTE. NUMERAL IN
FEDERAL RESERVE SEAL IS NOW CHANGED TO A LETTER.

BANK & CITY	A.B.P.	V.FINE	UNC.	BANK & CITY	A.B.P.	V.FINE	UNC.
☐ Boston	21.85	31.50	53.00	☐ Chicago	21.85	31.50	53.00
☐ New York	21.85	31.50	53.00	☐ St. Louis	21.85	31.50	55.00
☐ Philadelphia	21.85	31.50	53.00	☐ Minneapolis	21.85	31.50	55.00
☐ Cleveland	21.85	31.50	53.00	☐ Kansas City	21.85	31.50	55.00
☐ Richmond	21.85	31.50	53.00	☐ Dallas	21.85	31.50	60.00
☐ Atlanta	21.85	31.50	55.00	☐ San Francisco	21.85	31.50	55.00

SERIES OF 1928C—SIGNATURES OF WOODS-MILLS, GREEN SEAL
ONLY TWO BANKS ISSUED THIS NOTE.

BANK & CITY	A.B.P.	V.FINE	UNC.	BANK & CITY	A.B.P.	V.FINE	UNC.
☐ Chicago	28.00	55.00	225.00	☐ San Francisco	28.00	55.00	225.00

TWENTY DOLLAR NOTES (1934) FEDERAL RESERVE NOTES
(Small Size)   NOTE NO. 100A

FACE AND BACK DESIGN SIMILAR TO PREVIOUS NOTE.
"REDEEMABLE IN GOLD" REMOVED FROM OBLIGATION OVER
FEDERAL RESERVE SEAL. SIGNATURES OF JULIAN-MORGENTHAU,
GREEN SEAL.

BANK & CITY	GOOD	V.FINE	UNC.	BANK & CITY	GOOD	V.FINE	UNC.
☐ Boston	——	29.00	50.00	☐ St. Louis	——	30.00	47.00
☐ New York	——	29.00	47.00	☐ Minneapolis	——	30.00	55.00
☐ Philadelphia	——	29.00	47.00	☐ Kansas City	——	30.00	47.00

BANK & CITY	GOOD	V.FINE	UNC.	BANK & CITY	GOOD	V.FINE	UNC.
☐ Cleveland	——	29.00	47.00	☐ Dallas	——	30.00	47.00
☐ Richmond	——	29.00	47.00	☐ San Francisco ..	——	30.00	47.00
☐ Atlanta	——	29.00	47.00	☐ *San Francisco			
☐ Chicago	——	29.00	47.00	(HAWAII)	50.00	150.00	925.00

CURRIER & IVES PRINTS

ORIGIN: Nathaniel Currier began his career in lithography in 1828. At that time, he was apprenticed, at the age of 15, to Pendleton of Boston, one of the earliest American lithographic firms known. After five years, he left and engaged in various business ventures, one of which was with Stodart in New York. It was at this time in 1834 that the print "Dartmouth College" was published by Currier.

The venture with Stodart was short-lived; and, in 1835, Currier started his own firm at 1 Wall Street in New York. James Ives joined the firm in 1852 as a bookkeeper, after being recommended to Nathaniel Currier by his brother Charles, who also worked in the business. (Ives was married to Charles' sister-in-law.) The firm was located in New York City during its entire existence but occupied several locations over the years.

DESCRIPTION: The firm was unique in its ability to combine artistic talent, skilled craftsmanship, appropriate technology, and merchandising acumen into a successful business enterprise. Well-known artists of the day including Maurer, Palmer, Tait, and Worth were a few who were employed at various times. Appropriate attention to detail is manifest in the work as examination of a clipper ship print or a country scene will attest. Only the finest materials were used: stones from Bavaria (where lithography was invented), lithographic crayons from France, and colors from Austria. The firm contributed to technology by inventing a lithographic crayon, reputed to be superior to any others available anywhere. It also produced a lithographic ink, which contained beef suet, goose grease, white wax, castile soap, gum mastic, shellac, and gas black. Innovative merchandising techniques were used. Mass distribution and low cost were the keys to success. Cost was important. Uncolored prints sold for as little as six cents each and even large-colored folios sold for no more than three dollars. Anyone could afford a print at these prices. Prints were sold door-to-door by peddlers, in the streets by pushcart vendors, in geographically remote places through distributors, and even overseas through agents. Although an estimated ten million prints were sold, only a small percentage are in existence today.

The prints were published in various sizes but are commonly grouped into folio sizes shown below:

Very Small	Up to approximately 7″ x 9″
Small	Approximately 8.8″ x 12.8″
Medium	Approximately 9″ x 14″ to 14″ x 20″
Large	Anything over 14″ x 20″

The sizes pertain to the picture only, not to the margin around the picture. Often, print owners trimmed the margins of the pictures. Therefore, an uncut print is more valuable than a pared one.

Most of the prints were made in black and white and then handcolored. Although occasionally sold uncolored, usually a group of workers colored the prints by working from a professional artist's rendition. Because of this method, different colorings of the same print were found. Folio sizes very small, small, and medium were completed in this manner. However, the large folios were sometimes partially printed in color and then finished by hand, usually by only one artist.

Currier and Ives were successful men who worked well together. Currier retired in 1880 and died in 1888. Ives continued to run the business until his death in 1895. Although the sons of both men ran the business from 1895, it soon dissolved in 1907.

COMMENTS: Currier and Ives' prints are not only attractive and historically informative, but they represent a sound investment value. Studies indicate these prints have increased in value by 300 to 500 percent in the past twenty years. For example, the large folio "The Life of a Hunter—A Tight Fix" sold in 1928 for $3,000. Recently it sold at an auction for $7,500.

Currier and Ives prints are found in public and private collections. A large collection exists at a New York City museum which holds over 2,885 of their prints. However, no known collection contains all of the prints because previously unknown titles are uncovered occasionally.

RECOMMENDED READING: For further information you may refer to *The Official Price Guide to Collector Prints*, published by The House of Collectibles.

THE BEST FIFTY (small folio)

	Current Price Range		P/Y Average
☐ 1. The Express Train - 1790*	750.00	1000.00	770.00
☐ 2. American Railroad Scene - Snowbound - 187*	900.00	1200.00	920.00
☐ 3. Beach Snipe Shooting - 445	900.00	1100.00	920.00
☐ 4. Ice-boat Race on the Hudson - 3021	1000.00	1800.00	1100.00
☐ 5. Central Park in Winter - 953	900.00	1200.00	920.00
☐ 6. The Star of the Road - 5701	250.00	500.00	270.00
☐ 7. The High Bridge at Harlem, N. Y. - 2810*	250.00	400.00	270.00
☐ 8. Maple Sugaring, Early Spring in the Northern Woods - 3975	400.00	600.00	410.00
☐ 9. Shakers Near Lebanon - 5475	600.00	900.00	620.00
☐ 10. Winter Sports - Pickerel fishing - 6747	750.00	900.00	780.00
☐ 11. The American Clipper Ship Witch of the Wave - 115	600.00	800.00	620.00
☐ 12. Gold Mining in California - 2412	700.00	900.00	720.00
☐ 13. The Great International Boat Race - 2623	800.00	1000.00	820.00

American Homestead Winter *by Currier and Ives,* $460.00–$635.00

	Current Price Range		P/Y Average
☐ 14. Wild Turkey Shooting - 6677	400.00	600.00	420.00
☐ 15. Perry's Victory on Lake Erie - 4754	400.00	550.00	420.00
☐ 16. Washington at Mount Vernon, 1797 - 6515	250.00	350.00	270.00
☐ 17. The Whale Fishery, "Laying On" - 6626 ...	900.00	1200.00	920.00
☐ 18. Chatham Square, New York - 1020	450.00	600.00	470.00
☐ 19. Water Rail Shooting - 6567*	500.00	650.00	520.00
☐ 20. The Sleigh Race - 5554*	500.00	800.00	520.00
☐ 21. Franklin's Experiment - 2128*	300.00	500.00	320.00
☐ 22. Washington Crossing the Delaware - 6523*	250.00	350.00	270.00
☐ 23. American Homestead Winter - 172	400.00	600.00	420.00
☐ 24. Washington Taking Leave of the Officers of His Army - 6547	250.00	350.00	270.00
☐ 25. Steamboat Knickerbocker - 5727	250.00	350.00	270.00
☐ 26. Kiss Me Quick! - 3349*	200.00	250.00	220.00
☐ 27. On the Mississippi Loading Cotton - 4607	250.00	350.00	270.00
☐ 28. Bound Down the River - 627	350.00	500.00	370.00
☐ 29. American Whalers Crushed in the Ice - 205	800.00	1000.00	820.00
☐ 30. Dartmouth College - 1446*	1000.00	1300.00	1100.00
☐ 31. Terrific Combat Between the Monitor, 2 Guns, and the Merrimac, 10 Guns - 5996*	350.00	500.00	370.00
☐ 32. General Francis Marion - 2250	200.00	300.00	220.00
☐ 33. Art of Making Money Plenty - 275	200.00	300.00	220.00
☐ 34. Hon. Abraham Lincoln - 2895*	150.00	250.00	170.00
☐ 35. Gen. George Washington (with cape) - 2261*			
....	150.00	250.00	170.00

	Current Price Range		P/Y Average
☐ 36. Black Bass Spearing - 543	1100.00	1300.00	1200.00
☐ 37. Early Winter - 1652	1500.00	2000.00	1600.00
☐ 38. Woodcock Shooting - 6773*	450.00	600.00	470.00
☐ 39. "Dutchman" and "Hiram Woodruff" - 1640	600.00	700.00	620.00
☐ 40. Great Conflagration at Pittsburg, Pa. - 2581	500.00	600.00	520.00
☐ 41. Bear Hunting, Close Quarters - 446*	1500.00	2000.00	1600.00
☐ 42. The Destruction of Tea at Boston Harbor - 1571	600.00	800.00	620.00
☐ 43. Cornwallis is Taken - 1258	250.00	400.00	270.00
☐ 44. Landing of the Pilgrims at Plymouth, 11th Dec., 1620 - 3435*	200.00	300.00	220.00
☐ 45. The Great Fight for the Championship - 2613	300.00	500.00	320.00
☐ 46. Benjamin Franklin - 499*	150.00	300.00	170.00
☐ 47. Noah's Ark - 4494*	150.00	200.00	170.00
☐ 48. Black Eyed Susan - 551*	125.00	150.00	140.00
☐ 49. The Bloomer Costume - 574*	150.00	175.00	160.00
☐ 50. The Clipper Yacht "America" - 1173*	700.00	1000.00	720.00

THE BEST FIFTY (large folio)

	Current Price Range		P/Y Average
☐ 1. Husking - 3008	4000.00	8500.00	4500.00
☐ 2. American Forest Scene - Maple Sugaring - 157	3000.00	4500.00	3200.00
☐ 3. Central Park Winter - The Skating Pond - 954	3000.00	5000.00	3200.00
☐ 4. Home to Thanksgiving - 2882	7000.00	8000.00	7200.00
☐ 5. Life of a Hunter - A Tight Fix - 3522	12000.00	15000.00	12500.00
☐ 6. Life on the Prairie - The Buffalo Hunt - 3527	5500.00	6000.00	5600.00
☐ 7. The Lightning Express Trains Leaving the Junction - 3535*	5000.00	6500.00	5200.00
☐ 8. Peytona and Fashion - 4763	7000.00	8000.00	7200.00
☐ 9. The Rocky Mountains - Emigrants Crossing the Plains - 5196	7500.00	10000.00	7800.00
☐ 10. Trolling for Blue Fish - 6158	3000.00	4000.00	3200.00
☐ 11. Whale Fishery - The Sperm Whale in a Flurry - 6628*	7000.00	8000.00	7200.00
☐ 12. Winter in the Country - The Old Grist Mill - 6738	5500.00	7000.00	5700.00
☐ 13. American Farm Scenes No. 4 (Winter) - 136	2000.00	4000.00	2200.00
☐ 14. American National Game of Baseball - 180	8000.00	10000.00	8200.00
☐ 15. American Winter Sports - Trout Fishing on Chateaugay Lake - 210*	3000.00	4500.00	3200.00
☐ 16. Mink Trapping - Prime - 4139	7500.00	8000.00	7600.00
☐ 17. Preparing for Market - 4870*	1500.00	3000.00	1750.00
☐ 18. Winter in the Country - Getting Ice - 6737	5000.00	7500.00	5500.00
☐ 19. Across the Continent - Westward the Course of Empire Takes its Way - 33	7500.00	8000.00	7600.00
☐ 20. Life on the Prairie - The Trappers Defense - 3528	5500.00	6000.00	5700.00
☐ 21. The Midnight Race on the Mississippi - 4116*	2000.00	3500.00	2200.00

	Current Price Range		P/Y Average
☐ 22. The Road - Winter - 5171	6000.00	8000.00	6200.00
☐ 23. Summer Scenes in New York Harbor - 5876	2000.00	3000.00	2200.00
☐ 24. Trotting Cracks at the Forge - 6169	2000.00	3500.00	2200.00
☐ 25. View of San Francisco - 6409	4000.00	6000.00	4200.00
☐ 26. Wreck of the Steamship "San Francisco" - 5492	3500.00	4500.00	3700.00
☐ 27. Taking the Back Track "A Dangerous Neighborhood" - 5961	5000.00	5500.00	5200.00
☐ 28. American Field Sports - Flush'd - 149	1500.00	3000.00	1600.00
☐ 29. American Hunting Scenes - A Good Chance - 174	1500.00	3000.00	1600.00
☐ 30. American Winter Scenes - Morning - 208 ..	4000.00	6000.00	4200.00
☐ 31. Autumn in New England - Cider Making - 322	2500.00	3500.00	2600.00
☐ 32. Catching a Trout - "We Hab You Now, Sar" - 845	800.00	1000.00	850.00
☐ 33. Clipper Ship "Nightingale" - 1159	5500.00	7000.00	5700.00
☐ 34. The Life of a Fireman - The Race - 3519 ..	2000.00	4000.00	2200.00
☐ 35. Mac and Zachary Taylor - Horse Race - 3848	1000.00	2000.00	1100.00
☐ 36. New England Winter Scene - 4420	3500.00	5000.00	3600.00
☐ 37. Rail Shooting on the Delaware - 5054	3500.00	5000.00	3600.00
☐ 38. Snowed Up - Ruffed Gouse - Winter - 5581	3000.00	4000.00	3200.00
☐ 39. Surrender of General Burgoyne at Saratoga - 5907	3000.00	3500.00	3200.00
☐ 40. Surrender of Cornwallis at Yorktown - 5906	3000.00	3500.00	3200.00
☐ 41. Clipper Ship "Red Jacket" - 1165*	4000.00	5000.00	4200.00
☐ 42. American Winter Sports - Deer Shooting on the Shattagee - 209	3000.00	5000.00	3200.00
☐ 43. The Bark "Theoxana" - 371	1500.00	2500.00	1700.00
☐ 44. The Cares of a Family - 814*	2000.00	2500.00	2100.00
☐ 45. The Celebrated Horse Lexington - 887* ...	1600.00	1800.00	1700.00
☐ 46. Grand Drive - Central Park - 2481	2000.00	3000.00	2100.00
☐ 47. The Great Fire at Chicago - 2615	2000.00	3000.00	2100.00
☐ 48. Landscape, Fruit and Flowers - 3440	1500.00	2500.00	1600.00
☐ 49. The Life of a Fireman - The Metropolitan System - 3516	2000.00	4000.00	2100.00
☐ 50. The Splendid Naval Triumph on the Mississippi - 5659	750.00	1000.00	780.00

Note: Those titles followed by an asterisk are known to appear on more than one composition.

CUT GLASS

DESCRIPTION: Cut glass features deep prismatic cutting in elaborate, often geometrical designs. The edges are very sharp, thus allowing light to be refracted easily. Its high lead content makes it heavier than most blown glass. It also has a distinct bell tone when struck.

ORIGIN: It developed during the 16th century in Bohemia and was very popular until the invention of molded pressed glass in America about 1825 which was an inexpensive imitation of cut glass. It enjoyed a revival during the Brilliant period of cut glass in America which dated from 1876–1916.

PROCESS: The making of cut glass was a time consuming process requiring the patience and talent of master craftsmen. The glass was handblown of the finest 35–45% lead crystal and poured into molds to produce the shaped piece, called a blank. These blanks were anywhere from ¼"–½" thick in order to achieve the deep cutting which distinguished this glass from later periods. The resulting finished product was, therefore exceedingly heavy.

The cutting and polishing was accomplished in four steps. The first step involved making the desired pattern on the blank with crayons or paint. Next the deepest cuts were made by rough cutting. This was accomplished by pressing the blank on an abrasive cutting wheel of metal or stone which was lubricated by a small stream of water and sand. In the third step, the rough cuts were smoothed with a finer stone wheel and water only. Finally, polishing or "coloring" was done on a wooden wheel with putty powder or pumice, in order to produce the gleaming brilliant finish.

RECOMMENDED READING: For more in-depth information on cut glass, you may refer to *The Official Price Guide to Glassware*, and *The Official Identification Guide to Glassware*, published by The House of Collectibles.

	Current Price Range		P/Y Average
☐ **Ashtray,** rectangular	55.00	80.00	62.00
☐ **Ashtray,** richly cut, signed	80.00	110.00	88.00
☐ **Basket,** floral design, handle, 10″	210.00	260.00	225.00
☐ **Basket,** scalloped edge, handle, 6″	160.00	210.00	175.00
☐ **Basket,** floral and miter cut, twisted handle, 8″	170.00	195.00	172.00
☐ **Bell,** diamond and fan	110.00	135.00	112.00

Cut Glass

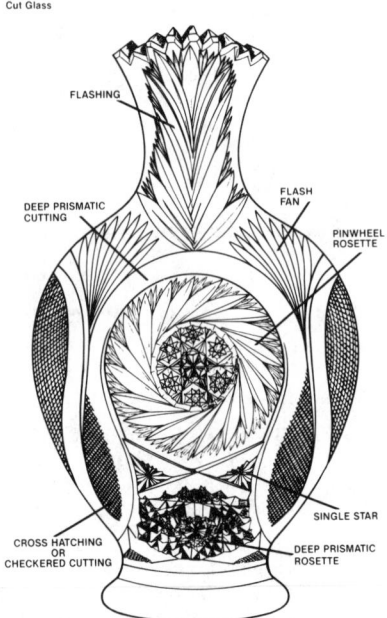

FLASHING

DEEP PRISMATIC
CUTTING

FLASH
FAN

PINWHEEL
ROSETTE

SINGLE STAR

CROSS HATCHING
OR
CHECKERED CUTTING

DEEP PRISMATIC
ROSETTE

PATTERN MOTIFS

	Current Price Range		P/Y Average
☐ **Bell,** star design	135.00	160.00	138.00
☐ **Bonbon,** diamond shape, 6″	70.00	95.00	78.00
☐ **Bonbon,** heart shape, 6″	80.00	110.00	88.00
☐ **Bonbon,** oval, 5¼″	28.00	38.00	30.00
☐ **Bonbon,** pedestal, pair	460.00	510.00	475.00
☐ **Candy Dish,** American, Clarke	90.00	140.00	110.00
☐ **Candy Dish,** sterling and crystal, Hawkes	160.00	210.00	175.00
☐ **Carafe,** block and fan	32.00	42.00	35.00
☐ **Carafe,** diamond and strawberry	185.00	210.00	188.00
☐ **Carafe,** hobstar and clover	55.00	80.00	62.00
☐ **Carafe,** prism and fan	80.00	110.00	88.00
☐ **Carafe,** Russian, starred buttons	235.00	335.00	275.00
☐ **Carafe,** water, Harvard, prism stem	110.00	135.00	112.00
☐ **Carafe,** water, hobstar and notched prism	80.00	110.00	88.00
☐ **Carafe,** water, pinwheel, crosscut diamond and flasked fan	90.00	120.00	98.00
☐ **Carafe,** water, pinwheel cut flowers	80.00	110.00	88.00
☐ **Carafe,** wine, hobstar and fan, sterling collar ..	135.00	160.00	138.00
☐ **Celery,** Harvard, Libbey	260.00	310.00	275.00
☐ **Celery,** hobstar and fan, signed Hawkes	135.00	160.00	138.00
☐ **Celery,** strawberry, diamond and fan, Hawkes	185.00	210.00	188.00
☐ **Champagne,** Russian, rayed star base	80.00	110.00	88.00

	Current Price Range		P/Y Average
□ **Compote,** Harvard, hobstar base, intaglio cut, 9″	310.00	360.00	325.00
□ **Compote,** hobstar, strawberry, diamond and fan, 8″	360.00	410.00	375.00
□ **Compote,** pinwheel, hobstar, prism cut, 7½″	135.00	160.00	138.00
□ **Compote,** square, signed Hoare	510.00	585.00	538.00
□ **Cordial,** crystal and silver, pair	760.00	835.00	780.00
□ **Cordial,** Russian	80.00	110.00	88.00
□ **Cordial,** sterling, blown glass	135.00	185.00	150.00
□ **Creamer,** hobstar	80.00	95.00	82.00
□ **Creamer,** pinwheel	55.00	70.00	58.00
□ **Creamer,** Waterford, c. 1930's	45.00	65.00	50.00
□ **Cruet,** Harvard, signed Hoare	160.00	185.00	162.00
□ **Cruet,** Middlesex	75.00	95.00	80.00
□ **Cruet,** prism, signed Libbey	155.00	175.00	155.00
□ **Cruet,** pyramid shape, 7½″	55.00	80.00	62.00
□ **Decanter,** Art Deco, pressed pattern of Chrysler Building	110.00	160.00	125.00
□ **Decanter,** Harvard, 8″	95.00	140.00	110.00
□ **Decanter,** hobstar, diamond and fan, cut stopper	160.00	185.00	162.00
□ **Decanter,** original stopper, numbered	185.00	210.00	188.00
□ **Decanter,** pineapple cut	110.00	135.00	112.00
□ **Decanter,** pineapple fan, brilliant cut	80.00	130.00	100.00
□ **Decanter,** pinwheel	185.00	210.00	188.00
□ **Dish,** cheese and cracker, signed Hoare	310.00	410.00	350.00
□ **Dish,** cheese and cracker, hobstar, strawberry and diamond	100.00	125.00	105.00
□ **Dish,** cheese, pinwheel	285.00	335.00	300.00
□ **Dish,** cheese, diamond and fan, covered	385.00	460.00	412.00
□ **Dish,** ice cream, hobstar	385.00	435.00	400.00
□ **Dish,** lemon, signed Hawkes	40.00	55.00	42.00
□ **Dish,** nut, signed Libbey, pair	285.00	335.00	300.00
□ **Dish,** olive, hobstar and comet	40.00	55.00	42.00
□ **Dish,** shell, signed Hoare	110.00	135.00	112.00
□ **Dish,** signed Omega	50.00	65.00	52.00
□ **Dish,** square, Imperal, signed Libbey	185.00	235.00	200.00
□ **Dish,** four sections, strawberry, and diamond point	160.00	210.00	175.00
□ **Dish,** condiment, heavily cut, c. 1900's	135.00	185.00	150.00
□ **Dish,** pedestal	285.00	335.00	300.00
□ **Glass,** etched, signed Libbey, pair	110.00	160.00	125.00
□ **Glass,** magnifying, Art Nouveau, sterling	135.00	185.00	150.00
□ **Glass,** magnifying, ivory handles	1250.00	1450.00	1300.00
□ **Glass,** magnifying, mother-of-pearl	135.00	185.00	150.00
□ **Goblet,** panel, prism cut	55.00	80.00	62.00
□ **Goblet,** prism cut, signed Hawkes	60.00	85.00	68.00
□ **Goblet,** Russian	110.00	135.00	112.00
□ **Goblet,** spiral pinwheel	40.00	55.00	42.00
□ **Goblet,** Vintage	55.00	80.00	62.00
□ **Inkwell,** crystal	235.00	310.00	262.00
□ **Inkwell,** silver and crystal	535.00	610.00	562.00
□ **Inkwell,** sterling lid, 2″	40.00	55.00	42.00

	Current Price Range		P/Y Average
☐ **Jar,** Art Nouveau, sterling lid	45.00	65.00	50.00
☐ **Jar,** candy, Hawkes, 11"	210.00	260.00	225.00
☐ **Jar,** mustard, signed Webb	55.00	80.00	62.00
☐ **Jar,** powder, Art Nouveau, hobstar and fan ...	110.00	135.00	112.00
☐ **Jar,** powder, Reine Des Fleurs	80.00	110.00	88.00
☐ **Jar,** powder, sterling lid, 3" x 3"	80.00	110.00	88.00
☐ **Jar,** tobacco, sterling top, 7"	135.00	160.00	138.00
☐ **Jug,** whiskey, Clarke	285.00	335.00	300.00
☐ **Knife Rest,** c. 1920's	22.00	32.00	25.00
☐ **Knife Rest,** ball ends, diamond cut	28.00	38.00	30.00
☐ **Knife Rest,** signed Hawkes	45.00	65.00	50.00
☐ **Lamp,** diamond cut, 17"	385.00	485.00	425.00
☐ **Lamp,** table, mushroom shade, 18"	485.00	585.00	525.00
☐ **Matchstrikes,** antique, pair..................	210.00	260.00	225.00
☐ **Muffineer,** sterling, cone shaped	80.00	130.00	100.00
☐ **Nappy,** hobstar and fan, signed Clarke	65.00	80.00	68.00
☐ **Nappy,** pinwheel	50.00	65.00	52.00
☐ **Nappy,** strawberry and diamond	45.00	60.00	48.00
☐ **Pitcher,** cider, prism and bull's eye, hobstar base, 8"	160.00	185.00	162.00
☐ **Pitcher,** claret, Encore by Strauss, 12"	260.00	310.00	275.00
☐ **Pitcher,** Harvard, signed Libbey, 8"	160.00	210.00	175.00
☐ **Pitcher,** hobstar and fan, 8"	160.00	210.00	175.00
☐ **Pitcher,** milk, Russian, starred buttons, 5"	360.00	435.00	380.00
☐ **Pitcher,** milk, deep cutting, twelve point star base, signed Hawkes, 5½"	185.00	235.00	200.00
☐ **Pitcher,** pinwheel, strawberry and diamond, 9"	135.00	160.00	138.00
☐ **Platter,** ice cream, oval, Russian	310.00	370.00	330.00
☐ **Punch Bowl,** two pieces, flower with star, box pattern	1250.00	1450.00	1300.00
☐ **Punch Bowl,** two pieces, signed Tuthill, 10½"	660.00	760.00	700.00
☐ **Relish Dish,** Harvard	95.00	125.00	100.00
☐ **Relish Dish,** hobstar, strawberry and diamond, 11½"	185.00	235.00	200.00
☐ **Relish Dish,** Royal, 7"	95.00	125.00	100.00
☐ **Rose Bowl,** Harvard, signed Libbey	310.00	360.00	325.00
☐ **Rose Bowl,** hobstar and fan, footed, 4"	185.00	235.00	200.00
☐ **Rose Bowl,** hobstar, diamond and fan	210.00	260.00	225.00
☐ **Salt and Pepper Shakers,** 6"	25.00	35.00	30.00
☐ **Stickpin,** antique cameo	160.00	185.00	162.00
☐ **Stickpin,** cameo	145.00	185.00	155.00

DAIRY COLLECTIBLES

DESCRIPTION: All items pertaining to the American dairy industry.

TYPES: Dairy collectibles include articles used on dairy farms such as pails, milking devices and churns, containers to transport and retail milk and other dairy products; and advertising items, brochures, signs generated by the dairy industry.

PERIOD: Though dairy farming in America dates to the early colonial era, collectibles available on the market date from the 1700s. Most of them are of the period from about 1850 to the early 1900s. This era ushered in large scale factory production of such items as milk cans and store bottles.

COMMENTS: This is another of various fields of collecting in which charm and historical appeal take precedence over immaculate condition.

	Current Price Range		P/Y Average
☐ **Bottle Filler,** three wooden legs, glass window at front, brass spigot, 36″ tall	27.00	34.00	30.00
☐ **Butter Churn,** Dazy Churn and Manufacturing Co., glass, model No. 40, made in St. Louis, square, four quart capacity, wood paddles	43.00	57.00	48.00
☐ **Centrifugal Butter Fat Tester,** Vermont Farm Machinery Co., Bellows Falls, Vermont, 100 revolutions per minute, embossed cover, brass gears and brass bottle holders, galvanized rack and tank, 8½″ x 6″ x 7″	90.00	115.00	98.00
☐ **Metal Sign,** Turner Centre Ice Cream, reads "It's Frozen Health," embossed black letters on yellow background, nailhole at top, 1928	90.00	105.00	95.00
☐ **Milk Bottle,** B & S Pasteurizing Co., Tamaque, Pennsylvania, glass, quart, round, slug plate . . .	6.00	8.00	7.00
☐ **Milk Bottle,** Bloomingdale Dairy Co., Inc., 136 to 40 Hunterdon St., Newark, New Jersey, glass, quart, round	7.00	10.00	8.20

	Current Price Range		P/Y Average
Milk Bottle, Chestnut Farm Chevy Chase Dairy, Washington, D.C., reads "Milk for Babies," glass, quart, round	6.00	8.00	7.00
Milk Bottle, D.A. Delano, Norway, Maine, "Tel. 6-24," glass, quart, round, slug plate	7.00	10.00	8.50
Milk Bottle, Edward Carlson, East Walpole, glass, quart, round	6.00	8.00	7.00
Milk Bottle, Granite Farm Pure Milk and Cream, Brunswick, Maine, glass, quart, round, slug plate	7.00	10.00	8.50
Milk Bottle, Laudholm Farms, Wells, Maine, glass, quart, round	7.00	10.00	8.50
Milk Bottle, The Lawson Milk Co., Akron, Ohio, glass, quart, round, slug plate	6.00	8.00	7.00
Milk Bottle, Petersburg Creamery, Petersburg, Ohio, reads "Safe Milk Every Morning," glass, quart, round	9.00	12.00	10.20
Milk Bottle, R.O. Stockman, Portland, Maine, glass, quart, round	6.00	8.00	7.00
Milk Bottle, Wonder Brook Farm, A.F. Smith, Kennebunk, Maine, glass, quart, round stubby style	9.00	12.00	10.25
Milk Bottle Cap, Parson's Jersey Dairy, plug type, 56 mm.	.10	.15	.12
Milk Bottle Cover, National Milk Co., Boston, aluminum with pouring lip	9.00	12.00	10.20
Milk Strainer, filter type, homemade filter holder	4.00	6.00	5.00
Porch Box, Blais Dairy, Lewiston, Maine, stenciled name, double box, holds eight milk bottles	22.00	28.00	24.00
Porch Box, Needham Dairy Inc., embossed double box, holds six milk bottles	20.00	26.00	22.00

DAUM NANCY GLASS

DESCRIPTION: August and Jean Daum of Nancy, France produced exquisite cameo glass, although they had never been recognized until recent years. Their work is similar to that of Gallé but the background colors differ; Daum-Nancy cameo glass often has orange and yellow grounds as contrasted to the cream ground so often used by Gallé. This glass was produced from 1900 through the 1920s.

RECOMMENDED READING: For more in-depth information on Daum Nancy glass you may refer to *The Official Price Guide to Glassware* and *The Official Identification Guide to Glassware,* published by The House of Collectibles.

Vase, Daum Nancy, *French Cameo glass, sterling base and feet, thistle motif, 5",* **$550.00-$650.00**

	Current Price Range		P/Y Average

☐ **Beaker,** flaring cylinder, gray shading to light pink and green, enameled black winter landscape, signed, 6" high, c. 1910 . . . . 600.00 800.00 610.00

☐ **Bottle,** compressed spherical body, inverted bell shaped lid, mottled gray shading to lavender, overlaid and enameled in lavender and green, gilding, cut with violets and leaves, strapwork on base, signed, 4" high, c. 1910 . . . . 700.00 800.00 710.00

☐ **Bottle,** perfume, stopper, ovoid shape flattened on two sides, tapering to cylinder neck, concave disc-shaped stopper, mottled blue background, overlaid, cut and enameled with yellow iris and green leaves, signed, 5½" high, c. 1910 . . . . . . 600.00 700.00 620.00

☐ **Bottle,** perfume, stopper, ovoid shape, short cylinder neck, fan-shaped stopper, gray background shading to darkish-yellow and pink, cut and enameled with wildflowers in blue, red, and gray, gilding, 3½" high, c. 1910 . . . . 550.00 650.00 565.00

☐ **Bowl,** elongated diamond shape, waisted shoulder, dipped rim, mottled pink and blue background, overlaid and enameled with flowers and leaves in blue, green, dark brown, signed, 12" high, c. 1910 . . . . 800.00 1000.00 850.00

☐ **Bowl,** enameled, short ovoid body, background of yellow sea and orange and grey sunset, overlaid with greyish-brown sailboats, signed, 5¼" high, c. 1900 . . . . 400.00 600.00 420.00

☐ **Bowl,** enameled, frosted and yellow background, cut with trailing violets and leaves enameled in light green and lavender, 4⅜" high, c. 1900 . . . 300.00 350.00 320.00

☐ **Bowl,** fish bowl shape, shading from green at neck to pale green at base, cut and enameled into bowl is river scene, signed, 5½" high, c. 1900 . . . . 350.00 450.00 375.00

☐ **Box,** covered, bulging circular, domed lid with knop finial, mottled brown and green with gilt foil inclusions, signed, 6" diameter, c. 1925 . . . . 400.00 500.00 420.00

☐ **Box,** covered, circular, domed lid, mottled gray background, overlaid in pink, green, red, cut with blossoms and leaves, signed, 3½" diameter, c. 1915 . . . . 300.00 500.00 325.00

☐ **Box,** covered, flattened circular lid, enameled gray winter scene, bowl enameled with river scene, opalescent background, signed, 6" diameter, c. 1910 . . . . 800.00 1000.00 825.00

☐ **Box,** covered, waisted spherical shape, domed lid, mottled aquamarine and gray shading to dark blue, overlaid in green and blue, cut with peacock feathers, signed, 6" diameter, c. 1910 . . . . 900.00 1100.00 935.00

☐ **Creamer,** ovoid shape, applied silver handle with foliage, silver flattened lid chased with lilies of the valley and leaves, opalescent, enameled scene with windmills and sailboats in charcoal, signed, 4¼" high, c. 1910 . . . . 600.00 800.00 625.00

	Current Price Range		P/Y Average

Dish, clover shape, mottled ochre, etched and enameled with columbines and leaves in rust and green, signed, 5¾" diameter, c. 1915 .... **400.00 600.00 450.00**

Ewer, elongated teardrop, applied loop handle, short circular foot, mottled yellow and orange, overlaid and enameled in red and green poppies and leaves, band of flowers around base, 9½" high, c. 1910 .... **800.00 1200.00 850.00**

Figure, woman in classical dress, standing on rectangular base, hand raised over head, glass shading progressively downward from light purple to green and dark purple, signed, 10" high, c. 1915 .... **3500.00 4500.00 3600.00**

Goblet, domed, cylinder stem with lobe, domed circular foot, cut with croix de Lorraine and hatched scrolls, enameled in red, gray, black, and white croix de Lorraine, heraldic crests, and thistles, gilding, signed, 4¼" high, c. 1890 .... **800.00 1000.00 830.00**

Lamp, domed shade with upper section lobed, on three-arm support of wrought-iron, baluster shape stand with knopped neck and circular spreading foot, deep blue shading to light blue with gold foil inclusions, signed, 18½" high, c. 1920 .... **1500.00 2000.00 1600.00**

Lamp, lobed domed shade supported by wrought-iron angular arms, baluster standard, knopped above the slightly domed foot, mottled yellow-brown background overlaid in lavender, cut with lake scene, signed, 14¾" high, c. 1910 .... **6000.00 7000.00 6100.00**

Lamp, lobed domed shade with uneven edge, supported by angular wrought-iron arms, baluster standard with spiraling grooves and knopped above slightly domed foot, mottled blue shading to green, standard mottled in green shading to blue-green and lavender, signed, 21½" high, c. 1915 .... **700.00 800.00 720.00**

Pitcher, ovoid shape, slightly flaring rim with small spout, scrolling handle, mottled blue shading to green, cut and enameled with wildflowers and leaves, signed, 3½" high, c. 1910 .... **700.00 800.00 720.00**

Pitcher, slender cylindrical body, flat shoulder, straight cylindrical neck, elongated spout, streaked burgundy sides overlaid in purple shading to blue, cut around neck and shoulder with scrolling strapwork against a tooled ground, sides tooled with lily blossoms and leaves, signed, 16½" high, c. 1900 .... **800.00 900.00 850.00**

Salt, circular bowl shape with two notched portions of the rim extending as handles, gray background, enameled Dutch scene of the seashore in gray, signed, 1¾" high, c. 1910 .... **300.00 400.00 320.00**

	Current Price Range		P/Y Average

☐ **Tumbler,** cylinder shape, expanding towards the rim, gray streaked with ochre, burgundy, and yellow, overlaid in ochre, green, yellow, blue, burgundy, and rust, cut with leafy branches with raspberries, signed, 5″ high, c. 1915 . . . . 600.00   800.00   610.00

☐ **Vase,** baluster shape tapering towards the neck, waisted neck and base, knopped base with spreading foot, mottled gray streaked with green and mustard background, etched and enameled with wildflowers, leaves, and grass in pink, green, and brown, signed, 16¾″ high, c. 1915 . . . . 625.00   775.00   615.00

☐ **Vase,** cylindrical, wide foot, spotted, gold and orange evenly to blue-green, signed, 25″ high . . . 770.00   800.00   760.00

☐ **Vase,** wide top tapers to bottom, pastoral scene, no animals shown, blue, gold and green, signed, 6″ high 435.00   500.00   465.00

DECOYS

TOPIC: A decoy is a representation of some animal used to lure others of that species within shooting range.

TYPES: Decoys most often represent waterfowl, but frog, fish, owl and crow decoys are not uncommon. Decoys can be sold, hollow or slatbodied. They can be either of the floating variety or the "stick-up" variety, which is driven into the ground.

PERIOD: Decoys produced after the mid-nineteenth century are most popular among collectors.

ORIGIN: American Indians have made and used decoys since 1000 A.D.

MAKERS: Famous decoy carvers include Ira Hudson, Charles Wheeler, Albert Laing and Mark Whipple.

MATERIALS: Decoys are usually carved out of wood, although metal and other materials are found.

COMMENTS: Enthusiasts usually collect decoys by carver, species or fly-way (the path of migration). Decoys made for actual use are more favored by collectors than those intended only for show.

TIPS: The condition of the paint on a decoy is a good indicator of age. Many cracked layers of paint mean that the decoy is probably old. Original paint is favored by collectors.

	Current Price Range		P/Y Average
☐ **B.W. Teal,** P. Wilcoxen	75.00	125.00	105.00
☐ **B.W. Teal,** glass eyes, pre-1900	1300.00	1700.00	1500.00
☐ **B.W. Teal,** preening, Ohio..................	50.00	100.00	87.50
☐ **Beach Duck,** papier-mache, paper label, Mackey	170.00	220.00	195.00
☐ **Beach Duck,** cork body, Thomas H. Gelston ..	125.00	175.00	150.00
☐ **Black Duck,** August mock drake, c. 1900	200.00	250.00	225.00
☐ **Black Duck,** Cobb Island, carved wing tips	175.00	225.00	200.00
☐ **Black Duck,** Dan English	525.00	575.00	550.00
☐ **Black Duck,** handcarved, c. 1900	90.00	110.00	100.00
☐ **Black Duck,** hollow, carved, Ken Anger	170.00	350.00	375.00
☐ **Black Duck,** hollow, carved, Stanley Grant	150.00	200.00	175.00
☐ **Black Duck,** hollow, carved, John Heisler	375.00	425.00	400.00
☐ **Black Duck,** hollow, carved, K. Peck	275.00	325.00	300.00
☐ **Black Duck,** hollow, carved, Harry V. Shourdes	150.00	190.00	170.00
☐ **Black Duck,** bird standing with wings spread, Ira Hudson	1500.00	1700.00	1600.00
☐ **Black Duck,** sleeping, set of five, original paint	850.00	1050.00	950.00
☐ **Black Duck,** swimming, Down East Decoy Co.	160.00	190.00	175.00
☐ **Blue Jay,** signed, A. Elmer Crowell	1400.00	1600.00	1500.00
☐ **Brant,** carved cedar	300.00	500.00	400.00
☐ **Brant,** Cobb Island, carved wings	200.00	250.00	200.00
☐ **Brant,** hollow, Harry Shourdes	175.00	300.00	250.00
☐ **Brant,** hollow, carved, New Jersey, carved wings	300.00	350.00	325.00
☐ **Brant,** Long Island, cork body	175.00	225.00	200.00
☐ **Brant,** Mason's			
☐ **Brant,** swimming, carved wings	200.00	240.00	220.00
☐ **Broadbill,** Chauncey Wheeler	300.00	360.00	330.00
☐ **Bufflehead,** drake, Doug Jester	115.00	145.00	130.00
☐ **Bufflehead,** drake, Ira Hudson	300.00	425.00	362.50
☐ **Bufflehead,** drake, California	50.00	125.00	100.00
☐ **Bufflehead,** glass eyes	650.00	1000.00	750.00
☐ **Bufflehead,** drake, hollow, carved, Charles Parker	300.00	360.00	330.00
☐ **Bufflehead,** drake, primitive, Oscar Ayers	115.00	145.00	130.00
☐ **Canada Goose,** Nathan Cobb	450.00	500.00	475.00
☐ **Canada Goose,** Hurley Conklin	650.00	750.00	700.00
☐ **Canada Goose,** John Furlow	275.00	325.00	300.00
☐ **Canada Goose,** solid, Madison Mitchell	185.00	225.00	180.00
☐ **Canada Goose,** L. Parker	325.00	500.00	300.00
☐ **Canada Goose,** Harvey V. Shourds	380.00	420.00	400.00
☐ **Canada Goose,** swimming, signed, c. 1880 ...	1900.00	2100.00	2000.00
☐ **Canvasback,** drake, balsa wood, Harry Megargy	90.00	120.00	105.00

	Current Price Range		P/Y Average
☐ **Canvasback,** drake, feeding, A. Elmer Crowell	415.00	475.00	445.00
☐ **Canvasback,** drake, Lohrman	125.00	175.00	155.00
☐ **Canvasback,** drake, Madison Mitchell	100.00	170.00	135.00
☐ **Canvasback,** drake, Michigan bobtail.........	190.00	220.00	205.00
☐ **Canvasback,** drake, Samuel Denny	245.00	285.00	265.00
☐ **Canvasback,** hen, Mason's	120.00	190.00	105.00
☐ **Canvasback,** hen, Frank Schmidt	250.00	310.00	300.00
☐ **Canvasback,** Michael Pavolich	125.00	175.00	175.00
☐ **Coot,** J.W. Johnson, 1960	50.00	90.00	80.00
☐ **Coot,** Mason's	300.00	330.00	315.00
☐ **Coot,** Benjamin J. Schmidt	170.00	200.00	185.00
☐ **Crow,** hollow, late 1800s	325.00	425.00	375.00
☐ **Crow,** hollow, carved, Charles H. Perdew Co.	275.00	375.00	350.00
☐ **Crow,** wooden, glass eyes, c. 1900	475.00	525.00	500.00
☐ **Curlew,** Barnegat	615.00	645.00	630.00
☐ **Curlew,** Cobb Island, running	760.00	790.00	775.00
☐ **Curlew,** Eskimo, carved wings, signed	740.00	780.00	760.00
☐ **Curlew,** Mason's	2800.00	3000.00	2900.00
☐ **Curlew,** sickle-billed, Harry Shourdes, contemporary	225.00	325.00	275.00
☐ **Dowitcher,** Long Island	275.00	325.00	300.00
☐ **Duck,** J. H. Whitney	90.00	120.00	105.00
☐ **Duck,** Labrador	770.00	790.00	780.00
☐ **Duck,** Pacific Northwest	45.00	75.00	60.00
☐ **Duck,** papier-mache	35.00	55.00	45.00
☐ **Eider duck,** primitive	160.00	180.00	170.00
☐ **Fish,** carved and painted, pair, 19th c.	340.00	360.00	350.00
☐ **Gadwell,** hen, Ken Anger	270.00	290.00	280.00
☐ **Golden Eye,** drake, Doug Jester	125.00	200.00	162.50
☐ **Golden Eye,** drake, Mason's	290.00	320.00	305.00
☐ **Golden Eye,** drake, Steven's Decoy Factory ..	400.00	440.00	420.00
☐ **Golden Eye,** hen, Harry Shourdes	130.00	160.00	170.00
☐ **Golden Eye,** hen, Bob White	325.00	375.00	350.00
☐ **Golden Plover**	75.00	90.00	82.50
☐ **Goose,** standing, aggressive stance, hollow, Prince Edward Island	300.00	500.00	475.00
☐ **Great Blue Heron,** sheet metal, painted	375.00	425.00	400.00
☐ **Gull,** with iron weight, J. W. Carter	2500.00	2700.00	2600.00
☐ **Heron,** primitive	650.00	750.00	700.00
☐ **Lesser Yellowlegs,** Bay Head	250.00	280.00	265.00
☐ **Lesser Yellowlegs,** Mason's	650.00	700.00	675.00
☐ **Lesser Yellowlegs,** William Matthews	315.00	335.00	325.00
☐ **Lesser Yellowlegs,** c. 1896	300.00	320.00	310.00
☐ **Mallard,** drake, J. N. Dodge Decory Factory ...	95.00	130.00	85.00
☐ **Mallard,** drake, Elliston	2400.00	2800.00	2600.00
☐ **Mallard,** drake, Old Illinois River	360.00	380.00	370.00
☐ **Mallard,** drake, Charles H. Perdew Co.	550.00	580.00	565.00
☐ **Mallard,** hen, Mason's	80.00	100.00	90.00
☐ **Mallard,** hen, Ward Brothers, c. 1920	220.00	250.00	235.00
☐ **Mallard,** papier-mache	25.00	30.00	27.50
☐ **Mallard,** drake, cork body	28.00	32.00	30.00
☐ **Merganser,** drake, red-breasted, Hurley Conklin	170.00	190.00	180.00

	Current Price Range		P/Y Average
☐ **Mallard,** crude, Kansas	25.00	45.00	37.50
☐ **Merganser,** hen, Doug Jester	500.00	540.00	520.00
☐ **Merganser,** Long Island	370.00	400.00	385.00
☐ **Merganser,** Harold Haertel	2900.00	3000.00	2950.00
☐ **Merganser,** primitive, American	150.00	200.00	175.00
☐ **Merganser,** red-breasted, drake	125.00	225.00	175.00
☐ **Merganser,** tack eyes	850.00	1200.00	850.00
☐ **Old-Squaw,** drake, Mark English	850.00	890.00	870.00
☐ **Owl,** balsa wood, glass eyes	480.00	500.00	490.00
☐ **Owl,** 19th c.	225.00	275.00	250.00
☐ **Pigeon,** English wood, Austin Johnson	275.00	350.00	312.50
☐ **Pigeon,** Lou Schifferell	275.00	295.00	285.00
☐ **Pintail,** drake, carved cedar	280.00	300.00	290.00
☐ **Pintail,** drake, carved wings and feathers	275.00	325.00	300.00
☐ **Pintail,** drake, A. Elmer Crowell	230.00	300.00	265.00
☐ **Pintail,** drake, Ira Hudson	850.00	890.00	870.00
☐ **Pintail Duck,** green beak	60.00	80.00	70.00
☐ **Pintail,** hen, Mason's	170.00	200.00	185.00
☐ **Pintail,** hen, Lem and Steve Ward	1500.00	2000.00	1750.00
☐ **Pintail,** hen and drake, L. T. Ward, pair	3000.00	3500.00	3250.00
☐ **Plover,** black-bellied, Cobb Island	390.00	410.00	400.00
☐ **Plover,** black-bellied, A. Elmer Crowell	1500.00	1700.00	1600.00
☐ **Plover,** black-bellied, William Matthews	340.00	380.00	360.00
☐ **Plover,** black-bellied, Charles E. Wheeler	1700.00	2100.00	1900.00
☐ **Redhead,** drake, Ben Schmidt			
☐ **Redhead,** hen, Frank Schmidt			
☐ **Redhead,** drake, Lloyd Parker	200.00	325.00	262.50
☐ **Redhead,** Michael Pavolich	125.00	175.00	175.00
☐ **Redhead,** drake, turned head, solid body	600.00	1000.00	900.00
☐ **Redhead,** cork body	180.00	200.00	190.00
☐ **Redhead,** drake, Thomas Gelston	140.00	160.00	150.00
☐ **Redhead,** drake, hollow, carved, signed	1400.00	1500.00	450.00
☐ **Redhead,** drake, sleeping, Mason's	340.00	370.00	355.00
☐ **Redhead,** hen, Nate Quillen	530.00	590.00	560.00
☐ **Ruddy Duck,** hen, L. T. Ward	150.00	170.00	160.00
☐ **Sanderling,** A. Elmer Crowell	830.00	860.00	845.00
☐ **Sanderling,** Taylor Johnson	280.00	300.00	290.00
☐ **Sandpiper,** Cobb Island	260.00	280.00	270.00
☐ **Sandpiper,** primitive	70.00	90.00	80.00
☐ **Scaup,** drake, Elliston	225.00	275.00	255.00
☐ **Scaup,** hen, F. Bach	250.00	300.00	275.00
☐ **Scaup,** drake, glass eyes	275.00	475.00	400.00
☐ **Scaup,** drake, Bart Clayton	170.00	190.00	180.00
☐ **Scaup,** drake, Henry Grant	600.00	640.00	620.00
☐ **Scaup,** drake, hollow, carved feathers	1800.00	2000.00	1900.00
☐ **Scaup,** drake, Roland Horner	440.00	460.00	450.00
☐ **Scaup,** drake, Joe King, hollow, carved	80.00	100.00	90.00
☐ **Scaup,** hen, Mason's	500.00	600.00	550.00
☐ **Scaup,** hen, Chauncey Wheeler	250.00	300.00	275.00
☐ **Shorebird,** carved head, glass eyes	380.00	400.00	390.00
☐ **Shorebird,** Dodge Decoy Factory	100.00	130.00	115.00
☐ **Snipe,** robin, Cobb Island	220.00	240.00	230.00
☐ **Snipe,** robin, Dodge Decoy Factory	220.00	230.00	225.00
☐ **Snipe,** robin, Joe King	270.00	290.00	280.00

	Current Price Range		P/Y Average
☐ **Snipe,** robin, primitive	120.00	130.00	125.00
☐ **Swan,** hollow, carved	900.00	950.00	925.00
☐ **Swan,** c. 1900	450.00	500.00	475.00
☐ **Widgeon,** A. Elmer Crowell	160.00	200.00	130.00
☐ **Widgeon,** c. 1880	170.00	190.00	180.00
☐ **Willet,** carved wings	400.00	500.00	450.00

DEPRESSION GLASS

DESCRIPTION: Colored glassware was machine-made during the Depression years of the late 1920s and early 1930s. The glass was available in ten cent stores, given away at filling stations, theatres, and used for promotional purposes. There are approximately 150,000 collectors and the popularity is steadily increasing each year. There are over eighty Depression Glass clubs that sponsor shows, with attendance in the thousands.

COMMENTS: Of the approximately 100 different patterns and colors produced, rose pink remains the favorite color. Luncheon sets of 16 pieces sold new for as low as $1.29. Today a dinner service, depending on the scarcity of the pattern, may cost from $100.00 to $1000.00.

RECOMMENDED READING: For more in-depth information on Depression Glass you may refer to *The Official Price Guide to Depression Glassware, The Official Price Guide to Glassware* and *The Official Identification Guide to Glassware,* published by The House of Collectibles.

BOWKNOT (Green)

☐ **Berry Bowl,** diameter 4 1/2″	6.50	9.50	7.25
☐ **Cereal Bowl,** 5 1/2″	9.00	12.00	10.00
☐ **Cup**	5.50	8.50	6.50
☐ **Salad Plate,** diameter 7″	6.00	8.00	6.00
☐ **Sherbet**	6.50	9.50	7.50
☐ **Tumbler,** 10 oz.	9.00	12.00	9.00
☐ **Tumbler,** footed, 10 oz.	9.00	12.00	9.00

	Current Price Range		P/Y Average

CIRCLE (Green—Hocking Glass Co.)

☐ **Bowl**, diameter 4 1/2″	2.00	4.00	2.50
☐ **Bowl**, diameter 8″	4.75	8.25	5.25
☐ **Creamer**	3.50	5.50	4.00
☐ **Cup**	1.50	3.50	2.00
☐ **Decanter**, handled	14.00	18.00	15.00
☐ **Dinner Plate**, diameter 9 1/2″	5.75	9.00	5.25
☐ **Juice Tumbler**, 4 oz.	2.50	4.50	3.00
☐ **Pitcher**, 80 oz.	15.00	19.00	16.00
☐ **Saucer**	1.00	2.50	.75
☐ **Sherbet**, diameter 3 1/8″	2.50	4.50	3.00
☐ **Sherbet**, diameter 4 3/4″	3.50	5.50	4.00
☐ **Sherbet Plate**, diameter 6″	1.00	3.00	1.50
☐ **Sugar Bowl**	3.50	5.50	4.00
☐ **Vase**, hat shape	16.00	19.00	17.00
☐ **Water Goblet**, 8 oz.	5.00	8.00	6.00
☐ **Water Tumbler**, 8 oz.	4.50	6.50	4.00
☐ **Wine Goblet**, height 4 1/2″	4.50	6.50	3.50

FOREST GREEN (Green—Anchor Hocking Glass Co.)

☐ **Ashtray**	2.50	4.00	2.50
☐ **Creamer**, flat	3.00	5.00	4.00
☐ **Cup**	2.00	3.50	1.75
☐ **Lunch Plate**, diameter 8″	4.00	6.00	3.50
☐ **Pitcher**, circular, 3 qt.	19.50	23.00	19.00
☐ **Platter**, rectangular	10.00	12.00	9.50
☐ **Salad Bowl**, diameter 7″	5.50	7.75	6.00
☐ **Salad Plate**, diameter 6 1/2″	1.25	2.25	1.75

Circle (Green-Hocking Glass Co.)

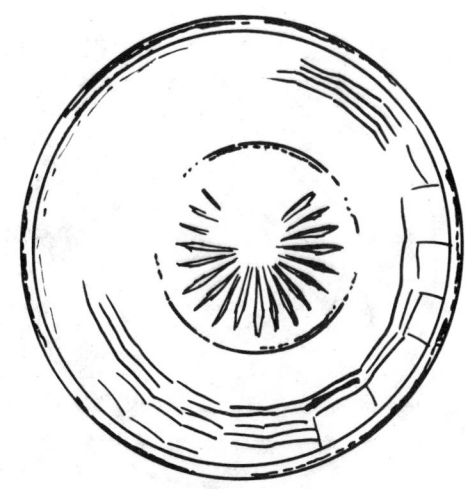

	Current Price Range		P/Y Average
☐ Saucer	1.00	2.50	1.00
☐ Soup Bowl, diameter 6″	5.00	7.00	6.00
☐ Tumbler, 5 oz.	1.75	2.50	1.75
☐ Vase, height 6″	3.00	5.00	3.25

GEORGIAN (Green—Federal Glass Co.)

	Current Price Range		P/Y Average
☐ Berry Bowl, diameter 4″	4.25	5.25	4.75
☐ Berry Bowl, diameter 7 1/2″	38.50	40.00	38.50
☐ Bowl, steep sided, diameter 6 1/2″	42.00	46.00	44.00
☐ Butter Dish, with cover	60.00	70.00	65.00
☐ Cereal Bowl, diameter 5 1/4″	12.00	14.00	13.00
☐ Creamer, pedestal foot, diameter 3″	7.00	9.00	8.00
☐ Creamer, pedestal foot, diameter 4″	8.00	10.00	9.00
☐ Cup	6.00	8.50	7.00
☐ Dinner Plate, diameter 9 1/4″	15.00	18.50	16.00
☐ Lunch Plate, diameter 8″	5.25	6.75	5.75
☐ Plate, central medallion and band on rim, diameter 9 1/4″	14.25	16.00	14.75
☐ Platter, tab handle, diameter 11 1/4″	42.00	46.00	44.00
☐ Saucer	1.75	3.00	2.25
☐ Sherbet Dish, stemmed	7.00	9.00	8.00
☐ Sherbet Plate, diameter 6″	2.25	3.25	2.75
☐ Sugar Bowl, pedestal foot, height 3″	7.00	9.75	8.00
☐ Sugar Bowl, pedestal foot, diameter 4″	8.25	9.25	8.75
☐ Sugar Lid, ...	21.00	23.00	22.00
☐ Tumbler, height 4″	33.00	36.00	34.50
☐ Tumbler, height 5 1/4″	56.00	62.00	59.00
☐ Vegetable Bowl, length 9″	42.00	46.00	44.00

Georgian (Green-Federal Glass Co.)

	Current Price Range		P/Y Average

HOLIDAY (Pink—Jeannette Glass Co.)

	Current Price Range		P/Y Average
☐ **Berry Bowl**	6.25	8.00	6.75
☐ **Butter Dish**	32.00	36.00	34.00
☐ **Candlesticks,** pair	53.00	60.00	49.00
☐ **Creamer**	5.25	7.00	5.75
☐ **Cup And Saucer**	7.25	8.25	7.75
☐ **Plate,** diameter 9"	8.75	9.75	9.25
☐ **Pitcher,** diameter 7"	23.00	26.00	24.50
☐ **Sherbet,** footed	2.75	4.00	2.75
☐ **Sugar And Creamer**	10.00	13.00	11.50
☐ **Tumbler,** footed, diameter 4"	23.00	26.50	24.50

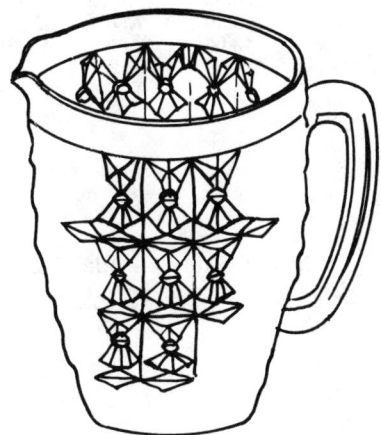

Holiday (Pink—Jeannette Glass Co.)

Moonstone (Opalescent Crystal-Anchor Hocking Glass Co.)

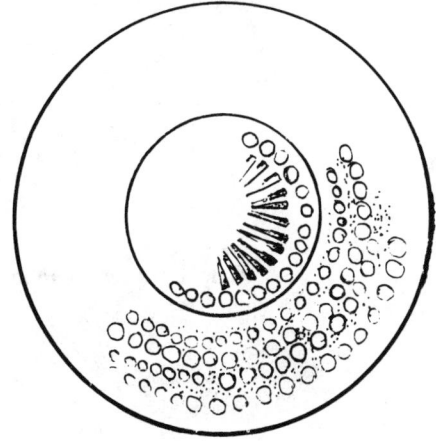

		Current Price Range		P/Y Average

MOONSTONE, (Opalescent Crystal—Anchor Hocking Glass Co.)

	Current Price Range		P/Y Average
☐ **Berry Bowl,** diameter 5″	6.50	9.50	6.50
☐ **Bon Bon,** heart shape	5.50	8.50	6.25
☐ **Bowl,** flat, diameter 7 1/2″	6.50	9.50	7.25
☐ **Bowl,** fluted edge, diameter 9″	11.00	14.00	12.00
☐ **Bowl,** fluted rim, with handle	5.50	8.50	6.25
☐ **Bud Vase,** height 5″	7.00	10.00	8.00
☐ **Candlesticks,** pair	13.00	17.50	14.00
☐ **Candy Jar,** with lid, diameter 5″	16.00	18.50	16.75
☐ **Cigarette Bowl,** with lid	13.00	16.00	13.75
☐ **Creamer**	4.50	7.50	5.25
☐ **Cup**	4.50	7.50	5.25
☐ **Dessert Bowl,** fluted rim, diameter 5″	4.50	7.50	5.25
☐ **Goblet,** height 5 1/2″	13.00	16.00	14.00
☐ **Lunch Plate,** diameter 8″	7.00	9.50	8.00

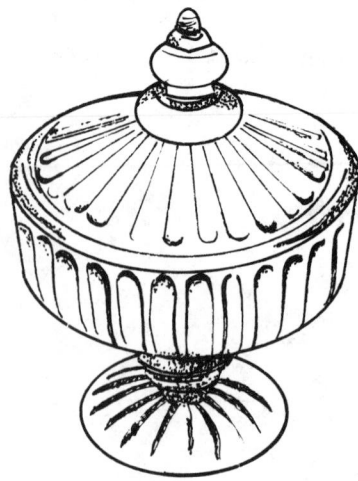

Ribbon (Green-Hazel Atlas Glass Co.)

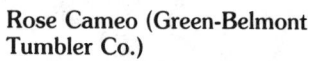

Rose Cameo (Green-Belmont Tumbler Co.)

	Current Price Range		P/Y Average
☐ **Puff Box,** with lid, diameter 4 1/2″	13.00	17.00	14.00
☐ **Relish Bowl,** two compartments, diameter 7″	8.00	12.00	9.00
☐ **Relish Dish,** clover shapes, three compartments	7.00	10.00	8.00
☐ **Sandwich Plate,** diameter 10″	14.00	18.00	14.00
☐ **Sherbet Dish,** pedestal foot	5.00	8.00	5.25

RIBBON (Green—Hazel Atlas Glass Co.)

☐ **Berry Bowl,** diameter 4″	2.00	4.50	1.50
☐ **Berry Bowl,** diameter 8″	6.50	12.00	5.50
☐ **Candy Dish,** with cover	22.00	29.00	19.00
☐ **Creamer,** pedestal foot	3.50	8.50	3.00
☐ **Cup**	1.50	3.50	2.00
☐ **Lunch Plate,** diameter 8″	1.00	3.00	1.50
☐ **Salt And Pepper**	13.00	18.00	14.00
☐ **Saucer**	.75	2.25	1.00
☐ **Sherbet Dish,** pedestal foot	3.00	5.25	2.50
☐ **Sherbet Plate,** diameter 6″	.50	2.00	.75
☐ **Sugar Bowl,** pedestal foot	2.00	4.00	2.50
☐ **Tumbler,** height 6″	5.25	8.50	5.00
☐ **Tumbler,** height 7″	6.25	9.50	6.00

ROSE CAMEO (Green—Belmont Tumbler Co.)

☐ **Berry Bowl,** diameter 4 1/2″	3.75	5.25	2.85
☐ **Cereal Bowl,** diameter 5″	5.00	7.00	5.25
☐ **Salad Plate,** diameter 7″	4.00	6.25	4.00
☐ **Sherbet Dish**	3.50	5.50	4.00
☐ **Tumbler,** diameter 5″	9.50	12.00	9.25

DISNEYANA

DESCRIPTION: Disneyana refers to all items made by or for Walt Disney Productions, the company that gave Americans Mickey Mouse, Donald Duck, Snow White and a host of other cartoon characters.

TYPE: There are many different types of Disney collectibles. Disney characters have been reproduced on every item from animated cels to dishes.

COMMENTS: Some hobbyists collect Disneyana by character or item, while others collect anything which features a Disney character. Older Mickey Mouse items are especially valuable, since this was the first character produced by the company.

ADDITIONAL TIPS: For more information, consult *The Official Price Guide to Collectible Toys,* published by The House of Collectibles.

	Current Price Range		P/Y Average
☐ **Aristocats, The,** Schmid, Walt Disney Prod., set of five figural music boxes, all play different tunes, height 6″	100.00	129.00	112.50
☐ **Baloo,** Walt Disney Prod., ceramic figurine of the "Jungle Book" bear, height 5 1/2″, c. 1965. ..	18.00	23.00	18.00
☐ **Bambi,** Anri, wooden music box, figures of Bambi and Thumper revolve on this Italian Disney item, c. 1971	82.00	105.00	95.00
☐ **Bambi And Thumper,** Schmid, pair of two pewter figurines, recent	30.00	40.00	30.00
☐ **Cinderella,** drinking glass, #8, red, yellow and blue, shows her being fitted for shoe, height 4 5/8″, c. 1950	8.00	11.00	6.00
☐ **Cinderella,** planter, ceramic	20.00	25.00	22.00
☐ **Clarabelle Cow,** drinking glass, full figure in red, seated in front of mirror primping, height 4 3/4″, c. 1930	24.00	28.00	22.50
☐ **Clarabelle Cow,** drinking glass, full figure in red, walking to the right, height 4 3/4″, c. 1930. ...	21.00	24.00	20.00
☐ **Clarabelle Cow,** drinking glass, full figure in red, height 4 3/8″	22.00	23.00	20.00
☐ **Dalmatians,** Schmid, ceramic figural "Playmates" music box, mother, father dog watching pups play, plays "Whistle A Happy Tune," first limited edition, height 6 1/2″, c. 1982	33.00	42.00	35.00
☐ **Dalmations,** Schmid, ceramic "Playmate" figurine, mother and father with pups, first edition "Mother's Day 1981," height 4 1/2″, c. 1981	20.00	23.00	18.00
☐ **Dalmatians,** pin back button, promoting Disney, re-release of movie, diameter 3 1/2″, c. 1979	11.00	18.00	6.00
☐ **Disney,** Ben Rickert, Inc., Snow White, Goofy, Mickey Mouse and Donald Duck, c. 1980	13.50	17.50	12.00
☐ **Disney,** Fort Productions, pewter collectible shovel spoon set, figures of Mickey, Minnie Donald and Goofy on handles, length 4 1/4″	24.00	34.00	25.00
☐ **Disney,** Fort Productions, silver plate collectible spoon set, four different with their names: Mickey, Minnie, Donald and Goofy on the handles, length 4″	26.00	30.00	25.00
☐ **Disney,** party baskets, plastic, features colorful figures of Mickey, Donald and Minnie, set of approximately 29 figures in original box, made by Best Toy Novelties, 7 1/2″ x 11″ x 4″.	125.00	150.00	120.00
☐ **Donald Duck and Nephews,** colorful rug, 21″ x 38″	100.00	130.00	95.00

	Current Price Range		P/Y Average

☐ **Donald Duck,** badge, "Happy Birthday Donald Duck 1934 –1984," enamel on metal, issued by the Disney channel, 1983 . . . . — 25.00 — 50.00 — 27.50

☐ **Donald Duck,** doll, Lenci, felt . . . . — 350.00 — 400.00 — 375.50

☐ **Donald Duck,** night light, ceramic, Walt Disney Productions . . . . — 32.00 — 52.00 — 42.00

☐ **Donald Duck,** night light, figure on black base, 9 1/2" . . . . — 55.00 — 65.00 — 53.00

☐ **Donald Duck,** paint box, c. 1930s . . . . — 13.00 — 23.00 — 20.50

☐ **Donald Duck,** watering can, tin, Walt Disney Enterprises, c. 1930s . . . . — 35.00 — 45.00 — 41.00

☐ **Donald Duck,** United China, Co., bisque and painted figurine, he's sitting in pool of water next to golf club, with ball on his head, height 3" . . . — 12.50 — 15.50 — 20.00

☐ **Donald Duck,** United China, Co., bisque hand painted figurine, in his bathing suit, ready to jump off diving board, height 4" . . . . — 13.00 — 16.00 — 10.00

☐ **Donald Duck,** bisque hand painted figurine, standing on surf board riding a wave, height 4" — 11.50 — 16.00 — 10.00

☐ **Donald Duck,** Morris Plastics, "The Bubble Duck," mouth clacks, blows bubbles, in original box, c. 1955 . . . . — 16.00 — 22.00 — 14.00

☐ **Donald Duck,** California Originals, ceramic canister cookie jar, Donald's Cookie Express, height 10", c. 1970 . . . . — 16.50 — 23.50 — 15.00

☐ **Donald Duck,** ceramic figural cowboy bank, height 6 1/2", c. 1940 . . . . — 47.00 — 52.00 — 44.50

☐ **Donald Duck,** ceramic figural milk pitcher, height 6 1/2", c. 1940 . . . . — 29.00 — 35.00 — 27.50

☐ **Dopey,** figurine, plaster, 14" high, c. 1930s . . . — 70.00 — 90.00 — 78.00

☐ **Dumbo,** California Originals, ceramic figural cookie jar, says "Dumbo's Greatest Cookies On Earth," height 12" . . . . — 25.00 — 43.00 — 24.00

☐ **Dumbo,** ceramic figural toothbrush holder, height 4", c. 1940 . . . . — 25.00 — 30.00 — 26.50

☐ **Dumbo,** ceramic planter, height 3 3/4", c. 1940 . . . . — 21.00 — 25.00 — 18.00

☐ **Dumbo,** Cameo Doll Co., composition figure, swiveling trunk and "Googlie Eyes," height 9", c. 1941 . . . . — 110.00 — 160.00 — 125.00

☐ **Dumbo,** Gare Mold Co., glazed figurine, height 9" . . . . — 35.00 — 40.00 — 32.50

☐ **Dumbo,** Schmid, pewter figurine . . . . — 28.00 — 32.00 — 25.00

☐ **Dumbo,** American Pottery, seated version of "Baby" Dumbo with Bonnet, #41 on bottom, height 5 1/2", c. 1940 . . . . — 55.00 — 65.00 — 55.00

☐ **Dumbo And Timothy,** Gare Mold Co., pair of figurines, height 9" . . . . — 35.00 — 42.00 — 33.50

☐ **Fantasia,** "Lionel Train" box car, depicts scenes from this Disney classic, from 1970s . . . . — 20.00 — 24.00 — 17.00

☐ **Goofy,** Schmid, pewter figurine, c. 1980 . . . . . . — 25.00 — 32.00 — 23.50

☐ **Goofy,** die cast and plastic auto, "Politoy," in pictorial box, marked #W5, c. 1965 . . . . — 11.50 — 13.00 — 9.50

Mickey Mouse Top, *8" diameter,* **$10.00-$20.00**

Mickey Mouse Handcar Set, *windup, metal handcar with
tracks,* **$550.00-$650.00**

	Current Price Range		P/Y Average

☐ **Goofy and Morty,** Schmid, ceramic Christmas ornament, height 3 1/2″, c. 1981 . . . .   12.00   16.50   12.00

☐ **Goofy, Morty And Huey,** Schmid, Christmas ceramic figural, sleigh ride music box, plays "We Wish You A Merry Xmas," first limited edition, height 7 1/4″, c. 1980 . . . .   27.00   30.00   28.50

☐ **Goofy And Wilbur,** Disney All Star Parade drinking glass, height 4 3/8″, c. 1939 . . . .   10.00   14.00   12.00

☐ **Grandma Duck,** die cast and plastic auto, "Politoy," Donald's grandma in 1/43rd scale, Italian, c. 1970 . . . .   12.00   18.00   12.00

☐ **Greedy Pig And Colt,** Disney All Star Parade drinking glass, red and black, height 4 3/8″, c. 1937 . . . .   8.50   13.50   9.25

☐ **Grumpy,** Christmas light bulb, c. 1940 . . . .   8.00   7.50   8.00

☐ **Horace Horsecollar,** drinking glass, full figure in red, bending over for coin, height 4 3/4″, c. 1930 . . . .   20.00   25.00   22.50

☐ **Horace Horsecollar,** juice glass, full figure in black, bending over for coin, height 3 1/2″, c. 1930 . . . .   14.00   18.00   16.00

☐ **Huey, Dewey, And Louie,** frosted glass figurine, Donald's three nephews, Italian, height 3 1/2″, c. 1970 . . . .   14.00   19.00   15.00

☐ **Jiminy Cricket,** Christmas light bulb, c. 1950   12.00   13.00   7.50

☐ **Jiminy Cricket,** drinking glass, in green with poem on back, height 4 3/8″ 18.00   23.00   18.00

☐ **Jiminy Cricket,** drinking glass, with poem on reverse side, height 4 3/4″, c. 1940 . . . .   17.00   24.00   20.00

☐ **Jiminy Cricket,** frosted glass figurine, Italian, first series, height 4 5/8″, c. 1970 . . . .   12.00   17.00   12.50

☐ **Jiminy Cricket,** Gare Mold, glazed Hi-gloss figurine, height 9″ 30.00   37.00   32.00

☐ **Jiminy Cricket,** Gund, vinyl and cloth hand puppet, in original box, c. 1960 . . . .   9.00   14.00   9.50

☐ **Jiminy Cricket,** oval "cameonyx" jewelry box, showing him in poses raised on cover, white on blue, height 6″, c. 1980 . . . .   37.00   44.00   40.00

☐ **Lady And Tramp,** double bisque figurine, having spaghetti dinner over candlelight, height 7″, c. 1970 . . . .   30.00   35.00   27.50

☐ **Lady And The Tramp,** Grolier bisque Christmas figurine in original box, c. 1980 . . . .   43.00   47.00   40.00

☐ **Mickey Mouse,** Page Productions, 50th birthday paint set in tin lithoed box, 45 large colors, length 9 1/2″ 10.00   15.00   10.00

☐ **Mickey Mouse,** 50th birthday pin back button, marked "Disneyland," diameter 3 1/2″, c. 1978 . . . .   9.00   14.00   8.00

☐ **Mickey Mouse,** Page of England, paint set, lithoed tin box, Mickey Mouse, Minnie, Morty, Ferdy, Goofy doing yard work, length 9 3/4″ . .   8.00   13.00   6.00

☐ **Mickey Mouse,** pie-eyed Santa full figure 7.00   10.00   10.00

☐ **Mickey Mouse,** pie-eyed Santa face 7.00   11.00   10.00

	Current Price Range		P/Y Average

☐ **Mickey Mouse,** pie-eyed "Telephone" 7.75 11.00 11.00

☐ **Mickey Mouse and Minnie,** pie-eyed on roller skates 11.50 15.00 14.50

☐ **Mickey Mouse,** pin back button, "Globe Trotters' Member," diameter 1 1/4", c. 1930 ...... 38.00 46.00 47.00

☐ **Mickey Mouse,** plastic figural head drinking cup, the bandleader in red, height 4", c. 1930 ..... 10.00 14.00 13.50

☐ **Mickey Mouse,** "Politoy," die cast plastic automobile, Italian, marked #W600, c. 1960 ...... 10.00 14.00 14.00

☐ **Mickey Mouse,** Royal Orleans, bisque figurine, dressed as Santa going down chimney, height 4", c. 1980 .... 11.50 16.00 18.00

☐ **Mickey Mouse,** recipe scrap book, premium by "Peter Pan Bread," height 6 1/4", c. 1930 .... 30.00 44.00 42.50

☐ **Mickey Mouse,** Colorforms, seed packets, c. 1977 .... 4.00 6.50 4.50

☐ **Mickey Mouse,** Bransford, silverplate spoon, has pie-eyed full figure of Mickey on handle, his name down the stem, length 5 1/2", c. 1930 13.00 19.00 15.00

☐ **Mickey Mouse,** set of three different Christmas pin back buttons, diameter 1 3/4" 5.00 7.00 7.00

☐ **Mickey Mouse,** Schmid, 50th birthday ceramic figural music box, Mickey in formal attire lighting candle on cake 41.00 50.00 47.00

☐ **Mickey Mouse,** Viletta, 50th birthday ceramic plate 80.00 89.00 85.00

☐ **Mickey Mouse,** Studios Giveaways, 50th birthday commemorative match box, box of 50, c. 1978 .... 40.00 80.00 55.00

☐ **Mickey Mouse,** Schmid, 50th birthday globe ornament, in box 14.00 18.50 14.50

☐ **Mickey Mouse and Donald Duck,** J. Chein and Co., tin sand pail, also shows Daisy and nephews at the zoo, height 4 1/2", c. 1940 .... 25.00 33.00 28.00

☐ **Mickey Mouse, Donald Duck And Goofy,** Masterwork, Bicentennial belt buckle, item laminated with colorful scene of the three of them marching and carrying flag as "Minutemen," c. 1976 .... 6.00 10.00 8.00

☐ **Mickey Mouse, Donald Duck And Goofy,** Schmid, ceramic Christmas ornament, height 3 1/2" 14.00 20.00 15.00

☐ **Mickey Mouse, Donald Duck And Goofy,** "Triple Bisque" Bicentennial figurine, depicting the three of them dressed as "Minutemen," marching and playing instruments, c. 1976 .... 290.00 415.00 390.00

☐ **Mickey Mouse, Donald Duck And Goofy,** Mattel, "Skediddlers" toys, set of three in original boxes, c. 1960 .... 40.00 48.00 47.00

☐ **Mickey Mouse, Donald Duck And Pluto,** "Patriot China" cup, shows them in a tug of war scene, c. 1930 .... 8.00 10.00 11.00

	Current Price Range		P/Y Average

☐ **Mickey Mouse And Goofy,** Schmid, Christmas ceramic figural "Happy Holidays" music box, Mickey and Goofy are holding wreaths around their necks, plays "Rudolph The Red Nosed Reindeer," height 7", c. 1981 . . . .   30.00   38.00   34.00

☐ **Mickey Mouse And Minnie Mouse,** Royal Orleans, bisque figurine with stocking caps, she's holding Christmas sock with Christmas package in it, he's holding a big Christmas package, c. 1980 . . . .   20.00   25.00   27.00

☐ **Mickey Mouse And Minnie Mouse,** bisque toothbrush holder, they're standing arm-in-arm, height 4 1/2", c. 1930 . . . .   85.00   94.00   85.00

☐ **Mickey Mouse And Minnie Mouse,** Schmid, "Caroling" pewter figurines, they're holding book marked "Noel" 26.00   32.00   33.00

☐ **Mickey Mouse And Minnie Mouse,** Dan Brechner, ceramic salt and pepper shakers, seated on a wooden park bench, height 4 1/2", c. 1950   30.00   41.00   40.00

☐ **Mickey Mouse And Minnie Mouse,** drinking glass, full figures in black on pink, height 5 7/8", c. 1950 . . . .   12.00   11.00   14.00

☐ **Mickey Mouse And Minnie Mouse,** "Nifty Nineties" double bisque figurine, Mickey's sporting striped coat, straw hat, bow-tie and cane, Minnie in polka dot dress with bow in hair 26.00   33.00   34.00

☐ **Pluto,** Walt Disney Productions, composition figural bank, sitting down with tongue hanging out, height 6 1/2" 11.50   14.00   15.00

☐ **Pluto And Goofy,** Radnor, set of two bone china thimbles, in box, c. 1970 . . . .   16.50   19.50   20.00

DOLLHOUSES

PERIOD: Dollhouses have been manufactured by toy companies since the Industrial Revolution. The most elaborate American dollhouses date from the Victorian period which is considered to be the "golden age" of toys.

COMMENTS: Many of the loveliest examples are handmade. Traditionally fathers and grandfathers have made dollhouses for their little girls, often a miniature version of their actual house.

ADDITIONAL TIPS: Because of the tremendous popularity of all types of miniature collectibles the demand for vintage dollhouses is at its greatest peak ever.

	Current Price Range		P/Y Average
☐ **Dollhouse,** Bliss, 13″	155.00	175.00	165.00
☐ **Dollhouse,** fireplaces in all rooms, simulated carved shingles, stucco exterior, late 1920s ...	730.00	830.00	780.00
☐ **Dollhouse,** lithographed, c. 1930	80.00	100.00	90.00
☐ **Dollhouse,** lithographed, wood, 2 wooden figures, 13″ L.	275.00	325.00	300.00
☐ **Dollhouse,** wood, faced with paper, painted, brick styled chimney, 17 1/2″ L.	90.00	110.00	100.00
☐ **Dutch Colonial,** wood, accessories, c. 1925 ..	475.00	575.00	520.00
☐ **English,** four rooms with staircase, two fireplaces, original, late 1800	850.00	950.00	900.00
☐ **French chateau-style,** windows on three sides, working door, c. 1890	650.00	750.00	700.00
☐ **German,** curtained windows, attic, steps leading to front door, c. 1890	1475.00	1575.00	1525.00
☐ **German castle,** 1/2″ to 1′ scale, molded after a late Gothic castle, c. 1875	2200.00	3200.00	2250.00
☐ **German,** small, embossed paper railing on second floor, unfurnished, c. 1900	310.00	360.00	335.00
☐ **Nineteenth century style,** roof shingled, clapboard sides, four rooms with hallways and staircase, two fireplaces, Victorian furnishings	3000.00	4000.00	3500.00
☐ **Swiss chalet style,** oak base on wheels, stenciled design on exterior, five rooms, Victorian furnishings, fourteen figures	2600.00	3600.00	3100.00
☐ **Tootsietoy**	35.00	45.00	40.00
☐ **Tudor style,** Schoenhut	300.00	340.00	320.00
☐ **Twentieth century style,** four rooms with hallways and staircase, conventional furnishings ..	270.00	370.00	325.00
☐ **Walt Disney,** six-room, metal	60.00	90.00	75.00

DOLLHOUSE FURNITURE

☐ **Bathtub,** tin, paint worn, 2 1/2″, late 19th c. ...	25.00	35.00	30.00
☐ **Bedroom suite,** four pieces: chairs, bureau ...	40.00	50.00	45.00
☐ **Bedroom suite,** three pieces, painted, c. 1920	50.00	80.00	65.00
☐ **Bowfront chest,** Tynietoy, scale	55.00	65.00	60.00
☐ **Broom holder,** tin, with brooms and dust pan	50.00	60.00	55.00
☐ **Dining table,** golden oak, scale 1″ to 1′	70.00	90.00	80.00
☐ **Drum table,** rosewood, top tilts, edge lines in velvet, 3″ Dia.	45.00	50.00	47.50
☐ **Fireplace,** open hearth, pine mantel	25.00	35.00	30.00
☐ **Hepplewhite sofa,** Tynietoy, scale	70.00	90.00	80.00
☐ **Ice cream parlor set,** 2 chairs with wire mesh seats, table 3 1/2″	50.00	55.00	52.50
☐ **Rope bed,** ticking mattress and pillow, 15 1/2″ x 10 1/2″	30.00	40.00	35.00

	Current Price Range		P/Y Average
☐ **Rug,** needlepoint, 3 1/2″ Dia.	12.00	16.00	14.00
☐ **Shaving mirror,** mahogany frame and stand, mirror beveled glass, 4″	35.00	45.00	40.00
☐ **Stove,** cast iron	70.00	90.00	80.00
☐ **Stove,** tin kitchen, with utensils 11″ H.	115.00	125.00	120.00
☐ **Teakettle,** brass with trivet	55.00	75.00	65.00
☐ **Victrola,** four-legs, painted wood, 4 1/2″	55.00	75.00	65.00

FINE MINIATURE FURNITURE

☐ **Chest of drawers,** George III, mahogany, late 18th c., 14″, H.	365.00	465.00	420.00
☐ **Chest of drawers,** George III style, mahogany, 10″ H.	110.00	120.00	115.00
☐ **Tea caddy,** George III, 4 1/2″, H., 18th c.	110.00	150.00	130.00
☐ **Victorian dining room set,** walnut table and sideboard with marble tops, upholstered chairs	240.00	290.00	265.00
☐ **Wing chair,** Federal, upholstered in brocade, 8 1/4″ H.	265.00	285.00	275.00

DOLLS

COMMENTS: Doll collecting has grown phenomenally in the last 25 years to become one of the top hobbies in the United States. Individual appeal seems to be the magic ingredient in the world of doll collecting. Some dolls made of common materials show exquisite workmanship and detailing, while others, made of fine porcelain bisque, are crudely fashioned.

ADDITIONAL TIPS: The prices of dolls cover such a wide range that any collector can find specimens to fit his budget. While the French and German fashion dolls are out of the financial reach of many collectors, most of the more recent composition dolls are relatively plentiful and inexpensive. Interesting and varied collections may be assembled by specializing in dolls of a certain era, a certain construction material, those dressed in similar nationalistic costumes, or all the various dolls made by a single manufacturer. Prices given are for dolls in excellent to mint original condition. Deductions must be made for any missing parts, worn-out or faded clothes, and broken or cracked heads.

RECOMMENDED READING: For more extensive information, see *The Official Price Guide to Dolls,* published by The House of Collectibles.

ALEXANDER

	Current Price Range		P/Y Average
☐ **Alexanderkin,** hard plastic, wears bathing suit, sandals, robe, square sunglasses, carries beach bag, 8.75″	75.00	150.00	80.00
☐ **Amy,** plastic sleep eyes, blonde looped curls, 14″	105.00	250.00	97.50
☐ **Cissy,** hard plastic, jointed at knees and elbows, long flowing yellow cape-style coat, sleep eyes, high heel open dress shoes, 21″	125.00	200.00	97.50
☐ **Laurie,** vinyl head, sleep eyes, sad, long eyelashes, black hair, wears double-breasted jacket, plaid trousers, 12″	40.00	150.00	13.50
☐ **Scarlett O'Hara,** vinyl, sleep eyes, long black glossy hair, satin gown with trimming, satin bonnet, wears cameo on a chain at the neck, marked Alexander 1961, 21″	400.00	700.00	120.00
☐ **Sleeping Beauty,** Disney special edition, 1959, 9″	195.00	495.00	350.00

Georgene Averill Doll, *Bonnie Babe, marked Copr. by Georgene Averill Germany, 16″,* **$850.00–$950.00**

	Current Price Range		P/Y Average

	Current Price Range		P/Y Average
☐ **M.I.B.**	445.00	595.00	475.00
☐ **Wendy,** hard plastic, sleep eyes, dressed as tennis player with racquet, skirt, opentoe shoes, 8″	85.00	110.00	102.50
☐ **Wendy Ann,** hard plastic, sleep eyes, puffy cheeks, blond hair, wears jacket and skirt of matching style, two buttons on jacket, 8″	85.00	200.00	75.00

ARMAND MARSEILLE

☐ **Bisque,** socket head set on toddler body, fully jointed construction, open mouth showing two teeth, fixed eyes, marked Armand Marseille/Germany 996/A. 3 M., 16″	130.00	180.00	155.00
☐ **Bisque,** socket head, sleep eyes, open mouth with two teeth, five-piece body, marked G.B. 327/A. 12 M. Germany, 21″	335.00	385.00	360.50
☐ **Bisque,** five-piece composition body, set eyes, open mouth showing four teeth and traces of others, marked A.M. 560a/DRGM R 232/1, 14″ ..	280.00	330.00	305.00
☐ **Bisque,** socket head, five-piece composition body, sleep eyes, open mouth with two teeth, marked Germany/971/A.4.M., 15″	90.00	140.00	115.00

ARRANBEE

☐ **Army Boy,** composition head and limbs, body stuffed with excelsior, molded hair, painted eyes, wears U.S. soldier's uniform of post-World War I era, featuring reproductions (in reduced size) of Lincoln cents for jacket buttons, 15″	95.00	150.00	85.00
☐ **Baby Marie,** vinyl head, vinyl arms and legs, plastic body, sleep eyes, molded hair, partially open mouth, shaped for insertion of nursing bottle, wears diaper, quilt jacket, 8 1/4″	5.00	7.00	5.00
☐ **Scarlet,** composition head, composition arms, legs and body, sleep eyes (green), long eyelashes, closed mouth, wears long ball gown of U.S. Civil War era and large bonnet, gown is trimmed with silk ribbons, marked R & B, 15″	65.00	115.00	59.50
☐ **Sonja Heinie,** composition head and body, brunette wig attached by adhesive, sleep eyes (brown), marked R & B, made in 1945, 21 1/4″	75.00	150.00	53.50
☐ **Taffy,** plastic, sleep eyes (green), marked R & B, made in 1954, 16 1/2″	65.00	125.00	61.00

FISHER PRICE

☐ **Audrey,** vinyl head, cloth body, rooted hair, painted eyes, blouse with small heart pattern, marked 168240, 1973, Fisher Price Toys, 14″	11.00	15.00	10.00

	Current Price Range		P/Y Average

☐ **Baby Ann,** vinyl head, cloth body, rooted blond hair, painted eyes, floral print dress with large sash ribbon, marked 60, 188460, 1973, Fisher Price Toys, 13 1/2" **10.00 14.00 9.00**

☐ **Elizabeth,** black, vinyl head, cloth body, rooted hair, closed mouth in semi-smile, painted eyes, marked 18, 168630, 1973, Fisher Price Toys, 13 1/2" **11.00 15.00 10.00**

☐ **Mary,** vinyl head, cloth body, rooted hair, up-turned eyes (painted), angelic facial expression, wears print dress and white apron, marked 168420, 1973, Fisher Price Toys, 14" **10.00 14.00 9.00**

☐ **Natalie,** vinyl head, cloth body, rooted hair, up-turned eyes (painted), grinning smile, marked 168320, 1973, Fisher Price Toys, 13 1/2" **11.00 15.00 10.00**

HASBRO

☐ **Baby Ruth,** vinyl head, stuffed body, vinyl hands, molded and painted features, blonde hair, rooted, sold originally with a tag reading Baby Ruth 1971, used as a premium by the Curtis Candy Co., 10" **5.00 7.00 5.00**

☐ **Flying Nun,** vinyl, brunette hair, rooted, molded and painted features, marked 1967 Hasbro, Hong Kong, 5" **12.00 20.00 11.50**

☐ **G.I. Joe,** Action Marine, plastic, molded hair, brown, brown eyes, painted, marked 7700, G.I. Joe TM Copyright by Hasbro Patent Pending, made in U.S.A., made in 1964, 11 1/2" **40.00 55.00 39.00**

IDEAL

☐ **Baby, Baby,** vinyl, rooted hair (blonde), fixed eyes (blue), nursing mouth, marked 115 Ideal, made in Hong Kong in 1974, 7" **7.00 10.00 6.00**

☐ **Baby Belly Button,** black, vinyl, black hair (rooted), painted features, brown eyes, smiling closed mouth, in the likeness of an infant, Baby Belly Button has a knob at its stomach which, when turned, makes the arms, legs and head move, dressed in a diaper and white lace-edged smock, marked Ideal Toy Corp., E9-2-H-165, made in Hong Kong in 1970, 9" **5.50 7.00 5.00**

☐ **Baby Big Eyes,** vinyl, blonde hair (rooted), sleep eyes (blue), closed mouth, marked Ideal Doll, made in 1954, 21" **45.00 56.00 42.00**

☐ **Snow White,** composition head, arms and legs, cloth body, molded and painted hair, molded and painted features, open mouth, eyes turned to side, marked Ideal, made c. 1939, 17 1/2" **70.00 85.00 65.00**

☐ **Tressy,** plastic/vinyl, black hair (rooted), sleep eyes (blue), pug nose, closed mouth, hair has "grow" feature (portion of wig is fitted inside head; when hair is pulled gently, it gives the ap-

	Current Price Range		P/Y Average

pearance of "growing" out of the scalp), marked 1969, Ideal Toy Corp., GH-18, also marked (on hip) with Patent No. 3162976, made in Hong Kong **8.00   10.00   7.00**

JUMEAU

☐ **Bebe Parie,** talker, bisque, sleep eyes (roundish), painted lashes on upper and lower lids, long arching brows, partially open mouth, narrow nose, joined at the elbows, talking mechanism operated by pullcord, says two words ("mama" and "papa"), date of manufacture unknown, probably c. 1895, 32" **950.00   1150.00   950.00**

☐ **Cody,** bisque, fixed eyes (medium size, dark), lightly painted lashes on upper and lower lids, naturalistic brows (slightly arched), closed mouth, thin pale lips, narrow nose with well-defined nostrils, long thin face, found dressed as a child or adult, marked 13, date of manufacture unknown, c. 1887, one of the most famous and sought-after of the Jumeau dolls, 26" **5,000.00   6,000.00   5,000.00**

☐ **Bisque,** fixed eyes (large, prominent, dark), painted lashes on the upper and lower lids, arching brows (rather bushy), partially open mouth (the lower lip much smaller than the upper), narrow nose, squarish jaw, conventional ears, representing a girl about 5 or 6 years of age, marked Depose E-3J, date of manufacture unknown, 10 1/2" **1000.00   1200.00   1000.00**

☐ **G.I. Joe,** Action Marine, plastic, molded hair, brown, brown eyes, painted, marked 7500, G.I. Joe, Copyright 1964 by Hasbro, Pat. No. 3,277,602, made in U.S.A., no problem distinguishing this 1967 version from the previous: the patent is no longer pending, a patent number is shown, 11 1/2" **21.00   25.00   19.00**

HEINRICH HANDWERCK

☐ **Bisque,** head with bisque shoulder plate, fixed eyes, large, almond shaped, short painted lashes on top of eye socket, much longer painted lashes beneath, open mouth showing teeth, wide nose, thick prominent eyebrows, roundish jaw, prominent ears, marked with the letters HcH and the mold number 5/0, additionally marked with a device which resembles an airplane propeller or a flower with two petals, date of manufacture unknown, but the absence of the word "Germany" from the marking would suggest a dating of pre-1892, 17" **230.00   300.00   270.00**

☐ **Bisque,** head with bisque shoulder plate, fixed eyes, medium large, partially open mouth showing teeth, long face with prominent cheeks and

	Current Price Range		P/Y Average

jaw, moderately arched eyebrows, representing a girl of 4 or 5 years of age, marked with a four-petaled flower and the letters HcH, and also with the mold number 9/0, date of manufacture unknown, but the absence of the word "Germany" from the marking would suggest a dating of pre-1892, 14 3/4" **200.00   300.00   250.00**

HORSMAN

☐ **Athlete,** mechanical, plastic/vinyl, molded and painted hair, molded and painted features, stands on platform, operates by spring-driven motor, marked Horsman 1967, 5 1/2" **7.00   9.00   6.00**

☐ **Babs,** composition, sleep eyes, blue, molded and painted hair, made in 1931, 10" **68.00   80.00   70.00**

☐ **Baby Chubby,** composition head, cloth body, composition arms and legs, molded and painted hair, reddish blonde, sleep eyes, blue, marked A-Horsman, made in 1940, 23" **30.00   40.00   32.50**

☐ **Bootsie,** black, plastic/vinyl, rooted hair, black, sleep eyes, brown, marked 1125-4-Horsman, made in 1969, 12" **30.00   35.00   32.50**

☐ **Campbell Kid,** composition body and head, molded and painted hair, painted shoes and socks, 1948, 12" **95.00   105.00   95.00**

☐ **Campbell Soup Kids,** plastic, boy in chef hat, girl with ribbon **27.00   34.00   27.00**

MATTEL
BARBIE AND BARBIE-RELATED

☐ **Barbie,** plastic, molded and painted features, bubble hairdo, wears red swimsuit (one piece), marked 850, made in 1962, 11 1/2" **330.00   430.00   380.00**

☐ **Barbie's Friend Christie,** black, plastic, molded and painted features, talker, brown hair (parted), wears knitted green shirt and red shorts, marked 1126, sold in 1968, 11 1/2" **120.00   150.00   100.00**

☐ **Bendable Ken,** plastic, molded and painted features, bendable legs, wears blue jacket and red trunks, marked 1020, sold in 1965, 12" **14.00   18.00   12.00**

☐ **Busy Barbie,** plastic, molded and painted features, wears checkered skirt and denim sunsuit, marked 3311, sold in 1972, 11 1/2" **7.00   10.00   6.00**

☐ **Chef Boy-Ar-Dee Barbie,** plastic, molded and painted features, painted lashes, wears green and red suit (one piece), marked 1190, sold in 1971, 11 1/2" **8.00   11.00   7.00**

DOORSTOPS

DESCRIPTION: Doorstops are small, heavy figures, usually made of iron, that are used to hold open doors.

ORIGIN: While things such as stones have always been used to prop open doors, the use of decorative figures for such a purpose dates to late 18th century England.

MATERIALS: Doorstops are usually made of cast iron that has been painted or bronzed. Some are made of other metals, and those made of brass tend to be the most valuable.

COMMENTS: Doorstops made prior to 1920 are the most collectible. Age, rarity and condition affect the price.

ADDITIONAL TIPS: The listings are alphabetical according to the figure. Measurements and descriptions follow as available. Unless otherwise noted, the doorstops are made of cast iron.

	Current Price Range		P/Y Average
☐ **Airedale**	35.00	45.00	37.00
☐ **American Eagle**	50.00	65.00	53.00
☐ **Aunt Jemima**	65.00	75.00	67.00
☐ **Basket of Flowers,** height 6 1/4″	17.00	26.00	19.00
☐ **Basket of Red Poppies,** height 8″, Hubley	25.00	35.00	28.00
☐ **Basket of Fruit,** height 10″, aluminum	20.00	28.00	22.50
☐ **Black Bear**	40.00	50.00	43.00
☐ **Boxer**	30.00	42.00	33.00
☐ **Bull**	35.00	45.00	37.00
☐ **Bulldog**	37.50	47.00	40.00
☐ **Campbell Kid,** with teddy bear	170.00	210.00	185.00
☐ **Cat,** black	28.00	35.00	30.00
☐ **Cat,** black, green eyes	40.00	50.00	43.00
☐ **Cat,** height 7″, seated, black body with green eyes, red mouth and yellow whiskers	80.00	100.00	87.00
☐ **Cat,** white, blue eyes, bell at throat, Hubley	80.00	100.00	87.00
☐ **Cockatoo,** height 7 1/2″, red, yellow and green paint, B. Noyes & Co.	55.00	75.00	62.00

	Current Price Range		P/Y Average
☐ **Cockatoo**	28.00	34.00	29.00
☐ **Colonial Lady,** height 11 1/2", black dress, holding yellow hat	40.00	55.00	42.00
☐ **Conestoga Wagon,** height 10"	60.00	80.00	67.00
☐ **Court Jester,** with animal	50.00	60.00	53.00
☐ **Dog,** Boston Terrier, height 8 1/2", length 7"	40.00	58.00	45.00
☐ **Dog,** Boston Terrier, height 9 1/2", length 8", facing left	65.00	80.00	70.00
☐ **Dog,** Cocker Spaniel	40.00	50.00	43.00
☐ **Dog,** German Shepherd	35.00	50.00	40.00
☐ **Dog,** Russian Wolf Hound, height 9 1/2", length 15 1/2"	130.00	155.00	138.00
☐ **Dog,** Scotty, length 10 1/4"	70.00	85.00	75.00
☐ **Doll,** with toy	40.00	50.00	43.00
☐ **Drum Major**	115.00	140.00	125.00
☐ **Elephant**	30.00	40.00	32.00
☐ **Fiddler,** with violin	33.00	40.00	34.00
☐ **Flowers,** in basket, solid brass	60.00	75.00	63.00
☐ **Fox,** brass	70.00	80.00	72.00
☐ **Frog,** solid bronze	92.00	115.00	95.00
☐ **Fruit,** in bowl	28.00	35.00	30.00
☐ **General Robert E. Lee,** height 7 1/4"	70.00	95.00	75.00
☐ **Girl,** height 11 3/8", standing, bonnet on head, holding skirt by hem, white and blue paint, B&H	100.00	120.00	105.00
☐ **Boy and Girl,** Dutch, Hubley	80.00	97.00	85.00
☐ **Golfer,** in knickers	140.00	165.00	150.00
☐ **Horses**	45.00	55.00	47.00
☐ **Indian,** riding horse	78.00	90.00	80.00
☐ **Jenny Lind,** height 4 1/2"	60.00	75.00	65.00
☐ **Kitten**	38.00	45.00	40.00
☐ **Lamb,** black	48.00	55.00	50.00
☐ **Lighthouse**	68.00	80.00	70.00
☐ **Lion**	40.00	55.00	47.00
☐ **Little Red Riding Hood and The Wolf,** pair	68.00	80.00	70.00
☐ **Mail Coach**	50.00	60.00	52.00
☐ **Mammy,** height 9"	110.00	135.00	115.00
☐ **Monkey**	40.00	50.00	42.00
☐ **Parrot**	28.00	35.00	29.00
☐ **Peacock**	78.00	95.00	85.00
☐ **Penguin,** height 10 1/2", black and white paint	73.00	90.00	79.00
☐ **Peter Rabbit,** height 11 3/4"	58.00	73.00	65.00
☐ **Popeye**	50.00	60.00	53.00
☐ **Punch,** with dog	92.00	115.00	95.00
☐ **Rabbit**	35.00	45.00	37.00
☐ **Red Riding Hood and Wolf**	68.00	85.00	75.00
☐ **Rooster**	50.00	60.00	52.00
☐ **Spanish Dancer**	45.00	53.00	47.00
☐ **Squirrel**	37.00	45.00	39.00
☐ **Stagecoach**	45.00	55.00	47.00
☐ **Tiger Lilies**	43.00	55.00	46.00
☐ **Windmill**	40.00	50.00	42.00
☐ **Wolf**	35.00	45.00	37.00
☐ **Woodpecker**	78.00	98.00	85.00

DUCK STAMPS

TOPIC: Duck Stamps are similar to hunting licenses in that the proceeds are used to procure and maintain refuges for waterfowl, and every waterfowl hunter over sixteen years of age must buy one from the government. The Duck Stamps themselves are not as collectible as the Duck Stamp prints, which the artist markets independently. Duck Stamps and the corresponding prints feature new pictures of waterfowl each year.

TYPES: Duck Stamps may be issued by either the state or the federal government. The listings given here are for federal Duck Stamp prints. Please refer to *The Official Price Guide to Collector Prints,* published by The House of Collectibles, for additional information and listings.

PERIOD: The first Duck Stamps and prints were issued by the federal government in 1934. The first state-issued stamps were released in 1971.

ORIGIN: The Duck Stamp program was begun as a response to a serious decline in the waterfowl population, resulting from loss of habitat.

COMMENTS: Many collectors frame both the print and its corresponding stamp. The second winning design is scarce; only 100 were issued. Because of this, no more than 100 complete sets of federal Duck Stamp prints can exist.

FEDERAL DUCK STAMP PRINTS

YEAR	PRINT DESIGN	ARTIST	MEDIUM	EDITION	CURRENT RETAIL PRICE
☐ 1934	MALLARDS	Ding Darling	Etching	300	**4,400.00**
☐ 1935	CANVASBACKS	Frank W. Benson	Etching	100	**6,800.00**
☐ 1936	CANADA GEESE	Richard E. Bishop	Etching	unlimited	**1,000.00**
☐ 1937	GREATER SCAUP	J. D. Knap	Gravure	260	**3,000.00**
☐ 1938	PINTAILS	Roland Clark	Etching	300	**3,700.00**
☐ 1939	GREEN WING TEAL	Lynn Bogue Hunt	Stone Litho	1st ed. 100	**6,200.00**
				2nd ed. 100	**5,700.00**

YEAR	PRINT DESIGN	ARTIST	MEDIUM	EDITION	CURRENT RETAIL PRICE
☐ 1940	BLACK DUCKS	Francis L. Jacques	Stone litho	1st ed. 30	**7,000.00**
				2nd ed. 30	**6,000.00**
				3rd ed. 200	**3,500.00**
☐ 1941	RUDDY DUCKS	E. R. Kalmback	Gravure (rev.)	100–110	**3,600.00**
			(reg.)	unknown	**1,300.00**
☐ 1942	WIGEON	A. Lassell Ripley (signed by Mrs. Ripley)	Etching	unlimited	**1,200.00**
☐ 1943	WOOD DUCKS	Walter E. Bohl	Etching	unlimited	**1,000.00**
				2nd ed.	**500.00**
☐ 1944	WHITE FRONT GEESE	Walter A. Weber	Stone litho (rev.)	100	**4,500.00**
				2nd ed. 200	**2,500.00**
				3rd ed. 90	**850.00**
☐ 1945	SHOVELERS	Owen J. Gromme	Gravure	250	**6,200.00**
☐ 1946	REDHEADS	Robert W. Hines	Stone litho	1st ed. 300	**2,000.00**
				2nd ed. 380	**150.00**
☐ 1947	SNOW GEESE	Jack Murray	Gravure	300	**2,400.00**
☐ 1948	BUFFLEHEADS	Maynard Reece	Stone litho	200	**1,200.00**
				150	**1,000.00**
				400	**600.00**
☐ 1949	GOLDEN EYES	Roger E. Preuss	Stone litho	250	**3,200.00**
☐ 1950	TRUMPETERS	Walter A. Weber	Gravure	1st ed. 250*	**1,500.00**
				2nd ed. 300	**400.00**
☐ 1951	GADWALL	Maynard Reece	Stone litho	1st ed. 250	**1,500.00**
				2nd ed. 400	**750.00**
☐ 1952	HARLEQUINS	John H. Dick	Stone litho	250*	**1,100.00**
☐ 1953	BLUE WING TEAL	Clayton B. Seagears	Stone litho	250*	**1,100.00**
☐ 1954	RING NECKS	Harvey D. Sandstrom	Stone litho	275	**1,100.00**
☐ 1955	BLUE GEESE	Stanley Stears	Etching	1st ed. 1st pr. 250	**1,100.00**
				1st ed. 2nd pr. 53	**1,100.00**
				2nd ed. 100	**600.00**
☐ 1956	MERGANSERS	Edward J. Bierly	Etching	1st ed. 325	**1,000.00**
				2nd pr. 125	**800.00**
☐ 1957	EIDERS	Jackson Miles Abbott	Stone litho	1st ed. 253	**1,100.00**
				500	**300.00**
☐ 1958	CANADA GEESE	Leslie C. Kouba	Stone litho	1st ed. 250	**1,100.00**
				2nd ed. 250	**1,000.00**
☐ 1959	LABRADOR DOG	Maynard Reece	Stone litho	1st ed. 400	**2,700.00**
				2nd ed. 300	**1,600.00**
				3rd ed. 400	**900.00**
☐ 1960	REDHEADS	John A. Ruthven	Litho	1st ed. 400	**1,000.00**
				2nd ed. 400	**600.00**
☐ 1961	MALLARDS	Edward A. Morris	Etching	275	**1,100.00**
☐ 1962	PINTAILS	Edward A. Morris	Etching	275	**1,100.00**
☐ 1963	BRANT	Edward J. Bierly	Etching	1st ed. 550	**1,000.00**
				2nd pr. 125	**800.00**
☐ 1964	NENE GEESE	Stanley Stearns	Stone litho	1st ed. 300	**1,100.00**
				2nd ed. 300	**700.00**
☐ 1965	CANVASBACKS	Ron Jenkins	Stone litho	1st ed. 700	**750.00**
				2nd ed. 100	**600.00**
				3rd ed. 250	**200.00**

STATE DUCK STAMPS

YEAR	PRINT DESIGN	ARTIST	MEDIUM	EDITION	CURRENT RETAIL PRICE
☐ 1966	WHISTLING SWANS	Stanley Stearns	Stone litho	1st ed. 300	**1,100.00**
				2nd ed. 300	**500.00**
☐ 1967	OLD SQUAWS	Leslie C. Kouba	Etching	275	**900.00**
☐ 1968	MERGANSERS	Claremont G. Pritchard	Stone litho	750	**1,100.00**
☐ 1969	SCOTERS	Maynard Reece	Stone litho	750	**1,000.00**
☐ 1970	ROSS GEESE	Edward J. Bierly	Photo litho-rem.	1,000	**3,200.00**
			-reg.	total	**2,500.00**
				2nd ed. 2,150	**150.00**
☐ 1971	CINNAMON TEAL	Maynard Reece	Stone litho	950	**5,200.00**
☐ 1972	EMPEROR GEESE	Arthur M. Cook	Photo litho-rem.	950	**4,000.00**
			-reg.	total	**2,800.00**
☐ 1973	STELLER'S EIDERS	Lee LeBlanc	Photo litho-rem.	1,000	**2,100.00**
			-reg.	total	**1,900.00**
☐ 1974	WOOD DUCKS	David A. Maass	Photo litho	unknown	**1,100.00**
☐ 1975	CANVASBACK DECOY	James Fisher	Photo litho-rem.	3,150	**1,100.00**
			-reg.	total	**950.00**
☐ 1976	CANADA GEESE	Alderson Magee	Photo litho with comp. pc.	1,000	**2,100.00**
			w/o comp. pc.	3,600	**1,000.00**
☐ 1977	ROSS' GEESE	Martin Murk	Photo litho-rem.	5,800	**750.00**
			-reg.	total	**600.00**
☐ 1978	HOODED MERGANSER	Albert Earl Gilbert	Photo litho-rem.	5,800	**1,100.00**
			-reg.	total	**550.00**
☐ 1979	GREEN WING TEAL	Ken Michaelson	Photo litho with comp. pc.		**600.00**
			-reg.		**450.00**
☐ 1980	MALLARDS	Richard Plasschaert	Photo litho	12,950	**600.00**
☐ 1981	RUDDY DUCKS	John Wilson	Photo litho	16,000	**300.00**
☐ 1982	CANVAS BACK	David Maass	Photo litho	22,250	**300.00**
☐ 1983	PINTAILS	Phil Scholer	Photo litho	17,000	
			w/medallion-	7,000	
			-rem.		**1,000.00**
			-reg.		**450.00**

EGGS

DESCRIPTION: Eggs are considered very beautiful art objects and are quite collectible.

VARIATIONS: Eggs are made for various purposes, from simple wooden darning eggs to jeweled egg boxes.

COMMENTS: The most famous eggs, prized for their beauty and rarity, are the Russian eggs created by Peter Carl Fabergé. Today the decorated Easter egg is the one most sought after by collectors. Prices tend to be reasonable.

ADDITIONAL TIPS: The listings are alphabetical according to type of egg, followed by description, manufacturer, year and price range.

For further information on eggs, contact The Egg Art Guild, 1174 Glenwood Dale, Cape St. Claire, MD 21408

	Current Price Range		P/Y Average
☐ **Art Glass Egg,** iridescent, large, Vanderbelt ..	35.00	45.00	37.00
☐ **Art Glass Egg,** pink, gold flowers	138.00	165.00	145.00
☐ **Box,** china, painted with flowers and birds, hinged lid, brass fittings, 9 1/2″	140.00	180.00	145.00
☐ **Easter Candy Container,** papier-mache, egg being drawn by rabbit, 4″	12.50	20.00	14.00
☐ **Easter Egg,** baby chick, Goebel, c. 1978	17.50	25.00	19.00
☐ **Easter Egg,** dove on cover, Wedgwood, c. 1977	60.00	75.00	63.00
☐ **Easter Egg,** glass, raised lettering	40.00	50.00	44.00
☐ **Easter Egg,** glass, undecorated, large set of four	40.00	50.00	44.00
☐ **Easter Egg,** porcelain, Royal Bayreuth, c. 1979	25.00	35.00	28.00
☐ **Easter Egg,** porcelain, floral decoration, Fursten-berg, c. 1974	20.00	30.00	23.00
☐ **Easter Egg,** silver and enamel, lilies and forget-me-nots, Faberge, by Ruckert, c. 1900	11750.00	14000.00	12000.00
☐ **Jewel case,** mother-of-pearl, gilded metal, egg "wheelbarrow"	68.00	85.00	72.00

Minton Emperor's Garden,
of the egg series,
1982, $95.00-$110.00

	Current Price Range		P/Y Average
☐ **Mary Gregory Glass Egg,** raised lettering and design	25.00	35.00	27.00
☐ **Milk Glass Egg,** raised lettering and design ...	30.00	40.00	32.00
☐ **Minton Emperor's Garden,** Royal Doulton, edition size 3500, 1982	100.00	115.00	103.00
☐ **Minton 19th Century,** Royal Doulton, edition size 3500, 1979.........................	80.00	100.00	85.00
☐ **Rouge Flambe,** Royal Doulton, edition size 3500, 1980	110.00	120.00	112.00
☐ **Vinaigrette,** ivory, screw lid with grill inside, English	175.00	250.00	185.00
☐ **Vinaigrette,** ivory, screw lid with grill inside, English	700.00	800.00	720.00
☐ **Vinaigrette,** silver and enamel, purple, gold, white, French	950.00	1300.00	1050.00
☐ **Wooden Egg,** pine, hen, painted	7.50	12.00	8.00

ELVIS PRESLEY MEMORABILIA

DESCRIPTION: Elvis Presley, a rock and roll legend, was one of the greatest influences on music. His twenty year career spanned from 1956 until his untimely death in 1977. Because of the millions of Elvis Presley fans throughout the world, any items belonging to the "King of Rock and Roll" are valuable among collectors.

TYPES: There are all kinds of Elvis memorabilia, from clothes, cars and contracts to autographed photos and school items. One of the largest collecting areas is his records.

COMMENTS: Some Elvis fans collect only his records while others collect all types of his memorabilia.

ADDITIONAL TIPS: For more information, consult *The Official Price Guide to Music Collectibles,* and *The Official Price Guide to Records,* published by The House of Collectibles.

MEMORABILIA

	Current Price Range		P/Y Average
☐ **Book,** *The Army Years* by Nick Corvino, 93 pages, clothbound, 5 1/2" x 8 1/2" .... **Fictionalized story of the years spent by Elvis in the army.**	5.00	7.00	6.00
☐ **Book,** *The Complete Elvis* by Martin Torgoff, paperback, 256 pages	9.00	12.00	10.50
☐ **Book,** *Elvis* by Dave Marsh, clothbound, 246 pages	30.00	40.00	35.00
☐ **Book,** *Elvis* by Albert Goldman, clothbound ...	13.00	17.00	15.00
☐ **Book,** *Elvis: The Final Years* by Jerry Hopkins, clothbound, 258 pages	11.00	15.00	13.00
☐ **Book,** *Elvis: The Illustrated Discography* by Martin Hawkins and Colin Escott, paperback.	5.00	7.00	6.00

	Current Price Range		P/Y Average
☐ **Book,** *Elvis: The Illustrated Record* by Roy Carr and Mick Farren, 12″ square format	11.00	15.00	13.00
☐ **Book,** *Elvis in His Own Words* by Mick Farren and Pearce Marchbank, paperback, 128 pages.	5.00	7.00	6.00
☐ **Book,** *Elvis: The Legend and the Music* by John Tobler and Richard Wooten, clothbound, 192 pages	10.00	13.00	11.50
☐ **Book,** *Elvis Presley: A Complete Reference* by Wendy Sauers, clothbound, 194 pages	16.00	20.00	18.00
☐ **Book,** *Elvis Presley Reference Guide and Discography* by John Whisler, clothbound, 250 pages	13.00	17.00	15.00
☐ **Book,** *Elvis Presley: A Study in Music* by Robert Matthew-Walker, paperback, 154 pages	5.00	7.00	6.00
☐ **Book,** *Elvis Presley News Diary* by Bill Johnson, 230 pages, spiral binding, 9 1/2″ x 12″, 1981	8.00	10.00	9.00
☐ **Book,** *The Illustrated Elvis* by W. A. Harbinson, 160 pages, softbound, 8″ x 10 1/2″	2.00	3.00	2.50
☐ **Book,** *Jailhouse Rock* by Lee Cotten and Howard A. DeWitt, clothbound, 368 pages	16.00	20.00	18.00
☐ **Book,** *Private Elvis,* author uncredited, 199 pages, softbound, 8 1/2″ x 11″, 1978	10.00	13.00	11.50
☐ **Book,** *Up and Down With Elvis Presley* by Marge Crumbaker and Gabe Tucker, clothbound, 254 pages	11.00	15.00	12.50
☐ **Book,** *When Elvis Died* by Neal Gregory and Janice Gregory, clothbound, 290 pages	12.00	16.00	14.00
☐ **Elvis Presley Child's Guitar,** plastic	28.00	38.00	33.00
☐ **Elvis Presley School Bag**	35.00	50.00	42.50
☐ **8x10 Photo with Guitar,** signed and inscribed, 1957	350.00	450.00	400.00
☐ **Printed Postcard Photo,** facsimile signature . .	5.00	8.00	6.50
☐ **Lifesize Cardboard Figure** of Elvis, c. 1961, used for theater promotion, full color	375.00	475.00	425.00
☐ **8x10 Color Photo,** signed	400.00	600.00	500.00
☐ **Signature on label** of 45rpm record - add $225–$300 to value of record as listed above.			
☐ **Signature on label** of 33 1/3 rpm long-play record—add $275–$375 to value of album as listed above.			
☐ **Signature on cover** of 33 1/3 rpm long-play album—add $300–$400 to value of album if record is present. If record is not present, cover alone is worth $300–$400.			
☐ **Elvis Presley Drinking Mug,** ceramic, picture on side	23.00	32.00	27.50
☐ **Handkerchief,** colored silk, illustrated	20.00	27.00	23.50
☐ **Typewritten Note** by Col. Tom Parker (his manager), signed	9.00	12.00	10.50
☐ **8x10 Photo,** unsigned, black and white	2.00	4.00	3.00
☐ **8 x 10 Motion Picture Still,** unsigned, black and white	1.50	3.00	2.25
☐ **8x10 Color Photo,** unsigned (not clipped from magazine or book)	6.00	10.00	8.00

	Current Price Range		P/Y Average
☐ 8x10 Motion Picture Still, unsigned, color	5.00	8.00	6.50
☐ 8x10 Motion Picture Still, black and white, signed	250.00	375.00	312.50
☐ 8x10 Motion Picture Still, color, signed	300.00	450.00	375.00
☐ Typewritten Letter, signed, 1/2 page	150.00	225.00	187.50
☐ Typewritten Letter, signed, 1 page	180.00	250.00	215.00
☐ Typewritten Letter, signed, 2 pages	275.00	375.00	325.00
☐ Handwritten Letter, signed, 1/2 page	275.00	375.00	325.00
☐ Handwritten Letter, signed, 1 page	450.00	600.00	525.00
☐ Handwritten Letter, signed, 2 pages	600.00	800.00	700.00
☐ Handwritten Letter, signed, 3 pages	750.00	1100.00	925.00
☐ Note in his handwriting, one line	150.00	200.00	175.00
☐ Signature on an otherwise blank sheet of paper or card	80.00	100.00	90.00
☐ Typewritten Letter to him from record company executive	40.00	50.00	45.00
☐ Typewritten Letter to him from motion picture executive	35.00	49.00	42.00
☐ Typewritten Letter to him from TV producer	31.00	42.00	36.50
☐ Typewritten Letter to him from music agent	29.00	39.00	34.00
☐ Typewritten Letter to him from U.S. Armed Forces	235.00	310.00	272.50
☐ Typewritten Letter to him from author seeking an interview	9.00	14.00	11.50
☐ Typewritten Letter to him from Ed Sullivan ..	140.00	200.00	170.00
☐ Draft Card issued to him by Selective Service	1750.00	3000.00	2375.00
☐ Magazine Cover with full color photo	.50	1.00	.75
☐ News Cuttings (most)	.50	2.00	1.25

Elvis Presley, *still, if signed would be worth considerably more,* **$1.50-$2.00**

	Current Price Range		P/Y Average

ELVIS PRESLEY—45 SINGLES

☐ **Sun 209** *That's All Right/Blue Moon of Kentucky*	195.00	350.00	322.50
☐ **210** *Good Rockin' Tonight/I Don't Care If the Sun Don't Shine*	175.00	275.00	225.00
☐ **215** *Milkcow Blues Boogie/You're a Heart-breaker*	250.00	375.00	312.50
☐ **217** *Baby Let's Play House/I'm Left, Your Right, She's Gone*	140.00	240.00	190.00
☐ **223** *Mystery Train/I Forgot to Remember to Forget*	130.00	240.00	175.00
☐ **RCA6357** *Mystery Train/I Forgot to Remember to Forget*	15.00	24.00	19.50
☐ **6380** *That's All Right/Blue Moon of Kentucky*	15.00	24.00	19.50
☐ **6381** *Good Rockin' Tonight/I Don't Care If the Sun Don't Shine*	15.00	24.00	19.50
☐ **6382** *Milkcow Blues Boogie/You're a Heart-breaker*	15.00	24.00	19.50
☐ **6383** *Baby Let's Play House/I'm Left, You're Right, She's Gone*	15.00	24.00	19.50
☐ **6420** *Heartbreak Hotel/I Was the One*	5.00	9.00	7.00
☐ **6540** *I Want You, I Need You, I Love You/My Baby Left Me*	5.00	9.00	7.00
☐ **6604** *Don't Be Cruel/Hound Dog*	5.00	9.00	7.00
☐ **6636** *Blue Suede Shoes/Tutti Frutti*	15.00	24.00	19.50
☐ **6637** *I Got a Woman/I'm Countin' on You*	15.00	24.00	19.50
☐ **6638** *I'm Gonna Sit Right Down and Cry Over You/I'll Never Let You Go*	15.00	24.00	19.50
☐ **6639** *Tryin' to Get to You/I Love You Because*	15.00	24.00	19.50
☐ **6640** *Blue Moon/Just Because*	15.00	24.00	19.50
☐ **6641** *Money Honey/One-Sided Love Affair*	15.00	24.00	19.50
☐ **6642** *Shake, Rattle and Roll/Lawdy Miss Clawdy*	15.00	24.00	19.50
☐ **6643** *Love Me Tender/Anyway You Want Me*	4.50	8.00	19.50
☐ **6800** *Too Much Playing For Keeps*	4.50	8.00	6.75
☐ **6870** *All Shook Up/That's When Your Heart-aches Begin*	4.50	8.00	6.75
☐ **7000** *Teddy Bear/Loving You*	4.50	8.00	6.75
☐ **7035** *Jailhouse Rock/Treat Me Nice*	4.50	8.00	6.75
☐ **7150** *Don't/I Beg of You*	4.50	8.00	6.75
☐ **7240** *Wear My Ring Around Your Neck/Doncha Think It's Time*	4.50	8.00	6.75
☐ **7280** *Hard Headed Woman/Don't Ask Me Why*	4.50	8.00	6.75
☐ **7410** *One Night/I Got Stung*	4.50	8.00	6.75
☐ **7506** *A Fool Such As I/I Need Your Love Tonight*	3.75	6.00	4.88
☐ **7600** *A Big Hunk O' Love/My Wish Came True*	3.75	6.00	4.88
☐ **7740** *Stuck on You/Fame and Fortune*	3.25	5.50	4.38
☐ **7740** *Stuck on You/Fame and Fortune (stereo single)*	70.00	125.00	91.50
☐ **7777** *It's Now or Never/A Mess of Blues*	3.25	5.50	4.38
☐ **7777** *It's Now or Never/A Mess of Blues (stereo single)*	70.00	125.00	97.50

	Current Price Range		P/Y Average
☐ **7810** *Are You Lonesome Tonight?/I Gotta Know*	3.25	5.50	4.38
☐ **7810** *Are You Lonesome Tonight?/I Gotta Know (stereo single)*	70.00	125.00	97.50
☐ **7850** *Surrender/Lonely Man*	3.25	5.50	4.38
☐ **7850** *Surrender/Lonely Man (stereo single)*	95.00	165.00	130.00
☐ **7880** *I Feel So Bad/Wild in the Country*	3.25	5.50	4.38
☐ **7880** *I Feel So Bad/Wild in the Country (stereo single)*	95.00	165.00	130.00
☐ **098** *His Latest Flame/Little Sister*	3.00	5.00	4.00
☐ **7968** *Can't Help Falling in Love/Rock-A-Hula-Baby*	3.00	5.00	4.00
☐ **7992** *Good Luck Charm/Anything That's a Part of You*	3.00	5.00	4.00
☐ **8041** *She's Not You/Just Tell Her Jim Said Hello*	3.00	5.00	4.00
☐ **8100** *Return to Sender/Where Do You Come From?*	3.00	5.00	4.00
☐ **8134** *One Broken Heart For Sale/They Remind Me Too Much of You*	3.00	5.00	4.00
☐ **8188** *Devil in Disguise/Please Don't Drag That Sting Around*	3.00	5.00	4.00
☐ **8234** *Kissin' Cousins/It Hurts Me*	3.00	5.00	4.00
☐ **8360** *What's I Say/Viva Las Vegas*	3.00	5.00	4.00
☐ **8400** *Such a Night/Never Ending*	3.00	5.00	4.00
☐ **8440** *Ask Me/Ain't That Loving You Baby*	3.00	5.00	4.00
☐ **8500** *Do the Clam/You'll Be Gone*	3.00	5.00	4.00
☐ **8585** *(Such An) Easy Question/It Feels So Right*	3.00	5.00	4.00
☐ **8740** *Tell Me Why/Blue Rider*	3.00	5.00	4.00
☐ **8780** *Frankie and Johnny/Please Don't Stop Loving Me*	3.00	5.00	4.00
☐ **8870** *Love Letters/Come What May*	3.00	5.00	4.00
☐ **8941** *If Every Day Was Like Christmas/How Would You Like To Be*	4.50	8.00	6.25
☐ **9056** *Indescribably Blue/Fools Fall in Love*	3.00	5.00	4.00
☐ **9115** *Long Legged Girl/That's Someone You Never Forget*	3.00	5.00	4.00
☐ **9287** *There's Always Me/Judy*	3.00	5.00	4.00
☐ **9341** *Big Boss Man/You Don't Know Me*	3.00	5.00	4.00
☐ **94258** *Guitar Man/High Heeled Sneakers*	3.00	5.00	4.00
☐ **9465** *U.S. Male/Stay Away Joe*	3.00	5.00	4.00
☐ **9547** *Let Yourself Go/Your Time Hasn't Come Yet Baby*	3.00	5.00	4.00
☐ **9600** *You'll Never Walk Alone/We Call on Him*	3.00	5.00	4.00
☐ **9610** *A Little Less Conversation/Almost in Love*	3.00	5.00	4.00
☐ **9670** *If I Can Dream/Edge of Reality*	2.75	4.50	3.62
☐ **9731** *Memories/Charro*	2.75	4.50	3.62
☐ **9741** *In The Ghetto/Any Day Now*	2.75	4.50	3.62
☐ **9747** *Clean Up Your Own Back Yard/The Fair is Moving On*	2.75	4.50	3.62
☐ **9764** *Suspicious Minds/You'll Think of Me*	2.75	4.50	3.62
☐ **9768** *Don't Cry Daddy/Rubberneckin'*	2.75	4.50	3.62

	Current Price Range		P/Y Average
☐ 9791 Kentucky Rain/My Little Friend	2.75	4.50	3.62
☐ 9835 The Wonder of You/Mama Liked the Roses	2.75	4.50	3.62
☐ 9873 I've Lost You/The Next Step is Love	2.75	4.50	3.62
☐ 9916 You Don't Have to Say You Love Me/Patch It Up	2.75	4.50	3.62
☐ 9960 I Really Don't Want To Know/There Goes My Everything	2.75	4.50	3.62
☐ 9980 Where Did They Go, Lord?/Rags to Riches	2.75	4.50	3.62
☐ 9985 Life/Only Believe	2.75	4.50	3.62
☐ 9998 I'm Leavin'/Heart of Rome	2.75	4.50	3.62
☐ 1017 It's Only Love/The Sound of Your Cry ...	2.75	4.50	3.62
☐ 0619 Until It's Time for You to Go/We Can Make the Morning	2.75	4.50	3.62
☐ 0672 An American Trilogy/The First Time I Ever Saw Your Face	2.75	4.50	3.62
☐ 0769 Burning Love/It's a Matter of Time	2.50	4.00	3.25
☐ 0815 Separate Ways/Always on My Mind	2.50	4.00	3.25
☐ 0910 Steamroller Blues/Fool	2.50	4.00	3.25
☐ 0088 Raised on Rock/For Ol' Time Sake	2.50	4.00	3.25
☐ 0196 I've Got a Thing About You Baby/Take Good Care of Her	2.50	4.00	3.25
☐ 0280 If You Talk in Your Sleep/Help Me	2.50	4.00	3.25
☐ 10074 Promised Land/It's Midnight	2.50	4.00	3.25
☐ 10191 My Boy/Thinking About You	2.50	4.00	3.25
☐ 10278 T-R-O-U-B-L-E/Mr. Songman	2.50	4.00	3.25
☐ 10401 Bringing It Back/Pieces of My Life	2.50	4.00	3.25
☐ 10601 Hurt/For the Heart	2.50	4.00	3.25
☐ 18057 Moody Blue/She Thinks I Still Care	2.50	4.00	3.25

EXTENDED PLAY (EP)

	Current Price Range		P/Y Average
☐ RCA 1254 Elvis Presley (double-pocket)	90.00	165.00	77.50
☐ 747 Elvis Presley	12.00	25.00	18.50
☐ 821 Heartbreak Hotel	14.00	27.00	20.50
☐ 830 Elvis Presley	14.00	27.00	20.50
☐ 940 The Real Elvis	14.00	27.00	20.50
☐ 965 Anyway You Want Me	14.00	27.00	20.50
☐ 4006 Love Me Tender	14.00	27.00	20.50
☐ 992 Elvis, Vol. I	14.00	27.00	20.50
☐ 993 Elvis, Vol. II	14.00	27.00	20.50
☐ 994 Strictly Elvis	14.00	27.00	20.50
☐ 1-1515 Loving You, Vol. I	14.00	27.00	20.50
☐ 2-1515 Loving You, Vol. II	14.00	27.00	20.50
☐ 4041 Just for You	14.00	27.00	20.50
☐ 4054 Peace in the Valley	12.00	25.00	18.50
☐ 4108 Elvis Sings Christmas Songs	14.00	27.00	20.50
☐ 4114 Jailhouse Rock	14.00	27.00	20.50
☐ 4319 King Creole, Vol. I	14.00	27.00	20.50
☐ 4321 King Creole, Vol. II	14.00	27.00	20.50
☐ 4325 Elvis Sails	27.00	48.00	32.50
☐ 4340 Christmas with Elvis	14.00	27.00	20.50

	Current Price Range		P/Y Average
☐ 4368 Follow That Dream	8.25	14.00	11.13
☐ 4371 Kid Galahad	8.25	14.00	11.13
☐ 4382 Easy Come, Easy Go	9.50	18.00	13.75
☐ 4383 Tickle Me	9.50	18.00	13.75
☐ 5088 A Touch of Gold, Vol. I (maroon label)	35.00	56.00	45.50
☐ 5088 A Touch of Gold, Vol. I (black label)	12.00	25.00	18.50
☐ 5120 The Real Elvis (reissue) (maroon label)	35.00	54.00	44.50
☐ 5120 The Real Elvis (reissue) (black label)	9.50	15.00	12.25
☐ 5121 Peace in the Valley (reissue) (maroon label)	35.00	54.00	44.50
☐ 5151 Peace in the Valley (reissue) (black label)	9.50	15.00	12.25
☐ 5122 King Creole, Vol. I (reissue) (maroon label)	35.00	54.00	44.50
☐ 5122 King Creole, Vol. I (reissue) (black label)	9.50	15.00	12.25
☐ 5101 A Touch of Gold, Vol. II (maroon label)	35.00	54.00	44.50
☐ 5101 A Touch of Gold, Vol. II (black label)	12.00	25.00	17.50
☐ 5141 A Touch of Gold, Vol. II (maroon label)	35.00	54.00	44.50
☐ 5141 A Touch of Gold, Vol. III (black label)	12.00	25.00	17.50
☐ 5157 Elvis Sails (reissue) (maroon label)	40.00	70.00	55.00
☐ 5157 Elvis Sails (reissue) (maroon label)	12.00	25.00	17.50

COMPACT 33'S

	Current Price Range		P/Y Average
☐ RCA 37-7850 Surrender/Lonely Man	48.00	115.00	81.50
☐ 37-7880 I Feel So Bad/Wild in the Country	75.00	175.00	125.00
☐ 37-7908 His Latest Flame/Little Sister	75.00	175.00	125.00
☐ 37-7968 Can't Help Falling in Love/Rock-A-Hula Baby	75.00	175.00	125.00
☐ 37-7992 Good Luck Charm/Anything That's Part of You	75.00	175.00	125.00
☐ 37-8041 She's Not You/Just Tell Her Jim Said Hello	90.00	250.00	170.00
☐ 37-8100 Return to Sender/Where Do You Come From?	90.00	250.00	170.00

LP'S

THE ALBUMS BELOW WERE FIRST ISSUED ONLY IN MONO

	Current Price Range		P/Y Average
☐ RCA 1254 (M) Elvis Presley	25.00	56.00	40.50
☐ 1382 (M) Elvis	25.00	56.00	40.50
☐ 1515 (M) Loving You	17.00	39.00	28.00
☐ 1035 (M) Elvis' Christmas Album (double-pocket)	75.00	190.00	82.50
☐ 1707 (M) Elvis' Golden Records	17.00	39.00	28.00
☐ 1884 (M) King Creole	17.00	39.00	28.00
☐ 1951 (M) Elvis' Christmas Album (reissue) (photo on back)	17.00	39.00	28.00
☐ 1990 (M) For LP Fans Only	24.00	56.00	40.00
☐ 2011 (M) A Date with Elvis (double pocket)	34.00	84.00	59.00
☐ 2011 (M) A Date with Elvis (single pocket)	17.00	39.00	28.00
☐ 2075 (M) Elvis' Golden Records, Vol. II	17.00	39.00	28.00

	Current Price Range		P/Y Average

THE ALBUMS BELOW HAVE EQUIVALENT VALUE IN MONO AND STEREO

	Current Price Range		P/Y Average
☐ 2231 (M) *Elvis is Back*	17.00	39.00	28.00
☐ 2256 (M) *G.I. Blues*	17.00	39.00	28.00
☐ 2328 (M) *His Hand in Mine*	12.00	29.00	20.50
☐ 2370 (M) *Something for Everybody*	17.00	39.00	28.00
☐ 2436 (M) *Blue Hawaii*	17.00	39.00	28.00
☐ 2523 (M) *Pot Luck*	17.00	39.00	28.00
☐ 2621 (M) *Girls! Girls! Girls!*	17.00	39.00	28.00
☐ 2697 (M) *It Happened at the World's Fair*	17.00	39.00	28.00
☐ 2697 (M) *Fun in Acapulco*	15.00	35.00	25.00
☐ 2765 (M) *Elvis' Golden Records, Vol. III*	15.00	35.00	25.00
☐ 2894 (M) *Kissin' Cousins*	15.00	35.00	25.00
☐ 2999 (M) *Roustabout*	15.00	35.00	25.00
☐ 3338 (M) *Girl Happy*	15.00	35.00	25.00
☐ 3450 (M) *Elvis for Everyone*	15.00	35.00	25.00
☐ 3468 (M) *Harum Scarum (with photo enclosed)*	20.00	35.00	27.50
☐ 3553 (M) *Frankie and Johnny*	17.00	39.00	28.00
☐ 3643 (M) *Paradise, Hawaiian Style*	15.00	35.00	25.00
☐ 3702 (M) *Spinout*	17.00	39.00	28.00
☐ 3758 (M) *How Great Thou Art*	15.00	35.00	25.00
☐ 3787 (M) *Double Trouble*	15.00	35.00	25.00

THE ALBUMS BELOW HAVE A HIGHER VALUE IN MONO

	Current Price Range		P/Y Average
☐ 3893 (M) *Clambake*	40.00	100.00	70.00
☐ 3893 (S) *Clambake*	17.00	39.00	28.00
☐ 3921 (M) *Elvis' Golden Records, Vol. IV*	90.00	240.00	165.00
☐ 3921 (S) *Elvis' Golden Records, Vol. IV*	17.00	39.00	28.00
☐ 3989 (M) *Speedway*	320.00	800.00	560.00
☐ 3989 (S) *Speedway*	17.00	39.00	28.00

EMBROIDERY

DESCRIPTION: Embroidery is decorative needlework using diverse threads such as silk, gold, wool or cotton stitched into any type of fabric including cloth or leather.

PERIOD: The most valuable and rarest embroidery work is from the 1700s. Embroidery pieces from the 1800s and 1900s are more readily available.

VALUE: The condition, workmanship, materials, design and age of a piece are equally important in determining value.

COMMENTS: Many hobbyists collect all types of embroidery while others collect by motif, stitch or country.

	Current Price Range		P/Y Average
□ **Embroidered Picture,** titled "Cornelia's Jewels," signed by Mary Beach of Saunders and Beach Academy, Dorchester, Massachusetts, embroidered and painted on silk, five figures in semi-classical style, inscription beneath, undated, c. 1830, 16 1/2″ x 16 1/2″	1800.00	2175.00	1975.00
□ **Embroidered Picture,** titled "Spring," anonymous, showing two women and a man in a field, one of the women seated, an overhanging tree nearby, place of origin not known, probably late 18th century or early 19th century, 16 1/2″ x 18″	625.00	750.00	670.00
□ **Embroidered Picture on Silk,** titled "Timoclea," signed by Harriet Valentine, a classical scene from the legend of Timoclea with numerous figures clad in robes, the embroidery done in chenille and silk thread, undated, c. 1840, 26″ x 36″	850.00	1075.00	920.00

Tea Cloth, *royal blue with white embroidery and crocheted trim, 1930s,* $10.00-$15.00

	Current Price Range		P/Y Average

□ **Embroidered Picture on Silk,** untitled, an American eagle with spread wings near the top, in the central portion a vignette of a World War I naval gunnery ship surrounded by flags, also cannon and anchor devices, probably made in the Orient for sale on the U.S. market at the time of World War I, c. 1918, 42″ x 25 1/2″ 450.00 575.00 500.00

□ **Needlework Map of Maryland,** also showing portions of New Jersey and Pennsylvania, signed by Harriet Beall, done in a variety of stitches and colors, undated, probably very early 19th century, 13″ x 17 1/2″ 800.00 1000.00 875.00

□ **Silk and Chenille Embroidered Floral Picture,** signed with initials "G.M.," worked in various colors of chenille thread against solid beige silk background, picturing a basket filled with an assortment of flowers, place of origin unknown, c. 1820, 22″ x 19″ 375.00 450.00 410.00

□ **Tent-Stitched Picture,** titled "Fishing Lady," shows lady at pond hooking fish while man stands by with hat in hand, various colors of wool thread woven into a canvas backing, Connecticut origin, mid 1700s, 16″ x 20″ 4475.00 5600.00 4800.00

□ **Yarn-sewn Wall Picture,** untitled, signed by Christine Wuerpel, showing a male and female rider in a sleigh being drawn across a snow-covered field by a light and dark horse, undated, c. 1880, 22″ x 33″ 325.00 425.00 365.00

EYEGLASSES

TOPIC: Eyeglasses are devices that enhance eyesight. They consist of one or two glass or plastic lenses, and a frame to help the user keep the lenses in front of his eyes.

TYPES: Common types of eyeglasses that collectors are interested in include the quizzing glass, scissors-glasses, temple spectacles and the lorgnette. The quizzing glass was an early version of the monocle. Scissors-glasses consisted of two eyepieces connected by a hinged handle that was held under the nose. Temple spectacles employ two bars that press against the temples; these are modern eyeglasses. The lorgnette is a pair of eyepieces with a handle on one side.

PERIOD: Although eyeglasses have been available since the 1200s, they did not come into general use until the 1780s.

COMMENTS: Wild styles of eyeglasses from the 1960s are currently in demand among collectors. Prices for these and other types of eyeglasses are still reasonable.

ADDITIONAL TIPS: Old eyeglasses can be found through Lions and Rotary Clubs, which collect eyeglasses for the needy. Optometrist offices are another good source for collectible specimens.

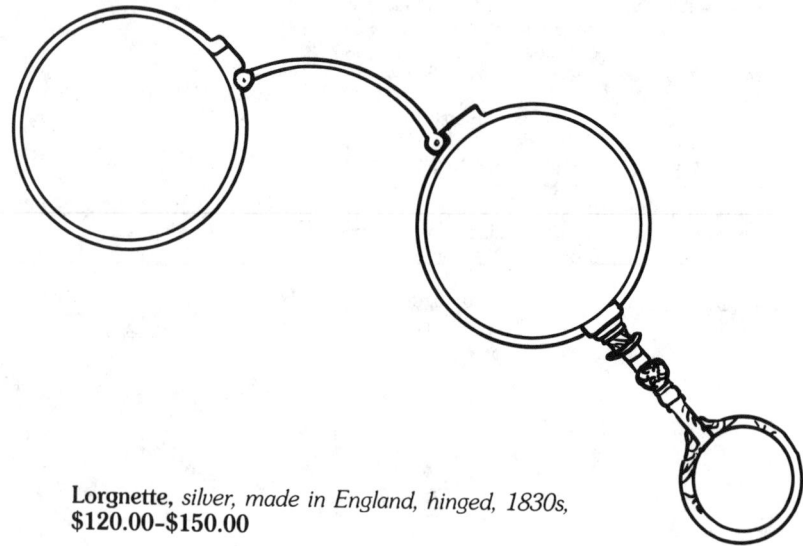

Lorgnette, *silver, made in England, hinged, 1830s,* $120.00–$150.00

	Current Price Range		P/Y Average
☐ **Harold Lloyd,** bone frame, c. 1920	60.00	78.00	69.00
☐ **Lorgnette,** English, gilded, c. 1840	130.00	150.00	140.00
☐ **Lorgnette,** mother-of-pearl, c. 1800	70.00	90.00	80.00
☐ **Lorgnette,** sterling silver, c. 1840	160.00	190.00	175.00
☐ **Lorgnette,** tortoiseshell, c. 1800	130.00	150.00	140.00
☐ **Magnifying,** plain silver frame, c. 1910	30.00	40.00	35.00
☐ **Monocle,** gold frame, silk cord, c. 1800	50.00	80.00	65.00
☐ **Quizzing,** monocle, gold and silver, c. 1800 ...	80.00	100.00	90.00
☐ **Scissor,** gold plated, ornate, c. 1880	85.00	95.00	90.00
☐ **Spectacles,** pinch, Art Deco, wire frame, c. 1930	60.00	80.00	70.00
☐ **Spectacles,** pinch, Edwardian, 16k gold	100.00	130.00	115.00
☐ **Spectacles,** pinch, hard rubber, c. 1860	65.00	85.00	75.00

	Current Price Range		P/Y Average
☐ **Spectacles,** pinch, sterling silver, c. 1920	85.00	105.00	95.00
☐ **Spectacles,** pinch, wire frame, c. 1920	63.00	83.00	73.00
☐ **Spectacles,** steel framed with ties, c. 1800 . . .	110.00	120.00	115.00
☐ **Spectacles,** steel framed, wire temples, c. 1800	100.00	130.00	115.00

CASES

☐ **Engraved Silver,** oval, clasp works, c. 1900 . .	140.00	160.00	150.00
☐ **Papier-mache,** with mother-of-pearl inlay, c. 1850–1860	145.00	175.00	160.00

EZRA BROOKS BOTTLES

DESCRIPTION: Ezra Brooks bottles are collector figural bottles manufactured by the Ezra Brooks Distilling Co., Frankfurt, Kentucky.

TYPES: Ezra Brooks produces figural bottles with themes from sports and transportation to antiques. The antique series includes an Edison phonograph and a Spanish cannon.

COMMENTS: Ezra Brooks rivals Jim Beam as one of the chief whiskey companies manufacturing figural bottles.

ADDITIONAL TIPS: For more information, consult *The Official Price Guide to Bottles, Old and New,* published by The House of Collectibles.

☐ **Alabama Bicentennial** (1976)	10.00	15.00	12.50
☐ **American Legion** (1971), distinguished embossed star emblem born out of WWI struggle. Combination blue and gold. On blue base	25.00	34.00	29.00
☐ **American Legion** (1972), Ezra Brooks salutes the American Legion, its Illinois Department, and Land of Lincoln and the city of Chicago, host of the Legion's 54th National Convention	60.00	70.00	65.00
☐ **American Legion** (1973), Hawaii, our fiftieth state, hosted the American Legion's 1973 annual Convention. It was the largest airlift of a mass			

Ezra Brooks Drum and Bugle
Conquistador, *(1971)*,
$10.00-$15.00

	Current Price Range		P/Y Average
group ever to hit the islands. Over 15,000 Legionnaires visited the beautiful city of Honolulu to celebrate the Legion's fifty-fourth anniversary	10.00	15.00	12.50
☐ **American Legion** (1977) Denver	20.00	30.00	25.00
☐ **American Legion** (1973) Miami Beach	8.00	12.00	10.00
☐ **Amvets** (1974) Dolphin	16.00	20.00	18.00
☐ **Amvet** (1973) Polish Legion	16.00	22.00	19.00
☐ **Antique Cannon** (1969)	5.00	8.00	6.50
☐ **Antique Phonograph** (1970), Edison's early contribution to home entertainment. White, black, "Morning Glory" horn, red. Richly detailed in 24k gold	8.00	12.00	10.00
☐ **Arizona** (1969), man with burro in search of "Lost Dutchman Mine", golden brown mesa, green cactus, with 22k gold base, "ARIZONA" imprinted	5.00	8.00	6.50
☐ **Auburn 1932** (1978) Classic Car	30.00	40.00	35.00
☐ **Badger No. 1** (1973) Boxer	14.00	20.00	17.00
☐ **Badger No. 2** (1974) Football	16.00	24.00	20.00
☐ **Badger No. 3** (1974) Hockey	16.00	24.00	20.00
☐ **Baltimore Oriole Wild Life** (1979)	35.00	45.00	40.00
☐ **Bare Knuckle Fighter** (1971)	6.00	10.00	8.00
☐ **Baseball Hall of Fame** (1973), baseball fans everywhere will enjoy this genuine Heritage China ceramic of a familiar slugger of years gone by	16.00	21.00	19.00

	Current Price Range		P/Y Average
☐ **Basketball Player** (1974)	8.00	12.00	10.00
☐ **Bear** (1968)	5.00	8.00	6.50
☐ **Bengal Tiger Wild Life** (1979)	32.00	40.00	36.00
☐ **Betsy Ross** (1975)	12.00	18.00	15.00
☐ **Big Bertha,** Nugget Casino's very-own elephant with a raised trunk, gray, red, white and black, yellow & gold trim. "Blanket" and stand	8.00	12.00	10.00
☐ **Big Daddy Lounge** (1969), salute to South Florida's "STATE" liquor chain, and "Big Daddy's" lounges. White, green, red	5.00	10.00	7.50
☐ **Bighorn Ram** (1973)	8.00	11.00	9.50
☐ **Bird Dog** (1971)	10.00	18.00	14.00
☐ **Bordertown,** Borderline Club where California and Nevada meet for a drink. Brown, red, white. Club Building with Vulture on roof stopper, and outhouse...............................	5.00	10.00	7.50
☐ **Bowler** (1973)	5.00	10.00	7.50
☐ **Brahma Bull** (1972)	12.00	18.00	15.00
☐ **Clown** (1978), Imperial Shrine	20.00	28.00	24.00
☐ **Club Bottle** (1973), the third commemorative Ezra Brooks Collector Club bottle is created in the shape of America, each gold star on the new club bottle represents the location of an Ezra Brooks Collectors Club	21.00	28.00	24.00
☐ **Clydesdale Horse** (1973), in the early days of distilling, Clydesdales carted the bottles of whiskey from the distillery to towns all across America	10.00	16.00	13.00
☐ **Colt Peacemaker** (1969), flask	4.00	8.00	6.00
☐ **Conquistadors,** tribute to a great drum & bugle corps, silver colored trumpet attached to drum	6.00	12.00	8.00
☐ **Conquistador's Drum & Bugle** (1972)	10.00	18.00	14.00
☐ **Corvette Indy Pace Car** (1978)	40.00	50.00	45.00
☐ **Maine Lobster** (1970), bottle in Lobster shape, complete with claws, pinkish-red color, bottle is sold only in Maine	20.00	28.00	24.00
☐ **Maine Lighthouse** (1971).................	16.00	20.00	18.00
☐ **Man-O-War** (1969), "Big Red" captured just about every major horse-racing prize in turfdom, replica of famous horse in brown and green, 22k gold base, embossed, "MAN-O-WAR"	10.00	16.00	13.00
☐ **M & M Brown Jug** (1975)	18.00	24.00	21.00
☐ **Map** (1972), U.S.A. Club Bottle	8.00	14.00	11.00
☐ **Masonic Fez** (1976)	10.00	18.00	14.00
☐ **Max** (1976), the hat, Zimmerman	25.00	30.00	27.50
☐ **Military Tank** (1971)	15.00	22.00	19.50
☐ **Minnesota Hockey Player** (1975)	18.00	22.00	20.00
☐ **Minuteman** (1975)	12.00	18.00	14.00
☐ **Missouri Mule** (1972), brown	12.00	15.00	13.50

	Current Price Range		P/Y Average

☐ **Moose** (1973) 22.00 30.00 26.00

☐ **Mr. Maine Potato** (1973), from early beginnings the people of Maine have built the small potato into a giant industry, today potatoes are the number one agricultural crop in the state, over thirty-six billion pounds are grown every year 6.00 10.00 8.00

☐ **Mr. Foremost** (1969), an authentic reproduction of the famous bottle-shaped symbol of Foremost Liquor stores, "Mr. Foremost" known for good wines and spirits, red, white and black 9.00 12.00 10.50

☐ **Mr. Merchant** (1970), JUMPING MAN, Whimsical, checkered-vest caricature of amiable shopkeeper, leaping into the air, arms outstretched, yellow, black 8.00 12.00 10.00

☐ **Motorcycle,** motorcycle rider and machine, rider dressed in blue pants, red jacket, with stars 'n stripes helmet, motorcycle black with red tank on silver base 8.00 12.00 10.00

☐ **Mountaineer** (1971), figure dressed in buckskin, holding rifle, "MOUNTAINEERS ARE ALWAYS FREE" embossed on base, bottle is hand-trimmed in platinum, one of the most valuable Ezra Brooks figural bottles 40.00 60.00 50.00

☐ **Mustang Indy Pace Car** (1979) 12.00 18.00 15.00

☐ **New Hampshire State House** (1970), 150-year old State House, embossed doors, windows, steps, eagle topped stopper, gray building with gold 10.00 14.00 12.00

☐ **Nebraska—Go Big Red!** (1972), genuine Heritage China reproduction of a game ball and fan, trimmed in genuine 24k gold 10.00 14.00 12.00

☐ **North Carolina Bicentennial** (1975) 10.00 14.00 12.00

☐ **Nugget Classic,** replica of golf pin presented to golf tournament participants, finished in 22k gold
.... 8.00 10.00 9.00

☐ **Oil Gusher,** bottle in shape of oil drilling rig, all silver, jet black stopper in shape of gushing oil 5.00 8.00 6.50

☐ **Old Capitol** (1971), bottle in shape of Iowa's seat of government when the corn state was still frontier territory, embossed windows, doors, pillars, "OLD CAPITOL/IOWA 1840–1857" on base, reddish color with gold dome stopper 15.00 22.00 19.00

☐ **Old Ez** (1977), No. 1, barn owl 45.00 55.00 50.00

☐ **Old Ez** (1978), No. 2, eagle owl 62.00 66.00 64.00

☐ **Old Ez** (1979), No. 3, snow owl.............. 40.00 45.00 42.50

☐ **Panda—Giant** (1972), Giant Panda ceramic bottle....................................... 14.00 18.00 16.00

☐ **Penguin** (1972), Ezra Brooks salutes the penguin with a genuine Heritage China ceramic figural bottle 8.00 12.00 10.00

☐ **Reno Arch** (1968), honoring the "biggest little city in the world", Reno, Nevada, arch shape with "RENO" embossed on yellow, front of bottle

	Current Price Range		P/Y Average

multi-color decal of: dice, rabbits foot, roulette wheel, slot machine, etc., white and yellow, purple stopper	5.00	10.00	7.50
☐ **San Francisco Cable Car** (1968)	10.00	16.00	13.00
☐ **Sailfish** (1971), leaping deep water Sailfish with a sword-like nose and large spread fin, blue-green luminous tones on green "waves" base	8.00	12.00	10.00
☐ **Salmon** (1971), Washington King	12.00	18.00	15.00
☐ **San Francisco Cable Car** (1968)	10.00	16.00	13.00
☐ **Sea Captain** (1971), salty old seadog, white hair and beard, in blue "captains" jacket with gold buttons and sleeve stripes, white cap, gold band, holding pipe, on "wooden" stanchion base	10.00	14.00	12.00
☐ **Senator** (1971), cigar-chomping, whistle-stopping State Senator, stumping on a platform of pure nostalgia, black "western" hat and swallow-tail coat, red vest, string tie, gold, black red, white	12.00	16.00	14.00
☐ **Senators of the U.S.** (1972), Ezra Brooks honors the Senators of the United States of America with this genuine Heritage Ceramic "Old Time" courtly Senator	12.00	16.00	14.00
☐ **Setter** (1974).............................	12.00	18.00	15.00
☐ **Shrine King Tut Guard** (1979)	30.00	38.00	34.00
☐ **Silver Saddle** (1973)	24.00	30.00	27.00
☐ **Silver Spur Boot** (1971), cowboy-boot shaped bottle with silver spur buckled on, "SILVER SPUR—CARSON CITY NEVADA" embossed on the side of boot, brown boot with platinum trim	8.00	14.00	11.00
☐ **1804 Silver Dollar** (1970), commemorates the famous and very valuable "1804 Silver Dollar," embossed replica of the Liberty Head dollar, platinum covered round dollar shaped bottle on black or white base	5.00	8.00	6.50

FANS

ORIGIN: Folding fans were popular and fashionable accessories for women of means during the 18th, 19th, and even into the early 20th centuries. Aside from the obvious function of being used to cool oneself, fans were used to show not only one's social position and wealth, but also for coquetry or flirting.

The Oriental version–like all Oriental artifacts–was a symbolic and functional device, essential to the proper code of daily living. Men as well as women utilized them, from the scented fans of the elderly, to the black and red implements of the military. A popular export item (particularly the delicate ivory fans, carved under water and much sought after as wedding gifts), fans served many functions in Oriental society. They were used for cooling of course, but also as an essential fashion accessory, for fanning flames, to direct military troops, as message carriers, in dances, stories, games and wrestling matches.

CONSTRUCTION: Folding fans were constructed in one of two ways. The more common method was the insertion of sticks into a pleated piece of material called a "leaf." Leaves were made of silk lace, paper, or even vellum (very thin goatskin). The other type of folding fan was called a "brise." The brise fan was made up of wide, overlapping sticks and joined by a ribbon. Nearly all fans of both types have scenes or designs painted on them.

Another type, considered quite stylish from the 1870s until about 1910, was the feather fan. Usually made of ostrich feathers, this type was quite perishable and is now relatively rare.

Beautifully drawn, painted, or inscribed, Oriental fans fell into two main structural categories. Women's fans were usually non-folding, consisting of a roundish piece of paper glued to a flat bamboo handle. Folding fans, used more extensively in ritual ceremonies, or by high born citizens, were made of paper or silk, with wooden, bamboo, ivory, or mother-of-pearl ribs.

ADDITIONAL TIPS: Because fans are not durable collectibles, their numbers tend to be rather low and prices accordingly high. Once a beautiful fan is acquired, the methods of display and preservation are vital factors. Special attention should be paid to store the item in an airtight container that screens out damaging ultraviolet rays. Most specimens do well when placed in a protective frame.

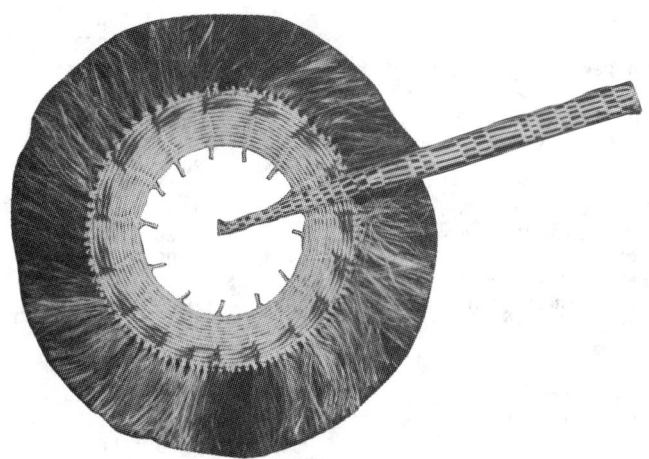

Fan, woven straw with tortoiseshell, 1920s, $8.00-$10.00

RECOMMENDED READING: For more in-depth information on fans you may refer to *The Official Price Guide to Oriental Collectibles,* published by The House of Collectibles.

	Current Price Range		P/Y Average
☐ **Advertising,** Hire's Root Beer, 6½", c. 1930	10.00	15.00	12.50
☐ **Advertising,** Homer's 5 Cigar, 7", c. 1910	10.00	15.00	12.50
☐ **Advertising,** lithographed, late 19th c.........	10.00	15.00	12.50
☐ **Black net,** with sequins	20.00	30.00	25.00
☐ **Bride's,** lace, hand painted	20.00	30.00	25.00
☐ **Bride's,** lace, sequins, ivory sticks	35.00	45.00	37.50
☐ **Brise,** child's, painted, ribbon and floral design	65.00	75.00	70.00
☐ **Brise,** gilded, painted with three vignettes, loop	130.00	160.00	145.00
☐ **Brise,** Regency, painted floral design, amber guards	120.00	130.00	125.00
☐ **Brise,** Regency, painted vase of flowers	40.00	60.00	50.00
☐ **Celluloid,** carved flower	40.00	60.00	50.00
☐ **Celluloid,** miniature	40.00	60.00	50.00
☐ **Celluloid,** Oriental design	20.00	30.00	25.00
☐ **Celluloid,** sequins, chiffon	45.00	50.00	47.50
☐ **Cockade,** silver and cut steel pique, middle quizzing glass	275.00	300.00	237.50
☐ **Feather,** celluloid sticks	45.00	55.00	50.00
☐ **Feather,** ivory sticks	100.00	140.00	120.00
☐ **Feather,** painted, c. 1870	100.00	110.00	105.00
☐ **Feather,** tortoiseshell sticks	100.00	110.00	105.00
☐ **Feather,** small, late 19th c.	120.00	130.00	125.00
☐ **Feather,** signed Duvelleroy, 19th c.	500.00	600.00	550.00
☐ **French,** painted, ivory sticks	175.00	185.00	170.00
☐ **French,** painted, tortoise sticks, sequins	175.00	185.00	170.00

		Current Price Range		P/Y Average
French, painted, signed Jolivet, 19th c.	500.00	700.00	600.00
French, painted, carved, signed	75.00	85.00	80.00
Garrett Snuff, advertising, paper, c. 1928	15.00	20.00	17.50
George Washington and Cherry Smash, lithographed	20.00	30.00	25.00
Gold edge, pink silk, ebony ribs	30.00	35.00	32.50
Hand painted, floral design, wood	20.00	30.00	25.00
Horn, carved, painted pansies, blue ribbon	100.00	130.00	115.00
Lacquered, black, silver flower	75.00	85.00	80.00
Lacquered, white, silver handle	55.00	65.00	60.00
Marabou feathers, satin, hand painted, 20″	125.00	145.00	135.00
Oriental, bamboo, 7″ x 20″, 1900s, signed Liang Zhuang-cheng	450.00	650.00	550.00
Oriental, bamboo and birds, 8″ x 23″, c. 1820–1875, signed by Hezhong	450.00	650.00	550.00
Oriental, bamboo, rock and trees, 6″ x 18″, c. 1910–1930, by Wu Hafan	8000.00	12000.00	1000.00
Oriental, bird and fruit blossoms, 6″ x 18″, c. 1620–1665, by Ren Yi	2050.00	3100.00	2500.00
Oriental, birds and bamboo, 6″ x 18″, c. 1830–1845, by Ren Yi	10000.00	12000.00	11000.00
Oriental, birds, flowers, rocks, bamboo, 6″ x 19″, c. 1820–1865, by Ren Yi	850.00	1250.00	1050.00
Oriental, blossom, 7″ x 21″, c. 1820–1875, by Hu Gongshou	450.00	650.00	550.00
Oriental, blossoms, 8″ x 21″, c. 1820–1875, by Hu Gongshou	550.00	750.00	650.00
Oriental, calligraphy, 7″ x 20″, c. 1820–1895, by Liu Rongsi	450.00	650.00	550.00
Oriental, calligraphy, 6″ x 21″, c. 1620–1665, by Yilin	1050.00	1250.00	1150.00
Oriental, city scene, 7″ x 20″, c. 1820–1875, by Wang Kun	450.00	650.00	550.00
Oriental, cricket and mulberries, 8″, x 21″, c. 1890–1910, by Wang Kun	15000.00	20000.00	17500.00
Oriental, egrets, 8″ x 21″, c. 1850–1895, by Wang Kun	6000.00	8000.00	7000.00
Oriental, female, 7″ x 21″, c. 1820–1875, figure preparing to mount horse, by Gu Luo	555.00	750.00	650.00
Oriental, flowers and wood, 6″ x 17″, c. 1505–1575	850.00	1050.00	950.00
Oriental, fruit and blossoms, 7″ x 21″, c. 1820–1875, by Deng Qichang	650.00	850.00	750.00
Oriental, immortal and goose, 6″ x 18″, c. 1930–1950, by Ren Yi	12000.00	15000.00	13500.00
Oriental, landscape and calligraphy, 7″ x 21″, c. 1890–1910, by PuRu	6000.00	8000.00	7000.00
Oriental, landscape, 7″ x 22″, c. 1720–1795, by Fang Shishu	1250.00	1550.00	1400.00
Oriental, landscape, 7″ x 20″, c. 1820–1890, by Dai Jian	350.00	550.00	450.00
Oriental, landscape, 7″ x 21″, c. 1820–1875, by Yongbo	550.00	750.00	650.00

	Current Price Range		P/Y Average
☐ **Oriental,** landscape, 7″ x 20″, 1620–1665, artist unknown	1550.00	2050.00	1800.00
☐ **Oriental,** landscape, 7″ x 20″, c. 1720–1795, by Huang Yi	1050.00	1250.00	1175.00
☐ **Oriental,** lohan, 7″ x 20″, c. 1820–1875, by Ren Xun	4000.00	6000.00	5000.00
☐ **Oriental,** lohans, 6″ x 18″, c. 1820–1875, signed Fanglan	650.00	850.00	750.00
☐ **Oriental,** lotus flower, 7″ x 20″, c. 1930–1950, by Zhang Daqian	25000.00	30000.00	27500.00
☐ **Oriental,** magnolia, 6″ x 18″, c. 1910–1930, by Shao'ang	3000.00	3500.00	3250.00
☐ **Oriental,** man and youth, 7″ x 20″, c. 1820–1875, by Fena Ning	450.00	650.00	550.00
☐ **Oriental,** man at table 7″ x 20″, c. 1820–1875, by Ren Xun	1250.00	1550.00	1375.00
☐ **Oriental,** mountain scene, 8″ x 22″, by Juru Bao	450.00	650.00	550.00
☐ **Oriental,** pavilions, 8″ x 21″, c. 1820–1875, artist unknown	2100.00	2550.00	2325.00
☐ **Oriental,** poem in character, 7″ x 20″, c. 1620–1665, by Jiang Jie	710.00	920.00	815.00
☐ **Oriental,** poem, 7″ x 22″, c. 1620–1665, by Shu Youzhang	550.00	650.00	600.00
☐ **Oriental,** poem, 8″ x 21″, c. 1820–1870, artist unknown	450.00	650.00	550.00
☐ **Oriental,** riverscape, 6″ x 20″, by Shu Youzhang	550.00	950.00	850.00
☐ **Oriental,** rocks and bamboo, 7″ x 21″, c. 1890–1910, artist unknown	350.00	500.00	425.00
☐ **Oriental,** sailboats, 6″ x 20″, 1505–1575, artist unknown	850.00	1250.00	925.00
☐ **Oriental,** scholar in a landscape scene, 6″ x 18″, c. 1890–1910, by PuRu	6000.00	8000.00	7000.00
☐ **Oriental,** the court, 75 x 2″, c. 1620–1675, artist unknown	250.00	350.00	300.00
☐ **Oriental,** tiger and priest, 8″ x 21″, c. 1820–1875, by Cao Hua	450.00	650.00	550.00
☐ **Oriental,** wiseman on the water, 7″ x 215, c. 1720–1795, by Bi Han	650.00	850.00	750.00
☐ **Oriental,** straw, lacquered handle	15.00	20.00	17.50
☐ **Oriental,** silk, Geisha figure	10.00	15.00	12.50
☐ **Ostrich plume,** tortoise shell sticks	50.00	60.00	55.00
☐ **Pearl sticks,** sequin design, 8″	35.00	45.00	40.00
☐ **Puzzle,** four scenes, two-way opening	150.00	170.00	160.00
☐ **Satin flower center,** carved, ivory sticks	150.00	170.00	160.00
☐ **Silk,** embroidered, ivory sticks	75.00	85.00	80.00
☐ **Silk,** hand painted animal figure and books	25.00	35.00	30.00
☐ **Silk,** hand painted figures and floral designs, original storage container	65.00	75.00	70.00
☐ **Silk,** Oriental design, ivory and bamboo	45.00	55.00	50.00
☐ **Souvenir Centennial,** historical buildings, 12″	100.00	110.00	105.00
☐ **Wedding,** ivory sticks, lace	65.00	75.00	70.00

FARM EQUIPMENT

DESCRIPTION: Farm equipment includes any implement used for agriculture.

TYPES: Farm equipment includes tractors, potato diggers, pitchforks, plows and cultivators.

PERIOD: Americans began using farm machinery during the early 1800s. Although farm equipment from the early years often consisted of impractical inventions that did not survive, those which did are highly collectible.

MAKER: In the 1800s and early 1900s, there were many manufacturers who later went out of business. The obscure company's equipment is usually more valuable due to rarity than an existing company's equipment. Rock Island Plow Company, the Minneapolis Threshing Machine Company and the Avery Manufacturing Company are examples of relatively obscure companies, while John Deere and International Harvester are companies which have existed since the 1800s.

	Current Price Range		P/Y Average
☐ **Avery steam engine,** 40 hp. with full extension wheels, 1912	1650.00	1850.00	1700.00
☐ **Baker steam engine,** 20 hp. single cylinder side mount, 1920	3250.00	3550.00	3350.00
☐ **Case Tractor,** model "C," 4 cylinder, rubber wheels, restored, good condition, c. 1927	800.00	1050.00	900.00
☐ **Case Tractor,** VAC model, rubber wheels, restored, good condition, c. 1931	360.00	510.00	420.00
☐ **Chilled Plow,** Richland Farm Implements, iron and oak, for two or three horses	150.00	250.00	200.00
☐ **International Harvester Tractor,** model "H," rubber wheels, restored, good condition, c. 1937	800.00	1050.00	900.00
☐ **John Deere Tractor,** model "B," rubber wheels, restored, good condition, c. 1935	420.00	620.00	500.00
☐ **Russell Traction Steam Machine,** 8 hp., restored	3550.00	4050.00	3750.00
☐ **Sattley's Timber Saw,** kerosene engine	1250.00	1450.00	1300.00

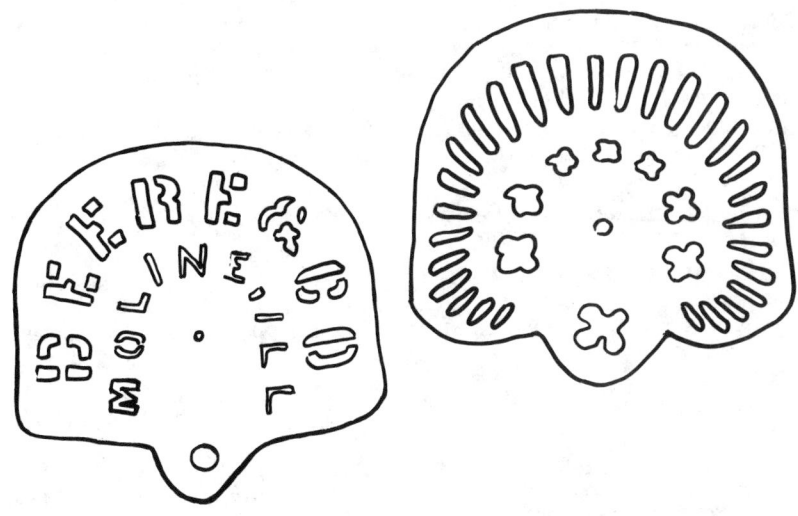

Left to Right: *tractor seat, iron, Deere & Co., Moline, ILL imprinted in seat,* **$20.00-$40.00;** *tractor seat, J.I. Case, Racine, WI, 1800s,* **$100.00-$120.00**

FIESTA WARE

DESCRIPTION: Fiesta Ware is a line of brightly colored pottery tableware introduced in 1935 by the Homer Laughlin China Company of East Liverpool, Ohio.

DESIGN: The design is a series of rings which graduate in size, with the smallest ring at the center and the greatest width between rings also at the center. This design is mostly used on the rims and at the center of items such as plates, bowls, etc. It is also used on pieces with small pedestal bases and on lids.

COLOR: The colors used for these wares are Fiesta red, rose, dark green, medium green, light green, chartreuse, yellow, old ivory, gray, turquoise and dark blue. Red is the most valuable.

COMMENTS: Fiesta began to be actively collected in the 1960s and a big surge of popularity followed in the next decade. Prices on the secondhand market zoomed from an average of 25¢ to 35¢ to the $5 to $10 range. This seemed unbelievable, because everyone knew Fiesta ware was very common—it had been one of the most widely manufactured tablewares of the 20th century. Nevertheless, buyer demand was strong, and with this kind of demand anything can happen to retail prices.

MARKS: Each piece, except a very few, is marked with the Fiesta trademark, either in the mold or an ink handstamped mark.

RECOMMENDED READING: For more in-depth information on Fiesta Ware you may refer to *The Official Price Guide to Pottery and Porcelain* and *The Official Identification Guide to Pottery and Porcelain*, published by The House of Collectibles.

	Current Price Range		P/Y Average
Blue			
☐ **Bowl,** dessert, 6", 1959	9.00	11.00	9.50
☐ **Bowl,** salad, 10", footed	65.00	75.00	68.00
☐ **Candleholders,** pair, spherical body on square base	62.00	72.00	64.00
☐ **Carafe**	28.00	32.00	29.00
☐ **Plate,** 13"	15.00	20.00	16.00
☐ **Tumbler,** footed	18.00	22.00	19.00
Gray			
☐ **Bowl,** dessert, 4½"	8.00	12.00	9.00
☐ **Bowl,** fruit, 5½"	8.00	12.00	9.00
☐ **Plate,** 9½"	7.00	9.00	8.00
Ivory			
☐ **Carafe,** three pint, cork seal top, 1940s	29.00	34.00	30.00
☐ **Creamer**	4.00	6.00	5.00
☐ **Gravy Boat**	16.00	22.00	17.00
☐ **Plate,** 6"	3.00	5.00	4.00
☐ **Plate,** 9½"	6.50	8.00	7.00
☐ **Plate,** 10½"	18.00	22.00	19.00
☐ **Plate,** 13"	9.00	15.00	10.00
☐ **Relish,** three compartments	40.00	50.00	42.00
☐ **Soup Plate,** scalloped rim	9.00	12.00	10.00
☐ **Tray,** relish, 1939	37.00	42.00	38.00
Light Green			
☐ **Bowl,** fruit, 5½"	6.00	8.00	7.00
☐ **Coffeepot,** lidded	25.00	30.00	26.00
☐ **Creamer,** ring handle, small pedestal base	6.00	8.00	7.00
☐ **Cup And Saucer**	10.00	15.00	11.00
☐ **Plate,** 11"	8.00	10.00	9.00
☐ **Platter,** 12"	9.00	12.00	10.00
☐ **Salt and Pepper Shakers**	9.00	12.00	10.00
☐ **Sauceboat,** handled, on small pedestal base, 1939	11.00	14.00	12.00
Medium Green			
☐ **Bowl,** dessert, 1959	22.00	27.00	23.00
☐ **Bowl,** fruit, 4¾", flared rim	22.00	27.00	24.00

	Current Price Range		P/Y Average
☐ **Cup And Saucer**	20.00	30.00	21.00
☐ **Tray,** utility, extended rim	11.00	14.00	12.00
Red			
☐ **Ashtray**	18.00	25.00	19.00
☐ **Coffeepot,** notched lid and handle, 1930s	52.00	62.00	53.00
☐ **Cup and Saucer**	13.00	16.00	14.00
☐ **Pitcher,** juice	20.00	30.00	22.00
☐ **Plate,** 6″	4.00	6.00	4.50
☐ **Plate,** 11″	10.00	15.00	11.00
☐ **Sugar And Creamer,** 1940s	13.00	17.00	14.00
☐ **Teapot,** large, holds eight cups, ring handle, 1930s	27.00	35.00	28.00
☐ **Teapot,** small, lidded	50.00	60.00	52.00
☐ **Tumbler,** footed	15.00	17.00	16.00
Turquoise			
☐ **Bowl,** 4½″	7.50	9.50	8.00
☐ **Carafe**	32.00	38.00	33.00
☐ **Creamer**	52.00	67.00	54.00
☐ **Mug**	22.00	27.00	24.00
☐ **Plate,** 10½″, three compartments, flared rim, 1940s	8.00	11.00	9.00
☐ **Platter,** 12″, oval, with extended rim, 1939	8.00	11.00	9.00
☐ **Relish,** three compartments	45.00	55.00	46.00
☐ **Soup Plate,** scalloped rim	9.00	12.00	10.00
☐ **Sugar Bowl,** lidded	10.00	14.00	11.00

Pitcher,
water, Fiesta pattern,
$20.00-$30.00

	Current Price Range		P/Y Average
☐ **Tray**	52.00	62.00	53.00
☐ **Tumbler,** footed	11.00	14.00	12.00
☐ **Tumbler,** 5 ounces, cylindrical	11.00	14.00	12.00
Yellow			
☐ **Ashtray,** floral design	20.00	30.00	21.00
☐ **Ashtray,** three impressions, 1930s	17.00	22.00	18.00
☐ **Bowl,** salad, 9½″, pronounced rim	27.00	32.00	29.00
☐ **Candleholders,** pair, tripod	32.00	34.00	33.00
☐ **Casserole,** French Baker	60.00	70.00	62.00
☐ **Casserole,** notched lid and plug handle	66.00	82.00	67.00
☐ **Coffeepot,** lidded	40.00	80.00	42.00
☐ **Creamer**	5.00	7.00	6.00
☐ **Creamer,** experimental, ring handle	22.00	27.00	23.00
☐ **Creamer,** yellow, on small pedestal base	9.00	12.00	10.00
☐ **Cup And Saucer**	10.00	15.00	11.00
☐ **Mug**	22.00	27.00	23.00
☐ **Pitcher,** juice, disk shape, handled	9.00	11.00	10.00
☐ **Pitcher,** water	20.00	30.00	21.00
☐ **Plate,** 6″	4.00	6.00	5.00
☐ **Plate,** 9½″	6.00	8.00	7.00
☐ **Plate,** 13″	12.00	16.00	13.00
☐ **Plate,** chop, 6″	6.00	8.00	7.00
☐ **Plate,** dessert, 6″	6.00	8.00	7.00
☐ **Platter,** 12″, oval	11.00	14.00	12.00
☐ **Soup Plate,** scalloped rim	9.00	12.00	10.00
☐ **Sugar Bowl,** lidded	9.00	12.00	10.00
☐ **Teapot,** lidded	35.00	45.00	36.00
☐ **Tray**	52.00	62.00	53.00
☐ **Tray,** utility, 1940s	8.00	11.00	9.00
☐ **Tumbler,** 5 ounces	11.00	14.00	12.00

FIRE FIGHTING EQUIPMENT

VARIATIONS: All types of fire fighting equipment is collected, from fire engines to fire marks, axes and buckets.

PERIOD: Organized fire fighting began in the late 1650s in the United States when citizens were asked to keep leather buckets in their homes to put fires out with.

COMMENTS: Much equipment used by firemen received heavy use, so today many early items are scarce. This accounts for price variations and the high price often placed on small items.

ADDITIONAL TIPS: The listings are in alphabetical order according to item. Following the item are descriptions, dates and price ranges.

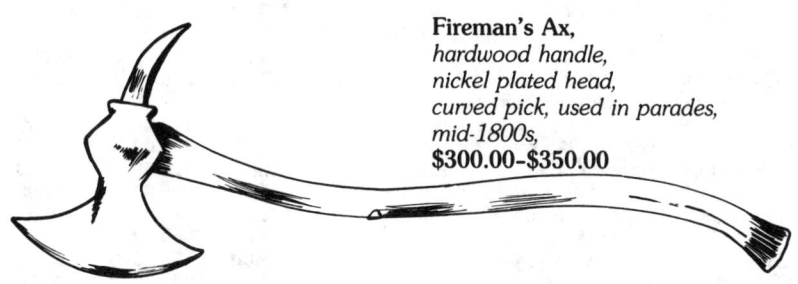

Fireman's Ax,
hardwood handle,
nickel plated head,
curved pick, used in parades,
mid-1800s,
$300.00–$350.00

	Current Price Range		P/Y Average
☐ **Axe,** nickel-plated head, c. 1850, ...	212.00	275.00	225.00
☐ **Banner,** for parades, with lantern, axe and trumpet	115.00	130.00	120.00
☐ **Bell,** brass, hand crank	275.00	350.00	300.00
☐ **Belt,** parade belt, leather	65.00	100.00	75.00
☐ **Belt,** parade belt, leather with black, white and red trim, shiled on buckle	35.00	50.00	38.00
☐ **Belt Buckle,** brass with fire engine engraved, c. 1970	68.00	85.00	72.00
☐ **Book,** *Our Fireman,* by A.E. Costello, history of New York fire departments, c. 1887	215.00	240.00	222.00
☐ **Bucket,** leather, decorated with helmet and hatchet	212.00	240.00	220.00
☐ **Bucket,** leather, painted	185.00	230.00	195.00
☐ **Bucket,** leather with red design	330.00	360.00	340.00
☐ **Bucket,** tin	30.00	40.00	32.00
☐ **Bucket,** with owner's name inscribed, 19th century	920.00	1500.00	970.00
☐ **Bucket,** wooden with iron bandings and leather strap handle, height 13″	20.00	30.00	23.00
☐ **Cap,** fireman's dress cap with badge	75.00	90.00	80.00
☐ **Extinguisher,** glass	52.00	70.00	57.00
☐ **Extinguisher,** brass	30.00	45.00	33.00
☐ **Extinguisher,** bulb shape	12.50	20.00	13.50
☐ **Extinguisher,** tin	13.00	23.00	14.00
☐ **Fire Bell,** nickel plated bronze, outside mechanism, mounted on board	180.00	220.00	195.00
☐ **Fire Engine,** American LaFrance, Auburn V-12 engine with ladders, siren, bell, c. 1944	1100.00	1400.00	1200.00
☐ **Fire Engine,** American LaFrance, 6 cyl., pumper, c. 1948	1350.00	1650.00	1400.00

	Current Price Range		P/Y Average
☐ **Fire Engine,** American LaFrance, 6 cyl., type 40 pumper, c. 1917	15000.00	18000.00	16500.00
☐ **Fire Engine,** American LaFrance, 6 cyl., type 75 pumper, c. 1924	2200.00	2600.00	2300.00
☐ **Fire Engine,** Chevrolet, 4 cyl., one ton, restored, excellent condition, c. 1927	4100.00	4500.00	4250.00
☐ **Fire Engine,** Ford, 8 cyl., restored, c. 1941	1750.00	2500.00	2000.00
☐ **Fire Engine,** Ford, F-6, V-8, equipped, c. 1948	1900.00	2500.00	2100.00
☐ **Fire Engine,** Ford, unrestored, c. 1947	1100.00	1400.00	1200.00
☐ **Fire Engine,** Seagrave, Model "A," 4 cyl., restored, c. 1928	16500.00	19500.00	17500.00
☐ **Fire Mark,** cast iron, c. 1860	240.00	280.00	250.00
☐ **Fire Mark,** hands clasped, Germantown National Fire, c. 1843	138.00	170.00	145.00
☐ **Fire Mark,** hydrant, F.A., brass plaque, c. 1817	200.00	240.00	210.00
☐ **Fire Mark,** hydrant, F.A., brass plaque, c. 1843	92.00	120.00	100.00
☐ **Fire Mark,** Insurance Co. of Florida, c. 1841	250.00	295.00	263.00
☐ **Fire Mark,** Mutual Assurance Co., iron plaque	125.00	175.00	140.00
☐ **Fire Mark,** Twentieth Century	38.00	60.00	45.00
☐ **Helmet,** aluminium with eagle finial	58.00	75.00	65.00
☐ **Helmet,** brass with eagle finial	225.00	275.00	240.00
☐ **Helmet,** hand painted shield, c. 19th century	525.00	575.00	540.00
☐ **Helmet,** leather, black embossed with brass eagle, c. 1889	88.00	120.00	95.00
☐ **Helmet,** leather, ornamental parade helmet, 18th century	675.00	750.00	700.00
☐ **Helmet,** leather, 6-seam, front shield	60.00	80.00	65.00
☐ **Helmet,** leather, white with eagle, 19th century	112.00	140.00	120.00
☐ **Helmet,** leather with trumpet finial	127.00	160.00	135.00
☐ **Helmet,** spike top, used for parades	135.00	170.00	142.00
☐ **Helmet,** three cornered, 19th century	1350.00	1650.00	1430.00
☐ **Honor Roll,** watercolor	312.00	350.00	320.00
☐ **Hose Nozzle,** brass, 12"	60.00	85.00	65.00
☐ **Hose Nozzle,** brass, 15"	78.00	108.00	85.00
☐ **Hose Nozzle,** copper, 25"	82.00	115.00	95.00
☐ **Horn,** brass	262.00	325.00	275.00
☐ **Lantern,** brass	100.00	175.00	120.00
☐ **Lantern,** nickel plated	80.00	95.00	83.00
☐ **Lantern,** wagon style with brass font	170.00	200.00	178.00
☐ **Spotlight,** nickel plated brass	160.00	180.00	165.00
☐ **Tickets,** fireman's benefit, 19th century	6.25	10.00	7.50
☐ **Trumpet,** brass, engraved	350.00	395.00	360.00
☐ **Trumpet,** nickel plated	138.00	170.00	148.00
☐ **Trumpet,** silver plated with red tassel	285.00	325.00	300.00
☐ **Trumpet,** sterling silver	438.00	500.00	450.00
☐ **Watch Fob,** copper	25.00	40.00	30.00
☐ **Watercolor Drawing,** pumpers, crowd, 19th century	385.00	440.00	400.00

FISHING TACKLE

DESCRIPTION: Rods, reels, flies and lures comprise the majority of collectible fishing tackle. The manufacture of fishing tackle did not begin in the United States until around 1810. Prior to that time, all fishing supplies were imported from Europe.

MAKERS: Reels made by J.F. and B.F. Meeks, B. Milam and Pfleuger are favored, as are rods made by Hiram Leonard. Flies, fake bait made by tying feathers, fur or other materials around the shaft of a hook, are also popular. There are over 5,000 patterns and sizes of flies, each with its own name. The manufacturer, or tier, of individual flies is very difficult to discern, unless the fly is in its original marked container.

Artificial Lure,
tin, "Arbogast,"
$5.00–$8.00

	Current Price Range		P/Y Average
☐ **Casting rod,** Heddon, split bamboo, 6', c. 1920	85.00	100.00	115.00
☐ **Casting rod,** split bamboo, straight handle, 5', c. 1800	45.00	55.00	50.00
☐ **Casting rod,** Tonkin, cane, 5½', c. 1900	55.00	65.00	60.00
☐ **Casting rod,** Union Hardware, 5', c. 1920	20.00	30.00	25.00
☐ **Casting rod,** Winchester, split bamboo, c. 1925	20.00	30.00	25.00
☐ **Creel fishing basket,** splint weave, pine lid, c. 1900	85.00	125.00	105.00

	Current Price Range		P/Y Average
□ **Creel fishing basket,** wicker with leather straps, c. 1880	115.00	165.00	140.00
□ **Fishhooks,** set of 50, c. 1910	20.00	24.00	22.00
□ **Flies,** English, set of 12, c. 1880	420.00	440.00	430.00
□ **Fly box,** metal, round, c. 1910	25.00	35.00	30.00
□ **Fly box,** wooden, 6" x 10", c. 1900	55.00	65.00	60.00
□ **Fly rod,** Heddon, split bamboo, 9½', c. 1922	65.00	75.00	70.00
□ **Fly rod,** H. L. Leonard, 8½', c. 1890	165.00	185.00	175.00
□ **Fly rod,** H. L. Leonard, 7', c. 1885	320.00	340.00	330.00
□ **Lure,** Heddon, wooden plug, Dowagiac Minnow	10.00	15.00	12.00
□ **Lure,** Heddon, wooden plug, Heddon's Minnow, #100 series	10.00	12.00	11.00
□ **Lure,** Heddon, wooden plug, Meadow Mouse, #4000 series	8.00	10.00	9.00
□ **Lure,** Shakespeare, wooden plug, Darting Shrimp, #135 series	13.00	15.00	14.00
□ **Reel,** Billinghurst, fly, nickel plated, c. 1869	190.00	250.00	220.00
□ **Reel,** Coxe, casting, aluminum, c. 1940	120.00	140.00	130.00
□ **Reel,** English fly, silver, c. 1850	520.00	620.00	570.00
□ **Reel,** Heddon, casting, silver, c. 1925	55.00	85.00	70.00
□ **Reel,** Hendryx, fly, brass, c. 1890	25.00	35.00	30.00
□ **Reel,** Leonard, fly, bronze, silver trim, c. 1878	470.00	570.00	520.00
□ **Reel,** Leonard, fly, silver, c. 1925	270.00	300.00	285.00
□ **Reel,** Meek, casting, brass, c. 1855	520.00	620.00	570.00
□ **Reel,** Meek, casting, silver, c. 1930	145.00	185.00	165.00
□ **Reel,** Meisselbach, casting, c. 1920	55.00	75.00	65.00
□ **Reel,** Meisselbach, fly, nickel plated, c. 1895	50.00	70.00	60.00
□ **Reel,** Meisselbach, trolling, wood, c. 1910	25.00	35.00	30.00
□ **Reel,** Milam, casting, brass, c. 1865	420.00	520.00	470.00
□ **Reel,** Milam, casting, silver, c. 1898	170.00	230.00	200.00
□ **Reel,** Mills, fly, nickel, c. 1895	120.00	170.00	145.00
□ **Reel,** Orvis, fly, nickel plated, c. 1874	120.00	170.00	145.00
□ **Reel,** Orvis, fly, solid silver, c. 1874	620.00	720.00	670.00
□ **Reel,** Pennell, casting, nickel plated, c. 1920	40.00	60.00	50.00
□ **Reel,** Pfleuger, casting, brass, c. 1910	25.00	35.00	30.00
□ **Reel,** Pfleuger, casting, silver, c. 1925	60.00	110.00	85.00
□ **Reel,** Pfleuger, fly, rubber, c. 1905	120.00	170.00	145.00
□ **Reel,** Pfleuger, trolling, brass, c. 1915	30.00	40.00	35.00
□ **Reel,** Pfleuger, trolling, silver, c. 1890	40.00	60.00	50.00
□ **Reel,** Sage, fly, solid silver, c. 1848	770.00	870.00	820.00
□ **Reel,** Shakespeare, casting, plastic, c. 1940	50.00	70.00	60.00
□ **Reel,** Shakespeare, casting, level wind, c. 1922	40.00	60.00	50.00
□ **Reel,** Shakespeare, universal, take down, c. 1922	40.00	60.00	50.00
□ **Reel,** Shipley, casting, brass, c. 1885	190.00	270.00	230.00
□ **Reel,** Snyder, casting, brass, c. 1820	520.00	670.00	595.00
□ **Reel,** South Bend, fly, aluminum, c. 1940	45.00	65.00	55.00
□ **Reel,** Talbot, casting, silver, c. 1920	95.00	145.00	120.00
□ **Reel,** Union Hardware, fly, nickel plated, c. 1920	35.00	55.00	45.00
□ **Reel,** Vom Hofe, fly, nickel, small, c. 1890	145.00	195.00	165.00
□ **Reel,** Vom Hofe, trolling, rubber, c. 1918	170.00	240.00	195.00

	Current Price Range		P/Y Average
☐ **Reel,** Yawman and Erbe, fly, aluminum, c. 1889	120.00	170.00	145.00
☐ **Reel,** Zwarg, trolling, rubber, c. 1950	195.00	275.00	235.00
☐ **Rod case,** wood, brass trim, 5', c. 1880	100.00	120.00	110.00
☐ **Steel casting rod,** Wards, telescopic, 9", c. 1922	35.00	45.00	40.00
☐ **Steel casting rod,** Wards, with case, agate guides, 5½', c. 1922	35.00	45.00	40.00
☐ **Tackle box,** wooden and brass trim, 14", c. 1910	55.00	65.00	60.00
☐ **Tackle box,** metal and brass trim, 16", c. 1925	55.00	65.00	60.00

FLASH GORDON

DESCRIPTION: Flash Gordon is a futuristic comic strip featuring Flash Gordon as the heroic figure conquering space.

ORIGIN: Alex Raymond produced Flash Gordon for King Features Syndicate. The strip first appeared in Sunday newspapers on January 7, 1934.

TYPES: Flash Gordon has appeared in many types of media from newspaper comic strips and comic books to movies. Items relating to any facet of the comic strip are collectible.

RECOMMENDED READING: For further information refer to *The Official Price Guide to Comic Books and Collectibles* and *The Official Price Guide to Science Fiction and Fantasy Collectibles,* published by The House of Collectibles.

☐ **Button,** Flash Gordon Dueling Ming, copyright by King Features Syndicate, signed by Alex Raymond	6.50	8.50	7.00
☐ **Christmas Card,** portrait of Flash Gordon surrounded by holly wreath, interior shows rocket ship, 1951	8.00	11.00	8.50
☐ **Christmas Light Covers,** made by Textolite under license from King Features Syndicate, set of eight, hard plastic with decal illustrations, contained in a stiff paper box with lithographed illus-			

Flash Gordon Signal Pistol, *The Screaming Signal Gun,*
$200.00-$400.00
Photo courtesy of Hake's Americana, York, PA.

	Current Price Range		P/Y Average
tration, all artwork by Alex Raymond (creator of Flash Gordon), undated, almost certainly 1930s	75.00	100.00	85.00
□ Individually	7.00	10.00	7.00
□ Compass, Flash Gordon Space Compass, flexible plastic band, white with red artwork, portrait in red, white and blue	20.00	25.00	20.75
□ Decals, Flash Gordon Easter Egg Decals, also features The Phantom and other characters, dated 1940............................	30.00	40.00	30.00
□ Figure, Flash Gordon, standing at attention, wood, 5″ tall	87.00	110.00	90.00
□ Figures, Flash Gordon Solar Commando, made by Premier, a lithographed card with three plastic figures, each 3″ tall, dated 1952, the card measures 6¾″ x 9¾″ and the price is for the intact card (the loose figures would sell for much less)	46.00	57.00	46.00
□ Gun, Flash Gordon Arresting Ray Gun, copyright by King Features Syndicate, maker unidentified, lithographed tin, red/yellow/blue with profile of Flash Gordon on butt, name in large letter on barrel	85.00	105.00	85.00

	Current Price Range		P/Y Average
☐ **Gun, Flash Gordon Radio Repeater,** lithographed tin, red, black and silver, illustrations of Flash Gordon along with planet and star. Bears a King Features copyright notice as licensee to Marx Toy Co., 4½" x 10"	190.00	230.00	197.00
☐ **Guns,** set of two ray guns made by Louis Marx, 1935, rare	1600.00	2100.00	1750.00
☐ **Record, Flash Gordon In The City Of Caves,** 78 r.p.m. Record Guild of America record, pictures disc on which both sides of the record comprise large pictures, dated 1948	65.00	85.00	70.00
☐ **Premium,** Kelloggs Pep Cereal, lithographed tin *button,* multicolored, 1940s	8.00	11.00	8.50
☐ **Premium,** Kelloggs Pep Cereal, lithographed tin *button,* portrait facing full front, based on drawing by Alex Raymond, 1946	25.00	30.00	27.50
☐ **Rocket Ship, Flash Gordon Rocket Fighter,** copyright by King Features Syndicate, manufacturer unidentified, clockwork, lithographed tin, red/yellow/black/white, 1937, 12½"	275.00	350.00	237.50
☐ **Rocket Ship,** Marx, lithographed tin, Flash Gordon seated in open cockpit with gun, wears crash helmet, 13"	110.00	140.00	122.00
☐ **T-Shirt,** Flash Gordon iron on	6.00	8.00	7.00

FLASKS

DESCRIPTION: Flasks are containers which have a broad body and narrow neck, often fitted with a closure. Usually they were used to hold alcoholic beverages.

TYPES: There were many variations of flask bottles produced including figural and portrait flasks.

PERIOD: Usually collectors search for flasks from the early 1800s through the early 1900s. Before 1810, few glass containers were manufactured.

COMMENTS: Flasks with portraits of Presidents or other politicians are highly sought after by collectors.

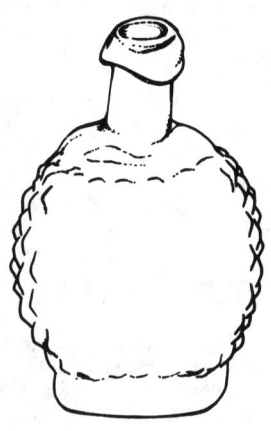

Poison Flask, *diamond motif, 4",* $55.00–$75.00

ADDITIONAL TIPS: For more information, consult *The Official Price Guide to Bottles, Old and New,* published by The House of Collectibles.

	Current Price Range		P/Y Average
☐ **A.G.W.L.,** under bottom, saddle flask, amber, ½ pint	15.00	25.00	20.00
☐ **All Seeing Eye,** star and large eye in center, under it A.D., in back, six-pointed star with arms, Masonic emblem, under it G.R.J.A., pontil, sheared top, amber, pint	230.00	300.00	265.00
☐ **Anchor Flask,** double ring, amber or clear, ½ pint, quart	30.00	40.00	35.00
☐ **Aquamarine,** pint	40.00	50.00	45.00
☐ **Baltimore Glass Works,** aqua, very thin glass, pontil, on back a stack of wheat	150.00	200.00	175.00
☐ **Baltimore Monument,** and under it Balto. door with step railing, in back sloop with pennant flying, sailing to right above it Fells below point, ½ pt. 3 ribbed on side, plain top, pontil, aqua, qt. (c. 1840)	125.00	175.00	150.00
☐ **Same as above, except plain bottom,**	115.00	145.00	130.00
☐ **B.P. & B.,** Yellow green, ½ pint	45.00	60.00	52.00
☐ **Bridgeton, New Jersey,** around a man facing to left, in back a man facing to the left with Washington around it, ribbed sides, sheared top, pontil, aqua, pint	80.00	100.00	90.00
☐ **Calabash,** Hunter and fisherman, aqua, quart	45.00	60.00	52.00
☐ **Chapman P., Balt., MD,** soldier with a gun on front, a girl dancing on a bar in back, sheared top, aqua, pint	160.00	200.00	180.00
☐ **Clasped Hands-Eagle Flask** (c. 1860–75), Union 13 stars, clasped hands, eagle above banner mark, "E", Wormer & Co., Pittsburg, aqua, quart	100.00	130.00	115.00
☐ **Clasped Hands-Eagle Flask** (c. 1860–75), deep golden amber, ½ pint	110.00	150.00	130.00

	Current Price Range		P/Y Average

☐ **Clasped Hands-Flask** (c. 1860–75), one with eagle and banner, above oval marked Pittsburgh, Pa., other cannon to left, flag and cannonballs, aqua, pint	80.00	100.00	90.00
☐ **Delicate powder blue**, ½ pint	40.00	50.00	45.00
☐ **18 diamond quilted flask**, green, 6¼″	115.00	135.00	125.00
☐ **Dog**, in center, in back man in uniform on a horse, pontil, sheared top, aqua, quart	120.00	155.00	137.00
☐ **Double Eagle** (eagles lengthwise), open pontil, olive green	110.00	150.00	130.00
☐ **Double Eagle**, aqua, pint	135.00	175.00	155.00
☐ **Double Eagle**, light green, pint	110.00	135.00	122.00
☐ **Double Eagle**, beneath unembossed oval, sheared top, pontil, amber, 6¼″	35.00	45.00	40.00
☐ **Double Eagle, Stoddard, N.H.**, olive or amber, pint	110.00	135.00	122.00
☐ **Duck Flask**, picture of a duck in water, under duck SWIM, above duck WILL YOU HAVE A DRINK, aqua, pint	140.00	160.00	150.00
☐ **Eagle**, on oval panels, 25 sun rays in ¼ circle around eagle head, 8 vertical bars on shield. End of olive branch & arrows under claws in oval frame with 23 small pearls around. T.W.D., in back full sailing to right. U.S. flag at reas., waves beneath frigate and in semi-circle beneath Franklin pt. 3 vertically ribbed on side, sheared top, pontil, aqua, (c. 1830)	125.00	175.00	150.00
☐ **Eagle**, and stag, aqua, ½ pint	175.00	225.00	200.00
☐ **Eagle**, and tree, aqua, pint	90.00	110.00	100.00
☐ **Flora Temple**, aqua, pint	200.00	250.00	225.00
☐ **Flora Temple**, handle, puce or amber, pint . . .	200.00	250.00	225.00
☐ **Florida Universal Store Bottle**, clear, pint	6.00	10.00	8.00
☐ **H. Frank, Pat'd. Aug. 6th 1879**, under bottom, two circles in center, reverse plain, ring top, ribs on sides	40.00	50.00	45.00
☐ **H. Frank, Pat. Aug. 6, 1872**, all on bottom, circular shaped flask, two circles in center on front, reverse side plain, wide rib on sides, ring neck, aqua, pint	45.00	60.00	52.00
☐ **Franklin & Franklin**, aqua, quart	130.00	170.00	150.00
☐ **Gen. Macarthur and God Bless America**, purple or green, ½ pint	12.00	18.00	15.00
☐ **G.H.A.**, Concord, N.Y. 1865, aqua, ½ pint	20.00	28.00	24.00
☐ **Girl For Joe**, girl on bicycle, aqua, pint	70.00	90.00	80.00
☐ **Granite Glass Co.**, in three lines, reverse Stoddard, N.H., sheared top, olive, pint	150.00	200.00	175.00
☐ **Guaranteed Flask**, clear or amethyst, 6¼″ . . .	6.00	10.00	8.00
☐ **Guaranteed Full**, clear, 6½″	8.00	12.00	10.00
☐ **History Flask**, label, aqua, side panels, 7¼″	15.00	22.00	18.00
☐ **Iron**, pontil, double collared, pint	40.00	50.00	45.00

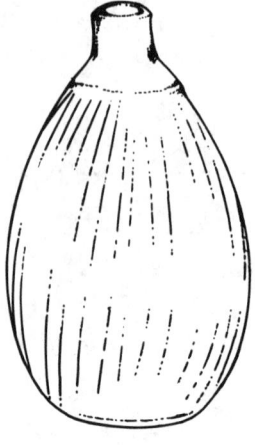

Pitkin Flask, *vertical ribbing, amber, 7",* **$55.00–$75.00**

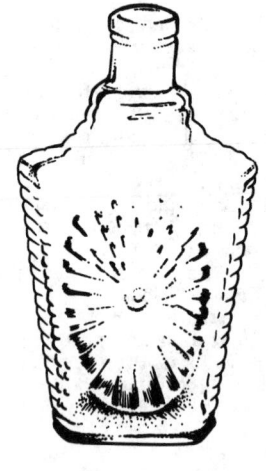

Keene Marlboro Street Glassworks, *sunburst design, green,* **$310.00–$390.00**

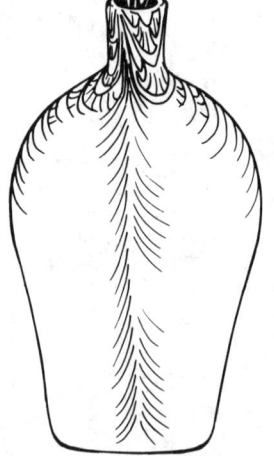

Nailsea Flask, *blue with white loopings, 6⅞",* **$200.00–$250.00**

	Current Price Range		P/Y Average
☐ **Isabella G.W.,** sheaf of wheat, pint	75.00	95.00	85.00
☐ **Jenny Lind,** with wreath, reverse picture of glass works, above is FISLERVILLE GLASS WORKS, wavy line on neck, pontil, tapered top, aqua, quart	110.00	150.00	130.00
☐ Same as above, except S. HUFFSY	60.00	80.00	70.00
☐ **Jenny Lind Lyre,** aqua, pint	110.00	150.00	130.00
☐ **L.C. & R. Co.,** on bottom, eagle in a circle, reverse plain, clear, ½ pint	40.00	50.00	45.00
☐ **Legendary Grandfather,** broken swirl pattern, reddish amber	110.00	150.00	130.00
☐ **Pike's Peak,** man with pack and cane walking to left, reverse eagle with ribbon in beak in oval panel, aqua, pint	100.00	150.00	125.00
☐ Same as above, except several colors	75.00	95.00	85.00
☐ **For Pike's Peak,** reverse side, man shooting a gun at a deer, aqua, 9½"	35.00	45.00	40.00
☐ **For Pike's Peak,** old rye, aqua, pint	35.00	45.00	40.00
☐ **Pittsburgh,** double eagle, aqua, pint	30.00	40.00	35.00
☐ **Pittsburgh, PA.,** in raised oval circle at base, with an eagle on front, back same except plain for label, aqua, applied ring at top, pint, 7½"	40.00	50.00	45.00
☐ **Pitkin type,** light green, pint	55.00	75.00	65.00
☐ **Pottery Flask,** figure of a man and horse, same on reverse side, pint	275.00	350.00	312.00
☐ **Railroad—Eagle Flask** (c. 1830–48), amber, pint	160.00	200.00	180.00
☐ **Railroad Flask** (c. 1860), on oval panels, horse drawing long cart on rail to right. Cart filled with barrels and boxes, under it Lowell and above it Railroad in back eagle facing left. Shield with 7 vertical & 2 horizontal bars on breast, 3 arrows in eagles left claw, olive branch in right, 13 large stars surround edge, ½ pt. 3 ver. ribbed on side, sheared top, pontil, O. amber	110.00	150.00	130.00
☐ **Railroad Flask,** designs on oval panels, crude locomotive to left on rail, embossed success to the Railroad, reading around locomotive-back but the line connecting the tender with rear wheel shows a slight break and E in success carries a conbex dot attached to the upper bar pt. 3 vertically ribbed on side, sheared top O. amber, (c. 1830)	120.00	175.00	147.00
☐ **Ravenna Glass Works—Star Flask** (c. 1857–60), Ohio, aqua, pint	150.00	190.00	170.00
☐ **Ravenna Glass Works,** in three lines, ring top, yellow green, pint	130.00	175.00	152.00
☐ **Ravenna,** in center, anchor with rope, under it GLASS COMPANY, ring top, aqua, pint	140.00	175.00	157.00
☐ **Ravenna Travelers Companion,** pontil, amber, quart	250.00	350.00	300.00

	Current Price Range		P/Y Average
☐ **Rehm Bros,** Bush & Buchanan Sts & O'Farrel & Mason Sts, in a sunken circle, ribbed bottom, two rings near shoulder, coffin type, metal and cork cap, clear or amethyst, ½ pint	100.00	145.00	122.00
☐ **Springfield G.W. and Cabin,** aqua, ½ pint . . .	65.00	85.00	75.00
☐ **Spring Garden,** in center, anchor, under it GLASS WORKS, reverse side, log cabin with a tree to the right, ring top, aqua, ½ pint	130.00	160.00	145.00
☐ **Stag and tree,** aqua, pint	65.00	85.00	75.00
☐ **Star—Cornucopia Flask,** star with a circle around it on shoulder, light amber, saddle flask, ½ pint	12.00	18.00	15.00
☐ **Stoddard,** double eagle, GRANITE GLASS CO., STODDARD, N.H. pontil, golden amber, pint . .	100.00	130.00	115.00
☐ **Willington—Eagle Flask** (c. 1860–72), bright green, pint	100.00	130.00	115.00
☐ Same as above, except olive amber, ½ pint . .	100.00	130.00	115.00
☐ **Willington Glass Co., West Willington, Conn.** on four lines, reverse eagle and shield, under it a wreath, on shoulder LIBERTY, amber, pint . .	100.00	130.00	115.00
☐ **Will You Take a Drink? Will a Duck Swim?** aqua, pint	150.00	175.00	162.00
☐ **Winter and Summer Flask,** tree with leaves and a bird on right side, above it SUMMER, reverse side tree without leaves and bird, above it WINTER, tapered top aqua, quart and pint	110.00	150.00	130.00
☐ Same as above, but with SUMMER on front and WINTER on back	100.00	130.00	115.00
☐ **Zanesville City Glass Works,** in oval panel, reverse plain, ring top, amber	100.00	130.00	110.00
☐ Same as above, except aqua	65.00	85.00	70.00

FOLK ART

DESCRIPTION: Originally the term used to describe painting and sculpture done by untrained artists, today the term is given to all handcrafted items.

TYPES: Various types of folk art sculpture include dolls, toys, animals, jewelry and bottlecap sculpture. Four types of folk art painting include: paintings done by stencil called theorems; drawings that display unique penmanship skills called calligraphic; frakturs, which were ornately designed certificates of birth, baptism or marriage; and mourning pictures, to commemorate the death of a loved one.

PERIOD: Folk art has no specific period; it is still made today.

ORIGIN: The original popularity of folk art dates to the 1920s and the first Folk Art exhibits at the Whitney Studio Club (later the Whitney Museum of American Art) and the Museum of Modern Art.

COMMENTS: Until the 1920s the value of folk art was largely ignored because its distortion of size and scale was not considered artistic. Today, such Americana collectibles are much sought after. Reasonably priced pieces can be found, especially those from the 19th and 20th centuries.

	Current Price Range		P/Y Average
□ **Banjo,** snake skin head, three string, 31″	60.00	80.00	63.00
□ **Barber's Pole,** with hitching post	152.00	178.00	155.00
□ **Bird,** cloth, Victorian	48.00	75.00	52.00
□ **Bird In Hoop,** green and yellow painted wood parrot perched in a wrought-iron hoop; 19th c., 14″	675.00	725.00	720.00
□ **Blanket Chest,** Chippendale, front is painted with a comport filled with red and yellow flowers and bordered with yellow floral vines on a painted red and black background, signed Miss H. Taylor in pencil inside lid, 19th c., 8″ x 19″ x 7¼″ ...	1000.00	1500.00	1200.00
□ **Boat,** model, wood, c. 1900	48.00	75.00	52.00
□ **Boot Jack,** wooden, unpainted	17.00	27.00	21.00
□ **Bottlecap Sculpture,** snake	162.00	190.00	165.00
□ **Bottlecap Sculpture,** carved heads of a man and woman, c. 1930	82.00	115.00	85.00
□ **Box,** hinged lid has three overlapping hearts carved, edge is painted black, green sponge decoration on bottom, 14″ x 9″ x 5″	75.00	95.00	84.50
□ **Bride's Box,** painted bentwood, late 18th c., 6½″ x 18¼″	395.00	495.00	445.00
□ **Butcher's Shop Sign,** carved pig painted pink-orange, inscribed MEAT in black letters, wrought-iron tail, iron suspension rings, c. 1930, 12″ x 26″	1400.00	1500.00	1435.00
□ **Candle Box,** pine planked construction, painted red, 14″	300.00	350.00	335.00
□ **Carving,** bird, wood, painted, 6″	40.00	60.00	45.00
□ **Cigar Store Indian,** Princess, c. 1880, 61″ ...	4500.00	5500.00	5000.00
□ **Coffee Pot,** Toleware, decorated with painted red flowers on green stems with yellow leaves, dark brown background, convex hinged lid, conical shape, 19th c., 8¼″	900.00	950.00	936.00
□ **Cow,** felt, painted face, 9″	30.00	40.00	32.00
□ **Cradle,** doll, pine, original paint, 18th c.	225.00	275.00	240.00
□ **Crock,** marked White's-Utica 3, decorated with a dark blue flower, stem and leaves, open top	160.00	185.00	174.00

	Current Price Range		P/Y Average
Decoy, swan, original paint, hollow construction, cedar	950.00	1075.00	1050.00
Decoy, wooden bluebill, glass eyes, weighted bottom, some bullet marks	35.00	55.00	48.00
Decoy, wooden bluebill, painted eyes, original paint	45.00	55.00	50.00
Decoy, wooden, Canadian Goose in gray, white, black and brown, 27"	40.00	50.00	46.00
Doll, dancer, jointed wood, hand operated, 14½", 19th c.	200.00	240.00	210.00
Doll, reversible face, dress and color, 14"	275.00	320.00	285.00
Face Mask, carved, man's face	125.00	145.00	130.00
Figure, black preacher, carved and painted wood, initials DC carved on chest, 10"	3000.00	3120.00	3085.00
Figure, cast-iron form of a woman holding two trays in her hands, painted polychrome, 12⅝" x 11"	1000.00	1100.00	1050.00
Flute, pine, 15"	60.00	80.00	65.00
Footstool, wooden, pumpkin top with two ends black and red underneath, 12" x 8" x 7"	55.00	75.00	67.50
Footstool, wooden with turned legs, square nailed construction, 10" x 9" x 6"	40.00	50.00	46.00
Fraktur, part printed, part hand-colored, Victorian frame	50.00	70.00	55.00
Game, checkered game board, splined, signed, 19" x 29"	82.00	115.00	85.00
Game, ring toss, 5 rings, c. 1900	52.00	80.00	60.00
Game, skittles, ornate steeple in center, 19th c.	200.00	250.00	220.00
Gate Post Finial, carved Statue of Liberty finial made of pine, wrought-iron crown spokes, traces of black and yellow polychrome, c. 1900, 19¾"	2500.00	3500.00	3000.00
Hooked Rugs, picture of dog in the middle encircled in dark blue with purple border, set of two, c. 1910, 45" x 26"	300.00	400.00	350.00
Hooked Rug, two black and two white horses on vertical striped background, 49" x 26"	150.00	250.00	190.00
Miniature, bookcase on chest, accessories, 11¾" x 9½"	160.00	200.00	170.00
Miniature, furniture, set of 3 chairs, painted	60.00	80.00	65.00
Miniature, windmill, wood, tin blades, 21"	75.00	100.00	80.00
Mourning Picture, embroidery on silk, 16" x 20"	338.00	365.00	345.00
Oil On Board, little girl in hooded cape, 7" x 9", c. 1820	125.00	175.00	130.00
Oil On Board, rat terrier with rat, 19th c.	275.00	325.00	290.00
Oil On Canvas, apples and book, 8" x 10"	390.00	425.00	400.00
Oil On Canvas, boy, girl, lamb, mid-19th c.	138.00	170.00	145.00
Oil On Canvas, fruit and bird, unframed, 24" x 18", c. 1835	550.00	650.00	570.00
Oil On Canvas, Irish Setter, 16" x 19", framed	325.00	380.00	340.00
Picture, cut paper, white cut into a design against a red background, c. 1850	425.00	500.00	450.00

	Current Price Range		P/Y Average
□ **Portraits,** man and woman (pair), unsigned, 19th c.	350.00	395.00	360.00
□ **Portrait,** miniature, on ivory, bust of man in coat, gold frame with leaves and flowers, 19th c.	1900.00	2400.00	2100.00
□ **Portraits,** pair, signed, G.H. Blackburn, 30" x 28" framed, c. 1886	325.00	375.00	335.00
□ **Rag Doll,** Amish, embroidered face	90.00	100.00	95.00
□ **Rag Doll,** Amish, faceless, Amish outfit	65.00	75.00	70.00
□ **Rag Doll,** handmade of floss eyes, nose, mouth and hair, blue and white dress, 11"	25.00	50.00	37.50
□ **Rag Doll,** made from a printed pattern, c. 1930s	40.00	50.00	46.00
□ **Rocking Horse,** wooden shoo-fly, with seat between sides of horse	100.00	200.00	145.00
□ **Sewing Stand,** to hang on wall, set of three spool holders on top shelf, hand carved diamond design around top border, carved heart and three initials on second shelf, natural pine darkened with time	55.00	75.00	64.00
□ **Shelves,** two shelves, stripped down with blue, red and gray showing, checkerboard showing on the bark, 10" x 14" x 4"	45.00	55.00	49.50
□ **Spreaders,** wooden, original mustard colored paint, set of two, 29"	20.00	30.00	24.00
□ **Storks,** carved and painted, c. 1910, 20", pair	380.00	420.00	410.00
□ **Toy,** baby rattle, hand carved, 9"	82.00	115.00	85.00
□ **Toy,** climbing clown, flat, made of cardboard in red and blue polka dots	17.00	25.00	21.50
□ **Toy,** "Froggie" of the Andy Devine Show, green, red, white and black rubber, 5"	10.00	20.00	14.50
□ **Toy,** monkey on pole, hand carved	72.00	100.00	75.00
□ **Toy,** pecking chicken, hand carved	62.00	85.00	65.00
□ **Toy,** rocking horse, handmade	62.00	85.00	65.00
□ **Toy,** sheep on wheels, hand carved	138.00	170.00	145.00
□ **Toy,** train, hand carved, painted, 23", 19th c.	112.00	135.00	115.00
□ **Whirligig,** black man made of wood wearing a yellow hat and jacket, red pants and black boots, paddle baffles on the arms, round base, Maine, early 20th c.	3900.00	4400.00	4190.00
□ **Whirligig,** cast iron, painted, man turning grindstone	475.00	545.00	490.00
□ **Whirligig,** wooden duck, glass eyes, mounted on a wood fence post	60.00	75.00	66.00
□ **Whirligig,** wooden Indian, carved and painted, 11½"	1700.00	1800.00	1750.00

FOOTBALL CARDS

DESCRIPTION: Football cards usually have the picture of a football player on one side and his statistics or biography on the other.

ORIGIN: The first football cards were produced by Goudey Gum in 1933.

MAKER: There are several companies who have produced football cards including Topps, Fleer, O-Pee-Chee and Bowman.

COMMENTS: Although the popularity of collecting football cards lags behind the well established baseball card hobby, football's tremendous popularity assures the growth of football card collecting.

ADDITIONAL TIPS: The most valuable cards to watch for are old sets, famous player cards and rookie cards. For more information, consult *The Official Price Guide to Football Cards,* published by The House of Collectibles. Keys to listings below are: VG —very good; PYM —prior year mint; VG—E —very good to excellent.

BOWMAN—1950 (2 1/16″ x 2½″, Numbered 1–144, Color)

			MINT	VG	PYM
☐		Complete Set	435.00	245.00	227.00
☐	1	**Doak Walker,** Detroit Lions back	8.00	2.50	4.70
☐	5	**Y.A. Tittle,** Baltimore Colts, quarterback	16.00	8.00	7.48
☐	6	**Lou Groza,** Cleveland Browns, tackle ...	13.00	6.50	5.35
☐	16	**Glenn Davis,** Los Angeles Rams, back ..	10.50	5.00	4.60
☐	27	**Sid Luckman,** Chicago Bears, quarterback	13.00	6.50	5.53
☐	45	**Otto Graham,** Cleveland Browns, quarterback	21.00	10.00	11.98
☐	78	**Dante Lavelli,** Cleveland Browns, end ...	6.50	3.25	3.90
☐	100	**Sammy Baugh,** Washington Redskins, quarterback	21.00	10.00	11.75
☐	132	**Chuck Bednarik,** Philadelphia Eagles, center	10.50	5.00	4.95

			MINT	VG	PYM

BOWMAN—1951 (2 1/16" x 3⅛", Numbered 1–144, Color)

			MINT	VG	PYM
☐		Complete Set	455.00	300.00	235.00
☐	2	**Otto Graham,** Cleveland Browns, quarterback...............................	18.00	9.00	10.65
☐	4	**Norm VanBrocklin,** Los Angeles Rams quarterback	15.00	7.50	6.60
☐	12	**Chuck Bednarik,** Philadelphia Eagles, center	10.50	5.00	5.05
☐	20	**Tom Landry,** New York Giants, back	33.00	16.00	10.65
☐	34	**Sammy Baugh,** Washington Redskins, quarterback	21.00	10.00	10.65
☐	75	**Lou Groza,** Cleveland Browns, tackle ...	10.50	5.00	8.18
☐	76	**Elroy Hirsch,** Los Angeles Rams, back	8.50	4.00	5.05
☐	102	**Bobby Layne,** Detroit Lions, quarterback	13.00	6.50	8.95
☐	105	**Joe Perry,** San Francisco 49ers, back ...	8.50	4.00	5.10

BOWMAN—1952 (2 1/16" x 3⅛", Numbered 1–144, Color)

			MINT	VG	PYM
☐		Complete Set	430.00	250.00	337.00
☐	1	**Norman Van Brocklin,** Los Angeles Rams, quarterback	21.00	7.00	9.98
☐	2	**Otto Graham,** Cleveland Browns, quarterback...............................	21.00	10.00	110.45
☐	16	**Frank Gifford,** New York Giants, back ..	45.00	20.00	11.85
☐	30	**Sammy Baugh,** Washington Redskins, quarterback	32.00	16.00	11.85
☐	78	**Bobby Layne,** Detroit Lions, quarterback	18.00	9.00	11.00
☐	127	**Ollie Matson,** Chicago Cardinals, back ..	18.00	9.00	5.68
☐	137	**Bob Waterfield,** Los Angeles Rams, quarterback	15.00	7.50	9.25
☐	142	**Tom Landry,** New York Giants, back	75.00	35.00	9.88

BOWMAN—1953 (2½" x 3¾", Numbered 1–96, Color)

			MINT	VG	PYM
☐		Complete Set	315.00	200.00	206.00
☐	9	**Marion Motley,** Cleveland Browns, back	7.00	3.50	3.75
☐	11	**Norm Van Brocklin,** Los Angeles Rams, quarterback	11.00	5.50	6.73
☐	21	**Bobby Layne,** Detroit Lions, quarterback	14.00	7.00	9.00
☐	26	**Otto Graham,** Cleveland Browns, quarterback...............................	14.00	7.00	10.65
☐	32	**Hugh McElhenny,** San Francisco 49ers, back................................	7.00	35.00	5.13
☐	43	**Frank Gifford,** New York Giants, back ..	24.00	12.00	10.60
☐	53	**Emlen Tunnel,** New York Giants, back ..	7.00	35.00	3.75
☐	88	**Leo Nomellini,** San Francisco 49ers, tackle...............................	7.00	3.50	3.75
☐	95	**Lou Groza,** Cleveland Browns, tackle ...	11.00	5.50	5.13

BOWMAN—1954 (2½" x 3¾", Numbered 1–128, Color)

			MINT	VG	PYM
☐		Complete Set	260.00	165.00	117.00
☐	6	**Joe Perry,** San Francisco 49ers, back ...	6.50	3.25	2.83

			MINT	VG	PYM
☐	7	**Kyle Rote,** New York Giants, end	5.00	2.50	3.08
☐	8	**Norm Van Brocklin,** Los Angeles Rams, quarterback	8.50	4.00	4.70
☐	23	**George Blanda,** Chicago Bears, quarterback	13.00	6.00	6.45
☐	40	**Otto Graham,** Cleveland Browns, quarterback	12.00	6.00	8.35
☐	42	**Y.A. Tittle,** San Francisco 49ers, quarterback	8.50	4.00	4.95
☐	53	**Bobby Layne,** Detroit Lions, quarterback	10.50	5.00	6.45
☐	55	**Frank Gifford,** New York Giants, back . .	18.00	9.00	8.35
☐	56	**Leon McLaughlin,** Los Angeles Rams, center	1.00	.60	.63

BOWMAN—1955 (2½″ x 3¾″, Numbered 1–160, Color)

☐		Complete Set	175.00	120.00	110.00
☐	7	**Frank Gifford,** New York Giants, back . .	15.00	7.50	7.98
☐	16	**Charley Conerly,** New York Giants, quarterback	3.75	1.85	1.75
☐	32	**Norm Van Brocklin,** Los Angeles Rams, quarterback	8.40	4.00	4.95
☐	37	**Lou Groza,** Cleveland Browns, tackle, kicker	6.00	3.00	4.60
☐	44	**Joe Perry,** San Francisco 49ers, back . . .	5.00	2.50	2.55
☐	52	**Pat Summerall,** Chicago Cardinals, end	5.00	2.50	2.80
☐	62	**George Blanda,** Chicago Bears, quarterback	8.00	4.00	5.88
☐	71	**Bobby Layne,** Detroit Lions, end	9.00	4.00	8.15

FLEER—1960 (2½″ x 3½″, Numbered 1–132, Color)

☐		Complete Set	110.00	67.50	56.50
☐	7	**Sid Gillman,** Los Angeles Chargers (AFL), coach	2.50	1.25	.74
☐	20	**Sammy Baugh,** New York Titans (AFL), coach	9.00	4.50	4.55
☐	58	**George Blanda,** Houston Oilers (AFL), quarterback/kicker	7.00	3.50	3.53
☐	66	**Billy Cannon,** Houston Oilers (AFL), back/end	2.50	1.25	1.90
☐	73	**Abner Haynes,** Dallas Texans (AFL), back	2.00	1.00	1.90
☐	76	**Paul Lowe,** Los Angeles Chargers (AFL), back	2.00	1.00	1.13
☐	116	**Hank Stram,** Los Angeles Chargers, (AFL), back	2.50	1.25	1.90
☐	118	**Ron Mix,** Los Angeles Chargers (AFL), tackle	3.00	1.50	1.90
☐	124	**Jack Kemp,** Los Angeles Chargers (AFL), quarterback	17.00	8.00	4.55

FLEER—1961 (2½″ x 3½″, Numbered 1–220, Color)

☐		Complete Set	155.00	90.00	113.00
☐	11	**Jim Brown,** Cleveland Browns, back	21.00	10.00	17.13

			MINT	VG	PYM
☐	30	**John Unitas,** Baltimore Colts, quarterback	8.50	4.00	5.70
☐	41	**Don Meredith,** Dallas Cowboys, quarterback	12.50	6.00	6.25
☐	69	**Kyle Rote,** New York Giants, end	2.50	1.25	1.90
☐	88	**Bart Starr,** Green Bay Packers, quarterback	6.50	3.25	4.40
☐	90	**Paul Horning,** Green Bay Packers, back	5.00	2.50	3.08
☐	117	**Bobby Layne,** Pittsburg Steelers, quarterback	6.50	3.25	4.25
☐	155	**Jack Kemp,** San Diego Chargers (AFL), quarterback	11.00	5.00	6.23
☐	166	**George Blanda,** Houston Oilers (AFL), quarterback/kicker	7.00	3.50	4.95

TOPPS—1956 (2⅝″ x 3⅝″, Numbered 1–120, Color)

			MINT	VG	PYM
☐		Complete Set	195.00	115.00	135.00
☐	6	**Norm Van Brocklin,** Los Angeles Rams, quarterback	7.50	3.75	4.25
☐	28	**Chuch Bednarik,** Philadelphia Eagles, center	5.00	2.50	2.83
☐	29	**Kyle Rote,** New York Giants, end	5.00	2.50	3.08
☐	36	**Art Donvan,** Baltimore Colts, tackle	3.50	1.75	1.90
☐	53	**Frank Gifford,** New York Giants, back ..	18.00	9.00	7.30
☐	60	**Lenny Moore,** Baltimore Colts, back	7.50	3.75	2.83
☐	78	**Elroy Hirsch,** Los Angeles Rams, end/back	5.00	2.50	2.83
☐	87	**Ernie Stautner,** Pittsburgh Steelers, tackle	3.50	1.75	1.63
☐	101	**Roosevelt Grier,** New York Giants, tackle	3.50	1.75	1.90
☐	110	**Joe Perry,** San Francisco 49ers, back ...	5.00	2.50	2.83

TOPPS—1957 (2½″ x 3½″, Numbered 1–154, Color)

			MINT	VG	PYM
☐		Complete Set	235.00	140.00	155.00
☐	11	**Roosevelt Brown,** New York Giants, tackle	3.00	1.50	1.50
☐	22	**Norman Van Brocklin,** Los Angeles Rams, quarterback	6.50	3.25	4.20
☐	28	**Lou Groza,** Cleveland Browns, tackle, kicker	4.50	2.25	2.70
☐	30	**Y.A. Tittle,** San Francisco 49ers, quarterback	6.00	3.25	5.00
☐	31	**George Blanda,** Chicago Bears, quarterback/kicker	6.50	3.25	7.20
☐	32	**Bobby Layne,** Detroit Lions, quarterback	6.50	3.25	7.45
☐	88	**Frank Gifford,** New York Giants, back ..	15.00	7.50	7.98
☐	119	**Barr Starr,** Green Bay Packers, quarterback	30.00	15.00	11.75
☐	151	**Paul Horning,** Green Bay Packers, back	30.00	15.00	11.80

		MINT	VG	PYM

TOPPS—1958 (2½″ x 3½″, Numbered 1–132, Color)

		MINT	VG	PYM
☐	Complete Set	165.00	85.00	135.00
☐ 2	**Bobby Layne,** Detroit Lions, quarterback	5.50	2.75	5.05
☐ 22	**John Unitas,** Baltimore Colts, quarterback	12.50	6.00	6.75
☐ 62	**Jim Brown,** Cleveland Browns, back	50.00	25.00	42.50
☐ 66	**Bart Starr,** Green Bay Packers, quarterback...................................	8.00	4.00	5.05
☐ 73	**Frank Gifford,** New York Giants, back ..	12.50	6.00	6.75
☐ 86	**Y.A. Tittle,** San Francisco 49ers, quarterback..................................	5.50	2.75	5.05
☐ 90	**Sonny Jurgensen,** Philadelphia Eagles, quarterback	15.00	7.50	6.75
☐ 122	**Hugh McElhenny,** San Francisco 49ers, back......................................	3.00	1.50	2.55
☐ 129	**George Blanda,** Chicago Bears, quarterback/kicker	5.50	2.75	5.05

TOPPS—1959 (2½″ x 3½″, Numbered 1–176, Color)

		MINT	VG	PYM
☐	Complete Set	145.00	72.00	118.00
☐ 1	**Johnny Unitas,** Baltimore Colts, quarterback..................................	12.50	5.00	6.38
☐ 5	**Hugh McElhenny,** San Francisco 49ers, back......................................	2.50	1.25	2.25
☐ 7	**Kyle Rote,** New York Giants, end	2.50	1.25	2.25
☐ 10	**Jim Brown,** Cleveland Browns, back	20.00	10.00	18.00
☐ 20	**Frank Gifford,** New York Giants, back ..	11.00	5.00	6.00
☐ 23	**Bart Starr,** Green Bay Packers, quarterback...................................	7.00	3.50	4.68
☐ 40	**Bobby Layne,** Pittsburg Steelers, quarterback...................................	5.00	2.50	5.03
☐ 82	**Paul Horning,** Green Bay Packers, back	5.00	2.50	3.95
☐ 130	**Y.A. Tittle,** San Francisco 49ers, quarterback..................................	5.00	2.50	3.83

TOPPS—1960 (2½″ x 3½″, Numbered 1–132, Color)

		MINT	VG	PYM
☐	Complete Set	120.00	70.00	83.60
☐ 1	**John Unitas,** Baltimore Colts, quarterback	12.00	4.00	5.53
☐ 23	**Jim Brown,** Cleveland Browns, back	20.00	10.00	16.25
☐ 51	**Bart Starr,** Green Bay Packers, quarterback...................................	7.00	3.50	4.96
☐ 74	**Frank Gifford,** New York Giants, back ..	11.00	5.00	5.53
☐ 87	**Chuck Bednarik,** Philadelphia Eagles, center	2.50	1.25	2.20
☐ 93	**Bobby Layne,** Pittsburgh Steelers, quarterback	5.00	2.50	4.45
☐ 113	**Y.A. Tittle,** San Francisco 49ers, quarterback..................................	5.00	2.50	3.25
☐ 114	**Joe Perry,** San Francisco 49ers, back ...	2.50	1.25	2.20
☐ 116	**Hugh McElhenny,** San Francisco 49ers, back......................................	2.50	1.25	2.20

		MINT	VG	PYM
TOPPS—1961 (2½″ x 3½″, Numbered 1–198, Color)				
☐	Complete Set	144.00	75.00	103.50
☐ 1	**John Unitas,** Baltimore Colts, quarterback	10.00	3.50	5.60
☐ 39	**Bart Starr,** Green Bay Packers, quarterback.................................	6.50	3.25	4.85
☐ 58	**Y.A. Tittle,** San Francisco 49ers, quarterback.................................	5.00	2.50	3.38
☐ 59	**John Brodie,** San Francisco 49ers, quarterback	5.00	2.50	2.75
☐ 71	**Jim Brown,** Cleveland Browns, back	20.00	10.00	18.50
☐ 77	**Cleveland Browns Action Card,** Jimmy Brown	6.50	3.25	7.33

FOSTORIA GLASS

ORIGIN: Founded in Fostoria, Ohio in 1887, Fostoria continues in production at their Moundsville, West Virginia factory today. Many of their lovely glassware lines are considered to be "elegant" depression era glass and these patterns are avidly sought by collectors today.

RECOMMENDED READING: For further information refer to *The Official Price Guide to Depression Glassware,* published by The House of Collectibles.

AMERICAN

This classic cube style design has become a favorite glass of collectors. Prices should escalate as a result of Fostoria's announcement that its manufacturing process will no longer include handwork. American was mostly made in crystal; some green, amber, blue and yellow was also made. Some pieces of American are still being produced.

	Current Price Range		P/Y Average
Appetizer, individual, 3¼″			
☐ crystal	15.00	40.00	20.00
Ashtray, square, 5″			
☐ crystal	17.00	25.00	19.00

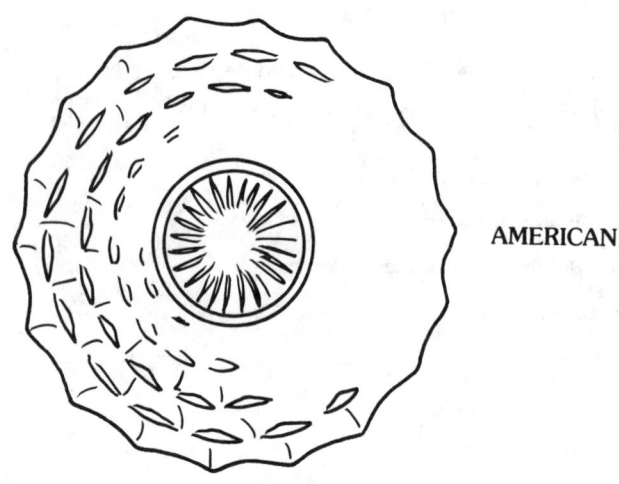

AMERICAN

	Current Price Range		P/Y Average
Baby Set, tumbler and bowl			
□ crystal	40.00	50.00	42.00
Banana Split Bowl, 9″			
□ crystal	28.00	42.00	32.00
Bell			
□ crystal	17.00	27.00	19.00
Bon Bon Dish, 3 toes, 6″			
□ crystal	8.00	13.00	9.50
Bowl, rolled edge, 11½″			
□ crystal	30.00	45.00	33.00
Bread And Butter Plate, 6″			
□ crystal	5.00	7.50	6.00
Bud Vase, footed, flared, 6″			
□ crystal	13.00	17.00	14.00
Bud Vase, footed, flared, 8½″			
□ crystal	20.00	26.00	21.00
Butter Dish, with lid, round			
□ crystal	95.00	108.00	98.00
Butter Dish, oblong, ¼ lb.			
□ crystal	30.00	40.00	32.00
Cake Plate, footed, 12″			
□ crystal	37.00	46.00	39.00
Candlesticks, pair, 3″			
□ crystal	22.00	35.00	25.00
Candlesticks, pair, 6″			
□ crystal	50.00	70.00	57.00
Centerpiece Bowl, 3 corners, 11″			
□ crystal	30.00	45.00	34.00

	Current Price Range		P/Y Average
Coaster, 3¾″			
☐ crystal	4.00	8.00	5.00
Cocktail Goblet, footed, 3 oz., 2⅞″			
☐ crystal	11.00	14.00	12.00
Cologne Bottle, 8 oz., 7½″			
☐ crystal	43.00	60.00	46.00
Comport, flat, 8½″			
☐ crystal	40.00	50.00	42.00
Comport, flat, 9½″			
☐ crystal	40.00	50.00	42.00
Condiment Tray, 4 sections			
☐ crystal	30.00	40.00	32.00
Cream Soup			
☐ crystal	20.00	30.00	22.50
Creamer, 9½ oz., 4¼″			
☐ crystal	9.00	14.00	11.00
Creamer, tea			
☐ crystal	6.00	9.00	7.00
Cup, footed, 7 oz.			
☐ crystal	6.00	10.00	7.00
Decanter, with stopper, 24 oz., 9¼″			
☐ crystal	68.00	85.00	72.00
Dinner Plate, 9½″			
☐ crystal	18.00	24.00	20.00
Finger Bowl, 4½″			
☐ crystal	17.00	24.00	18.00
Finger Bowl Plate, 6½″			
☐ crystal	8.00	12.00	9.00
Fruit Bowl, footed, 12″			
☐ crystal	85.00	110.00	90.00
Fruit Bowl, footed, 16″			
☐ crystal	60.00	90.00	68.00
Fruit Nappy, flared, 4¾″			
☐ crystal	8.00	12.00	9.00
Goblet, footed, 10 oz., 6⅞″			
☐ crystal	14.00	19.00	15.00
Goblet, low, 9 oz., 5½″			
☐ crystal	9.00	13.00	10.00
Handkerchief Box, with cover, 5½″ x 4½″ x 2″			
☐ crystal	110.00	140.00	115.00
Hurricane Lamp, 12″			
☐ crystal	70.00	80.00	72.00
Ice Bucket			
☐ crystal	40.00	50.00	42.00
Iced Tea Tumbler, footed, flared, 12 oz., 5¾″			
☐ crystal	13.00	17.00	14.00

	Current Price Range		P/Y Average
Jam Pot, with cover, 4½"			
□ crystal	40.00	50.00	42.00
Jelly Comport, regular, 4¼"			
□ crystal	12.00	18.00	13.00
Juice Tumbler, footed, 5 oz., 4¾"			
□ crystal	10.00	14.00	11.00
Lemon Dish, with cover, 5½"			
□ crystal	26.00	34.00	28.00
Mayonnaise Dish, with liner			
□ crystal	24.00	32.00	25.00
Mayonnaise Ladle			
□ crystal	10.50	14.50	11.50
Muffin Tray, handled			
□ crystal	21.00	29.00	22.50
Mustard Dish, with cover and spoon, 3¾"			
□ crystal	28.00	35.00	30.00
Napkin Ring			
□ crystal	5.00	8.00	6.00
Nappy, flared, 7"			
□ crystal	30.00	40.00	32.00
Nappy, flared, 9"			
□ crystal	30.00	45.00	33.00
Nappy, shallow, 7"			
□ crystal	27.00	35.00	28.00
Nappy, 3 corners, handle, 5"			
□ crystal	8.00	12.00	9.00
Oil Cruet, 7 oz., 6¾"			
□ crystal	35.00	45.00	37.00
Old Fashioned Tumbler, flat, 6 oz., 3⅜"			
□ crystal	9.00	13.00	10.00
Oyster Cocktail, 4½ oz., 3½"			
□ crystal	11.00	14.00	12.00
Pickle Jar, with cover, 6"			
□ crystal	135.00	165.00	142.00
Pitcher, with lip, 3 pints, 6½"			
□ crystal	45.00	55.00	47.00
Pitcher, with lip, ½ gallon, 8¼"			
□ crystal	70.00	80.00	72.00
Platter, oval, 12"			
□ crystal	60.00	70.00	62.00
Preserve Bowl, with cover and handle, 5½"			
□ crystal	30.00	45.00	33.00
Puff Box, with cover, 3" x 3" x 2⅞"			
□ crystal	68.00	85.00	72.00
Punch Bowl, with base, 3¾ gallons, 18"			
□ crystal	230.00	260.00	240.00

	Current Price Range		P/Y Average
Punch Cup, flared, 6 oz. ☐ crystal	6.00	9.00	7.00
Relish Tray, for olives, oval, 6″ ☐ crystal	8.00	12.00	9.00
Relish Tray, for pickles, oval, 8″ ☐ crystal	11.00	15.00	12.00
Relish Tray, oval, 3 sections, 11″ ☐ crystal	28.00	35.00	30.00
Rose Bowl, 3½″ ☐ crystal	13.00	22.00	15.00
Rose Bowl, 5″ ☐ crystal	18.00	25.00	19.00
Salad Plate, 8½″ ☐ crystal	13.00	17.00	14.00
Salt And Pepper, round bottom, 3½″ ☐ crystal	13.00	17.00	14.00
Salt Dish, individual ☐ crystal	3.00	7.00	4.00
Sandwich Plate, 11½″ ☐ crystal	20.00	30.00	22.00
Saucer ☐ crystal	2.50	4.50	3.00
Serving Bowl, with handle, 9″ ☐ crystal	20.00	30.00	22.00
Sherbet, low, flared, 5 oz., 3¼″ ☐ crystal	7.50	11.50	8.50
Sherbet, with handle, 4½ oz., 3½″ ☐ crystal	13.00	17.00	14.00
Sugar, tea ☐ crystal	5.50	8.50	6.00
Sugar, with cover and handle, 5¼″ ☐ crystal	19.00	25.00	21.00
Sugar Shaker, 4¾″ ☐ crystal	110.00	140.00	120.00
Sundae, 6 oz., 3⅛″ ☐ crystal	8.00	11.50	9.00
Sweet Pea Vase, 4½″ ☐ crystal	88.00	105.00	92.00
Toothpick, 2¼″ ☐ crystal	16.00	23.00	17.00
Urn, square, 7½″ ☐ crystal	30.00	40.00	32.00
Utility Tray, handled, round, 9″ ☐ crystal	21.00	29.00	22.00
Vase, 8″ ☐ crystal	32.00	45.00	34.00

	Current Price Range		P/Y Average
Vase, 10″			
☐ crystal	42.00	55.00	44.00
Vegetable Bowl, oval, 2 sections, 10″			
☐ crystal	27.00	37.00	30.00
Water Bottle, 44 oz., 9¼″			
☐ crystal	130.00	160.00	138.00
Water Tumbler, footed, 9 oz., 4⅜″			
☐ crystal	9.00	15.00	10.00
Wedding Bowl, pedestal, 6½″			
☐ crystal	28.00	37.00	30.00
Whiskey Tumbler, flat, 2 oz., 2½″			
☐ crystal	7.00	11.00	8.00
Wine Goblet, footed, 2½ oz., 4¾″			
☐ crystal	12.00	17.00	13.00

BAROQUE

Made in crystal, blue and yellow, this elegant pattern features ornamental scrolls and designs on simple, delicately scalloped pieces.

	Current Price Range		P/Y Average
Ashtray, oval			
☐ blue	14.00	18.75	14.00
☐ yellow	12.50	15.00	12.00
☐ crystal	7.00	10.00	8.00
Bowl, flared, 12″			
☐ blue	30.00	37.50	28.00
☐ yellow	24.00	32.00	22.00
☐ crystal	15.00	20.00	16.00
Bowl, handles, 10½″			
☐ blue	35.00	44.00	32.00
☐ yellow	29.00	38.00	28.00
☐ crystal	17.00	23.00	18.00

BAROQUE

	Current Price Range		P/Y Average
Bowl, oval, 6½"			
☐ blue	16.50	22.00	14.00
☐ yellow	14.00	18.50	12.00
☐ crystal	8.00	12.00	9.00
Bread And Butter Plate, 6"			
☐ blue	6.50	8.00	5.50
☐ yellow	4.75	6.50	4.00
☐ crystal	2.00	4.00	2.50
Cake Plate, handles, 10"			
☐ blue	24.00	28.00	21.00
☐ yellow	17.00	24.00	16.00
☐ crystal	11.00	14.00	12.00
Candelabra, 3 lights, 9¼"			
☐ blue	68.00	82.00	71.00
☐ yellow	54.00	66.00	56.00
☐ crystal	40.00	50.00	42.00
Candlesticks, 4"			
☐ blue	22.00	29.00	23.00
☐ yellow	18.00	22.00	19.00
☐ crystal	13.00	17.00	14.00
Candlesticks, 5½"			
☐ blue	26.00	34.00	28.00
☐ yellow	22.00	28.00	23.00
☐ crystal	18.00	22.00	19.00
Celery Dish, oval, 11"			
☐ blue	24.50	32.50	23.00
☐ yellow	16.00	22.00	15.00
☐ crystal	11.00	14.00	12.00
Cereal Bowl, 6"			
☐ blue	31.00	37.00	28.00
☐ yellow	25.00	29.00	21.00
☐ crystal	14.00	20.00	15.00
Cocktail Tumbler, footed, 3¾ oz., 3"			
☐ blue	15.00	20.00	16.00
☐ yellow	12.00	16.00	13.00
☐ crystal	8.00	12.00	9.00
Compote, 6½"			
☐ blue	18.00	22.00	19.00
☐ yellow	14.00	18.00	15.00
☐ crystal	8.00	11.00	10.00
Cream Soup			
☐ blue	26.00	34.00	28.00
☐ yellow	20.00	25.00	21.00
☐ crystal	14.00	19.00	15.00
Creamer, footed, 3¾"			
☐ blue	14.00	18.00	15.00
☐ yellow	11.00	14.00	12.00
☐ crystal	6.00	10.00	7.00

	Current Price Range		P/Y Average
Cruet, with stopper, 3½ oz., 5½"			
☐ blue	230.00	270.00	240.00
☐ yellow	230.00	270.00	240.00
☐ crystal	23.00	29.00	24.00
Dinner Plate, 9"			
☐ blue	29.00	37.50	28.00
☐ yellow	24.00	29.00	21.00
☐ crystal	13.00	17.00	14.00
Floating Garden Bowl, 10"			
☐ blue	35.00	45.00	37.00
☐ yellow	31.00	39.00	32.00
☐ crystal	21.00	29.00	22.00
Ice Bucket, metal handle			
☐ blue	78.00	97.00	82.00
☐ yellow	55.00	65.00	57.00
☐ crystal	31.00	39.00	32.00
Iced Tea Tumbler, 14 oz., 5¾"			
☐ blue	31.00	39.00	32.00
☐ yellow	25.00	30.00	26.00
☐ crystal	15.00	20.00	16.00
Juice Tumbler, 5 oz., 3¾"			
☐ blue	20.00	25.00	21.00
☐ yellow	18.00	22.00	19.00
☐ crystal	11.00	14.00	12.00
Luncheon Plate, 8"			
☐ blue	10.00	14.00	10.00
☐ yellow	8.50	12.00	8.00
☐ crystal	5.00	9.00	6.00
Mayonnaise, 5½"			
☐ blue	24.00	31.00	26.00
☐ yellow	20.00	24.00	21.00
☐ crystal	17.00	21.00	18.00
Nappy, 5"			
☐ blue	14.00	20.00	15.00
☐ yellow	11.00	15.00	12.00
☐ crystal	8.00	12.00	9.00
Old Fashioned Tumbler, 6¾ oz., 3½"			
☐ blue	21.00	29.00	22.00
☐ yellow	18.00	22.00	19.00
☐ crystal	11.00	14.00	12.00
Pickle Dish, 8¼"			
☐ blue	14.00	19.00	15.50
☐ yellow	11.00	16.00	12.00
☐ crystal	7.50	11.50	8.50
Pitcher, 44 oz.			
☐ blue	625.00	675.00	635.00
☐ yellow	525.00	575.00	535.00
☐ crystal	135.00	165.00	145.00

	Current Price Range		P/Y Average
Punch Cup, 6 oz.			
☐ blue	18.00	22.00	19.00
☐ crystal	6.00	9.00	7.00
Relish Tray, 3 sections, handled			
☐ blue	24.00	31.00	26.00
☐ yellow	20.00	25.00	21.00
☐ crystal	11.00	14.00	12.00
Rose Bowl, 3¾"			
☐ blue	27.50	35.50	28.00
☐ yellow	21.00	28.00	21.00
☐ crystal	13.00	17.00	14.00
Rose Bowl, 8¾"			
☐ yellow	26.00	34.00	28.00
Salad Plate, 7"			
☐ blue	8.50	13.00	8.00
☐ yellow	7.00	12.00	7.00
☐ crystal	4.00	7.00	5.00
Salt And Pepper Shakers			
☐ blue	100.00	133.00	110.00
☐ yellow	88.00	96.00	90.00
☐ crystal	30.00	40.00	32.00
Saucer			
☐ blue	4.50	6.50	5.00
☐ yellow	3.00	5.00	3.50
☐ crystal	1.00	3.00	1.50
Serving Plate, center handle, 11"			
☐ crystal	15.00	21.00	15.00
Sherbet, 5 oz.			
☐ blue	16.00	21.00	17.00
☐ yellow	12.00	16.00	13.00
☐ crystal	7.00	10.00	8.00
Sugar, footed, 3½"			
☐ blue	12.00	15.00	13.00
☐ yellow	9.00	13.00	10.00
☐ crystal	6.00	9.00	6.50
Tray, oval, 11¼"			
☐ blue	21.00	26.50	21.00
☐ yellow	16.00	21.00	16.00
☐ crystal	11.00	14.00	12.00
Vase, 8¼"			
☐ blue	26.00	34.00	28.00
☐ yellow	21.00	28.00	22.00
☐ crystal	16.00	20.00	17.00

COLONY

Colony was made from the 1920s to the 1970s. This pattern was mostly made in crystal, though other colors include green, blue and yellow.

	Current Price Range		P/Y Average
Almond Bowl, footed			
☐ crystal	3.00	5.00	3.50
Bowl, low foot, 9″			
☐ crystal	13.00	17.00	14.00
Candlestick, 9¾″			
☐ crystal	11.00	14.00	12.00
Candy Dish, with lid, 6½″			
☐ crystal 29.00	19.00	.00	
Celery Bowl, 11½″			
☐ crystal	11.00	14.25	11.50
Cocktail Goblet, 3½ oz., 4″			
☐ crystal	7.50	10.50	8.50
Creamer			
☐ crystal	6.50	9.50	7.50
Finger Bowl, 4¾″			
☐ crystal	5.00	8.00	6.00
Goblet, 9 oz., 5¼″			
☐ crystal	10.50	13.50	11.50
Oyster Cocktail, 4 oz., 3⅜″			
☐ crystal	7.00	10.00	8.00
Pickle Bowl, 9½″			
☐ crystal	8.50	11.50	9.50
Plate, 6″			
☐ crystal	1.50	3.50	2.00
Plate, 7″			
☐ crystal	2.00	4.00	2.50

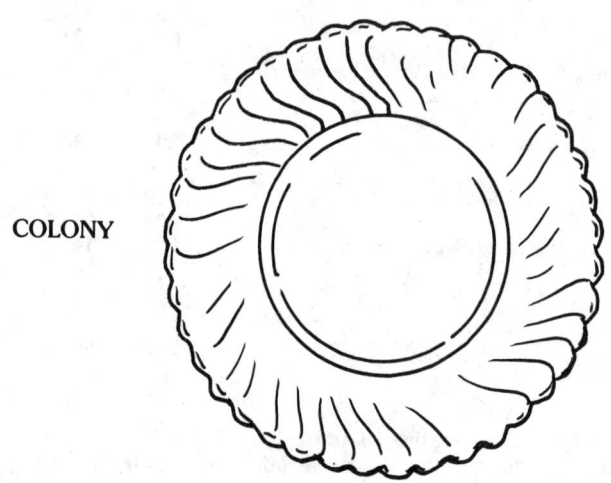

COLONY

	Current Price Range		P/Y Average
Plate, 8″			
☐ crystal	2.50	4.50	3.00
Plate, 9″			
☐ crystal	3.50	5.50	4.00
Plate, 10″			
☐ crystal	7.00	10.00	7.00
Sherbet, 5 oz., 3⅝″			
☐ crystal	7.50	11.50	8.50
Sugar			
☐ crystal	4.00	6.00	4.50
Tumbler, 5 oz.			
☐ crystal	6.50	9.50	7.50
Tumbler, 9 oz.			
☐ crystal	8.50	11.50	9.50
Tumbler, footed, 5 oz., 4½″			
☐ crystal	8.00	11.00	9.00
Tumbler, footed, 12 oz., 5¾″			
☐ crystal	10.00	13.00	11.00
Tumbler, 12 oz.			
☐ crystal	10.50	13.50	11.50
Vase, 8″			
☐ crystal	15.00	20.00	16.50
Wine Goblet, 3¼ oz., 4¼″			
☐ crystal	8.00	10.75	9.50

FAIRFAX

This plain simple pattern was made from the 1920s to the 1940s. Other patterns were created using Fairfax and adding a design.

FAIRFAX

	Current Price Range		P/Y Average
Ashtray			
☐ blue	19.00	23.00	19.00
☐ orchid	18.00	22.00	19.00
☐ pink	17.00	21.00	17.00
☐ green	17.00	21.00	17.00
☐ amber	11.00	15.00	12.00
Bon Bon Dish			
☐ blue	16.00	21.00	16.00
☐ orchid	15.00	20.00	16.00
☐ pink	14.00	18.00	14.00
☐ green	14.00	18.00	14.00
☐ amber	10.00	14.00	11.00
Bowl, footed, 11¾″			
☐ blue	22.00	26.00	22.00
☐ orchid	21.00	25.00	22.00
☐ pink	18.00	22.00	18.00
☐ green	18.00	22.00	18.00
☐ amber	13.00	17.00	14.00
Bowl, oval, 10½″			
☐ blue	26.00	31.50	26.00
☐ orchid	25.00	30.00	26.00
☐ pink	23.00	29.00	23.00
☐ green	22.00	28.00	23.00
☐ amber	15.00	20.00	16.00
Bread And Butter Plate, 6″			
☐ blue	3.50	5.50	4.00
☐ orchid	3.50	5.50	4.00
☐ pink	3.00	5.00	3.50
☐ green	3.00	5.00	3.50
☐ amber	2.00	4.00	2.50
Cake Plate, handles, 10″			
☐ blue	16.00	21.00	16.00
☐ orchid	15.00	20.00	16.00
☐ pink	14.00	18.00	14.00
☐ green	14.00	18.00	14.00
☐ amber	11.00	14.00	12.00
Candy Dish, with lid, 3 sections			
☐ blue	42.00	52.00	44.00
☐ orchid	42.00	52.00	44.00
☐ pink	33.00	41.00	34.00
☐ green	33.00	41.00	34.00
☐ amber	29.00	35.00	31.00
Cereal Bowl, 6″			
☐ blue	14.00	18.00	14.00
☐ orchid	13.00	17.00	14.00
☐ pink	12.00	15.00	12.00
☐ green	12.00	15.00	12.00
☐ amber	8.50	11.50	9.50
Cigarette Box			
☐ blue	31.00	39.00	33.00
☐ orchid	31.00	39.00	33.00

	Current Price Range		P/Y Average
☐ pink	23.00	33.00	25.00
☐ green	23.00	33.00	25.00
☐ amber	20.00	25.00	21.00
Claret Goblet, 4 oz.			
☐ blue	23.00	28.00	24.00
☐ orchid	23.00	28.00	24.00
☐ pink	20.00	25.00	21.00
☐ green	20.00	25.00	21.00
☐ amber	17.00	21.00	18.00
Coaster, 3½"			
☐ blue	5.00	7.00	5.50
☐ orchid	5.00	7.00	5.50
☐ pink	3.00	5.00	3.50
☐ green	3.00	5.00	3.50
☐ amber	2.00	4.00	2.50
Cocktail Goblet, 3 oz.,			
☐ blue	20.00	25.00	21.00
☐ orchid	20.00	25.00	21.00
☐ pink	18.00	22.00	19.00
☐ green	18.00	22.00	19.00
☐ amber	15.00	20.00	16.00
Compote, 7"			
☐ blue	20.00	25.00	21.00
☐ orchid	20.00	25.00	21.00
☐ pink	18.00	22.00	19.00
☐ green	18.00	22.00	19.00
☐ amber	14.00	18.00	15.00
Cordial Goblet, ¾ oz.			
☐ blue	26.00	34.00	28.00
☐ orchid	26.00	34.00	28.00
☐ pink	25.00	30.00	26.00
☐ green	25.00	30.00	26.00
☐ amber	21.00	26.00	23.00
Cream Soup			
☐ blue	12.00	15.00	13.00
☐ orchid	12.00	15.00	13.00
☐ pink	10.50	13.50	11.50
☐ green	10.50	13.50	11.50
☐ amber	8.50	11.50	9.50
Creamer, footed			
☐ blue	8.50	11.50	9.50
☐ orchid	8.50	11.50	9.50
☐ pink	6.50	9.50	7.50
☐ green	6.50	9.50	7.50
☐ amber	5.00	7.00	5.50
Cruet, footed, with handle			
☐ blue	112.00	140.00	117.00
☐ orchid	112.00	140.00	117.00
☐ pink	98.00	122.00	104.00
☐ green	98.00	122.00	104.00
☐ amber	82.00	98.00	85.00

	Current Price Range		P/Y Average
Cup, footed			
☐ blue	7.00	10.00	8.00
☐ orchid	7.00	10.00	8.00
☐ pink	4.50	7.50	5.50
☐ green	4.50	7.50	5.50
☐ amber	4.00	6.00	4.50
Dinner Plate, 10¼"			
☐ blue	26.50	31.50	26.00
☐ orchid	25.00	30.00	26.00
☐ pink	23.00	30.00	23.00
☐ green	23.00	30.00	23.00
☐ amber	18.00	22.00	19.00
Finger Bowl, 4⅝" x 2"			
☐ blue	13.00	17.00	14.00
☐ orchid	13.00	17.00	14.00
☐ pink	11.00	15.00	12.00
☐ green	11.00	15.00	12.00
☐ amber	8.50	11.50	9.50
Fruit Bowl, 5"			
☐ blue	7.50	11.50	8.50
☐ orchid	7.50	11.50	8.50
☐ pink	5.00	8.00	6.00
☐ green	5.00	8.00	6.00
☐ amber	5.00	7.00	5.50
Grill Plate, 10¼"			
☐ blue	15.00	20.00	16.00
☐ orchid	15.00	20.00	16.00
☐ pink	11.00	14.00	12.00
☐ green	11.00	14.00	12.00
☐ amber	8.50	11.50	9.50
Ice Bucket, with metal handle			
☐ blue	36.00	44.00	38.00
☐ orchid	36.00	44.00	38.00
☐ pink	31.00	39.00	33.00
☐ green	31.00	39.00	33.00
☐ amber	25.00	30.00	26.00
Luncheon Plate, 9½"			
☐ blue	8.50	11.50	8.50
☐ orchid	7.50	10.50	8.50
☐ pink	7.50	10.50	7.50
☐ green	7.50	10.50	7.50
☐ amber	6.00	8.00	6.50
Mayonnaise Dish			
☐ blue	13.00	17.00	14.00
☐ orchid	13.00	17.00	14.00
☐ pink	9.50	12.50	10.50
☐ green	9.50	12.50	10.50
☐ amber	7.50	10.50	8.50
Mayonnaise Ladle			
☐ blue	18.00	22.00	19.00
☐ orchid	18.00	22.00	19.00

	Current Price Range		P/Y Average
☐ pink	13.00	17.00	14.00
☐ green	13.00	17.00	14.00
☐ amber	13.00	17.00	14.00
Oyster Cocktail, footed, 5½ oz.			
☐ blue	14.50	18.50	15.50
☐ orchid	14.50	18.50	15.50
☐ pink	12.00	16.00	13.00
☐ green	12.00	16.00	13.00
☐ amber	8.50	11.50	9.50
Parfait, footed, 6½ oz.			
☐ blue	15.00	20.00	16.00
☐ orchid	15.00	20.00	16.00
☐ pink	12.00	16.00	13.00
☐ green	12.00	16.00	13.00
☐ amber	11.00	14.00	12.00
Pitcher, footed, 48 oz.			
☐ blue	175.00	220.00	180.00
☐ orchid	175.00	220.00	180.00
☐ pink	150.00	190.00	160.00
☐ green	150.00	190.00	160.00
☐ amber	120.00	150.00	127.00
Platter, oval, 15″			
☐ blue	43.00	53.00	45.00
☐ orchid	42.00	52.00	45.00
☐ pink	39.00	47.50	40.00
☐ green	39.00	47.50	40.00
☐ amber	32.00	39.00	33.00
Relish Tray, 2 sections, 8½″			
☐ blue	13.00	16.00	14.00
☐ orchid	13.00	16.00	14.00
☐ pink	11.00	14.00	12.00
☐ green	11.00	14.00	12.00
☐ amber	8.50	11.50	9.00
Relish Tray, 3 sections, 11½″			
☐ blue	20.00	25.00	21.00
☐ orchid	20.00	25.00	21.00
☐ pink	15.00	20.00	16.00
☐ green	15.00	20.00	16.00
☐ amber	11.00	14.00	12.00
Relish Tray, 3 sections, round			
☐ blue	15.00	20.00	16.00
☐ orchid	15.00	20.00	16.00
☐ pink	12.00	15.00	13.00
☐ green	12.00	15.00	13.00
☐ amber	8.50	11.50	9.50
Sauce Boat			
☐ blue	31.00	39.00	33.00
☐ orchid	31.00	39.00	33.00
☐ pink	26.00	34.00	28.00
☐ green	26.00	34.00	28.00
☐ amber	23.00	28.00	24.00

	Current Price Range		P/Y Average
Saucer			
☐ blue	2.50	4.50	3.00
☐ orchid	2.50	4.50	3.00
☐ pink	1.50	3.50	2.00
☐ green	1.50	3.50	2.00
☐ amber	1.50	3.50	2.00
Sherbet, low, 6 oz.			
☐ blue	14.00	17.00	15.00
☐ orchid	14.00	17.00	15.00
☐ pink	12.00	15.00	13.00
☐ green	12.00	15.00	13.00
☐ amber	11.00	14.00	12.00
Sherbet, tall, 6 oz.			
☐ blue	15.00	20.00	16.00
☐ orchid	15.00	20.00	16.00
☐ pink	12.00	16.00	13.00
☐ green	12.00	16.00	13.00
☐ amber	12.00	16.00	13.00
Soup Bowl			
☐ blue	15.00	20.00	16.00
☐ orchid	15.00	20.00	16.00
☐ pink	13.00	17.00	14.00
☐ green	13.00	17.00	14.00
☐ amber	11.00	14.00	12.00
Sugar, footed			
☐ blue	7.50	10.50	8.50
☐ orchid	7.50	10.50	8.50
☐ pink	6.00	8.00	6.50
☐ green	6.00	8.00	6.50
☐ amber	4.00	6.00	4.50
Tray, handle, 11″			
☐ blue	27.00	31.50	26.00
☐ orchid	27.00	31.50	26.00
☐ pink	20.00	25.00	21.00
☐ green	20.00	25.00	21.00
☐ amber	15.00	20.00	16.00
Tumbler, footed, 12 oz.			
☐ blue	18.00	22.00	19.00
☐ orchid	18.00	22.00	19.00
☐ pink	16.00	20.00	17.00
☐ green	16.00	20.00	17.00
☐ amber	14.00	18.00	15.00
Tumbler, footed, 9 oz.			
☐ blue	15.00	20.00	16.00
☐ orchid	15.00	20.00	16.00
☐ pink	12.00	16.00	13.00
☐ green	12.00	16.00	13.00
☐ amber	10.50	13.50	12.50
Tumbler, footed, 5 oz.			
☐ blue	12.00	16.00	13.00
☐ orchid	12.00	16.00	13.00

	Current Price Range		P/Y Average
☐ pink	9.50	12.50	10.50
☐ green	9.50	12.50	10.50
☐ amber	7.50	10.50	8.50
Tumbler, footed, 2½ oz.			
☐ blue	12.50	15.50	13.50
☐ orchid	12.50	15.50	13.50
☐ pink	9.50	12.50	10.50
☐ green	9.50	12.50	10.50
☐ amber	7.50	10.50	8.50
Water Goblet, 10 oz.			
☐ blue	20.00	25.00	21.00
☐ orchid	20.00	25.00	21.00
☐ pink	16.00	20.00	17.00
☐ green	16.00	20.00	17.00
☐ amber	15.00	18.00	16.00

JUNE

This understated, lacy pattern is built around a series of wide, bowknot motifs, separated one from the other by a trailing garland about the rim. It was issued in crystal, blue, topaz, and rose.

	Current Price Range		P/Y Average
Ashtray			
☐ yellow	27.00	34.00	32.00
☐ pink	27.00	34.00	32.00
☐ blue	27.00	34.00	32.00
☐ crystal	20.00	25.00	22.00
Baking Dish, egg shape, length 9″			
☐ yellow	70.00	80.00	72.50
☐ pink	40.00	45.00	42.00
☐ blue	50.00	60.00	55.00
☐ crystal	30.00	35.00	32.00
Bon Bon, stemmed			
☐ yellow	20.00	25.00	22.00
☐ pink	15.00	20.00	17.00
☐ blue	18.00	22.00	19.00
☐ crystal	10.00	14.00	11.00
Bouillon Bowl, pedestal foot with under-plate			
☐ pink	20.00	25.00	22.00
☐ yellow	20.00	25.00	24.00
☐ crystal	10.00	14.00	11.00
☐ blue	33.00	36.00	34.00
Bowl, diameter 10″			
☐ yellow	33.00	38.00	34.00
☐ pink	38.00	43.00	39.00
☐ blue	48.00	53.00	49.00
☐ crystal	22.00	28.00	24.00
Bread And Butter Plate, diameter 6″			
☐ yellow	5.00	7.00	6.00
☐ pink	5.00	7.00	6.00

	Current Price Range		P/Y Average
□ blue	6.00	8.00	7.00
□ crystal	4.00	6.00	5.00
Cake Plate, handled, diameter 10″			
□ yellow	33.00	38.00	34.00
□ pink	35.00	40.00	37.00
□ blue	43.00	48.00	46.00
□ crystal	23.00	28.00	24.00
Canape Plate			
□ yellow	12.00	15.00	13.00
□ pink	12.00	15.00	13.00
□ blue	14.00	15.00	16.00
□ crystal	8.00	10.00	9.00
Candlesticks, pair, height 2″			
□ yellow	33.00	38.00	34.00
□ pink	35.00	40.00	37.00
□ blue	40.00	45.00	42.00
□ crystal	28.00	33.00	29.00
Candlesticks, pair, height 3″			
□ yellow	35.00	40.00	37.00
□ pink	38.00	43.00	39.00
□ blue	45.00	50.00	46.00
□ crystal	30.00	35.00	32.00
Candlesticks, pair, height 5″			
□ yellow	40.00	45.00	42.00
□ pink	45.00	50.00	47.00
□ blue	55.00	60.00	56.50
Candy Jar, with lid, capacity two cups			
□ yellow	95.00	110.00	97.00
□ pink	105.00	115.00	107.50
□ blue	145.00	155.00	147.00
□ crystal	63.00	68.99	64.00
Candy Jar, with lid, capacity six cups			
□ yellow	70.00	90.00	75.00
□ pink	145.00	155.00	147.00
□ blue	145.00	155.00	147.00
□ crystal	40.00	50.00	45.00
Celery Dish, length 11″			
□ yellow	33.00	37.00	34.00
□ pink	33.00	38.00	34.00
□ blue	38.00	43.00	40.00
□ crystal	20.00	25.00	22.00
Centerpiece Bowl, oval, length 11″			
□ yellow	30.00	50.00	32.00
□ pink	40.00	50.00	42.00
□ blue	40.00	50.00	42.00
□ crystal	20.00	25.00	22.00
Cereal Bowl, diameter 6″			
□ yellow	25.00	30.00	27.00
□ pink	20.00	25.00	22.00
□ blue	23.00	27.00	24.50
□ crystal	14.00	16.00	15.00

	Current Price Range		P/Y Average

Cheese And Cracker Set

☐ yellow	30.00	35.00	32.00
☐ pink	40.00	44.00	42.00
☐ blue	40.00	44.00	42.00
☐ crystal	20.00	25.00	22.00

Chop Plate, diameter 12"

☐ yellow	35.00	40.00	37.00
☐ pink	35.00	40.00	37.00
☐ blue	40.00	45.00	42.00
☐ crystal	20.00	25.00	22.00

Condiment Bottle, footed, with stopper

☐ yellow	240.00	260.00	245.00
☐ pink	290.00	310.00	295.00
☐ blue	370.00	380.00	372.00
☐ crystal	145.00	155.00	148.00

Comport, diameter 5"

☐ yellow	22.00	38.00	23.00
☐ pink	30.00	34.00	30.00
☐ blue	30.00	34.00	30.00
☐ crystal	28.00	34.00	29.50

Comport, diameter 6"

☐ yellow	50.00	60.00	53.00
☐ pink	55.00	65.00	58.00
☐ blue	65.00	75.00	68.00
☐ crystal	38.00	43.00	39.50

Comport, diameter 7"

☐ yellow	55.00	65.00	58.00
☐ pink	60.00	70.00	63.00
☐ blue	80.00	90.00	83.50
☐ crystal	43.00	48.00	44.00

Comport, diameter 8"

☐ yellow	65.00	75.00	67.50
☐ pink	70.00	80.00	73.50
☐ blue	90.00	100.00	94.50
☐ crystal	57.00	63.00	58.50

Cordial Cup

☐ yellow	30.00	35.00	32.00
☐ pink	38.00	43.00	39.50
☐ blue	45.00	55.00	48.50
☐ crystal	20.00	25.00	22.00

Cordial Cup Saucer

☐ yellow	8.00	10.00	8.50
☐ pink	9.00	11.00	9.50
☐ blue	11.00	14.00	12.00
☐ crystal	6.00	8.00	7.00

Cordial Glass, stemmed

☐ yellow	62.00	68.00	63.00
☐ pink	55.00	65.00	58.00
☐ blue	68.00	73.00	69.00
☐ crystal	30.00	40.00	35.00

	Current Price Range		P/Y Average
Creamer, collar base			
☐ yellow	23.00	28.00	24.00
☐ pink	28.00	33.00	29.50
☐ blue	33.00	38.00	34.00
☐ crystal	20.00	25.00	22.00
Creamer, pedestal foot			
☐ yellow	16.00	18.00	17.00
☐ pink	16.00	18.00	17.00
☐ blue	20.00	22.00	21.00
☐ crystal	16.00	18.00	16.50
Cup, pedestal foot			
☐ yellow	20.00	22.00	21.00
☐ pink	20.00	25.00	22.00
☐ blue	25.00	30.00	26.00
☐ crystal	14.00	16.00	14.50
Decanter, with glass stopper			
☐ yellow	390.00	410.00	395.00
☐ pink	440.00	460.00	445.00
☐ blue	490.00	510.00	495.00
☐ crystal	290.00	310.00	295.00
Dessert Bowl, handled, diameter 8″			
☐ yellow	45.00	55.00	48.00
☐ pink	55.00	65.00	59.00
☐ blue	60.00	70.00	64.00
☐ crystal	38.00	43.00	39.00
Dinner Plate, diameter 9″			
☐ yellow	20.00	25.00	22.00
☐ pink	14.00	16.00	15.00
☐ blue	16.00	18.00	17.00
☐ crystal	11.00	14.00	11.50
Dinner Plate, diameter 10¼″			
☐ yellow	33.00	38.00	34.00
☐ pink	35.00	40.00	37.00
☐ blue	40.00	50.00	43.00
☐ crystal	23.00	28.00	24.00
Fan Vase, pedestal foot			
☐ yellow	90.00	100.00	94.00
☐ pink	95.00	105.00	98.00
☐ blue	120.00	130.00	124.00
☐ crystal	70.00	80.00	74.00
Finger Bowl			
☐ yellow	23.00	28.00	24.00
☐ pink	23.00	28.00	24.00
☐ blue	30.00	38.00	32.50
☐ crystal	15.00	20.00	17.00
Fruit Bowl, diameter 5″			
☐ yellow	18.25	21.50	18.00
☐ pink	16.00	21.50	16.00
☐ blue	20.00	25.00	22.00
☐ crystal	11.00	13.00	11.50

	Current Price Range		P/Y Average
Mayonnaise Compote			
☐ yellow	30.00	35.00	32.50
☐ pink	35.00	40.00	37.00
☐ blue	45.00	50.00	47.00
☐ crystal	25.00	35.00	28.00
Mint Dish			
☐ yellow	20.00	25.00	22.00
☐ pink	23.00	28.00	24.00
☐ blue	27.00	33.00	28.00
☐ crystal	14.00	18.00	15.00
Nappy, flat, diameter 7″			
☐ yellow	15.00	20.00	16.00
☐ pink	15.00	20.00	16.00
☐ blue	18.00	20.00	19.00
☐ crystal	10.00	14.00	11.00
Nappy, pedestal foot, diameter 6¼″			
☐ yellow	315.00	20.00	16.00
☐ pink	15.00	20.00	16.00
☐ blue	18.00	20.00	19.00
☐ crystal	10.00	14.00	11.00
Oil Cruet, pedestal foot			
☐ yellow	280.00	320.00	290.00
☐ pink	340.00	360.00	345.00
☐ blue	420.00	430.00	425.00
☐ crystal	140.00	160.00	150.00
Oyster Plate			
☐ yellow	20.00	24.00	22.00
☐ pink	20.00	24.00	22.00
☐ blue	28.00	32.00	30.00
☐ crystal	20.00	26.00	22.00
Parfait Glass			
☐ yellow	40.00	45.00	42.00
☐ pink	24.00	28.00	25.00
☐ blue	30.00	35.00	32.00
☐ crystal	18.00	20.00	19.00
Pitcher			
☐ yellow	340.00	360.00	345.00
☐ pink	340.00	360.00	345.00
☐ blue	465.00	485.00	470.00
Platter, diameter 11″			
☐ yellow	40.00	45.00	42.00
☐ pink	43.00	48.00	44.00
☐ blue	45.00	55.00	48.00
☐ crystal	30.00	40.00	34.00
Platter, diameter 15″			
☐ yellow	85.00	95.00	87.00
☐ pink	95.00	105.00	97.00
☐ blue	115.00	135.00	120.00
☐ crystal	55.00	65.00	58.00

	Current Price Range		P/Y Average
Relish Dish, two compartments, length 8¼″			
☐ yellow	20.00	24.00	21.50
☐ pink	25.00	30.00	26.00
☐ blue	25.00	30.00	26.00
☐ crystal	14.00	16.00	15.00
Sugar Bowl, small with lid			
☐ yellow	20.00	25.00	22.00
☐ pink	25.00	30.00	27.00
☐ blue	33.00	38.00	34.00
☐ crystal	20.00	25.00	22.00
Tray, loop handle, diameter 11″			
☐ yellow	33.00	38.00	34.00
☐ pink	38.00	43.00	39.50
☐ blue	45.00	55.00	49.50
☐ crystal	25.00	30.00	27.50
Tumbler, height 3½″			
☐ yellow	30.00	35.00	32.00
☐ pink	30.00	35.00	32.00
☐ blue	35.00	40.00	36.00
☐ crystal	20.00	30.00	22.00
Tumbler, height 5″			
☐ yellow	20.00	30.00	22.00
☐ pink	20.00	30.00	22.00
☐ blue	25.00	30.00	26.00
☐ crystal	14.00	16.00	15.00
Vase, height 7½″			
☐ yellow	95.00	100.00	97.50
☐ pink	95.00	100.00	97.50
☐ blue	185.00	205.00	187.50
☐ crystal	30.00	40.00	35.00
Water Glass, stemmed			
☐ yellow	20.00	30.00	22.50
☐ pink	30.00	35.00	32.00
☐ blue	28.00	33.00	29.50
☐ crystal	18.00	22.00	19.50
Whipped Cream Bowl, large			
☐ yellow	110.00	120.00	112.00
☐ pink	123.00	128.00	124.00
☐ blue	140.00	160.00	145.00
☐ crystal	65.00	85.00	70.00
Whipped Cream Bowl, small			
☐ yellow	18.00	22.00	19.00
☐ pink	20.00	25.00	22.00
☐ blue	23.00	28.00	24.00
☐ crystal	15.00	20.00	17.00
Whiskey Tumbler, shot, 2½ oz.			
☐ yellow	30.00	35.00	32.00
☐ blue	30.00	35.00	32.00
☐ pink	40.00	45.00	41.50
☐ crystal	20.00	25.00	22.00

	Current Price Range		P/Y Average

Wine Glass, stemmed
☐ yellow	40.00	45.00	42.00
☐ pink	35.00	40.00	37.00
☐ blue	45.00	50.00	47.00
☐ crystal	19.00	23.00	20.00

TROJAN

This is an interesting symmetrical pattern made up of spade-like motifs created by framing ridgework with a curly scroll, trapping a floral design that is reminiscent of a fleur-de-lis. These shapes alternate around the outer rim with draped scrollwork delicately drawn in low relief. The rest of the glass is plain, with no center medallions or base designs.

Ashtray, large
☐ pink	25.00	35.00	25.50
☐ yellow	25.00	35.00	25.50

Bon bon Bowl
☐ pink	10.00	20.00	12.00
☐ yellow	10.00	20.00	12.00

Bouillon Bowl, footed
☐ pink	15.00	26.50	15.00
☐ yellow	15.00	26.50	15.00

Cereal Bowl, diameter 6″
☐ pink	16.00	26.00	17.50
☐ yellow	16.00	26.00	17.50

Compote, height 6″
☐ pink	20.00	30.00	22.00
☐ yellow	20.00	30.00	22.00

Creamer, footed
☐ pink	15.00	25.00	16.50
☐ yellow	15.00	25.00	16.50

Dinner Plate, diameter 10¼″
☐ pink	25.00	35.00	26.50
☐ yellow	25.00	35.00	26.50

Finger Bowl, with liner
☐ pink	20.00	30.00	22.00
☐ yellow	20.00	30.00	22.00

Grill Plate, diameter 10″
☐ pink	25.00	35.00	26.50
☐ yellow	25.00	35.00	26.50

Luncheon Plate, diameter 8¾″
☐ pink	11.00	21.50	12.00
☐ yellow	11.00	21.50	12.00

Mayonnaise Bowl, with liner
☐ pink	25.00	35.00	26.50
☐ yellow	25.00	35.00	26.50

Parfait
☐ pink	24.00	34.00	25.00
☐ yellow	24.00	34.00	25.00

	Current Price Range		P/Y Average

Pitcher
☐ pink 225.00 300.00 235.00
☐ yellow 225.00 300.00 235.00

Platter, diameter 12″
☐ pink 28.00 38.00 30.00
☐ yellow 28.00 38.00 30.00

Platter, diameter 15″
☐ pink 40.00 50.00 42.00
☐ yellow 40.00 50.00 42.00

Relish Dish, diameter 8½″
☐ pink 10.00 20.00 12.00
☐ yellow 10.00 20.00 12.00

Relish Dish, three compartments
☐ pink 20.00 30.00 22.00
☐ yellow 20.00 30.00 22.00

Saucer
☐ pink 4.00 10.00 6.00
☐ yellow 4.00 10.00 6.00

Sherbet, height 4¼″
☐ pink 14.00 20.00 16.00
☐ yellow 14.00 20.00 16.00

Sugar Bowl, footed
☐ pink 15.00 25.00 17.00
☐ yellow 15.00 25.00 17.00

Tray, diameter 11″, center handle
☐ pink 25.00 35.00 26.50
☐ yellow 25.00 35.00 26.50

Tumbler, height 4½″
☐ pink 18.00 28.00 20.00
☐ yellow 18.00 28.00 20.00

Tumbler, height 5¼″
☐ pink 14.00 24.00 15.00
☐ yellow 14.00 24.00 15.00

Tumbler, height 6″
☐ pink 18.00 28.00 20.00
☐ yellow 18.00 28.00 20.00

Vase, height 8″
☐ pink 57.00 67.00 57.50
☐ yellow 57.00 67.00 57.50

Whipped Cream Tub
☐ pink 65.00 80.00 70.00
☐ yellow 65.00 80.00 70.00

VERSAILLES

This pattern was Fostoria's pride and joy during the time of the Depression and was expensive, given the economic conditions of the time. Now collectors have made it a favorite and the prices reflect it. It is a scrolled pattern, consisting of sprays of ornate curves around a stylized fern-like center. The variety of shapes is enormous with many interesting handles and lids. The glass is delicate, the moldwork excellent, the design well-conceived.

	Current Price Range		P/Y Average
Ashtray			
☐ blue	28.00	38.00	30.00
☐ green	22.00	32.00	23.00
☐ pink	22.00	32.00	22.00
☐ yellow	25.00	35.00	26.50
Bonbon Bowl			
☐ blue	12.00	22.00	14.00
☐ green	10.00	20.00	12.00
☐ pink	10.00	20.00	12.00
☐ yellow	10.00	20.00	12.00
Bouillon Bowl			
☐ blue	20.00	30.00	21.50
☐ green	15.00	25.00	17.00
☐ pink	15.00	25.00	17.00
☐ yellow	16.00	26.00	17.50
Bread and Butter Plate, diameter 6″			
☐ blue	5.00	11.00	5.00
☐ green	4.00	9.75	4.00
☐ pink	4.00	9.75	4.00
☐ yellow	4.00	9.75	4.00
Cereal Bowl, diameter 6″			
☐ blue	25.00	35.00	27.00
☐ green	18.00	28.00	20.00
☐ pink	18.00	28.00	20.00
☐ yellow	20.00	30.00	22.00
Chop Plate, diameter 13″			
☐ blue	33.00	43.00	35.00
☐ green	28.00	38.00	30.00
☐ pink	28.00	38.00	30.00
☐ yellow	30.00	40.00	32.00
Compote, height 6″			
☐ blue	28.00	38.00	30.00
☐ green	20.00	30.00	22.00
☐ pink	20.00	30.00	22.00
☐ yellow	25.00	35.00	26.00
Compote, height 7″			
☐ blue	33.00	43.00	34.00
☐ green	23.00	33.00	24.00
☐ pink	23.00	33.00	24.00
☐ yellow	28.00	38.00	30.00
Creamer, footed			
☐ blue	18.00	28.00	20.00
☐ green	13.00	23.00	15.00
☐ pink	13.00	23.00	15.00
☐ yellow	13.00	23.00	15.00

	Current Price Range		P/Y Average
Demitasse Cup and Saucer			
☐ blue	45.00	55.00	47.00
☐ green	20.00	30.00	22.00
☐ pink	20.00	30.00	22.00
☐ yellow	30.00	40.00	32.00
Decanter			
☐ blue	175.00	250.00	185.00
☐ green	125.00	200.00	135.00
☐ pink	125.00	200.00	135.00
☐ yellow	140.00	180.00	145.00
Finger Bowl, with liner			
☐ blue	25.00	35.00	26.50
☐ green	18.00	28.00	18.50
☐ pink	18.00	28.00	18.50
☐ yellow	23.00	33.00	24.50
Fruit Bowl, diameter 5″			
☐ blue	15.00	25.00	16.50
☐ green	12.00	22.00	14.00
☐ pink	12.00	22.00	14.00
☐ yellow	13.00	23.00	14.00
Ice Bucket			
☐ blue	77.00	87.00	80.00
☐ green	60.00	70.00	62.00
☐ pink	60.00	70.00	62.00
☐ yellow	73.00	84.00	74.50
Lemon Bowl			
☐ blue	12.00	22.00	14.00
☐ green	8.00	18.00	10.00
☐ pink	8.00	18.00	10.00
☐ yellow	10.00	20.00	12.00
Luncheon Plate, diameter 8¾″			
☐ blue	7.00	19.00	10.00
☐ green	7.00	17.00	7.50
☐ pink	7.00	17.00	7.50
☐ yellow	7.00	19.00	10.00
Mayonnaise Bowl, with liner			
☐ blue	45.00	55.00	47.00
☐ green	33.00	43.00	35.00
☐ pink	33.00	43.00	35.00
☐ yellow	38.00	48.00	40.00
Parfait			
☐ blue	28.00	38.00	30.00
☐ green	24.00	34.00	25.00
☐ pink	24.00	34.00	25.00
☐ yellow	25.00	35.00	26.50
Pitcher			
☐ blue	380.00	440.00	400.00
☐ green	240.00	280.00	245.00
☐ pink	240.00	280.00	245.00
☐ yellow	280.00	330.00	295.00

	Current Price Range		P/Y Average
Platter, diameter 12″			
☐ blue	38.50	49.00	40.00
☐ green	29.00	39.00	30.00
☐ pink	29.00	39.00	30.00
☐ yellow	34.50	44.00	34.50
Platter, diameter 15″			
☐ blue	58.00	68.00	59.50
☐ green	43.00	53.00	44.00
☐ pink	43.00	53.00	44.00
☐ yellow	45.00	55.00	46.50
Relish, diameter 8½″			
☐ blue	38.00	48.00	39.50
☐ green	28.00	38.00	32.00
☐ pink	28.00	38.00	32.00
☐ yellow	33.00	43.00	34.50
Sauce Boat and Underplate			
☐ blue	57.00	67.00	58.00
☐ green	43.00	53.00	44.00
☐ pink	43.00	53.00	44.00
☐ yellow	38.00	48.00	40.00
Saucer			
☐ blue	4.00	10.00	5.00
☐ green	3.00	9.00	4.00
☐ pink	3.00	9.00	4.00
☐ yellow	3.00	8.00	3.50
Soup Bowl, diameter 7″			
☐ blue	29.00	39.00	30.00
☐ green	24.00	35.00	24.50
☐ pink	24.00	35.00	24.50
☐ yellow	26.00	37.00	26.50
Sugar, footed			
☐ blue	18.00	28.00	20.00
☐ green	13.00	23.00	15.00
☐ pink	13.00	23.00	15.00
☐ yellow	13.00	23.00	15.00
Tray, diameter 11″, with center handle			
☐ blue	28.00	38.00	30.00
☐ green	18.00	28.00	20.00
☐ pink	18.00	28.00	20.00
☐ yellow	23.00	33.00	24.50
Tumbler, height 4½″, 5 oz.			
☐ blue	22.00	32.00	23.50
☐ green	18.00	28.00	21.50
☐ pink	18.00	28.00	21.50
☐ yellow	20.00	30.00	22.50
Tumbler, height 5¼″, 9 oz.			
☐ blue	23.00	33.00	24.50
☐ green	18.00	28.00	19.50
☐ pink	18.00	28.00	19.50
☐ yellow	19.50	29.50	20.00

	Current Price Range		P/Y Average
Tumbler, height 6″, 12 oz.			
☐ blue	25.00	35.00	26.50
☐ green	20.00	30.00	22.00
☐ pink	20.00	30.00	22.00
☐ yellow	23.00	33.00	24.50
Vase, height 8″			
☐ blue	123.00	153.00	127.50
☐ green	73.00	93.00	72.50
☐ pink	73.00	93.00	72.50
☐ yellow	90.00	125.00	97.50

FRANKOMA POTTERY

DESCRIPTION: Founded in 1933 by John Frank, the Frankoma Pottery continues to produce earthenwares made from Oklahoma clays to the present day. Located in Sapula, Oklahoma, the wares of this company are known for their color and durability.

TYPES: Many types of objects have been produced by Frankoma including jewelry, limited edition plates, miniatures, trivets, Christmas cards, sculpture, novelties and of course dinnerware.

RECOMMENDED READING: For more in-depth information you may refer to *The Official Price Guide to Pottery and Porcelain* and *The Official Identification Guide to Pottery and Porcelain,* published by The House of Collectibles.

☐ **Bowl, divided,** 11″, item #49d, peach glow,	6.00	8.00	7.00
☐ **Bowl,** 14 ounces	3.50	5.00	4.25
☐ **Creamer And Sugar,** 8 ounces, item #4a, peach glow	8.00	10.00	9.00
☐ **Cup,** item #4c, clay blue	4.00	5.50	4.75
☐ **Dish, butter,** item #4k, peach glow, lidded	7.00	10.00	8.50
☐ **Juice,** 6 ounces	3.00	4.00	3.50
☐ **Lazy Suzette,** 5 sections, on ball bearing base, made from 1957–1982	22.00	24.00	23.00
☐ **Pitcher,** item #4d, two quart, clay blue	9.00	12.00	10.50
☐ **Platter, serving,** 12⅞″, item #4p, clay blue	11.00	14.00	12.50

Mug, *1969, Nixon-Agnew Presidential,* $75.00–$85.00

	Current Price Range		P/Y Average
☐ **Plate, dinner,** 10", item #4f, peach glow	5.00	6.00	5.50
☐ **Pot,** 3 quart, lid, handled	16.00	18.00	17.00
☐ **Saucer,** 5¼", item #4e, clay blue	1.75	2.00	1.85
☐ **Soup Cup,** 11 ounces, ...	4.00	6.00	5.00
☐ **Spoon Holder,** 6"	3.00	5.00	4.00
☐ **Tumbler,** 12 ounces	4.00	6.00	5.00
☐ **Vegetable,** 24 ounces	5.00	7.00	6.00
☐ **Bowl, salad,** 20 ounces, item #7x1, woodland moss	6.00	8.00	7.00
☐ **Bowl, sugar,** item #7b, prairie green, unlidded	9.00	12.00	10.50
☐ **Bowl, vegetable,** one quart, item #7n, woodland moss....................................	7.00	9.00	8.00
☐ **Creamer and sugar,** items #7a, 7b, woodland mossand, C-shape handles, the sugar bowl's lid with a plug-type handle, the creamer featuring a vaulted pouring spout......................	13.00	16.00	14.50
☐ **Cup,** item #7c, woodland moss, sculptured handle	4.00	5.00	4.50
☐ **Dish, fruit,** 8 ounces, item #7xo, woodland moss	4.00	5.50	4.75
☐ **Dish, sauce,** 10 ounces, item #7s, desert gold, lidded	2.50	3.25	2.75
☐ **Mug,** item #7cl, woodland moss, modified loop handle	3.00	4.00	3.50
☐ **Pitcher,** item #7d, woodland moss, pot form with tall loop handle	10.00	14.00	12.00

	Current Price Range		P/Y Average
☐ **Plate,** 7"	3.00	4.00	3.50
☐ **Plate, dinner,** 9", item #7f, woodland moss ..	4.00	5.50	4.75
☐ **Plate,** 10"	6.00	8.00	7.00
☐ **Platter,** 13", shallow	7.00	10.00	8.50
☐ **Plate,** 15"	16.00	18.00	17.00
☐ **Platter,** 11"	5.00	6.00	5.50
☐ **Saucer,** 5", item #7e, woodland moss	2.75	3.75	3.25
☐ **Shakers,** salt and pepper	5.00	6.00	5.50
☐ **Teapot,** 2 cup	7.00	9.00	8.00
☐ **Teapot,** 6 cup, tall, short lip spout	10.00	12.00	11.00
☐ **Tray,** 9"	5.00	7.00	6.00

FRUIT CRATE LABELS

DESCRIPTION: The decorative labels that adorned the sides of wooden fruit crates have become popular collectables.

PERIOD: The oldest and most rare fruit crate labels date to the 1880s.

ORIGIN: Fruit crate labels were originally designed to attract potential fruit buyers. In the 1950s collecting such art work began when the use of decorated wooden crates declined.

COMMENTS: Rarity and design are the important variables with fruit crate labels. California labels are usually worth more than Florida labels, and orange labels usually have more ornate designs. Label designs changed over the years, and some collectors focus on labels that have undergone design changes.

ADDITIONAL TIPS: The listings are alphabetical according to fruit company name. Following names are descriptions of the label art, type of fruit and price range. Size of label and states are listed when available.

☐ **Ahtanum, WA.,** pear, three pears, mountains, stock label #947, pictorial	3.00	5.00	4.00
☐ **Airline, CA.,** citrus, globe with wings, stars in red, white and blue, 10" x 11"	.75	1.75	1.00
☐ **Airship, CA.,** citrus, pictures commercial airplane, royal blue, 10" x 11"	6.00	10.00	8.00

	Current Price Range		P/Y Average
☐ **Ak-Sar-Ben, CA.,** citrus, picture of oranges on a blue background, 10″ x 11″	.75	1.75	1.00
☐ **All American, WA.,** apple, flag type shield, patriotic appearance, blue background, pictorial ...	4.00	6.00	5.00
☐ **Altissimo, CA.,** citrus, pictures mountains in pink and blue on a blue sky background, dated 1918, 10″ x 11″	.75	1.75	1.00
☐ **All Year, CA.,** citrus, black border frames landscape scene, 12½″ x 8¾″	.50	1.50	1.00
☐ **Alpine Orchards, WA.,** pear, three pears, yellow, red, black background, pictorial.	2.00	4.00	3.00
☐ **Blue Mountain, WA.,** apple, silhouette of trees and mountains, one red and one golden apple in right corner, orange background, blue border ..	9.00	11.00	10.00
☐ **Blue Streak, WA.,** large red ribbon seal with two red apples, brown border	3.00	5.00	4.00
☐ **Blue Tip, CA.,** citrus, picture of a large feather, 9″ x 9″	.50	1.00	.74
☐ **Blue Winner, WA.,** apple, cowboy on horseback picking up an apple in a rodeo, blue and white background	3.00	5.00	4.00
☐ **Boa Vista Ranch, CA.,** apple, mountains, orchard and farm house, one red and one golden apple, blue border......................	1.50	3.50	2.50
☐ **Bolero, CA.,** apple, Spanish dancer with two guitarists, black background	4.50	6.50	5.50
☐ **Bounty, CA.,** pear, bright yellow background, blue and red lettering, blue border	1.00	3.00	2.00
☐ **Boy Blue, WA.,** apple, boy with horn, white lettering	3.50	5.50	4.50
☐ **Boy Blue, WA.,** pear, boy about to blow an old horn, blue background, white letters	2.50	4.50	3.50
☐ **Briant, WA.,** apple, Washington State map, white and blue lettering, blue background	1.00	3.00	2.00
☐ **Briskey, WA.,** apple, snowy scene from Naches Pass, mountains and two red apples, black background, blue border	2.00	4.00	3.00
☐ **Broadway, CA.,** pear, red and black lettering (old) graphic type, gold leaf, blue background, blue-green border	2.00	4.00	3.00
☐ **Bronco, CA.,** citrus, old stone litho of fully dressed cowboy riding a wild horse, very colorful	3.00	5.00	4.00
☐ **Brownie's, CA.,** citrus, pictures Brownies preparing orange juice against a yellow sun and blue background, 10″ x 11″	1.00	3.00	2.00
☐ **Buckaroo, WA.,** apple, cowboy breaking a bucking horse, mountains and desert, yellow sky ...	5.50	7.50	6.50
☐ **Buddy,** Michigan broker label, smiling baby, blue background, green border, 1920	3.50	5.50	4.50
☐ **Buffalo, CA.,** apple, angry looking buffalo, red lettering, blue background, green border	3.50	5.50	4.50

	Current Price Range		P/Y Average

☐ **Bunting, WA.,** apple, one red apple, ribbon sash through the center, red lettering, blue background 3.00 5.00 4.00

☐ **Butler's Pride, WA.,** apple, branch with large red apple, white lettering, graphic, blue background .75 2.75 1.50

☐ **Caledonia, CA.,** citrus, picture of Scotch thistles on plaid background, 10″ x 11″ .... .50 1.00 .74

☐ **Cal-Flavor, CA.,** citrus, oranges, blossoms and leaves against a woodgrained and black background, 10″ x 11″ 1.00 3.00 2.00

☐ **Cambria, CA.,** citrus, brown border frames a brown eagle and two torches against a blue background, 10″ x 11″ 1.00 3.00 2.00

☐ **Carefree, CA.,** citrus, pictures a girl with blonde hair laughing against a blue background, 10″ x 11″ 1.00 3.00 2.00

☐ **Carro Amano Aranci, CA.,** citrus, pictures Italian fruit peddler with a cart full of oranges, 10″ x 11″ 1.00 3.00 2.00

☐ **Chere Best, WA.,** apple, aqua inset with block lettering, blue background .... .75 2.75 1.50

☐ **Chief Joseph, WA.,** apple, large white arrow head with Chief Joseph's image in front of it, dressed in full headdress and beads, historic, red lettering, blue background 7.00 9.00 8.00

☐ **Cho Paka, WA.,** apple, trees, mountains, distant orchard scene, blue background 8.00 10.00 9.00

☐ **Circle A&F, WA.,** apple, yellow and black lettering, circle in center with A&F in white letters, black background 3.00 5.00 4.00

☐ **Clasen, WA.,** apple, old litho of orchard homes and Mt. Adams in the background, two red apples on a limb, red lettering, 40 Lbs. (old) 2.50 4.50 3.50

☐ **Cliff, WA.,** apple, rock cliffs with raging waterfall, span bridge over water with old sedan driving over it, orchard hills, blue sky and red lettering, brown border 3.00 5.00 4.00

☐ **Clipper, FL.,** citrus, three-masted schooner, 7″ x 7″ .... .75 1.75 1.00

☐ **Clipper Ship, WA.,** apple, large sailing ship on the ocean, blue background 17.50 19.50 18.50

☐ **Coed, CA.,** citrus, pictures smiling girl in graduate cap and gown against a purple background, 10″ x 11″ 1.00 3.00 2.00

☐ **Color Guard, WA.,** apple, blue bottom, yellow lettering, graphic, black background 2.00 4.00 3.00

☐ **Columbia, WA.,** apple, mountains, cliffs, Columbia River gorge, farm, houses, orchards, ghostly Statue of Liberty with torch in background (the torch is emitting a light on two large apples), blue background, beautiful, rare 45.00 47.00 46.00

☐ **Columbia Bell, WA.,** apple, patriotic dressed lady with crown and holding a drawn sword, one red apple, blue and white background 3.00 5.00 4.00

	Current Price Range		P/Y Average

☐ **Congdon Refrigerated, WA.,** apple, first edition label, one red apple frozen in a block of ice, art deco lettering, black background **15.00 17.00 16.00**

☐ **Congdon Refrigerated, WA.,** pear, pear frozen in a block of ice **4.00 6.00 5.00**

☐ **Corona Lily, CA.,** citrus, white and gold speckled lily against a black background, 10″ x 11″ **1.00 3.00 2.00**

☐ **Desert Bloom, CA.,** citrus, white, blooming yucca with desert greenery and mountains against a blue sky background, 10″ x 11″ **1.00 3.00 2.00**

☐ **Dewy Fresh, WA.,** apple, modern green leaf, fairy in leafy skirt holding a wand, believed to be one of the last labels printed, white and red background, 1956 . . . . **1.50 3.50 2.50**

☐ **Diamond, OR.,** apple, red diamonds in center with white letters saying Hood River Apples (cartoon of apple head man), green background . . **6.00 8.00 7.00**

☐ **Diamond, OR.,** pear, Mt. Hood scene, red diamond shipper is Apple growers service **2.00 4.00 3.00**

☐ **Diamond S, CA.,** pear, two horse heads, blue diamond, black-tan background **6.00 8.00 7.00**

☐ **Di Giorgio, CA.,** pear, two gold pears, white letters, dark blue background, light blue border . . **1.50 3.50 2.50**

☐ **Dinner Gong, WA.,** apple, one red apple with leaves and stem, black bottom, blue background **1.00 3.00 2.00**

☐ **Diving Girl, CA.,** apple, 1920s girl in swimming suit diving into the lake **6.50 8.50 7.50**

☐ **Dixie Boy, FL.,** citrus, picture of a black boy, 9″ x 9″ **2.00 4.00 3.00**

☐ **Don Juan, CA.,** pear, orchard scene in upper left corner, blue/black/red background **1.50 3.50 2.50**

☐ **Donnater, TX.,** citrus, pink grapefruit against a black background, 9″ x 9″ . . . . **.25 .75 .50**

☐ **Don't Worry, WA.,** apple, blond boy holding apple with bite out of it, written white letters, shiny black background **4.00 6.00 5.00**

☐ **Double A, CA.,** citrus, train supported by two capital letter As on a trestle, 10″ x 11″ . . . . . . **.75 1.75 1.00**

☐ **Duckwall, OR.,** apple, stone wall with a very colorful duck in front, red background **15.00 17.00 16.00**

☐ **Dunbar, OR.,** pear, cartoon pear skiing down snowy hill, yellow letter, blue sky **2.50 4.50 3.50**

☐ **Eagle, CA.,** pear, eagle and two pears, red lettering, blue background, yellow border **3.50 5.50 4.50**

☐ **Eatmor, WA.,** pear, 1920s boy in plaid knickers, holding a pear, red lettering, green background, rare **20.00 22.00 21.00**

☐ **Eat One, CA.,** citrus, pictures arrow pointing to an orange, aqua background, 10″ x 11″ **1.00 3.00 2.00**

☐ **Eatum, WA.,** apple, one red and one golden apple, yellow letters, graphic type label, blue and black background **1.00 3.00 2.00**

	Current Price Range		P/Y Average

□ **El Mejor, CA.**, citrus, pictures Sunkist orange, 10″ x 11″ .... .75 1.75 1.00

□ **Emerald Beauty, WA.**, pear, Spanish lady playing a guitar, rare 17.50 19.50 18.00

□ **Emerald Green, WA.**, apple, suit of armor head with shield with a large emerald on it, green background.................................... 3.00 5.00 4.00

□ **Empire, WA.**, apple, evaporated apples, old litho of mountains, orchards and trees 3.00 5.00 4.00

□ **Empire Builder, WA.**, apple, mountains, large warehouse, trucks, train orchards, large apple covered wagon and four oxen 1.50 3.50 2.50

□ **Endurance, CA.**, citrus, night scene pictures walking camels against a purple and black background, 10″ x 11″ 5.00 7.00 6.00

□ **Esperanza, CA.**, citrus, pictures a Senorita with a carnation in her hair, wearing a lace mantilla and holding a lace fan against a blue background, 10″ x 11″ .... .75 1.75 1.00

□ **Exeter, CA.**, citrus, Tulare Co. map against a multicolored background, 10″ x 11″ .... .75 1.75 1.00

□ **Fido, CA.**, citrus, white puppy with black spot against a black background, 12½″ x 8¾″ 9.00 11.00 10.00

□ **Fiesta, TX.**, citrus, girl dressed in gown against a black background, 10″ x 11″ .... .25 .75 .50

□ **Fillmore Crest, CA.**, citrus, blue border frames three oranges and green leaves against a turquoise background, 10″ x 11″ .... .75 1.75 1.00

□ **First Blue, WA.**, apple, photo of three apples, light blue and orange letters, on a yellow sash, blue background 1.50 3.50 2.50

□ **Flavor Crest.**, treasure chest full of red and golden apples (apple label from New York), blue background 5.00 7.00 6.00

□ **Florida Cowboy, FL.**, citrus, cowboy astride bucking bronco with diamond K brand palm trees in background, 9″ x 9″ 3.00 7.00 5.00

□ **Florita, CA.**, citrus, dancing senorita and two guitarists against a black background, 10″ x 11″ 3.00 5.00 4.00

□ **Flying V, WA.**, apple, photo of red apple, yellow written letters and A V with wings on it, blue background................................... 3.50 7.50 5.50

□ **Foothills, OR.**, pear, old stone litho of orchard, mountain, river and two pears 4.50 6.50 5.50

□ **For The Kids Of Austin, WA.**, apple, stock label, two red apples and a leafy limb, Kiwanis International insignia, tufted yellow, blue background 3.00 5.00 4.00

□ **Full O' Juice, CA.**, citrus, pictures half peeled orange and a glass of orange juice, lavender background, 10″ x 11″ 1.00 3.00 2.00

□ **Galleon, CA.**, citrus, galleon sailing on the open sea, sky background, 12½″ x 8¾″ 1.00 3.00 2.00

□ **Gladiola, CA.**, citrus, two gladiola sprays on a gold and tan background, 10″ x 11″ 1.00 3.00 2.00

	Current Price Range		P/Y Average
□ **Globes O' Gold, CA.**, citrus, pictures three oranges, blossoms, leaves, 10″ x 11″	.75	1.75	1.00
□ **Gold Buckle, CA.**, citrus, outline of a belt with a gold buckle frames an orchard scene against a blue background, 10″ x 11″	1.00	3.00	2.00
□ **Gold Circle, CA.**, pear, gold circle, yellow circle, two pears, graphic, blue background	2.00	4.00	3.00
□ **Kentucky Cardinal, KY.**, apple, three apples and a red cardinal on a blossoming apple limb, 1918 stone litho	17.50	19.50	18.50
□ **King David, CA.**, citrus, king with white beard in royal robes and crown, 10″ x 11″	1.00	3.00	2.00
□ **Kings Park, CA.**, citrus, pictures a waterfall and mountain stream, 10″ x 11″	1.00	3.00	2.00
□ **Lakecove, CA.**, pear, barefoot boy with straw hat on, leaning on a tree, lake and mountain	5.00	7.00	6.00
□ **Lake View, WA.**, apple, two goldens with a red apple between them, scene of the Pajaro Valley, old, blue background, green border	5.00	7.00	6.00
□ **Lamb, WA.**, apple, Lamb's first printing, lamb standing on a hillside with orchard mountain background, two red apples hanging over its head, blue/black border, 1920s artwork, beautiful	55.00	57.00	56.00
□ **La Reina, CA.**, citrus, hacienda scene with Spanish senorita holding a black fan against a blue background, 10″ x 11″	.50	1.50	1.00
□ **Lauree, CA.**, citrus, pictures oranges, berries, laurel leaves, blue background, 10″ x 11″	.50	1.50	1.00
□ **Laurie, CA.**, apple, little girl with an apple in each hand, she has a pink dress on, blue background, 1930s label, rare	10.00	12.00	11.00
□ **Leavenworth, WA.**, pear, two green pears with white letters, blue background	1.50	3.50	2.50
□ **Legal Tender, CA.**, citrus, pictures U.S. currency in a $250 bundle against a blue and black background, 10″ x 11″	1.00	3.00	2.00
□ **Lemonade, CA.**, citrus, three lemons in foreground, orchard scene in background, 12½″ x 8¾″	.25	.75	.50
□ **Lily, CA.**, citrus, two white calla lilies, green leaves on a black background, 10″ x 11″	1.00	3.00	2.00
□ **Lincoln, CA.**, citrus, portrait of Lincoln with oranges and leaves, 10″ x 11″	1.00	3.00	2.00
□ **Loch Lomond, CA.**, citrus, Scottish scene on blue and green plaid background, 10″ x 11″ ..	.50	1.50	1.00
□ **Loop Loop, WA.**, apple, Indian chief on a palomino horse, he is picking an apple from the horse's back	10.00	12.00	11.00
□ **Loot Of Ventura County, CA.**, citrus, multicolored, 10″ x 11″	1.00	3.00	2.00
□ **Lucky Lad, WA.**, apple, large red apple with image of the 1920s farm boy in front of it, gold letters, black background, green border	50.00	52.00	51.00

	Current Price Range		P/Y Average

☐ **Lure, WA.,** apple, image of a big, largemouth bass hooked on a fish plug, bright red letters, blue border **25.00 27.00 26.00**

☐ **Luxor, WA.,** apple, big red maltese cross with the name Luxor in white on it, blue background . . . **10.00 12.00 11.00**

☐ **M Brand, WA.,** apple, big blue M with some kind of gold lance behind it, red background, rare . . **7.00 9.00 8.00**

☐ **Nimble, CA.,** citrus, pictures an orange and blossoms against an orchard landscape, aqua background, 10″ x 11″ . . . . **.50 1.50 1.00**

☐ **Nob Hill, CA.,** pear, Metropolitan skyscrapers, autos and street cars **5.00 7.00 6.00**

☐ **Nuchief, WA.,** apple, little cartoon Indian chief with an apple in his right hand and a tomahawk in his left, says Apples from Washington State, blue background **4.00 6.00 5.00**

☐ **Orchard King, CA.,** citrus, orange, with crown, royal blue background, 10″ x 11″ . . . . **.50 1.50 1.00**

☐ **Orchard, OR.,** pear, old stone litho, Model T truck on a road, orchard and mountains, white background **5.00 7.00 6.00**

☐ **Oriole, CA.,** citrus, oriole perched on a branch with nearby orange, blossoms and leaves, black background, 10″ x 11″ **3.00 5.00 4.00**

☐ **Orland, CA.,** citrus, pictures old dam scene, 10″ x 11″ **4.00 6.00 5.00**

☐ **Our Pride, WA.,** apple, parrot sitting on a twig, one red apple, black background, blue border, copy 1923, 40 lbs. **5.00 7.00 6.00**

☐ **Outboard, WA.,** apple, modern race boat zooming across a lake; houses, orchards and mountains in the background, red lettering **17.50 19.50 18.50**

☐ **Ox Team, WA.,** apple, covered wagon pulled by a team, driver with whip in hand, desert in the background, red and green border, 1937 label **10.00 12.00 11.00**

☐ **Princess, CA.,** citrus, princess in royal robes and crown jewels, with grapefruits, leaves on a blue background, dated 1911 . . . . **1.50 2.50 2.00**

☐ **Pure Gold, CA.,** citrus, pictures prospector and his mule, blue background, 10″ x 11″ . . . . **.75 1.75 1.00**

☐ **Pyramid, Canada,** apple, three pyramids with river, palm trees, camel and rider, blue background **10.00 12.00 11.00**

☐ **Queen Esther, CA.,** citrus, elegant queen dressed in turquoise gown, golden crown, 10″ x 11″ **2.00 4.00 3.00**

☐ **Queen Fruits, WA.,** pear, two pears, old queen in full dress, blue background **10.00 12.00 11.00**

☐ **Quercus Ranch, CA.,** pear, orchard, sky, lake, mountains and two pears **3.00 5.00 4.00**

☐ **Rancheria, CA.,** pear, Indian Chief on horse by a maiden, teepees, black background **2.50 4.50 3.00**

☐ **Red Bird, CA.,** citrus, large red eagle, black background, 10″ x 11″ . . . . **.50 1.50 1.00**

Pacific Fruit & Produce Co., WA, *peaches,* $3.00–$6.00

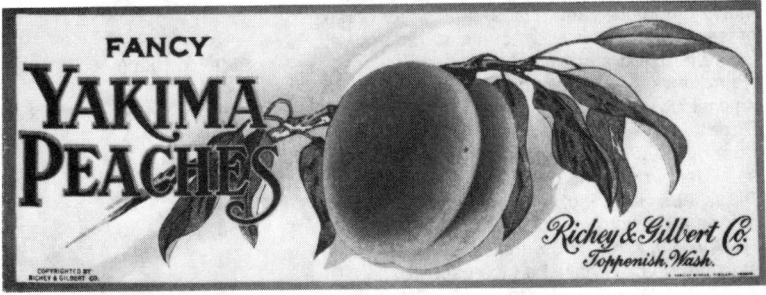

Top: Richey & Gilbert Co., WA, *peaches,* $3.00–$6.00; Bottom: Pacific Fruit & Produce Co., WA, *cantaloupes,* $3.00–$6.00

	Current Price Range		P/Y Average

☐ **Red Label, WA.,** apple, valley scene with town, roads, river and mountains, two large red apples in the sky, red border 15.00 17.00 16.00

☐ **Redlands Best, CA.,** citrus, four blue arrows pointing to big orange in center, 10″ x 11″ 2.00 4.00 3.00

☐ **Redman, WA.,** apple, Indian brave, behind him are cave drawings, two apples—one red and one golden, blue background 4.00 6.00 5.00

☐ **Red Peak, CA.,** citrus, landscape scene, 10″ x 11″ .... .50 1.50 1.00

☐ **Red Seal, WA.,** apple, red ribbon with old time red wax seal, two red apples, white letters, green background 2.00 4.00 3.00

☐ **Red Star, CA.,** apple, big red star in the center, red and white letters, black background, red border 4.00 6.00 5.00

☐ **Red Streak, WA.,** apple, two drawn apples, one red and one golden, red lightning streak shooting through the label, black background, red border 15.00 17.00 16.00

☐ **Red Wagon, WA.,** apple, cartoon boy pulling a red wagon full of red and golden apples, black background, yellow border 8.00 10.00 9.00

☐ **Red Winner, WA.,** apple, picture inset of Indian maiden in leather and beads, on a white horse, grassy plains, desert and mountains, red and yellow letters, red and white background 4.00 6.00 5.00

☐ **Reindeer, CA.,** citrus, reindeer and grove scene against a yellow background, 10″ x 11″ 2.00 4.00 3.00

☐ **Repetition, WA.,** apple, three identical boys in front of three identical boxes of apples with the same label on them, black background 10.00 12.00 11.00

☐ **Rider, FL.,** citrus, jockey in white and green silks astride a brown race horse, 9″ x 9″ .... .50 1.50 1.00

☐ **Rocky Hill, CA.,** citrus, Indian chief on horse standing on cliff against a blue background, 10″ x 11″ .... .50 1.50 1.00

☐ **Rose, WA.,** apple, two large red roses with thorns and leaves, white letters, blue background 3.50 5.50 4.50

☐ **Round Robin, OR.,** pear, big red robin standing on a hill, old, blue background 8.00 10.00 9.00

☐ **Royal Feast, CA.,** citrus, pictures orange, blossoms, dark blue leaves with two lions in black framed by a black checkered border, 10″ x 11″ .... .50 1.50 1.00

☐ **Royal Knight, CA.,** citrus, knight on horseback against a yellow background, 10″ x 11″ ...... .50 1.50 1.00

☐ **Rubaiyat, CA.,** citrus, pictures desert scene under a full moon, 10″ x 11″ .... .50 1.50 1.00

☐ **Safe Hit, TX.,** vegetables, 1920s baseball player hitting a ball, grandstand in the background, 7″ x 9″ 2.00 4.00 3.00

	Current Price Range		P/Y Average

☐ **Sails, WA.**, apple, large sailing ship in a rough choppy sea, yellow and red letters, blue background, red penline border, 40 lbs. .... | 5.00 | 7.00 | 6.00

☐ **Sam Birch, OR.**, apple, one red apple, yellow strip through the label with blue letters on it, blue background .... | 8.00 | 10.00 | 9.00

☐ **Sunshine Ranch, WA.** apple, large warehouse with Mt. Adams in the background at sunrise, letters in the orange sky say EAT GOOD APPLES FOR VITAMINS/EAT APPLES FOR HEALTH, blue border .... | 10.00 | 12.00 | 11.00

☐ **Sun Smile, CA.** pear, smiling face of the sun, blue letters, also a blue anchor, sunburst background .... | 3.00 | 5.00 | 4.00

☐ **Sun Sugared, OR.** pear, photo of an orange pear, black background .... | 1.00 | 3.00 | 2.00

☐ **Super Crisp, WA.** apple, two-and-a-half apples, one red and one golden; orchard, house, hill, writing in the sky, blue border, c. 1948 .... | 1.50 | 3.50 | 2.50

☐ **Super-Pak, WA.** apple, blue ribbon in a triangle with the lettering on it, black background ..... | 1.00 | 3.00 | 2.00

☐ **Sure Mark, CA.** pear, red stripes, blue background .... | 3.00 | 5.00 | 4.00

☐ **Surety, WA.** apple, stone litho of a steamship in a cove with pine trees, orchards, mountains, red sky with blue letters in the sky, in the corner it says "FROM TREE TO TRADE," a busy red lace type border .... | 5.00 | 7.00 | 6.00

☐ **Swan, WA.** apple, big white swan on the water, orange letters, black background .... | 6.00 | 8.00 | 7.00

☐ **Sweet Sue, WA.** apple, three red apples in the center of the label with an inset in front of them with 1920s lady's face, white letters, brown and green border .... | 9.00 | 11.00 | 10.00

☐ **Talisman, CA.** Citrus, three talisman roses against a blue and black background, 10″ x 11″ .... | 1.00 | 3.00 | 2.00

☐ **Tasty Treet, WA.** apple, three apples, two reds with one golden in the center, blue stripe with white lettering on it, on the tail of the last "t" it says YOUR TASTY TREAT TO HEALTH, black background .... | 1.50 | 3.50 | 2.00

☐ **The Dalls Cherries,** photo of cherries background with the printing on it, small lug label .. | .75 | 2.75 | 1.75

☐ **Tom Cat, CA.** citrus, black and white cat reclining on a pillow, 12 ½″ x 8 ¾″ .... | 20.00 | 30.00 | 25.00

☐ **Topaz, WA.** apple, there is a big topaz in the word topaz where the o should be, blue background .... | 2.50 | 4.50 | 3.50

☐ **Triton, WA.** apple, King Neptune sitting on a rock by the ocean holding a spear and an apple, he is wearing a gold crown, the sky is orange and pink, blue and light blue border .... | 5.00 | 7.00 | 6.00

Swan Apples, *black background, white swan,* **$7.00-$10.00**

Hi-Tone Pears, *red background, yellow pears, colorful orchard in center,* **$3.00-$5.00**

Tulip Apples, *black background, blue, orange and yellow tulips,* **$4.00-$6.00**

	Current Price Range		P/Y Average
☐ **Trojan, WA.** apple, Roman Gladiator with sword and shield in front of a man size red apple, he is standing on a globe of the world, with horse mounted gladiators on each side of him, black back round, blue border with a red penline border, rare	15.00	17.00	16.00
☐ **Trout, WA.** apple, white arrowhead with Indian brave's head in front of it, large Rainbow trout jumping in the center of the label, white lettering, blue background	2.50	4.50	3.50
☐ **Tulip, WA.** apple, three tulips, one red, one yellow and one blue, orange letters, black background	4.00	6.00	5.00
☐ **Uncle Sam, WA.** apple, has a repetition design of one apple, one American shield border and letters of white, also a stone litho of Uncle Sam with tophat in hand, green background	5.00	7.00	6.00
☐ **Valencia, CA.** apple, orchards, farms, hills, mountains, purple sky with lettering	3.00	5.00	4.00
☐ **Valley Queen Cantaloupes, WA.** half a cantaloupe on an Early American dinnerware plate, vase of flowers, farm valley and a plateau range	1.00	3.00	2.00
☐ **Vandalla, CA.** citrus, male peacock against a blue background, 10″ x 11″	.50	1.50	1.00
☐ **Velvet, CA.** citrus, Sunkist orange against draped blue velvet, dated 1929, 10″ x 11″	.50	1.50	1.00
☐ **Victoria, CA.** citrus, portrait of Queen Victoria, 10″ x 11″	1.00	3.00	2.00

FRUIT JARS

DESCRIPTION: Fruit jars are glass containers which were sold empty and were intended for use in the home preservation of food.

TYPES: There were several types of fruit jars produced including those with either the manufacturer's name or a decorative motif printed on the jar.

MAKER: One of the most familiar names in fruit jars is the Mason jar produced by John Landis Mason in the early 1800s. One of Mason's innovations was a zinc lid which provided greater air tightness.

COMMENTS: Fruit jars of the 1800s are highly collectible. Before 1810, few glass containers were manufactured.

ADDITIONAL TIPS: For more information, consult *The Official Price Guide to Bottles, Old and New,* published by The House of Collectibles.

Ball Fruit Jar,
Perfect Mason,
Aqua, c. 1960,
$3.00-$5.00

	Current Price Range		P/Y Average
☐ **Anchor Mason's,** patent in 3 lines, sheared top, Mason seal, qt., clear	35.00	45.00	40.00
☐ **Atlas EZ Seal,** in 3 lines all in a circle, sheared top, lightning seal, qt., aqua, lt. blue	13.00	18.00	15.00
☐ **Atlas E.Z,** seal all in 3 lines, under bottom Atlas E-Z seal, aqua pt. jar, clear or aqua	1.50	2.50	2.00
☐ **Atlas Improved Mason** (c. 1890's), glass lid, metal screw band, aqua or green	8.00	10.00	9.00
☐ **Atlas Mason's Patent** (c. 1900), zinc lid, olive green, quart	18.00	20.00	19.00
☐ **Atlas Mason's Patent Nov. 30, 1858,** zinc lid, olive green, 1/2 gallon	20.00	28.00	24.00
☐ **Atlas Mason's Patent Nov. 30th, 1858,** screw top, olive green, quart	20.00	28.00	24.00
☐ **Atlas Mason's Patent,** screw top, green, quart	4.00	6.00	5.00
☐ **Atlas Special** (c. 1910), screw top, clear or blue	6.00	8.00	7.00

	Current Price Range		P/Y Average

☐ **B & Co. Ld,** under bottom, stopper finish (neck) per glass stopper, cork jacket (English) 2 Sizes lt. green **2.00** **4.00** **9.00**

☐ **Baker Bros.** (c. 1865), wax sealer, groove ring, green or aqua, pint **30.00** **35.00** **32.50**

☐ **Ball,** vaseline glass, screw top, pint, quart **6.00** **8.00** **7.00**

☐ **Ball** (c. 1890), screw top, green, three sizes ... **7.00** **10.00** **8.50**

☐ **The Ball** (c. 1890), screw top, green, quart **7.00** **10.00** **8.50**

☐ **Ball** in script, Ideal, wire top clamp, clear, 3" or 4 ¾" **6.00** **8.00** **6.00**

☐ **Ball** in script, Ideal, in back, Pat. July 14, 1908, wire top clamp, green or clear, three sizes **5.00** **7.00** **6.00**

☐ **Ball Ideal Patd July 14 1988,** (error in date), blue green, pint **18.00** **24.00** **21.50**

☐ **Boyd Mason** (c. 1910), zinc lid, olive green, pint, quart **6.00** **8.00** **45.00**

☐ **Boyd Perfect Mason,** zinc lid, green, 1/2 pint, pint, quart **5.00** **7.00** **6.00**

☐ **Boyds Genuine,** Mason under bottom inside of diamond IG Co. sheared top, Mason seal, qt., aqua **3.00** **5.00** **4.00**

☐ **Braun Safetee Mason,** zinc lid, aqua **5.00** **7.00** **6.00**

☐ **Brayton & Co. A.P.,** In half moon, under it San Francisco, Cal. Pressed on laid on ring, Iron closure, William Haller, Patd. Aug. 7, 1860, aqua, quart **420.00** **510.00** **465.00**

☐ **Brelle Jar,** glass lid and wire clamp, wide mouth, clear, quart **20.00** **25.00** **17.50**

☐ **Brighton** (c. 1890), glass lid, metal wire clamp, clear, amber or amethyst, quart **70.00** **80.00** **55.00**

☐ **Geo. D. Brown & Co.** (c. 1875), glass lid and heavy metal clamp, green, quart **60.00** **70.00** **65.00**

☐ **The Burlington** (c. 1880), zinc band, clear or aqua **70.00** **80.00** **50.00**

☐ **Decker's Iowana,** glass lid and wire ball, clear, quart **3.00** **5.00** **4.00**

☐ **Dexter** (c. 1865), zinc band with glass insert, aqua, quart **30.00** **60.00** **45.00**

☐ **Diamond Fruit Jar,** glass lid and full wire bail, clear, quart **3.00** **5.00** **4.00**

☐ **Dictator D.D.I. Holcomb Patented Dec. 14th, 1869,** wax seal, blue, quart **75.00** **100.00** **87.00**

☐ **Dillon** (c. 1890), wax seal, round, aqua, quart **10.00** **12.00** **11.00**

☐ **Dominion** (c. 1886), zinc band and glass insert, round, clear, quart **75.00** **100.00** **87.00**

☐ **Dominion Widemouth Special,** zinc lid, round, clear, quart **2.00** **3.00** **2.50**

☐ **Doolittle, The Self Sealer,** glass lid, wide mouth, clear, quart **50.00** **75.00** **62.00**

☐ **Drey Ever Seal,** glass lid and full wire bail, clear or amethyst, quart **2.00** **3.00** **2.50**

☐ **Economy,** metal lid and spring wire clamp, amethyst, pint, quart, ½ gallon **2.50** **4.50** **3.50**

	Current Price Range		P/Y Average
☐ **Economy, Trade Mark,** clear or amethyst, quart	2.50	4.50	3.50
☐ **Economy, Trade Mark, Pat, June 9, 1903,** clear or amethyst, quart	2.50	4.50	3.50
☐ **E.G.Co.** (monogram) Imperial, clear, quart	9.00	12.00	10.50
☐ **Electric,** glass lid and wire bail, round, aqua, quart	10.00	12.00	10.50
☐ **Electric Fruit Jar** (c. 1900–15), glass lid and metal clamp, round, aqua, quart	60.00	70.00	65.00
☐ **Electroglas N.W.,** clear, quart	3.00	4.50	3.75
☐ **Empire,** in maltese cross, clear, quart	8.00	11.00	9.50
☐ **Empire** (c. 1860), glass stopper, deep blue, quart	55.00	75.00	65.00
☐ **The Empire** (c. 1866), glass lid with iron lugs to fasten it, aqua, quart	65.00	75.00	70.00
☐ **Erie Fruit Jar** (c. 1890), screw top, clear, quart	75.00	100.00	87.00
☐ **Erie Lightning,** clear, quart	20.00	25.00	22.50
☐ **Eureka** (c. 1864), wax dipped cork or other, extending neck, aqua, pint	35.00	45.00	40.00
☐ **Eureka, Pat. Feb 9th, 1864, Eureka Jar Co. Dunbar, W. VA.** (c. 1870), aqua, quart	14.00	20.00	17.00
☐ **Everlasting Improved Jar** (c. 1904), in oval, quart	15.00	20.00	17.50
☐ **Everlasting Jar** (c. 1904), glass lid and double wire hook fastener, round, green, pint, quart, 1/2 gallon	15.00	20.00	17.50
☐ **Excelsior** (c. 1880–90), zinc screw band and glass insert, aqua, quart	48.00	55.00	51.00
☐ **Gilberds Improved Jar** (c. 1885), glass lid and wire bail, aqua, quart	40.00	55.00	47.00
☐ **Gilberds Jar** (c. 1884), glass lid and screw band, aqua, quart	55.00	75.00	65.00
☐ **Gilchrist** (c. 1895), zinc lid and dome shaped opal liner, wide mouth, aqua green, quart	7.00	10.00	8.50
☐ **Glassboro** (c. 1880–1900), trademark, zinc band and glass insert, light to dark green, three sizes	15.00	20.00	17.50
☐ **Glassboro Improved** (c. 1880), wide zinc screw band and glass insert, aqua or pale green, quart	15.00	20.00	17.50
☐ **Glenshaw G. Mason,** (G in square), clear, quart	3.00	5.00	4.00
☐ **Globe,** glass lid, metal neck band, top wire bail and bail clamp, amber, green or clear, quart ...	12.00	18.00	15.00
☐ **Glocker, Pat. 1911 Other Pending Sanitary,** aqua, quart	12.00	15.00	13.50
☐ **Haines** (c. 1882), glass lid and iron clamp, green, quart	40.00	55.00	47.00
☐ **Haines Improved** (c. 1870), glass lid and top wire bail, aqua green, quart	175.00	200.00	187.00
☐ **Hamilton Glass Works,** green, quart	14.00	20.00	17.00
☐ **Hansee's Place Home Jar,** pat. Dec. 19 1899 under bottom, aqua, 7″	40.00	50.00	45.00

	Current Price Range		P/Y Average

☐ **Harris** (c. 1860), metal lid, ground top, deep green, quart **125.00 150.00 137.00**

☐ **Harris Improved** (c. 1875–1880), glass lid and iron clamp, green, quart **45.00 60.00 52.00**

☐ **Haserot Company** (c. 1915–1925), zinc lid, green, quart **12.00 15.00 13.50**

☐ **The Haserot Company, Cleveland Mason Patent,** screw top, ground top, green, quart **15.00 18.00 16.50**

☐ **E.C. Hazard & Co., Shrewsbury, N.J.,** wire clamp, aqua, quart **10.00 12.00 11.00**

☐ **Hazel,** glass lid and wire bail, aqua, quart **12.00 15.00 13.50**

☐ **Hazel-Atlas Lightning Seal,** full wire bail and glass lid, green, quart **6.00 10.00 8.00**

☐ **H. & D.** (c. 1915), glass top, metal band **5.00 7.00 6.00**

☐ **Helme's Railroad Mills,** amber, 7¾″ **12.00 15.00 13.50**

☐ **Helmes Railroad Mills,** amber, quart **12.00 16.00 14.00**

☐ **The Improved Hero,** glass top, metal band, green, base, Patd Nov. 26, 1867 . . . . **15.00 20.00 17.50**

☐ **Hero,** with cross and lightning at top, green, quart **25.00 30.00 27.50**

☐ **The Heroine,** wide zinc screw band and glass insert, light green, quart **25.00 30.00 27.50**

☐ **The High Grade,** zinc screw-on top, clear **20.00 25.00 22.50**

☐ **Kerr Economy Trade Mark,** Chicago on base, metal lid and narrow clip band, clear or amethyst, pint, quart **2.00 4.00 3.00**

☐ **Kerr Economy** in script, under it TRADE MARK, under bottom Kerr Glass Mfg. Co., Sand Spring, Okla., clear, 3¾″ **2.00 4.00 3.00**

☐ Same as above, except Chicago Pat. under bottom **2.00 4.00 3.00**

☐ **Kerr Wide Mouth Mason,** clear, ½ pint **15.00 22.00 18.00**

☐ **KG,** in oval, wire clamp, clear, quart **1.50 3.00 2.25**

☐ **The Kilner Jar,** zinc screw band and glass insert, clear, quart **2.00 4.00 3.00**

☐ **King,** full wire bail and glass lid, clear or amethyst, quart **10.00 12.00 11.00**

☐ **Kinsella True Mason** (c. 1874), zinc lid, clear, quart **6.00 8.00 7.00**

☐ **Kline Pat. Oct. 27, 1863,** a on glass stopper, aqua, quart with jar **100.00 150.00 125.00**

☐ **Kline A.** (c. 1863), glass fitting lid and clamp, aqua, quart **25.00 30.00 27.50**

☐ **Leotric,** in oval, glass lid, ground top, medium green, quart **8.50 10.00 9.25**

☐ **Lightning Trade Mark Registered U.S. Patent Office,** Putnam 4 on bottom, lid with dates, aqua, pint **2.00 4.25 3.12**

☐ **Lightning Trade Mark,** Putnam 199 on bottom, aqua, ½ gallon **6.00 8.00 7.00**

☐ Same as above, except wire and lid, pint **6.00 8.00 7.00**

☐ **Lightning Trademark,** glass top, round, aqua, 6″ **7.00 10.00 8.50**

	Current Price Range		P/Y Average

	Current Price Range		P/Y Average
☐ Same as above, except Putnam on base, aqua, quart, ½ gallon	8.00	11.00	9.50
☐ Same as above, except amber, pint, quart, ½ gallon	15.00	20.00	17.50
☐ **Lightning,** Putnam 824 under bottom, sheared top, aqua	9.00	12.00	10.50
☐ **Lindell Glass Co.** (c. 1870), wax sealer, amber, quart	70.00	100.00	85.00
☐ **Lockport Mason,** zinc top, aqua, ½ gallon ...	4.50	8.00	6.25
☐ **Lockport Mason, Improved,** zinc screw band, glass insert, aqua, quart	4.00	6.00	5.00
☐ **Lorillard & Co,** on base, glass top, metal clamp, amber, pint	12.00	15.00	13.50
☐ **P. Lorillard & Co.,** sheared top, amber, 6¼"	10.00	12.00	11.00
☐ **Lustre R.E. Tongue & Bros. Co. Inc. Phila.,** in circle or shield, wire clamp, quart	6.00	8.00	7.00
☐ **Mason's,** swirled milk glass, 7¼"	75.00	90.00	82.00
☐ **Mason's CG, Patent Nov. 30, 1858,** zinc lid, green, quart	5.00	8.00	6.50
☐ **Mason's-C-Patent Nov. 30th 1858,** green, 7"	10.00	12.00	11.00
☐ **Mason's Improved Butter Jar,** sheared top, aqua, ½ gallon	10.00	14.00	12.00
☐ **Mason's Improved,** ground top with zinc lid, quart, blue	7.00	14.00	10.00
☐ **Mason's Improved,** Hero F J Co. in cross above, zinc band and glass lid covered with many patent dates, earliest Feb. 12, '56, aqua	10.00	14.00	12.00
☐ **Mason's Improved,** zinc screw band and glass insert, aqua or green, pint	10.00	14.00	12.00
☐ **Mason's Keystone** (c. 1869), zinc screw band and glass insert, aqua, quart	15.00	20.00	17.50
☐ **Mason's "M" Patent Nov. 30th 1858,** green, 7"	5.00	8.00	6.50
☐ **Mason's,** under it "M" Patent Nov. 30th 1898, screw top, aqua, quart	11.00	15.00	13.00
☐ **Mason's Patent 1858,** zinc lid, amber or green, pint	15.00	20.00	17.50
☐ **Peerless,** wax dipped cork, green, quart	55.00	75.00	65.00
☐ **The Penn,** metal cap and wax seal, green, quart	30.00	35.00	32.50
☐ **Peoria Pottery,** metal top and wax seal, glazed brown stoneware, quart	15.00	18.00	16.50
☐ **Perfection,** double wire bail and glass top, clear, quart	35.00	40.00	37.50
☐ **The New Perfection,** clear or amethyst, ½ gallon	19.00	26.00	22.00
☐ **Perfect Seal,** full wire bail and glass top, clear, quart	4.00	6.00	5.00
☐ **Perfect Seal** in shield, Made in Canada, clear, quart	1.50	2.50	2.00
☐ **Pet,** glass stopper, green, quart	45.00	60.00	52.00
☐ **Pet,** glass stopper and wire bail, aqua, quart ..	30.00	35.00	32.50
☐ **H.W. Pettit, Wesville N.H.,** under bottom, ground top, aqua, quart	8.00	12.00	10.00

	Current Price Range		P/Y Average
☐ **The Goragas Pierie Co., Phila., Royal Peanu- tene,** sheared top, clear, quart	9.00	12.00	10.50
☐ **Pine Deluxe Jar,** full wire bail and glass top, clear, quart...............................	4.00	6.00	5.00
☐ **Pine** (P in square) Mason, zinc top, clear, quart	4.00	5.00	4.50
☐ **Porcelain Lined,** zinc top, aqua, quart........	15.00	20.00	17.50
☐ Same as above, except green, 2 gallon	12.00	17.00	14.50
☐ **Potter & Bodine Philadelphia,** in script, glass top and clamp, aqua, quart	85.00	95.00	90.00
☐ **Premium Coffeyville Kas.,** wire ring and glass top, clear or amethyst, quart	14.00	18.00	16.00
☐ **Premium Improved,** glass top and side wire clips, clear, quart...........................	15.00	20.00	17.50
☐ **Presto,** screw-on top, clear	2.50	3.25	2.82
☐ **Presto Fruit Jar,** screw-on top, clear	2.50	3.25	2.82

FURNITURE

(See Art Deco, Art Nouveau, Oriental Furniture, Shaker, and Wicker)

COMMENTS: Interest in antique and collectible furniture is growing, according to auction houses and dealers around the country. Record prices were realized for American Federal and Victorian period pieces this year. European furniture is also very strong. Experts feel that the current design trends featuring "country" and Victorian styles have had a major impact on this upward movement in the popularity of antique furniture. Also, prices for fine old pieces compare very favorably to the cost of new furniture.

RECOMMENDED READING: For more in-depth information on furniture you may refer to *The Official Identification Guide to Early American Furniture, The Official Identification Guide to Victorian Furniture, The Official Price Guide to Wicker, The Official Price Guide to Oriental Collectibles, The Official Guide to Buying and Selling Antiques and Collectibles* and *The Official Encyclopedia of Antiques and Collectibles,* published by The House of Collectibles.

Victorian Eastlake Renaissance Revival Bed, *walnut,*
1875, $750.00-$1000.00.
Photo courtesy of Wood's Auction, New Carlisle, OH.

	Current Price Range		P/Y Average
☐ **Adams Style,** English, armchairs, pair, walnut, squared back, open lyre splat, arms with beaded molding and bowfront, tapering reeded legs, 32″ high, 1900	2900.00	3100.00	400.00
☐ **Art Deco,** American, bedroom suite, five pieces, red and black laquer and chrome	825.00	1125.00	950.00
☐ **Art Deco,** desk, burl walnut, diamond parquetry veneer on sides and top, front and rear worked in design of three concentric veneer bands, 27″ high x 56″ longx 29″ wide	1850.00	2250.00	2050.00
☐ **Art Deco,** French, table, mahogany, rectangular sloped base inset with six copper dividers supporting two three-drawer units united by six copper supports bearing glass top, glass ball knobs, 33″ high x 50″ long x 16″ wide, 1920	765.00	975.00	865.00
☐ **Art Nouveau,** English, sideboard, mahogany, floral carved top section	600.00	700.00	650.00
☐ **Belter,** American Rococo, bedstead, carved rosewood, 1860	4000.00	8000.00	6000.00
☐ **Belter,** American Rococo, bureau with mirror, rosewood, very elaborate, 1860	10000.00	17000.00	7000.00

	Current Price Range		P/Y Average

☐ **Biedermeier,** credenza, inlaid walnut, rectangular top above three frieze drawers over three cupboard doors, raised on tapering square legs, 39″ high x 54½″ long x 17¾″ deep .... | 830.00 | 1250.00 | 1000.00

☐ **Brass,** canopy bed, knob and tube style, twin size, 81″ long x 43″ wide x 84″ high .... | 800.00 | 1200.00 | 1000.00

☐ **Chippendale,** American, architectural corner cupboard, upper molded applied arch, double glazed doors each with twelve panes, 103¼″ high x 63″ wide x 25″ deep, Maryland, 1760–1790 .... | 9000.00 | 11000.00 | 4000.00

☐ **Chippendale,** American, desk, slant-front, walnut, thumb molded slant lid opening, elaborately fitted interior, six serpentine front drawers over four thumb molded graduated drawers, 42½″ high x 41″ wide x 22″ deep, Pennsylvania, 1765–1795 .... | 9100.00 | 11,200.00 | 5500.00

☐ **Chippendale,** American, gaming table, serpentine shaped top, square corners, five ball and claw feet, New York, 28″ high x 32″ wide x 16¾″ deep, 1765–1785 .... | 27000.00 | 37,000.00 | 32000.00

☐ **Chippendale Style,** chest of drawers, mahogany, serpentine, four drawers, 1830 .... | 1000.00 | 1600.00 | 1300.00

☐ **Chippendale Style,** china cabinet, curved glass, pierced cornice above floral frieze, astragal doors, 1850s .... | 1750.00 | 2750.00 | 2250.00

☐ **Directoire,** dining table, mahogany, oval top, square tapering legs, Egyptian female busts, stamped Chaplus, 70″ wide, 1790 .... | 4000.00 | 5000.00 | 4500.00

☐ **Duncan Phyfe Style,** dining table, mahogany, re-eded edge top, three reeded legs, brass paws and casters, two leaves, English, 28½″ high x 46″ wide x 51″ diameter, early 20th century ... | 2800.00 | 3200.00 | 3000.00

☐ **Dutch,** curio shelf, hanging, three shelves above a two door cupboard base section, the doors with inlaid floral decoration, 34½″ x 22½″ x 6″, 1800 .... | 225.00 | 275.00 | 250.00

☐ **Eastlake,** bureau and matching bedstead, incised mahogany and walnut, bureau has gray marble top over three long drawers, mirror has stylized floral crest, bedstead is 5′2″ high x 4′9½″ wide .... | 425.00 | 525.00 | 450.00

☐ **Empire,** late, side chairs, set of six, tablet crest rail centering a panel flanked by scrolls and carved leafage, molded stiles over a trapezoidal slip seat on sabre legs, 32½″ high x 19″ wide x 21½″ deep .... | 6000.00 | 8000.00 | 3000.00

☐ **English,** provincial, chairs, set of six, oak, ladderback, last quarter 18th century .... | 2800.00 | 3200.00 | 3000.00

☐ **Federal,** chest of drawers, mahogany and birch veneer, 39″ high x 40″ wide, Massachusetts, 1790–1810 .... | 3000.00 | 4000.00 | 3500.00

	Current Price Range		P/Y Average

☐ **Federal,** Pembroke table, inlaid mahogany, square tapered legs with bell flower motifs, Baltimore, 28½" high x 29¾" wide x 19" deep **5500.00 7500.00 650.00**

☐ **Federal,** settee, bird's eye maple, tablet crest rail above three raking stiles connected by a horizontal rail, rush seat, turned legs, 33¼" high x 60" wide, New England, 1810–1830 .... **4000.00 5500.00 1000.00**

☐ **Federal,** settee, stenciled and ochre painted, rectangular crest rail decorated with cornucopia above spindle splats, plank seat raised on cylindrical legs joined by stretchers, 6' long, 1840 **675.00 875.00 750.00**

☐ **Federal,** side chair, painted, oval shaped back centering a pierced Prince of Wales splat, bowed seat square tapering legs, surface painted white with polychrome flowers, stems, feathers, bows and plumes, 35⅝" x 21¼" wide, Philadelphia, 1795–1800 .... **10000.00 18000.00 14000.00**

☐ **Federal,** side chairs, set of six, mahogany, heart shaped back, fan shaped reticulated splat, reeded legs, spade feet, New York, 1790–1800 **6500.00 8500.00 3000.00**

☐ **Federal Style,** bed, post, cherry, broken arch crest, 85" high x 60" wide **1100.00 1500.00 700.00**

☐ **French Provincial,** cupboard, walnut, hand carved, two double doors at top, two lower doors, scrolled legs, 56 ½" x 91" high, 18th century **3250.00 4250.00 3750.00**

☐ **French Provincial,** dresser, oak, two sections, upper section with carved crest above three open shelves, lower section with molded top above molded floral frieze, 78" high x 80" wide x 18" deep **1000.00 3000.00 2000.00**

☐ **George I,** bureau bookcase, red lacquer chinoiserie, 87" high x 44" wide, 1730 .... **5000.00 5800.00 5400.00**

☐ **George III,** chairs, dining, set of fourteen, mahogany, arched crest rail above a pierced interlaced splat, flared serpentine seat raised on molded square legs joined by stretchers **4500.00 5500.00 5000.00**

☐ **George III Style,** desk, partners, mahogany, gold embossed leather top above one long and two short drawers set upon two pedestals with three drawers each, 31" high x 59" wide x 41" deep, last quarter 19th century **1200.00 4100.00 1600.00**

☐ **Georgian,** armchair, open, mahogany, carved in the French manner, shaped upholstered back, serpentine front seat, cabriole legs, scrolled feet, 1770 .... **1800.00 2200.00 700.00**

☐ **Georgian,** English, library stand, burled walnut, adjustable tilting top, 49½" high x 18" wide x 14" diameter, 18th or early 19th century **2400.00 2800.00 2600.00**

☐ **Hepplewhite Style,** English, dining suite, eleven pieces, mahogany, table with two leaves, buffet, china cabinet, eight chairs **7000.00 8000.00 7500.00**

☐ **Irish,** cabinet, pine, raised panels, double doors, 1820 .... **850.00 950.00 900.00**

	Current Price Range		P/Y Average
☐ **Louis XIV Style,** armchairs, pair, oak, rectangular upholstered back, scroll arms, ball feet, 46″ high, late 19th century	1000.00	1400.00	500.00
☐ **Louis XV,** bergere, walnut, molded frame enclosing leather back and seat, decorated at back with cane work, raised on cabriole legs	2100.00	2950.00	600.00
☐ **Louis XV Provincial,** armoire, fruitwood, molded cornice above two grilled doors, raised on scrolled feet, 6′3″ high x 4′3″ long x 15″ deep	1150.00	2100.00	1500.00
☐ **Louis XV Provincial,** table, bedside, cherry, oblong top above a conforming frieze with full drawer and scalloped apron raised on cabriole legs, 28½″ high x 19½″ wide x 13½″ deep . .	3000.00	3600.00	700.00
☐ **Louis XV Style,** parlor set, settee, armchair and sidechair, giltwood, early 20th century	1200.00	2300.00	1200.00
☐ **Louis XVI Style,** mirror, easel type, silvered bronze, cartouche shaped frame cast with floral garlands and ribbon pendants, raised on scrolled feet, 19½″ high x 15½″ wide	700.00	800.00	750.00
☐ **Louis XVI Style,** parlor set, square back, beribboned crest bowfront seat, cream gessoed woodwork, brocade upholstery	800.00	1200.00	1000.00
☐ **Oak,** golden, armchair, pressed carving in back splat, upholstered seat, 38″ high x 27″ wide . .	140.00	225.00	170.00
☐ **Oak,** golden, china cabinet, curved front, mirrored back, three glass shelves, 87″ high x 44″ wide	625.00	825.00	700.00
☐ **Oak,** golden, dentistry cabinet, 54″ high x 36″ wide x 13″ deep	825.00	1100.00	900.00
☐ **Oak,** golden, dining table, round with center pedestal and four carved feet, 1 leaf, 30″ high x 42″ diameter, 1880	625.00	825.00	725.00
☐ **Oak,** golden, ice box, zinc lined, two doors, some chestnut, 42″ high x 35″ wide x 18″ deep	365.00	475.00	425.00
☐ **Oak,** golden, Morris Chair, 38″ high x 27″ wide x 28″ deep, 1880s	315.00	425.00	350.00
☐ **Oak,** golden, rocker, pressed carving	225.00	425.00	300.00
☐ **Oak,** golden, sideboard, mirrored, elaborate carvings, plain, quarter, and tiger stripe wood, 82″ high x 60″ wide	825.00	3300.00	1600.00
☐ **Queen Anne Style,** English, tea table, walnut, flip top, adjustable, brass pulls, two drawers, 22″ x 15″ x 30″ high	300.00	500.00	400.00
☐ **Queen Anne Style,** side chairs, set of four, spoon back, 1860	2100.00	2700.00	2400.00
☐ **Regency Credenza,** calamander, brass mounted parcel gilt, 36″ high x 6′ long x 15″ deep	3250.00	3750.00	1750.00
☐ **Regency,** English, dining chairs, set of ten, mahogany, rectangular molded crest rail, latticework slat, reeded back supports, tapering legs, spade foot, 34″ high x 20½″ wide x 18″ diameter . . .	5300.00	5900.00	5800.00
☐ **Regency,** games table, elm, inlaid, 44½″ wide, 1810	4000.00	5000.00	4500.00

	Current Price Range		P/Y Average

☐ **Regency Style,** dining chairs, set of ten, black lacquer and parcel gilt, faux bamboo turnings — **2875.00 3575.00 3225.00**

☐ **Sheraton Style,** bed, mahogany, queen size, four posters, carved and fluted columns, swan neck headboard **850.00 950.00 900.00**

☐ **Sheraton Style,** dining chairs set of twelve, painted, rounded back, open splat, painted serpentine front, 37½" high, early 20th century ... **2200.00 2700.00 1000.00**

☐ **Sheraton Style,** fern stand, pair, mahogany, square tops with notched corners, turned standards, raised on tripod bases, 36" high **325.00 375.00 350.00**

☐ **Sheraton Style,** sideboard, cornucopia inlay, single recessed cupboard below bowfronted central section, fluted malborough legs, 1840 **2850.00 3250.00 3050.00**

☐ **Sheraton Style,** table stand, mahogany, three tier, the top tier features galleried sides, fitted with an under drawer, 12" x 18" x 28" high ... **275.00 375.00 325.00**

☐ **Stickley, Gustav,** bookcase, oak, double doors, 56" high x 62" wide x 12¼" deep, 1907 ...... **2600.00 3100.00 2850.00**

☐ **Stickley, Gustav,** desk, slant front, oak, opens to fitted interior, 40" high x 29" wide x 17" deep, 1915 .... **425.00 475.00 450.00**

☐ **Stickley, Gustav,** table, dropleaf, oak, two hinged flaps, three drawers, 28" high x 16¼" deep, top is 43" long when extended, 1910 ... **600.00 700.00 650.00**

☐ **Thonet,** chaise lounge, bentwood, elaborate, caned frame, adjustable back, unsigned, 43½" x 21", 1898 .... **3000.00 3500.00 1200.00**

☐ **Victorian,** corner cabinet, rosewood, marquetry inlaid, top has beveled glass display cabinet, 79" high x 32" wide x 19" deep, late 19th century **1000.00 1800.00 1400.00**

☐ **Victorian,** hall tree, walnut and burl walnut, arched and thumb molded cornice above a central mirrored panel flanked by pilasters and brass lion head knobs, plinth base with single drawer flanked by wells, 9'8" high x 4'11" wide x 19½" deep, late 19th century **750.00 950.00 850.00**

☐ **Victorian,** parlor suite, six pieces, mahogany and burl walnut, includes settee, gentleman's armchair, lady's chair and three side chairs, settee is 6'8" long, late 19th century **1000.00 1900.00 1450.00**

☐ **Victorian,** pedestal table, oak round top, pedestal base with carved lion's mask, paw feet, 30" high x 62" diameter **1900.00 2100.00 500.00**

☐ **Victorian,** Renaissance Revival, American, bedroom suite, two pieces, dresser and bed, black walnut, dresser has white beveled marble top, ebony finish wood drawer pulls, elaborate mirror, both bed and dresser have carved bust of Columbia at top, raised panels in burl walnut, headboard is 93½" high x 61 ¼" wide, dresser is 102" high x 51½" wide x 21 ½" deep, made by Berkey and Gay, Grand Rapids, Michigan, 1870–1876 **3500.00 5000.00 4250.00**

	Current Price Range		P/Y Average
☐ **Victorian,** stool, walnut, covered in needlepoint	450.00	550.00	500.00
☐ **Victorian,** writing table, Carlton House, marquetry satinwood, 48″ wide, 19th century	5500.00	6500.00	6000.00
☐ **Welsh,** dresser, pine, upper section with wide valanced cornice over three narrow shelves, lower section with three short drawers, 78″ high x 58″ wide x 15¼″ deep, late 18th-early 19th century	1200.00	1900.00	1550.00
☐ **William and Mary,** desk, maple and pine, slant lid enclosing valanced compartments, drawers, and hidden compartment, block and turned legs, scalloped skirt, some restoration, New England, 39″ high x 22½″ wide x 15″ deep, 1740	3600.00	4300.00	4000.00

GALLÉ GLASS

DESCRIPTION: The greatest of all the French art glass makers was Emile Gallé, who directed the acclaimed Nancy School of Art in Nancy, France. This academy was formed to promote the great Art Nouveau movement in France. Nancy developed into a colony for the artisans of this movement.

Early in his career Gallé produced enamelled and gilded transparent amber, and also green, or white pieces using historical themes. In the mid-1880s, he began to make pieces decorated with realistic motifs drawn from the world of nature. Flora, fauna, and even insects appeared on transparent glass objects. Gallé is probably most famous for his exquisite cameo glass which he introduced in the 1890s. With improved mass production techniques, Gallé used acid to etch designs on cased glass and remove layers of glass, leaving bas-relief designs which were then further carved by hand. Emile Gallé died in 1904 and the quality of the work produced by his factory declined dramatically. He signed his glass "Gallé", after his death the mark "Gallé" appeared.

RECOMMENDED READING: For more in-depth information on Gallé glass you may refer to *The Official Price Guide to Glassware* and *The Official Identification Guide to Glassware,* published by The House of Collectibles.

	Current Price Range		P/Y Average
□ **Beaker,** cylinder shape, protruding horizontal rib around lower portion, sits on a gilt-bronze foot with scalloped design, pale blue background, overlaid in red, orange, and maroon, cut with an orchid and leaves, signed, 5 ¼" high, c. 1900	3500.00	4500.00	3550.00
□ **Beaker,** cylinder shape tapering towards base and rim, Islamic-like designs enameled in red, white, blue, mauve, and gray, on front side cut with cartouche enclosing a woman and birds, reverse side with oval panel enclosing a king, figures yellow, signed, 4 ¼" high, c. 1890	800.00	900.00	815.00
□ **Bottle,** pilgrim, flattened ovoid shape, waisted neck, canoe-shaped lip, yellow background, overlaid	2000.00	3000.00	2100.00
□ **Bowl,** circular with cylinder ridged foot, yellow background, overlaid in maroon, and beige, carved with a lakeside scene with sailboats in the background and trees, in the foreground, 9 ¼" diameter, c. 1900	3500.00	4500.00	3600.00
□ **Bowl,** cylinder shape, beige background, overlaid in amber and brown, cut with fruitladen and leafy branches in the foreground and trees and clouds in the background, signed, 9 ¼" diameter, c. 1900	1800.00	2500.00	1900.00

Vase,
frosted,
floral design,
signed Gallé, 4 ½",
$250.00-$300.00

	Current Price Range		P/Y Average

☐ **Bowl,** deep bulbous shape with ruffled flaring rim, deep yellow, enameled with a cross of Lorraine encircled by a garland of thistles in pale orange, ivory and gilt, signed, 9″ high, c. 1885 .... **800.00 900.00 815.00**

☐ **Bowl,** elongated ovoid, straight neck, gray background, carved iris blossoms and leaves in avocado, signed, 6 ½″ long, c. 1900 .... **300.00 500.00 320.00**

☐ **Bowl,** half-spherical shape with spreading cylinder foot, yellow background, cartouche in center, flowers and leaves in ivory, rose, green, and brown, gilt, decorative band around the rim, floral repousse around the bottom edge of the foot, signed, 9 ½″ diameter, c. 1895 .... **3000.00 3500.00 3100.00**

☐ **Bowl,** half-spherical with lobed lip, light gray background, frosted inside, overlaid in orange, cut with hanging grapes, signed, 4 ¾″ long, c. 1900 .... **450.00 550.00 475.00**

☐ **Bowl,** shallow with wide mouth, mottled amber shading pale to dark, green lower body, fire polished, signed, 5 ¼″ diameter, c. 1890 .... **600.00 800.00 625.00**

☐ **Bowl,** triangular shape, straight-sided, red background, overlaid in burgundy, cut with orange blossoms and leaves, signed, 4″ high, c. 1900 **300.00 500.00 310.00**

☐ **Box,** covered, circular, domed lid on top, yellow background, overlaid in red, cut flowers and vines, signed, 4 ⅛″ diameter, c. 1900 .... **600.00 700.00 610.00**

☐ **Box,** covered, circular shallow shape, flattened lid, light orange background, overlaid in blue, cut with morning glories, leaves and trailings, signed, 3″ diameter, c. 1900 .... **700.00 800.00 720.00**

☐ **Box,** covered, hexagonal, mottled gray, yellow, and pink background, overlaid in various shades of brown, cut with butterflies on lid, river scene with blossoming trees on box, signed, 6 ¾″ diameter, c. 1900 .... **550.00 800.00 550.00**

☐ **Box,** covered, cylinder body which tapers, yellow background with reddish brown overlay, carved branches with flowers and leaves, matching cover with three butterflies, box and cover signed, 2 ⅞″ diameter, c. 1900 .... **300.00 500.00 315.00**

☐ **Cordial Set,** decanter and six cups, decanter swollen ovoid body, short cylinder neck with spout, large applied handle, cups cylinder shape expanding towards the rims, mottled gray and yellow background, overlaid in bright red, cut with hanging grape vines with berries and leaves, signed, decanter 8 ½″ high, cups 2 ½″ high, c. 1900 .... **1700.00 1800.00 1750.00**

☐ **Decanter,** bell shape body with waisted shoulder, baluster, neck, trumpet-shaped stopper with flaring, scalloped rim, short circular foot, spiral ribbing, upper knop above shoulder and lower portion of body carved with wildflowers, green background, signed, c. 1895 .... **1800.00 2200.00 1850.00**

	Current Price Range		P/Y Average

☐ **Decanter,** tear drop shape, slightly domed foot, knopped neck, knopped flattened stopper, light amber background, enameled with lion on one side and fleur-de-lys on the other in white, black, and gray, applied bosses on sides, signed, 10 ½" high, c. 1895 .... **1500.00 2000.00 1600.00**

☐ **Dish,** leaf shape, scalloped rim which is rolled at two sides, light blue, enameled with dragonflies and lacy ribbons in red, pink, blue-gray, and black, gilding, signed, 12" long, c. 1895 .... **800.00 1200.00 840.00**

☐ **Ewer,** cylinder shape with tapering towards the base and the neck, uneven rim with rising spout, short circular foot, twining applied handle, amber background, enameled in dark rose and bright red with a cross of Lorraine and a blooming thistle with leaves, gilding, signed, 10 ½" high, c. 1900 .... **1200.00 1300.00 1250.00**

☐ **Ewer,** ovoid body, cylinder neck, applied handle, short circular foot, red and yellow, foil inclusions, carved with orchids and leaves, signed, 6 ¾" high, c. 1900 .... **3000.00 4000.00 3050.00**

☐ **Ewer,** ovoid shape, cylinder neck with spout, short circular foot, applied handle, pale yellow, transparent, enameled in pink, citron, green, and brown, gilt with wildflowers, signed, 7 ½" high, c. 1900 .... **800.00 900.00 810.00**

☐ **Ewer,** small, pear shape with slanted rim, spiral ribbing, small C-scroll handle, light amber background, enameled with berries and leaves in red and green, gilding around rim and handle, signed, 3 ½" high, c. 1900 .... **700.00 1000.00 750.00**

☐ **Flacon,** compressed spherical body, waisted bulbous neck tapering into cylinder below acorn-shaped stopper, pale blue background, overlaid in red, maroon, and deep rose, carved with hanging orchids and leaves, signed, 7 ¼" high, c. 1900 .... **6000.00 7000.00 6050.00**

☐ **Flacon,** spherical base, waisted and bulbous neck, applied handle, green background, enameled with landscape, signed, 3 ¼" high, c. 1900 .... **600.00 700.00 620.00**

☐ **Flacon,** pear shape, lobed, rectangular sections, flattened circular stopper, dark yellow background, enameled in off-white and black undulating bands, insects and geometric shapes, gilding, signed, 5 ½" high, c. 1890 .... **600.00 1000.00 630.00**

☐ **Flacon,** wide cylinder, flattened shoulders, slightly ribbed, short cylinder neck, flower-shaped stopper, green etched background, cut with flowers and leaves, touches of white enameling, cut in intaglio of ferns, signed, 4 ½" high, c. 1900 .... **800.00 1200.00 825.00**

	Current Price Range		P/Y Average

☐ **Lamp,** swollen conical shade, lower border lobed, standard in baluster shape, spreading foot, shade supported by three arms of bronze, pink and gray background, overlaid in violet shading to green, cut with primroses and leaves, signed, 22 ¼″ high, c. 1904–1914 . . . .   4500.00   5500.00   4600.00

☐ **Lamp base,** baluster shape, waisted neck, flaring foot, yellow background, overlaid in red, carved roses and leaves, signed, 16 ½″ high, c. 1900 . . . .   600.00   800.00   610.00

☐ **Sconces,** ovoid shape with flat top and lower section coming to a point, gilt-bronze lines the sides ending in a scrolling design at the rim and a small paneled design at the bottom, pale pink background, overlaid in purple, cut with scrolling morning glories, signed, 11″ high, c. 1900 . . . .   1200.00   1300.00   1250.00

☐ **Shade,** ceiling, half-spherical, flared rim, pale yellow background, overlaid in bright red, cut with cactus blossoms and leaves, signed, 21 ¼″ high, c. 1900 . . . .   1000.00   2000.00   1075.00

☐ **Shade,** ceiling, half-spherical, flaring rim, pale yellow background, overlaid in orange, red, yellow, and maroon, cut with branches with acorns, leaves and a squirrel, signed, 20″ diameter, c. 1910 . . . .   19000.00   21000.00   19100.00

☐ **Tumbler,** cylinder shape, tapering towards neck and base, light amber background, enameled with two dragonflies in red, pink, blue, green and white, carved pinwheels, signed, 4 ½″ high, c. 1900 . . . .   600.00   900.00   630.00

☐ **Vase,** baluster shape, swollen shoulders, slightly flaring foot, gray with orange streaked background, overlaid in orange, cut with chrysanthemums and leaves, signed, 7 ⅞″ high, c. 1900   800.00   1200.00   840.00

☐ **Vase,** baluster shape, trumpet base, mottled amber background, overlaid in purple, carved with delphiniums, signed, 17 ⅛″ high, c. 1900   700.00   1000.00   715.00

☐ **Vase,** baluster shape, waisted neck and foot, rolled foot, gray shading to turquoise background, overlaid in rose and avocado, cut with poppy blossoms, buds and leaves, signed, 11 ½″ high, c. 1904 . . . .   700.00   1000.00   725.00

☐ **Vase,** baluster shape, waisted neck, flaring foot, yellow background, overlaid in red, cut with poppies and leaves, signed, 8 ¾″ high, c. 1900 . . .   600.00   1000.00   650.00

☐ **Vase,** baluster shape, waisted neck, flaring rim, domed foot, off-white blackground, overlaid in red, cut with leafy branches and fuchias hanging, signed, 8″ high, c. 1900 . . . .   1500.00   2000.00   1575.00

☐ **Vase,** baluster shape, waisted neck with slightly flaring rim, spreading foot with knob, mottled amber shading to lavender, overlaid in dark amber shading to lavender, carved with iris blossoms and leaves, signed, 13 ¾″ high, c. 1900   1500.00   2000.00   1600.00

	Current Price Range		P/Y Average

☐ **Vase,** baluster shape with paneled sides, thick-walled, milky gray background, enameled with shells and plants, gilt, signed, 8 ½" high, c. 1900 .... 1100.00 1400.00 1150.00

☐ **Vase,** baluster shape with slightly everted rim, short rolled foot, gray opalescent background, overlaid in pink, rose, deep red, cut with wild roses and leaves, signed, 11 ¾" high, c. 1900 2000.00 2200.00 2050.00

☐ **Vase,** baluster shape, yellow and gray background, overlaid in red and burgundy, cut with primroses and leaves, signed, 14 ¼" high, c. 1900 .... 800.00 1200.00 850.00

☐ **Vase,** bud, compressed spherical body, thin cylinder neck, gray and lavender background, overlaid in lavender, cut with blossoms and leaves, polished, signed, 8 ½" high, c. 1900 .... 250.00 350.00 275.00

GAMES

TOPIC: Games are amusing activities that people participate in. The games that collectors are primarily interested in are board games, which are played on the decorated surface of a board or platform.

PERIOD: The first American board game was produced 1843 by W. and S.B. Ives Company. Monopoly, the most famous of all American games, was invented around 1934.

COMMENTS: From 1850 to 1920, games were created using lithography. Some parts were hand-painted. The most collectible board games were made by the Ives Company or the McLoughlin Brothers.

ADDITIONAL TIPS: American board games do not have a high survival rate. When selecting a collectible game, look for one in good condition and with all its pieces intact. For further information, please refer to *The Official Price Guide to Collectible Toys,* published by The House of Collectibles.

Puzzle, *map of the United States, by All Fair,* $7.50

	Current Price Range		P/Y Average
☐ **Across the Continent:** *The United States Game,* Parker Brother, board game, lid shows various modes of transportation including motorcycle and auto, game board when open measures 17" x 32 ½", 1922	115.00	150.00	140.00
Note: Apparently this game was in production a very long time. This is a 1922 version but the board has a 1901 copyright date.			
☐ **Age Cards,** Germany, seven cards, 2" x 2" ...	2.25	5.25	2.75
☐ **Air Mail,** Milton Bradley, c. early 1930's, roll marble across board with obstacles	30.00	40.00	32.00
☐ **Ally Sloper,** Milton Bradley, #4110 subtitled "A Splendid Game For Many Players," instructions in English and Spanish, colorful box, 6 ½" x 13", 1907	60.00	75.00	65.00
Note: Balls were thrown into a clown's mouth, in the style of amusement park games.			
☐ **Alphabet Game,** c. 1950's, "Pinkey Lee's" ...	7.00	14.00	5.00
☐ **Action Letters,** Parker Brothers, includes play money and cards, box lid has full color illustration of rabbits attending an auction, 5 ½" x 7 ½", 1900	130.00	160.00	142.00
☐ **Bear Game,** lithographed paper under glass, put knife and fork in bear's hands by shaking	22.50	32.50	24.00

	Current Price Range		P/Y Average
☐ **Ben Casey, M.D.,** Bing Crosby Productions, based on TV program, pictures Vincent Edwards on cover, box measures 9″ x 17 ½″, 1961	25.00	30.00	26.50
☐ **Bing Crosby's Call Me Lucky,** Parker Brothers, board game picturing Bing Crosby on cover, box measures 10″ x 20″, c. 1953	27.50	32.50	27.75
☐ **Bingo Game,** Germany, c. 1920s, twelve cards, wood numbers	3.00	6.00	3.50
☐ **Blackout,** World War II era, covered with glass, tin sides, shows planes about to bomb town, object: to cover windows with rolling shades	30.00	40.00	33.00
☐ **Blondie Card Game,** King Features Syndicate, deck of thirty six cards with playing instructions, in a box measuring 5″ x 6″, 1941	60.00	75.00	65.00
☐ **Chalk and Checkers,** The Ohio Art Company, #523, c. 1960's, metal, slate, plastic, eraser, chalk	7.00	12.00	8.00
☐ **Checker Board,** advertising giveaway for Preferred Accident Insurance Company, c. 1930s	8.00	12.00	9.00
☐ **Checkers,** empress, Japan, wood	2.00	5.00	2.50
☐ **Checkers,** The Ohio Art Company, #97, c. 1950s, tin, multicolored, Chinese, and regular checkers, diameter 13″	8.00	12.00	9.00
☐ **Chinese Checkers,** The Ohio Art Company, #535, 1960s, metal, marbles, multicolored	8.00	12.00	9.00
☐ **Chinese Checkers and Checkers,** The Ohio Art Company, #538, c. 1960s, metal board, glass marbles, plastic checker	13.50	18.50	15.50
☐ **Cinderella Game,** Bavaria, nine cards, 3″ x 3″	2.00	5.00	2.50
☐ **Collage football,** Milton Bradley, board game with moving pieces and instructions, lid has colored sketch of game action, 8″ x 16″, undated but uniforms worn by players in the lid picture suggest a dating of c. 1930	45.00	60.00	52.00
☐ **Dad's Puzzler,** J. W. Hayward, c. 1926, wood block puzzle game	15.00	20.00	16.00
☐ **Deluxe Chinese Checkers and Checkers,** The Ohio Art Company, #539, c. 1960s, metal board, glass marbles, plastic checkers, storage drawer, diameter 18″	22.00	27.50	23.00
☐ **Eddie Cantor Tell it To The Judge,** Parker Brothers	20.00	25.00	21.00
☐ **Education Board,** Brill Monfort Company, New York, multiply and divide, 12″ x 13″	6.00	12.00	7.00
☐ **Finance and Fortune,** Parker Brothers, board game inspired by Monopoly, box measures 10″ x 19″, c. 1936	25.00	30.00	26.00
☐ **Game of Chance,** c. 1940s, wooden box, disc that spins causes dice to tumble	75.00	95.00	82.00
☐ **Game of Venetian Fortune Telling,** Parker Brothers	6.00	11.00	8.00
☐ **Gee-Whiz Horse Race,** Wolverine, flywheel game, tin with steel wheel, horses race to flag	50.00	60.00	53.00

	Current Price Range		P/Y Average
□ **Goose Game,** dice, pegs, multicolored pictures, 15″ x 11″	10.00	15.00	11.00
□ **Heads Down,** puzzle game, under glass with tin sides, object: put trucks standing on heads, 3″ x 4″	20.00	30.00	23.00
□ **Hold the Fort,** Parker Brother, c. 1895, Civil War cover	35.00	45.00	40.00
□ **Horseshoe Set,** The Ohio Art Company, #531, c. 1950s, metal, vinyl, black, red	7.50	13.00	9.00
□ **Howdy Doody's Own Game,** Parker Brothers, lithographed box lid pictures characters from the TV program, box measures 7″ x 15″, c. 1950–1955	63.00	85.00	74.00
□ **Jolly Darkie Target Game,** McLoughlin, late 19th century, cardboard with colored lithographed covering, game in which the target is a likeness of a black man wide open mouth, 11 ½″	140.00	170.00	150.00
□ **Jolly Old Maid,** Parker Brothers	5.00	10.00	7.00
□ **Kick Back,** pinball game, spring action, board 15″ x 24″	20.00	30.00	23.00
□ **Koo Koo Choo Choo,** The Ohio Art Company, #647, c. 1960s, metal plastic, exploding train game, mechanical	13.00	23.50	15.00
□ **Let 'Em Have It,** World War II era, lithographed cover and game board with battle scenes	30.00	40.00	32.00
□ **Lightning Express,** Milton Bradley, game board part of box	22.00	28.00	24.00
□ **Man From U.N.C.L.E.,** Ideal Toy Co., based on TV program, Robert Vaughn and David McCallum on cover, hard plastic figures, box measures 10″ x 19 ½″, c.	32.50	42.50	33.00
□ **Mickey Mouse Club Magic Adder,** battery operated, red light turns on correct answer is given	18.00	22.00	18.00
□ **Money Box,** The Ohio Art Company, #121, c. 1950s, in, multicolored, rectangular, play coins, bills	8.50	12.50	9.50
□ **Mother Goose, E.L. Horsman,** contains fourteen cartoon pictures that must be assembled in playing the game, in box measuring 7″ x 9″, c. 1880–1890	200.00	300.00	230.00
□ **Old Maid,** Bavaria, nine cards, 2″ x 2″	2.00	5.00	2.50
□ **Perry Mason: Case Of Missing Suspect,** Transogram, based on TV program, pictures Raymond Burr on cover, box measures 10″ x 19 ½″, 1959	27.50	32.50	27.50
□ **Peter Coddles Visit to New York,** c. early 1900s, word game, lithographed cover, 5″ x 6″	12.00	18.00	14.00
□ **Picture Puzzle,** McLoughlin Brothers, New York, wood backed	35.00	45.00	38.00
□ **Pike's Peak or Bust,** Parker Brother, c. 1895	15.00	20.00	17.00
□ **Pollyana,** Parker Brothers, c. 1915, game board and cards, lithographed	30.00	40.00	33.00

	Current Price Range		P/Y Average

☐ **Queen of the Prom,** Barbie Doll Game, box measures 9″ x 22″, 1960 .... 25.00 30.00 26.50

☐ **Presidential Puzzle,** wooden playing pieces, race to White House by Herbert Hoover and Franklin D. Roosevelt, no indication of manufacturer, must have been retailed during the campaign of 1932 .... 50.00 65.00 56.00

☐ **Ralph Edwards' This Is Your Life,** Lowell Toy Manufacturing Corporation, board game, based on TV program, box measures 13½″ x 18″, c. 1958 .... 45.00 60.00 49.00

☐ **Ring Toss,** c. 1940s, wood, rope, post length 6″ 7.00 12.00 8.00

☐ **Roulette,** Reliable Toys, England, c. 1930's, roulette wheel, metal ball 35.00 45.00 39.00

☐ **Rubber Ball Shooting Gallery,** Schoenhut, c. 1910–1915, wood and cardboard covered in lithographed paper, bell rung by clown when shooter makes a direct hit, three additional targets, 16″ 360.00 420.00 380.00

☐ **Schley,** card game by Chaffee of New York, fifty two cards plus instructions in a cardboard box, based on the Spanish-American War adventures of Admiral Schley, box measures 5″ x 7″, 1899 100.00 130.00 112.00

☐ **Shoot-A-Loop-Marble Game,** Wolverine 18.00 22.00 20.00

☐ **Spinner,** lithographed box, 7″ x 7″ 12.00 18.00 14.00

☐ **Spudsie,** The Ohio Art Company, #514, c. 1960s, plastic, hotpotato game, length 7″ 5.00 10.00 6.00

☐ **Steeple Chase,** Bavaria, dice, marker, grand national, 15″ x 15″ 12.00 20.00 13.00

☐ **Table Golf,** The Ohio Art Company, #549, c. 1960s, metal, plastic, flet, putting green, hazards, golfers 15.00 25.00 16.00

☐ **The Spider and The Fly,** Waverly Toy Works, c. 1869, wood, glass cover, picture of spider and web, four felts, 4″ x 4″ 12.00 18.00 14.00

☐ **Through The Locks To The Golden Gate,** Milton Bradley, comes with spinners and wooden playing pieces, label pictures Panama Canal and 1915 Expo building 8.00 12.00 9.00

☐ **Tic Tac Toe,** Tahe Ohio Art Company, #528, c. 1960s, plastic, marbles 5.00 10.00 6.00

☐ **Tiddly Winks,** Milton Bradley, box 4″ x 5½″ .. 12.00 18.00 14.00

☐ **Touring,** Parker Brothers 8.00 12.00 10.00

☐ **Toy Soldiers And Battle game,** parker Brothers, lithographed paper on box, none standup paper soldiers, five wooden shells, and a wooden cannon 40.00 50.00 43.00

☐ **U.S. Map Puzzle,** Parker Brothers, c. 1907, wood backed, diecut, 12″ x 20″ 45.00 55.00 47.00

☐ **What's The Time,** Parker Brothers, c. 1898, lithographed cover, teacher hot to tell time 18.00 22.00 19.00

☐ **When My Ship Comes in,** Parker Brothers, c. 1888 .... 12.00 18.00 14.00

GARNIER BOTTLES

DESCRIPTION: Garnier bottles are collector figural and decorative liquor bottles produced by the Garnier Company.

ORIGIN: The Garnier Company began producing figural bottles in 1899.

COMMENTS: Garnier bottles produced prior to World War II are scarce. Some of the better known include the Cat, 1930; Clown, 1910; Country Jug, 1937; and Greyhound, 1930.

ADDITIONAL TIPS: For more information, consult *The Official Price Guide to Bottles, Old and New,* published by The House of Collectibles.

	Current Price Range		P/Y Average
☐ **Aladdin's Lamp** (c. 1963), silver, 6½″	38.00	48.00	42.00
☐ **Alfa Romeo 1913** (c. 1970), red body, yellow seats, black trim, 4″ x 10½″	15.00	25.00	20.00
☐ **Alfa Romeo 1929** (c. 1969), pale blue body, red seat, black trim, 4″ x 10½″	15.00	25.00	20.00
☐ **Alfa Romeo Racer** (c. 1969), maroon body, black tires and trim, 4″ x 10″	15.00	25.00	20.00
☐ **Antique Coach** (c. 1970), multicolor pastel tones, 8″ x 12″	15.00	25.00	20.00
☐ **Apollo** (c. 1969), yellow quarter-moon, blue clouds, silver Apollo Spaceship, 13½″	12.00	17.00	15.00
☐ **Aztec Vase** (c. 1965), "stone" tan, multicolor aztec design, 11¾″	8.00	14.00	11.00
☐ **Baby Foot-Soccer Shoe** (c. 1963), black with white trim, 3¾″ x 8½″	10.00	20.00	15.00
1962 soccer shoe—large	8.00	11.00	9.50
☐ **Baby Trio** (c. 1963), clear glass, gold base, 6¼″	7.00	10.00	8.50
☐ **Baccus-Figural** (c. 1967), purple, brown, flesh tones, 13″	12.00	16.00	14.00
☐ **Bahamas,** black policeman, white jacket, and hat, black pants, red stripe, gold details	16.00	26.00	21.00
☐ **Baltimore Oriole** (c. 1970), multicolor, green, yellow, blue, approx. 11″	10.00	16.00	13.00

Garnier Strawberries (1982),
decanter basket of ceramic
strawberries, contained
Strawberry liqueur.
$18.00-$26.00

	Current Price Range		P/Y Average
☐ **Bandit-Figural** (c. 1958), pin-ball shape, multi-color, 11½"	10.00	14.00	12.00
☐ **Bedroom Candlestick** (c. 1967), white with hand painted flowers, 11½"	32.00	42.00	37.00
☐ **Bellows** (c. 1969), gold and red, 4" x 14½" ..	14.00	21.00	17.50
☐ **Canada,** "Mountie" in red jacket, black jodphur, brown boots	11.00	14.00	12.50
☐ **Candlestick** (c. 1955), yellow candle, brown holder with gold ring, 10¾"	11.00	15.00	13.50
☐ **Candlestick Glass** (c. 1965), ornate leaves and fluting, 10"	16.00	23.00	20.00
☐ **Cardinal State Bird—Illinois** (c. 1969), bright red bird, green and brown "tree", 11½"	10.00	14.00	12.00
☐ **Cat, Black** (c. 1962), black cat with green eyes, 11½"	15.00	25.00	19.00
☐ **Chalet** (c. 1955), white, red, green, and blue, 9"	40.00	50.00	43.75
☐ **Chimney** (c. 1956), red bricks and fire, white mantle with picture, 9¾"	55.00	65.00	60.00

	Current Price Range		P/Y Average
☐ **Chinese Dog** (c. 1965), foo dogs, carved, embossed, ivory white on dark blue base, 11″ ...	15.00	25.00	20.50
☐ **Christmas Tree** (c. 1956), dark green tree, gold-decorated, white candles, red flame, 11½″	60.00	70.00	64.00
☐ **Classic Ashtray** (c. 1958), clear glass, round with pouring spout, 2½″	5.00	8.00	6.75
☐ **Clown Holding Tuba** (c. 1955), green clown with gold trim, 12¾″	15.00	25.00	20.00
☐ **Drunkard—Drunk on Lampost,** figure in top hat and tails holding "wavy" lampost, black red, blue, and white, 14¾″	20.00	30.00	26.00
☐ **Duckling Figural** (c. 1956), yellow duckling, white basket and red flowers, pink hat	18.00	26.00	22.50
☐ **Eiffel Tower** (c. 1951), ivory with yellow tones, 13½″	15.00	25.00	17.90
☐ **Fiat 500, 1913** (c. 1970), yellow body, red hub caps, black trim, 4″ x 10¾″	15.00	25.00	21.00
☐ **Flying Horse Pegasus** (c. 1958), black horse, gold mane and tail, red "marble" candle holder, 12″	50.00	60.00	54.00

GEORGE OHR POTTERY

DESCRIPTION: The George Ohr pottery holds a unique position among all American pottery wares. Ohr, of Biloxi, Mississippi, designed and manufactured all his products himself. He was totally unconcerned about what would appeal to the public. Rather than letting the public dictate taste to him, he dictated to the public—something which even the giant potteries would not dare to do. He took a totally casual attitude about whether or not anyone wanted to buy it. If there were no customers for one line of his products, he did not stop producing it. Instead, he made more and more, stockpiling it away, feeling certain that someday its real worth would be recognized. It is said he planned to sell his warehouse filled with pottery to the Smithsonian Institute in Washington D.C., so it could have the greatest collection of pottery in existence.

TYPE: The Ohr pottery is almost totally free hand work, like doodles done in clay, but some striking results were achieved. Ohr's boundless confidence in himself shows through in every piece. No matter how offbeat the idea or design, each item was created with masterful skill.

PERIOD: Ohr ran away from home when he was a young boy and worked as a ship chandler's assistant, among various odd jobs. He entered the pottery business in the early 1880s and continued producing items until 1906. Then he simply retired, without passing on any of his trade secrets.

COMMENTS: Today, among collectors, the Ohr pottery is loved by some and detested by others. This is the same response it received when it was being produced the only difference is that today the prices are higher. Some collectors are prejudiced against these products, believing that a potter of Ohr's background and character could not possibly have produced respectable work. The foolishness of this line of thinking can easily be seen, after examining other lives and personalities of the world's artists.

MARKS: Just like the wares themselves, George Ohr's markings followed no special pattern. He seems to have experimented with marks just as much as with designs and working procedures. Most pieces are marked G.E. OHR, BILOXI but this can be a small or large mark, in block or script lettering, by itself or in conjunction with numbers and legends of various kinds. Some of Ohr's pieces are dated—not only with the year, but the month and day on which the mold was ready for casting or on which the piece was fired. Ohr sometimes numbered his works like limited editions. But he had no real plan in that direction, either, and would begin numbering after many pieces had already left the kiln.

	Current Price Range		P/Y Average
☐ **Bowl,** 3½", beige, of squat form with cylindrical sides flaring out into a wide base, crimped along the lip and decorated with small ornaments along the base rim. Marked G.E. OHR, BILOXI, MISS. Believed to date from the late 19th or early 20th centuries	140.00	157.50	132.00
☐ **Bowl,** 2½", brown, of free form design giving the appearance of an ashtray with shaped rim, marked G.E. OHR, BILOXI, MISS. Believed to date from the late 19th or early 20th centuries	230.00	270.00	235.00
☐ **Bowl,** 2½", brown-green, of free form design giving the appearance of an ashtray, caved-in sides, high-gloss glaze. Marked G.E. OHR, BILOXI. Believed to date from the late 19th or early 20th centuries	620.00	750.00	625.00
☐ **Bowl,** 4", green and mud-brown flecked with very dark brown, circular. Marked G.E. OHR, BILOXI. Believed to date from the late 19th or early 20th centuries	310.00	375.00	315.00
☐ **Bowl,** 3¼", green and mud-brown, of squat free form design, Marked G.E. OHR, BILOXI, MISS. Believed to date from the late 19th or early 20th centuries	240.00	300.00	245.00

	Current Price Range		P/Y Average

☐ **Bowl,** 7 ″, various shades of brown, V-form with severely crimped sides. Marked GEO. E. OHR, BILOXI, MISS. Believed to date from the late 19th or early 20th centuries 320.00 385.00 325.00

☐ **Ink stand,** 6¼″, green streaked-glaze, in the form of a semi-rectangular artist's palette with thumb-hole and molded brush, the inkwell resting to one corner. The entire palette encircled by small beadwork at the rim. Marked G.E. OHR, BILOXI. Believed to date from the late 19th or early 20th centuries 330.00 370.00 335.00

☐ **Pitcher,** 5″, brown with green mottling, of free form design resembling a fish in which the tail is pierced and serves as the handle. Marked G.E. OHR. Believed to date from the late 19th or early 20th centuries 620.00 775.00 625.00

☐ **Teapot,** 3⅞″, brown and green splatter glaze, ovoid bulbous form with thumbprint designing, braided handle, disc-type lid. Marked GEO. E. OHR, BILOXI, MISS. Believed to date from the late 19th or early 20th centuries 720.00 850.00 725.00

☐ **Vase,** 7″, blue, of modified cylindrical form with a bulging shoulder and tall neck, molded design-work along the lip. Marked G.E. OHR. Believed to date from the late 19th or early 20th centuries 620.00 750.00 625.00

☐ **Vase,** 10″, blue, of basically cylindrical form widening out slightly at the bottom, very glossy glaze. Marked G.E. OHR BILOXI, MISS. Believed to date from the late 19th or early 20th centuries 500.00 570.00 525.00

☐ **Vase,** 3¼″, brown, bulbous shaped form with pinched and dented sides. Marked G.E. OHR, BILOXI, MISS. Believed to date from the late 19th or early 20th centuries 215.00 240.00 220.00

☐ **Vase,** 3½″, brown smear glaze, of bulbous form with crimped neck. Marked G.E. OHR. Believed to date from the late 19th or early 20th centuries 430.00 520.00 435.00

☐ **Vase,** 5¼″, burnt orange and green glaze, in cologne-bottle form with dome-shaped bowl, pinched neck and funnel-type neck and mouth. Marked GEO. E. OHR, BILOXI. Believed to date from the late 19th or early 20th centuries 200.00 250.00 210.00

☐ **Vase,** 5¼″, burnt orange and olive glaze with rust brown, of hurricane lamp form with a bulbous body and inverted dome neck, wide mouth. Decorated with the applied likeness of a caterpillar. Marked G.E. OHR. Believed to date from the late 19th or early 20th centuries 520.00 615.00 525.00

GINGER BEER BOTTLES

ORIGIN: Though Ginger Beer originated in the early 1800s in Great Britain, this section features only American Ginger Beer bottles. The heyday for Ginger Beer was from 1890 to the 1920s when the new production of grain beer won many fans. Some non-alcoholic Ginger Beer is still made today, however. Unless otherwise noted in the description, the ginger beer bottles listed are made of stoneware.

COMMENTS: The bottles and prices in this section were furnished by Sven Stau of Buffalo, NY. For further information on Ginger Beer bottles, please refer to The Illustrated Stone Ginger Beer, by Sven Stau, P.O. Box 1135, Buffalo, NY 14211.

RECOMMENDED READING: For further information refer to *The Official Price Guide to Bottles Old and New,* published by The House of Collectibles.

	Current Price Range		P/Y Average
☐ **Akron Ginger Beer Co.,** Akron, OH, English brewed Ginger Beer	13.00	18.00	14.00
☐ **Albany Bottling Company,** Albany, NY	13.00	18.00	14.00
☐ **G. Aste and Co., Inc.,** New York, NY, Josiah Russell's Olde Fashioned Stone Ginger Beer, paper label	13.00	18.00	14.00
☐ **Atlantic Bottling Works,** Buffalo, New York, Ginger Beer, green glass	3.00	7.00	3.50
☐ **Atlantic Bottling Works,** Buffalo, NY, pottery	95.00	110.00	96.00
☐ **Barnum's,** Niagara Falls, NY, brewed Ginger Beer	20.00	30.00	21.00
☐ **William Batt,** Tonawanda, NY, brewed Ginger Beer	20.00	30.00	21.00
☐ **C. Baumgartner,** McKeesport, PA, Ginger Beer	18.00	24.00	19.00
☐ **C. H. Bell,** Albany, NY, incised	48.00	52.00	49.00
☐ **Bradford Ginger Beer,** Bradford, PA, BGB	12.00	18.00	13.00
☐ **Henry Brown Co.,** Glendale, CA, Sierra Club Ginger Beer	22.00	26.00	23.00

	Current Price Range		P/Y Average
☐ **J. C. Buffum,** Pittsburg, PA, Ginger Beer	38.00	48.00	39.00
☐ **A. Carpenter and Co.,** Eastman Springs, MI/Chicago, IL, U.S.A., Stone Ginger Beer	22.00	27.00	23.00
☐ **Chelmsford Spring Co.,** Chelmsford, MA, Old English Ginger Beer	33.00	38.00	34.00
☐ **Cleverly's,** Syracuse, NY, English brewed Ginger Beer	16.00	23.00	17.00
☐ **Coburn, Lang and Co.,** Boston, MA, incised quart	62.00	78.00	63.00
☐ **Crescent Bottling Co.,** Alleghany, PA, the original brewed Ginger Beer, 2233 Wayne St.	18.00	24.00	19.00
☐ **Crown Ginger Beer Co.,** Cleveland, OH, English brewed Ginger Beer	10.00	15.00	11.00
☐ **Dr. Brown's,** New York, NY, Ginger Pop, incised	27.00	34.00	28.00
☐ **The Double Eagle Bottling Co.,** Cleveland, OH, Ginger Beer, with picture of double eagles	18.00	24.00	19.00
☐ **The Double Eagle Bottling Co.,** Cleveland, OH, with picture of double eagles, painted label, brown glass	3.00	7.00	4.00
☐ **Adrian Feyh,** New York, NY, incised	11.00	15.00	12.00
☐ **Flanigan and Murphy,** Syracuse, NY, brewed Ginger Beer	18.00	24.00	19.00
☐ **Friedler's,** Rochester, NY, high grade English brewed Ginger Beer	18.00	24.00	19.00
☐ **Frier's,** Niagara Falls, NY, Ginger Beer bottled by A. C. Freir	20.00	30.00	21.00
☐ **Gardner's,** Elmira, NY, Gardner's Old English style Ginger Beer	18.00	24.00	19.00
☐ **A. Goldstein,** Rochester, NY, celebrated Ginger Beer...................................	25.00	35.00	26.00
☐ **John J. Halloran Co.,** Syracuse, NY, imperial brewed Ginger Beer	13.00	18.00	14.00
☐ **Heyworth,** New Bedford, PA, brewed Ginger Beer...................................	22.00	28.00	23.00
☐ **Harry Hicks,** New Castle, PA, English brewed Ginger Beer	22.00	28.00	23.00
☐ **Hughes & Poticher,** Johnston, PA, English brewed Ginger Beer	22.00	30.00	23.00
☐ **Imperial Bottling Co.,** Buffalo, NY, English brewed Ginger Beer	16.00	22.00	17.00
☐ **International Drug Co.,** Calais, ME, Old Homestead Ginger Beer, height 6¾"	13.00	18.00	14.00
☐ **Jumbo Bottling Works,** Cincinnati, OH, Ginger Beer, with picture of elephant	48.00	56.00	49.00
☐ **Koenig Brewery,** Auburn, NY, Ginger Beer ...	33.00	38.00	34.00
☐ **Latter and Co.,** Seattle, WA, home brewed Ginger Beer..................................	18.00	30.00	19.00
☐ **Maurice Lewis,** Rochester, NY, high grade English style Ginger Beer, brown glass	8.00	12.00	9.00
☐ **Maurice Lewis,** Rochester, NY, high grade English brewed Ginger Beer	50.00	65.00	51.00
☐ **Louis Brass,** Lancaster, NY, brewed Ginger Beer....................................	18.00	24.00	19.00

	Current Price Range		P/Y Average
☐ **Lucas Bros.,** Auburn, NY, English brewed Ginger Beer	11.00	15.00	12.00
☐ **McCoy and Bushnell,** Watertown, NY	13.00	18.00	14.00
☐ **New York Bottling Works,** Syracuse, NY, R.D., high grade European style Ginger Beer	9.00	14.00	10.00
☐ **Niagara Bottling Co.,** Buffalo, NY, brewed F&M Ginger Beer	20.00	25.00	21.00
☐ **A. Noe and Son,** Sharpesburg, PA, improved Ginger Beer	13.00	18.00	14.00
☐ **Ohio Ginger Beer Co.,** Toledo, OH, Ginger Beer, brewed by English process	16.00	22.00	17.00
☐ **J. Oliver,** Savannah, GA, Ginger Pop, incised	28.00	35.00	29.00
☐ **J. Pabst,** Baltimore, MD	13.00	18.00	14.00
☐ **Painesville Mineral Springs Co.,** Painesville, OH	10.00	16.00	11.00
☐ **Pine and Co.,** Seattle, WA, home brewed Ginger Beer.	28.00	40.00	29.00
☐ **Ramroth,** Troy, NY, Ginger Beer, green glass	3.00	7.00	4.00
☐ **Rex Water Co.,** New York, NY, Sir Arthur's original Ginger Beer English brew, non-alcoholic . . .	22.00	29.00	23.00
☐ **Rochester Soda and Mineral Water Co.,** Rochester, NY, English brewed Ginger Beer	18.00	25.00	19.00
☐ **Rycroft Artic Soda Co., Ltd.,** Honolulu, Hawaii, Rycroft's old fashioned Ginger Beer, 9 fluid ounces	150.00	300.00	152.00
☐ **The M. Shouler Bottling Works,** Akron, OH, English brewed Ginger Beer, keep cool	13.00	19.00	14.00
☐ **Smith and Clody,** Buffalo, NY, brewed Ginger Beer, monogram brand	10.00	15.00	11.00
☐ **Southern English Ginger Beer Co.,** Jacksonville, FL, John's English brew Ginger Beer, with man holding mug, height 5½″	20.00	30.00	21.00
☐ **Spring Bottling Works,** Utica, NY, T&C Ginger Beer	18.00	24.00	19.00
☐ **Standard Water Co.,** Buffalo, NY, Ginger Beer	45.00	55.00	46.00
☐ **Stone Jug Beverage Co.,** Buffalo, NY, all American Gingerbru, painted label, brown glass	3.00	7.00	4.00
☐ **Dr. Swett's Root Beer,** Boston, MA, original Root Beer, registered	13.00	18.00	14.00
☐ **Tulley Bottling Co.,** Syracuse, NY, Gay's English brewed Ginger Beer	22.00	30.00	23.00
☐ **Vartray,** Buffalo, NY, brewed Ginger Beer, keep cold	10.00	15.00	11.00
☐ **Vimo Co.,** Cleveland, OH, English brewed Ginger Beer, non-alcoholic, improves with age	13.00	18.00	14.00
☐ **Washington Bottling Co.,** Baltimore, MD, genuine Brewed Ginger Beer, English Process	13.00	18.00	14.00
☐ **Washington Bottling Co.,** Baltimore, MD, Weiss Beer.	13.00	18.00	14.00
☐ **Washington Bottling Co.,** Washington, D.C., genuine brewed Ginger Beer English Process	13.00	18.00	14.00
☐ **Western Bottling Co.,** Buffalo, NY, WB	13.00	18.00	14.00

GOLF MEMORABILIA

TYPES: All types of golf memorabilia are collectible, from gloves to bags, balls, clubs, and autographs.

COMMENTS: Golf memorabilia collectors are not as large a group as collectors of baseball and football memorabilia. Most collectors seek golf clubs, and, as with most collectibles, age and rarity account for high prices.

ADDITIONAL TIPS: The listings are alphabetical according to item. For further information, contact the *Golf Collectors' Society,* 638 Wagner Road, Lafayette Hill, PA 19444.

	Current Price Range		P/Y Average
☐ **Driver,** wooden shaft, c. 1910	142.00	180.00	160.00
☐ **George Low Wizard 600 Putter,** flanged	490.00	720.00	610.00
☐ **Golf bag,** leather, c. 1930	220.00	265.00	240.00
☐ **Golf glove,** c. 1910	34.00	42.00	38.00
☐ **MacGregor R. Armour Set,** wood and irons, c. 1950	1070.00	1450.00	1200.00
☐ **Marathon Wards set,** wood and irons, c. 1922	238.00	312.00	275.00
☐ **Power build driver,** c. 1950	120.00	150.00	135.00
☐ **Putter,** wooden shaft, c. 1930	61.00	75.00	68.00
☐ **Putter,** two-way blade with wooden shaft, c. 1920	71.00	85.00	78.00
☐ **Reuter Bull's Eye putter**	100.00	150.00	125.00
☐ **Score card,** Master's Tournament	59.00	97.00	78.00
☐ **Golfer's Manual by H.B. Farnie,** c. 1857	625.00	725.00	675.00
☐ **Tommy Armour wedge,** c. 1959	168.00	212.00	190.00
☐ **Wedge,** Walter Hagen, c. 1930	112.00	137.00	125.00
☐ **Wilson,** Sam Snead set, woods and irons, c. 1940	458.00	542.00	500.00
☐ **Wilson,** R-20 wedge, c. 1930	168.00	212.00	190.00

GRANITEWARE

DESCRIPTION: Metal ware with an enamel coating, Graniteware often has a mottled or marbleized appearance. Most Graniteware is made for use in the kitchen.

PERIOD: 1870s to the present.

ORIGIN: First featured in 1876 at the Centennial Exposition in Philadelphia, Graniteware became popular immediately.

COMMENTS: Graniteware was made in large quantities and is still produced today. There is a fairly consistent demand for the ware, and prices are reasonably stable.

ADDITIONAL TIPS: The listings are in alphabetical order according to item. For further information on Graniteware, refer to *The Official Price Guide to Kitchen Collectibles,* published by The House of Collectibles.

	Current Price Range		P/Y Average
☐ **Basting Spoon,** green and cream mottled	8.00	15.00	9.00
☐ **Basting Spoon,** light blue, excellent condition, 13¼" long	12.00	18.00	12.50
☐ **Basting Spoon,** true blue enamelware, pointed bowl, threaded handle	7.00	9.00	8.00
☐ **Bathtub,** for baby, mottled, gray	70.00	80.00	75.00
☐ **Batter Bucket,** tin lid, handle	45.00	58.00	49.00
☐ **Bedpan,** gray, odorless tabbed cover	10.00	20.00	12.00
☐ **Biscuit Pan**	12.00	17.00	13.00
☐ **Bowl and Pitcher,** blue and white streaked, matched set	47.00	58.00	49.00
☐ **Bowl,** blue and white marbleized, mixing	11.00	17.00	12.00
☐ **Bowl,** blue and white swirl, mind condition, 7"	20.00	35.00	22.00
☐ **Bowl,** blue, deep	20.00	35.00	22.00
☐ **Bowl,** blue swirl, 9"	30.00	45.00	32.00
☐ **Bowl,** cereal, children's, pink with cobalt trim, rabbit decoration in bottom	10.00	25.00	11.00

	Current Price Range		P/Y Average
☐ **Bowl,** gray, mixing, 8″ diameter	5.50	9.00	6.00
☐ **Bowl,** gray, two quart, shallow sides	10.00	20.00	15.00
☐ **Bread Box,** white with blue swirls, circular, hinged lid	47.00	55.00	49.00
☐ **Bread Pan**	12.00	17.00	13.00
☐ **Bread Raiser,** gray mottled, tin lid with wooden knob, 18″ diameter	50.00	65.00	55.00
☐ **Bucket,** berry, blue and white marbleized swirls, small	12.00	18.00	15.00
☐ **Bucket,** berry, child's, gray, with lid, bail handle	55.00	70.00	56.00
☐ **Bucket,** berry, cobalt and white swirl	53.00	70.00	55.00
☐ **Bucket,** berry, cobalt diffused, mint condition	55.00	75.00	57.00
☐ **Coffee Boiler,** brown and white marbleized, dome lid, six quart	58.00	70.00	62.00
☐ **Coffee Boiler,** cobalt and white swirl	74.00	90.00	75.00
☐ **Coffee Boiler,** gray mottled, half moon shape, 5½″ handle, 9″ x 5″ x 4¾″	25.00	45.00	26.50
☐ **Coffee Boiler,** gray, strap and bail handles . . .	35.00	55.00	37.50
☐ **Coffee Boiler,** navy speckled with white, U.S. Navy, wire bail with wooden handle, mint condition, large	20.00	40.00	22.00
☐ **Coffee Pot,** black and white mottled, eleven quart, dome lid	26.00	37.00	29.00
☐ **Coffee Pot,** black and white, small	12.00	17.00	13.00
☐ **Coffee Pot,** blue and white, slant sides, moss rose decoration	65.00	95.00	67.00
☐ **Coffee Pot,** blue and white swirl	45.00	65.00	48.00
☐ **Coffee Pot,** blue and white swirl, gooseneck . .	65.00	75.00	65.00
☐ **Coffee Pot,** blue and white swirl, large	55.00	75.00	58.00
☐ **Coffee Pot,** blue, dome lid	30.00	50.00	32.00
☐ **Coffee Pot,** blue, large	55.00	70.00	58.00
☐ **Coffee Pot,** blue swirl	40.00	60.00	42.00
☐ **Coffee Pot,** blue, tin lid	40.00	60.00	42.00
☐ **Coffee Pot,** cobalt swirl, tin lid	45.00	60.00	47.00
☐ **Coffee Pot,** crystolite and white swirl, gooseneck, small	84.00	100.00	85.00
☐ **Coffee Pot,** cyrstolite and white swirl, small . . .	38.00	50.00	39.00
☐ **Coffee Pot,** gray	20.00	40.00	22.00
☐ **Coffee Pot,** gray, eight cup, enamel dome lid with hollow knob, straight spout	30.00	40.00	32.00
☐ **Coffee Pot,** gray mottled	30.00	45.00	32.00
☐ **Coffee Pot,** gray mottled, bail handle	40.00	60.00	42.00
☐ **Cup and Saucer,** toy, gray	25.00	35.00	30.00
☐ **Cup,** blue and white swirl	9.00	15.00	10.00
☐ **Cuspidor,** with ironware base, mottled gray . . .	20.00	29.00	24.00
☐ **Dinner Bucket,** gray, miner's	65.00	80.00	67.00
☐ **Dinner Pail,** gray, tin lid, round, striped mottling, wood and bail handle, large	60.00	80.00	62.00
☐ **Dinner Plate,** red and white marbleized, excellent condition	20.00	30.00	21.50
☐ **Dipper,** blue and white mottled, white interior, black rim	15.00	27.00	17.00

Braising Pot, *self basting with cover, 19th c.,* $30.00-$50.00

Coffeepot, *gray, 11" high,* $20.00-$40.00
(Photo courtesy of Lou McCulloch, Highland Heights, Ohio)

Depression Glass—Mayfair "Open Rose" by Hocking Glass, pink; Footed Ice Tea Tumbler, 5¼", **$26.00-$30.00;** Wine Goblet, 4½", **$46.00-$52.00;** deep, Flared Vegetable Bowl, **$10.00-$13.00;** Decanter, 32 oz., **$87.00-$95.00.**

Depression Glass—Moondrops by New Martinsville, red; Sugar Bowl, **$9.50-$11.00;** Creamer, **$9.50-$11.50;** Candleholder, **$57.50-$63.00;** Cocktail Shaker, **$20.00-$24.00.**

"Martele" Silver Vase and Plateau, Gorham (c. 1930), three swan-shaped handles, repoussé design of water lilies, marked, 13" high, 105 troy ounces net weight, **$24,000-$26,000.** Photo courtesy of Christie's, New York.

Seven-Piece Silver, Ivory and Bakelite Tea Service, by Jean Puiforcat (c. 1930), each item impressed "JEAN E. PUIFORCAT," tray diameter is 25", 295.5 troy ounces net weight, **$10,000-$11,000.** Photo courtesy of Christie's, New York.

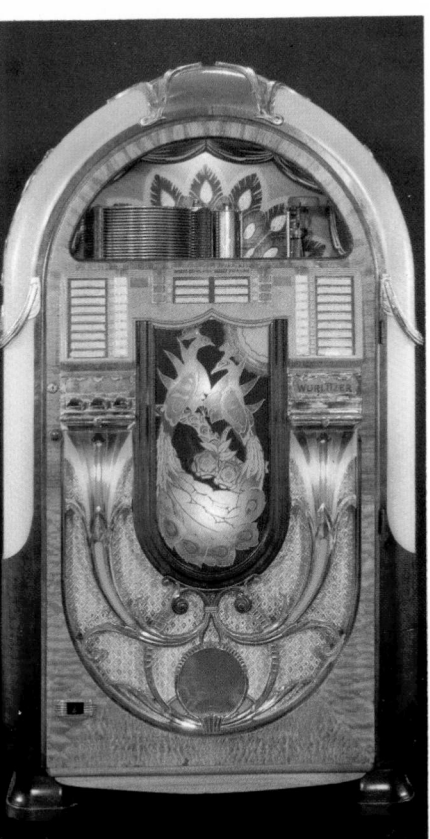

Wurlitzer 850 Jukebox
(c.1941). Also known as the Peacock, 5½'. 350 pounds, played 24 78rpm records, **$6500.00-$7200.00.** *Photo courtesy of JUKEBOX: THE GOLDEN AGE, Asian Humanities Press Publishers. Photograph by Kasuhiro Tsuruta.*

Rock-Ola 1428 *(c.1948), 5', 370 pounds, played 20 78rpm records, blond wood grain finish,* **$1500.00-$1900.00.** *Photo courtesy of JUKEBOX: THE GOLDEN AGE, Asian Humanities Press Publisher. Photograph by Kasuhiro Tsuruta.*

Roseville Pottery (TOP TO BOTTOM) *Blackberry 13" Console Bowl (c. 1933)*, **$160.00-$170.00;** ROW #2, *Donatello 12½" Vase (c. 1915)*, **$130.00-$140.00;** *Ferella 10" Vase (c. 1931)*, **$235.00-$250.00;** *Ming Tree 13" Vase (c. 1947)*, **$75.00-$90.00;** ROW #3, *Imperial 1" Basket Vase (c. 1924)*, **$60.00-$75.00;** *Aztec 9" Vase (c. 1905-07)*, **$210.00-$235.00;** *Laurel Vase (c. 1934)*, **$55.00-$70.00;** ROW #4, *Pine Cone Planter (c. 1931)*, **$42.00-$50.00;** *Persian 9" Candlestick (c. 1916)*, **$120.00-$130.00;** ROW #5, *Medallion Planter (pre-1916)*, **$82.00-$95.00;** *Ferella 6½" Vase (c. 1931)*, **$135.00-$155.00.**

Hull Pottery "Butterfly" Tea Set, *Sugar, Creamer and Pot, set of three,* **$45.00-$75.00.**

CEL—***The Band Concert***, *1935, Walt Disney Studios (Mickey's debut in color).*
Highest price ever paid for a cel at auction, **$24,000.**
Photo courtesy of Christie's, New York.

CEL—***The Flying Mouse***, *1934, Walt Disney Studios,* **$7,000.**
Photo courtesy of Christie's, New York.

Bracelet, *carved coral crossbone motif with hand clasp, c. 1840-1860,* **$800.00-$1000.00.**

Brooch, *human hair in "Prince of Wales" motif, gold frame, English, c. 1860,* **$250.00-$350.00.**

Pin and Earring Set, *hardstone agate cameos, Etruscan granulation on mountings, gold, English, c. 1860-1880,* **$1200.00-$1400.00.**

Cameo Brooch, *carved ivory in an Oriental motif, gold frame, c. 1860-1880,* **$350.00-$450.00.**

FUTURE COLLECTIBLE—
The Cabbage Patch Kids
are appearing on their own cereal
box, produced by Ralston.

FUTURE COLLECTIBLE—
The Rubik's Cube *was fun,*
but not easy.

FUTURE COLLECTIBLE—
Cougar, *is made from genuine Mt. St. Helens ash—manufactured by Martin's Ceramics in Morton, Washington.*

FUTURE COLLECTIBLE—
Jimmy Carter Walking Peanut, *the type of novelty political collectors look for.*

	Current Price Range		P/Y Average
☐ **Dipper,** blue and white swirl, two quart	12.00	18.00	12.50
☐ **Dipper,** blue and white Windsor, marbleized with long handle, 5″ diameter	22.00	35.00	26.00
☐ **Dipper,** cobalt and white swirl, mint condition, large	58.00	70.00	60.00
☐ **Dipper,** cobalt swirl, 1½ cup, enamel label reads E.W. Morse, Omega, 10	15.00	20.00	16.00
☐ **Dipper,** gray	18.00	30.00	19.00
☐ **Funnel,** gray, large	18.00	30.00	20.00
☐ **Funnel,** gray mottled, canning jar, strap handle, rough edges	8.00	15.00	9.50
☐ **Funnel,** gray mottled, hollow handle, excellent condition, 4½″ diameter, 5″ long	18.00	28.00	18.50
☐ **Funnel,** gray mottled, hollow side handle, near mint condition, 7″ long, 5½″ diameter	20.00	30.00	22.00
☐ **Funnel,** gray mottled, strap handle, very old, very good overall condition, 3¾″ diameter, 4½″ long, small	18.00	28.00	18.50
☐ **Funnel,** gray, small	10.00	20.00	12.00
☐ **Funnel,** white with black trim, 4″	12.00	18.00	13.00

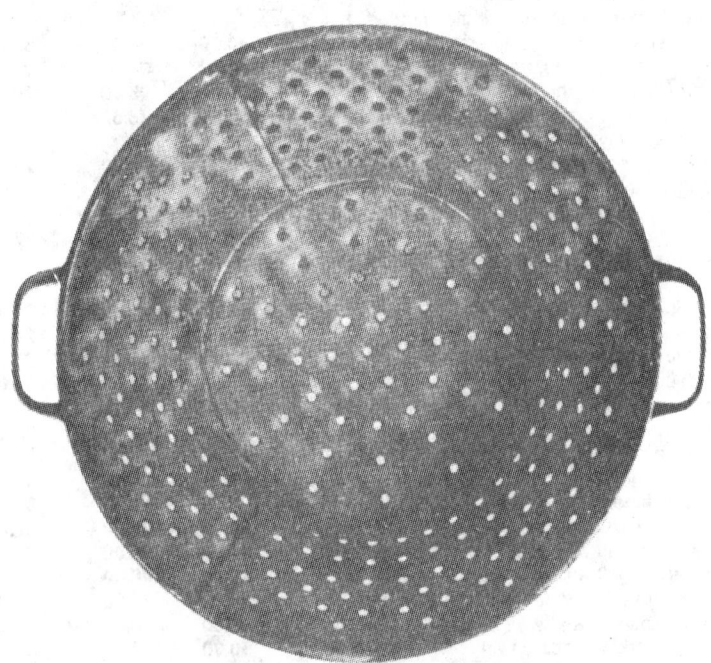

Colander, *blue, 11″,* $20.00-$35.00

	Current Price Range		P/Y Average
☐ **Grater,** cheese, steel handles	34.00	45.00	36.00
☐ **Ham Boiler,** blue and white, bail handle, oval, white liner, 19″ x 9″	22.00	30.00	24.00
☐ **Heater,** kerosene, blue and white mottled, bail handle, 20″	48.00	58.00	53.00
☐ **Invalid Feeder,** gray, gooseneck spout	10.00	25.00	12.00
☐ **Iron,** Coleman gas, blue and white swirl	30.00	45.00	32.00
☐ **Iron,** Coleman, turquoise, nickel over brass tank, nickel over steel base	25.00	35.00	27.00
☐ **Kerosene Stove,** table top, gray, very fancy, ornate nickel coated trim, includes one quart nickel plated brass teakettle with ornate gooseneck spout and lid, bell shaped bottom, wood and bail handle, tray with raised rim, made by George Haller, 11″ diameter	350.00	425.00	375.00
☐ **Ladle,** black and white mottled, 12″	9.00	14.00	9.50
☐ **Ladle,** cobalt, 12″	10.00	15.00	10.50
☐ **Ladle,** cup size	10.00	15.00	12.00
☐ **Ladle,** dumpling, turquoise and white	30.00	45.00	33.00
☐ **Ladle,** dumpling, white....................	10.00	18.00	11.00
☐ **Ladle,** gray, pierced, enamel, label reads			
☐ **Lunch Bucket,** gray and white mottled, black rim, miner's style, 24″ diameter	50.00	60.00	52.00
☐ **Lunch Bucket,** white, tin handle and lid	25.00	35.00	27.00
☐ **Lunch Pail,** gray, three piece	70.00	95.00	72.00
☐ **Measure,** gray, one cup	60.00	75.00	62.00
☐ **Measure,** gray mottled, strap handle, hand-riveted lip, some chips, very old	18.00	30.00	20.00
☐ **Measure,** gray mottling, good old seams, hollow handle, marked 1 Qt. Liquid, near mint condition	35.00	45.00	37.50
☐ **Measure,** gray, quart, handle, wide lip, embossed lines.....................................	20.00	30.00	22.00
☐ **Pan,** blue, 9″	30.00	45.00	33.00
☐ **Pan,** blue and white swirl, round, 8″	25.00	38.00	27.00
☐ **Pan,** blue, round, 8″	25.00	38.00	26.00
☐ **Pan,** blue, round, 11″	15.00	30.00	17.00
☐ **Pan,** blue swirl,, 11″	20.00	40.00	22.00
☐ **Pan,** blue swirl, round, 8″	20.00	35.00	22.00
☐ **Pan,** blue swirl, round, 9″	28.00	40.00	29.50
☐ **Rice Ball,** gray	160.00	180.00	165.00
☐ **Roaster,** blue and white mottled	37.00	48.00	38.00
☐ **Roaster,** brown and white swirl	35.00	50.00	37.00
☐ **Roaster,** cobalt and white swirl	37.00	50.00	38.00
☐ **Roaster,** cobalt and white, three-piece	120.00	140.00	122.00
☐ **Roaster,** oval, gray, flat side handles, small ...	20.00	30.00	22.00
☐ **Roaster,** oval, gray, two handles	16.00	30.00	19.00
☐ **Roaster,** turkey, cobalt swirl................	50.00	80.00	55.00
☐ **Skillet,** aqua and white swirl	73.00	90.00	75.00
☐ **Skillet,** egg, gray, enamel over iron, five eyes, long handle	75.00	95.00	80.00

	Current Price Range		P/Y Average
☐ **Skillet,** dark blue and white swirl, 12″, large ...	50.00	60.00	52.00
☐ **Teapot,** robin's egg blue and white speckled, Britannia Metal, hinged cover and spout, fancy handle, Manning-Bowman Co.	145.00	175.00	150.00
☐ **Teapot,** white and blue speckled	38.00	50.00	39.50
☐ **Teapot,** white with pewter trim	145.00	170.00	147.50
☐ **Teapot,** wooden knob, "S" curved spout	16.00	34.00	18.00

GREETING CARDS

TYPES: All types of Christmas greeting cards were produced in 1843. However the tradition of giving greeting cards didn't take hold until 1860, with the introduction of small visiting greeting cards.

MAKERS: Popular publishers of cards in Marcus Ward & Co., DeLaRue & Co., Raphael Tuck & Co. and L. Prang and Co.

COMMENTS: Greeting cards from the 19th century are the most beautiful and the most sought after. Greeting cards are easy to find and most are reasonably priced.

ADDITIONAL TIPS: The listings are alphabetical according to type of greeting. Also see the section in this book on Valentines.

☐ **Christmas,** "A Merry Christmas and Happy New Year," children playing under Christmas tree, c. 1870's	4.00	7.25	4.75
☐ **Christmas,** "A Merry Christmas to you All," family strolling through snow-blanketed woodland, c. 1880	5.50	8.50	7.00
☐ **Christmas,** blue fringed, golding, birds and flowers, c. 1880	25.00	50.00	30.00
☐ **Christmas,** child in 19th century, bonnet	3.50	7.50	5.00
☐ **Christmas,** children and farm scene	3.50	6.50	5.00
☐ **Christmas,** flowers and birds, Merry Christmas and Happy New Year, 4 pages	9.50	21.00	14.00
☐ **Christmas,** Fold out Christmas card, Santa Claus	11.50	17.00	14.00

Greeting Card, *Christmas ad for Raphael Tuck & Sons,* **$28.00-$30.00**
Photo courtesy of Lou McCulloch, Highland Heights, OH 44143.

	Current Price Range		P/Y Average
☐ **Christmas,** Fold out Christmas card, Nativity scene, c. 1820	7.50	12.50	9.00
☐ **Christmas,** "Hail, Day of Joy," card by L. Prang and Co., angel kneeling with dove on finger, c. 1870's	15.00	20.00	16.00
☐ **Christmas,** "Here Comes the New Year with Lots of Good Cheer," child with Christmas tree and toys, c. 1870	11.00	17.50	13.00
☐ **Christmas,** "Here, Open the Door," card by Kate Greenaway, young messenger boy knocking on door, c. 1880	40.00	55.00	43.00

	Current Price Range		P/Y Average

☐ **Christmas,** ice pond, boy putting skates on a girl, fringed and embroidered, German 9.00 13.00 11.00

☐ **Christmas,** "Merry Christmas and Happy New Year," children romping in snow, church in background, c. 1860 .... 4.50 6.75 5.00

☐ **Christmas,** "Merry Christmas to You All," card by L. Prang and Co., brown suited Santa in chimney, square, c. 1880's 22.00 31.00 24.00

☐ **Christmas,** "My Lips May Give a Message," card by Kate Greenaway, young girl holding letter, c. 1880 .... 40.00 55.00 43.00

☐ **Christmas,** Pop up Christmas card, ice skating scene, England, c. 1890 .... 22.00 30.00 25.00

☐ **Christmas,** Prang's American Third Prize Christmas Card, designed by C. C. Coleman, oriental scene 18.00 26.00 21.00

☐ **Christmas,** Victorian Christmas card, paper lace border surrounds season's greeting, c. 1800's 10.00 16.00 13.00

☐ **Christmas,** "Wishing You a Happy New Year," card by L. Prang and Co., folded, young girl on front, old man on back, fringed, tied with tasseled cord, c. 1884 .... 24.00 34.00 27.00

☐ **Christmas,** "Wishing You a Merry Christmas," card by L. Prang and Co., fireplace scene, cat and kittens looking up chimney, square, c. 1880's 21.00 29.00 24.00

☐ **Christmas,** "With Best Christmas Wishes," card by Raphael Tuck and Sons, young girl holding spray of flowers, c. late 1800's 12.00 18.00 15.00

☐ **Christmas,** "With the Season's Greetings," card by W. S. Coleman, girl on swing (back view), c. 1890 .... 7.50 13.00 9.75

☐ **Easter,** angels on front, by Whitney, New York, 19th century 4.00 6.00 5.00

☐ **Easter,** Bible verses, birds, late 19th century .. 3.00 6.00 4.50

☐ **Easter,** booklet, poem, cross with flowers, German 2.00 5.00 3.00

☐ **Easter,** child coming out of egg, gold fringed .. 6.00 10.00 8.00

☐ **Easter,** cross on reef in sea, by Carter and Karrick, 19th century 4.00 8.00 6.00

☐ **Easter,** floral cross on front, German, 19th century 4.50 6.50 5.50

☐ **Easter,** girl climbing out of an egg shelf, fringed German, 19th century 8.50 15.00 12.00

☐ **Easter,** religious, floral, Tuck 10.00 18.00 14.00

☐ **Greetings,** cupid with ribbon holding flowers, 19th century 7.00 15.00 10.00

☐ **Greetings,** heads of children in flower pot, 19th century 1.00 4.00 2.00

☐ **Greetings,** Shakespeares, "Heaven Give You Many Merry Days," 19th century 3.00 6.00 4.00

☐ **Happy Birthday,** blue fringed, floral design, c. 1880 .... 15.00 25.00 18.00

	Current Price Range		P/Y Average
☐ **Happy Birthday,** booklet, flowers, 19th century	3.00	6.00	4.00
☐ **Happy Birthday,** children, 19th century	2.00	4.00	3.00
☐ **Happy Birthday,** maroon floral, fringed, 19th century	14.00	20.00	16.00
☐ **Happy Birthday,** maroon fringed, flowers	8.00	12.00	10.00
☐ **New Year,** girl holding bird under palm tree, 19th century	3.00	6.00	4.00
☐ **Religious,** blue fringed, 19th century	3.00	6.00	4.00
☐ **Religious,** eggs and feathers, c. 1880	7.00	12.00	9.00
☐ **Religious,** embossed card, "I Go to Prepare A Place for You"	1.00	2.00	1.50
☐ **Religious,** Welcome to Happy Morn, 19th century	4.50	6.50	5.50
☐ **Season's Greetings,** card shaped like fan	2.50	5.00	3.50
☐ **Season's Greetings,** mechanical, boy with flowers, 19th century	15.00	25.00	20.00
☐ **Season's Greetings,** river and small boat, 19th century	4.00	8.00	5.50
☐ **Valentine,** American, heart shaped, lace, c. 1905	9.00	16.00	9.50
☐ **Valentine,** American, honeycomb, "Cupid's Temple of Love," c. 1928	8.00	16.00	8.50
☐ **Valentine,** American, Maggie and Jiggs, c. 1940	4.00	12.00	4.25
☐ **Valentine,** American, Popeye, c. 1940	4.00	10.00	4.25
☐ **Valentine,** Art Nouveau, heart shaped folder ..	4.50	6.50	4.75
☐ **Valentine,** Carrington, folder, lace, c. 1937	1.50	4.50	1.75
☐ **Valentine,** Comic Valentine, the "Hat Trimmer," Elton and Co., New York, illustration of glum-looking woman sewing hat, with verse, c. 1860	22.00	30.00	22.50
☐ **Valentine,** "Dainty Dimples" series, per card ..	3.00	8.00	3.25
☐ **Valentine,** Easel Valentine, fold back, free standing, c. early 1900s	34.00	44.00	35.00
☐ **Valentine,** German, five layer, pulldown, religious sentiment, flowers	45.00	65.00	46.00
☐ **Valentine,** German, large ship, mechanical pulldown	55.00	85.00	56.00
☐ **Valentine,** German, pulldown, children, c. 1915	4.50	10.00	4.15
☐ **Valentine,** German, pulldown, gold	10.00	20.00	11.00
☐ **Valentine,** German, pullout and stand up cottage, c. 1910	7.00	15.00	7.50
☐ **Valentine,** German, pullout and stand up steam boiler, c. 1910	12.00	18.00	12.50
☐ **Valentine,** German, stand up, little girl holding opening parasol..........................	15.00	25.00	15.50
☐ **Valentine,** German, three layers, pulldown, lavender, pink, gold, green, c. 1920	6.50	15.00	7.00
☐ **Valentine,** Gibson Art, paper doll mechanical stand up, little girl holding doll, German	20.00	35.00	21.00
☐ **Valentine,** "Hearts Are Ripe," children picking heart shaped apples from tree	3.00	7.00	4.00
☐ **Valentine,** H. Dobbs and Co., "Pillar Post," illustration of mailbox, c. 1800	22.00	27.00	23.00

	Current Price Range		P/Y Average
☐ **Valentine,** "It Must Be Fine, To Have a Valentine," from "Valentine Wishes" series	7.00	12.00	7.50
☐ **Valentine,** "Lady Killer," comic valentine by A. J. Fisher, NY, c. 1850	29.00	39.00	30.00
☐ **Valentine,** McLoughlin, folder, no lace, c. 1905	5.00	12.00	5.50
☐ **Valentine,** McLoughlin, three layer, silver, white, lace, c. 1880	5.00	12.00	5.50
☐ **Valentine,** McLoughlin, three layer, white, gold, lace, c. 1880	5.00	12.00	5.50
☐ **Valentine,** Mansell, lace, handwritten verse, c. 1946	75.00	100.00	78.00
☐ **Valentine,** Mansell, lace paper, lovers in a park, heavily ornamented, white with silver, c. 1855	44.00	54.00	45.00
☐ **Valentine,** Mansell, cameo embossing, two lovers walking along woodland path, c. 1845	39.00	49.00	40.00
☐ **Valentine,** Mechanical, set of fifteen, c. 1920	34.00	44.00	35.00
☐ **Valentine,** Mechanical, "Such is Married Life," c. 1950	39.00	49.00	40.00
☐ **Valentine,** Mechanical, various animals, c. 1930	10.00	15.00	11.00
☐ **Valentine,** Mechanical, Walt Disney character, c. 1930	17.00	24.00	18.00
☐ **Valentine,** Meek & Son, Gibson Girl (from photo), surrounded by lace in various ornamental patterns, cherub heads, c. 1890	54.00	65.00	55.00
☐ **Valentine,** Meek, layered folder, lace, c. 1870	8.00	15.00	9.00
☐ **Valentine,** "Temple of Love'," from Raphael Tuck's "Betsy Beauties" series, young girl chasing butterfly	5.00	9.00	6.00
☐ **Valentine,** "To My Valentine," from Raphael Tuck's "Innocence Abroad" series, two young children, brief verse	5.00	8.00	6.00
☐ **Valentine,** "To My Wife," embossed woman, hearts and flowers, cutout flowers tied with satin ribbon, real lace surrounds cutout heart, c. 1936	11.00	16.00	12.00
☐ **Valentine,** Tuck, folder, heart shaped, little girl on front	4.00	10.00	5.00
☐ **Valentine,** Victorian, fold out, paper lace	20.00	25.00	21.00

GRUEBY POTTERY

DESCRIPTION: This very prestigious art pottery manufacturer was in business rather briefly, a total of 16 years. In that time, it rose to the top of its market, was considered one of the foremost trend-setters, and established an enviable reputation for creativity and quality. Its years of operation (from 1891 to 1907) coincided with the glory years of art pottery, when it not only made a resounding public splash but influenced other crafts and arts. Grueby ware was expensive and was intended for a limited audience. Grueby did so well that, in a sense, it put itself out of business. The Tiffany Co. of New York, which had been selling fine jewelry and decorative glassware for many years, decided to add art pottery to its inventory. Rather than selling the products of another manufacturer, Tiffany would consider nothing less than manufacturing its own pottery. Since Grueby had the outstanding reputation in the industry, Tiffany approached the company with purchase offers. The purchase plan was completed in 1907 and thereafter all Grueby pottery was manufactured and sold under the name of Tiffany.

TYPE: Grueby had as diverse a line as any art pottery manufacturer. Its products included vases, ornamental wares of various kinds including statuettes, and decorative tiles.

MARKS: The majority of Grueby ware carries not only a factory stamp but an artist's marking as well. There are several variations of the company mark, which fall into two basic categories: straight-line and circular. The straight-line mark will sometimes read GRUEBY POTTERY and, directly beneath this in lettering of a slightly smaller size BOSTON, U.S.A.

RECOMMENDED READING: For more in-depth information you may refer to *The Official Price Guide to Pottery and Porcelain* and *The Official Identification Guide to Pottery and Porcelain,* published by The House of Collectibles.

	Current Price Range		P/Y Average
☐ **Bowl,** 4½″, greenish brown glaze (mottled), pressed bulbous form, bearing an impressed factory mark	180.00	210.00	195.00

	Current Price Range		P/Y Average

☐ **Bowl,** 6½″ x 5″, matte blue, thick glaze 325.00 335.00 330.00
☐ **Inkwell,** 3¾″, floral sterling silver overlay, hinged silver cover, bulbous body, marked sterling 500.00 550.00 525.00
☐ **Paperweight,** 4″, matte green glaze, c. 1904 140.00 150.00 145.00
☐ **Tile,** 4″, windmill design 120.00 130.00 125.00
☐ **Tiles,** 4″, set of 4, plain, solid color 65.00 75.00 67.50
☐ **Tile,** 6″, grape motif 65.00 75.00 67.50
☐ **Tile,** 6¼″ square, blue, decorated with a painting of green flowers, bearing an impressed factory mark and an artist's initials. Probably early 1900's 310.00 385.00 347.00

Note: It should be mentioned that when such items occur for sale in groups, such as half a dozen of the same design, the price per tile is higher than for a single specimen. This is because their decorative uses are greater when one has a number of them.

☐ **Tile, Horse,** 6¼″ square, pastel blue, decorated with a painting of a white horse, bearing an impressed factory mark and an artist's initials. Probably early 1900s 285.00 345.00 315.00
☐ **Tile, landscape,** 4″ square, chiefly green and beige, bearing an impressed factory mark and hand-inked artist's initials P.S. Late 19th to early 20th centuries 140.00 165.00 147.00

Note: While Rookwood was selling its huge tile murals (more than a yard square), Grueby was doing a good business with these small individual tiles. Naturally, each pattern was turned out in the thousands, since it would take hundreds just to cover a single wall. Nevertheless, they aren't common—because when the houses they decorated came down, the tiles were destroyed with them.

☐ **Vase,** bulbous base, purple glaze 280.00 310.00 295.00
☐ **Vase,** 3¼″, green, flared neck, rounded lip, thick glaze 150.00 175.00 145.00
☐ **Vase,** 4¼″, green, molded loaf design, bulbous body, signed with initials 300.00 350.00 325.00
☐ **Vase,** 5¾″, brown glaze (speckled), of flattened spherical form with short neck, bearing an impressed factory mark. c. 1900 .... 310.00 385.00 347.50
☐ **Vase,** 6¼″, green glaze, bulbous bowl with a tall squared cylindrical neck, bearing an impressed factory mark and artist's initials. Late 19th century to early 20th century 435.00 535.00 485.00
☐ **Vase,** 6¼″, light blue matte glaze, c. 1900 .... 160.00 170.00 165.00
☐ **Vase,** 7″, blue glaze 315.00 335.00 325.00
☐ **Vase,** 7″, green, of modified ovoid form with molded panels encircling the body, bearing an impressed factory mark and artist's initials. Late 19th century to early 20th century 480.00 570.00 525.00

	Current Price Range		P/Y Average
□ **Vase,** 7½", green, ovoid flask-style form with pinched neck, decorated by Lillian Newman, bearing an impressed factory mark. c. 1898/1901	540.00	620.00	580.00
□ **Vase,** 8", matte green glaze, molded with buds on stems above leaves, artist-signed, c. 1900	260.00	280.00	270.00
□ **Vase,** 8½", bulbous body, 3-handled, matte green glaze, leaf design	850.00	1000.00	925.00
□ **Vase,** 10", green, decorated by Ruth Erickson, impressed factory mark, artist's initials, c. 1900	1250.00	1650.00	1450.00
□ **Vase,** 11", green, molded with leaves	290.00	310.00	300.00
□ **Vase,** 11", matte green glaze, molded with bud and leaf motif, artist-signed	530.00	580.00	555.00
□ **Vase,** 12½", green, cylindrical shape, leaf and bud motif, stamped and numbered 161	750.00	850.00	800.00

HALL CHINA

DESCRIPTION: Hall's best known dinnerwares were in white or cream usually with a gilt border and decorated with soft pastel flowers. This was the standard line which found new customers in each succeeding generation. In addition, it manufactured numerous other styles in creative patterns, including solid-color wares with richly painted decoration.

INNOVATIONS: This giant of the dinnerware industry was noteworthy not only for the volume of its sales and variety of its patterns, but because it produced the first leadless glaze in the trade. This resulted in strong hardpaste wares with non-porous surfaces which required only a single trip through the firing kiln. Not only were labor costs reduced, but the sales impact was enormous. Hall could authentically claim it was manufacturing chinaware by the same process used in China centuries earlier. The ancient Oriental potters fired their wares only once.

MARKS: There are numerous marks and variations of them, sometimes accompanied by trade names applying to the different lines. The earlier markings were very simple compared to those of later eras, usually consisting of nothing more than the words HALL'S CHINA arranged in a plain circular frame, containing a mold or pattern number at the center. This was sometimes accompanied by

MADE IN U.S.A. directly beneath the stamp. Later, the name Hall was placed in a rectangular frame with wider border, with a small R in a circle beneath it (signifying registration as a trademark). A more elaborate marking reads HALL'S SUPERIOR QUALITY KITCHENWARE in a rectangular frame with bars above and beneath. There are also many retailers' marks to be encountered on the Hall products.

RECOMMENDED READING: For more in-depth information on Hall China you may refer to *The Official Price Guide to Pottery and Porcelain* and *The Official Identification Guide to Pottery and Porcelain,* published by The House of Collectibles.

Autumn Leaf salt and pepper range shakers, *made by Hall for Jewel Tea, pair,* **$13.00–$15.00**

AUTUMN LEAF (Introduced 1933)

Hall produced this pattern in 1933 for the Jewel Tea Company.

	Current Price Range		P/Y Average
☐ **Baker,** 9½"	14.00	16.00	15.00
☐ **Bowl,** 3½"	4.50	6.50	5.00
☐ **Bowl,** 5"	5.50	8.50	6.50
☐ **Bowl Set,** 6", 7½" 9¼", mixing	30.00	34.00	32.00
☐ **Bowl,** 6½"	8.50	11.00	9.00
☐ **Bowl,** 8"	10.00	12.00	11.00
☐ **Casserole,** covered, round	24.00	27.00	25.50
☐ **Casserole Set,** covered, three pieces	55.00	60.00	57.50
☐ **Coffeepot,** covered, metal insert	37.00	40.00	38.50
☐ **Cookie Jar,** covered, c. 1936–39	70.00	75.00	72.50

	Current Price Range		P/Y Average
☐ **Creamer,** ruffled	11.00	13.00	11.00
☐ **Creamer And Sugar,** covered sugar, pair	22.00	26.00	24.00
☐ **Cup And Saucer** pair	6.75	8.50	7.50
☐ **Custard Cups,** set of six	30.00	34.00	32.00
☐ **Dish,** 7½", swirl design	6.75	8.50	7.50
☐ **Dish,** covered	95.00	105.00	100.00
☐ **Dish,** gravy	10.00	12.00	11.00
☐ **Dish,** pickle	12.00	15.00	13.50
☐ **Dish,** with lid	24.00	28.00	26.00
☐ **Jar,** cover and underplate, three piece set	50.00	58.00	54.00
☐ **Pitcher,** 6"	15.00	20.00	17.50
☐ **Pitcher,** ice lip	27.00	33.00	30.00
☐ **Plate,** 6"	3.50	6.50	5.25
☐ **Plate,** 7"	5.50	7.50	6.50
☐ **Plate,** 8"	6.25	8.50	7.50
☐ **Plate,** 9"	7.25	9.50	8.50
☐ **Plate,** 9½"	6.50	8.50	7.50
☐ **Plate,** 10"	10.00	12.00	11.00
☐ **Plate,** 13", oval	13.00	16.00	14.50
☐ **Salad Bowl,** c. 1937	12.00	15.00	13.50
☐ **Saucer**	2.25	4.50	3.50
☐ **Sauce,** 5½"	5.25	6.75	6.50
☐ **Shakers,** salt and pepper, pair, c. 1933	32.00	35.00	33.50
☐ **Stove Set,** 4 pieces	28.00	32.00	30.00
☐ **Sugar**	4.50	6.50	5.50
☐ **Teapot,** covered	50.00	58.00	54.00
☐ **Vegetable Dish,** covered	30.00	35.00	32.50
☐ **Vegetable Dish,** 10½", oval, open	13.00	16.00	14.50

BLUE BOUQUET (Introduced early 1950s)

Hall produced this pattern for the Standard Coffee Company, discontinuing production in the mid-1960s.

☐ **Baker**	12.00	15.00	12.50
☐ **Ball Jug #3**	18.00	28.00	18.50
☐ **Bread and Butter Plate,** 6"	1.75	3.25	2.50
☐ **Cake Stand**	10.00	13.00	11.00
☐ **Casserole,** covered	22.00	32.00	22.50
☐ **Cereal Bowl,** 6"	4.50	6.50	5.00
☐ **Coffeepot**	42.50	52.50	44.00
☐ **Creamer**	5.50	8.50	6.50
☐ **Cup**	4.00	5.50	4.25
☐ **Custard Cup**	5.50	8.50	6.00
☐ **Dinner Plate,** 9"	4.50	6.50	5.00
☐ **Fruit Bowl,** 5½"	3.50	4.75	4.00
☐ **Gravy Boat**	15.00	20.00	15.50
☐ **Luncheon Plate,** 8¼"	4.00	5.00	4.00
☐ **Mixing Bowl,** 6"	5.75	10.00	6.25
☐ **Mixing Bowl,** 7½"	12.00	18.00	12.50
☐ **Mixing Bowl,** 8½"	12.00	18.00	12.50
☐ **Pitcher**	12.00	15.00	12.50
☐ **Platter,** 11"	12.00	18.00	12.50
☐ **Platter,** 13"	15.00	20.00	15.50

	Current Price Range		P/Y Average
☐ **Salad Bowl,** 9"	11.00	15.00	11.50
☐ **Salt and Pepper Shakers,** pair	15.00	20.00	15.50
☐ **Saucer**	1.00	2.75	1.80
☐ **Soup Bowl,** 8½"	9.00	13.00	9.50
☐ **Soup Tureen**	50.00	70.00	55.00
☐ **Sugar Bowl,** with lid	9.00	13.00	9.50
☐ **Teapot,** Aladdin shape	38.00	42.00	39.00
☐ **Vegetable Bowl,** 9¼"	18.00	24.00	18.50

CAMEO ROSE (Introduced 1950s)

Hall produced this pattern for the Jewel Tea Company.

☐ **Bread and Butter Plate,** 6½"	1.75	2.50	1.80
☐ **Butter Dish,** covered	25.00	35.00	26.00
☐ **Casserole,** covered, two tab handles	20.00	30.00	21.00
☐ **Cereal Bowl,** 6"	3.00	4.25	3.50
☐ **Creamer**	5.75	7.00	6.00
☐ **Cup**	5.00	6.00	5.25
☐ **Dessert Plate,** 8"	2.50	3.50	2.80
☐ **Dinner Plate,** 10"	4.50	6.50	4.40
☐ **Fruit Bowl,** 5¼"	2.25	3.25	2.45
☐ **Gravy Boat**	10.00	15.00	11.00
☐ **Luncheon Plate,** 9¼"	3.50	4.35	3.50
☐ **Platter,** 11"	8.00	11.00	9.00
☐ **Platter,** 13"	10.00	13.00	11.00
☐ **Relish Dish,** 9"	7.00	9.00	8.00
☐ **Salt and Pepper Shakers,** pair	10.00	15.00	11.00
☐ **Saucer**	1.00	1.50	1.30
☐ **Soup Bowl**	5.00	7.00	5.50
☐ **Sugar Bowl,** covered	8.00	13.00	8.50
☐ **Teapot**	28.00	38.00	29.00
☐ **Vegetable Bowl,** oval	8.00	11.00	8.50
☐ **Vegetable Bowl,** round, 9"	8.00	11.00	8.50

CROCUS (Introduced 1930s)

☐ **Baker**	14.00	19.00	14.50
☐ **Ball Jug #3**	25.00	30.00	25.50
☐ **Bean Pot,** with lid	45.00	52.00	45.50
☐ **Bread and Butter Plate,** 6"	1.75	3.50	2.00
☐ **Butter Dish,** covered, large, rare	325.00	385.00	300.30
☐ **Cereal Bowl,** 6"	3.50	6.00	4.00
☐ **Creamer**	6.50	8.50	7.00
☐ **Cup**	4.00	6.00	4.50
☐ **Custard Cup**	3.00	4.35	3.50
☐ **Dinner Plate,** 9"	3.50	6.25	4.00
☐ **Drip Jar**	20.00	24.00	21.00
☐ **Dripolator,** china	90.00	100.00	91.00
☐ **Fruit Bowl,** 5½"	3.00	3.75	2.50
☐ **Gravy Boat**	15.00	19.00	15.50
☐ **Luncheon Plate,** 8¼"	3.50	5.25	4.00
☐ **Mixing Bowl,** 6"	7.00	9.00	7.25

	Current Price Range		P/Y Average
☐ Mixing Bowl, 7½″	9.00	11.00	9.50
☐ Mixing Bowl, 9″	12.00	15.00	12.50
☐ Mug	20.00	30.00	21.00
☐ Pie Plate	10.00	13.00	11.00
☐ Platter, 11¼″	10.00	13.00	11.00
☐ Platter, 13¼″	11.00	14.00	12.00
☐ Refrigerator Jar, rectangular	20.00	26.00	21.00
☐ Refrigerator Jar, square	20.00	25.00	21.00
☐ Salad Bowl, 9″	10.00	13.00	11.00
☐ Saucer	1.50	2.50	1.50
☐ Soup Bowl, 8½″	8.00	11.00	9.00
☐ Sugar Bowl, covered.....................	8.00	13.00	9.00
☐ Teapot	20.00	30.00	21.00
☐ Tidbit Server, 3 tier	28.00	33.00	29.00
☐ Tureen, covered	60.00	80.00	61.00
☐ Vegetable Bowl, oval	10.00	13.00	11.00

MORNING GLORY (Introduced 1940s)

Hall produced this kitchenware line for the Jewel Tea Company.

☐ Bowl, 6″	5.00	9.00	5.50
☐ Bowl, 7½″	8.00	13.00	8.50
☐ Bowl, 9″	12.00	17.00	12.50
☐ Coffeepot, drip, china	55.00	70.00	56.00
☐ Custard Cup	3.50	6.25	3.50
☐ Teapot, Aladdin shape	35.00	47.00	36.00

MUMS

☐ Bread and Butter Plate, 6″	.75	1.50	1.00
☐ Casserole	28.00	33.00	29.00
☐ Cereal Bowl, 6″	4.00	5.75	4.25
☐ Creamer..................................	5.00	6.50	5.25
☐ Cup	3.50	4.75	3.75
☐ Custard Cup	2.50	3.75	3.00
☐ Dinner Plate	4.50	5.75	4.60
☐ Fruit Bowl, 5½″	3.00	4.25	3.25
☐ Luncheon Plate, 8¼″	2.50	3.75	3.00
☐ Platter, 11″	11.00	13.00	11.50
☐ Platter, 13″	13.00	15.00	13.50
☐ Salad Bowl, 9″	9.00	13.00	9.50
☐ Salt and Pepper Shakers, pair	10.00	12.00	10.50
☐ Saucer	.75	1.50	1.00
☐ Soup Bowl, 8½″	6.00	7.50	6.25
☐ Sugar Bowl, covered.....................	9.00	11.00	9.25
☐ Teapot	50.00	58.00	52.00

ORANGE POPPY (Introduced 1933)

Hall produced this dinnerware line for the Great American Tea Company.

☐ Baker	10.00	14.00	11.00

	Current Price Range		P/Y Average
☐ Ball Jug #3	14.00	16.00	15.00
☐ Bean Pot, covered, one handle..............	35.00	40.00	36.00
☐ Bowl, 6"	6.00	9.00	7.00
☐ Bowl, 7½"	8.00	10.00	9.00
☐ Bowl, 9"	12.00	15.00	12.50
☐ Bowl, 10"	15.00	21.00	15.50
☐ Bread and Butter Plate, 7"	3.00	6.00	3.50
☐ Bread Box, metal.........................	40.00	48.00	41.00
☐ Cake Plate	10.00	13.00	10.50
☐ Canisters, set of four, metal	30.00	38.00	31.00
☐ Casserole, covered, oval, 8"	18.00	25.00	18.50
☐ Casserole, 11", covered, oval	55.00	70.00	56.00
☐ Casserole, covered, two handles, round	15.00	21.00	15.50
☐ Coffeepot	30.00	42.00	31.00
☐ Creamer	6.00	7.50	6.25
☐ Cup	3.50	5.50	4.25
☐ Custard Cup	13.00	15.00	13.50
☐ Drip Jar	13.00	15.00	13.50
☐ Dessert Plate, 7¾"	4.00	6.00	4.25
☐ Dinner Plate, 9"	5.00	6.50	5.25
☐ Fruit Bowl	3.25	4.50	3.75
☐ Platter, 11¼"	11.00	15.00	11.50
☐ Platter, 13¼"	15.00	19.00	15.50
☐ Pretzel Jar, covered	45.00	52.00	46.00
☐ Refrigerator Jar, oval, one loop handle on top	20.00	28.00	21.00
☐ Salad Bowl, 9"	9.00	11.00	9.50
☐ Salt and Pepper Shakers, pair	5.00	10.00	5.50
☐ Saucer	1.25	2.75	1.60
☐ Sifter, metal	15.00	19.00	15.50
☐ Soup Bowl, 8½"	8.00	11.00	8.50
☐ Spoon...................................	30.00	38.00	31.00
☐ Sugar Bowl, covered......................	10.00	15.00	10.50
☐ Teapot, Bellvue shape	80.00	90.00	81.00
☐ Teapot, Boston Shape	30.00	35.00	31.00
☐ Teapot, Doughnut shape	80.00	95.00	81.00
☐ Teapot, Melody shape	80.00	90.00	81.00
☐ Teapot, Streamline shape	40.00	48.00	41.00
☐ Teapot, Windshield shape	60.00	70.00	61.00
☐ Vegetable Bowl, 9¼"	18.00	24.00	19.00

PASTEL MORNING GLORY (Introduced 1930s)

☐ Ball Jug #3	20.00	24.00	21.00
☐ Bean Pot, covered, one handle..............	40.00	50.00	41.00
☐ Bowl, oval	13.00	15.00	14.00
☐ Bread and Butter Plate, 6"	2.50	4.50	3.00
☐ Casserole, covered, closed tab handles	25.00	30.00	26.00
☐ Cereal Bowl, 6"	5.00	6.00	5.50
☐ Creamer	6.00	8.00	6.50
☐ Cup	4.00	5.50	4.25
☐ Dinner Plate, 9"	6.00	8.00	6.25
☐ Drip Jar	14.00	16.00	14.50
☐ Fruit Bowl, 5½"	4.00	5.50	3.75
☐ Gravy Boat	18.00	24.00	18.50

	Current Price Range		P/Y Average
☐ Luncheon Plate, 8¼″	3.50	5.00	3.50
☐ Platter, 11″	12.00	15.00	12.50
☐ Platter, 13″	15.00	19.00	15.50
☐ Salad Bowl, 9″	10.00	13.00	10.50
☐ Salt and Pepper Shakers, pair	15.00	20.00	15.50
☐ Saucer	1.50	2.25	1.75
☐ Soup Bowl, 8½″	9.00	11.00	9.50
☐ Sugar Bowl, covered	10.00	15.00	11.00

RED POPPY (Introduced early 1950s)

Hall produced this dinnerware line for Grand Union Tea Company.

	Current Price Range		P/Y Average
☐ Ball Jug #3	20.00	28.00	21.00
☐ Baker	13.00	15.00	14.00
☐ Bowl, 6″	8.00	10.00	9.00
☐ Bowl, 7½″	10.00	15.00	11.00
☐ Bowl, 9″	15.00	19.00	15.00
☐ Bread and Butter Plate, 6″	1.50	2.70	1.70
☐ Cake Plate	10.00	14.00	11.00
☐ Cereal Bowl, 6″	4.00	6.00	4.25
☐ Coffeepot	15.00	18.00	16.00
☐ Creamer	6.00	7.50	6.25
☐ Cup	4.50	5.50	4.75
☐ Custard Cup	3.00	4.00	3.25
☐ Dessert Plate, 7″	3.00	4.00	3.25
☐ Dinner Plate, 10″	6.50	7.50	6.75
☐ Fruit Bowl, 5½″	3.50	4.50	3.60
☐ Gravy Boat	18.00	24.00	18.50
☐ Luncheon Plate, 9¼″	5.00	6.25	5.50
☐ Platter, 11″	12.00	14.00	12.50
☐ Platter, 13″	15.00	17.00	15.50
☐ Salad Bowl, 9″	9.00	11.00	9.50
☐ Salt and Pepper Shakers, set	6.00	9.00	6.50
☐ Saucer	1.00	2.10	1.40
☐ Soup Bowl	9.00	11.00	9.25
☐ Sugar Bowl, covered	9.00	11.00	9.25
☐ Teapot, Aladdin shape	30.00	38.00	31.00
☐ Teapot, New York shape	30.00	38.00	31.00
☐ Vegetable Bowl, oval 10″, ...	15.00	19.00	16.00

ROSE PARADE (Introduced 1940s)

	Current Price Range		P/Y Average
☐ Baker	10.00	15.00	11.00
☐ Bean Pot, covered, tab handles	30.00	38.00	31.00
☐ Bowl, 6″	8.00	10.00	9.00
☐ Bowl, 7½″	10.00	15.00	11.00
☐ Bowl, 9″	12.00	16.00	12.50
☐ Casserole, covered, tab handles	15.00	19.00	15.50
☐ Creamer	5.00	9.00	5.50
☐ Custard Cup	4.25	6.00	4.50
☐ Drip Jar	14.00	19.00	15.00
☐ Pitcher, 5″	10.00	16.00	11.00

	Current Price Range		P/Y Average
☐ **Pitcher,** 6½"	15.00	19.00	16.00
☐ **Pitcher,** 7½"	20.00	26.00	21.00
☐ **Salad Bowl,** 9"	10.00	13.00	10.50
☐ **Salt and Pepper Shakers,** pair	10.00	15.00	10.50
☐ **Sugar Bowl,** covered	6.00	9.00	6.25
☐ **Teapot,** four cup	15.00	22.00	16.00
☐ **Teapot,** six cup	18.00	25.00	18.50

ROSE WHITE (Introduced 1940s)

☐ **Baker**	8.00	13.00	8.50
☐ **Bean Pot,** covered, tab handles	25.00	34.00	25.50
☐ **Casserole,** covered, tab handles	18.00	24.00	18.50
☐ **Creamer**	5.50	7.25	6.25
☐ **Custard Cup**	4.00	6.00	4.50
☐ **Drip Jar,** covered, tab handles	10.00	14.00	10.50
☐ **Pitcher,** 5"	10.00	15.00	10.50
☐ **Pitcher,** 6½"	12.00	17.00	12.50
☐ **Pitcher,** 7½"	14.00	21.00	14.50
☐ **Salad Bowl,** 9"	8.00	11.00	8.50
☐ **Salt and Pepper Shakers,** pair	10.00	12.00	10.50
☐ **Sugar Bowl,** covered	4.00	6.00	4.50
☐ **Teapot,** four cup	14.00	19.00	14.50
☐ **Teapot,** six cup	17.00	24.00	17.50

ROYAL ROSE (Introduced 1940s)

☐ **Ball Jug** #3	20.00	28.00	22.00
☐ **Casserole,** covered	18.00	23.00	19.00
☐ **Drip Jar,** covered	14.00	19.00	14.50
☐ **Mixing Bowl,** 6"	7.00	10.00	7.50
☐ **Mixing Bowl,** 7½"	10.00	14.00	11.00
☐ **Mixing Bowl,** 8½"	12.00	15.00	12.50
☐ **Salt and Pepper Shakers,** pair	12.00	18.00	12.50
☐ **Teapot**	25.00	33.00	25.50

SERENADE (Introduced 1930s)

Hall produced this dinnerware pattern for the Eureka Tea Company.

☐ **Bowl,** 6"	5.25	7.25	6.00
☐ **Bowl,** 7¼"	8.00	10.00	8.25
☐ **Bowl,** 9"	11.00	15.00	11.25
☐ **Bread and Butter Plate,** 6"	1.25	2.25	1.50
☐ **Casserole,** covered	20.00	26.00	21.00
☐ **Cereal Bowl,** 6"	4.50	5.50	5.00
☐ **Coffeepot**	15.00	19.00	16.00
☐ **Cup**	3.50	4.50	4.25
☐ **Dinner Plate,** 9"	3.25	6.50	4.00
☐ **Fruit Bowl,** 5½"	3.00	4.50	3.50
☐ **Gravy Boat**	15.00	19.00	15.50
☐ **Luncheon Plate,** 8¼"	3.50	4.35	4.25
☐ **Platter,** 11"	11.00	15.00	11.50

	Current Price Range		P/Y Average
☐ Platter, 13″	13.00	15.00	13.50
☐ Pretzel Jar, covered, tab handles	40.00	48.00	41.00
☐ Salad Bowl, 9″	6.75	11.00	8.00
☐ Salt and Pepper Shakers, pair	15.00	20.00	15.50
☐ Saucer	1.50	2.95	1.75
☐ Soup Bowl, 8½″	8.00	10.00	8.50

SILHOUETTE (Introduced 1930s)

☐ Baker	10.00	13.00	10.50
☐ Ball Jug #3	25.00	32.00	25.50
☐ Bread and Butter Plate, 6″	6.25	7.25	6.25
☐ Casserole Dish, covered	20.00	25.00	21.00
☐ Cereal Bowl, 6″	6.00	7.25	6.25
☐ Coffeepot, drip, china	100.00	120.00	1.01
☐ Cup	4.70	7.25	6.00
☐ Dinner Plate, 9¼″	5.50	6.50	5.75
☐ Drip Jar, covered	10.00	15.00	10.50
☐ Fruit Bowl, 5½″	3.50	4.50	3.25
☐ Luncheon Plate, 8¼″	4.00	5.00	4.00
☐ Mug	20.00	30.00	21.00
☐ Pitcher	15.00	25.00	15.50
☐ Platter, 11″	10.00	13.00	10.50
☐ Platter, 13″	15.00	19.00	15.00
☐ Pretzel Jar, covered, closed tab handles	40.00	50.00	41.00
☐ Refrigerator Jar, covered, rectangular	15.00	18.00	15.50
☐ Refrigerator Jar, covered, square	20.00	28.00	21.00
☐ Salt and Pepper Shakers, pair	8.00	15.00	5.50
☐ Salad Bowl, 9″	8.00	10.00	8.50
☐ Saucer	1.30	2.15	1.40
☐ Soup Bowl, 8½″	9.00	11.00	9.50
☐ Sugar Bowl, covered	10.00	13.00	10.50
☐ Teapot, New York shape	45.00	55.00	45.50

SPRINGTIME

☐ Ball Jug #3	20.00	28.00	21.00
☐ Bread and Butter Plate, 6″	1.25	2.00	1.50
☐ Casserole, covered, two tab handles, thick	20.00	26.00	21.00
☐ Cereal Bowl, 6″	70.00	80.00	71.00
☐ Coffeepot, drip, china	4.00	6.00	4.25
☐ Creamer	4.00	4.75	3.25
☐ Cup	5.00	6.00	5.25
☐ Dinner Plate, 9¼″	10.00	13.00	11.00
☐ Drip Jar, thick	10.00	13.00	11.00
☐ Fruite Bowl, 5½″	3.50	4.25	3.50
☐ Gravy Boat,	15.00	19.00	15.00
☐ Luncheon Plate, 8¼″	3.25	4.00	3.95
☐ Pie Plate	10.00	15.00	11.00
☐ Platter, 11″	11.00	13.00	11.25
☐ Platter, 13″	13.00	15.00	13.50
☐ Salad Bowl, 9″	9.00	11.00	9.50
☐ Salt and Pepper Shakers, pair	15.00	20.00	15.50
☐ Saucer	1.00		1.15

	Current Price Range		P/Y Average
☐ **Soup Bowl**, 8½″	7.00	8.50	7.75
☐ **Sugar Bowl**, covered	9.00	13.00	9.25

TULIP

Hall produced this dinnerware line for the Cook Coffee Company.

☐ **Baker**	10.00	15.00	10.50
☐ **Bread and Butter Plate**, 6″	1.25	2.25	1.45
☐ **Cereal Bowl**, 6″	4.00	5.00	4.25
☐ **Coffeepot**, drip, china	65.00	75.00	65.50
☐ **Creamer**	4.50	7.00	4.25
☐ **Cup**	3.50	5.00	3.75
☐ **Custard Cup**	3.50	5.00	3.75
☐ **Dessert Plate**, 7″	2.50	3.50	3.00
☐ **Dinner Plate**, 10″	5.00	7.00	5.50
☐ **Drip Jar**	13.00	15.00	13.50
☐ **Fruit Bowl**, 5½″	3.25	4.35	3.35
☐ **Gravy Boat**	14.00	19.00	14.50
☐ **Luncheon Plate**, 9″	3.25	5.50	3.75
☐ **Mixing Bowls**, nesting set of three, thick	30.00	40.00	31.00
☐ **Platter**, 11″	12.00	14.00	12.50
☐ **Platter**, 13″	13.00	17.00	13.50
☐ **Salad Bowl**, 9″	8.00	10.00	8.25
☐ **Salt and Pepper Shakers**, pair	8.00	12.00	8.25
☐ **Saucer**	.85	1.55	.85
☐ **Soup Bowl**, 8½″	8.00	10.00	8.25
☐ **Sugar Bowl**, covered	10.00	15.00	11.00

WILDFIRE (Introduced 1950s)

Hall produced this dinnerware line for the Great American Tea Company.

☐ **Baker**	8.00	11.00	8.25
☐ **Bread and Butter Plate**, 6″	2.10	3.25	2.15
☐ **Casserole**, covered, tab handles	20.00	30.00	21.00
☐ **Cereal Bowl**, 6″	4.50	5.75	4.75
☐ **Coffeepot**	20.00	28.00	21.00
☐ **Creamer**	5.00	7.00	5.50
☐ **Cup**	4.00	5.00	4.50
☐ **Custard Cup**	4.00	5.50	4.50
☐ **Dessert Plate**, 7″	3.50	5.00	4.00
☐ **Dinner Plate**, 10″	4.50	5.50	4.65
☐ **Drip Jar**	10.00	15.00	10.25
☐ **Egg Cup**	20.00	28.00	21.00
☐ **Fruit Bowl**, 5½″	3.25	3.75	3.50
☐ **Gravy Boat**	10.00	15.00	11.00
☐ **Mixing Bowl**, large	18.00	24.00	18.50
☐ **Mixing Bowl**, medium	8.00	11.00	8.50
☐ **Mixing Bowl**, small	6.00	8.00	6.25
☐ **Pie Plate**	8.00	11.00	8.50
☐ **Platter**, 11″	8.00	11.00	8.50
☐ **Platter**, 13″	10.00	13.00	10.50
☐ **Salad Bowl**, 9″	8.00	11.00	8.50

	Current Price Range		P/Y Average

☐ Salt and Pepper Shakers, pair	15.00	20.00	15.50
☐ Saucer	2.50	3.50	3.00
☐ Soup Bowl, 8½"	8.00	11.00	8.25
☐ Sugar Bowl, covered......................	8.00	11.00	8.25
☐ Teapot, Aladdin shape	30.00	35.00	31.50
☐ Tidbit Tray, 3-tier	20.00	28.00	21.00

WILD POPPY (Introduced 1930s)

☐ Baker	13.00	15.00	13.50
☐ Bean Pot, covered, one loop handle	50.00	58.00	51.00
☐ Canister	55.00	65.00	56.00
☐ Casserole, oval	20.00	25.00	21.00
☐ Creamer...................................	6.00	8.00	6.50
☐ Custard Cup	3.50	5.25	4.00
☐ Mixing Bowls, set of three	20.00	28.00	21.00
☐ Salt and Pepper Shakers, pair	20.00	28.00	21.00
☐ Sugar Bowl, covered......................	8.50	12.00	8.50
☐ Teapot, four cup	40.00	48.00	41.00
☐ Teapot, six cup	40.00	48.00	41.00

YELLOW ROSE

☐ Baker	9.00	13.00	9.50
☐ Bread and Butter Plate, 6"	1.50	2.50	1.25
☐ Casserole, covered	15.00	19.00	15.50
☐ Cereal Bowl, 6"	3.75	4.75	3.85
☐ Coffeepot, drip, Norse shape	35.00	42.00	36.00
☐ Creamer...................................	4.50	7.50	5.00
☐ Cup	3.75	5.00	4.00
☐ Custard Cup	2.00	3.50	2.25
☐ Dinner Plate, 9"	4.25	5.25	4.15
☐ Fruit Bowl, 5½"	3.00	4.25	3.15
☐ Gravy Boat	10.00	18.00	10.50
☐ Luncheon Plate, 8¼"	3.25	4.25	3.50
☐ Platter, 11"	8.00	11.00	8.25
☐ Platter, 13"	10.00	13.00	10.50
☐ Salad Bowl, 9"	8.00	11.00	8.50
☐ Salt and Pepper Shakers, pair	15.00	20.00	15.50
☐ Saucer	1.35	2.50	1.75
☐ Soup Bowl, 8½"	7.50	8.50	7.75
☐ Sugar Bowl, covered......................	8.00	11.00	8.25
☐ Teapot, New York shape	25.00	34.00	25.50

HANDGUNS

TOPIC: A handgun is a firearm designed to be held and fired with one hand.

TYPES: There are several common varieties of handguns. Flintlocks are muzzleloaded. They utilize a hammer holding a flint that strikes a springloaded frizzen/pan cover to produce ignition. A revolver is a handgun with a revolving cylinder containing multiple chambers. A semi-automatic ejects the spent case and cycles a new round into the chamber using the energy of the fired round. It only fires one shot with each pull of the trigger. A singleshot has no magazine, and thus can fire only one shot.

PERIOD: Firearms made before 1898 are considered antiques.

COMMENTS: Collecting handguns is an expensive hobby which nevertheless attracts many enthusiasts. New guns as well as antiques help fill many collections, since antiques may be out of the price range of many people.

ADDITIONAL TIPS: For more information and extensive listings, please refer to *The Official Price Guide to Antique and Modern Firearms,* and *The Official Price Guide to Collector Handguns,* written by David Byron and published by The House of Collectibles. The following listings are for revolvers only.

	VG	EXC.	Prior Year EXC. Value
☐ ".357 Magnum", 357 magnum, 6 shot, various barrel lengths, adjustable sights, target hammer, target grips, modern	310.00	460.00	440.00
☐ ".357 Magnum", .357 magnum, 6 shot, various barrel lengths, adjustable sights, modern	250.00	290.00	385.00
☐ 125 Anniversary, .45 colt, single action army, commemorative, blue with gold plating, cased, curio	450.00	715.00	700.00
☐ Agent, .38 special, 6 shot, parkerized, 2″ barrel, light weight, modern	115.00	155.00	150.00
☐ Agent, .38 special, 6 shot, blue, 2″ barrel, lightweight, modern	155.00	230.00	225.00
☐ Agent, .38 special, 6 shot, nickel plated, 2″ barrel, lightweight, modern	155.00	225.00	220.00

COLT

Patterson, NJ 1836–1841; Whitneyville, CT 1847–1848; Hartford, CT 1848–present.

	VG	EXC.	Prior Year EXC. Value
☐ **Carolina Charter Tercentennial,** .22 L.R.R.F., and .45 Colt set, Frontier Scout & S.A.A., commemorative, blue with gold plating, 4¾" barrel, cased, curio	675.00	1025.00	1050.00
☐ **Chamizal Treaty,** .22 L.R.R.F., and .45 Colt set, Frontier Scout and S.A., commemorative, blue with gold plating, 4¾" barrel, cased, curio	200.00	290.00	310.00
☐ **Chamizal Treaty,** .22 L.R.R.F., and .45 Colt set, Frontier Scout and S.A.A., commemorative, blue with gold plating, cased, curio	1200.00	1850.00	1995.00
☐ **Chamizal Treaty,** .45 Colt, single action army, commemorative, blue with gold plating, 5½" barrel, cased, curio	775.00	1100.00	1200.00

REMINGTON ARMS CO.

Eliphalet Remington, Herkimer County, NY 1816–1831; Ilion, NY 1831 to date; E. Remington & Sons, 1856; Remington Arms Co., 1888; Remington Arms U.M.C. Co., 1910; Remington Arms Co., 1925 to date; Ilion, N.Y.

	VG	EXC.	Prior Year EXC. Value
☐ **Iroquois,** .22 L.R.R.F., 7 shot, solid frame, spur trigger, single action, unfluted cylinder, antique	225.00	350.00	320.00
☐ **Model 1875,** .44–40 WCF, single action, Western style, solid frame, antique	700.00	1150.00	1075.00
☐ **Model 1875,** .45 Colt, single action, Western style, solid frame, antique	650.00	1100.00	1000.00
☐ **Model 1890,** .44–40 WCF, single action, Western style, solid frame, antique	950.00	1750.00	1700.00
☐ **Smoot #1,** .30 short R.F., 5 shot, solid frame, spur trigger, single action, antique	170.00	255.00	245.00

	VG	EXC.	Prior Year EXC. Value
☐ **Smoot #2,** .32 short R.F., 5 shot, solid frame, spur trigger, single action, antique	150.00	235.00	220.00
☐ **Smoot #3,** .38 long R.F., 5 shot, solid frame, spur trigger, single action, birdhead grip, antique	200.00	325.00	300.00
☐ **Smoot #3,** .38 long R.F., 5 shot, solid frame, spur trigger, single action, saw handle grip, antique	210.00	350.00	335.00
☐ **Smoot #4,** .38 S & W, 5 shot, solid frame, spur trigger, single action, no ejector housing, antique	150.00	235.00	220.00
☐ **Iroquois,** .22 L.R.R.F., 7 shot, solid frame, spur trigger, single action, fluted cylinder, antique . . .	200.00	320.00	295.00

RUGER

Sturm, Ruger & Co., Southport, CT.

	VG	EXC.	Prior Year EXC. Value
☐ **.22 L.R.R.F.,** Western style, single action, blue, lightweight, early model, modern	255.00	350.00	335.00
☐ **"Magna-port IV",** .44 magnum, Western style, single action, commemorative, modern	950.00	1450.00	1400.00
☐ **"Magna-port V",** .44 magnum, Western style, single action, commemorative, modern	995.00	1750.00	1700.00
☐ **Bearcat,** .22 L.R.R.F., Western style, single action, blue, brass grip frame, modern	160.00	235.00	225.00
☐ **Bearcat,** .22 L.R.R.F., Western style, single action, blue, aluminum grip frame, early model, modern	185.00	280.00	265.00
☐ **Blackhawk,** .30 Carbine, Western style, single action, blue, new model, modern	145.00	175.00	170.00
☐ **Blackhawk,** .30 Carbine, Western style, single aciton, blue, modern	160.00	225.00	220.00
☐ **Blackhawk,** .357 magnum, Western style, single action, blue, new model, modern	140.00	170.00	165.00
☐ **Blackhawk,** .357 magnum, Western style, single action, blue, modern	160.00	225.00	220.00
☐ **Blackhawk,** .357 magnum, Western style, single action, blue, flat-top frame, early model, modern	335.00	450.00	435.00
☐ **Blackhawk,** .357 magnum, Western style, single action, blue, 10" barrel, ...	495.00	700.00	675.00
☐ **Super Single Six,** .22LR/.22 WMR Combo, Western style, single action, blue, new model, modern	100.00	145.00	140.00
☐ **Super Single Six,** .22L/.22 WMR Combo, Western style, single action, blue, new model, 9½" barrel, modern	100.00	145.00	140.00
☐ **Super Single Six,** .22R/.22 WMR Combo, Western style, single action, blue, modern	140.00	185.00	175.00
☐ **Super Single Six,** .22LR/.22 WMR Combo, Western style, single action, blue, 9½" barrel, modern	150.00	195.00	185.00

	VG	EXC.	Prior Year EXC. Value
□ **Super Single Six,** .22LR/.22 WMR Combo, Western style, single action, stainless steel, new model, modern	140.00	170.00	165.00
□ **Redhawk, .44** magnum, double action, stainless, interchangeable sights, swingout cylinder, modern	185.00	280.00	275.00

SMITH & WESSON

Started in Norwich, CT in 1855 as Volcanic Repeating Arms Co., reorganized at Springfield, MA as Smith & Wesson in 1857: (Volcanic Repeating Arms moved to New Haven, CT in 1856 and was purchased in 1857 by Winchester Repeating Arms Co.) Smith & Wesson at Springfield, MA to date.

	VG	EXC.	Prior Year EXC. Value
□ **.32 Double Action,** .32 S & W, 1st model, top break, 5 shot, straight-cut sideplate, rocker cylinder stop, antique	950.00	1450.00	1400.00
□ **.32 Double Action,** .32 S & W, 2nd model, top break, 5 shot, irregularly-cut sideplate, rocker cylinder stop, antique	150.00	210.00	200.00
□ **.32 Double Action,** .32 S & W, 3rd model, top break, 5 shot, irregularly-cut sideplate, antique	140.00	190.00	180.00
□ **.32 Double Action,** .32 S & W, 4th model, round-back trigger guard, top break, 5 shot, irregularly-cut sideplate, modern	125.00	175.00	170.00
□ **.32 Double Action,** .32 S & W, 5th model, round-back trigger guard, top break, 5 shot, irregularly-cut sideplate, front sight forged on barrel, modern	125.00	175.00	170.00
□ **Hand Ejector,** .32 S & W long, 1st model, solid frame, swing-out cylinder hammer, actuated cylinder stop, target sights, double action, modern.	330.00	495.00	485.00

===

HARLEQUIN WARE

ORIGIN: Harlequin tableware was introduced by the Homer Laughlin Pottery Company in 1938 and continued to be produced until 1964.

DESCRIPTION: The Harlequin wares are similar to Fiesta, having bright colors and simple shapes. They have an Art Deco flair with the same series of rings, but they are not on the rim. Instead, they appear farther into the center, after a thin band with no design.

COLORS: The colors used on Harlequin are tangerine, salmon, forest green, medium green, light green, chartreuse, Harlequin yellow, gray, turquoise, mauve blue, maroon and spruce green.

MARKS: Harlequin was not marked.

RECOMMENDED READING: For more in-depth information on Harlequin tableware you may refer to *The Official Price Guide to Pottery and Porcelain* and *The Official Identification Guide to Pottery and Porcelain,* published by The House of Collectibles.

	Current Price Range		P/Y Average
Blue			
☐ Bowl, salad, 7″, shallow, no rings	5.00	7.00	5.50
☐ Bowl, fruit, 5½″, flared rim	3.00	5.00	3.50
☐ Creamer, inverted dome shape, with pointed handles	4.00	6.00	4.25
☐ Cup, coffee, with pointed handle	6.00	10.00	6.25
☐ Plate, 6″, recessed center	1.25	2.50	1.50
☐ Plate, 7″, recessed center	1.50	2.75	1.75
☐ Platter, 13″, oval, recessed center	4.50	8.00	4.75
☐ Sugar Bowl, inverted dome shape, with lid	5.00	8.00	5.25
Chartreuse			
☐ Bowl, 5″, flared rim........................	3.00	5.00	3.25
☐ Cup, cream, soup, with two pointed handles ...	3.00	5.00	3.25
☐ Saucer, with recessed ring for cup	1.00	2.00	1.25
Gray			
☐ Bowl, salad, 7″, shallow, no rings	6.00	8.00	6.25
☐ Casserole, with lid	20.00	26.00	21.00

Harlequin Dinnerware By Homer Laughlin Company, *1978 reissue in commemoration of the 100th anniversary of Woolworth and Co.,* **$30.00-$40.00**

	Current Price Range		P/Y Average
□ Creamer, inverted dome shape, with pointed handles	4.00	6.00	4.25
□ Cup, cream, soup, with two pointed handles ...	5.00	9.00	5.25
□ Plate, 6", recessed center	1.25	2.50	1.50
□ Plate, 7", recessed center	1.25	2.50	1.50
□ Plate, 9", recessed center	3.00	4.00	3.25
□ Plate, 10", recessed center	4.00	6.00	4.25
□ Sauceboat, oblong, squared, with handle	6.00	8.00	6.25
Harlequin Yellow			
□ Ashtray, basketweave	17.00	22.00	17.50
□ Baker, 9", oval, with lid and pointed handles ..	5.00	8.00	5.50
□ Bowl, salad, 7", shallow, no rings	6.00	10.00	6.25
□ Casserole, with lid	18.00	24.00	18.50
□ Creamer, inverted dome shape, with printed handles	2.00	5.00	2.25
□ Dish, nut, 3", basketweave design	5.00	8.00	5.25
□ Eggcup, on pedestal base	5.00	11.00	5.25
□ Jug, water, with handle	11.00	14.00	11.25
□ Plate, 6", recessed center	1.25	2.50	1.50
□ Plate, 7", recessed center	1.50	2.75	1.75
□ Plate, 9", recessed center	3.00	4.00	3.25
□ Plate, 10", recessed center	4.00	6.00	4.25
□ Salt And Pepper Shakers, inverted dome shape, on small pedestal base	3.00	8.00	3.25
□ Sugar Bowl, with lid	3.00	8.00	3.25
□ Teacup, inverted dome shape, with pointed handles	4.00	6.00	4.25
□ Teapot, inverted dome shape, with pointed handles	16.00	21.00	16.50

	Current Price Range		P/Y Average

Maroon

☐ Ashtray, with three impressions	17.00	22.00	17.50
☐ Bowl, fruit, 5½", flared rim	3.00	5.00	3.25
☐ Casserole, with lid	24.00	40.00	25.00
☐ Dish, nut, 3", basketweave design	4.00	7.00	4.25
☐ Jug, 22 ounce, cylindrical with pointed handle	7.00	12.00	7.50
☐ Plate, 6", recessed center	1.25	2.50	1.50
☐ Platter, 11", oval, recessed center	5.50	8.40	6.00
☐ Sugar Bowl, with lid	5.50	8.40	6.00
☐ Teapot, with handles	13.00	17.00	13.50

Mauve Blue

☐ Bowl, salad, 7", shallow, no rings	6.50	10.50	7.00
☐ Bowl, fruit, 5½", flared rim	3.35	5.85	3.60
☐ Baker, oval, with lid and pointed handles	5.25	8.50	5.75

Medium Green

☐ Creamer, inverted dome shape, with pointed handles	4.30	6.50	4.85
☐ Plate, 10", recessed center	3.30	6.50	3.75

Red

☐ Ashtray, basketweave, with three impressions	17.00	22.00	17.50
☐ Bowl, fruit, 5½", flared rim	3.25	5.25	3.50
☐ Butter Dish, with cover	22.00	27.00	22.50

HARMONICAS

DESCRIPTION: A harmonica is a rectangular instrument with air slots. Musical tones are produced by blowing air into the slots.

PERIOD: Harmonicas were first produced in the 1800s.

COMMENTS: Material, maker and rarity play important roles in determining the value of a harmonica.

☐ **Angel's Clarion,** made by Weiss, 28 holes, brass reed plates, c. 1900	35.00	50.00	42.00
☐ **"Baseball Club Band Mouth Organ,"** 32 bell metal reeds, two sound horns, 1920s	10.00	15.00	12.50

Harmonica, *Germany, 4½", 1800s*, $35.00–$45.00
(photo courtesy of © The Metropolitan Museum of Art, The Crosby Brown Collection of Musical Instruments, 1889)

	Current Price Range		P/Y Average
☐ **Bell Harmonica (Richter),** 10 single holes, brass reed plates, German silver covers, extended ends, one bell	30.00	40.00	35.00
☐ **As Above,** with two bells	35.00	45.00	40.00
☐ **Bohm's Professional Harmonica,** 10 single holes, 20 brass reeds, 1890s	25.00	35.00	30.00
☐ **Bohm's Jubilee Harmonica,** 10 single holes, 20 brass reeds, brass reed plates, c. 1900	20.00	25.00	22.50
☐ **Bohm's Sovereign,** 5½" x 1½", 16 double holes, 32 steel reeds, nickel covers	20.00	25.00	22.50
☐ **The Brass Band Clarion,** by Weiss, 10 single holes, 20 reeds, c. 1900	25.00	35.00	30.00
☐ **Columbian Exhibition Harmonica,** 10 single holes, nickel reed plates and covers, bronzed wood	60.00	80.00	70.00
☐ **Concert Harmonica,** two bells, 10 double holes with 40 reeds, brass reed plates, engraved German silver covers	45.00	60.00	52.00
☐ **Doerfel's International,** made of celluloid, 10 double holes, 40 reeds, brass reed plates	50.00	65.00	57.00
☐ **Doerfel's New Best-Quality Harmonika,** 48 steel and bronze reeds, brass reed plates, in original box	11.00	15.00	13.00
☐ **Doerfel's Patent Universal Harp,** made of celluloid, 10 single holes, 20 reeds, brass reed plates, one of the earliest celluloid harmonicas, 1890s	40.00	50.00	45.00
☐ **Duss Band Harmonica,** 14 double holes, 28 metal reeds set on brass plates, nickel covers, 4¾", 1920s	15.00	20.00	17.50
☐ **Duss Band Tremelo,** three-in-one harmonica, each tuned to a different key, 32 double holes, 96 reeds, brass reed plates, nickel covers, 8¾", post-World War I	20.00	25.00	22.50
☐ **Duss Full Concert Harmonica,** 10 single holes, 40 reeds on brass plates, nickel covers, 4½"	10.00	15.00	12.50
☐ **Carl Essbach's French Harp #44,** 10 single holes, 20 German silver reeds, brass reed plates, nickel covers	14.00	20.00	17.00

	Current Price Range		P/Y Average
☐ **European Brass Band Harmonica,** 10 double holes, 40 reeds, brass reed plates	40.00	50.00	45.00
☐ **European,** 10 single holes, white metal reed paltes with steel reeds, 1890s	20.00	25.00	22.50
☐ **High Art,** 16 double holes, 32 reeds, brass plates, curved mouthpiece, nickel covers, 4" ..	10.00	15.00	12.50
☐ **Hohner Auto Harmonica,** shaped like auto, 14 double holes, 28 reeds, metal cover	25.00	35.00	30.00
☐ **Hohner Concert Harmonica,** marked "Ulm 1871–Philadelphia 1873," 20 double holes, 80 reeds, brass reed plates, nickel covers, 1890s	20.00	300.00	250.00
☐ **Hohner Double Side Harmonica,** 64 reeds, brass plates, steel covers, nickel-plated, 1920s	25.00	35.00	30.00
☐ **Hohner "Grand Auditorium,"** 16 double holes, 32 reeds, brass reed plates, nickel covers	130.00	200.00	165.00
☐ **M. Hohner Harmonica,** 10 single holes, brass reed plates, c. 1900	20.00	30.00	25.00
☐ **Hohner Harmonica,** 20 double holes, 80 reeds, brass reed plates, nickel covers, c. 1900	70.00	90.00	80.00
☐ **Hohner,** harp shaped, 14 double holes, 28 tremolo reeds, brass plates, nickel-plated covers, 4⅝"	20.00	30.00	25.00
☐ **M. Hohner's Newest And Best Full Concert Harmonica,** 10 double holes, 40 reeds, brass reed plates, nickel covers	45.00	60.00	52.00
☐ **Hohner,** 10 double holes, 40 reeds, brass reed plates, nickel covers	70.00	90.00	80.00
☐ **"The Improved Emmet,"** 10 single holes, brass reed plates, nickel-plated covers, 1890s	35.00	45.00	40.00
☐ **Ludwig Harmonica,** double sided with 10 holes and 20 reeds on each side, 1890s	55.00	75.00	65.00
☐ **Ludwig Harmonica,** Richter Pattern, 10 single holes, 20 reeds, 1890s	30.00	40.00	35.00
☐ **Ludwig Harmonica,** 20 double holes, 40 brass reeds, heavy brass reed plates and nickel covers, c. 1900	65.00	85.00	75.00
☐ **Gebruder Ludwig's "Professional Concert Mouth Organ,"** 10 double holes, 40 reeds, brass reed plates, German silver covers	60.00	80.00	70.00
☐ **"The New Troubador,"** 20 single holes, ten on each side, c. 1897	25.00	35.00	30.00
☐ **"The Prairie Queen,"** 10 single holes, steel and bronze reeds, nickel-plated reed plates and covers	40.00	60.00	50.00
☐ **"The Quadruple Reed Mouth Organ,"** 160 reeds, inscribed "House Music, Best Harp for Artists from Ocean to Ocean," 7¼"	15.00	20.00	17.50
☐ **"Radio Band" Harmonica,** two sets of reeds, pitched in different keys, in the original box, 1920s	10.00	15.00	12.50
☐ **"Radio Band Jazz Mouth Organ,"** novelty harmonica in shape of flashlight with horn at end, sold in U.S. 11", 1929	15.00	20.00	17.50

	Current Price Range		P/Y Average
☐ **"Reveille Mouth Organ,"** nickel-plated covers, c. 1925	6.00	8.00	7.00
☐ **Richter "C,"** 10 single holes, brass reed plates, nickel covers	14.00	20.00	17.00
☐ **"The Silver-Tongued Richter,"** 10 double holes, brass reed plates, nickel covers	42.00	60.00	51.00
☐ **Sousa's Band Harmonica,** 10 single holes, 20 brass reeds, 4", c. 1900	25.00	35.00	30.00
☐ **Sousa Band Harmonica,** 20 holes, 40 brass reeds, 4¾", c. 1900	35.00	50.00	42.00
☐ **"World's Fame,"** 10 single holes, 20 reeds, brass plates, nickel covers, 4"	5.00	10.00	7.50

HEISEY GLASS

ORIGIN: The A.H. Heisey Glass Co. was established in the 1860s at Newark Ohio, by a partnership which included George Duncan and Daniel C. Ripley. It manufactured cut and pressed wares.

DESCRIPTION: Heisey Glass is of a high quality and many patterns are called "elegant depression glass"

COMMENTS: The Heisey Collectors of America Inc. publishes The Heisey News, a newsletter with information on patterns history of Heisey and advertisements. Address: Box 27, Newark O H 43055.

RECOMMENDED READING: For further information refer to *The Official Price Guide to Depression Glass* published by House of Collectibles.

Bowl, footed, diameter 11", floral			
☐ crystal	14.00	16.00	14.50
☐ cobalt	250.00	300.00	265.00
Candlestick, height 6"			
☐ crystal	73.00	78.00	74.00
☐ green	145.00	155.00	147.50
☐ pink	100.00	120.00	105.00
☐ yellow	130.00	140.00	132.50

IPSWICH,
A.H. Heisey.

This distinctive pattern was produced on blank #1405 in crystal, green (Moongleam), pink (Flamingo), yellow (Sahara), cobalt and Alexandrite.

	Current Price Range		P/Y Average
Candy Jar, with lid			
☐ crystal	38.00	43.00	39.50
☐ green	240.00	260.00	245.00
☐ pink	140.00	160.00	145.00
☐ yellow	190.00	210.00	195.00
Champagne Goblet, 5 oz.			
☐ crystal	10.00	12.00	11.50
Cocktail Goblet, 4 oz.			
☐ crystal	10.00	12.00	11.50
Cocktail Shaker, with strainer and stopper			
☐ crystal	140.00	160.00	145.00
☐ green	440.00	460.00	445.00
☐ pink	240.00	260.00	245.00
☐ yellow	340.00	360.00	345.00
Creamer			
☐ crystal	14.00	16.00	14.50
☐ green	32.00	42.00	34.00
☐ pink	22.00	32.00	24.00
☐ yellow	28.00	34.00	31.50
Cruet, with stopper, footed, 2 oz.			
☐ crystal	48.00	55.00	50.00
☐ green	85.00	95.00	78.00
☐ pink	65.00	75.00	68.00
☐ yellow	75.00	85.00	78.00
Finger Bowl, with underplate			
☐ crystal	14.00	16.00	14.50
☐ green	40.00	44.00	41.50
☐ pink	25.00	29.00	26.50
☐ yellow	34.00	40.00	35.50
Goblet, 10 oz.			
☐ crystal	14.00	16.00	14.50
Pitcher, 64 oz.			
☐ cobalt	300.00	350.00	315.00
☐ crystal	95.00	115.00	95.00

	Current Price Range		P/Y Average
☐ green	400.00	450.00	415.00
☐ pink	140.00	160.00	145.00
☐ yellow	190.00	210.00	195.00
Sherbet, 4 oz.			
☐ crystal	8.00	10.00	7.50
☐ green	20.00	27.00	21.50
☐ pink	17.00	22.00	18.00
☐ yellow	20.00	27.00	21.50
Plate, square, diameter 8″			
☐ crystal	15.00	20.00	17.50
☐ green	25.00	32.00	
☐ pink	22.00	27.00	
☐ yellow	26.00	32.00	
Sugar Bowl			
☐ crystal	15.00	20.00	16.50
☐ green	30.00	37.00	31.50
☐ pink	27.00	32.00	27.00
☐ yellow	36.00	42.00	37.00
Tumbler, curved rim, 10 oz.			
☐ crystal	8.00	12.00	9.50
☐ green	28.00	35.00	30.00
☐ pink	24.00	30.00	25.00
☐ yellow	27.00	35.00	28.00
Ashtray, 4″			
☐ crystal	5.00	10.00	6.00
Basket, footed, 10″			
☐ crystal	125.00	135.00	125.00
Bowl, 4″			
☐ crystal	14.00	22.50	15.00
Bowl, flat, 8″			
☐ crystal	13.00	17.50	13.50
Buffet Plate, 21″			
☐ crystal	33.00	43.00	34.00

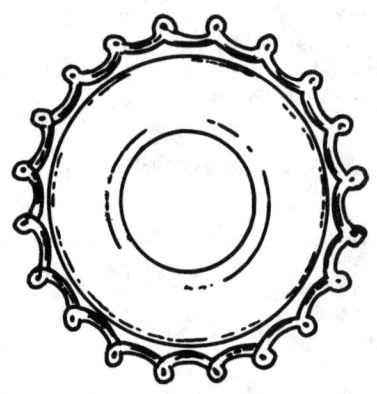

LARIAT,
A.H. Heisey.

This unique pattern was produced on blank #1540 and features pronounced circular loops around exterior rims. It was primarily made in crystal and very infrequently in black.

	Current Price Range		P/Y Average

Cake Plate, rolled edge, 12″
☐ crystal 18.00   25.00   19.50

Candlestick, two candles
☐ crystal 11.00   16.00   12.00

Fruit Bowl, 12″
☐ crystal 15.00   20.00   15.00

Gardenia Bowl, 13″
☐ crystal 18.00   25.00   19.00

Goblet, 9 oz.
☐ crystal 10.00   14.00   11.00

Goblet, blown, 10 oz.
☐ crystal 12.00   16.00   12.50

Salad Plate, 7″
☐ crystal 7.00   12.00   6.00

Salad Plate, 8″
☐ crystal 8.00   12.00   9.00

Salt and Pepper Shakers, pair
☐ crystal 140.00 160.00 145.00

Sandwich Plate, two handles, 14″
☐ crystal 28.00   38.00   30.00

Saucer
☐ crystal 3.00   6.00   4.00

Sherbet, low, 6 oz.
☐ crystal 4.00   10.00   5.00

Basket, #500, 5″
☐ crystal 48.00   58.00   50.00
☐ pink 68.00   78.00   70.00
☐ yellow 83.00   93.00   85.00
☐ green 78.00   88.00   80.00
☐ orchid 105.00 120.00 110.00

Bonbon Dish, upturned sides, #1229, 6″
☐ crystal 4.00   9.00   5.00
☐ pink 7.00   12.00   8.00

OCTAGON,
A.H. Heisey.

Featuring a geometric simplicity, this pattern was produced on blank #500, #1229, and #1231. Colors found are crystal, pink (Flamingo), yellow (Sahara), green (Moongleam), orchid (Hawthorne), amber (Marigold) and very rarely, smoke (Dawn).

	Current Price Range		P/Y Average
□ yellow	9.00	15.00	10.00
□ green	11.00	18.00	12.00
□ orchid	14.00	23.00	15.00
Cheese Dish, two handles, #1229, 6"			
□ crystal	4.00	10.00	5.00
□ pink	7.00	15.00	8.00
□ yellow	9.00	16.00	10.00
□ green	11.00	20.00	12.00
Grapefruit Bowl, 6½"			
□ crystal	8.00	15.00	9.00
□ pink	13.00	20.00	14.00
□ yellow	15.00	25.00	16.00
□ green	14.00	20.00	15.00
□ orchid	19.00	28.00	20.00
Hors d'oeuvre Plate, #1229, 13"			
□ crystal	14.00	24.00	15.00
□ pink	19.00	29.00	20.00
□ yellow	24.00	34.00	25.00
□ green	29.00	38.00	30.00
□ orchid	34.00	44.00	35.00
Plate, 6"			
□ crystal	3.00	9.00	4.00
□ pink	5.00	15.00	6.00
□ yellow	7.00	17.00	8.00
□ green	9.00	19.00	10.00
□ orchid	11.00	21.00	12.00
Ashtray			
□ crystal	4.50	10.50	5.00
□ pink	30.00	39.00	30.00
□ yellow	20.00	29.00	20.00
□ green	35.00	45.00	35.00
□ cobalt	40.00	49.00	40.00
Beer Mug, 12 oz.			
□ crystal	24.00	34.00	25.00
□ pink	185.00	200.00	190.00
□ yellow	195.00	220.00	200.00
□ green	240.00	260.00	250.00
□ cobalt	270.00	285.00	275.00

OLD SANDWICH,
A.H. Heisey.

Produced on blank #1404, this pattern is found in crystal, pink (Flamingo), yellow (Sahara), green (Moongleam) and cobalt.

	Current Price Range		P/Y Average

Beer Mug, 18 oz.
☐ crystal	28.00	38.00	29.00
☐ pink	220.00	240.00	225.00
☐ yellow	245.00	265.00	248.00
☐ green	290.00	320.00	295.00
☐ cobalt	320.00	340.00	324.00

Claret Goblet, 4 oz.
☐ crystal	9.00	18.00	10.00
☐ pink	15.00	24.00	16.50
☐ yellow	17.50	26.00	18.50
☐ green	20.00	29.00	22.00
☐ cobalt	88.00	100.00	91.50

Cocktail Goblet, 3 oz.
☐ crystal	8.00	17.00	8.50
☐ pink	14.00	23.00	15.50
☐ yellow	16.00	25.00	17.50
☐ green	19.00	27.00	20.50

Compote, 6″
☐ crystal	28.00	38.00	29.00
☐ pink	68.00	78.00	69.00
☐ yellow	74.00	84.00	74.50
☐ green	78.00	88.00	79.00

Cup
☐ crystal	7.00	14.00	8.00
☐ pink	11.00	21.00	12.50
☐ yellow	13.00	21.00	14.50
☐ green	16.00	26.00	17.50

Decanter, with stopper
☐ crystal	60.00	80.00	65.00
☐ pink	155.00	175.00	158.50
☐ yellow	165.00	185.00	168.50
☐ green	175.00	195.00	178.50
☐ cobalt	320.00	350.00	325.00

Finger Bowl
☐ crystal	8.00	16.00	9.00
☐ pink	12.00	21.00	11.50
☐ yellow	15.00	25.00	14.50
☐ green	18.00	28.00	17.50

Flower Bowl, oval, footed, 12″
☐ crystal	25.00	35.00	26.50
☐ pink	48.00	58.00	49.00
☐ yellow	58.00	68.00	59.00
☐ green	68.00	78.00	69.00

Flower Bowl, round, footed, 11″
☐ crystal	24.00	34.00	26.00
☐ pink	39.00	48.00	39.50
☐ yellow	48.00	58.00	49.50
☐ green	58.00	68.00	59.50

Iced Tea Tumbler, 12 oz.
☐ crystal	9.00	18.00	10.50
☐ pink	16.00	25.00	17.00

	Current Price Range		P/Y Average
☐ yellow	21.00	30.00	21.50
☐ green	26.00	35.00	27.50
Iced Tea Tumbler, footed, 12 oz.			
☐ crystal	9.00	18.00	10.50
☐ pink	16.00	25.00	17.00
☐ yellow	21.00	30.00	22.50
☐ green	26.00	35.00	27.50
Juice Tumbler, 5 oz.			
☐ crystal	3.00	12.00	4.50
☐ pink	11.00	20.00	12.50
☐ yellow	14.00	23.00	15.50
☐ green	19.00	28.00	21.00
Oyster Cocktail Goblet, 4 oz.			
☐ crystal	3.00	12.00	4.50
☐ pink	9.00	18.00	9.50
☐ yellow	10.00	19.00	10.00
☐ green	12.00	21.00	12.50
Parfait			
☐ crystal	8.00	16.00	9.50
☐ pink	14.00	22.00	14.50
☐ yellow	19.00	29.00	19.50
☐ green	24.00	34.00	24.50
Pilsner Glass, 8 oz.			
☐ crystal	10.00	20.00	11.50
☐ pink	23.00	33.00	24.50
☐ yellow	28.00	38.00	29.50
☐ green	33.00	43.00	34.50
Pilsner Glass, 10 oz.			
☐ crystal	13.00	23.00	14.50
☐ pink	26.00	36.00	27.50
☐ yellow	30.00	40.00	31.50
☐ green	36.00	46.00	37.50
Pitcher, 64 oz.			
☐ crystal	55.00	85.00	60.00
☐ pink	115.00	145.00	120.00
☐ yellow	120.00	150.00	125.00
☐ green	125.00	155.00	130.00
Pitcher, ice lip, 64 oz.			
☐ crystal	63.00	73.00	64.50
☐ pink	120.00	150.00	124.00
☐ yellow	125.00	155.00	130.00
☐ green	130.00	160.00	135.00
Plate, square, 6"			
☐ crystal	4.00	11.00	4.75
☐ pink	8.00	16.00	8.75
☐ yellow	10.00	18.00	10.50
☐ green	13.00	21.00	13.50
Plate, square, 7"			
☐ crystal	4.00	11.00	4.50
☐ pink	10.00	18.00	9.50

	Current Price Range		P/Y Average
☐ yellow	13.50	21.50	12.50
☐ green	14.50	24.00	14.50
Plate, square, 8″			
☐ crystal	6.00	13.00	7.00
☐ pink	12.00	18.00	11.50
☐ yellow	15.00	23.00	14.50
☐ green	17.00	27.00	17.50
Salt and Pepper Shakers, pair			
☐ crystal	28.00	38.00	29.50
☐ pink	38.00	48.00	39.50
☐ yellow	48.00	58.00	49.50
☐ green	58.00	68.00	59.50
Saucer			
☐ crystal	6.00	15.00	7.50
☐ pink	10.00	19.00	9.50
☐ yellow	12.00	21.00	11.50
☐ green	14.00	23.00	13.50
Bouillon Bowl, two handles, 5″			
☐ crystal	5.00	14.00	6.50
☐ pink	9.00	18.00	10.50
☐ green	11.00	20.00	12.50
Bouillon Underplate, 6¾″			
☐ crystal	2.00	9.00	3.50
☐ pink	5.00	12.00	6.50
☐ green	7.00	14.00	8.50
Bowl, 4″			
☐ crystal	4.00	13.00	5.50
☐ pink	7.00	16.00	8.50
☐ green	9.00	18.00	10.50
Cereal Bowl, 6½″			
☐ crystal	4.00	13.00	5.50
☐ pink	9.00	18.00	10.50
☐ green	11.00	20.00	12.50
Champagne Goblet, 5 oz.			
☐ crystal	4.00	13.00	5.50
☐ pink	9.00	18.00	10.50
☐ green	11.00	20.00	12.50

PLEAT AND PANEL,
A.H. Heisey.

Produced on blank #1170, this very simple pattern is found in crystal, pink (Flamingo) and green (Moongleam).

	Current Price Range		P/Y Average
Cheese and Cracker Set, 10½″			
☐ crystal	19.00	28.00	20.50
☐ pink	29.00	37.00	30.50
☐ green	34.00	43.00	35.50
Compote, covered, footed, 5″			
☐ crystal	24.00	33.00	25.50
☐ pink	44.00	53.00	45.50
☐ green	54.00	63.00	55.50
Creamer, institutional			
☐ crystal	4.00	13.00	5.50
☐ pink	9.00	18.00	10.50
☐ green	14.00	23.00	15.50
Cruet, with stopper, 3 oz.			
☐ crystal	16.00	25.00	17.50
☐ pink	29.00	38.00	30.50
☐ green	34.00	43.00	35.50
Cup			
☐ crystal	4.00	13.00	5.50
☐ pink	9.00	18.00	10.50
☐ green	14.00	23.00	15.50
Jelly Bowl, two handles, 5″			
☐ crystal	5.00	14.00	6.50
☐ pink	9.00	18.00	10.50
☐ green	11.00	20.00	12.50
Lemon Bowl, covered, 5″			
☐ crystal	9.00	18.00	10.50
☐ pink	13.00	22.00	14.50
☐ green	15.00	24.00	16.50
Luncheon Plate, 8″			
☐ crystal	4.00	13.00	5.50
☐ pink	9.00	18.00	10.50
☐ green	11.00	20.00	12.50
Marmalade Jar, 4¾″			
☐ crystal	6.00	15.00	7.50
☐ pink	11.00	20.00	12.50
☐ green	16.00	25.00	17.50
Nappy, 4½″			
☐ crystal	4.00	13.00	5.50
☐ pink	7.00	16.00	8.50
☐ green	8.00	17.00	9.50
Nappy, 8″			
☐ crystal	9.00	18.00	10.50
☐ pink	14.00	23.00	15.50
☐ green	16.00	25.00	17.50
Pitcher			
☐ crystal	30.00	40.00	32.00
☐ pink	50.00	60.00	52.00
☐ green	65.00	75.00	67.00

	Current Price Range		P/Y Average
Pitcher, ice lip			
☐ crystal	40.00	50.00	42.50
☐ pink	60.00	70.00	62.50
☐ green	75.00	85.00	72.50
Plate, 6″			
☐ crystal	2.00	9.00	3.50
☐ pink	5.00	12.00	6.50
☐ green	7.00	14.00	8.50
Platter, oval, 12″			
☐ crystal	16.00	25.00	17.50
☐ pink	29.00	38.00	30.50
☐ green	34.00	43.00	35.50
Sandwich Plate, 14″			
☐ crystal	14.00	23.00	15.50
☐ pink	24.00	33.00	25.50
☐ green	29.00	38.00	30.50
Saucer			
☐ crystal	2.00	9.00	3.50
☐ pink	4.00	11.00	5.50
☐ green	5.00	12.00	6.50
Ashtray, square, 3″			
☐ crystal	11.00	20.00	12.50
Bonbon Dish, two handles, 7″			
☐ crystal	9.00	18.00	10.50
☐ green	29.00	38.00	30.50
Bread Plate, 7″			
☐ crystal	9.00	18.00	10.50
Buffet Plate, 18″			
☐ crystal	24.00	33.00	25.50
Butter Dish, covered			
☐ crystal	55.00	75.00	60.00
Candleholder, one candle			
☐ crystal	14.00	23.00	15.50

PROVINCIAL,
A.H. Heisey.

Reminiscent of Early Thumbprint pattern glass, Provincial was produced on blank #1506 in crystal and green.

	Current Price Range		P/Y Average
Candleholder, three candles			
☐ crystal	34.00	43.00	35.50
Candy Box, covered, footed, 5½"			
☐ crystal	80.00	100.00	85.00
☐ green	220.00	240.00	225.00
Iced Tea Tumbler, footed, 12 oz.			
☐ crystal	14.00	23.00	15.50
☐ green	39.00	48.00	41.00

HOLIDAY DECORATIONS

DESCRIPTION: The category of holiday decorations encompasses all holidays and all manner of decorations. The most popular collectibles are, of course, the delightful ornamentations of Christmas.

BACKGROUND: Christmas ornaments became popular in the 1870s. Previously, Christmas trees were decorated with homemade ornaments. Today collectors especially prize early figures of Santa and figural light bulbs.

COMMENTS: The following is merely a sampling of the more unusual holiday items available on the market today. All are listed alphabetically according to their respective holidays.

TIPS: For further information, refer to the directory located in the front of this book.

CHRISTMAS

☐ **Angel,** cardboard, Dresden-type	200.00	250.00	230.00
☐ **Angel,** from the Danbury mint, 4"	15.00	45.00	31.00
☐ **Angel,** paper, die-cut, trimmed with tinsel	8.00	16.00	13.50
☐ **Angel,** wax, wings are made of spun glass	45.00	70.00	59.00
☐ **Button,** "Merry Christmas," Santa with pack in household Christmas scene, lithographed tin ..	25.00	50.00	32.50
☐ **Button,** "Santa Claus Gave This To Me," 1½"	25.00	50.00	32.50
☐ **Button,** shows Santa reading a book titled "Good Boys—Good Girls," 1¼"	25.00	50.00	32.50

	Current Price Range		P/Y Average
☐ **Cards,** comic characters, in original box, c. 1940s	30.00	35.00	32.00
☐ **Creche,** papier mache, stable made of wood, set of seventeen figures, c. 1930s	90.00	100.00	96.00
☐ **Decoration,** folding, life size Santa Claus, c. 1920s	100.00	150.00	125.00
☐ **Decoration,** Santa Claus doll, has pack, holds tree, composition, 1910	90.00	100.00	95.00
☐ **Figural Light Bulb,** Santa Claus holds tree, drum, doll and horn, c. 1920s, 5″	105.00	125.00	115.00
☐ **Lights,** bells on a string	8.00	16.00	12.00
☐ **Ornament,** baby in basket, cardboard, Dresden-type	40.00	65.00	57.00
☐ **Ornament,** ball, blown glass, decorated with wire tinsel, 3″	4.00	11.00	7.25
☐ **Ornament,** basket of flowers	9.00	11.00	9.00
☐ **Ornament,** boat, blown glass	25.00	30.00	27.50
☐ **Ornament,** bugle, blown glass	16.00	21.00	19.00
☐ **Ornament,** camel, cardboard, Dresden-type	25.00	40.00	33.50
☐ **Ornament,** candy cane	13.00	16.00	14.50
☐ **Ornament,** church, blown glass	18.00	28.00	22.00
☐ **Ornament,** clown, blown glass, inscribed "My Darling," pale pink costume with silver collar, 4″	15.00	25.00	18.50
☐ **Ornament,** coiled like a snake, blown glass, metallic silver and blue	15.00	25.00	18.50
☐ **Ornament,** cornucopia, gauze, on front a diecut Santa, loop made of tinsel	13.00	20.00	17.25
☐ **Ornament,** Dutch girl	26.00	31.00	28.00
☐ **Ornament,** ear of corn	45.00	55.00	50.00
☐ **Ornament,** elf, blown glass	22.00	34.00	28.00
☐ **Ornament,** elf sitting on a mushroom	27.00	32.00	27.75
☐ **Ornament,** enamel daisy on heart	27.00	32.00	27.50
☐ **Ornament,** gold and white ball with woodpecker	27.00	32.00	27.50
☐ **Ornament,** icicle with cotton batting	22.00	32.00	28.00
☐ **Ornament,** reindeer with cotton batting	70.00	100.00	82.50
☐ **Ornament,** Santa Claus, celluloid, white and red	8.00	13.00	10.00
☐ **Ornament,** snowman, with cotton batting	70.00	95.00	84.50
☐ **Ornament,** star, tin	15.00	25.00	21.00
☐ **Ornament,** Teddy Bear	20.00	25.00	22.00
☐ **Ornament,** Victorian Christmas stocking	65.00	70.00	66.50
☐ **Ornaments,** pine cones, blown glass, set of three	16.00	26.00	20.00
☐ **Plate,** child's ABC's, features children and snowman	55.00	62.00	57.00
☐ **Print,** Father Christmas, chromo lithograph, die punched, c. 1890s	16.50	26.50	21.00
☐ **Santa,** blow glass, three dimensional, Santa holds a pine tree, 4½″	25.00	50.00	37.50
☐ **Santa Claus Costume,** c. 1920s	30.00	40.00	36.00
☐ **Seals,** full sheets, 1934–38	6.00	11.00	8.50

	Current Price Range		P/Y Average
☐ **Snowflake,** Gorham, 1972 and 1973 issues ...	25.00	45.00	35.00
☐ **Three Light,** Santa Claus has bag over one shoulder, handpainted, 4½″	95.00	105.00	100.00

EASTER

☐ **Easter Egg Candy Containers,** red, gold and white	20.00	30.00	24.00
☐ **Easter Eggs,** blown glass..................	4.00	12.00	9.00

HALLOWEEN

☐ **Hat,** decorated, orange and black crepe paper	6.00	10.00	7.50
☐ **Jack-O-Lantern,** tin	75.00	126.00	95.00
☐ **Mask,** black cat, paper, round eyes, 11″ x 8″	12.00	20.00	17.00
☐ **Mask,** clown, paper, red, black and yellow, 8½″ x 9″	5.50	16.00	12.00
☐ **Mask,** devil, horns and pointed ears, 11″ x 8″	12.00	20.00	16.50
☐ **Mask,** Grandma, paper, glasses and bonnet, black, white, yellow, pink and blue, 11″ x 8″ ..	12.00	20.00	16.50
☐ **Mask,** pirate, paper, eyepatch and earrings, red, black and yellow, 9″ x 8″	5.50	16.00	12.50
☐ **Mask,** pumpkin, paper, dark eyes and eyebrows, 11″ x 8″	12.00	20.00	16.50
☐ **Mask,** witch, paper, red, black and yellow, 9″ x 8″..	5.50	16.00	13.00
☐ **Mask,** Wizard of Oz, made by Par-T-Mask, excellent condition	205.00	305.00	250.00
☐ **Noisemaker,** with face, lithographed tin, c. 1920s, 10″ x 4″	55.00	75.00	65.00

THANKSGIVING

☐ **Candlesticks,** cornucopia shape, ceramic, pair, 3½″	5.00	10.00	7.00
☐ **Candlesticks,** pilgrims, ceramic, 2½″, pair	6.00	10.00	8.00
☐ **Centerpiece,** turkey, Hallmark, c. 1940s	7.00	12.00	9.00
☐ **Cornucopia,** papier mache, c. 1910–20	7.00	17.00	10.00
☐ **Cornucopia,** made of wicker	5.00	10.00	7.00

VALENTINES DAY

☐ **Candlesticks,** cupids, ceramic	9.00	15.00	11.00

HULL POTTERY

DESCRIPTION: Since 1903 the Hull Pottery Co. has produced a diverse range of products. Though the firm did not work exclusively in artware, its production of art pottery rivaled that of its leading competitors. Its jugs, pitchers and vases, sometimes of heroic proportions, are typical examples of the flamboyant art pottery era. Prices for these are high. However, many Hull creations can be purchased modestly in fields other than art pottery, such as the containers it made for after-shave lotion in the 1930's. Something in the neighborhood of 11,000,000 of these were produced and retailed across the country for the Shulton Company. The diligent hobbyist will learn to inspect every item for a Hull marking, because the firm made wares of every conceivable description. Destroyed by fire in 1950, the factory was reopened in 1952 and is still active.

MARKS: The marking practices of this manufacturer were rather confusing. Most of the artware is stamped with numbers, which, suggest edition sizes: 100, 200, 300 and so on. Actually, it has nothing to do with the quantity manufactured, but relates to a coding system in which each color was referred to by an assigned number. Some Hull pottery has a paper label. The usual marking is HULL ART U.S., sometimes HULL U.S.A. When the name is spelled without the first letter capitalized, this points to a manufacturing date of 1952 or later. This practice was not instituted after that date.

RECOMMENDED READING: For more in-depth information on Hull, you may refer to *The Official Price Guide to Pottery and Porcelain* and *The Official Identification Guide to Pottery and Porcelain,* published by The House of Collectibles.

CAMELIA

	Current Price Range		P/Y Average
☐ **Basket,** shape # 107, 8″	65.00	70.00	72.50
☐ **Pitcher,** shape # 102, 8½″	30.00	40.00	35.00
☐ **Pitcher,** shape # 105, 7″	50.00	60.00	55.00
☐ **Pitcher,** shape # 128, 4¼″	25.00	30.00	27.50
☐ **Planter,** shape # 113, 7″	35.00	38.00	36.50
☐ **Swan,** shape # 102, 8½″	40.00	45.00	42.50
☐ **Vase,** shape #122, 6¼″	25.00	28.00	26.50
☐ **Vase,** shape # 123, 6½″, flattened	35.00	40.00	37.50

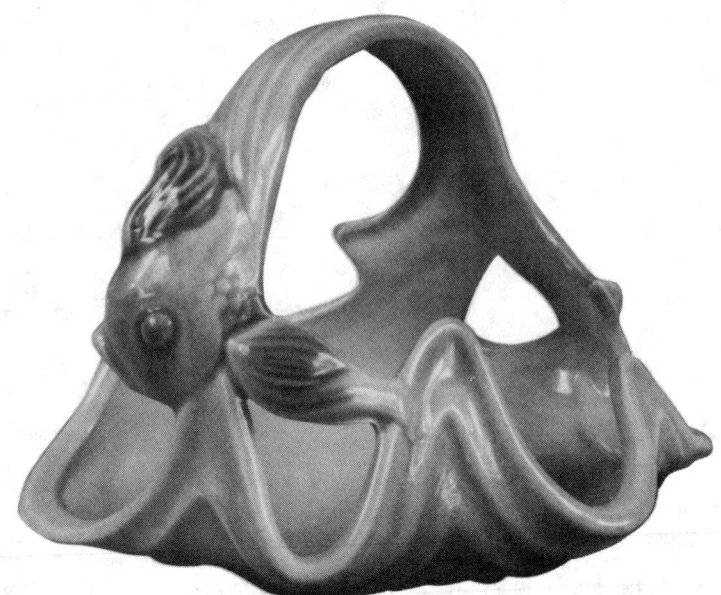

Basket, *Ebb Tide pattern, fish shape handle,*
$30.00-$35.00

	Current Price Range		P/Y Average
☐ **Vase,** shape # 126, 8″, hand shape, matte white	50.00	60.00	57.50
☐ **Vase,** shape # 127, 4½″	20.00	25.00	22.50
☐ **Vase,** shape #136, 6¼″	30.00	35.00	32.50
☐ **Vase,** shape #138, 6¼″	30.00	35.00	32.50

CONTINENTAL

	Current Price Range		P/Y Average
☐ **Basket,** shape # USA 55, orange, c. 1959 ...	20.00	30.00	25.00
☐ **Candleholder,** shaped # USA 61, 3½″, blue, c. 1959	20.00	30.00	25.00
☐ **Console Bowl,** shape # USA 51, 8″, persimmon, c. 1959	25.00	30.00	27.50
☐ **Planter,** shape # USA 68, 6″, green, c. 1959	20.00	30.00	25.00
☐ **Vase,** shape # USA 57, 14″, gourd shape, green, c. 1959	20.00	30.00	25.00
☐ **Vase,** shape # USA 58, 13¾″, persimmon, c. 1959	20.00	30.00	25.00
☐ **Vase,** shape # USA 59, 15″, green, c. 1959 ..	25.00	30.00	27.50
☐ **Vase,** shape # USA 60, 15″, blue, c. 1959 ...	30.00	40.00	35.00
☐ **Vase,** shape # 66, 6″, bud, persimmon, c. 1959	35.00	40.00	37.50

	Current Price Range		P/Y Average

HOUSE AND GARDEN

☐ **Beer Mug,** 3½", brown	3.00	5.00	4.00
☐ **Creamer,** marked Hull oven proof, brown	9.00	12.00	10.50
☐ **Creamer,** shape # 518, brown	3.50	5.50	4.50
☐ **Creamer,** shape # 518, green	9.00	11.00	10.00
☐ **Coffee Mug,** 3½", brown	3.00	6.00	4.50
☐ **Milk Pitcher,** 6¾", brown	8.00	12.00	10.00
☐ **Mug,** 3½", brown and orange	2.00	4.00	3.00
☐ **Pitcher,** 9½", brown	12.00	15.00	13.50
☐ **Shaker,** 3½", matte finish, brown	2.50	4.00	3.25
☐ **Saucer,** 6", brown	1.00	3.00	2.00
☐ **Sugar,** marked Hull oven proof, with cover, brown	8.00	11.00	10.50
☐ **Sugar,** shape # 519, green	9.00	12.00	10.50

OPEN ROSE

☐ **Basket,** shape # 501, 7½", pink and blue, c. 1949	65.00	70.00	67.50
☐ **Cornucopia,** shape # 511, 11½", blue and peach, c. 1949	65.00	70.00	67.50
☐ **Cornucopia,** shape # 522, 4½", peach, c. 1949	20.00	25.00	22.50
☐ **Cornucopia,** shape # 522, 4½", pink, c. 1949	20.00	25.00	22.50
☐ **Creamer,** shape # 111, 5", white, c. 1949 ...	25.00	30.00	27.50
☐ **Pitcher,** shape # 128, 4¾", matte, white, c. 1949	12.00	14.00	13.00
☐ **Pitcher,** shape # 505, 6½", peach, and blue, c. 1949	35.00	40.00	37.50
☐ **Planter,** shape # 514, 4", peach, c. 1949	20.00	30.00	25.00
☐ **Planter,** # 521, 7", peach and blue, c. 1949	35.00	40.00	37.50
☐ **Vase,** shape # 127, 4", pink and blue, c. 1949	20.00	25.00	22.50
☐ **Vase,** shape # 143, 8½", pink and blue, c. 1949	28.00	32.00	30.00
☐ **Vase,** shape # 502, 6½", suspended, blue and pink, c. 1949	35.00	40.00	37.50
☐ **Vase,** shape # 502, 6½", suspended, pink, c. 1949	35.00	40.00	37.50
☐ **Vase,** shape # 509, 6½", blue and cream, c. 1949	25.00	30.00	27.50
☐ **Vase,** shape # 513, 6½", pink, c. 1949	35.00	70.00	50.00
☐ **Vase,** shape # 515, 8½", pink and blue, c. 1949	40.00	45.00	42.50
☐ **Watering Can,** shape # 50T, 6½", with cover, beige, c. 1949	22.00	30.00	26.00

POPPY

☐ **Vase,** shape # 404, 4¾", peach, c. 1944	22.00	25.00	23.50
☐ **Vase,** shape # 602, 6½", c. 1944	35.00	40.00	37.50
☐ **Vase,** shape # 606, 6½", c. 1944	30.00	40.00	35.00
☐ **Vase,** shape # 606, 6½", pink and blue, c. 1944	45.00	50.00	47.50

	Current Price Range		P/Y Average
☐ **Vase**, shape # 607, 8½″, pink base, blue top, c. 1944	65.00	70.00	67.50
☐ **Vase**, shape # 607, 8½″, blue base, pink top, c. 1944	65.00	70.00	67.50
☐ **Vase**, shape # 607, 4¾″, pink and blue, c. 1944	25.00	30.00	27.50
☐ **Vase**, shape # 608, 4¾″, c. 1944	25.00	30.00	27.50
☐ **Vase**, shape # 611, 6¼″, c. 1944	30.00		40.0035.00
☐ **Vase**, shape # 611, 6½″, pink and blue, c. 1944	45.00	50.00	47.50
☐ **Vase**, shape # 612, 6½″, c. 1944	30.00	40.00	35.00
☐ **Wall Pocket**, shape # 609, 9″, pink and blue, c. 1944	45.00	50.00	47.50

RED RIDING HOOD

☐ **Bank**, 6¾″, shaped like red, c. 1938	275.00	300.00	287.50
☐ **Butter Dish**, 7″ x 5½″, with cover, c. 1939 ...	250.00	300.00	275.00
☐ **Cannister**, c. 1937	200.00	300.00	250.00
☐ **Cookie Jar**, c. 1937	80.00	90.00	85.00
☐ **Creamer**, 5″, c. 1945	45.00	50.00	47.50
☐ **Jam Jar**, c. 1940	35.00	45.00	40.00
☐ **Pitcher, 8″, c. 1937**	75.00	85.00	80.00
☐ **Salt And Pepper**, 3″, shaped like red, c. 1940	18.00	22.00	20.00
☐ **Salt And Peppers**, 5½″, shaped like red, c. 1941	30.00	40.00	35.00

SERENADE

☐ **Ashtray**, shape # S23, 13″, blue, c. 1957	20.00	22.00	21.00
☐ **Ashtray**, shape # S23, 14″, blue, c. 1957	15.00	18.00	16.50
☐ **Basket**, shape # S4, hat shape, yellow, c. 1957	25.00	30.00	27.50
☐ **Basket**, shape # 85, 6″, yellow, c. 1957	20.00	30.00	25.00
☐ **Basket**, shape # S14, blue, c. 1957	65.00	70.00	67.50
☐ **Candy Dish**, shape # S3, with cover, turquoise, c. 1957	24.00	28.00	26.00
☐ **Console Bowl**, shape # S9, 6″, blue, c. 1957	28.00	32.00	30.00
☐ **Creamer**, shaped S18, pink, c. 1957	20.00	30.00	25.00
☐ **Dish**, shape # S3, on pedestal, yellow, c. 1957	15.00	17.00	16.00
☐ **Hat Vase**, shape # S4, yellow, c. 1957	12.00	15.00	13.50
☐ **Pitcher**, shape # S2, 6½″, pink, c. 1957	10.00	14.00	11.50
☐ **Pitcher, shape # S21, pink, 1957**	40.00	45.00	42.50
☐ **Pitcher**, shape # 67, 10½″, blue, c. 1957	20.00	25.00	22.50
☐ **Pitcher**, shape # 67, 10½″, pink, c. 1957	22.00	24.00	23.00
☐ **Vase**, shape # S1, 6″, yellow, c. 1957	18.00	22.00	20.00
☐ **Vase**, shape # S1, 6½″, yellow, c. 1957	11.00	15.00	13.00
☐ **Vase**, shape # S11, rectangular, blue with gold, c. 1957	50.00	55.00	52.50

THISTLE

☐ **Vase**, shape # USA51, 6½″, blue, c. 1940 ...	35.00	36.00	35.50
☐ **Vase**, shape # USA51, 6½″, pink, c. 1940 ...	35.00	38.00	36.50

	Current Price Range		P/Y Average
☐ **Vase,** shape # USA52, 6½", yellow, c. 1940	30.00	34.00	32.00
☐ **Vase,** shape # USA53, 6½", blue, c. 1940 ...	35.00	38.00	36.50
☐ **Vase,** shape # USA53, 6½", pink, c. 1940 ...	35.00	40.00	37.50
☐ **Vase,** shape # USA52, 6½", blue, c. 1940 ...	35.00	40.00	37.50
☐ **Vase,** shape # USA54, 6½", blue, c. 1940 ...	30.00	35.00	32.50

HUMMELS

DESCRIPTION: Hummels are ceramic figurines, usually of children engaged in some activity.

ORIGIN: Berta Hummel, an artist and nun, was the creator of Hummels. In 1935, with the help of the Franz Goebel factory, the first figurine was produced.

MARKS: Although there are variations, all marks fall into one of six basic groups which include Crown Mark (CM), 1935–1949; Full Bee, 1950–1958; Stylized Bee; 1956–1963; 3-line mark, 1963–1972; Goebel/V (V-G), 1972–1979; and Goebel, 1979-present.

ADDITIONAL TIPS: Fore more information, consult *The Official Price Guide to Hummel Figurines and Plates,* published by The House of Collectibles.

ACCORDION BOY

☐ **185,** Full Bee trademark, 5–6"	224.00	234.00	105.00
☐ **185,** Stylized Bee trademark 5–6"	148.00	158.00	105.00
☐ **185,** 3-line mark trademark, 5–6"	98.00	111.00	87.00

ANGEL DUET

☐ **261,** 3-line mark trademark, 5"	325.00	355.00	340.00
☐ **261,** Goebel/V trademark, 5"	95.00	105.00	100.00
☐ **261,** Goebel trademark, 5"	88.00	98.00	93.00

APPLE TREE BOY

☐ **142/3/0,** Stylized Bee trademark, 4–4¼"	95.00	115.00	105.00
☐ **142/3/0,** Goebel trademark, 4–4¼"	65.00	172.00	68.00
☐ **142/2/1,** Goebel trademark, 6–6¾"	105.00	116.00	110.00

	Current Price Range		P/Y Average

THE ARTIST

□ **304,** 3-line trademark, 5½"	325.00	355.00	340.00
□ **304,** Goebel/V trademark, 5½"	110.00	120.00	115.00
□ **304,** Goebel trademark, 5½"	94.00	104.00	99.00

BAKER

□ **128,** CM trademark, 4¾–5"	350.00	385.00	235.00
□ **128,** Stylized Bee trademark, 4¾–5"	110.00	120.00	100.00
□ **128,** Goebel/V trademark, 4¾–5"	82.00	90.00	62.00

BE PATIENT

□ **197/2/0,** Goebel/V trademark, 4¼–4½"	95.00	105.00	100.00
□ **197/1,** Full Bee trademark, 6–6¼"	250.00	275.00	262.00
□ **197/1,** Goebel/V trademark, 6–6¼"	115.00	125.00	120.00

Baker, 128, *Full Bee Trademark, 4¾"–5",* **$200.00-$220.00**

	Current Price Range		P/Y Average

BIRD WATCHER

☐ **300,** Goebel/V trademark	130.00	145.00	137.00
☐ **300,** Goebel trademark, 5″	100.00	110.00	105.00

BOOTS

☐ **140/0,** Goebel/V trademark, 5–5½″	82.00	90.00	86.00
☐ **143/1,** Goebel/V trademark, 6½–6¾″	150.00	165.00	157.00
☐ **143,** Stylized Bee trademark, 6¾″	300.00	330.00	315.00

BOY WITH HORSE

☐ **117,** CM trademark, 3½″	125.00	135.00	130.00
☐ **117,** 3-line trademark, 3½″	30.00	35.00	32.00
☐ **117,** Goebel trademark, 3½″	26.00	30.00	28.00

BUSY STUDENT

☐ **367,** Stylized Bee trademark, 4¼″	260.00	285.00	272.00
☐ **367,** 3-line trademark, 4¼″	110.00	120.00	115.00
☐ **367,** Goebel trademark, 4¼″	72.00	80.00	76.00

CELESTIAL MUSICIAN

☐ **188,** CM trademark, 7″	750.00	800.00	775.00
☐ **188,** Stylized Bee trademark, 7″	200.00	220.00	210.00
☐ **188,** Goebel/V trademark, 7″	130.00	140.00	135.00

CHICK GIRL

☐ **57/0,** Stylized Bee trademark, 7″	125.00	135.00	130.00
☐ **57/0,** Goebel/V trademark, 3½″	75.00	85.00	80.00
☐ **57/1,** 3-line trademark, 4¼″	150.00	160.00	155.00

CINDERELLA

☐ **337,** Goebel/V trademark, 4¼″	120.00	130.00	125.00
☐ **337,** Goebel trademark, 4½″	115.00	120.00	117.00

CLOSE HARMONY

☐ **336,** 3-line trademark, 5¼–5½″	350.00	370.00	360.00
☐ **336,** Goebel/V trademark, 5¼–5½″	140.00	150.00	130.00
☐ **336,** Goebel trademark, 5¼–5½″	125.00	135.00	130.00

CONFIDENTIALLY

☐ **314,** 3-line trademark, 5¾″	600.00	630.00	615.00
☐ **314,** Goebel/V trademark, 5¾″	105.00	115.00	110.00
☐ **314,** Goebel trademark, 5¾″	94.50	105.00	100.00

FEATHERED FRIENDS

☐ **344,** 3-line trademark, 4¾″	250.00	260.00	255.00
☐ **344,** Goebel/V trademark, 4¾″	120.00	130.00	125.00

	Current Price Range		P/Y Average
☐ **344,** Goebel trademark, 4¾"	110.00	125.00	117.00

FEEDING TIME

☐ **199/0,** Goebel, trademark, 4¼–4½"	88.00	98.00	93.00
☐ **199/1,** Goebel/V trademark, 5½–5¾"	105.00	115.00	110.00
☐ **199,** trademark, 5¾"	480.00	530.00	505.00

FLOWER VENDOR

☐ **381,** 3-line trademark, 5¼"	350.00	370.00	360.00
☐ **381,** Goebel/V trademark, 5¼"	110.00	120.00	115.00
☐ **381,** Goebel trademark, 5¼"	100.00	120.00	110.00

GOOD FRIENDS

☐ **183,** Full Bee trademark, 4–4¼"	250.00	275.00	262.00
☐ **182,** 3-line trademark, 4–4¼"	120.00	125.00	122.00
☐ **182,** Goebel trademark, 4–4¼"	83.00	90.00	86.00

GOOD HUNTING

☐ **307,** Stylized Bee trademark, 5"	250.00	270.00	260.00
☐ **307,** 3-line trademark, 5"	175.00	185.00	180.00
☐ **307,** Goebel trademark, 5"	94.00	105.00	99.00

HAPPINESS

☐ **86,** CM trademark, 4½–5"	245.00	275.00	260.00
☐ **86,** Stylized Bee trademark, 4½–5"	100.00	120.00	110.00
☐ **86,** Goebel/V trademark, 4½–5"	60.00	80.00	70.00

HELLO

☐ **124/0,** Stylized Bee trademark, 5¾–6¼"	150.00	170.00	160.00
☐ **124/0,** Goebel/V trademark, 5¾–6¼"	85.00	95.00	90.00
☐ **124/1,** Goebel/V trademark, 6¾–7"	110.00	120.00	110.00

IN TUNE

☐ **414,** Goebel trademark, 3¼"	120.00	140.00	130.00

JOYFUL

☐ **53,** trademark, 3½–4¼"	295.00	330.00	312.00
☐ **53,** Stylized Bee trademark, 3½–4¼"	75.00	95.00	85.00
☐ **53,** Goebel/V trademark, 3½–4¼"	50.00	70.00	60.00

KNITTING LESSON

☐ **256,** 3-line trademark, 7½"	275.00	295.00	285.00
☐ **256,** Goebel/V trademark, 7½"	240.00	260.00	250.00
☐ **265,** Goebel trademark, 7½"	220.00	240.00	230.00

	Current Price Range		P/Y Average

LET'S SING

☐ **110/0,** Stylized Bee trademark, 3–3¼″	90.00	110.00	100.00
☐ **110/0,** Goebel trademark, 3–3¼″	55.00	65.00	60.00
☐ **110/1,** Stylized Bee trademark, 3½–4″	125.00	135.00	130.00

LOST SHEEP

☐ **68/2/0,** Stylized Bee trademark, 4¼–4½″	110.00	120.00	115.00
☐ **68/2/0,** Goebel/V trademark, 4¼–4½″	65.00	75.00	70.00
☐ **68/0,** 3-line trademark, 5½″	110.00	120.00	115.00

MADONNA WITHOUT HALO

☐ **46/0,** 3-line trademark, 10¼–10½″	75.00	85.00	80.00
☐ **46/1,** 3-line trademark, 11¼–12″	100.00	110.00	105.00
☐ **46/111,** 3-line trademark, 16¼–16¾″	200.00	220.00	210.00

MISCHIEF MAKER

☐ **342,** 3-line trademark, 5″	350.00	375.00	362.00
☐ **342,** Goebel/V trademark, 5″	120.00	140.00	130.00
☐ **342,** Goebel trademark, 5″	110.00	130.00	120.00

THE PHOTOGRAPHER

☐ **178,** CM trademark, 4¾–5¼″	495.00	545.00	525.00
☐ **178,** Stylized Bee trademark, 4¾–5¼″	195.00	227.00	212.00
☐ **178,** Goebel/V trademark, 4¾–5¾″	112.00	127.00	120.00

PUPPY LOVE

☐ **1,** CM trademark, 5–5¼″	345.00	385.00	365.00
☐ **1,** Stylized Bee trademark, 5–5¼″	145.00	175.00	160.00
☐ **1,** Goebel/V trademark, 5–5¼″	80.00	100.00	90.00

RING AROUND THE ROSIE

☐ **348,** Line trademark, 6¾″	1750.00	1950.00	1850.00
☐ **348,** Goebel/V trademark, 6¾″	1500.00	1700.00	1600.00
☐ **348,** Goebel trademark, 6¾″	1310.00	1500.00	1400.00

STREET SINGER

☐ **131,** CM trademark, 5–5½″	295.00	335.00	315.00
☐ **131,** Stylized Bee trademark, 5–5½″	115.00	124.00	125.00
☐ **131,** Goebel/V trademark, 5–5½″	73.00	87.00	80.00

SURPRISE

☐ **94/3/0,** Stylized Bee trademark, 4–4½″	120.00	140.00	95.00
☐ **94/3/0,** Goebel/V trademark, 4–4½″	70.00	90.00	80.00
☐ **94/1,** Stylized Bee trademark, 5¼–5½″	170.00	200.00	185.00

	Current Price Range		P/Y Average
TO MARKET			
☐ **49/3/0,** Stylized Bee trademark, 4″	145.00	175.00	160.00
☐ **49/3/0,** Goebel/V trademark, 4″	80.00	100.00	90.00
☐ **49/0,** Goebel/V trademark, 5–5½″	125.00	155.00	140.00
WATCHFUL ANGEL			
☐ **194,** Full Bee trademark, 6¼–6¾″	348.00	378.00	365.00
☐ **194,** 3-line trademark, 6¼–6¾″	174.00	196.00	185.00
☐ **194,** Goebel trademark, 6¼–6¾″	136.50	154.00	146.00
WEARY WANDERER			
☐ **204,** CM trademark, 5½–6″	498.00	548.00	525.00
☐ **204,** Stylized Bee trademark, 5½–6″	198.00	218.00	210.00
☐ **204,** Goebel/V trademark, 5½–6″	98.00	108.00	105.00

HUTCHINSON BOTTLES

DESCRIPTION: Hutchinson bottles are containers with a unique stopper which consists of a rubber disc held between two metallic plates attached to a spring stem.

ORIGIN: The Hutchinson bottle was produced by Charles A. Hutchinson, Chicago, in the late 1870s.

COMMENTS: Hutchinson bottles are not decorative. They were last manufactured in 1912.

ADDITIONAL TIPS: Prices on Hutchinson bottles vary more sharply by geographic locale than prices for other types of collectible bottles. For more information, consult *The Official Price Guide to Bottles, Old and New,* published by The House of Collectibles.

☐ **Anchor, The Bottling Works, Cincinnati, Ohio,** all in a circle, in center of it an anchor, in back registered bottle never sold in 2 lines, on base D, panels base 6¾″ aqua	17.00	24.00	21.00

	Current Price Range		P/Y Average

☐ **Anchor, The Bottling Works, Cincinnati, Ohio,** all in a circle, in center, anchor, aqua, 7″ ..... | 15.00 | 20.00 | 17.50

☐ **Anchor Steam Bottling Works, Shawnee, Oklahoma,** all in a circle, in center an anchor, anchor on base, clear, 6¾″ .... | 15.00 | 20.00 | 17.50

☐ **A. Anchor Steam Bottling Works, Shawnee, Oklahoma,** all in a circle, aqua, 6¾″ .... | 45.00 | 65.00 | 55.00

☐ **Andrae, G. Port Huron, Michigan,** all in a circle, blue, 6¾″ .... | 25.00 | 35.00 | 30.00

☐ **Anniston, Alabama,** Coca-cola in block letters, aqua, 7¾″ .... | 100.00 | 130.00 | 115.00

☐ **City Bottling Works, Braddock, Pennsylvania,** all in a circle, aqua, 6½″ .... | 13.00 | 18.00 | 15.00

☐ **City Brewing Co., Wapakonet, Ohio,** in moon letter, aqua, 7″ .... | 13.00 | 18.00 | 15.00

☐ **CityIce,** in center, & Bottling Works, GEORGETOWN, under Texas, all in a circle, aqua, 6½″ | 12.00 | 17.00 | 14.50

☐ **Decker Bottling, Dayton, Ohio,** on 3 panels bottle, aqua, 7″ .... | 19.00 | 25.00 | 22.00

☐ **Dels & Tibbals, Lima, Ohio,** all in a circle, aqua, 7″ .... | 12.00 | 17.00 | 15.00

☐ **Delaney & Co. Bottlers, Plattsburg, New York,** all in a circle, aqua, 7″ .... | 12.00 | 17.00 | 15.00

☐ **Delaney & Young, Eureka, California,** all in a circle, pale blue, 6½″ .... | 15.00 | 20.00 | 17.50

☐ **Erts,J. M., Poughkeepsie, New York,** all in a circle, Reg. on base E. under bottom, clear, 7″ .. | 12.50 | 17.50 | 16.00

☐ **Esposito G., Phiade,** all in a circle, aqua, 6¾″ | 12.50 | 17.50 | 14.50

☐ **Eureka California Soda Water Co., San Francisco,** in center of it, a bird, light green, 6¾″ | 16.00 | 23.00 | 20.00

☐ **Evenchick Bros. Bottling Works, Cleveland, Ohio,** in center an Eagle, all in a circle, aqua, 7″ .... | 15.00 | 20.00 | 17.50

☐ **Ewa Bottling Work,** in a horse shoe letters, under it H.T., Panels base, clear, 7½″ .... | 70.00 | 90.00 | 81.00

☐ **As Above,** also aqua.................... | 80.00 | 105.00 | 94.00

☐ **Excelsior Bottling Co., Bloomington, Illinois,** all in a circle, under bottom E.B. Co., aqua, 7″ | 14.00 | 20.00 | 17.00

☐ **Excelsior Bottling Co., Clarksburg, West Virginia,** all in a circle, aqua, 6¾″ .... | 12.00 | 17.00 | 14.50

☐ **Excelsior Bottling Works, Houston, Texas,** all in a circle, aqua, 7¼″ .... | 15.00 | 20.00 | 17.50

☐ **F.A.B.,** in a large horse shoe, in center, Galveston, TX near base, aqua, 7½″ .... | 12.00 | 17.00 | 14.50

☐ **Fargo, The Mineral Springs, Co.,** in a horse shoe in center of it Pure & Clean, Warren O., clear, 6⅝″ .... | 12.00 | 17.00 | 14.50

☐ **Felbrath, H. Peoria, Illinois,** all in a circle at base S.B. & Co., aqua, 7″ .... | 12.00 | 17.00 | 14.50

☐ **Fidelity Bottling Works,** Reg. Monroe, La. all in a circle, panels base, under bottom, Fidelity, aqua 7″ .... | 15.00 | 20.00 | 17.50

☐ **5th Ward Bottling Works, Houston, Texas,** in center 5th Ward, aqua, 7¾″ .... | 15.00 | 20.00 | 17.50

Delta Mfg. Co. Trade Mark, Delta *(in triangle), Greenville, Miss., rounded shoulders, short neck stopper, aqua, 7½",* **$12.00-$17.00**

Capital S.W. Co., *Columbus, Ohio, rounded shoulders, shortneck stopper, aqua, 7¼",* **$12.00-$17.00**

Elephant Steam Bottling Works, *Birmingham, Ala., all on front under line drawing of elephant, aqua, 6½",* **$14.00-$19.00**

	Current Price Range		P/Y Average

☐ **Finley And Son,** in ½ moon letters in center 1893, under it Bottlers, 1806 D St. N.W. Washington, D.C. in black, T.B.N.T.B.S., under bottom F, aqua, 6½″ **15.00 20.00 17.50**

☐ **Fischer And Co., Santa Fe, New Mexico,** all in a circle, aqua, 6¼″ **15.00 20.00 17.50**

☐ **Lauterback, John,** letters in a horse shoe, under it Springfield, Ill., on base N.B.B.G. Co., 46, aqua, 7⅛″ **12.00 17.00 14.50**

☐ **Lavin, M.F., Ashlley, Pennsylvania,** letters in a horse shoe, under it Reg., light blue, 6¾″ **12.00 17.00 14.50**

☐ **Lawrence, Louis, Manaimo, B.C.,** all in a circle, aqua, 7½″ **16.00 23.00 20.00**

☐ **Mahaska Bottling Works,** all in a circle, clear, 7″ **12.00 17.00 14.50**

☐ **Mahaska Bottling Works,** all in a circle, aqua, 6¾″ **12.50 17.50 15.00**

☐ **Manfield Bottle Works, Manfield, Arkansas,** all in a circle, "M" etc. under bottom, light green, 6½″ **15.00 20.00 17.00**

☐ **Manhattan, The, Bottling Co., Chicago, Illinois,** center, trade mark horse head, Registered under bottom Trademark Registered in center head, aqua, 6¾″ **16.00 23.00 20.00**

☐ **Manhattan, The, Bottling Co.,** trademark registered Chicago, Ill. all in a circle, central horse head, aqua, 6½″ **12.50 17.50 15.00**

☐ **Marietta Bottling Works, Marietta, Georgia,** all in a circle, clear, 7″ **12.00 17.00 14.50**

☐ **Marietta Bottling Works, Marietta, Oklahoma,** all in a circle, panels base, aqua, 7¼″ **72.00 96.00 83.00**

☐ **Marion Bottling & Ice Cream Co.,** made from Mo-Cola, original Coca-Cola Formula not an imitation, Ocala, Fla. all in a circle, aqua, 6¾″ ... **12.00 17.00 14.50**

☐ **Marion Bottling & Ice Cream Co.,** made from Mo-Cola original, Coca-Cola Formula, not an imitation, all in a circle, clear, 6¼″ **55.00 75.00 65.00**

☐ **Marion Bottling Works, Fairmont, West Virginia,** all in a circle, aqua, 6¾″ **12.00 17.00 14.50**

☐ **Markowitz, L., Brunswick, Georgia,** in 3 lines in back T.B.T.B.R., aqua, 7⅝″ **16.00 23.00 20.00**

☐ **Marsh, J.I., Portsmouth, O.,** all in a circle, aqua, green, 6¼″ **12.00 17.00 14.50**

☐ **Omaha Bottling Co.,** in 2½ moon lines under it Omaha Nebr. "O" under bottom, light aqua, 6½″ **16.00 23.00 20.00**

☐ **Ottenville, E. "MC",** in 2 lines, under bottom "25", cobalt, 6″ **65.00 85.00 75.00**

☐ **Ottenville, Nashville, Tennessee,** all in a circle, blue **33.00 42.00 38.00**

☐ **Ottenville, E.,** "McC" on base, "25" under bottom, cobalt, 6″ **67.50 85.00 76.00**

	Current Price Range		P/Y Average
☐ **Ottenville, Nashville, Tennessee,** blue, 6½″	67.50	85.00	76.00
☐ **Pablo & Co.,** man in a canoe and dog, T.B.N.S., etc. N.O., aqua, 7″	33.00	42.00	38.00
☐ **Pablo & Co., J.,** in center, man in canoe with dog, Trade Mark, on base T.B.N.S. Seltzer & Mineral Mfg. Nos.-475–477 & 479 St. Claude, St. N.D.	17.00	23.00	20.00

ICART PRINTS

MAKER: Louis Icart was born in the small southern French city of Toulouse. This city was the home of many famous French artists, the most famous being Henri de Toulouse-Lautrec. In this atmosphere Icart became aware of the fine arts. He began his sketching at the early age of six and by the age of fifteen was sketching designs for costumes. As a fashion artist he was quite successful.

With the outbreak of World War I, Icart went to the front as a soldier. Not completely abandoning his desire as an artist, he would sketch and etch on any available material. At the end of the war, with encouragement from friends, Icart began to make prints of the etchings he had made during this period. When they were published, they became an immediate international success.

TECHNIQUE: Icart's works demonstrate a mastery of dry point, line etching, aquatint, and their variations. Icart produced up to 500 prints each of over one thousand subjects. However, his works are scarce, because many have been lost or destroyed.

MARKS: Most Icart prints are easily identified. Most bear his hallmark which is usually located near the edge of the print. The picture below is his hallmark in actual size.

His signature is also easily identifiable, although subject to forgery and sometimes found on lithographic reproductions of his prints.

Earlier works will have his signature but may not bear the hallmark. Most will, however, bear the stamp of his gallery, an oval shape with the letters EM for l'estampe moderne. It is possible to have an original Icart with no hallmark at all, but this is rare.

The prints are usually numbered in the traditional manner of a first number representing the number of the print, then a slash mark followed by a second number. This second number represents the number of prints in the edition (excluding artist's proofs and hors commerce prints if they exist). For example 75/120 means the print is number seventy-five of an edition of one hundred and twenty prints.

Icart pulled two editions frequently, one for Europe and one for American distribution. Sometimes the number is preceded by the letter "A" for an American edition; as in the example a 75/120. All prints were not numbered.

RECOMMENDED READING: For further information, refer to *The Official Price Guide to Collector Prints* published by The House of Collectibles.

ADDITIONAL TIPS: The following is a listing of prints with current prices compiled from dealer's price lists across the country. These prices are for mint prints (perfect or near perfect), and of course, prices vary from one area of the country to another.

Coursing II *by Louis Icart*

TITLE	PRICE RANGE	
☐ After The Raid	1,550.00	2,000.00
☐ Above the Wings	1,850.00	2,250.00
☐ Amazonia	4,500.00	5,000.00
☐ Angry Buddha	800.00	
☐ Apache Dancer	750.00	
☐ Arabian Nite (1926)(Masked nude rear)	850.00	
☐ Attic Room	1,100.00	
☐ Arrival (Woman entering doorway)	700.00	
☐ Autumn Leaves	850.00	
☐ Backstage	750.00	
☐ Ballerina with roses	750.00	
☐ Bathing beauties	1,500.00	2,000.00
☐ Before the Raid	2,500.00	3,000.00

TITLE	PRICE RANGE	
☐ Bird of Prey (Woman with eagle)	1,800.00	2,000.00
☐ Bird Seller	850.00	
☐ Black Fan	750.00	
☐ Birth of Venus	2500.00	
☐ Blue Book	750.00	
☐ Blue Buddha	750.00	
☐ Blue Broken Jug	750.00	
☐ Blue Parasol	750.00	
☐ Bo Peep	750.00	
☐ Bubbles	1200.00	1,500.00
☐ Butterfly Falls	1,200.00	
☐ Carmen	750.00	
☐ Cassanova	950.00	
☐ Champs (Girls in buggy)	850.00	
☐ Charm of Montmarte	750.00	
☐ Chestnut Vendor	850.00	
☐ Clipped Wings	850.00	
☐ Cinderella	850.00	
☐ Coach, The	750.00	
☐ Conchita	1,500.00	
☐ Courage France	2,000.00	2,500.00
☐ Coursing II	850.00	1,250.00
☐ Coursing III	850.00	1,250.00
☐ Cat with paw in fishbowl	750.00	
☐ Dame Rose	750.00	
☐ Dancer (Finale)	750.00	
☐ D'Artagnan	850.00	
☐ Date Tree	750.00	
☐ Dear Friends	1,250.00	
☐ December	850.00	

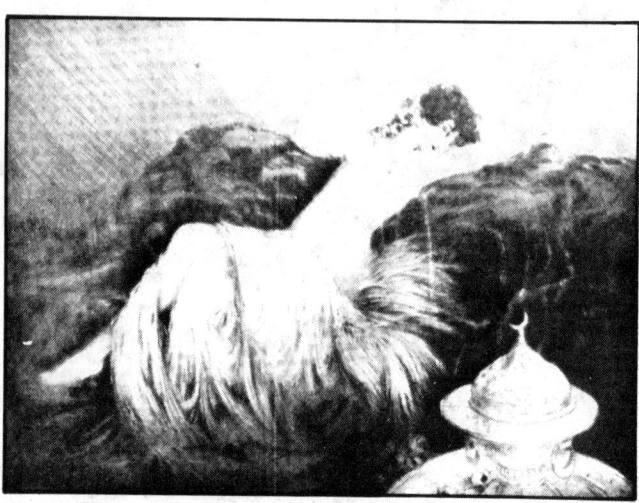

Fumee - Smoke *by Louis Icart*

TITLE	PRICE RANGE	
☐ Defense of the Homeland	1,950.00	2,250.00
☐ Descending Coach	700.00	
☐ Dollar	500.00	
☐ Don Juan	950.00	
☐ Dream Waltz	1,200.00	1,400.00
☐ Ecstacy	1,500.00	2,000.00
☐ Embrace	750.00	
☐ Eve(Nude)(Large Oval)	1,400.00	1,500.00
☐ Fair Dancer	750.00	
☐ Faust	900.00	1,000.00
☐ Favorites The	950.00	
☐ Fashion Early	850.00	
☐ Feeding Time	750.00	
☐ Finlandia	850.00	1,000.00
☐ Flower Vendor	750.00	
☐ Follies	3,000.00	4,000.00
☐ Forbidden Fruit	800.00	
☐ Fountain, The	1,000.00	1,500.00
☐ Four Dears	950.00	
☐ From From	850.00	
☐ France de Foyer	1,800.00	2,000.00
☐ French Bus	950.00	1,400.00
☐ French Doll	750.00	
☐ Gatsby 1920's	750.00	
☐ Gay Senorita	850.00	
☐ Gay Trio	1,850.00	2,000.00
☐ German Eagle	1,850.00	2,000.00
☐ Girl in Crinoline	800.00	
☐ Golden Veil	1,500.00	
☐ Goosed	700.00	
☐ Grande Eve	7,000.00	7,500.00
☐ Green Broken Jug	750.00	
☐ Guardian	900.00	
☐ Gust of Wind	1,250.00	
☐ Happy Birthday	1,200.00	1,500.00
☐ Recollections (Woman at desk)	750.00	850.00
☐ Red Alcove	750.00	
☐ Red Riding Hood	850.00	900.00
☐ Reflections Pool	1,500.00	1,800.00
☐ Repose	5,000.00	
☐ Ritz, The	1,500.00	2,000.00
☐ Salome	750.00	
☐ Sappho	750.00	
☐ Scherazade	800.00	
☐ Seashell (Nude woman on shell)	1,500.00	2,000.00
☐ Secrets or Blue Book	750.00	
☐ Singing Lesson	850.00	
☐ Sleeping Beauty	950.00	1,250.00
☐ Smoke	1,350.00–	1,500.00
☐ Speed (Woman and greyhound)	1,500.00–	1,800.00
☐ Sofa	7,500.00	
☐ Spanish Dancer	850.00	
☐ Spilled Apples	750.00	
☐ Springtime	900.00	

TITLE	PRICE RANGE	
☐ Summer Music	600.00	
☐ Swans	1,500.00	2,000.00
☐ Sweet Mystery	950.00–	1,250.00
☐ Symphony in Blue	850.00	
☐ Symphony in White	1,200.00	1,500.00
☐ Tennis	900.00	1,000.00
☐ Three of Four Seasons	900.00	
☐ The Coach (There are several versions)	750.00	
☐ Tosca	850.00	950.00
☐ Thoroughbreds (Woman with horse, Rare)	3,500.00	4,000.00
☐ Treasure Chest	600.00	
☐ Trenches	2,250.00	2,500.00
☐ Two Beauties	5,500.00	
☐ Unmasked	1,200.00	
☐ Venetian Nights	900.00	
☐ Venus (Companion to Eve)	1,500.00	2,500.00
☐ Victory in the Skies	2,250.00	
☐ Victory Wreath (Soldier holding woman holding wreath up in air, WWI)	2,500.00	2,250.00
☐ View of Montmartre	750.00	

INKWELLS AND INKSTANDS

TOPIC: Inkwells are containers for holding ink. They were used in the days before pens had their own ink supply. An inkstand is composed of two or more inkwells and a tray. Other accessories are often included.

PERIOD: Most of the collectible inkwells and inkstands date from the 1800s and early 1900s.

ORIGIN: These items have been in use for over 4,500 years.

MATERIAL: Glass is the most common material for collectible inkwells and inkstands. Other popular materials include stone, metal, wood, pottery, and porcelain.

COMMENTS: Many collectors focus on glass inkwells and inkstands. The variety and beauty of these pieces make them wonderful collectibles.

ADDITIONAL TIPS: It is rare to find an inkwell with an intact separate glass cover. These pieces are valuable. Inkstands with numerous accessories in good condition are worth the most.

INKWELLS

	Current Price Range		P/Y Average
☐ **Brass,** Art Deco, glass insert	55.00	65.00	55.00
☐ **Brass,** crab, glass insert, hinged lid	85.00	105.00	95.00
☐ **Brass,** cups on brass, tray, 6" x 9", c. 1900s.	225.00	275.00	250.00
☐ **Brass,** devil, German, c. 1900	80.00	98.00	89.00
☐ **Brass,** horse, two milk glass inserts, 5½" x 9½"	115.00	135.00	125.00
☐ **Brass,** scrollwork, porcelain insert, square	80.00	98.00	89.00
☐ **Brass,** shape of kettle, Japanese, 2½", 1800s	230.00	260.00	245.00
☐ **Brass,** Victorian, two glass inserts	80.00	100.00	90.00
☐ **Bronze,** Art Deco, glass insert, silver inlay	85.00	110.00	95.00
☐ **Bronze,** Art Nouveau, ornate sailing vessel . . .	145.00	165.00	150.00
☐ **Bronze,** Art Nouveau, woman's head with flowing hair for lid	140.00	177.50	155.00
☐ **Bronze,** clay pot of natural flowers	140.00	170.00	155.00
☐ **Cast iron,** car, two glass inserts, 5½" x 10" . .	150.00	180.00	165.00
☐ **Cast iron,** cat's head, 4", c. 1800s	225.00	275.00	250.00
☐ **Cast iron,** globe, Columbian Exposition	60.00	80.00	70.00

Inkwell, *ceramic, made in France, marked Imperial,*
$55.00-$75.00

	Current Price Range		P/Y Average
☐ **Cloisonne,** stone wall and tray, 7", c. 1900s ..	110.00	130.00	120.00
☐ **Delft,** lion, Germany, 7½" x 9"	170.00	190.00	180.00
☐ **Delft,** windmill, Germany, 3" x 3½", c. 1800s	100.00	130.00	115.00
☐ **Glass, Cut,** eagle finial on brass lid, c. 1800s	160.00	210.00	185.00
☐ **Glass, Cut,** hinged crystal lid	100.00	126.00	113.00
☐ **Glass, Cut,** sterling silver lid, 2"	100.00	130.00	115.00
☐ **Glass, Pressed,** chair with cat on cushion, 4", c. 1800s	150.00	190.00	170.00
☐ **Glass,** blue, hinged brass lid, 2½"	160.00	180.00	170.00
☐ **Glass,** sterling silver overlay	100.00	120.00	110.00
☐ **Glass,** umbrella shape, c. 1800s	225.00	275.00	250.00
☐ **Glass And Bronze,** Tiffany Favrile, mosaic, height 3", c. 1910	1300.00	1500.00	1400.00
☐ **Glass And Bronze,** Tiffany Favrile, mosaic, iridescent cover, height 4", c. 1910	1100.00	1400.00	1250.00
☐ **Marble,** blue and gray, cherubs, French, 4" ...	150.00	190.00	170.00
☐ **Metal,** enameled, camel, glass insert, c. 1900s	180.00	240.00	210.00
☐ **Metal,** enameled, camel, glass, insert, c. 1900s	180.00	240.00	210.00
☐ **Metal,** enameled, floral motif, Chinese, c. 1800s	120.00	150.00	135.00
☐ **Metal,** enameled, gold and brass trim, glass inset	60.00	80.00	70.00
☐ **Milk glass,** cat on iron base, 5"	140.00	160.00	150.00
☐ **Milk glass,** dogs on iron base, 4"	120.00	140.00	130.00
☐ **Papier Mache,** Japanned, gold figures, black lacquer, length 8½", c. 1800s	80.00	100.00	90.00
☐ **Pewter,** blue pottery insert, 9", c. 1820	160.00	180.00	170.00
☐ **Pewter,** dome rolltop, 5"	80.00	110.00	95.00
☐ **Pewter,** pear with bees on tray, Kayserzinn ...	225.00	255.00	240.00
☐ **Pewter,** round, 6½"	100.00	130.00	115.00
☐ **Porcelain,** Limoges, gilded, floral motif, hinged top	70.00	85.00	77.50
☐ **Porcelain,** boy wearing hat, French, 12", c. 1880s	150.00	170.00	160.00
☐ **Porcelain,** hinged lid, painted flowers	70.00	100.00	85.00
☐ **Porcelain,** Victorian woman, 4"	60.00	78.00	69.00
☐ **Silver-Plated,** figural, dog's head, hat is inkwell cover	55.00	65.00	60.00
☐ **Silver-Plated,** Tiffany Studios, pine needle design on white glass, 5½"	90.00	100.00	95.00
☐ **Soapstone,** carved dog on stand, Italian, 8", 1700s	120.00	140.00	130.00
☐ **Stoneware,** dark red glaze, roped edge, four pen holes, signed, 5"	135.00	155.00	145.00
☐ **Stoneware,** round, chiseled edge	50.00	68.00	59.00
☐ **Wood,** carved, Black Forest deer	135.00	155.00	145.00
☐ **Wood,** glass insert, four pen holes, 4"	60.00	80.00	70.00
☐ **Wood,** porcelain insert, 3"	50.00	68.00	59.00

INKSTANDS

☐ **Brass,** with two milk glass ink bottles, hinged lid, height 2½"	85.00	95.00	90.00

	Current Price Range		P/Y Average
□ **Bronze,** crab and shell, Tiffany Studios, 7", c. 1910	2000.00	2500.00	2250.00
□ **Bronze,** French, gilded, shell boat pulled by swan, oval stand, length 11¼", c. 1800s	400.00	500.00	450.00
□ **Iron,** horse, brass cap, 5"	45.00	65.00	55.00
□ **Silver,** Austrian, oval, pierced, panel feet, beaded rim, length 11⅜", c. 1795	900.00	1100.00	1000.00
□ **Silver,** engraved, Paul de Lamerie	5250.00	6250.00	5750.00
□ **Silver, George III,** rectangular, panel feet, cut-glass receptacles, length 11", c. 1800	1200.00	1500.00	1350.00
□ **Silver, George IV,** flowers, oblong, paw feet, c. 1822	4500.00	4800.00	4650.00
□ **Silver,** Georgian	900.00	1300.00	1100.00
□ **Wood,** J. R. Chappell, 3¾"	60.00	80.00	70.00

INSULATORS

DESCRIPTION: Insulators are the nonconducting glass figures used to attach electrical wires to poles.

ORIGIN: The first insulator was invented in 1844 for a telegraph line.

COMMENTS: Insulators became collectible after World War II. Old electrical lines with insulators were taken down during the early post war stages of urban development.

Color, age and design determine value. Threadless insulators are older, more rare and usually more valuable than threaded ones.

Clear glass is most common. Colors, including green, milk white, amber, amethyst and cobalt blue are more valuable.

ADDITIONAL TIPS: The listings are alphabetical according to manufacturer. Other information including color and size is also included.

□ **A.G.M.,** amber, 3¾" x 2¾"	12.00	24.00	18.00
□ **A.T.&T. Co.,** aqua, single skirt, 2⅛" x 3¾", c. 1900	7.00	12.00	9.00
□ **A.T.& T. Co.,** aqua, 3⅜"	7.00	12.00	9.00
□ **A.T.& T. Co.,** aqua, two-piece, 2¾" x 3⅝" ...	5.00	8.00	6.50

	Current Price Range		P/Y Average
☐ **A.T.& T. Co.,** green, single skirt, 2½″ x 3¾″ ..	5.00	12.00	7.50
☐ **Agee,** clear amethyst, 3⅝″ x 2¾″	12.00	16.00	14.00
☐ **American Insulator Co.,** aqua, double petticoat, 4⅛″ x 3⅛″	10.00	14.00	12.00
☐ **Armstrong,** amber 4″ x 3¼″	10.00	14.00	12.00
☐ **Armstrong,** No. 5, clear, double petticoat, 3⅛″ x 3¾″	5.00	8.00	6.50
☐ **A.U. Patent,** green, 4⅜″ x 2¾″	29.00	39.00	33.00
☐ **B. & O.,** aqua, 3⅞ x 3¼″	29.00	39.00	34.00
☐ **B.F.G. Co.,** aqua, 4″ x 3½″	39.00	49.00	44.00
☐ **B.G.M. Co.,** clear amethyst, 3⅜″ x 2¼″	17.00	25.00	21.00
☐ **Barclay,** aqua, double petticoat, 3″ x 2¼″	17.00	25.00	21.00
☐ **Boston Bottle Works,** aqua, 4⅛″ x 3″	44.00	54.00	48.00
☐ **Brookes, Homer,** aqua, 3¾″ x 2¾″	21.00	31.00	26.00
☐ **Brookfield,** No. 36, aqua, green, 3⅞″ x 3⅛″	12.00	18.00	15.00
☐ **Brookfield,** No. 45, aqua, green, 4⅛″ x 3⅛″	7.00	12.00	9.50
☐ **Brookfield,** No. 55, aqua, green, 4″ x 2½″ ...	12.00	18.00	14.00
☐ **Brookfield,** No. 83, aqua, green, 4″ x 3⅛″ ...	17.00	25.00	21.00
☐ **Brookfield,** dark olive green, double petticoat, 3¾″ x 4″	7.00	12.00	8.50
☐ **Brookfield,** green, double petticoat, 3 3/16″ x 3⅝″, c. 1865	7.00	12.00	8.50
☐ **B.T. Co. of Canada,** clear, amethyst, 3½″ x 2⅛″	15.00	25.00	20.00
☐ **B.T. Co. of Canada,** aqua, green, 3¼″ x 2⅜″	12.00	16.00	14.00
☐ **C. & P. Tel Col.,** aqua, green, 3½″ x 2⅜″	10.00	14.00	12.00
☐ **C.E.L.,** amethyst, 4⅛″ x 2¾″	12.00	16.00	14.00
☐ **C.E.N.,** amethyst, 3¼″ x 2½″	34.00	44.00	39.00
☐ **C.G.I.,** clear, amethyst, 3½″ x 2⅛″	21.00	27.00	24.00
☐ **Cable,** aqua, green, 4½″ x 3¼″	23.00	30.00	26.00
☐ **California,** aqua, green, 3½″ x 2⅛″	23.00	30.00	26.00
☐ **California,** clear, amethyst, 4⅜″ x 3½″	32.00	40.00	37.00
☐ **California,** clear, amethyst, 4⅛″ x 3¼″	5.00	10.00	7.50
☐ **California,** CK-162, purple, double petticoat, 3¾″ x 4″	7.00	12.00	9.50
☐ **Canadian Pacific,** blue, green, aqua, 3⅝″ x 2¾″	44.00	54.00	49.00
☐ **Canadian Pacific,** clear, amethyst, 3½″ x 2¾″	15.00	20.00	17.00
☐ **Castle,** aqua, 3⅞″ x 2½″	44.00	54.00	49.00
☐ **Chester,** aqua, 4″ x 2⅜″	48.00	58.00	53.00
☐ **Columbia,** aqua, green, 3¾″ x 4″	38.00	48.00	33.00
☐ **Derflinger, T.N.I.,** aqua, green, 4″ x 3½″	17.00	25.00	21.00
☐ **Dominion** No. 9, amber, aqua and clear, 3¾″ x 2½″	3.00	6.00	4.50
☐ **Duquesne,** aqua, green, 3⅜″ x 2⅜″	30.00	40.00	35.00
☐ **Dwight,** aqua, 4″ x 3″	30.00	40.00	35.00
☐ **E.C. & M. Co.,** green, 4″ x 2½″	23.00	30.00	26.50
☐ **Electrical Supply Co.,** aqua, green, 3⅝″ x 2⅝″	30.00	40.00	35.00
☐ **Folembray,** No. 221, olive green, 2⅝″ x 3⅜″	38.00	48.00	43.00
☐ **Gayner,** 36-190, aqua, 3¾″ x 3¼″	10.00	14.00	12.00
☐ **Gayner,** green, double petticoat, 3 3/16″ x 3⅞″	23.00	30.00	27.00

	Current Price Range		P/Y Average
☐ **H.G. Co.**, amber, double petticoat, 3¼″ x 3¾″	12.00	16.00	14.00
☐ **H.G. Co. Petticoat,** aqua, green, 3¾″ x 3¾″	5.00	8.00	6.50
☐ **H.G. Co. Petticoat,** clear, 4⅛″ x 3¼″	10.00	14.00	12.00
☐ **Hawley,** aqua, 3¼″ x 2¼″	15.00	20.00	17.50
☐ **Hemingray,** No. 2 Cable, aqua, green, 4″ x 3⅝″	22.00	30.00	26.50
☐ **Hemingray,** No. 7, aqua, green, 3½″ x 2½″ ..	3.00	6.00	4.50
☐ **Hemingray,** No. 8, aqua, green, 3⅜″ x 2⅜″ ..	14.00	18.00	16.00
☐ **Hemingray,** No. 9, aqua, single skirt, 2¼″ x 3½″	17.00	23.00	20.00
☐ **Hemingray,** No. 10, clear, single skirt, 2⅝″ x 3½″	12.00	16.00	14.00
☐ **Hemingray,** No. 16, green, single skirt, 2⅞″ x 4″	3.00	6.00	4.50
☐ **Hemingray,** No. 19, aqua, double petticoat, 3¼″ x 3″	28.00	38.00	33.00
☐ **Hemingray,** No. 25, aqua, green, 4″ x 3¼″ ...	14.00	20.00	17.00
☐ **Hemingray,** No. 95, aqua, green, 3⅝″ x 2⅞″	34.00	40.00	37.00
☐ **Hemingray Beehive,** green, double petticoat, 3⅛″ x 4⅜″	17.00	23.00	20.00
☐ **Hemingray Petticoat,** cobalt blue, 4″ x 3¼″	30.00	40.00	35.00
☐ **Hemingray Transportation,** green, 4½″ x 3¼″	23.00	30.00	26.00
☐ **Isorex,** clear, black, green, blue, 5½″ x 3½″	5.00	8.00	6.50
☐ **Jeffery Mfg. Co.,** aqua, 3⅝″ x 2¾″	30.00	40.00	35.00
☐ **Jumbo,** aqua, 7¼″ x 5¼″	21.00	27.00	25.00
☐ **Knowles Cable,** aqua, green, 4″ x 3⅝″	32.00	40.00	36.00
☐ **Fred M. Locke,** No. 14, aqua, 4⅜″ x 3⅛″	21.00	27.00	24.00
☐ **Fred M. Locke,** No. 21, aqua, green, 4″ x 4″	5.00	8.00	6.50
☐ **Lynchburg,** No. 10, aqua, green, 3⅜″ x 2¼″	7.00	14.00	10.50
☐ **Lynchburg,** No. 31, aqua, green, 3½″ x 2⅜″	7.00	12.00	9.50
☐ **Lynchburg,** No. 44, aqua, single skirt, 2¼″ x 3⅝″	10.00	14.00	12.00
☐ **Lynchburg,** No. 44, 4″ x 3⅝″	5.00	8.00	6.50
☐ **Maydwell,** No. 9, clear, aqua, 3⅝″ x 2⅛″	5.00	8.00	6.50
☐ **Maydwell,** No. 9, clear, single skirt, 2⅛″ x 3½″	5.00	8.00	6.50
☐ **Maydwell,** No. 16, amber, 3⅞″ x 2¾″	5.00	8.00	6.50
☐ **Maydwell,** No. 20, white milk glass, 3⅝″ x 3⅛″	21.00	27.00	24.00
☐ **McLaughlin,** No. 9, green, single skirt, 2¼″ x 3⅝″	12.00	16.00	14.00
☐ **McLaughlin,** No. 16, amber, aqua, green, 3⅝″ x 2⅝″	5.00	10.00	7.50
☐ **McLaughlin,** No. 19, aqua, 3¾″ x 3¼″	3.00	6.00	4.50
☐ **McLaughlin,** No. 42, aqua, 4″ x 3⅝″	5.00	10.00	7.50
☐ **McLaughlin,** No. 62, aqua, 3⅝″ x 3⅝″	7.00	11.00	9.00
☐ **Mershon,** aqua, 5″ x 5½″	31.00	38.00	34.50
☐ **Monogram H.I. Co.,** aqua, 4½″ x 3⅛″	21.00	27.00	24.00
☐ **Mulford & Biddle,** aqua, 3¼″ x 2⅝″	34.00	40.00	37.00
☐ **N.E.G.M. Co.,** aqua, green, 3½″ x 2⅛″	14.00	18.00	16.00
☐ **N.E.G.M. Co.,** aqua, 3½″ x 3¼″	17.00	23.00	20.00
☐ **N.E.T. & T. Co.,** aqua, green, 3⅝″ x 2⅜″	5.00	8.00	6.50
☐ **N.E.T. & T. Co.,** blue, 3½″ x 3″	12.00	16.00	14.00

	Current Price Range		P/Y Average
☐ **Noleak,** aqua, green, 4″ x 4″	31.00	36.00	33.00
☐ **O.V.G. Co.,** aqua, 3½″ x 2¼″	7.00	12.00	10.00
☐ **O.V.G. Co.,** aqua, green, 3½″ x 2¼″	12.00	16.00	14.00
☐ **Pettingel Anderson Co.,** aqua, 4″ x 2¾″	17.00	23.00	20.00
☐ **Pony,** blue, 3⅛″ x 2⅜″	21.00	27.00	24.00
☐ **Postal,** aqua, green, 4⅛″ x 3½″	15.00	18.00	16.50
☐ **Pyrex,** carnival glass, 3⅛″ x 3¾″	17.00	23.00	20.00
☐ **Pyrex,** carnival glass, 3″ x 3¾″	12.00	16.00	14.00
☐ **Pyrex,** double threads, carnival glass, 2⅝″ x 4¼″	14.00	18.00	16.00
☐ **S.B.T. & T. Co.,** aqua, green, 3½″ x 2¼″	14.00	18.00	16.00
☐ **Santa Ana,** aqua, green, 4¼″ x 4¾″	28.00	35.00	31.50
☐ **Standard,** clear, amethyst, 3⅝″ x 2¾″	12.00	16.00	14.00
☐ **Star,** aqua, single skirt, pony, 2⅜″ x 3½″	7.00	10.00	8.50
☐ **Sterling,** aqua, 3¼″ x 2¼″	14.00	18.00	16.00
☐ **T.C.R.,** aqua, 4″ x 3¾″	12.00	16.00	14.00
☐ **T.H.E. Co.,** aqua, 4″ x 3⅛″	29.00	35.00	32.00
☐ **Thomas,** brown pottery, 2½″ x 1⅛″	5.00	10.00	7.50
☐ **Transportation,** No. 2, aqua, 4¼″ x 2⅞″	21.00	27.00	24.00
☐ **U.S. Tel. Co.,** aqua, 3¾″ x 2⅜″	14.00	18.00	16.00
☐ **V.M.R. Napoli,** aqua, green, 4″ x 2¾″	12.00	16.00	14.00
☐ **W.F.G. Co.,** clear, amethyst, 3½″ x 2⅛″	14.00	18.00	16.00
☐ **W.G.M. Co.,** clear, amethyst, 3½″ x 2¼″	23.00	30.00	26.00
☐ **W.G.M. Co.,** clear, amethyst, 3⅞″ x 3⅛″	17.00	23.00	20.00
☐ **W.V.,** No. 5, aqua, 4¼″ x 2¾″	17.00	23.00	20.00
☐ **Westinghouse,** aqua, green, 3⅛″ x 2⅜″	27.00	33.00	30.00
☐ **Whitall Tatum,** amber, 3⅞″ x 3¼″	12.00	16.00	14.00
☐ **Whitall Tatum,** 512-A, amber, red, 3½″ x 3⅝″	5.00	10.00	7.50

IRONS

TYPES: Various types of collectible irons include: the charcoal iron; the box iron which featured a heated metal slug placed inside the hollow iron; and the sadiron, a solid iron that was heated on the hearth or stove. In 1871 Mary Potts invented a detachable handle for the sadiron. The Potts iron led to self-heating irons fueled with gasoline or cooking gas. These were dangerous and unsatisfactory. The electric iron was patented in 1882.

ORIGIN: Irons were used in Asia for centuries before their 17th century Western introduction.

COMMENTS: Collectible irons are still reasonably priced. Collectors should seek odd shaped irons.

ADDITIONAL TIP: The listings are alphabetical according to type of iron.

	Current Price Range		P/Y Average
☐ **Alcohol Iron,** wooden handle, c. 1880	65.00	80.00	70.00
☐ **Box Iron,** heated slug, c. 1890	45.00	65.00	53.00
☐ **Box Iron,** English, heated slugs, c. 1800	82.00	125.00	90.00
☐ **Box Iron,** solid brass, punch decoration on top surface, height 5″ x 4½″	105.00	117.00	110.00
☐ **Charcoal Iron,** brass fittings, chimney vent ...	70.00	90.00	75.00
☐ **Charcoal Iron,** twisted handle, chimney vent ..	75.00	90.00	78.00
☐ **Charcoal Iron,** wooden handle	42.00	50.00	45.00
☐ **Charcoal Iron,** wooden handle, c. 1890	45.00	60.00	48.00
☐ **Charcoal Iron,** wooden iron, with trivet	65.00	80.00	69.00
☐ **Flat Iron,** all iron	6.00	7.50	6.50
☐ **Flat Iron,** bail handle	8.00	12.00	10.00
☐ **Flat Iron,** charcoal, chimney vent, c. 1860	29.00	40.00	33.00
☐ **Flat Iron,** hollow handle	29.00	40.00	33.00
☐ **Flat Iron,** metal handle, c. 1860	29.00	40.00	35.00
☐ **Flat Iron,** no handle, asbestos	4.00	6.00	5.00
☐ **Flat Iron,** no handle, Blass and Drake, Newark, New Jersey, height 6″	4.00	6.00	5.00
☐ **Flat Iron,** red, small, c. 1877	45.00	50.00	47.00
☐ **Flat Iron,** removable handle, c. 1870	29.00	38.00	32.00
☐ **Flat Iron,** rope handle	28.00	35.00	30.00
☐ **Flat Iron,** stone body, metal handle, c. 1850 ..	45.00	60.00	50.00
☐ **Flat Iron,** wooden handle, child's, c. 1860	29.00	40.00	33.00
☐ **Flat Iron,** wooden handle, large	34.00	45.00	36.00
☐ **Fluting Iron,** brass rollers, with black enamel and red and gold stripes, two slugs, height 9″	85.00	95.00	89.00
☐ **Fluting Iron,** double, with holder	65.00	80.00	68.00
☐ **Fluting Iron,** Geneva, c. 1870s	50.00	65.00	57.00
☐ **Gasoline Iron,** Coleman	28.00	38.00	30.00
☐ **Gasoline Iron,** wooden handle, c. 1910	55.00	70.00	58.00
☐ **G.E. Electric Iron,** c. 1905	39.00	50.00	42.00
☐ **G.E. Electric Iron,** c. 1920	34.00	45.00	37.00
☐ **Iron,** for a child, glass base, wooden handle ..	4.75	6.25	5.50
☐ **Laundry Stove,** cast iron, double burner	170.00	220.00	190.00
☐ **Laundry Stove,** cast iron, single burner	120.00	180.00	135.00
☐ **Laundry Stove,** fancy cast iron, c. 1895	500.00	600.00	520.00
☐ **Nickel Plated Iron**	24.00	37.00	27.00
☐ **Polishing Iron,** oval shaped, c. 1845	48.00	58.00	52.00
☐ **Sadiron,** alcohol iron, nickel plated, black wooden handle, Foote Manufacturing Co., Dayton, Ohio................................	47.00	55.00	50.00
☐ **Sadiron,** for child, removable wooden handle, 2″ x 4″	40.00	52.00	45.00
☐ **Sadiron,** waffle pattern on bottom, "Genoa" ..	30.00	37.00	33.00
☐ **Tailor's Iron**	34.00	45.00	37.00
☐ **Travel Iron,** asbestos	29.00	40.00	33.00

IRONWARE

DESCRIPTION: Nineteenth century kitchenware and other household items were often made of iron because of its durability.

COMMENTS: Ironware usually can be found for fairly low prices. Marked pieces are of greater value and importance. Dates on ironware do not always stand for the year made: some dates stand for the year the patent was issued.

Oiling or polishing old ironware decreases its value.

ADDITIONAL TIPS: The listings are alphabetical according to item.

For further information, refer to *The Official Price Guide to Kitchen Collectibles,* published by The House of Collectibles.

	Current Price Range		P/Y Average
IRONWARE			
☐ **Anvil,** regulation type, antique	1400.00	1800.00	1650.00
☐ **Apple Parer,** with clamp, cast iron, Simplex Company	27.50	43.00	32.50
☐ **Apple Parer,** Double Quick model	27.50	43.00	32.50
☐ **Apple Parer,** Sinclair & Scott Company	27.50	43.00	32.50
☐ **Apple Parer,** cast iron, c. 1870	27.50	43.00	32.50
☐ **Apple Parer,** cast iron, c. 1900	27.50	43.00	32.50
☐ **Apple Parer,** cast iron, Apple Parer Company, c. 1880	19.00	62.50	54.00
☐ **Apple Parer,** pares, cores, and slices	19.00	27.00	22.00
☐ **Apple Parer,** Hudson Parer Company	26.00	32.00	27.00
☐ **Apple Parer,** cast iron, F.A. Walker, c. 1870s	19.00	57.50	45.00
☐ **Apple Parer,** Rocking Table Company	19.00	52.50	32.00
☐ **Apple Parer,** White Mountain Company	19.00	50.00	39.00
☐ **Apple Peeler**	40.00	49.00	42.00
☐ **Apple Segmenter,** bolt type, cast iron, patented 1869	25.00	37.50	29.00
☐ **Asparagus Buncher,** cast iron, on walnut board	140.00	175.00	156.00

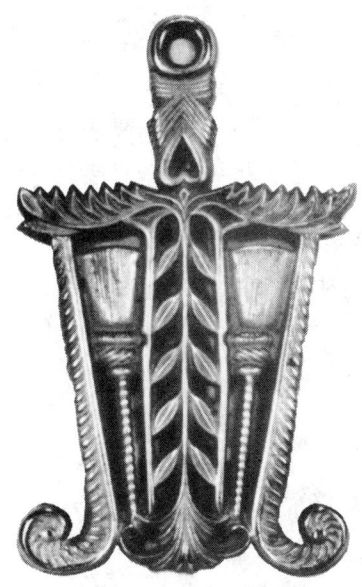

Trivet, *nickel plated iron, c. 1900,*
$15.00-$20.00
Photo courtesy of Lou McCulloch,
Highland Heights, OH, 44133

	Current Price Range		P/Y Average
☐ **Balance Scales,** forged, hook on top, 13″	20.00	40.00	30.00
☐ **Basket Spit,** spun iron basket with andiron hooks to hold meat	80.00	125.00	105.00
☐ **Basket,** fireplace grate, cast iron, c. 1900, 11″ long	120.00	180.00	126.00
☐ **Bathtub,** hammered tin alloy, c. 1820	500.00	625.00	575.00
☐ **Bedwarmer,** with wooden handle, 36″	60.00	80.00	64.00
☐ **Bird Spit,** wrought iron, legged with hooks and drip pan	90.00	130.00	110.00
☐ **Bookends,** bronzed, profile of Abraham Lincoln, 4¾″	13.00	17.00	15.50
☐ **Bowl,** cast iron, diameter 9″, depth 3″	50.00	60.00	53.00
☐ **Bowl,** cast iron, flared sides, flat bottom, round spove, early 19th century, top 12″, height 3½″	160.00	185.00	167.00
☐ **Broiler,** "Reliable", cast iron, c. 1893	40.00	60.00	42.00
☐ **Broiler,** wrought iron, for fireplace, legged, round, 14″ diameter	58.00	75.00	68.00
☐ **Broiler,** wrought iron, rectangular	40.00	55.00	49.00
☐ **Butcher Flesh Fork,** wrought iron, length 15″	35.50	41.00	36.50
☐ **Butcher Set,** strainer and ladle, wrought iron, length 20″	60.00	70.00	63.00
☐ **Butter Tester,** iron pin, 17½″ long	10.00	20.00	12.50
☐ **Cabbage Cutter,** cast iron and wood, sided ...	45.00	55.00	48.00
☐ **Cabbage Cutter,** cast iron blades on wooden board, 33″ long	30.00	45.00	37.00
☐ **Candle Dip,** early 19th century	200.00	250.00	210.00
☐ **Candleholder,** cast iron, 7″ high	70.00	95.00	78.00

	Current Price Range		P/Y Average
☐ **Candleholder,** cast iron, c. 1800, 7¾" high ...	90.00	115.00	99.00
☐ **Candleholder,** forged iron, English, c. 1800, 11" high	250.00	400.00	315.00
☐ **Candleholder,** forged iron, wall type, c. 1600	90.00	115.00	101.00
☐ **Candleholder,** forged iron, c. 1700	70.00	85.00	78.00
☐ **Candleholder,** forged iron with spike, wall type, c. 1600	175.00	225.00	199.00
☐ **Meat Chopper,** cast iron, tin, painted wood, c. 1865	17.00	16.00	12.00
☐ **Meat Chopper,** cast iron, with crank handle, clamps, c. 1900	11.00	16.00	13.00
☐ **Meat Chopper,** cast iron, with crank handle, clamp, Universal Company, c. 1900	13.00	16.00	15.00
☐ **Meat Chopper,** twin blades, Enterprise Company, c. 1900	12.00	16.00	15.00
☐ **Meat Hook,** tinned iron, c. 1890	12.00	16.00	13.50
☐ **Meat Slicer,** crank handle, clamp-on table type, circular blade	9.00	13.50	11.25
☐ **Meat Tenderizer,** cast iron, c. 1892	10.00	25.00	13.00
☐ **Pan,** iron and tin alloy, rolled sheet for soap-making, 10" diameter	50.00	60.00	53.00
☐ **Paring Knife,** steel blade, wood handle, Dunlap Company	3.00	5.75	3.50
☐ **Pastry Blender,** wood nickeled iron, 1915 to 1940	8.75	16.00	9.75
☐ **Pastry Jigger,** cast iron, octagonal shape, 5½" diameter, c. 1700	40.00	45.00	42.00
☐ **Pastry Marker,** late 19th century	9.00	16.00	11.75
☐ **Pea Huller**	37.50	37.50	20.00
☐ **Pea Sheller,** clamp on type	16.00	26.00	17.00
☐ **Peel,** cast iron, hook end, shovel head, open handle, hand cast, antique	45.00	60.00	53.00
☐ **Peel,** wrought iron, hook end, shovel head for use in fireplace	50.00	65.00	58.00
☐ **Peel,** wrought iron, knob end, shovel head, open handle grip	60.00	75.00	68.00
☐ **Pot Hook,** wrought iron hook with wood handle	11.00	25.75	15.00
☐ **Raisin Seeder,** cast iron	16.00	30.00	17.00
☐ **Raisin and Grape Seeder,** clamp on, Enterprise Company	20.00	35.00	26.00
☐ **Raisin and Grape Seeder,** c. 1890	28.00	38.00	29.00
☐ **Raisin and Grape Seeder,** inscribed "Wet your Raisins", c. 1895	28.00	38.00	29.00
☐ **Rug Beater,** wire pattern with wood handles, c. 1920	11.00	25.50	14.00
☐ **Rug Beater,** wire, including handle, spade shape, c. 1850	12.00	26.00	15.00
☐ **Rushlight,** iron, 10" high, c. 1850	120.00	175.00	131.00
☐ **Rushlight,** iron, 12" high, c. 1750	540.00	750.00	580.00
☐ **Rushlight,** iron, 8½" high	90.00	125.00	105.00
☐ **Rushlight,** iron, snake head, 11" long, c. 1750	275.00	400.00	315.00
☐ **Rushlight,** oak pedestal, 10" high, c. 1750	275.00	400.00	315.00
☐ **Rushlight,** yew pedestal, 8½" high, c. 1850 ..	275.00	400.00	315.00

	Current Price Range		P/Y Average
☐ **Sausage Stuffer,** cast and sheet iron, gears ..	30.00	45.00	37.00
☐ **Sausage Stuffer**	38.00	50.00	42.00
☐ **Saratoga Potato Chipper,** clamp on type, crank handle	18.00	23.50	21.00
☐ **Sugar Cutter,** nippers, shears, for snipping pointed or square shaped, solid mounds of sugar	78.00	100.00	79.00
☐ **Sugar Devil,** iron, for use with brown sugar, cut off hardened lumps	75.00	95.00	84.00
☐ **Sugar Nips,** late 19th century	19.00	30.00	21.00
☐ **Tailors Iron,** European origin, mid 19th century, 9″ long	15.00	27.00	18.00
☐ **Tallow Dipper,** wrought, 18th century, 25″ long	380.00	412.00	388.00
☐ **Tea Kettle,** ironstone, English, c. 1870	42.00	53.00	47.00
☐ **Tenderer Steak,** iron, wood, c. 1870	9.00	13.00	9.50
☐ **Toaster**	155.00	180.00	181.00
☐ **Toaster,** two slices, supported by three legs, comes with handle, 17″ long	135.00	150.00	139.00
☐ **Trivet,** lacy cast iron, six pointed and circular motif, mid 19th century	78.00	95.00	79.99
☐ **Trivet,** leaf and scroll	95.00	115.00	99.00
☐ **Trivet,** letters...........................	20.00	30.00	21.00
☐ **Trivet,** lyre	35.00	43.00	37.00
☐ **Trivet,** Maltese emblem	32.00	40.00	35.00
☐ **Trivet,** Masonic emblem	42.00	55.00	47.00
☐ **Trivet,** moose	13.00	20.00	15.00

JEWELRY

PERIOD: Some of the major style periods for jewelry include 18th century Georgian, 19th century Victorian, Art Nouveau and Art Deco.

COMMENTS: Usually the value of a piece of jewelry depends on the quality of material used. Designer status also accounts for some high prices. To judge material quality, the collector should use a loupe, an eyepiece magnifier. A 10-power loupe is recommended. A touchstone should be used to assess gold content in jewelry.

ADDITIONAL TIPS: The following listings are alphabetical according to item of jewelry.

For further information, refer to *The Official Price Guide to Antique Jewelry,* published by The House of Collectibles.

Bracelet, *snake and leaf motif, three garnets in snake head, seed pearls and turquoise leaf, 9K gold, English, c. 19th Century,* **$1550.00-$1750.00**

BRACELETS—BANGLE GOLD

	Current Price Range		P/Y Average
☐ **Pair Bangles,** emerald-cut black onyx in center with a row of genuine Oriental seed pearls on either side, c. late 19th century	3500.00	3750.00	3550.00
☐ **Pair Narrow Bangles,** pave Oriental seed pearls in top half of each bracelet, gold, c. 1860	1550.00	1750.00	1600.00
☐ **Plaited Bangle,** Etruscan granulation ends, gold, c. 1870	1450.00	1550.00	1500.00
☐ **Ribbon Motif,** pave turquoise, seed pearl borders, silver, c. 1820	2650.00	3100.00	2800.00
☐ **Rose Diamonds,** in silver, blue enamel oval center with seed pearls, seed pearls collet-set around center of bracelet, gold, c. 1850	2200.00	2750.00	2300.00
☐ **Rose Diamonds,** gold, c. 1880	800.00	1050.00	850.00
☐ **Sandwich Bangle,** inner gold band, woven hair, outer gold band cutout oval designs on front of bangle, 9K gold, English, c. late 19th century	450.00	500.00	467.00
☐ **Wide Bangle,** opaque black enamel, 14K gold, American, Victorian	600.00	700.00	645.00
☐ **Woven Bangle,** with slide and end with cabochon opals, old mine diamonds, black enamel leaf motif, gold, c. 1850	2550.00	2850.00	2700.00

BROOCHES—ANIMAL AND BUG

☐ **Swallow,** 70 old mine diamonds, ruby in head, silver, c. 1850	1750.00	2000.00	1800.00
☐ **Swallow,** rose diamonds in feathers, rubies in eyes, blue, black and white enamel, gold, silver, c. 1860	2750.00	3200.00	2875.00
☐ **Swallows,** rose diamond body and wings in silver topped gold, gold safety pin, c. 1830	950.00	1050.00	965.00
☐ **Turtle,** emerald eyes, cabochon opal body surrounded with diamonds, gold, c. 1935	2000.00	2200.00	2100.00
☐ **Turtle,** six rose diamonds, 36 demantoid garnets, gold, c. early 20th century	550.00	650.00	600.00
☐ **Turtle,** round diamonds, cushion-cut sapphires, silver topped gold, c. 1860	1100.00	1650.00	1300.00
☐ **Winged Lion,** Etruscan granulation, Gothic revival, gold, c. 1860-80	1450.00	1550.00	1465.00

Winged Lion, *Etruscan granulation, Gothic revival, gold, c. 1860–80.* **$1450.00-$1550.00**

Geometric engraved motif, *gold plate on sterling silver, American, c. 1894–1895,* **$45.00-$55.00**

	Current Price Range		P/Y Average

BABY PIN

☐ **"BABY"** raised letter motif, gold front, American, c. 1894-1895	40.00	50.00	44.00
☐ **"BABY"** raised letter motif, gold front, American, c. 1894-1895	45.00	55.00	50.00
☐ **Cutout Motif,** engraved, gold front, American, c. 1894-1895	45.00	50.00	43.00
☐ **Same as above but gold filled**	25.00	30.00	29.50
☐ **"DARLING"** cutout letter motif, gold front, American, c. 1894-1895	45.00	55.00	49.00
☐ **Flower Motif,** engraved, one round garnet, one seed pearl, gold front, American, c. 1894-1895	55.00	60.00	57.50
☐ **Flower Motif,** blue enamel, 14K gold, American, c. 1894-1895	60.00	65.00	60.00
☐ **Flower Motif,** enamel, 14K gold, American, c. 1894-1895	60.00	75.00	64.00
☐ **Flower Motif,** engraved, 14K gold, American, c. 1894-1895	60.00	65.00	65.00
☐ **Same as above but gold filled**	30.00	35.00	32.00
☐ **Flower Motif,** enamel, sterling silver, American, c. 1896	45.00	55.00	50.00

EARRINGS—DIAMOND

☐ **Leaf and Flower Dangle Motif,** rose diamonds, silver, c. 1820-1840	1550.00	1750.00	1600.00

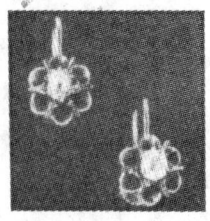

Single Stone Motif, *old mine diamonds, 14K gold, c. 1900,* **$350.00-$400.00**

Fleur-De-Lis Motif, *natural pearls, old mine and rose diamonds, gold, platinum, c. 19th century,* **$10,500.00-$12,600.00**

	Current Price Range		P/Y Average
☐ **Leaf and Flower Motif,** two pear-shape rose diamonds, round rose diamonds, silver back gold, c. 1790	4200.00	4600.00	4200.00
☐ **Star Motif,** blue enamel, rose diamonds, gold, c. 1850	1200.00	1450.00	1200.00
☐ **Straight Line Dangle Motif,** rose diamonds, gold, c. 1800	1550.00	1750.00	1620.00
☐ **Wreath Motif,** two old mine diamonds, rose diamonds, silver, c. 18th century	1550.00	1750.00	1600.00

EARRINGS—GEMSTONE

	Current Price Range		P/Y Average
☐ **Knot Motif,** almandine garnets, 15K gold, c. 1855–60	400.00	450.00	420.00
☐ **Cluster Motif,** garnets, gold, c. 1860	225.00	275.00	230.00
☐ **Cluster Motif,** garnets, gold, American, c. 1895	250.00	275.00	260.00
☐ **Cluster Motif,** cabochon turquoise, seed pearl center, enamel, gold, contemporary posts, c. 1860	250.00	300.00	270.00
☐ **Cube Motif,** engraved, onyx, gold, American, c. 1895	70.00	95.00	77.00
☐ **Cube Motif,** gold, American, c. 1895	65.00	75.00	70.00
☐ **Emeralds:** step-cut, gold, c. 1790	2400.00	2650.00	2400.00
☐ **Filigree Motif,** round moonstone centers, round sapphires, white gold, maker: Tiffany & Co.	550.00	600.00	550.00
☐ **Flower Motif,** onyx, gold, American, c. 1895	100.00	125.00	110.00
☐ **Flower Motif,** onyx, gold, American, c. 1895	100.00	125.00	110.00
☐ **Flower Motif,** onyx, gold, American, c. 1895	100.00	125.00	110.00
☐ **Flower Motif,** pearl, gold, American, c. 1895	200.00	225.00	200.00

	Current Price Range		P/Y Average
☐ **Flower Motif,** rubies, gold, American, c. 1895	150.00	175.00	160.00
☐ **Flower Motif,** pearl, gold, American, c. 1895 ..	135.00	160.00	142.50
☐ **Flower Motif,** pearls, gold, American, c. 1895	100.00	125.00	110.00
☐ **Flower Motif,** rubies, gold, American, c. 1895	135.00	160.00	140.00
☐ **Flower Motif,** coral, gold, American, c. 1895 ..	140.00	170.00	140.00
☐ **Flower Motif,** garnets, gold, c. 1850–60	450.00	500.00	465.00

JIM BEAM BOTTLES

DESCRIPTION: Jim Beam Bottles refer to the figural liquor containers first issued in the 1950s by the James B. Beam Distilling Company, Kentucky.

ORIGIN: The company was founded in 1778 by Jacob Beam. The firm now bears the name of Jacob Beam's grandson, Colonel James B. Beam.

TYPES: The company produces a variety of themes including The Executive Series, Regal China Series, and Political Figures Series.

COMMENTS: Early Beam bottles made before the figural series are also collectible. In 1953, the company produced its first figural decanter. When the decanters sold well, Beam began producing decorative bottles on a large scale.

ADDITIONAL TIPS: For more information, consult *The Official Price Guide to Bottles, Old and New,* published by The House of Collectibles.

☐ **The Big Apple,** 1979, apple shaped bottle with embossed Statue of Liberty on the front with New York City in the background and the lettering "The Big Apple" over the top	10.00	15.00	12.50
☐ **Bing Crosby 36th,** 1976, same as the Floro de Oro except for the medallion below the neck. Urn-shaped bottle with pastel wide band and flowers around the middle. Remainder of bottle is shiny gold with fluting and designs	28.00	36.00	32.00
☐ **Ernie's Flower Cart,** 1976, replica of an old-fashioned flower cart used in San Francisco. Wooden cart with movable wheels. In honor of Ernie's Wines and Liquors of Northern California	22.00	30.00	25.50

"Boxer," *Jim Beam 1964 Presidential Decanter,* **$27.00-$30.00**

	Current Price Range		P/Y Average
☐ **Falstaff,** 1979, replica of Sir John Falstaff with blue and yellow outfit holding a gold goblet. Second in the Australlian Opera Series. Music box which plays "Va, vecchio, John." Limited edition of 1000 bottles.	250.00	350.00	300.00
☐ **Fantasia Bottle,** c. 1971, this tall, delicately handcrafted Regal China decanter is embellished with 22 karat gold and comes packaged in a handsome midnight blue and gold presentation case lined with red velvet. 16¼″	12.00	18.00	15.00
☐ **Fiesta Bowl,** c. 1973, the second bottle created for the Fiesta Bowl. This bottle is made of genuine Regal China, featuring a football player on the front side. 13¼″	10.00	16.00	13.00
☐ **Figaro,** c. 1977, figurine of the character Figaro from the opera "Barber of Seville. Spanish costume in beige, rose, and yellow. Holds a brown guitar on the ground in front of him. Music box plays an aria from the opera	300.00	350.00	325.00
☐ **Hawaiian Open,** c. 1973, the second bottle created in honor of the United Hawaiian Open Golf Classic. Of genuine Regal China designed in the shape of a golf ball featuring a pineapple and airplane on front, 11″	6.00	10.00	8.00
☐ **Hawaiian Open,** c. 1974, genuine Regal China bottle commemorating the famous 1974 Hawaiian Open Golf Classic, 15″	6.00	10.00	8.00

	Current Price Range		P/Y Average

Hawaii Paradise, 1978, commemoraties the 200th Anniversary of the landing of Captain Cook. Embossed scene of a Hawaiian resort framed by a pink garland of flowers. Black stopper, 8¾" 20.00 28.00 24.00

Hemisfair, c. 1968. the Lone Star of Texas crowns the tall gray and blue "TOWER OF THE AMERICAS." "THE LONE STAR STATE" is lettered in gold over a rustic Texas scene. The half map of Texas has "HEMISFAIR 68—SAN ANTONIO." Regal China, 13" 6.00 10.00 8.00

Hoffman, c. 1969, the bottle is in the shape of "HARRY HOFFMAN LIQUOR STORE" with the Rocky Mountains in the background. Beam bottles, and "SKI COUNTRY—USA" are in the windows. Reverse: embossed mountain & ski slopes with skier. Regal China, 9" 4.00 8.00 6.00

Short Timer, 1975, brown army shoes with army helmet sitting on top. Produced for all who have served in the armed forces, 8" 28.00 34.00 31.00

Shriners, 1975, embossed camel on front of bottle in blue, green, and brown with bright red blanket flowing from the camel's saddle. A gold scimitar and star centered with a fake ruby is on the back. 10½" 15.00 20.00 17.50

Shriners' Pyramid, 1975, white and brown pyramid with embossed emblems on the sides, 5" 12.00 16.00 14.00

Tall Dancing Scot, c. 1964, a small Scotsman encased in a glass bubble in the base dances to the music of the base. A tall pylon shaped glass bottle with a tall stopper. No dates on these bottles. Glass, 17" 12.00 18.00 15.00

Tavern Scene, c. 1959, two "beer stein" tavern scenes are embossed on sides, framed in wide gold band on this round decanter. Regal China, 11½" 65.00 75.00 70.00

Telephone, 1975, replica of a 1907 phone of the Magneto Wallset type which was used from 1890 until the 1930s, 9½" 55.00 65.00 60.00

Ten-Pin, 1980, designed as a bowling pin with two red bands around the shoulder and the neck. Remainder of the pin is white, screw lid, 12" .. 4.00 8.00 6.00

Thailand, c. 1969, embossed elephant in the jungle and "THAILAND—A NATION OF WONDERS" on the front. Reverse: A map of Thailand and a dancer. Regal China, 12½" 4.00 8.00 6.00

Thomas Flayer 1907, 1976, replica of the 1907 Thomas Flyer, 6-70 Model K "Flyabout," which was a luxury car of its day. Comes in blue or white. Plastic rear trunk covers the lid to the bottle 50.00 60.00 55.00

Volkswagen Commemorative Bottle, two colors, c. 1977, Commemorating the Volkswagen Beetle ... the largest selling single production

	Current Price Range		P/Y Average
model vehicle in automotive history. Handcrafted of genuine Regal China, this unique and exciting bottle will long remain a memento for bottle collectors the world over, 14½″	30.00	36.00	33.00
☐ **Washington State Bicentennial,** 1976, patriot dressed in black and orange holding drum. Liberty bell and plaque in front of drummer, 10″	12.00	20.00	15.00
☐ **Waterman,** 1980, in pewter or glazed. Boatman at helm of his boat wearing rain gear. Glazed version in yellow and brown, 13½″	150.00	200.00	175.00

JUKEBOXES

DESCRIPTION: A coin operated phonograph that automatically plays records is a jukebox.

PERIOD: The most collectible jukeboxes were manufactured from 1938 to 1948.

MAKER: The most popular machines were manufactured by Wurlitzer. They were prized for their imaginative cabinetry and see through mechanisms. Favored models are the 850, 950 and 1015.

ADDITIONAL TIPS: For more information, consult *The Official Price Guide to Music Collectibles,* published by The House of Collectibles.

	Current Price Range		P/Y Average
☐ **AMI Model A,** 40 tune selections, called "Mother of Plastic," lights up, "jewels" on front of case, c. 1948	1250.00	2500.00	2000.00
☐ **AMI Model FR,** 20 tune selections, simple wood case in an Art Deco style, top glass panel is record mechanism and tune cards, c. 1932	350.00	520.00	400.00
☐ **AMI "Singing Tower,** 10 tunes, looks like an Art Deco skyscraper, 6′ H., c. 1941	2500.00	3000.00	2750.00
☐ **AMI "Top Flight,"** 20 tune selections, straight rectangular case, metal trim, rounded speaker opening, lights up, c. 1936	400.00	750.00	500.00

	Current Price Range		P/Y Average

□ **Capehart Jukebox,** early example, simple rectangular oak case, glass panels to view mechanism, decorative grill, 1930s 500.00 750.00 620.00

□ **Filben "Maestro,"** 30 tune selections, very space age design, plastic top section, 1940s .. 1000.00 1500.00 1250.00

□ **Gabel's Charme,** 18 tune selections, all wood rectangular case, selection dial, some case decoration, tune cards inside clear glass window 300.00 500.00 400.00

□ **Mills "Empress" Model 910,** 20 tune selections, rounded wood case, large plastic panels, small window to view tune cards, lights up 1250.00 1750.00 1500.00

□ **Mills Jukebox,** 12 tune selections (78rpm), arranged in a "Ferris Wheel" effect, wood case, some decoration, dial tune selector, volume control, doors open on front top of case, speaker grill in bottom, 1930s 500.00 1250.00 750.00

□ **Mills "Throne of Music,"** 20 tune selections, plastic panels, very similar in appearance to "Empress" 1000.00 1500.00 1250.00

□ **Packard Pla-Mor (Capehart),** 24 tune selections, plastic and wood, large viewing window in top front, decorative grill in base, tune selection cards on wheel, coin mechanism in top center 800.00 1500.00 1000.00

□ **Rock-Ola "Luxury Light-Up,"** 20 tune selections, large rounded corners case, orange and green plastic panels, push button tune selector in center, tune cards under plastic panel, decorative grill panel and trim 2000.00 2500.00 2250.00

□ **Rock-Ola "Multi-Selector,"** 12 tune selections, clear glass, top front panel to view mechanism, push button tune selection, simple walnut case and front grill, c. 1935 .... 500.00 800.00 600.00

□ **Rock-Ola "Rocket" Model 1434,** 50 tune selections, push button, simple grill, colored panels, dome, top covers record mechanism, colored corner panels, 1950s 550.00 1250.00 750.00

□ **Rock-Ola "Rhythm King,"** 12 tune selections, wood base, plain case, viewing window to see mechanism, c. 1938 .... 750.00 1250.00 1000.00

□ **Rock-Ola Style 1426,** 20 tune, "Classic" style, push buttons, revolving lights, plastic, viewing window, c. 1947 .... 1700.00 2250.00 2050.00

□ **Seeburg Audiophone,** 8 disc records, plain rectangular case, oval glass opening on top front, "Ferris Wheel" type mechanism with 8 turntables, speaker on door in front, c. 1928. .... 600.00 1000.00 800.00

□ **Seeburg "Commander,"** 20 tune selections, "Space Age" 1930s look, plastic front, sides, top, decorative trim mouldings, button next to each tune card, c. 1940 .... 800.00 1500.00 1000.00

□ **Seeburg P147 (P148),** 20 tune selections, "washing machine" case style, plastic panels, c. 1947 .... 800.00 1200.00 1000.00

Rock-Ola, *style 1422,* *"Magic Glo,"* 1940s, **$1250.00–$2000.00**

	Current Price Range		P/Y Average
☐ **Seeburg "Symphonoia,"** 12 tune selections, rectangular plain case style, window to view mechanism, selector dial, c. 1936	600.00	1250.00	750.00
☐ **Seeburg "Symphonoia Classic,"** 20 tune selections, push button, mainly wood and red plastic panels in front and top corners, decorative trim, lights up, c. 1938	800.00	1200.00	620.00
☐ **Seeburg "Symphonoia Regal,"** 20 tune selections, plastic panels, tune cards in top section (no viewing of mechanism), c. 1940	1000.00	1500.00	1250.00
☐ **Wurlitzer Model P 10,** 10 tune selections, rectangular wooden case, simple lines, glass window, tune selector dial, simple front grill on bottom, early version of "Simplex," c. 1934	300.00	550.00	400.00
☐ **Wurlitzer Model 35,** 12 tune selections, more elaborate walnut case, art deco style, clear glass front window to view mechanism, 1930s	400.00	550.00	400.00
☐ **Wurlitzer Counter Model 61,** 12 tune selection, wood base and sides, some plastic (comes with floor stand), c. 1938–39	1500.00	2500.00	1500.00
☐ **Wurlitzer Counter Model 81,** 12 tune selections, wood base and sides, curving plastic panels, graceful front grill, small viewing window with tune selection cards, push buttons, 1940s	1500.00	2500.00	1500.00
☐ **Wurlitzer Model 416,** 16 tune selections, simple wood case, tune selector dial, rounded front corner columns, decorative front grill over speaker, 1930s	400.00	550.00	350.00

	Current Price Range		P/Y Average
☐ **Wurlitzer Model 616 Simplex,** 16 tune selections, wood case, rounded rectangular style, simple lines, clear glass top front viewing panel, tune selector dial, decorative grill, 1930s	800.00	1800.00	1000.00
☐ **Wurlitzer Model 700,** 24 tune selections, wood case, plastic panels on front corners and top, push button tune selections, decorative metal-grill, c. 1940	1000.00	2500.00	1750.00
☐ **Wurlitzer Model 750,** 24 tune selections, "Classic" style, plastic panels, viewing window, push buttons, c. 1937–40	2300.00	3500.00	2500.00
☐ **Wurlitzer Model 800,** 24 tune selections, wood trim and base, large orange and red plastic corner side and top panels, decorative grill, clear glass panel to view mechanism and tune selections, lights up, c. 1940	1500.00	3000.00	2250.00
☐ **Wurlitzer "Victory,"** 24 tune selections, distinctive design, wood case, multicolored glass panels along front with musical instruments, harlequins, etc., small half circle viewing window, push buttons, decorative grill with colored panels behind, c. 1942–43	2000.00	3750.00	2500.00
☐ **Wurlitzer Model 1015,** 24 tune selections, "Classic" style, revolving lights in plastic bubble tubes, viewing window, c. 1946–47	3500.00	6500.00	5750.00

KNIVES

MAKER: Well-known knife manufacturers include Russell, Case, Winchester and Remington.

COMMENTS: Most collectors of American knives are interested in specific types, including seaman's knives, military knives, knives adapted for hand-to-hand combat and bowie knives.

ADDITIONAL TIPS: Two prices are given for the knife section. The manufacturers, listed in alphabetical order, make a variety of knives so the prices indicate the range for each manufacturer.

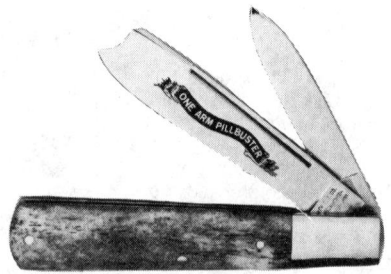

Parker, *One Arm Pillbuster, genuine stag, 3⅞"*, **$30.00-$40.00**

For more complete information, refer to *The Official Price Guide to Collectors Knives,* published by The House of Collectibles.

	Current Price Range		P/Y Average
☐ **A-1 Novelty Cutlery** Canton, OH	10.00	120.00	60.00
☐ **Ack Cutlery Co.** Freemont, OH	40.00	100.00	40.00
☐ **Adams & Bros.**	55.00	130.00	55.00
☐ **Adams & Sons**	40.00	100.00	55.00
☐ **Adolph Blaich,** San Francisco, CA	20.00	175.00	80.00
☐ **Adolphuis Cutlery Co.,** Sheffield, England	10.00	70.00	30.00
☐ **Aerial Mfg. Co.,** Marionette, WI	10.00	115.00	50.00
☐ **Akron Cutlery Co.,** Akron, OH	30.00	70.00	40.00
☐ **Alamo,** Japan	3.00	7.00	4.00
☐ **American Cutlery Co.,** U.S.A.	17.00	38.00	22.00
☐ **American Cutlery Co.,** Germany	9.00	22.00	13.00
☐ **Armstrong Cutlery Co.,** Germany	6.00	12.00	8.00
☐ **Arnex (stainless),** Solingen, Germany	4.50	10.00	7.00
☐ **Atenback,** Swanswork, Germany	10.00	50.00	28.00
☐ **Atlantic Cutlery Co.,** Germany	12.00	25.00	16.00
☐ **Autopoint,** Chicago, IL	3.00	8.00	5.00
☐ **Banner Cutlery Co.,** Germany	12.00	25.00	17.00
☐ **Banner Knife Co.**	12.00	25.00	17.00
☐ **A.F. Bannister & Co.,** New Jersey	3.00	45.00	23.00
☐ **Barhep,** Solingen, Germany	6.00	10.00	8.00
☐ **Barlett Tool Co.,** Newark, NY	18.00	70.00	35.00
☐ **Barrett & Sons**	6.00	65.00	30.00
☐ **Barton Bros.,** Sheffield, England	15.00	45.00	50.00
☐ **Bassett,** Derby, CT	8.00	25.00	15.00
☐ **Bastian Bros. Co.,** Rochester, NY	25.00	65.00	40.00
☐ **R. Bunting & Sons** Sheffield	75.00	500.00	280.00
☐ **Burkinshaw Knife Co.** Pepperell, MA	35.00	300.00	100.00
☐ **Frank Buster Cutlery Co.**	10.00	1000.00	460.00
☐ **Butler Bros.** Chicago, IL	15.00	85.00	45.00
☐ **Camden Cutlery Co.,** Germany	25.00	100.00	60.00
☐ **Camillus Cutlery Co.** Camillus, NY	8.00	110.00	50.00
☐ **Camillus,** New York, NY	5.00	25.00	15.00
☐ **Camp Buddy,** USA	8.00	25.00	16.00
☐ **Camp King**	8.00	25.00	16.00
☐ **Continental Cutlery Co.** Kansas City, MO	25.00	65.00	45.00
☐ **Cook Bros.**	75.00	125.00	100.00

	Current Price Range		P/Y Average
☐ **Copper Bros.**	8.00	18.00	13.00
☐ **Delux**	6.00	15.00	10.00
☐ **Depend-on-me-Cutlery Co.**, New York	7.00	35.00	20.00
☐ **E.A.A.** Solingen, Germany	5.00	10.00	7.00
☐ **E.F. & Co.**	65.00	90.00	75.00
☐ **Eagle**	20.00	35.00	26.00
☐ **Eagle Cutlery Co.**	65.00	300.00	180.00
☐ **Eagle Knife Co.**, U.S.A.	30.00	300.00	160.00
☐ **Eagle Pencil Co.**	5.00	15.00	10.00
☐ **Eagleton Knife Co.**	20.00	125.00	70.00
☐ **Emmon Hawkins Hardware**	15.00	100.00	55.00
☐ **Empire Knife Co.** Winsted, CT	30.00	300.00	160.00
☐ **Empire,** Winsted, CT	30.00	300.00	160.00
☐ **Emrod Co.**, Germany	4.00	15.00	9.00
☐ **Wm. Enders Mfg. Co.**, U.S.A.	15.00	125.00	68.00
☐ **Faulkhiner & Co.** Germany	10.00	20.00	14.00
☐ **Favorite Knife Co.** Germany	4.00	25.00	14.00
☐ **Hibbard, Spencer, & Bartlett** Chicago, IL	10.00	350.00	170.00
☐ **Hickory**	4.00	200.00	100.00
☐ **Highcarbon Steel**, U.S.A.	10.00	150.00	90.00
☐ **Higler & Sons**	15.00	75.00	45.00
☐ **Hike Cutlery Co.** Solingen, Germany	10.00	35.00	22.00
☐ **Hill Bros.**	20.00	60.00	40.00
☐ **Honk Falls**, Napanoch, NY	35.00	900.00	450.00
☐ **Imperial Knife Co.** Providence, RI	2.00	75.00	38.00
☐ **Imperial,** Mexico	1.00	3.00	2.00
☐ **Imperial,** Germany	6.00	26.00	15.00
☐ **Joseph Allen & Sons**	10.00	250.00	120.00
☐ **K.I.E.**, Sweden	3.00	15.00	10.00
☐ **Ka-Bar**, U.S.A.	10.00	600.00	300.00
☐ **Kabar**, U.S.A.	10.00	300.00	150.00
☐ **Kamp Cutlery Co.** Germany	5.00	15.00	9.00
☐ **Kamp Huaser** Plumacher, Germany	15.00	60.00	37.00
☐ **Murcott**, Germany	5.00	25.00	16.00
☐ **R. Murphy**, Boston, MD	15.00	25.00	21.00
☐ **New Port Cutlery Company** Germany	12.00	18.00	15.00
☐ **Newton Premier** Sheffield	10.00	25.00	16.00
☐ **New York Knife Company** Walden, NY	25.00	1000.00	500.00
☐ **Norsharp**	10.00	35.00	24.00
☐ **N. American**, Wichita, KS	10.00	55.00	32.00
☐ **Olcut**, Olean, NY	45.00	300.00	145.00
☐ **Old Cutlery** Olean, NY	17.00	130.00	65.00
☐ **Old American Knife**, U.S.A.	10.00	35.00	19.00
☐ **Old Hickory (Ontario Knife Company)**	4.00	12.50	8.00
☐ **Parker-Frost**	10.00	200.00	100.00
☐ **Wm. & J. Parker**	110.00	400.00	200.00
☐ **Petters Cutlery Company** Chicago, IL	25.00	85.00	45.00
☐ **Phoenix Knife Co.** Phoenix, NY	10.00	135.00	70.00
☐ **Pic**, Germany	3.00	8.00	6.00
☐ **PIC**, Japan	2.00	5.00	4.10
☐ **Pine Knot**, U.S.A.	35.00	300.00	150.00
☐ **Pine Knot** James W. Price	45.00	400.00	200.00
☐ **C. Platts & Sons** Andover, NY	40.00	800.00	400.00
☐ **Platts Bros.**, Union, NY	75.00	800.00	890.00

	Current Price Range		P/Y Average
☐ Poor Boy	5.00	100.00	50.00
☐ Pop Cutlery Co. Camillus, NY	5.00	20.00	10.00
☐ Quick Point (Winchester stamped on back of tang)	53.00	78.00	63.00
☐ R.J. Richter, Germany	4.00	15.00	8.00
☐ Ring Cutlery, Japan	1.00	5.00	3.50
☐ Rivington Works	15.00	65.00	37.00
☐ Rizzaro Estilato, Milan, Italy	35.00	75.00	57.00
☐ Roberts & Johnson & Rand St. Louis, MO	15.00	75.00	40.00
☐ Robertson Bros. & Co. Louisville, KY	15.00	300.00	150.00
☐ Robeson, Germany	25.00	75.00	40.00
☐ Robeson, Rochester, NY	15.00	400.00	210.00
☐ Robeson, Suredge	10.00	125.00	60.00
☐ Sizeker Manstealed, Germany	10.00	15.00	14.00
☐ Sliberstein Laporte & Co.	35.00	65.00	45.00
☐ Simmons Hardware Co. Germany	25.00	300.00	150.00
☐ Simmons Hardware St. Louis, MO	20.00	300.00	150.00
☐ Simmons Warden White Co. Dayton, OH	15.00	75.00	60.00
☐ Spartts, England	35.00	90.00	60.00
☐ Spear Cutlery Co., Germany	10.00	25.00	16.00
☐ Spring Cutlery Co. Sheffield	15.00	125.00	50.00
☐ Springer, Japan	4.00	15.00	8.00
☐ Standard Cutlery Co. Germany	5.00	25.00	15.00
☐ Thomas Turner & Co. Sheffield, England	16.00	175.00	100.00
☐ United, Germany	3.00	10.00	8.00
☐ Universal Knife Co. New Britain, CT	15.00	35.00	25.00
☐ Utica Co., Czechoslovakia	12.00	35.00	24.00
☐ Utica Cutlery Co. Utica, NY	10.00	150.00	90.00
☐ Utica Knife Co., U.S.A.	10.00	150.00	90.00
☐ V. K. Cutlery Co., Germany	5.00	15.00	9.00
☐ Valley Falls Cutlery Co.	15.00	75.00	45.00
☐ Valley Forge Cutlery Co.	20.00	95.00	50.00
☐ Valor, Germany	3.00	15.00	8.00
☐ Valor, Japan	3.00	15.00	8.00
☐ Van Camp, U.S.A.	3.00	100.00	51.00
☐ Van Camp H & I Co., U.S.A.	15.00	300.00	150.00
☐ Van Camp Indianapolis, IN	15.00	300.00	150.00
☐ Van Camp, Germany	10.00	30.00	19.00
☐ Vanco, Indianapolis, IN	5.00	35.00	19.00
☐ Vernider, St. Paul, MN	5.00	25.00	19.00
☐ John Watts, Sheffield	15.00	30.00	24.00
☐ Webster, Sycamore Works U.S.A.	10.00	35.00	22.00
☐ Webster Cutlery Co., Germany	5.00	15.00	9.00
☐ Weck, N.Y.	15.00	65.00	35.00
☐ Wedgeway Cutlery Co.	14.00	35.00	27.00
☐ Weed & Co., Buffalo	35.00	75.00	52.00
☐ G. Weiland, New York	5.00	25.00	18.00
☐ Marshall Wells Hardware Co.	39.00	130.00	155.00
☐ H. C. Wentworth & Son Germany	5.00	35.00	20.00
☐ Weske Cutlery Co. Sandusky, OH	15.00	35.00	19.00
☐ Westaco, Boulder, CO	30.00	64.00	45.00
☐ Wester, B. C.	5.00	35.00	25.00
☐ Wester Bros., Germany	35.00	250.00	100.00
☐ Wester Stone, Inc., U.S.A.	15.00	116.00	50.00
☐ Western, Boulder, CO	50.00	520.00	240.00

LALIQUE

DESCRIPTION: Rene Lalique first achieved fame as a maker of Art Nouveau jewelry in the 1890s. He experimented with glass and incorporated it into his jewelry designs. His fame as a glassmaker, however, came as a result of his commission by Coty Parfums to produce decorative bottles for their fragrances. His most famous work was produced during the Art Deco period and included illuminated, frosted glass sculpture, vases and even car hood ornaments.

ADDITIONAL TIPS: The current resurgence of interest in the Art Deco period has caused the exquisite jewelry and glassware of Lalique to skyrocket in price.

RECOMMENDED READING: For more in-depth information on Lalique, you may refer to *The Official Price Guide to Glassware, The Official Price Guide to Antique Jewelry* and *The Official Identification Guide to Glassware,* published by The House of Collectibles.

	Current Price Range		P/Y Average
☐ **Ashtray,** circular form, wide flat rim, amber, molded in high relief with scarabs with leaves, signed, 5¼″ high, c. 1925	300.00	500.00	350.00
☐ **Ashtray,** square, stepped corners, frosted, molded with interweaving bands—one plain, the other of daisies, signed, 10″ long, c. 1925	400.00	600.00	425.00
☐ **Bottle,** compressed spherical, short cylinder neck, ovoid stopper, green, molded with protruding ruffled fan designs, signed, 2½″ high, c. 1925	400.00	600.00	425.00
☐ **Brooch,** sculptured lady with bat wings, translucent blue enamel, gold, maker: Lalique, French, c. 1900	5700.00	6700.00	6200.00
☐ **Buckle,** rectangular shape with rounded corners, amber, molded and pierced with two twining cobras with open mouths, signed, 1¾″ long, c. 1925	800.00	1000.00	810.00

	Current Price Range		P/Y Average

☐ **Centerpiece,** round bowl with large looped-shaped handles with pierced scrolls, frosted handles molded with leaping gazelles, signed, 18½" long, c. 1925 .... **800.00 1200.00 825.00**

☐ **Chandelier,** domed shape, clear, molded with three bands of grape clusters and vines, pierced, signed, 13¾" diameter, c. 1925 .... **800.00 1000.00 850.00**

☐ **Chandelier,** domed shade, pierced and supporting four hooks, molded in high relief with peaches and leaves, 15" diameter, c. 1930 .... **1000.00 1400.00 1000.00**

☐ **Chandelier,** domed shape shade, frosted, molding on exterior of bouquets of primroses, brown wash, signed, 12" diameter, c. 1925 .... **600.00 800.00 615.00**

☐ **Clock,** flat panel with arched crest, molded with two females in classical dress holding garland circling etched circular clock face, on rectangular base silver painted, on four ball feet, 15¼" high, c. 1925 .... **8000.00 10000.00 8500.00**

☐ **Clock,** flattened rectangular frame, expands into rectangular base, clear, molded in low relief with birds perched in cherry branches, signed, 6" high, c. 1930 .... **800.00 1000.00 815.00**

☐ **Clock,** flattened rectangular, stepped rectangular base, clear, background of molded flowers, molded swallows flying in black enamel, signed, 6" high, c. 1925 .... **600.00 800.00 610.00**

☐ **Clock,** flattened square, clear and frosted, molded with nude females swimming, signed, 4½" high, c. 1925 .... **400.00 600.00 425.00**

☐ **Clock,** rectangular shape, frosted, pierced, molded with sparrows perched on leafy branches, signed, 6" high, c. 1925 .... **800.00 1000.00 800.00**

☐ **Decanter,** bell shape, short neck, clear, slightly domed stopper with molded branches of berries and leaves, signed, 8½" high, c. 1930 .... **600.00 800.00 650.00**

☐ **Decanter,** double-cone shape, flaring neck, teardrop on stem stopper, clear, molded with leaves radiating in bands, black ring around neck, signed, 11¼" high, c. 1925 .... **150.00 200.00 160.00**

☐ **Decanter,** ovoid shape, molded in pattern of blossoms on one side, the other flattened side has a large molded blossom, stopper in shape of disc with blossom design, signed, 8" high, c. 1925 .... **300.00 500.00 325.00**

☐ **Necklace,** priestess motif, green and blue enamel, bar link chain, gold, 3¾" long, Art Nouveau, maker: Rene Lalique, French, c. late 19th **35000.00 40000.00 37500.00**

☐ **Pendant,** flattened triangular shape with rounded corners, mold on one side with scrolling branches with berries, pierced for stringing, signed, 2" long, c. 1925 .... **800.00 1200.00 810.00**

	Current Price Range		P/Y Average

☐ **Pendant,** medallion motif, obverse: warrior with griffin, reverse: a lady, gold, Art Nouveau, maker: Rene Lalique, c. 1900 . . . . 1000.00 1200.00 1100.00

☐ **Tray,** perfume, rectangular shape with five apertures, blossom-shaped stoppers, clear, molded with pattern of thistle branches, 8¾" long, c. 1930 . . . . 600.00 800.00 600.00

☐ **Vase,** molded, opalescent, urn shape, molded with pattern of thistles and leaves, 8½" high, c. 1925 . . . . 500.00 600.00 550.00

☐ **Vase,** opalescent, cylinder shape, flaring rim, molded with eucalyptus leaves and berries, 6½" high, c. 1925 . . . . 300.00 500.00 325.00

☐ **Vase,** opalescent, trumpet shape, frosted background, molded with bands of overlapping leaves, signed, 5⅛" high, c. 1925 . . . . 300.00 500.00 325.00

☐ **Vase,** ovoid body, rimmed neck, frosted, molded in high relief with grasshoppers and blades of grass, green and blue wash, signed, c. 1925 . . 1000.00 1400.00 1100.00

☐ **Vase,** ovoid body, short cylinder neck, amber, molded in relief with archers hunting flying birds, signed, 10¾" high, c. 1930 . . . . 2000.00 3000.00 2200.00

☐ **Vase,** ovoid body, short cylinder neck, dark amber, molded frieze of nude men with bows and arrows hunting birds in flight, signed, 10½" high, c. 1925 . . . . 2000.00 3000.00 2200.00

LAMPS AND LIGHTING FIXTURES

TYPES: There are many different types of lighting fixtures, from grease burning to kerosene to electric. Styles of lamps and other fixtures may be named for the designer who innovated them or a distinctive feature of the lamp itself. For instance, the "Emeralite" light is a green glass shaded office lamp.

PERIOD: Lamps and lighting fixtures have been popular since the early 1700s. Collectors focus on the periods that saw significant developments in the field, such as the Art Nouveau period.

ORIGIN: Clay oil lamps have existed for at least 2000 years.

MAKERS: The most prominent makers of lamps and lighting fixtures are Tiffany, Quezal, Handel and Pairpoint. These companies produced some of the finest and most artistic lamps in existence.

COMMENTS: Although few individuals collect lamps and lighting fixtures as a hobby, these items are eagerly sought as accent pieces. Many lamps, especially the most expensive ones, are works of art as much as functional pieces.

ADDITIONAL TIPS: These listings are arranged according to the type of lighting fixture. Lamps by such distinctive makers such as Tiffany and Handel are grouped together.

LAMPS AND LIGHTING DEVICES

	Current Price Range		P/Y Average
☐ **Angle Lamp,** brass, double lacquered	195.00	280.00	235.00
☐ **Argand Lamp,** American Empire, bronze, cut glass shade	225.00	335.00	250.00
☐ **Art Nouveau Figural Lamp,** white paint, metal	175.00	220.00	190.00
☐ **Astral Lamp,** English, classical column, floral motif frosted shade, square base, 17⅜″ H., c. 1838	1100.00	1400.00	1250.00
☐ **Betty Lamp,** tin, with hanger	100.00	115.00	95.00
☐ **Boudoir Lamp,** Art Deco, Austrian porcelain, figural, fabric shade	60.00	90.00	75.00
☐ **Boudoir Lamp,** Blanc de Chine, figural base, 11½″ H. base	40.00	65.00	47.50
☐ **Bradley and Hubbard,** caramel shade, signed base, 24″ H.	560.00	700.00	625.00
☐ **Candelabrum,** Art Nouveau, bronze, figural, two lights, pate de verre shades, 20½″ H.	1200.00	1400.00	1300.00
☐ **Carriage Lamps,** brass, clear glass and red reflector lenses	290.00	325.00	300.00
☐ **Ceiling Light Fixture,** Art Deco, bronze and onyx, inverted pyramid, bronze mounts, 35″ H., c. 1933	550.00	660.00	575.00
☐ **Ceiling Light Fixture,** pressed glass, hobnail	60.00	100.00	80.00
☐ **Chandelier,** brass and pressed glass, three lights, crystal bulbs, 24″ diameter	110.00	165.00	130.00
☐ **Chandelier,** bronze, six arms, French, 21″ diameter	65.00	110.00	80.00
☐ **Chandelier,** crystal and brass, prisms and swags, 18″ diameter	60.00	75.00	65.00
☐ **Chandelier,** Dresden, porcelain, nine arms, 24″ diameter	2400.00	3200.00	2800.00
☐ **Chandelier,** Florent, gilt metal, five lights, 17″ diameter	175.00	240.00	200.00
☐ **Chandelier,** Louis XV style, cut glass shade	1000.00	1200.00	1100.00
☐ **Chandelier,** milk glass and cranberry overlay, prisms, five arms, 20″ diameter	125.00	215.00	160.00

	Current Price Range		P/Y Average
Chandelier, porcelain and d'ore bronze, six arms, blue, white and gold, 27″ diameter	180.00	260.00	220.00
Chandelier, tin circle, fifteen candle sockets, 21″ diameter	365.00	450.00	300.00
Chandelier, Victorian, kerosene lamp with hurricane shade, 42″ H.	280.00	350.00	310.00
Chinese Lamp, bronze, urn form, low-relief dragon, 30″ H............................	190.00	250.00	210.00
Courting Lamp, pewter, clear and frosted front, 4″ H.	100.00	125.00	105.00
Desk Lamp, goose neck, quezel art glass shade in trumpet form, iridescent, 15″ H., late 1800s	165.00	200.00	175.00
Emeralite Lamp, brass, green glass globe, square brass base, 13″ H., c. 1920	120.00	155.00	130.00
Floor Lamp, French, bronze, reeded shaft, Dresden flowers	90.00	125.00	100.00
Floor Lamp, oak, carved diamond shaft, crossbar base	50.00	80.00	60.00
Gas Sconces, pair, handwrought, French	300.00	360.00	330.00
"Gone With the Wind" Lamp, umbrella shade with cupids and foliage, brass foot, 20″ H.	295.00	325.00	300.00
"Gone With the Wind" Lamp, grape pattern with green leaves, 22″ H...................	550.00	600.00	550.00
"Gone With the Wind" Lamp, magnolia blossoms handpainted, 24″ H.	595.00	685.00	625.00
"Gone With the Wind" Lamp, red glass with red bull's eye, 28½″ H.	695.00	750.00	725.00
Handel Desk Lamp, square trunk base, swing porcelain shade, 15″ H.	320.00	400.00	360.00
Handel Table Lamp, glass and metal, reverse painted, 24½″ H.	2500.00	2700.00	2600.00
Handel Table Lamp, art glass shade, cylindrical base with handles, 24½″ H.	700.00	800.00	750.00
Handel Table Lamp, Persian bordered glass shade, 22″ H.	1450.00	1650.00	1550.00
Hanging Lamp, brass with chocolate glass panels, 14″ H.	75.00	90.00	75.00
Hanging Lamp, cranberry with prisms	700.00	800.00	750.00
Hanging Lamp, striped with canopy, 13″ H....	175.00	225.00	200.00
Hanging Lamp, light fixture, brass and crystal, three lights, crystal bulbs, 19½″ H............	50.00	90.00	60.00
Hurricane Lamp, pair 11″ H.	50.00	60.00	45.00
Kerosene Lamp, Bohemian crystal, brass shaft, white marble base, cut flowers, red, 22″ H. ...	65.00	95.00	75.00
Kerosene Lamp, cabbage case pattern	65.00	85.00	70.00
Kerosene Lamp, country store fixture, brass front..................................	140.00	160.00	150.00
Kerosene Lamp, green pattern, milk glass base	90.00	110.00	90.00
Kerosene Lamp, hanging fixture, cranberry glass with brass frame	225.00	275.00	250.00
Kerosene Lamp, hobnail pattern	40.00	50.00	40.00
Kerosene Lamp, table, Lincoln Drape pattern, amber	110.00	150.00	130.00

	Current Price Range		P/Y Average
☐ **Kerosene Lamp,** table, overlay glass, 13″ H.	675.00	775.00	725.00
☐ **Miner's Safety Lamp,** brass and iron, red lens, #1000	115.00	155.00	130.00
☐ **Oil Lamp,** dogtooth	45.00	50.00	35.00
☐ **Oil Lamp,** Hall & Son, brass, tiered square base, frosted vintage globe, 26″ H.	280.00	375.00	320.00
☐ **Oil Lamp,** green depression glass	45.00	55.00	45.00
☐ **Oil Lamp,** Victorian, aqua milk glass square pedestal base, hurricane chimney, 23″ H., late 1800s	35.00	55.00	40.00
☐ **Oriental Lamp,** elephant, bronze, wood base, 19¾″ H.	410.00	580.00	490.00
☐ **Pairpoint,** butterflies and roses, signed base and shade, 10″ Dia.	1100.00	1300.00	1200.00
☐ **Peg Lamp,** brass burner, 6″ H.	80.00	100.00	80.00
☐ **Peg Lamp,** ribbed glass with brass candlesticks, pair	160.00	210.00	175.00
☐ **Railroad Switch Lamp,** four lenses, red and green, type 1880	50.00	90.00	60.00
☐ **Railroad Switch Lamp,** Handlan, St. Louis, four lenses	55.00	85.00	65.00
☐ **Student Lamp,** double brass, green glass shade with original chimney	550.00	595.00	535.00
☐ **Student Lamp,** hanging double, burnished, green shade	675.00	775.00	725.00
☐ **Student Lamp,** single brass front, milk glass shade	320.00	370.00	345.00
☐ **Table Lamp,** American Empire, brass, glass prisms, cut frosted shade	700.00	800.00	750.00
☐ **Table Lamp,** "Arrow Root," leaded glass shade with bronze base, 25½″ H.	8500.00	10500.00	9500.00

LANTERNS

☐ **Auto Lantern,** brass, oil burning, 14½″ H.	110.00	140.00	118.00
☐ **Barn Lantern,** Peter Gray, Boston	110.00	155.00	125.00
☐ **Buggy Dashboard Lantern,** kerosene	25.00	35.00	27.00
☐ **Candle Lantern,** sheet metal painted black, 16¼″ H.	65.00	85.00	75.00
☐ **Carriage Lantern,** brass trim, pair	340.00	400.00	370.00
☐ **Chien Lung Period Lantern,** porcelain, gourd form, pierced pedestal base, teak stand, hexagonal, 18″ H., late 1700s.	320.00	400.00	360.00
☐ **Chinese Junk Lantern,** brass, oil	55.00	70.00	56.00
☐ **Coach Lantern,** pierced, 17½″ H.	170.00	210.00	190.00
☐ **Continental Lantern,** brass and tin, finials, 9½″ H., c. 1800s	400.00	600.00	500.00
☐ **Dietz Driving Lantern,** red glass in rear, 7½″ H.	135.00	170.00	145.00
☐ **Kerosene Lantern,** brass base and top engraved "Joseph Gavett, Roxbury," 17″ H.	250.00	300.00	275.00
☐ **Kerosene Lantern,** Dietz red reflector	34.00	42.00	33.00
☐ **Miner's Lantern,** tin and brass, 5½″ H., Jan. 10, 1882	28.00	44.00	32.50

ACL Railroad Lantern, *clear globe*, $35.00-$55.00

	Current Price Range		P/Y Average
☐ **Paul Revere Lantern,** tin with swirled punched holes	160.00	190.00	175.00
☐ **Railroad Lantern,** Nazi, marked with Swastika	25.00	45.00	30.00
☐ **Railroad Lantern,** New York City, red or clear globe	20.00	35.00	22.50
☐ **Railroad Lantern,** San Francisco, clear globe	25.00	55.00	40.00
☐ **Skater's Lantern,** brass with glass globe	75.00	100.00	87.50
☐ **Ship's Lantern,** copper, pair, 16″ H.	270.00	320.00	295.00
☐ **Wagon Lantern,** clamp-on type with rear red reflector	30.00	40.00	30.00
☐ **Wood Lantern,** rare second material	160.00	190.00	175.00

MINIATURE LIGHTING DEVICES

☐ **Acorn Burner,** brass, 6″ H.................	70.00	90.00	75.00
☐ **Acorn Burner,** milk glass, white, embossed with iris, clear glass chimney	180.00	220.00	200.00
☐ **Acorn Burner,** opaline glass base and chimney, house scene	190.00	240.00	115.00
☐ **Acorn Burner,** tin.........................	22.00	30.00	23.00
☐ **Artichoke,** red satin......................	55.00	75.00	60.00
☐ **Aventurine,** green, glass base	45.00	65.00	50.00
☐ **Banquet Lamp,** blue, glass, jeweled base, 10″ H.	270.00	350.00	310.00
☐ **Bristol,** blue enamel flowers, 6½″ H.	80.00	110.00	95.00
☐ **Bristol type,** hexagonal base, figures on sides	120.00	170.00	145.00
☐ **Bullseye Lamp,** by U.S. Glass Co.	50.00	60.00	50.00
☐ **Christmas Tree Lamp,** clear glass	90.00	100.00	90.00

	Current Price Range		P/Y Average
☐ **Coreopsis,** green band base	50.00	60.00	50.00
☐ **Cosmos,** clear glass, painted base	20.00	30.00	25.00
☐ **Cosmos,** floral motif, 8″ H.	280.00	440.00	360.00
☐ **Cosmos,** pink band base	40.00	50.00	45.00
☐ **Daisy,** by U.S. Glass	80.00	90.00	85.00
☐ **Fleur de Lis,** milk glass, by Eagle Glass Co. . .	280.00	320.00	300.00
☐ **Greek Key,** clear glass	42.00	52.00	47.00
☐ **Kerosene Lamp,** pressed glass, daisy motif . .	35.00	45.00	40.00
☐ **Lincoln Drape Lamp**	70.00	80.00	75.00
☐ **Melon Lamp,** yellow cased glass	60.00	70.00	65.00
☐ **Milk Glass,** chimney top with fluted stem, footed base, 5½″ H.	180.00	230.00	205.00
☐ **Night Lamp,** ribbed base	55.00	75.00	65.00
☐ **Nutmeg Burner,** brass saucer, 2″ H. . . . . : . .	70.00	100.00	85.00
☐ **Nutmeg Burner,** clear glass base and chimney	45.00	55.00	50.00
☐ **Oil Lamp,** Greek Key	30.00	40.00	35.00
☐ **Oil Lamp,** swirl base and chimney, metal handle, 6″ H., c. 1940s	12.00	18.00	15.00
☐ **Star Lamp,** painted . . . . /.	40.00	60.00	50.00
☐ **Night Lamp,** swirl, narrow	40.00	50.00	45.00
☐ **Skating Lamp,** brass, link chain, 8″ H.	65.00	85.00	75.00
☐ **Table Lamp,** beehive, Pairpoint, 14½″ H.	450.00	600.00	525.00

LENOX

DESCRIPTION: Lenox China was founded on May 18, 1889 by Jonathan Coxon, Sr. and Walter Scott Lenox, who had met when both were employed by Ott & Brewer. The original name of the company was the Ceramic Art Company, and Coxon was its president with Lenox as secretary/treasurer and art director. Company activities in the early years included production of both decorated and undecorated wares. By the end of the C.A.C. period, they were producing around 600 different shapes decorated both in standard and original fashion. The emphasis was on giftware instead of dinnerware, and many of the more interesting Lenox collectibles date from this time. With the formation of Lenox, Inc., in 1906, dinnerware production was greatly expanded. Hand-painting, although it would continue for another half-century, became less important than transfer decoration. By the time of World War II, the company had produced more than 3,000 different shapes decorated with thousands of different designs. Since World War II, the company has added crystal bone china, and oven-proof ware to their list. The china is now made in Pomona, NJ, and new corporate headquarters were recently opened in Lawrenceville, NJ. The Lenox corporate umbrella now covers a diversified group of companies making everything from school rings to candles.

MARKS: Lenox marks are extremely complicated. For a complete discussion refer to *The Official Price Guide to Pottery and Porcelain* and *The Official Identification Guide to Pottery and Porcelain,* published by The House of Collectibles.

Pitcher, *shape #352, transition mark,* **$340.00–$395.00**

	Current Price Range		P/Y Average
□ **Bouillon Cup and Saucer,** shape #628, transfer decorated with vegetables, gold trim, Lenox palette mark	23.00	28.00	25.00
□ **Bouillon Cup and Saucer,** shape #628, undecorated, Lenox wreath mark	15.00	20.00	17.00
□ **Bouillon Cup and Saucer,** shape #633, undecorated, Lenox wreath mark	13.00	16.00	14.75
□ **Butter Pat,** item #176, 3″, hand-painted little pink roses with gold trim, Lenox wreath mark	35.00	38.00	36.00
□ **Butter Pat,** item #176, 3″, gold trim, C.A.C. lavender palette mark	20.00	23.50	22.00
□ **Butter pat,** item #177, 3¼″, round, scalloped rim similar to that of item #178, undecorated, Lenox palette mark	14.00	16.00	15.00
□ **Butter Pat,** item #178, 3¼″, hand-painted with small pink roses, gold trim, transition mark	34.00	38.00	36.00
□ **Butter pat,** item #178, 3¼″, gold trim, Lenox palette mark	19.00	23.50	21.00

	Current Price Range		P/Y Average

☐ **Butter Pat,** item #178, 3¼", undecorated and unmarked **7.00**   **8.00**   **7.50**

☐ **Candlesticks,** shape #147, 10½", high, embossing, undecorated, Lenox wreath mark, pair   **110.00**   **120.00**   **115.00**

☐ **Candlesticks,** shape #147, 10½", high, brushed gold trim, Lenox wreath mark, pair . . .   **115.00**   **125.00**   **120.00**

☐ **Chocolate Pot,** shape #107, 8" high, beautifully done floral design on shaded background, gold trim, signed W. H. Morley, transition mark **420.00**   **470.00**   **435.00**

☐ **Cigarette Box,** shape #2424, plain green, Lenox wreath mark **29.00**   **33.00**   **31.50**

☐ **Cigarette Box,** shape #2424, white with Lenox Rose trim, Lenox wreath mark **43.00**   **48.00**   **44.50**

☐ **Cigarette Holder,** shape #2635, 3" high, relief laurel wreath on base, coral, Lenox wreath mark **19.00**   **23.50**   **22.00**

☐ **Cigarette Holder,** shape #2635, 3" high, relief laurel wreath on base, blue, Lenox wreath mark **19.00**   **23.50**   **22.00**

☐ **Coffeepot,** shape #108, 8" high, hand-painted, scattered wild flowers, nicely done gold trim, artist signed and dated, C.A.C. lavender palette mark **135.00**   **150.00**   **142.50**

☐ **Cup and Saucer,** Shape #2, 2¼", ribbed design, fancy handle, gold trim, Lenox palette mark **35.00**   **38.00**   **36.00**

☐ **Cup and Saucer,** shape #3, 2¼", six panels with fish scale design, fancy handle, undecorated, C.A.C. lavender palette mark **50.00**   **55.00**   **53.00**

☐ **Desk Set, Three-pieces,** unmarked rolling blotters, two-compartment standing letter holder (6" x 8"), and covered inkwell with 5" underplate, monochromatic blue Delft type scene with houses, children, etc., artist's initials, transition mark and Tiffany & Company mark **650.00**   **720.00**   **675.00**

☐ **Fern Pot,** shape #181, 6¼", round shape, ruffled rim, speckeld gold trim, C.A.C. lavender palette mark, several flecks on rim **110.00**   **120.00**   **115.00**

☐ **Fern Pot,** shape #182, 6¼", same basic shape as #181 but rim is scalloped as well as ruffled, pale lavender exterior, gold trim on rim, C.A.C. pink palette mark **170.00**   **195.00**   **180.00**

☐ **Horn of Plenty,** shape #70, 4½" high, plain white, Lenox wreath mark **32.00**   **35.00**   **33.00**

☐ **Jug,** shape #271, 8" tall, undecorated, Lenox palette mark **58.00**   **63.00**   **60.00**

☐ **Jug,** shape #271, 8" tall, badly decorated with wheat stalks on mottled background, artist initialed, Lenox palette mark **90.00**   **100.00**   **92.00**

☐ **Ladle Rest/Sugar Bowl,** shape #72½, 4½", diameter, undecorated, Lenox wreath mark **35.00**   **38.00**   **36.00**

☐ **Loving Cup,** shape #258, three-handled, undecorated, Lenox palette mark **85.00**   **95.00**   **90.00**

	Current Price Range		P/Y Average

☐ **Match Holder,** shape #2425, undecorated, Lenox wreath mark **42.00 47.50 45.00**

☐ **Match Holder,** shape #2425, gold trim, Lenox wreath mark **42.00 47.50 43.00**

☐ **Muffineer,** shape number unknown, hand-painted flowers, Lenox wreath mark **70.00 75.00 73.00**

☐ **Mug,** shape #251, 4⅞″ high, gold trim on handle and rims, gold monogram on front, Lenox palette mark **42.00 47.50 45.00**

☐ **Mug,** shape #251, 4⅞″ high, blue bands top and bottom and blue on handle, mediocre central scenic section, C.A.C. lavender palette mark . . **85.00 95.00 90.00**

☐ **Pitcher,** shape #24, 5″ high, undecorated, C.A.C. brown palette mark **110.00 120.00 115.00**

☐ **Pitcher,** shape #24, 5″ high, gold trim on handle and brushed gold near rims, C.A.C. wreath mark, eggshell thin **20.00 23.50 21.00**

☐ **Sugar and Creamer,** shape #38, creamer 4″, sugar 4½″ diameter, raised gold paste trim, C.A.C. lavender palette mark **170.00 195.00 180.00**

☐ **Teapot,** shape #946, 3¾″, hand-painted roses, pink on one side, red on the other, gold trim, artist signed, Lenox palette mark **62.00 70.00 65.00**

☐ **Tea Strainer,** shape #339, hand-painted roses and gold trim, transition mark **270.00 320.00 295.00**

☐ **Tobacco Jar,** shape #328, 7½″ high, hand-painted Indian smoking peace pipe, Lenox palette mark **180.00 220.00 190.00**

☐ **Tray,** shape #983, 11⅜″ x 7⅛″, rounded-off corners, gold trim, Lenox palette mark **70.00 78.00 75.00**

☐ **Shot Glass,** shape #269, tiny ears or corn hand-painted on front, gold trim, Lenox palette mark **30.00 32.50 31.00**

☐ **Vase,** item #27, 7½″ high, bulbous bottom, white top with coral bottom, Lenox wreath mark, see photo **35.00 38.00 36.00**

☐ **Vase,** item #27, 7½″ high, bulbous bottom, beige matte finish with raised gold paste work, lavender palette C.A.C. mark **110.00 120.00 115.00**

LICENSE PLATES

MATERIAL: Pre-1910 license plates were made of various materials, including leather. Since then, plates have been made of metal.

COMMENTS: License plates are the first auto collectible to attract widespread interest. Some collectors focus on plates from the same state, while others collect plates in chronological order. Older plates show changes in design, size and color. Because of materials used, most plates are not in mint condition.

ADDITIONAL TIPS: The following sampling of license plates is listed alphabetically by state. The year follows.

	Current Price Range		P/Y Average
☐ **Arkansas,** 1932	17.50	26.00	18.50
☐ **California,** 1930	17.50	26.00	18.50
☐ **Connecticut,** 1915	80.00	90.00	85.00
☐ **Iowa,** 1932	22.50	38.00	27.00
☐ **Maine,** 1920	7.50	14.00	9.00
☐ **Kansas,** 1933	13.50	20.00	15.00
☐ **Massachusetts,** 1915	22.50	38.00	27.00
☐ **Rhode Island,** 1926	12.50	18.00	14.00
☐ **Wisconsin,** 1925	12.50	18.00	14.00
☐ **Michigan,** good condition, 1916	50.00	60.00	52.00
☐ **Ohio,** good condition, 1922	60.00	70.00	62.00
☐ **Pennsylvania,** 1908	55.00	65.00	60.00

LIGHTNING ROD ORNAMENTS

TOPIC: A lightning rod ornament is a glass ball that has a hole through its middle. This allows it to be placed on a lightning rod for decoration. These ornaments resemble very large Christmas ornaments except for the hole going all the way through the ball. Other decorations for lightning rods, such as ornamental tips to surmount the rod, are also collected, though much more rarely.

TYPES: Lightning rod ornaments can be classified by type of glass or shape. Spheres are the most common shape, although the teardrop and the doorknob forms are not unusual.

PERIOD: Most of the collectible balls were produced between 1880 and 1910. Lightning rod ornaments were just coming into vogue in the mid-1800s.

MATERIALS: These items were almost exclusively made of glass. Porcelain is seen very rarely.

COMMENTS: Lightning rod ornaments can be exquisitely beautiful and they are well suited to display. Since few individuals are aware of them and collect them, prices are relatively low for most items.

ADDITIONAL TIPS: These specimens can be cleaned with a mild solution of soapsuds. After cleaning, they may be rubbed with olive oil on a rag to make them sparkle.

	Current Price Range		P/Y Average
☐ **Diddie Blitzer,** mercury glass ball	80.00	100.00	90.00
☐ **Electra ball,** amber/brown	40.00	48.00	44.00
☐ **Hawkeye,** brick red	120.00	150.00	135.00
☐ **Mercury glass,** gold-toned, 4½" Dia.	30.00	36.00	33.00
☐ **Milk glass,** doorknob ball, orange	250.00	280.00	265.00
☐ **Moon and star ball,** red	60.00	70.00	65.00

LINCOLNIANA

DESCRIPTION: Lincolniana is memorabilia dealing with Abraham Lincoln, America's 16th President.

TYPES: There are all types of Lincoln Memorabilia from photographs to campaign ribbons.

PERIOD: Lincoln served as president from 1861 to 1865. He was assassinated by actor John Wilkes Booth on April 14, 1865 at Ford's Theater in Washington. Most of Lincoln's collectibles are items dealing with his political life.

	Current Price Range		P/Y Average
☐ **Advertising Poster,** carte-de-visite photograph of Lincoln mounted as the centerpiece of an advertising poster, advertises a Providence, R.I. salvage dealer's business seeking to buy "papers, rags and junk metals."	45.00	60.00	51.00
☐ **Banner,** cotton, bust portrait with no wording in white and black, marked Joseph Rhein, Detroit, undated, probably post-assassination, 36" x 48"	400.00	500.00	430.00
☐ **Cabinet Card,** with applied albumen photo print, card consists of lengthy eulogistic text, marked Bancroft, Philadelphia, photo is 2½" x 3½", card overall is 9" x 14", 1865	170.00	200.00	180.00
☐ **Ferrotype,** bearded Lincoln pictured, brass frame	140.00	160.00	150.00
☐ **Locket,** with albumin portrait photograph, tortoiseshell, oval, Lincoln bearded, probably from the 1860 campaign, 1¼" x 1¾"	160.00	190.00	172.00
Note: The presence or absence of a beard is one certain method of placing at least an approximate date on Lincoln portraits. He began growing the beard in late 1860.			
☐ **Medal,** copper, profile bust with wording, "Repub Cand for Pres/Prot(ector) to Amer Industry, Free Homes for Free Men," from the 1860 campaign	40.00	55.00	47.00

	Current Price Range		P/Y Average

☐ **Medal For Funeral,** white metal (imitation silver), pictures willow tree and urn with wording, "Died by the Hands of a Rebel Assassin," black silk ribbon at top **40.00 55.00 46.00**

☐ **Medal,** North Western Sanitary Fair, bronze, profile bust facing right, official U.S. Mint issue struck in early 1865 before his assassination **250.00 350.00 280.00**

Note: The "sanitary fairs," held in various cities during the Civil War, were glorified carnivals whose proceeds went to buy medicine and clothing for Union troops.

☐ **Medal,** white metal (imitation silver), profile bust with wording, "A Foe to Traitors, No Compromise With Armed Rebels," probably from first year of Civil War **60.00 80.00 68.00**

☐ **Merchant's Token,** brass, Stoner and Shroyer. Dry Goods, Adamsville, Ohio, portrait bust facing right **230.00 280.00 250.00**

Note: Merchant tokens, given to customers in place of pennies when change was scarce, where issued profusely during the Civil War in all eastern and midwest cities. This is one of the rarer examples and has a much higher value than most.

☐ **Paperweight,** Zanesville tile **35.00 45.00 39.00**

☐ **Photograph,** carte-de-visite by Matthew Brady, half length seated portrait with hands resting on arms of ornate armchair, marked "Brady's National Photographic Portrait Galleries, 352 Pennsylvania Avenue, Washington, D.C.," dated January 8, 1864 .... **500.00 600.00 540.00**

☐ **Photograph,** John Wilkes Booth, rare **125.00 135.00 130.00**

☐ **Photograph,** Lincoln and family, taken by Joseph Hoover, 1866 .... **85.00 100.00 92.00**

☐ **Photograph,** Lincoln's Tomb, three soldiers stand guard at front, taken by F.W. Ingmire ... **50.00 60.00 55.00**

☐ **Picture,** Lincoln and wife Mary Todd, small ... **40.00 50.00 45.00**

☐ **Print,** portrait within oval by Kellogg, dove of peace with wording "Justice, Liberty, Equality," 12" x 16" **90.00 115.00 103.00**

☐ **Ribbon,** silk, made in Switzerland, multicolor, beardless Lincoln pictured, "A. Lincoln, President", written underneath picture, 1861 .... **650.00 700.00 675.00**

☐ **Ribbon,** silk, made in Switzerland, "With Charity to all, with malice for none," written above portrait of Lincoln, weeping Columbia with face buried in U.S. flag below portrait. **250.00 300.00 275.00**

☐ **Stereo Card,** image # 1312 in the "Photographic War History" series published by Taylor & Huntington after the Civil War in 1880s, from an original stereo plate done by Mathew Brady in 1864 .... **250.00 275.00 262.00**

Envelope, *Civil War design, Lincoln and overall bicolored motif,*
$75.00–$100.00
(photo courtesy of © Lou McCulloch, Highland Heights, OH)

	Current Price Range		P/Y Average
☐ **Stereo Photograph,** box at Ford's Theater occupied by Lincoln at the time of his assassination, from the Anthony series with number 3403, made from a Matthew Brady negative	75.00	95.00	83.00
☐ **Stereo Photograph,** chair in which Lincoln was seated at time of assassination, from the Anthony series with number 3406, made from a Brady negative	75.00	95.00	82.00
☐ **Stereo Photograph,** funeral procession of Abraham Lincoln passing through Philadelphia (Broad Street), unmarked, housed in a flat yellow mat	160.00	190.00	172.00
☐ **Stereo Photograph,** funeral procession of Abraham Lincoln passing through New York (lower Broadway), from the Anthony series with number 2954	160.00	190.00	172.00
☐ **Statue,** glass, Gillinder and Sons for the 1876 Centennial Exposition, portrait bust of Lincoln, 6″	320.00	365.00	335.00
☐ **Stereo Photograph,** half length portrait from the Anthony Prominent Portraits series, numbered 2968, housed in a mount	700.00	900.00	765.00
☐ **Tintype,** bearded Lincoln, 2¼″ x 3⅞″, rare . . .	450.00	500.00	475.00
☐ **Tintype,** taken by Mathew Brady, 1860, 3¾″ x 2½″	750.00	800.00	775.00

LUNCH BOXES

DESCRIPTION: The colorful lunch boxes used by school children are avidly sought by collectors. Usually these boxes feature comic and science fiction characters. Lunch boxes from the 1950s–1980s are particularly interesting.

ADDITIONAL TIPS: Condition is extremely important and rust, scratches or dents will lower value dramatically.

RECOMMENDED READING: For further information refer to *The Official Price Guide to Science Fiction and Fantasy Collectibles* and *The Official Price Guide to Comic Books and Collectibles,* published by The House of Collectibles.

Star Trek, *Paramount Pictures,* $50.00–$60.00

	Current Price Range		P/Y Average
☐ **Battlestar Galactica,** made by Aladdin, 7″ x 7¾″	9.00	12.00	10.50
☐ **Bionic Woman**	4.00	6.00	5.00
☐ **Captain Astro**	10.00	12.00	11.00
☐ **Enterprise,** on the side with scenes from the television show Aladdin-Hump Backed, 1978	50.00	70.00	60.00
☐ **Flying Nun,** Screengems made by Aladdin, lithographed tin, illustration of Sally Field, 1968	10.00	15.00	11.00
☐ **Green Hornet**	9.00	11.00	10.00
☐ **Jungle Book,** Walt Disney Productions, lithographed tin, illustration of Mowgli, the Jungle Boy and other characters	7.00	10.00	8.25
☐ **King Kong,** Dino deLaurentis, lithographed tin, 1977	9.00	12.00	9.75
☐ **Kirk,** on one side, King-Seely Thermos Co., from the motion picture, Spock and McCoy on the other side, thermos captioned "Star Trek," 1979	10.00	15.00	12.50
☐ **Marvel Comics Super Heroes,** Marvel Comics Group, Aladdin, illustrations of The Fantastic Four, Thor, Spiderman and Captain Marvel, with vinyl thermos, 1976	12.00	16.00	13.00
☐ **Return of The Jedi,** 1983	6.00	8.00	7.00
☐ **Space 1999,** metal	5.00	7.00	6.00
☐ **Superman,** Adco-Liberty Manufacturing Co./Superman Corp./National Periodical Publications, lithographed tin, artwork shows Superman battling robot with planes circling around, 6″ x 9″, c. 1940–50	120.00	150.00	130.00

Note: Artwork could be Wayne Boring; hard to tell for certain as a number of the Superman artists used very similar styles.

	Current Price Range		P/Y Average
☐ **The Empire Strikes Back,** 1980	8.00	10.00	9.00
☐ **U.F.O.,** Century 21 Merchandising Company, lithographed tin, 1973	12.00	17.00	13.45

LUNCH BOX AND THERMOS SETS

☐ **Batman**	25.00	27.00	26.00
☐ **Battlestar Galactica**	8.00	10.00	9.00
☐ **Green Hornet**	20.00	22.00	21.00
☐ **Land Of The Giants**	12.00	15.00	13.50
☐ **Lost in Space,** metal	30.00	35.00	32.00
☐ **Monsters**	8.00	10.00	9.00
☐ **Planet Of The Apes,** metal	10.00	12.00	11.00
☐ **Space Capsule,** 1960	8.00	10.00	9.00
☐ **Space 1999**	10.00	12.00	11.00
☐ **Star Trek,** 1968	50.00	60.00	55.00
☐ **Superman,** 1967	12.00	15.00	13.50
☐ **UFO,** metal	8.00	10.00	9.00

THERMOS

☐ **Astronauts,** plastic	4.00	6.00	5.00
☐ **Batman**	10.00	12.00	11.00
☐ **Munsters**	10.00	12.00	11.00
☐ **Planet Of The Apes**	4.00	6.00	5.00
☐ **Tom Corbett Space Cadet,** Aladdin, bearing the copyright notice of Rockhill Radio, imprinted with a brightly colored illustration, 6½", 1952	20.00	25.00	21.00

LUXARDO BOTTLES

DESCRIPTION: Luxardo bottles are figural decanters produced by the Luxardo Company of Torreglia, Italy. They were first imported to America in 1930.

TYPES: Luxardo produces both glass and majolica figural bottles. Classical and natural history themes dominate the decorative bottles.

COMMENTS: Luxardo bottles are often blends of a variety of colors. This careful blending of colors attracts collectors.

ADDITIONAL TIPS: For more information, consult *The Official Price Guide to Bottles, Old and New,* published by The House of Collectibles.

	Current Price Range		P/Y Average
☐ **Alabaster Fish,** figural, c. 1960–67–68	19.00	26.00	22.00
☐ **Alabaster Goose,** figural, c. 1960–67–68, green and white, wings, etc.	19.00	26.00	22.00
☐ **Apple Figural,** c. 1960, yellow apple, green leaves	10.00	15.00	13.50
☐ **Assyrian Ash Tray Decanter,** c. 1961, gray, tan and black	16.00	22.00	19.00
☐ **Autumn Wine Pitcher,** c. 1958, hand painted country scene, handled pitcher	30.00	40.00	35.00
☐ **Babylon Decanter,** c. 1960, dark green and gold	16.00	23.00	19.50
☐ **Baby Amphoras,** c. 1956, six hand painted miniature bottles, set vari-colored	16.00	23.00	19.50
☐ **Florentine Majolica,** c. 1956, round handled decanter, painted pitcher, yellow, dragon, blue wings	21.00	27.00	24.50
☐ **Gambia,** c. 1961, black princess, kneeling holding tray, gold trim, 10¾"	14.00	19.00	16.50
☐ **Golden Fakir,** seated snake charmer, with flute and snakes, gold	26.00	37.00	32.00
☐ **1961, Fakir 1960,** black and gray	26.00	37.00	32.00
☐ **Gondola,** c. 1959, highly glazed "abstract" gondola and gondolier in black, orange and yellow, stopper on upper prow, 12¾"	21.00	27.00	24.50
☐ **Same as above,** miniature, 4½"	11.00	16.00	14.50
☐ **Gondola,** c. 1960, same as 1959, stopper moved from prow to stern	14.00	19.00	16.50
☐ **Same as above,** miniature	11.00	15.00	13.00
☐ **Grapes,** pear figural	24.00	34.00	29.00
☐ **Opal Majolica,** c. 1957, two gold handles, translucent opal top, pink base, also used as lamp base, 10"	14.00	19.00	16.50
☐ **Penguin,** Murano glass figural, c. 1968, black and white penguin, crystal base	26.00	37.00	32.00
☐ **Pheasant,** red and gold figural, c. 1960, red and gold glass bird on crystal base	23.00	35.00	28.00
☐ **Pheasant,** Murano glass figural, c. 1960, red and clear glass on a crystal base	26.00	37.00	32.00
☐ **Primavera Amphora,** c. 1958, two handled vase shape, with floral design in yellow, green and blue, 9¾"	14.00	19.00	17.00
☐ **Puppy,** Cucciolo glass figural, c. 1961, amber and green glass	26.00	37.00	32.00
☐ **Puppy,** Murano glass figural, c. 1960, amber glass, crystal base	26.00	37.00	32.00
☐ **Silver Blue Decanter,** c. 1952–55, hand painted silver flowers and leaves	22.00	28.00	25.00
☐ **Silver Brown Decanter,** c. 1952–55, hand-painted silver flowers and leaves	26.00	37.00	32.00

Luxardo Calypso Girl, *figural, (c. 1962), black, West Indian girl, flower headdress in bright color,* **$14.00-$19.00**

	Current Price Range		P/Y Average
☐ **Sir Lancelot,** c. 1962, figure of English knight in full armor with embossed shield, tan-gray with gold, 12″	14.00	19.00	16.50
☐ **Spring-Box Amphora,** c. 1952, vase with handle, leaping African deer with floral and lattice background, black, brown, 9¾″	14.00	19.00	16.50
☐ **Squirrel,** glass figural, c. 1968, amethyst colored squirrel on crystal base	30.00	40.00	35.00
☐ **Sudan,** c. 1960, two handle classic vase, incised figures, African motif in browns, blue, yellow and gray, 13½″	14.00	19.00	16.50
☐ **Torre Rosa,** c. 1962, rose tinted tower of fruit, 10¼″	16.00	24.00	20.00
☐ **Torre Tinta,** c. 1962, multicolor tower of fruit, natural shades	16.00	24.00	20.00
☐ **Tower of Fruit,** majolicas, Torre Bianca, c. 1962, white and gray tower of fruit, 10¼″	16.00	24.00	20.00
☐ **Tower of Fruit,** c. 1968, various fruits in natural colors, 22¼″	16.00	24.00	20.00

MAGAZINES

DESCRIPTION: Magazines are periodicals usually containing articles and illustrations.

TYPES: There are many types of magazines including nature, sports, home, garden and news.

COMMENTS: Hobbyists enjoy magazine collecting because periodicals capture a part of history. Magazines detail world events which make interesting reading decades later.

ADDITIONAL TIPS: Many hobbyists collect the issues of only one magazine such as Life, National Geographic or Playboy. Others collect magazines topically buying periodicals with photographs and articles about their favorite Hollywood stars, Presidents or sports heroes. Another way to collect magazines is by subject.

RECOMMENDED READING: For extensive information on a wide variety of magazines refer to *The Official Price Guide to Paperbacks and Magazines,* published by The House of Collectibles.

	Current Price Range		P/Y Average
☐ **American Museum of Natural History Bulletin.** Volumes 1–16, loose as issued, 1881–96	225.00	300.00	275.00
☐ Lot consisting of bound copies of Volumes 1–6, 8–14, 16, 18, 60, 62, 69, 85, and 96	135.00	200.00	150.00
☐ **American Museum of Natural History Bulletin.** Volume 37, bound in buckram	10.00	13.50	12.00
☐ **American Musicological Society Journal.** 1948	2.75	4.00	3.25
☐ **American Musicological Society Journal.** Volumes 1–14, cloth bound, 1948–61	325.00	400.00	350.00
☐ **American Naturalist.** Volumes 1–95, a complete set bound in boards with linen spines, some of the earlier volumes bound in marbled boards with black leather spines, condition G VG, 1867–1961	3200.00	4500.00	3500.00

House Beautiful, *September, 1926,* $4.00–$6.00

	Current Price Range		P/Y Average
☐ **American Naturalist.** Volume 1, bound, 1867	26.00	32.00	28.00
☐ **American Neptune.** Volumes 1–21, bound in cloth, 1941–61	600.00	700.00	625.00
☐ **American Neptune.** Individual issues, 1941–50	4.00	5.50	4.25
☐ **American Neurological Association.** Transactions. Volumes 59–81, bound in buckram, some volumes soiled. 1933–56	260.00	320.00	275.00
☐ **American Notes and Queries.** Volumes 1–9, lacking nine issues, loose as issued, 1888–92	40.00	45.00	42.00
☐ **American Oil Chemists' Society Journal.** Volumes 24–36, lacking several issues, loose as issued, 1947–59	200.00	260.00	235.00
☐ **Argosy.** 1882–90	4.00	5.50	4.75
☐ **Argosy.** 1891–1900	3.25	4.50	3.75
☐ **Argosy.** 1901–10	275	4.00	3.50
☐ **Argosy.** 1911–20	2.25	3.25	2.75
☐ Lot of 156 issues, some duplicates, loose as issued, a few with covers lacking, 1941–57	40.00	50.00	43.00
☐ Complete run, bound in various bindings, condition mostly good, 1881–1978	1675.00	2350.00	1775.00
☐ **Arizona Highways.** 1955–60	4.00	5.50	
☐ **Arizona Highways.** 1961–65	3.25	5.00	4.00
☐ **Atlantic Monthly.** 1950–59	2.75	3.25	3.00
☐ **Atlantic Monthly.** 1960–69	2.00	2.75	2.25
☐ **Atlantic Monthly.** 1970	1.25	2.00	1.75
☐ **Audubon Magazine.** 1950–55	4.50	7.00	6.00

	Current Price Range		P/Y Average
☐ **Audubon Magazine.** 1956–60	4.00	6.00	
☐ Lot consisting of 331 mixed issues (some duplicates), loose as issued, 1906–58	1350.00	2000.00	1400.00
☐ **Baseball Magazine, The.** 1923 (per issue)	12.00	16.00	13.00
☐ **Baseball Magazine, The.** 1955 (per issue)	3.25	4.50	4.00
☐ **Better Homes and Gardens.** Issue of June 1928	6.75	9.00	8.00
☐ **Better Homes and Gardens.** 1950–60	3.25	4.50	3.75
☐ **Better Homes and Gardens.** 1961–70	2.25	3.25	3.00
☐ **Boy's Life.** 1945–55	3.25	4.50	3.75
☐ Lot consisting of 61 different issues, 1919–68	325.00	450.00	375.00
☐ **Century Illustrated Monthly Magazine.** Bound volume, 1916	65.00	95.00	70.00
☐ **Child Life.** 1936 (per issue)	4.00	5.50	4.75
☐ **Colliers.** Complete set, bound in half morocco, 1888–1957	2750.00	3250.00	2900.00
☐ **Colliers.** Bound volume, half cloth, soiled, Jan.–June 1936	25.00	32.00	28.00
☐ **Colliers.** Individual issues, 1951	4.50	6.00	5.00
☐ **Commentary.** Bound volume, 1966	27.00	32.00	29.00
☐ **Cosmopolitan.** With Harrison Fisher covers . . .	7.75	13.50	8.00
☐ **Cosmopolitan.** 1890–99	16.75	25.00	18.50
☐ **Cosmopolitan.** 1900–10	13.50	20.00	15.50
☐ **Cosmopolitan.** 1911–20	12.00	16.75	14.00
☐ **Cosmopolitan.** 1921–30	2.75	10.00	6.75
☐ **Country Gentleman.** 1853–60	7.75	13.00	8.25
☐ **Country Gentleman.** 1861–70	6.75	11.00	8.25
☐ **Country Gentleman.** 1871–80	4.00	6.75	5.00
☐ **Dileneator, The** 1873–80	5.50	7.75	6.25
☐ **Dileneator, The.** 1881–90	4.50	6.75	5.25
☐ Mixed lot of 46 issues, prior to 1900	135.00	200.00	150.00
☐ **Etude, The.** 1900–10	1.35	2.75	2.00
☐ **Family Circle.** 1950–59	1.00	1.35	1.25
☐ **Family Circle.** 1960–69	.75	1.00	.85
☐ **16 bound volumes, cloth, various years 1940's–60's**	65.00	75.00	68.00
☐ **Field & Stream.** 1896–1900	2.75	4.00	3.00
☐ **Field & Stream.** 1901–10	2.25	3.25	3.00
☐ **Field & Stream.** 1911–20	2.00	2.75	2.50
☐ **Field & Stream.** 1921–30	1.00	2.75	1.75
☐ **Godey's Lady's Book.** Bound volume, 1842 . .	40.00	45.00	42.50
☐ **Godey's Lady's Book.** Bound volumes, half roan. 1841, 1845, 1846, 1851–57	325.00	400.00	375.00
☐ **Godey's Lady's Book.** Single issues, 1844–53	5.50	7.75	6.25
☐ **Godey's Lady's Book.** Single issues, late 1860's	2.75	4.00	3.00
☐ **Godey's Lady's Book.** Bound volumes, complete, three-quarters green leather, scuffed, some covers extracted, 1881–97	300.00	375.00	310.00
☐ **Good Housekeeping.** 1920–29	5.50	6.75	5.75
☐ **Good Housekeeping.** 1930–39	3.25	4.50	3.50
☐ **Good Housekeeping.** 1940–49	2.25	3.25	3.00
☐ **Harper's Bazaar.** Bound volume, 1871	55.00	65.00	57.00

	Current Price Range		P/Y Average
☐ **Harper's Bazaar.** Bound volume, 1884	42.00	55.00	45.00
☐ **Harper's Bazaar.** Single issues, 1893	4.00	5.50	4.50
☐ **Harper's Monthly.** 1850, per issue	6.75	9.00	7.75
☐ **Harper's Monthly.** 1851–55	11.00	20.00	14.50
☐ **Harper's Monthly.** Bound volumes, December–May, 1881, December–May, 1881	32.50	42.50	45.00
☐ **Harper's Weekly.** Complete run, bound, bindings vary, early volumes in half leather, most later ones in buckram, 1857–1916	2000.00	2600.00	2100.00
☐ **Harper's Weekly.** Single issues, 1850	5.50	7.75	6.10
☐ **Harper's Weekly.** April 21, 1860 (Stephen Douglas on cover reproduced from Mathew Brady photo)	27.50	32.50	30.00
☐ **Harper's Weekly.** Single issues, 1860–65	5.50	40.00	
☐ **Harper's Weekly.** Bound volume, January–June, 1865	135.00	200.00	
☐ **Harper's Weekly.** 26 mixed issues, 1861–77 ..	110.00	135.00	115.00
☐ **Harper's Weekly.** Single issues, 1866–80	2.75	20.00	12.50
☐ **Harper's Weekly.** Most issues after 1880	2.00	6.75	4.50
☐ **Harper's Weekly.** St. Louis Fair issue, April 30, 1904	9.00	13.50	10.00
☐ **House Beautiful.** 1930–39	2.00	3.00	2.25
☐ **Ladies Home Journal.** 1890–99	2.00	6.75	4.50
☐ **Ladies Home Journal.** 1900–10	1.75	6.75	3.50
☐ **Ladies Home Journal.** 1911–20	2.75	7.75	5.00
☐ **Ladies Home Journal.** 1921–30	1.75	6.76	5.00
☐ **Ladies Home Journal.** 426 mixed issues, loose as issued, 1902–47	1100.00	1300.00	1250.00
☐ **Ladies Home Journal.** Loose as issued, complete year 1970	6.75	7.75	7.00
☐ **Ladies Home Journal.** Loose as issued, complete year 1978	4.50	6.00	5.00
☐ **Leslie's Weekly, Frank's.** Most issues 1890–99	2.00	3.25	2.25
☐ **Leslie's Weekly, Frank's.** 1900–10	1.75	2.75	2.00
☐ **Leslie's Weekly, Frank's.** 1911–20	1.35	2.00	1.75
☐ **Liberty.** 1924–30	1.35	2.00	1.75
☐ **Liberty.** 1931–40	1.00	2.75	1.95
☐ **Life.** Bound in cloth, covers removed, ex-library copy, Volume 1, No. 1, 1936	20.00	26.00	24.00
☐ **Life.** Most single issues (except very early numbers), 1930's	6.75	16.75	14.00
☐ **Life.** Single issues, 1940–45	11.00	16.00	12.00
☐ **Life.** Single issues, 1946–50	4.00	11.00	8.00
☐ **Life.** Single issues, 1960–65	2.00	4.00	3.00
☐ **Life.** Bound volume, January–June, 1951	45.00	60.00	50.00
☐ **Batch of mixed issues (old and new Life), total of 431 copies, about 100 duplicates, some covers lacking, 1887–1956**	550.00	675.00	600.00
☐ **Literary Digest.** 1910–29	.75	1.25	1.00
☐ **Literary Digest.** Issues with Norman Rockwell covers, 1920's	4.50	6.00	5.25
☐ **Literary Digest.** 1930–38	.75	1.00	.80
☐ **Literary Digest.** Bound volume, full year, 1935	6.75	7.75	7.00

	Current Price Range		P/Y Average
☐ **Look.** Single issues, 1930's	6.75	9.50	8.00
☐ **Look.** Single issues, 1940's.	4.50	6.75	5.00
☐ **Lot of 321 issues, good condition, 1941–70**	400.00	540.00	450.00
☐ **McCall's.** 1873–1910	4.50	11.00	
☐ **McCall's.** 1911–20	4.00	6.75	
☐ **McCall's.** 1921–30	2.75	4.50	
☐ **McCall's.** 1931–40	2.25	4.00	
☐ **McCall's.** Volume 43, bound, 1966	7.75	11.00	
☐ **McCall's.** Volume 53, bound, 1975	7.00	10.00	8.00
☐ **Mentor, The.** Personality issue, bound in half leather, owner's name on spine, June 1928	13.50	16.75	15.00
☐ **Modern Priscilla.** 1887–99	2.00	3.25	2.50
☐ **Modern Priscilla.** Bound volume, 1891	18.00	22.00	19.50
☐ **Modern Priscilla.** Bound volume, 1896	20.00	26.00	24.00
☐ **Modern Priscilla.** Individual issues, 1921–30	4.50	6.00	5.00
☐ **Motion Picture.** Pre–1920 issues	13.50	20.00	15.00
☐ **Motion Picture.** 1921–30	11.00	16.00	14.00
☐ **Motion Picture.** 1931–40	10.00	13.50	12.00
☐ **Motion Picture.** 1941–50	4.50	7.00	5.50
☐ **Motion Picture.** 1951–60	2.00	3.25	3.00
☐ **Motion Picture News.** Pre–1930 issues	5.50	6.75	6.25
☐ **National Geographic.** Volume 1, No. 1 (1880)	550.00	675.00	600.00
☐ **National Geographic.** Volume 1, No. 2	200.00	325.00	275.00
☐ **National Geographic.** March 1898	45.00	60.00	50.00
☐ **National Geographic.** Most issues 1908–12	13.50	20.00	14.00
☐ **National Geographic.** Bound volumes with covers intact:			
☐ **No. 1, four issues, (1888–89)**	1350.00	2000.00	1400.00
☐ **No. 2, five issues, (1890–91)**	400.00	540.00	450.00
☐ No. 3, five issues, (1891–92)	600.00	700.00	625.00
☐ No. 6, Nine issues, (1894–95)	600.00	700.00	625.00
☐ **Nature.** Issues prior to 1920	1.00	2.00	1.75
☐ **Nature.** 1920–29	.75	1.35	1.00
☐ **Needlecraft.** Individual issues, 1909	1.35	4.50	2.50
☐ **Needlecraft.** 1910–19	1.35	4.00	3.00
☐ **Needlecraft.** 1920–29	.75	1.00	.95
☐ **Newsweek.** 1950–55	2.00	3.25	2.25
☐ **Newsweek.** 1956–60	1.75	2.75	2.10
☐ **Newsweek.** 1961–65	1.35	2.00	1.75
☐ **Newsweek.** 1966–70	1.00	1.35	1.10
☐ **Peterson's Magazine.** Bound in one-quarter roan, 1843 full year	54.00	65.00	56.00
☐ **Peterson's magazine.** Individual issues, 1844	4.50	6.00	5.00
☐ **Peterson's Magazine.** Individual issues, 1861	4.00	5.50	5.00
☐ **Photoplay.** Individual issues, 1920–29	16.75	26.00	18.50
☐ **Photoplay.** Complete year, bound in two volumes, half red leather, 1925	175.00	225.00	195.00
☐ **Photoplay.** Complete year, bound in two volumes, cloth, scuffed, 1927	160.00	200.00	175.00
☐ **Photoplay.** Bound in orange buckram, ex-library, 1928, Jan.–June	60.00	70.00	65.00
☐ **Photoplay.** Individual issues, 1930–39	12.00	16.00	14.00
☐ **Photoplay.** Individual issues, 1940–49	7.75	11.00	10.00

	Current Price Range		P/Y Average
☐ **Pictorial Review.** Most single issues, World War I era................................	2.75	5.50	4.50
☐ **Popular Mechanics.** 1900–10	1.35	2.00	1.75
☐ **Popular Mechanics.** 1960–69	.75	.85	.75
☐ **Popular Science.** Pre–1900 issues	.85	1.65	1.00
☐ **Popular Science.** 1901–10	1.35	2.00	1.50
☐ **Popular Science.** 1911–30	1.50	2.25	2.00
☐ **Prairie Farmer, The.** 1920–29	1.00	2.00	1.50
☐ **Puck.** Issues of the early 1900's	4.00	6.75	5.00
☐ **Reader's Digest.** Individual issues, 1930's	.75	1.35	1.00
☐ **Reader's Digest.** 1940–60	.50	1.00	.75
☐ **Reader's Digest.** Bound volumes, half imitation leather, gilt tops, 1948–66..................	110.00	160.00	120.00
☐ **Saturday Evening Post.** Individual issues, 1900–09	4.00	6.75	5.00
☐ **Saturday Evening Post.** 1911–20 (except with Rockwell covers)..........................	4.50	6.00	5.00
☐ **Saturday Evening Post.** 1921–30 (except with Rockwell covers)..........................	4.00	6.00	5.00
☐ **Saturday Evening Post.** 1931–40 (except with Rockwell covers)..........................	2.75	4.00	3.00
☐ **Mixed lot of 1,628 issues, in 23 cardboard cartons, mostly good condition, a few duplicates, late 19th-century to 1960's**	1350.00	2000.00	1395.00
☐ **Complete year, bound in four folio volumes, three-quarters brown pigskin with sailcloth sides, gilt tops, 1951**	160.00	200.00	175.00
☐ **Scientific American.** Individual issues, 1950–60	1.25	1.75	1.50
☐ **Scribner's Monthly.** World War I era, individual issues	.50	.75	.65
☐ **Scribner's Monthly.** Bound volume, 1879	7.75	10.00	8.00
☐ **Sports Afield.** Most single issues, 1890–1940	3.25	6.75	5.00
☐ **St. Nicholas.** Mixed lot of 36 issues, a few with covers missing, 1890–99	65.00	100.00	75.00
☐ **Woman's Home Companion.** 1900–10	4.00	6.75	5.00

MAPS

TOPIC: Printed maps showing the layout of the land were printed as early as the mid–1400s. Later maps featured landmarks, altitudes, territorial boundaries and even more specialized information such as mineral deposits. Of course, the most common map found today is the road map.

TYPES: Maps can be traditional or "bird's eye" perspective of a town or other small area. "Bird's eye" maps feature the town as seen from one point in space, while traditional maps are not done in perspective.

PERIOD: Artistically and historically, maps from the 1600s are the most desirable. For the purposes of the average collector, however, most specimens date from the 1800s.

COMMENTS: Maps are collected both for their beauty and their historical importance. Often maps reflect the misconception people had about distances and relationships between land forms.

ADDITIONAL TIPS: Since maps with margins are worth more than those that have been trimmed down, examine the margin area carefully to determine its condition. Also look for creases caused by careless handling, since these lessen the value of the map. Condition is very important in the map collecting field. For more information, please refer to *The Official Price Guide to Paper Collectibles,* published by The House of Collectibles.

	Current Price Range		P/Y Average
☐ **A Map of the Most Inhabited Part of New England,** containing the Provinces of Massachusetts Bay and New Hampshire with the Colonies of Connecticut and Rhode Island, colored outlines, two section, each measuring 21″ x 39½″, Paris, after the original by M. Le Rouge, 1777	460.00	510.00	485.00
☐ **A Map of New England and New York,** shows southwest to Chesapeake Bay, sold by Thomas Basset and Richard Chiswell, uncolored, 16½″ x 21½″, London, 1676	460.00	560.00	510.00

Atlas, *North America, J. Olney's Atlas, engraved by D. Robinson, 1829,* **$40.00-$45.00**
Photo courtesy of Lou McCulloch, Highland Heights, OH 44143.

	Current Price Range		P/Y Average

☐ **A Map of Virginia and Maryland,** sold by Thomas Basset and Richard Chiswell, Uncolored, 17″ x 22¼″, London, 1676 . . . . — 460.00 / 560.00 / 510.00

☐ **America,** engraved, 11″ x 14″, Frankfurt, Merian, second quarter of the seventeenth century . . . . — 300.00 / 350.00 / 315.00

☐ **America,** engraved, based on Mercator's maps, 14¾″ x 19″, Amsterdam, Hondius, 1631 . . . . . . — 725.00 / 925.00 / 760.00

☐ **America,** engraved, based on Mercator's maps, illustrations of sailing vessels and sea monsters, inset of "Terra Incognita," 15″ x 20″, Amsterdam, Jansson, second quarter of the seventeenth century . . . . — 800.00 / 1100.00 / 900.00

☐ **America,** engraved, bordered with likeness of native costumes and dignitaries (one identified as "King of Florida"), shows and names Martha's Vineyard, portrays California as a island, Atlantic Ocean is identified as "The North Sea," Pacific Ocean is "The South Sea," 15½″ x 20″, London, Speed, 1626 . . . . — 2000.00 / 3000.00 / 2275.00

☐ **America,** engraved, has California as an island, 19″ x 23½″, Amsterdam, Allard, c. 1690–1710 — 750.00 / 1000.00 / 825.00

☐ **America,** engraved, shows California as an island, 19″ x 22″, London, Senex, c. 1720 . . . . . . — 600.00 / 800.00 / 650.00

☐ **America,** engraved, shows routes of Cortez, Drake and Mendana, illustrations of native birds and manners of the Indians, 19½″ x 22″, Augsburg, Seutter, c. 1735 . . . . — 700.00 / 900.00 / 750.00

☐ **America,** engraved, uncolored, 18″ x 21″, Nuremburg, Hasius, 1746 . . . . — 700.00 / 1000.00 / 790.00

☐ **British And French Dominions in North America,** engraved, a large wall map consisting of eight separate sheets, each sheet 26″ x 19″, price is for full set, London, Jefferys and Faden, c. 1765 . . . . — 8000.00 / 10000.00 / 8275.00

☐ **California,** engraved, shows it as an island in the Pacific crudely shaped, illustrations of wildlife, 18″ x 26″, Paris, DeFer, 1720 . . . . — 1500.00 / 2000.00 / 1575.00

☐ **Caroline Meridionale et Partie de la Georgia,** Par le Chevr. Bull . . . Chevr. Bryan, et de Brahn . . . colored outlines, two sheets, each measuring 29″ x 42″, A Paris, chez Le Rouge, 1777 . . . . . — 460.00 / 510.00 / 485.00

☐ **Carte de la Floride Occidentale et Louisiana,** shows coast of Louisiana to westward of New Orleans, the coasts of Mississippi and Alabama, all but the southern tip of Florida, and the Bahamas, mainly uncolored, 21″ x 54¾″, Paris, Le Rouge, 1777 . . . . — 210.00 / 270.00 / 240.00

☐ **Carte des Troubles de l'Amerique Levee,** Par Ordre du Chevalier Tryon, Capitaine General et Gouverneur de la Province de New-York Ensemble la Province de New-Jersey, Par Sauthier et Ratzer, traduit de l'Anglois, from Montreal south to Delaware Bay and Cape Henlopen and from

	Current Price Range		P/Y Average

Salem and Marblehead (northeast of Boston) westward to part of Lake Ontario, colored outlines, 29" x 21", Paris, Le Rouge, 1778 . . . . — 275.00 / 325.00 / 300.00

☐ **Chicago,** lithographed, very detailed street plan, most streets renamed since then but still recognizable, 22½" x 37½", New York, Talcott, 1836 . . . . — 1500.00 / 1900.00 / 1625.00

☐ **Chignecto Bay,** engraved, 14" x 22½", London, Jefferys, 1755 . . . . — 450.00 / 600.00 / 510.00

☐ **English Colonies And Canada,** engraved, 18½" x 23½", Amsterdam, Visscher, c. 1680 — 1200.00 / 1600.00 / 1350.00

☐ **Les Cotes aux Environs de la Riviere de Misisipi Descouvertes par Mr. de la Salle en 1683 et reconnues par M. le Chevallier d'liberville en 1698 et 1699,** par N. de Fer, Geographe de Monseigneur le Dauphine, shows the present Gulf states, the Bahamas, Cuba and part of Mexico, colored, 9" x 13", Paris, 1705 . . . . — 275.00 / 325.00 / 300.00

☐ **Map of Louisiana, Mississippi and Alabama,** colored, 18¾" x 25", Philadelphia, A. Finley, 1827 . . . . — 85.00 / 115.00 / 100.00

☐ **Map of Maine, New Hampshire and Vermont,** colored, 18¾" x 25", Philadelphia, A. Finley, 1826 . . . . — 125.00 / 175.00 / 150.00

☐ **Map of Massachusetts, Connecticut and Rhode Island,** colored, 18¾" x 24¾", Philadelphia, A. Finley, 1826 . . . . — 85.00 / 115.00 / 100.00

☐ **Map of North and South Carolina and Georgia,** colored, 18¾" x 24¾", Philadelphia, A. Finley, 1827 . . . . — 85.00 / 115.00 / 100.00

☐ **Map of Pennsylvania, New Jesey and Delaware,** colored, 18¾" x 24¾", Philadelphia, A. Finley . . . . — 85.00 / 115.00 / 100.00

☐ **Map of Reconnaissance Exhibiting the Country between Washington and New Orleans,** The Routes examined in reference to a contemplated National Road between those two cities, mostly uncolored, 21¾" x 28", N.p., 1826 . . . . — 85.00 / 115.00 / 100.00

☐ **Map of the State of Missouri and Territory of Arkansas,** colored, 18¾" x 25", Philadelphia, A. Finley, 1826 . . . . — 100.00 / 140.00 / 120.00

☐ **Map of Virginia and Maryland,** colored, 18¾" x 25", Philadelphia, A. Finley, 1827 . . . . — 85.00 / 115.00 / 100.00

☐ **Nouvelle Carte des Cotes des Carolines (North and South) . . . du Cap Fear a Sud Edisto,** Levees et Sondees par N. Pocock en 1770, traduites de l'Anglois, uncolored, 21" x 29¼", A Paris, chez Le Rouge, 1777 . . . . — 230.00 / 300.00 / 265.00

☐ **Philadelphia,** engraved, includes detailed street plan as well as surrounding villages (Germantown, Derby, Frankfort), Quaker meeting houses, 18" x 23½", Augsburg, Scull and Heap, 1777 — 900.00 / 1150.00 / 985.00

	Current Price Range		P/Y Average

☐ **Russian America,** (Alaska and surrounding territory), engraved, grossly inaccurate in many respects, 18″ x 25″, Paris, Delisle, c. 1780 ..... **800.00 1000.00 875.00**

☐ **Russian America,** (Alaska and surrounding territory), engraved, 19″ x 25″, St. Petersburg (now Leningrad), Von Staehlin, 1784 .... **400.00 550.00 470.00**
Note: This was a refutation of the Delisle map of Russian America published earlier in Paris, which was so inaccurate that it caused embarrassment to the Russians.

☐ **United States,** engraved, colored, titled "National Map of the American Republic," 24″ x 34″, Philadelphia, Mitchell, 1843 .... **350.00 450.00 380.00**

☐ **United States,** engraved, ornamental border with vignettes of major cities, 69″ x 85″, New York, Calvin Smith, 1853 .... **1000.00 1250.00 1100.00**

☐ **United States,** engraved, 16″ x 21″, Paris, Bouchon, 1825 .... **150.00 200.00 165.00**

☐ **United States,** engraved, 48″ x 56″, London, Arrowsmith, 1795 .... **1350.00 1625.00 1475.00**

☐ **United States of America,** colored, 17¼″ x 22¼″, engraved by B. Tanner, Philadelphia, 1827 .... **75.00 125.00 100.00**

☐ **Virginia, Maryland** ... par Fry et Jefferson ... augmente a Paris, chez Le Rouge, 1777, partly colored outlines, 29″ x 40½″ **400.00 520.00 460.00**

☐ **Virginiae Partis Australis, et Floridae Partis Orientalis,** shows from Chesapeake Bay to a small part of present northeastern Florida, cartouche of Indians and ships at sea, colored outlines, 18½″ x 23″, Amsterdam, Blaeu, c. 1640 **325.00 375.00 350.00**

☐ **World,** engraved, insets of Arctic and Antarctic, Niger River shown in Africa (its existence was only speculation at that time), 19″ x 22″, Paris, Delisle, 1700 .... **800.00 1000.00 835.00**

☐ **World,** engraved, titled "A New and Accurate Map of the World," two large hemispheres surrounded by illustrations of the elements, solar and lunar eclipse, portraits of Drake, Cavendish, Magellan and Noort (first four explorers to circle the globe), 15½″ x 20½″, London, Speed, 1651 .... **2000.00 2500.00 2200.00**

☐ **World,** engraved, typical world map of that era with Europe and Eastern Asia fairly accurate and distortions in North and South America, 20″ x 26″, Holland, Vander Leyden, c. 1720 .... **800.00 1000.00 885.00**

☐ **World,** woodcut, figures of the Twelve Winds, 11″ x 13½″, Basle, Sebastian Munster, 1540 **600.00 775.00 650.00**

☐ **World,** woodcut, titled "Charta Cosmographica," shows the world opened out and laid flat in one continuous section, illustrations off sailing vessels and allegorical subjects, South America recognizable but North America blundered, 8″ x 12″, Antwerp, Gemma Frisius, 1584 .... **700.00 900.00 775.00**

MARBLEHEAD POTTERY

ORIGIN: Marblehead Pottery was organized by Dr. Herbert J. Hall of Marblehead, Massachusetts. Marblehead Pottery started as a therapeutic resource for invalids until size forced it to branch out on its own. In 1916, it was bought by artist Arthur Baggs.

DESCRIPTIONS: The ware produced was heavy and dark using colors like gray, brown, blue and yellow. Later, a cream colored ware with multicolored decoration was introduced and included a new line of children's pieces. The company ceased production in 1936.

MARKS: Backstamps include a sailing ship with a M and P on opposite sides and a monogram of Arthur E. Baggs.

	Current Price Range		P/Y Average
☐ **Bowl,** 6″, dark blue glaze	35.00	45.00	37.00
☐ **Candlestick,** 3″, blue glaze, pair	75.00	90.00	77.00
☐ **Pitcher,** 4¾″, dark blue glaze	50.00	65.00	52.00
☐ **Planter,** turquoise glaze, artist signed, 1934 . . .	225.00	250.00	230.00
☐ **Tile,** 6½″ x 6½″, brown and yellow glaze, floral motif, rare	150.00	170.00	155.00
☐ **Vase,** 3½″, bulbous shape, gray matt with blue flecks	70.00	80.00	75.00
☐ **Vase,** 6″, black glaze	400.00	450.00	410.00
☐ **Vase,** 6½″, green glaze	40.00	50.00	42.00
☐ **Vase,** 7″, cylinder shape, tree motif, gray and green glaze, artist signed	275.00	325.00	280.00
☐ **Vase,** 7″, dark blue glaze	50.00	60.00	55.00
☐ **Wall Pocket,** blue glaze	50.00	60.00	55.00

MARBLES

TYPES: Most common are glass marbles. Antique marbles were made of steel, porcelain, clay, agate, onyx, rose quartz and carnelian. Marble was rarely used. Most marbles measure from ½″ to 1½″ in diameter. Larger ones were used for other types of games.

PERIOD: The most collectible marbles were handmade in Germany before World War I, though some were also made in America during that time. Since World War I most marbles have been machine made and hold little interest for the collector.

COMMENTS: Marble value is not based on age. Material, beauty, design and rarity are the variables. Most common are marbles made of crockery, stone or clay. Limestone marbles are more rare. Agate marbles are valuable, as are one-of-a-kind "end of day" marbles which were made of leftover glass scraps.

ADDITIONAL TIPS: The listings are alphabetical according to type of marble. For more marble information, refer to *The Official Price Guide to Collectible Toys,* published by The House of Collectibles.

	Current Price Range		P/Y Average
☐ **Carpet Bowl,** black on white, diameter 3¼″ ..	45.00	55.00	48.00
☐ **Double Ribbon,** one with red, yellow and white, one blue and white, wide ribbons, yellow and white outer strands, diameter 1¾″	60.00	70.00	62.00
☐ **Granite,** large dark brown and gray paint beauty, diameter 3″	75.00	87.00	78.00
☐ **Ivory,** ivory sphere, diameter 2″	8.00	12.00	10.00
☐ **Latticinio Swirl,** white core with four outer bands, two red and white, two green and yellow, diameter 1⅜″	30.00	40.00	34.00
☐ **Latticinio Swirl,** white core with six very bright outer bands, three green and white, three red and yellow, diameter 1⅜″	60.00	70.00	65.00
☐ **Latticinio Swirl,** yellow core with many outer bands, each having red, white, blue and yellow, diameter 1½″	60.00	70.00	64.00

	Current Price Range		P/Y Average

☐ **Latticinio Swirl,** white core with four multicolored outer bands, diameter 1½″ 60.50 70.00 **64.00**

☐ **Latticinio Swirl,** yellow core, six outer bands, three red and blue, three red and green, diameter 1⅝″ 60.00 70.00 **65.00**

☐ **Latticinio Swirl,** yellow core with four wide outer bands of blue, white and yellow, diameter 1⅝″ 45.00 55.00 **50.00**

☐ **Latticinio Swirl,** white core with six outer bands, three blue and white, three red and white, diameter 1⅝″ 55.00 65.00 **60.00**

☐ **Latticinio Swirl,** yellow core with six wide outer bands, three white, one blue, one green, one red, diameter 1¾″ 75.00 85.00 **80.00**

☐ **Latticinio Swirl,** yellow core with wide red, blue and green outer bands, diameter 1¾″ 55.00 65.00 **53.00**

☐ **Latticinio Swirl,** white core with eight outer bands, four red, two blue and white, two green and white, diameter 1⅞″ 85.00 95.00 **90.00**

☐ **Latticinio Swirl,** white core with four wide outer bands one with yellow and blue, one with red and yellow, diameter 1⅞″ 85.00 95.00 **90.00**

☐ **Latticinio Swirl,** white core with blue bands, narrow yellow alternate bands, diameter 1⅞″ 90.00 110.00 **100.00**

☐ **Open Core,** wide bands, two red and white, one blue and white, one green and white, yellow outer strands, diameter 1¾″ 85.00 95.00 **80.00**

☐ **Open Core,** four very wide bands, yellow and red, yellow and green, blue and white, red and white with four sets of three outer strands, two white and two yellow, core fills the marble, diameter 1¾″ 85.00 95.00 **88.00**

☐ **Open Core,** four multicolored center bands, four sets of three yellow outer strands, diameter 1⅞″ 85.00 95.00 **90.00**

☐ **Open Core,** two red and two blue center bands, four sets of three white outer strands, gray glass, diameter 1⅞″ 60.00 70.00 **65.00**

☐ **Open core,** three wide center bands, three sets of four yellow outer strands, diameter 2″ 90.00 110.00 **100.00**

☐ **Open Core,** four wide multicolored central bands, yellow and white outer strands, diameter 2″ 85.00 95.00 **87.00**

☐ **Pottery,** modern, handpainted, glazed, diameter 1½″ 12.00 18.00 **14.00**

☐ **Pottery,** modern, handpainted, glazed, diameter 2″ 18.00 24.00 **20.00**

☐ **Ribbon Swirl,** single very wide ribbon core with two wide sets of yellow outer strands, diameter 2½″ 70.00 80.00 **72.00**

☐ **Solid Core,** triple layer, center core white with narrow red, blue and green overlay stripes, narrow yellow outer strands, diameter 1½″ 50.00 60.00 **54.00**

	Current Price Range		P/Y Average
☐ **Solid Core,** double twist, diameter 1⅝"	67.00	77.00	69.00
☐ **Solid Core,** double twist with red, white, blue and green core, yellow outer strands, diameter 1¾"	72.00	82.00	74.00

MAXFIELD PARRISH PRINTS

DESCRIPTION: Maxfield Parrish was a successful American illustrator and artist during the early 1900s.

TYPES: Parrish did ads for various national companies, magazines covers and many limited edition prints. A popular collector's item is Parrish's Collier Magazine covers.

PERIOD: Parrish's popularity reached extraordinary heights until the 1940s. His work regained popularity in the 1960s.

ADDITIONAL TIPS: This section only lists Parrish's prints. For additional information, consult *The Official Price Guide to Collector Prints,* published by The House of Collectibles.

	Current Price
☐ **Above The Balcony,** knaves and maidens in garden	35.00
☐ **Air Castles,** nude in bubbles	125.00
☐ **Aladdin In Cave Of 40 Thieves,** 12" x 16¼", on quality paper	85.00
☐ **Aladdin And The Lamp,** 10" x 12"	70.00
☐ **Ancient Trees,** large oak tree by lake	95.00
☐ **Argonauts, In Quest of the Golden Fleece, The**	40.00
☐ **Atlas,** giant holding up sky	70.00
☐ **Arizona,** landscape of mountain-rich blues 11" x 13"	40.00
☐ **Aucassin Seeks Nicolotte,** knight on horse, Bookplate SM	18.00
☐ **Autumn,** maiden standing on hilltop	75.00
☐ **Below the Balcony,** knaves and maidens in garden	35.00
☐ **Bookplate,** John Cox-His Book	20.00
☐ **Brazen, The Boatman,** 10" x 12"	70.00

	Current Price
☐ **Brown And Bigelow Landscape,** the village church, 24″ x 27″	175.00
☐ **Cadmus Showing the Dragons Teeth,** 10″ x 12″	40.00
☐ **Canyon,** maiden in canyon, 12″ x 5″	130.00
☐ **Circles Palace,** maiden standing on porch	40.00
☐ **Cleopatra,** rare, large	500.00
☐ **Community Plate,** 11″ x 13″, 1918	25.00
☐ **Contentment,** large Edison Mazda Calendar	375.00
☐ **Dawn,** maiden sitting on rock, Mazda print	42.00
☐ **Daybreak,** nude and maiden on porch, small size	125.00
☐ **Daybreak,** large size	200.00
☐ **Dinkey Bird,** nude on swing, 13½″ x 18″, 1904	125.00
☐ **Djer-Kiss Ad,** Maiden on swing in forest, 10½″ x 14″	40.00
☐ **Dreaming,** nude sitting under oak, medium size	225.00
☐ **Dreaming,** large size	400.00
☐ **Dream Castle in the Sky,** 9″ x 12″	35.00
☐ **Duchess at Prayer,** illustration for L'Allegro, 10″ x 15″, 1901	20.00
☐ **Ecstasy,** maiden standing on rock, small size	125.00
☐ **Ecstasy,** large Edison Mazda Calendar	500.00
☐ **Enchantment,** maiden standing on stars at night, 9½″ x 20½″, large ..	400.00
☐ **Errant Pan, The,** Pan sitting by stream, 6″ x 8″, small	25.00
☐ **Evening,** nude sitting on rock in lake	135.00
☐ **Evening,** nude sitting in lake, 13″ x 17″	80.00
☐ **Fisherman And The Geni, The,** 10″ x 12″	65.00
☐ **Florentine Fete,** maidens in garden, 10″ x 16″	30.00
☐ **Garden of Allah,** 3 maidens sitting in garden, medium size	125.00
☐ **Garden of Allah,** Large Edison Mazda Calendar	275.00
☐ **Garden Of Opportunity, The,** prince and princess	325.00
☐ **Garden of Opportunity Triptyk,** 10″ x 13″	50.00
☐ **Golden Hours,** maidens in forest, Large Edison Mazda Calendar	350.00
☐ **Hilltop,** youths sitting on mountain, medium size House of Art	200.00
☐ **Hilltop,** large size, House of Art	450.00
☐ **Hilltop,** small size	75.00

Garden of Allah *by Maxfield Parrish,* **$95.00–$190.00**

	Current Price
☐ **His Christmas Dinner,** tramp having dinner	50.00
☐ **Interlude,** maidens sitting in garden playing lutes	110.00
☐ **Isola Bella Scene,** 9″ x 10″	16.00
☐ **Jason and His Teacher Chiron The Centaur,** 1910	35.00
☐ **King of the Black Isles,** king on throne, on quality paper 9 x 11	70.00
☐ **Kings Son, The,** Arab in garden by fountain	40.00
☐ **Knaves and Maidens,** conversing in garden	50.00
☐ **Lamplighters, The,** Mazda Calendar, 9″ x 13″, 1924	90.00
☐ **Lampseller of Bagdad, The,** maiden on steps, Mazda Calendar	350.00
☐ **Land of Make-Believe, The,** maiden to garden	20.00
☐ **Little Princess, The,** princess sitting by fountain	18.00
☐ **Lute Players,** small size, House of Art	60.00
☐ **Lute Players,** large size, House of Art	400.00
☐ **Milkmaid, The,** maiden walking in Mountain	20.00
☐ **Morning,** maiden sitting on rock, 13″ x 16″	120.00
☐ **Night Call,** bare breasted girl in surf, 6″ x 8″	25.00
☐ **October—1900,** woman in long gown holding fruit draped in her gown, large orange moon behind her head, 18″ x 23″	25.00
☐ **Old Romance,** nude sitting in pool, 6″ x 8″	45.00
☐ **Old King Cole**	375.00
☐ **Pandora's Box,** maiden sitting by large box	70.00
☐ **Pierrot,** clown with lute and gorgeous golds in water, sky glittering, 1912	110.00
☐ **Pool of the Villa D'Este,** nude boy lying down besides luminous pool, 7¼″ x 10¾″	18.00
☐ **Pipe Night,** comical men with pipes and coffee urns sitting facing each other at table, 9″ x 12½″	25.00
☐ **Post standing,** by river in forest	25.00
☐ **Potpourri,** nude in garden picking flowers	40.00
☐ **Primitive Man,** unique salesman's sample, 4¾″ x 7½″	45.00
☐ **Prince Goodad,** pirates on boat	70.00
☐ **Prince, The,** from Knave of Hearts, 10″ x 12½″, very rare	125.00
☐ **Prosperina,** maiden in the sea, 10″ x 12″	70.00
☐ **Providing It By The Book,** 2 gents at table	18.00
☐ **Queen Guinare,** maiden on porch, 10″ x 12″	70.00
☐ **Reveries,** two maidens sitting by fountain	35.00
☐ **Reveries,** Large Edison Mazda Calendar	200.00
☐ **Sandman, The,** sandman with full moon, 6″ x 7½″	30.00
☐ **Scribners One Of The Wise Men,** 10″ x 11½″	18.00
☐ **Search For The Singing Tree**	35.00
☐ **Sea Nymphs,** 12″ x 14″, 1914	45.00
☐ **Seven Green Polls At Cintra,** 6″ x 8″	25.00
☐ **Shepherd With Sheep,** 8½″ x 13½″	18.00
☐ **Ship In Ocean,** 11″ x 13½″	35.00
☐ **Sinbad And The Cyclops,** 10″ x 12″	35.00
☐ **Sing A Song Of Sixpence,** 9″ x 21″	425.00
☐ **Singing Tree, The,** 10″ x 12″	40.00
☐ **Stars,** House of Art, medium size, nude sitting on Rock	300.00
☐ **Stars,** House of Art, large size, nude sitting on Rock	525.00
☐ **Story From Phoebus,** 8″ x 10″, 1901	16.00
☐ **Sunlit Valley,** scenic of river and mountains	125.00
☐ **Sunrise,** Edison Mazda Calendar Top	125.00
☐ **Sunrise,** Edison Mazda Calendar, rare, large	500.00

	Current Price
☐ **Swifts Ham Ad**, Jack Sprat and wife	40.00
☐ **Turquoise Cup, The**, Gent sitting in Villa	18.00
☐ **Twilight Had Fallen**, two figures on beach	25.00
☐ **Valley of Diamonds**, Arab in Valley	35.00
☐ **Venetian Lamplighter**, Edison Mazda Calendar, 1924	85.00
☐ **Villa D'Este**, nude sitting by pool	30.00
☐ **Walls of Jasper**, youth and castle, 12″ x 14″	85.00
☐ **Waterfall**, small Edison Mazda Calendar	125.00
☐ **Waterfall**, large Edison Mazda Calendar	550.00
☐ **White Birch**, farmer under large birch	35.00
☐ **Wild Geese**, girl on Rock, 13″ x 16″	120.00
☐ **Knave Of Hearts Book**, mint	600.00
☐ **Dreamlight**, maiden sitting on swing in forest, large Edison Mazda Calendar, 9½″ x 20½″, 1925, large	475.00

McCOY POTTERY

DESCRIPTION: This 20th century company is noted both for its artware and general lines of tableware, as well as decorative pieces and utilitarian pottery of many kinds. The majority of its fine artware, now so avidly sought, was produced in its earlier years of operation prior to 1930. As was the case with a number of other firms, a cutback on artware production became necessary during the Depression of the 1930s, because only essential merchandise was sought by the public. Brush-McCoy's lines of popular-priced wares fared extremely well in stores throughout the nation. They were continued and expanded in the 1940s and 1950s with many sales registered by mail order via the major catalogue houses. Today the available variety of Brush-McCoy wares for the collector is overwhelming, offering something for just about all tastes and budgets. There are even many pieces of very recent vintage, going back to the 1960s.

HISTORY: Brush-McCoy Pottery was first established as the J.W. McCoy Pottery Company, located in Roseville, Ohio—the heart of Ohio "clay country." From all available evidence, it seems that the company got off to an ambitious start when it was incorporated in 1899. J.W. McCoy reportedly had $15,000 capital at the outset, then two years later had multiplied this investment to $100,000.

In 1909, George Brush joined the organization after a pottery works he had been operating was ruined by fire. However, it was not until two years later that the name became Brush-McCoy. J.W. McCoy was not an office holder in the newly reorganized Brush-McCoy Pottery Co. Two reasons could be attributed to his lack of interest. In 1910, McCoy and son Nelson founded The Nelson McCoy Sanitary Stoneware Co., also in Roseville, Ohio. There is also speculation that McCoy's health was failing since he died three years later. After McCoy's death in 1914, Nelson McCoy served on the Brush-McCoy Board of Directors until 1918. The name McCoy was dropped from the company name in 1925.

MARKS: Many different marks were used by this company for its various lines. In its earlier days and up to the Depression, it rarely marked any of its art pottery, and therefore identification must be made on the basis of style. Later, its artware was customarily marked. The more commonly found mark (used on later wares) is the name *BRUSH* in block capitals with flourishing serifs on the first and last letters. This is above the initials *USA*. There are several varieties of this mark. The variations are not of great help in dating as they were often used simultaneously. Several of the marks of this organization, both early and late, made a play on the word "Brush," picturing artists' brushes. These would sometimes be accompanied by an inkwell or a palette. Beginning in the late 1930's, it was customary for the object's mold number to appear in the mark. The collector of Brush-McCoy is certain to learn far more from studying the works themselves than from studying the marks.

	Current Price Range		P/Y Average
☐ **Ashtray,** frogs, 6½", mud brown, green and marble-white, a pair of frogs, seated at either side of a shallow bowl tray, their heads turned upward and moutns open (the open mouths designed as rests for cigars or cigarettes), the frogs have alternate stripes of brown and pale green on their legs	7.00	9.00	8.00
☐ **Ashtray,** turtle, 5", ivory-white and various reddish hues mixed with brown, the form of a standing turtle	5.00	6.75	5.50
☐ **Bank,** Emigrant, Golden Eagle	12.00	13.00	12.50
☐ **Bank,** frog, 3½", forest green and yellow, a bullfrog seated on a circular platform with ribbed edge, both are green, with yellow highlights	24.00	27.50	25.00
☐ **Bank,** 7¼", Williamsburg, gray with original pen holder	11.00	13.00	11.50
☐ **Basket,** 9" x 7", green and brown, marked 1/29/3C	10.00	12.00	10.50
☐ **Bean Pot,** high gloss brown, marked 1/21/3A	6.00	7.00	6.25
☐ **Bean Pot,** with lid, 2 quart, brown, marked H59/1	21.00	24.00	22.00
☐ **Birdbath Ornament,** frog, 8", beige and slate purple with gray, a frog seated on a tree stump, slate purple with hints of gray, his chest a pale cream-beige, the tree stump is a somewhat deeper beige with slate purple streaking to suggest wood texture	30.00	35.00	30.00

	Current Price Range		P/Y Average

☐ **Birdbath Ornament,** frog, 7½", marble-white, a pair of frogs, one standing with legs crossed, the other seated with hand on knee . . . . — 24.00 — 28.00 — 26.00

☐ **Bookends,** pair of birds, marked 161/2/3 . . . . — 17.50 — 18.50 — 18.00

☐ **Bookends, "Wise Bird,"** 7", burnt orange, lavender and yellow, an owl wearing spectacles, holding an open book and reading, he perches upon a stump and faces a lectern which forms the support of each bookend, pair . . . . — 70.00 — 85.00 — 71.00

☐ **Same as above,** but single bookend . . . . — 28.00 — 33.00 — 29.00
Note: Since single specimens could easily be mistaken for figurines, the value is somewhat higher than for most single bookends.

☐ **Bowl,** 8", bright canary yellow, modified pot form with molded banding, giving the appearance of graduated sections joined together, small handles . . . . — 7.00 — 10.00 — 7.50

☐ **Bowl,** 2½", shape #133, cream white, pink and rose red, inverted dome form, decorated with narrow ribbing vertically encircling the body . . . — 5.00 — 7.00 — 5.50

☐ **Bowl,** 2½", yellow and brown, footed, marked 1/65/4A . . . . — 3.00 — 4.00 — 3.25

☐ **Bowl,** 4¾", big red roses, gold trim, side handled, four footed, scalloped rim . . . . — 7.00 — 8.00 — 7.25

☐ **Bowl,** 5" x 2¼", maroon with one handle . . . . . — 4.00 — 5.00 — 4.25

☐ **Bowl,** 5¾", high gloss black . . . . — 2.00 — 3.00 — 2.25

☐ **Bowl,** 5¾", high gloss maroon . . . . — 2.00 — 3.00 — 2.10

☐ **Bowl,** 5¾" x 2", yellow . . . . — 2.00 — 3.00 — 2.10

☐ **Bowl,** 5 4/5", turquoise, vertical lines and chevrons . . . . — 3.25 — 4.00 — 3.00

☐ **Bowl,** 10", pink and gray with flecking . . . . — 7.00 — 8.00 — 7.25

☐ **Bowl,** shape #195, ivory white streaked with jade green, to appear like carved ivory, inverted cap form, with molded decoration beneath the rim . . . . — 6.00 — 8.00 — 6.25

☐ **Bowl,** 10" wide, slate white, inverted dome form, with flared lip, decorated with a wide central black band, blocked at either side by a similar but narrower band . . . . — 7.00 — 10.00 — 7.25

☐ **Box, hanging salt,** 4½", cream white with a wooden hinged lid, cylindrical form flattened at the back (to fit flush with a wall), decorated with vertical molded fluting, at the front a cartouche with the word "SALT" . . . . — 23.00 — 27.00 — 24.00

☐ **Box, hanging salt,** 4½", marble-white and blue, with a wooden hinged lid, half-cylindrical form (flattened at the back to fit flush against a wall), with pierced hanger, decorated with a triple horizontal blue band, with the word "SALT" printed in black script characters . . . . — 43.00 — 49.00 — 44.00

☐ **Box, hanging salt,** 6¼" x 4¼", marble-white and blue, with a wooden hinged lid, rectangular shape with pierced hanger, also set with feet for optionally standing, decorated with stenciled mo-

	Current Price Range		P/Y Average

tifs in the upper left and lower right corners of the front panel, in blue, with the word "SALT" printed in black script characters **38.00 44.00 39.00**

☐ **Box, hanging salt,** 6½″ x 4½″, marble-white and blue, with a wooden hinged lid, rectangular shape with pierced hanger, also set with feet for optionally standing, decorated with a modified Greek key emblem at top and bottom of front panel, with the word "SALT" printed in black script characters **41.00 47.00 42.00**

☐ **Centerpiece,** 9¾″ x 6″ x 2″, green, rectangular shape, ribbing scoring, center crosstrip with leaf relief and hole for candle **8.75 10.00 7.25**

☐ **Console Bowl,** 6½″, splotchy maroon and chartreuse, marked H127/4B **7.00 8.00 7.25**

☐ **Cookie Jar,** antique auto, steel gray, bone white and yellow, form of a touring car of World War I vintage, with convertible top, the body is steel gray and the top white, wheel spokes are yellow, the lid is formed by the convertible top **20.00 26.00 19.00**

☐ **Cookie Jar,** antique stove, white **10.00 12.00 11.00**

☐ **Cookie Jar,** apple **10.00 12.00 11.00**

☐ **Cookie Jar,** "Balloon Boy," cream white with yellow, green and other colors, representing a boy dressed like a child of the 1920's holding two balloons in his left hand. He wears a moss-green jacket, blue knickers, yellow shoes and a yellow boater hat. The balloons are magenta and pastel blue. The jar's lid is formed by his head and upper shoulders, including the balloons **14.00 17.00 15.00**

☐ **Cookie Jar,** bananas **18.00 20.00 19.00**

☐ **Cookie Jar,** bear **22.00 25.00 23.00**

☐ **Cookie Jar,** bear, marked 95/1/1 .... **25.00 30.00 26.00**

☐ **Cookie Jar,** bear with cookies in pocket **20.00 22.00 21.00**

☐ **Planter, Turtle,** shape #205, pale lavender and beige, a standing turtle, wearing a long-sleeve sweater with ribbed collar and knitted cap, the planter is formed by the turtle's shell, World War II era **3.00 5.00 3.25**

☐ **Planter, Turtle,** #740, 8″ x 4½″, glossy green and bronze **10.00 12.00 10.50**

☐ **Planter,** twin shells, 8½″ x 3″ x 3½″, glossy yellow, marked H 199/1A **6.00 7.00 6.25**

☐ **Planter, "Twin Swans,"** bone white with black and pink, a pair of swans, face to face, their heads touching in such a manner that their necks create a heart-shaped outline, back of each hollowed out as a planter, manufactured in early 1940s **7.00 9.00 7.20**

☐ **Planter,** white, marked C2/23/6 .... **8.00 9.00 8.50**

☐ **Planter,** window box, 4″ x 8″, maroon **5.00 6.00 5.50**

☐ **Planter,** window box, 6½″ x 3¼″, glossy dark green, basketweave pattern **5.00 6.00 5.50**

	Current Price Range		P/Y Average

☐ **Planter,** window box, 6½" x 3¼", glossy turquoise with leaf relief 4.00 5.00 4.25

☐ **Planter,** window box, 7" x 4½", pedestal base, glossy dark green, marked H 213/3C 3.50 4.50 3.75

☐ **Planter,** window box, 8" x 4½", glossy dark green with swirls, footed, marked H 215/7C ... 6.00 7.00 6.25

☐ **Planter,** window box, 9" x 3½" x 3", pale blue over turquoise with scallops and vertical ribbing 5.00 6.00 5.50

☐ **Planter,** wishing well 8.00 9.00 8.25

☐ **Planter,** wishing well, green and gray, rare 14.00 15.00 14.50

☐ **Planter,** wood grain, 6¼", green and gold, marked C2/34/1D 4.00 5.00 4.25

☐ **Planter,** 3½" x 4½", gold ribbed panels 2.00 3.00 2.50

☐ **Planter,** 4½", white with vertical ribbing and horizontal ripples 2.00 3.00 2.50

☐ **Planter,** 6½" x 3", black, footed 3.00 4.00 3.50

☐ **Planter,** 7" x 2", high gloss green with diagonal ridges and sculptured scrolls 3.00 4.00 3.25

☐ **Planter,** 7" x 2", ivory with curlicue relief 3.00 4.00 3.25

☐ **Planter,** 7" x 4½" x 3", green zig-zag rim with mosaic sides 4.00 5.00 4.25

☐ **Planter,** 8⅜" x 4" x 4", glossy turquoise with swirled ribbing, footed 5.00 6.00 5.15

☐ **Planter,** 8½" x3½" x 2¾", cream with rose decal, footed 4.00 5.00 4.25

☐ **Planter,** 10", white oval shaped 3.00 4.00 3.25

☐ **Planter,** #66, Chinese, 5½", black with hand painted decoration, marked C1/37 .... 6.50 7.50 6.75

☐ **Planter,** #711, double flower pot, 10" x 5", two-tone green with applied yellow swallow, attached saucer, marked 1/79/711 .... 7.00 8.00 7.10

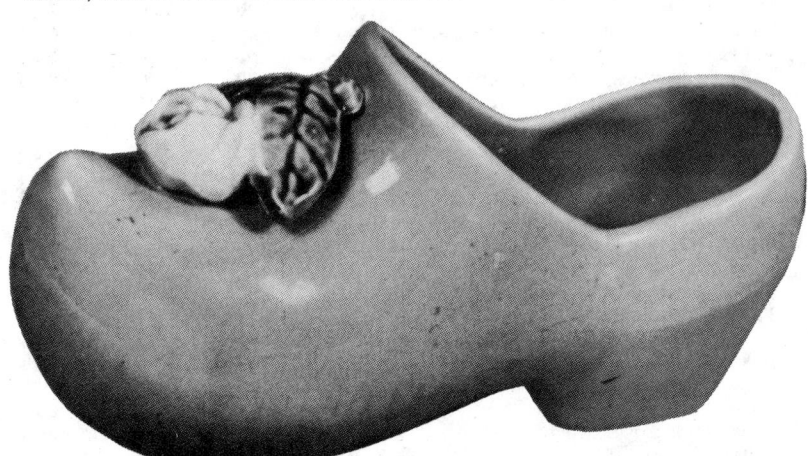

Planter, *shoe, blue with white flower,* $6.00-$7.00

	Current Price Range		P/Y Average
☐ **Planter,** #1302, oval, 10" x 9" 3", glossy dark green, three footed	4.50	5.50	4.65
☐ **Radio Receiver,** 9½" x 3", a ceramic bug (a beetle) which contained a radio receiver, contained a crystal receiver, value as stated is for a specimen without the receiver	95.00	112.00	97.00
☐ **Rolling pin,** marble-white and black, with turned wooden holders, cylindrical form with foliage designs stenciled at either end	130.00	150.00	134.00
☐ **Vase, "Wise Bird,"** 8", deep mahogany brown with yellow and touches of green, an owl perched on a stump next to a hollow tree trunk (which forms the vase), the owl is dark brown with some black coloring to highlight the texturing of its feathers, both the stump and the lower part of the tree trunk are yellow with tones of pale and deep green	23.00	27.00	24.00
☐ **Vase,** 5½", yellow with side handles, footed . .	3.50	4.50	3.75
☐ **Vase,** 6", glossy green with side handles and vertical ribbing, footed	5.00	6.00	5.25
☐ **Vase,** 6", lavender, swirled	5.00	6.00	5.25
☐ **Vase,** 6", white, marked H 62/2/1	8.00	9.00	8.25
☐ **Vase,** 6" x 5" x 3", glossy green with brown flecks, marked H 221/5B	5.00	6.00	5.25
☐ **Vase,** 6" x 5½" x 6½", yellow flowers on pink, footed, marked H 185/3B	6.00	7.00	6.25
☐ **Vase,** 7", orchid swirled and footed, marked C1/81/4A	5.00	6.00	5.25
☐ **Vase,** 7¼", pink, four ribs, footed	5.00	6.00	5.25
☐ **Vase,** 8", green and blue with ribbing and diamond medallions	7.00	8.00	7.25
☐ **Vase,** 8", green with ribbing and side handles	6.00	7.00	6.25
☐ **Vase,** 8", pink with ribbing and side handles . .	6.00	7.00	6.25
☐ **Vase,** 8", pink with side handles	3.00	4.00	3.25
☐ **Vase,** 8", white with side handles	3.00	4.00	3.25
☐ **Vase,** 8" x 7", yellow flowers, marked H 155/2B	9.00	10.00	9.50
☐ **Vase,** 8½", maroon with stylized leaves and side handles, footed	7.00	8.00	7.25
☐ **Vase,** 8¾", pink with bird in relief, handled, footed	6.50	7.50	6.75
☐ **Vase,** 9", cream, marked H/191/2B	7.00	8.00	7.10
☐ **Vase,** 9", flared yellow with handles, footed . . .	6.00	7.00	6.10
☐ **Vase,** 9", glossy green with ribbing, handled and footed, marked H 197/3C	7.00	8.00	7.25
☐ **Vase,** 9", glossy pink, square footed	7.00	8.00	7.25
☐ **Vase,** 9", glossy turquoise, square footed	7.00	8.00	7.25
☐ **Vase,** 9", green with square pedestal base . . .	6.00	7.00	6.25
☐ **Vase,** 9¼", glossy green with ribbing, handles, footed, marked C1/11/2A	6.00	7.00	6.25
☐ **Vase,** 9¼", green and brown with grapes, marked C1/43/4B	13.00	14.00	13.25

	Current Price Range		P/Y Average
☐ **Vase,** 9¼", turquoise, side handles	6.00	7.00	6.25
☐ **Vase,** 10", green, decorated with long leaves, side handles, marked H 199/5/2	10.00	11.00	10.50
☐ **Wall Ornament,** 8", white, cream-white and brown, in the form of a cone, at the front of which is a figure of a perched owl, the cone is brown and has molded leaves at the sides, intended to give the appearance of a tree trunk, the owl is chiefly white with touches of brown and yellow	24.00	29.00	25.00
☐ **Wall Ornament,** yellow, pale blue and rust brown, vertical rectangular plaque with a sculptured mermaid, tail upturned, holding a shell which serves as a rest for jewelry	13.00	16.00	14.00
☐ **Wall Ornament, boxer dog,** caramel brown with violet-brown, touches of yellowish beige, extremely realistic modeling of a standing boxer dog, set against a textured background, with storage compartment	14.00	17.00	15.00

MENUS

DESCRIPTION: Collectible menu types include board menus, printed wall menus, novelty, decorated or autographed menus, White House menus and those that commemorate special events.

COMMENTS: Though fun and fairly easy to collect, the value of menus depends on their age, rarity and decoration. Board menus, written and hung on wooden boards, date to the 18th and 19th century and are quite valuable. White House menus, especially those from inaugural ball dinners, are sought after. Special menus, made to commemorate a special event, were often painted or hand lettered on special material. Menus from famous restaurants of New York, Hollywood, New Orleans and Paris are favorites of collectors.

ADDITIONAL TIPS: Menu prices vary greatly in price. The following price sampling is alphabetized according to type of menu.

☐ **Board Menu,** California, 1850–1880	1800.00	2800.00	2300.00
☐ **Board Menu,** California, 1880–1910	550.00	850.00	700.00

	Current Price Range		P/Y Average
☐ **Board Menu,** Midwestern U.S., 1860–1890 ...	800.00	1200.00	1000.00
☐ **Board Menu,** Midwestern U.S., 1890–1910 ...	270.00	420.00	330.00
☐ **Board Menu,** New England, pre–1800	1000.00	1400.00	1200.00
☐ **Board Menu,** New England, 1800–1859	800.00	1200.00	1000.00
☐ **Board Menu,** New York City, pre–1800	1400.00	1900.00	1600.00
☐ **Board Menu,** New York City, 1800–1850	900.00	1400.00	1100.00
☐ **Board Menu,** Southern states, 1800–1850	3000.00	4000.00	3200.00
☐ **Board Menu,** Southwestern, U.S., 1890–1910	460.00	710.00	520.00
☐ **Famous Restaurants,** menus from the heyday of noted restaurants in New York, Hollywood, New Orleans, Paris	5.50	15.00	8.00
☐ **Hand-painted Bill Of Fare,** unnamed tavern, believed to be Midwest. Flat-cut wooden board with decorative top (spindles at either side), the board painted cream color, lettering in black ink applied with a thin brush, more than 100 items listed, overall size 22″ x 31″, c. 1875	1800.00	2500.00	2000.00
☐ **Leheigh Valley Railroad,** dinner menu, picture of Lehigh Valley Railroad tugboat on front cover, c. 1950–1960	4.00	5.00	4.40
☐ **Lond Boar's Head Coffee House,** paper wall menu, c. 1820	220.00	260.00	240.00
☐ **New York Central,** dinner menu advertising the Grand Central Art Galleries, various examples of this menu exist with different works of art on the cover	3.00	4.00	3.50
☐ **New York Central,** dinner menu from "The James Whitcomb Riley," color cover picturing steam loco pulling the train	6.00	8.00	6.80
☐ **New York Central,** World War II "Victory" menu with large V for Victory	5.00	7.00	5.90
☐ **Norddeutscher Lloyd Bremen,** ocean liner dinner menu, c. 1900–1910	2.50	3.50	3.00
Note: This was the forerunner of the steamship company now known as North German Lloyd.			
☐ **Silver Star Cafe,** (location unknown, thought to be southwestern U.S.), hand-lettered bill of fare on wooden board. The board shellacked and painted over in various colors with decorations, artistic lettering, etc. Few dishes listed, along with house rules. 18½″ x 33 2/3″, c. 1910	600.00	800.00	700.00
☐ **Steamship Menus,** from major steamship lines	2.00	8.00	5.00
☐ **Washington Inn,** (probably New Hampshire or Vermont), hand-lettered bill of fare on thick wooden board. The board is whitewashed, with list of dishes and prices lettered in dark brown paint. Corners worn down, some of the painted surface cracked, 13″ x 18½″ x 1½″, c. 1835	550.00	700.00	625.00

Menus, *color artwork, 1890s,* **$12.00-$35.00**

MILITARY COLLECTIBLES

DESCRIPTION: Military memorabilia encompasses items pertaining to all branches of the military.

COMMENTS: Some hobbyists collect military memorabilia by type of item, for example badges or swords, while others collect by military branch like the Navy, Army or Air Force.

ADDITIONAL TIPS: For more information, consult *The Official Price Guide to Military Collectibles,* published by The House of Collectibles.

Whistle, *England, World War I,* **$15.00–$20.00**

	Current Price Range		P/Y Average

BADGES AND OTHER INSIGNIA

☐ **Aerial Gunner badge,** World War II	40.00	45.00	42.00
☐ **Airship Pilot badge,** c. 1921. Authorized in 1921, a dirigible took the place of the balloon in this badge	175.00	200.00	185.00
☐ **Bombardier badge,** World War II	40.00	45.00	42.00
☐ **Combat (Aircraft) Observer badge,** World War II	50.00	55.00	52.00
☐ **Command Pilot badge,** World War II	55.00	60.00	57.00
☐ **Flight Surgeon's badge,** c. 1943	60.00	65.00	62.00

SWORDS

☐ **Army Foot Artillery sword,** model 1833. Brass scaled grip cast in one piece with a short cross guard with plain disk finials. Blade marked with the American Eagle and "N.P. AMES SPRING-FIELD." An American Eagle appears on the pommel. Hilt attached to the tang of the blade by three iron traverse rivets	169.00	185.00	173.00
☐ **Army Officer's sword,** model 1850. Based on French army model, half basket hilt in gilt with gilt wire wrapped leather covered grips. Phrygian helmet pattern pommel, blade single edge and slightly curved, polished black leather scabbard with gilt/brass fittings	210.00	230.00	220.00
☐ **Army Officer's sword,** model 1902. Generally similar to the above except that the grips are notched on the inside for the fingers. Full back strap, simple rounded semicap pommel with small caspan top, "D" shape knuckle guard divides into three parts as it becomes the guard. Turned down tear shape finial, nickled scabbard	141.00	175.00	153.00

UNIFORMS

☐ **Army Air Force Officer's Blouse.** U.S. buttons and cuff braid. Officer's U.S. and winged propellor collar insignia. Pilot's silver wings	55.00	60.00	55.00
☐ **Army Enlisted Man's Field Jack,** World War II. So-called "Eisenhower jacket of stout OD material. Two pleated pockets. Concealed button front. Embroidered 1st Division patch on left shoulder	25.00	29.00	25.00
☐ **Army Enlisted Man's Issue Blouse.** World War I, 89th Division, patch on upper left sleeve. Bronze U.S. enlisted device on right collar and Signal Corps device on left side. Single overseas chevron	50.00	55.00	51.00
☐ **Marine Corps Enlisted Man's Coat,** World War II period. Green coat with four bronze Marine Corps buttons down the front and on each of four pockets. Marine Second Division patch on upper			

	Current Price Range		P/Y Average

left shoulder. Corporal's stripes and one enlistment stripe on each sleeve. Red "Ruptured Duck" discharge device on green backing on right breast **25.00**   **27.00**   **25.00**

☐ **Marine Sergeant OD Wool Blouse,** World War I period. Four pockets closed with bronze Marine Corps buttons as are pockets. Blouse has high collar with rare collar ornaments consisting of disk bearing Marine Corps emblem. Sergeant's chevrons **90.00**   **98.00**   **92.00**

MILITARY MEDALS AND DECORATIONS

TOPIC: Decorations are individual awards for specific acts of gallantry, valor or exceptional meritorious service. On the other hand, medals are given in quantity to many individuals for participation in battles or war. However, at least one decoration, the U.S. Medal of Honor, while strictly a decoration, has the word "medal" in its title.

TYPES: There are numerous different awards given for outstanding service. The highest award the United States gives is the Medal of Honor.

MATERIALS: Bronze is extremely common, although many other valuable metals are used.

COMMENTS: In connection with the collecting of decorations and medals given by the United States, it should be noted that Federal law prohibits the sale of such awards but does permit them to be offered on a trade basis. In buying such items, it is required that an article or articles of trade, such as stamps, be exchanged.

ADDITIONAL TIPS: For further information, please refer to *The Official Price Guide to Military Collectibles,* published by The House of Collectibles.

	Current Price Range		P/Y Average

CANADA

☐ **Efficiency Medal,** George VI	50.00	70.00	60.00
☐ **Forces Decoration,** Elizabeth II	60.00	80.00	70.00
☐ **Forces Decoration,** George VI	120.00	140.00	130.00
☐ **General Service Medal,** 1866–1870	375.00	400.00	387.50
☐ **General Service Medal,** 1870, Red River	1000.00	1300.00	1150.00
☐ **Korean War Medal,** 1951	40.00	60.00	50.00
☐ **Medal of Bravery,** instituted 1972, circular medallion with maple leaf	160.00	190.00	175.00
☐ **Memorial Cross,** Elizabeth II	50.00	70.00	55.00
☐ **Military Cross,** Korea	120.00	160.00	140.00

GERMANY (IMPERIAL)

☐ **Baden Leopold Medal.** (for service in the Franco-Prussian War) With 1870–1871 bar	75.00	95.00	85.00
☐ **Baden World War I Honor Medal.** Medal inscribed "For Baden's Honor," dated 1914–1918	38.00	58.00	45.00
☐ **Bavarian 1870 Cross for Volunteer Nurses**	220.00	300.00	260.00
☐ **Bavarian Order of Military Merit,** 4th Class, with swords	135.00	155.00	145.00
☐ **Bavarian 10 Year Service Medal**	20.00	25.00	22.00
☐ **Brunswick Order of Henry the Lion,** 3rd Class	400.00	440.00	420.00
☐ **Grand Cross to the Iron Cross,** 1914	1000.00	1200.00	1100.00
☐ **Hesse Order of Philip the Good,** 4th Class . .	200.00	240.00	220.00

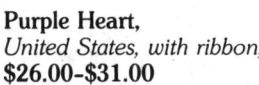

Purple Heart,
United States, with ribbon,
$26.00-$31.00

	Current Price Range		P/Y Average
☐ **Iron Cross,** 1st Class, 1870	410.00	460.00	435.00
☐ **Iron Cross,** 1st Class, World War I, pin back	60.00	80.00	70.00
☐ **Iron Cross,** 2nd Class, World War I, with ribbon	32.00	52.00	40.00
☐ **Iron Cross,** 2nd Class, 1870 (Franco Prussian War), with 25 year oak leaf	130.00	150.00	140.00
☐ **Saxon Order of Albert,** 4th Class, with swords, ribbon	140.00	170.00	155.00
☐ **Wilhelm I Commemoration Medal**	18.00	28.00	23.00
☐ **Wurttemberg Medal for Veterans,** wars of 1793–1815	85.00	105.00	90.00
☐ **Wurttemberg Silver Medal for Bravery,** World War I. This offering was for the medal together with the award certificate	90.00	110.00	100.00

GREAT BRITAIN

☐ **Air Force Medal,** World War I	375.00	475.00	425.00
☐ **Air Force Medal,** World War II	300.00	350.00	325.00
☐ **Albert Medal,** heroic actions on land or sea, oval bronze medallion surmounted by crown, classified according to monarch who made presentation:			
☐ **Edward VI**	1700.00	1800.00	1750.00
☐ **Elizabeth II**	1600.00	1700.00	1650.00
☐ **George V**	1600.00	1700.00	1650.00
☐ **George VI**	1600.00	1700.00	1650.00
☐ **Victoria**	1700.00	1900.00	1800.00
☐ **Allied Victory Medal,** Air	27.50	37.50	30.00
☐ **Allied Victory Medal,** awarded to all members of combat battalions in World War I, C.E.F. ...	27.50	37.50	30.00
☐ **Allied Victory Medal,** Naval	27.50	37.50	30.00
☐ **Anglo-Boer War Medal**	70.00	90.00	80.00
☐ **Arctic Medal,** 1857	250.00	300.00	275.00
☐ **Baltic Medal,** 1854–1855	90.00	100.00	95.00
☐ **Colonial Auxiliary Forces Officers Decoration,** G.R.V. (George V)	80.00	90.00	85.00
☐ **Colonial Auxiliary Forces Officers Decoration,** V.R.I. (Victoria)	95.00	115.00	100.00
☐ **Conspicuous Gallantry Medal,** World War II	2600.00	2700.00	2650.00
☐ **Crimea Medal,** one bar "SEBASTOPOL"	85.00	95.00	90.00
☐ **Defense Medal,** 1939–1945	4.00	7.00	5.50
☐ **Distinguished Conduct Medal,** Korea	700.00	725.00	712.00

UNITED STATES

☐ **Air Force Commendation Medal**	25.00	35.00	30.00
☐ **Airman's Medal**	25.00	35.00	30.00
☐ **American Campaign Medal**	20.00	30.00	25.00
☐ **American Defense Service Medal**	20.00	30.00	25.00
☐ **American Defense Medal,** 1939–1946	9.00	15.00	11.00
☐ **Armed Forces Reserve Medal**	15.00	21.00	18.00
☐ **Army Commendation Medal**	16.00	22.00	19.00
☐ **Bronze Medal,** California, Spanish-American War, #1758	90.00	120.00	105.00

	Current Price Range		P/Y Average
☐ **Bronze Star,** "Boys Remember The Maine" ..	15.00	25.00	20.00
☐ **Dewey Relic Medal,** bronze, 1899	50.00	70.00	60.00
☐ **Distinguish Military Service,** New Jersey, silver	20.00	30.00	25.00
☐ **Gettysburg Veteran Model,** 1893, bronze	25.00	35.00	30.00
☐ **Good Conduct Medal,** Navy, 1920	40.00	60.00	50.00
☐ **Join Services Commendation Medal**	35.00	45.00	40.00
☐ **Korean Service Medal**	14.00	20.00	17.00
☐ **Legion of Merit,** Commander Degree, complete with neck ribbon and lapel pin	190.00	230.00	210.00
☐ **Legion of Merit,** Legionnaire Degree	40.00	50.00	45.00
☐ **Marine Corps Expeditionary Medal**	28.00	38.00	33.00
☐ **Marine Corps Good Conduct Medal**	25.00	35.00	30.00
☐ **Marine Corps Reserve Medal**	20.00	30.00	25.00
☐ **Marine Corps Yangtze Service Medal**	40.00	48.00	44.00
☐ **Medal For Humane Action** (Berlin Air Lift) ...	25.00	35.00	30.00
☐ **Medal Of Honor** (Air Force), cased, recent issue	580.00	680.00	630.00
☐ **Medal Of Honor,** Civil War, bronze	1550.00	1850.00	1650.00
☐ **Mexican Service Medal,** Navy and Marine Corps, 1911–1917	62.00	72.00	65.00
☐ **Navy Good Conduct Medal**	30.00	38.00	34.00
☐ **Navy Reserve Medal**	19.00	29.00	24.00
☐ **New Jersey Volunteer Medal,** Spanish-American War, 1898.....................	75.00	95.00	80.00
☐ **Purple Heart,** with ribbon bar	29.00	39.00	34.00
☐ **Sampson Medal** (Navy)	70.00	80.00	75.00
☐ **Second Nicaraguan Campaign,** Marine Corps, 1926–1930	170.00	200.00	185.00
☐ **Service Medal,** World War I, Connecticut	17.50	22.00	18.00
☐ **Service Medal,** World War I, New York, silver	40.00	50.00	45.00
☐ **Silver Star**	60.00	80.00	70.00
☐ **Spanish War Service Medal,** #18367	40.00	50.00	45.00
☐ **Veteran Soldier Medal,** bronze, 1861–1865 ..	10.00	20.00	15.00
☐ **Victory Medal,** World War II	5.00	10.00	7.50
☐ **Vietnam Service Medal**	14.00	18.00	16.00
☐ **World War I Victory Medal.** (Battle and sector clasps increase value)	25.00	35.00	30.00
☐ **World War II Victory Medal**	20.00	30.00	25.00

MINING COLLECTIBLES

DESCRIPTION: All memorabilia pertaining to mining operations in the U.S., such as deeds, bills of sale, stock certificates, sales brochures, posters, etc.; books on the history of mining; and actual objects used in connection with mining, such as tools, dynamite detonators, helmets, lanterns and the like.

MAKER: As the items involved are so diverse, so too are their origins and the persons responsible for them. Mining gear and equipment was usually commercially manufactured, and by the 1890s could even be ordered from mail order catalogues. It was sold by the trading posts in mining towns.

ADDITIONAL TIPS: Some items have premium value because of the specific mine or locality to which they relate; others because they happen to be more elaborate than others, such as a mining stock certificate which carries a large steel engraving.

	Current Price Range		P/Y Average
☐ **Alabama.** Geological Survey of. Report on the Coal Measures of Blount Mountain. 80 pages. Montgomery, 1893	25.00	38.00	33.00
☐ **Arizona.** Minerals of Arizona. Their Occurrence and Association: with notes on their composition. By William P. Blake, Tucson, 1909	22.50	31.50	25.00
☐ **Atrato Mining And Developing Co.,** for working the Atrato and Quito Rivers, in the Province of Choco, State of Cauca . . . Colombia. 16 pages. Portland, ME, 1882	25.00	38.00	30.00
☐ **Battle Creek Gravel Mining Co.** (Custer County, Dakota). Prospectus for private distribution only. N.Y., 1880	31.00	44.00	36.00
☐ **Best and Belcher Mine.** Virginia City, NV. Report of operations, 1889	8.00	12.00	10.00
☐ **California, G.A. Barton, Assayer.** Memorandum of bullion deposited, 1880	20.00	30.00	25.00

	Current Price Range		P/Y Average

☐ **California Water And Mining Co.,** 1880 prospectus. Folding map and four-page leaflet. N.Y., 1880 . . . . **50.00 75.00 65.00**

☐ **Canada Consolidated Gold Mining Co.,** at Marmora, Ontario, report upon the property of the. By Richard F. Rothwell. N.Y., 1880 . . . . **31.00 44.00 36.00**

☐ **Chemical Gold And Silver Ore Reducing Co.** Prospectus and statement, with letter from Dr. J.C. Ayer. 16 pages. N.Y., 1865 . . . . **25.00 38.00 30.00**

☐ **Chester Mining Co.,** Report on the Property of the. Located in Chester Township, Canada East, Boston, 1864 . . . . **31.00 44.00 35.00**

☐ **Copper Falls Mine, Keweenaw Co., Michigan.** Report on the. By M.E. Wadsworth. Boston, 1879 . . . . **25.00 38.00 34.00**

☐ **Cripple Creek Gold Fields.** Placer Lodes. 31 pages. Colorado Springs, 1892 . . . . **80.00 100.00 90.00**

☐ **Deer Island Silver Mining Comp't.** Report of Professor W.F. Stewart, on the property of the Company at Deer Isle . . . Maine. Portland, ME, 1880 . . . . **31.00 44.00 36.00**

☐ **Diamonds.** Catalogue of the Collection of Rough Diamonds, now on Exhibition (at Tiffany and Co.). 23 pages. N.Y., 1885 . . . . **31.00 44.00 38.00**

☐ **Gardner Mountain Copper Mining Co.** of Winterport, Waldo County, Maine. Bylaws and list of officers of the. Portland, 1897 . . . . **10.00 15.00 12.00**

☐ **Gold Fields of St. Domingo, The.** With a description of the agricultural, commercial and other advantages . . . containing some account of . . . cities, rivers, bays and harbors. By W.S. Courtney. N.Y., 1860 . . . . **35.00 48.00 42.00**

☐ **Gold In Canada.** St. Francis Gold Mining Company of Canada. Portland, ME, 1881 . . . . **38.00 50.00 44.00**

☐ **Gould And Curry Mine.** Virginia City, NV. Report of operations, 1888 . . . . **8.00 12.00 10.00**

☐ **Harshaw Mining Co., Arizona.** Prospectus of the. N.Y., 1879 . . . . **50.00 75.00 65.00**

☐ **Holiday Mining Co.** General Land Office, Colorado. Mining certificate, 1884 . . . . **37.00 47.00 40.00**

☐ **Hulbert, Edwin J.** Calument-Conglomerate Discovery, 1864. Rome, Italy, 1899 . . . . **22.50 31.50 26.00**

☐ **Iron.** The Future Sites of the Principal Iron Production in the World. By Edward Atkinson. Baltimore, 1890 . . . . **28.00 38.00 33.00**

☐ **Janin, Louis.** Report . . . on the Harshaw Mining Property, Harshaw Mining District, Patagonia Mountains, Arizona. N.Y., 1879 . . . . **44.00 56.00 48.00**

☐ **King, Clarence.** Copy of Official Letter . . . to the . . . San Francisco and New York Mining and Commercial Company, Discovering the new Diamond Fields to be a Fraud. N.p., n.d. (San Francisco, 1873?) **125.00 185.00 140.00**

	Current Price Range		P/Y Average
☐ **Maine Silver Mining.** The Consolidated Hampden Silver Mining Company. 24 pages. Bangor, 1880	25.00	38.00	30.00
☐ **Michigan.** Annual Report of the Inspector of Mines of Gogebic County, Michigan. By Clarence M. Boss, Lansing, 1892	44.00	56.00	50.00
☐ **Michigan Mining School.** A Paper on the. Prepared by Director M.E. Wadsworth Houghton. Lansing, 1894	25.00	38.00	32.00
☐ **Nevada.** Biennial Report of the State Mineralogist of the State of. For 1873 and 1874. Carson City, 1875	125.00	185.00	145.00
☐ **Nevada Mining.** Report by William C. Prescott, Esq., March 8, 1865, on the Uncle Sam Senior and Gold Canon Silver Mines of the Comstock Lode in Nevada. N.p., n.d. (San Francisco, 1866)	125.00	185.00	145.00
☐ **Nevada Mining.** Statement and Reports concerning the Uncle Sam Senior and Gold Canon Silver Lodes, in Nevada. Boston, 1865	90.00	155.00	125.00

MOLDS

DESCRIPTION: Molds are used to hold certain foods while they harden or gel. The food item retains the mold form or design.

VARIATIONS: There are many kinds of molds including butter, chocolate and sugar. Molds are made of wood, copper, tin, iron and graniteware.

COMMENTS: Popular collectibles, molds are often sought after by kitchen collectors. Prices of molds vary greatly, depending on rarity, condition and material.

ADDITIONAL TIPS: The listings are alphabetized according to type of mold or type of material. Descriptions and price ranges follow.

☐ **Buttermold,** apple, wooden	336.00	350.00	343.00
☐ **Buttermold,** eagle with branch, 3″ diameter, wooden	236.00	250.00	243.00

	Current Price Range		P/Y Average
Buttermold, eagle, maple, round, wooden	215.00	260.00	230.00
Buttermold, eagle, wingtip to wingtip, c. 1800s, wooden	131.00	175.00	145.00
Buttermold, eight, number, wooden	79.00	90.00	83.00
Buttermold, encircled cross and lily, wooden	79.00	90.00	83.00
Buttermold, partridge in a pear tree, wooden	436.00	460.00	443.00
Buttermold, parrot on perch, wooden	210.00	230.00	215.00
Buttermold, c. 1890, wooden	63.00	75.00	67.00
Buttermold, hen, wooden	179.00	195.00	185.00
Buttermold, peaches, wooden	146.00	160.00	150.00
Buttermold, peony, wooden	452.00	460.00	455.00
Buttermold, pigeon, wooden	79.00	99.00	85.00
Buttermold, pineapple, seratted edge, 3¾", diameter, wooden	52.00	72.00	60.00
Buttermold, pine cone and leaf, wooden	83.00	90.00	87.00
Buttermold, pine cones in basket, wooden ...	32.00	40.00	35.00
Buttermold, pine twig stamp, wooden	32.00	40.00	35.00
Buttermold, pine twigs, wooden	42.00	50.00	45.00
Buttermold, plum, wooden	252.00	320.00	265.00
Buttermold, potted tree, wooden	89.00	100.00	93.00
Buttermold, primitive, wooden	73.00	90.00	80.00
Buttermold, caveman, wooden	105.00	115.00	110.00
Buttermold, name, wooden	226.00	255.00	230.00
Buttermold, ram and floral design, 4" diameter, wooden	387.00	400.00	390.00

Buttermold, *pineapple motif,* $50.00–$60.00

	Current Price Range		P/Y Average
☐ **Buttermold,** wooden	189.00	200.00	193.00
☐ **Buttermold,** Uncle Remus, wooden	179.00	210.00	181.00
☐ **Buttermold,** rooster, wooden	138.00	150.00	140.00
☐ **Buttermold,** rose and bud, factory made, 3″ diameter, wooden	37.00	50.00	40.00
☐ **Buttermold,** rosebuds, c. 1880s, 2″ diameter, wooden	84.00	110.00	90.00
☐ **Buttermold,** rose, with leaves, factory made, wooden	37.00	50.00	40.00
☐ **Buttermold,** round, four pattern repeat, wooden	37.00	50.00	40.00
☐ **Buttermold,** initials, wooden	188.00	200.00	193.00
☐ **Buttermold,** name, wooden	176.00	200.00	185.00
☐ **Buttermold,** sea shell, wooden	189.00	200.00	193.00
☐ **Buttermold,** sheaf stamp, wooden	42.00	55.00	47.00
☐ **Buttermold,** sheaf of wheat, hand carved, 3″ diameter, wooden	47.00	70.00	50.00
☐ **Buttermold,** sheep, with handle, wooden	141.00	160.00	145.00
☐ **Buttermold,** shell, ring border, c. 1800s, 3″ diameter, wooden	121.00	135.00	126.00
☐ **Buttermold,** fern, factory made, 2″ diameter, wooden	32.00	65.00	40.00
☐ **Buttermold,** flower, wooden	47.00	75.00	50.00
☐ **Buttermold,** flower and leaf, jagged edge, wooden	268.00	350.00	280.00
☐ **Buttermold,** ship, wooden	341.00	370.00	350.00
☐ **Buttermold,** single fish, wooden	263.00	300.00	270.00
☐ **Buttermold,** single pine, wooden	31.00	45.00	33.00
☐ **Buttermold,** single pine twig, wooden	31.00	45.00	33.00
☐ **Buttermold,** single strawberry, wooden	37.00	50.00	40.00
☐ **Buttermold,** six-leaf flower, c. 1830s, 3½″ diameter, wooden	52.00	80.00	60.00
☐ **Buttermold,** six motif, wooden	131.00	140.00	135.00
☐ **Buttermold,** six-pointed star, carven, carven	99.00	115.00	105.00
☐ **Buttermold,** six-sided lyre, wooden	131.00	145.00	135.00
☐ **Buttermold,** snowflake, wooden	42.00	52.00	45.00
☐ **Buttermold,** star, wooden	57.00	65.00	60.00
☐ **Buttermold,** sunburst, wooden	73.00	90.00	75.00
☐ **Buttermold,** sunflower, wooden	131.00	160.00	136.00
☐ **Buttermold,** sunflower with leaves, c. 1800s, wooden	68.00	80.00	72.00
☐ **Buttermold,** swirls and flowers, wooden	436.00	535.00	450.00
☐ **Buttermold,** three feathers, wooden	105.00	115.00	107.00
☐ **Buttermold,** three leaf fern, maple, 5″ diameter, wooden	55.00	65.00	60.00
☐ **Buttermold,** three twigs, factory made, 3″ diameter, wooden	37.00	50.00	40.00
☐ **Buttermold,** thistle, wooden	47.00	60.00	50.00
☐ **Buttermold,** tobacco foliage, wooden	94.00	100.00	94.00
☐ **Buttermold,** Tree of Life, 3″ diameter, wooden	126.00	180.00	135.00
☐ **Chocolate,** turkey, tin	20.00	25.00	15.00
☐ **Chocolate,** hen, tin, German	20.00	30.00	25.00
☐ **Copper,** bird	32.00	48.00	35.00

	Current Price Range		P/Y Average
☐ **Copper,** bundt	95.00	115.00	98.00
☐ **Copper,** Easter egg, rabbit	55.00	70.00	60.00
☐ **Copper,** jelly or pudding	53.00	75.00	58.00
☐ **Copper,** quart size	32.00	47.00	35.00
☐ **Copper,** pint size	29.00	42.00	32.00
☐ **Copper,** circular base with fruit or floral motif, quart size	31.00	45.00	33.00
☐ **Copper,** circular base, with fruit or floral motif, pint size	15.00	28.00	17.00
☐ **Copper,** twelve tube, c. 1860	129.00	155.00	135.00
☐ **Copper,** pan	138.00	160.00	142.00
☐ **Copper,** pan, iron, handle, hanging eye	149.00	170.00	153.00
☐ **Copper,** dull finish, copper handles, 6″ x 20″ diameter	149.00	170.00	152.00
☐ **Copper,** iron handle, 13″, diameter	68.00	80.00	70.00
☐ **Graniteware,** barley sheaf	27.00	36.00	29.00
☐ **Graniteware,** corn	24.00	32.00	26.00
☐ **Graniteware,** food, grey, 9″, circular	25.00	36.00	28.00
☐ **Graniteware,** gelatin, pineapple	15.00	25.00	18.00
☐ **Graniteware,** pudding, blue and white swirl, ring	37.00	60.00	40.00
☐ **Graniteware,** strawberry and grapes	32.00	40.00	36.00
☐ **Graniteware,** tube	15.00	25.00	18.00
☐ **Ice Cream,** Ace of Clubs, pewter	25.00	35.00	30.00
☐ **Ice Cream,** Ace of Spades, pewter	25.00	35.00	30.00
☐ **Ice Cream,** airplane, pewter	25.00	45.00	38.00
☐ **Ice Cream,** American flag, pewter	30.00	42.00	36.00
☐ **Ice Cream,** apple, pewter	25.00	35.00	30.00
☐ **Ice Cream,** aster, pewter	25.00	38.00	32.00
☐ **Ice Cream,** ball, pewter	15.00	25.00	20.00
☐ **Ice Cream,** banana, pewter	25.00	36.00	31.00
☐ **Ice Cream,** battleship, pewter	42.00	52.00	46.00
☐ **Ice Cream,** bell, pewter	25.00	35.00	30.00
☐ **Ice Cream,** grapes, pewter	25.00	35.00	30.00
☐ **Ice Cream,** Calla Lily, pewter	25.00	35.00	28.00
☐ **Ice Cream,** carnation, pewter	30.00	40.00	35.00
☐ **Ice Cream,** cat, pewter	28.00	38.00	32.00
☐ **Ice Cream,** chicken, pewter	30.00	42.00	36.00
☐ **Ice Cream,** crysanthemum, pewter	28.00	36.00	32.00
☐ **Ice Cream,** cupid, pewter	35.00	45.00	40.00
☐ **Ice Cream,** daisy, pewter	25.00	35.00	30.00
☐ **Ice Cream,** doves, pewter	28.00	38.00	32.00
☐ **Ice Cream,** Easter Lily, pewter	25.00	35.00	30.00
☐ **Ice Cream,** egg, pewter	20.00	32.00	26.00
☐ **Ice Cream,** engagement ring, pewter	25.00	35.00	29.00
☐ **Ice Cream,** football, pewter	25.00	35.00	30.00
☐ **Ice Cream,** George Washington, pewter	45.00	55.00	50.00
☐ **Ice Cream,** harp, pewter	35.00	45.00	38.00
☐ **Ice Cream,** heart, pewter	25.00	35.00	30.00
☐ **Ice Cream,** heart with cupid, pewter	25.00	35.00	30.00
☐ **Ice Cream,** hyacinth, pewter	25.00	35.00	30.00
☐ **Ice Cream,** Liberty Bell, pewter	35.00	45.00	30.00
☐ **Ice Cream,** mutton chop, pewter	27.00	37.00	32.00

	Current Price Range		P/Y Average
☐ **Ice Cream**, ocean liner, pewter	35.00	45.00	40.00
☐ **Ice Cream**, orange, pewter	25.00	35.00	28.00
☐ **Ice Cream**, peach, pewter	25.00	35.00	28.00
☐ **Ice Cream**, pear, pewter	25.00	35.00	28.00
☐ **Ice Cream**, petunia, pewter	25.00	35.00	30.00
☐ **Ice Cream**, potato, pewter	25.00	35.00	30.00
☐ **Ice Cream**, pumpkin, pewter	25.00	35.00	28.00
☐ **Ice Cream**, rose, pewter	25.00	35.00	30.00
☐ **Ice Cream**, rosebud, pewter	30.00	40.00	34.00
☐ **Ice Cream**, Santa Claus, pewter	35.00	45.00	40.00
☐ **Ice Cream**, smoking pipe, pewter	30.00	40.00	34.00
☐ **Ice Cream**, stork with baby, pewter	30.00	40.00	35.00
☐ **Ice Cream**, turkey, pewter	28.00	38.00	31.00
☐ **Ice Cream**, wedding bell, pewter	30.00	40.00	28.00
☐ **Ice Cream**, wedding ring, pewter	25.00	35.00	28.00
☐ **Iron Mold**, ice cream, apple	20.00	30.00	22.00
☐ **Iron Mold**, ice cream, automobile	58.00	68.00	60.00
☐ **Iron Mold**, Albany Troy Foundry, c. 1750	108.00	185.00	115.00
☐ **Iron Mold**, cheese, porcelain and metal	58.00	70.00	60.00
☐ **Iron Mold**, Dariel, cast iron, c. 1870s	26.00	55.00	30.00
☐ **Iron Mold**, for ice cream, heart and cupid pattern	40.00	50.00	42.00
☐ **Iron Mold**, for ice cream, locomotive	68.00	80.00	72.00
☐ **Iron Mold**, for ice cream, pumpkin	38.00	50.00	40.00
☐ **Iron Mold**, for ice cream, rabbit, two part hinged	46.00	60.00	48.00
☐ **Iron Mold**, cast iron, two piece, 11″ long	99.00	120.00	103.00
☐ **Iron Mold**, rabbit, cast iron, two piece, mirror image	37.00	50.00	39.00
☐ **Maple Sugar**, bird	6.00	12.00	8.00
☐ **Maple Sugar**, cookie boy	5.00	9.00	7.00
☐ **Maple Sugar**, cookie girl	6.00	12.00	8.00
☐ **Maple Sugar**, cow	6.00	10.00	8.00
☐ **Maple Sugar**, crouching rabbit	6.00	12.00	8.00
☐ **Maple Sugar**, duck	5.50	10.50	7.50
☐ **Maple Sugar**, elephant	6.00	12.00	8.00
☐ **Maple Sugar**, horse	6.00	12.00	8.00
☐ **Maple Sugar**, horse and bear	12.00	18.00	14.50
☐ **Maple Sugar**, horse and pig	12.00	18.00	14.50
☐ **Maple Sugar**, lion	6.00	12.00	8.00
☐ **Maple Sugar**, pig	5.00	7.50	10.00
☐ **Maple Sugar**, rooster	6.00	12.00	8.00
☐ **Maple Sugar**, rooster and duck, two imprints	12.00	18.00	14.50
☐ **Maple Sugar**, rooster and turkey, two imprints	12.00	18.00	14.50
☐ **Maple Sugar**, sheep, two imprints	5.00	7.50	10.00
☐ **Maple Sugar**, sheep and pig, two imprints	12.00	18.00	14.50
☐ **Maple Sugar**, squirrel	6.00	12.00	8.00
☐ **Maple Sugar**, turkey and duck, two imprints	10.00	18.00	14.50
☐ **Tin Mold**, bread or pudding, 11″ long	37.00	48.00	39.00
☐ **Tin Mold**, fluted edge handle, 3″ long	15.00	25.00	18.00
☐ **Tin Mold**, ice cream, c. 1880	26.00	53.00	29.00
☐ **Tin Mold**, jelly, c. 1890	26.00	53.00	29.00
☐ **Tin Mold**, lion, with base, 6″ long	23.00	35.00	28.00

	Current Price Range		P/Y Average
☐ **Tin Mold,** embossed design gives relief on cheese, grape pattern, 6″ long	30.00	50.00	35.00
☐ **Tin Mold,** pierced tin, heart shaped, for cheese, 19th century	16.00	25.00	18.00
☐ **Tin Mold,** tubed, c. 1890	11.00	16.00	12.00

MOVIE COSTUMES

DESCRIPTION: Costumes worn by movie actors and actresses are sought after collectibles.

COMMENTS: Costumes are difficult to find and acquire. Most are one of a kind creations which makes them quite valuable.

The best way to locate costumes is through auction houses and private dealers. A studio label is usually sewn in the garment, and often the star's name or the designer's name will be on a label.

ADDITIONAL TIPS: The listings are in alphabetical order according to item. For further information on movie memorabilia, refer to *The Official Price Guide to Radio, Movie and TV Collectibles.*

☐ **Coat,** men's from MGM wardrobe, gray wool, ¾ length, lined, c. 1950s	65.00	85.00	75.00
☐ **Coat,** men's, from MGM wardrobe, MGM label, green with beige ruffles at end of sleeves, satin lined, c. 1950s	65.00	85.00	75.00
☐ **Coat,** worn by Gene Kelly in "The Black Hand," brown, 1950	180.00	225.00	190.00
☐ **Coat,** worn by Lana Turner in "The Bad And The Beautiful," fur, knee length, hood, lined	150.00	250.00	200.00
☐ **Court Gown,** worn by Linda Darnell in "Forever Amber," heavy cut green velvet with lace trim, 1954	350.00	450.00	375.00
☐ **Dress,** worn by Susan Hayward, in "I'll Cry Tomorrow," designed by Helen Rose, black crepe dress, flares at waist, 'v' neck in back, 1956 ..	300.00	600.00	450.00

	Current Price Range		P/Y Average
□ **Gown,** from MGM wardrobe, designer Ben Reig, black chiffon, bustle sewed in, lace, sequins and rhinestones trimmed on bustle, c. 1950s	150.00	250.00	200.00
□ **Gown,** from MGM wardrobe, no label, orange satin, large satin bow, c. 1950s	125.00	250.00	187.00
□ **Gown,** from MGM wardrobe, polyester, satin lined, sequined jacket, blue, c. 1950s	50.00	75.00	87.00
□ **Gown,** worn by Anne Baxter in "My Wife's Best Friend," silver and white in the style of a Joan of Arc costume, 1952	18.00	23.00	20.00
□ **Gown,** worn by Ava Gardner in "Lone Star," satin bodice, pink tulle ball gown, 1952	130.00	170.00	145.00
□ **Gown,** worn by Betty Grable in "The Farmer Takes A Wife," designed by William Travilla, pink, chiffon, ribbon trim, sequins attached	300.00	500.00	400.00
□ **Gown,** worn by Deborah Kerr in "An Affair To Remember", designed by Charles LeMaire, strapless, chiffon, black sequins, full length slip of satin, corset sewn into garment	300.00	400.00	350.00
□ **Gown,** worn by Debra Paget in "Prince Valiant", designed by Charles LeMaire, double layer blue over lavender chiffon	200.00	275.00	237.00
□ **Gown,** worn by Greer Garson in "Price and Prejudice," polka dot, 1940	160.00	180.00	165.00
□ **Gown,** worn by Jayne Mansfield in "The Girl Can't Help It," designed by Charles LeMaire, blue rayon crepe, beaded, 1956	500.00	600.00	550.00
□ **Gown,** worn by Loretta Young in "Mother Is A Freshman," designed by Kay Nelson, green silk chiffon over pale yellow half-slip, ribbon accents, 1949	175.00	225.00	200.00
□ **Gown,** worn by Marilyn Monroe, designed by William Travilla, white wool, flared from knee, metallic threaded piping throughout pattern, lined ...	400.00	600.00	500.00
□ **Gown,** worn by Marilyn Monroe in "Don't Bother To Knock," designed by William Travilla, orange silk chiffon, 1952	350.00	450.00	400.00
□ **Gown,** worn by Susan Hayward in "I'll Cry Tomorrow," rose chiffon, sequined, designed by Helen Rose, 1955	1000.00	1200.00	950.00
□ **Gown,** worn by Susan Hayward in "Untamed," lime green, 1955	130.00	170.00	115.00
□ **Gown,** worn by Mary Pickford in "The Taming of the Shrew," green silk with gold and silver edging, 1929	500.00	700.00	575.00
□ **Jacket,** bolero style, men's, from MGM wardrobe, MGM label, brown with tan labels and sleeves, satin lined, c. 1950s	40.00	60.00	50.00
□ **Jacket,** waist style, men's, from MGM wardrobe, MGM label, gray wool, satin lined, c. 1950s ...	40.00	50.00	45.00
□ **Leotard And Skirt,** worn by Betty Grable in "When My Baby Smiles at Me," 1948	60.00	80.00	65.00
□ **Military Coat And Pants,** worn by Rock Hudson in "Ice Station Zebra," 1968	160.00	200.00	170.00

	Current Price Range		P/Y Average
☐ **Military Shirt,** worn by William Holden in "The Bridge on the River Kwai," 1957	100.00	125.00	90.00
☐ **Military Shirt,** worn by Cliff Robertson in "P.T. 109," 1963	38.00	48.00	42.00
☐ **Navy Shirt,** worn by Henry Fonda in "Mr. Roberts," 1955	150.00	175.00	145.00
☐ **Pants,** riding, women's, from MGM wardrobe, beige wool, gold braid design on front and back, c. 1950s	40.00	50.00	45.00
☐ **Pants,** riding, women's, from MGM wardrobe, no label, beige wool, pant legs trimmed, c. 1950s	25.00	45.00	35.00
☐ **Pants,** women's, from MGM wardrobe, MGM label, black with white trim and red rhinestones, c. 1950s	50.00	75.00	63.00
☐ **Pants,** women's, from MGM wardrobe, MGM label, black wool, braided work on lower half, c. 1950s	45.00	55.00	50.00
☐ **Pants,** women's, from MGM wardrobe, MGM label, black wool with purple, pink, orange and yellow tassels attached, c. 1950s	45.00	55.00	50.00
☐ **Robe,** worn by June Allyson in "A Woman's World," pink cotton, 1954	25.00	35.00	29.00
☐ **Space Suit,** worn by Keir Dullea in "2001: A Space Odyssey," 1968	1600.00	2000.00	1500.00
☐ **Suite Dress,** worn by Greer Garson in "Scandal at Scourie," blue, 1953	20.00	25.00	22.00
☐ **Surgical Gown,** worn by Chad Everette in "Medical Center"	80.00	100.00	80.00
☐ **Toga,** worn by Esther Williams in "Jupiter's Darling," white with gold trim, 1955	180.00	220.00	185.00
☐ **Tuxedo,** worn by Elvis Presley in "Double Trouble," MGM label, three pieces including jacket, vest and pants, black wool	600.00	800.00	700.00

MOVIE POSTERS

DESCRIPTION: Movie posters are pictures of various sizes which advertise a motion picture.

TYPES: In 1909, the Motion Picture Patents Company standardized the size and purpose of posters. Currently, there are seven poster sizes including lobby card, 11″ x 14″; window card, 14″ x 22″; display card, 22″ x 28″; insert, 14″ x 36″; one sheet poster, 27″ x 41″, two sheet poster, 30″ x 40″ and three sheet poster, 41″ x 81″.

ORIGIN: The Lumiere Brothers of France produced the first movie posters in 1895. The posters featured scenes from the movie as well as pictures of the audience viewing the movie.

COMMENTS: Today, fine poster art is becoming very collectible. Factors that determine a poster's value include the death of a great performer, a new version of an old movie and rarity.

ADDITIONAL TIPS: Classic movies like *Phantom of the Opera* or *Gone With the Wind* will always command high prices. Currently, the market is showing an increased interest in western posters, especially those picturing John Wayne, and horror film posters.

For more information, consult *The Official Price Guide to Radio, TV and Movie Memorabilia,* published by The House of Collectibles.

LOBBY CARDS
(Individual 11″ x 14″)

	Current Price Range		P/Y Average
☐ **Abbott and Costello Meet Frankenstein,** 1948, Universal Pictures, Bud Abbott, Lou Costello, Bela Lugosi, Lon Chaney, scene card	20.00	32.00	25.00
☐ **Christopher Columbus,** 1949, Universal Pictures, Fredric March, title card	8.00	15.00	12.00
☐ **Christopher Strong,** 1933, RKO Radio Pictures, Katharine Hepburn, scene card	120.00	145.00	132.00
☐ **Cimarron Kid,** 1952, Universal Pictures, Audie Murphy, title card	8.00	12.00	10.00

Grand Hotel, *1932,* ©*Metro-Goldwyn-Mayer, Greta Garbo, John Barrymore,*
$1200.00-$1300.00
Photo courtesy of Poster City, Orangeburg, NY

	Current Price Range		P/Y Average
☐ **Colossus of New York, The,** 1958, Paramount Pictures, John Baragrey, Mala Powers, Otto Kruger, scene card	3.00	7.00	4.00
☐ **Comanche Station,** 1960, Columbia Pictures, Randolph Scott, title card	4.00	8.00	5.00
☐ **Come Live With Me,** 1941, Metro-Goldwyn-Mayer, James Stewart, Hedy Lamarr, title card	27.00	40.00	32.00
☐ **Holiday For Lovers,** 1959, Twentieth Century-Fox, Clifton Webb, Jane Wyman, Jill St. John, Carol Lynley, Paul Henreid, Gary Crosby, Jose Greco, title card	5.00	10.00	6.50
☐ **Homecoming,** 1948, Metro-Goldwyn-Mayer, Clark Gable, Lana Turner, scene card	15.00	27.00	25.00
☐ **Hopalong Cassidy Returns,** 1936, Paramount Pictures, William Boyd, scene card	27.50	40.00	32.00
☐ **House of Wax,** 1953, Warner Brothers, Vincent Price, Phyllis Kirk, Frank Lovejoy, Charles Bronson, scene card	25.00	40.00	33.00
☐ **How To Marry a Millionaire,** 1953, Twentieth Century-Fox, Marilyn Monroe, Betty Grable, Lauren Bacall, title card	35.00	50.00	40.00
☐ **Humoresque,** 1946, Warner Brothers, John Garfield, Joan Crawford, scene card	27.50	40.00	30.00
☐ **Hunchback of Notre Dame, The,** 1957, Allied Artists, Gina Lollabrigida, Anthony Quinn, scene card	4.00	8.00	5.00

	Current Price Range		P/Y Average

☐ **I Want To Live,** 1958, United Artists, Susan Hayward, scene card 5.00 12.00 10.00

☐ **I Wanted Wings,** 1941, Paramount Pictures, Ray Milland, William Holden, Wayne Morris, Brian Donlevy, Veronica Lake, scene card 30.00 45.00 35.00

☐ **I Was a Teenage Frankenstein,** 1957, American International, Whit Bissell, Phyllis Coates, scene card 10.00 20.00 14.00

LOBBY CARDS
(Complete Sets Of Eight 11″ x 14″ Lobby Cards)

☐ **Abdication, The,** 1974, Warner Brothers, Peter Finch, Liv Ullman 5.00 12.00 9.00

☐ **Across 110th Street,** 1972, United Artists, Anthony Quinn, Yaphet Kotto, Anthony Franciosa 5.00 12.00 9.00

☐ **City Beneath The Sea,** 1953, Universal Pictures, Robert Ryan, Mala Powers, Anthony Quinn, Suzan Ball 10.00 32.00 20.00

☐ **Clay Pigeon,** 1971, Metro-Goldwyn-Mayer, Telly Savalas, Robert Vaughn, John Marley, Burgess Meredith 5.00 12.00 8.00

☐ **Cold Turkey,** 1971, United Artists, Dick Van Dyke 5.00 12.00 8.00

☐ **Come Back, Little Sheba,** 1953, Paramount Pictures, Burt Lancaster, Shirley Booth, Terry Moore, Richard Jaeckel 22.50 35.00 25.00

The Misleading Lady,
*1932, © Paramount Pictures,
Claudette Colbert, Edmund Lowe,*
$350.00-$400.00

	Current Price Range		P/Y Average

☐ **Come Fill the Cup,** 1951, Warner Brothers, James Cagney 25.00   38.00   30.00

☐ **Docks of New Orleans,** 1948, Monogram Pictures, Roland Winters, Mantan Moreland, Victor Sen Young 50.00   75.00   60.00

☐ **Don't Get Personal,** 1941, Universal Pictures, Hugh Herbert, Mischa Auer, Jane Frazee 20.00   30.00   25.00

☐ **Don't Knock the Twist,** 1962, Columbia Pictures, Chubby Checker, Gene Chandler, The Carroll Brothers, Linda Scott, The Dovells, Vic Dana 15.00   25.00   20.00

☐ **Dragnet,** 1954, Warner Brothers, Jack Webb   25.00   37.00   32.00

☐ **Farewell To Arms, A,** 1958, Twentieth Century-Fox, Rock Hudson, Jennifer Jones, Vittorio De-Sica 18.00   28.00   25.00

☐ **Finger of Guilt,** 1956, RKO Radio Pictures, Richard Basehart, Mary Murphy 7.00   15.00   10.00

☐ **First Texan, The,** 1956, Allied Artists, Joel McCrea 10.00   20.00   15.00

☐ **Forty Carats,** 1973, Columbia Pictures, Liv Ullman, Edward Albert, Gene Kelly, Binnie Barnes   4.00   10.00   8.00

INSERTS
(14″ X 36″)

☐ **Abbott and Costello Go to Mars,** 1953, Universal Pictures, Bud Abbott and Lou Costello 50.00   65.00   55.00

☐ **Abbott and Costello Meet Dr. Jekyll and Mr. Hyde,** 1953, Universal Pictures, Bud Abbott and Lou Costello, Boris Karloff 95.00   115.00   100.00

It Happened One Night,
1934, ©*Columbia Pictures,*
Clark Gable, Claudette Colbert,
$500.00-$600.00

	Current Price Range		P/Y Average

☐ **Abominable Snowman of the Himalayas, The,** 1957, Twentieth Century-Fox, Forrest Tucker, Peter Cushing 12.00 18.00   14.00

☐ **Accused, The,** 1949, Paramount Pictures, Loretta Young, Robert Cummings 20.00 25.00   22.00

☐ **Atomic Man, The,** 1956, Allied Artists, Gene Nelson, Faith Domergue 12.00 18.00   14.00

☐ **Colossus of Rhodes, The,** 1961, Metro-Goldwyn-Mayer, Rory Calhoun 8.00 15.00   10.00

ONE-SHEET POSTERS
(27" X 41")

☐ **All American Co-Ed,** 1941, United Artists, Francis Langford, Johnny Downs, Marjorie Woodworth, Noah Berry, Jr., Esther Dale, Harry Langdon, The Tanner Sisters 15.00 23.00   18.00

☐ **All Fall Down,** 1962, Metro-Goldwyn-Mayer, Eva Marie Saint, Warren Beatty, Karl Malden, Angela Lansbury, Brandon de Wilde 5.00 10.00   8.00

☐ **All the Young Men,** 1960, Columbia Pictures, Alan Ladd, Sidney Poitier, black and white 1.00 3.50   2.50

☐ **Allotment Wives,** 1945, Monogram Pictures, Kay Francis, Paul Kelly 5.00 10.00   8.00

☐ **Corridors of Blood,** 1963, Metro-Goldwyn-Mayer, Boris Karloff 7.50 14.00   10.00

☐ **Corregidor,** 1943, Producers Releasing Corp., Otto Kruger, Elissa Landi 15.00 20.00   17.00

☐ **Cosmic Man, The,** 1959, Allied Artists, Bruce Bennett, John Carradine 25.00 35.00   30.00

WINDOW CARDS
(22" X 28")

☐ **Abandon Ship,** 1957, Columbia Pictures, Tyrone Power, duo-tone 27.50 35.00   30.00

☐ **Absent-Minded Professor, The,** 1961, Walt Disney Productions, Fred MacMurray, Nancy Olson, Keenan Wynn, Tommy Kirk, duo-tone .. 5.00 15.00   10.00

☐ **Across the Sierras,** 1941, Columbia Pictures, Wild Bill Elliott 5.00 10.00   8.00

☐ **Adam Had Four Sons,** 1941, Columbia Pictures, Ingrid Bergman, Warner Baxter, Susan Hayward, Fay Wray 50.00 75.00   60.00

☐ **Adventures of Huckleberry Finn, The,** 1960, Metro-Goldwyn-Mayer, Tony Randall, Patty McCormack, Neville Brand 3.00 8.00   5.00

☐ **Agent For H.A.R.M.,** 1966, Universal Pictures, Mark Richman 5.00 15.00   10.00

☐ **Dangerous Intruder,** 1945, Producers Releasing Corp., Charles Arnt, Veda Ann Borg 5.00 10.00   8.00

☐ **Dark Command, The,** 1940, Republic Pictures, John Wayne, Claire Trevor 10.00 20.00   15.00

☐ **David and Goliath,** 1969, Allied Artists, Orson Welles 8.00 12.00   9.00

MUSIC BOXES

DESCRIPTION: This section deals with cylinder music boxes. The cylinder has an arrangement of tiny metal pins that pluck the teeth of a tuned metal comb as the cylinder revolves. This causes the tune to play.

PERIOD: Cylinder music boxes were popular from the mid–1800s to 1890.

ORIGIN: The cylinder music box originated in 18th century Switzerland.

COMMENTS: With the advent of the disc music box and other forms of home entertainment, cylinder music boxes lost some of their popularity. Today such music boxes are quite collectible.

ADDITIONAL TIPS: Listings are alphabetical according to music box maker. Descriptions of the boxes are included.

For more complete music box listings refer to *The Official Price Guide to Music Collectibles,* published by The House of Collectibles.

	Current Price Range		P/Y Average
☐ **Conchon (Switzerland)** 6 tune 11″ cyl, mandoline zither attachment, operatic selections, veneered and decorated case, inlaid lid, base molding, tune sheet	1200.00	1600.00	1400.00
☐ **Dawkins,** 6 tune 13¼″ cyl, interchangeable, burled walnut, gold painted decoration, inlay on cover, tune card, one cylinder	2250.00	2500.00	2300.00
☐ 10 tune 8¼″ cyl, with 5 bells, walnut with inlay decoration	1250.00	2000.00	1700.00
☐ 12 tune 13″ cyl, drum, bell, wood block, inlay on cover, tune card, large case	1750.00	2500.00	2300.00
☐ **Ducommon Girod,** 4 tune 8″ cyl, simple case, inlay on lid	750.00	1500.00	1200.00
☐ 6 tune 6″ cyl, simple case, tune sheet, stop/start and change levers, c. 1880	500.00	1000.00	800.00
☐ 6 tune 11¼″ cyl, c. 1840, walnut case, three control levers, simple case style	600.00	800.00	725.00

	Current Price Range		P/Y Average
☐ 6 tune 13″ cyl, 7 bells, drum with eight beaters, stop/start and change levers, 123 tooth comb, single spring barrel with crank, burl walnut veneer with some decoration	1500.00	2000.00	1700.00
☐ 8 tune 16¼″ cyl, 3 bells, castanet, inlaid case, full glass inner lid	1500.00	2000.00	1800.00
☐ 12 tune 19″ cyl, rosewood veneered case with enamel and brass inlay decoration, operatic selections, tune sheet	1500.00	2500.00	2100.00
☐ **J. Manger & Co. (Switzerland),** 8 tune 13″ cyl, interchangeable cylinders (10), c. 1880, 6 bells with bee strikers, two piece comb, four spring barrels, crank wind outside, speed adjustment, ornate case decoration with ebony, fruitwood and mother-of-pearl decoration, inner glass lid, matching storage table, with two drawers side-by-side for cylinder storage, turned legs	8500.00	11000.00	9800.00
☐ **Mermod Fréres (St. Croix, Switzerland),** 4 tune 6″ cyl, simple rosewood case, inner glass lid, ornate tune card, stop/start and change levers, late 19th century	500.00	1000.00	700.00
☐ 6 tune 3½″ cyl, c. 1900, crank wind, simple wood case with decal decoration	200.00	400.00	300.00

Regina Disc Music Box,
*style #50, table model,
serpentine case,
mahogany,* **$2800.00-$3750.00**

	Current Price Range		P/Y Average

☐ 6 tune 7½" cyl, simple case, inner glass lid, some decorations on case, tune card **750.00 1250.00 1100.00**

☐ 6 tune 7½" cyl, interchangeable cyl, inlaid rosewood, tune in

☐ **Lecoultre (Geneva, Switzerland),** 2 tune, SNUFF BOX, tortoise shell case, c. 1860–1880 **1250.00 1500.00 1300.00**

☐ 4 tune 8¼" cyl, key wind, early plain box, instant stop and change levers **750.00 1000.00 800.00**

☐ 4 tune 12" cyl, 3" wide diameter cyl, keywind, pianoforte, inlaid lid, tune card, 16" long **3250.00 3750.00 3400.00**

☐ 6 tune 8" cyl, keywind, simple case **750.00 1000.00 825.00**

☐ 6 tune 11" cyl, simple case, some decoration, 18" long case, inner glass lid, lever wind **1000.00 1500.00 1200.00**

☐ **Paillard,** 2 tune 1¾" cyl, Musical Photograph Album, c. 1900. Art Nouveau case decoration, single comb, album sits on ornate corner feet **100.00 300.00 200.00**

☐ 4 tune 19" cyl, 3" diameter cyl, glass inner lid, Sublime-Harmony, interchangeable cyls (2), 47" case **3500.00 5000.00 4000.00**

☐ **Rivenc,** 6 tune 13" cyl, interchangeable cyls (5), tune card, zither attachment, double spring barrel, burled walnut panels on walnut case, inner glass lid, matching table with storage drawer for extra cylinders, turned legs, mother-of-pearl, ebony and brass decoration **4000.00 6000.00 5000.00**

☐ 6 tune 13" cyl, interchangeable 4" wide ("fat") cylinders, simple case style with some decoration **2750.00 4000.00 3400.00**

☐ 8 tune 6" cyl, duplex cylinder box (cylinders placed end to end), two combs, inlaid floral decorations on lid, marquetry borders on lid and sides **2000.00 3250.00 2650.00**

☐ 8 tune 11" cyl, interchangeable cyls, stop/start and change levers, mandolin attachment, tune indicator, brass figures of griffons, tune card, burled walnut case inlaid with satinwood swallows **1250.00 3500.00 2000.00**

☐ 17½" cyl, with organ, basket case **1000.00 1500.00 1275.00**

LINDER MUSIC BOXES—MAKERS UNKNOWN

☐ 3 tune 4¼" cyl, walnut, very simple, unadorned box **500.00 750.00 650.00**

☐ 4 tune 3⅝" cyl, small box, mahogany (or walnut), decoration on lid, small inside glass lid, tune card, tune indicator **400.00 600.00 500.00**

☐ 4 tune 5" cyl, simple case design, 11½" long **400.00 650.00 510.00**

☐ 4 tune 6" cyl, simple case, tune card, 12" long **750.00 1000.00 825.00**

☐ 4 tune 7¾" cyl, key wind, sectional comb, single comb, simple case style **750.00 1500.00 1200.00**

NAUTICAL MEMORABILIA

DESCRIPTION: Nautical memorabilia refers to any items about sailing including figureheads, anchors, windlasses, deadeyes and navigational and weather instruments.

TYPES: The types of objects included in this area are varied and include not only items salvaged from ships, but paper items such as ship lists, posters, and ship logs; articles created by sailors; and paintings of ships.

PERIOD: Collectors will usually find items dating from the 1800s. Items before that time are rare and usually housed in museums.

COMMENTS: Nautical memorabilia has only recently become popular collectible items. Now it is so universally popular that the finer items are very valuable on the collectible market. Yet, the determined hobbyist will still succeed in finding items. Ship salvage yards are an excellent place to search for nautical gear.

Telescope, *American, brass, rosewood, early 1800s, 17″*, $200.00–$300.00

	Current Price Range		P/Y Average
☐ **Bill of Lading,** partially printed, Liverpool to Boston, on the ship John and Phiebe, 1799, 5″ x 9½″	13.00	17.00	15.00
☐ **Book,** *Sailing Craft* by Edwin Schpettle, published in New York in 1928, cloth bound, 786 pages	90.00	115.00	100.00
☐ **Deadeye,** wood braced with iron, c. 1860	70.00	90.00	80.00
☐ **Diver's Helmet,** brass with glass viewing shield, some iron and nickel components, complete with partial shoulder plate, late 1800s	300.00	375.00	335.00

	Current Price Range		P/Y Average

☐ **Document,** British Brig Geffrared enters the Port of San Francisco, large document headed Inward Foreign Entry, 1854 . . . .   35.00   45.00   40.00

☐ **Document,** Entry of Merchandise from Valpariso to San Francisco on the ship Bark Orient, partially printed, 1853, 14″ x 17″ 35.00   45.00   40.00

☐ **Lithograph,** Coleman's Line Clipper Ship, in the form of a huge card, undated, 9″ x 12″ 450.00   550.00   500.00

☐ **Oil Painting,** Clipper Ship by Antonio Jacobsen, oil on board, dated 1915, 16″ x 12″ 1600.00   2000.00   1800.00

☐ **Oil Painting,** Sailing in Philadelphia Harbor by James E. Buttersworth, oil on panel, 5¾″ x 9¼″ 4000.00   5500.00   4600.00

☐ **Print,** two ships at sea, marked Seamen's Bank for Savings, New York, 1962, 15½″ x 22″ 20.00   25.00   22.00

☐ **Sailor's Foot Locker,** made of rough pine joined with copper braces at the sides and back, decorated with simple incised carving of port scenes and several crude representations of sailing ships, 39″ wide x 19″ deep x 18″ high, undated, c. 1875 . . . .   350.00   450.00   400.00

☐ **Ship's Compass,** in cherrywood box with lid, brass fittings, made in England, undated, c. 1820 . . . .   400.00   500.00   450.00

☐ **Ship's Log,** Nantucket whaler, 168 pages, some sketches of whales and harpooning in margins, binding loose, stained, dated 1884 . . . .   500.00   650.00   570.00

☐ **Ship's Wheel,** mahogany, well preserved condition, mid to late 1800s, overall diameter including grips 39″ 550.00   675.00   610.00

☐ **Ship's Wheel,** rosewood and brass, mid 1800s, overall diameter including grips 44½″ 700.00   900.00   800.00

☐ **Trade Sign Figure,** The Little Navigator, carved and painted wood, figure of a man in stove-pipe hat holding navigational instrument, c. 1860, 27½″ 600.00   750.00   660.00

NEEDLEWORKING TOOLS

DESCRIPTION: The often exquisite sewing utensils used by past generations are sought after collectibles today.

COMMENTS: While most needleworking tools are collectible, and fairly easy to find, thimbles are the most popular. They vary in price and were made in silver, porcelain and plastic with advertising slogans, but cut glass thimbles are the most valuable and the most rare. Scissors are also sought after, as are workboxes and small cases.

ADDITIONAL TIPS: The listings are alphabetical according to sewing item. Prices follow.

	Current Price Range		P/Y Average
☐ **Basket,** wicker, 12" H	22.50	29.00	23.00
☐ **Darner,** foot-form, patented, wood, double ended	2.50	4.50	3.75
☐ **Darner,** glass, red	31.00	40.00	32.00
☐ **Darner,** glove, sterling silver	44.00	54.00	46.00
☐ **Darner,** wood, spring clip	1.50	3.50	2.75
☐ **Darner,** sock, brown	31.50	39.00	33.00
☐ **Needlebook,** embossed lithograph decoration on cover	10.00	16.00	12.00
☐ **Needle Case,** brass	16.00	22.00	18.00
☐ **Needle Case,** carved ivory	36.00	44.00	38.00
☐ **Needle Case,** sterling silver	27.00	34.00	28.00
☐ **Needle Case,** tortoise shell	85.00	110.00	92.00
☐ **Pincushion,** ball shaped, black alternating with red and white check, hangs on a ribbon, 19th century	35.00	50.00	39.00
☐ **Pincushion,** ivory, pedestal base	48.00	60.00	52.00
☐ **Pincushion,** patchwork, 8"	16.50	22.00	18.00
☐ **Pincushion,** sterling silver	120.00	160.00	130.00
☐ **Pincushion,** tomato shape in red satin with green felt leaves, 5½" diameter, 9" high	50.00	65.00	53.00
☐ **Scissors,** embroidery, stork, silver plate, 3" L	31.50	39.00	33.00
☐ **Sewing Bird,** brass	49.00	60.00	52.00

	Current Price Range		P/Y Average

☐ **Sewing Bird,** brass, clamp-on, large with cushion	165.00	215.00	275.00
☐ **Sewing Bird,** iron, 6″ L	35.00	45.00	37.00
☐ **Sewing Bird,** sterling silver, 6″ L	46.50	60.00	48.00
☐ **Sewing Machine,** Singer, heavy duty	260.00	340.00	300.00
☐ **Sewing Machine,** White, Cleveland, Ohio, early 1900s	150.00	190.00	170.00
☐ **Spinning Wheel,** Norwegian, paint decorated, small	205.00	255.00	220.00
☐ **Spool Cabinet,** Eureka, walnut, 22 drawers, 16 with glass	1250.00	1800.00	1350.00
☐ **Spool Cabinet,** Brooks, four-drawer	312.00	375.00	320.00
☐ **Stencil,** copper, Old English alphabet, used to make needlework design	8.00	16.00	10.00
☐ **Tape Measure,** clock	75.00	100.00	83.00
☐ **Tape Measure,** duck and hen	40.00	52.00	42.00
☐ **Tape Measure,** figural turtle, sterling, brass enamel	57.00	77.00	67.00
☐ **Tape Measure,** owl	26.00	34.00	28.00
☐ **Tape Measure,** papoose, original box	14.50	20.00	15.50
☐ **Tape Measure,** rabbit	36.00	45.00	38.00
☐ **Tape Measure,** vault	26.00	35.00	28.00
☐ **Tatting Shuttle,** tortoise shell	15.00	23.00	16.00
☐ **Thimble,** brass	18.50	26.00	20.00
☐ **Thimble,** celluloid	8.50	13.00	9.50
☐ **Thimble,** engraved bird, large size, 14k gold ..	82.00	110.00	85.00
☐ **Thimble,** gold with leather case	95.00	125.00	105.00
☐ **Thimble,** sterling silver marked with star trademark, in leather box	45.00	60.00	48.00
☐ **Thimble,** sterling silver	47.50	62.00	50.00
☐ **Thimble,** tortoise shell and sterling silver	107.00	135.00	115.00
☐ **Thimble Holder,** wooden acorn with hinged leaf top	55.00	80.00	62.00
☐ **Thimble Holder,** celluloid, with thread holder	16.50	25.00	18.00

NEWCOMB COLLEGE POTTERY

DESCRIPTION: Pottery making and decorating became the chief specialty at the art department of Newcomb College in New Orleans. Its efforts in the field were launched in 1896. As all the work was performed under expert guidance and at a pace much slower and more conducive to artistic achievement than that of a commercial factory, some very noteworthy results were obtained. Most of the Newcomb pottery is brilliant. Its level of quality is consistently high and the decorating reflects imagination and spirit. Since its works were never produced in large quantities, they ranked as collectors' items almost from the beginning. Lovers of fine art pottery have been seeking out Newcomb products for at least 80 years.

COMMENTS: The Newcomb Pottery operations were headed by Dr. Ellsworth Woodward and Mary G. Sheerer. Newcomb wares carry underglaze designs, picturing subjects from nature. Local subject-matter predominates, as the objective was to have students paint "from life" rather than from pictures in books (which was usually the case in commercial potteries). Thus the designs present an intriguing panorama of the flowers, leaf types, birds, etc. of Louisiana.

MARKS: There are normally five marks on any given piece. First is the general mark of Newcomb, which will appear either as a white-on-black vase with the initials N.C., or consist merely of those initials without symbolization (the N resting within the C). Another variety of the mark has NEWCOMB COLLEGE spelled out. Additionally, the piece will (or should) carry a potter's mark, an artist's or decorator's mark, a recipe mark, and finally a registration mark. The purpose of using potters' marks was to identify which works were produced by the students. The artists' marks were more elaborate than those of the potters, consisting usually of boldly drawn initial letters within geometrical frames. Obviously, the students took some inspiration in signing their names from the practices of artists at commercial art pottery factories. The recipe mark is a single capital letter, which relates to a book of clay mixtures used by the class.

RECOMMENDED READING: For further information, you may refer to *The Official Price Guide to Pottery and Porcelain,* published by The House of Collectibles.

	Current Price Range		P/Y Average
□ **Bowl,** painted flowers, applied roses and leaves	105.00	115.00	110.00
□ **Candlesticks,** 7¼", pair, trumpet shape, matte lavender glaze with green and rose, c. 1925 ..	350.00	375.00	360.00
□ **Trivet,** floral motif, signed Sadie Irvine	200.00	220.00	205.00
□ **Vase,** 4", green, lavender and rose, high gloss finish	235.00	245.00	240.00
□ **Vase,** 5", white and yellow flowers, green leaves around rim and sides, blue background, signed Sadie Irvine	555.00	575.00	260.00
□ **Vase,** 5", floral motif, dark blue band on neck continuing to light blue on bulbous body, matte glaze, signed Sadie Irvine, c. early 20th century	390.00	410.00	395.00
□ **Vase,** 5", ovoid, narcissi and leaf motif, pale cream matte glaze on blue matte background, artist signed, c. 1910	610.00	630.00	615.00
□ **Vase,** 6", moon shining through trees motif, blue background, signed Henrietta Bailey	1450.00	1475.00	1455.00
□ **Vase,** 6", white floral motif, blue background, signed Henrietta Bailey	720.00	750.00	725.00
□ **Vase,** 8", floral motif, signed Henrietta Bailey	500.00	525.00	505.00
□ **Vase,** 8", pale gray and beige glaze on purple, background, blossoming dogwood branches motif, signed Sarah Irvine, c. 1910	720.00	740.00	725.00

NEWSPAPERS

DESCRIPTION: Newspapers are daily or weekly papers which contain news events, features and advertising.

TYPES: The types of newspapers that are valuable are those with major events headlining its pages. One of the most valuable twentieth century newspapers is that carrying the premature "Dewey defeats Truman" headline.

ADDITIONAL TIPS: Prices are for whole issues, not just front pages. Front pages alone are worth less than the prices shown. For more information, consult *The Official Price Guide to Paper Collectibles,* published by The House of Collectibles.

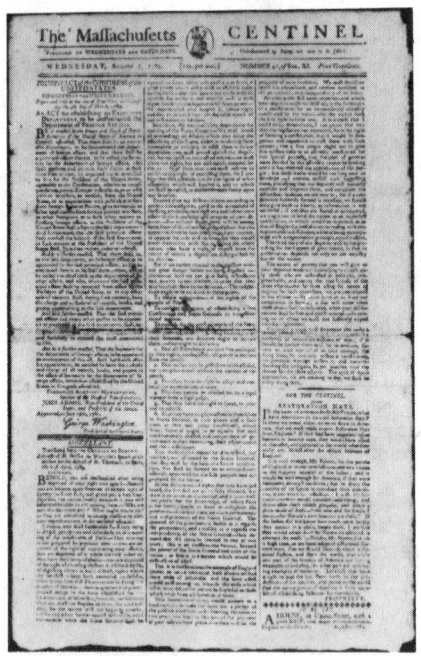

Newspaper, *facsimile signature of George Washington, 1789,* **$35.00–$50.00**
Photo courtesy of Lou McCulloch, Highland Heights, OH 44143.

ASSASSINATIONS

	Current Price Range		P/Y Average
☐ **Archduke Francis Ferdinand**	7.75	11.50	9.67
☐ **James Garfield Shot** (still alive)	11.50	16.50	13.50
☐ **James Garfield dies of wound**	5.75	6.75	6.25
☐ **Mahatma Gandhi**	4.00	5.75	4.87
☐ **Mrs. Indira Gandhi,** Denver Post, news of attack without definite word on her condition	1.00	1.50	1.50
☐ **John F. Kennedy**	20.00	30.00	25.00
☐ **Robert Kennedy Shot** (still alive)	5.75	6.75	6.25
☐ **Robert Kennedy dies of wound**	4.00	5.75	4.87
☐ **Martin Luther King, Jr.**	4.00	5.75	4.87

	Current Price Range		P/Y Average
☐ **Abraham Lincoln**	115.00	170.00	142.00
☐ **Huey Long**	6.75	7.75	7.25
☐ **Huey Long** —New Orleans paper	10.00	13.50	11.75
☐ **William McKinley Shot** (still alive)	11.50	16.50	13.50
☐ **William McKinley dies of wound**	6.75	7.75	7.25
☐ **Benito Mussolini**	25.00	35.00	29.00
☐ **Anwar Sadat**	.75	1.00	.87
☐ **Leon Trotsky,** (early report, stating he had been shot)	9.00	12.00	10.00
☐ **Leon Trotsky,** (corrected report, stating he was bludgeoned with hammer)	7.00	10.00	7.50

ATTEMPTED ASSASSINATIONS

☐ **Charles DeGaule**	1.35	2.00	1.67
☐ **Gerald Ford**	.65	.95	.80
☐ **Hitler,** attempt by concealed bomb fails, London Daily Telegraph	8.00	11.00	9.25
☐ **Franklin D. Roosevelt**	4.00	5.50	4.75
☐ **Harry S. Truman**	2.75	4.00	3.38
☐ **Gov. George Wallace**	2.00	3.25	2.62
☐ **Pope John-Paul II**	.75	1.00	.87

RESULTS OF PRESIDENTIAL ELECTIONS

☐ **1860,** Lincoln/Douglas	33.75	47.25	40.50
☐ **1864,** Lincoln/McClellan	27.50	40.00	33.75
☐ **1868,** Grant/Seymour	8.00	13.50	10.50
☐ **1872,** Grant/Greeley	8.00	13.50	10.50
☐ **1876,** Hayes/Tilden	6.75	10.75	8.75
☐ **1880,** Garfield,/Hancock	6.75	10.75	8.75
☐ **1884,** Cleveland/Blaine	6.75	10.75	8.75
☐ **1888,** Harrison/Cleveland	6.75	10.75	8.75
☐ **1892,** Cleveland/Harrison	6.75	10.75	8.75
☐ **1896,** McKinley/Bryan	8.00	12.25	10.00
☐ **1900,** McKinley/Bryan	8.00	12.25	10.00
☐ **1904,** Roosevelt/Parker	6.75	10.75	8.75
☐ **1908,** Taft/Bryan	5.50	9.50	7.50
☐ **1912,** Wilson/Roosevelt/Taft	8.00	12.25	10.00
☐ **1916,** Wilson/Hughes	5.50	9.50	7.50
☐ **1920,** Harding/Cox	4.00	6.75	5.37
☐ **1924,** Coolidge/Davis	2.75	4.75	3.75
☐ **1928,** Hoover/Smith	2.75	4.75	3.75
☐ **1932,** Roosevelt/Hoover	5.50	9.50	7.50
☐ **1936,** Roosevelt/Landon	4.00	6.75	5.37
☐ **1940,** Roosevelt/Wilkie	4.00	6.75	5.37
☐ **1944,** Roosevelt/Dewey	4.00	6.75	5.37
☐ **1948,** Truman/Dewey	4.00	6.75	5.37
Note: Papers carrying premature "Dewey Defeats Truman" headlines are worth as much as $200. The New York Times was not one of them.			
☐ **1952,** Eisenhower/Stevenson	2.75	4.75	3.75
☐ **1956,** Eisenhower/Stevenson	2.00	3.50	2.75
☐ **1960,** Kennedy/Nixon	8.00	12.25	10.00
☐ **1964,** Johnson/Goldwater	2.00	3.50	2.75

	Current Price Range		P/Y Average
☐ **1968,** Nixon/Humphrey	2.00	3.50	2.75
☐ **1972,** Nixon/McGovern	2.00	3.50	2.75
☐ **1976,** Carter/Ford..........................	1.35	2.75	2.05
☐ **1980,** Reagan/Carter	1.00	1.50	1.25
☐ **1984,** Reagan/Mondale	.75	1.00	—

DEATHS OF CELEBRATED PERSONS (WHOLE PAPER)

☐ **Jack Benny**	1.35	2.75	2.05
☐ **Charlie Chaplin**	2.75	4.75	3.75
☐ **Winston Churchill**	4.00	6.75	5.37
☐ **Calvin Coolidge**	2.75	4.50	3.62
☐ **Charles DeGalle**.....................	2.00	3.00	2.50
☐ **Edward VII**	2.75	4.50	3.62
☐ **Adolph Eichmann** (Executed)	5.50	9.50	7.50
☐ **Dwight D. Eisenhower**	2.00	3.50	2.75
☐ **Judy Garland**	13.50	20.00	16.50
☐ **Warren Harding**	2.75	4.75	3.75
☐ **Adolph Hitler** (unconfirmed)	20.00	27.00	24.00
☐ **Herbert Hoover**	2.00	3.50	2.75
☐ **Lyndon Johnson**	1.35	2.75	2.05
☐ **Nikita Khrushchev**	2.00	3.50	2.75
☐ **John Lennon**	1.00	1.50	1.25
☐ **Ethel Merman,** New York Times	1.00	1.50	1.50
☐ **Marilyn Monroe**	16.00	23.50	20.00
☐ **Elvis Presley**.........................	12.00	16.00	14.00
☐ **Queen Victoria**	13.50	20.00	16.50
☐ **Franklin D. Roosevelt**	13.50	20.00	16.50
☐ **Theodore Roosevelt**	5.50	9.50	7.50
☐ **William H. Taft**	2.75	4.00	3.37
☐ **Harry Truman**	2.00	3.50	2.75
☐ **John Wayne**	.65	1.00	.82
☐ **Woodrow Wilson**	4.00	6.75	5.37

NEWS EVENTS

☐ **Aaron Burr Slays Alexander Hamilton in Pistol Duel**	100.00	130.00	112.00
☐ **Alan Ameche Scores TD In Overtime As Colts Defeat Giants For NFL Championship,** Baltimore Sun	4.00	6.00	5.00
☐ **Astronauts Killed in Fire**	4.00	6.50	5.25
☐ **Atomic Bomb Dropped on Nagasaki**	33.75	45.50	39.57
☐ **Battle of Little Big Horn**	130.00	190.00	160.00
☐ **Billy The Kid Slain By Pat Garrett**	60.00	80.00	67.00
Note: This was not treated as "front page" news by most newspapers; it received just a paragraph in some. The lengthier and more prominent the coverage, the more valuable.			
☐ **Body of Bobby Greenlease Found,** kidnap victim, Kansas City Times	4.00	6.00	5.00
☐ **Brooklyn Dodgers Play First Night Game And Are Victims Of No-Hit Pitching By John VanderMeer,** New York Daily Mirror	5.00	7.00	5.75

	Current Price Range		P/Y Average
☐ Burning of Morro Castle	10.00	15.00	11.75
☐ Coolidge Sworn In As President Following Death of Harding	22.00	30.00	25.00
☐ Disaster Of Excursion Boat "General Slocum" With 1,000 Killed	50.00	70.00	60.00
☐ Jack Johnson Knocks Out James J. Jeffries To Retain Heavyweight Title, New York Times, lengthy report with byline of John L. Sullivan (former heavyweight champion)	50.00	65.00	56.75
☐ Bonnie and Clyde Shot	40.00	45.00	42.50
☐ John Wilkes Booth Slain	37.50	50.00	43.50
☐ Caryl Chessman Executed	2.60	4.50	3.50
☐ Chicago Fire	100.00	125.00	112.50
☐ Chicago Fire — Chicago newspaper	450.00	650.00	550.00
☐ Coronation of Elizabeth II	4.00	6.50	5.25
☐ D-Day	20.00	26.00	23.00
☐ John Dillinger Shot	33.00	40.00	36.00
☐ Germany Surrenders (World War II)	20.00	26.00	23.00
☐ John Glenn Orbits Earth..................	6.50	10.50	8.50
☐ Bruno Hauptmann Executed	52.00	65.00	58.00
☐ Hindenberg Explodes	52.00	65.00	58.00
☐ Jesse James Killed	70.00	100.00	85.00
☐ Japan Surrenders	26.00	32.00	29.00
☐ John F. Kennedy Inaugurated	6.50	10.50	8.50
☐ Lee Harvey Oswald Slain By Jack Ruby	10.00	15.00	11.25
☐ Charles Lindbergh Baby Kidnapped	45.00	60.00	52.00
☐ Charles Lindbergh Crosses Atlantic	100.00	160.00	130.00
☐ Marilyn Monroe Marries Joe DiMaggio	15.00	20.00	17.00
☐ Moon Landing (first, 1969)	20.00	26.00	23.00
☐ Mount St. Helens Erupts, 1981, Seattle Post-Intelligencer	3.00	4.00	3.25
☐ Police Storm Hideout of Simbionese Liberation Army, Slay Donald DeFreese, Los Angeles Times	2.00	3.00	2.20
☐ Power Failure Blacks Out East Coast of U.S., Newark Star Ledger	3.00	4.00	3.50
☐ Richard Nixon Resigns	7.25	10.50	9.05
☐ Pearl Harbor Attacked	26.00	40.00	33.00
☐ Prince Charles/Princess Diana's Marriage ..	1.00	1.50	1.25
☐ Russian Sputnik Launched	15.00	22.00	19.00
☐ 1929 Stock Market Crash	52.00	65.00	58.50
☐ Titanic Sinks...........................	78.00	105.00	91.00
☐ Triangle Shirtwaist Factory Fire	13.00	20.00	17.00
☐ Truman Relieves General MacArthur of Korean Command	10.00	15.00	12.00

NILOAK POTTERY COMPANY

DESCRIPTION: The products of this 20th century art pottery are highly creative. Prior to closing in 1946, Niloak sold decorative wares with very simple shapes, whose textures resembled marble. All the shapes and styles were inspired by so-called primitive work, by the ancient Greeks and Romans and especially by the American Indians. The Niloak pottery is essentially old classic redware, the same type you find in museums, but with the drastic difference of a marbleized texture. To achieve an even more natural, striking appearance, the company decided to stop using exterior glazes. Thus, most of the Niloak pottery has a glaze on the inside only. This interior glaze was considered necessary from a utilitarian point of view, in the event any owner wanted to keep liquids in them. It is highly doubtful, though, if anyone did more with Niloak creations than to display them as decorative objects of art. They were dazzlers, especially in a setting with subdued lighting.

Today, Niloak has become a favorite art pottery with collectors. It never fails to intrigue the general public, too, though there are many who instinctively believe it to have an Indian origin.

HISTORY: Niloak products were developed in an old family pottery business in 1909 in Benton, Arkansas, when the company was being run by Charles D. Hyten. Charles was the son of J.H. Hyten, who had come to Arkansas from Iowa many years earlier to establish a pottery works. Niloak was nothing more than an experiment at the factory when it was initially produced. The word "niloak" is kaolin spelled backwards, kaolin being the special clay which serves as chief ingredient in porcelain. Since Niloak pottery was about as opposite to porcelain as any ware could be, the use of this name was appropriate. Clays of various colors taken from the neighborhood around Benton went into Niloak. They were blended on the wheel so that one streaked into another leaving traces of unblended color creating the striated or marbleized effect.

Hyten made arrangements with a jewelry shop in Benton to show some of his strange new creations on consignment. They aroused interest and very soon the Hyten Pottery became the Niloak Pottery Company. Distribution was made to the leading market areas of the country, but Niloak never expanded to the point of actually mass producing its wares. The firm's most successful decade was the 1920s. Like other art potteries it was hit hard by the depression and never regained momentum, though it managed to survive into the 1940s.

MARKS: Niloak pottery will either have an impressed mark or a circular paper label, reading simple *NILOAK POTTERY.* The mark is contained in a collar and is printed in plain block letters. Paper labels became standard with Niloak in its later years. As with other pottery bearing paper labels, the labels sometimes came loose, leaving the item without any indication of its origin. A more elaborate form of the mark reads *FROM THE NILOAK POTTERIES AT BENTON, ARKANSAS.* Some pieces carry model numbers and some do not. It is incorrect to refer to these as MOLD numbers, since the Niloak ware was always thrown on the wheel, not pressed from molds.

HYWOOD (Introduced 1930s)

This line was less expensive to produce. It was finished with either high gloss or semi-matte glazes.

	Current Price Range		P/Y Average
☐ **Ewer,** 10", brown and green semi-matte glaze, eagle molded on side	30.00	35.00	32.00
☐ **Pitcher,** miniature	12.00	14.00	13.00
☐ **Vase,** matte white glaze	130.00	140.00	132.00
☐ **Vase,** 6", applied handles, matte glaze	32.00	37.00	34.00
☐ **Vase,** 7½", matte rose glaze	38.00	43.00	39.00
☐ **Vase,** 8", two handled, scalloped rim, rose to blue glaze	48.00	55.00	49.00

MISSION WARE (Introduced Early 1900s)

This line is the most desirable of Niloak's production. It features hand-thrown clay decoration in various colors.

	Current Price Range		P/Y Average
☐ **Bowl,** 10", earth tone swirls	65.00	75.00	67.00
☐ **Holder,** match, swirls	40.00	45.00	42.00
☐ **Vase,** 3½", swirls	37.00	43.00	38.00
☐ **Vase,** 4", dark blue, cream and blue swirls	40.00	50.00	41.00
☐ **Vase,** 4½", tan and blue swirls	48.00	55.00	49.00
☐ **Vase,** 5", brown, blue and cream swirls	37.00	42.00	38.00
☐ **Vase,** 5½", blue and brown swirls	40.00	45.00	41.00
☐ **Vase,** 5½", blue and white swirls	45.00	62.00	56.00
☐ **Vase,** 6", bulbous body, flared rim, swirls	55.00	62.00	56.00
☐ **Vase,** 6", swirls	40.00	45.00	41.00
☐ **Vase,** 6¾", brown, tan, ivory and blue swirls ..	60.00	65.00	61.00
☐ **Vase,** 9", swirls	92.00	100.00	93.00
☐ **Vase,** 10", swirls	130.00	140.00	131.00

NIPPON

DESCRIPTION: Nippon porcelain ware is the result of an American tariff act in the late 19th century which required imports to be marked with the country of their origin. Nippon ware is something of an enigma to all but experienced collectors as it also represents Satsuma, Noritake, Imari and other Japanese wares of a certain period. Nippon ware really is quite beautiful combining a relatively contemporary look with old style craftsmanship and exquisite taste.

COMMENTS: Nippon was not a popular collectible until the mid 1950s. It is still possible to find Nippon porcelain in flea markets, thrift shops, yard sales, attics or Grandma's china closet. Really choice pieces are difficult to locate, however, as the owners withhold them from the market to increase their value, or because of sentimental attachment.

MARKS: Nippon marks most frequently depict an M within a green wreath, and the word "Nippon" printed in curved letters underneath. There are many, many variations, however. By the early 20th century, the Nippon emblem was replaced with "Japan," thus ending an era.

ADDITIONAL TIPS: Typical of any lucrative collectible field, Nippon ware has been faked and reproduced on the antique market. Items are arranged according to function, material and color.

RECOMMENDED READING: For more in-depth information on Nippon you may refer to *The Official Price Guide to Oriental Collectibles,* published by The House of Collectibles.

	Current Price Range		P/Y Average
MISCELLANEOUS			
☐ **Ashtray,** 3″ in diameter, c. 1900s, autumnal hues, horse, trees, lake shore motif, green M mark	17.00	28.00	22.00
☐ **Ashtray,** 4″ in diameter, c. 1900s, round shape, geometric motif in raised enamel	28.00	47.00	34.00
☐ **Bowl,** c. 1900s, strawberries, leaves and flowers, leaf shaped handle	260.00	300.00	285.00

	Current Price Range		P/Y Average

☐ **Box,** 2″ high, c. 1900s, blue, gold-raised motif, green M mark 75.00 125.00 100.00

☐ **Candy Bowl,** c. 1900s, hand painted scene of palm trees, lake with sailboat, mountains in pastel colors, beaded gold trim around outer rim, two pierced, upturned handle 50.00 70.00 60.00

☐ **Bowl,** 7″ in diameter, c. 1900s, blue, white background, pink, red floral medallions, handles, green M mark 12.00 20.00 16.00

☐ **Bowl,** 8″ in diameter, c. 1900s, enameled, raised chestnut motif, handles, green M mark 22.00 31.00 26.00

☐ **Bowl,** 9″ in diameter, c. 1900s, bisque, walnut motif, green M mark 55.00 100.00 75.00

☐ **Bowl,** 9″ in diameter, c. 1900s, mustard color, hand painted, M wreath, blue mark, gold, jewels, rose motif 39.00 77.00 50.00

☐ **Bowl,** 9″ in diameter, c. 1900s, red, black, figural, scenic, floral motif, green, red border, unmarked 43.00 82.00 60.00

☐ **Candy Bowl,** 6″ square, c. 1900s, beaded, gold rim, blown out sides, two gold handles, floral design, purple, green, yellow and brown, pastel background 72.00 90.00 80.00

☐ **Desk Set,** c. 1900s, five pieces, tray, round pen point holder, covered stamp box, ink well, no lid, blotter, scenic cameos, gold around the cameos edges, bodies raised blue dots of enamel 225.00 265.00 245.00

☐ **Dresser Set,** c. 1900s, 7″ tray, stoppered bottle 3″ high, small and larger covered patch boxes, round, trimmed in gold, on white 50.00 70.00 60.00

☐ **Ewer,** 10″ high, c. 1900s, bulbous body, band of violets, greens and violets, cabinet item, unmarked 170.00 195.00 180.00

☐ **Ewer,** 12″ high, 1900s, bulbous body, long 5½″ neck, handle extends from body to neck, folial center piece, red and violet 210.00 290.00 250.00

☐ **Fruit Bowl,** 9″ in diameter, c. 1900s, handles, scalloped gold rim, geometric designs, wide beaded gold ribbons, hand painted red flowers and buds outlined in gold, signed with the blue leaf mark 75.00 95.00 80.00

☐ **Hat Pin Holder,** c. 1900s, gold, floral detail on dark blue background 37.00 53.00 42.00

☐ **Humidor,** 4″ high, c. 1900s, bisque finish, gray, trimmed in gold, scene depicts playing cards .. 435.00 500.00 450.00

TABLE SERVICE

☐ **Candy Dish,** 7″ x 5″, c. 1900s, oval shape, hand painted M wreath, green mark, scenic motif, two open work handles 38.00 50.00 40.00

☐ **Celery Dish or Spooner,** 9″ x 4″, c. 1900s, satin finish, small houseboat with sail, docked on shore with brush on both sides, faint windmill in

	Current Price Range		P/Y Average

background, variety of colors, gold tracing on ends on sides, flowers, leaves, raised gold dots **22.00** **30.00** **25.00**

☐ **Cocoa Set,** c. 1900s, main pot, six cups, saucers, lid top and bottom, in turquoise blue, offset with bands of gold dots, main portion of body has sprays and individual roses, cups and saucers turquoise **290.00** **340.00** **300.00**

☐ **Coffee Set,** 9″ high, c. 1900s, pot, five cups, saucers, demitasse size, satin scenic, grays, white skyline pink, rose, green M mark **135.00** **150.00** **140.00**

☐ **Compote,** 3″ high, c. 1900s, moriage, green background, floral insects, medallion of new post office building, Chicago, Oriental China Nippon mark **65.00** **80.00** **70.00**

☐ **Compote,** 5″ x 12″, c. 1900s, bisque, Indian in a birch bark canoe aiming a rifle, yellows and greens, handles gold, gold tracings, the scene surrounded on the inside of the bowl by pictographs **120.00** **150.00** **140.00**

☐ **Cookie Server,** 10″ in diameter, c. 1900s, yellow background, floral motif, gold handle, M mark **25.00** **35.00** **30.00**

☐ **Cream and Sugar Set,** c. 1900s, hand painted flowers, leaves, beaded gold trim around top rims, gold trim on handles and finial **45.00** **60.00** **50.00**

☐ **Creamer,** c. 1900s, gold foliage motif, handle, hand painted Nippon mark **12.00** **16.00** **14.00**

☐ **Creamer,** 4″ high, c. 1900s, light blue background, white floral motif, Greek key motif, square handle, pedestal base, green M mark .. **60.00** **80.00** **70.00**

☐ **Cruets,** 6″ high, c. 1900s, cream background, oriental garden motif, M mark (pair) **75.00** **95.00** **85.00**

☐ **Cup,** 3″ high, c. 1900s, gold, grape, vine, leaf motif, green M mark **14.00** **22.00** **18.00**

☐ **Cups and Saucers,** c. 1900s, multicolored floral motif, art nouveau, green M mark **7.00** **11.00** **9.00**

☐ **Demitasse Set,** c. 1900s, porcelain, pot, five cups, saucers, pink, art deco, black outline, marked Nippon, queen **120.00** **150.00** **130.00**

☐ **Dish,** 6″ in diameter, c. 1900s, cream background, raised gold, multicolors, M mark **12.00** **18.00** **14.00**

☐ **Dish,** 7″ x 6″, c. 1900s, gold background, floral, foliage motif, M mark **25.00** **35.00** **30.00**

☐ **Dish,** 7″ wide, c. 1900s, moriage, fish shape, red background, mythical bird motif, bordered, unmarked **60.00** **80.00** **70.00**

☐ **Dish,** 8″ x 6″, c. 1900s, brown and tan panel, pink and white floral motif, gold handle, cover, rising sun mark **45.00** **75.00** **55.00**

☐ **Dish,** 12″ x 6″, c. 1900s, yellow, tan floral motif, green stems, black ribbons, lined in gold, green M mark **9.00** **15.00** **12.00**

☐ **Egg Cup,** c. 1900s, white background, blue and amber butterflies **21.00** **26.00** **23.00**

	Current Price Range		P/Y Average

☐ **Egg Warmer,** 5½″ in diameter, c. 1900s, green M in wreath 100.00   125.00   115.00

☐ **Jar,** 4″ high, c. 1900s, multicolored floral, gold green M mark 20.00   35.00   30.00

☐ **Napkin Ring,** c. 1900s, satin finish, scene of windmill 65.00   85.00   75.00

☐ **Nut Set,** c. 1900s, main bowl, four individual nut cups on legs, small flowers traced in gold line 35.00   45.00   40.00

☐ **Plate,** 5″ in diameter, c. 1900s, floral motif, art nouveau, green M mark 6.00   9.00   7.00

☐ **Plate,** 6″ in diameter, c. 1900s, gold outlined, oval floral medallions, blue mark 35.00   55.00   45.00

☐ **Plate,** 7″ in diameter, c. 1900s, child holds bouquet, blue M mark 13.00   19.00   15.00

☐ **Plate,** 7″ in diameter, c. 1900s, children playing, elephant motif, hand painted Nippon 18.00   25.00   23.00

☐ **Plate,** 8″ in diameter, c. 1900s, gold raised enamel leaves, vines, oval medallions, green M mark 22.00   28.00   25.00

☐ **Plate,** 10″ in diameter, c. 1900s, multicolored floral motif, green M mark 18.00   27.00   21.00

☐ **Plate,** 10″ in diameter, c. 1900s, raised gold, red floral motif, pierced handles, marked 60.00   80.00   70.00

☐ **Platter,** 11″ in diameter, autumn scene of lake, trees, leaves turning brown, path leading to the forest, two applied handles, moriage decoration 70.00   90.00   80.00

☐ **Salt and Pepper Shakers,** designs filled with white enamel, salt is open bowl type 25.00   35.00   30.00

☐ **Salt and Pepper Shakers,** 2″ high, c. 1900s, pink floral, foliage motif, gold handles, rising sun mark 22.00   28.00   25.00

☐ **Salt Dip,** c. 1900s, multicolored floral motif, gold outline on rims and handles, green M mark ... 13.00   19.00   15.00

☐ **Sardine Set,** 6′14″ long, c. 1900s, three pieces, with figural sardine, sprigged on top green M in wreath 135.00   170.00   145.00

☐ **Spoon Holder,** c. 1900s, floral motif, two handles, M mark 40.00   60.00   50.00

OCCUPIED JAPAN

DESCRIPTION: Collectibles from this category represent Japanese exported items made after World War II, when Japan was "occupied" by a foreign country for the first time in history. The term "occupied" was essential to Japanese economic recovery. Hostile feelings toward the Eastern nation still ran high for many years after the war; people absolutely refused to buy anything with "Made in Japan" as its trademark, believing that American dollars could not go to a more unworthy cause than to support a country responsible for such economic, personal, and political worldwide upheaval. Since Japanese exports still retained such superior craftsmanship, beauty and aesthetic symmetry despite the scarcity of materials and manpower, the trademark "Occupied Japan," assured consumers, that they were in no way contributing their hard earned dollars to the menacing powers of the pre-war era.

COMMENTS: Like Nippon, Occupied Japanese items are steadily growing in value as collectibles, and more and more dealers are scrambling to supply these items to their Orientalia buyers. Identification is fairly simple of course; the trademark is self explanatory. Do not be put off by Westernized motifs and design; the Japanese were, after all, in a state of national transition marking the beginning of their conversion to Westernized ideals and modes of living.

Items are arranged according to category. In large sections, these are further broken down according to type of object. Within the listings, articles are alphabetically arranged by size, smallest to largest.

RECOMMENDED READING: For more in-depth information on Occupied Japan, you may refer to *The Official Price Guide to Oriental Collectibles,* published by The House of Collectibles.

FIGURINES

	Current Price Range		P/Y Average
ANIMALS			
☐ **Bird,** 2″ high, perched on two books, yellow, green and blue wings, red tail	6.00	7.25	6.50
☐ **Bird,** 2″ x 3″ long, tan body, red head, multicolor wings, black tail	9.00	11.50	10.50

	Current Price Range		P/Y Average

☐ **Bird,** 3″ high, yellow body, red beak, brown base 6.50 8.00 7.25

☐ **Bird,** 3″, white wings, yellow crest, blue and green base 9.00 11.50 10.00

☐ **Bird,** 3½″ high, perched on branch, yellow body, tan wings and tail, blue breast 8.00 10.50 9.25

☐ **Bird,** 3½″ x 3″, red head, white and gold body, yellow tail, gold trim, on floral branches 8.00 10.50 9.25

☐ **Bird,** 4½″ x 4¾″ long, cocked head, long yellow beak, rose body, grey wings, raised tail 16.00 19.00 17.50

☐ **Bird,** 4¾″ high, perched on stump 11.00 13.00 12.00

☐ **Bird,** 5″ high, perched on tree stump, leaves on base 10.00 12.25 11.00

☐ **Boxer,** 3″ high, grey, standing 8.50 10.00 9.25

☐ **Crane,** 4″ high, blue and yellow out-stretched wings 7.00 8.50 7.75

☐ **Dog,** 2″, black spotted, long nose and ears, seated 6.00 8.50 7.50

CHILDREN

☐ **Alpine Girl,** 4½″ high, black hat, green dress, lavender apron 7.00 9.00 8.00

☐ **Boy,** 4″ high, blue turban, green jacket, gold and white pants, red shoes, carrying two bottles and a basket of fruit 11.00 13.50 12.00

☐ **Boy,** 4″ high, green hat, red feather, white shirt, brown shorts, seated on bench playing violin .. 9.00 12.50 10.50

Lamps, *pair,* $70.00-$90.00

	Current Price Range		P/Y Average

☐ **Boy,** 4″ high, holding basket of apples, duck at feet **8.50** **10.25** **9.35**

☐ **Boy,** 4½″ high, blue hat, brown knickers, toy boat in hands **7.00** **9.00** **8.00**

COUPLES— Two Figures On Pedestal Base

☐ **Colonial Lady And Gent,** 3″ x 4″, lady sitting with fan, man in long coat standing **10.00** **12.25** **11.00**

☐ **Colonial Lady And Gent,** 3½″ high, man holding hat, lady in long skirt **10.00** **12.25** **11.00**

☐ **Colonial Lady And Gent,** 3½″ x 4½″, lady seated with musical instrument, man standing **10.00** **12.25** **11.00**

☐ **Colonial Lady and Gent,** 3¾″ high, seated gent in blue cape, black hat, yellow breeches, standing lady in red bodice, green bustles, yellow and blue ruffled dress **11.00** **15.00** **13.00**

☐ **Colonial Lady and Gent,** 4″ x 3½″, white, gold trim, lady holds open fan, man holds book **13.00** **15.50** **14.00**

☐ **Colonial Lady and Gent,** 4¼″ high, dancing, lady in green bodice, blue bustles, yellow skirt, gent in blue coat, red breeches **13.00** **15.50** **14.00**

☐ **Colonial Lady and Gent,** 4¼″ high, seated lady in green flowered skirt, standing gent in red jacket, flowered vest, blue pants, holds hat ... **13.00** **15.50** **14.00**

☐ **Colonial Lady and Gent,** 4½″ high, gent in red coat, flowered ascot, striped breeches, seated lady in pink bodice, blue bustles, flowered skirt **14.00** **16.50** **15.00**

☐ **Colonial Lady and Gent,** 4½″ high, seated, gent in blue cape, green jacket, white pants, holds rose, arm around lady in red bodice, orange bustle, flowered white skirt, flower basket **14.00** **16.50** **15.00**

☐ **Colonial Lady and Gent,** 4½″ x 5¼″, lady seated playing musical instrument, man standing playing musical instrument **12.00** **14.25** **14.00**

☐ **Colonial Lady and Gent,** 4¾″ high, holding hands **14.50** **16.25** **15.00**

☐ **Colonial Lady and Gent,** 4¾″ x 3″, man wears cape, standing, lady is seated **14.50** **16.25** **15.00**

OCEAN LINER COLLECTIBLES

DESCRIPTION: Ocean Liner collectibles are items pertaining to steam powered sea vessels, chiefly commercial ocean liners.

TYPES: Menus, schedules, postcards, brochures, ashtrays or any part of the ship are types of items that can be included in a collection of ocean liner memorabilia.

COMMENTS: Usually collectors are interested in the ships which attracted the most notoriety. These include Britain's Queen Mary and Queen Elizabeth, France's Normandie and the White Star ships which include the Titanic, Olympic, Brittanic and Oceanic.

	Current Price Range		P/Y Average
☐ **Advertising Broadside,** one sheet, Pacific Mail steamships from New York to San Francisco, the ship Colon, 1889, 7″ x 11″	175.00	225.00	200.00
☐ **Advertising Lithograph,** Starnis Excursions, New York, four pictures in one, lithographed by Donaldson Brothers, undated, c. 1875, very large size	1000.00	1400.00	1175.00
☐ **Ashtray,** aluminum, Holland-America lines, c. 1950, 4⅜″	2.00	3.00	2.50
☐ **Ashtray,** from the liner France, cobalt glass, gold picture of steamship, 4½″	7.00	10.00	8.00
☐ **Bath Towels,** set of two, Queen Elizabeth I, 22″ x 40″	35.00	45.00	39.00
☐ **Brochure,** Cruises on Holland-America line, fold-out, multicolored, undated	1.50	2.00	1.75
☐ **Cuspidor,** porcelain, Eastern Steamship Lines, marked "Ye Olde Ivory, Buffalo China, Marine, Made Especially for ESS Co. for Thompson Winchester Co., Boston," 7½″	20.00	26.00	23.00
☐ **Faucet Knob,** brass and porcelain, Queen Mary	40.00	55.00	46.00

	Current Price Range		P/Y Average
☐ **Life Preserver,** Queen Elizabeth II, with original white rope attached	70.00	90.00	80.00
☐ **Menu,** Leonardo DaVinci, three sheet foldout on stiff paper, c. 1970	1.50	2.00	1.75
☐ **Newspaper,** Chicago Tribune, 1954 with front page story of the wreck of the Andria Doria ...	2.50	3.50	3.00
☐ **Pamphlet,** Pacific Coast Official Railway and Steamship Guide, timetables and ads from San Francisco businesses, vignette of steam and sail ship on cover, 140 pages, 1891	80.00	100.00	90.00
☐ **Playing Cards,** Cunard Line, Goodall, gold edges, linen finish, full deck, c. 1915	20.00	30.00	23.00
☐ **Playing Cards,** Lamport and Holt Steamship Line, full deck	20.00	30.00	23.00
☐ **Playing Cards,** SS Norway, Norwegian Caribbean Line, full deck	6.00	8.00	6.50
☐ **Toy Model of Lusitania,** lightweight brass, cast unpainted, c. 1920, 4½" long	60.00	80.00	70.00

OLD COMMONWEALTH

ORIGIN: Old Commonwealth is produced by J.P. Van Winkle and Son. The company, which began operating in 1974, is one of the newest companies producing collector decanters filled with high quality whiskey.

TYPES: Most of the company's decanters are produced in regular and miniature sizes.

COMMENT: The company's decanters are easily identified by the titles placed on front plaques on most pieces.

ADDITIONAL INFORMATION: For more information, consult *The Official Price Guide to Bottles, Old & New,* published by The House of Collectibles.

☐ **Alabama Crimson Tide** (1981), University of Alabama symbol, front of elephant thrusting through a large red A, elephant's foot propped on top of a football, "Crimson Tide" printed on the front	35.00	45.00	40.00

Old Commonwealth Coal Miner, (1982), *#2, mini, man stands with pick in one hand and a lantern in the other, blue mining outfit with red kerchief, plaque reads "Old Time Coal Miner,"* **$15.00–$20.00**

	Current Price Range		P/Y Average
☐ **Bulldogs** (1982), the mascot of the Georgia Bulldogs, front portion of a bulldog stands in the center of a large G with one front paw propped on a football	45.00	55.00	50.00
☐ **Chief Illini** (1979), #1, the mascot for the University of Illinois, warrior stands with arms up and spread wide, dressed in beige buckskin and ceremonial warbonnet	72.00	78.00	75.00
☐ **Chief Illini** (1981), #2, the mascot of the University of Illinois, warrior running with arms flung back to the sides, dressed in beige buckskins and orange feathered headdress, a large letter "I" in orange and blue stands behind him	50.00	60.00	55.00

	Current Price Range		P/Y Average

☐ **Cottontail** (1981), jumping rabbit lands on front feet with hind feet extended in the air, short stump 35.00 45.00 40.00

☐ **Coal Miner** (1975), #1, man stands holding shovel in one hand, and other hand on jacket, bucket of coal at his feet 90.00 120.00 105.00

☐ **Mini, (1980)** 40.00 60.00 50.00

☐ **Coal Miner** (1976), #2, man stands with pick in one hand and a lantern in the other, wears blue mining outfit with red kerchief, plaque reads "Old Time Coal Miner" 30.00 40.00 35.00

☐ **Mini** (1982) 12.00 18.00 15.00

☐ **Coal Miner** (1977), #3, miner kneels on one leg, holding a shovel in one hand and coal in the other hand, bucket of coal at his feet 30.00 40.00 35.00

☐ **Mini, (1981)** 12.00 18.00 15.00

☐ **Coal Miner-Lunch Time** (1980), #4, miner sits eating lunch, red apple in one hand, wears blue overalls and red miner's hat 35.00 45.00 40.00

☐ **Elusive Leprechaun** (1980), leprechaun sits on top of a pot of gold with arms wrapped around bent knees, wears dark green hat and boots, and red jacket 35.00 45.00 40.00

☐ **Fisherman, "A Keeper,"** (1980), old man sits holding fish in both hands, his pole tucked in one arm, fishing tackle sits on the ground 35.00 45.00 40.00

☐ **Golden Retriever** (1979), dog sits with game laying between front feet 30.00 40.00 35.00

☐ **Kentucky Thoroughbreds** (1976), red mare and colt with dark manes and tails, prancing on blue grass 30.00 40.00 35.00

☐ **L.S.U. Tiger** (1979), the mascot for Louisiana State University, ferocious tiger stands with front legs resting on stone structure, a football under one paw, "LSU" in yellow on structure 45.00 55.00 50.00

OLD SLEEPY EYE POTTERY

DESCRIPTION: Old Sleepy Eye is an interesting pottery produced by Western Stoneware Company of Monmouth, Illinois. Sleepy Eye ware sports an Indian head motif. The name "Old Sleepy Eye" refers to an Indian chief whose tribe lived in Minnesota. The town of Sleepy Eye, Minnesota, was named after him.

TYPES: The common color of this line was cobalt blue on white. Other colors such as brown on white, solid green, solid brown and green on white are rare.

ADDITIONAL TIPS: Also scarce are pieces produced by the Weir Pottery Company of Monmouth, Illinois which merged with six other companies in 1906 to form the Western Stoneware Company.

	Current Price Range		P/Y Average
☐ **Mustache Cup,** cobalt blue on white, rare	2500.00	3000.00	2550.00
☐ **Pitcher,** 4″, cobalt blue on white, "monmouth" printed below spout, Indian head on handle, 1920s	1000.00	1100.00	1050.00
☐ **Pitcher,** 5¼″ cobalt blue on gray, Indian head on handle, 1915	210.00	245.00	205.00
☐ **Pitcher,** 5¼″, cobalt blue on yellow, Indian head on handle	750.00	780.00	755.00
☐ **Pitcher,** 7¾″, cobalt blue on white, Indian head on handle, early 1900s	200.00	225.00	205.00
☐ **Pitcher,** 7¾″, solid green	1300.00	1400.00	1325.00
☐ **Pitcher,** flemish blue on gray, standing Indian	950.00	1050.00	955.00
☐ **Stein,** 7¾″, brown on white	750.00	800.00	760.00
☐ **Stein,** any stein made for the Board of Directors Western Stoneware Co. from 1968 to 1973, each	280.00	320.00	285.00

OLD WEST MEMORABILIA

DESCRIPTION: Old West memorabilia generally refers to the cowboy era which existed in the western United States during the 1800s.

TYPES: Old West memorabilia comprises a wide range of items, the most common being cowboy gear. Items dealing with outlaws, Indians and ghost towns are also widely collected.

PERIOD: Many of the collectible Old West items date from the 1800s.

ADDITIONAL TIPS: A good source for identifying Old West collectibles is through catalogs of the 1800s, which can be bought through auction houses or dealers specializing in Old West collectibles.

	Current Price Range		P/Y Average
☐ **Arrest Warrant,** state of California, Sacramento, February 7, 1876, warrant from Executive Department signed by Governor William Irwin for arrest of Christian Henke, fugitive from Missouri wanted for grand larceny, 11″ x 16″	43.00	57.00	50.00
☐ **Belt Buckle,** tradesman's belt buckle in cast brass, found at California ghost town, c. 1860	70.00	90.00	80.00
☐ **Bill Heads,** San Francisco merchants, price shown is for a typical bill head with vignette illustration dating from 1870 to 1890	2.00	3.00	2.50
☐ **Book,** *Reminiscences of a Ranger* by Horace Bell, published in Los Angeles in 1881, cloth bound, 457 pages	250.00	300.00	275.00
☐ **Book,** *The Log of a Cowboy* by Andy Adams, published in Boston in 1903, 387 pages, bound in pictorial cloth	70.00	90.00	80.00
☐ **Book,** *They Died With Their Boots On* by Thomas Ripley, published in New York in 1935, cloth bound, 285 pages	110.00	140.00	120.00
☐ **Boot Heel Plate,** iron, shaped like horseshoe, late 19th century	6.00	8.00	7.00
☐ **Button,** ranger's button from Ft. Fetterman, Wyoming	1.00	1.50	1.25

No.247.853   1879.

J. Beck.
Spurs.

Patented *July 29.*
1879.

Spurs, *Thomas Beck, Dallas TX, Steel, 4" x 3",*
1879, $120.00-$150.00
(photo courtesy of ©Bret Farnum)

	Current Price Range		P/Y Average
☐ **Cartridge Box,** brass, found in Wyoming, some corrosion	8.00	10.00	9.00
☐ **Cattle Skull,** sun bleached skull of steer found on Arizona plains, teeth intact, horns missing, shellacked	40.00	50.00	45.00
☐ **Check,** Idaho Territory, Bank of Idaho, J.T. Morgan and Co., Bankers, Blackfoot, Idaho, unused check with a pair of vignettes, one of them showing a cowboy roping a steer, undated, c. 1885	4.00	6.00	5.00
☐ **Check,** Virginia City, Nevada, Agency of the Bank of California, has two revenue stamps and signature of John Mackay, 1870	50.00	70.00	60.00
☐ **Check,** Wells Fargo, drawn on Wells Fargo and Co.'s bank in San Francisco, undated, signed by J. Hyman	13.00	17.00	15.00
☐ **Contract for Mail Route,** State of California, from North San Juan to North Bloomfield, issued to John Hogan, one half is a printed list of instructions, 1870, 13" x 16½"	26.00	34.00	30.00
☐ **County Warrant,** Mono County, California, relating to the paying of a bill, 1877	13.00	17.00	15.00
☐ **Fork,** nickel silver, stamped Fort D.A., Russell, Wyoming	9.00	12.00	10.00
☐ **Knapsack Hook,** brass, found in Wyoming, 19th century	1.50	2.00	1.75
☐ **Magazine,** *The Galaxy,* New York, March, 1873, with article "Life on the Plains" by General George Armstrong Custer	25.00	35.00	30.00

	Current Price Range		P/Y Average

☐ **Map,** hand-drawn survey map of Dakota Territory, executed by Charles W. Irish for the C. & N.W. Railroad, 1880, on a roll measuring 6′ x 19″ . . . . — 600.00 / 800.00 / 700.00

☐ **Nail,** iron, hand forged, square head, 19th century . . . . — 1.00 / 1.50 / 1.25

☐ **Newspaper,** *U.S. Telegraph,* Washington, D.C., for July 10, 1832, with reports of Black Hawk War . . . . — 10.00 / 13.00 / 11.00

☐ **Oil Painting,** Bringing in the Saddle Stock by Gordon Phillips, oil on canvas, 20th century, 22″ x 30″ . . . . — 2200.00 / 3000.00 / 2600.00

☐ **Pamphlet,** *Marshall's Gold Discovery,* a lecture by John S. Hittell, published in San Francisco, 20 pages, 1893, 9″ x 6″ . . . . — 42.00 / 58.00 / 50.00

☐ **Pay Warrant,** Columbia, Texas, certificate entitling Robert Middleton to pay off $48 for six months employment by Paratts Company in 1836, countersigned by paymaster, 3½″ x 7″ — 40.00 / 50.00 / 45.00

☐ **Pistol Hammer,** from unidentified percussion pistol, iron with subdued engraving . . . . — 3.00 / 4.50 / 3.75

☐ **Proclamation,** appointment of deputy sheriff, state of Colorado, county of El Paso, W.R. Buergelin is appointed a Deputy Sheriff, signed by George G. Birdsall, Sheriff of El Paso County, 1913, 7″ x 8¼″ . . . . — 18.00 / 23.00 / 20.00

☐ **Reward Poster,** the state of California offers $200 for the arrest of Frank Revada for the crime of murder of Thomas Leahey at Williams' ranch in the county of Mono, 1892, 9″ x 14″ . . . . — 130.00 / 180.00 / 150.00

☐ **Spoon,** nickel silver, stamped Fort D.A., Russell, Wyoming . . . . — 9.00 / 12.00 / 10.50

☐ **Spurs,** pair, brass, six-pointed stars, moderately to heavily corroded, place of manufacture unknown, c. 1880 . . . . — 30.00 / 35.00 / 32.00

☐ **Ticket,** Montana Stage and Railroad ticket, three part ticket of the North Western Overland Mail Line and the Northern Pacific Railroad, unused, undated, 19th century, 3″ x 6″ . . . . — 9.00 / 12.00 / 10.50

☐ **Voting List,** Great Register of the County of Mono, California, lists all registered voters, 46 pages, undated, 19th century, 9″ x 12″ . . . . — 90.00 / 115.00 / 103.00

☐ **Way Bill,** Ft. Apache Stage Line, list of passengers and freight, vignette of wagon and team of horses, 1901, 7″ x 17″ . . . . — 23.00 / 28.00 / 25.00

OPERA MEMORABILIA

COMMENTS: Items from the well-known artists, Enrico Caruso, Nicolai Gedda; well-known opera houses, The Metropolitan Opera House; and well-known operas are the most sought after and collectible. Opera recordings are fairly readily available, though many collectors seek 78 r.p.m. records.

ADDITIONAL TIPS: The listings are alphabetical according to item.

For more complete listings and information, see *The Official Price Guide to Music Collectibles,* published by The House of Collectibles.

	Current Price Range		P/Y Average
☐ **Album Cover,** autographed by Kirsten Flagstad, records missing	60.00	75.00	65.00
☐ **Annual,** Metropolitan Opera Annual, signed by Regine Crespin	12.00	15.00	13.00
☐ **Book,** Bubbles, autographed by Beverly Sills	30.00	40.00	33.00
☐ **Book,** Songs of Stephen Foster, signed by John Charles Thomas	27.00	37.00	28.00
☐ **Bracelet,** gold colored costume bracelet worn by Leontyne Price	60.00	75.00	63.00
☐ **Brochure,** opera company brochure signed by Regina Resnik, c. 1952	8.00	12.00	10.00
☐ **Calling Card,** signed by Enrico Caruso	65.00	85.00	70.00
☐ **Check,** endorsed by John Brownlee	10.00	13.00	11.00
☐ **Christmas Card,** autographed by Anna Moffo.	21.00	26.00	23.00
☐ **Contract,** opera company contract signed by Patrice Munsel	30.00	40.00	33.00
☐ **Contract,** opera contract signed by Giuseppe Deluca	70.00	90.00	80.00
☐ **Contract,** record company contract signed by Robert Merrill	42.50	52.50	44.00
☐ **Contract,** signed by Richard Tucker	70.00	95.00	80.00
☐ **Earrings,** once belonged to Zinka Milanor	60.00	80.00	70.00
☐ **Envelope,** addressed by Dorothy Kirsten, contents missing	12.00	16.00	13.00

Theatrical Program, *Adelina Patti, farewell tour,* $25.00-$35.00

	Current Price Range		P/Y Average
☐ **Fan,** used by Grace Moore	30.00	40.00	33.00
☐ **Gloves,** pair of long silver gloves worn by Patrice Munsel in an opera production, with letter of authentication	42.00	50.00	46.00
☐ **Helmet,** reputedly worn by Birgit Nilsson in a production	79.00	100.00	85.00
☐ **Letter,** handwritten in Russian by Fyodor Chaliapin	430.00	560.00	450.00

	Current Price Range		P/Y Average
☐ **Libretto,** opera libretto signed by Cesare Siepi	13.00	18.00	15.00
☐ **Libretto,** opera libretto signed by Helen Traubel	13.00	18.00	15.00
☐ **Magazine,** *Opera News,* signed by Justino Diaz who is on the cover	25.00	35.00	28.00
☐ **Magazine Cover,** signed by Joan Sutherland	25.00	35.00	28.00
☐ **Magazine Cover,** signed by Richard Tucker, c. 1962	20.00	26.00	22.00
☐ **Menu,** signed by Enrico Caruso, c. 1915	170.00	210.00	170.00
☐ **Menu,** signed by Joan Sutherland	8.00	12.00	10.00
☐ **Menu,** signed by Lorenzo Alvary	9.00	16.00	11.00
☐ **Photograph,** autographed photo of Beverly in costume from Daughter of the Regiment, 8″ x 10″	25.00	35.00	27.00
☐ **Photograph,** autographed by Charles Anthony, 8″ x 10″	10.00	15.00	11.50
☐ **Photograph,** autographed photo of Dorothy Kirsten, 8″ x 10″	55.00	70.00	65.00
☐ **Photograph,** autographed photo of Enrico Caruso in Rigoletto costume, 5″ x 7″	155.00	195.00	150.00
☐ **Photograph,** autographed portrait of Enrico Caruso, c. 1906, 8″ x 10″	190.00	225.00	200.00
☐ **Photograph,** autographed portrait of Fyodor Chaliapin, c. 1925, 5″ x 7″	185.00	265.00	200.00
☐ **Photograph,** autographed photo of James Melton in costume, 8″ x 10″	23.00	35.00	27.00
☐ **Photograph,** autographed photo of John Brownlee in Rigoletto costume, c. 1940, 8″ x 10″ ...	25.00	32.00	26.00
☐ **Photograph,** autographed photo of Jussi Bjoerling in Boheme costume, 8″ x 10″	25.00	35.00	28.00
☐ **Photograph,** autographed photo of Leontyne Price in Costume, 8″ x 10″	30.00	40.00	33.00
☐ **Photograph,** autographed photo of Lorenzo Alvary, 8″ x 10″	10.00	15.00	11.50
☐ **Photograph,** autographed photo of Nadine Conner	21.00	26.00	22.00
☐ **Photograph,** autographed photo of Rosalind Elias, 8″ x 10″	11.00	15.00	12.00
☐ **Photograph,** autographed photo of Tito Gobbi, c. 1959, 8″ x 10″	30.00	37.00	32.00
☐ **Pinback Button,** "Beverly Sills Is a Good High," red and white, c. 1975	3.50	4.50	3.50
☐ **Poster,** advertising appearance of Salvatore Baccaloni, c. 1940	13.00	18.00	14.50
☐ **Poster,** autographed opera poster of Nicolai Gedda	23.00	32.00	35.00
☐ **Poster,** Metropolitan Opera poster, Emperor Jones, signed by Lawrence Tibbett	250.00	325.00	275.00
☐ **Poster,** Metropolitan Opera poster featuring Enrico Caruso	245.00	340.00	260.00
☐ **Program,** concert program, signed by Roberta Peters	10.00	15.00	12.00
☐ **Program,** Metropolitan Opera, signed by Frances Alda	26.00	38.00	29.00

	Current Price Range		P/Y Average
☐ **Program,** Metropolitan Opera, signed by Kirsten Flagstad	35.00	45.00	38.00
☐ **Program,** Metropolitan Opera House, pre-1900	10.00	14.00	12.00
☐ **Program,** Metropolitan Opera House, 1901–1910	8.00	12.00	10.00
☐ **Program,** Metropolitan Opera House, 1911–1920	6.00	10.00	8.00
☐ **Program,** Metropolitan Opera House, 1921–1930	5.00	9.00	7.00
☐ **Program,** Metropolitan Opera House, 1931–1940	4.00	6.00	5.00
☐ **Program,** Metropolitan Opera House, 1941–1950	3.00	5.00	4.00
☐ **Program,** Metropolitan Opera House, 1951–1960	2.00	4.00	3.00
☐ **Program,** Metropolitan Opera House, 1961–1970	1.00	2.50	1.50
☐ **Program,** opera program, signed by Jan Peerce	12.00	18.00	14.00
☐ **Score,** from Traviata, signed by Lily Pons	30.00	40.00	33.00
☐ **Sheet Music,** Some Enchanted Evening, signed by Ezio Pinza	35.00	48.00	38.00
☐ **Sheet Music,** When Irish Eyes Are Smiling, signed by John McCormack	85.00	110.00	90.00
☐ **Signature,** on a card of Cesare Siepi	4.00	5.50	4.50
☐ **T-Shirt,** with likeness of Leontyne Price	8.00	11.00	9.25

ORIENTAL FURNITURE

DESCRIPTION: Oriental furniture differed from European furniture in several ways:

1) It was lower.

2) It was built to be arranged against walls, never jutting out or dividing a room.

3) It was built to conceal daily functions; writing tables folded into cabinets, chests were used for clothes, tables as altar frontals.

4) It was joined by grooves, not nails, and rarely glue.

CONSTRUCTION: Hardwood, particularly rosewood, was the preferred furniture material in more northerly climates, and bamboo or lacquer in the warmer southerly regions. Oriental furniture cannot really be typified much more than this. It was ornate, it was simple, some pieces were of superior workmanship, others fell apart easily.

ADDITIONAL TIPS: Up until now, Oriental furniture has represented only a small percentage of the Oriental collectibles market, although that trend seems to be changing. Now would be a good time to purchase some of these interesting relics, before prices are swept upwards and out of the sight of the average collector.

RECOMMENDED READING: For more in-depth information on Oriental furniture you may refer to *The Official Price Guide to Oriental Collectibles,* published by The House of Collectibles.

	Current Price Range		P/Y Average
☐ **Altar Coffer,** Chinese, rectangular with drawers, carved scrolls and dragons, Huang Huali, 60″ x 32″ x 19″	6150.00	8100.00	6300.00
☐ **Altar Table,** Chinese, carved hardwood, rectangular, apron pierced with fruit carvings, trestle supports, 82″ x 35″ x 17″, 19th century	1850.00	2250.00	1900.00
☐ **Altar Table,** Chinese, carved rectangular, top features scrolled ends above apron, slender legs, Hongmu, 57″ x 32″ x 15″, 19th century	1625.00	2250.00	1575.00
☐ **Altar Table,** Chinese, low rosewood with marble inset top, maroon finish, pierced apron panels, mask and flame carved knees, scrolled feet, 25″ x 8″ x 5″	110.00	175.00	90.00
☐ **Altar Table,** rosewood, carved pierced apron, phoenix bird motif, 46″ x 23″ x 15¼″	850.00	1250.00	1005.00
☐ **Armchair,** Chinese, simple toprail above splat carved with medallion, seat features cane matting, Jigi Mu, 17th century	4375.00	6250.00	4400.00
☐ **Armchair,** hardwood, intricately carved in high relief, dragon and serpent motif, cabriole legs, 40″ high, 19th century	1025.00	1175.00	1200.00
☐ **Armchair,** hardwood, carved back, coiling dragon amidst clouds, panel with a phoenix, lathed arms, cabriole legs, 19th century	800.00	1100.00	800.00
☐ **Armchair,** teakwood, horseshoe shape, pierced trelliswork decoration, 20th century	460.00	515.00	450.00
☐ **Bar,** mahogany, hinged top, reliefed landscape decor, footed, 40″ high, 20th century	625.00	630.00	650.00
☐ **Bed,** hardwood, headboard, foot fretted design, high polish, 32″ high, 19th century	1450.00	1625.00	1475.00
☐ **Bed,** fruitwood, carved canopy, paneled sides, frieze borders, 8′ high, 19th century	3200.00	4300.00	3225.00
☐ **Bed,** Chinese, carved hardwood, paneled backrest, open arms with carved fretwork, carved fretwork base, silk cushions, 65″ x 29″ x 43″, 19th century	2625.00	3650.00	2300.00
☐ **Bench,** rosewood, inlaid cane top, straight legs, 22″ high, 20th century	6750.00	7500.00	7000.00

	Current Price Range		P/Y Average

☐ **Box,** tiered, Chinese Export, black and gold lacquer, oval shaped with compartments, 11″ high, 19th century **615.00 900.00 635.00**

☐ **Breakfront,** Chinese, teakwood, upper section has double glass doors with two shelves and mirrored back, bottom features carved double doors, 6′3″ x 2′10″ x 16″ **925.00 1220.00 950.00**

☐ **Cabinet,** bamboo, four legs, 19th century **350.00 450.00 375.00**

☐ **Cabinet,** burlwood, open shelves, bamboo doors and drawers, 48″ high, 19th century **3550.00 3900.00 3575.00**

☐ **Cabinet,** camphorwood, carved top, Chinese, 18″ x 13″ **200.00 215.00 195.00**

☐ **Cabinet,** Chinese design Chippendale, lighted, 74″ high **15200.00 17150.00 15650.00**

☐ **Chaise,** Chinese, hardwood, carved, high back with openwork medallion carving, rectangular arms with openwork carving, long rectangular seat, short legs with scrollwork, 54″ x 77″ x 27″ **725.00 1050.00 775.00**

☐ **Chaise,** hardwood, long back panel, carved design, low legs, 37″ high, 19th century **3150.00 3700.00 3725.00**

☐ **Chest,** camphor, heavily carved with sailing ships in landscape, hinged cover, 34″ x 16″ x 19″ .. **265.00 370.00 300.00**

☐ **Chest,** cedar lined, oak exterior, elaborate allover carving, decorative scalloped brass lock with floral and leaf chasing, stepped bracket feet, 40″ x long, 21″ deep, 23″ high **430.00 610.00 450.00**

☐ **Chest on Chest,** Chinese, black lacquer, mother-of-pearl inlay fish, trees, bats, kites, birds, animals, two double doors, bracket feet, 31″ wide, 16″ deep, 50″ high, 19th century **1550.00 2175.00 1575.00**

☐ **Clothes Cupboards,** Chinese, doors, shelves and drawers, some fruit carving, brass lockplates and hinges, Han Mu, pair, 8′7″ x 49″ x 21″ ... **2100.00 32500.00 40000.00**

☐ **Commode,** 19th century **1025.00 1550.00 1250.00**

☐ **Console Tables,** Chinese, black lacquer, gilt decoration, half-moon shape with gilt painted landscape, fret and foliate border, shaped apron with four legs with scrolled flanks, 31″ x 34″ x 17″, 19th century **6700.00 9850.00 9000.00**

☐ **Cupboard,** Chinese, Ming style, hardwood, rectangular, molded edges, hinged doors, square stiles form feet, 62″ x 31″ x 16″ **1250.00 1575.00 1300.00**

☐ **Cupboard,** Korean, elm, rectangular, paneled front features drawers and doors, 68″ x 44″ ... **750.00 1000.00 800.00**

☐ **Daybed,** Chinese Export, mahogany with canework, carved roll supports, caned lid that opens, drawers, 7′ long, 19th century **5500.00 8200.00 5575.00**

☐ **Desk,** burlwood, carved decoration on top, squared simple legs, three top drawers, brass fittings, 33″ high, 19th century **3675.00 4150.00 3750.00**

☐ **Dining Chair,** hardwood, knobbed ends, sculptured borders, 29″ high, 18th century **3000.00 3375.00 3200.00**

	Current Price Range		P/Y Average

☐ **Dining Table,** hardwood, rectangular top, two medallion decorations on surface, 32″ high, 19th century 730.00 925.00 800.00

☐ **Dining Table,** rectangular, geometric carved border, 36″ high, 20th century 815.00 950.00 900.00

☐ **Dining Room Set,** Chinese, teakwood and blond Honduran mahogany, table has Chinese dragon carving and plate glass top, six side chairs have straight legs, upholstered seats, table is 72″ long, 42″ wide, 29″ high, 20th century 525.00 815.00 575.00

☐ **Display Cabinets,** Chinese, painted lacquer, rectangular with assortment of shelves, a pair of pierced lattice doors and drawers, decorated with gilt phoenix and dragon medallions, 75″ x 36″ x 15″, 19th century, pair 5000.00 7000.00 5500.00

☐ **Dressing Table,** Padouk wood, carved, 3′ wide 725.00 765.00 750.00

☐ **Dressing Table,** rectangular top, three drawers, above two pedestals with three drawers each, drawer fronts lacquered in red and gold, 30″ x 4′6″ 600.00 720.00 600.00

☐ **Etagere,** hardwood, rectangular top, scrolled design, shelves open and with sliding doors, gilded decoration, 40″ high, 19th century 415.00 525.00 450.00

☐ **Etagere,** huoli, veneer inset, trellis supports, scroll work, 40″ high, 19th century 3150.00 4200.00 3300.00

☐ **Game Table,** Chinese, hardwood, carved, rounded and shaped top with raised border, apron contains four drawers, supported by an x-form stand and hipped legs, 32″ high, 19th century 1150.00 1650.00 1200.00

☐ **Game Table,** hardwood, drawers all around, x-shaped brackets, 32″ high, 20th century 1025.00 1175.00 1225.00

☐ **Garden Seat,** hardwood, round marble inlaid seat, 20″ high, 20th century 1025.00 1175.00 1225.00

☐ **Garden Seat,** green lacquered wood, landscape decor, 19″ high 950.00 1175.00 1050.00

☐ **Garden Seat,** Chinese, barrel shape, mahogany, five supports and floor stretcher, piercing on apron and legs and beading at the borders, inset handpainted porcelain top depicts storks in floral landscape, artist's seal, 14″ diameter, 18″ high 215.00 400.00 225.00

☐ **Headboard,** hardwood, red lacquer and gilt decoration, elaborately carved with birds and foliage, 60″ high, 19th century 2025.00 2550.00 2150.00

☐ **Lamp,** patinated, polished bronze, 19th century 925.00 1050.00 975.00

☐ **Lantern,** bronze, lidded, pierced grate, 22″ high, 19th century 1450.00 1875.00 1525.00

☐ **Lantern,** metal, gilded, relief design, set of four, 18″ high, 19th century 1550.00 1800.00 1750.00

☐ **Loveseat,** Chinese, carved hardwood, rectangular, spindleback sides and apron, round legs joined by stretchers and footrest, 36″ x 33″ x 19″ 3275.00 4300.00 3300.00

	Current Price Range		P/Y Average

☐ **Pedestal,** Chinese, teakwood, inset white marble circular top, pierced tendril and floral apron, curved legs, 12″ diameter, 36″ high . . . . — 320.00 / 510.00 — 350.00

☐ **Pedestal,** Chinese, teakwood, pierced and carved apron and curved legs, 16″ diameter, 37″ high . . . . — 425.00 / 530.00 — 450.00

☐ **Pedestal,** Chinese, teakwood, round top with marble inlay, beaded border, carved and pierced floral apron, high cabriole legs, x-form base, 11″ diameter, 36″ high . . . . — 430.00 / 600.00 — 450.00

☐ **Screen,** coromandel, four panels, front of each decorated with various landscape, figural and pagoda scenes, back decorated with birds and flowers, 72″ x 72″ . . . . — 525.00 / 725.00 — 550.00

☐ **Screen,** hardwood, four panels, carved figural domestic scenes, each panel measures 72″ high by 17⅞″ wide, 20th century . . . . — 1600.00 / 2625.00 — 1650.00

☐ **Screen,** Chinese, black lacquered wood, four panels, figures in garden scene, border features dragons, 9′ x 88″ . . . . — 1725.00 / 2250.00 — 1800.00

☐ **Settee,** Chinese, Ming style, rosewood, horseshoe shape with shell and whorl open arm terminations, open back with two curved splats, featuring carved Taoist and Greek key motifs, straight legs, single loose Shou embroidered cushion in two-tone gold, 50″ long, 20th century . . . . — 1225.00 / 1650.00 — 1275.00

☐ **Pair of Matching, open armchairs** to above settee . . . . — 1225.00 / 1650.00 — 1275.00

☐ **Settee,** Southeast Asian, mahogany, finely carved all over, floral, leaf and scroll design on sides, back and apron, back panel has carved landscape scene with train of elephants, scrolled arm terminals, plank seat for cushion, stylized paw feet, 70″ long, 26″ deep, 33″ high . . . . — 850.00 / 1250.00 — 900.00

☐ **Matching Cocktail Table,** to above settee, 50″ long, 24″ deep, 16″ high . . . . — 310.00 / 520.00 — 360.00

☐ **Side Chairs,** Chinese, shaped top rail, paneled splat, openwork apron, legs joined by stretchers, foot rest, Hongmu, pair . . . . — 1225.00 / 1475.00 — 1325.00

☐ **Side Chairs,** Chinese, simple design of top rail and plain splat, cane seat joins to shaped brackets and tapered legs, Hongmu, 19th century . . — 465.00 / 670.00 — 495.00

☐ **Side Chairs,** Chinese, Ming style, hardwood, four chairs, shaped top rails, each splat has a different floral carving, solid seat, square legs, stretchers and foot rest, 19th century . . . . — 1550.00 / 2100.00 — 1650.00

☐ **Side Table,** Chinese, Ming style, hardwood, shaped rectangular top, plain apron, carved flanks support legs joined by double stretchers, 49″ x 30″ x 15″ . . . . — 650.00 / 1050.00 — 900.00

☐ **Side Tables,** Chinese, Ming style, inlaid square top, shaped stretchers on square legs, hoofed feet, 16″ x 20″, 19th century . . . . — 815.00 / 1000.00 — 900.00

	Current Price Range		P/Y Average
□ **Stand,** hardwood with mother-of-pearl inlay, claw feet, carved decor, 36" high, 20th century	600.00	650.00	610.00
□ **Stand,** hardwood, round shape, red lacquer, 24" high, 19th century	1850.00	2100.00	1925.00
□ **Stand,** hardwood, three shelves, key work frieze, 31" high, 19th century	950.00	1200.00	1050.00
□ **Stool,** Chinese, painted black lacquer, barrel shaped, with landscape scenes, mock ring handles, 19" high, 19th century	825.00	1050.00	900.00
□ **Stool,** eight sided, scroll feet, frieze decor, 18" high, 19th century	1050.00	2015.00	1250.00
□ **Stool,** Chinese, carved barrel shape, top inlaid above pierced apron, Hongmu, 10" high, 19th century	625.00	915.00	675.00
□ **Table,** burlwood, geometric frieze, scroll toes, 36" high, 19th century	450.00	1075.00	900.00
□ **Table,** burlwood, leather inset top, side table on simple squared legs, 20" high, 19th century ...	2100.00	2385.00	2250.00
□ **Table,** burlwood, turned legs, squared supports, polished top, 16" high, 19th century	725.00	850.00	750.00
□ **Table,** cinnabar, highly ornate, tall, decor overall, lacquered, 30" high, 18th century	7100.00	8250.00	7150.00

ORIENTAL PAINTINGS

COMMENTS: Early Chinese paintings consisted of mostly landscapes, though later works incorporated people, animals, court scenes, portraits and calligraphy. Paintings were done on a variety of materials including silk and paper.

RECOMMENDED READING: For further information refer to *The Official Price Guide to Oriental Collectibles,* published by The House of Collectibles.

	Current Price Range		P/Y Average
□ **Album,** Chinese, ink and color on paper, eight leaves in album, various landscapes, Yuan Bei, 8" x 11", 19th century	1475.00	1825.00	1500.00
□ **Album,** Chinese, ink and color on paper, twelve leaves, Chinese erotica, 7" x 6", 19th century	650.00	825.00	675.00

	Current Price Range		P/Y Average

☐ **Album,** Chinese, ink and color on paper, twelve leaves, animals and vegetables, 10″ x 6″, 20th century **290.00 420.00 300.00**

☐ **Fan Painting,** Chinese, ink and color on gold paper, scenic view of figure on bridge, by Chen Guan, 7″ x 20″, 17th century **1575.00 2550.00 1600.00**

☐ **Fan Painting,** Chinese, ink and color on paper, house scene with scholar and attendant, Hua Yan, 6″ x 20″, 18th century **1050.00 1375.00 2000.00**

☐ **Fan Painting,** Chinese, ink and color on paper, scenic view, Pu Ru, 7″ x 20″, 20th century **680.00 865.00 725.00**

☐ **Fan Painting,** Chinese, ink and color on paper, vegetables, Wang Xuetao, 7″ x 21″, 20th century **680.00 865.00 685.00**

☐ **Fan Painting,** Chinese, ink on gold paper, scenic landscape with two figures, Bian Wenyu, 6″ x 19″, 17th century **2750.00 4175.00 2575.00**

☐ **Hanging Scroll,** Chinese, ink on paper, running script calligraphy, Wang Wenzhi, 48″ x 15″, 18th century **750.00 1050.00 750.00**

☐ **Hanging Scroll,** Chinese, ink on paper, scene with flower, rock and bamboo, Fang Xun, 55″ x 19″, 18th century **2050.00 2525.00 2075.00**

☐ **Hanging Scroll,** Chinese, ink on paper, scenic view, Pu Ru, 36″ x 13″, 20th century **865.00 1100.00 910.00**

☐ **Hanging Scroll,** Chinese, ink on paper, scenic view with flowers, rocks and bamboo, Jian Ting Xi, 51″ x 19″, 18th century **2050.00 4025.00 2150.00**

☐ **Hanging Scroll,** Chinese, ink on paper, two fish, Li Ku Chan, 27″ x 19″, 20th century **775.00 975.00 800.00**

☐ **Hanging Scroll,** Chinese, ink on satin, scenic landscape, Cai Jia, 39″ x 26″, 18th century . . . **4050.00 6025.00 4150.00**

☐ **Hanging Scroll,** Chinese, ink on satin, scenic landscape, Fa Ruozhen, 90″ x 19″, 17th century **22100.00 25100.00 22500.00**

☐ **Hanging Scroll,** Chinese, ink on silk, bamboo, 63″ x 19″, 18th century **1050.00 1275.00 1175.00**

☐ **Hanging Scroll,** Chinese, ink on silk, landscape, gold color, Qiang Guozhong, 25″ x 14″, 17th century **15100.00 19050.00 15550.00**

☐ **Hanging Scroll,** Chinese, ink on silk, Lohan, 52″ x 33″, 17th century **1825.00 2310.00 1925.00**

☐ **Hanging Scroll,** Chinese, ink on silk, scenic landscape, Wang Jian, 18″ x 10″, 17th century **11100.00 14025.00 12000.00**

☐ **Hanging Scroll,** Chinese, ink on silk, scenic view, by Dong Qichang, 42″ x 21″, 16th century **9025.00 12050.00 9550.00**

☐ **Hanging Scroll,** Chinese, ink on silk, scenic view, Mingshan Qingyong, 73″ x 40″, 17th century **5050.00 7025.00 5275.00**

☐ **Hanging Scroll,** Chinese, ink on silk, scenic view of trees and water, Pu Ru, 14″ x 23″, 20th century **1210.00 1525.00 1300.00**

	Current Price Range		P/Y Average
☐ **Hanging Scroll,** Chinese, rubbing of calligraphy, repainted in gold, Qing Gaozong, 62″ x 29″, 18th century	725.00	1015.00	775.00
☐ **Portraits,** Chinese, ink and color on silk, ancestor portraits, pair, 57″ x 36″, 18th century	3050.00	5015.00	2250.00
☐ **Portraits,** Chinese, ink and color on paper, Deities, pair, 56″ x 29″, 19th century	825.00	1015.00	900.00

ORIENTAL PRINTS

COMMENTS: The method of color printing that became popular in Japan, or at least widely adopted by publishers of illustrated books, bore little relationship to Western lithography—the artform of Currier and Ives. Nor could it be directly linked to any of the earlier Western efforts in color printing. Originating c. 1765, it involved the cutting of numerous duplicate blocks to achieve "nishiki-e"; brocade-like pictures. To the Japanese, who had not painted in oils on canvas, colored prints were likened to woven fabrics. It was not unusual for two or three dozen blocks, or even more, to be cut for a single picture. Each was used to print a particular color shade which the printer was responsible for applying. Each color hue, some of them differing so slightly that none but a keen eye could distinguish it, was applied in such a way that subtle blends and tonal effects could be achieved. So delicate was this work that every step had to be carried out flawlessly; cutting the blocks, choosing colors, mixing them, applying them to the blocks, and pulling impressions. The alignment in printing could not be off by even a millimeter, without destroying visual quality. Considering that each was printed by hand, without machinery of any kind, this was surely a proof of dedication and innate skill.

RECOMMENDED READING: For further information refer to *The Official Price Guide to Oriental Collectibles,* published by The House of Collectibles.

☐ **The Basket of Medlar Fruit,** artist: Paul Jacoulet; carver: Maeda; printers: Fujii, Onodera, pencil signature, published May 23, 1950, 18″ x 14″	150.00	300.00	175.00

	Current Price Range		P/Y Average

☐ **Chinese Mask Seller,** artist: Paul Jacoulet; carver: Maeda; printers: Honda, Uchikawa, Ogawa, pencil signature, published December 30, 1940, 18″ x 14″ **350.00 550.00 375.00**

☐ **Chinese Puppets,** artist: Paul Jacoulet; carver: Yamagishi; printer: Urushibara, pencil signature, published April 29, 1935, 18″ x 14″ **450.00 650.00 475.00**

☐ **Jade Lady,** artist: Paul Jacoulet; carver: Maeda; printers: Honda, Uchikawa, pencil signature, published February 2, 1940, 18″ x 14″ **600.00 900.00 625.00**

☐ **The Love Letter,** artist: Paul Jacoulet; carver: Maeda; printers: Onodera, Honda, pencil signature, published May 1955, 18″ x 14″ **650.00 850.00 675.00**

☐ **The Miraculous Catch,** artist: Paul Jacoulet; carver: Maeda; printers: Honda, Uchikawa, pencil signature, published December 12, 1939, 18″ x 14″ **350.00 550.00 375.00**

☐ **Sawara Fisherman,** artist: Paul Jacoulet; carver: Maeda; printers: Honda, Fujii, pencil signature, published January 15, 1936, 18″ x 14″ **400.00 600.00 425.00**

☐ **Shepherds Of The High Mountains,** artist: Paul Jacoulet; carver: Maeda; printer: Ogawa, pencil signature, published April 20, 1941, 18″ x 14″ **300.00 500.00 325.00**

☐ **The Water Pipe,** artist: Paul Jacoulet; carver: Maeda; printer: Onodera, pencil signature, published December 31, 1952, 18″ x 14″ **300.00 500.00 325.00**

☐ **Winter Flowers,** artist: Paul Jacoulet; carver: Maeda; printers: Onodera, Honda, pencil signature, published June 1955, 18″ x 14″ **400.00 600.00 425.00**

☐ **Young Girl of Saipan And Hibiscus Flowers,** artist: Paul Jacoulet; carver: Yamagishi; printer: Urushibara, pencil signature, published June 30, 1934, 18″ x 14″ **200.00 425.00 225.00**

ORIENTAL TEXTILES

DESCRIPTION: Collectible Oriental textiles are based primarily upon silk, and silk brocade products, though satin, cotton and gauze are also acceptable. Silk garments were cherished and given special treatment over other materials. They were reserved mainly for special occasions.

MATERIAL: Silk was a carefully kept secret of the Chinese for many centuries, and even today there are only a few places in the world where it can be successfully cultivated (the United States is not one of them). For years envious countries—particularly Japan, which prized the textile as an essential commodity during warm weather—believed silk was made from some kind of plant, like flax or cotton. The real secret lay with a simple moth, who happened to lay her eggs on the leaves of a mulberry tree. When the eggs hatched and the silkworms appeared, they would steadily eat the leaves of their birthplace, before wrapping themselves in a gorgeous, very strong cocoon comprised of around 1000 yards of silken thread filament. Nevertheless, it takes thousands of silkworms to make one yard of silk, which is one reason it is still such an expensive natural fabric. In the old days the silken filaments were woven on hand looms and distributed to a very profitable foreign trade. Now power looms are used for the same purposes, but silkworms continue to be raised in carefully monitored incubators and are our only source to this valuable commodity.

COMMENTS: Prized Oriental textiles frequently feature some type of embroidery, stitched in satin or silk thread in colorful motifs. Small personal items can often be found in good condition, as can whole garments or swatches of fabric. Often collectors like to mount their finds within frames as gorgeous wall hangings—care must be taken, however, to avoid direct sunlight. The main problem with old silks is not that they fall apart, but that they fade so easily.

The main clothing articles in Oriental wardrobes included kimono, jackets, chuba (longer than a jacket, shorter than a robe), robes, obi (sash), hakama (loose trousers), fun dashi (loin cloth) and the mo (apron).

RECOMMENDED READING: For more in-depth information on Oriental textiles, you may refer to *The Official Price Guide to Oriental Collectibles,* published by The House of Collectibles.

Japanese Robe, *1820–50,* **$1700.00-$1800.00**
(photo courtesy of Marc Bernsau, Sanford, ME, 1984)

CEREMONIAL

	Current Price Range		P/Y Average
☐ **Altar Frontal,** 30″ long, c. 1800s, red silk, gold stitched dragon, lotus bat motif	750.00	975.00	865.00
☐ **Altar Frontal,** 32″ long, c. 1800s, blue silk, gold stitched floral motif	550.00	972.00	660.00
☐ **Altar Robe,** 40″ x 70″, c. 1900s, silk, rectangular, embroidered figurines, marked	975.00	990.00	975.00
☐ **Badge,** 10″ x 11″, c. 1800s, blue satin, blue green, orange, white stitches, duck motif	375.00	475.00	425.00
☐ **Badge,** 12″ x 12″, c. 1800s, gold satin, multicolored stitches, pheasant motif	325.00	425.00	375.00
☐ **Badge,** 12″ x 12″, c. 1800s, satin, multi-colored stitches, egret shape, floral motif	215.00	310.00	260.00
☐ **Badge,** 12″ x 12″, c. 1800s, silk, bird shape, multicolored stitches	160.00	215.00	200.00
☐ **Banner,** 8″ x 26″, c. 1700s, yellow damask, dragon, loud motif, Korean	800.00	975.00	875.00
☐ **Court Robe,** 50″ long, c. 1770s, red silk, embroidered cranes, flowers, fruit, butterflies, waves, emblems	1075.00	1285.00	1175.00
☐ **Court Vest,** 50″ long, c. 1800s, black satin, embroidered, bats, clouds, birds, dragons, waves	1200.00	1625.00	1375.00
☐ **Holy Robe,** 58″ x 65″, c. 1800s, yellow damask, embroidered dragons, clouds and bird motifs . .	2300.00	3250.00	2850.00
☐ **Robe,** 1600s, ceremonial, brilliant floral and dragon motif	375.00	400.00	398.00

	Current Price Range		P/Y Average
☐ **Throne Back Cover,** 25″ x 15″, yellow satin, embroidered lotus, foilage, bat, fan, bamboo motif	480.00	570.00	525.00
☐ **Warrior Outfit,** 60″ long,c. 1700s, multicolored brocade, embroidered gold floral motif.	675.00	875.00	775.00

DECORATIVE

	Current Price Range		P/Y Average
☐ **Embroidery,** 9″ x 23″, c. 1900s, beige background, multicolored, vase with flowers motif, brocade border	25.00	32.00	28.00
☐ **Embroidery,** 10″ x 24″, c. 1900s, beige background, multicolored bird, floral motif, brocade border	43.00	52.00	48.00
☐ **Embroidery,** 12″ x 12″, c. 1600s, multicolored satin, oval shape, embroidered floral, foliage motifs	475.00	675.00	575.00
☐ **Embroidery,** 12″ x 13″, c. 1900s, multicolored background, floral, bird, butterfly motif, brocade border	22.00	32.00	28.00
☐ **Embroidery,** 13″ x 26″, c. 1900s, beige background, hand stitched black border, multicolored vase, incense burner, floral motif	85.00	110.00	100.00
☐ **Embroidery,** 13″ x 26″, c. 1900s, beige background, multicolored bird motif, brocade border	65.00	105.00	90.00
☐ **Embroidery,** 15″ x 12″, c. 1600s, multicolored satin, oval shape, embroidered bird, tree motifs	475.00	675.00	675.00
☐ **Pillar Hanging,** peach, silk, embroidered dragons, birds, clouds, religious emblems, 90″ x 60″, 18th century	8800.00	11250.00	10025.00
☐ **Silk,** Chinese, beige ground, red rose with green stem, 60″ wide, 2 yards long	160.00	210.00	198.00
☐ **Silk,** Chinese, brown ground, profuse raised gold and silver covering entire piece, 39″ wide, 7 2/3 yards long	220.00	310.00	275.00
☐ **Silk,** bolt, Chinese, copper ground, overall geometric embroidered design in gold and silver thread, 28½″ wide, 14 yards long	220.00	310.00	265.00
☐ **Silk,** bolt, Chinese, emerald/sapphire, brilliant color, woven pattern of large circular discs, 31″ wide, 19 1/3 yards long	265.00	365.00	300.00
☐ **Silk,** Chinese, gold ground with exquisite dragon embroidery work in blue and gold, 72″ wide, 7 yards long	115.00	160.00	145.00
☐ **Silk,** Chinese, gold with scalloped and floral designs, 26½″ wide, 9 1/3 yards long	115.00	160.00	145.00
☐ **Silk,** bolt, Chinese, royal purple, pagoda design pattern, 31″ wide 18 1/3 yards long	220.00	315.00	275.00
☐ **Silk,** bolt, Chinese, tan field, embroidered gold thread designs, 39½″ wide, 5 2/3 yards long			
☐ **Silk,** Chinese, yellow and gold Oriental designs, 31″ wide, 4 1/3 yards long	60.00	100.00	80.00
☐ **Silk Cover,** pink embroidered floral, fowl, tree motif, 9′ x 6′, 19th century	1200.00	1550.00	1350.00

	Current Price Range		P/Y Average
☐ **Table Frontal,** red gauze embroidered floral fruit motif, 35″ x 34″, 19th century	275.00	365.00	325.00
☐ **Table Frontal,** red silk, embroidered gold elephant motif, 40″ x 30″, 18th century	380.00	565.00	410.00
☐ **Tapestry,** sheared velvet, lake, toreii gate, pine tree hills, Japanese, 70″ x 92″, 20th century ..	525.00	650.00	595.00
☐ **Wall Hanging,** blue brocade, embroidered gold dragon motif, 90″ x 60″, 18th century	8500.00	11000.00	9700.00
☐ **Wall Hanging,** silk, multicolored, child, dragon, fungus, wave motif, 40″ x 60″, 20th century ...	2175.00	2650.00	2300.00

GARMENTS

	Current Price Range		P/Y Average
☐ **Obi,** silk, multicolored, bird, branch, floral motif, 13″ wide, 20th century.....................	725.00	935.00	825.00
☐ **Obi,** silk, multicolored, fans, floral motif, 13″ x 13″, 20th century	900.00	1600.00	1200.00
☐ **Obi,** silk, multicolored fans, scrolls, folded papers motif, 13″ x 12″, 20th century	430.00	520.00	495.00
☐ **Obi,** silk, multicolored, ferns, and mums motif, 6″ x 9″, 20th century........................	170.00	210.00	185.00
☐ **Obi,** silk, multicolored, floral, cart, crane, 13″ x 13″, 20th century	530.00	625.00	575.00
☐ **Obi,** silk, multicolored, kirin, bamboo, floral motif, 6″ x 36″, 20th century	210.00	315.00	275.00
☐ **Obi,** silk, multicolored peacocks, fans, cranes, pine, mums motif, 12″ x 12″, 20th century	210.00	315.00	285.00
☐ **Obi,** silk, multicolored, phoenix, crane motif, 12″ x 12″, 20th century........................	630.00	750.00	700.00
☐ **Obi,** silk, multicolored, phoenix, garden house, trees motif, 6″ x 9″, 20th century	170.00	215.00	195.00
☐ **Obi,** silk, multicolored, pine, plum, bamboo, sea waves, tortoise shell, clouds, cranes motif, 11″ x 13″, 20th century	215.00	310.00	285.00
☐ **Obi,** silk, red background overlapping decorated balls, gold geometric motif, leaves and flowers, 9″ x 9″, 20th century	170.00	215.00	195.00

FLOOR COVERINGS

	Current Price Range		P/Y Average
☐ **Carpet,** Chinese, blue field with center scenic design, border also features landscape design, very simple, and clear, 13′2″ x 9′10″, 20th century	3800.00	5175.00	4400.00
☐ **Carpet,** Chinese, 9′ x 12′, 20th century	3200.00	4100.00	3600.00
☐ **Carpet,** Chinese, 12′ x 9′, brown background, floral and foliage motif	1300.00	1600.00	1400.00
☐ **Carpet,** Chinese, cream field features design of octagons and medallions with foo dogs, birds and flowers, maze-work border, 18′9″ x 12′11″, 20th century	4750.00	7150.00	5750.00
☐ **Carpet,** Chinese, cream field features design of octagons and medallions with foo dogs and floral blossoms, floral borders, 8′2″ x 6′7″, 20th century	750.00	1000.00	800.00

	Current Price Range		P/Y Average
☐ **Carpet,** Chinese, cream field features woven squares, a rose flower is contained in each square, open black border, 11′7″ x 8′10″, 20th century	3400.00	4600.00	4000.00
☐ **Carpet,** Chinese, cream field with all over design featuring flowers and scenic medallions, maze-work border, 10′4″ x 6′, 20th century	1375.00	1725.00	2070.00
☐ **Carpet,** Chinese, cream field with octagon design, medallions feature design of flowers and animals, maze-work and floral borders, 17′10″ x 8′8″, 20th century	2700.00	3350.00	3025.00
☐ **Carpet,** Chinese, dark blue background, clouds and foliage motif, 12′ x 8′	1600.00	2100.00	1850.00
☐ **Carpet,** Chinese, dark blue background, flowery medallion, 16′ x 13′, 19th century	22000.00	31000.00	26000.00
☐ **Carpet,** Chinese, dark blue background, floral motif, 12′ x 8′	1150.00	1400.00	1200.00
☐ **Carpet,** Chinese, dark blue background, flower clusters, animal motifs, 12′ x 8′10″, 20th century	2700.00	3200.00	2900.00
☐ **Carpet,** Chinese, floral motif, gold borders, 9′ x 12′	975.00	1225.00	1025.00
☐ **Carpet,** Turkish, pale green background, orange-yellow medallion, tree and floral patterned border, 13′ x 11′, 19th century	1650.00	2175.00	1850.00
☐ **Carpet,** Turkish, red background, a green medallion of floral motif, green border, 12′4″ x 11′, 20th century	3350.00	4350.00	3550.00
☐ **Carpet,** Turkish, red brown background, white border, 12′ x 6′, 19th century	2275.00	3100.00	2675.00
☐ **Carpet,** Turkish, red, pink background, white border, lozenge shaped, 10′ x 5′, 19th century	6500.00	8500.00	7500.00
☐ **Carpet,** Turkish, red, pink background, yellow medallion, floral border, 15′ x 10′, 20th century	1900.00	2300.00	2000.00
☐ **Carpet,** Turkish, yellow background, flower medallions, blue floral and foliage border, 13′ x 10′, 19th century	2675.00	3150.00	2875.00
☐ **Mat,** Chinese, pure white background, flower bouquets, sitting birds, pink and red border, 4′ x 2′	115.00	160.00	145.00
☐ **Mat,** Chinese, pure white trailing tendril and floral border, blue background, 4′ x 2′	475.00	675.00	525.00
☐ **Mat,** Chinese, purple medallion, fruit blossoms on orange background, flower and foliage border, blue, 3′8″ x 13′	565.00	675.00	585.00
☐ **Mat,** Chinese, yellow orange background, flower medallions, orange border, 4′ x 3′	850.00	975.00	900.00
☐ **Mat,** Chinese, yellow background, sitting goat and goose, butterflies, red border, 5′ x 3′	465.00	585.00	525.00
☐ **Mat,** Chinese, yellow background, white inner and outer borders, 5′ x 3′	800.00	1050.00	900.00
☐ **Mat,** Chinese, yellow medallion flower sprigs, white border, 5′ x 3′	1150.00	1425.00	1225.00

	Current Price Range		P/Y Average

☐ **Mat,** Chinese, yellow, wreathed medallion enclosing bat, blooming flowers, white background, two borders in white, 3'8" x 2', 19th century . . . 675.00 875.00 725.00

FUNCTIONAL

☐ **Blanket,** c. Turkish, green, maroon, white, embroidery, vine motif, 6'8" x 5', 20th century 2250.00 3200.00 2750.00

☐ **Chair Panel,** orange satin, seascape, dragon, phoenix motif, 70" x 20", 17th century 1175.00 1625.00 1425.00

☐ **Chair Panel,** orange velvet, lotus, phoenix motif, 70" x 22", 18th century 675.00 875.00 725.00

☐ **Chair Panel,** pink brocade, dragon phoenix, bird motif, 70" x 25", 18th century 1750.00 2635.00 2025.00

☐ **Cushion Covers,** yellow brocade, embroidered dragon, cloud motif, 40" x 40", 19th century . . 650.00 850.00 750.00

☐ **Pillow Cover,** yellow satin, embroidered red flowers, green foliage motif, 20" x 20", 19th century 390.00 560.00 450.00

☐ **Pillow Covers,** Chinese, silk, embroidered with dragons in orange and mauve on ivory ground, 28" x 86" (pair) 115.00 160.00 140.00

RUGS

☐ **Rug,** Caucasian, red background, figures, blue border, 8' x 5', 20th century 4300.00 5500.00 4800.00

☐ **Rug,** Caucasian, red, blue background brown foliage, floral border, 9'8" x 4', 19th century 3400.00 4375.00 3800.00

☐ **Rug,** Caucasian, red, blue background, dark red border, 6' x 3'8", 19th century 1150.00 1600.00 1400.00

☐ **Rug,** Caucasian, red floral background, white border, 6'8" x 4', 19th century 3200.00 3650.00 3400.00

☐ **Rug,** Caucasian, white background, dark blue border, 5' x 3', 19th century 2200.00 2650.00 2350.00

☐ **Rug,** Chinese, beige background, floral, vases, butterfly motif, green border, 11' x 8', 20th century 1375.00 1825.00 1525.00

☐ **Rug,** Chinese, beige background, hotel motif, multicolored design, bordered, 7' x 5', 20th century 1100.00 1550.00 1350.00

☐ **Rug,** Chinese, beige background, Lignum vitae, animal motif, 5' x 7', 20th century 1600.00 2000.00 1800.00

☐ **Rug,** Chinese, blue, 9' x 12', 20th century 325.00 385.00 345.00

☐ **Rug,** Chinese, blue background, butterflies, trees, birds, blue and gold medallion, bordered blue, 5' x 3', 19th century 900.00 1275.00 1175.00

☐ **Rug,** Chinese, blue background, central medallion, silk borders, 4' x 6', 20th century 1625.00 2075.00 1825.00

☐ **Rug,** Chinese, blue background, immortal, cloud motif, signed, 5' x 3', 19th century 1550.00 1850.00 1650.00

☐ **Rug,** Chinese, blue background, flowers, white border, 8' x 5' 1625.00 2100.00 1900.00

	Current Price Range		P/Y Average
☐ **Rug,** Chinese, blue field, center medallion with dragon, flower motif on each side of medallion, trellis design border, 5'8" x 5'8", 20th century	2150.00	2600.00	2300.00
☐ **Rug,** Chinese, blue field, phoenix surrounded by fretwork and flowers, ivory border of flowers, 6'1" x 3'6", 20th century	1125.00	1375.00	1225.00
☐ **Rug,** Chinese, dark blue background, cross motif, multicolored borders, 6' x 4', 20th century	630.00	750.00	700.00
☐ **Rug,** Chinese, dark blue background, floral medallion, blue floral motif, 17' x 11', 19th century	420.00	530.00	485.00
☐ **Rug,** Turkish, background pure white bands of foliage and connecting medallions, red border, fringed, 8' x 4', 19th century	5200.00	6300.00	6000.00
☐ **Rug,** Turkish, background, red star shaped medallion, slanted border, 4' x 3', 19th century . . .	3200.00	4375.00	3900.00
☐ **Rug,** Turkish, blue background, yellow medallion floral patterned borders, 6'9" x 4'8", 19th century	2175.00	2650.00	2475.00
☐ **Saddle Cover,** Afghanistan, dark blue background, multicolored guard borders, 3' x 3', 20th century	1250.00	1400.00	1350.00
☐ **Saddle Cover,** Chinese, background red, bat motif, white border, 4'6" x 2'	1225.00	1550.00	1350.00
☐ **Saddle Cover,** Chinese, patterned background, two round medallions, bordered with fruit and foliage motif, 9'8" x 9'2"	1225.00	1550.00	1350.00

OTT & BREWER POTTERY

ORIGIN: The company which was later to be known as Ott & Brewer was founded in May 1863, by Bloor, Ott and Booth. Booth left the business in 1864, and his part of the company was bought by Garret S. Burroughs. Due to illness, Burroughs also lasted only one year. It was at this point that John Hart Brewer entered the firm, and items which are marked "O.B.B." could mean Bloor, Ott & Booth, Bloor, Ott & Burroughs, or Bloor, Ott & Brewer.

Isaac Broome came to Ott & Brewer in 1875 or 1876 and greatly expanded the parian line there. Many of his items were shown at the Philadelphia exposition in 1876.

DECORATION: Ott & Brewer used the full range of decorating methods on their wares, including transfer decoration of various types (primarily on their non-porcelain wares), hand-painting, gold paste, Royal Worcester "cloisonne" style artwork, and Irish Belleek type pearlized glazes. Pate-sur-pate work was done there, primarily by a man named Saunders. (Where is all that pate-sur-pate now?)

PRICES: Ott & Brewer Belleek has never been cheap. The recent rise in prices has eliminated the middle class collector. Most collectors do not distinguish between the ivory porcelain and the true Belleek, although most are aware that items with the crown marks can be a little heavier than those with the crescent marks. There is also little difference in pricing between the two types. (Remember that although the true Belleek is thinner, the ivory porcelain is older.)

Non-porcelain items are still found at popular prices, although this situation may not last. As more O&B Belleek becomes unreachable, the granite wares and cream-colored wares will become more interesting to collectors. This could raise prices.

Parian items and pieces signed by Broome are the most expensive. During the past year, the only known sale of a Broome item was the egg shown in the color section. It sold for $1,200. It is marked with a variation of mark F, and has the date 1877 and the Broome signature. Expect to pay a minimum of $1,500 for a marked parian bust.

RECOMMENDED READING: For further information refer to *The Official Price Guide to Pottery and Porcelain,* published by The House of Collectibles.

NON-PORCELAIN WARES

	Current Price Range		P/Y Average
☐ **Cracker Jar,** granite ware, oxblood color, hand-done sponged gold clouds covering jar and lid, gold trim on finial and handles somewhat worn, marks A and C	120.00	140.00	130.00
☐ **Cracker Jar, same as above,** except green background and not marked	80.00	95.00	85.00
☐ **Plates,** 9½", hand-painted game birds, colored rims with sponged gold finish, one rim copper color and the other gray, pencil line gold banding on outer rim and on shoulder, crazing on surface, otherwise perfect, marks A and C on one plate, mark A only on the other, see photo of one plate, pair	120.00	140.00	132.00
☐ **Vase,** 9", slightly rounded shape, hand-painted red and pink flowers on green background, marks A and C in green	115.00	130.00	121.00

Note: Expect to pay a minimum of $65 for any decorated piece of Ott & Brewer opaque ware. Earlier samples of this type of item are usually crazed, and this is not held against them where value is concerned.

Plate, *game bird*

PORCELAIN ITEMS

	Current Price Range		P/Y Average

No attempt will be made to differentiate between ivory porcelain and true Belleek.

☐ **Basket,** 6″, rustic handle, raised gold paste trim in thistle pattern on beige matte finish, mark I, see photo in color section	600.00	700.00	640.00
☐ **Chocolate Pot,** 12″, green bottom section, top section has raised gold paste trim in several shades of gold, on bottom section, top section has raised gold paste trim in several shades of gold, gold trim on dragon handle and spout and on finial and rims, mark I	700.00	820.00	770.00
☐ **Cup and Saucer,** after dinner size, gold paste trim, mark K and Tiffany & Co. mark, saucer only marked, gold is not the same color on the cup as on the saucer for some reason, but it is obvious the pieces belong together	115.00	130.00	122.00
☐ **Cup and Saucer,** after dinner size, plain shape, spray of raised enamel flowers across front of cup, smaller spray on back, two sprays on saucer, pearlized pink interior, gold trim on rims and handle, mark J with New Orleans inscription, saucer broken in half and glued back together	135.00	155.00	145.00
☐ **Cup and Saucer,** Tridacna pattern, teacup size, pearlized yellow interior, gold trim on handle and rims, mark K	150.00	175.00	167.00
☐ **Cup and Saucer,** Tridacna pattern, boullion, pearlized pink interior, gold trim on handle and rims, mark K, small fleck on underside of saucer	140.00	170.00	145.00

	Current Price Range		P/Y Average

☐ **Cup and Saucer,** cactus pattern, teacup size, pearlized white finish, gold trim on handle and rim, crack in handle .... | 120.00 | 140.00 | 130.00

☐ **Cup and Saucer,** after dinner size, enamel ribbon design, gold trim, mark I .... | 180.00 | 220.00 | 192.00

☐ **Ewer,** double spouted, rustic handle, top section covered with gold, bottom section has hand-painted coral colored water lilies, two small chips on top section, mark I .... | 750.00 | 850.00 | 800.00

☐ **Ewer,** raised gold paste cattail pattern, two turtle figurines applied to side of piece, turtles and coral handle decorated in green and gold, small fleck on one of the turtles, mark I .... | 800.00 | 1000.00 | 920.00

☐ **Ewer,** 8″, bulbous shape, raised gold paste in thistle pattern on beige matte finish, gold trim on handle and rims, mark I .... | 650.00 | 750.00 | 700.00

☐ **Ewer,** similar in size and shape to the one with turtles listed above, hand-painted water lilies outlined in gold, handle is formed like stem to buds and leaves which are applied near the rim, piece has been totally devastated in the back and is held together with glue, damage does not show very much in front, handle badly cracked so piece has to be picked up by the body, mark I ...... | 210.00 | 255.00 | 230.00

☐ **Ewer,** 7″, shaped like a vinegar cruet, raised gold paste trim in chrysanthemum design on beige matte finish, mark K .... | 385.00 | 455.00 | 420.00

☐ **Ewer,** 8″, melon-ribbed, white glazed background with gold paste trim in oak leaf pattern, mark I, spider crack in bottom of piece .... | 170.00 | 200.00 | 187.50

☐ **Shell,** raised on coral and seashell base, pearlized pink interior to shell, gold trim on rim and on base, one of the small shells that form the base has been broken off, mark I .... | 400.00 | 470.00 | 430.00

☐ **Shell,** 1½″ high, 3¼″ wide, (handle included), very delicate and thin, forked handle and two small shell feet decorated in gold, gold trim on rim, little shells are misplaced so the item wobbles ever so slightly, mark I .... | 90.00 | 110.00 | 97.50

☐ **Shell,** similar to one above but with no handle, pearlized blue interior, mark J .... | 90.00 | 110.00 | 100.00

☐ **Shoe,** 5″, hand-painted small flowers in scatter pattern, gold trim, marks I and J .... | 400.00 | 470.00 | 430.00

☐ **Sugar and Creamer,** cactus pattern, pearlized finish, gold trim on rim, bronze trim on handles, mint condition, mark I .... | 385.00 | 455.00 | 415.00

☐ **Sugar and Creamer,** Tridacna pattern, pearlized pink inside, gold trim on handles and rims, mark J .... | 265.00 | 325.00 | 285.00

☐ **Sugar and Creamer,** ruffled top sugar, creamer fits inside of sugar, raised gold paste trim in oak leaf pattern on beige matte finish, mark K ..... | 310.00 | 410.00 | 350.00

	Current Price Range		P/Y Average

☐ **Vase,** 7″, beautiful hand-painted orchid, raised gold paste work, openwork handles, raised on small openwork feet one of which is damaged, probably had a lid at one time which is no longer present, mark K **400.00 470.00 430.00**

☐ **Vase,** 7″, calla lily shape on rustic base, applied leaf on side helps support the lily, pearlized ivory interior, leaf pale lavender, gold trim on rim and on base section, a few small rough spots, mark I **680.00 885.00 725.00**

☐ **Vase,** 10″, bulbous bottom with long neck, hand-painted yellow and brown flowers, raised gold trim, mark I **525.00 625.00 570.00**

☐ **Vase,** 12″, bulbous bottom with long narrow square neck, green background with raised gold paste trim done in at least five different shades ranging all the way from a silver color to a bronze, mark I **875.00 1075.00 995.00**

☐ **Vase,** 12″, bulbous bottom with long neck, hand-painted roses outlined in gold on high-glaze white finish, small repaired spot on top, mark H **600.00 700.00 620.00**

☐ **Vase,** 10″, double-handled, raised gold paste in three shades of gold, mark J **525.00 625.00 575.00**

☐ **Watering Can,** 7½″, raised gold paste trim on beige matte finish, damage to spout, mark I ... **375.00 475.00 400.00**

OWLS

ORIGIN: The owl was first used as a decoration on coins in ancient Greece.

COMMENTS: A popular collectible, owls have been used on emblems, shields and beginning in the 19th century, on decorative items.

ADDITIONAL TIPS: The listings are alphabetical according to item. Following the items is a description, followed by maker, date, and other information as available.

	Current Price Range		P/Y Average
☐ **Bookends,** rookwood, tan glaze, pair	120.00	160.00	130.00
☐ **Book Rack,** expanding, cast brass, two owls	36.00	46.00	40.00

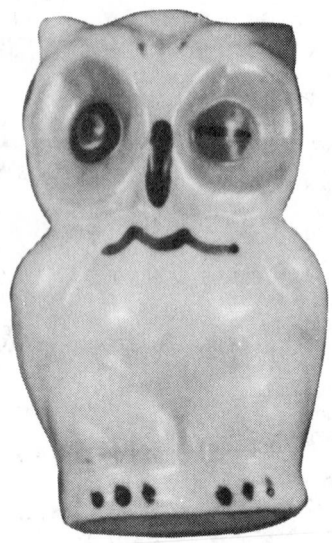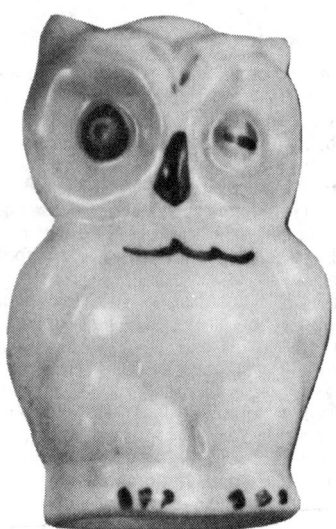

Salt and Pepper Shakers, *white with tan trim, winking eye, shawnee pottery.* **$8.50–$12.50**

	Current Price Range		P/Y Average
☐ **Chatelaine,** wire plaque, link chains, silver plated	140.00	170.00	150.00
☐ **Cookie Jar,** tan and white, one eye closed, Shawnee Pottery Company	10.00	15.00	12.00
☐ **Doorstop,** carved wood with glass eyes, c. 1920s	21.50	30.00	24.00
☐ **Fairy Lamp,** bisque, owl face, glass eyes, 4½″ high	165.00	240.00	185.00
☐ **Figurine,** carved wooden owl	55.00	75.00	65.00
☐ **Figurine,** character owl in checked shawl with ermine collar, Royal Doulton	775.00	875.00	825.00
☐ **Figurine,** Great Horned Owl, ceramic	40.00	60.00	50.00
☐ **Figurine,** Great Horned Owl, porcelain, Royal Copenhagen	450.00	550.00	500.00
☐ **Figurine,** veined owl, Rouge Flambe, Royal Doulton, No. 2249	310.00	360.00	340.00
☐ **Figurine,** wise old owl in red cloak with ermine collar	425.00	525.00	475.00
☐ **Inkwell,** alabaster, owl on pile of books, 19th century	125.00	175.00	150.00
☐ **Jar,** Atterbury, opal glass, inserted red eyes, 7″ high	125.00	165.00	135.00
☐ **Jar,** owl on a pedestal, pastel bisque, head is the jar lid, Royal Doulton-Lambeth	390.00	440.00	400.00
☐ **Painting,** primitive, two owls, late 19th century	107.00	140.00	117.00
☐ **Paperweight,** crystal, round, frosted horned owl, copper engraving	425.00	525.00	475.00

	Current Price Range		P/Y Average

	Current Price Range		P/Y Average
☐ **Pitcher,** owl design, etched, clear green glass	30.00	45.00	35.00
☐ **Plate,** "1981 First Light - Great Horned Owl, The Prowlers of the Clouds Series," by Larry Toschik	60.00	70.00	65.00
☐ **Plate,** "1981 His Golden Throne - Screech Owl, The Prowlers of the Clouds Series," by Larry Toschik	60.00	70.00	65.00
☐ **Print,** Baby Saw-Whet Owls, released 1981, by Guy Coheleach	30.00	60.00	45.00
☐ **Print,** Barn Owl, released, 1980, by Owen J. Gromme	100.00	120.00	105.00
☐ **Print,** Barred Owl, released 1982, by Guy Coheleach	120.00	140.00	130.00
☐ **Print,** Burrowing Owl, released 1975, by Arthur Singer	30.00	60.00	45.00
☐ **Print,** "Eyes of the Night," Great Horned Owl, released 1979 by Owen J. Gromme	100.00	115.00	105.00
☐ **Print,** Great Horned Owl, released 1974, by Roger Tory Peterson	150.00	200.00	175.00
☐ **Print,** Great Horned Owl, released 1979, by Jill Fogelsong	50.00	75.00	60.00
☐ **Print,** Long-Eared Owl, released 1976, by James A. Carson	85.00	100.00	90.00
☐ **Print,** Oval Owl, released 1978, by Stan Brod	45.00	60.00	50.00
☐ **Print,** Pigmy Owl, released 1972, by Peter Parnall	30.00	180.00	80.00
☐ **Print,** Richardson's Owl, released 1972, by Peter Parnall	30.00	215.00	150.00
☐ **Print,** Screech Owls, by E. Gordon West	30.00	45.00	37.00
☐ **Print,** Screech Owl, released 1972, by Gene Gray	25.00	50.00	35.00
☐ **Print,** Snowy Owls, released 1979, by Charles Frace	65.00	95.00	75.00
☐ **Print,** Snowy Owl, released 1972, by Roger Tory Peterson	175.00	575.00	250.00
☐ **Print,** Spectacled Owl, released 1979, by Jill Fogelsong	100.00	150.00	125.00
☐ **Purse,** mesh, diamonds, rubies, gold, owl motif frame, Art Nouveau, c. 1890	23000.00	25000.00	24000.00
☐ **Salt and Pepper Shakers,** tan and white, one eye closed, Shawnee Pottery Company	8.00	14.00	11.00
☐ **Sculpture,** Snowy Owl, female, by Robert Jefferson, Royal Doulton, 1974	2150.00	2400.00	2250.00
☐ **Sculpture,** Snowy Owl, male, by Robert Jefferson, Royal Doulton, 1974	1750.00	2000.00	1850.00
☐ **Stick-Pin,** 14K gold, c. 1895	70.00	80.00	75.00
☐ **Stick Pin,** gold, two diamond chip eyes, 14K gold	140.00	175.00	155.00
☐ **Stick Pin,** gold filled, c. 1895	30.00	40.00	35.00
☐ **Vase,** hand painted owl profile, tan and brown, Weller Hudson	1050.00	1200.00	1100.00
☐ **Vase,** primitive owl design, pottery, Avon Pottery	800.00	950.00	850.00

PAPER COLLECTIBLES

TOPIC: This section covers business correspondence, celebrity items, checks and documents. For listings of other paper items such as autographs or books, please refer directly to those individual sections.

TYPES: There is a huge variety of paper items that people collect. If the item is of historical importance it probably has value for collectors.

COMMENTS: Collectors of paper goods specialize as to the type of item they collect, since the field is too vast for general collecting.

ADDITIONAL TIPS: For further information and listings, please refer to *The Official Price Guide to Paper Collectibles,* published by The House of Collectibles.

BUSINESS CORRESPONDENCE

	Current Price Range		P/Y Average
☐ **California Aeronautics Firm,** 651 letters covering the period January to June 1938, a few of later date, some stained or damaged, in three plywood flip-top cartons with lettered labels (one carton broken)	150.00	170.00	160.00
☐ **Chicago Ice-House,** 421 letters covering the period December 1890 to July 1896, some invoices, etc. included	90.00	120.00	105.00
☐ **Connecticut Clock Manufacturer,** 68 letters covering the period September 1851 to January 1852, bound in a half morocco case	180.00	220.00	200.00
☐ **Massachusetts Leather Goods Manufacturer,** 81 letters covering the period July to October 1870, loose, some letters have a page or more missing	65.00	85.00	75.00
☐ **New York Cigar Wholesaler,** 223 letters covering the period April 1889 to October 1889	48.00	68.00	58.00
☐ **New York Optical Goods Company,** 17 letters, 1862	85.00	105.00	95.00

Advertising, *booklet and blotters, c. 1930s,* **$2.00-$5.00**
Photo courtesy of Lou McCulloch, Highland Heights, OH 44143.

	Current Price Range		P/Y Average

☐ **Parisian Hat Manufacturer,** 367 letters (plus miscellaneous bills, a few photos and design sketches) covering the period August 1906 to March 1907, enclosed in a buckram folder 55.00 65.00 60.00

☐ **Tiffany & Co., New York Fancy Goods Retailer,** 891 letters (plus promotional items, notes, memos, etc.) of 1911–1915, enclosed in six cardboard felt-lined cases 850.00 1050.00 950.00

CELEBRITY ITEMS

☐ **Amos and Andy Map of Weber City,** Pepsodent radio premium, 1935 .... 38.00 48.00 43.00

☐ **Amos and Andy,** 8″ x 10″ photo, n.d., c. 1935 13.00 17.00 15.00

☐ **Amos and Andy,** four page brochure about the program, c. 1935 .... 13.00 17.00 15.00

☐ **Astaire, Fred,** brochure of Fred Astaire Dance School, c. 1954 .... 2.00 3.00 2.50

☐ **Hopalong Cassidy Western Magazine,** Vol. 1, No. 2, colored cover, published by Best Books, 162 pages, Winter, 1951 .... 60.00 70.00 65.00

☐ **Hopalong Cassidy with Cole Bros. Circus,** souvenir program, color cover, 32 pages, 1950 25.00 35.00 30.00

☐ **Hopalong Cassidy Coloring Book,** Abbott Publishing Co., 10″ x 15″, unused, 1950 .... 18.00 22.00 20.00

☐ **Hopalong Cassidy Returns,** by Clarence E. Mulford, colored cover, "Pocket Book", 250 pages, published 1946 .... 10.00 12.00 11.00

☐ **Doomed Caravan Featuring William Boyd,** lobby card for motion picture, 1942 .... 25.00 30.00 27.50

☐ **Hopalong Canasta,** boxed game, includes deck of Hoppy cards, score sheet, rules and plastic card holder designed as a saddle, 1950 ...... 35.00 45.00 40.00

☐ **Judy Garland,** "Wizard of Oz" scrapbook belonging to her, containing numerous press cuttings and other memorabilia 1000.00 1200.00 1100.00

☐ **Judy Garland,** "Over the Rainbow", musical arrangement prepared for her, for motion picture "Wizard of Oz" 2700.00 3100.00 2900.00

☐ **Judy Garland,** "A Star is Born," first-draft copy of the Moss Hart script for motion picture in which she starred 1400.00 1600.00 1500.00

☐ **Judy Garland,** telegram sent by her to Louis B. Mayer, 1945 .... 300.00 340.00 320.00

☐ **"Shirley Temple—in Warner Bros. Pictures,"** 5″ x 7″ photo sold originally as a picture frame insert, probably about 1940 .... 10.00 14.00 12.00

☐ **"Love, Shirley Temple,"** printed card sent in reply to fan request for photo, listing prices of various photos 10.00 14.00 12.00

☐ **"Shirley Temple Grows Up,"** cover story from Life magazine, 1942 .... 11.00 15.00 13.00

	Current Price Range		P/Y Average

☐ **Shirley Temple Edition of the Littlest Rebel,** Random House, 214 pages with photo illustrations taken from movie stills, 1939 .... 8.00 12.00 10.00

☐ **Rudolph Valentino,** full color embossed cigar box label, 7″ x 9″ 11.00 16.00 13.50

☐ **Jane Withers—Her Life Story,** Whitman picture book, 32 pages, 1936 .... 18.00 22.00 20.00

CHECKS, CELEBRITY

☐ **Authors; Maxwell Anderson,** n.d.	16.00	24.00	20.00
☐ **Susan B. Anthony,** 1889	22.00	28.00	25.00
☐ **Henry W. Beecher,** 1884	16.00	26.00	21.00
☐ **John Fiske,** 1889	10.00	14.00	12.00
☐ **FitzGreen Halleck,** 1846	8.00	12.00	10.00
☐ **Military; G. T. Beauregard,** three checks dating 1878–1880	23.00	29.00	26.00
☐ **John A. Dix,** filled out by a clerk but signed by him, 1836	8.00	12.00	10.00
☐ **Admiral R. P. Hobson,** 1911	4.00	6.00	5.00
☐ **General Henry Knox,** 1792	35.00	42.00	38.50
☐ **John A. Logan,** 1879	8.00	12.00	10.00
☐ **Partly printed (red and black) check on the Treasurer of the Confederate States,** made out to an officer, signed by Captain Barksdale, Richmond, 1861	10.00	14.00	12.00
☐ **Winfield Scott,** 1827	20.00	26.00	23.00
☐ **Winfield Scott,** 1851	17.00	23.00	20.00
☐ **Statesmen; Robert Morris,** 1812	8.00	14.00	10.00
☐ **James Oliver,** two checks, 1896	8.00	14.00	10.00
☐ **Gerrit Smith,** 1871	5.00	9.00	7.00
☐ **Andrew Stevenson,** two checks, both 1828 ..	8.00	12.00	10.00
☐ **Charles Summer,** 1871	7.00	8.00	7.50
☐ **John Cleves Symmes,** 1797	13.00	17.00	15.00
☐ **Daniel Webster,** on Corcoran and Riggs bank, 1845	27.00	37.00	32.00
☐ **Gideon Wells,** on Riggs and Co., 1869	7.00	9.00	8.00
☐ **Theatrical; George Burns,** 1955	25.00	35.00	30.00
☐ **Enrico Caruso,** Hudson Trust Co., NY, 1920 ..	45.00	55.00	50.00
☐ **Lotta Crabtree,** 1888	17.00	23.00	20.00
☐ **Erroll Flynn,** 1941	35.00	45.00	40.00
☐ **Cary Grant,** 1966	25.00	30.00	27.50
☐ **Victor Herbert,** Corn Exchange Bank, NY, 1924	20.00	28.00	24.00
☐ **Marilyn Monroe,** 1951	300.00	380.00	340.00
☐ **Elvis Presley,** 1963	420.00	520.00	470.00

CHECKS, NON-CELEBRITY

☐ **Pre –1800**	20.00	26.00	23.00
☐ **1800–1830**	13.00	17.00	15.00
☐ **1831–1859**	9.00	13.00	11.00
☐ **1860–1889**	6.00	10.00	8.00
☐ **1890–1910**	3.00	5.00	4.00

	Current Price Range		P/Y Average

DOCUMENTS

☐ **Amherst, Jeffrey,** Commander-in-chief in North America (1759), military document signed, one page, 1774	210.00	260.00	235.00
☐ **Audubon, John James,** artist, legal document signed, Henderson Circuit Court, Kentucky, five pages, 1820	850.00	1050.00	950.00
☐ **Bacon, Nathaniel,** (1593–1660), holograph document signed, on behalf of Oliver Cromwell, 1656	125.00	155.00	140.00
☐ **Bacon, Sir Francis,** document signed as Baron Verulam, two pages, large folio, repaired, February 11, 1618	1300.00	1800.00	1550.00
☐ **Burke, Edmund,** document signed as Paymaster General of the Forces, one page, April 10, 1782	90.00	120.00	105.00
☐ **Carleton, Sir Guy,** Governor of Quebec, document signed, two pages, 1789	150.00	210.00	180.00
☐ **Cary, Robert,** document signed, one page, 1622	65.00	85.00	75.00
☐ **Catherine the Great,** Empress of Russia, document signed, with the great seal attached, decorating an officer for outstanding service, 1785	270.00	370.00	320.00
☐ **Catherine de Medici,** document signed, vellum, 9″ x 19″, one page, 1579	120.00	270.00	195.00
☐ **Charles IX,** King of France, document signed, a record of gifts and payments by the king, two pages, 1567	200.00	260.00	230.00
☐ **Chase, Samuel,** Maryland signer of the Declaration of Independence, holograph document signed, about 100 words, silked	220.00	260.00	240.00
☐ **Choate, Rufus,** lawyer, document signed, Boston, one page, 1845	18.00	22.00	20.00
☐ **Christian IV,** (1577–1648), King of Norway and Denmark, vellum document, signed, 1647	100.00	130.00	115.00
☐ **Clemenceau, Georges,** Premier of France, document signed, Paris, two pages, 1912	130.00	150.00	140.00
☐ **Coleridge, Samuel Taylor,** poet, document signed, folio, June, two pages, 1805	130.00	150.00	140.00
☐ **Cromwell, Richard,** Lord Protector of England, document on vellum, one page, December 16, 1658	320.00	380.00	350.00
☐ **Cutler, Manasseh,** Ohio pioneer, short holograph document signed, Ipswich, 1773	90.00	110.00	100.00
☐ **DeLesseps, Ferdinand,** official document, signed by Queen Victoria, August, 1870	125.00	145.00	135.00
☐ **Dudley, Robert,** Earl of Leicester, 1532–88, Proclamation signed as Governor of the Netherlands, 16″ x 12″, 1586	480.00	580.00	530.00
☐ **Dummer, Jeremiah,** holograph document signed, Boston, 1701	170.00	210.00	190.00
☐ **Elizabeth I of England,** vellum document signed, June, 1559, one page, quarto, 9″ x 12″	2100.00	2600.00	2350.00

	Current Price Range		P/Y Average
☐ **Elizabeth I,** vellum document, unsigned but bearing a good impression of her Great Seal, attached to the document with silken twine, fleece-lined case, 7″ x 4½″	1400.00	1600.00	1500.00
☐ **Ellery, William,** signer of the Declaration of Independence from Rhode Island, document signed, 5″ x 7″, 1768	80.00	120.00	100.00
☐ **Evelyn, John,** English diarist, vellum document, 1654	160.00	200.00	180.00
☐ **Francis of Sales,** Saint. document signed, 10½″ x 14″	620.00	720.00	670.00

PAPER DOLLS

COMMENTS: Paper dolls were first produced in the 1400s and first used as children's toys in the late 1700s. Collectors usually specialize in two ways either by antique examples or by specific types such as celebrity, advertising, works of favorite artists or companies.

A paper doll's collectibility depends upon several factors including artist, subject, age, construction, condition and size. Because paper dolls have been produced for such a long time, examples from the 1800s in excellent condition can be readily found.

MAKERS: Some companies which produced paper dolls include Whitman, Colorforms, Childrens Press, Avalon Industries, American Toy Works, Samuel Gabriel Sons and Co., Dennison Manufacturing Co. and Saalfield Co.

RECOMMENDED READING: For further information you may refer to *The Official Price Guide to Paper Collectibles,* published by The House of Collectibles.

☐ **Bride and Groom,** 1970 Whitman book #1989, punchouts, pink cover, uncut	8.00	12.00	10.00
☐ **Bride and Groom,** England, 1971, combination coloring book and paper dolls, two dolls, assorted outfits, uncut	2.00	8.00	6.00
☐ **Candy Stripers,** 1973 Saalfield	2.00	6.00	4.00
☐ **Captain Big Bill,** 1956 Samuel Lowe, uncut ...	2.00	4.00	3.00

	Current Price Range		P/Y Average

☐ **Career Girls,** 1942 Samuel Lowe, uncut ...... | 12.00 | 18.00 | 14.00

☐ **Career Girls,** by Doris Lane Butler, 1944 Whitman Book #973, three dolls—Ann, Marty, and Dottie, cloth-like outfits .... | 20.00 | 30.00 | 25.00

☐ **Career Girls,** 1950 Samuel Lowe, uncut ...... | 10.00 | 16.00 | 14.00

☐ **Carmen, Rita Hayworth,** 1948, two dolls, assorted outfits, thin cover, uncut .... | 45.00 | 55.00 | 50.00

☐ **Carmen Miranda,** 1942 Whitman #995, uncut | 80.00 | 90.00 | 85.00

☐ **Carmen Miranda,** 1942 Whitman #995, two dolls, twenty outfits, fourteen accessories, cut | 16.00 | 24.00 | 20.00

☐ **Carmen Miranda,** 1952 Saalfield #1558, two dolls, assorted outfits, cut .... | 16.00 | 18.00 | 14.00

☐ **Carmen Miranda Paper Dolls,** by Tom Tierney, one doll, assorted costumes, uncut .... | 2.00 | 6.00 | 4.00

☐ **Dress-up Doll Book,** by Sally de Frehn Ogg, 1953 Treasure book #T-167, five dolls, assorted outfits to be colored, uncut .... | 20.00 | 30.00 | 25.00

☐ **Dr. Kildare Play Book,** Samuel Lowe, uncut .. | 2.00 | 6.00 | 4.00

☐ **Dr. Kildare and Nurse Susan,** #2740, based on TV show, punch-outs, three dolls, assorted outfits, uncut .... | 20.00 | 30.00 | 25.00

☐ **Dolls Across the Sea,** by Queen Holden, 1969 Platt and Munk, Hans, Ingrid, Yvonne, and Juliane, foreign costumes, boxed, uncut .... | 8.00 | 12.00 | 10.00

☐ **Dolls For All Seasons—Rosy Ruth,** by Raphael Tuck, one doll with three dresses and one hat | 70.00 | 80.00 | 75.00

☐ **Dolls Of All Nations—Russia,** Boston Sunday Globe, uncut .... | 12.00 | 16.00 | 14.00

☐ **Dolls Of Other Lands,** 1968 Watkins, six dolls, forty-two costumes .... | 5.00 | 10.00 | 8.00

☐ **Dolly Dingle's Friend Sunny,** August 1926, Sunny Spear—boy doll, doll, and ball, cut ..... | 6.00 | 10.00 | 8.00

☐ **Dolly Dingle's Friends Return,** June 1926, Marie-Louise, backed, cut .... | 8.00 | 12.00 | 10.00

☐ **Dolly Dingle's Little Friend Junior Allen And Tinker,** May 1924, three suits, two hats, cut ... | 4.00 | 8.00 | 6.00

☐ **Dolly Dingle's Little Friend Mary Lamb With Fancy Dress Costumes,** April 1924, cut ...... | 6.00 | 10.00 | 8.00

☐ **Dolly Dingle's Little Friend Tottie,** September 1926, one doll, costume and hat, dress and coat, dog, cut .... | 4.00 | 10.00 | 6.00

☐ **Dolly Dingle's World Flight,** June 1932, four dresses, uncut .... | 8.00 | 12.00 | 10.00

☐ **Dolly Dingle's World Flight in Italy,** December 1932, boy doll, three costumes, uncut .... | 8.00 | 12.00 | 10.00

☐ **Dolly Dingle's World Flight In Italy,** December 1932, Italian doll, cut .... | 3.00 | 8.00 | 5.00

☐ **Dolly Dingle's World Flight in Russia,** March 1933, one doll, pets, uncut .... | 8.00 | 12.00 | 10.00

☐ **Dolly Dingle's World Flight in Sweden,** February 1933, boy, costumes, uncut .... | 8.00 | 12.00 | 10.00

☐ **Dolly Dingle's World Flight in Switzerland,** September 1931, uncut .... | 8.00 | 12.00 | 10.00

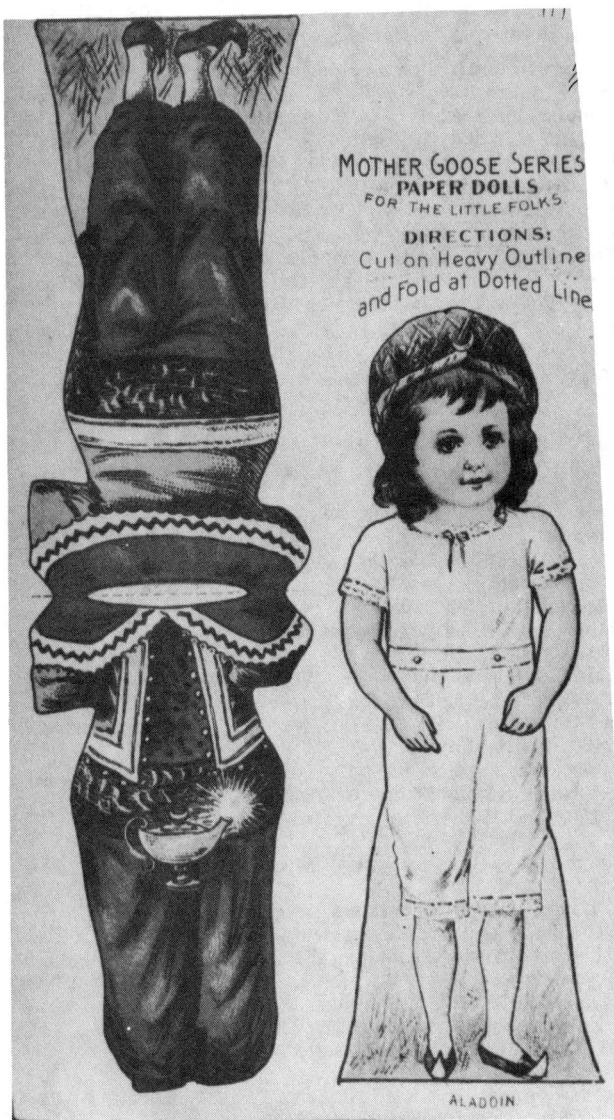

Mother Goose series, *c. 1885,* **$5.00–$8.00**
Photo courtesy of Lou McCulloch, Highland Heights, OH 44143.

	Current Price Range		P/Y Average

☐ **Dolly Dingle's Young Visitor,** November 1929, one doll, four dresses, shoes, cut . . . . — 3.00 — 8.00 — 5.00

☐ **Donna Reed,** 1959 Saalfield #4412, two dolls, assorted clothes, folder, cut . . . . — 10.00 — 18.00 — 14.00

☐ **Doris Day,** 1952 Whitman book #210325, statuette dolls, assorted outfits, folder, uncut . . . . . . — 60.00 — 70.00 — 65.00

☐ **Doris Day,** 1952 Whitman book #210325, dolls and assorted costumes, folder, cut . . . . — 10.00 — 18.00 — 12.00

☐ **Doris Day,** 1952 Whitman book #1179, two dolls, assorted costumes and clothes, cut . . . . . — 30.00 — 40.00 — 35.00

☐ **Doris Day,** 1954 Whitman book #1179:15, two dolls, eight pages of outfits, uncut . . . . — 70.00 — 80.00 — 75.00

☐ **Doris Day,** 1955 Whitman book #1952, statuette dolls, assorted clothes, folder, uncut . . . . . — 60.00 — 70.00 — 65.00

☐ **Doris Day,** 1956 Whitman book #1952, assorted outfits, uncut . . . . — 40.00 — 50.00 — 45.00

☐ **Dorothy Provine,** 1962 Whitman book #1964, one doll, assorted outfits, folder with handle, uncut . . . . — 30.00 — 40.00 — 35.00

☐ **Dorothy Provine,** 1962 Whitman #1964, two dolls, assorted clothes, cut . . . . — 10.00 — 18.00 — 14.00

☐ **Dottie Darline,** real wavy hair, front and back clothes, boxed, cut . . . . — 2.00 — 8.00 — 6.00

☐ **Hayley Mills In Summer Magic,** 1963 Whitman book #1966, one doll, assorted costumes, folder with handle, uncut . . . . — 40.00 — 50.00 — 45.00

☐ **Hayley Mills in Summer Magic,** 1963 Whitman book #1966, assorted outfits, folder with handle, cut . . . . — 20.00 — 30.00 — 25.00

☐ **Hayley Mills In That Darn Cat,** 1965 Whitman book #1955, one doll, assorted clothes, uncut — 40.00 — 50.00 — 45.00

☐ **Hayley Mills In the Moon Spinners,** 1964 Whitman book #1960, one doll, assorted clothes, uncut . . . . — 40.00 — 50.00 — 45.00

☐ **Hansel and Gretel Push Out Book,** 1954 Whitman . . . . — 10.00 — 18.00 — 14.00

☐ **Happy Days Playset Characters,** various scenes, characters, and props based on the T.V. series, such as Arnold's Drive In, and Fonzie's motorcycle . . . . — 2.00 — 8.00 — 6.00

☐ **Happy Family,** 1973 Samuel Lowe, uncut . . . . — 2.00 — 6.00 — 4.00

☐ **Happy Holiday,** reprint of Carmen Miranda, Saalfield book #2722, two dolls, assorted outfits, uncut . . . . — 20.00 — 30.00 — 25.00

☐ **Happiest Millionaire,** 1967 Saalfield . . . . — 5.00 — 10.00 — 8.00

☐ **Happy Birthday,** 1939 Merrill, uncut . . . . — 25.00 — 35.00 — 30.00

☐ **Happy Bride,** 1967 Whitman book #1958, four dolls, 1960s-styled clothes, uncut . . . . — 12.00 — 18.00 — 14.00

☐ **Hedy Lamarr,** 1942 Merrill #3482, two dolls, twenty-two outfits, twenty-nine accessories, uncut . . . . — 20.00 — 30.00 — 25.00

☐ **Hedy Lamarr,** 1942 Merrill #3482, two dolls, five outfits, accessories, cut . . . . — 2.00 — 6.00 — 4.00

	Current Price Range		P/Y Average

☐ **Hedy LaMarr,** 1951 Saalfield, uncut . . . . — 25.00 / 35.00 / 30.00

☐ **Hee Haw,** punch-out, by George and Nan Pollard, 1971 C.B.S. Artcraft book #5139, Gunilla, Lulu, Kathy, and Jeannie, uncut . . . . — 8.00 / 12.00 / 10.00

☐ **In Old New York,** 1957 Saalfield book #4411, coloring and paperdolls, book, two dolls, assorted costumes, uncut . . . . — 25.00 / 35.00 / 30.00

☐ **In Old New York,** Saalfield book #1772, two dolls, two pages of costumes, thin cover, uncut — 20.00 / 30.00 / 25.00

☐ **In Our Background,** 1941 Samuel Lowe, uncut . . . . — 15.00 / 25.00 / 20.00

☐ **Jack and Jill,** book #1561, four dolls, animals, assorted storyland costumes, uncut . . . . — 12.00 / 18.00 / 14.00

☐ **Jackie and Caroline,** #107, cut . . . . — 30.00 / 40.00 / 35.00

☐ **Jack With the Magic Eyes,** by Queen Holden, 1963 James and Jonathan #9301-P, large doll, discs on eyes, uncut . . . . — 40.00 / 50.00 / 45.00

☐ **Journey Friends, Toy From Germany,** by Ann Eshner, Jack and Jill set, December 1952, uncut . . . . — 2.00 / 8.00 / 6.00

☐ **Judy,** 1951 Merrill, uncut . . . . — 5.00 / 10.00 / 8.00

☐ **Judy and Jim,** by Hilda Miloche and Wilma Kane, Simon and Shuster, assorted outfits . . . . — 40.00 / 50.00 / 45.00

☐ **Judy Garland,** by Queen Holden, 1940 Whitman book #999, two dolls, large assortment of outfits, cut . . . . — 45.00 / 55.00 / 50.00

☐ **Judy Garland,** 1945 Whitman #996, uncut . . . — 85.00 / 95.00 / 90.00

☐ **Judy Garland Paper Dolls,** by Tom Tierney, three dolls—Garland as a teenager, young adult, and mature, thirty costumes from a number of her films, uncut . . . . — 2.00 / 6.00 / 4.00

☐ **Judy Holiday,** 1954 Saalfield book #159110, three dolls, four pages of clothes, thin cover, uncut . . . . — 45.00 / 55.00 / 50.00

☐ **Julia,** 1968 Saalfield, uncut . . . . — 5.00 / 10.00 / 8.00

☐ **Julie Andrews,** 1958 Saalfield, uncut . . . . — 15.00 / 25.00 / 20.00

☐ **June Allyson,** 1950 Whitman book #970, two dolls, assorted outfits, cut . . . . — 25.00 / 35.00 / 30.00

☐ **June Allyson,** 1950/1952 Whitman book #119015, eight pages of clothes, uncut . . . . . . — 70.00 / 80.00 / 75.00

☐ **June Allyson,** 1953 Whitman book #1173:15, two dolls, eight pages of dresses and costumes, uncut . . . . — 70.00 / 80.00 / 75.00

☐ **June Allyson,** 1953 Whitman #1173, punch-out dolls, three pages of clothes, cut . . . . — 15.00 / 25.00 / 20.00

☐ **June Allyson,** 1953 Whitman book #1173, two dolls, assorted clothes, cut . . . . — 30.00 / 40.00 / 35.00

☐ **June Allyson,** 1957 Whitman book #2089, two dolls, six pages of clothes, uncut . . . . — 70.00 / 80.00 / 75.00

☐ **June Allyson,** 1960s Watkins/Strathemore book #1820, two statuette dolls, one in green, one in pink and gray, assorted clothes, uncut — 60.00 / 70.00 / 65.00

☐ **June Bride,** by Art Tanchon, 1946 Stephens Company book #136, uncut . . . . — 18.00 / 22.00 / 20.00

	Current Price Range		P/Y Average

☐ **June Bride,** by Art Tanchon, c. 1940s, six dolls cut from front and back covers, numerous outfits, cut 8.00 12.00 10.00

☐ **June and Stu Erwin with Jackie and Joyce,** stars from (Trouble With Father), 1954 Saalfield book #159210, thin cover, uncut 40.00 50.00 45.00

☐ **Jungletown Jamboree,** Samuel Lowe, uncut 2.00 4.00 3.00

☐ **Junior Miss,** 1942 Saalfield book #250, large dolls, uncut 18.00 22.00 20.00

☐ **Junior Prom,** 1942 Saalfield, uncut 10.00 18.00 14.00

☐ **Karen Goes To College,** 1955 Merrill, uncut .. 5.00 10.00 8.00

☐ **Kate Greenaway Paper Dolls,** by Kathy Albert, four dolls, twenty-eight costumes as created by Kate Greenaway, Victorian England styles, uncut 2.00 6.00 4.00

☐ **Kathie, Sallie and Mimi,** three statuette dolls, bathing suits and outfits, cut 4.00 10.00 8.00

☐ **Keepsake Folio—Mini Doll,** 1964 Samuel Lowe, uncut 5.00 10.00 7.00

☐ **Keepsake Folio—Trudy Doll,** 1964 Samuel Lowe, uncut 15.00 20.00 16.00

☐ **Kelly Sisters,** 1944 Saalfield book #2466, reprint of Shirley Temple book #1783–1939, thin cover, cut 30.00 40.00 35.00

☐ **Kewpies,** 1963, large-sized Skootles on cover, two smaller kewpies on back cover, assorted clothes, uncut 20.00 30.00 25.00

☐ **Kewpies in Kewpieville,** 1966 Saalfield, Rose O/Niel's dolls 16.00 24.00 20.00

☐ **Kewpie Kin,** by Joseph Kallus, 1967 Saalfield book #4413, punch-out, wrap-around dresses, blue cover, uncut 12.00 18.00 14.00

☐ **Kiddie Circus,** Saalfield, uncut 2.00 6.00 4.00

☐ **Little Ballerina,** 1969 Whitman book #1963, four dolls, assorted outfits, comes in folder, uncut 2.00 8.00 5.00

☐ **Little Brothers and Sisters,** 1953 Whitman, four dolls, assorted outfits 2.00 8.00 5.00

☐ **Little Cousins,** 1940 Samuel Lowe, uncut 5.00 10.00 8.00

☐ **Little Dolls,** 1972 Samuel Lowe 2.00 4.00 3.00

☐ **Little Fairy,** 1951 Merrill book #154715, four children with assorted costumes, uncut 20.00 30.00 25.00

☐ **Little Fairy,** 1951 Merrill book #1547, four dolls, assorted costumes, cut 12.00 18.00 14.00

☐ **Little Folks Dolls Set,** c. 1900s, Milton Bradley #4727, three True-Life dolls—two older girls and one young girl, three sheets of colored clothing, twenty-five sheets of clothes to color, uncut ... 60.00 70.00 65.00

☐ **Little Girls,** 1969 Samuel Lowe, uncut 2.00 4.00 3.00

☐ **Little Kitten to Dress,** 1942 Samuel Lowe, uncut 10.00 16.00 13.00

☐ **Little Joy San,** McCalls, October 1919, one doll, Japanese girl, dress, toy, lantern 4.00 8.00 6.00

	Current Price Range		P/Y Average

	Current Price Range		P/Y Average
☐ **sorted outfits, uncut**	12.00	18.00	14.00
☐ **Party Time,** 1952 Whitman	5.00	10.00	8.00
☐ **Pat Boone,** 1959 Whitman book #1968, two statuette dolls in folder, assorted clothes, uncut	30.00	40.00	35.00
☐ **Pat Boone,** 1959 Whitman #1985, cut	20.00	30.00	25.00
☐ **Patches and Petunia,** by Betty Bell Rea, 1937 Saalfield book #2160, large doll, assorted clothes, cut	12.00	18.00	14.00
☐ **Patchwork,** 1971 Saalfield, uncut	2.00	6.00	4.00
☐ **Patchy Annie,** 1962 Saalfield, uncut	2.00	6.00	4.00
☐ **Pat Crowley,** 1955 Whitman book #2050, two dolls, eight pages of clothes, uncut	60.00	70.00	65.00
☐ **Patience and Prudence,** 1959 Abbott book #1807, two dolls, assorted outfits, thin cover, uncut	30.00	40.00	35.00
☐ **Patti Doll Book,** 1961 Samuel Lowe, cut	2.00	4.00	3.00
☐ **Pat The Stand Up Doll With Front and Back Dresses,** 1946 Lowe book #1042, assorted clothes, uncut	30.00	40.00	35.00
☐ **Patti Page,** 1958 Abbott book #1804, two dolls, assorted outfits, thin cover, uncut	30.00	40.00	35.00
☐ **Patty Duke,** 1964 Whitman #1991, two dolls, folder, cut	10.00	18.00	14.00
☐ **Patty Duke,** 1965 Whitman book #1991:59, two dolls, six pages of punch-out clothes, uncut ...	45.00	55.00	50.00
☐ **Polly Pal,** 1976 Samuel Lowe, uncut	2.00	4.00	3.00
☐ **Preschool,** 1958, Saalfield, uncut	5.00	10.00	8.00
☐ **Pretty As A Rose,** 1963 Saalfield, uncut	5.00	10.00	8.00
☐ **Prince And Princess,** Saalfield book #4464, combination coloring book and paper dolls, punch-outs, horse and rider, medieval costumes, uncut	30.00	40.00	35.00
☐ **Princess Diana Paper Doll Book of Fashion,** by Clarissa Harlow and Mary Anna Bedford, numerous outfits—formal and informal—for Princess Diana and Prince Charles, including Emmanuel wedding gown, forty-page book, 9″ x 11″	5.00	10.00	8.00
☐ **Prom Home Permanent,** 1952 Samuel Lowe, uncut	10.00	18.00	14.00
☐ **Puppy And Kitty Cutouts,** 1938 Florence Salter, twenty-one pieces of clothing	10.00	18.00	14.00
☐ **Queen Elizabeth I Paper Dolls,** Bellerophon, authentic costumes with great detail, to be colored, uncut	2.00	6.00	4.00
☐ **Quiz Kids,** 1942 Saalfield, uncut	25.00	35.00	30.00
☐ **Raggedy Ann,** by Ethel Hays Simms, Saalfield book #369, thin cover, uncut	20.00	30.00	25.00
☐ **Raggedy Ann,** 1970 Whitman	2.00	6.00	4.00
☐ **Raggedy Ann and Raggedy Andy,** 1961 book #1728, two dolls, yellow cover, uncut	8.00	12.00	10.00

	Current Price Range		P/Y Average

☐ **Raggedy Ann And Raggedy Andy,** by Ethel Hays Simms, 1961 Saalfield book #2715, both Raggedies on front cover, Marcella on back, uncut 20.00 30.00 25.00

☐ **Raggedy Ann And Raggedy Andy,** by Ethel H. Simms, coloring and paper doll book, 1944 Saalfield book #4409, Marcella and the Raggedies, uncut 30.00 40.00 35.00

☐ **Raggedy Ann and Raggedy Andy Sticker Kit Circus,** 1941, #546, sticker pictures to make the Raggedies, animals, and clown 15.00 25.00 20.00

☐ **Ranch Family,** 1957 Merrill, uncut 5.00 10.00 8.00

☐ **Rave Doll Dressing Book,** England, possibly based on T.V. show (The Avengers), uncut ... 10.00 15.00 12.00

☐ **Ricky Nelson,** 1959 Whitman book #2081, two dolls, six pages of clothes, uncut 45.00 55.00 50.00

☐ **Ricky Nelson,** 1959 Whitman #2081, punch-out dolls, assorted outfits, cut 10.00 18.00 14.00

☐ **Ride A Pony-Judy And Jill,** 1944 Merrill, uncut 5.00 10.00 8.00

☐ **Rita Hayworth,** 1942 Merrill book #3478, two dolls, assorted outfits, uncut 65.00 75.00 70.00

☐ **Rita Hayworth,** 1942 Merrill book #3478, two dolls, with thirteen outfits for one and twelve outfits for the other, cut 10.00 18.00 14.00

☐ **Robin Hood,** 1973 Walt Disney, press-out finger puppets, scenery and castle, uncut 12.00 18.00 14.00

☐ **Robin Hood And Maid Marian,** Saalfield book #2784, assorted costumes, die-cut covers, uncut 40.00 50.00 45.00

☐ **School Friends,** 1955–60 Merrill book #1556, three dolls—Linda, Bobbie, and Diane, dresses and cowgirl suits, uncut 12.00 18.00 14.00

☐ **School Girl,** 1942 Saalfield book #2400, large dolls, assorted clothes, uncut 30.00 40.00 35.00

☐ **Schoolmates,** 1947 Saalfield, uncut 8.00 12.00 10.00

☐ **Sesame Street Characters,** 1976 Whitman, Big Bird, Oscar, Cookie Monster, and more 2.00 8.00 6.00

☐ **Seven And Seventeen,** 1954 Merrill book #3441, four dolls, assorted clothes, cut 12.00 18.00 14.00

☐ **Seven Children,** by Queen Holden, large assortment of clothes, cut 40.00 50.00 45.00

☐ **Shari Lewis,** 1958 Saalfield, uncut 15.00 25.00 20.00

☐ **Shari Lewis And Her Puppets,** 1960 Saalfield, uncut 5.00 10.00 8.00

☐ **Sheree North,** 1957 Saalfield book #1728, front and back dolls, four pages of dresses, thin cover, uncut 45.00 55.00 50.00

☐ **Sherlock Bones,** 1955 Samuel Lowe, uncut .. 2.00 4.00 3.00

☐ **Sherry and Terry,** Lowe book #1847, Kewpie-style dolls, uncut 4.00 10.00 8.00

☐ **Shirley Temple,** advertising give-away, c. 1930s, front and back doll, blue plaid dress, white collar, black tie 20.00 30.00 25.00

	Current Price Range		P/Y Average

☐ **Shirley Temple,** 1934 Saalfield book #2112, four dolls, assorted clothes, numerous accessories, uncut 70.00 80.00 75.00

☐ **Shirley Temple,** 1934 Saalfield book #2112, four dolls, assorted outfits, cut 30.00 40.00 35.00

☐ **Shirley Temple,** 1937 Saalfield book #1761, two toddler dolls, two dresses, cut 30.00 40.00 35.00

☐ **Shirley Temple,** die-cut 1942 teenage set, two dolls, yellow formal, assorted outfits, thin cover, uncut 125.00 175.00 150.00

☐ **Shirley Temple,** c. 1950s Gabriel #300, statuette doll, snap-on clothes, real picture faces, numerous outfits, cut 20.00 30.00 25.00

☐ **Shirley Temple,** 1958 Saalfield book #5110, statuette doll, assorted dresses, folder, cut 40.00 50.00 45.00

☐ **Shirley Temple,** 1976 Whitman book #1986, one doll, assorted clothes, pink tote bag for clothes, uncut 8.00 12.00 10.00

☐ **Shirley Temple—Her Movie Wardrobe,** 1938, one doll in pink slip, assorted outfits, cut 50.00 60.00 55.00

☐ **Sparkle Plenty,** baby from the Dick Tracy comic strip, 1948 .... 20.00 30.00 25.00

☐ **Sports Time,** 1952 Whitman book #2090, blonde doll in white slip, uncut 12.00 18.00 14.00

☐ **Square Dance,** 1950 Saalfield #2717, five dolls, six pages of costumes, uncut 10.00 18.00 14.00

☐ **Stand Up Dolls,** c. 1960s Artcraft, six dolls ... 2.00 6.00 4.00

☐ **Star Babies,** 1945 Merrill, uncut 12.00 18.00 14.00

☐ **Star Time,** c. 1960s book #1317, reprint of book from 1950s, six dolls, parts of Butterfly Ballet and Ice Carnival, assorted costumes, uncut 12.00 18.00 16.00

☐ **Star Trek,** 1975 Saalfield book #C2272, activity book, punch-out, stand-up dolls, Captain Kirk, Mr. Spock, Dr. McCoy, Lt. Uhura, and Sulu 4.00 10.00 8.00

PAPERWEIGHTS

TYPES: Millefiori weights contain arrays of small ornamental glass beads or stems arranged in a striking pattern. They are quite colorful. Sulfides are ceramic relief plaques encased in glass. Many other artistic types of paperweights were made, and souvenir paperweights featuring some company or place are also common, though not as desirable.

PERIOD: Paperweights were not seen before the 1700s; they are a recent item. The most important paperweights were made in the 1800s.

MAKERS: Clichy, Baccarat and St. Louis are all important producers of artistic glass paperweights. Prices for famous makers like these are high, although less known craftsmen can also produce exquisite items.

MATERIALS: For the most part, glass is the medium used for artistic paperweights. Functional weights are rarely made of metal.

COMMENTS: The weight of the specimen is not an indication of quality. Rather, the name of the maker and the level of artistry evident determine the value of a paperweight.

ADDITIONAL TIPS: Famous makers like Clichy, Baccarat and St. Louis sometimes put their initials on one of the canes in a millefiori weight. This makes certain specimens easy to identify.

	Current Price Range		P/Y Average
☐ **Baccarat,** millefiori canes, 1847, 2½″ diameter	600.00	660.00	630.00
☐ **Baccarat,** Primrose, pink, red and green, 3″ diameter	200.00	250.00	225.00
☐ **Baccarat,** sulfide, Eleanor Roosevelt	50.00	100.00	75.00
☐ **Baccarat,** sulfide, John Kennedy	225.00	275.00	250.00
☐ **Baccarat,** sulfide, Will Rogers	150.00	200.00	175.00
☐ **Banford, Ray,** stylized roses, c. 1974	275.00	325.00	300.00
☐ **Bonnel,** pine key	40.00	60.00	50.00
☐ **Coca-Cola,** blue lettering, dome	13.00	19.00	16.00
☐ **Crider,** most designs, large	40.00	50.00	45.00
☐ **Crider,** most designs, small	25.00	35.00	30.00
☐ **Davis, Jim,** bell shape, swirl design	14.00	18.00	16.00
☐ **Davis, Jim,** bird shape, large	10.00	15.00	12.50

	Current Price Range		P/Y Average
☐ **Davis, Jim,** bird shape, small	5.00	7.00	6.00
☐ **Davis, Jim,** five flowers in vase	20.00	28.00	24.00
☐ **Gentile,** bubble, clear, small	5.00	8.00	6.50
☐ **Gentile,** butterfly, small	13.00	15.00	14.00
☐ **Gentile,** cabbage leaf	16.00	18.00	17.00
☐ **Gentile,** Elks lodge	14.00	16.00	15.00
☐ **Gentile,** five petaled flower, colored, small	7.00	8.00	7.50
☐ **Gentile,** millefiori butterfly and flower	40.00	50.00	45.00
☐ **Gentile,** millefiori heart	20.00	39.00	30.00
☐ **Gentile,** millefiori pinwheel	30.00	40.00	35.00
☐ **Gentile,** mushroom, colored, small	12.00	16.00	14.00
☐ **Gentile,** Remember Pearl Harbor	22.00	30.00	26.00
☐ **Gentile,** sign of the Zodiac	14.00	18.00	16.00
☐ **Gentile,** spotted pattern	12.00	14.00	13.00
☐ **Gentile,** tear drop bubble, clear	13.00	14.00	13.50
☐ **Gentile,** three lilies	13.00	15.00	14.00
☐ **Gentile,** white goose	15.00	20.00	17.50
☐ **Hamon, Bob,** millefiori cane weight, signed . . .	70.00	80.00	75.00
☐ **Kaziun, Charles,** miniature, floral motif, pedestal, 2" high	400.00	430.00	415.00
☐ **New England Glass Co.,** posy bouquet, millefiori canes, 2⅝" diameter	440.00	500.00	470.00
☐ **Oriental,** flower, elongated pedestal, 5½" tall	25.00	31.00	28.00
☐ **Oriental,** open rose, 3½" tall	25.00	30.00	27.50
☐ **Oriental,** stemmed apple, 2⅞" tall	15.00	22.00	18.50
☐ **Oriental,** two frogs, 4" tall	20.00	26.00	23.00
☐ **Perthshire,** sunflower, 1979, 3⅛" diameter . . .	140.00	170.00	155.00
☐ **St. Clair,** apple, crimped	15.00	20.00	17.50
☐ **St. Clair,** bell with five flowers	10.00	14.00	12.00
☐ **St. Clair,** crimped	8.00	12.00	10.00
☐ **St. Clair,** floral design with five flowers	14.00	20.00	17.00
☐ **St. Louis,** dahlia, star cut base, 2⅛" diameter	1000.00	1100.00	1050.00
☐ **St. Louis,** fruit in a basket, 2⅞" diameter	2000.00	2200.00	2100.00
☐ **St. Louis,** King Tut mask, 1979	270.00	330.00	300.00
☐ **Tiffany,** favrile, red sides with internal yellow blossoms, 1906	4500.00	5500.00	5000.00
☐ **Tiffany,** favrile scarab, 4½" long, c. 1900	440.00	600.00	520.00
☐ **Vandermark,** latticinio design	50.00	60.00	55.00
☐ **Ysart Paul,** clematis in lattininio basket, 2⅞" diameter	500.00	600.00	550.00
☐ **Ysart, Paul,** fish with multicolored sea bed, 3" diameter	450.00	550.00	500.00

PATTERN GLASS

ORIGIN: Glass historians are still undecided as to whether the Americans or the British first invented pressed glass. Small objects and feet for footed bowls were first hand pressed in England in the early 1800s, but this method was crude compared to the mechanical process which later evolved. Pressing glass with machinery to produce a wide range of glass objects appears to have originated in America. Glass companies began producing pressed glass in matching tableware sets during the 1840s.

COMMENTS: Although identification of pieces is mainly by pattern name, the novice collector will have some confusion in this area. This is due to the fact that most of the original names have been discarded by advanced collectors who have renamed the pattern in descriptive terms. For the most part these collectors have found it impossible to attribute most patterns to a particular maker.

ADDITIONAL TIPS: Although pattern glass was originally made to imitate cut glass, you will have no problem differentiating one from the other. Despite the similarities, pattern glass lacks the deep faceted appearance of cut—the edges of the patterns look rounded, the earlier pieces contain many imperfections—bubbles, lumps, impurities, and sometimes cloudiness.

MARKS: Manufacturers' marks are exceedingly rare and there are few catalogs available from the period before 1850. By studying the old catalogs that do exist, along with shards found at old factory sites, some sketchy information has been provided. But because patterns were so quickly copied by the competition, absolute verification of the manufacturer is impossible.

REPRODUCTIONS: Reproductions can pose a definite problem to the beginning pattern glass collector. Two very popular patterns, Bellflower and Daisy and Button, have been reproduced extensively. With careful, informed scrutiny, you will be able to detect the dullness and lack of sparkle characteristic of remakes. If the reproduction was made from a new mold (formed from an original object), the details will not possess the clarity and preciseness of the original article.

RECOMMENDED READING: For more in-depth information on pattern glass you may refer to *The Official Price Guide to Glassware* and *The Official Identification Guide to Glassware,* published by The House of Collectibles.

	Current Price Range		P/Y Average

BAKEWELL BLOCK

❏ **Celery**	100.00	107.00	96.00
❏ **Champagne**	100.00	108.00	95.00
❏ **Creamer**	165.00	175.00	160.00
❏ **Decanter**	135.00	145.00	131.00
❏ **Spooner**	70.00	80.00	60.00
❏ **Sugar Bowl,** covered	90.00	100.00	80.00
❏ **Tumbler,** bar	90.00	100.00	81.00
❏ **Whiskey Tumbler,** handle	105.00	115.00	100.00
❏ **Wine**	70.00	80.00	64.00

CANADIAN

❏ **Butter,** with cover	60.00	70.00	62.50
❏ **Celery**	45.00	55.00	47.50
❏ **Compote,** high, with cover	65.00	75.00	67.50
❏ **Compote,** low	45.00	65.00	55.00
❏ **Cordial**	42.00	52.00	42.50
❏ **Creamer**	42.00	52.00	42.50
❏ **Goblet**	55.00	65.00	57.50
❏ **Jam Jar**	50.00	60.00	55.00
❏ **Milk Pitcher,** large	85.00	95.00	87.50
❏ **Milk Pitcher,** small	70.00	80.00	72.50
❏ **Plate,** diameter 6½″	48.00	60.00	47.50
❏ **Plate,** diameter 7½″	60.00	70.00	65.50
❏ **Sauce,** flat	18.00	21.00	16.50
❏ **Sauce,** footed	22.00	32.00	22.50
❏ **Spooner**	40.00	50.00	42.50
❏ **Sugar,** with cover	65.00	75.00	67.50
❏ **Water Pitcher,** large	90.00	100.00	95.00
❏ **Water Pitcher,** small	70.00	80.00	72.50
❏ **Wine Glass**	50.00	60.00	52.50

DIAMOND THUMBPRINT

❏ **Butter Dish,** covered	147.00	157.00	145.00
❏ **Cake Stand**	220.00	250.00	222.00
❏ **Celery**	180.00	190.00	175.00
❏ **Champagne Glass,** rare	230.00	250.00	220.00
❏ **Creamer**	125.00	140.00	120.00
❏ **Compote,** footed, scalloped edge	42.00	52.00	42.00
❏ **Decanter,** no stopper, pint size	75.00	80.00	75.00
❏ **Decanter,** original stopped, quart size	150.00	165.00	150.00
❏ **Goblet,** rare	350.00	365.00	345.00
❏ **Honey Dish**	17.00	22.00	15.00
❏ **Sauce Dish**	11.00	16.00	11.00
❏ **Spooner**	80.00	90.00	75.00
❏ **Sugar Bowl,** covered	150.00	170.00	155.00
❏ **Tumbler**	100.00	110.00	95.00

	Current Price Range		P/Y Average
☐ **Waste Bowl**	85.00	95.00	80.00
☐ **Water Pitcher,** rare	350.00	370.00	362.00
☐ **Whiskey Tumbler,** handled	275.00	300.00	280.00
☐ **Wine Glass,** rare	220.00	240.00	205.00
☐ **Wine Jug,** places for holding glasses	750.00	950.00	800.00

FLUTE

☐ **Ale Glass**	30.00	40.00	28.00
☐ **Bottle,** bitters	30.00	37.00	28.00
☐ **Bowl,** scalloped edge	30.00	38.00	27.00
☐ **Candlesticks,** pair	40.00	50.00	37.00
☐ **Champagne**	30.00	35.00	27.00
☐ **Compote,** open, diameter 8″	32.00	38.00	30.00
☐ **Decanter,** quart	50.00	56.00	47.00
☐ **Egg Cup,** single	17.00	21.00	13.00
☐ **Egg Cup,** double	30.00	35.00	28.00
☐ **Goblet**	30.00	40.00	25.00
☐ **Honey Dish**	16.00	21.00	13.00
☐ **Lamp**	70.00	77.00	67.00
☐ **Mug**	50.00	60.00	48.00
☐ **Pitcher,** water	60.00	70.00	65.00
☐ **Salt,** footed	20.00	25.00	17.00
☐ **Sauce,** flat	15.50	20.00	12.00
☐ **Sugar Bowl,** open	27.00	35.00	25.00
☐ **Tumbler**	28.00	34.00	27.00
☐ **Whiskey,** handled	25.00	33.00	23.00
☐ **Wine**	25.00	30.00	23.00

LEE

☐ **Celery Dish**	110.00	120.00	105.00
☐ **Champagne Glass**	140.00	148.00	135.00
☐ **Creamer**	130.00	140.00	125.00
☐ **Decanter**	75.00	90.00	75.00
☐ **Goblet**	135.00	145.00	130.00
☐ **Sugar Bowl,** covered	130.00	140.00	125.00
☐ **Tumbler**	100.00	110.00	96.00

MINERVA

☐ **Butter,** with cover	110.00	115.00	112.50
☐ **Cake Plate,** diameter 12″	115.00	125.00	117.50
☐ **Compote,** high	85.00	110.00	95.00
☐ **Compote,** low	75.00	100.00	78.00
☐ **Compote,** with lid	70.00	75.00	72.50
☐ **Creamer**	65.00	85.00	67.50
☐ **Goblet,** small	75.00	85.00	75.50
☐ **Goblet,** large	90.00	100.00	95.00
☐ **Jam Jar,** with cover	85.00	95.00	87.50
☐ **Plate,** tab handled	65.00	75.00	67.50
☐ **Platter,** oval	50.00	60.00	52.50
☐ **Pickle Dish,** oval, says "Love's Request is Pickles"	40.00	50.00	42.50

	Current Price Range		P/Y Average
☐ **Relish Dish,** three compartment	35.00	45.00	37.50
☐ **Sauce,** flat	25.00	35.00	27.50
☐ **Sauce,** footed	30.00	35.00	32.50
☐ **Spooner**	40.00	50.00	42.50
☐ **Sugar**	75.00	85.00	77.50
☐ **Sugar,** with cover	90.00	100.00	92.50
☐ **Water Pitcher**	125.00	135.00	130.00

PICKET

☐ **Butter,** with cover	70.00	80.00	75.00
☐ **Celery**	50.00	60.00	50.00
☐ **Compote,** high, with cover	60.00	70.00	65.00
☐ **Compote,** low	45.00	55.00	47.50
☐ **Creamer**	47.50	57.00	49.00
☐ **Goblet**	55.00	60.00	57.50
☐ **Jam Jar**	46.00	52.00	46.00
☐ **Pickle Dish,** with cover	45.00	55.00	47.50
☐ **Salt**	20.00	30.00	25.00
☐ **Spooner**	30.00	40.00	28.00
☐ **Sugar,** with cover	52.00	55.00	53.00
☐ **Toothpick**	35.00	40.00	37.50
☐ **Tumbler**	40.00	50.00	42.50
☐ **Water Pitcher**	65.00	75.00	67.50
☐ **Wine Glass**	32.50	42.00	35.00

SCROLL

☐ **Butter**	30.00	40.00	32.50
☐ **Celery**	30.00	40.00	35.00
☐ **Compote,** high	25.00	30.00	32.50
☐ **Compote,** low	20.00	30.00	22.50
☐ **Creamer**	27.50	32.50	27.50
☐ **Egg Cup**	30.00	40.00	32.50
☐ **Goblet**	17.00	22.00	17.50
☐ **Relish Bowl**	20.00	30.00	22.50
☐ **Salt**	17.00	22.00	17.50
☐ **Sauce,** flat	12.00	14.00	11.00
☐ **Sauce,** footed	20.00	30.00	25.00
☐ **Spooner**	22.00	30.00	24.00
☐ **Sugar,** with cover	30.00	40.00	32.50
☐ **Water Pitcher**	40.00	60.00	45.00
☐ **Wine Glass**	22.00	32.50	24.00

PENS AND PENCILS

TYPES: Pens can be either dip pens, the earliest type, fountain pens or ball-point pens. Dip pens are the style of modern calligraphy pens: a pointed nib is dipped in ink and used quickly. Fountain pens contain their own ink supply, as do ball-points. Pencils are either traditional or mechanical.

PERIOD: The fountain pen, which is the most collectible type, experienced its heyday in the 1920s and 1930s.

ORIGIN: The fountain pen was invented in the 1880s by Lewis Waterman.

MAKERS: The big names in pen and pencil production are Waterman, Parker, Conklin, Sheaffer and Wahl. All of these companies produced fine pens that are currently in great demand by collectors.

COMMENTS: As mentioned before, few ball-point or dip pens are collected by modern enthusiasts. Also, collectors focus on post-1880 specimens.

ADDITIONAL TIPS: Rarity and condition are very important; the second more so than the first. Historical importance may also play a part, though only in isolated instances.

	Current Price Range		P/Y Average
☐ **Autopoint,** gold filled, 1930s	12.00	18.00	15.00
☐ **Blaisdell,** green, gold plated trim, pencil, 1920s	10.00	20.00	15.00
☐ **Century,** Durapoint, red woodgrain, marbeled, 1928	125.00	175.00	150.00
☐ **Chilton,** cream and gold, marbled, gold plated trim, golf pencil, 1930	20.00	30.00	25.00
☐ **Conklin,** 2P black chased hard rubber, crescent filler, 1918	25.00	40.00	32.50
☐ **Conklin,** Endura, orange, lever filler, gold plated trim, 1920s	30.00	40.00	35.00
☐ **Conklin,** Nozak, gray and red pearl, gold plated trim, 1931	25.00	45.00	35.00

	Current Price Range		P/Y Average
☐ **Cross,** 1888	60.00	70.00	65.00
☐ **Doric,** pearly lined nickle plated trim, pencil, 1935	20.00	40.00	35.00
☐ **Dunn,** sterling silver, fine point, 1922	110.00	150.00	130.00
☐ **Eversharp,** green, chrome gold banded cap, 1951	25.00	35.00	30.00
☐ **Eversharp,** Skyline, black, 1945	15.00	20.00	17.50
☐ **Lincoln,** red, marbled, 1926	25.00	40.00	32.50
☐ **Majestic,** black and cream, 1930s	25.00	35.00	30.00
☐ **Parker,** # 51, Blue Diamond, black, gold plated trim, Lustraloy cap, 1945	32.00	52.00	42.00
☐ **Parker,** Deluxe Challenger, gold plated trim, 1930s	30.00	40.00	35.00
☐ **Parker,** Duofold, gold pearl and black, gold plated trim, 1939	50.00	60.00	55.00
☐ **Parker,** Duofold Sr., Big Red, gold plated trim, 1924	100.00	150.00	125.00
☐ **Parker,** Duofold Jr., black, gold plated trim, 1927	35.00	40.00	37.50
☐ **Parker,** gold filled metal, button filler, 1926 . . .	50.00	70.00	60.00
☐ **Parker,** Lady Duofold, red, gold plated trim . . .	30.00	50.00	40.00
☐ **Parker,** Pastel, blue, gold plated trim, 1926 . . .	35.00	45.00	40.00
☐ **Parker,** silver plate, pencil, 1921	60.00	70.00	65.00
☐ **Parker,** Vacumatic, black, 1947	25.00	35.00	30.00
☐ **Peerless,** black and cream, gold plated trim, lever filler, 1930	20.00	30.00	25.00
☐ **Peerless,** lever filler, gold plated trim, black veined cream, 1920s	18.00	28.00	23.00
☐ **Pilot,** black lacquer and hand painted design, gold fittings, Japanese	50.00	70.00	60.00
☐ **Rider,** black, eye dropper filler, # 6 nib Mabie Todd	50.00	100.00	75.00
☐ **Royal,** Parker Duofold imitation, yellow, gold plated trim, 1928	35.00	45.00	40.00
☐ **Sanford and Bennett,** black, eye dropper filler, 1904	30.00	50.00	40.00
☐ **Sheaffer,** 5–30, black, lever filler, gold plated trim, ladies', 1930s	15.00	25.00	20.00
☐ **Sheaffer,** Balance, pearl and black marbled, pencil, 1931	40.00	60.00	50.00
☐ **Sheaffer,** black, gold plated trim, pencil, 1925	30.00	45.00	37.50
☐ **Sheaffer,** Lifetime, black and pearl, lever filler, gold plated trim, 1932	90.00	110.00	100.00
☐ **Sheaffer,** sterling silver, early feed, ladies, lever filler, 1916	40.00	50.00	45.00
☐ **Sheaffer,** Triumph, striped, plunger filled, 1946	30.00	45.00	37.50
☐ **Swann,** solid gold 14K, fine point, 1920s	60.00	80.00	70.00
☐ **Wahl,** # 4, gold filled metal, 1924	80.00	100.00	90.00
☐ **Wahl,** lever filler, gold filled, 1926	35.00	45.00	40.00
☐ **Wahl-Eversharp,** gold filled metal, pen and pencil set, 1924	100.00	130.00	115.00
☐ **Waterman,** # 52, black chased hard rubber, nickle plated trim, 1923	20.00	30.00	25.00

	Current Price Range		P/Y Average
☐ **Waterman,** #412, orange with silver overlay, eye dropper filler, 1905	330.00	370.00	350.00
☐ **Waterman,** #452, gothic sterling silver, 1925	120.00	130.00	125.00
☐ **Waterman,** #554, lower end covered, solid 14K gold, gothic, 1928	430.00	470.00	450.00
☐ **Waterman,** #5116, Ink View, gray pearl, gold plated trim, 1939	40.00	50.00	45.00
☐ **Waterman,** black, chased hard rubber, pencil, 1920	15.00	25.00	20.00
☐ **Waterman,** Taperite, gold filled cap, 1946	20.00	30.00	25.00

PHONOGRAPHS

DESCRIPTION: An instrument that reproduces sound by the use of a needle playing on a cylinder record or flat disc.

PERIOD: Thomas Edison invented the phonograph in 1877 and was issued a patent in 1878.

MAKER: There were several major manufacturers of phonographs including Columbia Phonograph Company, North American Phonograph Company and Berliner Gramophone Company which later became RCA Victor. Lesser known companies which produced phonographs included Vitaphone, Euphonic and Echophone.

COMMENTS: Although all types of phonographs are valuable, collectors especially seek those with the visible sound horn. Collectors also search for obscure company's phonographs.

ADDITIONAL TIPS: For more information, consult *The Official Price Guide to Music Collectibles,* published by The House of Collectibles.

☐ **Apollo (Disc),** table model, plain oak case, outside blue fluted metal (painted), horn, crank wind, plays 78rpm records, Apollo, Jr. reproducer (sound box) European maker	250.00	360.00	340.00

Edison Triumph, *with polyphone attachment*

	Current Price Range		P/Y Average
☐ **Apollo Floor Model (Disc),** highly styled fruitwood case, curved legs, storage for records, cover lifts to reveal turntable, nickel plated exposed parts, European maker	285.00	390.00	275.00
☐ **Adler (Disc) "Box Camera"** style portable, tone arm fits into opening in cover, "horn" is drawer in the cover which opens out on one side to form a horn, turntable is three spokes which open out to hold record, hand crank, 7″ x 4″ x 7″	125.00	210.00	170.00
☐ **Aretino (Disc),** table model, rear mount horn bracket, 3″ spindle, morning glory horn	250.00	520.00	375.00
☐ **Aux-E-To-Phone,** c. 1903 (Disc), sold in U.S. by Victor, mahogany floor cabinet with carved and gold decoration, uncovered 12″ turntable on top with outside brass bell horn, operates on Electro-Pneumatic principle, reed sound box, motor drive, triple spring (simpler case variations)	2500.00	3550.00	3200.00

	Current Price Range		P/Y Average

(EMILE) BERLINER GRAM-O-PHONES (Canada) F.L.

☐ **Berliner "Standard" Gram-O-Phone Type A (Disc),** simple oak case on wood base, top crank wind, 7" turntable, plays 7" and 10" Berliner records, brass bell horn 16" long, nickel plated metal parts, metal horn support with wood "tone arm", reproducer attached at end of tone arm and horn (Clark/Johnson Reproducer), very similar to Victor Type "B" Trademark machine **1500.00   2750.00   2400.00**

☐ **Berliner "Ideal" Type B (Disc),** oak case with heavy base and top moulding, side crank wind, double spring, 7" turntable, plays 7" and 10" records, 16" brass bell horn, nickel plated metal parts, wood and metal horn support and "tone arm" **1000.00   1300.00   1200.00**

☐ **Brunswick (Disc),** console floor model deluxe, "The Beaux Arts", walnut case, decorative moulding, 45" high, electrically powered, on legs, turntable on one side, storage for discs on the other. (Brunswick made many period cabinet styles) **350.00   450.00   400.00**

☐ **Brunswick Model 200,** c. 1923 (Disc). Floor model oak (mahogany) disc phonograph, oval shaped grill opening with fret work, storage in base for discs, 12" turntable, reproducer head rotates to play either lateral or vertical cut records (inside horn). Case variations in floor models . .   **100.00   250.00   200.00**

☐ **Busy-Bee Grand,** c. 1905 (Disc). Oak, simple case table model with front mount horn support for large 8 petal Morning Glory horn (red or blue with gold), reproducer attached at end of horn (No "tone arm"), plays Busy-Bee records only. (Some variation in placement of horn and bracket and decal.) **350.00   575.00   420.00**

☐ **Busy-Bee "Queen"** c. 1906 (Cylinder). Oak case, plain, lyric reproducer, small ribbed horn (also: front crane supported ribbed horn), Busy-Bee decal on front, (see Columbia Jewel "Type BK") **350.00   450.00   400.00**

☐ **Cameraphone (Disc),** very small portable phonograph in the shape of an old box camera, leather covered case, simulated tortoise shell (resonator), horn, metal spoke turntable fold out, very compact, good volume (Variations in case, some wood, some covered in black material), plays 78 rpm discs **125.00   150.00   140.00**

CAPITOL PHONO LAMP

☐ **Capitol Phono Lamp (Disc),** metal base large table lamp, fringed shade opens up to reveal disc turntable and tone arm **500.00   1200.00   900.00**

	Current Price Range		P/Y Average

CARYOLA HAT BOX PHONOGRAPH

☐ **Caryola Hat Box Phonograph (Disc),** flat style rounded case portable disc phonograph ...... | 75.00 | 150.00 | 100.00 |

COLIBRE

☐ **Colibre "Box Camera" Portable (Disc),** black metal case .... | 100.00 | 150.00 | 130.00 |

☐ **Columbia Type A.** c. 1897 (cylinder). Oak case and cover (plain), nickel plated and black painted metal parts with gold and red decoration, open ended mandrel, small belled horn, plays 2-minute cylinder records, "Graphophone" decal, black reproducer, early version made in Washington, later in New York

☐ **Washington** .... | 400.00 | 600.00 | 520.00 |
☐ **New York** .... | 300.00 | 425.00 | 380.00 |

☐ **Columbia Type AA,** c. 1901 (cylinder). Small case, ornate mouldings, oak, large ribbon decal, exposed mechanism nickel plated, horizontally placed reproducer, 14" horn with bell, Eagle reproducer .... | 275.00 | 375.00 | 295.00 |

☐ **Columbia Type AB,** "McDonald Graphophone" (cylinder). Open works, key wind, mounted on oak base (fancy moulding and decoration) plays regular 2-minute cylinders and 5" Grand cylinders, 5" mandrel fits over the smaller one, nickel plated works and belled horn, Heavy Eagle, (later Model "D" reproducer) .... | 750.00 | 1250.00 | 900.00 |

☐ **Columbia Type AD,** c. 1901 (cylinder). Oak "Home Grand" cabinet, plays regular 2-minute cylinders and grand cylinders, 5" mandrel fits over 2" mandrel, nickel plated works, six spring motor (very, very rare), (see Columbia Home Grand for case description) .... | 1000.00 | 1500.00 | 1300.00 |

☐ **Columbia Type AF,** (cylinder). Plays concert and regular cylinders .... | 2000.00 | 3000.00 | 2650.00 |

☐ **Columbia Type AG** (see Grand AG and Concert Grand AG)

☐ **Columbia Eagle Type B,** c. 1897 cylinder. Open works mounted on oak base with cover, nickel plated mechanism, "Graphophone" decal on cover, double spring, plays 2-minute wax cylinders, Aluminum Eagle Reproducer, small black horn (no bell) or ear tubes .... | 250.00 | 500.00 | 400.00 |

☐ **Columbia Elite (Disc),** table model mahogany square shaped inside horn style, front grill flaps forward for volume control, top cover, aluminum tone arm, plays 78 rpm records .... | 100.00 | 150.00 | 130.00 |

☐ **Columbia Grafonola Type #25A (Disc),** c. 1920s, floor model, oak, 39½" high, triple spring, Garrand motor, 12" turntable, tone arm rotates

	Current Price Range		P/Y Average

on ball bearings, #7 reproducer, automatic brake, simple straight case lines, 5 shelf storage for discs, vertically louvered speaker grill . . . . . .

□ **Davis Corner Phonograph (Disc),** mahogany finish triangular shaped floor model disc phonograph, on high legs, top cover, cloth covered speaker on one side, wood tone arm, 12″ turntable . . . .

□ **Decca Junior Portable Style JC (Disc),** leather covered case with carrying handle, end of tone arm folds down from center of "Horn" in cover of case, 8″ turntable, exposed metal parts nickel plated (many variations of portables by Decca and other companies) . . . .

□ **Duplex Phonograph Company (Disc),** plain oak table model case style, corner columns, "Duplex" decal, two brass bell horns coupled to one reproducer, metal horn bracket, holds both horns, small turntable . . . .

□ **Edison Amberola Model IV,** c. 1913 (cylinder) floor model, Mission oak style, open shelf for storage under phonograph, single spring, traveling reproducer, belt driven, simple straight case and front grill . . . .

□ **Edison Amberola Model V,** c. 1912 (cylinder), table model with cover, simple case and grill, mahogany (oak), single spring, stationary mandrel, automatic stop, traveling reproducer connected to swivel arm, Diamond Model "B" reproducer, worm and gear driven . . . .

□ **Edison Amberola Model 50** (cylinder), table model, mahogany (or oak), wooden front grill, 15″ case, double spring, worm and gear driven, Diamond Model "C" reproducer . . . .

□ **Edison "Class M" Electric ("Victor"),** (Cylinder), early version of the Edison "Balmoral". 2-volt battery operated, table model, oak case, exposed metal parts finished in black with gilt decoration and nickel Edison Automatic Reproducer, recorder, shaving device, 14″ brass horn or two way hearing tube . . . .

Item	Current Price Range Low	Current Price Range High	P/Y Average
on ball bearings...	125.00	250.00	200.00
Davis Corner Phonograph	300.00	600.00	500.00
Decca Junior Portable	100.00	185.00	160.00
Duplex Phonograph Company	1000.00	1750.00	1500.00
Edison Amberola Model IV	650.00	850.00	775.00
Edison Amberola Model V	375.00	750.00	500.00
Edison Amberola Model 50	225.00	400.00	300.00
Edison "Class M" Electric	2750.00	4000.00	3400.00

PHOTOGRAPHS

TYPES: Photographs are usually one of four varieties: daguerreotypes, ambrotypes, tintypes or modern paper prints. Ambrotypes and tintypes are less valuable but are often collected. Three varieties of pictures made from negatives are original prints, later prints or reproductions. Original prints are those made by the photographer, or someone in his employ, shortly after taking the negative. Later prints are made from the original negative at a later date, sometimes fifty or more years later. Reproductions are made by making a new negative from the photo print. In most instances, original prints are most desired by collectors.

PERIOD: Photographs taken during the 1800s are most in demand by collectors. Early 1900s scenes, especially of the outdoor environment, are becoming more popular.

ORIGIN: The daguerroetype was invented in 1839 by Louis Daguerre.

MAKERS: Works by famous photographers such as Edward Curtis, Mathew Brady, Alfred Stieglitz and Carleton Watkins all command high prices in the collector market.

COMMENTS: Value is determined by age and subject matter. Of course the quality of the print in important; it must be in good condition to merit its full value.

TIPS: For further information, please refer to *The Official Price Guide to Paper Collectibles,* published by The House of Collectibles.

	Current Price Range		P/Y Average
☐ **Arbus, Diane,** "Bishop By The Sea, L.A. Cal.," silver print, matted, 14¾″ x 15″, 1964, printed after the photographer's death by Neil Selkirk, date unknown	350.00	400.00	375.00
☐ **Arbus, Diane,** "Parlor, Xmas, Levittown," 1962, silver print, signed, matted and framed, 12¾″ x 12¼″, 1962, the specific printing date unknown	1825.00	1925.00	1850.00

Engagement Picture,
sepia tones, Fox Studios,
Chicago, January, 1915,
$5.00-$10.00

	Current Price Range		P/Y Average
☐ **Avedon, Richard,** "Portrait of Buster Keaton," silver print, signed, matted and framed, this photograph was used in the book "Avedon" (1970), a collection of the photographer's works, 20″ x 24″, 1952, printed in 1970	2250.00	2750.00	2500.00
☐ **Bell, Charles M.,** "The Delegation of Sioux Chiefs to Ratify the Sale of Lands in Dakota to the U.S. Government," albumen print, arched top, mounted, framed, 12″ x 21″, December 1889, the specific date unknown	525.00	575.00	550.00
☐ **Bellocq, E. J.,** "Storyville Portrait," printing, out paper, mounted, matted and framed, 10″ x 8″, 1911–13, printed in the early 1970s by Friedlander	225.00	275.00	250.00
☐ **Booth, Edwin,** as Cardinal Richelieu, carte-de-visite by Sarony	17.00	23.00	19.00
☐ **Brandt, Bill,** "Race-Goers," silver print, mounted, signed, 13¼″ x 11½″, printed later, the specific date unknown	325.00	345.00	335.00
☐ **Brady (Mathew) Studio,** album containing 1,120 mounted prints on 119 pages, mostly carte-de-visite size, almost all identified, some measuring 8″ x 10″, includes 18 U.S. Presidents, 84 Union officers, 66 Confederate officers, 11 Confederate statesmen, 130 American statesmen and authors, 95 European statesmen and royalty, etc., small folio, full leather, c. 1860s	13000.00	17000.00	15000.00

	Current Price Range		P/Y Average

☐ **Brassaï,** "Conchita With an Admirer at the Place D'Italie," silver print, signed, 11½" x 9", 1930s, printed later, the specific date unknown **1550.00 1650.00 1600.00**

☐ **Brassaï,** "Lovers in a Park," silver print, signed, 12" x 9½", 1930s, printed later, the specific date unknown **950.00 1000.00 975.00**

☐ **Bravo, Manuel Alvarez,** "La Buena Fama Durmiendo," silver print, signed, matted, 7⅛" x 9½", 1938, printed later, the specific date unknown **550.00 600.00 575.00**

☐ **Brazil and Mexico,** album of 60 mounted photographs, folio, half leather, c. 1870 .... **150.00 200.00 175.00**

☐ **Briquet, A.,** group of 14 mounted photos, ranging from 5" x 8" to 8" x 10", showing indians, views of Mexico City, etc., c. 1875 .... **300.00 400.00 350.00**

☐ **British Snapshots,** album with over 100 small amateur snapshots, mostly 3½" x 4½", showing views of Oxford, Chester, Devonshire, etc., boards, back cover lacking **45.00 55.00 50.00**

☐ **Bunker Hill Monument,** carte-de-visite, historical information printed on reverse **9.00 12.00 10.00**

☐ **Business and Commerce,** collection of over 40 mounted photos showing shops, factories, work crews, wagons and other aspects of 19th-century American commerce, mostly from Connecticut, sizes 13" x 16" and smaller, mixed condition, c. 1880s–1910 .... **85.00 125.00 105.00**

☐ **Callahan, Harry,** "Eleanor, Chicago," silver print, signed, matted, 7⅜" x 7", 1948, printed later, the specific date unknown **480.00 530.00 505.00**

☐ **Callahan, Harry,** "Ivy Tentacles on Glass," silver print, signed, framed, 8" x 10", c. 1952, printed later, the specific date unknown **425.00 475.00 450.00**

☐ **Canada and Alaska,** group of 32 stereograms, some colored lithoprints, by various photographers, showing Yukon Gold Rush and other subjects, 3¼" x 7", mostly c. 1890s **45.00 65.00 55.00**

☐ **Cunningham, Imogen,** "Magnolia Blossom," silver print, mounted, matted, 10" x 12⅝", 1925, printed after the photographer's death in 1976 **425.00 475.00 450.00**

☐ **Cunningham, Imogen,** "Portrait of Alfred Stieglitz," silver print, mounted, signed, matted and framed, 9⅜" x 7⅜", 1934, printed later, probably in the 1970s **600.00 700.00 650.00**

☐ **Daguerreotype,** ninth-plate portrait of young man in tall silk hat, reverse side states "Boston Daguerreotype Co., Tyler & Co." Ad states, "Portraits, 25 cents & upwards. 600 Executed Daily, by the Double Camera, Two at a Pop. Beware of Imitators." c. late 1840s **56.00 84.00 65.00**

☐ **Daguerreotype,** quarter-plate portrait of James R. Swift, a sailor. In an old frame, c. 1840s ... **140.00 210.00 185.00**

	Current Price Range		P/Y Average

☐ **Daguerreotypes,** two sixth-plate daguerreotypes by Holmes of 289 Broadway, one of a young man in tall hat, the other a woman, N.Y., c. 1847 .... **56.00 84.00 70.00**

☐ **Dassonville, William,** "The Great Beach, San Francisco," silver print, signed, 8″ x 10″, 1912–17, printed before 1934 .... **400.00 450.00 410.00**

☐ **Dassonville, William,** "Standard Oil Storage Tank, Richmond, CA," silver print, signed, matted, 10″ x 8″, late 1920s/early 1930s, printed before 1934 .... **350.00 400.00 365.00**

☐ **Dassonville, William,** "Study in Black and White, No. 11," silver print, signed, matted, 9½″ x 7″, early 1920s, printed before 1924. .... **525.00 575.00 550.00**

☐ **Dassonville, William,** "Study of Iris," platinum print, signed, 7⅜″ x 4⅜″, early 1900s, the specific printing date unknown **575.00 625.00 600.00**

☐ **Dassonville, William,** "Yosemite, Cathedral Rocks," platinum print, signed, matted, 6″ x 8″, 1907–8, the specific printing date unknown **250.00 300.00 275.00**

☐ **Dater, Judy,** "Imogen and Twinka at Yosemite," silver print, mounted, signed, matted and framed, 9½″ x 7⅝″, 1974, printed later, the specific date unknown **600.00 675.00 650.00**

☐ **De Meyer, Baron,** photo of an actress in royal medieval dress, 9½″ x 7½″, signed "DeMeyer," c. 1924 .... **210.00 280.00 250.00**

☐ **Joyce, Paul,** "Bill Brandt, Brassai and Ansel Adams," platinum print, matted, 7⅛″ x 9½″, 1976, printed c. 1980 .... **300.00 350.00 325.00**

☐ **Karsh, Yousuf,** "Portrait of George Bernard Shaw," silver print, mounted, matted, 12⅝″ x 10¼″, 1943, the specific printing date unknown **400.00 475.00 450.00**

☐ **Karsh, Yousuf,** "Portrait of Picasso," silver print, mounted, 19¾″ x 15⅞″, 1954, printed later, the specific date unknown **825.00 925.00 900.00**

☐ **Karsh, Yousuf,** "Portrait of Winston Churchill," silver print, mounted, 19¾″ x 15⅞″, 1941, printed later, the specific date unknown **740.00 810.00 775.00**

☐ **Kertesz, Andre,** "Chez Mondrian," silver print, matted, 23⅞″ x 19⅝″, 1925, printed later, the specific date unknown **1350.00 1550.00 1450.00**

☐ **Kertesz, Andre,** "Hungry," three plates from A Hungarian Memory (N.Y., 1980, an edition of 100), the first "Boskay Ter," the second "Budafok," and the third "Duna Haraszti," silver prints, matted, each approximately 7¾″ x 9¼″, c. 1920 .... **475.00 525.00 500.00**

☐ **Koudelka, Josef,** "Gypsy with His Horse," silver print, 9¼″ x 14⅛″, 1960s, printed in the 1970s **350.00 400.00 365.00**

	Current Price Range		P/Y Average

Krause, George, Print of an old woman walking on a narrow sidewalk, 4½" x 6". Signed on verso. N.d. . . . . 140.00 | 210.00 | 190.00

Kuhn, Heinrich, "Portrait of a Young Girl," gum bichromate print, mounted, matted, framed, 11" x 9", 1911, the specific printing date unknown 1000.00 | 1100.00 | 1050.00

Lange, Dorothea, portrait of young woman in black shawl, 7½" x 6½", c. 1930 . . . . 350.00 | 500.00 | 425.00

Lartigue, Jacques-Henri, "Donkey-Drawn Racing Carts," silver print, matted and framed, 6⅞" x 14⅛", early 1900s, printed later, the specific date unknown . . . . 200.00 | 240.00 | 235.00

Lartigue, Jacques-Henri, "Lartigue's Parents at Point de-L'Arche, Normandy," silver print, matted, 9½" x 12⅝", 1902, printed later, the specific date unknown . . . . 575.00 | 625.00 | 585.00

Lartigue, Jacques-Henri, "Zissou Takes Off in His 'ZYZ 24,' Rouzat," silver print, matted and framed, 9½" x 13¼", printed later, the specific date unknown . . . . 685.00 | 755.00 | 700.00

Lynes, George Platt, "Bill Miller," a group of three portraits, silver prints, one matted, each approximately 9¼" x 7½", 1942–46, the specific printing dates unknown . . . . 900.00 | 1075.00 | 1000.00

Lyon, Danny, "Clearing Land," silver print, signed on back, matted, 9" x 13¼", c. 1970–80 . . . . 240.00 | 290.00 | 260.00

Mapplethorpe, Robert, "Cowboy, San Francisco," silver print, 14½" x 13¾", c. 1976, the specific printing date unknown . . . . 750.00 | 800.00 | 775.00

Meyerowitz, Joel, "Provincetown," a group of six photographs, five from the Porch Series and one from the Bay/Sky Series, C prints, framed, each approximately 7¾" x 9¾", 1976–77, printed c. 1976 . . . . 1700.00 | 1800.00 | 1725.00

Michals, Duane, "Magritte," silver print, matted, 4⅞" x 7¼", 1965, printed later in an edition of 100, the specific date unknown . . . . 400.00 | 450.00 | 425.00

Monsen, Frederick I, "Children of the Desert, Rio Grande, New Mexico," silver print, mounted, title label on the mount, matted, 18⅝" x 13⅛", 1920s, the specific printing date unknown . . . . . 145.00 | 185.00 | 150.00

Moon, Karl, "Home from the Hunt," silver print, triple-mounted, 11⅜" x 14⅜", 1920s, the specific printing date unknown . . . . 400.00 | 450.00 | 425.00

Morse, Samuel F.B., lantern slide reproduction of Bogardus' famous portrait of Morse with his Daguerreotype camera by his side, 3¼" x 4¼", c. 1880 . . . . 56.00 | 70.00 | 60.00

Mortensen, William, "Henri," silver print, incorporating etching texture, mounted, 13½" x 10½", 1930s, the specific printing date unknown . . . . 400.00 | 450.00 | 425.00

	Current Price Range		P/Y Average

☐ **Mortensen, William,** "The Young Scholar," silver print incorporating texture, mounted, 13¼" x 10¼", 1938, the specific printing date unknown
.... 325.00 350.00 340.00

☐ **Musicians,** group of 14 carte-de-visites portraits of European musicians, both from life and paintings, by various photographers, c. 1860s–70s 42.00 56.00 50.00

☐ **Muybridge, Eadweard J.,** panorama of San Francisco. Series of albumen prints mounted accordion style, with identification of 221 landmarks, in original cloth binder, overall size 7½" x 84", San Francisco, 1877 .... 2100.00 2800.00 2500.00

☐ **Nahr, M.,** "Portrait of Gustav Klimt," silver print, framed, 5" x 3¾", c. 1908, the specific printing date unknown 350.00 400.00 375.00

☐ **Naval,** album of 46 photos showing French and British naval vessels and crews, by Gale and Polden, Ltd., c. 1905 .... 56.00 84.00 65.00

☐ **New York,** 72 stereograms of New York City, Niagara Falls, etc., 3½" x 7", c. 1880s–1910.... 56.00 84.00 70.00

☐ **Newton, Helmut,** "Two Models in Rue Aubriot, Paris," silver print, signed, matted, with copyright stamp, 13¼" x 9", 1975 .... 575.00 675.00 600.00

☐ **Notable Americans,** album with 42 small oval portraits of W. H. Seward, Stephen Douglas, John Brown, H. W. Beecher, others, c. 1860s 84.00 124.00 95.00

☐ **Orkin, Ruth,** "Lauren Bacall at St. Regis Hotel, N.Y.C.," C print, signed, matted and framed, 9" x 13⅜", c. 1950, printed in 1979. .... 125.00 185.00 135.00

☐ **O'Sullivan, Timothy,** "Black Canon, Colorado River, from Camp 8, Looking Above," albumen print, 7¾" x 10⅝", c. 1873 .... 1100.00 1300.00 1200.00

☐ **Palestine,** 12 mounted albumen prints by G. Brogi. Views of Jaffa, Bethlehem, Nazareth, etc. Each about 8" x 10", c. 1860s 210.00 280.00 240.00

☐ **Parker, Olivia,** "Miss Appleton's Shoes," silver print, matted, signed by the photographer, framed, 6¼" x 5", 1976, printed in 1977 ...... 350.00 400.00 360.00

☐ **Pennsylvania,** 63 stereograms of views in Philadelphia and elsewhere in Pennsylvania, 3½" x 7", c. 1870s–90s 56.00 84.00 70.00

☐ **Pennsylvania,** 85 photos, mostly in original mounts. Farm houses, cities, churches, etc., 5" x 7" and 8" x 10", c. 1870s–1900 .... 115.00 165.00 145.00

☐ **Philippines,** 56 photos of Manila and environs, in a half leather album. Mostly 8½" x 10½", c. 1880s 280.00 420.00 350.00

☐ **Photochromes,** 14 color reproductions of views in Egypt, Tunisia, and some in Europe, 6½" x 9" and 8" x 11", c. 1900 .... 42.00 56.00 47.00

☐ **Portrait,** full-plate miniature case housing hand-colored portrait of Elizabeth de G. Kane, c. 1860s
.... 56.00 84.00 75.00

	Current Price Range		P/Y Average

☐ **Presidents and Assassin,** eight photos, including three carte-de-visites of Lincoln, photographer unidentified, portrait of J. W. Booth, others, c. 1860s .... 70.00 — 105.00 — 90.00

☐ **Rail Disaster,** 10 photos by G. W. Freeland showing scenes of storm and train wreck of October 4, 1877, Milford, NJ, 6″ x 9″ and 7″ x 9″, all on printed mounts .... 81.00 — 121.00 — 90.00

☐ **Revels, Hiram,** cabinet card from Mathew Brady's National Photographic Galleries, Washington, D. C., showing profile of Revels (senator from Mississippi), 6½″ x 4¼″, c. 1870 .... 115.00 — 165.00 — 145.00

☐ **Reward Poster,** broadside advertising $1,000 reward for capture of James Burns, charged with robbing Post Office in Brooklyn, N.Y. Mounted on poster is a carte-de-visite of Burns. Overall size 9″ x 5½″, Brooklyn, 1883 .... 56.00 — 84.00 — 75.00

☐ **Rhodesia,** album of 20 photos of botanical experiments, crops, etc., in Rhodesia. Dated 1914 .... 42.00 — 56.00 — 48.00

☐ **Robertson, James,** mounted albumen print believed to be by Robertson but not positively identified, showing view of the Parthenon with young top-hatted man standing near, 10¼″ x 15″, on mount 17″ x 21″, c. 1857 .... 280.00 — 420.00 — 325.00

☐ **Roth Sanford,** "Portrait of James Dean," silver print, photographer's copyright stamp on back, 13½″ x 10¾″, 1955 .... 225.00 — 275.00 — 250.00

☐ **Rothstein, Arthur,** "Farm Isolated By a Flooding of the Shenandoah," silver print, Resettlement Administration photograph, 8″ x 7½″, c. 1930–40 .... 125.00 — 150.00 — 130.00

☐ **San Francisco,** group of five mounted photos of views in San Francisco: Cliff House, Sutro Heights, Golden Gate, and Fort Point, Band Stand, Seal Rocks, 5¼″ x 8½″, c. 1870s ..... 105.00 — 140.00 — 130.00

☐ **Savage, Charles R.,** three carte-de-visites of Indians, c. 1870s .... 115.00 — 165.00 — 140.00

☐ **Spirit Photographs,** 10 photos of male medium demonstrating levitation, ectoplasm. "Marjorie the Medium, 10 Lime Street, Boston," 7″ x 5″, c. 1935 .... 56.00 — 84.00 — 70.00

☐ **Smith, W. Eugene,** "Prop Violins From Limelight," silver print, signed, matted, 10½″ x 13½″, 1951 .... 1200.00 — 1450.00 — 1325.00

☐ **Stereograms,** 72 cards by Keystone View Co., mostly of scenes in Africa, India, and Sweden, 3½″ x 7″, c. 1900 .... 56.00 — 70.00 — 60.00

☐ **Stieglitz, Alfred,** photo, "Sunlight and Shadow," 8″ x 10″, (negative made 1889, date of print unknown) .... 140.00 — 210.00 — 350.00

☐ **Stieglitz, Alfred,** photo, "The Steerage," 8″ x 10″, (negative made 1907, date of print unknown) .... 140.00 — 210.00 — 325.00

	Current Price Range		P/Y Average
☐ **Tintype,** tintype a young boy, nicely tinted, in quarter-plate case, issued by Critchlow and Co., c. 1857	70.00	105.00	85.00
☐ **Tintype,** black Couple in semi-formal dress, photographer unidentified, c. 1870, set of two	40.00	50.00	45.00
☐ **Tintype,** man smoking cigar, seated, with dog by his side, his right hand rests across dog's shoulder, photographer unidentified, c. 1865–70	12.00	16.00	14.00
☐ **Tintype,** two boys with pet cat, in a paper mat, photographer unidentified, c. 1870	22.00	28.00	26.00
☐ **Tintype,** two military bandsmen, full dress, standing alongside their trumpets, photographer unidentified, 4″ x 5½″, Civil War era or slightly later, large	90.00	105.00	95.00

PIPES

DESCRIPTION: A pipe is an item used for smoking which consists of a tube with a bowl and mouthpiece at opposite ends.

ORIGIN: American Indians are believed to be the first known people to make pipes. Europeans picked up the custom from them during the 1500s.

MATERIAL: Clay, porcelain and wood are different materials used to produce pipes. Meerschaum, a white clay, was discovered during the middle 1600s. This soft clay produced beautiful pipes that are highly prized collectors' items today.

COMMENTS: Meerschaum pipes carved in Vienna during the 19th and 20th centuries, pipes made by famous German porcelain factories during the 18th century and briar pipes produced in the early 1900s by famous British pipe makers like Alfred Dunhill of London and Comoy's of London are some of the most sought after pipes by collectors.

ADDITIONAL TIPS: Factors to consider when searching for collectible pipes are design, maker and user. Value is added when a notable person owns the pipe, a famous company produces the pipe, or the pipe is intricately designed.

CLASSIC PIPE SHAPES

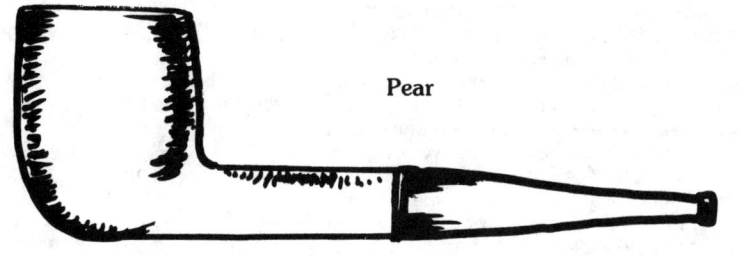

Pear

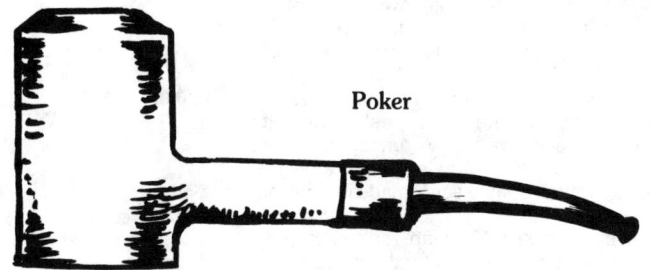

Poker

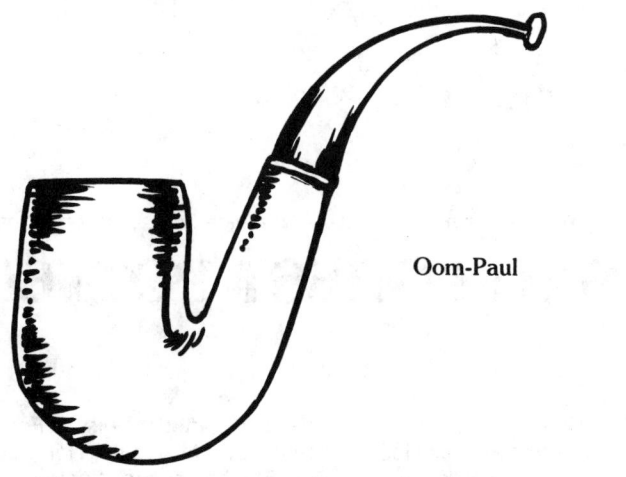

Oom-Paul

	Current Price Range		P/Y Average
Corn Cob, American, large tapering bowl with light incised carving, grayish patina, 1890s	21.00	27.50	22.00
Ivory, the bowl in oval form carved with an oriental scene of peasants carrying trays and buckets, with intricate leaf and vinework, 1870s	200.00	250.00	220.00
Meerschaum, bowl carved in the likeness of a female figure with flowing hair, cherrywood stem, horn mouthpiece, age uncertain	60.00	80.00	70.00
Meerschaum, British "bull dog" type soldier's pipe from World War I, carved with the date 1915 and word "Dardanelles," plated ferrule	31.50	42.50	36.00
Meerschaum, large size, fully sculptured bowl in the likeness of a female head and neck, in a leather case, 1870s	80.00	100.00	90.00
Meerschaum, large tapering bowl carved with a cavalier's face at the front, small figures of elks at sides, the top carved as the rim of an elaborate feathered hat, in the original polished mahogany case with inlaid bone ornaments, 1830s	500.00	650.00	560.00
Meerschaum, "Sherlock Holmes" style with curved stem and heavy bowl, undecorated but highly polished with fine graining, in the original cedar case lined in white satin, made in England, 1920s	42.00	52.50	45.00
Porcelain, Imperial German soldier's pipe, crowned cross and painted floral wreath, cherry stem and horn mouthpiece, 1914	75.00	95.00	85.00

PISGAH FOREST POTTERY

DESCRIPTION: Walter Stephen and C.P. Ryman started the Pisgah Forest Pottery in 1913. The company was located at the foot of Mt. Pisgah, North Carolina. Although this partnership dissolved in 1916, Stephen began to produce pottery again in 1920. Currently, the firm is still producing wares.

The company produced many types of pieces including vases, jugs, tea sets and mugs.

MARKS: Early pieces are marked Stephen or W.B. Stephen with either a raised figure of a potter at his wheel or without. After 1926, "Pisgah Forest" was the mark used. Again, the potter figure was sometimes used with this mark.

RECOMMENDED READING: For further information, refer to *The Official Price Guide to Pottery and Porcelain,* published by The House of Collectibles.

Bowl, *5"*, $30.00-$40.00

	Current Price Range		P/Y Average
☐ **Bowl,** 3", flat, very bulbous shaped body	25.00	45.00	35.00
☐ **Vase,** 4¾", green and pink, 1948	42.50	55.00	44.50
☐ **Vase,** 5", bulbous body, green, three handled	25.00	37.00	27.00
☐ **Vase,** 6", red and green, collared neck	42.50	50.00	44.50
☐ **Vase,** 6", white and creme glaze	152.50	180.00	156.00

PLATES

DESCRIPTION: Collector plates have a painting or design usually by a well-known or studio artist portrayed on its face.

TYPES: There are two types of limited edition collector plates. Either the number of plates or the number of production days is limited.

PERIOD: Collector plates first began with the 1895 blue and white porcelain Christmas plate by Bing and Grondahl. Companies have been producing collector plates since that time.

COMMENTS: Most plate collectors display their plates as artwork and derive the same sense of pleasure and satisfaction from them that they would from original paintings, except at a small fraction of the cost of a painting. Yet, plates usually appreciate at a phenomenal rate.

ADDITIONAL TIPS: For more information, consult *The Official Price Guide to Collector Plates,* published by The House of Collectibles.

	Issue Price	Current Price
☐ **Accent on Art,** Mother Goose Series, 1978, Jack and Jill, artist: Oscar Graves, production quantity 5,000	80.00	80.00
☐ **American Express,** Four Freedoms Series, 1976, Freedom of Worship, production: one year	37.50	38.00
☐ **American Express,** Four Freedoms Series, 1976, Freedom from Want, production: one year	37.50	38.00
☐ **American Express,** Four Freedoms Series, 1976, Freedom from Fear, production: one year	37.50	38.00
☐ **American Express,** Four Freedoms Series, 1976, Freedom of Speech, production: one year	37.50	38.00
☐ **American Legacy,** Children to Love Series, 1982, Sandy, artist: Sue Etem, production quantity 10,000	60.00	125.00
☐ **American Rose Society,** All-American Rose Series, 1975, Arizona, production quantity 9,800	39.00	128.00
☐ **American Rose Society,** All-American Rose Series, 1983, Sweet Surrender, production quantity 9,800	49.00	51.00

Uncle Tad's Cats Series
"Walter's Window," 1981,
Thaddeus Krumeich,
Anna-Perenna,
$85.00-$87.00

Uncle Tad's Cats Series
"Princess Aurora, Queen
of the Night," 1981
Thaddeus Krumeich
Anna-Perenna
$80.00-$82.00

	Issue Price	Current Price
☐ **Anna-Perenna,** Romantic Loves Series, 1979, Romeo and Juliet, artist: Frank Russell and Gertrude Barrer, production quantity 7,500	95.00	110.00
☐ **Artists of the World,** The DeGrazia Children of the World Series, 1976, Los Ninos, artist: Ted DeGrazia, signed, production quantity 500	100.00	2675.00
☐ **Artists of the World,** The DeGrazia Children of the World Series, 1979, The Flower Boy, artist: Ted DeGrazia, signed, production quantity 500	100.00	605.00

	Issue Price	Current Price
☐ **Artists of the World,** The Prowlers of the Clouds Series, 1981, First Light, artist: Larry Toschik, production quantity 5,000	55.00	57.00
☐ **Bareuther,** Christmas Series, 1971, Toys for Sale, artist: Hans Mueller, production: one year	12.75	27.00
☐ **Bareuther,** Thanksgiving Series, 1971, First Thanksgiving, production quantity 2,500	13.50	35.00
☐ **Bing and Grondahl,** Christmas Series, 1895, Frozen Window, artist: Frans August Hallin, production: one year	.50	4000.00
☐ **Bing and Grondahl,** Christmas Series, 1896, New Moon, artist: Frans August Hallin, production: one year	.50	2000.00
☐ **Bing and Grondahl,** Christmas Series, 1920, Hare in Snow, artist: Achton Friis, production: one year	2.00	95.00
☐ **Bing and Grondahl,** Christmas Series, 1985, Christmas Eve at the Farmhouse, artist: Edward Jensen, production: one year	54.50	54.50
☐ **Blue Delft,** Single Release, 1972, Olympiad	12.00	16.00
☐ **Blue Delft,** Single Release, 1972, Apollo 11	6.00	9.00
☐ **Briant, Paul and Sons,** Seven Sacraments Series, 1982, The Gift of the Spirit, artist: Terry Clark, production quantity 2,000	110.00	110.00
☐ **California Porcelain, Inc.,** Now is the Moment Series, 1984, Be Still, artist: Carolyn Blish, production quantity 12,500	35.00	35.00
☐ **Canadian Collector Plates,** Discover Canada Series, 1979, Sawmill Kings Landing, artist: Keirstead, production quantity 10,000	98.00	350.00
☐ **Carmel Collection,** Memories of the Heart Series, 1984, Petals, artist: Elizabeth Maxwell, production quantity 15,000	28.50	29.00
☐ **Daum,** Famous Musicians Series, 1971, Mozart, production quantity 2,000	75.00	75.00
☐ **Dave Grossman Designs,** Margaret Keane Series, 1977, My Kitty, artist: Margaret Keane, production quantity 5,000	25.00	32.00
☐ **Elegance of Bronze,** Knapp Series, 1978, Navajo Madonna, production quantity 2,500	250.00	285.00
☐ **Fenton Art Glass,** Christmas in America Series, 1970, Little Brown Church in Vale, production: one year	12.50	100.00
☐ **Fenton Art Glass,** Mother's Day Series, 1972, Madonna of the Goldfinch, production: one year	12.50	48.00
☐ **Franklin Mint,** Currier and Ives Series, 1977–79 American Forest Scene, artist: Currier and Ives, production quantity 1,836	39.50	45.00
☐ **Goebel Collection,** Hummel Annual Series, 1972, Globe Trotter, artist: M.I. Hummel, production: one year	32.50	180.00
☐ **Gorham Collection,** Julian Ritter Series, 1977, Falling Love, artist: Julian Ritter, set of four, production quantity 5,000	100.00	95.00
☐ **Gorham Collection,** Leaders of Tomorrow Series, 1981, Future Farmer, artist: Leon Jansen, production quantity 9,800	50.00	51.00
☐ **Hackett American Collector,** Wondrous Years Series, 1981, After the Rains, artist: Rudy Escalera, production quantity 5,000	39.50	40.00
☐ **Hamilton Collection,** Gardens of the Orient Series, 1983, A Winter's Repose, artist: Shunsuke Suetoni, production: less than one year	19.50	20.50

	Issue Price	Current Price
☐ **Haviland and Parlon,** Tapestry Series I, 1971, Unicorn in Captivity, production quantity 12,000	35.00	195.00
☐ **Hibel Studios,** David Series, 1981, David the King, artist: Edna Hibel, production quantity 5,000	275.00	275.00
☐ **Hoyle Products,** Bavarian Forest Series, 1981, Deer, production quantity 7,500	150.00	150.00
☐ **JM Company,** Love Series, 1980, Love's Serenade, artist: Hal Reed, production quantity 5,000	50.00	50.00
☐ **Porsgrund,** Christmas Series, 1974, The Shepherds, artist: Gunnar Bratlie, production: one year	15.00	41.00
☐ **Rockwell Museum,** American Family Series, 1978, Baby's First Step, artist: Norman Rockwell, production quantity 9,900	28.50	80.00
☐ **Rockwell Museum,** American Family Series II, 1980, Sweet Dreams, artist: Norman Rockwell, production quantity 22,500	35.00	35.00
☐ **Royal Cornwall,** Exotic Birds of Tropizue Series, 1981, Greater Sulfer-Crested Cockatoo, artist: Konrad Hack, production quantity 19,500	49.50	50.00
☐ **Royal Devon,** Norman Rockwell Christmas Series, 1977, The Big Moment, artist: Norman Rockwell, production: one year	27.50	82.00
☐ **Vague Shadows,** Nature's Harmony Series, 1982, Peaceable Kingdom, artist: Gregory Perillo, production quantity 12,500	100.00	100.00

PLAYER PIANOS

DESCRIPTION: A self-playing instrument that uses suction, that is controlled by a paper roll passing over a bar, to produce sound.

TYPES: The three types of player mechanisms used through the 1930s are Welte-Mignon, Duo-Art and Ampico.

COMMENTS: Note the reputation of the piano manufacturer, the type of player mechanism used in the piano and whether the piano is restored when determining the value of any player piano.

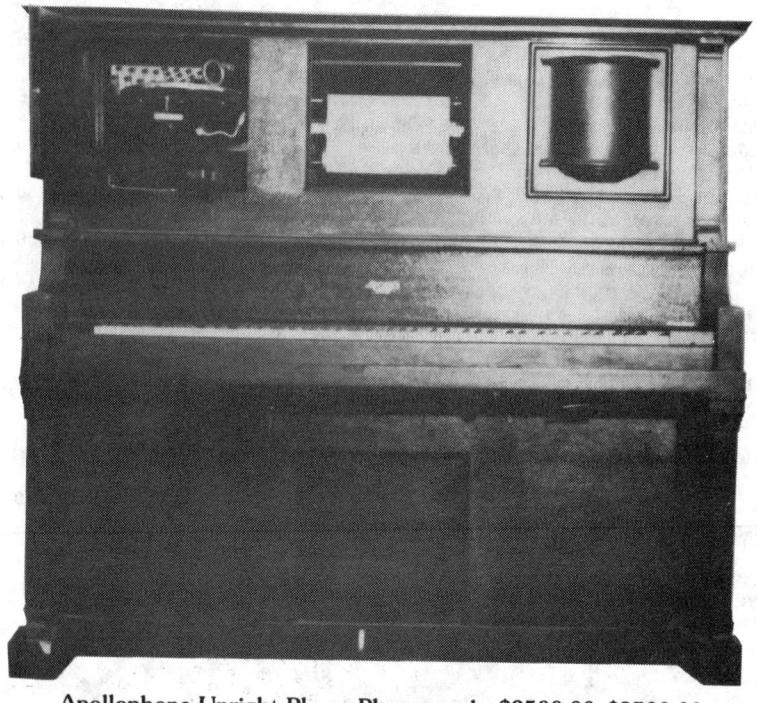

Apollophone Upright Player-Phonograph. $2500.00–$3500.00

ADDITIONAL TIPS: For more information, consult *The Official Price Guide to Music Collectibles,* published by The House of Collectibles.

	Unrestored	Restored
☐ **Aeriola Players,** Made by Aeolian	150.00– 250.00	2500.00– 2750.00
☐ **Aldrich Piano Co.,** used the Aeolian Player mechanism or the Simplex Player mechanism	250.00	2000.00
☐ **Angelus,** player action affiliated with the Premier Grand Piano Corp. It used what was called the "Artistyle" system of expression and is found in many pianos, e.g. Wilcox and White, Emerson, Lindemann, George Norris. Early examples were push-up players. (See sections on "Reproducing Expression Pianos" and "Push-Up Players" for examples, and see individual listings for values.)		
☐ **Apollo Piano Co. (IL),** used foot pump player actions made by Melville and Simplex in their pianos	200.00– 275.00	2000.00– 2500.00
☐ **Bachman Piano Company,** used the Standard Player mechanism	200.00	2250.00
☐ **Bailey Piano Company (N.Y.),** used the Bjur Bros. Player mechanism	200.00	2150.00

	Unrestored	Restored
☐ **Behning & Sons Pianos Co. (N.Y.),** used the Behning or Standard Player mechanisms	225.00–275.00	2250.00–2750.00
☐ **Behr Bros. and Co. (N.Y.),** used their own player mechanism, also the Standard Player mechanism and the Auto deluxe Welte-Mignon Reproducing mechanism	200.00–500.00	2000.00–3000.00
☐ With Welte mechanism	400.00–600.00	2750.00–4000.00
☐ **Concertone,** player made by Mansfield Piano Co. (NY) for their pianos	250.00	2500.00
☐ **Derivas and Harris (NY),** used Standard and Simples player mechanisms	150.00–250.00	2500.00–2750.00
☐ **Elburn Music Co. (Kansas City, MO),** used the Aeolian Player mechanism	250.00	2500.00
☐ **Grinnell Bros. (Detroit, MI),** used the Aeolian and Lester Player mechanisms	250.00–300.00	2500.00–3000.00
☐ **Grunet-Hupfeld Solophonola,** regular upright player, foot pump (see also Hupfeld, Ludwig)	350.00	3500.00
☐ **Harrison Piano,** used the Kimball Regular Player mechanism	250.00	2000.00
☐ **Livingston Pianos,** controlled by Weaver Piano Co. (York, PA). Made a line of players	250.00	2500.00–2700.00
☐ **Lorraine Pianos,** made for the Field-Lippman Piano Stores (St. Louis, MO). Sold a line of popular priced player pianos	250.00	2500.00
☐ **Norris and Hyde,** used the National Air-O-Player mechanism	250.00	2500.00
☐ **Pianola,** trademark name used by Aeolian for their Player Pianos	200.00–250.00	2500.00–2750.00
☐ **Sterling Piano Co. (CT),** used their own and the Standard Player mechanisms. The Sterling mechanism also found in Harvey, Huntington, Mendelssohn and other pianos	250.00	2500.00–3250.00
☐ **Walters Piano Co. (Long Island, NY),** made pianos under several names among them Bloomingdale Bros. Used Standard, H. C. Bay and Strauch Bros. player mechanisms.....................................	250.00–350.00	2750.00–3500.00

PLAYING CARDS

TYPES: Standard playing cards feature a king, a queen and a jack as the court subjects on a face card. The subjects will differ on a nonstandard deck. Tarot cards are also very collectible; they are used in fortune-telling.

ORIGIN: Playing cards are believed to have first appeared in the Far East around the 1100s. Printed playing cards probably were developed in Switzerland around 1430.

COMMENTS: Age usually determines value, although the quality of the artwork will have some influence. Very old playing cards do not often appear on the collectible market.

Playing Card, *Kinney Tobacco Co., 1889,* $16.00–$20.00

	Current Price Range		P/Y Average
☐ **Advertising,** Lorrilard Splendid Cut Plug Tobacco, 52 cards plus joker, American Playing Card Co., backs in red/white/blue, c. 1880, believed to be the earliest American advertising deck with pictorial backs	155.00	210.00	170.00

	Current Price Range		P/Y Average

- **Advertising,** souvenir of the 11th Annual Convention of the United Drug Co., 52 cards, each with photographs of Rexall club officers, 1913 — 150.00 / 200.00 / 165.00
- **American Indian Souvenir Playing Cards,** 52 cards plus joker and title card, Lazarus and Melzer, 1900 — 82.50 / 110.00 / 89.00
- **Art Nouveaux,** deck depicts turn of the century artists, Grimaud, 1900 — 4.50 / 7.00 / 6.00
- **At Sea,** 52 cards, Congress, gold borders — 20.00 / 25.00 / 21.75
- **Barking Dog,** pinochle deck, Standard Playing Card Co., gold edges, c. 1910 — 18.00 / 23.00 / 20.00
- **Bezique,** Samuel Hart, square corners, one way courts, believed to be pre-Civil War — 110.00 / 150.00 / 125.00
- **Bicycle Bridge,** 52 cards plus joker, United States Playing Card Co., c. 1945 — 8.00 / 11.25 / 8.35
- **Brown Derby,** 52 cards plus two jokers, each card has caricature of a show business personality (including Ronald Reagan), 1951 — 26.00 / 34.00 / 29.00
- **Canary Playing Cards,** 52 cards plus joker, backs have black and white picture of lady with long curls and large hat, c. 1910 — 12.00 / 16.00 / 13.50
- **Chicago World's Fair,** deck, c. 1934 — 15.00 / 21.00 / 18.00
- **Chinese Art Treasures,** double deck — 13.00 / 18.00 / 15.50
- **Circus World Museum Souvenir Deck,** 52 cards, backs picture Buffalo Bill's Wild West Show, c. 1970–1980 — 6.75 / 8.50 / 7.00
- **Civil War Pack,** Union Playing Cards, American Card Co., NY, 2-color, eagles, stars, flags, shields, suits — 550.00 / 850.00 / 700.00
- **Coca-Cola,** double deck — 6.00 / 11.00 / 7.50
- **Culbertson's Own,** 52 cards, Russell, each card has bridge tips printed on it, 1932 — 25.00 / 32.00 / 28.00
- **Cupid's Secret,** 52 cards, gold edges, 1907 — 20.00 / 25.00 / 22.25
- **Deck,** 52 cards, Andrew Dougherty, tiny picture of card in two corners, c. 1870 — 120.00 / 200.00 / 160.00
- **Deck,** Andrew Dougherty, NY, Owen Jones designs, c. 1880 — 53.00 / 135.00 / 90.00
- **Deck,** 36 cards, two information cards, The Game of Kings, Adams, NY, portraits of British monarchs, 1845 — 220.00 / 320.00 / 270.00
- **Double Action,** 52 cards, 1935 — 32.50 / 42.75 / 34.00
- **Fish Up,** 52 cards plus two jokers, Creative Playing Card Co., all have cartoon backs with fishing themes, 1963 — 7.00 / 10.00 / 8.25
- **Fleet Wing Gasoline,** advertising deck, c. 1910 — 16.00 / 22.00 / 19.00
- **Flinch Cards,** c. 1910 — 25.00 / 30.00 / 27.50
- **France Royale,** double deck, by Piatnik — 8.00 / 11.00 / 9.50
- **French Suited Pack,** L.I. Cohen, large size, gold trim, mint — 220.00 / 320.00 / 270.00
- **Grover Cleveland,** campaign deck, reprint of 1888 issue — 3.25 / 7.50 / 5.00

	Current Price Range		P/Y Average
Gypsy Witch, fortune telling deck	10.00	15.00	12.50
Hard-A-Port-Cut Plug, tobacco premium, 52 cards plus joker, c. late 1880s	170.00	350.00	260.00
Hollyhocks, 52 cards, Dougherty, 1921	13.00	17.00	14.50
Huntress, 52 cards, Andrew Dougherty, gold edges, ace of spades is neutral	13.00	17.00	14.75
Illuminated Deck, 52 cards, A. Dougherty, all pips gold outlined in style of medieval cards, Civil War era, considered one of the classic American packs	200.00	250.00	220.00
Indian Wars, 52 cards, Humphrey, with black spades, red hearts, yellow diamonds, blue clubs, rare	1300.00	1600.00	1425.00
Jack Daniels, 1972 edition	4.00	7.00	5.50
Jaws, double deck, Stancraft, motion picture inspired with shark reverses, c. 1978	6.00	11.00	8.65
Mardi Gras, deck, reprint of 1925 issue	3.50	7.00	5.10
Nixon, politicards, 1971 edition	8.75	13.00	10.25
Panama Souvenir Cards, 53 plus information cards, USPC, real photos, c. 1908	40.00	80.00	60.00
Picturesque Canada, 52 cards plus joker, backs picture Chateau Frontenac	20.00	26.50	23.00
Picturesque Nova Scotia, 52 cards plus joker, Canadian Playing Card Co., Montreal, illustrated on both sides, c. 1920	25.00	35.00	29.00
Rita, double deck in double box, total of four jokers	25.00	33.00	28.75
Sebago, pinochle deck, Dougherty, gold edges, World War I era	12.00	17.00	13.25
Serenader, 52 cards, Russell, gold edges	10.00	12.00	11.00
Shooting The Rapids, 52 cards, 1910	70.00	100.00	83.00
Souvenir Of The Canary Islands, 52 cards, Fournier, 1973	10.50	16.00	12.50
Steamboats, 52 cards plus joker, U.S. Printing Co., pre-1900	50.00	65.00	56.00
Texas Souvenir Deck, 52 cards plus joker, gold edges, c. 1900–1910	75.00	100.00	83.00
Uncle Sam's Cabinet, 1901	30.00	40.00	35.00
Vanity Fair Transformation Deck, United States Playing Card Co., America's first true transformation deck, 1895	450.00	650.00	550.00
Verkehrvelt Tarock, reproduction of 1810 edition, "Topsy Turvy Animal Tarot"	50.00	70.00	60.00
Washable Plastic Deck, 52 cards plus joker, Dale, c. 1950	7.50	11.00	8.25
W.C. Fields, 52 cards plus two jokers, J.L. Brown, scenes from his movies on courts and aces plus booklet with hints on cheating, 1971	13.00	17.00	15.00

POLICE MEMORABILIA

DESCRIPTION: Police memorabilia includes any items pertaining to the policeman or a police station from ephemera to toys and paintings.

PERIOD: The early 1800s saw the first use of paid policemen in America. It wasn't until the middle 1800s that police uniforms were used. During the early years of police duty, the officers carried items that were later outlawed. These items, such as a bully club with nails, are sought after by collectors.

TYPES: All types of police memorabilia from different law enforcement agencies including city police, sheriffs, rangers and private guards are collected especially uniforms, badges, night sticks and headgear.

MAKER: Most police badges from the 19th and early 20th centuries were produced by either the Waterbury Button Company of Waterbury, CT or Danbury Button Company of Danbury, CT.

COMMENTS: The type of material, style changes and rarity play important roles in determining value of police collectibles.

	Current Price Range		P/Y Average
☐ **Badge,** Bangor Police 3, Bangor, Maine, silver, star in center with openwork around it, c. 1900	90.00	110.00	97.00
☐ **Badge,** Boston Police, embossed brass, first issue, pictures Justice with scales and date 1630, large size, issued 1853–1854, 4″	310.00	412.00	340.00
☐ **Badge,** Chief of Police, western, made from a Mexican silver coin of the 1800s with engraved wording added and a pin on the back	225.00	275.00	250.00
☐ **Badge,** Federal Protective Service Police, 1981 Inauguration of the President (Ronald Reagan), gold and blue, special badge worn on that occasion only	182.50	240.00	197.00
☐ **Badge,** Fire Police, place of origin unknown, brass with light silver overlay, shield shape with wording on thin banners at top and bottom, c. 1880	35.00	45.00	40.00

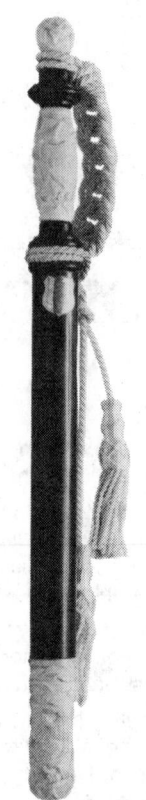

Presentation Police Baton, *rosewood, handcarved ivory sections, gold plate inset inscribed "Presented to Sgt. William McCarthy, Jan. 8, 1901," original silk cord and tassel, 22½",* **$200.00-250.00**

(photo courtesy of ©Alfred J. Young Collection, NYC)

	Current Price Range		P/Y Average
☐ **Badge,** Metropolitan Police Conference, New York City, enamel, shield shape, a special occasion badge worn by officers to gain admission to a function, date of origin unknown	22.50	26.50	22.00
☐ **Badge,** Newark, New Jersey, Police #189, brass with applied numerals, shield shape, c. 1890 . .	67.50	87.50	72.00
☐ **Badge,** New Bedford Police, Massachusetts, brass with silver overlay, circular, word "Police" in large letters near bottom	36.00	44.00	39.00
☐ **Badge,** New York City Department of Correction Elevator Operator, gold washed	47.50	47.50	39.00
☐ **Badge,** Office of the Sheriff, Jacksonville Police, The Bold New City of the South, enameled bronze, illustration of skyline of Jacksonville, Florida on large elaborate shield shaped badge, early 1900s	35.00	45.00	35.00
☐ **Badge,** P. Morton, Police Chief, Ashland, New Hampshire, gilt copper, large with ornate eagle at top, c. 1910	45.00	55.00	49.00

	Current Price Range		P/Y Average

☐ **Badge,** Railroad Police, New York, New Haven and Hartford Railroad, brass with black enamel, pointed at top and bottom, late 1800s **75.00 95.00 82.00**

☐ **Badge,** Saco Police, Maine, brass with silver overlay, plain incised lettering, shield shape, late 1800s or early 1900s **44.75 60.00 50.00**

☐ **Badge,** Safety Patrol, Providence, brass with silver overlay and containing a small celluloid insert, spreadwing eagle at top, cross at center, late 1800s **28.00 35.00 29.00**

☐ **Badge,** Sheriff's Officer, Camden County, New Jersey, brass with inlaid enamel, star shape, early 1900s **36.00 44.00 38.00**

☐ **Badge,** Waltham Police, Massachusetts, plated silver, beehive center, shellwork at sides, large pin **82.50 105.00 88.00**

☐ **Badge,** White House Police, Honorary Badge, gold filled, engraved "with best wishes, Harry S. Truman," c. 1945–1952 .... **200.00 300.00 230.00**

☐ **Badge,** White House Police Chief, second issue (1940–1951), 10K golf face **250.00 350.00 285.00**

☐ **Brass Knuckles,** iron, stamped Loudons Patent, Oct. 20, 1885, three joined loops for fitting over the first three fingers **42.00 52.00 45.00**

☐ **Coat,** frock type worn by Providence (R.I.) police force, 19 buttons, c. 1900 .... **90.00 115.00 102.00**

☐ **Flask,** in shape of nightstick or "billy club," glass with screw on tin lid, dark brown to resemble wood, said to have been carried by some police in Victorian era to circumvent orders against drinking on duty, 10½", c. 1850–1860 .... **100.00 130.00 110.00**

☐ **Handcuffs,** nickel plated, oval shaped connected by rectangular loop links, working order with key, c. 1925 .... **27.00 35.00 30.00**

☐ **Hat,** felt, bonnet type as worn by many metropolitan forces in the 1890s, oil cloth strap, badge in front states "Precinct Three" but no further details **130.00 160.00 142.00**

☐ **Hat,** straw, for summer wear by an unidentified metropolitan force, c. 1915 .... **62.50 82.50 67.00**

☐ **Helmet,** New York City Police Force, iron, dome shape, painted dark blue, name "Edwards" and number "261" written inside in white paint, c. 1885 .... **150.00 200.00 165.00**

☐ **Nightstick,** rosewood, unmarked, rubber grip, leather thong, c. 1935, 21" **15.00 20.00 17.00**

☐ **Nightstick,** wood with metal weighted end, leather strap, 17½", c. 1910 .... **31.50 42.50 35.00**

☐ **Photograph,** Springfield (Massachusetts) Police Department group photo in uniform with accessories, mounted, 7½" x 10", 1891 .... **95.00 117.50 101.75**

☐ **Toy,** Patrol wagon with two horses, four police figures, moveable wheels, 1890s, 13" **300.00 350.00 325.00**

POLITICAL BUTTONS

DESCRIPTION: Political buttons usually have a portrait of a politician produced on them and a pin attached to the back.

TYPE: There are several types of buttons produced including celluloids and jugates, which are buttons having both presidential and vice presidential candidates pictured.

MATERIAL: Early pictures used on the pin back buttons from the late 1800s and early 1900s were printed on paper with a metal backing and covered with celluloid. By 1920, pictures were lithographed to the metal with the plastic covering omitted.

ADDITIONAL TIPS: Celluloids and jugates are both sought after collector's items. Rarity plays one of the most important factors in determining the value of political buttons.

	Current Price Range		P/Y Average
☐ **Bryan/Kern Jugate,** picture of eagle, multicolored	245.00	290.00	265.00
☐ **Coolidge,** lithographed tin, blue and white	14.00	18.00	15.50
☐ **Coolidge/Davis Jugate,** celluloid, black and white, ⅞″	36.50	45.00	39.25
☐ **Eugene Chafin for President,** 1908 Prohibition Party candidate, ⅞″	40.00	55.00	45.00
☐ **Eugene Debs,** celluloid, red, white and black	70.00	100.00	80.00
☐ **Franklin Roosevelt,** celluloid, "We Are Going to Win This War," red, white and blue, 1½″	14.00	18.25	16.75
☐ **Franklin Roosevelt,** "New Deal, Cowlitz County, Washington," red, white, blue and black	92.50	117.50	100.00
☐ **Governor Franklin D. Roosevelt,** "The People's Choice for President," 1932, brass 1¼″	19.50	24.50	21.00
☐ **Hoover,** black and white, 1¼″	30.00	40.00	33.00
☐ **Hoover/Curtis Jugate,** lithographed tin, red, white and blue, 2½″	110.00	140.00	120.00
☐ **I Like Ike,** lithographed tin, red lettering on white background, no illustration, used in 1952	1.65	3.25	2.50

	Current Price Range		P/Y Average

☐ **Landon for President Club,** red trim 15.00   20.00   17.00

☐ **Lucky Willkie,** red letters on white background, no illustration, used for the 1940 Republican candidacy of Wendell Willkie 6.00   10.50   8.50

☐ **Lyndon Johnson/Hubert Humphrey Jugate,** "Let us Continue," 1964 campaign, ⅞" 38.00   46.00   41.00

☐ **McKinley,** celluloid, red, white and black, "An Honest Dollar Earned and Spent at Home" . . .   65.00   85.00   72.00

☐ **McKinley/Theodore Roosevelt Jugate,** photos in brass shell with flags in red, white and blue, used in 1900 campaign 24.00   30.00   25.00

☐ **Nixon/Lodge, Jugate,** lithographed tin, from campaign of 1960 which Richard Nixon lost to John Kennedy 1.50   1.90   1.20

☐ **Ronald Reagan for Governor,** lithographed tin, white border 2.15   3.25   2.30

☐ **Smith/Robinson Jugate,** lithographed tin, from 1928-campaign 20.00   30.00   23.00

☐ **Stevenson,** celluloid, blue and white, shoulder length portrait, reading 1960 beneath 52.25   68.00   56.00

☐ **Support FDR,** Elect Satini Secretary of State, local button from Massachusetts, blue and white, 1936 . . . .   14.00   18.25   14.00

☐ **Taft,** oval, celluloid, red, white, blue and green   31.50   36.75   32.00

☐ **Taft/Sherman Jugate,** celluloid, multicolored   35.00   43.00   38.00

☐ **Truman,** lithographed tin, pictures dome of U.S. Capitol, mentions his running mate Barkley 14.50   19.25   15.00

☐ **Willkie,** white and black with shoulder length portrait, wording "For President" at top 18.75   22.50   18.00

☐ **Wilson/Dunne Jugate,** celluloid, blue and white, 1¼" 55.00   70.00   62.00

☐ **Young Republican Hoover League,** blue and white, not illustrated 29.00   35.00   30.00

POLITICAL MEMORABILIA

COMMENTS: Every political campaign from dog catcher to President produces memorabilia. In addition to the familiar campaign buttons, there is sure to be literature of all types, including posters, pictures, brochures and newspaper ads. Collectors naturally place the highest values on items pertaining to historic statesmen but even the memorabilia from campaigns of recent Presidents is highly favored by hobbyists.

	Current Price Range		P/Y Average
☐ **"America's Pride,"** colored and embossed cigar box label. Pictures George Washington, 7″ x 9″, c. 1910	6.75	13.50	7.00
☐ **Bottom Is Out Of The Full Dinner Pail, The,** Postcard, 1908	9.50	16.50	10.00
☐ **Back To The Farm—Three Strikes And Out,** Anti-Bryan cartoon postcard	13.50	20.00	14.00
☐ **Dee Lighted,** a postcard picturing Teddy Roosevelt, 1905.	6.75	13.50	7.00
☐ **"First Banner,"** cigar box label picturing Washington, an eagle and a shield. 7″ x 10″	6.75	13.50	7.00
☐ **F.D.R.,** paper window poster, 8″ x 11″	6.75	11.00	7.00
☐ **F.D.R., "Rain Or Shine,"** paper poster, 8″ x 11″	11.00	16.00	12.00
☐ **"Gold Water—The Right Drink For The Conservative Taste,"** cardboard carton that once held six cans of soda; soda cans missing, 1964	16.00	24.00	17.00
☐ **"Great Issues And National Leaders, The Voter's Guide For the Campaign Of 1908,"** book, with photos on cover of Taft and Bryan	8.00	11.00	9.00
☐ **"Horace Greeley,"** photo printed on heavy cardboard, set into brass frame	9.00	13.50	10.00
☐ **"I Like Ike,"** 3″ x 3½″ sticker, 1952 or 1956	6.75	9.00	7.00
☐ **"Interview, The,"** Playboy Magazine folder with 2½″ button, "Carter Talks in Playboy." 1976 campaign	6.75	11.00	7.00

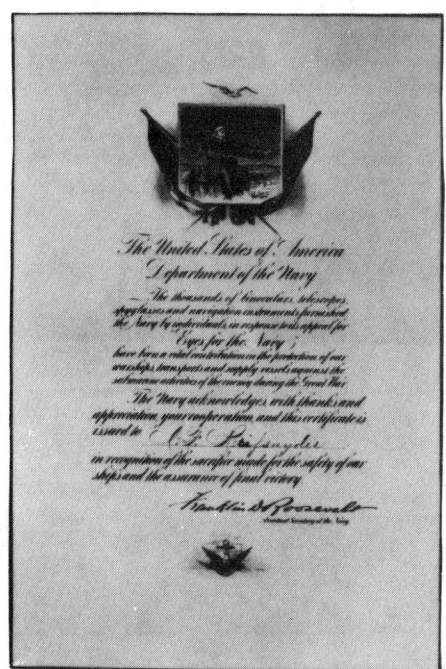

Document, *Donation of Binoculars as "Eyes for the Navy" by FDR, 1918,* **$40.00–$50.00**
Photo courtesy of Lou McCulloch, Highland Heights, OH 44143.

	Current Price Range		P/Y Average
☐ **"I Think We've Got Another Washington And Wilson Is His Name,"** song sheet, 1915	13.50	20.00	14.00
☐ **"Let's Back Nixon,"** 4″ x 6″ paper sticker showing Nixon pointing his finger at Khrushchev. 1960 campaign	13.50	20.00	14.00
☐ **"Lincoln Bouquet,"** colored and embossed cigar box label. 6″ x 10″. c. 1910	6.75	13.50	7.00
☐ **"Lieut.-General Winfield Scott, Faithful To The Last,"** 19th century ferrotype photo by Abbot, set in brass frame, 1½″ x 1¾″	27.00	40.00	28.00
☐ **Nation's Choice, The,** embossed postcard picturing Taft and Sherman	6.75	11.00	7.00
☐ **"Never Swap Horses When You're Crossing A Stream,"** song sheet with portrait of Woodrow Wilson, 1916	13.50	20.00	14.00
☐ **Next Occupant Of The White House,** campaign postcard for William J. Bryan	6.75	11.00	7.00
☐ **"One World,"** by Wendell L. Wilkie, autographed copy of book, 1943	13.50	20.00	14.00

Political, *General Grant carte de visite,* **$20.00-$25.00**
Photo courtesy of Lou McCulloch, Highland Heights, OH 44143.

	Current Price Range		P/Y Average
☐ **Our Next President William H. Taft: Glory And Prosperity For Our Country,** colored postcard picturing Taft	6.75	11.00	7.00
☐ **Our Next President,** full color picture of the Capitol with Taft pictured in the corner. Postcard, 1908.	6.75	11.00	7.00
☐ **Our Next President And Vice President,** postcard picturing Taft and Sherman.	6.75	11.00	7.00
☐ **"Puck" Magazine,** issue contains two large political cartoons, one of Teddy Roosevelt, 1906 ..	9.00	13.50	10.00
☐ **"U.S. Grant,"** photo printed on heavy cardboard, set into brass frame	9.00	13.50	10.00
☐ **"Vote Democratic,"** paper window sticker, 4" x 4". c. 1948	6.75	11.00	7.00
☐ **William Howard Taft For President,** tinte photo on white background	6.75	11.00	7.00

POSTCARDS

DESCRIPTION: Postcards are cards with a picture on one side and a place to write a message on the other. Postcards can also be mailed without an envelope.

PERIOD: Postcard collecting began in Europe in 1902 and by 1906 Americans were purchasing them at the rate of 700 million a year. The postcard boom dropped off around 1914 but began again in the 1960s.

TYPES: Hobbyists usually collect postcards by subject with the most popular portraying transportation, political events and advertising.

COMMENTS: The cards from pre-World War I are highly valuable. Artist, signature and category are items that determine value.

	Current Price Range		P/Y Average
☐ **Bosselman,** Eastern States, color, undivided back	7.00	10.00	8.25
☐ **Clinton & Close,** The Iron Ore Docks of Toledo, color, undivided back	7.00	10.00	8.25
☐ **Detroit Photo Co.** #9100, Indias Amate-cas/Mexico, color, undivided back	6.00	8.00	6.85
☐ **Erker #221,** Levee Scene, color, undivided back	5.00	7.50	6.00
☐ **Erker #246,** Soulard Market, color, undivided back	5.00	7.50	6.00
☐ **Erker #250,** Wabash Freight Station, color, un-divided back	5.00	7.50	6.00
☐ **Holmes & Warren,** Branding Calves, two-tone, undivided back	5.00	7.50	6.00
☐ **Illinois Postcard Co.,** Indian Encampment on River Bank, color, undivided back	5.00	7.50	6.00
☐ **Leighton,** "Indians," Chief Spotted Tail, color, undivided back	5.00	7.50	6.00
☐ **Louis Levy,** Horse Drawn Double Decker Buses in London's Ludgate Circus, color, divided back	6.00	8.50	7.00
☐ **MacFarlane,** "Wild West" Series, Fur Canoe, color, undivided back	10.00	14.00	11.25

Postcards, *Left: Gruss aus of postman—the pouch attachment contains views of Bremen; Right: A postcard street seller of 1910,* **$5.00–$20.00** *Photo courtesy of Lou McCulloch, Highland Heights, OH 44143.*

	Current Price Range		P/Y Average
☐ **MacFarlane,** "Wild West" Series, Red River Carts, color, divided back	10.00	14.00	11.25
☐ **Miller,** Two Crow Papooses, black and white, undivided back	5.00	7.50	6.00
☐ **Morris & Kirby,** A Beef Herd on Water, black and white, undivided back	6.25	8.50	6.85
☐ **Ridley,** "Wild West" Series, A Roper, two-tone, undivided back, artwork by Charles M. Russell	20.00	25.00	22.00
☐ **Ridley,** "Wild West" Series, Antelope Hunting, two-tone, undivided back, artwork by Charles M. Russell	22.00	28.00	24.00

	Current Price Range		P/Y Average
☐ **Samuel Cupples,** "German Tyrolean Alps" Series, Red Roof Tower at Left of Mountains	15.00	20.00	17.00
☐ **Samuel Cupples,** "German Tyrolean Alps" Series, Residence House at Roof Square	15.00	20.00	17.00
☐ **Samuel Cupples,** "German Tyrolean Alps" Series, The Village Square	15.00	20.00	17.00
☐ **Samuel Cupples,** Oklahoma Building, color, undivided back	7.00	10.00	6.75
☐ **Sunday Post Dispatch (St. Louis),** Missouri State Building, color, undivided back, c. 1900	7.00	10.00	6.75
☐ **Tammen,** Home Sweet Home, color, undivided back	11.00	15.00	12.50
☐ **Underwood & Underwood,** Austrian Cavalry Patrol Crossing River, color	7.00	10.00	8.20
☐ **Valentine,** The Westmount Club of Montreal, color, divided back	6.00	8.00	6.75

PREMIUMS

DESCRIPTION: Premiums are advertising giveaways used to promote a company's product.

ORIGIN: Premiums proved to be quite successful for radio during the 1930s to 1940s. Giveaways were also used to a smaller extent on television and for some foods like cereal or Cracker Jacks.

COMMENTS: Radio premiums, which comprise a large portion of the premium collector market, are more readily available in the Midwest than on the East or West Coast. There were many successful radio shows originating in cities like Detroit, Chicago, Cincinnati and Kansas City, therefore prices are generally lower in these areas than in New York or Los Angeles.

ADDITIONAL TIPS: Paper items are considered more valuable than metal objects simply because paper does not hold up through the years like metal. Character popularity, type of item and rarity are important factors to consider in the premium market.

For additional information, consult *The Official Price Guide to Radio, TV and Movie Memorabilia,* published by The House of Collectibles.

Left to Right: Little Orphan Annie, *ceramic cup, Ovaltine premium,* **$5.00-$10.00;** *and* **Quaker Oats** *mug, Quaker Oats premium,* **$2.00-$5.00**

	Current Price Range		P/Y Average
☐ **Amos 'N Andy,** cardboard figure, 1931 Pepsodent premium, Amos driving cab	17.00	25.00	20.00
☐ **Bobby Benson,** code rule, 1935 Hecker-H-O premium, cardboard	95.00	115.00	105.00
☐ **Buck Rogers,** Wilma Pendant, 1930s Cream of Wheat premium	50.00	75.00	60.00
☐ **Buck Rogers,** birthstone initial ring, 1939 Popsicle Pete premium	100.00	150.00	125.00
☐ **Captain Midnight,** Membership Manual, 1941 Ovaltine premium, secret squadron, 12 page manual	110.00	120.00	117.50
☐ **Captain Midnight,** Mirro-Flash Code-O-Graph, 1946 Ovaltine premium	22.00	30.00	24.00
☐ **Captain Tim,** Ivory Stamp Club Album, 1934 Ivory Sopa premium, 72 page	8.00	12.00	10.00
☐ **Captain Video,** Flying Saucer Ring, 1950s Powerhouse candy bar premium	60.00	75.00	66.00
☐ **Captain Video,** photo ring, 1950s, Powerhouse candy bar premium	50.00	60.00	55.00
☐ **Death Valley Days,** 1931 Story of Death Valley, 1931 Borax premium, 24 page book with photos of radio show cast, history of Death Valley and map	13.00	19.00	16.50
☐ **Dick Tracy,** flashlight, 1939 Quaker Oats premium, pocket size	35.00	45.00	40.00
☐ **Dizzy Dean,** Winners Club Member Pin, late 30s Post Cereal premium	18.00	22.00	20.00
☐ **Eddie Cantor,** cards, 1935 Pebeco toothpaste premium, trick cards and instructions	30.00	40.00	35.00
☐ **Fibber McGee and Molly,** cast photo, 1940s Johnson Wax premium	19.00	24.00	22.00
☐ **Flash Gordon,** movie serial button, 1930s theater giveaway	75.00	100.00	87.50

	Current Price Range		P/Y Average
☐ **Junior Detective,** Junior Detective Corps Captain Badge, 1933 Post Toasties premium, brass badge	13.00	17.00	15.00
☐ **Lone Ranger,** blackout kit, 1943 Kix premium, rare	90.00	110.00	100.00
☐ **Lone Ranger,** Membership Badge, 1935 Silvercup Bread premium	35.00	45.00	40.00
☐ **Lone Wolf,** manual, 1932 Wrigley gum premium, 32 page book has illustrations, shows picture writing and gives secret signs and signals of the Lone Wolf Tribe	95.00	110.00	95.00
☐ **Lum and Abner,** badge, 1936 radio premium; walking weather prophet badge	20.00	30.00	25.00
☐ **Melvin Purvis,** badge, 1936 Post Toasties Corn Flakes premium	15.00	25.00	20.00
☐ **Radio Orphan Annie,** pin, 1934 Ovaltine premium	15.00	25.00	20.00
☐ **Radio Orphan Annie,** pin, 1935 Ovaltine premium	20.00	30.00	25.00
☐ **Radio Orphan Annie,** pin, 1937 Ovaltine premium, Sunburst decoder	10.00	20.00	15.00
☐ **Radio Orphan Annie,** puzzle, 1933 Ovaltine premium	60.00	75.00	67.50
☐ **Sekatary Hawkins,** membership card, 1932 Ralston premium, has oath on back, rare	35.00	45.00	40.00
☐ **SGT Preston,** celluloid membership button, 1950s Quaker premium	65.00	75.00	70.00
☐ **Sky King,** microscope, 1947 Peter Pan Peanut Butter premium, has four specimens for viewing, instructions	75.00	100.00	80.00
☐ **Tarzan Of The Apes,** book, 1935 Sears premium, Hal Foster art, rare	20.00	35.00	25.00
☐ **Tom Mix,** badge, 1945 Ralston premium	45.00	50.00	45.00
☐ **Tom Mix,** bandana, 1933 Ralston premium, rare	75.00	100.00	85.00
☐ **Tom Mix,** book, 1935 Ralston premium, titled "Tom Mix On The Trail Of The Terrible Six" ..	15.00	25.00	20.00
☐ **Tom Mix,** booklet, 1934 National Chicle Gum premium, 8 page illustrated booklet	15.00	25.00	20.00
☐ **Tom Mix,** bracelet, 1947 Ralston premium	25.00	35.00	30.00
☐ **Tom Mix,** button, 1946 Ralston premium	10.00	15.00	10.00
☐ **Tom Mix,** catalog, 1933 Ralston premium, 24 page illustrated manual gives life of Tom Mix ..	60.00	75.00	70.00
☐ **Tom Mix,** six gun decoder, 1941 Ralston premium	57.00	65.00	60.00
☐ **Tom Mix,** identification bracelet, 1947 Ralston premium	27.50	35.00	30.00
☐ **Tom Mix,** Brass Compass Magnifier, 1940 Ralston premium	30.00	40.00	35.00
☐ **Tom Mix,** Straight Shooter paper face mask of Tom, 1930s Ralston premium	35.00	45.00	40.00
☐ **Tom Mix,** Straight Shooter bangle bracelet, 1930s Ralston premium	75.00	85.00	80.00

	Current Price Range		P/Y Average
☐ **Tom Mix,** Straight Shooter Luck Sterling Silver Charm, 1936 Ralston premium	35.00	45.00	40.00
☐ **Tom Mix,** Straight Shooter Gold Ore charm, rectangular, 1941 Ralston premium	45.00	50.00	47.00
☐ **Tom Mix,** telephone set, 1938 Ralston premium	40.00	52.00	48.00
☐ **The Flash,** lithographed pinback button, 1940s comic premium	45.00	60.00	52.00
☐ **U.S. Jones Cadets,** pinback button, 1940s comic premium	65.00	75.00	70.00
☐ **Uncle Ezra,** giveaway photo, c. 1935 Alka-Seltzer premium giveaway from station EZRA, in Elkhart, IN	10.00	15.00	12.50
☐ **Welch's Sugar Daddy,** comic character cards, c. 1950s Welch's premium, full color, set of 50 different cards	65.00	77.00	71.00
☐ **Wizard of Oz,** books, 1933 Jello premium, "Ozma," "The Little Wizard"	50.00	60.00	55.00
☐ **Wonder Woman,** lithographed pinback button, 1940s comic premium	45.00	60.00	52.00

PRINTS

DESCRIPTION: Often referred to as limited edition or collector prints, this type of artwork is completed by a printmaking process.

TYPES: The three common forms of printmaking are original lithography, offset lithography or serigraphy. Original lithographs are made from hand drawn stones or plates. The artist paints directly on the stone or plate. The artist must reverse his drawing so when it is transferred to the paper, it will be viewed in the proper perspective. An offset lithograph is a photomechanical reproduction of the original work. Serigraph or silk screening is a method of printing using a squeegee. The squeegee forces the ink through a screen in which a stencil forms the area where the ink will go.

COMMENTS: Several factors are used to compile prices for collector prints including authenticity, subject, condition, size, artist's workmanship, printing technique, and quality of material.

ADDITIONAL TIPS: This section is organized by artist, followed by the name of the print, release date, edition number, size and publisher or distributor. The listing also tells if the print is signed and numbered (s/n), numbered only (n/o) or signed only (s/o).

For more information, consult *The Official Price Guide to Collector Prints,* published by The House of Collectibles.

Money To Spend *by Jay Schmidt*

	Issue Price	Current Price
☐ **Adamson, Harry,** Winging In-Pintails, rel. 1971, ed. 450, s/n, 17″ x 25″, pub Wild Wings, Inc.	50.00	675.00
☐ **Allison, Betty,** Cascades In Shade, rel. 1979, ed. 1,000, s/n, 15″ x 30″	40.00	80.00
☐ **Antis, Harry,** Whitetail Buck, rel. 1970, ed. 500, s/n, 24″ x 30″	25.00	60.00
☐ **Baize, Wayne,** Lazy Summer Days, rel. 1974, ed. 2,500, s/o, 27″ x 15″, pub Frame House Gallery, Inc.	30.00	125.00
☐ **Balke, Don,** Barn Owl, rel. 1976, ed. 1,000, s/n, 20″ x 26″, distributor Masterpiece Moulding and Frame	40.00	100.00
☐ **Bama, James,** Ken Hunder, Working Cowboy, rel. 1974, ed. 1,000, s/n, 21″ x 24″, pub Greenwich Workshop	55.00	375.00
☐ **Barber, John,** Atlantic Sentinel, ed. 750, s/n, 18″ x 28″, distributor Commodore Art Publishing	40.00	200.00
☐ **Bateman, Robert,** Cheetah with Cubs, rel. 1978, ed. 950, s/n, 21″ x 27″, pub Mill Pond Press, Inc.	95.00	175.00

	Issue Price	Current Price
☐ **Bergsma, Jody,** First Boat Boy, rel. 1979, ed. 1,000, s/o, 8″ x 10″, pub Bergsma Illustrations	3.00	40.00
☐ **Bierly, Edward,** Winter Woods, rel. 1977, ed. 600, s/n, 24″ x 32″, pub EJB Editions	100.00	350.00
☐ **Bollar, Sean,** Red-Headed Woodpecker, rel. 1975, ed. 800, s/n, 12″ x 16″, pub Pandion Gallery Ltd.	24.00	30.00
☐ **Boren, James,** Rainy Day at Hillsboro, rel. 1977, ed. 950, s/n, 20″ x 27″, pub Mill Pond Press, Inc.	75.00	185.00
☐ **Boutwell, George,** Fence Line, rel. 1970, ed. 1,000, s/n, 5″ x 7″, pub George Boutwell	1.00	15.00
☐ **Burger, Howard,** back home, rel. 1975, ed. 1,000, s/n, 18″ x 20″, pub Paul Sawyier Galleries, Inc.	30.00	250.00
☐ **Chapple, Dave,** Backwater Mallards, rel. 1978, ed. 150, etching, pub Etchings, Etc.	90.00	150.00
☐ **Coheleach, Guy,** Great Blue Heron, rel. 1968, ed. 2,500, s/o, 22½″ x 26″, pub Frame House Gallery	40.00	75.00
☐ **Combes, Simon,** Facing The Wind, rel. 1980, ed. 1,500, s/n, 32″ x 22″, pub Greenwich Workshop	75.00	120.00
☐ **Cowan, John,** Sunken Blind, ed. 600, s/n, 22″ x 28″, pub Meredith Long & Company	85.00	650.00
☐ **Crandall, Jerry,** Smoke Up Ahead, rel. 1977, ed. 450, s/n, 20″ x 30″, pub Guildhall, Inc.	60.00	450.00
☐ **Day, Ray,** Mail Pouch Barn, plate 1, rel. 1973, ed. 500, s/n, 20″ x 24″, distributor Masterpiece Moulding And Frame	15.00	100.00
☐ **Dodson, Larry,** Springtime in Elijay, rel. 1975, ed. 1,000, s/n, 18″ x 19″, pub Swan Graphics, Inc.	20.00	175.00
☐ **Dunnington, Tom,** American Bald Eagle #1, rel. 1971, ed. 4,700, s/o, 32″ x 23″, pub Cottage Hill Wildlife Art	30.00	60.00
☐ **Dye, Burton,** Country Afternoon, rel. 1977, ed. 1,000, s/n, 15″ x 21″, pub Burton Dye Prints	30.00	40.00
☐ **Faner, Ron,** Keeper of the Owls, rel. 1980, ed. 375, s/n, 26″ x 33″, pub Frame House Gallery	100.00	185.00
☐ **Farnsworth, Imogene,** Bengal Tiger, rel. 1973, ed. 1,000, s/n, 20″ x 24″	35.00	750.00
☐ **Ferrandiz, Juan,** He Seems to Sleep, rel. 1981, ed. 450, s/n, 18″ x 11″, pub Schmid Bros.	125.00	400.00
☐ **Forbes, Bart,** Shaker Girl, ed. 150, s/n, 22″ x 30″, pub Salt Creek Graphics	150.00	250.00
☐ **Forrest, Christopher,** Woody's Rest, rel. 1983, ed. 300, s/n, 21″ x 27″, pub Hang Ups, Inc.	250.00	300.00
☐ **Frace, Charles,** African Leopard, rel. 1981, ed. 12,500, s/o, 16″ x 20″, pub American Masters Foundation	25.00	35.00
☐ **Frisino, Louis,** single mallard, ed. 500, s/n, 11″ x 14″, pub Russell A. Fink	15.00	30.00
☐ **Getsinger, Joseph,** Antique Show, ed. 175, s/n, 10″ x 15″, etching, pub Joseph Getsinger Enterprises	20.00	30.00
☐ **Gill, Lunda,** Lundy in the Sand, rel. 1972, ed. 1,000, s/n, 31″ x 23″, pub Frame House Gallery	35.00	100.00
☐ **Granstaff, Bill,** At East, rel. 1973, ed. 200, s/n, 12″ x 16″, pub Granstaff Prints Ltd.	12.00	100.00
☐ **Gray, Gene,** Eastern Gray Squirrel, rel. 1968, ed. 5,000, s/o, 22″ x 18″	8.00	110.00
☐ **Haney, Enoch,** Spirit of Osceola, ed. 1,500, s/n, pub American Indian Arts Collection	40.00	175.00

	Issue Price	Current Price
☐ **Harm, Ray,** American Butterflies, rel. 1966, ed. 5,000, s/o, 22″ x 17″, pub Frame House Gallery	10.00	75.00
☐ **Harper, Bret,** Consider the Lillies, rel. 1975, ed. 250, s/n, 12″ x 20″, pub Frame House Gallery	20.00	40.00
☐ **Harper, Charles,** Ladybug, rel. 1968, ed. 500, s/n, 15″ x 20″, pub Frame House Gallery	20.00	250.00
☐ **Hibel, Edna,** Bouquet, ed. 101, s/n, 13″ x 19″, pub Jar Publishers	85.00	550.00
☐ **Hughes, Allen,** Returning Woodies, rel. 1975, ed. 750, s/n, 18″ x 23″, pub Swan Graphics, Ltd.	65.00	100.00
☐ **Joyce, Marshall,** Sea Ghost, rel. 1979, ed. 950, s/n, 20″ x 24″, pub Mill Pond Press Inc.	85.00	110.00
☐ **Maass, David,** Wild Wings Logo-Greenwing Teal, rel. 1981, ed. 950, s/n, pub Wild Wings, Inc.	75.00	100.00
☐ **Martin, Bernard,** Eastern Bluebird, rel. 1974, ed. 500, s/n, 16″ x 18″, pub Bernard Martin	20.00	200.00
☐ **McGaughy, Clay,** Bachelor, rel. 1970, ed. 500, s/n, 34″ x 27″, pub Arts Limited, Inc.	50.00	300.00
☐ **Moore, Wayland,** America's Champion, rel. 1977, ed. 500, s/n, 40″ x 30″, pub Felicie, Inc.	200.00	800.00
☐ **Nute, Cherrie,** Governor's Mansion, rel. 1975, ed. 1,000, s/n, 25″ x 22″, pub Foxfire Fine Arts, Inc.	25.00	150.00
☐ **Parker, Ron,** Raccoon Pair, rel. 1982, ed. 950, s/n, 21″ x 17″, pub Mill Pond Press, Inc.	95.00	120.00
☐ **Parnall, Peter,** Fox, rel. 1972, ed. 1,500, s/n, 28″ x 21″, pub Greenwich Workshop	60.00	150.00
☐ **Perillo, Gregory,** Madre, rel. 1977, ed. 500, s/n, 22″ x 28″, pub Vague Shadows Limited	125.00	300.00
☐ **Peterson, Roger Tory,** Baltimore Oriole, rel. 1973, ed. 450, s/n, 18″ x 18″, pub Mill Pond Press, Inc.	150.00	300.00
☐ **Preuss, Roger,** American Widgeon, rel. 1958, ed. 1,140, s/ in plate, 38″ x 48″, pub Wildlife of American	15.00	130.00
☐ **Reece, Maynard,** Bobwhites, rel. 1964, ed. 950, 14″ x 18″	20.00	650.00
☐ **Ren, Chuck,** The Mountain Men, rel. 1981, ed. 600, s/n, 22″ x 24″, pub Grey Stone Press	75.00	150.00
☐ **Sander, Tom,** From Cover, rel. 1977, ed. 500, s/n, 24″ x 30″, pub Frame House Gallery	40.00	115.00
☐ **Sawyer, Paul,** Elkhorn Creek Scene, rel. 1965, ed. 1,000, n/o, pub Sawyier Galleries, Inc.	15.00	45.00
☐ **Singer, Arthur,** Peregrine Falcon, rel. 1978, ed. 800, s/n, 37″ x 18″, pub Frame House Gallery	60.00	115.00
☐ **Sloan, Richard,** Eastern Bluebird, rel. 1968, ed. 5,000, s/o, 22″ x 28″, pub Nature House, Inc.	30.00	400.00
☐ **Solberg, Morton,** Chippewa Lake, rel. 1978, ed. 1,000, s/n, 29″ x 22″, pub Greenwich Workshop	65.00	115.00
☐ **Spencer, Irene,** Beyond the Sun, ed. 400, s/n, pub Irene Spencer	185.00	400.00
☐ **Timberlake, Bob,** Ella's Cupboard, rel. 1971, ed. 250, s/n, pub The Heritage Company	35.00	500.00
☐ **Vickers, Mary,** Age of Innocence, rel. 1970, ed. 200, s/n, pub Art Spectrum	40.00	325.00
☐ **Ward, Edward,** Caribe, rel. 1981, ed. 175, s/n, 11″ x 13″, pub Ed Ward	18.00	24.00

	Issue Price	Current Price
☐ **Wilson, Charles Banks,** New Rich, rel. 1939, ed. 10, 14″ x 10″, pub Charles Banks Wilson	5.00	250.00
☐ **Wright, David,** A Way of Life, ed. 1,500, s/n, 19″ x 25″, pub Grey Stone Press	40.00	80.00

PUPPETS

TYPES: There are four basic puppet types: hand puppets are controlled by puppeteers who wear puppets on their hands; rod puppets have rods attached to their jointed legs, arms and head; shadow puppets are flat and are used behind a screen or sheet to cast shadows; and marionettes or string puppets have much detail and are usually large.

COMMENTS: Made for the theatre and for children's toys, puppets have been collected since the 1920s. Those made before 1920 are currently the most valuable, but those from the 1930s and 1940s are usually easier to find and just as collectible.

ADDITIONAL TIPS: The listings are alphabetical and placed under puppet-type subheads. Ventriloquist dummies are also included here.

For further information on puppets, contact The Puppeteers of America, Inc., 2311 Connecticut Ave., NW #501, Washington, D.C. 20008.

HAND PUPPETS

	Current Price Range		P/Y Average
☐ **Figure of an old woman,** wearing long dress and apron, carved wood head, painted, French or Swiss, late 18th or early 19th c.	610.00	725.00	650.00
☐ **Oliver J. Dragon,** of the "Kukla, Fran and Ollie" television program, the original puppet made and used by Burr Tilstrom, c. 1940's	7000.00	9000.00	8000.00
☐ **Policeman,** old style uniform and hat, the head carved of balsa wood, painted and gilded, American, first quarter of the 20th c.	175.00	225.00	200.00
☐ **Punch,** long crooked nose, red cheeks, brightly colored costume, porcelain head and hands, chipped, probably English, mid-Victorian	1250.00	1550.00	1350.00

	Current Price Range		P/Y Average

MARIONETTES

☐ **"Black Sambo,"** composition head and hands, checkered shirt, brown striped pants, brown jacket, in original box with 78 r.p.m. phonograph record, America, 11½″ H., c. 1947 . . . . | 75.00 | 95.00 | 85.00

☐ **"Buffalo Bill,"** composition head, dressed in western outfit, belt with two guns, one hand missing, signs of wear, 46″ H. . . . . | 1600.00 | 2000.00 | 1800.00

☐ **Figure in the likeness of a skeleton,** painted wood, may be Mexican, 16½″ H., first half of the 20th c. . . . . | 450.00 | 550.00 | 500.00

☐ **Figure of a dragon,** entirely of wood, green, purple and other colors, prominent eyes, Chinese, 56″ H., 20th c. . . . . | 1050.00 | 1350.00 | 1150.00

☐ **Figure of Satan,** papier-mache head, garishly painted, the body made of red plush, wooden shoes, carved wooden pitchfork, 29″ H., 20th c.
. . . . | 850.00 | 1150.00 | 950.00

☐ **Figure of a woman,** possibly a princess, silk attire in multicolors, composition head, Japanese modern . . . . | 85.00 | 105.00 | 95.00

☐ **Fish, carved and painted wood,** moveable lower jaw, fins and tail, approx. 2′ H. . . . . | 512.00 | 575.00 | 543.00

☐ **Howdy Doody,** replica of the TV puppet, reduced size sold in toy stores in the early 1950's, 12″ H. . . . . | 82.00 | 110.00 | 93.00

☐ **Howdy Doody,** the original puppet used when the TV program first appeared on the air in 1948
. . . . | 20000.00 | 30000.00 | 25000.00

☐ **Man with round face,** buldging eyes, in tuxedo, American, carved and painted wooden face, 37″ H., 20th c. . . . . | 1050.00 | 1350.00 | 1200.00

ROD PUPPETS (Operated By Sticks)

☐ **Man on a horse,** stuffed bodies, papier-mache heads . . . . | 425.00 | 525.00 | 475.00

☐ **Monkey with smiling face,** long arms, rods attached to arms, 21″ H. . . . . | 350.00 | 450.00 | 400.00

VENTRILOQUIST "DUMMIES"

☐ **Jerry Mahoney,** composition head and hands, a small but exact replica, American, 21″ H., c. 1950 (was not sold with phonograph record) . . | 105.00 | 135.00 | 120.00

☐ **Jerry Mahoney,** composition head and hands, wearing suit and white shirt, American, 32″ H., c. 1950 . . . . | 180.00 | 220.00 | 200.00

☐ **As above,** in original suitcase-like carrying case with phonograph record . . . . | 350.00 | 450.00 | 400.00

	Current Price Range		P/Y Average

☐ **Original Charlie McCarthy dummy** of radio fame, head of carved wood (for a long while Edgar Bergen worked with just a single model of Charlie, then made another in case something happened to the first) 32500.00 47500.00   40000.00

☐ **Original Jerry Mahoney** used by Paul Winchell, head of carved wood. Jerry was by far the best designed of all the "famous dummies," with many special features 8500.00 11500.00   10000.00

QUILTS

DESCRIPTION: Quilts have been absorbed into the category of Folk Art, though their creators seldom intended them as works of art. Early America, and especially early rural America, thrived on its self-sufficiency: its ability to cultivate foodstuffs and manufacture the necessities of everyday life. Quilts are one example (of many) of our ancestors using their creative skills and their sense of thrift: oddments of fabric were cut and sewn into various patterns, to make clothing, bed coverings, etc. Not only was some money saved, but the owner was sure to possess a very unique "original," which made the shopkeeper's merchandise seem pale by comparison.

COMMENTS: Collecting specimens of old quilts was once a very restricted hobby, which seemed destined never to get beyond rural New England, Pennsylvania and some other areas. It has blossomed to full flower today, aided by museum interest and antique shows. On the whole, Amish quilts are the leaders in hobbyist appeal and in value, though they are not invariably the most valuable. The self-contained Amish community (of western Pennsylvania) was intent on "doing for itself," unconcerned about what was fashionable in the world's eyes; its quilts are ample testimony to its artistic spirit.

☐ **Arkansas Star,** 1930s, cotton, blocks are pieced with various solid colors for star points, prints for center of star, set in blocks of unbleached muslin, lattice strips of yellow, red, white and green print, solid red corner blocks and border, unbleached muslin backing which has been turned up and

Doll Quilt, *patchwork, wool,* **$30.00–$40.00**

	Current Price Range		P/Y Average
machine stitched to form binding, leaf and vine quilting design on lattice strips, never washed, excellent condition, 85″ x 67″	150.00	155.00	150.00
□ **Baseball,** cotton, all-over pattern made of gingham and calico, many colors, good light and dark contrast, border on one end, no setup blocks or strips, good condition, 70″ x 73″	130.00	155.00	142.00
□ **Bowtie,** cotton, pieced 5″ red bowties set in white squares alternate diagonally with gold and white blocks, wide inner white border with cable quilting, red outer border with diagonal quilting, white muslin back and binding, good used condition, 65″ x 81″	190.00	215.00	197.00
□ **Bowtie,** cotton, pieced 7″ blocks of various old calicoes, set up with beige print, border on two sides in same beige print, unbleached muslin back, some damage, 70″ x 84″	90.00	115.00	96.00
□ **Butterfly Applique,** cotton, sixty 5″ x 4½″ butterflies pieced of solid color percale, coordinating print and black percale body with embroidered antennae, appliqued to white block with black button hole stitching, gold percale strips, border and binding, lavender percale backing, fine fancy quilting, good used condition, 70″ x 75″	150.00	175.00	162.00

	Current Price Range		P/Y Average

☐ **Butterfly Applique,** 1930s, cotton, each butter-fly pieced with various coordinating prints and solids, appliqued onto unbleached muslin blocks with running stitch in black embroidery threat, set up lattice, strips in yellow and white print, smaller butterflies in blocks form border, unbleached muslin binding and backing, lovely quilting, never washed, excellent condition, 76″ x 80″ **180.00 200.00 190.00**

☐ **Cactus Basket,** also called basket of scraps, cotton, blocks are pieced in purple calico and pink gingham with white muslin background, set diagonally with squares of light lime-yellow cal-ico, lime yellow binding, unbleached muslin back, very good condition, 80″ x 68″ **130.00 155.00 140.00**

☐ **Checkerboard,** cotton, 13″ blocks are pieced with various old calicoes, chambrays and ging-hams, set diagonally with yellow, red and black calico print blocks, unbleached muslin back, ma-chine stitched binding, fan quilting, very good condition, 82″ x 60″ **100.00 125.00 112.00**

☐ **Colonial Tulip Applique,** 1930s, cotton, tulips are of solid lavender and lavender, purple and white print, green leaves and stems, hand appli-qued onto sixteen inch square unbleached mus-lin blocks, lavender binding, diagonal quilting, no set-up strips or border, never washed, excellent condition, 77″ x 85″ **170.00 195.00 180.00**

☐ **Double Irish Chain With Shamrocks,** cotton, al-ternating 2″ squares of solid red and green, larger white blocks with appliqued green sham-rocks, green binding, white backing, good used condition, 72″ x 85″ **200.00 225.00 210.00**

☐ **Double T,** Ohio Amish, cotton sateen, blue, tur-quoise, mauve and green pieced TS are set in diamond block arrangement, deep blue back-ground, blue border with cable stitching, bright green, binding **675.00 725.00 700.00**

☐ **Double Wedding Ring,** 1930s, cotton, pieced rings of various prints and solids, squares where rings meet are solid blue and solid yellow, white background, blue binding, straight rather than scalloped edges, intricate spider web quilting in medium blue thread, good used condition, 70″ x 84″ **130.00 155.00 140.00**

☐ **Double Wedding Ring,** 1930s, cotton, rings and squares where rings meet are all made of various color prints, white background and backing, green binding, good used condition, 86″ x 75″ **195.00 215.00 200.00**

☐ **Dresden Plate,** 1930s, cotton, each 12″ plate is pieced from calico prints and hand appliqued to solid pink blocks, darker pink background, never washed, excellent condition, 65″ x 82″ **90.00 115.00 100.00**

	Current Price Range		P/Y Average

☐ **Dresden Plate,** 1930s, cotton, prints and solids appliqued by hand to white muslin background, centers of plates are yellow and so are lattice strips, borderless, white backing and binding, diagonal quilting, excellent condition, 69″ x 89″ — 150.00 175.00 160.00

☐ **Embroidered Flowers In A Basket,** .cotton, 1938, four blocks with embroidered red, gold, blue and purple flowers, green leaves in large brown handled basket, three large embroidered flowers surround each basket, green squares placed diagonally between white triangular pieces form lattice strips which separate the four large embroidered blocks, inner border matches lattice strips, outside border of larger white and green triangular pieces with green pieces forming scalloped edge, green binding, unbleached muslin back, lovely handwork, never washed, very good condition, 86″ x 79″ 225.00 250.00 235.00

☐ **Embroidered State Flowers,** cotton, forty eight pink blocks are each embroidered with state flower and abbreviated state name, solid red, pastel pink and pastel blue lattice strips separate the blocks, blue corner blocks, dark pink, backing, very good condition, 85″ x 67″ 150.00 175.00 160.00

☐ **Flower Applique,** cotton, two shades of pink form four petal flowers with buds, green leaves, large dramatic repetition, very intricate quilting with swag border forming corner teardrops, never washed, excellent condition 450.00 475.00 460.00

☐ **Flower Applique,** Ohio, 1950, cotton, original design, red and pink calico flowers with yellow centers, green calico leaves and stems, each flower is surrounded by four leaves and curved stems with four buds, white background with tan band in border, signed and dated with quilters name, town and date in ink on back 650.00 675.00 660.00

☐ **Flower Baskets,** 1930s, cotton, assorted calico prints form pieced baskets on white background, good quilting between baskets, good used condition 200.00 225.00 210.00

☐ **Flower Wreath Applique,** crib, cotton, pink and blue flowers form wreath in center of white background, cable quilted border, new blue binding — 250.00 275.00 260.00

☐ **Flyfoot,** 1920s, cotton, large 15″ blocks are pieced with various prints having backgrounds, solid pink cotton is used for the foot, solid green lattice set-up strips, pink corner blocks, green binding, green and white polka dot backing with green, red and yellow apples and green leaves, crossing lines quilting, good handwork never washed, excellent condition, 90″ x 73″ 100.00 125.00 110.00

	Current Price Range		P/Y Average

☐ **Four Patch,** Indiana Amish, 1910, cotton, tan, black, yellow are pieced to form each of the four patches, indigo blue background and border with light blue band 800.00   825.00   810.00

☐ **Grape Vine Wreath,** applique, cotton, deep red grapes, dark green leaves form large wreath which covers entire off-white background of top, applique done by old machine stitching, hand quilted, cotton seeds throughout batting, never washed, excellent condition 475.00   500.00   485.00

☐ **Hexagon,** cotton, 1½" hexagons made of pastel, 1930s, percale prints and solids, 5" solid pink percale border, white backing, pink binding, crossing lines quilting, very good condition, 74" x 85" 150.00   175.00   160.00

☐ **Hole In The Barn Door,** Amish, cotton, wine pieced pattern mounted on black diamond blocks, medium blue blackground, medium blue border with black band and binding, quilted in white thread 550.00   575.00   560.00

☐ **Indiana Puzzle,** also called monkey wrench, cotton, solid white and bright red, machine bound, fan quilting, never washed, good condition, 75" x 85" 140.00   165.00   150.00

☐ **Jacob's Ladder,** cotton, made entirely of two old calico prints, one red and the other dark green, set diagonally in rows with no set-up strips or blocks in between, green calico border with cable quilting, very good condition, 78" x 79" 350.00   375.00   360.00

☐ **Jeweled Chain,** 1930s, cotton, pieced with various 1¼" squares of various cotton prints set with larger areas of white fancy quilted muslin, narrow inside border of white muslin, 2¾" outside border composed of 1¼" printed squares arranged diagonally with white triangular pieces, good used condition, 90" x 71" 250.00   275.00   260.00

☐ **Johnny In The Corner In A Garden Maze,** Indiana, cotton, red pieced geometric pattern, slate blue background, gold back and binding, never washed, mint condition 375.00   400.00   385.00

☐ **LeMoyne Star,** cotton, each 9" square block contains a star which is pieced of alternating dark and light calicoes, chambrays, and ginghams surrounded by solid light orange background, set up diagonally with indigo blue and white geometric print, unbleached muslin back, never washed, excellent condition, 78" x 85" 170.00   195.00   180.00

☐ **LeMoyne Star,** 1930s, cotton, 9" star blocks are pieced with various prints on solid green background, green binding, whitebacking, fine quilting, never washed, very good condition, 80" x 71" 150.00   175.00   160.00

	Current Price Range		P/Y Average

☐ **Log Cabin,** cotton, blocks are pieced with old calico prints, red border, navy, white and red print backing, lovely quilting, good used condition, 66″ x 80″ **175.00 195.00 182.00**

☐ **Lone Star,** 1930s, cotton, pieced large star is made of various percale prints, background and backing are solid green, machine stitched, binding, crossing lines design quilting, good used condition, 82″ x 85″ **225.00 250.00 235.00**

☐ **Nine Patch,** Ohio Amish, crib, cotton sateen, pieced wine squares form pattern, black black-ground and border, wine binding, new **75.00 85.00 80.00**

☐ **Nine Patch,** Pennsylvania Amish, wool, pieced with burgundy, plum, brown, navy and teal, loden green background, wine blocks in footend corners, wide green border with tulip quilting **600.00 625.00 610.00**

☐ **Nine Patch,** Pennsylvania, crib, various old prints, form blocks, background is pieced from mostly pink prints, used condition with some fading and wear **85.00 90.00 87.00**

☐ **Oak Leaf Applique,** nine repeats, four yellow-green leaves with four gold flowers, gold eight point star in center of each repeat, vine and bud border, good used condition **300.00 325.00 310.00**

☐ **Picture Frame,** Ohio Amish, cotton, solid black with bright blue band in border, bright blue binding, exceptional quilting, very contemporary . . . **250.00 275.00 260.00**

☐ **Plain,** Iowa Amish, cotton sateen, one solid piece of celery green sateen, exceptional quilting . . . **350.00 375.00 380.00**

☐ **Rainbow Tile,** also called Diamond Field, bright prints and solids are pieced to form pattern, unbleached muslin backing, machine stitched binding, never washed **100.00 125.00 110.00**

☐ **Rising Star,** cotton, large 13″ blocks pieced with old calicoes, ginghams and solid percales, solid turquoise percale lattice strips and narrow border, backing is white, turquoise, gold and black print, diagonal line quilting, good used, 66″ x 79″ **80.00 100.00 90.00**

☐ **Rose Applique,** cotton, large oval design of roses, buds, stems and leaves in two shades of green and four shades of pink hand appliqued using whipstitch in matching thread, embroidered veins in leaves, white background and binding, fine quilting in shell, feather, diagonal lines and other designs, white binding, scalloped edges on two sides, excellent condition, 60″ x 85″ **130.00 155.00 145.00**

☐ **Shooting Star,** 1920s, cotton, tiny old rose print calico and white muslin is pieced to form blocks which are set diagonally with squares of pieced white, tan and rose prints, rose calico inside border on two sides with narrow outside white border on all sides, white cotton backing, lovely quilting, good used, 76″ x 80″ **190.00 215.00 200.00**

	Current Price Range		P/Y Average

☐ **Squares,** Ohio Mennonite, crib, 1″ bands of wine, green, olive and black are pieced to form squares with black centers, black background, fifteen squares with black border **300.00 325.00 315.00**

☐ **Star String,** cotton, large four point stars are pieced with various 1930s print and solids, large, solid pink diamond shaped pieces between stars and border, pink binding, unbleached muslin backing, diagonal line quilting, never washed, excellent condition, several years old, 68″ x 69″ **150.00 175.00 162.00**

☐ **Streak Of Lightning,** crib, cotton, pieced solid red, white, and blue zig-zag pattern, red binding, good used condition **350.00 375.00 362.00**

☐ **T Block,** cotton, old solid red and white blocks recently pieced with additional white cotton to form 10″ blocks, white binding and backing, fine quilting, never washed, very good condition, 94″ x 72″ **180.00 200.00 190.00**

☐ **Texas Star,** also called Dolly Madison Star and Star Garden, 1930s, cotton, all over pattern consisting of 6″ pieced yellow stars, green, white and black print binding, solid yellow backing, good used condition **170.00 195.00 185.00**

☐ **Triple Irish Chain,** 1893, pieced with solid red and white, 1¾″ squares, inside red border, outside white border, white binding and backing, quilted in lines only one half inch apart, embroidered date Dec. 25, 1893, very good condition, 73″ x 68″ **325.00 350.00 333.00**

☐ **Wild Goose Chase,** cotton, blocks are pieced with triangles of old ginghams, calicoes, chambrays and solids, strips between rows of triangular pieces are solid aqua, unbleached muslin back, aqua binding, nice diagonal quilting, never washed, good condition, 82″ x 72″ **150.00 175.00 162.00**

RADIOS

TYPES: Most collectors seek vintage radio types including: early radio sets that required headphones; battery operated loudspeaker models; and loudspeaker models that ran on house currents. Even some transistor models are collectible today.

PERIOD: Collectible radios date from 1920, the start of commercial radio broadcasting.

COMMENTS: Most valuable are working radios with all of their original parts. Though they are expensive, large console models are sought after.

ADDITIONAL TIPS: The radio listings are in alphabetical order.

	Current Price Range		P/Y Average
☐ **A.C. Dayton Co.,** crystal set, c. 1923	120.00	155.00	135.00
☐ **A.C. Dayton Co.,** Super Six, c. 1924	148.00	190.00	160.00
☐ **Adams-Morgan,** Paragon Regen, c. 1921	218.50	260.00	230.00
☐ **Adams-Morgan,** R10 Short Wave, c. 1921	268.00	320.00	280.00
☐ **Atwater Kent,** #10, c. 1923	265.00	330.00	302.50
☐ **Beaver Baby Grand,** c. 1924	125.00	160.00	135.00
☐ **Crosley,** Vim, c. 1922	305.00	370.00	330.00
☐ **Crosley,** X, c. 1922	215.00	255.00	345.00
☐ **Crosley,** Pup, c. 1925	310.00	370.00	340.00
☐ **Crosley,** 5-38, c. 1926	210.00	265.00	242.50
☐ **DeForest,** D6, c. 1923	315.00	365.00	340.00
☐ **DeForest,** D10, c. 1923	405.00	465.00	435.00
☐ **DeForest,** Everyman, crystal, c. 1923	230.00	270.00	250.00
☐ **Federal,** 58DX, c. 1922	418.00	468.00	440.00
☐ **Federal,** 57DX, c. 1922	395.00	445.00	420.00
☐ **Federal,** 61DX, c. 1923	413.00	458.00	435.00
☐ **Freshman,** Masterpiece, c. 1924	255.00	305.00	280.00
☐ **Grebe,** CR6, c. 1919	495.00	565.00	530.00
☐ **Grebe,** CR5, c. 1921	285.00	335.00	310.00
☐ **Grebe,** Synchrophase, c. 1925	400.00	450.00	425.00
☐ **Lafayette,** ivory deco, plastic case	27.00	42.00	31.50
☐ **Magnavox,** TRF-5, c. 1925	250.00	350.00	300.00
☐ **Philco,** 551, c. 1928.....................	145.00	165.00	155.00
☐ **Philco,** 525, c. 1929.....................	100.00	120.00	110.00

	Current Price Range		P/Y Average
☐ **Philco,** Super-heterodyne Cathedral, c. 1931 ..	130.00	150.00	140.00
☐ **Philco Transistone,** portable, maroon and brown plastic case, leather handle	26.75	42.75	31.00
☐ **RCA,** Radiola X, c. 1925	420.00	470.00	450.00
☐ **RCA,** Radiola 26, c. 1925	515.00	575.00	530.00
☐ **RCA,** Radiola c. 1923	170.00	210.00	185.00
☐ **RCA,** Radiola special, c. 1923	175.00	225.00	200.00
☐ **RCA,** Aeriola Jr. (crystal), c. 1922	140.00	170.00	155.00
☐ **Zenith,** 835, c. 1932	150.00	200.00	175.00

RAILROADIANA

DESCRIPTION: Any items that pertain to the railroad make up railroadiana. This includes items from the steam powered, diesel and electric eras.

TYPES: Paper and hardware are the two basic types of railroadiana. The most collected paper item is the timetable while uniforms are an especially sought after hardware item.

ADDITIONAL TIPS: Some collectors obtain any object of railroadiana while others specialize in such areas as dining car items, ashtrays or keys.

☐ **Ashtray,** Erie, glass, diamond in center	7.00	10.00	8.00
☐ **Ashtray,** New York Central Railroad, crystal, blue, pictures diesel	15.00	19.00	16.00
☐ **Beer Mug,** Chessie System, glass, side logo with illustration of cat	7.00	10.00	8.00
☐ **Booklet,** New York, New Haven and Hartford, "Arranged Freight Train Service," c. 1920–1930	7.25	10.25	8.20
☐ **Brochure,** Erie Railroad, "The Erie Limited," with timetables and maps, 8½″ x 11″, 1929	6.25	8.25	6.90
☐ **Candle Holders,** Pennsylvania Railroad, silver plated, 3½″, pair.........................	200.00	250.00	220.00
☐ **Cordial Glass,** New York Central System, tall, side logo	9.50	12.50	10.50
☐ **Cordial Glass,** Santa Fe, etched glass	14.00	18.00	15.00
☐ **Cordial Glass,** 20th Century Limited, embossed glass	16.00	20.00	17.00

Railroad Spot Carbide Lantern, $30.00

	Current Price Range		P/Y Average
☐ **Dessert Fork,** New York Central Railroad, "New Pattern" by Hall and Elton, silver, 6½"	16.00	20.00	17.00
☐ **Folder,** Union Pacific, "Along the Union Pacific Railroad," c. 1930–1940	3.25	4.25	3.45
☐ **Formal Dinner Fork,** New York Central Railroad, "King's Pattern", silver, 8"	15.00	19.00	16.00
☐ **Horseradish Pot Holder,** Pennsylvania Railroad, glass and silver plated (two pieces), dated 1926	100.00	130.00	110.00
☐ **Juice Glass,** Chesapeake and Ohio, embossed glass, wording "For Progress"	8.00	10.75	8.75
☐ **Juice Glass,** New York Central Railroad, embossed glass, side marked, 6 oz.	6.00	8.00	6.50
☐ **Liquor License,** New York State, issued to New York Central Railroad, 8 x 11", c. 1960	4.50	6.00	5.10
☐ **Map,** New York Central System, color, 1924 ..	11.00	15.00	12.75
☐ **Menu,** Burlington Northern, Beverage List, 4 sided folder, states "form 2813", undated	2.25	3.25	2.75
☐ **Menu,** Burlington Northern, Breakfast, folder, April, 1970, 5" x 7"	2.25	3.25	2.75
☐ **Menu,** California Zephyr Lines, Cable Car Room cocktail menu, 4 sided folder, 1968	2.75	3.75	3.00
☐ **Menu,** Silver Meteor (Amtrack), Breakfast, 4-sided folder, October, 1962	4.00	6.00	4.75
☐ **Menu,** Wabash Railroad, undated	2.00	3.00	2.35
☐ **Napkin,** Rock Island Line, linen with logo	3.50	4.50	4.00

	Current Price Range		P/Y Average
☐ **Pass,** Maine Central Railroad, 1898	6.75	8.75	7.50
☐ **Pass,** Memphis and Little Rock Railroad Co., 1883	7.00	9.00	8.00
☐ **Pass,** Milwaukee and Northern, 1888	7.00	9.50	8.00
☐ **Pass,** Lake Shore and Western, 1882	7.00	9.00	8.00
☐ **Pass,** Lake Shore and Western, 1887	7.00	9.00	8.00
☐ **Pass,** Minneapolis and St. Louis, 1896	6.75	8.75	7.50
☐ **Pass,** Minneapolis and St. Louis, 1900	6.50	8.50	7.25
☐ **Pass,** Minneapolis, St. Paul and Sault Ste. Marie, 1895	7.00	9.00	7.75
☐ **Pass,** Missouri, Kansas and Texas Railway, 1889	7.00	9.00	8.00
☐ **Pass,** Missouri Pacific Railway Co., 1894	6.75	8.75	7.50
☐ **Pass,** Missouri Pacific Railway Co., 1898	6.75	8.75	7.50
☐ **Pass,** New York, Chicago and St. Louis Railroad, 1895	6.75	8.75	7.50
☐ **Placard,** Delaware and Western, "Switch Carefully," 3½" x 7"	1.00	1.35	1.00
☐ **Placard,** Delaware and Western, "Warning, Poisonous Fumes, Heated Car," 9½" x 9½"	2.00	3.00	2.40
☐ **Poster,** Brotherhood of Railroad Trainmen, various scenes in the life and deathof a rail employee, final scene shows window receiving death benefit check, c. 1900–1910, 22" x 28"	75.00	100.00	87.00
☐ **Poster,** New York Central, "Low Fare Excursions to Watkins Glen, July 12, 1931," 6" x 15"	4.50	5.25	5.00
☐ **Poster,** New York Central, "State Fair, Syracuse, September 7 to 12, 1931," fare chart plus list of events and attractions, 7" x 14"	4.50	6.00	5.15
☐ **Poster,** New York Central, "Weekend Excursion, Rochester to Montreal, Quebec, and Return," schedule plus points of interest, c. 1930	4.25	5.25	4.85
☐ **Serving Spoon,** New York Central Railroad, "King's Pattern", silver, 8"	15.00	19.00	16.00
☐ **Stock Certificate,** Market Street Railway Co., San Francisco, green and black with eagle vignette, c. 1925	9.00	12.00	10.00
☐ **Sugar Bowl,** Pennsylvania Railroad, silver plated with raised keystone emblem, dated 1929, 4"	80.00	100.00	88.00
☐ **Timetable,** Angelina and Neches River System, July, 1938	9.00	12.00	10.00
☐ **Timetable,** Ashley Drew and Northern System, December, 1938	11.00	14.00	12.00
☐ **Timetable,** Atlanta Birmingham and Coast Line System, November, 1936	9.00	12.00	10.00
☐ **Timetable,** Atlanta and West Point, Western Railway of Alabama, September, 1942	7.50	10.50	8.00
☐ **Timetable,** Baltimore and Ohio, Baltimore Division, October, 1965	3.50	5.00	4.15
☐ **Timetable,** Baltimore and Ohio, Buffalo Division, October, 1965	3.50	5.00	4.16
☐ **Timetable,** Baltimore and Ohio, Chicago Terminal, April, 1969	2.75	3.75	2.90

	Current Price Range		P/Y Average

❏ **Timetable,** Baltimore and Ohio, Cumberland Division, October, 1970 .... | 3.75 | 5.25 | 4.15
❏ **Timetable,** Baltimore and Ohio, Maryland Division, January, 1974 .... | 3.75 | 5.25 | 4.15
❏ **Timetable,** Baltimore and Ohio, Monogah Division, October, 1965 .... | 3.75 | 5.25 | 4.15
❏ **Timetable,** Baltimore and Ohio, St. Louis Division, April, 1967 .... | 3.75 | 5.25 | 4.15
❏ **Timetable,** Barre and Chelsea Railroad System, September, 1949 .... | 7.25 | 10.50 | 8.00
❏ **Timetable,** Beaver/Meade/Englewood, October, 1956 .... | 7.25 | 10.50 | 8.00
❏ **Timetable,** Belfast and Moosehead Lake System, April, 1953 .... | 4.50 | 6.00 | 5.10
❏ **Timetable,** Bennetsville and Cheraw Railroad System, May, 1939 .... | 11.00 | 14.00 | 12.00
❏ **Timetable,** Blue Ridge Railway System, May, 1942 .... | 8.00 | 11.00 | 9.00
❏ **Timetable,** Bonhomie and Hattiesburg System, November, 1928 .... | 13.00 | 17.00 | 14.00
❏ **Timetable,** Bonhomie and Hattiesburg System, April, 1954 .... | 7.00 | 10.00 | 8.00
❏ **Timetable,** Boston and Albany Railroad, poster style with large woodcut, c. 1870–1880, 18½″ x 24″ .... | 50.00 | 65.00 | 56.00
❏ **Timetable,** Boston Terminal Co., South Station, April, 1954 .... | 4.50 | 6.00 | 5.10
❏ **Timetable,** Central New Jersey Railroad, Central Division, September, 1953 .... | 5.25 | 7.25 | 5.75
❏ **Timetable,** Central New Jersey Railroad, Central Division, October, 1955 .... | 5.25 | 7.25 | 5.75
❏ **Timetable,** Central New Jersey Railroad, Central Division, October, 1961 .... | 4.75 | 6.25 | 5.20
❏ **Timetable,** Central New Jersey Railroad, Pennsylvania Division, April, 1959 .... | 5.25 | 7.75 | 6.10
❏ **Timetable,** Central Vermont System, April, 1964 .... | 4.75 | 6.25 | 5.00
❏ **Timetable,** Central Terminal of Toledo System, February, 1958 .... | 4.75 | 6.25 | 5.00
❏ **Timetable,** Charleston and Western Carolina System, April, 1946 .... | 8.00 | 11.00 | 9.20
❏ **Timetable,** Chicago and Alton, Northern Division, September, 1929 .... | 14.00 | 19.00 | 15.50
❏ **Timetable,** Chessie System, Covington and Cincinnati Elevated Railroad, April, 1941 .... | 8.00 | 11.00 | 9.00
❏ **Timetable,** Chessie System, Covington and Cincinnati Elevated Railroad, April, 1961 .... | 4.75 | 6.25 | 5.25
❏ **Timetable,** Chessie System, Ashland and Russell-Hocking Division, April, 1961 .... | 3.75 | 5.25 | 4.25
❏ **Timetable,** Chessie System, Cincinnati and Chicago Division, April, 1966 .... | 3.75 | 5.25 | 4.25
❏ **Timetable,** Chessie System, Grand Rapids-Saginaw Division, October, 1965 .... | 3.75 | 5.25 | 4.25

	Current Price Range		P/Y Average
☐ **Timetable,** Chessie System, Hinton Division, April, 1961	4.75	6.25	5.50
☐ **Timetable,** Chessie System, Hinton and Huntington Division, April, 1966	3.75	5.25	4.50
☐ **Timetable,** Erie Railroad, Wyoming and Jefferson Division, April, 1939	7.25	10.50	8.25
☐ **Timetable,** Erie Railroad, New York Division, April, 1660	4.75	6.25	5.35
☐ **Timetable,** Ft. Worth and Denver, Wichita Falls and Amarillo Division, October, 1936	9.00	12.00	10.00
☐ **Timetable,** Ft. Worth and Denver, Wichita Falls and Amarillo Division, December, 1942	7.00	10.00	8.00
☐ **Timetable,** Ft. Worth and Denver, Wichita Falls and Amarillo Division, October, 1945	6.00	8.00	6.75
☐ **Timetable,** Ft. Worth and Denver, Wichita Falls and Amarillo Division, June, 1949	6.50	8.50	7.25
☐ **Timetable,** Ft. Worth and Denver, Wichita Falls and Amarillo Division, June, 1954	5.50	7.25	6.25
☐ **Timetable,** Galveston Houston and Henderson, April, 1928	11.00	14.00	12.00
☐ **Timetable,** Galveston Houston and Henderson, December, 1932	9.00	12.00	10.00
☐ **Timetable,** Gulf Mobile and Ohio, Southern Division, October, 1940	7.50	10.50	8.75
☐ **Timetable,** Gulf Mobile and Ohio, Southern Division, January, 1952	5.25	7.25	6.25
☐ **Timetable,** Gulf Mobile and Ohio, Western Division, September, 1948	7.00	10.00	8.00
☐ **Timetable,** Gulf Mobile and Ohio, Western Division, April, 1960	4.85	6.50	5.75
☐ **Timetable,** Gulf and Ship Island Railroad System, June, 1930	11.00	14.00	12.00
☐ **Timetable,** Harlem Line, operating between Grand Central Depot and Mott Haven (Manhattan to Bronx, New York), broadside poster with rules on reverse side, c. 1881	8.00	11.00	9.25
Note: The Harlem Line with its short borough-to-borough runs was the direct ancestor of the subway train in New York City			
☐ **Timetable,** Houston and Texas Central System, March, 1960	18.00	23.00	19.00
☐ **Timetable,** Houston Belt and Terminal System, August, 1926	9.00	12.00	10.00
☐ **Timetable,** Houston Belt and Terminal System, October, 1933	8.00	11.00	9.00
☐ **Timetable,** Houston Belt and Terminal System, April, 1943	6.00	8.00	6.75
☐ **Timetable,** Houston Belt and Terminal System, January, 1948	5.00	7.00	5.50
☐ **Timetable,** Houston Belt and Terminal System, January, 1965	4.50	6.00	5.00
☐ **Timetable,** Houston Belt and Terminal System, December, 1972	3.75	5.50	4.10

	Current Price Range		P/Y Average

□ **Timetable,** Illinois Central, Louisville Division, August, 1900 . . . .   23.00   28.00   25.00

□ **Timetable,** Illinois Central, Louisville Division, September, 1950 . . . .   5.00   7.00   5.60

□ **Timetable,** Illinois Central, Louisville Division, September, 1953 . . . .   4.50   6.00   5.00

□ **Timetable,** Illinois Central, Louisville Division, October, 1958 . . . .   4.50   6.00   5.00

□ **Timetable,** Illinois Central, Paducah Division, April, 1972 . . . .   3.50   5.00   4.10

□ **Timetable,** Illinois Central, St. Louis Division, July, 1919 . . . .   18.00   23.00   19.00

□ **Timetable,** Illinois Central, St. Louis Division, June, 1923 . . . .   14.00   19.00   15.50

□ **Timetable,** Illinois Central, St. Louis Division, January, 1931 . . . .   9.00   12.00   10.00

□ **Timetable,** Illinois Central, St. Louis Division, October, 1965 . . . .   3.75   5.50   4.15

□ **Timetable,** Illinois Central, St. Louis Division, April, 1967 . . . .   3.75   5.50   4.15

□ **Timetable,** Illinois Central Gulf, Kentucky Division, January, 1978 . . . .   3.75   5.50   4.15

□ **Timetable,** Illinois Central Gulf, Mississippi Division, April, 1976 . . . .   3.75   5.50   4.15

□ **Timetable,** Illinois Central Gulf, Missouri Division, April, 1976 . . . .   3.75   5.50   4.15

□ **Timetable,** Illinois Central Gulf, Midwest Division, October, 1978 . . . .   2.75   4.25   2.85

□ **Walter's Clipboard,** Pennsylvania Railroad, silver plated with raised keystone emblem at top, 8¾" 170.00   200.00   180.00

□ **Water Glass,** Baltimore and Ohio, embossed glass, side logo with diesel and steam locomotives, 6 oz. 14.00   18.00   15.00

□ **Water Glass,** Baltimore and Ohio, embossed glass, pictures Capitol Dome, undated 9.00   12.00   10.00

□ **Water Glass,** New York Central Railroad, embossed glass, side marked, 10 oz. 9.00   12.00   10.00

□ **Water Glass,** Santa Fe, embossed glass, 8 oz.   6.00   8.00   6.60

□ **Water Glass,** 20th Century Limited, embossed glass, 8 oz. 18.00   23.00   19.25

□ **Water Glass,** Union Pacific, crest at side, 8 oz.   3.75   5.50   4.00

□ **Wine Glass,** New York Central Railroad, embossed glass, side marked, 4 oz. 7.00   10.00   8.15

□ **Wine List,** Burlington Northern, with insert, undated 2.00   3.00   2.35

RAZORS

MATERIALS: Most commonly, razor handles are made of wood, hard rubber and imitation bone. Finer razors had handles of ivory, bone or sterling silver.

COMMENTS: As with most collectibles, old and rare razors are the most valuable. Along with flea markets and antiques shops, knife shows often feature razors.

ADDITIONAL TIPS: The listings in this section are alphabetical according to manufacturer. When the manufacturer isn't known, the razor is listed by type.

	Current Price Range		P/Y Average
☐ **Amber,** straight razor, high carbon steel blade with gold plated end, extra full hollow grinding, transparent celluloid handle, ½″ wide blade (narrower than standard)	9.00	12.00	10.50
☐ **Antonio Tadros,** straight edge	8.50	12.00	10.00
☐ **Army/Navy,** straight razor, Wardlow English steel blade, three-quarter hollow grinding, oval handle of black hard rubber, ¾″ wide blade (wider than standard), commercially sold razor of World War I era said to be duplicate of military issue	10.00	13.00	11.50
☐ **Barber,** straight edge in original box	51.50	60.00	53.00
☐ **Cattaraugus Cutlery Co.** with "The Sovereign's Own" imprint	22.50	30.00	26.50
☐ **Chip-A-Way Cutlery Co., England** with "Chip-A-Way" imprint	10.50	13.50	12.00
☐ **Colquhoun and Cadman, Sheffield** with "Little Favorite" imprint	6.50	9.50	8.00
☐ **Curvit,** for women, in flannel pouch	4.00	10.00	6.00
☐ **Electric Cutlery, New York** with "Arlington" imprint	6.50	9.50	8.00
☐ **Elsener, Switzerland** with "Ideal" imprint	7.50	10.50	9.00
☐ **Euchler,** straight, with bakelite handle	6.00	10.00	8.00

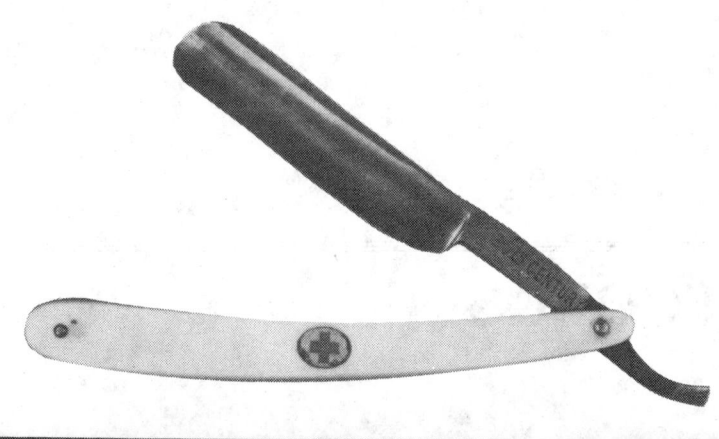

Straight Razor, *Red Injun, ivory celluloid handle, made in Germany, original box,* **$35.00-$40.00**

	Current Price Range		P/Y Average
□ **Ever-Ready,** safety razor, c. 1920–1930	5.00	7.00	6.00
□ **Favorite,** straight razor, Wardlow English steel blade, extra full hollow grinding, plain handle of hard black rubber, ⅝″ wide blade	8.00	11.00	9.50
□ **Genco Barber,** straight razor, extra full hollow grinding, celluloid handle in imitation of golden oak, ⅝″ wide blade	16.00	21.00	18.25
□ **Genco Heavy,** Geneva Cutlery Co., straight razor, full hollow grinding, plain hard black rubber handle with nickel silver ends, ⅝″ wide blade	12.00	17.00	14.50
□ **Gillette New Standard,** safety razor, triple silver plating	7.00	10.00	8.35

□□===□□===□□===□□===□□===□□===□□===□□===□□===□□===□□

RECORDS

TYPES: There are two primary types of records: 45s and LPs. A 45 is a small record that usually features one song on each side. It turns on the turntable at a rate of 45 revolutions per minute; thus, the name. An LP is a long playing album that has several songs on each side. It turns at a rate of 33 revolutions per minute.

PERIOD: Records from the 1950s and 1960s are most popular among collectors.

MATERIALS: Records are almost exclusively made of vinyl. Rare platinum and gold specimens are produced occasionally for superstars, but these almost never make it into the collectible market.

COMMENTS: Rare releases by famous groups and singers are in great demand. Bands like The Beatles and The Rolling Stones command top prices for scarce recordings.

ADDITIONAL TIPS: For further information and listings, please refer to *The Official Price Guide to Records,* published by The House of Collectibles.

	Current Price Range		P/Y Average
□ **Abba,** Atlantic, #3035, Watch Out Waterloo/Dance While the Music Still Goes On	2.00	5.00	3.00
□ **Addeo, Nicky,** Selsom, #104, Over the Rainbow/Gool #2	22.00	42.00	27.00
□ **Beatles,** Decca, #9-31382, My Bonnie/The Saints	375.00	860.00	500.00
□ **Beatles,** Vee Jay, #581, From Me to You/Please Me (Promo)	35.00	75.00	50.00
□ **Bluesology,** Fontana, #594, Times are Getting Tougher, featuring Elton John	23.00	40.00	27.00
□ **Clovers,** Rainbow, #122, Yes Sir, That's my Baby/When You Come Back to Me	160.00	285.00	190.00
□ **Creedence Clearwater Revival,** Scorpio, #412, Porterville/Call It Pretending	15.00	29.00	19.00
□ **Danny and the Juniors,** Singular, #711, At the Hop/Sometimes	39.00	65.00	42.00

	Current Price Range		P/Y Average
☐ **Fats Domino,** Imperial, #5058, The Fat Man/Detroit City Blues	27.00	46.00	42.00
☐ **Dominoes,** Federal, #12001, Chicken Blues, Do Something to Me	65.00	125.00	75.00
☐ **Dominoes,** Federal, #12010, Harbor Lights/No Says My Heart............................	180.00	325.00	215.00
☐ **Five Blobs,** Columbia, #41250, The Blob/Saturday Night in Tijuana	5.00	8.50	7.00
☐ **Five Jades, The,** Pyramid. #163, Are You Sorry/Let There Be You	50.00	90.00	65.00
☐ **Jackson 5,** Steeltown, #681, You've Changed/Big Boy	17.00	28.00	18.00
☐ **Jerry Landis (Paul Simon),** MGM, #12622, Anna Belle/Loneliness.....................	17.00	29.00	25.00
☐ **Little Richard,** RCA, #4392, Taxi Blues/Every Hour	76.00	128.00	120.00
☐ **Manhattan Transfer,** Atlantic, #3636, Birdland/Shaker Song	3.00	4.75	3.00
☐ **Elvis Presley,** Sun, #215, Milkcow Blues Boogie/You're A Heartbreaker	275.00	450.00	310.00
☐ **Elvis Presley,** RCA, #7506, A Fool Such As I/I Need Your Love Tonight	4.00	7.00	4.85
☐ **Robins, Crown,** #106, I Made A Vow/Double Crossin' Baby	46.00	80.00	72.00

RED WING POTTERY

DESCRIPTION: Red Wing Stoneware Company was founded in 1878 in Red Wing, Minnesota. It was one of the earliest midwestern potteries outside of Ohio. Pottery factories straying from the eastern Ohio region were usually doomed to an early failure, but Red Wing showed remarkable staying power. As the population of the area increased, its production increased, and the business thrived. The concept of expanding its line beyond stoneware was first explored in the early 1920s when the market for pottery in general broadened out as never before. The first new item put into production at that time was a line of flowerpots, followed in later years by artware cookie jars, jugs, trays, candleholders and vases. Also, a general line of dinnerware was added to the factory's schedule in the depression years to take up slack from the loss of artware sales. The best years for Red Wing art pottery were from the middle 1920s to the early 1930s.

MARKS: Red Wing manufactured under its own name and also as Rumrill sometimes spelled RumRill. When the RumRill mark is used, it will generally be with the second R capitalized. The Red Wing housemarks changed through the years. If one includes the early stoneware markings a long list would be necessary to record them all. In the era of its art pottery, there were at least three distinctive marks. One consisted of the wording RED WING ART POTTERY arranged in a circle with ART at the center and other symbols or decoration. An impressed mark from the 1930s states simply RED WING followed by the mold or model number. The most elaborate mark is a badge, with the company name in bold script lettering in Art Deco style.

Pitcher, *green mottled glaze,* $35.00–$40.00

	Current Price Range		P/Y Average
☐ **Ashtray,** salmon tinged with lavender, semi gloss, of roughly circular form in the shape of a horse's head and neck, with a shellwork design at the lower portion, marked RED WING U.S.A.	15.00	18.00	16.00
☐ **Bowl,** console, item #B-2014, red, semi-gloss, of freeform shape, low-slung, with bird's-wing molding at the sides, marked RED WING U.S.A.	12.00	15.00	12.75

	Current Price Range		P/Y Average

☐ **Candleholder,** item #B-1411, blue, high gloss, of roughly rectangular form with shaped sides, giving the appearance of an ashtray, marked RED WING U.S.A. **4.00   5.00   4.00**

☐ **Candleholder,** item #B-1412A, cedar brown, high gloss, of free form oval design pinched at one end, marked RED WING U.S.A. **8.00   10.00   9.35**

☐ **Candlestick,** item #1558, green, semi gloss, of shaped cylindrical form, flared at the top, composed of a set of four oval pillars joined together in freeform composition, marked RED WING U.S.A. **9.00**

☐ **Jug,** pastel beige, matte glaze, of spherical form with mouth and pouring spout positioned to one side, C-shape handle, marked RUM RILL **22.00   25.00   22.75**
Note: Red Wing produced a considerable amount of work for the Rum Rill Pottery Co. It is collected both by Red Wing enthusiasts and those who specialize in the Rum Rill products.

☐ **Planter,** item #5018, blue, matte glaze, of rectangular form with sloping sides, marked RED WING U.S.A. **8.00   10.00   9.25**

☐ **Planter,** item #1463, dark green, high gloss, shaped oval form with sculptured rim to give the appearance of carved rockstone, marked RED WING U.S.A. **11.00   13.00   12.00**

☐ **Planter,** item #1264, salmon, semi-gloss, of lampshade form with shaped fluted sides, marked RED WING U.S.A. **8.00   10.00   9.00**

☐ **Planter,** item #835, sea green, matte glaze, of oval form, low-slung, decorated at the sides with loopwork, marked RED WING U.S.A. **8.00   10.00   9.00**

☐ **Sign, "True China By Red Wing,"** bone white, matte glaze, rectangular with raised lettering. Show window sign for dealers selling the Red Wing Line. (Not offered for public sale.) **52.00   68.00   60.00**

☐ **Sugar and Creamer,** items #262 and #263, ivory white, matte glaze, decorated with molded figures of grape bunches highlighted with touches of burgundy coloring, marked RED WING U.S.A. **27.00   32.00   30.00**

☐ **Vase,** item #404, elephant gray, semi-gloss, of flattened tubular form with tripled molded banding and a flattened vertical panel rising the entire height of the body, red interior, marked RED WING U.S.A. **10.00   12.00   11.00**

☐ **Vase,** item #1357, elephant gray, semi-gloss, fluted panels, scrolled handles at either side, with molded leafwork at the base, marked RED WING U.S.A. **10.00   12.00   11.00**

☐ **Vase,** item #1197, blue, matte glaze, bulbous bowl with wide shaped neck, no lip, the neck fluted to form a corrugated design, the bowl decorated with small molded stars, marked RED WING U.S.A. **11.00   13.00   11.75**

ROBOTS

COMMENTS: There is a tremendous amount of activity in this area of toy collecting. The best place to see toy robots is at an antique toy show. Condition is very important in this field.

RECOMMENDED READING: For further information refer to *The Official Price Guide to Toys* and *The Official Price Guide to Science Fiction and Fantasy Collectibles,* published by The House of Collectibles.

	Current Price Range		P/Y Average
☐ **Action Packed Robot,** made in Japan, battery operated, lithographed tin with plastic arms and feet, doors on chest open to reveal machine guns, turns as he walks, 11½″	75.00	95.00	85.00
☐ **Action Robot,** made in Hong Kong, all plastic, guns mounted on either side of head, 10″	16.00	25.00	20.00
☐ **Apollo Astroid Robot,** made by Durham Japan, plastic with silver-colored radar screen that rotates as he walks, 6″	30.00	37.00	33.00
☐ **Artoo-Detoo,** Kenner Corp., stuffed toy of the little robot in Star Wars, 100% polyester with painted features and moveable legs	7.50	9.75	7.00
☐ **Atomic Robot,** maker unidentified, clockwork, tin, primitive styling with "tin can" appearance, lithographed dials, walks 7″	275.00	325.00	260.00
☐ **Big Max Robot,** made by Remco, all plastic, battery powered, robot hoists loads by electromagnet, places them on belt which deposits them into truck, was featured in 1958 Sears Roebuck catalogue	187.50	227.50	177.50
☐ **Lightan GB-38,** made in Orient with all Oriental lettering on box (but with U.S. patent numbers), looks like a gold covered cigarette case when closed but opens up into a robot which features a small telescope	27.50	38.50	26.50

Attacking Martian, *hips swivel, moves forward and back,* **$100.00–$180.00**

	Current Price Range		P/Y Average
☐ **Lightan GB-42,** made in Orient with all Oriental lettering on box (but with U.S. patent numbers), looks like a gold covered cigarette case but folds out to form a robot, has small wheels and fires projectiles	35.00	45.00	31.50
☐ **Looky the See-Through Take-Apart Robot,** made in Hong Kong, plastic, price for specimen in original carton with cellophane window front	32.50	37.50	31.00
☐ **Marvelous Mike Electromatic Tractor,** Saunders, lithographed tin, robot seated in tractor which he operates, carries patent date of 1954, 13″ in length by 8 ½″ high	130.00	160.00	119.50
☐ **Mechanical Mighty Robot,** made by Noguchi of Japan, lithographed tin, clockwork, walks and sparks (sparks appear on TV-like screen on robot's chest), key is affixed, 5½″	175.00	215.00	162.00
☐ **Microman,** maker not identified, made in Orient with Oriental lettering on box, five robots, one with wings, which can be assembled into one large robot or used separately	50.00	61.00	45.00

	Current Price Range		P/Y Average

☐ **Mr. Machine,** Ideal, all plastic, clockwork, caricature robot with tophat and smiling face, visible motor, large attached key at back, chirps, opens and closes his mouth, rolls forward, moves arms up and down, 1977, 17″ **30.00 39.00 31.00**
This toy was also made in a metallic version.

☐ **Mr. Monster,** Play Value Toys, made in Hong Kong, battery operated, plastic, walks and moves arms and legs, lights blink, radar screen on top of head revolves, 9″ **70.00 90.00 74.00**

☐ **Robot 2050,** no indication of maker, probably Oriental, metal and plastic, clockwork, light in chest blinks as he walks, 11″ **35.00 45.00 34.00**

☐ **Sir Galaxy Radio Control Robot,** Mattel, made in Hong Kong, remote control, walks, can change direction, makes beeping sounds, and projects operator's voice when spoken into remote control unit, 16″ **95.00 125.00 105.00**

☐ **Smoking Spaceman Robot,** Linemar Industries, tin, battery powered, eyes blink, mouth smokes, lighted pistons with domes, battery boxes located in legs, 12″, 1950s **900.00 1150.00 850.00**

☐ **Son Of Garloo,** Marx, made in Japan, clockwork, green, bat-like face with open mouth and prominent teeth, 5¾″ **110.00 162.50 87.00**

☐ **Spaceman,** made in Japan, lithographed tin, clockwork, walks and swings arms, 8″ **175.00 220.00 145.00**

☐ **Super Space Commander,** made by S.H. of Japan, battery powered, plastic, very similar to Video Robot (see below) but with different face, eyes are round and protruding, 10½″ **38.00 49.50 37.50**

☐ **Tinman Robot From The Wizard of Oz,** Remco, battery operated, plastic with decals, reads "Tin Man Robot" on chest, has gear panel, reverses direction when he bumps into something, 21″, 1969 .... **205.00 260.00 210.00**

☐ **Unnamed,** made in Japan, lithographed tin, has human face, TV screen for chest, wire projecting from head, 11½″ **90.00 120.00 70.00**

☐ **Unnamed,** made by Yone of Japan, lithographed tin, clockwork, miniature robot with broad shoulders and domed head, key affixed at right side, 3¾″ **16.00 21.00 10.00**

☐ **Video Robot,** made in Japan, body has "TV" screen for chest, wrench-like hands, box reads, "Walks Forward, Catches 'Scene of the Moon' on Big Screen," 9½″ **17.50 22.75 18.00**

ROOKWOOD

DESCRIPTION: Rookwood pottery features large, bold underglaze painting which gives the wares the appearance of oil painting on porcelain.

PERIOD: Rookwood manufactured pottery from 1879 to 1967. Its heyday was from 1890–1930.

ORIGIN: Rookwood was founded in 1879 in Cincinnati, Ohio. While other manufacturers of the day made stoneware, Rookwood strove to design artistic ware and maintain high quality. Rookwood proved that the buying public would buy American art pottery instead of European pottery.

MARKS: Products bore a factory artist mark, and they sometimes bore a clay mark, size mark and process mark as well. Those with a process mark are always worth a premium.

COMMENTS: In terms of length of operation, pieces manufactured and collector interest, Rookwood is the leader of art pottery makers. Rookwood vases are the most famous and popular. While prices for Rookwood pottery are fairly high, the market has stabilized in recent years.

ADDITIONAL TIPS: The listings are alphabetical by item. For more complete information on Rookwood, refer to *The Official Price Guide to Pottery and Porcelain,* published by The House of Collectibles.

	Current Price Range		P/Y Average
☐ **Box,** 5″, pink, slip-painted floral decor, by Vera Tischler, dated 1923	175.00	225.00	205.00
☐ **Box,** 5½″, Z glaze, modeled grapes on cover, green shades to blue, by K. Shirayamano, dated 1905	200.00	300.00	255.00
☐ **Bookends,** 5½″, item #2695, green, in the form of sailing ships, with an impressed factory mark and the initials of artist William P. McDonald, dated 1936................................	150.00	180.00	170.00
☐ **Bookends,** 5½″, item #2695, turquoise, in the form of a yacht, by William P. McDonald, dated 1925	95.00	120.00	110.00

	Current Price Range		P/Y Average
□ **Bookends,** 6″, blue, highly glazed, models of owls, by Margaret Helen McDonald, dated 1940	110.00	125.00	117.50
□ **Bookends,** 6″, green, glazed finish, models of horses, by Margaret Helen McDonald, dated 1940	150.00	200.00	170.00
□ **Creamer,** item #547, turquoise, matte finish, dated 1940	20.00	25.00	22.00
□ **Dish,** 5″, cameo glaze, peach shades to green, white flowers, log shape, dated 1890	115.00	125.00	117.50
□ **Ewer,** 5¼″, item #626/W, dark brown standard factory glaze with silver overlay, modified tankard form, decorated with a slip-painting of flowers and foliage by Anna M. Valentien (signed with initials), bearing an impressed factory mark and the date 1892	775.00	950.00	855.00
□ **Figurine,** goat, 6¼″, item #6170, white, matte finish, impressed Louise Abel, dated 1945	65.00	75.00	70.00
□ **Figurine,** 4½″, woman reclining on high glaze green tray	75.00	85.00	81.00
□ **Ginger Jar,** 3½″, item #1321E, pink, with lid	70.00	80.00	76.00
□ **Honey Jug,** 4¾″, bisque, light brown, intaglio clover design, by H. Wendroth, dated 1883 ...	140.00	160.00	147.50
□ **Jardiniere,** 10¾″, light brown glaze, orange slip-painted poppies, by Matthew Daly, dated 1892	1000.00	1250.00	1150.00

Vase, *c. 1949*

	Current Price Range		P/Y Average

□ **Jardiniere,** 11⅞″, in diameter, dark brown, standard factory glaze, decorated with floral blossoms by Matthew Daly (signed with initials), bearing an impressed factory mark and the date 1891 . . . . 520.00   610.00   555.00

□ **Jug,** 6½″, dark brown, standard factory glaze, bearing the molded seal of Cincinnati, Ohio on one side and the molded seal of the state of Ohio on the other, with an impressed factory mark and the date 1888 . . . . 700.00   875.00   800.00

□ **Plaque,** 5″ x 9″, vellum glaze, painted with a seascape during a snowfall by Lenore Asbury (signed with full name), bearing an impressed factory mark and the date 1919, mounted in a wooden frame for wall hanging. (The frame is not included in the above measurement.) 710.00   850.00   760.00

□ **Tray,** 10½″, brown matte finish with leaves and acorns with a rook, dated 1922 . . . . 170.00   190.00   180.00

□ **Vase,** 6″, item #2032, pink, matte finish, turned, dated 1923 . . . . 50.00   55.00   50.00

□ **Vase,** 6″, lavender shades to mauve, slip-painted pansies, by Sara Sax, dated 1904 . . . . 710.00   810.00   725.00

□ **Vase,** 6″, pink uncrazed glaze, lavender floral decoration, by F. Rothenbush, dated 1922 . . . . 135.00   155.00   140.00

□ **Vase,** 6″, slip-painted tiger lilies, standard glaze, by Grace Hall, dated 1905 . . . . 610.00   710.00   660.00

□ **Vase,** 6″, white, slip-painted birds and flowers, by Kay Ley, dated 1946 . . . . 510.00   610.00   560.00

□ **Vase,** 6¾″, item #80B, dark brown, standard factory glaze, decorated with a slip-painting in the Dutch 17th century manner of a gentleman in period costume by Sturgis Laurence (signed with initials), impressed factory mark and the date 1898 . . . . 4210.00   4910.00   4400.00

□ **Vase,** 6¾″, purple, slip-painted iris and crocus design, by Laura E. Lindeman, dated 1903 . . . . 760.00   860.00   800.00

ROSEVILLE POTTERY

HISTORY: The Roseville factory opened up in 1885 in Roseville, Ohio. It was operated by George Young, C.F. Allison and other partners, and got off to a modest beginning as a maker of general stoneware lines. Cuspidors were among its early products. In 1902, the factory bought out an old stoneware plant in Zanesville, and soon began making art pottery at Zanesville. This phase of its operations overshadowed the stoneware business at Roseville. In 1910, the Roseville arm of the company was closed down. After this, all manufacturing was at Zanesville, but the name Roseville Pottery Co. was retained. Because it had already built up a number of lines of moderately-priced ware, Roseville was not hurt as much by the 1930s financial depression as Rookwood. It nevertheless did feel the pinch; sales declined and never again reached their peak of the 1920s and earlier years. In 1954, Roseville went out of business.

DESCRIPTION: Roseville called its artware Rozane, a name coined from ROseville and ZANEsville. At first all the products were in deep brown, similar to those being produced by Rookwood. Soon the shades were lightened and variety was worked into the pottery. Various lines were introduced, including "Egypto," "Mongol," "Woodland," "Mara," and "Royal." Although, water pitchers, jugs, lamp bases, ashtrays, and a full array of other decorative products were made, the main line was vases.

MARKS: Most of the art pottery is marked Rozane or Rozane Ware, in conjunction with an artist's mark. There might be another mark indicating the line from which the piece has come. Apparently one of the earliest marks used at Zanesville was a three-line block-letter arrangement reading ROSEVILLE POTTERY CO., ZANESVILLE, O. On much of the earlier ware, the name ROZANE WARE is enclosed in a circular border, with a banner beneath giving the line name (MONGOL, ROYAL, etc.). A figure of a rose appears within the circle. This mark was heavily outlined and always impressed into the ware. Sometimes the marking was done by circular paper labels, which had decorative borders. These labels carried printing in red ink, which is often blurry and poorly centered.

RECOMMENDED READING: For more in-depth information on Roseville, you may refer to *The Official Price Guide to Pottery and Porcelain,* published by The House of Collectibles.

Vase, *Roseville, Sunflower pattern,*
$90.00-$100.00

	Current Price Range		P/Y Average
☐ **Antique Green Matt,** wall pocket, 10″, triangular shape, no trim, no mark	115.00	140.00	125.00
☐ **Apple Blossom Cornucopia,** shape #321, 6″, green....................................	28.00	32.00	27.00
☐ **Autumn,** pitcher, 8½″, orange, with light-brown design, bulbous, with handle, no mark	645.00	755.00	645.00
☐ **Azurean,** vase, 9″, landscape scene which covers most of the vase, egg-shaped, narrowing at the neck, no mark	1700.00	1800.00	1735.00
☐ **Bittersweet,** planter, shape #828, 10″	32.00	36.50	32.00
☐ **Bleeding Heart,** jardiniere, shape #651, 10″, pink	232.00	262.00	240.00
☐ **Bushberry,** hanging basket, green with berries and leaves	65.00	75.00	70.00
☐ **Carnelian I,** compote, 9½″ x 7″ x 3¾″, pink with dark blue drip, marked RV	45.00	50.00	48.00
☐ **Carnelian II,** bowl, 3″ x 8″, pink with green, purple with yellow drip.......................	39.00	45.00	40.00
☐ **Clematis,** basket, 7″, brown	46.00	53.00	47.50
☐ **Colonial,** soap dish, 4″ with lid, mottled green, spherical, lid has small handle, no mark	100.00	110.00	102.50
☐ **Dogwood,** vase, 8″, green, marked RV	75.00	80.00	77.00
☐ **Florentine,** console set, 10″ bowl, 2″ candle-holders, rare blond, set	85.00	90.00	85.00
☐ **Foxglove,** bookends, shape #10, pink and blue, pair	77.00	83.00	75.00

	Current Price Range		P/Y Average

☐ **Freesia,** vase, shape #117, 6", green 31.00 37.00 32.00
☐ **Fuchsia,** ewer, shape #902, 10½", green and brown 78.00 85.00 82.00
☐ **Fujiyama,** vase, yellow flowers and stems, lined in yellows, lighthouse shape, marked Fuhiyama, stamped in ink 800.00 1000.00 935.00
☐ **Holland,** mug, 4", white and gray, with embossed figure, simple shape, no mark 42.00 50.00 46.00
☐ **Imperial I,** bowl, 9", with handle 32.00 36.00 33.50
☐ **Imperial II,** vase, 5½", yellow, bee-hive shape, no mark 90.00 110.00 98.00
☐ **Ixia,** basket, shape #346, 10", green 95.00 120.00 115.00
☐ Jonquil, jardiniere, 9½" x 7" x 4½", ... 260.00 320.00 275.00
☐ **Juvenile,** baby plate, 8", green bane, duck in tall hat with untied shoes, signed RV 60.00 67.00 64.00
☐ **Landscape,** pitcher, early 63.00 70.00 66.00
☐ **Luffa,** candlesticks 4½", brown with original seal, pair 130.00 150.00 140.00
☐ **Lustre,** vase, 10", pink, cylindrical, no trim, paper label, black 49.00 60.00 55.00
☐ **Magnolia,** conch, shape #453, 6", brown 38.00 45.00 42.50
☐ **Matt Green,** vase, 4" x 5", marked H 1/170/bot 2/2 .... 30.00 35.00 33.00
☐ **Ming Tree,** ashtray, shite 37.00 42.00 38.50
☐ **Montacello,** console, oval, 13" x 3", blue 127.00 155.00 135.00
☐ **Morning Glory,** pot, 5", aqua background, with two small handles, bell shape, with a flare at the trim, no mark 120.00 143.00 132.00
☐ **Old Ivory,** humidor, 6", light blue tint, with lid, spherical on a small base, no mark 155.00 175.00 163.00
☐ **Peony,** mug, shape #2, 3½", green 30.00 34.00 31.00
☐ **Persian,** sugar bowl, 4", with lid and two handles, four-sided, no mark 47.00 50.00 48.00
☐ **Poppy,** planter, shape #336-5, 8½" x 2½', pink 40.00 45.00 42.00
☐ **Rosecraft Vintage,** wall pocket, brown with fruit and grapevines 75.00 90.00 80.00
☐ **Rozane Olympic,** vase, 14½", three large thick feet, design of Persia and Ionia yoked to the Chariot of Xesxes, urn shape, with a cylindrical neck, marked ROZANE POTTERY stamped in ink 4500.00 5000.00 4400.00

ROYAL DOULTON

DESCRIPTION: Royal Doulton figures are ceramic works of art. Although the English company produces other items, its HN series is the best known.

ORIGIN: The Royal Doulton Company began in the early 1800s by John Doulton. The HN series was introduced in 1913 and named after Harry Nixon, head colorist at the time.

TYPES: Besides their figurines, there are many different Royal Doulton collectibles including toby jugs, plates, limited editions and bird and animal figures.

MARKS: Royal Doulton figures are identified by the HN prefix followed by numbers in a chronological sequence.

COMMENTS: Subjects in the HN series are highly diverse representing the works of many different artists at different time periods. This series is good for topical collecting.

ADDITIONAL TIPS: HN figures one through twenty-six are listed. These are among the earliest Royal Doulton figures and usually the most desirable to collectors.

For more information, consult *The Official Price Guide to Royal Doulton,* published by The House of Collectibles.

	Current Price Range		P/Y Average
☐ HN 27, Madonna of the Square	1650.00	1800.00	1725.00
☐ HN 28, Motherhood	1750.00	2000.00	1850.00
☐ HN 29, The Sleepy Scholar	1750.00	2000.00	1850.00
☐ HN 30, Motherhood	2250.00	2500.00	2325.00
☐ HN 31, The Return of Persephone	4000.00	5000.00	4400.00
☐ HN 32, Child and Crab	1750.00	2000.00	1800.00
☐ HN 33, An Arab	1600.00	1900.00	1850.00
☐ HN 34, Moorish Minstrel	2000.00	2200.00	2100.00
☐ HN 35, Charley's Aunt (1st version)	700.00	800.00	750.00
☐ HN 36, The Sentimental Pierrot	1750.00	1900.00	1825.00
☐ HN 37, The Coquette	2500.00	3000.00	2720.00
☐ HN 38, The Carpet Vendor (1st version)	2750.00	3000.00	2850.00

Odds And Ends,
HN1844,
$800.00–$900.00

	Current Price Range		P/Y Average
HN 100—HN 299 ANIMAL AND BIRD MODELS			
☐ **HN 300,** The Mermaid	850.00	1000.00	925.00
☐ **HN 301,** Moorish Piper Minstrel	2750.00	3000.00	2850.00
☐ **HN 302,** Pretty Lady	1350.00	1600.00	1450.00
☐ **HN 303,** Motherhood	2250.00	2500.00	2350.00
☐ **HN 304,** Lady with Rose	1650.00	1800.00	1725.00
☐ **HN 305,** A Scribe	850.00	1000.00	925.00
☐ **HN 306,** Milking Time	2750.00	3000.00	2850.00
☐ **HN 307,** The Sentimental Pierrot	1750.00	1900.00	1825.00
☐ **HN 308,** A Jester (2nd version)	1250.00	1500.00	1350.00
☐ **HN 309,** A Lady of the Elizabethan Period (2nd version)	1750.00	2000.00	1875.00
☐ **HN 424,** Sleep	2000.00	2200.00	2100.00
☐ **HN 425,** The Goosegirl	2750.00	3000.00	2900.00
☐ **HN 426,** A Jester (1st version)	1250.00	1500.00	1325.00
☐ **HN 427,** One of the Forty (9th version)	1100.00	1200.00	1150.00
☐ **HN 428,** The Bouquet	1550.00	1700.00	1625.00
☐ **HN 429,** The Bouquet	1550.00	1700.00	1625.00
☐ **HN 430,** A Princess	2750.00	3000.00	2925.00
☐ **HN 431,** A Princess	2750.00	3000.00	2815.00
☐ **HN 432,** Puff and Powder	2000.00	2200.00	2100.00
☐ **HN 433,** Puff and Powder	2000.00	2200.00	2100.00
☐ **HN 434,** Marie (1st version)	2250.00	2500.00	2375.00

SAMPLERS

DESCRIPTION: Samplers are needlework pieces using a variety of stitches.

TYPES: Most common are samplers that feature the alphabet along with the name of the girl who did the work, the date and some decoration. Specialized samplers, which are more rare, feature such designs as maps, genealogy and mourning scenes.

PERIOD: The oldest samplers date back to 16th century England, while the oldest American samplers date to the 18th century.

ORIGIN: Samplers were first made by schoolgirls as part of their schoolwork.

COMMENTS: Most samplers found today date from the 18th to the mid-19th centuries. European samplers tend to be less valuable than American ones, though value is determined by color choice, design, needlework ability and condition.

A sampler on a colored background is usually more valuable than one on a natural linen colored background. Samplers with personal inscriptions and bright scenes are also sought after. A sampler in its original frame adds to its value.

ADDITIONAL TIPS: The listings are in alphabetical order according to sampler design.

	Current Price Range		P/Y Average
☐ **Adam and Even,** in good condition, c. 1740 ..	35000.00	37000.00	35000.00
☐ **Alphabet,** 19th century	700.00	1200.00	900.00
☐ **Alphabet,** script and block letters, c. 1800	900.00	1200.00	1050.00
☐ **Alphabet and Flowers,** c. 1855	350.00	500.00	425.00
☐ **Alphabet and Numbers,** c. 1842	350.00	500.00	400.00
☐ **Alphabet,** bands of alphabets, floral panels, red, green, blue and brown stitches on linen, c. 1840	1200.00	1400.00	1250.00
☐ **Alphabet,** bands of alphabets, inscription, c. 1800	1300.00	1500.00	1350.00

Sampler, *wool and linen, Nova Scotia, c. 1840s, 17",* **$1000.00–$2000.00**

	Current Price Range		P/Y Average
☐ **Alphabet,** bands of alphabets and numbers, vine borders and flowering urns, c. 1820	400.00	550.00	475.00
☐ **Alphabet,** geometric designs, long horizontal shape, c. 1680	1600.00	2400.00	1800.00
☐ **Alphabet,** three bands of alphabets, dog, cat, house, c. 1840	500.00	700.00	575.00
☐ **Alphabet,** wool stitches on linen, 19th century	450.00	600.00	525.00
☐ **Cain and Abel,** c. 1800	850.00	1050.00	925.00
☐ **Farmhouse,** with "God Bless This House," c. 1840	600.00	800.00	700.00
☐ **Patriotic,** "The Union Forever," nineteenth century	1000.00	1400.00	1180.00
☐ **Landscape,** house and paths, probably from New England	1100.00	1450.00	1250.00
☐ **Landscape,** house, birds, cow, c. 1830	700.00	900.00	800.00
☐ **Landscape,** trees, flowers and animals, inscription, c. 1840	500.00	800.00	650.00
☐ **Scene,** farmyard with animals, c. 1820	800.00	1000.00	875.00
☐ **Scene,** snowy landscape, probably New England, c. 1820–1840	1300.00	1700.00	1475.00
☐ **Scene,** "View of Walton's Inn," large building, walled garden, figures, animals, c. 1810	2000.00	2900.00	2400.00
☐ **Traditional,** c. 1830	375.00	475.00	400.00
☐ **Tree,** with various flowers, bright colors, 18th century	750.00	950.00	850.00

SATURDAY EVENING GIRLS

COMMENTS: Teenage girls belonging to the Saturday Evening Girls Club of Boston, Massachusetts produced this pottery. Although the company was called Paul Revere Pottery, many collectors refer to the pottery as Saturday Evening Girls or S.E.G. since this is usually the mark found on the ware.

Under the direction of Edith Brown, the girls made a wide variety of ware including vases, bowls, pitchers, jars, mugs, candlesticks, tiles and children's dishes.

The pottery closed in 1942, ten years after Edith Brown's death.

MARKS: S.E.G. placed in a bowl design is often used. Also used was a paper label of a man on a horse and Revere Pottery printed underneath.

	Current Price Range		P/Y Average
☐ **Bowl,** 5½″, silver and blue flecks, marked S.E.G.	65.00	75.00	62.00
☐ **Bowl,** speckled motif, footed, marked S.E.G. . .	70.00	80.00	72.00
☐ **Egg Cup,** blue, chicken motif	40.00	50.00	42.00
☐ **Pitcher,** 3½″, cream background, tree, mountain and sky scene, marked S.E.G.	340.00	360.00	345.00
☐ **Plate,** 8″, yellow, marked S.E.G.	20.00	30.00	22.00
☐ **Plate,** rabbit motif in center, marked S.E.G. . . .	280.00	310.00	285.00
☐ **Vase,** 15″, green glaze, marked S.E.G., 1915	240.00	260.00	245.00

SCHOENHUT DOLLS AND TOYS

COMMENTS: When Albert Schoenhut arrived in America from Wurttenberg Germany at the age of 17, he was already an accomplished wood carver. The Schoenhut family had been wood carvers in Germany for generations. Albert continued this family tradition, teaching the trade to his six sons and, in the 1870s, the Schoenhut family opened a toy factory in Philadelphia, Pennsylvania. However, it was not until 1911 that he began to market his unique all-wood dolls. These first Schoenhut dolls had swivel necks and spring jointed bodies with a hole in the bottom of each foot, which permitted the use of a stand for display purposes.

When Albert Schoenhut died in 1912, his sons carried on the Schoenhut doll and toy business. In 1913, Albert's oldest son designed a bent-limb baby and toddler doll, and in the 1920s a less expensive elastic jointed doll was introduced into production. Before it ceased operation in the 1930s, Schoenhut also marketed a fully jointed, all composition doll.

RECOMMENDED READING: For further information consult *The Official Price Guide to Collectible Toys* and *The Official Price Guide to Antique and Modern Dolls* published by The House of Collectibles.

	Current Price Range		P/Y Average
☐ **Acrobat,** wooden toy man, hinged at hips, tall molded red fez and tassel, goatee and moustache, two-piece brown patterned cotton suit, 7″	60.00	70.00	63.00
☐ **Baby,** all wood, molded wooden head, doweled bent limb wooden body, painted blue eyes, open/closed moth, 12″	350.00	450.00	350.00
☐ **Baby,** bent limb, blonde skin wig, closed mouth, 11″	350.00	400.00	365.00

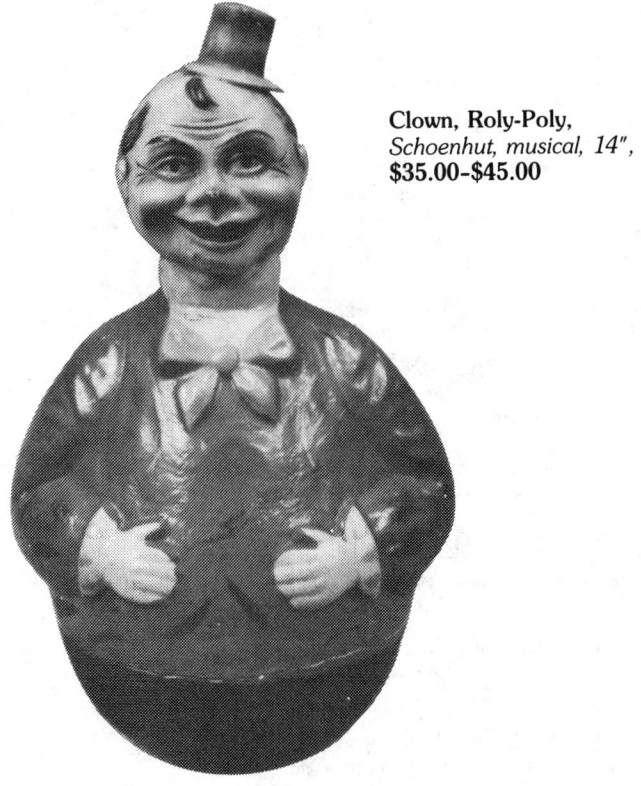

Clown, Roly-Poly,
Schoenhut, musical, 14″,
$35.00-$45.00

	Current Price Range		P/Y Average
☐ **Baby,** wooden head, bent limb body, painted eyes, no eyebrows, closed mouth, individually modeled fingers, dark skin tone, wearing a vertically striped infant's suit with rounded collar and tam o'shanter cap, marked H.E. Schoenhut/1913, 14½″	200.00	250.00	215.00
☐ **Baby Character,** wooden head, jointed wooden body, brown intaglio eyes, original wig, pouty mouth, original clothes and shoes, 21″	1200.00	1300.00	1200.00
☐ **Baby,** wooden construction carved features, ball-joint body, painted eyes, open mouth, layette suit with bonnet, c. 1911, 12″	300.00	400.00	325.00
☐ **Boy,** carved wooden head and spring jointed wood body, painted brown eyes, with blonde wig, two-piece black velvet suit and white shirt, paint peeling across fahe, marks: Schoenhut Doll Pat. Jan. 17'11, USA, 14″	95.00	100.00	200.00

	Current Price Range		P/Y Average
☐ **Boy,** sombre face, blonde wig, sailor suit, 16″	350.00	400.00	365.00
☐ **Boy,** spring jointed, bald, painted blue eyes, partially open mouth	400.00	450.00	410.00
☐ **Boy,** wooden, blue painted eyes, closed pouty mouth, striped woolen suit, marked head and marked incised body	550.00	650.00	550.00
☐ **Circus Clown,** wooden, striped cotton suit in green, pink, and white, large red feet, 8″	90.00	100.00	92.00
☐ **Dolly Face,** brown mohair wig, 22″	275.00	325.00	295.00
☐ **Dolly Face,** red pigtail mohair wig, sticker, 17″	225.00	275.00	240.00
☐ **Dolly Face,** 15½″	400.00	450.00	420.00
☐ **Female Acrobat,** wood, painted eyes, molded and painted hair, jointed at neck, arms and legs, wearing a fabric outfit of pink and green, 8″ . . . Note: sold as an accessory in the company's Humpty Dumpty Circus set.	250.00	300.00	265.00
☐ **Girl,** all-wood, jointed wooden body, blue intaglio eyes, brown wig, dressed in sailor suit, 16″ . . .	625.00	725.00	600.00
☐ **Girl,** character, wooden head, jointed wooden body, pouty, brown wig, painted features, original clothes, 16″	900.00	1000.00	950.00
☐ **Girl,** molded brown pulled over ears and tied in back with molded blue ribbon, fully jointed wooden body, painted blue eyes, pink gingham dress, 16″	975.00	1175.00	900.00
☐ **Girl,** sombre face, blonde wig, 15″	350.00	400.00	360.00
☐ **Lady Bareback Rider,** bisque head, painted blue eyes, brown hair, pink and green outfit, 7½″	425.00	475.00	440.00
☐ **Pouty,** wooden head on spring jointed wooden body, painted blue intaglio eyes, new blonde human hair wig, wearing pink checked pinafore over white lace trimmed blouse, nose rub, discreet retouching of face, marks: oval label reads "Schoenhut Doll, Pat. Jan. 17th, 1911 U.S.A., 14″	275.00	300.00	270.00
☐ **Ringmaster,** wood, painted eyes, molded and painted hair with mustache and whiskers, jointed at neck, arms and legs, representing a circus ringmaster in traditional costume with tall hat, vest, tailed jacket and black polished riding boots, 8″ . . . . Note: sold as an accessory in the Humpty Dumpty Circus set.	250.00	300.00	245.00
☐ **Rolly Dollys,** clown, 9″	100.00	150.00	120.00
☐ **Rolly Dollys,** policeman, 7″	90.00	110.00	98.00
☐ **Toddler,** brown, mohair wig, painted eyes, partially open mouth, 11″	350.00	450.00	365.00
☐ **Walker,** wooden head, jointed wooden five piece body, painted blue eyes, blonde mohair wig, open/closed mouth, sailor suit, paper label	400.00	575.00	425.00
☐ **Walker,** wooden, original mohair wig, blue painted eyes, closed pouty mouth, walker body, cute sailor suite, marked head and body, 16½″	695.00	850.00	650.00

	Current Price Range		P/Y Average

□ **Walker,** wood, spring jointed, carved head, blue ribbon headband with bow in back, brown intaglio eyes, Schoenhut stick in back, original sailor suit, underwear and shoes, 14" ....

	Current Price Range		P/Y Average
Walker	1500.00	1700.00	1450.00

SCOUTING

DESCRIPTION: Scouting memorabilia includes items for scouting groups including Boy Scouts, Cub Scouts, Camp Fire Girls, Brownies and Girl Scouts.

TYPES: All types of scouting treasures are considered collectible, from cloth badges to metal neckerchief rings and tools, backpacks, uniforms and manuals.

ORIGIN: Englishman Sir Robert S.S. Baden-Powell is the original founder of Boy Scouts and Girl Scouts in England.

The development of scouting in America is due to Daniel Carter Beard, William Boyce and James E. West for Boy Scouts of America, and Juliette Gordon Low for Girl Scouts of America. Both groups are separate and distinct.

COMMENTS: There are more collectors of Boy Scout treasures than of Girl Scout memorabilia. Prices are reasonable and fairly stable.

For more complete information, refer to *The Official Price Guide to Scouting Collectibles,* published by The House of Collectibles.

	Current Price Range		P/Y Average
□ **Ash Tray,** Kit Carson House, Philmont, 1950 ..	7.00	8.50	7.25
□ **Bank,** Conn., has another scout behind kettle, 1915	250.00	325.00	275.00
□ **Bank,** tin lithographed scout, 1912	22.00	28.00	23.50
□ **Binoculars,** tan leather, 1920's	77.00	88.00	79.00
□ **Blotter,** BSA/Coca-cola, "Be Prepared, Be Refreshed"	6.00	8.00	7.00
□ **Belt,** belt and buckle, gun medal, 1930's	7.50	9.50	8.00
□ **Bookends,** bronze metal, Girl Scout feeding rabbit....................................	20.50	26.00	21.00
□ **Bookends,** metal, first class Emblem 6" x 6"	24.00	32.00	26.00
□ **Bookmark,** green and gold, first class emblem, BSA National Council	4.25	5.50	4.75

Badge Sash, $3.00-$7.50

	Current Price Range		P/Y Average
☐ **Books,** Holy Bible, early BSA seal on cover ...	45.00	57.00	47.00
☐ **Cachet Cover,** Boy Scout stamp club, 1932 ..	9.00	11.00	9.50
☐ **Calendar Holder,** cast metal, BSA perpetual, first class emblem	18.50	22.00	19.25
☐ **Camera,** Official 7-Piece flash camera kit	12.00	17.00	13.00
☐ **Canteen,** Wearever seamless, felt cover, 1930's	17.00	22.00	18.00
☐ **Cards,** 65 BSA job description cards, 1949–1962	5.00	7.00	5.50
☐ **Collar Monogram,** BSA, brass collar monograms, 1920's	40.00	60.00	46.00
☐ **Comb,** Official BSA comb and clippers in a case	4.00	7.00	5.00
☐ **Compass,** Sylva pathfinder, BSA	2.00	4.00	2.50
☐ **Cut Outs,** Camping with the Scouts, gummed paper in book form, 1930's	22.00	27.00	23.00
☐ **Drum,** "Boy Scout Drum" tin, 6″ round 3½″ high, 1908	40.00	60.00	44.00
☐ **Figurine,** Head Scout, signaller, arms move, 2″	18.00	24.00	20.00
☐ **Figurine,** Kenner doll, Craig Cub Scout	15.00	21.00	17.00
☐ **Figurine,** Scout with pack and rifle, cardboard, 6″ high	4.50	5.50	4.75

	Current Price Range		P/Y Average
☐ **Figurine,** Lead Scout kneeling, frying eggs	11.00	14.00	12.00
☐ **Figurine,** Scout plastic figure, tree and flagpole, 3″	8.50	11.00	9.25
☐ **First Aid Kit,** Bauer and Black, gray, oval belt loop kit, rare, 1932	20.00	27.00	22.00
☐ **First Aid Kit,** Johnson and Johnson, swing clasp, 1942	16.00	22.00	17.50

SCRIMSHAW

TOPIC: Scrimshaw is artwork done on bone.

TYPES: Scrimshaw can be carved or painted. Carved scrimshaw, which seldom has any painted decoration, is mostly in the nature of little trinkets—boxes, pins or forks, for example. Painted scrimshaw is done directly on the tooth or bone. It is accomplished by scratching the design into the surface with needles, then working India ink into the scratches.

MATERIALS: Whalebone is the most commonly found material, followed by walrus tusk. Occasionally a low-grade ivory such as whale tooth is used.

COMMENTS: The age, size, artistic quality, subject matter and state of preservation all go into determining the value of scrimshaw.

☐ **Box,** whalebone and wood, 10″ L.	540.00	790.00	650.00
☐ **Bust of Man,** 4″ H.	150.00	250.00	200.00
☐ **Cane,** dove on knob, brass tip, 38″ H.	380.00	480.00	430.00
☐ **Carpenter's Molding Plane,** 9½″ L.	540.00	640.00	590.00
☐ **Carpenter's Square,** teakwood handle	160.00	200.00	180.00
☐ **Corset Stays,** whalebone, home scenes, 14″ L.	200.00	250.00	225.00
☐ **Hammer,** dolphin on handle, 7″ L.	270.00	330.00	300.00
☐ **Horn,** 10″ L., c. 19thg c.	210.00	250.00	230.00
☐ **Napkin Holder,** with cats	60.00	80.00	60.00
☐ **Pie Crimper,** fancy with rosewood handle	180.00	220.00	200.00
☐ **Walrus' Tusk,** cribbage board	900.00	1200.00	1050.00
☐ **Walrus' Tusk,** dagger, 10″ L.	130.00	170.00	150.00

Powderhorn, *scrimshaw, 1700s,* $4500.00–$4700.00
(photo courtesy of © Marc Bernsau, Sanford, ME, 1984)

	Current Price Range		P/Y Average
☐ **Walrus' Tusk,** Indians, 6″ L.	680.00	880.00	780.00
☐ **Walrus' Tusk,** mother and child on swing, 11″ L.	470.00	630.00	550.00
☐ **Whale's Tooth,** crucifix, 6″ L.	290.00	390.00	340.00
☐ **Whale's Tooth,** eagle and flag, 5″ L.	580.00	780.00	680.00
☐ **Whale's Tooth,** children playing	590.00	810.00	700.00
☐ **Whale's Tooth,** whaling scene, 5″ L.	700.00	900.00	780.00

SEARS-ROEBUCK CATALOGS

COMMENTS: Sears Roebuck catalogs were first collected in the 1960s. They are still popular and prices, especially for rare or mint copies, tend to be high.

CONDITION: Condition standards for such catalogs are fairly liberal, because they were large, soft bound and received much use.

ADDITIONAL TIPS: The listings are in chronological order with a price range.

Sears Catalog,
general catalog no. 111,
50¢ cover price,
1902, **$100.00-$125.00**

	Current Price Range		P/Y Average
☐ **1897,** general catalogue, Chicago, IL	200.00	250.00	220.00
☐ **1899,** general catalogue	175.00	225.00	200.00
☐ **1900–1910,** most editions, food, groceries, to-bacco	50.00	65.00	55.00
☐ **1902,** general catalogue #111, 50¢ cover price	130.00	150.00	130.00
☐ **1902,** general catalogue, 1969 reprint (Crown Pub., NY)	10.00	15.00	12.00
☐ **1905,** general catalogue	130.00	155.00	140.00
☐ **1906,** general catalogue	145.00	175.00	155.00
☐ **1907,** general catalogue, 1,240 pages	150.00	185.00	160.00
☐ **1908,** general catalogue, 1,232 pages	175.00	200.00	185.00
☐ **1910,** general catalogue, spring and summer, 1,182 pages	180.00	210.00	185.00
☐ **1911–1920,** most editions, food, groceries, to-bacco	45.00	60.00	47.00
☐ **1916,** furniture	65.00	90.00	73.00
☐ **1922,** general catalogue, spring and summer ..	125.00	145.00	135.00
☐ **1926,** general catalogue, autumn and winter ...	110.00	130.00	120.00
☐ **1931,** general catalogue, spring and summer ..	110.00	140.00	125.00
☐ **1944,** general catalogue, autumn and winter ...	80.00	110.00	95.00
☐ **1947,** Christmas catalogue	45.00	60.00	53.00
☐ **1949,** general catalogue, autumn and winter ...	40.00	55.00	47.00
☐ **1951,** business equipment	10.00	15.00	11.00
☐ **1951,** Christmas catalogue	35.00	45.00	40.00
☐ **1955,** general catalogue, spring and summer ..	27.00	40.00	32.00

	Current Price Range		P/Y Average
☐ **1960,** Christmas catalogue	20.00	30.00	25.00
☐ **1963,** general catalogue, autumn and winter ...	18.00	28.00	23.00
☐ **1965–1975,** general catalogues, most editions	13.00	20.00	14.00

SHAKER

DESCRIPTION: The Shakers were a socio-religious organization formed in the 18th century. A very disciplined group with purity as the basis of their beliefs, Shaker doctrines were precise and leadership was strict.

PERIOD: Shaker items were made from the early 19th century to the 20th century. Most pieces date to the mid-19th century, when Shaker communities were at their largest.

ORIGIN: A combination of the English Quaker Church and the French Prophets, the first Shaker society was formed in England in 1747. Formally called "The United Society of Believers in Christ's Second Appearing," they were nicknamed "Shakers" because of the devotional dancing they did in religious services.

Englishwoman Ann Lee became their first spiritual leader and led a group to America in 1776 where they attracted many converts.

COMMENTS: All Shaker products were made for practical use and they symbolized Shaker beliefs of purity, unity, simplicity and utility. Shakers used fine building techniques and did not hide carpentry details. Such details add charm and grace to Shaker pieces.

While much Shaker furniture was made for their own use, some was made for commercial sale.

ADDITIONAL TIPS: The listings are alphabetical according to item. Descriptions, dates and price ranges follow.

☐ **Almanac,** 1885	65.00	85.00	75.00
☐ **Basket,** double handle, 7″	125.00	165.00	130.00
☐ **Basket,** cover, red-painted handle	232.00	280.00	250.00
☐ **Basket,** draining	85.00	110.00	95.00

	Current Price Range		P/Y Average
Bed, plain headboard with rounded edges, square legs with wooden casters, usually made of pine, c. 1850	450.00	550.00	400.00
Bed, plain headboard and footboard, springs, carved wooden legs with casters, c. 1850	650.00	750.00	700.00
Bonnet, woven with straw	150.00	190.00	170.00
Bookcase, combination secretary and bookcase in two parts, simple molding, shelves, drawers, late 19th century	850.00	1000.00	925.00
Box, oval or round, made of wood with overlapping, tapered fingers	145.00	180.00	150.00
Box, 8½" oval	120.00	175.00	130.00
Box, 10½" oval	137.50	175.00	150.00
Box, pincushion	210.00	270.00	230.00
Box, sewing	232.00	280.00	250.00
Bucket, wood with handle and lid, 12" high	127.50	160.00	140.00
Bucket, 1 gallon, dove-tailed, fair condition	13.00	30.00	15.00
Candlestand, round top, tapering pedestal, cabriole legs and snake feet, 19th century	300.00	450.00	325.00
Chair, ladderback side chair, seat is either rush, wood splint or woven tape, 19th century	420.00	675.00	500.00

Shaker Pantry Boxes, *set of five, ea.,* **$110.00–$175.00**

	Current Price Range		P/Y Average

	Current Price Range		P/Y Average
☐ **Chair,** ladderback armchair, mushroom post arms, tapering legs, seat usually of woven tape, 19th century	525.00	775.00	625.00
☐ **Chair,** rocking side chair, 19th century	550.00	750.00	650.00
☐ **Chair,** rocking armchair, 19th century	700.00	900.00	800.00
☐ **Chair,** rocking armchair with shawl rail, late 19th century	850.00	1000.00	925.00
☐ **Chair,** dining, modified ladderback, built low so it could be placed under the dining table when not in use, 19th century	750.00	850.00	800.00
☐ **Chest,** blanket, storage, lifting top, drawers, c. 1830	600.00	800.00	700.00
☐ **Chest,** storage, work, case has two drawers and one door, plain top with hinged drop leaves	620.00	775.00	675.00
☐ **Chest,** tall, several drawers with top drawers in pairs, early 19th century	975.00	1250.00	1100.00
☐ **Chest,** drawers with side cabinet	800.00	950.00	875.00
☐ **Clothes Hanger**	70.00	90.00	80.00
☐ **Clothes Hanger,** six-peg	55.00	75.00	65.00
☐ **Comb,** wood	26.00	34.00	30.00
☐ **Cradle,** simple carving, shaped hood, carved handholds and rockers, c. 1800	550.00	700.00	625.00
☐ **Cupboard,** two sets of doors on top of each other, simple molding and slight cornice, c. 1850	970.00	1275.00	1100.00
☐ **Desk,** slanted work area with opening lid, pedestal, cabriole legs, snake feet, c. 1850	600.00	850.00	775.00
☐ **Desk,** high, made for Shaker deacons, identical sets of everything so it could be shared, 19th century	975.00	1200.00	1100.00
☐ **Dry Sink,** rectangular drawer, doors, round sink, splashboard, corner shelf, c. 1850	500.00	750.00	625.00
☐ **Dust Pan**	60.00	80.00	70.00
☐ **Foot Stool,** decorated	232.00	285.00	260.00
☐ **Hay Winder With Rope**	52.50	80.00	67.50
☐ **Jelly Cupboard,** red stained wood, c. 1890	525.00	625.00	575.00
☐ **Pegboard,** wood	210.00	270.00	230.00
☐ **Plantation Desk**	900.00	1200.00	1100.00
☐ **Rack,** spice dryer	190.00	230.00	210.00
☐ **Rocker,** ladderback, mushroom arms, splint seat	750.00	1000.00	850.00
☐ **Sap Bucket,** Enfield, New Hampshire	47.50	60.00	53.00
☐ **Sewing Stand,** sliding drawers so two people can use it at the same time, pedestal, cabriole legs, 19th century	550.00	750.00	650.00
☐ **Sewing Stand,** similar to desk with many small drawers, large work area, c. 1850	770.00	920.00	825.00
☐ **Sideboard,** doors, work area, top board, 19th century	775.00	975.00	875.00
☐ **Soap Shaver**	102.50	130.00	115.00
☐ **Spinning Wheel**	325.00	400.00	370.00
☐ **Steps,** utility, also called one-stepper, two-stepper, etc.	250.00	350.00	300.00

	Current Price Range		P/Y Average
☐ **Table,** dining, trestle table with plank top, 19th century	975.00	1225.00	1100.00
☐ **Table,** drop leaf, plain skirt, 19th century	450.00	550.00	500.00
☐ **Table,** oval, top overlaps frame, often used in Shaker shops, 19th century	475.00	600.00	500.00
☐ **Table,** square, drawer, dove tailed skirting, c. 1850	525.00	675.00	575.00
☐ **Washstand,** rectangular, dovetailed, boards shaped wash area, one drawer, 19th century ..	450.00	550.00	500.00

SHAWNEE POTTERY

DESCRIPTION: The Shawnee Pottery Company was founded in 1937 in Zanesville, Ohio. Its first president was Addis Hull Jr., of the Hull pottery family, which had been one of the leading factories in neighboring Crooksville. Discovering an Indian arrow on the grounds when the factory was being readied for opening led to the company being called Shawnee. Shawnee played up the Indian theme at various times in its history, notably with its line of corn-pattern dinnerware. This famous set, in yellow and green, was textured on every piece to resemble an ear of corn. It was officially known as Corn King, then as Corn Queen beginning in the mid 1950s. The final year of the Shawnee operations was 1961.

MARKS: The trademarks used by Shawnee usually carry the letters U.S.A., together with the factory name and a mold number. A low mold number is not necessarily an indication of early production. Most pieces of Shawnee figureware and such novelties as toy banks, ashtrays, etc., can be easily dated (approximately) on the basis of style. The vases are a little more difficult to accurately date, but a collector who makes educated guesses will probably score more hits than misses.

RECOMMENDED READING: For more in-depth information on Shawnee pottery, you may refer to *The Official Price Guide to Pottery and Porcelain* and *The Official Identification Guide to Pottery and Porcelain,* published by The House of Collectibles.

CORN LINE (Introduced Early 1940s)

Perhaps the company's most popular line, this pattern was called Corn King before 1954. After the company installed John Bonistall as the new president, he changed the glaze to a darker green and renamed the line Corn Queen. The mark and number remained the same.

	Current Price Range		P/Y Average
☐ **Butter Dish,** covered, marked Shawnee U.S.A. #72	25.00	30.00	26.00
☐ **Bowl,** large, marked Shawnee U.S.A. #6	12.00	16.00	13.00
☐ **Bowl,** mixing, marked Shawnee U.S.A. #5	10.00	14.00	11.00
☐ **Bowl,** small, marked Shawnee U.S.A. #94	8.00	12.00	9.00
☐ **Casserole,** 11", covered, marked Shawnee U.S.A. oven proof #74	25.00	35.00	26.00
☐ **Casserole,** covered, marked Shawnee U.S.A. oven proof #73	30.00	40.00	31.00
☐ **Cookie Jar,** lidded, marked Shawnee U.S.A. #66	45.00	55.00	46.00
☐ **Mug,** marked Shawnee U.S.A. #69	10.00	15.00	11.00
☐ **Pitcher,** 8½", marked Shawnee U.S.A. #71	24.00	34.00	25.00
☐ **Pitcher,** small, marked Shawnee U.S.A. #70	8.00	11.00	9.00
☐ **Plate,** dinner, marked Shawnee U.S.A. #68	9.00	14.00	10.00
☐ **Platter,** marked Shawnee U.S.A. oven proof #96	14.00	18.00	15.00
☐ **Relish,** oblong, marked Shawnee U.S.A. #79	14.00	18.00	5.00
☐ **Saucer,** marked Shawnee U.S.A. #91	4.00	7.00	5.00
☐ **Shakers,** 3½", salt and pepper, pair, no mark	10.00	14.00	11.00
☐ **Shakers,** 5½", salt and pepper, no mark	13.00	16.00	14.00
☐ **Sugar Bowl,** covered, marked Shawnee U.S.A. #78	7.00	12.00	8.00

Dish, *Corn King Pattern,* $30.00–$40.00

	Current Price Range		P/Y Average
☐ **Teacup,** marked Shawnee U.S.A. #90	4.00	6.00	5.00
☐ **Teapot,** covered, marked Shawnee U.S.A. #75	25.00	32.00	26.00

MISCELLANEOUS

	Current Price Range		P/Y Average
☐ **Cookie Jar,** white and brown owl, one eye closed, marked U.S.A.	9.00	11.00	10.00
☐ **Cookie Jar,** white cat, red bow, marked patented U.S.A.	30.00	35.00	32.00
☐ **Cookie Jar,** white pig, dressed as a farmer, marked U.S.A.	28.00	32.00	30.00
☐ **Figurine,** 6″, tan and white terrier	7.00	9.00	8.00
☐ **Lamps,** 12″, pair, white with gold trim, grape motif	45.00	50.00	47.00
☐ **Lamps,** pair, green, oriental man motif, marked with paper label	38.00	44.00	42.00
☐ **Lamps,** pair, tall, cylindrical shape, white with gold trim, flower design, marked with paper label	38.00	42.00	40.00
☐ **Lamp,** white and brown dog standing beside blue box, marked U.S.A.	10.00	12.00	11.00
☐ **Pitcher,** 7½″, sailor boy, red pants, blue shirt and cap, marked Shawnee U.S.A. #46	16.00	18.00	17.00
☐ **Pitcher,** 8″, girl, hat makes spout, marked Bo Peep U.S.A.	20.00	24.00	21.50
☐ **Pitcher,** white chicken, open mouth forms spout, tail is handle, marked chanticleer U.S.A.	20.00	25.00	22.00
☐ **Pitcher,** white elephant, tail makes handle, trunk is spout, marked patented U.S.A.	26.00	30.00	28.00

Cookie Jar, *pig,*
$35.00-$40.00

	Current Price Range		P/Y Average
☐ **Pitcher,** white pig, open mouth is spout, tail forms handle, marked patented Smiley U.S.A.	24.00	28.00	26.00
☐ **Planter,** blue and white deer standing by brown, red and white tree trunk, marked U.S.A. #535	10.00	12.00	11.00
☐ **Planter,** blue goose, marked U.S.A.	7.00	10.00	8.00

SHEET MUSIC

DESCRIPTION: Sheet music is a musical composition.

COMMENTS: Condition and rarity determine the value of sheet music. Specimens are not always in top condition due to music store stamps, tape marks, staples, binder holes and ownership signatures. Worn copies sell for considerably less than those in good or mint condition.

ADDITIONAL TIPS: Often prices in major hobby marketplaces such as New York and California are higher than prices in more remote areas. Collectors should also beware of high prices placed on sheet music at flea markets.

For more information, consult *The Official Price Guide to Radio, TV and Movie Memorabilia,* or *The Official Price Guide to Music,* both published by The House of Collectibles.

	Current Price Range		P/Y Average
☐ **Arm in Arm,** words by Ned Washington, music by Frances Zinman and Victor Young, inset Arthur Tracy, the Street Singer, c. 1932	2.25	3.00	2.50
☐ **The Army Air Corps,** words and music by Robert Crawford, pub. Carl Fischer, 1942 edition ..	2.25	3.00	2.50
☐ **(I've Got The) Blue Ridge Blues,** lyric by Chas. A. Mason, music by Chas. S. Cooke and Richard Whiting	2.25	4.00	3.15
☐ **Honey Hula,** Hawaiian Waltz Song, words and music by Fred Fisher, pub. Fred Fisher, c. 1921	3.00	4.00	3.25
☐ **Hummingbird,** words and music by Don Robertson, photo Les Paul and Mary Ford, pub. Ross Jungnickel, c. 1955	2.25	3.00	2.50

	Current Price Range		P/Y Average
☐ **Looking at the World (Thru Rose Colored Glasses),** by Tommie Malie and Jimmy Steiger, inset Jack Osterman, pub. Weil, c. 1926	2.25	3.00	2.50
☐ **Mambo Italiano,** by Bob Merrill, inset Rosemary Clooney, pub. Ryan Music, c. 1954	2.25	3.00	2.50
☐ **The Midnight Fire Alarm,** by Harry J. Lincoln, arr. by E. T. Paul (colored litho)	30.00	40.00	35.00
☐ **Our Bungalow of Dreams,** by Tommie Malie, Charlie Newman and Joe Verges, pub. Ted Browne, inset Baby Dorothy Johnson, c. 1927	1.25	2.00	1.70
☐ **The Poor People of Paris,** by Marguerite Monnot, pub. Reg Connelly, c. 1954	3.00	4.00	3.50
☐ **Shine on Harvest Moon,** words and music by Nora Bayes and Jack Norworth	2.25	3.00	2.50
☐ **The Shrine of St. Cecilia,** words by Carroll Loveday, music by Jokern, pub. Braun, c. 1940	2.50	3.00	2.70
☐ **Star Dust,** words by Mitchell Parish, music by Hoagy Carmichael, pub. Mills, c. 1929	3.00	4.00	3.35
☐ **The Little Fishies (Itty Bitty Poo),** by Saxie Dowell, c. 1939	2.50	4.00	3.00
☐ **Time on My Hands,** words by Harold Adamson and Mack Gordon, music by Vincent Youmans, pub. Miller, c. 1930	2.00	4.00	3.00
☐ **Ti-Pi-Tin,** music and Spanish lyrics by Maria Grever, English lyrics by Raymond Leveen, photo Horace Heidt, pub. Feist, c. 1938	2.00	4.00	3.00
☐ **To Be Worthy of You,** words by Benny Davis, music by J. Fred Coots	2.00	4.00	3.00

SHENANDOAH VALLEY POTTERY

DESCRIPTION: The Shenandoah Valley in Maryland and Virginia became known for its varied, brightly colored pottery. The most notable of the many potters was Peter Bell, Jr., who operated in Hagerstown, Maryland and then Winchester, Virginia from 1800–1845. Bell's sons John, Solomon and Samuel also started potteries. John established his pottery at Waynesboro, Pennsylvania in 1833, while Solomon and Samuel began a pottery in Strasburg, Virginia. Their descendants continued to run the potteries in the early 20th century. Shenandoah Valley redware pottery is eagerly sought by collectors because of the colorful glazes found in each piece.

MARKS: Although the Shenandoah Valley Pottery includes several companies, the concentration here is on the Bell family. Since both father and sons owned their own companies, the marks are made up of several names. They include: S. Bell & Son, Strasburg; S. Bell, Strasburg; John Bell, Waynesboro, Pennsylvania; Solomon Bell, Strasburg; or Upton Bell, Waynesboro, Pa.

	Current Price Range		P/Y Average
☐ **Bowl,** 15″, white, handled, marked S. Bell & Son, Strasburg	420.00	435.00	425.00
☐ **Cuspidor,** 6¾″ redware with cream, green and brown	200.00	210.00	205.00
☐ **Flowerpot,** 8″, brown and green, flared body, marked S. Bell & Sons, Strasburg	140.00	160.00	142.00
☐ **Flowerpot,** 8″, bulbous body, scroll design, cream, green and brown, handled, marked S. Bell & Son	320.00	340.00	322.00
☐ **Dish,** 9″, marked Upton Bell, Waynesboro, Pa.	145.00	165.00	148.00
☐ **Dish,** 10″, circular shape, green, orange and cream, marked S. Bell & Son, Strasburg	540.00	560.00	545.00
☐ **Figurine,** 3½″, lamb, sleeping position, cream, green and brown	1725.00	1775.00	1730.00
☐ **Figurine,** 4″, dog, yellow, orange and brown, oval base	1350.00	1375.00	1355.00
☐ **Figurine,** 8″, dog, seated, basket and bottle in mouth, black and brown	2300.00	2350.00	2310.00
☐ **Figurine,** 9″, dog, cream and black, marked John Bell, Waynesboro, Pennsylvania	1150.00	1450.00	1155.00
☐ **Jar,** 4¾″, cylinder body, straight sides, narrow neck, white, green and brown with redware	370.00	385.00	365.00
☐ **Jar,** 9½″, gray with three blue floral designs on shoulder, marked S. Bell & Son, Strasburg, c. 1882	130.00	140.00	132.00
☐ **Jar,** 9½″, blue flower design, marked Solomon Bell, Strasburg	190.00	200.00	185.00
☐ **Pitcher,** 6½″, brown and green, marked S. Bell, Strasburg	345.00	355.00	347.00
☐ **Pitcher,** 9″, handled, gray and green, angels and grapevine motif, marked John Bell, Waynesboro, Pennsylvania	850.00	885.00	855.00
☐ **Pitcher,** 10¼″, bulbous green body, tall brown neck, marked John Bell, Waynesboro, Pennsylvania	540.00	560.00	545.00
☐ **Pitcher,** 10½″, cylinder shape, one handle, green, brown and cream	670.00	685.00	672.00
☐ **Pitcher,** 16″, bulbous body, small handles, flower design, marked Solomon Bell, Strasburg	380.00	400.00	380.00

SHIP MODELS

TOPIC: Ship models are small replicas of ships that may or may not have actually been full-size sailing vessels.

TYPES: There are four main types of ship models: the wright's model, the sailor's model, the collector's model and the kit model. The wright's model is made by a shipwright (a ship builder) as a working model for an actual ship. The sailor's model is one made while the sailor served on that actual ship, for the purpose of selling when the ship called at port or for presentation to a relative. A collector's model is one made long after the ship itself was constructed, and often after it ceased to exist, by using photographs or drawings in books. Finally, a kit model is built from components and directions furnished in a commercially sold kit.

COMMENTS: Wright's models are the most desirable and expensive. Sailor's models may be crude, but they are highly regarded by collectors. The value of a collector's model is determined by age, size, intricacy of detail and state of preservation.

ADDITIONAL TIPS: Models of steamships, no matter how big or how nicely done, are not as valuable in the collector market as sailing vessels.

	Current Price Range		P/Y Average
☐ **American cargo ship "Explorer,"** masts and sails, mounted on a metal base, well-preserved except for portions of the rigging, 27″ L., c. 1880	700.00	900.00	800.00
☐ **American gunner "Victory,"** meticulous workmanship, some detail work damaged, overall well-preserved, mounted on a new stand made of polished walnut, 41″ L., c. 1900	1400.00	1900.00	1650.00
☐ **American battleship "Kentucky,"** the hull carved from a solid block of wood, painted, traces of original paint, one mast restored, the sails not original, mounted on a wooden platform painted deep blue, 19″ L., c.1870	1100.00	1500.00	1300.00

	Current Price Range		P/Y Average

☐ **American battleship "Maine,"** the guns made of real brass, figures of seamen in carved wood, tins and crates on board, the work of a master modeler, 24″ L., c. 1890 .... **2500.00 3000.00 2750.00**

☐ **American cargo ship "Explorer,"** masts and sails, mounted on a metal base, well-preserved except for portions of the rigging, 27″ L., c. 1880 .... **900.00 1200.00 1050.00**

☐ **American gunner "Victory,"** meticulous workmanship, some detail work damaged, overall well-preserved, mounted on a new stand made of polished walnut, 41″ L., c. 1900 .... **1700.00 2200.00 1950.00**

☐ **English battleship "Great Harry,"** brass guns, made largely of oak, some components of other wood, gilded work with most of the original gilding intact, rare model, probably English or Scottish, of a ship dating to the 16th c., 57 ″ L., c. 1810 **6100.00 9100.00 7600.00**

☐ **English liner "Titanic,"** wood and metal painted in various shades of gray, mounted on wooden stand, American or English, 32″ L., recent **850.00 1100.00 975.00**

☐ **English liner "Queen Mary,"** wood and metal, scale built by a modeler down to the smallest detail, rubber life preservers, scale-built lifeboats, etc., mounted on a copper and wood stand with engraved nameplate, 55″ L., c. 1940 .... **3900.00 5300.00 4600.00**

☐ **English schooner "Admiral V,"** 26″ L., c. 1900 .... **450.00 590.00 520.00**

☐ **German-built model of an unnamed sailing ship,** 15th c. design, well detailed, weathered wood, wormholes, some parts restored, unmounted, c. 1750–1800 .... **2200.00 3200.00 2700.00**

☐ **Model of an early Viking sailing ship,** 10th or 11th c. A.D., wood and canvas, probably German (not entirely accurate in design), 31″ L., c. 1860 .... **1900.00 2300.00 2100.00**

SHIRLEY TEMPLE DOLLS

COMMENTS: Child star Shirley Temple captured the heart of America during the 1930s and 40s. There is a tremendous interest in Shirley Temple collectibles today and a huge variety of items to choose from. Dolls are listed here.

RECOMMENDED READING: For in-depth information on all kinds of Shirley Temple collectibles refer to *The Official Price Guide to Radio, TV and Movie Memorabilia, The Official Price Guide to Collectible Toys* and *The Official Price Guide to Antique and Modern Dolls,* published by The House of Collectibles.

	Current Price Range		P/Y Average
IDEAL			
☐ **Shirley Temple,** Captain January, c. 1982, 8″	23.00	29.00	22.50
☐ **Shirley Temple,** Heidi, c. 1982, 8″	23.00	29.00	22.50
☐ **Shirley Temple,** Heidi, c. 1982, 12″	34.00	45.00	35.00
☐ **Shirley Temple,** Little Colonel, c. 1982, 8″	23.00	29.00	22.50
☐ **Shirley Temple,** Little Colonel, c. 1982, 12″ ..	35.00	45.00	35.00
☐ **Shirley Temple,** Little Miss Marker, c. 1983, 8″	15.00	18.00	12.50
☐ **Shirley Temple,** Little Miss Marker, c. 1983, 12″	19.00	25.00	17.50
☐ **Shirley Temple,** Littlest Rebel, c. 1982, 8″	23.00	29.00	22.50
☐ **Shirley Temple,** Poor Little Rich Girl, c. 1983, 8″	13.00	18.00	12.50
☐ **Shirley Temple,** Poor Little Rich Girl, c. 1983, 12″	17.00	22.00	17.50
☐ **Shirley Temple,** Rebecca of Sunnybrook Farm, c. 1983, 8″	13.00	18.00	12.50
☐ **Shirley Temple,** Rebecca of Sunnybrook Farm, c. 1983, 12″	17.00	22.00	17.50
☐ **Shirley Temple,** Stand Up and Cheer, c. 1982, 8″	22.00	27.00	22.50
☐ **Shirley Temple,** Stowaway, c. 1982, 8″	22.00	27.00	22.50
☐ **Shirley Temple,** Stowaway, c. 1982, 12″	33.00	43.00	35.00
☐ **Shirley Temple,** Susannah of the Mounties, c. 1983, 8″	13.00	19.00	12.50

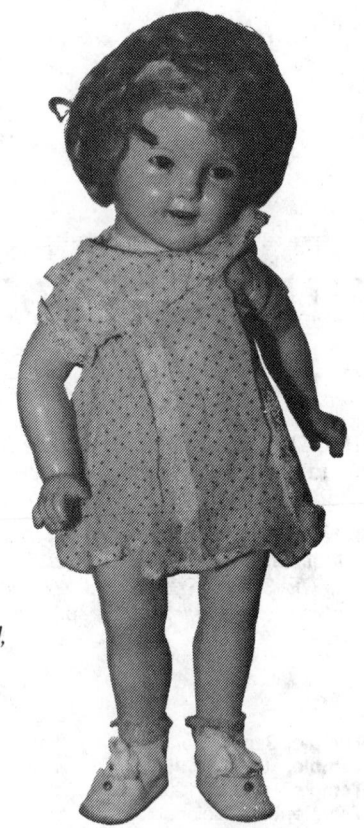

Shirley Temple, *Ideal, composition, c. 1930,* **$560.00-$660.00**

	Current Price Range		P/Y Average
☐ **Shirley Temple,** Susannah of the Mounties, c. 1983, 12″	19.00	26.50	19.00
☐ **Shirley Temple,** Wee Willie Winkle, c. 1983, 8″	12.00	17.00	12.50
☐ **Shirley Temple,** Wee Willie Winkle, c. 1983, 12″	17.00	22.00	17.50
☐ **Shirley Temple,** all composition, 27″	300.00	360.00	330.00
☐ **Shirley Temple,** all composition, 25″	175.00	200.00	187.00
☐ **Shirley Temple,** all composition, 23″	155.00	200.00	165.00
☐ **Shirley Temple,** all composition, 18″	125.00	150.00	135.00
☐ **Shirley Temple,** all composition, 17″	120.00	140.00	133.00
☐ **Shirley Temple,** all composition, 16″	120.00	140.00	133.00
☐ **Shirley Temple,** all composition, 15″	105.00	135.00	120.00
☐ **Shirley Temple,** all composition, 13″	75.00	90.00	75.00

	Current Price Range		P/Y Average

☐ **Shirley Temple,** all composition, 11″ 170.00 190.00 175.00

☐ **Shirley Temple,** all composition, jointed, blonde curly mohair wig, brown sleep eyes, open mouth, six teeth, Heidi style dress and pinafore not original, c. 1938, marked on head and body: 13 SHIRLEY TEMPLE, 22″ 530.00 580.00 550.00

☐ **Shirley Temple,** all composition jointed neck, shoulders and hips, green sleep eyes, open smiling mouth, original full blonde mohair wig styled in ringlets, original red and white polka dot dress, marked: Original Shirley Temple dress tag, head and body signed Shirley Temple, 25″ 740.00 780.00 750.00

☐ **Shirley Temple,** character, vinyl head, plastic body, jointed shoulders and hips, rooted hair painted eyes, smiling mouth, red-polka dot dress, original, mint, 16″ 75.00 85.00 75.00

☐ **Shirley Temple,** composition, curly top, Shirley pin, polka dotted red and white dress, c. 1935, 22″ 560.00 660.00 600.00

☐ **Shirley Temple,** composition, jointed body, glazed eyes, blonde wig, open smiling mouth, original clothes, marked on head and body: 13 SHIRLEY TEMPLE, 13″ 460.00 560.00 500.00

☐ **Shirley Temple,** composition, jointed body, glazed eyes, blonde wig, open smiling mouth, original clothes, marked on head and body: 13 SHIRLEY TEMPLE, 25″ 740.00 840.00 750.00

☐ **Shirley Temple,** composition, pink organdy dress, snap dress, 15″ 300.00 350.00 300.00

☐ **Shirley Temple,** original, ruffled lace dress, 22″ 500.00 600.00 540.00

☐ **Shirley Temple,** vinyl and hard plastic jointed neck, shoulders and hips, rooted blonde hair, green sleep eyes, smiling mouth with four porcelain teeth, dimples, original mint condition, petite 1957 model with complete wardrobe, all clothing tagged Shirley Temple, flannel nightgown with cap, pink ballet dress, two piece plaid dress with cap, Swiss dirndl, sunglasses and Shirley Temple pin and purse, wearing a pale yellow organdy dress, marked: Ideal Doll ST-12, 12″ 220.00 230.00 222.00

☐ **Shirley Temple,** vinyl head, jointed vinyl body, vinyl wig, sleep eyes, sheer blue gown, c. 1950, 17″ 125.00 140.00 130.00

☐ **Shirley Temple,** vinyl, print dress, marked: Ideal, 12″ 90.00 100.00 90.00

SHOTGUNS

TOPIC: A shotgun is a firearm that has a long, smooth barrel and fires "shot" (small pellets held together in a cartridge).

TYPES: A shotgun can be of many types, such as double barrel, semi-automatic, singleshot, slide action, bolt action or percussion. A double barrel shotgun has two barrels, which can be side-by-side or over-under. A semi-automatic ejects the spent case and cycles the new round into the chamber using energy from the fired round. A singleshot has no magazine and can only fire one shot. Slide action is a repeating action which uses a reciprocating forestock connected to the breechbolt. Bolt action is done manually by moving a reciprocating breechbolt. Percussion refers to the use of a percussion cap to ignite the powder charge.

ORIGIN: Firearms were developed in Europe.

MAKERS: Prominent manufacturers include Browning, Marlin, Remington and Winchester.

COMMENTS: Documented evidence of historical significance increases a gun's value to a marked degree. Any collectible firearm, even if in poor condition, should fetch at least twenty to thirty percent of the highest price given. Refinished guns are worth significantly less than their unrefinished counterparts which are still in good condition.

ADDITIONAL TIPS: For more information, please refer to *The Official Price Guide to Antique and Modern Firearms* by David Byron, published by The House of Collectibles.

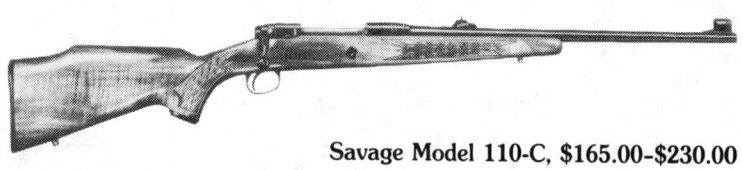

Savage Model 110-C, $165.00–$230.00

	Current Price Range		P/Y Average

BROWNING

SHOTGUN, DOUBLE BARREL, OVER—UNDER

☐ **Citori,** 12 gauge, trap grade, vent rib, checkered stock, modern	435.00	575.00	550.00
☐ **Citori,** 12 and 20 gauges, standard grade, vent rib, checkered stock, modern	425.00	550.00	535.00
☐ **Citori,** 12 and 20 gauges, skeet grade, vent rib, checkered stock, modern	435.00	575.00	550.00
☐ **Citori International,** 12 gauge, trap grade, vent rib, checkered stock, modern	485.00	625.00	600.00
☐ **Citori International,** 12 gauge, skeet grade, vent rib, checkered stock, modern	485.00	625.00	600.00
☐ **Citori Grade II,** various gauges, hunting model, engraved, checkered stock, single selective trigger, modern	670.00	885.00	850.00
☐ **Citori Grade II,** trap and skeet models, add 10%.			
☐ **Citori Grade V,** various gauges, fancy engraving, checkered stock, single selective trigger, modern	900.00	1400.00	1350.00

WINCHESTER REPEATING ARMS COMPANY

SHOTGUN, DOUBLE BARREL, OVER-UNDER

☐ **Model 101,** 12 gauges, trap grade, Monte Carlo stock, single trigger, automatic ejector, engraved, modern	575.00	750.00	675.00
☐ **Model 101,** 12 gauges, trap grade, single trigger, automatic ejector, checkered stock, engraved, modern	575.00	750.00	675.00
☐ **Model 101,** 12 gauges, Mag. 3″, vent rib, single trigger, automatic ejector, checkered stock, engraved, modern	550.00	725.00	650.00
☐ **Model 101,** various gauges, skeet grade, single trigger, automatic ejector, checkered stock, engraved, modern	575.00	750.00	675.00
☐ **Model 101,** various gauges, featherweight, single trigger, automatic ejector, checkered stock, engraved, modern	575.00	750.00	675.00
☐ **Model 101,** 3 gauges set, skeet grade, single trigger, automatic ejector, checkered stock, engraved, modern	1100.00	1650.00	1325.00
☐ **Model 101 Field,** various gauges, vent rib, single trigger, automatic ejector, checkered stock, engraved, modern	500.00	725.00	612.00

SILHOUETTES

TOPIC: Silhouettes are profiles cut out of one color paper and attached to a background of contrasting color. They can have detail added in chalk, pen or watercolors.

PERIOD: Silhouettes became popular in the 1700s and did not fall from popular favor until the middle of the 1800s.

MAKERS: Famous silhouette artists include Martha Anne Honeywell, William Henry Brown, Sanders Nellis and Auguste Edouart. Any silhouette bearing the name of Jean Millette is a fake; this was a name created by forgers.

COMMENTS: The value of a silhouette depends on the age, quality and size of the specimen; the notoriety of the subject is also very important. Any information marked on the silhouette increases its value.

ADDITIONAL TIPS: Modern and semi-modern silhouettes are not valued in the collector market.

	Current Price Range		P/Y Average
☐ **Aaron Burr,** bust portrait, black watercolor. Signed Jos. Wood, dated 1812, 3″ x 2¾″	390.00	450.00	420.00
☐ **Admiral,** unidentified, English wax, bowled glass, gilt rim, 3½″ diameter	185.00	215.00	195.00
☐ **Charles Carroll Of Carrollton** (last surviving signer of the Declaration of Independence), holding trowel and cane, dated 1828, 13″ x 10″ ...	260.00	390.00	325.00
☐ **Civil War Officer,** unidentified, violet paper against light pink background, matted and framed, believed to be of Virginia origin, 5½″ x 4″, c. 1865	195.00	260.00	220.00
☐ **Hon. Henry Clay,** bust portrait, inscribed J. W. Jarvis, dated 1810, 8″ x 6¼″	95.00	160.00	140.00
☐ **Couple,** in double frame, 19th-century	285.00	315.00	300.00
☐ **Double Portrait,** of gentleman and lady, full length figures. Signed Aug. Edouart, dated 1844, 9″ x 7⅛″, Edouart was the Stradivari of silhouettists	225.00	325.00	275.00

Portrait Silhouettes of Governor and Mrs. S.W. Kearney, *1840s,*
$400.00-$500.00

	Current Price Range		P/Y Average
☐ **Elderly Man,** unidentified, half-length profile. c. 1880	95.00	130.00	115.00
☐ **Miss Elizabeth Frobiser,** clad in bonnet, dress and white pantalettes. Signed Frith, dated 1821	325.00	390.00	380.00
☐ **Gentleman,** wearing top hat, landscape setting. Signed Aug. Edouart, dated 1829, 8⅞″ x 6⅝″	285.00	360.00	320.00
☐ **Alexander Hamilton,** bust portrait wearing frilled smock. Signed J. W. Jarvis, dated 1804, 4½″ x 3½″	520.00	650.00	575.00
☐ **Gentleman,** unidentified, English wax, 18th century style, 1¼″ high	290.00	320.00	305.00

SILVER

DESCRIPTION: Silver collectibles include all objects made of silver.

TYPES: All types of items are made from silver including tableware, household ornaments, artwork and jewelry.

MAKERS: American silverware includes both factory merchandise and items made by individual craftsmen. Some chief manufacturers include Gorham, Reed and Barton, Towle, Wallace, Rogers, Oneida, Reliance, Kirk and International.

MATERIALS: Silver is always alloyed with base metal, usually copper, in manufacturing. This is done to provide durability, as silver in its pure state is soft and vulnerable. The grade of silver is determined by the amount or percentage of alloy material contained. Sterling silver, the traditional American grade for silverware, is .925 fine.

ADDITIONAL TIPS: For more information, consult *The Official Price Guide to American Silver and Silver Plate,* published by The House of Collectibles.

VERSAILLES—STERLING

GORHAM-1898–INACTIVE

	Current Price Range		P/Y Average
☐ Bouillon Spoon	27.50	34.00	27.00
☐ Citrus Spoon	40.00	45.00	37.00
☐ Cocktail Fork	28.00	32.00	25.00
☐ Cream Soup Spoon	48.00	52.00	47.00
☐ Cream Soup Spoon, small	37.50	42.00	35.00
☐ Demitasse Spoon	22.00	27.00	22.00
☐ Dessert Spoon	42.50	47.00	40.00
☐ Dinner Fork	47.00	52.00	45.00
☐ Dinner Knife	57.00	62.00	55.00
☐ Five O'Clock Teaspoon	15.00	21.00	16.00
☐ Fruit Knife	37.00	42.00	35.00
☐ Ice Cream Spoon	42.00	47.00	40.00
☐ Iced Tea Spoon	52.00	57.00	50.00
☐ Luncheon Fork	37.00	42.00	35.00

Punch Bowl, *Tiffany "Chrysanthemum," c. 1895, diameter 17", 114 ounces,* **$7250.00**

	Current Price Range		P/Y Average
☐ **Luncheon Knife**	45.00	50.00	43.00
☐ **Salad Fork**	47.00	53.00	45.00
☐ **Steak Knife**	37.00	43.00	35.00
☐ **Teaspoon**	21.00	27.00	19.00
☐ **Berry Spoon,** large	127.50	135.00	125.00
☐ **Carving Fork**	67.50	75.00	65.00
☐ **Cheese Scoop,** large	145.00	155.00	145.00
☐ **Cold Meat Fork,** buffet fork	112.50	125.00	110.00
☐ **Fish Fork**	40.00	45.00	40.00
☐ **Fish Knife**	37.50	45.00	35.00
☐ **Flat Server**	30.00	35.00	30.00
☐ **Gravy Ladle**	100.00	110.00	95.00
☐ **Ice Cream Fork**	40.00	45.00	40.00
☐ **Jelly Server,** large	135.00	145.00	135.00
☐ **Lettuce Fork**	95.00	100.00	95.00
☐ **Nut Picks**	27.50	35.00	25.00
☐ **Olive or Pickle Fork**	45.00	50.00	45.00
☐ **Pie Server**	40.00	45.00	40.00
☐ **Soup Ladle**	250.00	260.00	250.00
☐ **Sugar Shell**	37.00	45.00	35.00
☐ **Sugar Tongs**	45.00	50.00	45.00
☐ **Tablespoon/Serving Spoon**	52.50	58.00	50.00

STAMPS

DESCRIPTION: Stamps are small pieces of printed paper, issued by post offices for the prepayment of postage. In most cases they have a gummed back which, when moistened, adheres to a letter or parcel. All U.S. stamps have had gummed backs, but certain early foreign stamps needed to be glued. In modern times, all stamps have had "perforations" by which they can easily be separated from each other. The first stamps of many nations including the U.S. did not have perforations, and had to be cut apart with scissors. These are called "imperforates". Due to the scissor cutting, which was rarely methodical, some "imperforates" have much larger or straighter margins than others.

ORIGIN: Postage stamps were introduced by Great Britain in 1840, and soon thereafter by other nations, the U.S. following in 1847. Prior to the first federally issued U.S. stamps, several city postmasters issued their own stamps. This was done in New York and St. Louis, as well as else-where. These are called "postmasters' provisionals" and are very rare in most cases.

MAKER: Today, all U.S. stamps are printed by the U.S. Department of Printing and Engraving in Washington, D.C. Our early stamps were printed under contract by private firms.

COMMENTS: Frequently called "the hobby of kings" (largely because of Britain's George V, an avid collector), stamp collecting is now enjoyed by more than 20 million persons in this country and a much larger total worldwide.

CONDITION AND CARE: It is vital to consider the condition of a stamp before purchasing it. Points such as a bent corner, a missing perforation, or a heavy cancel can greatly reduce the value of a stamp.

ADDITIONAL TIPS: Learn about the hobby before venturing after rarities or unusual pieces. Get a good magnifying glass and handle your stamps with tongs rather than fingers. Subscribe to one of the stamp periodicals and visit stamp shows if you have the opportunity.

More detailed information on stamps and their current values is available in *The Official Blackbook Price Guide of U.S. Stamps,* published by The House of Collectibles.

Scott No.			Fine Unused Each	Ave. Unused Each	Fine Used Each	Ave. Used Each
GENERAL ISSUES						
1847. FIRST ISSUE						
□ 1	5¢	Red Brown...............	—	4550.00	1265.00	1000.00
□ 2	10¢	Black	—	18260.00	3440.00	2650.00
1875. REPRODUCTIONS OF 1847 ISSUE						
□ 3	5¢	Red Brown...............	2575.00	1975.00	—	—
□ 4	10¢	Black	3355.00	2500.00	—	—
1851–56. REGULAR ISSUE—IMPERFORATE						
□ 5A	1¢	Blue (Ib)	—	—	3500.00	2725.00
□ 6	1¢	Blue (1a)	—	—	4200.00	3415.00
□ 7	1¢	Blue (II).................	700.00	520.00	300.00	135.00
□ 8	1¢	Blue (III)	—	—	625.00	1150.00
□ 8A	1¢	Blue (IIa)	—	1325.00	800.00	620.00
□ 9	1¢	Blue (IV)	440.00	350.00	135.50	90.00
□ 10	3¢	Orange Brown (I)	—	1200.00	100.00	75.00
□ 11	3¢	Dull Red (I)	290.00	195.00	14.00	10.00
□ 12	5¢	Red Brown (I)	—	—	1600.00	1025.00
□ 13	10¢	Green (I).................	—	—	940.00	675.00
□ 14	10¢	Green (II)	—	1150.00	435.00	350.00
□ 15	10¢	Green (III)	—	1120.00	390.00	280.00
□ 16	10¢	Green (IV)	—	—	1575.00	1250.00
□ 17	12¢	Black	—	1500.00	340.00	295.00
1857–61. SAME DESIGNS AS 1851–56 ISSUE—PERF. 15						
□ 18	1¢	Blue (I)	1000.00	650.00	550.00	350.00
□ 19	1¢	Blue (Ia)	—	—	2500.00	1825.00
□ 20	1¢	Blue (II).................	645.00	430.00	260.00	200.00
□ 21	1¢	Blue (III)	—	2475.00	1200.00	850.00
□ 22	1¢	Blue (IIIa)...............	695.00	525.00	300.00	210.00
□ 23	1¢	Blue (IV)	—	1400.00	410.00	270.00
□ 24	1¢	Blue (V)	175.00	135.00	50.00	40.00
□ 25	3¢	Rose (I)	—	650.00	50.00	29.00
□ 26	3¢	Dull Red (II)	160.00	80.00	12.00	8.00
□ 26A	3¢	Dull Red (IIa)	195.00	150.00	30.00	22.00
□ 27	5¢	Brick Red (I)	—	5750.00	1100.00	780.00
□ 28	5¢	Red Brown (I)	—	1350.00	460.00	315.00
□ 28A	5¢	Indian Red (I)	—	—	1200.00	900.00
□ 29	5¢	Brown (I)	910.00	600.00	340.00	215.00
□ 30	5¢	Orange Brown (II)	1150.00	675.00	1150.00	780.00
□ 30A	5¢	Brown (II)	600.00	360.00	300.00	220.00
□ 31	10¢	Green (I).................	—	3700.00	610.00	400.00
□ 32	10¢	Green (II)	1580.00	1125.00	240.00	180.00
□ 33	10¢	Green (III)	1510.00	1100.00	250.00	200.00
□ 34	10¢	Green (IV)	—	—	1425.00	1065.00

Scott No.						Fine Unused Each	Ave. Unused Each	Fine Used Each	Ave. Used Each
☐ 35	10¢	Green (V)				320.00	185.00	140.00	100.00
☐ 36	12¢	Black (I)				465.00	310.00	140.00	100.00
☐ 36b	12¢	Black (II)				440.00	325.00	175.00	120.00
☐ 37	24¢	Gray Lilac				900.00	625.00	350.00	230.00

1893. COLUMBIAN ISSUE (N-H ADD 95%)

Scott No.						Fine Unused Each	Ave. Unused Each	Fine Used Each	Ave. Used Each
☐ 230	1¢	Blue	310.00	230.00		75.00	45.00	.80	.50
☐ 231	2¢	Violet	300.00	200.00		55.00	38.00	.13	.09
☐ 231c	2¢	"Broken Hat"	520.00	400.00		120.00	90.00	1.25	1.00
☐ 232	3¢	Green	500.00	320.00		110.00	85.00	35.00	23.00
☐ 233	4¢	Ultramarine	900.00	700.00		165.00	120.00	13.73	12.00
☐ 234	5¢	Chocolate	1075.00	825.00		180.00	135.00	18.00	15.00
☐ 235	6¢	Purple	975.00	775.00		175.00	125.00	62.00	50.00
☐ 236	8¢	Magenta	1000.00	650.00		170.00	115.00	20.00	15.00
☐ 237	10¢	Black Brown	1675.00	1275.00		300.00	215.00	15.00	12.00
☐ 238	15¢	Dark Green	2950.00	2300.00		445.00	320.00	145.00	115.00
☐ 239	30¢	Orange Brown	4000.00	3000.00		650.00	475.00	250.00	180.00
☐ 240	50¢	Slate Blue	4600.00	3750.00		775.00	570.00	300.00	210.00
☐ 241	$1	Salmon	—	—		2580.00	2000.00	1075.00	710.00
☐ 242	$2	Brown Red	—	—		2800.00	1875.00	900.00	610.00
☐ 243	$3	Yellow Green	—	—		4600.00	3545.00	1625.00	1200.00
☐ 244	$4	Crimson Lake	—	—		6500.00	4500.00	2250.00	1600.00
☐ 245	$5	Black	—	—		6775.00	4965.00	2465.00	1250.00

Scott No.			Mint Sheet	Plate Block	Fine Unused Each	Fine Used Each
1969. W. C. HANDY—MUSICIAN						
☐ 1372	6¢	Multicolored	10.00	1.25	.20	.06
1969. SETTLEMENT OF CALIFORNIA						
☐ 1373	6¢	Multicolored	10.00	1.25	.20	.06
1969. MAJOR JOHN WESLEY POWELL—GEOLOGIST						
☐ 1374	6¢	Multicolored	10.00	1.25	.20	.06
1969. ALABAMA STATEHOOD						
☐ 1375	6¢	Red, Yellow, Brown	10.00	1.25	.20	.06
1969. XI INTL. BOTANICAL CONGRESS						
☐ 1376	6¢	Multicolored	—	—	2.10	.10
☐ 1377	6¢	Multicolored	—	—	2.10	.10
☐ 1378	6¢	Multicolored	—	—	2.10	.10
☐ 1379	6¢	Multicolored	—	—	2.10	.10
1969. DARTMOUTH COLLEGE CASE						
☐ 1380	6¢	Green	14.00	1.50	.22	.06
1969. PROFESSIONAL BASEBALL CENTENARY						
☐ 1381	6¢	Multicolored	15.00	1.50	.30	.07

Scott No.			Mint Sheet	Plate Block	Fine Unused Each	Fine Used Each

1969. INTERCOLLEGIATE FOOTBALL CENTENARY

| ☐ 1382 | 6¢ | Red & Green | 14.00 | 1.50 | .30 | .06 |

1969. DWIGHT D. EISENHOWER MEMORIAL

| ☐ 1383 | 6¢ | Blue, Black & Red | 10.00 | 1.50 | .30 | .06 |

1969. CHRISTMAS ISSUE

| ☐ 1384 | 6¢ | Multicolored | 12.00 | 5.00 | .30 | .06 |

1969. HOPE FOR THE CRIPPLED

| ☐ 1385 | 6¢ | Multicolored | 13.50 | 1.50 | .30 | .06 |

1969. WILLIAM M. HARNETT PAINTING

| ☐ 1386 | 6¢ | Multicolored | 10.00 | 1.50 | .30 | .06 |

1970. COMMEMORATIVES

1970. NATURAL HISTORY

☐ 1387	6¢	Multicolored	—	—	.25	.12
☐ 1388	6¢	Multicolored	—	—	.25	.12
☐ 1389	6¢	Multicolored	—	—	.25	.12
☐ 1390	6¢	Multicolored	—	—	.25	.12

1970. MAINE STATEHOOD SESQUICENTENNIAL

| ☐ 1391 | 6¢ | Multicolored | 15.00 | 1.50 | .32 | .06 |

1970. WILDLIFE CONSERVATION—BUFFALO

| ☐ 1392 | 6¢ | Black on Tan | 15.00 | 1.50 | .32 | .06 |

1970–74. REGULAR ISSUE

☐ 1393	6¢	Blue Gray	20.00	1.25	.18	.07
☐ 1393D	7¢	Light Blue	22.00	1.50	.20	.07
☐ 1394	8¢	Black, Blue, Red	22.00	1.50	.20	.07

Scott No.			Fine Unused Plate Blk	Ave. Unused Plate Blk	Fine Unused Each	Ave. Unused Each	Fine Used Each	Ave. Used Each

1939. GOLDEN GATE INTERNATIONAL EXPOSITION (N-H ADD 25%)

| ☐ 852 | 3¢ | Bright Purple | 3.90 | 3.50 | .25 | .20 | .12 | .07 |

1939. NEW YORK WORLD'S FAIR (N-H ADD 20%)

| ☐ 853 | 3¢ | Deep Purple | 3.90 | 3.00 | .25 | .20 | .12 | .07 |

1939. WASHINGTON INAUGURATION SESQUICENTENNIAL (N-H ADD 20%)

| ☐ 854 | 3¢ | Bright Red Violet | 8.00 | 7.00 | .35 | .25 | .16 | .10 |

1939. BASEBALL CENTENNIAL (N-H ADD 20%)

| ☐ 1855 | 3¢ | Violet | 10.00 | 7.00 | .70 | .55 | .12 | .09 |

Scott No.			Fine Unused Plate Blk	Ave. Unused Plate Blk	Fine Unused Each	Ave. Unused Each	Fine Used Each	Ave. Used Each

1939. 25TH ANNIVERSARY PANAMA CANAL (N-H ADD 20%)

| ☐ 856 | 3¢ | Deep Red Violet .... | 10.50 | 8.25 | .50 | .35 | .15 | .09 |

1939. COLONIAL PRINTING TERCENTENARY (N-H ADD 20%)

| ☐ 857 | 3¢ | Rose Violet .... | 5.00 | 4.00 | .30 | .25 | .12 | .09 |

1939. 50TH ANNIVERSARY OF STATEHOOD (N-H ADD 20%)

| ☐ 858 | 3¢ | Rose Violet .... | 5.00 | 4.00 | .35 | .29 | .12 | .09 |

1940. FAMOUS AMERICANS SERIES AMERICAN AUTHORS (N-H ADD 20%)

☐ 859	1¢	Bright Blue Green	3.50	2.60	.15	.10	.08	.08
☐ 860	2¢	Rose Carmine	3.50	2.75	.20	.16	.14	.10
☐ 861	3¢	Bright Red Violet	6.00	4.85	.22	.17	.10	.07
☐ 862	5¢	Ultramarine	50.00	32.00	1.00	.75	.40	.32
☐ 863	10¢	Dark Brown	165.00	135.00	6.00	4.00	2.15	3.15

AMERICAN POETS (N-H ADD 20%)

☐ 864	1¢	Bright Blue Green	6.00	4.50	.18	.15	.20	.16
☐ 865	2¢	Rose Carmine	6.50	5.00	.18	.14	.12	.08
☐ 866	3¢	Bright Red Violet	10.00	8.00	.25	.20	.10	.07
☐ 867	5¢	Ultramarine	50.00	40.00	1.25	.95	.43	.32
☐ 868	10¢	Dark Brown	150.00	130.00	7.25	6.00	5.25	3.00

AMERICAN EDUCATORS (N-H ADD 20%)

| ☐ 869 | 1¢ | Bright Blue Green .... | 6.75 | 5.00 | .30 | .22 | .16 | .14 |
| ☐ 870 | 2¢ | Rose Carmine .... | 7.00 | 5.25 | .32 | .18 | .16 | .14 |

STANGL POTTERY

HISTORY: Stangl was an outgrowth of the Fulper Pottery Company of Flemington, New Jersey. In 1910, J.M. Stangl assumed the post of ceramic engineer at Fulper and was directly responsible for much of its creative work during the next two decades. During the 1920s, Fulper, with its business rapidly expanding, bought out the old Anchor Pottery Company factory in Trenton. When the main Fulper plant was destroyed in a fire in 1929, the firm was reorganized as Stangl Pottery and Trenton became its headquarters. The Stangl Pottery Company was taken over by Pfaltzgraff, a division of Susquehanna Broadcasting Company of York, Pennsylvania in July 1878.

DESCRIPTION: The Stangl Pottery Company was one of the later producers of fine artware and dinnerware. Among its best-known works are the famous "Stangl birds" a series of statuettes released during the early part of World War . These charming pieces were produced in limited numbers, probably because of the war, and are now valuable "finds". Stangl was also well known for its fine vases with rich colors and satiny glazes, similar to the wares turned out by Grueby (and then by Tiffany, which acquired Grueby) some 30 or 40 years earlier.

MARKS: It appears as though the first mark used by the Stangl Pottery Company was STANGL USA, without periods between the initial letters. This was followed by a series of others, including an oval mark in which the trade name of the line appears at the center, with MADE IN TRENTON, U.S.A. beneath. A more elaborate version has the name STANGL, TRENTON, N.J. within an oval, accompanied by such wording as HAND-PAINTED, OVEN PROOF, COUNTRY GARDEN or HAND-PAINTED, GRANADA GOLD, denoting different lines of ware.

RECOMMENDED READING: For more in-depth information on Stangl Pottery you may refer to *The Official Price Guide to Pottery and Porcelain,* published by The House of Collectibles.

Cockatoo, *medium,* $40.00–$50.00

COUNTRY GARDEN

Double outer border of solid band accompanied by scalloped band; with printed pictures of various flowers, stems and leaves.

	Current Price Range		P/Y Average
☐ **Bowl,** cereal	4.00	5.00	4.50
☐ **Bowl,** fruit	4.00	5.00	4.50
☐ **Bowl,** 7", oval, tulip and daffodil design	8.00	10.00	9.00
☐ **Creamer**	5.00	6.00	5.40
☐ **Cup and Saucer,** tulip design	5.00	6.00	5.40
☐ **Mug,** festival	4.00	5.00	4.50
☐ **Plate,** 6", dahlia	4.00	5.00	4.50
☐ **Plate,** 8", tigerlily and bell motif	5.00	6.00	5.40
☐ **Plate,** 9¼", country life, circular	20.00	25.00	22.25
☐ **Sugar,** covered	7.00	8.00	7.70

FRUIT

Narrow solid outer border, enclosing a scalloped border, with (on plates) a brightly colored inner border and printed pictures of grapes, cherries, etc.

☐ **Bowl,** sugar, lidded	7.50	10.00	8.00
☐ lacking lid	5.50	7.00	5.40
☐ **Cup**	5.50	7.00	5.40
☐ **Pot,** bean, lidded	26.00	31.00	28.00
☐ **Saucer**	3.25	5.00	3.50
☐ **Salt and Pepper**	10.00	13.00	10.70

MAGNOLIA

A borderless ware, very brightly colored, with printed pictures of magnolia blossoms, stems, leaves and buds.

☐ **Coffee Warmer**	15.00	17.00	16.00
☐ **Plate,** dinner, 8¼"	5.00	6.00	5.40
☐ **Saucer**	2.00	3.00	2.60
☐ **Shakers,** pair	10.00	12.00	11.00

ORCHARD SONG

A borderless ware, decorated with printed pictures of various fruits brightly colored.

☐ **Plate,** 5"	2.00	3.00	2.60
☐ **Plate,** 6"	3.00	4.00	3.50
☐ **Plate,** dinner 8", pink cosmos	4.00	5.00	4.50
☐ **Plate,** dinner, 10¼", starflower	5.00	6.00	5.40
☐ **Pitcher,** 5¾", white and beige terra rose	11.00	14.00	12.50
☐ **Tray,** relish	5.00	7.00	6.00

	Current Price Range		P/Y Average

STAR FLOWER

❏ **Plate,** 6″	4.00	5.00	4.50
❏ **Plate,** 10″	6.00	8.00	7.00
❏ **Saucer**	4.00	5.00	4.50

TERRA ROSE

❏ **Bowl,** 7″, blue, covered	12.00	15.00	13.00
❏ **Bowl,** 10″, green	8.00	12.00	10.00
❏ **Cake Stand,** 8″, green	15.00	21.00	17.50

STAR TREK COLLECTIBLES

DESCRIPTION: Star Trek Collectibles include all items dealing with or made for the Television series, cartoon series or its movies.

ORIGIN: Star Trek, a science fiction space thriller, began as a television series which ran from 1966 to 1969. After its cancellation, the series was syndicated and by 1978 was shown 300 times per day worldwide. A cartoon series was produced which ran from 1972 to 1974. *Star Trek: The Motion Picture* and *The Wrath of Khan* were two Star Trek movies.

TYPES: There are all kinds of Star Trek memorabilia, including animated cels, toys, costumes, books and household ware.

COMMENTS: After the television series, Star Trek Fan Clubs, magazines and conventions sprang up worldwide. With more fans interested in these collectibles, the prices are rising into the double digits.

ADDITIONAL TIPS: For more information, consult *The Official Price Guide to Star Trek and Star Wars Collectibles,* published by The House of Collectibles.

Star Trek Adventure Set,
*made by Colorforms
under license from
Paramount Pictures Corp.,
punch-out cardboard figures
of characters, 1975,*
$5.00-$7.00

	Current Price Range		P/Y Average

BOOKS

☐ **Abode of Life, The,** L. Correy, Captain Kirk must try to help the hostile citizens of Mercan against their own sun, paperback, Pocket Books, 1982 — 2.00 | 3.00 | 2.25

☐ **Advanced Information on 1966–67 Programming: Star Trek,** 12 page booklet, prepared by NBC sales planning division in New York, includes two pictures of Spock, both show Spock's appearance more human than Vulcan, outline of the series as it was formed at the time of the second pilot, "Where No Man Has Gone Before" — 30.00 | 60.00 | 39.00

☐ **Best of Trek, The,** W. Irwin and G. Love, volume #1, interviews, convention close ups, close up on special effects, compiled from Trek, the magazine for Star Trek fans, 1974 .... — 2.00 | 3.00 | 2.25

☐ **Chekov's Enterprise,** W. Koenig, a personal journal of the making of *Star Trek-The Motion Picture,* the off camera camaraderie of the cast and crew in a personal on-the-set-diary, paperback, Pocket Books, 1980 .... — 8.00 | 12.00 | 10.00

☐ **Come and Be With Me,** L. Nimoy, poetry, Blue Mountain Arts, paperback .... — 8.00 | 12.00 | 10.00

☐ **Covenant of the Crown, The,** H. Weinstein, The Galaxy's hope to live long and prosper falls under the shadow of the Klingons, paperback, Pocket Books, 1981 .... — 2.00 | 3.00 | 2.35

	Current Price Range		P/Y Average
☐ **Death's Angel,** K. Sky, Star Trek novel, paperback, Bantam Books, April, 1981	10.00	15.00	12.00
☐ **Making of Star Trek II, The Wrath of Khan, The,** Allan Asherman, behind-the-scenes story of Star Trek's greatest adventure, paperback, Pocket Books, 1982	10.00	15.00	12.50
☐ **Star Trek Annual,** BBC Productions, a series, 1972 to date, comics and other articles, hard cover, Western Publishing.			
☐ **1973–75**	15.00	25.00	20.00
☐ **1976–80**	10.00	20.00	14.00
☐ **1981–83**	6.00	12.00	9.00
☐ **Star Trek Maps,** an introduction to navigation, Jeff Maynard, background and technical material about navigating with the Enterprise, four charts of the Federation, Klingon, and Romulan Zones, in portfolio, Bantam Books, 1980	30.00	50.00	37.50
☐ **Star Trek Medical Manual,** Eileen Palestine, a reference to Vulcan Physiology; Medical time line, chart of Diseases and Drugs, Ballantine Books, 1977	20.00	25.00	22.00

CARDS

AMERICAN GUM CARDS

☐ **Fantasy Trading Card Co.,** Star Trek-The Wrath of Khan, 30 card set, color photos, no stickers, no captions, print run limited to 7,500 possible sets, 1982, 5″ x 7″			
☐ **Set**	15.00	20.00	17.90
☐ **Kirk** with book under arm	.50	1.00	.80
☐ **Sulu**	.50	1.00	.80
☐ **Scott**	.50	1.00	.80
☐ **Uhura**	.50	1.00	.80
☐ **Kirk**	.50	1.00	.80
☐ **David Marcus**	.50	1.00	.80
☐ **Topps Photo Cards,** Star Trek, 88 card set, color photos from television show, "captain log" on back with narrative and character profiles, 2½″ x 3½″, 1976.			
☐ **Set**	50.00	100.00	77.50
☐ **1 The U.S.S. Enterprise**	1.00	2.00	1.25
☐ **2 Captain James T. Kirk**	1.00	2.00	1.25
☐ **3 Dr. "Bones" McCoy**	1.00	2.00	1.25
☐ **4 Science Officer Spock**	1.00	2.00	1.25
☐ **5 Engineer Scott**	1.00	2.00	1.25
☐ **6 Lieutenant Uhura**	1.00	2.00	1.25
☐ **7 Ensign Chekov**	1.00	2.00	1.25
☐ **8 The Phaser—Tomorrow's Weapon**	1.00	2.00	1.25
☐ **9 The Shuttle Craft**	1.00	2.00	1.25
☐ **10 Opponents**	1.00	2.00	1.25

	Current Price Range		P/Y Average

MAGAZINES

☐ **All About Star Trek Fan Clubs,** Ego Enterprises, New York, NY, series of five fanzines with complete membership information plus biographies, portraits, episodes and conventions, first published, Dec. 1976.

☐ #1	8.00	12.00	10.00
☐ #2–5	4.00	8.00	6.00

☐ **American Cinematographer,** ASC Holding Corp., Hollywood, California, Vol. 61, No. 2, Feb. 1980, issue devoted to a look behind the scenes of Star Trek, The Motion Picture 15.00 25.00 20.00

☐ **Vol. 63, No. 10,** Oct. 1982, "Special Effects For Star Trek III" 4.00 8.00 5.75

☐ **Biography of Majel Barrett,** Lincoln Enterprises, star who played Nurse Chapel, pamphlet .... .50 .75 .65

STAR WARS COLLECTIBLES

DESCRIPTION: Star Wars collectibles include all items made for or about the three Star Wars movies.

ORIGIN: *Star Wars,* a space fantasy, is the name of a movie released in the 1980s. Because of its popularity, two other movies were produced including *The Empire Strikes Back* and *Return of the Jedi.*

TYPES: All types of movie articles and promotional items were produced including posters, toys, patches, household ware and action figures.

COMMENTS: The three Star Wars movies were big hits with movie audiences worldwide. Thousands of Star Wars fans keep the collectible market booming.

ADDITIONAL TIPS: For more information, consult *The Official Price Guide to Star Trek and Star Wars Collectibles,* published by The House of Collectibles.

	Current Price Range		P/Y Average

BOOKS

☐ **Star Wars, The Adventures of Luke Skywalker,** G. Lucas, 16 pages color section, the original story that the saga is based on, Ballantine paperback, 1976.

☐ **First Edition,** no color pages	6.00	10.00	8.75
☐ **Later Editions**	2.00	3.00	2.65

☐ **Art of The Empire Strikes Back, The,** V. Bullock and V. Hoffman, a celebration of the artistic and technical accomplishment of the famous space epic, over-sized softcover, Ballantine, 1981 ...

	15.00	20.00	17.75

☐ **Art of Star Wars, The,** C. Titelman, a full script of the original movie illustrated with stills and artists' conceptions, oversized softcover, Ballantine, 1979 ....

	15.00	20.00	18.00

☐ **Art of Return of the Jedi,** a full script of the movie illustrated with storyboards and artists' conceptions, overzided softcover, Ballantine, 1983 ....

	18.00	20.00	19.50

☐ **Empire Strikes Back, The,** D. Glut, an adaptation of the movie in novel form, following the adventures of Leia, Luke, Han, and Darth Vader, paperback, Ballantine, 1980 ....

	2.00	3.00	2.60

Press Book,
The World of Star Wars,
Lucasfilm Ltd., 1981,
10½" x 16", **$35.00-$45.00**

	Current Price Range		P/Y Average

CARDS

TOPPS GUM CARDS
☐ **Star Wars, First Series,** Blue Borders, Cards 1–66

☐ **Complete set**	20.00	30.00	26.50
☐ **Second Series,** Red Borders, cards 67–132			
☐ **Complete set**	15.00	25.00	21.00
☐ **Third Series,** Yellow Borders, cards 133–198			
☐ **Complete set**	15.00	25.00	21.00

MAGAZINES

☐ **Cinefantastique,** F.S. Clark Publishers, the magazine with a "sense of wonder," Vol. 12, No. 5 and 6, July/August, 1982, "Star Trek II" and "The Revenge of the Jedi"	6.00	10.00	8.25
☐ **Vol. 6, No. 4, Vol. 7, No. 1,** double issue, "Making Star Wars" 23 interviews with the actors, technicians and artists	20.00	25.00	22.50
☐ **No. 26,** May/July, behind the scenes with Star Wars material, a color Star Wars center spread	4.00	6.00	5.00

POSTERS

☐ **Concert Poster,** Twentieth Century-Fox, shows musical adaptation of C-3PO and Artoo Detoo, used to announce concerts of Star Wars musical score, 2' x 3'	200.00	250.00	227.00
☐ **Empire Strikes Back Poster Album,** Bantha tracks, an official Star Wars fan club publication, featuring all the characters	5.00	8.00	6.50

SHEET MUSIC

☐ **Music Book,** The Empire Strikes Back, Lucasfilm Ltd., 1980, includes "Star Wars" (main theme), "The Imperial March" (Darth Vader's theme), "Yoda's Theme", "Han Solo and the Princess", "May The Force Be With You", and "Finale", numerous pictures with captions	8.00	10.00	9.00
☐ **Music Book,** Star Wars, 20th Century Fox Film Corporation, 1977, includes "Main Title" (piano solo), "Main Title" (sketch score), "Princess Leia's Theme" (piano solo), "Cantina Band" (sketch score), numerous pictures with extensive cutlines	8.00	10.00	9.00

STEINS

DESCRIPTION: Steins are ornately decorated large mugs with a lid.

ORIGIN: Although steins were produced in the thirteenth century, they are extremely rare. In fact, steins from the thirteenth through the seventeenth centuries are usually found in museums. Collectors seek steins from the 1800s and 1900s.

MANUFACTURERS: Steins produced by the Villeroy & Bock Company of Mettlach, Germany are especially valuable. Collectors also seek steins manufactured by Merkelbach & Wick and Simon Peter Gerz.

COMMENTS: Since few steins were produced in America, they are rare and sought after by collectors. Quality, condition and maker are all items which determine value.

	Current Price Range		P/Y Average
□ **Art Nouveau,** copper and brass, 14″	110.00	130.00	110.00
□ **Bacchus,** silver, Sheffield, 11½″	580.00	675.00	605.00
□ **Character,** drunken monkey, Musterschutz, one litre	400.00	465.00	415.00
□ **Crying Radish,** Musterschutz, 3/10 litre	450.00	550.00	475.00
□ **David And Goliath,** handle with four finger holes, ½ litre	590.00	670.00	605.00
□ **Firefighting Scene,** pewter top, ½ litre	340.00	390.00	330.00
□ **Happy Turnip,** Musterschutz, 3 litre	490.00	565.00	500.00
□ **Ivory,** battle scene, carved, 13¾″	2375.00	2950.00	2500.00
□ **Lithophanes,** clown, ½ litre	400.00	485.00	415.00
□ **Lithophanes,** German scene, 6½″	110.00	130.00	110.00
□ **Mettlach,** No. 1527, ½ litre	575.00	675.00	580.00
□ **Mettlach,** No. 1675, Heidelberg, ½ litre	500.00	585.00	515.00
□ **Mettlach,** No. 1934, soldiers, inlaid lid	650.00	825.00	720.00
□ **Mettlach,** No. 2002, Munich, ½ litre	400.00	460.00	415.00
□ **Mettlach,** No. 2038, Black Forest, ½ litre	3900.00	4400.00	4000.00
□ **Mettlach,** No. 2082, inlaid top, featuring Robin Hood character firing crossbow	1250.00	1450.00	1325.00
□ **Mettlach,** No. 2136, Brewmaster, ½ litre	350.00	425.00	365.00
□ **Mettlach,** No. 2181, Pug, ½ litre	350.00	425.00	365.00

Beer Stein, *Germany, porcelain with pewter lid, decorated with trio of merry makers in relief, 1900s,* **$175.00-$250.00**

	Current Price Range		P/Y Average
☐ **Mettlach,** No. 2277, inlaid top, castle and clock tower	425.00	525.00	460.00
☐ **Mettlach,** No. 2333, dancing gnomes, pewter top	135.00	160.00	145.00
☐ **Mettlach,** No. 2388, pretzel, ½ litre	490.00	575.00	500.00
☐ **Mettlach,** No. 2833F, inlaid top, tavern scene of men toasting, brick wall motif around base	370.00	450.00	385.00
☐ **Mettlach,** No. 2958, bowling, 16″	775.00	925.00	780.00
☐ **Monk,** Gesetzlicht, ½ litre	200.00	230.00	200.00
☐ **Pewter,** Kayserzinn, 10″	190.00	220.00	190.00
☐ **Porcelain,** pewter top, blacksmith crest	180.00	220.00	185.00
☐ **Pottery,** figural top, Roman soldier on sides . .	150.00	180.00	155.00
☐ **Pottery,** Marzi Remi, tavern scene	35.00	49.00	39.00
☐ **Pottery,** pewter top, border of grapes on top edge, seated men and women talking	55.00	70.00	62.00
☐ **Pottery,** pewter top, eagle crest in oval medallion	85.00	120.00	97.00

	Current Price Range		P/Y Average
❏ **Pottery,** pewter top, monks drinking, keg taps border bottom	80.00	120.00	93.00
❏ **Pottery,** soldier figural top, relief, featuring Diana, Mars and Minerva	100.00	140.00	114.00
❏ **Puss In Boots,** 6½″	55.00	70.00	61.00
❏ **Regimental,** 18th Infantry, 1 litre	340.00	400.00	360.00
❏ **Regimental,** Franco-Prussian War, 1 litre	340.00	400.00	360.00
❏ **Schlitz Beer,** ceramic, 7½″	33.00	39.00	34.00
❏ **Singing Pig,** Musterschutz, ¼ litre	340.00	410.00	360.00
❏ **Stoneware,** pewter top, blue saltglaze	100.00	140.00	109.00
❏ **Stoneware,** pewter top, blue saltglaze, band of musicians outdoors	110.00	140.00	117.00
❏ **Stoneware,** pewter top, blue saltglaze, hunters	100.00	120.00	105.00

STEREOGRAPHS

BACKGROUND: Stereographs were first introduced in the U.S. on glass. Those stereographs (or stereo cards, views) made before 1858 are easiest to place. They are unusually thin, and in most French and English examples, they have no identifying signatures or titles.

Those stereographs with a revenue stamp on the back can be easily dated between 1864–1866, when the U.S. taxed many minute luxuries. In 1868, many publishers listed the views in a particular stereographic series by underlining or outlining a card number or title.

After 1880, stereographs that were curved came on the market since it was believed that it carried a more three dimensional quality.

COMMENTS: A stereograph's value is determined by condition, subject, rarity, photographer and age. Of course, a series or set is usually more valuable than an individual card.

ADDITIONAL TIPS: Listed below is a sampling of stereographs recently purchased, or found, on today's market. They are listed alphabetically by category. For further information, please contact National Stereoscopic Association, Box 14801, Columbus, OH 43214.

Photographica, stereograph, c. 1880, **$3.00-$15.00.**
*Photo Credit: Lou McColloch, Highland Heights, OH
44143.*

	Current Price Range		P/Y Average

CELEBRITIES

☐ **William Jennings Bryan,** In New York City, Keystone Davis #15539	15.00	25.00	20.00
☐ **Calvin Coolidge,** with cabinet, Keystone Davis #26303, rare	45.00	55.00	49.50
☐ **Major Doolittle,** Keystone Davis #28031	30.00	40.00	34.50
☐ **Thomas Alva Edison,** Keystone Davis #V28007	45.00	55.00	49.50
☐ **Henry Ford,** Keystone Davis #28023	45.00	55.00	49.50
☐ **Herbert Hoover,** Keystone Davis #28012	15.00	35.00	25.00
☐ **Charles Lindberg,** next to plane, Keystone Davis #32062T	25.00	35.00	29.50
☐ **John D. Rockefeller,** Keystone Davis #V11961	10.00	30.00	19.50
☐ **Evangelist Billy Sunday**	7.00	12.00	9.50

EVENTS

☐ **Boxer Rebellion**	3.50	7.00	4.50
☐ **Chicago Fire of 1871**	3.00	9.00	7.00
☐ **Civil War,** set of 75	385.00	430.00	400.00
☐ **Mill Creek Flood of 1874**	3.00	5.00	3.75
☐ **San Francisco Earthquake**	10.00	20.00	15.00
☐ **Spanish American War**	3.00	12.00	9.00
☐ **Wedding,** of Tom Thumb, by Anthony Brady, c. 1860s	75.00	125.00	102.00
☐ **World War I,** set of 100	125.00	175.00	145.00

	Current Price Range		P/Y Average

PLACES

☐ **China,** set of 100	325.00	375.00	345.00
☐ **Death Valley,** Keystone Davis #32666	4.00	8.00	5.50
☐ **France,** set of 30	40.00	50.00	46.00
☐ **New York City,** views of various landmarks, set of eight	30.00	50.00	41.50
☐ **Philadelphia,** by James Cremer, 19th century, set of five	20.00	30.00	24.75
☐ **United States,** set of five	20.00	30.00	24.50
☐ **Virginia City,** Nevada, by C.E. Watkins	60.00	80.00	69.50
☐ **World Tour,** set of 200	275.00	325.00	305.00
☐ **Yosemite Falls,** by C.E. Watkins	19.00	30.00	22.50

MISCELLANEOUS

☐ **Household Scene,** hand tinted, features children, 19th century, set of nine	20.00	30.00	28.00
☐ **Nineteenth Century,** time capsule, by Anthony, Gardner and Bierstadt, set of 50	75.00	125.00	95.00
☐ **Nude,** woman, black and white, rare	9.50	15.00	12.50
☐ **Six Men Who Circled The Earth,** Keystone Davis #26408T, set of six	15.00	25.00	19.50

STOCK CERTIFICATES

DESCRIPTION: Stock certificates are printed paper documents designating ownership of shares in a company.

TYPES: Some hobbyists collect stock certificates according to the nature of the business like railroad or mining, while others collect all types including canceled, elaborately illustrated and unissued certificates.

PERIOD: Stocks from the 1800s are the most common collected by hobbyists.

ADDITIONAL TIPS: For more information consult *The Official Price Guide to Paper Collectibles,* published by The House of Collectibles.

	Current Price Range		P/Y Average

AUTOMOBILE INDUSTRY

☐ **Academy Motor Sales & Service, Incorporated,** green and black, vignette of an eagle, unissued 10.00   14.00   12.25

☐ **China Motor Corporation,** incorporated in Panama, green and black, Chinese Char's on top, no vignette, unissued 3.50   4.50   4.00

☐ **Durante Motors Incorporated,** subscription Warrant, ornate green, no vignette, 1931 . . . . .   18.00   22.00   19.35

☐ **Ford International Capital Corporation,** $1000 bond, magenta border, vignette of an old Ford, 1969 . . . .   10.00   14.00   12.10

MINING

☐ **Acacia Gold Mining Company,** black on white, vignette of a wildflower, 1901 . . . .   6.50   8.50   7.50

☐ **Acme Uranium Mines, Incorporated,** allegorical vignette of female and two males, 1950's   3.60   4.50   4.20

☐ **Ahmeek Mining Company,** green on green, sharp certificate, vignette of two beavers 5.00   7.00   6.20

☐ **Gould & Curry Mining Company,** mines in Nevada, black on white, no vignette, 1927 . . . .   6.00   9.00   7.00

Stock Certificate, *Western Maryland Railway Company*
Photo Courtesy of Lou McCulloch, Highland Heights, OH 44143

	Current Price Range		P/Y Average
□ **Hudson Bay Mining & Smelting Limited,** blue, vignettes of a dog sled, mine and airplane, 1946	14.00	17.00	16.00
□ **Island Creek Coal Company,** brown, vignette of coal mining on top, undated but issued	6.00	9.00	7.50

OIL AND GAS INDUSTRY

□ **Burk Pipe Lines & Refining Company,** green border and seal, no vignette, 1920	2.00	4.00	3.10
□ **Brookline Oil Company,** orange border, vignette of a big oil well field, 1938	4.00	6.00	5.00
□ **Clarno Basin Oil Company,** brown, gold seal, three vignettes of oil, gushers and oil fields, 1930	8.00	12.00	10.00
□ **Crusader Oil & Gas Company,** blue and pink on white, vignette of a helmeted knight, 1960	6.00	9.00	7.25
□ **Hale Petroleum Company,** green border, no vignette, 1918...............................	3.00	4.00	3.60

STOVES

PERIOD: Collectible stoves are those made in the 19th and early 20th centuries.

ORIGIN: Kitchen ranges with ovens were first made in the early 19th century. Before that time most cooking was done over an open fire.

COMMENTS: Stoves are usually sought after by kitchen enthusiasts. In 1850 the first gas cookers appeared on the market. Electric cookers were introduced in 1894 and stoves didn't come with thermostats until 1923.

ADDITIONAL TIPS: The listings include a description of each stove and the price range. For more complete information, refer to *The Official Price Guide to Kitchen Collectibles,* published by The House of Collectibles.

Cook Stove, *cast iron, 1890s,* $300.00-$600.00

	Current Price Range		P/Y Average
☐ **Stove,** Acme, Sunburst, hardcoal base burner, silver nickel swing top, a dome, artistic urn, tea kettle attachment, smoke collar, large double front doors, ash door with screw register, nickeled foot rails and base	900.00	1050.00	995.00
☐ **Stove,** Acme, Triumph, polished blue plate, high warming closet, coal feed pouch and broiler door, wood feed door, duplex grate, fire box, oven thermometer, reservoir tanks, early 20th century . .	3050.00	3600.00	3120.00
☐ **Stove,** cast iron, small, hot plate underneath cover that comes off, three footed, European make, early 20th century, 15″ x 38″ surface area	460.00	550.00	472.00
☐ **Stove,** Excelsior, small, rounded shape, burns wood or coal	95.00	128.00	98.00
☐ **Stove,** European make, cast iron, fully nickel plated, openworked cover, removeable for stoking, early 20th century, 17″ x 37″	835.00	1200.00	840.00
☐ **Stove,** European make, some brass and copper, numerous tiles, 65″ high	1200.00	1500.00	1250.00
☐ **Stove,** European, stands on hearth that comes out, enameled in green, hot plate, openworked cover, early 20th century, 17″ x 45″	465.00	550.00	472.00
☐ **Stove,** European make, enameled in dark red, handle in the shape of a winged creature, early 20th century, 27″ x 11″	510.00	675.00	525.00
☐ **Stove,** Franklin, stands on three legs, brass tip on top, bird, fruit and flower motifs, 35″ x 42″ surface area	160.00	220.00	162.00

	Current Price Range		P/Y Average

Stove, Norwegian, with burning box at the base, three sections above, each holding a hot-plate, late 19th century, 26" x 78"	830.00	1200.00	840.00
Stove, Norwegian, woodburning, cast iron, black leading, early 20th century, 16" x 58"	360.00	440.00	368.00
Stove, Scandinavian make, cast iron, a trio of ovens above hearth, wooden base, late 18th century, 88" x 30"	5600.00	7000.00	5750.00
Stove, Scandinavian make, mid 19th century, 55" x 35"	1300.00	1700.00	1450.00
Stove, Sears, step, two burners on top and one double burner on step, surface area 14" x 22", 24" high, early 20th century	1250.00	1750.00	1450.00
Stove, Sears, woodburning	35.00	44.00	36.00
Stove, Wehrle, combination stove, four hole, coal and wood, pig iron, rococo design, four slightly splayed legs, early 20th century	800.00	1200.00	840.00
Stove, Wehrle, see through door, early 20th century, 66" high	2100.00	2500.00	2345.00
Stove, Westminster, green enamel, removable hearth, early 20th century, 28" x 28"	625.00	800.00	630.00
Stove, Wildwood, return flue Todd stove, rococo design, silver nickeled ornaments, smoke collar, swing top, early 20th century	410.00	500.00	416.00
Stove, Windsor, gas, porcelain lined, colors of blue and white enamel	325.00	600.00	350.00
Stove, wood burning, old, ornate	95.00	107.00	99.00

ACCESSORIES

Stove Handles, iron coated with porcelain, early 20th century	15.00	22.00	19.00
Stove Lid Lifters, factory made, coil handle ..	7.00	16.00	8.50
Stove Lid Lifters, hand wrought	10.00	22.00	8.50
Stove Poker, wire handled, curved, bent	9.00	16.00	8.50
Stove Poker, wire handled, straight sided	9.00	16.00	8.50

SUPERMAN

DESCRIPTION: Items pertaining to the comic book character Superman are collectible.

TYPES: Toys, games, comic books, newspaper strips, original comic art, and premiums are some examples of Superman memorabilia.

PERIOD: The comic book Superman first appeared in 1938. It was created by Jerry Siegel and Joe Shuster.

COMMENTS: Besides comic books, Superman was portrayed in a television series, radio series and motion pictures.

Superman Krypto-Ray Gun, *Daisy Manufacturing Company,* $80.00–$90.00

	Current Price Range		P/Y Average

☐ **Badge,** movie promotional, emblem shaped (for Superman I) . . . . | 3.00 | 4.00 | 3.25

☐ **Bank,** dime register bank, lithographed tin, square, picture of Superman facing left, breaking chain by expanding his chest . . . . | 95.00 | 120.00 | 102.00

☐ **Belt Buckle,** tin, blue and red on silvered brass, half-length portrait, name at bottom, 1940 . . . . . | 90.00 | 115.00 | 102.00

☐ **Birthday Card,** You're Ten Today, Birthday Greetings From Superman, copyright by Superman, Inc., 1940s . . . . | 15.00 | 20.00 | 15.00

☐ **Button,** Kelloggs Pep Cereal premium, lithographed tin, multicolored, 1940s . . . . | 8.00 | 11.00 | 8.50

☐ **Button,** Muscle Building Club, lithographed tin, head and chest portrait, c. 1940 . . . . | 80.00 | 110.00 | 87.50

☐ **Button,** Superman of America, club button given to members of the Supermen of America, shows him breaking chains across his chest, 1939 . . . | 38.00 | 50.00 | 40.00

☐ **Clothing,** Superman the Movie T-shirt, with iron-on, made in four different colors, has full standing portrait . . . . | 6.00 | 8.00 | 7.00

☐ **Clothing,** T-shirt with iron-on, made in four different colors, pictures American flag . . . . | 6.00 | 8.00 | 7.00

☐ **Clothing,** T-shirt with iron-on, made in four different colors, has wording "Run, Jump, Fly." . . . . | 6.00 | 8.00 | 7.00

☐ **Clothing,** T-shirt with iron-on, has "S" symbol | 6.00 | 8.00 | 7.00

☐ **Cookie Jar,** California Originals, ceramic, figural, painted, shows him leaving phone booth after switching from Clark Kent identity, 1970s . . . . . | 25.00 | 32.00 | 25.50

☐ **Decoder,** Superman's Secret Code, premium from Action Comics sent to members of the Supermen of America club, 1938–1942 . . . . | 52.00 | 67.00 | 51.00

☐ **Doll,** made by The Toy Works, stuffed fabric, full length with cape, 25½" . . . . | 22.00 | 28.00 | 24.00

☐ **Figure,** Ideal, composition and wood, painted, with cape, one of the earliest Superman figures, 13" . . . . | 350.00 | 450.00 | 350.00

☐ **Figure,** Syrocco, 1940s, 5¾" . . . . | 200.00 | 250.00 | 182.00

☐ **Figure,** Brass Hanging Ornament, shows him standing on top of world, 4" . . . . | 2.50 | 3.50 | 3.00

☐ **Food Carton,** Superman Candy Coated Peanuts, box only, illustrated lid, multicolors, 1966, 5½" . . . . | 20.00 | 27.00 | 23.00

☐ **Mug,** tankard type, made by California Originals, ceramic, high relief, painted, 1978 . . . . | 23.00 | 30.00 | 22.50

☐ **Music Box,** made by Price, ceramic, figural, late 1970s, 7" . . . . | 25.00 | 33.00 | 25.50

☐ **Novelty,** Glow-in-the-Dark picture, shows him riding on a bomb with airplanes in background, 9" x 11" . . . . | 25.00 | 32.00 | 25.00

☐ **Pencil Case,** stiff paper, maroon and silver, illustration at top, 8¼" . . . . | 37.00 | 46.00 | 40.00

☐ **Pendant,** lithographed tin, movable arms, 1970s, 2½" . . . . | 4.00 | 6.00 | 5.00

	Current Price Range		P/Y Average
□ **Pen,** fountain pen, small colored decal of Superman standing with hands on hips, c. 1942	34.00	42.00	36.00
□ **Phonograph Record,** Superman and the Magic Ring, set of two seven-inch 78 r.p.m. records, Musette label, contains story that was broadcast on the radio with original radio cast, accompanied by a booklet, c. 1947	53.00	67.00	45.00
□ **Purse,** yellow, 1966	31.00	40.00	31.00
□ **Vehicle,** Supermobile, made by Corgi of Great Britain, diecast metal, bearing the number 265	9.00	12.00	10.25

TELEPHONES

DESCRIPTION: A telephone is a device which converts sounds into electrical impulses which are then transmitted by wire.

ORIGIN: Telephones were first installed for public use in the U.S. in 1877. This form of communication was developed by Alexander Graham Bell.

ADDITIONAL TIPS: Many small independent companies produced telephones which are highly collectible today. These companies include Stromberg Carlson Telephone Manufacturing Company, Manhattan Electrical Supply Company and Strowger Automatic Telephone Exchange.

□ **Adapter Plug,** modular receiver for four prongs, World War I era............................	3.00	4.00	3.50
□ **Back Cup For Transmitter,** brass, patented November 1910, 3″	4.00	6.00	5.00
□ **Bell,** from wall phone, single, solid brass with hole in center, dome shape, c. 1895	7.00	10.00	8.25
□ **Candlestick Phone,** Western Electric, brass with black paint, cord missing, all internal parts intact, some scuffing to paint, c. 1928	2.00	2.50	2.20
□ **Clapper Cover,** brass, c. 1915	3.00	4.50	3.65
□ **Directory,** 1881 Boston Telephone Directory, 56 pages with paper cover, gives list of subscribers plus ads for various phone equipment	250.00	325.00	285.00

Pay Telephone,
3 slot, 1930,
$75.00–$95.00

	Current Price Range		P/Y Average
☐ **Magneto Wall Phone,** box style, cabinet of golden oak, quarter sawn, early 1900s, 21″ high by 9″ wide	200.00	250.00	220.00
☐ **Magneto Wall Phone,** box style, cabinet of walnut, quarter sawn, 1900s, 21″ high by 9″ wide	170.00	215.00	185.00
☐ **Mouthpiece From Candlestick Phone,** black, c. 1925	2.50	3.50	3.00
☐ **Mouthpiece From Candlestick Phone,** brass, c. 1930	18.00	23.00	20.00
☐ **Mouthpiece From Wood Magneto Phone,** black, early 1900s	2.50	3.50	3.00
☐ **Pay Phone,** wall model, wood and brass, bells and crank at top, receiver hangs at left side, mouthpiece stationary at center, slots for deposit of coins of various denominations, c. 1900	500.00	700.00	600.00
☐ **Receiver,** outside terminal, 1882, 7½″	50.00	65.00	57.00
☐ **Receiver Cap,** Stromberg Carlson, 1¾″	10.00	14.00	12.00
☐ **Shelf For Wall Mounted Phone,** oak, late 1800s	18.00	23.00	20.00
☐ **Shelf For Wall Mounted Phone,** oak, late 1800s	18.00	23.00	20.00
☐ **Swivel Bracket,** Kellog, early 1900s, 4½″	5.00	7.00	6.00
☐ **Swivel Transmitter,** small, all brass except for mouthpiece, front casting, c. 1901, five ounces	12.00	16.00	14.00
☐ **Transmitter,** Kellog type, brass, 1910 patent date, 7″	15.00	20.00	17.00
☐ **Transmitter,** Western Electric, brass back cup, brass front plate with brass cap nuts, 1910 patent date, 8½″	15.00	20.00	17.00

TELEVISION MEMORABILIA

COMMENTS: Since the television industry itself is still rather young, collecting TV memorabilia is a relatively new hobby. It probably first emerged as part of the nostalgia craze in the 1970s. But its current popularity may be attributed to the recent market explosion of video tape recorders. With these, viewers can record and watch popular old TV programs that may no longer run. This often sparks an interest in collecting memorabilia from these shows.

RECOMMENDED READING: For further information refer to *The Official Price Guide to Radio, TV and Movie Memorabilia,* published by The House of Collectibles.

Howdy Doody Television Crayons and Pictures, *shadow box coloring set,* **5" x 6½", $4.00-$9.00** *Photo courtesy of Hake's Americana, York, PA.*

	Current Price Range		P/Y Average
☐ **Addams Family, The,** card game, Milton Bradley, 1965	12.50	15.00	14.00
☐ **Addams Family, The,** ½ hour, 16mm original print, "Morticia the Writer"	35.00	45.00	40.00
☐ **All In The Family,** original TV soundtrack, first album	5.00	8.00	6.75
☐ **Archies, The,** paper doll, Sabrina	12.00	15.00	14.00
☐ **Archies, The,** paper doll, other Archies character	12.00	15.00	14.00
☐ **Batman,** Batman flashlight, 1976	3.50	5.00	4.00
☐ **Batman,** fork, metal 6½", Imperial, 1966	18.00	23.00	21.00
☐ **Batman,** hair brush, plastic figural handle, white bristles, 8½", Avon, 1976	20.00	25.00	22.00
☐ **Batman,** plastic assembly kit, Robin the Teen Wonder, Aurora, 1974	22.00	25.00	23.00
☐ **Batman,** Robin flashlight, 1976	3.50	5.00	4.50
☐ **Beverly Hillbillies, The,** card game, "Set back," Milton Bradley, 1963	15.00	20.00	17.00
☐ **Beverly Hillbillies, The,** Magic Eyes story set	4.00	6.00	5.00
☐ **Bonanza,** album, "Party Time"	15.00	18.00	17.00
☐ **Bonanza,** Big Little Book, The Bubble Gum Kid, Whitman, 1967	3.50	4.00	3.50
☐ **Bonanza,** Hoss Cartwright doll	25.00	32.00	27.00
☐ **Bonanza,** jigsaw puzzle, Ponderosa Ranch	5.00	7.00	6.25
☐ **Bonanza,** lunch pail with thermos, Alladin, 1963	7.50	9.00	8.00
☐ **Bonanza,** movie viewer, National Broadcasting Co., Inc.	13.00	16.00	14.25
☐ **Bonanza,** paperback, The Living Legend of Bonanza, 7" x 10"	8.00	10.00	9.00
☐ **Bonanza,** paperback, One Man with Courage, Media Books, 1966	7.00	9.00	8.25
☐ **Dark Shadows,** comic book, #4	1.25	1.75	1.50
☐ **Dark Shadows,** glossy color TV still, Jonathan Frid, 8" x 10"	5.25	8.00	6.50
☐ **Dark Shadows,** gum card	2.00	3.00	3.40
☐ **Dark Shadows,** original TV soundtrack, Philips	20.00	25.00	22.00
☐ **Davy Crockett,** ceramic wall vase	15.00	20.00	17.00
☐ **Davy Crockett,** character pocket knife	6.50	8.50	7.00
☐ **Ed Sullivan Show, The,** glossy color TV still, The Beatles, 8" x 10"	5.00	8.50	6.95
☐ **Flintstones, The,** cookie jar, glazed ceramic, 12", Hanna-Barbera	65.00	85.00	75.00
☐ **Hawaiian Eye,** original TV soundtrack, Warner Brothers	8.00	12.00	10.00
☐ **Hogan's Heroes,** Peri-peeper periscope, ID card, badge	10.00	13.00	11.00
☐ **Hopalong Cassidy,** dental kit, Dr. West's, 8" x 9"	25.00	35.00	27.50
☐ **Hopalong Cassidy,** Ingraham alarm clock	148.00	160.00	155.00
☐ **Hopalong Cassidy,** leather belt	12.00	16.00	14.00
☐ **Hopalong Cassidy,** milk container, c. 1955, half gallon	8.00	10.00	9.25

	Current Price Range		P/Y Average

☐ **Hopalong Cassidy,** milk container, c. 1955, quart	6.00	9.00	7.75
☐ **Hopalong Cassidy,** milk container, c. 1955, pint	2.00	4.00	3.00
☐ **Hopalong Cassidy,** pinback button, Hopalong and Topper	7.50	10.00	8.25
☐ **Hopalong Cassidy,** record album	30.00	35.00	32.00
☐ **Hopalong Cassidy,** Viewmaster reel #956, "The Cattle Rustler"	4.00	12.00	8.50
☐ **Hopalong Cassidy,** wallet, 3½″ x 4½″	8.00	12.00	9.75
☐ **Howdy Doody,** figural ear muffs	18.00	25.00	22.00
☐ **Howdy Doody,** plastic Jack-in-the-box, 5″ high	20.00	25.00	23.00
☐ **Howdy Doody,** paper bag, fudge bar	6.00	10.00	7.50
☐ **Howdy Doody,** plate	16.00	20.00	18.00
☐ **Howdy Doody,** shadow box, for coloring, 5½″ x 6″	4.00	9.00	7.00
☐ **Immortal, The,** 1 hour, 16mm original print, "My Brother"	72.00	80.00	76.00
☐ **Invaders, The,** UFO model kit, Aurora, 1968	15.00	20.00	17.00
☐ **Ironsides,** graphic, Raymond Burr, Sunday supplement from the Pittsburgh Press; color cover, January 26, 1958	1.50	2.50	2.10
☐ **It Takes A Thief,** paperback, #1	1.00	3.50	2.70
☐ **Johnny Quest,** ½ hour, 16mm original print, "Antarctica"	25.00	30.00	28.00
☐ **Kojak,** playing cards, set of 56, color, original cast, Monty Gum	15.00	18.00	16.50
☐ **Lassie,** hardcover book, The Secret of The Smelter's Cave, Whitman, 1968	5.00	7.00	6.25
☐ **Laugh-In,** original TV soundtrack, Epic	4.00	7.00	6.00
☐ **Leave It To Beaver,** graphic, Sunday supplement from the Pittsburgh Press, color cover, September 6, 1959	2.00	4.00	3.10
☐ **Lone Ranger, The,** holsters, fiberboard, set of 2, 11″, c. 1945	15.00	25.00	20.00
☐ **Lone Ranger, The,** ink blotter, 3½″ x 8″	5.00	10.00	7.75
☐ **Man From U.N.C.L.E., The,** Corgi car	45.00	60.00	51.00
☐ **Man From U.N.C.L.E., The,** deck of cards	8.00	10.00	9.75
☐ **Man From U.N.C.L.E., The,** doll accessory	8.00	15.00	11.00
☐ **Man From U.N.C.L.E., The,** 50¢ Giant Wonder Book	2.00	5.00	4.00
☐ **Man From U.N.C.L.E., The,** halloween costume (rare item), bids usually solicited.			
☐ **Man From U.N.C.L.E., The,** hardcover book, Whitman, (2 issued)	3.00	7.00	3.95
☐ **Man From U.N.C.L.E., The,** lobby card	5.00	7.00	5.70
☐ **Man From U.N.C.L.E., The,** LP album	10.00	20.00	14.75
☐ **Man From U.N.C.L.E., The,** MGM promotional still	5.00	7.00	6.00
☐ **Man From U.N.C.L.E., The,** model kit	20.00	30.00	22.00
☐ **Man From U.N.C.L.E., The,** movie poster	15.00	20.00	18.75
☐ **Man From U.N.C.L.E., The,** paperback, 41 in the series #20–23 are rarest	5.00	7.00	6.50

Gene Autry and His Wonder Horse "Champion" Viewmaster
Reel #950, $7.00–$14.00.

(photo courtesy of Hake's Americana, York, PA)

	Current Price Range		P/Y Average
☐ **Man From U.N.C.L.E., The,** paperback, "ABC's Of Espionage"	1.00	3.50	2.25
☐ **Superman,** card game, Ideal, 1966	15.00	20.00	17.00
☐ **Superman,** copy of TV script, "Murder On Stage 13"	20.00	25.00	22.00
☐ **Superman,** copy of TV script, "Close Shave"	20.00	25.00	
☐ **Superman,** copy of TV script, "The Defeat Of Superman"	20.00	25.00	22.50
☐ **Superman,** copy of TV script, "The Deadly Rock"	18.00	23.00	20.00
☐ **Superman,** copy of TV script, "The Phantom Ring"	18.00	23.00	20.00
☐ **Superman,** copy of TV script, "Stamp Day for Superman"	25.00	30.00	27.00
☐ **Superman,** identification card, 2½" x 3½" 1947	15.00	20.00	18.00
☐ **Superman,** toothbrush, battery operated	65.00	75.00	71.00
☐ **Twilight Zone, The,** game	12.00	17.00	16.00
☐ **Twilight Zone, The,** graphic, Rod Serling, Sunday supplement from the Pittsburgh Press, color cover, September 27, 1959	2.50	3.50	3.00
☐ **Twilight Zone, The,** original TV soundtrack, CBS	25.00	30.00	27.50
☐ **Three Stooges, The,** puppet	10.00	15.00	12.00
☐ **Untouchables, The,** ½ hour, 16mm original print, "Canada Run"	95.00	115.00	110.00
☐ **Voyage To The Bottom Of The Sea,** Magic Eyes story set	4.00	6.00	5.10

	Current Price Range		P/Y Average
☐ **Wagon Train,** gum card, #46 Ward Bond, #47 Robert Horton, #48 The Warning, #49 Scouting Mission, #50 Gun Fight, Topps, 1958	1.00	1.25	1.00
☐ **Wagon Train,** hardcover book, Wagon Train, Whitman, 282 pages, 1959	6.50	8.50	7.75
☐ **Wagon Train,** record with picture sleeve, Mitch Miller and Orchestra, 45 rpm, 1957	7.50	9.00	8.00
☐ **Waltons, The,** paper doll	12.00	15.00	14.00
☐ **Wild, Wild West, The,** comic book, #3	5.00	7.00	6.00
☐ **Wild, Wild West, The,** writing tablet	5.00	7.00	6.00
☐ **Winky Dink And You,** magic television kit, 10″ x 14″	40.00	50.00	45.00
☐ **WKRP in Cincinnati,** glossy color TV still, cast portrait, 8″ x 10″	4.00	7.00	5.00
☐ **Woody Woodpecker,** tray puzzle	5.00	7.00	6.00
☐ **Yogi Bear,** wind-up toy	18.00	22.00	20.00
☐ **You Asked For It,** ½ hour, 16mm original print, "Knute Rockne presented by Pat O'Brien"	55.00	70.00	62.50
☐ **Zorro,** comic book, #960	9.00	12.00	10.75
☐ **Zorro,** comic book, Walt Disney, 1961	5.00	7.00	6.25
☐ **Zorro,** gum card, Topps, 1958	1.00	2.00	1.40
☐ **Zorro,** hardcover book, Whitman, 1957	10.00	12.00	11.00

THEATRICAL MEMORABILIA

COMMENTS: Items from every phase of the theater are highly collectible and are beginning to command high prices among hobbyists.

RECOMMENDED READING: For further information refer to *The Official Price Guide to Paper Collectibles,* published by The House of Collectibles.

☐ **Book,** *Songs of Stephen Foster,* signed by John Charles Thomas	25.00	35.00	26.00
☐ **Broadway Playbill,** *Advise and Consent,* 1961	1.50	3.00	1.75
☐ **Broadway Playbill,** *Amadeus,* 1981	2.00	3.50	1.75

	Current Price Range		P/Y Average
☐ **Broadway Playbill,** *American Buffalo,* 1977 ...	1.50	3.00	1.75
☐ **Broadway Playbill,** *Annie Get Your Gun,* 1966	1.50	3.00	1.75
☐ **Broadway Playbill,** *Any Wednesday,* 1964	1.50	3.00	1.75
☐ **Broadway Playbill,** *Bell, Book and Candle,* 1951	1.50	3.00	1.75
☐ **Broadway Playbill,** *Bells are Ringing,* 1957 ...	1.50	3.00	1.75
☐ **Broadway Playbill,** *Brigadoon,* 1948	1.50	3.00	1.75
☐ **Broadway Playbill,** *Chicago,* 1976	1.50	3.00	1.75
☐ **Broadway Playbill,** *Coco,* 1970	1.50	3.00	1.75
☐ **Broadway Playbill,** *Dear Liar,* 1960	1.50	3.00	1.75
☐ **Broadway Playbill,** *Diary of Anne Frank,* 1955	1.50	3.00	1.75
☐ **Broadway Playbill,** *Eddie Fisher at the Winter Garden,* 1962..........................	1.50	3.00	1.75
☐ **Broadway Playbill,** *Fiddler on the Roof,* 1977	1.50	3.00	1.75
☐ **Broadway Playbill,** *Forty Carats,* 1969	1.50	3.00	1.75
☐ **Broadway Playbill,** *Golden Boy,* 1964	1.50	3.00	1.75
☐ **Broadway Playbill,** *Grease,* 1976	1.50	3.00	1.75
☐ **Broadway Playbill,** *Guys and Dolls,* 1953	1.50	3.00	1.75
☐ **Broadway Playbill,** *Hamlet,* 1964	1.50	3.00	1.75
☐ **Broadway Playbill,** *I Remember Mama,* 1944	3.50	4.00	1.75
☐ **Broadway Playbill,** *Irene,* 1974	1.50	3.00	1.75
☐ **Broadway Playbill,** *Life with Father,* 1940	1.50	3.00	1.75
☐ **Broadway Playbill,** *Look Back in Anger,* 1958	1.50	3.00	1.75
☐ **Broadway Playbill,** *Master Harold and the Boys,* 1982	1.50	3.00	1.75
☐ **Broadway Playbill,** *Much Ado About Nothing,* 1959	1.50	3.00	1.75
☐ **Broadway Playbill,** *No Strings,* 1963	1.50	3.00	1.75
☐ **Broadway Playbill,** *No Time for Sergeants,* 1956	1.50	3.00	1.75
☐ **Broadway Playbill,** *One Touch of Venus,* 1944	3.50	5.00	1.75
☐ **Broadway Playbill,** *On the Town,* 1971	1.50	3.00	1.75
☐ **Broadway Playbill,** *Over Here,* 1974	1.50	3.00	1.75
☐ **Broadway Playbill,** *Pippin,* 1972	1.50	3.00	1.75
☐ **Broadway Playbill,** *Play it Again, Sam,* 1969	1.50	3.00	1.75
☐ **Broadway Playbill,** *Plaza Suite,* 1970	1.50	3.00	1.75
☐ **Broadway Playbill,** *Private Lives,* 1975	1.50	3.00	1.75
☐ **Broadway Playbill,** *Same Time Next Year,* 1975	1.50	3.00	1.75
☐ **Broadway Playbill,** *Sugar Babies,* 1979	1.50	3.00	1.75
☐ **Broadway Playbill,** *Sunday in New York,* 1963	1.50	3.00	1.75
☐ **Broadway Playbill,** *Sweeney Todd,* 1979	1.50	3.00	1.75
☐ **Broadway Playbill,** *There's a Girl in My Soup,* 1968	1.50	3.00	1.75
☐ **Broadway Playbill,** *They're Playing Our Song,* 1979	1.50	3.00	1.75
☐ **Broadway Playbill,** *Tribute,* 1978	1.50	3.00	1.75
☐ **Broadway Playbill,** *Under the Yum Yum Tree,* 1960	1.50	3.00	1.75
☐ **Broadway Playbill,** *Witness for the Prosecution,* 1956	1.50	3.00	1.75

	Current Price Range		P/Y Average
☐ **Broadway Playbill,** *Woman of the Year,* 1982	1.50	3.00	1.75
☐ **Brochure,** opera company brochure signed by Regina Resnik, c. 1952	8.00	12.00	8.50
☐ **Calling Card,** signed by Enrico Caruso	60.00	80.00	61.00
☐ **Contract,** opera company contract signed by Patrice Munsel	30.00	40.00	31.00
☐ **Contract,** opera contract signed by Giuseppe Deluca	70.00	90.00	71.00
☐ **Contract,** record company contract signed by Robert Merrill	40.00	50.00	41.00
☐ **Letter,** handwritten in Russian by Fyodor Chaliapin	430.00	560.00	435.00
☐ **Libretto,** opera libretto signed by Cesare Siepi	13.00	18.00	14.00
☐ **Libretto,** opera libretto signed by Helen Traubel	13.00	18.00	14.00
☐ **Magazine Cover,** signed by Joan Sutherland	25.00	35.00	26.00
☐ **Menu,** signed by Enrico Caruso, c. 1915	170.00	210.00	162.00
☐ **Menu,** signed by Joan Sutherland	8.00	12.00	9.00
☐ **Menu,** signed by Lorenzo Alvary	9.00	16.00	10.00
☐ **Photograph,** autographed photo of Beverly in costume from Daughter of the Regiment, 8″ x 10″	25.00	35.00	26.00
☐ **Photograph,** autographed by Charles Anthony, 8″ x 10″	10.00	15.00	11.00
☐ **Photograph,** autographed photo of Dorothy Kirsten, 8″ x 10″	55.00	75.00	56.00
☐ **Photograph,** autographed photo of Enrico Caruso in Rigoletto costume, 5″ x 7″	155.00	195.00	150.00
☐ **Photograph,** autographed portrait of Enrico Caruso, c. 1906, 8″ x 10″	190.00	225.00	185.00
☐ **Photograph,** autographed portrait of Fyodor Chaliapin, c. 1925, 5″ x 7″	185.00	265.00	190.00
☐ **Photograph,** autographed photo of James Melton in costume, 8″ x 10″	23.00	35.00	25.00
☐ **Photograph,** autographed photo of John Brownlee in Rigoletto costume, c. 1940, 8″ x 10″ ...	25.00	32.00	25.00
☐ **Photograph,** autographed photo of Jussi Bjoerling in Boheme costume, 8″ x 10″	25.00	35.00	28.00
☐ **Photograph,** autographed photo of Leontype Price in costume, 8″ x 10″	30.00	40.00	31.00
☐ **Photograph,** autographed photo of Lorenzo Alvary, 8″ x 10″	10.00	15.00	12.00
☐ **Photograph,** autographed photo of Nadine Conner	21.00	26.00	22.00
☐ **Photograph,** autographed photo of Rosalind Elias, 8″ x 10″	11.00	15.00	12.00
☐ **Photograph,** autographed photo of Tito Gobbi, c. 1959, 8″ x 10″	30.00	37.00	32.00
☐ **Poster,** advertising appearance of Salvatore Baccaloni, c. 1940	13.00	18.00	14.00
☐ **Poster,** autographbed opera poster of Nicolai Gedda	23.00	32.00	24.00
☐ **Poster,** Darkest Russia, 20″ x 30″, 1895	135.00	165.00	140.00
☐ **Poster,** *A Happy Little Home,* 40″ x 80″, 1895	225.00	300.00	230.00

	Current Price Range		P/Y Average
□ **Poster,** *East Lynne*, 30″ x 40″, early 1900s ...	165.00	210.00	170.00
□ **Poster,** *Girl of the Golden West*, 20″ x 30″ ...	60.00	75.00	65.00
□ **Poster,** *In Gay Atlantic City*, 30″ x 40″, 1890	300.00	375.00	320.00
□ **Poster,** *In Old Kentucky*, 30″ x 40″, 1897	275.00	330.00	280.00
□ **Poster,** Metropolitan Opera poster, *Emperor Jones*, signed by Lawrence Tibbett	250.00	325.00	255.00
□ **Poster,** Metropolitan Opera poster featuring Enrico Caruso	240.00	340.00	235.00
□ **Poster,** *Saved from the Sea*, 40″ x 80″, 1895	145.00	195.00	150.00
□ **Poster,** *William Gillette's Private Secretary*, 20″ x 30″, 1900	90.00	120.00	95.00
□ **Program,** concert program, signed by Roberta Peters	10.00	15.00	15.00
□ **Program,** Metropolitan Opera, signed by Frances Alda	26.00	38.00	30.00
□ **Program,** Metropolitan Opera, signed by Kirsten Flagstad	35.00	45.00	40.00
□ **Program,** Metropolitan Opera House, pre-1900	10.00	14.00	11.00
□ **Program,** Metropolitan Opera House, 1901–1910	8.00	12.00	9.00
□ **Program,** Metropolitan Opera House, 1911–1920	6.00	10.00	7.00

THIMBLES

TOPIC: Thimbles are small fingertip protectors used during sewing.

MATERIALS: Porcelain and silver are the most popular materials for making thimbles.

COMMENTS: Designs of thimbles are very diverse; the decorations on many thimbles are so exquisite that collectors may devote themselves solely to the painted porcelain or other varieties.

ADDITIONAL TIPS: Since thimbles are very difficult to date accurately, their decoration and design remain paramount to most collectors. Some individuals focus on advertising thimbles, while others prefer the artistic type.

	Current Price Range		P/Y Average
☐ **Beer Company Advertising,** porcelain, set of three	2.50	3.00	2.75
☐ **Currier & Ives,** porcelain, blue and white, set of four	1.00	1.50	1.25
☐ **Damron,** Butterfly, cystal	10.00	18.00	14.00
☐ **Delft,** blue, Holland	5.00	10.00	7.50
☐ **Friia,** goldplate, presidents	5.00	10.00	7.50
☐ **General Store Advertising,** porcelain, set of four	3.25	3.75	3.50
☐ **Goldplate Cloisonne,** Disney character	5.00	10.00	7.50
☐ **Hummel,** Apple Girl, porcelain	16.00	26.00	21.00
☐ **Hurley,** Calico Cuties, porcelain	12.00	20.00	16.00
☐ **Lefton,** porcelain, floral motif, set of three	.75	1.25	1.00
☐ **Limoges,** bird motif, porcelain	10.00	18.00	14.00
☐ **Partrige,** bisque, gold raised lettering, signed Joel	15.00	20.00	17.50
☐ **Silver,** engraved scenic design	21.00	26.00	24.00
☐ **Silver,** engraved scenic design on border	15.00	18.00	16.50
☐ **Silver,** hallmarked	25.00	35.00	30.00
☐ **Silver,** size 9	7.00	13.00	10.00
☐ **Silver,** size 6, star trade mark	20.00	26.00	23.00
☐ **Spode,** Heavenly cherubs, china	25.00	35.00	30.00
☐ **Tobacco Company Advertising,** porcelain, set of three	2.50	3.00	2.75
☐ **Whiskey Company Advertising,** porcelain, set of three	2.50	3.00	2.75

THIRD REICH COLLECTIBLES

DESCRIPTION: Items relating to the German Nazi government headed by Adolph Hitler from 1933 to 1945.

COMMENTS: Far from being sympathizers of the Third Reich and its policies, collectors of this memorabilia are usually concerned only with its historical significance.

Nazi Sun Helmet, *with tan (khaki) cover, early model,* **$80.00–$90.00**

ADDITIONAL TIPS: For more information, consult *The Official Price Guide to Collectibles of the Third Reich,* published by The House of Collectibles.

	Current Price Range		P/Y Average
☐ **Belt Buckle Pistol,** four short .22 caliber barrels are concealed behind a large heavy brass buckle attached to a heavy black belt. When a release is tripped the hinged buckle swings down and the barrels swing out.Each barrel is fired by slight pressure on a small trigger. On the front of the buckle appears the Nazi Party insignia of an eagle grasping a wreath encircling a swastika	17500.00	19400.00	18200.00
☐ **Goblet of Honor For Distinguished Achievements in the Air War,** silver, cup section is attached to a wide collar and base. The obverse of the cup part has raised figures of eagles in combat. The reverse has a large Iron Cross in raised relief.			
☐ **Goblet of Honor,** Uncased	1200.00	1400.00	1290.00
☐ **Goblet of Honor,** Cased. Very rarely offered.	3000.00	4500.00	3700.00
☐ **Goering's Wedding Sword,** large, heavy sword with genuine damascus blade. On one side in raised gold letters appears "10 APRIL 1935 DIE REICHSLUFTWAFFE IHREM OBER-FEFEHL-SHABER" (The National Air Force to its Commander-in-Chief). On the other side of the			

	Current Price Range	P/Y Average

blade appears "GETREU DEM FUHRER FUR VOLK UND REICH" (Loyal to the Fuhrer for the People and Nation) . . . . **VERY RARE**

☐ **Goering Leaded and Stained Glass Plaque,** this beautiful piece intended for hanging is reputed to have been a wedding gift from Adolph Hitler to Herman Goering and his new bride. Of circular form the principal motif consists of two shields one bearing Goering's coat of arms and the other the arms of his bride, A banner between the helmet crest of each coat of arms bears the legend "10 APRIL 1935," the date of the wedding, in Gothic letters. The background is composed of an intricate floral design. A wreath encircles the plaque . . . . **VERY RARE**

☐ **Goering Yacht,** this yacht was a wedding present to Herman Goering from the German automobile industry. Tastefully decorated and appointed throughout. The white hull on the bow of each side bears in color the Goering arms . . . . **VERY RARE**

☐ **Hitler's Pocket Watch,** silver cased pocket watch with the authentication that it belonged to Adolph Hitler. Plain white face with black Arabic numerals and gold hour and second hands . . .   3500.00   4000.00   3700.00

☐ **German Order,** the cross patee is of black enamel with raised gold edges within which are gold oak leaves. The cross design itself resembles the shape of the well known Iron Cross. A gold party eagle, swastika and wreath appears between the arms of the cross. The obverse center of the cross is occupied by a gold wreath encircling a white enamel disk upon which appears a circular red enameled band bearing in gold the legend "National Sozialistische D.A.P." (National Socialist German Workers Party) all in capital Roman letters. In the center of the band is a black enameled swastika. The reverse of the cross is generally the same except that there is a second edging of gold in lieu of the oak leaf border and the central disk is of black enamel upon which appears the signature of Adolph Hitler engraved in gold . . . . **VERY RARE**

☐ **Salver of Honor for Distinguished Achievements in Action Badge,** broad rim about a rather shallow dish, the rim had raised edging on both outer and inner sides. A design of widely spaced oak leaves and laurel sprigs in raised relief decorated the surface of the rim. In the center of the dish in raised design is a Luftwaffe eagle grasping a large swastika. Behind the swastika are crossed field marshall batons. On two scrolls above the eagle appear the name and rank of the receiver of the award. Under the baton design appears a long curved scroll bearing the legend "IN

	Current Price Range		P/Y Average

ANERIKENNUNG HERVORRAGENDER KAMP-
FLEISTUNGEN" (In recognition of distinguished
achievements in action) in raised Roman Letters
.... **3500.00 4000.00   3700.00**

☐ **SS First Type Field Cap,** black cloth trimmed
with white piping about the tip of the cap and
about the upper and lower band. On the front appears the Party eagle, wreath and swastika over
a skull and cross bones, all in silver color. Has
waterproof lining and leather sweatband. Has
paper RZM label **1350.00 1500.00   1410.00**

☐ **Luftwaffe Chaplain's DAK Tropical Cap.** Tan
cloth cap with cloth covered visor and silver piping, At top front of cap is Bevo Eagle, swastika
and wreath and cockade. Enclosing the cockage
is an inverted purple "V." Between the apex of
the "V" and the eagle is a silver embroidered
Gothic cross **500.00   600.00   540.00**

TIFFANY GLASS

MAKER: Louis Comfort Tiffany produced decorative accessories in glass, pottery and metal from the 1880s through the 1920s. He grew up in affluence, the
son of the famous jeweler, Charles Louis Tiffany, founder of Tiffany and Company of New York. Louis studied art abroad as a young man and spent ten years
pursuing a career as a fine artist, achieving some success as a painter, but not
the worldwide recognition he sought. He decided to enter the new field of interior decoration where he quickly gained enormous fame. While the foremost
exponent of the Art Nouveau movement in America, Tiffany did not strictly ad-
here to its precepts. Fascinated with the exotic and ornate, Tiffany's unique
sense of design and great love of beauty produced a style unlike any other.
It was his goal to bring beauty and artistic appreciation into every home in America. In his older years Tiffany's popularity declined as America moved into the
streamlined world of the Art Deco period. There was a tremendous resurgence
of interest in his work in the 1960s and now his decorative pieces are avidly
sought by collectors.

PERIOD: Louis Comfort Tiffany was a well known decorator by the 1880s and a devotee of the infant Art Nouveau movement in America. The Art Nouveau style was a rebellion against the imitativeness of the Victorian period and the mass production of the Industrial Revolution. It came out of the Arts and Crafts movement in England and the belief of its founder, William Morris, that all decorative arts should be handmade. The Art Nouveau style is characterized by a return to nature in motifs executed by sensual, flowing lines with a heavy oriental influence.

CHARACTERISTICS: Tiffany had been collecting ancient glass for years and was particularly captivated by the iridescence found on ancient glass as a result of chemical changes. In 1880 he obtained a patent for his "favrile" glass, favrile meaning handmade. Gold chloride was used either in the glass or as a spray to achieve the iridized gold sheen which characterized favrile. Indeed, Tiffany's colored glass was incredibly deep and true in its color due to the use of expensive metal oxides which produced the most intense colors. His blown glass was reheated as many as twenty times to achieve the desired effect. He absolutely believed that the decoration in glass must be a part of the glass itself, not applied externally.

TYPES: Tiffany Studios produced a wide range of decorative accessories in glass, enamel pottery and bronze. However, Tiffany is most remembered for his exquisite art glass which was fashioned into leaded glass lamp shades and windows, vases, bowls, screens, tableware, desk sets and jewelry boxes, to name just a few.

COMMENTS: Tiffany lamps are commanding astronomical prices these days and as a result, many forged marks are appearing. Therefore deal only with an established dealer if you are considering an expensive purchase. Furthermore, be suspicious if you should run across bargain prices for Tiffany items. They probably aren't genuine.

RECOMMENDED READING: For more in-depth information on Tiffany glass, you may refer to *The Official Price Guide to Glassware* and *The Official Identification Guide to Glassware,* published by The House of Collectibles.

	Current Price Range		P/Y Average
☐ **Bottle,** scent, bulbous body, teardrop-shaped neck, short circular foot, flattened knopped stopper, silvery-blue iridescent, c. 1899–1928	300.00	400.00	325.00
☐ **Bowl,** circular with paneled sides, scalloped rim, dark blue iridescent, 7″ diameter, c. 1928	5000.00	6000.00	4200.00
☐ **Bowl,** Favrile, circular expanding towards rim, incurvative rim, clear, white paperweight flowers with orange and yellow, green leaves, signed, 4¾″ diameter, c. 1925	2000.00	3000.00	2100.00
☐ **Bread plates,** Favrile, circular, wide flat rim with ruffling, green shading to opalescent ribbing in the center, 8″ diameter, c. 1920, set of six	600.00	700.00	625.00
☐ **Candlestick,** elongated candle socket, openwork, green background, thin cylinder stem, flattened circular foot, 22½″ high, c. 1892–1920	600.00	700.00	625.00

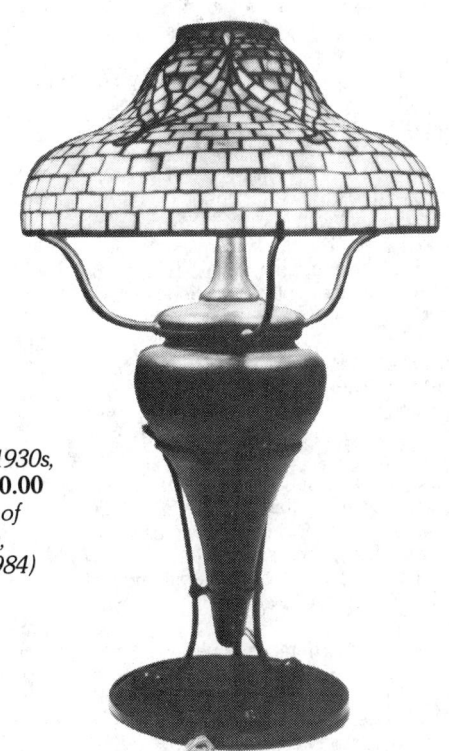

Tiffany Lamp, *1930s,*
$6000.00–$6200.00
*(photo courtesy of
©Marc Bernsau,
Sanford, ME, 1984)*

	Current Price Range		P/Y Average
□ **Candlestick,** free form, indented swirls and flared sides, iridescent amber, signed, 9½″ high c. 1906	600.00	800.00	700.00
□ **Clock,** carriage, Favrile, rectangular shape, green sides overlaid with bronze filigree in grapevine pattern, angular handle at top, stepped rectangular base, 8″ high, c. 1900	1400.00	1600.00	1500.00
□ **Compote,** circular shape, spiraling bands, scalloped rim, amber iridescent, 4⅛″ high, c. 1892–1928	175.00	225.00	200.00
□ **Decanter And Stopper,** double-gourd shape body, circular foot, slender tapering neck, flared rim, amber-colored body, lily pad with tendrils continuing into base, flattened knopped stopper, signed, 11″ high, c. 1904	800.00	900.00	700.00
□ **Desk Set,** includes a pair of bookends, a pentray, a letter rack, a rocker blotter, four-corner blotter ends, a pen knife, an inkwell, a calendar holder, and a paper clip, abalone pattern, c. 1899–1920	800.00	1200.00	850.00

	Current Price Range		P/Y Average

☐ **Lamp,** cone-shaped shade, bronze cylinder standard with fluted sections, flaring circular foot, bands running vertically and horizontally of striated ochre, band of opalescent turtle-back tiles in amber iridescent, 24⅜" high, c. 1899–1920 — 7000.00 / 8000.00 / 7500.00

☐ **Lamp,** desk, domed shade, irregular border, slightly domed finial with bud tip, baluster standard expanding, molded with leaves separating at base, rolled foot with openwork, five feet, shade with pattern of laburnum blossoms and leaves in yellow, ochre, green, blue, lavender and brown, 29" high, c. 1899–1920 — 35000.00 / 45000.00 / 40000.00

☐ **Lamp,** desk, domed shade, pivots on a harp-shaped support, flaring base, foot molded in petals, blue-green iridescent background, loops and trails in silvery-blue iridescence, signed, 18" high, c. 1899–1920 — 1400.00 / 1600.00 / 1500.00

☐ **Lamp,** desk, Favrile, cone-shaped shade, flattened dome finial, gilt-bronze Romanesque standard with scrolling foliage and two bands of glass bosses in green, shade with mottled yellow background and borders, graduated bands of medallions in green, blue, and red, 19¾" high, c. 1899–1920 — 14000.00 / 16000.00 / 13000.00

☐ **Lamp,** desk, Favrile, domed shade, wide bell-shaped finial, cylinder flaring base in open-work honeycomb pattern of bronze, mottled blue shading to mottled green background, band of spread winged dragonflies, ochre bodies, yellow, green, and blue wings, green cabochons set above, 31" high, c. 1899–1920 — 35000.00 / 45000.00 / 36000.00

☐ **Lamp,** dome shade, emerald green background, with pattern of cherry blossoms and leaves in pink and olive green, mounted on three serpentine supports, ribbed stand in cylinder shape, circular gadroon base, five ball feet, 22" high, c. 1899–1920 — 5000.00 / 7000.00 / 5200.00

☐ **Vase,** compressed spherical body, long, slender cylinder neck expanding to slightly bulbous above body, opalescent, brown and amber lappets, pale yellow background, 11¾" high, c. 1905 — 1200.00 / 1600.00 / 1250.00

☐ **Vase,** cylindrical body, sloping shoulder, waisted neck, circular foot, amber body with amber and tan swirls and loop design, signed, 12" high — 900.00 / 1100.00 / 950.00

☐ **Vase,** cylindrical body, sloping shoulder, waisted neck, circular foot, amber body with amber and tan swirls and loop design, signed, 12" high — 3500.00 / 4500.00 / 3600.00

☐ **Vase,** elongated ovoid shape, paneled sides, short circular foot, casing around neck in blue and amber and yellow iridescent design, overlapping lappets, signed, 8" high, c. 1921 — 3500.00 / 4500.00 / 3600.00

	Current Price Range		P/Y Average
☐ **Vase,** elongated tulip-shaped body, triangular section, tapering to cylinder stem, slightly domed foot, opalescent, striated amber iridescent and green feathering, 6″ high, c. 1905	900.00	1100.00	915.00

TIFFANY POTTERY

COMMENTS: Louis Comfort Tiffany, one of America's most illustrious artists known primarily for his work with glass, also produced pottery, jewelry and paintings.

Tiffany first showed his pottery at the St. Louis Exposition in 1904. Both Tiffany and Company and Tiffany Studios produced pottery with production ceasing by 1920.

MARKS: LCT is a mark often found on Tiffany Pottery. Other backstamps include variations of the inscription "L.C. Tiffany Favrile Pottery." Some pieces are also marked with code numbers or letters.

☐ **Bowl,** 7″, collared foot and neck with bulbous body, blue, marked LCT	500.00	550.00	510.00
☐ **Vase,** 6″, narrow base, bulbous shoulders, very narrow neck, green and maroon, marked LCT	500.00	600.00	510.00
☐ **Vase,** 6½″, yellow exterior, green interior, marked LCT	350.00	450.00	360.00
☐ **Vase,** 9¾″, long cylindrical shape, berry and leaf motif, green	600.00	700.00	610.00
☐ **Vase,** 11″, waisted cylindrical shape, artichoke leaf motif molded on bottom half of piece, cream and green exterior, blue and green interior, marked LCT	900.00	1100.00	920.00
☐ **Vase,** 20½″, narrow foot and neck with bulbous shoulders, leaf motif, green	1000.00	2000.00	1100.00

TIN

TYPES: All types of tin items are sought after collectibles. This section concerns tin kitchen utensils.

COMMENTS: A light, fusible metal, tin was often used to coat other metals. Early pieces were usually soldered together. Prices are fairly reasonable.

ADDITIONAL TIPS: The listings are alphabetical according to item. For further information, refer to *The Official Price Guide to Kitchen Collectibles,* published by The House of Collectibles.

Candle Mold, *tin,* **$20.00**

	Current Price Range		P/Y Average
☐ **Miniature,** washing machine, children's toy, glass and tin	23.00	33.00	26.00
☐ **Miniature,** cook stove, children's toy, electric, Kingston Products Co., c. 1920	52.00	70.00	60.00
☐ **Miniature,** cook stove, electric, says "Lil Orphan Annie," c. 1920	63.00	80.00	70.00
☐ **Miniature,** eggbeater, 5" long	4.00	8.00	5.00
☐ **Mixing Spoons,** slotted bowl, hanging hole	5.00	12.00	7.00
☐ **Mixing Spoons,** slotted bowl, says "Rumford Cake Mix," c. 1900	10.00	18.00	13.00
☐ **Mixing Spoons,** slotted bowl, bottle opener on handle end, advertising slogans	10.00	18.00	13.00
☐ **Mixing Spoons,** perforated bowls, wooden handles, c. 1900	8.00	12.00	9.00
☐ **Mixing Spoons,** hanging loop, shaped bowls, very long	7.00	12.00	8.00
☐ **Mixing Spoons,** set ranging from one half teaspoon to two tablespoons, Rumford Company	10.00	18.00	14.00
☐ **Mold,** bread or pudding, 11" long	37.00	50.00	41.00
☐ **Mold,** fluted edge handle, 3" long	18.00	28.00	21.00
☐ **Mold,** icecream, c. 1880	30.00	55.00	45.00
☐ **Mold,** jelly, c. 1890	30.00	55.00	38.00
☐ **Mold,** lion, with base, 6" long	32.00	56.00	40.00
☐ **Mold,** embossed design gives relief on cheese, grape pattern, 6" long	30.00	50.00	38.00
☐ **Mold,** pierced tin, heart shaped, for cheese, 19th century	22.00	31.00	24.00
☐ **Mold,** tubed, c. 1890	12.00	19.00	15.00
☐ **Muffin or Cupcake Pan,** six cups, tin and steel alloy, c. 1870	29.00	45.00	35.00
☐ **Muffin or Cupcake Pan,** twelve cups, tin and sheet iron, c. 1890	17.00	22.00	18.00
☐ **Muffin or Cupcake Pan,** eight cups, push out function, c. 1910	19.00	26.00	21.00
☐ **Muffin Rings,** c. 1870s	3.00	7.00	4.00
☐ **Nurser,** tin can, lidded with handle, spout	105.00	140.00	115.00
☐ **Nutmeg Grater,** wood handles, c. 1900, 4" long	60.00	90.00	71.00
☐ **Nutmeg Grater,** circular handmade drum type	20.00	33.00	24.00
☐ **Oven, Biscuit,** self powered with charcoal, hinged lid, legged	135.00	150.00	139.00
☐ **Oven, Roasting,** for use in fireplace, sits on hearth, with spit	160.00	185.00	171.00
☐ **Pail,** lard, c. 1890, tin, bail handles	40.00	60.00	47.00
☐ **Pail,** lunch, with cups and dishes	50.00	65.00	52.00
☐ **Pail,** lunch, domed style, with dishes and cup	90.00	110.00	96.00
☐ **Pail,** lunch, round, handle, 6" diameter	22.00	35.00	25.00
☐ **Pail,** milk, round, late 1800s	35.00	50.00	39.00
☐ **Pail,** milk, convex, dark brown, c. 1890	40.00	55.00	46.00
☐ **Pail,** baker's, heart shape, c. 1890, 13" long	55.00	70.00	61.00
☐ **Pastry Board,** with hanging loop, trough, 18" long	150.00	175.00	160.00
☐ **Pastry Board,** tinned sheet iron, comes with rolling pin, hanging loop	265.00	290.00	275.00

	Current Price Range		P/Y Average

□ **Pastry Board,** with rolling pin cradle, 22" x 18½"
.... 150.00 165.00 154.00
□ **Pie Lifter,** wire tines, heavy tin 10.00 16.00 12.00
□ **Pie Lifter,** tin with wooden handle 12.00 18.00 14.00
□ **Pie Lifter,** shovel-type, wooden handle, round shape 10.00 20.00 12.00
□ **Pie Lifter,** c. 1900 .... 15.00 25.00 19.00
□ **Pie Pan,** says "Crisco," c. 1920 .... 10.00 20.00 12.00
□ **Pie Pan,** says "Balto. Pie Bakery" 15.00 25.00 19.00
□ **Pie Plate,** c. 1880........................... 5.00 11.00 6.50
□ **Pitcher, Water,** large globe shape, 8 quart size, set with six tumblers 60.00 75.00 66.00
□ **Pitcher, Water,** sloping sides, flared lip, quart size 25.00 40.00 30.00
□ **Pitcher, Water,** sloping sides, hinged lid, quart size 30.00 45.00 34.00
□ **Plate Warmer,** handle, legs, bowl shape 90.00 120.00 97.00
□ **Plate Warmer,** box shape, legs, handle, coor 135.00 160.00 145.00
□ **Plate Warmer,** cylindrical shape, handle, lid, plate 24.00 31.00 25.00
□ **Popcorn Popper,** hinged lid, rectangular, wooden handle, c. 1800 .... 50.00 65.00 55.00
□ **Popcorn Popper,** plain, 19th century, factory made 15.00 25.00 18.00
□ **Pot,** egg shape, loop for hanging, lid with hinge 25.00 40.00 29.00
□ **Pot Chain,** mesh circles for pot cleaning 5.00 10.00 7.00
□ **Pot Chain,** mesh circles for pot cleaning, with steel blade scraper 7.00 12.00 9.00
□ **Pot Chain,** simple single ring style 4.00 9.00 5.00
□ **Press, Food,** c. 1930, zinc plated iron 25.00 40.00 29.00
□ **Press, Meat Loaf,** tin with wood frame, top handle 40.00 55.00 47.00
□ **Press, Wine,** perforated tin with wood frame, round 45.00 60.00 49.00
□ **Pudding Mold,** pan shaped, lidded, late 19th century 10.00 16.00 13.00
□ **Pudding Mold,** cylindrical shape, two quart size, cover 11.00 15.00 12.50
□ **Pudding Mold,** cylindrical shape, two quart size, cover, scalloped mold 16.00 22.00 17.50
□ **Pudding Mold,** oval, scalloped border, one quart 10.00 16.00 12.00
□ **Pudding Mold,** oval, serrated rim, 1½" quart 14.00 20.00 15.00
□ **Pudding Mold,** oval, tulip in center, two quart 17.00 22.00 18.00
□ **Roaster,** black tin, c. 1890 .... 22.00 28.00 24.00
□ **Roasting Oven,** swing backtop, handles on side, two back feet, original insert pan, reflector type, 11" x 10" x 9½" 100.00 120.00 110.00
□ **Rolling Pin,** tin body, wooden handles, rare ... 40.00 55.00 42.00
□ **Salt Box,** hanging............................ 18.00 28.00 22.00
□ **Salt Box,** with raised letters, "SALT" 20.00 30.00 23.00
□ **Sander,** cylinder, dark finish, 2½" 15.00 20.00 17.50

	Current Price Range		P/Y Average
Sausage Gun, tapering tube with wood plunger, loop for hanging	30.00	43.00	33.00
Sausage Gun, tavern size, 4″ long	62.00	75.00	65.00
Sausage Stuffer, tin with wooden press	26.00	30.00	27.00
Scoops, curved handle, 5″ long	10.00	18.00	14.00
Scrapple Pan, tinned iron, Pennsylvania Dutch	615.00	675.00	630.00
Shaker, tin, salt or spice, Norton Brothers, 1890	13.00	17.00	14.00
Shoe Sole Templates, tin, six different sizes, early 20th century	37.00	49.00	40.00
Sieves, perforated tin, c. 1900	10.00	20.00	14.00
Sifter, says "Kewpie," 3″ high	25.00	35.00	28.00
Skillet, mid 19th century	50.00	65.00	53.00
Skimmer, large shallow bowl, wooden handle, hanging loop	10.00	20.00	14.00
Skimmer, for candle wax, shallow bowl with perforated cover, wood handle	13.00	18.00	14.00
Skimmer, milk, perforated and stamped, c. 1890s	8.00	11.00	9.00
Skimmer, stamped tin, 19th century	8.50	11.00	9.50
Spice Boxes, set of six little boxes with tray, wood handle, tin construction	55.00	70.00	62.00
Spice Boxes, six square with tray and nutmeg grater, wood handle	60.00	75.00	63.00
Spice Box, set of seven, enameled tin, tray with lid	70.00	90.00	76.00
Spice Box, tray, japanned, strap handle	30.00	42.00	31.00
Steam Cooker, tall cylindrical shape, hinged lid, handle, 12″ diameter	35.00	50.00	41.00
Strainer, perforated tin bowl with wood handle	25.00	40.00	31.00
Strainer, hinged for extending to fit different sized bowls, c. 1870......................	12.00	20.00	14.00
Strainer, cone shape, handle loop for hanging	10.00	18.00	12.00
Strainer, meat pudding, tin, handmade, two pieces	41.00	49.00	43.00
Stove Board, c. 1890	15.00	30.00	18.00
Sugar Scoop, shovel head, handle strap, loop for hanging	14.00	20.00	16.50

TINTYPES

DESCRIPTION: Early photographs, usually but not exclusively portraits, made by a special process distinctive from other photographs of their era.

TYPES: The most familiar tintype is a portrait measuring approximately 2½ by 3½ inches, though tintypes of larger and smaller sizes exist. This size became standard as it permitted the photographer to make four different exposures on one plate. These are known as "Quarter-Plate" tintypes.

PERIOD: The tintype process was short lived. It was invented in 1856 and declined by the 1870s.

MATERIALS: Tintypes were exposed from metal plates whose surfaces had been coated with varnish. This was the point of departure from earlier processes, which had used silver coating.

COMMENTS: Tintypes are the earliest photographs widely available on the collector market at moderate prices. Anonymous portraits of anonymous persons are collected simply as specimens of pioneer photography, and are of interest even if no identification can ever be made of the photographer, subject, or locale. Of great appeal are topical specimens such as photos of Civil War soldiers and officers and circus performers.

ADDITIONAL TIPS: Today there are specialist dealers who regularly stock early photographs, including tintypes, but fine selections may also be found at auction sales of photographica and Americana.

	Current Price Range		P/Y Average
☐ **Actress,** ¼ plate of Ella Rathbun in a dancing pose, enclosed in a pink and red cardboard mat, c. 1885	42.00	53.00	46.00
☐ **Anonymous Domestic Portrait,** husband and wife, wife seated in ornate chair, husband standing with hand on her shoulder, 1865	11.00	15.00	13.00
☐ **Anonymous Portrait,** middle aged man with frock coat, eyeglasses, sideburns, head and shoulders view, mounted in a wood frame with oval opening, 1860s	11.00	15.00	13.00

	Current Price Range		P/Y Average

☐ **Bishop Baker,** Abbot & Co., commercially issued tintype picturing abolishionists and ministers, 1863, 1½″ x 1½″ **15.00 20.00 17.00**

☐ **Boy With Dog,** 1/6 plate, black dog on fringed chair, uncased **13.00 17.00 14.75**

☐ **Civil War Infantryman Loading Musket,** 1/6 plate, standing three quarter portrait holding M1861 musket and ramrod, cased **190.00 230.00 205.00**

☐ **Civil War Officer,** whole plate, three quarter length portrait holding bayoneted rifle over right shoulder **90.00 115.00 102.00**

☐ **Commodore DuPont,** Abbot & Co., commercially issued tintype, printed reverse, 1864 . . . .   **40.00 55.00 46.00**

☐ **Coney Island (New York),** 1/6 plate, roller skaters from "Coney Rink" **27.00 35.00 30.00**

☐ **Croquet Players,** 1/6 plate, distant view of players against wooded background, housed in a pink paper mat **20.00 25.00 22.00**

☐ **Cyclist,** 1/6 plate, man wearing bowtie stands next to his cycle, uncased, c. 1890 . . . .   **15.00 20.00 17.00**

☐ **Farm House,** whole plate, family gathered outside frame farm house, uncased, unmounted, c. 1870s **60.00 80.00 67.00**

☐ **Female Pilot,** woman in aviator outfit standing alongside early aircraft, housed in a decorated cardboard mat with shield and the word "Greetings," World War I era **32.00 39.00 34.00**

☐ **Foreign Costume,** large tintype portrait of man wearing Eastern European or Turkish national costume, full length **22.00 28.00 24.50**

☐ **Gamblers,** 1/6 plate, half length portraits of two men playing cards at a small table, uncased . .   **30.00 38.00 33.50**

☐ **General Burnside,** Abbot & Co., commercially issued tintype, printed reverse, 1864 . . . .   **45.00 60.00 51.00**

☐ **General Halleck,** Abbot & Co., commercially issued tintype, printed reverse, 1864 . . . .   **40.00 55.00 46.00**

☐ **General Walbridge,** Abbot & Co., commercially issued tintype picturing abolishionists and ministers, 1863, 1½″ x 1¼″ **15.00 20.00 17.00**

☐ **Grocer In Wagon,** 1/6 plate, man driving wagon which reads "City Grocery," pulled by horse, half case **50.00 65.00 56.00**

☐ **Hunter,** ¼ plate, full length portrait of man in dress suit with rifle over his left shoulder **23.00 30.00 26.00**

☐ **Louis Blenker,** Abbot & Co., Union commercially issued tintype, printed reverse, 1864 . . . .   **40.00 55.00 44.00**

☐ **Pair of Union Cavalry Soldiers,** wearing jackets and trousers, one has broadbrim hat with cavalry boots, a quarter-plate tintype **68.00 85.00 74.00**

☐ **Patriot,** ¼ plate of man standing next to large American flag, probably made during Civil War to show patriotism **36.00 44.00 39.00**

	Current Price Range		P/Y Average
☐ **Post-Civil War,** officer in dress uniform, 1870s	35.00	45.00	39.00
☐ **Rev. Theodore Parker,** Abbot & Co., commercially issued tintype picturing abolitionists and ministers, c. 1863, 1½″ x 1¼″	15.00	20.00	17.00
☐ **Soldier and Wife Seated on Ornate Victorian Sofa,** quarter plate tintype	45.00	60.00	49.00
☐ **Tennis Players,** 1/6 plate, group shot of six persons with racquets and balls, half case, c. 1880	35.00	45.00	39.00
☐ **Union Chaplain William Bryan,** 1/6 plate, half length portrait with shoulder bars and clerical collar, housed in a gutta percha case, dated March 26, 1863	200.00	250.00	215.00
☐ **Union Corporal,** 1/6 plate, half length seated portrait with right arm resting on table, cased	70.00	100.00	82.00
☐ **Union Soldier,** young, seated in front of photography backdrop	30.00	40.00	34.00
☐ **Violin Player,** 1/6 plate, young man holding violin and bow, gutta percha case	50.00	60.00	53.50
☐ **Watermelon Feast,** 1/6 plate, group shot of seven people (white) eating watermelon, c. 1880	15.00	20.00	17.00
☐ **Zouave,** 1/6 plate tinted, half length portrait, housed in an embossed contemporary case ...	110.00	140.00	115.00
☐ **Bust Portrait,** Union soldier, in uniform, mounted in frame with oval opening	32.00	40.00	35.00

TOBACCO JARS

DESCRIPTION: The tobacco jar is generally a combination of a humidor and pipe holder.

MATERIALS: Tobacco jars are made from a variety of items including wood, china, pottery, iron and other metals.

COMMENTS: Many tobacco jars were not only functional but quite ornately decorated. Sculptured heads, figures or animals are commonly found on tobacco jars.

ADDITIONAL TIPS: Price ranges listed are for original jars in good condition.

	Current Price Range		P/Y Average
☐ **Arab,** wearing headdress, 7″ H.	60.00	75.00	67.50
☐ **Boy,** bisque, 6¾″ H.	60.00	75.00	67.50
☐ **Buffalo,** pottery, Dedare ware	220.00	265.00	240.00
☐ **Bulldog,** Bristolware tan colored ceramic	60.00	75.00	65.00
☐ **Devil's Head,** red, bee on side of head	50.00	65.00	57.00
☐ **Elephant,** Majolica	90.00	115.00	102.50
☐ **Egyptian Queen,** exotic face, very colorful, 4″ H.	80.00	100.00	90.00
☐ **Frog With Pipe**	85.00	110.00	97.00
☐ **Girl's Face,** with light hair, hat functions as cover	85.00	110.00	97.00
☐ **Human Skull**	95.00	120.00	107.00
☐ **Indian Chief,** Majolica, feathered headdress, 10″ H.	95.00	120.00	107.00
☐ **Indian Head,** mahogany, top of head is lid, 1900s, 7″	130.00	160.00	145.00
☐ **Jester With Dog,** Staffordshire, 9½″ H.	250.00	300.00	275.00
☐ **Lion's Head,** Austrian hallmarks	50.00	70.00	60.00
☐ **Man,** with derby hat, pipe in mouth, Austrian ..	50.00	70.00	60.00
☐ **Man,** with skull cap, English pottery	95.00	120.00	97.00
☐ **Monk,** fat with laughing face, bisque chinaware	65.00	85.00	75.00
☐ **Monkeys,** face on lid and around base	140.00	175.00	157.00
☐ **Old Salt Sea Captain,** with cap and pipe	90.00	115.00	102.50
☐ **Owl,** Majolica, 7″ H.	55.00	75.00	65.00
☐ **Pipes On Cover,** pink and green pottery	70.00	95.00	82.50
☐ **Pirate,** shirt and hat, Majolica	95.00	120.00	107.00
☐ **Ram's Head,** Majolica	90.00	115.00	102.50
☐ **Royal Bayreuth,** tapestry ware, cows in field	275.00	340.00	302.00
☐ **Sea Captain,** pipe in mouth, Majolica	100.00	135.00	117.50

TOOLS

DESCRIPTION: A tool is a device used by hand. Those who use tools include carpenters, farmers, plumbers, cabinetmakers and wheelwrights.

TYPES: There are several different types of tools but woodworking tools which include planes, saws, measuring implements, augers, bits, and bladed instruments are the items most sought after by collectors.

COMMENTS: Handmade tools of the 1800s and factory produced tools of the early 1900s are the most desirable among collectors.

ADDITIONAL TIPS: Some hobbyists collect tools by type while others collect by craft. An entire collection could be comprised of tools used only by a shipwright or it could contain every type of bladed instrument from various occupations.

	Current Price Range		P/Y Average
☐ **Brace,** metal and wood, set screw holds bits (handturned handles), 1850s	35.00	50.00	42.00
☐ **Brace,** metal and wood, set screw holds bits, 1880s	20.00	29.00	23.50
☐ **Brace,** polished steel with beech head, "Peugeout Freres"	41.00	49.00	43.00
☐ **Brace,** Sheffield, beechwood, unplated, "Coca Cola" head	90.00	115.00	97.00
☐ **Brace,** two-post cage head, 17″	240.00	260.00	245.00
☐ **Brace,** walnut with brass trim, English mark, bit spring broken, 1820s	90.00	120.00	105.00
☐ **Brace,** wrench, adjustable, "P. Lowentraut, Newark, NJ, Pat. 1877"	90.00	100.00	93.00
☐ **Brace,** wrought iron, lignum vitae head, 10″ . . .	37.00	42.00	38.00
☐ **Buzz,** cooper's, beechwood, 14″	46.00	51.00	47.00
☐ **Caliper,** boxwood with brass screw and wingnut	32.00	38.00	33.50
☐ **Caliper,** brass, 22″	80.00	90.00	83.00
☐ **Caliper,** dancing legs, iron, 3½″	41.00	49.00	43.00
☐ **Caliper,** dancing legs, iron, 4¼″	51.00	59.00	52.50
☐ **Caliper,** wrought, 10″ x 14″	13.00	18.00	14.00
☐ **Carpenter's Square,** walnut handle, 10½″ . . .	3.75	8.75	6.00
☐ **Chisel,** marked, "Charles Buck—Cast Steel," brass ferrule, blade ⅞″ W., maple with leather, handle striking surface, 1900s	7.00	10.00	8.50
☐ **Chisel,** mortise, swan neck lock, boxwood handle, ½″ x 22″	46.00	54.00	48.50
☐ **Chisel,** sizing, lathe, "Buck Bros." 21″ long . . .	39.00	47.00	40.50
☐ **Clamp,** all wood, two "bolts," 5″ jaw, marked "William J. Hood, maker, Valley Falls, R.I.," 1870s	14.00	19.00	16.50
☐ **Clamp,** picture frame, cast bronze	70.00	80.00	72.00
☐ **Clamp,** screw type, round, "coca bola" nut, 11″	37.00	45.00	40.00
☐ **Cloth Tape,** in leather case, "Lufkin," 50′	13.00	18.00	13.50
☐ **Cloth Tape,** surveyor's, leather case, 50″ long	8.50	12.00	9.00
☐ **Plane,** plow, beechwood with slide arm and wooden screws	50.00	60.00	52.00
☐ **Plane,** rabbet, cast iron, 9″	90.00	100.00	93.00
☐ **Plane,** rounding, adjustable, wood with wrought cutter, 5″ x 10″	128.00	142.00	131.00
☐ **Plane,** Sargent, #3415, 15″ length	31.00	39.00	33.00
☐ **Plane,** Sargent, #5026, low angle block	25.00	35.00	30.00

	Current Price Range		P/Y Average

	Current Price Range		P/Y Average
Plane, sash, adjustable, wood screw adjustments, "E. W. Carpenter, Lancaster," dated 1831	140.00	160.00	145.00
Plane, sash filletster, brass trim	103.00	116.00	107.00
Plane, side bead, beechwood, "Woodrow & Co., Salisbury"	22.00	28.00	23.50
Plane, side bead, double iron, beechwood, "A. Cumings, Boston"	62.00	72.00	65.00
Plotting Scale, ivory, 1⅜" x 6"	46.00	52.00	47.00
Plow, adjustable with filletster bed and two fences, Miller's Patent #41, Stanley Rule & Level Co., emblem on iron	440.00	460.00	445.00
Plow, book binder's, wood, 12" x 16"	103.00	117.00	107.00
Plumb Bob, brass, turnip shape, 2½" diameter, 9" long	41.00	49.00	43.00
Plumb Bob, brass with steel tip, 5½" long	90.00	100.00	93.00
Plumb Bob, iron, turnip shape, 2"	7.00	9.00	7.50
Pointer, dowel, 7"	10.50	14.00	11.00
Punch, Grommet, 5" x 8"	46.00	53.00	47.50
Router, beechwood, brass sole, 12" long	37.00	43.00	38.00
Router, circular sash, cherrywood, 13" long	70.00	80.00	72.00
Router, coach maker's, steel plate and fence, 14"	15.00	19.00	16.00
Router, coach maker's, wrought iron, blade 1½"	20.00	24.00	21.00
Router, coach maker's, wrought iron, 22"	25.00	31.00	27.00
Router, coach maker's double, fruitwood, 18" long	158.00	173.00	161.00
Saw, pad type, beechwood handle, marked "Phila."	20.00	25.00	22.00
Saw, salt, zinc blade, 20"	57.00	63.00	58.00
Saw, two-edged, 25"	8.00	12.00	10.00
Saw Wrest, 18" long	28.00	32.00	29.00
Scale, lumber, hand marked, brass end	26.00	31.00	27.00
Scale, lumber, J. Chatillon & Son, New York, in yellow paint, "200," black, 1800s	60.00	90.00	75.00
Scale, lumber, octagonal cane-style	37.00	43.00	38.50
Scale, map, boxwood, beveled edges, 2" x 6"	26.00	31.00	27.50
Scale, steelyard, reversible, two hooks on "Heavy" measure, hand-forged, 1820s	50.00	70.00	60.00
Scorper, long handled with curved blade, 34" long	45.00	55.00	47.50
Scorper, long handled, wrought iron, curved blade 4¼"	60.00	70.00	62.00
Screwdriver, Primitive Yankee model	20.00	30.00	25.00
Screwdriver, Winchester, brass ferrule, 9"	20.00	25.00	23.75
Screwdriver, Winchester, wood handle, 10½"	12.00	17.00	14.50
Screw Plate, 16 sizes, 8¼" long	22.00	28.00	23.50
Screw Plate, 20 sizes, 9½" long	22.00	28.00	23.50
Screw Plate, 28 sizes, 14" long	30.00	38.00	31.50
Scribe, beech with brass facing and trim	9.00	12.00	10.50
Scribe, handmade, beech and mahogany, no inches	7.00	10.00	8.50

	Current Price Range		P/Y Average
☐ **Scribe,** rosewood with brass facings and trim	22.00	29.00	25.00
☐ **Shave,** basket maker, splint, adjustable blade 4", 12"	80.00	90.00	83.00
☐ **Shave,** brass, right and left radius cutters, 10"	16.00	20.00	17.00
☐ **Shave,** head, cooper's, beechwood with steel bottom, 12"	46.00	52.00	47.00
☐ **Sheller,** corn, Shaker, 9" x 24"	118.00	132.00	121.00
☐ **Shoe Fastener,** marked Peninsular Hand Tool. Mfg. by Parker Mfg. Co., Boston, wood box, 10" x 5" x 1½"	45.00	55.00	50.00
☐ **Shovel,** carved from one piece, maple or chestnut, grain shovel, c. 1840–1880	18.00	25.00	21.50
☐ **Shovel,** snow shovel, handmade, wood with tin trim, c. 20th c.	12.00	17.00	14.50
☐ **Slide Rule,** maple and mahogany, hand lettered	41.00	49.00	43.00
☐ **Spear,** eel, 5" wide, 10" long	41.00	49.00	43.00
☐ **Spear,** eel, wrought iron, 4½" x 10"	42.00	48.00	43.00
☐ **Spear,** eel, wrought iron, 7" wide, 17" long	50.00	60.00	52.00
☐ **Spear,** tobacco	13.00	17.00	14.00
☐ **Splitting Froe,** 12" blade	19.00	24.00	21.00
☐ **Splitting Wedge,** wooden top with iron ring	16.00	20.00	17.00
☐ **Spoke Shave,** beechwood, 10"	12.00	16.00	14.00
☐ **Square,** boxwood with brass ends and joints, folding, 6" x 6"	47.00	52.00	48.00
☐ **Square,** folding, with metal clamps along corner as locking device	22.00	28.00	23.00
☐ **Square,** plumb, cabinet maker's, mahogany, 7½" x 10"	46.00	54.00	48.00
☐ **Square,** plumb, cabinet maker's, mahogany, 10" x 13"	80.00	90.00	82.00
☐ **Stove,** charcoal, tinsmith's, tin with handle	31.00	39.00	33.00
☐ **Straight Edge,** saw maker's, 20" long	41.00	49.00	43.00
☐ **Straight Edge,** wallpaper hanger's, brass edges, 6" long	57.00	63.00	58.00
☐ **String Winder,** bentwood, 12"	50.00	60.00	53.00
☐ **Tape Measure,** marked Chesterman, Sheffeld, Eng. Pat. '09, made metal and cloth, 100', brass fittings and handle, polished leather case, 5½" diameter	15.00	25.00	20.00
☐ **Threading Die,** blacksmith's, four sizes, diamond faceted bolt, 21"	32.00	38.00	33.50
☐ **Threading Die,** blacksmith's, 26" length	18.00	22.00	19.00
☐ **Traveler,** wheelwright's, wrought iron wheel with wooden handle, 6" diameter	20.00	24.00	21.00
☐ **T Square,** architect's, adjustable, mahogany with brass, 37"	26.00	30.00	27.00
☐ **T Square,** rosewood handle, brass plate and three-pointed diamond inlay, stamped "OWO," blade, 7½" x 1¾", 1890s	14.00	19.00	16.50
☐ **T Square,** rosewood handle, brass plate and four-leaf clover inlay, "JM" carved in handle, blade 12" x 2⅛", 1880s	17.00	23.00	20.00

	Current Price Range		P/Y Average

□ **T Square,** rosewood handle, "Miller's Falls, Made in U.S.A.," #1438, brass plate, 8" x 1½", 1920s .... | 9.00 | 12.00 | 10.50

□ **Try Square,** marked Wm. Marples & Son, made of brass and rosewood, 11" blade .... | 8.00 | 11.00 | 9.50

□ **Try Square,** Stanley, handle made of brass and rosewood, 4" blade, rare .... | 15.00 | 20.00 | 17.50

□ **Twybill,** wrought iron, European style .... | 240.00 | 260.00 | 245.00

□ **Vise,** pin, 4¼" .... | 18.00 | 22.00 | 19.00

□ **Wheelwright's Traveler,** wrought iron, 6" diameter .... | 32.00 | 38.00 | 33.00

□ **Whetstone,** lift-off lid, oak case, 7" .... | 6.00 | 10.00 | 8.50

□ **Wrench,** adjustable, "Boynton's Pat. June, 14, 1887," 13" .... | 41.00 | 49.00 | 43.00

□ **Wrench,** American Beauty, 8" .... | 9.50 | 12.50 | 10.00

□ **Wrench,** Bemis & Call Co., 8" .... | 7.00 | 9.00 | 7.50

□ **Wrench,** Bemis & Call Co., 11" .... | 16.00 | 20.00 | 17.00

□ **Wrench Brace,** marked "P. Lowentraut, Newark, 1877 Patent" .... | 85.00 | 100.00 | 91.00

□ **Wrench,** Carll, Pat. May 6, 1913, 10" .... | 13.00 | 17.00 | 14.00

□ **Wrench,** monkey, A-1, pat'd., 1900 and 1908, miniature, 2" opening, c. 1910 .... | 5.00 | 7.50 | 6.75

□ **Wrench,** monkey, with inset handles made of wood, 6½" .... | 4.00 | 10.00 | 6.00

□ **Wrench,** monkey, walnut (no metal parts), 15" | 37.00 | 45.00 | 40.00

□ **Wrench,** Neverslip, 9" .... | 9.50 | 12.50 | 10.00

□ **Wrench,** Rogers, Printz & Co., Warren, PA, 9" | 24.00 | 30.00 | 25.50

□ **Wrench,** socket, set #14, open end and socket wrenches in oak case, "Frank Mossberg Co., Attleboro, Mass." .... | 80.00 | 90.00 | 82.00

□ **Wrench,** Superior Wrench Company, 9" ...... | 12.00 | 16.00 | 13.00

□ **Wrench,** Tokyo Tatag, 4½" .... | 7.00 | 9.00 | 7.50

□ **Wrench,** Trojan Wrench, L.A., CA, 11" .... | 19.00 | 23.00 | 20.00

□ **Wrench,** wagon wrench, hand-forged, curved body, 1840s .... | 12.00 | 17.00 | 14.50

□ **Wrench,** Wakefield #19, 8" .... | 6.00 | 8.00 | 6.50

TOY CARS

TOPIC: Toy cars are scaled-down models of automobiles. The detail on them can be extremely intricate, with working windshield wipers and rubber tires, or it can be minimal. Toy cars as a rule do not run under their own power.

PERIOD: Collectible toy cars date back to around 1910.

MAKERS: Corgi, Dinky, Matchbox and Tootsietoy are major names in the production of toy cars. Other less well known companies are F & F Corporation, Gamda Koor, Hubley and Play Art.

COMMENTS: Large toy cars are generally more valuable than smaller ones. Whether the car does what it was designed to do is immaterial, since it is mainly for display and not play.

ADDITIONAL TIPS: Most collectors do not play with their miniature toy cars, because the value of the item depends greatly on condition. Restored specimens have little value on the collector market. For additional information, please refer to *The Official Price Guide to Collectible Toys,* published by The House of Collectibles.

	Current Price Range		P/Y Average
☐ **No. 9E AMX Javelin,** c. 1972, green body, orange interior, silver trim	4.00	5.00	4.25
☐ **No. 9F Ford Escort RS 2000,** c. 1978, white body, black trim, "Shell" decal	3.00	4.00	3.25
☐ **No. 10F Plymouth "Granfury" Police Car,** c. 1979, white body, white interior, silver base ...	3.00	4.00	3.75
☐ **No. 12A Land Rover,** c. 1955, green body, silver trim	4.00	5.00	8.00
☐ **No. 12B Land Rover (Series II),** c. 1959, olive green body, tow hook	12.00	15.00	7.50
☐ **No. 12C Safari Land Rover,** c. 1966, green body, white interior	6.00	8.00	6.50
☐ **No. 12F Citroen CX,** c. 1980, light blue body, yellow interior, silver base	2.00	3.00	4.75

James Bond Aston Martin #271, $5.00-$7.00
Photo courtesy of Dick Starr.

	Current Price Range		P/Y Average
☐ **No. 13E Baja Buggy,** c. 1972, green body, black trim	2.00	3.00	3.00
☐ **No. 14A Daimler Ambulance,** c. 1956, cream body, silver trim, Red Cross decal	12.00	15.00	11.50
☐ **No. 14B Daimler Ambulance,** c. 1958, cream and silver, Red Cross decal	12.00	15.00	9.50
☐ **No. 14C Bedford Lomas Ambulance,** c. 1962, white body, white interior, silver trim	6.00	8.00	6.50

TOOTSIETOY

PREWAR CARS 1910–1933

☐ **No. 4258 Limousine,** c. 1911	25.00	30.00	28.50
☐ **No. 4570 Ford, Model T Open Tourer,** c. 1915	35.00	45.00	35.00
☐ **No. 4629 Yellow Cab Sedan,** c. 1923	25.00	30.00	11.50
☐ **No. 4636 Coupe,** c. 1920	25.00	30.00	17.50
☐ **No. 4655 Ford, Model A Coupe,** c. 1928	35.00	40.00	25.00
☐ **No. 4656 Buick Coupe in Tinplate Garage,** c. 1931	85.00	100.00	65.00
☐ **No. 4657 Buick Sedan in Tinplate Garage,** c. 1931	85.00	100.00	57.50
☐ **No. 4666 Bluebird I, Daytona Record Car,** c. 1932	20.00	25.00	17.00
☐ **No. 5101 "Andy Gump" Roadster,** c. 1932 ..	100.00	125.00	75.00
☐ **No. 5102 "Uncle Walt" Roadster,** c. 1932 ...	125.00	135.00	125.00
☐ **No. 5103 "Smitty" Motorcycle with Sidecar,** c. 1932	100.00	125.00	75.00
☐ **No. 5104 "Moon Mullins" Police Wagon,** c. 1932	100.00	125.00	75.00

	Current Price Range		P/Y Average
☐ No. 5105 "Kayo" Ice Wagon, c. 1932	90.00	110.00	75.00
☐ No. 5106 "Uncle Willy" Rowboat, c. 1932 ...	90.00	110.00	55.00
☐ No. 6001 Buick, Roadster, c. 1927	40.00	45.00	35.00
☐ No. 6002 Buick, Roadster, c. 1927	40.00	45.00	35.00
☐ No. 6003 Buick, Brougham, c. 1927	40.00	45.00	35.00
☐ No. 6004 Buick, Sedan, c. 1927	40.00	45.00	27.50
☐ No. 6005 Buick, Closed Touring Car, c. 1927	40.00	45.00	47.50
☐ No. 6101 Cadillac, Roadster, c. 1927	40.00	45.00	55.00
☐ No. 6102 Cadillac, Coupe, c. 1927	40.00	45.00	55.00
☐ No. 6103 Cadillac, Brougham, c. 1927	40.00	45.00	45.00
☐ No. 6104 Cadillac, Sedan, c. 1927	40.00	45.00	45.00
☐ No. 6105 Cadillac, Closed Touring Car, c. 1927	40.00	45.00	45.00
☐ No. 6201 Chevrolet, Roadster, c. 1927	40.00	45.00	45.00
☐ No. 6202 Chevrolet, Coupe, c. 1927	40.00	45.00	45.00
☐ No. 6203 Chevrolet, Brougham, c. 1927	40.00	45.00	45.00

POSTWAR CARS

Reissues

☐ No. 230 Sedan	10.00	15.00	12.50
☐ No. 231 Coupe	10.00	15.00	12.50
☐ No. 232 Touring Car	10.00	15.00	12.50
☐ No. 233 Roadster	10.00	15.00	12.50
☐ No. 237 Insurance Patrol	12.00	14.00	13.00
☐ No. 239 Station Wagon	11.00	13.00	12.00
☐ No. 1016 Torpedo Roadster	15.00	20.00	17.50
☐ No. 1017 Torpedo Coupe	15.00	20.00	17.50
☐ No. 1018 Torpedo Sedan	15.00	20.00	17.50
☐ No. 1042 Insurance Patrol	20.00	22.00	11.00

3 Inch Models

☐ Chevrolet, Belair, c. 1955	8.00	10.00	6.50
☐ Ford Custom Convertible, c. 1949	8.00	10.00	8.50
☐ Ford Customline, c. 1955	8.00	10.00	6.50
☐ Ford Custom Sedan, c. 1949	8.00	10.00	9.50
☐ Ford Falcon, c. 1960	4.00	5.00	9.50
☐ Ford Fairlane Convertible, c. 1956	8.00	10.00	6.50
☐ Ford Ranch Wagon, c. 1954	8.00	10.00	6.50
☐ Ford Station Wagon, c. 1960	12.00	15.00	7.50
☐ Ford Thunderbird, c. 1955	12.00	15.00	9.50
☐ Hot Rod, c. 1960	4.00	5.00	12.50
☐ Jaguar, D-Type, c. 1954	7.00	9.00	7.50
☐ Jaguar, XK120, c. 1950	9.00	11.00	9.50
☐ Jeep, CJ3, Army, c. 1950	3.00	9.00	9.50
☐ Jeep, CJ3, Civilian, c. 1950	3.00	4.00	10.50
☐ MG TF, Sports Car, c. 1954	11.00	13.00	12.50
☐ Nash Metropolitan, c. 1954	20.00	25.00	10.50
☐ Plymouth Belvedere, c. 1958	6.00	7.00	9.50
☐ Plymouth Sedan, c. 1950	8.00	10.00	6.50
☐ Studebaker Champion, c. 1947	20.00	25.00	12.50
☐ Studebaker Lark Convertible, c. 1960	10.00	12.00	10.50
☐ Triumph TR5, c. 1956	9.00	11.00	9.50
☐ Willy's Jeepster, c. 1948	12.00	15.00	9.50
☐ Volkswagen Bug, c. 1960	6.00	8.00	7.00

	Current Price Range		P/Y Average
4 Inch Models			
☐ **Buick, Experimental Roadster,** c. 1942	10.00	15.00	35.00
☐ **Chevrolet Ambulance,** c. 1950	20.00	22.00	21.50
☐ **Chevrolet, Corvette,** c. 1954	15.00	20.00	12.50
☐ **Chevrolet, Fleetmaster,** c. 1946	15.00	20.00	13.50
☐ **Chrysler, 300 Convertible,** c. 1959	12.00	14.00	12.50
☐ **Chrysler, Windsor Convertible,** c. 1941	20.00	25.00	22.50
☐ **Ford, Ranch Wagon,** c. 1954	15.00	20.00	22.50
☐ **Ford, Thunderbird,** c. 1955	20.00	25.00	22.50
☐ **Jeep, CJ3, Army,** c. 1950	4.00	5.00	17.50
☐ **Jeep, CJ3, Civilian,** c. 1950	4.00	5.00	19.50
☐ **Mercury,** c. 1949	15.00	20.00	13.00
☐ **Mercury, Custom Sedan,** c. 1952	20.00	25.00	19.00
☐ **Mercury, Fire Chief's Car,** c. 1949	20.00	25.00	25.00

TOY SOLDIERS

TOPIC: Toy soldiers are miniature figures of military personnel.

TYPES: Soldiers, officers, medical personnel and related figures are all collected avidly.

PERIOD: Figures from the World Wars are most popular, and the majority of the pieces were manufactured in the mid-20th century. Toy soldiers can date back to the late 1800s.

MAKERS: Major producers of toy soldiers are Barclay and Manoil. Many other manufacturers are also prominent.

MATERIALS: Lead, plastic and metals are usually used.

COMMENTS: Collectors have recently become more interesting in this field. Many collect a certain set of figures, while others focus on soldiers from a certain era.

ADDITIONAL TIPS: For further information, please refer to *The Official Price Guide to Collectible Toys,* published by The House of Collectibles.

AMERICAN MADE TOY SOLDIERS

	Current Price Range		P/Y Average

AUBURN RUBBER

☐ **Soldier,** Indiana, rubber, kneeling, machine gunner	6.00	11.50	7.00
☐ **Soldier,** Indiana, rubber, painted, marching, rifle held diagonally	6.00	11.50	7.00

BARCLAY—EARLY 20TH CENTURY

☐ **Cook,** New Jersey, lead, painted, standing, holding dinner	11.00	17.00	13.00
☐ **Doctor,** New Jersey, lead, painted, standing, in uniform, holding bag	11.00	17.00	13.00
☐ **Doctor,** New Jersey, lead, painted, standing, treating wounded soldier	16.00	22.00	18.50
☐ **Doctor,** New Jersey, #760, lead, painted, standing, with stethoscope	8.00	13.50	9.50
☐ **Nurse,** New Jersey, lead, painted, kneeling ...	11.00	17.00	12.50
☐ **Soldier,** New Jersey, #766, lead, painted, lunging, butt of rifle raised	7.00	17.00	12.00
☐ **Soldier,** New Jersey, #766, lead, painted, lunging, butt of rifle raised	11.00	17.00	12.00
☐ **Soldier,** New Jersey, #769, lead, painted, sitting, peeling potatoes	9.00	15.00	11.00

BARCLAY—MID 20TH CENTURY

☐ **Soldier,** New Jersey, #938, pod foot, lead, painted, throws bomb, in uniform	6.00	11.00	7.00
☐ **Soldier,** New Jersey, #947, lead, painted, pod foot, standing, aiming, marksman	2.50	6.00	3.00

Machine Gunner with Helper, *Manoil,* $5.00-$15.00
Photo courtesy of Hake's Americana, York, PA.

	Current Price Range		P/Y Average

Soldier, New Jersey, #948, lead, unpainted, pod foot, running, with rifle	2.50	6.00	3.00
Soldier, New Jersey, #974, lead, painted, pod foot, kneeling, anti-aircraft gunner	2.50	6.00	3.00
Soldier, New Jersey, #988, lead, painted, pod foot, marching, gun on back	2.50	6.00	3.00
Soldier, New Jersey, #991, lead, painted, pod foot, flame thrower	7.00	13.50	8.00

GREY IRON

Sailor, Pennsylvania, #14, cast iron, painted, in uniform, armed	8.00	15.50	9.00
Officer, Naval, Pennsylvania, #14AW, cast iron, painted, in uniform	10.00	20.00	12.00
Officer, U.S., Pennsylvania, #3, cast iron, painted, one of three pieces	9.00	18.00	10.50

MANOIL—MID 20TH CENTURY

General, New York, #45/15, lead, painted, on base, at attention, saluting, in uniform	38.00	60.00	43.00
Soldier, New York, #45/7, lead, painted, marching, holding flag	7.00	12.00	8.00
Soldier, New York, #45/8, lead, painted, marching, parade	11.00	17.00	12.50
Soldier, New York, #45/9, lead, painted, standing, at ease, with rifle	17.00	27.00	18.00
Soldier, New York, #45/10, lead, painted, at attention, rifle upright	11.00	22.00	13.00
Soldier, New York, #45/11, lead, painted, kneeling, aiming rifle upwards	22.00	33.00	25.00
Soldier, New York, #45/12, lead, painted, standing, aiming tommygun	17.00	22.00	18.00
Soldier, New York, #45/13, lead, painted, kneeling, aiming bazooka	11.00	22.00	12.00
Soldier, New York, #45/14, lead, painted, lying flat, with shell	28.00	45.00	33.00

MARX

Army Combat Training Center, U.S., #2654, plastic	90.00	100.00	93.00
Army Training Center, U.S., #4122, plastic ..	100.00	120.00	105.00
General Grant, plastic	3.50	7.00	4.00
Soldier, Union, plastic, advancing, with bayonet	2.50	4.00	3.00
Soldier, Union, plastic, crawling, with rifle	2.50	4.00	3.00
Soldier, Union, plastic, wounded	2.50	4.00	3.00

MULTIPLE PLASTICS CORPORATION

Officer, American Revolution, plastic	5.00	9.00	6.00
Soldier, American Revolution, plastic, advancing, bearing flag	2.50	6.00	3.00
Soldier, American Revolution, plastic, kneeling, firing	2.50	6.00	3.00
Soldier, American Revolution, plastic, kneeling, loading rifle	2.50	6.00	3.00

	Current Price Range		P/Y Average
☐ **Soldier,** American Revolution, plastic, mounted, sans horse	2.50	4.00	3.00

ENGLISH-MADE TOY SOLDIERS

BRITAINS LTD.

☐ **Air Force,** U.S., set #2044, metal, painted, eight pieces	95.00	115.00	99.00
☐ **Armed Forces,** Royal, set #240, lead, painted, approximately eighteen pieces	200.00	300.00	225.00
☐ **Artillery,** set #1730, metal, painted, seven pieces, standing, kneeling, at attention	60.00	75.00	50.00

TOY TRAINS

TOPIC: Toy trains are scaled-down models of locomotives and stock cars. They are designed to be operational on miniature tracks in miniature landscapes.

TYPES: The two major types of trains are distinguished by track size. The space between the outermost rails of the tracks will measure 2⅛″ if the set is standard gauge. This measurement will be 1¼″ if the set is 0 gauge. Other sizes are common, but these are the most popular.

PERIOD: Toy trains were first made in the late 1800s. They reached a peak of popularity in the 1940s and 1950s.

MAKERS: The primary manufacturers of toy trains in the United States were Lionel Corporation, American Flyer Manufacturing Company, Ives Corporation and Louis Marx and Company.

MATERIALS: Trains are commonly made of tinplate, cast iron, aluminum or plastic.

COMMENTS: Toy train collecting is an expensive hobby. Collectors may focus on a particular manufacturer, size or period of trains. The most valuable specimens were made prior to the second World War.

ADDITIONAL TIPS: The serious collector does not play with his trains; they are for display only. Use will result in wear and tear that lowers the value of the set. For more information and extensive listings, please refer to *The Official Price Guide to Collectible Toys,* published by The House of Collectibles.

	Current Price Range		P/Y Average

AMERICAN FLYER

NARROW GAUGE TRAIN SETS

☐ **#3107, baggage car #3150, pullman car #3161, observation car #3162,** train length 31″, oval track 61″ x 31″	300.00	350.00	325.00
☐ **No. 1329, Major Leaguer,** locomotive and tender #3193, tank car #3018, sand car #3016, automobile car #3015, caboose #3017, train length 45″, oval track 61″ x 31″	275.00	325.00	325.00
☐ **No. 1332, The Little American,** locomotive #1094, pullman car #1123, observation car #1124, train length 21″, curved track, 83″	400.00	500.00	425.00

NARROW GAUGE LOCOMOTIVES

☐ **No. 3192 Locomotive and Tender,** runs forward only, single headlight, black with brass trim, 12″	90.00	110.00	95.00
☐ **No. 3194 Locomotive and Tender,** manual control reverse, tender has eight wheels, 14¾″ . . .	100.00	125.00	110.00
☐ **No. 3195 Locomotive,** runs forward only, single headlight, black with brass trim	75.00	85.00	80.00
☐ **No. 3198 Locomotive,** manual control reverse, black with brass trim	150.00	300.00	175.00

NARROW GAUGE ROLLING STOCK

☐ **No. 1106 Log Car,** four wheels (single truck), 6½″	8.00	12.00	9.00
☐ **No. 1109 Sand Car,** four wheels (single truck), 5½″	6.00	10.00	7.00
☐ **No. 1110 Box Car,** four wheels (single truck), 5½″	6.00	8.00	7.00

STANDARD GAUGE

Train Sets

☐ **Freight Set,** diesel locomotive #4680 engine with tender, tank car #4010, mechanics car #4022, caboose #4017	1100.00	1400.00	1200.00
☐ **Freight Set,** electric locomotive #4692 with golden state tender, cattle car #4020, gondola #4017, boxcar #4018, caboose #4021	1600.00	2000.00	1750.00
☐ **Freight Set,** Hiawatha locomotive with tender, lumber, crane, gondola, tank and caboose	700.00	750.00	725.00
☐ **Passenger Set,** electric locomotive #4000, with baggage #4040, America coach, Pleasantview observation car, green, yellow, black and white	700.00	750.00	725.00
☐ **Passenger Set,** electric locomotive #4643 0-4-0, American coach, Pleasantview observation, green	300.00	400.00	325.00

	Current Price Range		P/Y Average

	Current Price Range		P/Y Average
☐ **Passenger Set,** Franklin locomotive 4-4-0, with two coaches #20, overland express baggage car #30	250.00	260.00	255.00
☐ **Passenger Set,** locomotive and tender, Columbus baggage #24773, Hamilton vista dome #24813, Washington observation #24833, silver cars with red stripe	175.00	225.00	195.00

Locomotives

☐ **No. 88 Franklin Locomotive,** with tender	80.00	100.00	90.00
☐ **No. 290 Electric Locomotive,** 4-6-2	65.00	75.00	65.00
☐ **No. 300 Reading Lines Locomotive,** with tender	40.00	60.00	45.00
☐ **No. 301 Reading Lines Locomotive,** with tender	30.00	35.00	32.00
☐ **No. 302 Reading Lines Locomotive,** plastic body	30.00	35.00	32.00
☐ **No. 303 Electric Locomotive,** 4-4-0, plastic body	45.00	55.00	48.00
☐ **No. 307 Reading Lines Locomotive,** with tender, plastic body	40.00	60.00	50.00
☐ **No. 312 Electric Locomotive,** 4-6-2, with tender	35.00	40.00	37.00
☐ **No. 322 New York Central Locomotive,** 4-6-4, with 12-wheel tender	140.00	160.00	145.00
☐ **No. 360A Diesel Locomotive,** with tender 364B	130.00	140.00	135.00
☐ **No. 370 Diesel Locomotive,** twin motor, with tender	65.00	85.00	70.00
☐ **No. 812 Texas Pacific Switcher**	210.00	230.00	215.00
☐ **No. 21206 San Francisco Diesel AA**	110.00	125.00	115.00
☐ **No. 21573 New Hampshire Diesel AA**	295.00	315.00	300.00

Rolling Stock

☐ **No. 20 Western Type Franklin Coach**	33.00	40.00	35.00
☐ **No. 30 Western Type Franklin Car**	38.00	45.00	40.00
☐ **No. 38 Overland Express**	43.50	50.00	45.00
☐ **No. 40 Western Type Baggage Express Car**	39.00	44.00	42.00
☐ **No. 625G Gulf Tank Car**	22.50	30.00	25.00
☐ **No. 628 Lumber Car,** W.L., metal base	14.50	16.00	15.00
☐ **No. 629 Cattle Car,** maroon	19.00	25.00	22.00
☐ **No. 630 Caboose,** with lights	5.50	7.00	6.00
☐ **No. 630 Caboose,** dark red	12.95	15.00	14.00
☐ **No. 631 T & P Gondola,** green	7.50	12.00	10.00
☐ **No. 632 Hopper,** dark gray	5.50	7.00	6.00
☐ **No. 633 B & O Box car,** red and white	21.00	24.00	23.00
☐ **No. 634 Searchlight Car**	15.00	17.00	16.00
☐ **No. 636 Depressed Center Cable Car,** 12 wheel	22.50	26.00	25.00
☐ **No. 637 Katy Box Car,** yellow and black	25.00	27.00	26.00
☐ **No. 637 Katy Box Car,** light yellow	32.00	36.00	35.00
☐ **No. 638 Caboose, A.F.L.,** red	7.50	9.00	8.00
☐ **No. 639 Box Car,** light yellow	29.00	22.00	26.00

TRADE CARDS

DESCRIPTION: Trade cards are usually made of very stiff paper advertising a business, product or service.

ORIGIN: Trade cards are an outgrowth of advertising handbills.

ADDITIONAL TIPS: Be wary of specimens that are heavily stained, torn or wrinkled. Light soiling is to be expected as are small pinholes in the upper corners. It was a frequent practice to post trade cards with thumbtacks.

	Current Price Range		P/Y Average
❏ **Ayers' Cherry Pectoral,** J.C. Ayers Co., Lowell, Massachusetts, girl on front, list of ailments on back	1.50	2.00	1.70
❏ **Ayers' Sasaparilla,** J.C. Ayers Co., Lowell, Massachusetts, picture of two women with children and dog on front	1.50	2.50	1.95
❏ **C.I. Hood & Co.,** Lowell, Massachusetts, telephone series, testimonials on reverses, price for group	5.00	7.00	6.00
❏ **Columbia Bicycles,** pictures cyclists on highwheelers riding at night, with lanterns	13.00	17.00	14.50
❏ **Dobbins' Soap,** six cards illustrating Shakespeare's "Six Ages of Man"	13.00	17.00	14.50
❏ **Freese's Clementine Glue,** has two illustrations, one vertical at left, the other in a circular medallion at right, wording above, 1885	4.00	6.00	5.00
❏ **Hall's Vegetable Sicilian Hair Renewer,** Nashua, New Hampshire, testimonials on reverse side, portrait of girl on front	1.25	1.75	1.50
❏ **Horseford's Self-Raising Bread Preparation,** Rumford Chemical Works, Providence, R.I.	1.00	1.50	1.20
❏ **Hoyt's Cologne,** perfumed card picturing large frog, 1883	2.00	2.50	2.20
❏ **Jumbo,** P.T. Barnum's famous circus elephant	5.00	6.00	5.45
❏ **Latest Novelty, Secret Motto Ring,** unillustrated but for engravings of ring in each of the four corners, decorative border like early paper money, ornamental lettering, 1870s	6.50	8.50	7.50

	Current Price Range		P/Y Average

☐ **Minard's Liniment, King of Pain,** pictures black man riding mule cart, reverse side lists various complaints for which product is supposedly effective 2.50 3.50 2.90

☐ **Nature's Remedy—Vegetine—The Blood Purifier,** girl 1.25 1.75 1.50

☐ **Page's Glue,** humorous card showing men stuck to bench with maker's product, printed by Bufford, 1890 .... 6.50 8.50 7.25

☐ **Ponds Extract Co.,** New York, gives cures on reverse side 1.25 1.75 1.50

☐ **Rising Sun Stove Polish,** pictures delivery boy stealing a kiss from housewife who has just finished polishing stove, 1890 .... 6.50 8.50 7.25

☐ **Rough On Rats,** E.R. Wells, Jersey City, New Jersey, reads "A 15¢ Box Will Keep Your House Free." 1.00 1.25 1.10

☐ **Tarrant's Seltzer Aperient,** little girl and sewing basket, cures on reverse side 1.50 2.00 1.60

☐ **Waterbury Watch Co.,** shows multi-panel illustrated story in cartoon format, picture of watch at upper right, vertical format, 1884 .... 15.00 20.00 17.00

☐ **Willimantic Thread,** pictures Brooklyn Bridge, printed by Forbes Lithography Co. 9.00 12.00 10.25

☐ **Worcester Salt,** card in the form of a pair of eyeglasses with eye holes at the center, 1885 .... 11.00 14.00 12.00

☐ **World's Largest Fruithouse,** pictures tall building that looks like a hotel, 1885 .... 7.00 9.00 8.00

TRADE CATALOGS

DESCRIPTION: Catalogs issued by manufacturers, wholesalers and retail merchants are called trade catalogs.

CARE AND CONDITION: Since many of the early specimens are rare, allowances are made for their condition. Usually trade catalogs received a great deal of use making it difficult for collectors to find them in excellent condition.

ADDITIONAL TIPS: Watch for specialized catalogs which pertain to one subject rather than general merchandise catalogs.

	Current Price Range		P/Y Average
Automobile Supplies, Sears, Roebuck and Co., Chicago, 112 pp, 1913	22.00	28.00	25.00
Bicycles, Tires, Motorcycle and Bicycle Accessories, Edwards and Crist Co., Chicago and Philadelphia, 122 pp, 1923	22.00	30.00	26.00
Blymyer Bells for Churches, Schools, Colleges, Court Houses, Fire Alarms, Factories, Farms, Plantations, Etc., Cincinnati Bell Foundry Co., Cincinnati, 31 pp, 1916	20.00	25.00	22.50
Bottling Supplies and Household Utensils, Consumers Products Company, Brooklyn, N.Y., 20 pp, 1927	9.00	12.00	10.00
Brooms, The Most Modern Broom Manufacturing Plant in the World, Hamburg Broom Works, Hamburg, Pennsylvania, 28 pp, 1911	8.00	11.00	10.00
Busiest House in America, illustrated catalogue of general merchandise, 640 pp, 1908	60.00	80.00	70.00
Civil Engineers' and Surveyors' Instruments, W. and L.E. Gurley, Troy, New York, 34 pp, 1878	45.00	60.00	55.00
Columbia Bicycles, Pope Manufacturing Co., Hartford, Connecticut, 31 pp, 1897	33.00	41.00	37.00
Counting Machines, W.N. Durant, Milwaukee, 20 pp, c. 1905	22.00	30.00	26.00
Descriptive and Illustrated Catalogue, Iron Cutting Shears, Bolt Forging Machinery, Pawtucket Manufacturing Co., Central Falls, Rhode Island, 74 pp, 1892	32.00	40.00	36.00
Florence Home Needle-Work, Nonotuck Silk Co., Florence, Massachusetts, 96 pp, 1891 . . .	13.00	17.00	15.00
Galvanized Patent Stock Trough, Foltz Manufacturing and Supply Co., Hagerstown, Maryland, 8 pp, c. 1902, price list of pig and other livestock troughs	6.50	8.50	7.00
Great Western Gun Works, Catalogue #40, J.H. Johnston Co., Pittsburgh, 64 pp, 1888	45.00	60.00	55.00
Hand-Book and Illustrated Catalogue of the Engineers' and Surveyor's Instruments of Precision, C.L. Berger and Sons, Boston, 212 pp, 1902	40.00	50.00	45.00
Hersey Water Meters, price list, Hersey Manufacturing Co., South Boston, Massachusetts, 7 pp, 1908	4.00	5.00	4.50
Hibbard Baskets, price list, Hibbard Basket Works, Lyons, New York, 12 pp, 1900	14.00	18.00	16.00
High Grade Bicycles, Special Catalogue, Cash Buyers' Union, Chicago, 40 pp, 1895	35.00	45.00	40.00
Illustrated Catalogue of Metal Broom Locks and Braces, M. Gould's Son and Co., Newark, New Jersey, 16 pp, 1906	16.00	20.00	18.00

	Current Price Range		P/Y Average
☐ **Jaros Hygienic Wear,** I. Jaros, New York, 79 pp, 1890	23.00	28.00	25.00
☐ **Keating Bicycles,** 1896 Catalogue, Keating Wheel Co., Holyoke, Massachusetts, 32 pp ...	25.00	30.00	27.50
☐ **Masonic Lodge Supplies,** Catalogue #2, Henderson Ames Co., Kalamazoo, Michigan, 110 pp, 1905	25.00	32.00	28.00
☐ **Photographic Card Stock,** A.M. Collins Manufacturing Co. price list, Philadelphia, 47 pp, 1898	25.00	32.00	28.00
☐ **Powell Brothers Shoe Co.,** Spring Catalogue, New York, 49 pp, 1902	11.00	15.00	13.00
☐ **Prices Current,** Soda Fountain Supplies, Fuller and Fuller Co., Chicago, 189 pp, c. 1906	25.00	32.00	28.00
☐ **Prices Current,** Patent Medicines, Propritary Articles, Plasters, Antiseptic Dressings, Etc., Fuller and Fuller Co., Chicago, 189 pp, c. 1906	17.00	21.00	19.00
☐ **Saddlery and Horse Furnishings,** Carriage and Sleigh Trimmings, James Bailey Co., Portland, Maine, 1913, 7″ x 10″	30.00	40.00	35.00
☐ **Schoenhut's Marvelous Toys,** A. Schoenhut Company, Philadelphia, 36 pp, 1904	90.00	115.00	102.00
☐ **Vertical Gas,** Gasoline, Kerosene and Distillate Engines for All Power Purposes, Fairbanks, Morse and Co., Chicago, 32 pp, 1904	10.00	14.00	12.00
☐ **Washington Stoves and Ranges,** Grey and Dudley Hardware Co., Nashville, Tennessee, 110 pp, c. 1918	20.00	25.00	22.00

TRUCKS

ORIGIN: The U.S. trucking industry dates to the early twentieth century when trucks were tested in New York for their capacity, speed and economy.

MAKERS: The best-known truck makers include Dodge, Ford, General Motors Corporation and International Harvester.

COMMENTS: Pick-up trucks are currently among the most collectible trucks. Rare trucks are always sought after and the collectible truck industry is rising in popularity.

ADDITIONAL TIPS: These listings are alphabetical according to the truck maker. Following the make is the date of manufacture, model, type of engine, type of body and price range. Prices do vary according to the condition of the truck. For further information, see *The Official Price Guide to Cars, Trucks and Motorcycles,* published by The House of Collectibles.

GMC—1948 "Pickup, FC-100", $2750.00-$3500.00
Photo courtesy of General Motors Corporations, Pontiac, MI.

YEAR	MODEL	ENGINE	BODY	F	G	E
DODGE						
1930	Stake Truck	(V) 8 cyl. Flathead	1½ Ton	2100	2450	2700
1936	Dump		Garwood	2000	2300	2500
1936	Humpback	(V) 8 cyl. 318	Deluxe Package	3500	4000	4500
1937	Pickup	Slant 6	¾ Ton	1950	2200	2600
1938	Humpback	(V) 8 cyl. 350	½ Ton	3000	3200	3500
1947	WC Pickup	Slant 6	½ Ton	2000	2400	2700
1948	Tow	6 cyl., 5-Speed		1700	2000	2300
1950	Pickup	(V) 8 cyl.	Long Bed	2500	2750	3000
1950	Pickup	6 cyl.	½ Ton, Slant Bed	2250	2500	2800
1953	Pickup	3-Speed	½ Ton, Short Bed	2200	2500	2800
1953	Pickup	4-Speed	½ Ton	2300	2500	2800
FORD						
1920	Model A	4 cyl.	C. Cab	4500	4900	5300
1923	Model T	4 cyl.	Short Back	4200	4500	4900
1925	Model TT	2-Speed	1 Ton	3500	3800	4200
1925	Stake	4 cyl.	1 Ton	3200	3500	3900
1928	Tow	2-Speed	Shortbed	1950	2450	2800
1930	Flatbed	4 cyl.	1½ Ton	1200	1500	1800

YEAR	MODEL	ENGINE	BODY	F	G	E
1931	Model A		½ Ton	4000	4300	4600
1931	Model AA	4-Speed		3800	4100	4400
1931	Model AA	(V) 8 cyl.	Short Box	4000	4200	4500
1932	Flatbed	4 cyl.	1½ Ton	2000	2200	2400
1933	Stake Truck	AB Motor	Grainbed	2000	2450	2700
1934	Pickup	(V) 8 cyl.	Sidemount	2800	3000	3300
1935	Panel	(V) 8 cyl., automatic		3000	3400	3900

TV GUIDES

DESCRIPTION: *TV Guide* is a weekly magazine which includes local television listings and articles about Hollywood stars.

PERIOD: The nationally distributed editions of *TV Guide* began in 1953. Before 1953, there were local forerunners.

COMMENTS: Issues which have popular Hollywood stars on the cover are usually more valuable than other editions. Editions with Lucille Ball, Ronald Reagan and Elvis Presley on the cover are highly valued by collectors.

ADDITIONAL TIPS: For more information, consult *The Official Price Guide to Radio, TV and Movie Memorabilia,* published by The House of Collectibles.

	Current Price Range		P/Y Average
☐ **April 3–9, 1953,** issue #1, photo of Lucille Ball's baby on cover, with small photo of Lucy in upper right corner, headline "Lucy's $50,000,000 Baby." This referred to the fact that many episodes of "I Love Lucy" in late 1952 and early 1953 were built around Lucy's pregnancy, and the fact that the baby ("Little Ricky") became an instant TV star. Though the issue is labeled #1, it was actually not the first issue of TV Guide, as regional issues had been published previously; it was the first coast-to-coast issue, and the first with a glossy cover	140.00	160.00	145.00
☐ **April 10–16, 1953,** issue #2, Jack Webb on cover	50.00	65.00	55.00

	Current Price Range		P/Y Average

☐ **April 17–23, 1953,** issue #3, caricatures of Lucille Ball, Arthur Godfrey, Milton Berle, Sid Caesar and Imogene Coca on cover . . . . 20.00 27.50 — 23.00

☐ **April 24–30, 1953,** issue #4, Ralph Edwards on cover . . . . 22.50 30.00 — 25.00

☐ **May 1–7, 1953,** issue #5, Eve Arden on cover 36.00 45.00 — 39.00

☐ **May 8–14, 1953,** issue #6, Arthur Godfrey on cover . . . . 25.00 35.00 — 28.00

☐ **May 22–28, 1953,** issue #8, Red Buttons on cover . . . . 20.00 30.00 — 24.00

☐ **June 12–18, 1953,** issue #11, Eddie Fisher on cover . . . . 15.00 25.00 — 19.00

☐ **June 19–25, 1953,** issue #12, Ed Sullivan on cover . . . . 10.00 20.00 — 14.00

☐ **July 3–9, 1953,** issue #14, Perry Como on cover . . . . 8.00 15.00 — 11.00

☐ **July 17–23, 1953,** issue #16, Lucille Ball and Desi Arnez on cover . . . . 25.00 35.00 — 29.00

☐ **July 24–30, 1953,** issue #17, caricature of Groucho Marx on cover . . . . 25.00 37.00 — 30.00

☐ **August 14–20, 1953,** issue #20, Patti Page on cover . . . . 15.00 25.00 — 19.00

☐ **August 21–27, 1953,** issue #21, Mary Hartline and Claude Kirchner of Super Circus on cover 25.00 35.00 — 29.00

☐ **August 28–September 3, 1953,** issue #22, Jane and Audrey Meadows on cover . . . . 12.50 20.00 — 14.00

☐ **October 2–8, 1953,** issue #27, Red Skelton on cover . . . . 17.00 23.00 — 19.00

☐ **October 16–22, 1953,** issue #29, TV beauty contestants on cover . . . . 10.00 20.00 — 14.00

☐ **October 23–29, 1953,** issue #30, Arthur Godfrey on cover . . . . 14.00 17.00 — 15.00

☐ **October 30–November 5, 1953,** issue #31, Beulah Witch, Kukla and Ollie on cover . . . . 15.00 25.00 — 19.00

☐ **June 27–July 3, 1959,** issue #326, Lloyd Bridges on cover, with article on the death of George Reeves (who had played "Superman" on TV) . . . . 32.00 40.00 — –

☐ **November 7–13, 1959,** issue #345, Jack Benny on cover . . . . 7.50 15.00 — –

☐ **December 12–18, 1959,** issue #350, Danny Thomas on cover . . . . 7.00 10.00 — –

☐ **January 9–15, 1960,** issue #354, Jane Wyatt on cover . . . . 17.00 23.00 — –

☐ **February 27–March 4, 1960,** issue #361, Robert Stack on cover . . . . 14.00 17.00 — –

☐ **May 7–13, 1960,** issue #371, Elvis Presley on cover . . . . 70.00 85.00 — –

☐ **June 11–17, 1960,** issue #376, Cast of Bachelor Father on cover . . . . 3.00 9.00 — –

☐ **August 13–19, 1960,** issue #385, Nick Adams on cover . . . . 32.00 40.00 — –

☐ **October 15–21, 1960,** issue #394, Carol Burnett on cover . . . . 17.00 23.00 — –

	Current Price Range		P/Y Average
☐ **January 28–February 3, 1961,** issue #409, Ron Howard on cover (as young boy—pre-"Happy Days")	17.00	23.00	–
☐ **May 27–June 3, 1961,** issue #426, Ronald Reagan on cover	27.00	35.00	–
☐ **July 1–7, 1961,** issue #431, The Flintstones on cover	22.00	29.00	–
☐ **December 16–22, 1961,** issue #455, Richard Chamberlain on cover	7.00	10.00	–
☐ **January 6–12, 1962,** issue #458, Vince Edwards on cover	10.00	14.00	–
☐ **March 10–16, 1962,** issue #467, Jack Paar on cover (he hosted "The Tonight Show" before Johnny Carson)	14.00	17.00	–
☐ **April 21–27, 1962,** issue #473, Connie Stevens on cover	14.00	17.00	–
☐ **November 10–16, 1962,** issue #502, Beverly Hillbillies on cover	14.00	17.00	–
☐ **December 12–18, 1964,** issue #611, Julie Newmar on cover	9.00	12.00	–
☐ **January 2–8, 1965,** issue #614, The Munsters on cover	18.00	23.00	–
☐ **March 6–12, 1965,** issue #623, David Janssen on cover	14.00	17.00	–
☐ **September 11–17, 1965,** issue #650, Fall Preview Issue (these are always a premium item for collectors	45.00	40.00	–
☐ **October 16–22, 1965,** issue #655, Red Skelton on cover	6.00	9.00	–
☐ **November 13–19, 1965,** issue #659, Joey Heatherton on cover	9.00	12.00	–
☐ **December 11–17, 1965,** issue #663, F Troop on cover	10.00	14.00	–
☐ **January 1–7, 1966,** issue #666, Carol Channing on cover	6.00	9.00	–

UNCLE SAM AND STATUE OF LIBERTY COLLECTIBLES

TOPIC: Uncle Sam and Statute of Liberty items are highly collectible, and rare, on the Americana market. Most items range from toys to posters, souvenirs o postcards.

ORIGIN: Uncle Sam originated in the 19th century, and became solidly established as a national symbol during the Civil War. Uncle Sam, as we know him oday, was created by Thomas Nast in his *Harper's Weekly* drawings, and lames Montgomery Flagg's World War I recruiting poster.

The Statue of Liberty was brought to America in 1876 as a gift from France. Next year, she will celebrate her 100th year of providing safe harbor to millions of Americans. For this gala event, she is currently receiving a much needed efurbishing.

COMMENTS: Authentic Statue of Liberty and Uncle Sam items are extremely are on today's market. Be careful of careless reproductions and fakes. The next two years should provide a wealth of Statue of Liberty collectibles that will be cherished for years to come.

ADDITIONAL TIPS: For further information, please contact *The Statue of Liberty Commemorative Corp.;* their address is listed in the directory section of his book.

	Current Price Range		P/Y Average
] **Ashtray,** Uncle Sam, glazed china	50.00	70.00	62.00
] **Bookmark,** Statue of Liberty, silk, Paris, 1878	65.00	70.00	67.00
] **Commemorative Plate,** Statue of Liberty, Pickard China	150.00	—	—
] **Costume,** Uncle Sam, traditional cloth coat and pants, applied stars, painted straw hat, three pieces	50.00	100.00	76.00

	Current Price Range		P/Y Average
☐ **Doll,** Uncle Sam, bisque, c. 1890s	850.00	950.00	880.00
☐ **Doll,** Uncle Sam, papier mache and cloth, 20″, c. 1910	100.00	150.00	125.00
☐ **Fan,** Uncle Sam, with flag, paper	5.00	10.00	7.00
☐ **Mail Box Holder,** Uncle Sam, cut out wood, 75½″, c. 1920–1940	40.00	60.00	52.00
☐ **Model,** Statue of Liberty, bronze casting of original model, limited edition, 1985	2600.00	—	—
☐ **Sign,** Uncle Sam, carved and painted wood, flat, on a black base made of steel, 77½″	720.00	975.00	835.00
☐ **Whirligig,** United States, painted red, white, black and blue, wood, 10″	350.00	450.00	400.00

VALENTINES

ORIGIN: Valentines have been given for centuries. The first Valentines were handwritten and homemade statements of love and affection. Commercial Valentines were produced by the end of the 18th century.

MAKERS: Popular Valentine makers and companies include, Whitney, Taft, Strong, Tuck, Mansell, and others.

COMMENTS: Handmade Valentines are quite desirable and quite rare. Period Valentines are also sought after, such as those from the Civil War, Victorian era, or the World Wars.

ADDITIONAL TIPS: The listings are in alphabetical order according to country of origin, type of Valentine or company, depending on available information.

☐ **American,** heart shaped, lace, c. 1905	9.00	16.00	12.00
☐ **American,** honeycomb, "Cupid's Temple of Love," c. 1928	8.00	16.00	12.00
☐ **American,** Maggie and Jiggs, c. 1940	4.00	12.00	8.00
☐ **American,** Popeye, c. 1940	4.00	10.00	6.50
☐ **Art Nouveau,** heart shaped folder	4.50	6.50	5.50
☐ **Carrington,** folder, lace, c. 1937	1.50	4.50	3.00
☐ **Comic Valentine,** the "Hat Trimmer," Elton and Co., New York, illustration of glum-looking woman sewing hat, with verse, c. 1860	22.00	30.00	25.00

Valentine Postcard,
1911, $2.00-$3.00

	Current Price Range		P/Y Average
"Dainty Dimples" series, per card	3.00	8.00	4.00
Easel Valentine, fold back, free standing, c. early 1900s	34.00	44.00	38.00
German, 5 layer, pulldown, religious sentiment, flowers	50.00	67.00	55.00
German, large ship, mechanical pulldown	55.00	85.00	70.00
German, pulldown, children, c. 1915	5.00	11.00	6.50
German, pulldown, gold	11.00	21.00	15.00
German, pullout and stand up cottage, c. 1910	7.00	15.00	12.00
German, pullout and stand up steam boiler, c. 1910	13.25	19.00	14.00
German, stand up, little girl holding opening parasol	16.25	27.00	20.00
German, three layers, pulldown, lavendar, pink, gold, green, c. 1920	7.00	16.00	8.50
Gibson Art, paper doll mechanical stand up, little girl holding doll, German	20.00	35.00	27.00
"Hearts Are Ripe," children picking heart shaped apples from tree	3.00	7.00	5.00
H. Dobbs and Co., "Pillar Post," illustration of mailbox, c. 1800	22.00	27.00	23.50
"It Must Be Fine, To Have a Valentine," from "Valentine Wishes" series	7.00	12.00	9.00
"Lady Killer," comic valentine by A.J. Fisher, N.Y., c. 1850	29.00	39.00	33.00

	Current Price Range		P/Y Average
☐ **McLoughlin,** folder, no lace, c. 1905	5.00	12.00	7.00
☐ **McLoughlin,** three layer, silver, white, lace, c. 1880	5.00	12.00	7.50
☐ **McLoughlin,** three layer, white, gold, lace, c. 1880	5.00	12.00	7.50
☐ **Mansell,** lace, handwritten verse, c. 1846	75.00	100.00	85.00
☐ **Mansell,** lace paper, lovers in a park, heavily ornamented, white with silver, c. 1855	44.00	54.00	48.00
☐ **Mansell,** cameo embossing, two lovers walking along woodland path, c. 1845	39.00	49.00	43.00
☐ **Mechanical,** set of fifteen, c. 1920	34.00	44.00	38.00
☐ **Mechanical,** "Such is Married Life," c. 1850 ..	39.00	49.00	43.00
☐ **Mechanical,** various animals, c. 1930	10.00	15.00	12.00
☐ **Mechanical,** Walt Disney character, c. 1930 ...	17.00	24.00	20.00
☐ **Meek & Son.,** Gibson Girl (from photo), surrounded by lace in various ornamental patterns, cherub heads, c. 1890	54.00	65.00	58.00
☐ **Meek,** layered folder, lace, c. 1870	8.00	15.00	12.00
☐ **"Temple of Love,"** from Raphael Tuck's "Betsy Beauties" series, young girl chasing butterfly ..	5.00	9.00	7.00
☐ **"To My Valentine,"** from Raphael Tuck's "Innocence Abroad" series, two young children, brief verse	5.00	8.00	6.00
☐ **"To My Wife,"** embossed woman, hearts and flowers, cutout flowers tied with satin ribbon, real lace surrounds cutout heart, c. 1936	11.00	16.00	12.00
☐ **Tuck,** folder, heart shaped, little girl on front .	4.00	10.00	6.50
☐ **Victorian Valentine,** fold out, paper lace	20.00	25.00	22.00
☐ **Whitney,** embossed paper in pattern, a child delivering a note to a lady, with original embossed envelope, c. 1870	39.00	49.00	43.00
☐ **Whitney,** folder, lace, c. 1920	3.50	8.00	6.00
☐ **Whitney,** heart shape, World War I soldier valentine	5.00	13.00	8.00
☐ **Whitney,** three layer, Art Nouveau design, lace, gold, pink, rose, hearts, c. 1912	15.00	30.00	23.00
☐ **Whitney,** three layer, lace, Art Deco, children	4.50	6.50	5.50
☐ **Whitney,** three layer, lace, Art Nouveau	10.00	18.00	14.00
☐ **Whitney,** three piece, heart shaped, little girls	1.75	3.50	2.10

VAN BRIGGLE

DESCRIPTION: Van Briggle was one of the earliest and most successful art potteries in the west. Founded in 1901 and located in Colorado Springs, it acquired a grasp on the western market from Denver to San Francisco which nearly equaled the hold that Rookwood had on the east. Van Briggle's wares perfectly reflected the western taste. They weren't frilly or delicate like the Old World porcelains. Instead, they had a rugged charm. Their creative shapes suggested the gnarled limbs of old trees, driftwood, cactus, and other products of nature. They proved to be quite an influence on the potters of the east who adapted some of Van Briggle's innovative ideas into their own wares. Color used by Van Briggle also suggested the West. They included Mountain Craig (green to brown), Midnight (black), Moonglo (off-white), Persian Rose, Turquoise Ming, and Russet. In terms of its importance to the art pottery movement, Van Briggle stands very high. It continues in operation to the present day.

MARKS: The first and most famous mark used by this firm consisted of the letters AA, the initials of the first names of Van Briggle and his wife, Anne. It was used in conjunction with an incised mark reading VAN BRIGGLE, scratched by hand into the ware itself. The date of production usually accompanied these markings, and often (especially at a later period) a stock number. Sometimes, the word ORIGINAL appears along with the mark. HAND CARVED is likewise found, occasionally, along with the factory mark on pieces with raised decoration.

RECOMMENDED READING: For more in-depth information on Van Briggle pottery you may refer to *The Official Price Guide to Pottery and Porcelain* and *The Official Identification Guide to Pottery and Porcelain,* published by The House of Collectibles.

	Current Price Range		P/Y Average
☐ **Ashtray,** 5⅜″, rose, spiral interior	20.00	30.00	25.00
☐ **Ashtray,** 6¾″, trapezoid shape, turquoise ming	20.00	28.00	24.00

	Current Price Range		P/Y Average
☐ **Bookends,** pair, rams, red and blue glaze	130.00	140.00	135.00
☐ **Bowl,** 3″, acorn form, brown, c. 1915	140.00	160.00	150.00
☐ **Bowl,** 3″, rose, butterfly decor	60.00	70.00	65.00
☐ **Bowl,** 3½″, rose glaze, cherry, leaf and vine motif	80.00	90.00	85.00
☐ **Bowl,** 4″, flat, small base, brown, leaf motif across top, c. 1917	80.00	90.00	85.00
☐ **Bowl,** 4″, red, leaf motif across top, c. 1914 ..	30.00	40.00	35.00
☐ **Bowl,** 5″, rose, scalloped rim, flared ends	20.00	28.00	24.00
☐ **Bowl,** 5½″, green, floral and leaf motif	110.00	120.00	115.00
☐ **Bowl,** 6″, acorn and leaf motif across top, marked III	30.00	40.00	35.00
☐ **Bowl,** 6″, flat, yellow, leaf motif, c. 1903	450.00	480.00	465.00
☐ **Bowl,** 6″, rose, swirled ivy motif	32.00	38.00	35.00
☐ **Bowl,** 12½″, rose glaze, leaf motif	200.00	220.00	210.00
☐ **Bowl,** pattern #283, 10½″, small base flaring out to shoulder, shoulder slopes inward to rim, moonglo background, blue flower and stem motif, c. 1906	150.00	170.00	160.00
☐ **Bowl,** pattern #678, 2″, bulbous shape, band of berries and leaves across top, pink and green, c. 1908	140.00	160.00	150.00
☐ **Bowl,** pattern #903D, 8½″, frog and dragonfly motif, turquoise ming	65.00	75.00	70.00
☐ **Candlesticks,** 6″, pair, rose, double tulip motif	30.00	40.00	35.00
☐ **Conch,** 9″, turquoise ming, marked 42	30.00	40.00	35.00

Vase, Van Briggle,
Loreli Pattern,
$75.00-$85.00

	Current Price Range		P/Y Average
Creamer, 2", hexagon, turquoise ming	12.00	18.00	15.00
Cup, 3½", six incised panel lines, turquoise ming, c. 1917	30.00	38.00	34.00
Figurine, 3", elephant, on base, yellow and brown	30.00	40.00	35.00
Figurine, 4", donkey, turquoise ming	30.00	40.00	35.00
Figurine, 4", elephant, rose, triangular ears ...	70.00	80.00	75.00
Figurine, 4¼", elephant, turquoise ming, trunk raised	30.00	40.00	35.00
Figurine, 6", detailed girl grinding corn, on base, turquoise ming	30.00	40.00	35.00
Figurine, 8", cat, sits on base, tail curled around body, long neck	50.00	60.00	55.00
Figurine, 8½", rearing horse, on stand, brown	45.00	55.00	50.00
Figurine, 9¾", owl on stump, brown	275.00	300.00	287.50
Lamp, 18", flat base, narrow neck, running horse motif, red	65.00	75.00	70.00
Lamp, 20", bulbous base, narrow middle, bulbous top, moonglo	45.00	55.00	50.00
Mug, 4¾", unglazed, c. 1908	180.00	190.00	185.00
Ornament, 1978, 4", has word "noel" on front, limited to 1,000, natural glaze	27.00	32.00	29.00
Ornament, 1980, 3", oval, angel blowing trumpet, words "The Herald" on front, natural glaze, limited to 1,000	20.00	25.00	22.50
Paperweight, 3½", rabbit, green and brown ..	60.00	70.00	65.00
Pitcher, 3", moonglo	18.00	25.00	22.00
Pitcher, 3½", bulbous body, handled, collared neck, turquois ming, c. 1908	140.00	160.00	150.00
Pitcher, 11", bulbous base, slender body and neck, slender handle, turquoise ming	50.00	60.00	55.00
Planter, 9", blue, floral motif	32.00	42.00	37.00
Planter, 12½", rose shell form	47.00	52.00	50.00
Plaque, 4½", oval, rise glaze, Indian head design	50.00	60.00	55.00
Vase, 2", bulbous body, red, leaf and stem motif, c. 1919	50.00	60.00	55.00
Vase, 2", rose, c. 1918	80.00	90.00	85.00
Vase, 3", bulbous body, narrow neck, small opening, red background, blue butterfly motif, c. 1921	65.00	75.00	70.00
Vase, 3", flared rim, feather motif, turquoise ming	20.00	25.00	22.50
Vase, 4", rose, ivy and floral motif	30.00	40.00	35.00
Vase, 4", rose, tulip shaped, scalloped rim	15.00	25.00	20.00
Vase, 4", rose, c. 1917	135.00	145.00	140.00
Vase, 4½", rose, butterfly motif	80.00	90.00	85.00
Vase, 4¾", ivy and floral motif, turquoise ming	20.00	30.00	25.00
Vase, 5", bulbous body, collared neck, green, leaf motif, c. 1908	75.00	85.00	80.00
Vase, 5", rose, floral motif	28.00	35.00	32.00
Vase, 5", rose and green, floral motif, c. 1905	390.00	410.00	400.00

	Current Price Range		P/Y Average
☐ **Vase,** 5¼″, rose, heart shaped, ivy motif	30.00	38.00	34.00
☐ **Vase,** 7″, cylinder shape, collared neck, turquoise ming, c. 1916	240.00	260.00	250.00
☐ **Vase,** 8″, bulbous body, narrow neck, two handled, red and blue, leaf motif, c. 1920	45.00	55.00	50.00
☐ **Vase,** 8¾″, moonglow, bird of paradise motif	20.00	30.00	25.00
☐ **Vase,** 9″, rose, flower and leaf motif	65.00	75.00	70.00

VANITY FAIR LITHOGRAPHS

DESCRIPTION: Vanity Fair was a weekly periodical published in London from 1860 to 1914. Each issue featured a lithograph depicting an influential man or woman usually in a satirical fashion.

TYPES: The Vanity Fair lithographs covered every topic imaginable, from ambassadors and boxers to ministers and criminals.

PROCESS: Lithography is a printing process from which the image to be printed accepts ink while the blank area repels it.

COMMENTS: Two of the most famous Vanity Fair artists were SPY (Leslie Ward) and APE (Carlo Pilligrini).

ADDITIONAL TIPS: This section is arranged by topic followed by the name of the work, year produced, artist and price. For more information, consult *The Official Price Guide to Collector Prints,* published by The House of Collectibles.

	Current Price
☐ **Ambassadors From England,** Diplomacy, 1873, unsigned	18.00
☐ **Ambassadors from England,** Siam, 1879, artist SPY	18.00
☐ **Americans,** An Arbitrator, 1872, unsigned	20.00
☐ **Americans,** Captain, Tanner, Farmer, 1872, unsigned	26.00
☐ **Americans,** President of the New York, 1889, artist SPY	20.00
☐ **Americans,** The New President, 1913, artist HESTER	24.00
☐ **Automobile Devotees,** Steam, 1907, artist SPY	24.00

	Current Price
⬜ **Aviators,** The Deutsch Prize, 1901, artist GEO HUM	80.00
⬜ **Boxers,** A Good Lightweight, 1877, artist SPY	24.00
⬜ **Businessmen and Empire Builders,** Manchester, 1875, artist APE	18.00
⬜ **Businessmen and Empire Builders,** Long John, 1910, artist QUIP	24.00
⬜ **Businessmen and Empire Builders,** Sir Horace, J.P., 1909, artist SPY	18.00
⬜ **Clergy,** The Chief Rabbi, 1904, artist SPY	36.00
⬜ **Clergy,** A Fashion Canon, 1898, artist FTD	16.00
⬜ **Freemasons,** The Lord Mayor, 1902, artist SPY	14.00
⬜ **Game Hunters,** Pointers, 1885, artist SPY	30.00
⬜ **Horse Trainers,** Sollie, 1910, artist HCO	16.00
⬜ **Jockeys,** Top of the List, 1906, artist SPY	40.00
⬜ **Legal,** Dick, 1900, artist SPY	40.00
⬜ **Legal,** The Majesty of the Law, 1870, artist APE	40.00
⬜ **Literary,** Waterloo, 1883, artist T	20.00
⬜ **Music,** English Tenor, 1892, artist LIB	24.00
⬜ **Music,** Wagnerian Opera, 1899, artist, WAG	24.00
⬜ **Newspapermen,** New York Herald, 1884, artist NEMO	20.00
⬜ **Orientals, Li,** 1896, artist GUTH	20.00
⬜ **Photographers,** East Birmingham, 1902, artist SPY	36.00
⬜ **Policemen,** Criminal Investigation, 1883, artist SPY	18.00
⬜ **Politicians,** The Kent Gang, 1885, artist APE	14.00
⬜ **Politicians,** A Sticker, 1908, artist SPY	20.00
⬜ **Prime Ministers,** The Greatest Liberal, 1869, artist APE	20.00
⬜ **Red Robe Judges,** The Recorder, 1903, artist SPY	60.00
⬜ **Rowing,** Pembroke, 1888, artist, HAY	30.00
⬜ **Royalty,** Oh Child, Mayst Thou, 1905, artist GUTH	20.00
⬜ **Shipping Officials,** Plymouth, 1888, artist SPY	14.00
⬜ **Theater,** The St. James's, 1909, artist MAX	20.00
⬜ **Turf Devotees,** Bunny, 1876, artist SPY	20.00
⬜ **Turf Devotees,** Sundown Park, 1891, artist SPY	20.00
⬜ **Yachting Devotees,** Alisa, 1896, artist MILLER	20.00

WATCHES

DESCRIPTION: Collectible watches include both the pocket and wrist style. Fobs which attached to pocket watches are another valuable item.

TYPES: All types of watches are collectible, including 1930s Walt Disney character children's wristwatches, 1920s men and women's wristwatches and European pocket watches.

COMMENTS: Watches are available from antique dealers, pawnshops and flea markets. Even inoperative watches can be quite valuable after repair.

ADDITIONAL TIPS: Age, manufacturer, movement's complexity and accuracy, design and material are all factors which determine the value of a watch.

Purse Watch, *black enamel, opening and closing the sliding case winds the watch, face marked "Chronometer, Movado," silver, Swiss, c. 1930,*
$325.00–$425.00

	Current Price Range		P/Y Average
☐ **Pocket Watch,** size 12 Hamilton, 19 jewels, model 900, 14K yellow gold in mahogany box, arabic dial, floral seal on back	400.00	500.00	450.00
☐ **Pocket Watch,** size 16 Hamilton, 17 jewels, model 974, arabic dial with red 5's, case made of Illinois nickel, 1918	50.00	70.00	60.00
☐ **Pocket Watch,** size 18 Hampden, bridge model, gold train, 1904	35.00	45.00	40.00
☐ **Pocket Watch,** size 16 Ingersoll Buck, 1922 . .	13.00	17.00	15.00
☐ **Pocket Watch,** size 16 Ingersoll Yankee, 1933	16.00	20.00	18.00
☐ **Pocket Watch,** size 16 New England Scout, gun metal case with duplex movement	45.00	60.00	52.00
☐ **Pocket Watch,** size 18 Seth Thomas, Philadelphia silverode arabic dial, case, 1912	40.00	55.00	46.00
☐ **Pocket Watch,** size 10 Waltham, 7 jewels, gold filled floral train model, 1894	65.00	80.00	72.00
☐ **Pocket Watch,** size 12 Waltham Ensign, 7 jewels, roman dial, 1897	65.00	80.00	72.00
☐ **Pocket Watch,** size 6 Waltham Seaside, gold train model with roman dial and case, "warranted 20 years," 1902	75.00	95.00	85.00
☐ **Pocket Watch,** size 18 Waltham, leaver set, stem wind, 17 jewels, demascenced, roman dial, case, 1903	70.00	85.00	76.00
☐ **Pocket Watch,** size 11 Lignes Girard Perregaux, 15 jewels automatic, model 300 case, stainless	35.00	45.00	40.00
☐ **Wristwatch,** Bugs Bunny, made by Lafayette under license from Warner Brothers, colored dial, in display box	25.00	33.00	28.00
☐ **Wristwatch,** Mary Marvel, has copyright of Fawcett Publications and is made in Switzerland, picture of Mary Marvel on dial, 1948	125.00	150.00	135.00
☐ **Wristwatch,** Mighty Mouse, made in Switzerland, pictorial dial, red vinyl band, dates from 1960s	11.00	15.00	12.50

	Current Price Range		P/Y Average
☐ **Wristwatch,** Superman, made by Dabs under license from National Periodical Publications, child size, with wrist strip, boxed, mid to late 1970s	20.00	25.00	21.00

WATERFORD CRYSTAL

ORIGIN: Waterford, the most famous Irish glass, was made from 1783 until 1850. Produced at the Waterford Glass House, an establishment formed by brothers George and William Penrose, Waterford is known for its fine cutting, lovely clarity and design.

DESCRIPTION: Blank items were cut by a revolving iron wheel combined with sand and a water trickle. Cuts were then polished with a soft powder. After 1800 glass cutters used a wider variety of cutting strokes to make an even more brilliant product. Manufacturers most often marked their glass with raised words under the base; Waterford items are marked "Penrose Waterford." The color of Waterford is much whiter than other Irish glass, though it is often mistakenly thought to have a blue tinge.

PERIOD: Much Waterford was imported from 1790 to 1850 and popular import items were decanters, glasses, lamps, chandeliers, candlesticks and candelabra. However, the characteristic Waterford items, most often associated with Ireland and Irish glass, include covered vases and jars for food, large serving bowls, oil and vinegar bottles, glasses, jugs and salts.

A new company was started at Waterford in the late 1940s. Along with a variety of fine cut glass items, they also make some copies of the original Waterford pieces. The Waterford crystal listed here was produced during this period.

RECOMMENDED READING: For further information refer to *The Official Price Guide to Glassware,* published by The House of Collectibles.

☐ **Ashtray,** vesicas on sides, starcut base, 1¼″ high, 7″ diameter	20.00	60.00	35.00
☐ **Bowl,** fruit, spiked diamond panels flank cut-fans in reserves, notched rim, cut crescents, signed, 3½″ high, 8″ diameter	110.00	150.00	130.00

	Current Price Range		P/Y Average

Bowl, fruit, spiked diamonds with panels and thumbprints, tapered sides, signed, 4½″ high, 12″ diameter .... 70.00 · 130.00 · 100.00

Bowl, fruit, tapered sides, cut vesieas on sides and base, round shape, 3½″ high, 8″ long .... 80.00 · 110.00 · 90.00

Bowl, fruit, tapered sides, cut stars within a square design, notched rim, round shape, signed, 4″ high, 7¾″ diameter .... 45.00 · 85.00 · 65.00

Bowl, notched diamonds, notched and paneled edge, starcut design on base, oblong shape, signed, 4¼″ high, 13½″ long .... 80.00 · 130.00 · 100.00

Bowl, salad, cut diamond design, notched edge, starcut base on tapered base, signed, 4¼″ high, 10″ diameter .... 80.00 · 130.00 · 100.00

Bowl, salad, marquise shape with daisy and button motif, flared rim, cylindrical shape, signed, 3¾″ high, 9″ diameter .... 80.00 · 110.00 · 90.00

Bowl, salad, slanted sides, cut zigzag vesicas, starcut design on base, round, signed, 4″ high, 8½″ diameter .... 80.00 · 110.00 · 90.00

Bowl, wide diamond cut band, pinwheel cut in pedestal base, signed, 3″ high, 10¼″ diameter 80.00 · 120.00 · 90.00

Candlesticks, starcut design on bases, 6″ high .... 55.00 · 80.00 · 65.00

Compote, spiked diamond band, cut fans around scalloped rim, starcut design on base, signed, 5½″ high, 5½″ diameter .... 80.00 · 110.00 · 90.00

Compote, spiked diamond band with thumprint band, round, notched rim, notched base, signed, 6″ high, 7½″ diameter .... 130.00 · 160.00 · 140.00

Compotes, pair, notched thumbprint, lid has spiral finials, base is six-sided, 14½″ high .... 150.00 · 250.00 · 200.00

Decanter, cut diamonds with sunburst design, thumbprints, notched neck, starcut design stopper, signed .... 65.00 · 90.00 · 75.00

Decanter, paneled neck, base has cut sawtooth band, signed, 11½″ high .... 80.00 · 110.00 · 95.00

Dish, round shape spiked diamond bands, ball finial, starcut design on base, signed, 6″ high, 6″ diameter .... 55.00 · 80.00 · 65.00

Dishes, pair, star design in center, 3½″ diameter .... 35.00 · 50.00 · 40.00

Jar, marmalade, pedestal base, 6″ high ...... 55.00 · 75.00 · 60.00

Jar, starcut design on lid, cut crosses and panels, signed, 3¾″ high .... 90.00 · 165.00 · 125.00

Mug, notched sides, 4½″ high .... 55.00 · 70.00 · 60.00

Mugs, marquise shapes alternate with cane design in reserves, starcut design on base, signed, set of four, 4½″ high .... 90.00 · 160.00 · 120.00

Napkin Ring, cut diamond pattern .... 20.00 · 30.00 · 25.00

Vase, cut diamond design, cylindrical shape, 6″ high .... 35.00 · 55.00 · 40.00

Vase, cut diamond panels with tapered sides, cylindrical shape, 10″ high .... 80.00 · 130.00 · 100.00

	Current Price Range		P/Y Average
☐ **Vase,** fine panels of double shield form notching, cylindrical shape, signed, 8″ high	40.00	80.00	55.00
☐ **Vase,** trumpet shape, grid design formed from cut vesicas, starburst design on base, signed, 10″ high	110.00	150.00	130.00

WEATHER VANES

MAKERS: The two best known makers of weather vanes were Cushing and White of Waltham, MA, and the J. Howard Company of East Bridgewater, MA.

MATERIALS: Weather vanes are usually made of copper, sheet iron or wood.

COMMENTS: The most valued weather vanes are those handmade of sheet copper before 1850. These are mostly museum pieces. Most collectors seek factory made weather vanes of copper hammered in iron molds. These date to the 19th and early 20th centuries. Three dimensional weather vanes are rare. More common among collectors are silhouettes cut from sheet iron. Condition, beauty and rarity decide prices of weather vanes. Many reproductions have been made from original molds.

ADDITIONAL TIPS: The listings are alphabetical according to weather vane figure. A description, date and price range follow.

	Current Price Range		P/Y Average
☐ **American Eagle,** with spread wings mounted on wooden block	700.00	900.00	775.00
☐ **Automobile,** open roadster, intricate detail, heavy copper, gilded gold leaf, full bodies, 26″ L.	475.00	650.00	525.00
☐ **Automobile,** open top, complete with goggled old green patina navigator and driver, heavy copper, full bodied, 24″ L.	1050.00	1400.00	1150.00
☐ **Banneret,** banner pierced with a letter, applied decorations, sheet metal and copper, 19th century	700.00	900.00	750.00
☐ **Banneret and Scroll,** ornately gilded copper, 3′ L.	110.00	150.00	125.00

	Current Price Range		P/Y Average
Beaver, Quebec, made of tin, c. 1860	1250.00	1700.00	1400.00
Cannon, mounted on spoked gun carriage, reinforced barrel and stand, copper	200.00	275.00	215.00
Chicken, old decorations made of tin with iron rods	850.00	1200.00	950.00
Cow, mounted on 20½" arrow, 9½" L.	175.00	275.00	225.00
Cow, molded copper, weathered, 19th century	1900.00	2300.00	2000.00
Cricket, copper with red glass eyes	250.00	350.00	275.00
Crowing Cock, made of copper, 28½" L.	1200.00	1600.00	1400.00
Deer, running buck with curved antlers, full-bodied, copper, old green patina with traces of old gilt, 50" L.	335.00	500.00	400.00
Dog, full figure of a retriever, molded copper, c. 1870	3500.00	5000.00	4000.00
Donkey Cart, three men riding donkey cart, painted metal, 19th century	800.00	1000.00	875.00
Dragon, winged beast with snake-like tail, crouching on stand above scrolled direction indicators, 54" L.	250.00	350.00	300.00
Eagle, American eagle in flight, molded and gilded copper mounted on cast iron, 19th century	700.00	900.00	800.00
Eagle, hollow copper, spreadwing, 24" W., c. 19th century	1400.00	2000.00	1600.00
Eagle, clawed feet resting on ball, old green patina, 5' wing span	205.00	250.00	220.00
Eagle, perched on sphere, cast iron with directional lettering	1250.00	1750.00	1450.00
Eagle, spread in flight, wings and head tilted up, molded copper, 19th century	250.00	350.00	275.00
Fish, contemporary folk art, painted galvanized tin, 18" L.	60.00	80.00	70.00
Fish, copper, 26" L.	1050.00	1400.00	1150.00
Fiske Running Horse, black hawk #201, 33" L.	4200.00	6000.00	5200.00
Flag, unfurled 48-star banner with pointed standard	140.00	180.00	160.00
Fox, running, scrolled pointers, copper, full-bodied, 30" L.	210.00	280.00	235.00
Fox and Hound, hound chasing fox, full-bodied figures, molded copper, c. 1880	8000.00	10000.00	8500.00
Goose, cast iron, 23" wing span	750.00	1050.00	900.00
Grasshopper, molded copper and cast iron, 19th century	1200.00	2300.00	1600.00
Greyhound, long-legged animal standing on reinforced pedestal, ¾ full-bodied, green patina, 30" L.	197.00	250.00	220.00
Hackney Horse, full-bodied horse, in a prance, molded copper, 19th century	3000.00	4000.00	3500.00
Heraldic Arrowwith Loins, wrought iron with scrolling base	325.00	475.00	400.00
Horse, elegant standing horse, molded copper, 19th century	1900.00	2300.00	2000.00

	Current Price Range		P/Y Average
Horse, full-bodied in a trot, molded and gilded copper with some paint, 19 century	700.00	900.00	775.00
Horse, full-bodied, running, 19th century	650.00	850.00	750.00
Horse and Arrow, gold globe	375.00	500.00	425.00
Horse and Rider, hollow copper, directional roof finial	2600.00	3400.00	3000.00
Horse and Rider, silhouettes, rider has top hat and one arm raised, painted sheet metal	700.00	900.00	750.00
Horse and Sulky, running horse pulling cart, molded copper	700.00	900.00	775.00
Indian, full-bodied, detailed Indian chief with bow and arrow, molded copper, 19th century	700.00	900.00	750.00
Indian, profile of Indian with bow and arrow, painted sheet iron, 19th century	400.00	600.00	500.00
Locomotive with Tender, large model of late 19th c. railroad machine, full-bodied copper, 5' L.	350.00	450.00	300.00
Lion, large head with carved mane, copper, ¾ full-bodied, 4' L.	237.00	325.00	275.00
Peacock, full-bodied, copper, 19th century	2600.00	2900.00	2700.00
Pig, molded and gilded copper pig, c. 1880 ...	8500.00	10500.00	9000.00
Race Horse with Jockey, Kentucky thoroughbred, full-bodied copper, 32" L.	350.00	450.00	300.00
Railroad, engine car, painted sheet metal	675.00	875.00	750.00
Rooster, full-bodied copper, c. 1880	2250.00	2400.00	2300.00
Rooster, full-bodied game rooster, molded copper, c. 1880	1200.00	1700.00	1400.00
Ram, full-bodied, molded copper, 19th century	2700.00	3700.00	3000.00
Rooster, molded and painted copper, c. 1880	2700.00	3700.00	3000.00
Rooster, painted metal	450.00	600.00	500.00
Rooster, strutting, molded copper, 19th century	1200.00	1700.00	1400.00
Sailing Vessel, painted green	315.00	400.00	350.00
Standing Indian, original zinc finish, single direction indicator	480.00	600.00	515.00
Winged Horse, with arrow, carved wood	650.00	850.00	750.00

WICKER

DESCRIPTION: Wicker is the general term for pieces made of woven rattan, cane, dried grasses, willow, reed or other pliable material.

PERIOD: The wicker heyday in the U.S. was from about 1860 to 1930.

ORIGIN: Wicker can be dated to about 4000 B.C., when the Egyptians used it. The interest in wicker in the U.S. began in the 1850s.

MAKERS: Cyrus Wakefield and the Heywood Brothers were the best known wicker manufacturers. They later joined to become the Heywood-Wakefield Company. Other companies include American Rattan Company and Paine's Manufacturing Company.

COMMENTS: While 19th century wicker is more valuable, pieces from the 1920s and 1930s are also very collectible and easier to find. Natural finish wicker is most desirable and less common pieces are the most sought after.

ADDITIONAL TIPS: For more information on wicker, see *The Official Price Guide to Wicker,* published by The House of Collectibles.

	Current Price Range		P/Y Average
☐ **Basket,** sewing, natural finish, c. 1880	165.00	225.00	180.00
☐ **Basket,** sewing, natural finish, loop design on bottom shelf, crisscross weave on basket, c. 1880	250.00	325.00	275.00
☐ **Basket,** sewing, natural finish, rare curlicue and spool design on basket, large birdcage design at middle of brace, c. 1880	300.00	425.00	330.00
☐ **Chair,** fancy, white, often used as a photographer's chair, four rows of wooden beadwork in backrest and scrollwork at bottom right, c. 1890	675.00	850.00	700.00
☐ **Chair,** high, natural finish, c. 1880	250.00	325.00	275.00
☐ **Chair,** high, white, wooden tray and footrest, c. 1880	275.00	375.00	300.00

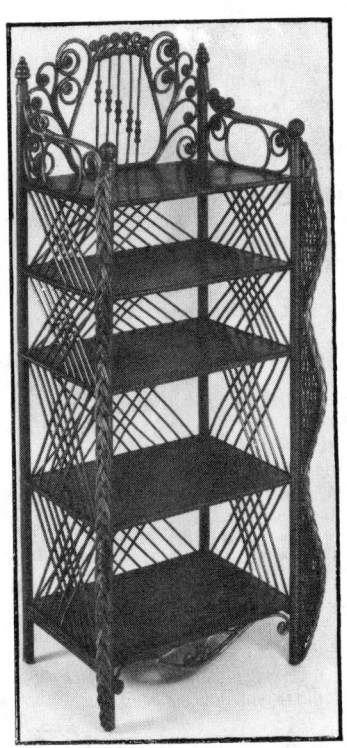

Music Stand, *natural finish, rare, lyre motif at top embellished with curlicues, reed latticework, thick braiding, turned wood frame, c. 1890s,* **$675.00–$900.00**
Photo courtesy of The Wicker Garden.

	Current Price Range		P/Y Average
☐ **Chair,** Morris, rare, serpentine arms and back, cushions, c. 1890	900.00	1200.00	1000.00
☐ **Chair,** piano, natural finish, rare, adjustable seat, birdcage design on back braces, turned wooden legs, c. 1880	500.00	700.00	550.00
☐ **Chair,** side chair, natural finish, intricate weaving and unique use of wooden beadwork set into the back, c. 1880	385.00	485.00	400.00
☐ **Chair,** side chair, natural finish, elaborate fancywork set into back panel, c. 1890	235.00	325.00	250.00
☐ **Chair,** side chair, natural finish, tall back employs canewrapped squares, birdcage design on back and legs, horizontally woven seat, c. 1880	200.00	285.00	230.00
☐ **Chair,** side chair, white, full circle shell-back design, woven reed seat, c. 1880	350.00	400.00	365.00

	Current Price Range		P/Y Average
☐ **Chair,** turkish, natural finish, closely woven arms and seat, wooden beadwork under arms and seat, c. 1890	325.00	400.00	340.00
☐ **Crib,** standing, natural finish, drop-side panel, flower motif set into headboard, c. 1870	1200.00	1500.00	1300.00
☐ **Crib,** swinging, natural finish, elaborate fancywork, canopy, c. 1890	1000.00	1400.00	1200.00
☐ **Doll Buggy,** natural finish, wickerwork emphasizes flowing design, silk parasol, wooden wheel has metal rims, c. 1880	350.00	450.00	375.00
☐ **Hanging Music Rack,** natural finish, elaborate scrollwork, c. 1880	225.00	350.00	250.00
☐ **Lounge,** natural finish, rare upholstered design, c. 1890	900.00	1500.00	1100.00
☐ **Rocker,** child's, natural finish, serpentine back and arms, wooden beadwork, c. 1890	200.00	300.00	225.00
☐ **Rocker,** platform, natural finish, curved backrest, serpentine back and arms, c. 1890	525.00	650.00	550.00
☐ **Rocker,** platform, white, serpentine, arms and arched platform, c. 1890	600.00	750.00	625.00
☐ **Rocker,** natural finish, chevron-shaped back panel, serpentine back and arms, turned wooden legs, c. 1890	275.00	375.00	300.00
☐ **Rocker,** natural finish, crisscross beadwork, serpentine back and arms, c. 1890	450.00	625.00	500.00
☐ **Rocker,** natural finish, leaf motif set into back panel, hand-caned seat, c. 1880	475.00	575.00	500.00
☐ **Rocker,** natural finish, spider-web caned back panel, c. 1880	275.00	350.00	300.00
☐ **Rocker,** white, banjo motif set into back panel, loop design on back and arms, c. 1880	400.00	575.00	450.00
☐ **Rocker,** white, circular braidwork, spider-web cane back panel, c. 1880	400.00	550.00	475.00
☐ **Sofa,** divan, natural finish, rolled backs and arms employ wooden beadwork, rosette arm tips, set-in cane seat, c. 1890	800.00	1000.00	875.00
☐ **Sofa,** settee, natural finish, serpentine back and arms, closely woven back panel, turned-wood legs, c. 1890	750.00	900.00	800.00
☐ **Sofa,** settee, white, peacock design dominates back panel, birdcage legs, c. 1880	950.00	1300.00	1000.00
☐ **Stand,** music stand, natural finish, oak shelves, beveled mirror, c. 1890	1500.00	2000.00	1700.00
☐ **Stand,** music, white, angled sides, two reed shelves, ball feet, c. 1890	250.00	350.00	280.00
☐ **Stand,** washstand, white, side towel racks, rustic design, tightly woven back, crisscross legs, c. 1880	350.00	500.00	400.00
☐ **Stool,** piano, white, circular woven reed seat, c. 1890	200.00	285.00	225.00
☐ **Stool,** ottoman, white, closely woven top, round rosette design on both ends, c. 1890	175.00	245.00	180.00
☐ **Table,** end table, white, large center birdcage design, c. 1890	225.00	325.00	260.00

	Current Price Range		P/Y Average
☐ **Table,** oblong table, white, wooden beadwork, c. 1890	285.00	350.00	300.00
☐ **Table,** round, white, cabriole legs, wooden beadwork frames top and bottom shelf, c. 1890	500.00	750.00	575.00
☐ **Table,** square, white, closely woven top, beadwork set into skirting, c. 1880	300.00	385.00	330.00

WOOD

TYPES: While many types of wood items are highly sought after collectibles, this section lists wooden kitchen utensils.

COMMENTS: Wooden utensils are most commonly made of maple. Other woods used include cedar, pine, hickory, ash and oak. Prices vary depending on item and type of wood.

ADDITIONAL TIPS: The listings are alphabetized according to item. For further information, refer to *The Official Price Guide to Kitchen Collectibles,* published by The House of Collectibles.

☐ **Apple Butter Bucket,** bail handle, c. 1850, 10″ long	110.00	140.00	120.00
☐ **Apple Butter Paddle,** paddle stirrer, perforated spatula, 60″ long	50.00	75.00	63.00
☐ **Apple Butter Paddle,** drilled holes, 30″ long ..	65.00	85.00	72.00
☐ **Apple Butter Scoop,** maple, c. 1850s	260.00	300.00	265.00
☐ **Apple Drying Rack,** open slats, three sided, legged, c. 1870	125.00	150.00	135.00
☐ **Apple Parers,** clamp, clank, two gears, drip board	200.00	225.00	210.00
☐ **Apple Peelers,** hardwood gears, c. 1700s	225.00	250.00	230.00
☐ **Apple Peelers,** crank handle, two size, belt driven gears	175.00	188.00	177.00
☐ **Apple Peelers,** wooden with iron gears, 7″ x 14″	170.00	200.00	178.00
☐ **Barrel,** nutmeg storage, enameled yellow, 4″ diameter.......................................	35.00	50.00	41.00
☐ **Barrel,** for pickles, staved, three concentric wooden bands, 12″ x 20″	35.00	60.00	40.00

Yarn Winder, *with counter,* $95.00

	Current Price Range		P/Y Average
☐ **Bandbox,** egg shaped, plain, 5″ long	70.00	95.00	83.00
☐ **Bread Peel,** poplar, long handle, mid 1800s, 54″ long	82.00	100.00	88.00
☐ **Bread Raiser,** with lid, tin, 12″ long	50.00	70.00	58.00
☐ **Broom,** flat, birch splint, bound with iron, spindled, maple handle	163.00	185.00	171.00
☐ **Broom,** oak splint	78.00	99.00	85.00
☐ **Bucket,** oak, for well	48.00	60.00	52.00
☐ **Bucket,** sap, 9¼″ diameter	150.00	175.00	160.00
☐ **Bucket,** mincemeat, lid, concave, 11″ diameter	88.00	105.00	93.00
☐ **Bucket,** sugar, floor standing, red	270.00	300.00	280.00
☐ **Bucket,** sugar, stave constructed, enameled, 13″ diameter	128.00	140.00	133.00
☐ **Bucket,** sugar, loop handles, lid, flat handle, c. 1890, 5″ diameter	175.00	200.00	179.00
☐ **Bucket,** water, one piece wood, side handles, rope bail	110.00	130.00	117.00

	Current Price Range		P/Y Average
Bucket, tin top, walnut, "S" shaped legs, 17" diameter	160.00	185.00	170.00
Bung Pusher, barrel, all wood, with lid and stem	15.00	24.00	19.00
Butcher's Block, sycamore, decoratively carved	720.00	750.00	730.00
Butter Churn, cylinder type, white cedar, one gallon capacity	62.00	80.00	68.00
Candlestick, adjustable stem, English, c. 1790, 8" high	1450.00	1560.00	1470.00
Candlestick, walnut, c. 1760, 6" diameter	300.00	340.00	314.00
Clothes Wringer, crank, handle and roller	18.00	30.00	22.00
Coaster, oak, English, c. 1810, 12" diameter	1100.00	1250.00	1150.00
Coaster, 18th century, treen, octagonal	225.00	260.00	235.00
Coffee Grinder, box type	90.00	110.00	97.00
Coffee Grinder, lap, oak	80.00	95.00	86.00
Coffee Grinder, lap, cherry box, brass fittings, crank	95.00	115.00	103.00
Coffee Grinder, lap type, handled, cherry	100.00	120.00	106.00
Coffee Grinder, wood, carved handle	70.00	89.00	76.00
Coffee Grinder, drawer, wooden base	85.00	100.00	92.00
Coffee Grinder, 19th century, wooden, French maker	82.00	110.00	95.00
Coffee and Spice Mill, c. 1760, 9" high	1300.00	1450.00	1355.00
Coffee Mill, hand crank, iron blade, storage box	60.00	80.00	67.00
Colander, wooden, circular, c. 1700s	280.00	310.00	291.00
Cookie Board, carved pattern, walnut, 8" long	70.00	90.00	78.00
Cookie Board, walnut construction, grape relief design, 9" long	20.00	30.00	22.00
Cookie Board, divided into squares, different molded design, 6" long	24.00	36.00	27.00
Lemon Squeezer, 11"	25.00	35.00	30.00
Lemon Squeezer, all wood construction, short handle, ridged press	22.00	31.00	25.00
Lemon Squeezer, on frame, indentation and drain holes, three turned legs, mid 18th century	150.00	250.00	120.00
Lemon Squeezer, hinged, all wood	30.00	45.00	35.00
Lemon Squeezer, hinged, wood frame, wood and ceramic, hinged, press is perforated	30.00	45.00	33.00
Lemon Squeezer, wood and tin, hinged, perforated	30.00	43.00	33.00
Lemon Squeezer, wood and nickel alloy, juicer is perforated	35.00	50.00	41.00
Lemon Squeezer, wooden, on stand, 14" x 9"	113.00	138.00	118.00
Lemon Squeezer, 8" long	52.00	68.00	56.00
Lemon Squeezer, 9" long	62.00	78.00	67.00
Mortar and Pestle, bird's eye maple, early	80.00	100.00	88.00
Muffineer, Tunbridge ware, c. 1790	180.00	210.00	195.00
Noggin, wood, carved decor, 8" high	175.00	210.00	195.00
Noodle Board, wooden circle with paddle handle, 24" long	82.00	96.00	85.00

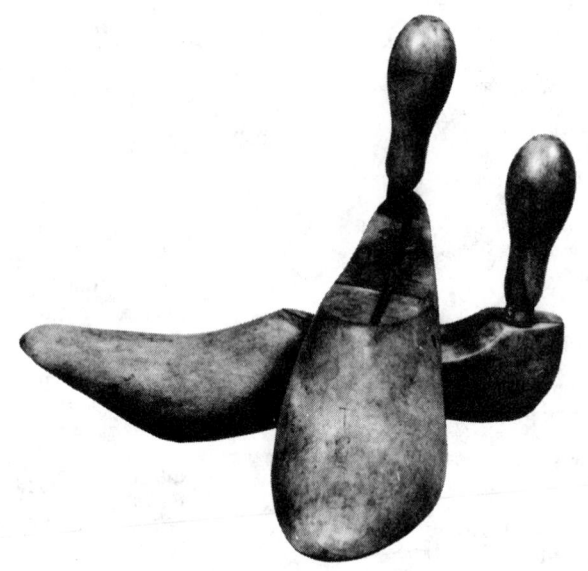

Wooden Shoe Trees, *pair*, $5.00

	Current Price Range		P/Y Average
☐ **Noodle Roller,** maple, perforated crank, c. 1840, 21″ long	67.00	99.00	70.00
☐ **Noodle Rolling Pin**	15.00	25.00	18.00
☐ **Notion Cabinet,** oak counter, pegged construction, framed compartments	495.00	525.00	512.00
☐ **Nutcracker,** bear's head, 9″ long	70.00	85.00	73.00
☐ **Nutcracker,** wood with iron presses, c. 1650, 5½″ long	350.00	380.00	363.00
☐ **Nutcracker,** large size, c. 1750, 10″ long	190.00	215.00	200.00
☐ **Nutcracker,** 18th century	225.00	250.00	231.00
☐ **Toddy Stick,** pestle style, hand carved, turned wood	12.00	20.00	14.00
☐ **Toddy Sticks,** early 19th century	20.00	42.00	32.00
☐ **Washtub,** oak slats, natural varnish, 23″ long	75.00	100.00	82.00
☐ **Whisk Broom,** Fuller Brush Company, 8″ long	45.00	60.00	50.00
☐ **Wooden Box,** Shaker	200.00	230.00	210.00
☐ **Wood Frame Churn,** windmill paddles, side turn handle, 15″ high	220.00	250.00	230.00
☐ **Wooden Shovel,** grain	285.00	310.00	295.00
☐ **Wood Churn,** staved, dasher, four gallon capacity	225.00	260.00	238.00
☐ **Wooden Wash Bowl,** chestnut, c. 1790	145.00	170.00	155.00
☐ **Wool Comb,** carved handle, 13″	15.00	30.00	20.00

	Current Price Range		P/Y Average
❏ **Yarn Winder,** box-type, spindle suspended on spike over box, turns in circular motion, 18″ ...	30.00	50.00	40.00
❏ **Yarn Winder,** duck feet	110.00	135.00	120.00
❏ **Yarn Winder,** floor model, spindled legs, yard counter, knobbed end	90.00	120.00	103.00
❏ **Yarn Winder,** maple	115.00	140.00	120.00

WORLD'S FAIR COLLECTIBLES

DESCRIPTION: World's Fair collectibles are items issued in conjunction with World's Fairs.

TYPES: The types of items produced are numerous and include booklets, ashtrays, fans, postcards, letter openers and keychains.

ORIGIN: The first large fair held in America was the Centennial of 1876. It was followed in 1892 by the Columbia Exposition which was held in Chicago.

❏ **Ashtrays,** New York World's Fair, 1964, set of three, metal, each pictures the Unisphere accompanied by different scenes in full color. trimmed in gold, 4″ diameter	3.50	5.00	4.10
❏ **Coaster,** New York Worlds's Fair, 1939, sirocco, pictures Administration Building in relief, 4″ ...	4.00	6.00	4.90
❏ **Commemorative Coin,** Columbian Exposition, 1892, silver 25¢ coin, valid as legal tender in the U.S., picturing Isabella of Spain on front and kneeling figure on back, coin is dated 1893 as the fair ran two years an it was not issued until the second year. A quantity of 24,214 were produced. Price is for an "uncirculated" specimen showing no signs of wear	400.00	500.00	450.00
❏ **Lamp,** New York World's Fair, 1939, white	16.00	20.00	18.00
❏ **Official Guide,** New York World's Fair, 1939 ..	12.00	16.00	14.00

	Current Price Range		P/Y Average
☐ **Official Guide,** New York World's Fair, 1964, original edition for the opening season of the fair, published by Time, Inc.	9.00	12.00	10.50
☐ **Official Guide,** New York World's Fair, 1964, guide is the revised edition for the 1965 season, states "All New for 1965," published by Time, Inc.	9.00	12.00	10.50
☐ **Pillow Cover,** New York World's Fair, 1964, satin, pictures Unisphere and fair scenes, fringed	7.00	10.00	8.20
☐ **Plate,** New York World's Fair, 1964, pictures Unisphere	7.00	10.00	8.00
☐ **Salt Shaker,** New York World's Fair, 1964, pictures Unisphere	2.50	3.50	3.00
☐ **Tumblers,** New York World's Fair, 1964, set of 8, each commemorates a different building at the fair, 6⅝"	32.00	38.00	35.00

COLLECTIBLES FOR THE FUTURE

THE 1980s — COLLECTIBLES FOR THE FUTURE

By Charles J. Jordan

Charles J. Jordan, author of this special feature section of *The Official 1987 Price Guide to Antiques and Collectibles,* is a nationally known expert on collectibles, having appeared on 200 radio and television programs around the country on the subject of collecting. He is the author of *What To Save From the '80s,* published by Ballantine Books of New York. Mr. Jordan and his wife, Donna, serve as consulting editors for The House of Collectibles.

The future is here now. Never is that expression more true than when applied to the collectibles field. Literally, tomorrow's collectibles are all around us today. The challenge is recognizing what among the myriad of items that surround us will be the highly sought-after souvenirs of the '80s.

The nice thing about collecting is that it has a track record. Certain types of items, which surface from time to time, decade in and decade out, historically find welcome places in the hands of collectors. All one needs to do is look back at a copy of *Hobbies* magazine from the '30s to realize how long collecting has been ingrained in the American consciousness. Little did people then realize the potential worth of the Mickey Mouse wristwatch on sale at the local Five and Ten store in town for under a dollar. That same period, someone could have stopped by a music store and sought out a stack of up-and-coming recordings of the Glenn Miller Orchestra on Brunswick records. Miller was mired in relative obscurity at the time, but in just a few more years he would switch record labels and become a giant name during the big-band era. Today, Miller Brunswicks are actively sought by record collectors.

The point is, as you are reading these words, similar items are out there—"sleepers" to be awakened out of their state of collectible suspended animation by the unfolding events of the future. While it is all but impossible to recognize all the hottest items of tomorrow today, a little collecting know-how applied to the right areas could place you in an enviable position of having a head start on tomorrow. And, if you play your cards right, you can be a hero with your grandchildren, passing on to them a virtual time capsule of valuable objects.

In some cases, however, you need not wait that long to see the toils of your efforts gain in value. Numerous objects which have been produced since 1980 either through design or by error, are already commanding good stipend money. Most, however, are far from reaching their full maturity and can still be had for a reasonable amount of cash out-of-pocket. (Not all of these items have begun to experience value appreciation and, in those cases, the price listed represents the most recent retail purchase price available.)

This special section of The House of Collectibles' *The Official 1987 Price Guide to Antiques and Collectibles* offers you a glimpse ahead, with your passport to the future being the objects of today.

BASEBALL COLLECTIBLES

DESCRIPTION: The field of sports collecting is often considered as the third most popular form of collecting in the country, only behind stamps and coins. The average baseball collector is a male in his early 30s, although the field enjoys popularity among the widest age bracket seen in the collecting world today.

TYPES: The most popular forms of baseball collectibles are baseball cards, with an estimated half-million collectors actively accumulating gum cards today. Other forms of paper sports collectibles, such as game programs and back issues of sports periodicals, show up in vast quantities at sports collecting shows. More affluent collectors go after actual objects from professional baseball, such as uniforms, baseballs signed by players, bats, and other artifacts associated with the great names in baseball. During the '80s, the porcelain limited edition field made great inroads into the sports collecting world through a series of successful autographed collector plates featuring leading players.

COMMENTS: The 1980s have seen two major developments that will be collected by sports enthusiasts in the years to come: the 1981 baseball strike and the emergence of Pete Rose as a bonafide sports immortal after surpassing Ty Cobb's hits record in 1985.

ADDITIONAL TIPS: When dealing with baseball cards, remember to look for error cards—hastily produced gum cards which spell the name of a player incorrectly, feature the wrong player beneath a name, or contain statistical inaccuracies. After a Federal Court ruled that the king of card producers, Topps, was monopolizing the major-league market and consequently opened the doors in 1981 to allow other producers, chiefly Fleer and Donruss, to enter the field, many errors resulted as the two producers rushed to get their cards out to collectors. Also, rookie cards, picturing players who come out of the gate strong, are good areas of speculation.

	CURRENT PRICE RANGE	
□ **Dwight Gooden Rookie Card,** Topps, 1985, sold in gum pack for 35 cents	5.00	
□ **Fernando Valenzuela Rookie Card,** first season was 1981	2.00	
□ **Glenn Hubbard Card,** Fleer, 1985, unusual card picturing Hubbard with boa constrictor wrapped around his shoulder	1.00	3.00
□ **Graig Nettles Error Card,** Fleer, 1981, part of regular series sold in pack of 17, third baseman for the New York Yankees, incorrectly identified as "Craig." Mistake was corrected during printing, but one out of every 33 cards distributed contained the misspelling of his first name	5.00	8.00
□ **"I Survived the 49 Day Baseball Strike" T-shirt,** white with red letters, features the words "49 Day" within a baseball . .	10.00	12.00
□ **Pete Rose Ceramic Baseball Card,** measures 3¼" x 5", outlined in platinum, manufactured by Gartlan Associates, Huntington Beach, California. Total of 4192 personally autographed by Rose	39.00	
□ **Pete Rose Ceramic Plaque,** titled "Desire to Win," measures 8½" x 10", with wood frame, manufactured by Gartlan Associates, Huntington Beach, California. Total of 4192 personally autographed by Rose	75.00	
□ **Pete Rose Collector Plate,** titled "The Best of Baseball" by artist Ted Sizemore, trimmed in platinum, manufactured by Gartlan Associates, Huntington Beach, California. Total of 4192 personally autographed by Rose	100.00	
□ **Pete Rose Porcelain Figurine,** created by Hal Reed, measures 6¾" supported by wood base, manufactured by Gartlan Associates, Huntington Beach, California. Total of 4192 personally autographed by Rose	125.00	
□ **Reggie Jackson Collector Plate,** 1982, art by Christopher Paluso, manufactured by Hackett American of Huntington Beach, California. A total of 10,000 individually numbered plates. Jackson autographed 464 (for special "Home Run" series). First baseball player on collector plate, signed $100, unsigned $60	60.00	100.00

BROOKLYN BRIDGE

DESCRIPTION: In May of 1983, the Brooklyn Bridge, once heralded as "the eighth wonder of the world," marked its 100th anniversary. The occasion saw a rush of centennial items hit the market which added credence to the old expression about "buying the Brooklyn Bridge."

TYPES: Editions of New York papers dated May 25, 1983, and commemoratives ranging from T-shirts and posters to a $2000 diamond-studded, gold-plated bridge pin are among the items which were hawked during the centennial.

COMMENTS: While the Brooklyn Bridge is world-renowned, having been at the time of its construction the largest suspension bridge in the world, it is especially revered by New Yorkers. Consequently, the highest prices which will forever be paid for Brooklyn Bridge memorabilia will be by New York collectors. By the same token, a good place to sell Brooklyn Bridge collectibles you might have is in the classified section of a New York newspaper.

ADDITIONAL TIPS: In the case of '80s Brooklyn Bridge souvenirs, look for the limited edition items to appreciate the most rapidly in number. Among these are top-dollar items, like original silk-screened centennial posters signed by Andy Warhol (priced for $1500) and pieces of the original granite and cable removed from the Brooklyn Bridge during renovation and marketed during the anniversary.

	CURRENT PRICE RANGE	
☐ **Brooklyn Bridge Granite,** measures 2½" x 2" x ¼", manufactured by Bridgestone Corporation in 1983. Actual piece of bridge's anchorage granite, each stone carried a "diamond-engraved" black and bronze plaque and came packaged in a gift box bearing the official seal of the Brooklyn Bridge Centennial Commission	14.95	
☐ **Brooklyn Bridge Poster,** measures 34 ¼" x 22", manufactured by Dover Publications, Inc., Mineola, N.Y. in 1983. Includes reproduction of two 19th century views of the bridge and sold as a promotional piece for Mary J. Shapiro's *A Picture History of the Brooklyn Bridge*	7.00	10.00
☐ *New York Post,* May 25, 1983 edition, marking the centennial of the Brooklyn Bridge with headline reading "Happy Birthday!"	2.00	4.00

CABBAGE PATCH DOLLS

DESCRIPTION: There are two forms of Cabbage Patch dolls being collected: the original dolls made and signed by their creator, Xavier Roberts and sold through his Cleveland, Georgia shop called Babyland General Hospital, and the mass-marketed dolls produced by Coleco. Both forms of these popular additions to 1980 toy boxes are commanding premium prices and are the subject of column after column of classified advertising in leading collecting journals.

TYPES: The success of Cabbage Patch dolls from the start has been the pitch that no two dolls are exactly alike. Roberts originals were different, as each was handmade, whereas Coleco accomplished this through computerization. Variations came in the form of color of hair, eyes, skin, addition of freckles, glasses, teeth, lack of hair, style of clothes, and placement of dimples—just like real kids.

COMMENTS: No other toy of the 1980s enjoyed greater popularity than Cabbage Patch dolls. This is fueled by the fact that the dolls were being purchased not only for children, but by adults, for themselves, as well. Industry spokesmen agree that the Cabbage Patch Kids are the biggest thing to hit the doll industry since Barbie and Ken.

ADDITIONAL TIPS: Just like retaining the pedigree papers for a thoroughbred show dog, it is important that individual adoption papers (another of Roberts' ideas carried through by Coleco) remain with dolls. The dolls were the hottest items in toy stores during Christmas 1983; consequently dolls from this year, when news of parents efforts to acquire them made headlines, can be expected to command higher prices with each passing year.

	CURRENT PRICE RANGE
☐ **Cabbage Patch Kids Boy Doll,** manufactured by Coleco in 1985, described as "bald, big ears."	65.00
☐ **Cabbage Patch Kids Freckled Girl Doll,** manufactured by Coleco in 1983	175.00
☐ **Cabbage Patch Kids Magazine,** premier issue, winter 1985. Published by Butterick Company, Inc., New York	2.50
☐ **Cabbage Patch Kids Twins,** manufactured by Coleco in 1985, with pacifiers	150.00
☐ **Xavier Roberts 1981 Cabbage Patch Boy Doll,** signed by its creator	450.00

COMIC BOOKS

DESCRIPTION: Comic books enjoy an immense popularity with collectors who attend numerous comic book conventions held all over the country yearly. Here they attend seminars held by noted cartoonists, as well as buy, swap, and sell favorite titles. Most comic books on the secondary market are moderately priced.

TYPES: Super hero comics, including the long list of active titles being produced by Marvel and DC comics, remain a staple among serious collectors. Comics based on popular movies and television series are also popular.

COMMENTS: During the 1980s, comic books became more aware of the world around them. Women super heros made important inroads in the field through the emergence of characters like the She-Hulk, as well as the Dazzler—who fights crime while wearing disco roller skates. A popular woman comic character from the past, Katy Keene, the fashion queen, was revived by Red Circle Comics Group in the '80s. Another trend was the unusual appearance of famous religious personages appearing in a series of comics produced by Marvel.

ADDITIONAL TIPS: During the decade, efforts were made to revive 3-D comics, which originally enjoyed considerable popularity in the 1950s. As comics from that period now command anywhere from $60 to $200 in top condition, it would be wise to pick up a cache of some of the new versions around today—but be sure to save the glasses as well.

	CURRENT PRICE RANGE	
☐ **Battle for a Three-Dimensional World,** published by 3D Cosmic Publications, North Hollywood, California, in 1982. Included 3D glasses. Art by Jack Kirby, written by Ray Zone	2.00	4.00
☐ **Dazzler,** published by Marvel Comics Group, New York, in March 1981, Vol. 1, No. 1	1.25	2.50
☐ **Katy Keene Special,** published by Red Circle Comics Group, New York, in September 1983, Vol 1, No. 1. Comprised of reprints from the original series spanning 1950–1961	1.00	1.50
☐ **Mother Theresa of Calcutta,** published by Marvel Comics Group, New York, in 1985. The reporter is back and this time Mother Theresa is his beat.	1.25	1.75
☐ **She-Hulk,** published by Marvel Comics Group, New York, in February 1980, Vol. 1, No. 1	1.00	2.00
☐ **The Life of Pope John Paul II,** published by Marvel Comics Group, New York, in 1982. Details the life of the Pope through the eyes of a newspaper reporter	1.50	2.00

ELVIS PRESLEY

DESCRIPTION: During his lifetime (1935–1977), Elvis Aaron Presley was known as "The King of Rock 'n' Roll." His popularity has continued even after his death, evidenced by the wide assortment of merchandise which accompanied the 50th anniversary celebration of his birth in January of 1985.

TYPES: RCA Victor released a couple of special promotional records during the decade, which saw limited circulation. Limited-edition collector items, including collector plates, whiskey decanters, and watches, were among the assortment of items produced in conjunction with the golden anniversary of Presley's birth.

COMMENTS: There are 94 active Elvis Presley fan clubs in existence around the globe today. Most of the original Presley fans are presently in their early to mid-40s—a prime expendable income age bracket. Consequently, the value of Presley memorabilia can expect to peak over the next five years.

ADDITIONAL TIPS: As Presley achieved fame through his records, collectors of Presleyana say that recordings remain the prime items to be had. Look for RCA Victor to continue releasing new Presley never-before released recordings from time to time, as well as devising new ways to repackage previously released recordings.

**CURRENT
PRICE RANGE**

☐ **Elvis Commemorative Gold Watch,** issued to mark Presley's 50th birthday by Bradley Time of New York, in 1985. Timepiece accentuated with a relief portrait of Elvis cast on gilt finish "coin" set in 18-karat gold case. Available in either mens' or ladies' models produced in limited editions consisting of 1,985 each **1985.00**

☐ **Elvis Doll,** vinyl, 19"-doll attired in white suit with gold trim, white boots and colored scarf. Accessories included a finger ring, belt buckle, and hand-held microphone. Made by World Doll, Inc., of New York, ...   **90.00**

☐ **Elvis Doll,** made by World Doll, Inc., of New York, N.Y. Measures 17" high with porcelain head, hands, and legs, with a "poseable" body. Doll attired in a gold lamé suit and gold boots. Each was numbered as part of a limited edition **225.00**

☐ **Elvis Doll,** made by World Doll, Inc., of New York, N.Y. All porcelain figure and measures 17" high, costumed in an "Aloha Hawaii" outfit studded with rhinestones, a diamond in the belt buckle, and scarf from Presley's personal wardrobe. Only 750 numbered pieces were produced, and each came with an authentic ticket from Elvis Presley's last concert **2500.00**

☐ **Record, 45 rpm,** The Impossible Dream/American Trilogy, white record sleeve with word "Elvis" on it. Produced by RCA Victor and given away free at the Elvis Presley home in Tupelo, Mississippi, in August 1982. Only 7500 copies were given away, and this record was never commercially released **200.00   300.00**

☐ **Record, 45 rpm,** Baby, Let's Play House/Hound Dog, first record to carry the "Elvis 50" logo on it. Produced by RCA Victor in August 1984. Record sleeve showed Elvis Presley appearing at the Mississippi-Alabama Dairy Show in September 1956. Record pressed on gold vinyl, and 12,000 were sold in Tupelo and Memphis before the record company halted further distribution due to poor sound quality. Not reissued **25.00   30.00**

☐ **Special Issue Commemorative Plate,** features montage of Presley images, trimmed in 24-karat gold. Limited to an edition of 10,000. Produced by Nostalgia Collectibles, North Brook, Illinois, in 1985 ....   **45.00**

HALLEY'S COMET

DESCRIPTION: It was the most anticipated celestial event of the decade, but due to unfavorable conditions, the sight of Halley's Comet making its return trip to the earth was something most of us missed. Nevertheless, the once-every-76-years occurrence will be most remembered for the hype it received via the mass-media, as well as through a multitude of Halley's Comet mementoes pushed onto the market.

TYPES: Most of these were the products of a few ambitious companies. These included commemorative coins, bumper stickers, T-shirts, tote-bags and reproduction Comet Pills. A rash of comet-related books were published during the mid-'80s.

COMMENTS: As could be expected, the visit by Halley's Comet in 1985–86 had Americans looking back at items produced during the famous comet's last visit to our skies in 1910. Items which became most desirable were those which saw local distribution, such as legendary bottles of Comet Pills sold to the gullible, at the time, in various corners of the country, guaranteeing protection from the "poisonous gases" as the comet swept by.

ADDITIONAL TIPS: The most desirable items of the '80s will be those which saw similar limited or localized distribution, such as clever promotional tie-ins ("Comet Madness Sales" signs from stores and car dealerships, for example), local newspaper articles containing recollections of the comet's 1910 visit by senior citizens, and brochures on comet programs at local planetariums.

	CURRENT PRICE RANGE
☐ **Booklet,** *Mr. Halley's Comet,* published in 1984 by Sky Publishing Corporation, Cambridge, MA. Billed as "Everyone's Complete Guide to Seeing the Celestial Event."	2.00
☐ **Bronze Medallion,** measures 1.5″ and bears a phrase which translates from Latin as "Save us from the evil of the comet." Marketed by Halley's Comet Watch '86	12.00
☐ *Also was offered in silver for $32.50; in gold for $325.00.*	
☐ **Comet Halley Poster,** distributed by Halley's Comet Watch '86 of Vincentown, New Jersey, in 1985. Includes diagrams of orbit of comet and portrait of Edmond Halley	6.95
☐ **Drinking Glasses,** set of four, 12-ounce tumblers featuring a frosted Halley's Comet logo. Marketed by Halley's Comet '86, Vincentown, New Jersey	12.95
☐ **Halley's Comet Calendar,** commissioned by the Halley's Comet Society of London in a limited edition for 1985–86 and sold through Halley's Comet Watch '86 in Vincentown, New Jersey. Contains historic information of the comet, and includes illustrations with viewing information for each of the 24 months	9.95

MAGAZINES

DESCRIPTION: Few other forms of collectibles better document their times than magazines. Capturing the tenure of the day through their topical articles and vintage advertising, they are popular forms of printed memorabilia.

TYPES: Among the more popular traditional periodicals with collectors are pictorials, news weeklies, travel journals, satirical and humor magazines, and men's magazines, as well as those which cover the motion picture and entertainment world.

COMMENTS: Magazines continued to document the many aspects of life during the '80s with an increasing number of specialty periodicals hitting the newsstands. The decade has also seen a goodly amount of parody publications emerge, poking fun at everything from *TV Guide* to the *New York Times Book Review*. Given the penchant of popularity parodies have enjoyed with collectors, the bumper crop of magazine mimmicks should fare well in the future.

ADDITIONAL TIPS: More often than not, the most important factor in determining the value of a magazine is what appears on its cover. Pictures of Presidents, sudden disasters, leading motion picture personalities, and anniversary issues (including, during the '80s, observing the 20th anniversary of the Kennedy assassination and Beatlemania) are surefire good bets. Celebrated typographical errors, especially if made on a cover, generate a lot of interest as conversation pieces with magazine buffs. Also, on occasion, a magazine makes use of a publishing gimmick, such as when *National Geographic* ran its first holographic cover in 1984. These also are earmarked for future value.

	CURRENT PRICE RANGE	
☐ *National Geographic Hologram Cover,* March 1984 issue. First of its kind showing a laser-sculpted image of an eagle. Run in conjunction with stories on lasers and holography ...	10.00	
☐ *National Geographic Hologram Cover,* November 1985 issue. The magazine's second holographic cover shows a skull dating back one to two million years. Published in conjunction with an article entitled "The Search for Early Man."	8.00	
☐ *Not Quite TV Guide,* parody published by Crown Publishers Inc., New York, in 1983	3.95	
☐ *Penthouse Magazine, Vanessa Williams,* September 1984 issue. This is the issue which contained nude pictures of the reigning Miss America and led to her forfeiting her crown ...	6.00	8.00
☐ *Time Magazine Error Cover,* March 13, 1983 edition containing a typographical error in a teaser headline in the upper right-hand corner of its cover: the "r" from the word "Control" is missing in the line "A New Plan For Arms Control." Error copies were replaced with corrected editions, and only a few were known to have reached the public's hands	40.00	50.00

MICHAEL JACKSON

DESCRIPTION: One of the 1980s pop music superstars, Michael Jackson, began as a child lead singer for a group consisting of he and his brothers, the Jackson Five. During the early '80s, Michael emerged as a star in his own right, breaking numerous music industry records with his smash solo album, "Thriller," released in 1983. During the height of Jacksonmania, he was called "the greatest thing to hit the pop-music spinoff market since the Beatles."

TYPES: Beside the compulsory posters, buttons and T-shirts, Jacksonmania also brought forth numerous variations of the single white glove Michael adopted as his trademark. There was also a much publicized doll, as well as postage stamps issued by the British Virgin Islands honoring Jackson.

COMMENTS: As a gauge of Jackson's popularity, mementoes associated with him made it all the way to some of New York's venerable auction galleries, commanding substantial closing bids.

ADDITIONAL TIPS: During 1985, Jackson dropped out of sight for the most part. At that time, Jackson memorabilia could be had for a song. He finally made it back into the charts early in 1986 with the release of his third solo album. In view of Jackson's remarkable impact on music during the early '80s, Jackson's place in the collectibles future seems secure.

	CURRENT PRICE RANGE	
☐ **Autographed Glove,** brought up for bids by Charles Hamilton Galleries of New York on November 29, 1984. Listed as lot number 107 and identified as "White Glove Autographed by Michael Jackson." Reportedly signed by Michael and his brother, Jermaine, after being presented to Michael by his personal elevator operator at a New York hotel.	250.00	300.00
☐ **Michael Jackson Doll,** produced by LJN Toys of New York, N.Y. in 1984. Measures 12″, and is attired in his Grammy Awards outfit, including sequin glove and socks, and holds a microphone	8.00	10.00
☐ **Michael Jackson Poster,** measures 45″ x 35″, produced in 1982 by CBS Inc. Issued to record stores to promote the release of his album "Thriller." Shows Michael reclining in white suit with tiger cub on knee	20.00	30.00
☐ **Michael Jackson Stamps,** issued by the British Virgin Islands in 1985, consisting of a set of eight postage stamps depicting Jackson	4.00	6.00
☐ **Promotional Award for "Thriller",** sold in June 1985 at Sotheby's in New York. Consists of a platinum album surrounded by three gold rpm's and a letter written by Jackson, all encased in a plexiglass frame with a photo of the pop star	2200.00	

NEWSPAPERS

DESCRIPTION: In times of national or international events of sudden magnitude, the very first thing people gravitate toward are those tangible chroniclers, newspapers. While national newspapers featuring banner headlines usually command the best prices, often state or local papers are more desirable if they detail a local story of national interest (such as Washington state papers covering the eruption of Mount St. Helens in May of 1980).

TYPES: Other than banner headline stories, other collectible newspapers include final editions and error headlines.

COMMENTS: When saving a worthy paper, it is important to remember to retain the entire issue, as the front page story (such as the reelection of President Reagan in 1984) is jumped to the inside, or reflected in other stories within the paper. Collectors prefer entire editions. Also, storage of papers is crucial to their future value. Store papers flat and in an open position. Papers left folded in half will get a brown stain at the fold and diminish their value. It is preferable to store newspapers in a large acid-free box with a lid, which will not only protect them from the sunlight, but also diminish the chances of acidification.

ADDITIONAL TIPS: When a person hits the headlines in a big way, write to the newspaper in that individual's hometown or birthplace, asking to buy a copy. Many collectors realize that such papers will generate considerable interest in the future. When Ronald Reagan was elected President, *The Dixon Evening Telegraph* (Illinois) received so many requests for its November 5, 1980 edition, detailing Reagan's victory, that it was forced to go back on press. Dixon, it turns out, was Reagan's boyhood hometown.

CURRENT
PRICE RANGE

☐ *Chicago Sun-Times* Error, printed during the Republican National Convention in 1980. It prematurely (and inaccurately) announced a Republican ticket of Ronald Reagan for President and former President Gerald R. Ford for Vice President. (Former President Ford was never seriously interested, and George Bush was ultimately selected.) The *Call-Chronicle* of Allentown, PA printed a similar erroneous headline regarding a Reagan-Ford ticket 50.00

☐ *The New York Times,* dated November 7, 1984. Ronald Reagan was swept to victory via a crushing defeat of his Democratic opponent, Walter Mondale, yet *The New York Times,* showing its traditional restraint, announced "Reagan the Apparent Victor." 2.00   3.00

☐ *Washington Star,* final edition, dated August 7, 1981. With this edition, the newspaper ended 128 years of continuous service
.... 10.00   12.00

OLYMPICS

DESCRIPTION: Olympic memorabilia collecting is a truly international hobby, with active collectors situated in the far-flung corners of the globe. Olympic collectibles received a boost in this country during the 1980s as a result of the twenty-third Olympiad being held in Los Angeles, the first summer games held in the United States in more than a half-century.

TYPES: One of the most popular forms of collectibles are Olympic pins from the various participating countries, including mascot pins from the given games. Original printed materials produced for spectators of the games, such as programs, special passes, and tickets, are also prized by Olympics buffs. During the Los Angeles games, limited edition posters and collector plates enjoyed considerable popularity. These games also prompted the United States to issue its first gold coin in 50 years, a commemorative piece minted in honor of the event.

COMMENTS: The United States boycotted the 1980 Moscow Olympics and, as a result, very few items picturing the official mascot of the games, Misha the Bear, found their way into this country. The Los Angeles games unleashed an avalanche of merchandise bearing either that year's mascot, Sam the Eagle, or the official "Star in Motion" emblem of the twenty-third Olympiad.

ADDITIONAL TIPS: In wading through the mire of merchandise produced in connection with the Los Angeles games, specialists in this field advise collectors to go after the limited edition items. The best prices will be obtainable in the southern California area, as remains the case with items from the 1932 Los Angeles games. For people residing in that part of the country, the 1984 Olympics will be remembered as the biggest event of the 1980s.

	CURRENT PRICE RANGE	
☐ **Cap,** white with red trim on brim, made by Clossco Action Headwear, and features Sam the Eagle and words "Los Angeles" and "1984 Olympics"	4.00	6.00
☐ **Collector Plate,** "Tribute" plate, keystone of an eight-plate series produced by Rudy Escalera (selected by the L.A. Organizing Committee as official Commemorative Plate Artist of the twenty-third Olympiad. Plate features a collage of athletes in action, highlighting a woman torch-bearer	50.00	
☐ **Key Chain,** in the shape of Sam the Eagle, holding torch, measures 3 1/3" and bears the copyright of the Los Angeles Olympic Committee	1.00	3.00
☐ **Limited Edition Poster,** a 24" x 34" poster featuring a Robert Rauschenberg design using the 1984 Olympic Games' official symbol, "The Stars in Motion." It pictures a panorama of people, places, and events reflecting the contemporary world. Produced by Knapp Communications Corporation. Unsigned	30.00	
☐ **Limited Edition Poster,** same as the above, but signed by Rauschenberg as part of a limited edition series of 750	250.00	
☐ **Twenty-third Olympiad $10 Gold Coin,** issued in 1984, this was the first gold coin issued by the U. S. Mint in 50 years. Depicts male and female runners carrying the Olympic torch aloft	352.00	
☐ **Twenty-third Olympiad Silver Coin,** issued in 1983, "The Discus Thrower" is the first U. S. commemorative silver dollar issued for collectors since 1900	32.00	
☐ **Twenty-third Olympiad Silver Coin,** follow-up coin, depicting the Olympic structure that graces the entrance to the Los Angeles Coliseum	32.00	

PIECES OF HISTORY

DESCRIPTION: From time to time, items identified as actual parts of well-known landmarks, ships, spacecrafts, and such are marketed through the efforts of some clever entrepreneur. These items were often secured during renovation work and touted as the ultimate in "conversation pieces." The 1980s has produced a good number of them.

TYPES: These bits of history turn up, more often than not, encased in a paperweight. Others have been attached to posters, framed with appropriate art under glass or Lucite, or simply issued in its original form with information about the item attached directly to it or inscribed on a separate base.

COMMENTS: While most of these items appeal to the specialty collectors from the given areas of their origin (space exploration collectors would collect pieces of Skylab, for example), a few collectors (this writer being one of them) will collect any legitimate item billed as a piece of history.

ADDITIONAL TIPS: These artifacts appear like flashes in the pan in the collecting world. To acquire a goodly amount, a collector has to be fast on his feet and quick with his checkbook. Most are offered for a very short time, "while supply lasts," and once they are gone, usually the company which produced them is also.

	CURRENT PRICE RANGE
☐ **Genuine Piece of Golden Gate Bridge Cable,** marketed by a San Francisco outfit called "A Smith Called Bob." Cut to 3-inch lengths, the tightly wrapped pieces were painted orange, and delivered with a wooden display stand and certificate of authenticity	12.95
☐ **Portion of Hollywood Sign,** a total of 30,000 pieces were marketed by Hank Berger Enterprises, Inc., of Hollywood, CA. Each piece attached to descriptive print and framed.	29.95
☐ **Skylab Lucite Pyramid,** produced by P. S. Enterprises, Inc., of Pittsburgh, PA. Contains an authenticated Skylab fragment (approximately one inch square), suspended over the official Skylab mission emblem	65.00
☐ **Space Shuttle Tile,** produced in 1981 by Noble House of Cupertino, CA. Half-inch wafer taken from sheet of material used on first Space Shuttle. Packaged in foil-stamped plastic cases	7.75
☐ **State Street Paperweight,** manufactured by the Great Street Emporium of Oak Park, IL. Piece of Chicago's famous thoroughfare encased in leaded glass. Affixed to the base of each paperweight is a sepia tone of State Street as it looked in 1913	19.95

POLITICS

DESCRIPTION: A very popular form of collecting, Presidential memorabilia receives a boost of publicity once every four years via the massmedia. Political memorabilia during the 1980s centered largely on items from the 1980 Carter and Reagan campaigns, and the 1984 Reagan and Mondale campaigns.

TYPES: While buttons generate the greatest interest here, banners, bumper stickers, autographs, and other political accoutrements enjoy various degrees of interest with political buffs.

COMMENTS: Jimmy Carter memorabilia is far more common from his first Presidential campaign, in 1976, than seen during the 1980 election year, when Carter's popularity plummetted. Ronald Reagan items are more abundant from the 1984 campaign than those dated from 1980, largely because of Reagan's immense popularity nationally during his reelection bid. More supporters meant more paraphernalia produced and distributed.

ADDITIONAL TIPS: Buttons of a humorous nature, many which surface at the national conventions, are very popular with collectors. More information is available by writing to the Carter Political Items Collectors, P. O. Box 1414, Decatur, GA 30030, and the Reagan Political Items Collectors, Rt. 1, Box 258-B, Denison, TX 75020.

	CURRENT PRICE RANGE	
☐ **Anti-Mondale Button, "Fritzbusters,"** modelled after similar pins released to promote the 1984 film "Ghostbusters," which showed a cartoon of a ghost with a void symbol superimposed over it. The ghost on the Fritzbusters pin resembles Walter Mondale. Popular item at the Republican National Convention. Six-inch size.	10.00	
☐ **Democratic National Convention Button,** humorous. Button reads "How is the 1980 Democratic National Convention Like a Mount St. Helens Volcano?" Button came with an attached sack containing Mount St. Helens volcanic dust.	6.00	8.00
☐ **Jimmy Carter Knife,** medium size and white, showing a donkey and reading "Carter 1980." Produced by the Case Knife Company	30.00	40.00
☐ **Nancy Reagan Paper Doll Book,** published in 1983 by Dover Publications, Inc., of New York. Book features one cut-out doll and 31 fashions drawn by illustrator Tom Tierney	3.50	
☐ **"Teddy Kennedy" Bear,** a 1980 version of the venerable teddy bear, this item was produced by Wes Soderstrom of Woodland Hills, CA. Features life-like face of Massachusetts Senator, made of soft vinyl and traditional furry bear body.	49.50	

ROBOTS

DESCRIPTION: Robots have long been a favorite with collectors of toys and science fiction. During the 1980s, the robot market literally took a new twist with the advent of changeable robots—clever toys which start out looking like one thing (often a vehicle of some sort) and, with a couple of twists and turns of jointed parts, are transformed into something totally different, like a giant robot warrior.

TYPES: Three lines of changeable robots dominated the market during the 1980s: Hasbro's Transformers, the Tonka Corporation's GoBots, and Matchbox Toy's Voltron series. These toys, among the hottest items in toy stores at the mid-decade point, were available in many sizes and variations.

COMMENTS: Of the latest breed of robots, those likely to be the more difficult to acquire in the future will be the higher-priced models, such as the deluxe Voltron III, which retails for just under $60.

ADDITIONAL TIPS: The success of these forms of toys brought many spinoffs. The most successful, the Transformers, was the hottest in the licenses spinoff business, with Transformer clothes, boots, watches, and other items marketed. In December 1985, 51 different companies were producing 121 products bearing the Transformers logo. A small group of these would round out one's collection.

	CURRENT PRICE RANGE
☐ **GoBot Space Shuttle,** changes from spacecraft to robot. Made by Tonka in 1985	3.39
☐ **Transformer Dinobot,** changes from a dinosaur to a robot. Made by Hasbro in 1985	12.99
☐ **Voltron III Robot,** with articulated arms, flexible knees, and "human face." Produced by Matchbox in 1985.	12.99
☐ **Voltron III, The Deluxe Lion Set,** includes five lion robots with moveable parts that combine to form a large Voltron III robot. Produced by Matchbox in 1985	59.99

ROYAL WEDDING

DESCRIPTION: On July 29, 1981, Prince Charles, the heir-apparent to the throne of England, married Lady Diana Spencer in what was called the social event of the decade. Prince Charles and Princess Diana memorabilia include items dating from the courtship and the wedding, as well as post-wedding items, some of which heralded the birth of their first child, William.

TYPES: Items produced in this country and abroad included austere commemoratives such as medallions, coins, plates, and clocks, as well as humorous items, such as a drinking mug bearing a likeness to Prince Charles, with an oversized ear serving as its handle.

COMMENTS: Some collectors consider Royal Wedding memorabilia as good as money in the bank, as the collecting of artifacts detailing members of the Royal Family goes back almost as far as the Windsor family tree.

ADDITIONAL TIPS: While a literal avalanche of Royal Wedding items were unleashed in England in advance of the nuptials, fewer items were produced in this country, and are consequently more scarce. Experts say that some of the higher-priced items from either country, as well as those of a humorous vein, will be the items to watch for future appreciation in value.

	CURRENT PRICE RANGE	
☐ **Bone China Plate,** produced in 1981 by the Franklin Mint. Features a floral arrangement designed by noted British botanical artist Mary Grierson and was crafted by Royal Doulton. The bouquet is framed with a border of royal blue, edged with 22-karat gold trim. A cartouche bearing the monograms of the couple appears in the lower portion of the plate	75.00	
☐ **Goblet,** issued by the Franklin Mint in 1981. Limited to an edition of 950, it is identifiable by the three feathers symbol from the coat of arms of the Prince of Wales incorporated into its stem	1950.00	
☐ **Royal Baby Paper Doll Book,** complete title, "The Royal Baby: The Private Life of His Royal Highness Prince William," published in November 1983 by Pocket Books of New York.	4.95	
☐ **Royal Wedding Postal Commemorative Booklet,** printed by the British post office, this glossy 12-page publication contained 14-pence and 25-pence official wedding British postage stamps (released July 22, 1981), encased on its cover	5.00	8.00
☐ **Sterling Silver Cameo,** a Franklin Mint product dated from 1981. This pendant bears a portrayal of the symbols of the British monarchy, together with the individual symbols representing Charles and Diana, all set on a mirror background. Carries the words "Prince Charles and Lady Diana, 29 July 1981." Produced in an edition of 35,750.	45.00	

STAR TREK MOVIES

DESCRIPTION: "Star Trek" was a popular television series originally aired between 1966 and 1969. During the 1980s, three full-length feature films were released: "Star Trek: The Motion Picture" (1980), "The Wrath of Khan" (1982), and "The Return of Spock" (1984).

TYPES: The movies have produced traditional forms of cinemabilia, such as sound track albums, posters, gum cards, and souvenir booklets. Also produced were dolls and a very successful series of collector plates.

COMMENTS: The first of the three "Star Trek" movies released was roundly panned. Manufacturers lost a bundle on products as a result of the bad reviews. The second and third films were critical and commercial successes. However, after being burned by the first film, many manufacturers ceased producing "Star Trek" items. As a result, spinoff toys from these three films are more difficult to acquire than might initially be believed.

ADDITIONAL TIPS: Specialists predict that the collector plates represent good investments for the future, as do sound track albums from the films, copies of the annual "Star Trek" calendar, and anything being made of ceramics or metal.

	CURRENT PRICE RANGE	
☐ **Calendar,** published by Pocket Books in 1982 and featuring photographs from the first motion picture	10.00	12.00
☐ **Dr. McCoy Collector Plate,** second in series. Issued by Ernst Enterprises, Escondido, California	29.50	
☐ **Enterprise Blueprint,** by David Kimble and released in conjunction with "Star Trek: The Motion Picture." Shows exterior detail only of the Enterprise bridge, a Klingon ship and bridge, and more	10.00	30.00
☐ **Kirk Doll,** manufactured by MEGO. One of six 12″ dolls in a series released in conjunction with "Star Trek: The Motion Picture" (1980)	50.00	60.00
☐ **Spock Collector Plate,** first in a series debuting in 1984. Features painting of the famous Vulcan by Susie Morton, and issued by Ernst Enterprises, Escondido, California	29.50	

STAR WARS SEQUELS

DESCRIPTION: After the immense popularity of the original motion picture, "Star Wars," in 1977, two sequels were released in the 1980s: "The Empire Strikes Back" and "Return of the Jedi."

TYPES: Basic forms of cinemabilia, as well as toys, dolls and costumes.

COMMENTS: These films rank among the most commercially exploited series of all time, and a multitude of merchandise was produced during the 1980s.

ADDITIONAL TIPS: Look for the more expensive items to break away from the myriad of products. Also, seek out the more ephemeral items—promotional tie-ins with McDonald's, for example. These items were available for only a short period of time and are already difficult to acquire in many cases.

	CURRENT PRICE RANGE	
☐ **Book,** *The Empire Strikes Back,* by Archie Goodwin and Al Williamson, illustrators, from the screenplay by L. Brackett and L. Kasdan. Published in paperback form by Marvel Comics Group in 1980	5.00	7.00

	CURRENT PRICE RANGE	
☐ **Prerelease Publicity Poster,** one-sheet issued in advance of the third in the Star Wars series, identifies film as "Revenge of the Jedi." Subsequently changed to "Return of the Jedi," original posters were the hottest forms of cinemabilia in February 1983. An estimated 9,000 were distributed to movie theaters and the official Star Wars Fan Club	100.00	400.00
☐ **Star Wars Belt,** manufactured by Lee. Red and black stretch belt with metal buckle which reads, "Return of the Jedi." . . .	2.50	3.50
☐ **Yoda Cap,** from "The Empire Strikes Back," with soft, sculpted velour ears, tufts of "authentic hair," and an embroidered "YODA," patch	14.95	
☐ **Yoda Hand Puppet,** made by Kenner, features finely sculpted head and hands which can be manipulated. Measures 8½″ in height	8.00	10.00

STATUE OF LIBERTY

DESCRIPTION: In 1986, the Statue of Liberty marked its centennial amid much excitement. For two years preceding the anniversary, the statue—originally called "Liberty Enlightening the World"—was the subject of a large-scale refurbishing.

TYPES: Always a popular souvenir, models of the Statue of Liberty took on new dimensions during the centennial, with a reproduction offered for every pocketbook. One of these was made from actual portions of the metal work and cement base discarded during the renovations.

COMMENTS: The Statue of Liberty is a universally recognized symbol around the globe, and collectibles produced in its image are sure to appreciate in value, joining a list of past models of Frederic Auguste Bartholdi's most famous creation (a metal copy from the late 19th century sold at Christie's in New York for $121,000 in 1985).

ADDITIONAL TIPS: A collection of humorous postcards lampooning the famous lady of New York Harbor and produced during the centennial era are good candidates for your "what to save" box.

	CURRENT PRICE RANGE	
☐ **Statue of Liberty Collector Plate,** features watercolor painting by artist Renee Faure entitled "Symbols of Freedom and Hope." Made by Heinrich/Villeroy & Boch of West Germany	38.00	
☐ **Statue of Liberty First Day Cover Stamp,** measures 6 1/2″ x 3 5/8″. Produced by Fleetwood of Cheyenne, Wyoming, and featuring U.S. postage stamp honoring sculptor Frederic Bartholdi on 150th anniversary of his birth. Postmarked in New York on July 18, 1875. Cover features full-color painting by artist Shannon Stirnwels	1.00	5.00

	CURRENT PRICE RANGE	
☐ **Statue of Liberty Model,** measures 26″ high. Cast of thirty pounds of solid American bronze, and sculpted and signed by Bonita Thien Knickmeyer. Produced in a limited edition of 5,000 by Liberty Bronze, Inc., of St. Louis. Statuary brown $595.00; weathered copper green $645.00.	595.00	645.00
☐ **Statue of Liberty Model,** measures 15″ high. Produced of materials removed from the actual statue during renovations. Marketed by Mader's Tower Gallery of Milwaukee during centennial era	39.50	
☐ **Statue of Liberty Poster,** measures 20″ x 28″. Published by *Welcome To New York City,* NY. Reproduction of drawing "Projected Statue of Liberty for New York Harbor," originally published in *Harper's* in 1875	5.00	15.00

TEDDY BEARS

DESCRIPTION: Teddy bears are stuffed animals said to have first been created simultaneously in this country and Germany early in this century. The American origin began after a couple from Brooklyn created a bear in honor of a publicized incident involving President Teddy Roosevelt and a bear during a hunting trip in 1906. The European Teddy was created by the Steiff Company of Germany about the same time.

TYPES: Bears are being produced in the 1980s in various sizes by Steiff, Gund, Alresford, Hermann and others. Largely through the efforts of Workman Publishing, a large selection of Teddy Bear stationery, puzzles, Christmas ornaments, and a very popular annual calendar are available.

COMMENTS: The Teddy Bear was catapulted back into the public eye largely through the publicity accorded the release of "The Teddy Bear Catalog," authored by Peggy and Alan Bialosky and published by Workman in 1980.

ADDITIONAL TIPS: Look for bears which imitate living personalities. In 1980, for example, a teddy bear appeared on the market garbed in a basketball uniform and named "Kareem Abdul-Jabear."

	CURRENT PRICE RANGE
☐ **Alresford's "British Bobbie,"** came clad in uniform, complete with shoes. Body made of soft, short hair, medium color beige. Non-jointed, stands 32″ high. Issued in 1982.	85.00
☐ **Hermann's Traditional Bear,** measures 24″ high, butterscotch in color, fully jointed, mohair, 1982	100.00
☐ **Teddy Bear Calendar,** published in 1984 by Workman of New York, New York. Features 1983 Teddy Bear calendar contest winners.	5.95

CURRENT
PRICE RANGE

☐ **The 100th Anniversary Steiff, "Papa,"** a reproduction of the original Steiff Teddy Bear introduced in 1903. Produced in a limited edition of 7,000. Measures 18″ tall, and made of honey mohair, felt pads, and embroidered nose 500.00

☐ **The 101st Anniversary Steiff, "Mama and Baby,"** designed to complement "Papa" bear. Made of honey-colored mohair, fully jointed, with felt pads. "Mama" measures 16″ high, "Baby" measures 6″ high. Came as a set................. 185.00

WORLD'S FAIRS

DESCRIPTION: During the 1980s, the South played host to two internationally sanctioned world's fairs—the Knoxville World's Fair of 1982 and the Louisiana World Exposition of 1984. Both fairs saw the marketing of a vast assortment of souvenirs, many which will find their place among the illustrious assemblage of world's fair miscellany dating back to the mid-19th century.

TYPES: Clocks and watches are traditionally some of the most desirable items. Souvenir books, flags, pins, postcards, posters, and medallions are but a few of the items to found in this field.

COMMENTS: While the Knoxville and Louisiana fairs fell far short of their anticipated draw, both will remain favorites with World's Fair collectors in this country. The simple fact is that, despite the large numbers of items produced, so few people attended the fairs that few items actually were circulated.

ADDITIONAL TIPS: Two collecting groups exist for the benefit of collectors of World's Fair memorabilia: the Exposition Collectors—Historians Organization (ECHO), 1436 Killarney, Los Angeles, CA 90065, and the World's Fair Collectors' Society, Inc., 148 Poplar St., Garden City, New York 11530.

CURRENT
PRICE RANGE

☐ **Book,** *The 34th World's Fair Exposition,* published by Chrome Yellow Press of Gainesville, Florida, in September 1982. The first 1,000 copies were autographed and numbered by Clayton Cottrell, who provided the background information for this pictorial volume. Features photographs by Jerry B. Reed, documenting the 1982 Louisiana World Exposition. 14.95

☐ **Desk Flag,** produced for the Louisiana World Exposition, designed by Robert Whitney in spring 1982. Measures 4″ x 6″, and includes logo from the exposition 2.00

☐ **Mantel Clock,** measures 10″ high and 6″ wide, copying the famous Doric-Mosaic clock of 1880. Made of mahogany, walnut, and polished brass. Individually numbered at the bottom of the World's Fair logo. Produced by Wagner Time, Inc., of Barrington, Illinois 99.99

☐ **Neck Tie,** produced for the Louisiana World Exposition, and came in navy or maroon. 10.00

**CURRENT
PRICE RANGE**

Pocket Watch, sold by Wagner Time, Inc., of Barrington, Illinois, in 1982, and produced by Westclox, a division of General Time Corp. The face contains the letters "Worlds Fair 82" in place of the usual numerals. Also carries the fair's theme, "Energy Turns the World." **21.95**

READER SURVEY

The House of Collectibles continually seeks to improve, expand, and update the material in *The Official Price Guide Series*. The assistance and cooperation of numerous collectors and dealers have added immeasurably to the success of the books in this series. Please take a few seconds and give us your help so we can provide you with information needed to become a successful collector.

Name _____ Phone ( ) _____

Address _____

City _____ State _____ Zip _____

Age Group: ☐ under 18 ☐ 18-24 ☐ 25-34 ☐ 35-44 ☐ 45-54 ☐ 55 & over

Title of book purchased _____

Date of purchase _____

Name & address of bookshop _____

_____

Reason for purchase: ☐ I was looking for a book about this subje
☐ I had the previous edition.   ☐ I saw it advertised.
☐ I saw it in a public library.   ☐ It was recommended to me.

Do you plan to buy the new revised
edition of this book when it's published? ☐ Definitely ☐ Probably ☐ No

Did you have difficulty locating a bookshop
that carries The House of Collectibles titles? ☐ Yes ☐ No

Is this the first House of
Collectibles book that you've purchased? ☐ Yes ☐ No

Is there any way you feel this book could be improved? _____
_____
_____

How do you feel this book compares with other books about the same subject?
_____
_____

Check the publisher's catalogue at the back of this book, then tell us:
are there any titles you'd like to see added to our series? _____
_____

Would you consider yourself primarily a:
☐ Collector ☐ Dealer ☐ Investor ☐ Home Decorator ☐ General Reader

Do you have any information not included
in the book but which you think should be? ☐ Yes ☐ No

If you do, would you be interested
in becoming a contributor to a future edition? ☐ Yes ☐ No
(If your answer is yes, we'll be contacting you with full details on how you can become an "Official Member" of the world's largest hobby publishing team!)

☐ Please send me the following price guides—
☐ I would like the most current edition of the books listed below.

THE OFFICIAL PRICE GUIDES TO:		
☐ 465-8	**American Silver & Silver Plate** 4th Ed.	10.95
☐ 482-8	**Antique Clocks** 3rd Ed.	10.95
☐ 283-3	**Antique & Modern Dolls** 3rd Ed.	10.95
☐ 287-6	**Antique & Modern Firearms** 6th Ed.	11.95
☐ 271-X	**Antiques & Other Collectibles** 6th Ed.	9.95
☐ 289-2	**Antique Jewelry** 5th Ed.	11.95
☐ 270-1	**Beer Cans & Collectibles,** 3rd Ed.	7.95
☐ 262-0	**Bottles Old & New** 9th Ed.	10.95
☐ 255-8	**Carnival Glass** 1st Ed.	10.95
☐ 453-4	**Collectible Cameras** 2nd Ed.	10.95
☐ 277-9	**Collectibles of the Third Reich** 2nd Ed.	10.95
☐ 281-7	**Collectible Toys** 3rd Ed.	10.95
☐ 490-9	**Collector Cars** 6th Ed.	11.95
☐ 267-1	**Collector Handguns** 3rd Ed.	11.95
☐ 290-6	**Collector Knives** 8th Ed.	11.95
☐ 266-3	**Collector Plates** 4th Ed.	11.95
☐ 476-3	**Collector Prints** 6th Ed.	11.95
☐ 489-5	**Comic Books & Collectibles** 8th Ed.	9.95
☐ 433-X	**Depression Glass** 1st Ed.	9.95
☐ 472-0	**Glassware** 2nd Ed.	10.95
☐ 492-5	**Hummel Figurines & Plates** 5th Ed.	9.95
☐ 451-8	**Kitchen Collectibles** 2nd Ed.	10.95
☐ 291-4	**Military Collectibles** 5th Ed.	11.95
☐ 268-X	**Music Collectibles** 5th Ed.	11.95
☐ 491-7	**Old Books & Autographs** 6th Ed.	10.95
☐ 298-1	**Oriental Collectibles** 3rd Ed.	11.95
☐ 297-3	**Paper Collectibles** 5th Ed.	10.95
☐ 276-0	**Pottery & Porcelain** 5th Ed.	11.95
☐ 263-9	**Radio, T.V. & Movie Memorabilia** 2nd Ed.	11.95
☐ 288-4	**Records** 7th Ed.	10.95
☐ 485-2	**Royal Doulton** 4th Ed.	10.95
☐ 280-4	**Science Fiction & Fantasy Collectibles** 2nd Ed.	10.95
☐ 477-1	**Wicker** 3rd Ed.	10.95
THE OFFICIAL:		
☐ 445-3	**Collector's Journal** 1st Ed.	4.95
☐ 365-1	**Encyclopedia of Antiques** 1st Ed.	9.95
☐ 369-4	**Guide to Buying & Selling Antiques** 1st Ed.	9.95
☐ 414-3	**Identification Guide to Early American Furniture** 1st Ed.	9.95
☐ 413-5	**Identification Guide to Glassware** 1st Ed.	9.95
☐ 448-8	**Identification Guide to Gunmarks** 2nd Ed.	9.95
☐ 412-7	**Identification Guide to Pottery & Porcelain** 1st Ed.	9.95
☐ 415-1	**Identification Guide to Victorian Furniture** 1st Ed.	9.95

THE OFFICIAL (POCKET SIZE) PRICE GUIDES TO:		
☐ 473-9	**Antiques & Flea Markets** 3rd Ed.	3.95
☐ 442-9	**Antique Jewelry** 2nd Ed.	3.95
☐ 264-7	**Baseball Cards** 5th Ed.	4.95
☐ 488-7	**Bottles** 2nd Ed.	4.95
☐ 468-2	**Cars & Trucks** 2nd Ed.	4.95
☐ 260-4	**Collectible Americana** 1st Ed.	4.95
☐ 294-9	**Collectible Records** 3rd Ed.	4.95
☐ 469-0	**Collector Guns** 2nd Ed.	4.95
☐ 474-7	**Comic Books** 3rd Ed.	3.95
☐ 486-0	**Dolls** 3rd Ed.	4.95
☐ 292-2	**Football Cards** 5th Ed.	4.95
☐ 258-2	**Glassware** 2nd Ed.	4.95
☐ 487-9	**Hummels** 3rd Ed.	4.95
☐ 441-0	**Military Collectibles** 2nd Ed.	3.95
☐ 480-1	**Paperbacks & Magazines** 3rd Ed.	4.95
☐ 443-7	**Pocket Knives** 2nd Ed.	3.95
☐ 479-8	**Scouting Collectibles** 3rd Ed.	4.95
☐ 439-9	**Sports Collectibles** 2nd Ed.	3.95
☐ 494-1	**Star Trek/Star Wars Collectibles** 3rd Ed.	3.95
☐ 493-3	**Toys** 3rd Ed.	4.95
THE OFFICIAL BLACKBOOK PRICE GUIDES OF:		
☐ 284-1	**U.S. Coins** 24th Ed.	3.95
☐ 286-8	**U.S. Paper Money** 18th Ed.	3.95
☐ 285-X	**U.S. Postage Stamps** 8th Ed.	3.95
THE OFFICIAL INVESTORS GUIDE TO BUYING & SELLING:		
☐ 496-8	**Gold, Silver and Diamonds** 2nd Ed.	9.95
☐ 497-6	**Gold Coins** 2nd Ed.	9.95
☐ 498-4	**Silver Coins** 2nd Ed.	9.95
☐ 499-2	**Silver Dollars** 2nd Ed.	9.95
THE OFFICIAL NUMISMATIC GUIDE SERIES:		
☐ 481-X	**Coin Collecting** 3rd Ed.	9.95
☐ 254-X	**The Official Guide to Detecting Counterfeit Money** 2nd Ed.	7.95
☐ 257-4	**The Official Guide to Mint Errors** 4th Ed.	7.95
☐ 256-6	**The Official Hewitt-Donlon Price Guide to Small Size Paper Money** 15th Ed.	7.95
☐ 162-4	**Variety & Oddity Guide of U.S. Coins** 8th Ed.	4.95
SPECIAL INTEREST SERIES:		
☐ 506-9	**From Hearth to Cookstove** 3rd Ed.	17.95
☐ 370-8	**Lucky Number Lottery Guide** 1st Ed.	3.50
☐ 504-2	**On Method Acting** 8th Printing	6.95
	TOTAL	

SEE REVERSE SIDE FOR ORDERING INSTRUCTIONS

FOR IMMEDIATE DELIVERY

VISA & MASTER CARD CUSTOMERS

ORDER TOLL FREE!
1-800-638-6460

This number is for orders only; it is not tied into the customer service or business office. Customers not using charge cards must use mail for ordering since payment is required with the order — sorry no C.O.D.'s.

OR SEND ORDERS TO ▐ ▐ ▐ ▐ ▐ ▐

THE HOUSE OF COLLECTIBLES, 201 East 50th Street
New York, New York 10022

─── **POSTAGE & HANDLING RATE CHART** ───

TOTAL ORDER/POSTAGE	TOTAL ORDER/POSTAGE	
0 to $10.00 - **$1.25**	$20.01 to $30.00 - **$2.00**	$50.01 & Over -
$10.01 to $20.00 - **$1.60**	$30.01 to $40.00 - **$2.75**	**Add 10% of your total order**
	$40.01 to $50.00 - **$3.50**	(Ex. $75.00 x .10 = $7.50)

Total from columns on reverse side. Quantity_____ $ _____

| | Check or money order enclosed $_____ (include postage and handling)

| | Please charge $_____ to my: | | MASTERCARD | | VISA

Charge Card Customers Not Using Our Toll Free Number Please Fill Out The Information Below.

Account No. (All Digits) _____ Expiration Date _____

Signature_____

NAME (please print) _____ PHONE _____

ADDRESS _____ APT. # _____ (10)

CITY _____ STATE _____ ZIP _____

DESCRIPTION	PURCHASED	COST	SOLD	PRICE	CONDITION

DESCRIPTION	DATE PURCHASED	COST	DATE SOLD	PRICE	CONDITION